Ex Libris

Randy Manning

MANUAL OF
Bulbs

THE NEW ROYAL HORTICULTURAL SOCIETY DICTIONARY

MANUAL OF
Bulbs

Consultant Editor JOHN BRYAN
Series Editor MARK GRIFFITHS

TIMBER PRESS
Portland, Oregon

Derived from
The New Royal Horticultural Society Dictionary of Gardening
Editor in Chief Anthony Huxley
Editor Mark Griffiths, Managing Editor Margot Levy
in four volumes, 1992.

First published 1995 by Macmillan Reference Books
a division of Macmillan Publishers Limited
25 Eccleston Place, London SW1W 9NF
and Basingstoke

Associated companies around the world

First published in North America in 1995 by
Timber Press, Inc.
The Haseltine Building
133 S.W. Second Avenue, Suite 450
Portland, Oregon 97204, U.S.A.

ISBN 0-88192-339-7

Printed and bound in Great Britain by
Butler & Tanner Ltd, Frome and London

Contents

Preface

In the fourth edition of his *Gardener's Dictionary* (1743), Philip Miller lists 23 'sorts' of *Allium*, 23 of *Crocus*, 32 *Lilium* and 46 *Narcissus*; of *Tulipa* he observes that there is 'no end of their numbers' – a disclaimer that holds good for each of these genera as they appear, some 250 years later, in *The New Royal Horticultural Society Dictionary of Gardening*. Miller's bulb count, surprisingly high, underscores the perennial popularity of bulbous plants and the classic status of some genera in particular – bulbs like the lily and narcissus that come down to us from antiquity steeped in symbolism, the bulbs of early herbals, and the buried treasures, like saffron and the tulip, that returned with silks and spices from the earliest Eastern explorations. It was a bulb that created one of the world's most notorious futures markets: much has been written on the tulip boom, mostly drawing attention to its odd mixture of fashion, greed and hubris, but it was equally one of the most resounding explosions of interest in ornamental plants and in their development through horticulture. That interest, true of so many bulbs today, is captured by Addison writing in 1710 of an episode when he was forced to shelter from the rain with a group of gentlefolk:

> My curiosity was raised when I heard the names of Alexander the Great and Artaxerxes; and as their talk seemed to run on ancient heroes, I concluded there could not be any secret in it; for which reason, I thought I might very fairly listen to what they said. I was surprised to hear one say that he valued the Black Prince more than the Duke of Vendosme. I heard the second affirm with great vehemence, that if the Emperor of Germany was not going off, he should like him better than either of them. He added that though the season was so changeable, the Duke of Marlborough was in blooming beauty. I was wondering to myself from whence they had received this odd intelligence: especially when I heard them mention the names of several other generals, as the Prince of Hesse and the King of Sweden, who, they said, were both running away. To which they added, what I entirely agreed with them in, that the Crown of France was very weak. ... At last, one of them told the company, if they would go along with him, he would show them a Chimney-Sweeper and a Painted Lady in the same bed, which he was sure would very much please them.

The rain passes and our correspondent, reeling from this heady political debate, is invited into the garden where he discovers 'that the kings and generals they had mentioned were only so many tulips'. That conversation, in much the same form, the same enthusiasm, the same cultivar connoisseurship, can still be heard today; indeed, it has been extended to take in the riches of the Cape and North America and the subtleties of the snowdrop, brooding Arisaemas, the cyclamen, American amaryllids and begonias. 'Knowing one's onions' has become an altogether harder task, with over 150 ornamental species, varieties and cultivars of *Allium* currently available in the United Kingdom.

From the crystal-fragile bells of the Snowdon Lily high on a Welsh crag, to the world's largest unbranched inflorescence, the Titan Arum from Sumatra, the diversity of bulbs is a remarkable testament to the ability of plants to meet environmental challenges. Too often this diversity has been enjoyed in gardens at the expense of *biodiversity*. In 1991, Patti Hagan reported in the *Wall Street Journal* that

> the (bulb) industry has exploited Turkey pre-eminently as a vast, free-dig, open-pit bulb mine: 71 million anemones, 20 million cyclamen, 62 million leucojums, 111 million winter aconites, 200 million snowdrops were extracted from Turkey in the '80s, without any documentable attempt to leave behind a viable bulb population for future harvest.

The bulb fields of the Mediterranean, Middle East and Central Asia are not alone in yielding up their pre-packed glories. In the United States, the Tennessee Department of Conservation has recorded that at least 600,000 wild-collected trilliums were lost to that State in 1989 alone. It has often been remarked that the deep appeal of bulbs lies in the mystery of their annual renewal, their resurrection. By refusing to purchase wild-collected bulbs and by promoting sustainable methods of propagation and conservation, both *in* and *ex situ*, we have the power to secure that cycle of renewal indefinitely – better bulb bounty than bulb booty.

This Manual aims to describe the botany, qualities and culture of the majority of cultivated ornamental bulbs. It excludes strictly economic plants and Orchidaceae, a family replete with storage organs but customarily treated as distinct from 'bulbous plants' even in the broadest sense. 'Bulbs' is taken here to encompass all plants that possess swollen, largely subterranean, storage organs – true bulbs, corms, true tubers, stem tubers, root tubers, tubercles and (some) fleshy roots, rhizomes and caudices. It is a generous definition, pulling together plants as polarized as *Bongardia* and *Babiana*, *Ranunculus* and *Rhodohypoxis*, *Salvia* and *Scilla*, and one made broader still by the widespread botanical and horticultural view which sees most herbaceous, petaloid monocots collectively as 'bulbs', even when, as in the case of *Maianthemum*, their storage capacity may be slight and the vessel slender. The Liliaceae – arguably the most important family among the bulbs – has undergone much revision and reclassification since the 1980's. In this work, the older and broader concept of Liliaceae is maintained because of its familiarity to horticulturists. The families into which it has been split are indicated for each genus in parenthesis after the traditional family, e.g. *Colchicum* Liliaceae (Colchicaceae); *Trillium* Liliaceae (Trilliaceae).

Much of the text of this Manual derives from *The New RHS Dictionary of Gardening*. The Introduction, however, is newly written by John Bryan. All thanks are due to him for sharing not only his unique understanding of the nature and nurture of bulbous plants, but also his encyclopaedic knowledge of the group. The accounts of genera are the work of many hands, but a special debt of gratitude is owed to those who made major taxonomic and horticultural contributions – Rupert Bowlby, C.D. Brickell, B.L. Burtt, L.E. Codd, Philip Damp, J. Doorenbos, Graham Duncan, Derek Fox, Diana Grenfell, Christopher Grey-Wilson, John Grimshaw, Alan Leslie, Brian Mathew, Victoria Matthews, Simon Mayo, Alan Meerow, Diana Miller, Martyn Rix, W.T. Stearn and Philip Swindells. The task of preparing and editing the accounts has been made possible only through the great kindness of Dr Brent Elliott and his colleagues at the Lindley Library, and by the Keeper and Librarian of the Royal Botanic Gardens, Kew.

The publishers wish to thank those artists whose drawings first appeared in *The New RHS Dictionary* and are reproduced here: Christine Grey-Wilson (*Cyclamen*; *Eranthis*; *Gladiolus*; *Narcissus*; *Tulipa*), Vana Haggerty (*Dahlia*), Christine Hart-Davies (*Anigozanthos*), Joanna Langhorne (*Arisaema*; *Fritillaria*; *Iris*; *Lilium*; *Nomocharis*; *Tricyrtis*), Lindsay Middleton (*Galanthus*), Bryan Poole (*Hemerocallis*) and Clare Roberts (*Kniphofia*). New artwork for this volume has been produced by Camilla Speight, Shirley Wheeler and Vana Haggerty. The care and style with which they have approached each subject will be readily appreciated by all devotees of bulbous plants and botanical art. At Macmillan, the text was processed by Mick Card, who deserves warm thanks, as do Joseph Spooner, who, inter alia, decoded the enigma of *Ipheion*, and, as ever, Margot Levy.

Mark Griffiths   London 1995

Introduction

Many years ago, I had the good fortune to be a student at Wisley, The Royal Horticultural Society's garden, during the first year of a scholarship awarded by the RHS and the Worshipful Company of Gardeners. At Wisley, I admired the many bulbs in the Rock Garden and especially appreciated the lilies growing on Battleston Hill. In my second year I studied in the Netherlands. Is it any wonder that I became fascinated by bulbs? If there was any hesitation, it was dispelled by my 10 years in Oregon, working with that father of the modern lily, Jan de Graaff.

Lilies and onions, along with many other plants, are true bulbs, having leaves adapted for storage. Cut into an onion and the rings of leaves are, one might say, transparently apparent. A corm is a stem modified for storage. Roots can also be modified for storage, as in a tuber, while a rhizome is a swollen underground stem from the tip(s) of which shoots emerge. When the word 'bulbs' is used, the tendency is to think of all of these adaptations, true bulbs, rhizomes, corms and tubers together – and correctly perhaps, as all these are plants that have a portion of themselves modified for storage. Many genera, and many thousands of species are involved in 'Bulbs' in the broadest sense.

It seems that over the years, various factors have played their part in deciding which species are regarded as 'bulbs'. I say 'regarded' advisedly, as certain species, which could quite correctly be placed in this category, are not. Factors not connected with the actual form (of the rootstock or stem of the plants in question) have in the past, played an important part in such considerations. Today these factors are still influential, often resulting in cases of rather artificial delineation. If, as in the case of *Liatris*, nurseries propagate a species with subterranean storage organs, but market it as an *herbaceous perennial*, few of the plants thus produced will find their way into bulb catalogues, into the bulb section of a general catalogue, or even into the gardening consciousness as *bulbs*.

Several examples of such plants come to mind. *Liatris* will often have corms; *Anigozanthos* has rhizomes described as 'stout', and which certainly function as 'bulbs' in their fire- and drought-stricken habitat. *Kniphofia* is a genus containing thickly rhizomatous species, and *Salvia yunnanensis* might well feel slighted, being in a genus where there are few, if any other 'bulbous' plants (it has rhizomatous stems and filiform tubers). Conversely, there is general acceptance that *Clivia* and *Agapanthus* should be grouped with 'bulbs', but, again, this distinction has arisen because of criteria other than those imposed by a strict botanical examination, and while parts of these plants are, to a certain degree, modified to overcome periods when moisture may be in short supply, it is stretching a point to call them 'bulbs'.

I was surprised, when researching genera for my two-volume work *Bulbs* (1989), to find that many species of *Pelargonium* had tuberous rootstocks. I asked myself the question why is a bulb a bulb? What determines such? A plant adapts its development, form and life cycle, in order to survive the environment in which it finds itself. Climate is the one factor of paramount importance here, and has the greatest possible influence. This factor matters because climate is not always conducive for the growth and even the survival of the plant. This may not pertain to each and every growing season, but at least from time to time.

Certain species, in overcoming the life-threatening force of fire, use it to their advantage and produce seeds that require exposure to this element and to smoke in order to germinate. Often the seed will be protected to such an extent, that even if the parent is destroyed, the seed will survive. Bulbs native to areas where summer fires occur complete their cycle during that period when fires are not prevalent, or they have a rootstock that can easily survive a fast-moving fire.

In October 1994, I was in South Africa, during springtime when many flowers can be enjoyed. I heard there had been fires in the Rotary Flower Reserve at Hermanus, not far from Cape Town. While the fires had passed through the area just a short time before my visit, I found the wonderful flowers of *Pillansia templemanii* in full glory. This species seldom flowers *except* after fire. What surprised me was just how quickly these plants came into full flower. I wondered how one would cultivate this plant in a garden. I suspect that piling dry straw around the plants and lighting the straw might do the trick. Obviously changes in the cells are triggered when temperatures are raised to a level as would be experienced in a fire. But why? Could it be that after a fire, the competition young seedlings of *Pillansia* face would be lessened? Grasses and certain of the fynbos, would be reduced so that the young plants get off to a good start in life – the fire presents a great window of opportunity, in fact, *Pillansia* is ideally suited for the area where it grows.

'Bulbs' have a common attribute, a common denominator – namely, they possess the ability to overcome periods when conditions are hostile and to select the most opportune time for growth. The tulip is dormant when snow covers the ground and when, if it were in growth, it would be exposed to unrelenting heat without adequate moisture to sustain it. It will complete its entire annual growth cycle in the one window of opportunity that the climate provides.

It is not difficult to understand why, at a certain period of the year, the majority of bulbs should become self-sufficient, self-contained, self-sustaining organisms. But for a while, one species did baffle me. The plant in question was a *Scadoxus* species closely confined to the rain forest at Victoria Falls in Zimbabwe. Surely its bulbous habit could not have evolved to counter a lack of moisture? Nor was temperature a factor here, as during the season when the river is not in flood and the rain forest is not supplied with rain, the temperature is pleasant in the 60°F range. There is also adequate light, so I pondered for quite a while why this species should be a bulb, and then a possible reason came to mind.

Roots of plants (unless especially adapted) need air. Saturated soil contains little air. When the mighty Zambesi river is in full spate, the ground is saturated. The trees, mostly species of *Ficus*, reduce the amount of light available. Thus, even in this lush warm area, there is a time when conditions are not entirely favourable for this bulb's growth - it is just too wet. The bulb becomes dormant during this time. It comes to life in very early spring (a much drier time) and finishes its annual cycle prior to the summer's heavy downpours created by the spray from the falls. The area that receives the rain is clearly defined, as is the habitat of this bulb. Did this plant develop its pattern of growth in response to the climate, or was its life cycle such that it found itself able to grow well in this particular environment?

It can be appreciated from these examples that within the ranks of 'bulbs', there can be found plants suitable for many different and unusual situations. Their form varies correspondingly. The height to which bulbs grow in a season varies greatly, from the towering *Dahlia imperialis* (over 12 feet) to the little *Crocus* that barely pops out of the ground. Almost any colour found in the plant kingdom can be found in the flowers of bulbs. Tulips were so called because of the many varied colours of the turbans (Turkish, *tulbend*) known to Ogier Ghiselin de Busbecq, Ambassador of the Holy Roman Emperor to Suleiman the Magnificent. Encountering these plants for the first time on his journey to Constantinople in 1554, he understood why his guide likened their many colours and outlines to the turbans that would have been seen everywhere in that part of the world. The Turkish name for a tulip is *Lâle* and I can imagine the mix-ups that might have occurred with lilies if this name had been used by Busbecq's guide.

Because they survive so well and grow in diverse climates, appearing and then disappearing, it is no wonder that bulbs entered into the lore of man. In heraldry, medicine, art and folklore, not to mention the kitchen, bulbs have played, important roles. Potatoes and onions are perhaps not thought of as 'bulbs' but they are, and what delightful dishes we would miss if we could not enjoy these vegetables.

This brings me to another point. There seems to be a division between plants grown in the vegetable garden and those grown in borders and flower beds. Garden plants have for too long been classified by *where* we grow them, an artificial division. We seem to forget that many plants were first introduced for their ornamental value, and then found their way into the vegetable garden. The attractive merits originally seen in them are forgotten. But how many plants grown in vegetable gardens find their way into ornamental gardens? – some but not many. Once they are commonly grown in either one or the other type of garden, plants seldom seem to cross back to the other. True, many species of *Allium* are grown as ornamentals, but why are not chives used more frequently as an ornamental – to edge a path for example? They are a delight when in flower, hardy and so easy to grow. Equally, why are *Gladiolus* flowers not used in the kitchen more frequently? Fill them with crab or chicken and they make colourful and attractive hors d'oeuvres.

The genetic potential of certain bulbous genera has been extensively but by no means exhaustively explored. Modern hybrids of lilies, tulips, dahlias and gladiolus prove that, with well thought out breeding programmes, exciting new cultivars can be developed. There are other genera of bulbous plants that merit the attention of the hybridizer, many not even considered or, as yet, not widely grown in gardens.

But even without hybrids, the potential for species to prove themselves plants of great commercial horticultural merit can not yet be said to have been fully appreciated. Only recently have *Rhodohypoxis* been introduced on the market as attractive pot plants. On the other hand, why have *Lachenalia* and *Velthemia* fallen out of favour with growers? These genera have so many great features, lovely colours and forms, are long-lasting in flower, and are not difficult to grow.

Today we are conscious of the need to be careful with toxic chemicals in the garden. Bulbs may sometimes be attacked by pests and diseases, but they are (for the most part) robust and remarkably trouble-free. Certain bulbs, those that we can rely upon to return year after year without great expenditure of labour, are worth their weight in gold. Lilies are an example. I have seen 20-year-old plantings, that each year are still vigorous, and putting on eye-stopping displays.

The lily is one example of a genus of bulbous plants so extensively developed by gardeners that it has warranted a horticultural classification for the plethora of hybrids and cultivars it has spawned. These classifications change from time-to-time to accommodate new advances in breeding. The classification of tulips has changed in the recent past. Notice was taken of the changes in the popularity of certain classes. While at one time classed under Cottage or Single Late Tulips, the Viridiflora Tulips now stand as a section by themselves. If such changes were not undertaken, problems would arise in exhibitions and competitions. It is only right that like be compared with like – as the saying goes, one should compare apples with apples.

Another change which I think should take place in the near future is to the Horticultural Classification of lilies. Certain new introductions of Asiatic Hybrids are neither clearly outward facing nor truly pendent, sometimes seeming to fall into one and sometimes the other division. One thing is certain – they are not upright, so why not have two divisions instead of three: 'Upright Facing' and 'Outward and Pendent'? With the Trumpet lilies there have been many fine introductions resulting from crosses with Orientals. Deserving of a new classification? I think so, and then we have to consider the Longiflorum Hybrids.

The bulb industry can rightly be proud of its heritage. It can be justifiably pleased that great efforts are being made to preserve wild species, a little late perhaps, but it is happening, so as to restrict the plundering of wild sources of bulbs. In this way generations yet unborn will have the thrill of seeing these plants in their native habitat. The valuable gene pool these wild species contain has, without doubt, such great potential that even today, we can not begin to appreciate or fully understand it. What lies ahead with our bulbous plants? They are, and have been for generations, appreciated. I think this will continue to be the case and indeed feel that these wondrous plants still contain many secrets that we can not envisage, even in our wildest imaginations. It is probable that species yet unused in any breeding programme may unlock miracles of colour, form, fragrance, disease-resistance, and attributes as yet unknown.

Over the years I have often remarked that we do not pay sufficient attention to the natural habitat of bulbs. We read that they are native to this or that part of the world. Do we take the time to find out the climate that they enjoy at home? Do we know who introduced them and when? Do we know if they have been used in the medicine of the people of their native lands, to increase fertility, for example, or to ward off evil spirits? Bulbs have remarkable stories to tell, they might be silent, but they are not without the ability to evoke thought and discussion, admiration and wonder, sadness perhaps in their passing out of flower, and great joy and anticipation as they emerge from their sleep, and once again unfurl their banners of colour. Exasperating, challenging, bulbs evoke so many emotions. No wonder there was 'Tulipmania'; no wonder that a bulb emerged as *the* symbol of grace and purity – the Madonna Lily. No wonder ancient civilizations featured them on their pottery, on the walls of temples, and regarded them as having magical powers.

I have not mentioned cultural requirements of bulbs here. This is deliberate. I think that far too often, too much care is taken with plants. Most certainly we should provide the temperatures required and we should plant at the correct time and depth, but far too often we overwater, overfeed and over-emphasize the 'exact' needs of plants we grow. In the wild, they do not receive such special treatment. It is written, 'Consider the lilies of the field, how they grow; they toil not neither do they spin: and yet I say unto you, that even Solomon in all his glory was not arrayed like one of these.' Points to keep in mind.

Take the dry tuber of an *Anemone* in your hand. Would any person, not knowing what it was, be able to imagine the beauty that it contains? Can many things remain dry for so long a time, and then produce such glory? They are indeed like wound-up clocks that just need a little impetus to start ticking and then help us to beguile away the hours.

Such cultural matters as planting depths should be respected, but they should serve as guides and must be adapted to individual situations. In cold, clay soil you might plant at a lesser depth, in warmer, sandy soils a little deeper. Such is often written, but the gardener must use common sense as well. In a warm location in the garden, would you plant more deeply or not as deeply, given that the soil was the same in both warm and colder locations? Allowances for the reflected heat from a wall, or from a hard surface, the chances of additional water being given to the plants by the run-off from a hard surface – all are factors to be kept in mind.

Bulbs lend themselves to many landscape uses. They are beautiful planted in drifts in woods – can anyone not admire a swathe of bluebells, or a host of daffodils? Such natural plantings are a delight. Spring-flowering bulbs on display, as at the Keukenhof gardens at Lisse in the Netherlands are glorious. The bulb fields in springtime, are a spectacular patchwork quilt of colour and form. Tulips in flower beds, or lilies among shrubs, add interest, often when the other plants in the border are not in flower. Likewise, container-grown bulbs are commonly seen growing on decks and patios, but the use of bulbs in the garden should not stop with planting in a way that can be termed 'conventional'.

I encourage gardeners to experiment with variously shaped groupings. A diagonal swathe of yellow tulips arising out of, or intermingled with, a bed of red or pink tulips can be striking. *Muscari* planted among roses give interest and colour prior to the roses coming into flower. Crocus can be planted in lawns; gladiolus among summer-flowering annuals to give a vertical accent (their foliage alone is quite dramatic, and then almost as a bonus they put on an eye-stopping display of colour). Bold and imaginative, unusual and exciting, bulbs lend themselves to such plantings. Even in the same location in the border, crocus can be followed by daffodils, followed by tulips, followed by lilies, dahlias or cannas. A bulb corner, if you will, because after all, few bulbs seem to object to the presence of other plants in their fraternity. Whatever the design, bulbs can, indeed should be, an important part of the planting scheme, adding interest and colour.

Today we have many formulas of fertilizer available. In days past, we raised great plants and made up our own formulas using blood meal, dried blood, sulphate of ammonia, hoof and horn, bonemeal, sulphate and muriate of potash. People seem to forget the basics, but they are still valid today – nitrogen for growth and foliage colour, phosphates for bud formation and hardiness, and potash for the general health of the plant. We want growth in the spring, followed by balanced growth, and then to augment hardiness and the general health of the bulb. In containers where we have to water frequently, nitrogen is quickly leached, so reduce the amount given at each feeding but increase the number of feedings.

In this *Manual of Bulbs*, you will find information which provides the essential points to remember when growing bulbs. It is however important that the grower should build upon this solid foundation of knowledge by adding ingredients culled from experience.

There is much to learn, much to enjoy. Growing plants and especially bulbs is so worthwhile. On decks, on patios, in the home, there are bulbs suitable for every location, every climate and – just as important – every pocketbook. One might add that no matter what the decorative scheme of a residence, ancient or ultra modern, there are bulbs that will compliment the style. Bulbs are indeed both ancient and modern.

Bulbs, mysterious in so many ways, just what does occur inside them while they are dormant? What secrets do they contain? What can we do to appreciate fully their thousands of species? Bulbs have evoked such questions for as long as they have been cultivated: our future will undoubtedly be made brighter and more colourful by their continued presence in our gardens, in our lives.

John E. Bryan

Bulb Cultivation

BULB BIOLOGY

Bulbs, corms, tubers and rhizomes are all storage organs developed to carry a plant through dormancy during seasons of adverse weather conditions – usually drought combined with extremes of heat or cold. While most true bulbs and corms belong to the three great families of petaloid monocots – Amaryllidaceae, Iridaceae and Liliaceae – tubers, rhizomes and even a caudex thickened to resemble a tuber may be found in other plant families. Thus in the Berberidaceae, *Bongardia*, *Gymnospermium* and *Leontice* produce swollen subterranean tubers; *Dahlia* in the Compositae and *Ranunculus* (Ranunculaceae) bear clustered true tubers; certain asclepiads and pelargoniums form swollen caudices, *Oxalis* scaly bulbs.

Strictly, the *bulb* is a specialized storage organ growing below the soil or occasionally protruding above it. It consists of a basal plate from which spring the roots and a compressed stem resembling a bud with an embryo shoot or a complete embryo flower, enclosed by a series of fleshy scales. Each scale is a swollen modified leaf or swollen leaf base in which food materials are stored, ensuring survival in periods unfavourable to growth. In bulbs such as narcissus, tulip and onions, the scales are tightly packed, completely encircling those within, and not readily separated. The bulb is typically enclosed in a papery tunic which may be green in above-ground bulbs but is otherwise brown, black, translucent or fibrous, even forming a reticulated pattern. The tunic-cover protects the bulbs from surface damage and drying. The roots are usually produced annually, but may be perennial as in *Muscari* or biennial as in *Iris* subgenus *Scorpiris*.

Bulbs of fritillaries and lilies produce modified scale leaves only, not covered with a protective tunic and therefore more susceptible to drying. Lilies usually produce a large number of scales which are often narrow, very fleshy and easily removed, whereas fritillaries are made up of only two or three scales, often tightly packed, or else may consist of a rather small core surrounded by numerous tiny 'rice grains', these being loosely attached swollen scales which fall away with the slightest disturbance. If this happens the parent bulb is weakened and may not flower. Another distinguishing feature of this kind of bulb is that new roots are made during summer and persist through the dormant period. The genus *Tulbaghia* grows from a clump of small bulbs firmly attached to a continuous basal plate, which is sometimes regarded as a rhizome.

Tunicate bulbs fall into three categories based on the bulb's formation and growth habit. The tulip – one kind – dies after flowering and is renewed annually by the development of one or more new daughter bulbs arising from buds in the axils of the bulb scales, or on the extremities of short stolons: the true, aerial leaves provide the energy for the formation of the new bulbs. Annually renewed bulbs such as tulips are composed entirely of modified leaves (true scales), the foliage leaves being produced by the apical flowering or vegetative shoot. Daffodil bulbs, however, contain both true scales and swollen leaf bases and persist for several years. The bulb perennates through the development year-on-year of a new bulb from the main growing point together with the production of lateral offset bulbs, thus providing a continuous succession of new bulbs in various stages of development. *Hippeastrum* is an example of the third bulb type, composed entirely of swollen leaf bases and remains perennial. This is achieved by the continuous formation of new primordial bulbs as its centre; such bulbs may take three seasons before flowering. The leaf bases are progressively pushed further to the outside of the bulb, where they will finally form the dry papery tunic.

A *corm* is a solid food storage organ formed from the thickened underground base of a stem, usually within some overlapping papery scale-like leaves called a tunic arising from the segments of the corm and completely covering it. The tunic is formed from the dried-off bases of the leaves, protecting the corm against injury and preventing water loss. Corms differ from bulbs in being solid. Single

Bulbs and corms (a) *Lilium* (b) *Cardiocrinum giganteum* (c) *Narcissus* (d) *Lilium* (stoloniferous)
(e) *Hyacinthus* (f) *Fritillaria imperialis* (g) *Notholirion* (h) *Colchicum* (i) *Gladiolus* (j) *Tulipa* (k) *Crocosmia*
(l) *Galanthus* (m) *Crocus* (n) *Tritonia* (o) *Freesia*

or multiple buds arise from the upper surface, with annual roots growing from the base, often form-ing flowering shoots with lateral buds arising between the segments or nodes forming two opposite rows down the corm. In most cormaceous Iridaceae the corm is annual, the new corm forming at the base of the current season's stem on top of the old corm, which withers away. Cormaceous Liliaceae form new corms at the side of the old, more in the nature of a bulbous offset. In the Iridaceae, corm-lets are often produced freely from the base or top of the corm, or at the end of long underground stolons or even in the leaf axils. In a few groups, such as garden montbretias and their allies, the reserves are not fully used annually so that there is a tight cluster of several years' degenerating corms sitting one behind the other. In this way corms are naturally replaced each year and can increase in number depending on how many stems are produced from the original corm.

Corms can also form a number of cormels or cormlets (miniature corms), often arising between the old and new corms which develop when the plant is in flower. Plants that produce corms are found extensively in the Iridaceae and include *Babiana*, *Chasmanthe*, *Crocosmia*, *Crocus*, *Freesia*, *Gladiolus*, *Ixia*, *Lapeirousia*, *Moraea*, *Romulea*, *Sparaxis*, *Tritonia*, *Tigridia* and *Watsonia*. Depending upon the hardiness of the plants and the locality in which they are grown, corms may need to be lifted and stored over the dormant period. In climates with cool, dull summers, some of the more tender plants such as *Freesia*, *Sparaxis* and *Tigridia* may not develop corms strong enough to survive unless they are grown under protection.

The more tender cormous plants should ripen readily and be ready for lifting given a well-man-aged fertile soil that receives some degree of sun-baking toward the end of the growing season. Allow foliage to wither before lifting. Lifted corms should be cleaned of surplus soil, placed in slat-ted containers ensuring good air circulation and put into a warm (30°C/87°F) environment for about 12 hours. This will allow easier separation of remnant top growth, old shrivelled corms and cormels from the newly formed corms. Grade and discard damaged and diseased corms, treat with an appro-priate fungicide and return to a warm (30°C/87°F) and humid (80% RH) environment for a further 7-10 days. Besides allowing the wounded surfaces caused by the separation process to heal, this treatment will reduce the incidence of fusarium corm rot and avoid excessive drying out of the corms. After this 'curing' process, place corms in a cool (5°C/40°F) well ventilated environment until planting the following season.

Tuberous roots are underground storage organs that are effectively swollen roots. Their external and internal physiology is the same as a root's with the inability to produce adventitious buds except at the proximal end, where they typically form a 'crown'. The tuberous root develops during germination as a swelling on the emerging radicle of a seedling plant; this increases in size to form a single structure; adventitious buds are formed on its surface. Annually produced tuberous roots include *Dahlia* spp., *Dioscorea* spp., *Ipomoea batatas* and *Ranunculus asiaticus*. Swellings occur on the lateral roots arising from the crown during the growing season and may form a cluster of tuberous roots attached to a central stem. Besides ensuring the survival of the plant over the dor-mant period, such structures will provide the major source of energy for the developing shoot sys-tem during the spring. Once the food has been used up the swollen structure dies and disintegrates. New tuberous roots will be formed during the growing season to continue the cycle.

True tubers superficially resemble tuberous roots but each has an arrangement of buds over its surface and all the internal parts of a typical stem – pith, cortex and a vascular system – which a tuberous root does not. Tubers often develop from the tips of rhizomes, forming swollen starch-filled structures. A great many tubers may form from one plant, for example, in the case of the potato, *Solanum tuberosum*; their function, like that of the tuberous root, is to ensure the sur-vival of the plant over the dormant period and provide a ready source of energy for the developing shoots arising from the axillary buds during the spring. Such structures are generally formed annu-ally and disintegrate once the food reserves are depleted; new tubers are formed during the growing season. Plants that produce true tubers are few and include *Caladium* spp., *Helianthus tuberosus* (Jerusalem artichoke), *Nymphaea* spp. (waterlilies), *Solanum tuberosum* (potato), *Tropaeolum* spp. (especially *T. tuberosum*) and *Ullucus tuberosus*.

Stem tubers differ from those already described in being perennial and increasing in size each sea-son. Typical examples are *Anemone coronaria*, *Begonia* Tuberhybrida Hybrids and *Cyclamen*, all of which produce more or less circular tubers, in the latter two, regular and flattened. These produce leaf and flowers shoots from the upper side and roots which may be produced from either side or both.

Some plants produce *tubercles*, small aerial tubers located in the leaf axils and formed from the axillary buds. Tubercles are naturally formed near the end of the growing season as day lengths shorten. Examples include *Begonia grandis* ssp. *evansiana* and *Dioscorea bulbifera,* which is an unusual type of yam, the aerial tubers being eaten in preference to the root tubers. *Ceropegia linearis* ssp.*woodii,* which has swollen, tuber-like stem bases, also produces small tubers on the stems (which appear to grow right through the tubers).

Whereas bulbs, corms and tubers are single organs that remain (more or less) in one place, a *rhizome* is usually a wandering underground or soil-surface organ, often spreading widely. Structurally, it is a modified stem, swollen with stored nutrients to enable the plant to make rapid growth when conditions are favourable after a period of rest or after physical disturbance. It typically has nodes and internodes, with shoots and roots arising from the apex and from adventitious buds: as the rhizome lengthens at its apex the oldest part eventually becomes exhausted. Such structures are often clothed with remnants of enveloping leaf-bases, each defining an area of a potential bud and giving the rhizome a segmented appearance, especially at the youngest point.

Rhizomes vary in form and habit. Some plants (for instance the bearded irises of horticulture) have markedly swollen rhizomes growing on the surface of the ground, some have similar roots but growing below ground, like *Zantedeschia* and *Hedychium*. Others, such as *Anemone nemorosa,* are more slender and live below the surface. Asparagus, peony and rhubarb form 'crown' rhizomes which increase in size annually but produce very little extension growth. This contrasts with *Maianthemum* , which produces slender rhizomes with long internodes, allowing the plant to spread rapidly. Rhizome scales (modified leaves) are sometimes conspicuous, as in *Achimenes.*

GENERAL CULTURE

In the wild, most 'bulbs' grow with their shoulder from 5cm/2in. to 25cm/10in. or more below ground level as a protection from extremes of weather and marauding animals. A notable exception is *Urginea maritima,* which in its mild sea-level Mediterranean habitat can safely grow with its huge bulb exposed, protected from animal depredation by its toxicity. There are also a very few true bulbous epiphytes from the tropics, of which *Lilium arboricola* from Burma and *Hippeastrum calyptratum* from Brazil are examples. In cultivation many bulbs, such as *Lilium candidum* and even *Hyacinthoides hispanica,* are seen with the upper surface exposed. This is usually because bulbs from nutrient-poor soils in the wild respond to the richer conditions of cultivation by producing excessive basal offsets which push the mother bulb to the surface, a particularly good example being *Nerine sarniensis* which grows in nature many inches deep in impoverished soil. For different reasons, *Cyclamen* tubers, so far below soil level in the wild, bring themselves to the surface in cultivation. Conversely, the tubers of *Arum* usually sink. Other deep-growing tubers, as in some *Corydalis* spp., may be planted at any convenient depth.

Popular horticultural bulbs (daffodils, tulips, hyacinths, crocuses, etc.) can be planted in the open ground in the autumn, at a depth of twice the height of the bulb, and then left to look after themselves. Many *Lilium* spp. and hybrids (especially those that are stem-rooting), some *Fritillaria* spp. (especially *F. imperialis* and its cultivars) and certain amaryllids *(Pancratium illyricum, P.maritimum* and *Amaryllis belladonna* are examples) require deep planting to 15cm/6in. over the top of the bulb, the lilies requiring very rich soil. Rich, well drained soil is appreciated by most bulbs, as is an autumn mulch with garden compost or leafmould. Animal manure should be avoided or only used when very well rotted. It is of the greatest importance when tidying in the garden not to remove bulb foliage until it begins to die back naturally, likewise to keep container-grown bulbs in growth until natural dieback starts.

When horticultural bulbs are grown in pots or bowls for indoor decoration, they should be planted with the nose above soil level. Standard soilless composts may be used unless it is the intention to keep the bulbs in top condition for future years, in which case grow them in free-draining containers in a richer mixture. *Lilium* must always be planted with the top of the bulb below the surface of the soil in deep containers. The grower of more specialized bulbs will generally be giving the collection a degree of protection appropriate to the geographical situation. This may take the form of planting direct into a bulb frame or glasshouse border, or in containers which are best plunged in sand on the greenhouse staging or in the frame. Whether the containers are of clay or plastic depends upon the preferences and requirements of the owner, who must bear in mind that the soil in clay pots dries out more quickly so that the roots are drawn to the damper areas adjacent to the clay. With plastic pots, soil is in greater danger of becoming waterlogged, but a relatively smaller pot may be used since the root spread is more even.

There are two basic types of potting medium. Type 'A' is a high-fertility loam-based medium, like John Innes No.3, which can be varied according to the individual grower's preferences as much as to the plant's requirements. The medium may be given extra porosity by the addition of leafmould, sharp grit/sand or one of the numerous varieties of plastic or clay pellets. A general slow-release fertilizer with trace elements may be helpful, especially for Amaryllidaceae. Type 'B' is usually soilless and will usually involve peat or a peat substitute. The soilless mixtures are either general-purpose with a near-neutral pH level, or they are made up to be 'ericaceous', i.e. with a low pH. Although soilless mixes are generally enriched, it is often advisable to add a long-acting fertilizer with trace elements. Annual repotting is advisable when soilless mixtures are used, but in any case particular attention must be given to regular feeding if bulbs are to go for more than a year without repotting.

For bulbs outside the usual horticultural range, the grower must have a good knowledge of the plant's origin and of its conditions in the wild – it is usually helpful to match cultural requirements with habitat types and geographical range. Allowances must be made for the more equable climate of other parts of the world's temperate zones, where many bulbs considered difficult in Britain and the US may thrive (a tantalizing example is *Lycoris*), whereas *Galanthus* and many *Narcissus* may be difficult away from Europe. In much of Northeast America the more tender bulbs may not survive in the open.

Group 1. Mediterranean area, West and Central Asia and California. Bulbs from these areas experience a cool, moist winter, when growth takes place, followed by dormancy during a hot and dry summer, so planting should be done in the autumn. Even if there is little or no top growth during the winter, their roots are active and must be kept watered. Flowering takes place from the autumn (sometimes before the leaves appear) through to late spring. For pot-grown plants the often advocated 'baking' in hot sun during summer dormancy should be treated with caution: this applies especially to plants with roots that do not die off, such as *Muscari*, *Iris* subgenus *Scorpiris*, *Cyclamen graecum*, when the roots cannot reach the deeper and more sheltered soil levels where they would penetrate in the wild. It should be noted that certain high-altitude plants (for instance the rhizomatous Oncocyclus irises) may start into growth with the first autumn rains and then go into 'green dormancy' under the winter's snow – a regime difficult to simulate in cultivation, although Dutch commercial growers have succeeded in adjusting the date of initiation of autumn growth until later in the season and then allowing growth to continue unchecked. There are also problems with some snow-melt plants such as *Fritillaria alburyana:* these grow and flower very rapidly as the snow cover melts. Potting medium 'A' suits most of the bulbs in Group 1, which includes such important genera as *Calochortus, Colchicum, Crocus, Fritillaria, Narcissus, Scilla, Sternbergia, Tulipa* and many others.

Group 2. Temperate woodlanders, especially those from Japan and North America, but also including Himalayan and Chinese spp. The growth cycle for these is very much the same as for the last group, but cooler and damper conditions are required during the summer. The aim is dappled shade in a site where the plants will not be dried out by the sun and where tree roots will prevent waterlogging of the soil. Neutral to acid soil is essential for many of the North American and Japanese spp., including *Lilium* and the rhizomatous *Trillium.* Those from the Himalayas and China, including some *Arisaema, Fritillaria* and *Lilium,* often thrive even in a limy soil. Mulching with leafmould or bark chippings helps to maintain the right conditions while suppressing the surrounding vegetation in the wild garden or woodland. For container-grown plants attention must be given to adequate shading.

Group 3. Bulbs from the winter rainfall areas of the Cape Province, South Africa, the world's richest bulbous flora. Many species are confined in the wild to a very few localities and sometimes to only one site: many are seriously endangered. Limited populations of new species even from such conspicuous and well known genera as *Gladiolus* and *Moraea* are still being discovered, and are immediately in danger of extinction. A good knowledge of their requirements is essential in order to maintain safe populations of these endangered plants in cultivation throughout the world.

Growth occurs during the cool, wet, winter months, with flowering in the spring, although a few may flower in the autumn before their leaves emerge. Flowering is much influenced in the wild by climatic factors, including natural fires. The soils are often on the acid side and usually poor in nutrients, especially nitrates. In the northern hemisphere these plants must be brought into 'phase' for the reversed seasons. This is easy with seeds, which should be planted in late summer or early autumn. Bulbs and corms, which are usually received from nurseries when growth is starting during the northern spring, should be kept growing in a cool, shady place until growth dies down. It is then essential to allow 4–8 weeks dormancy in a warm, dry spot before bringing them into growth for the ensuing winter. For established plants, winter watering should start in late summer. In non-Mediterranean temperate climates only a few (*Gladiolus, Nerine, Romulea, Schizostylis*) are reliably hardy or robust enough to withstand the winter (their growing season) without protection, but they make superb plants for the nearly frost-free greenhouse. In many temperate regions of the southern hemisphere South African bulbs are important plants for the open garden, indeed some (including *Watsonia*) have naturalized in parts of Australia.

Composts of type 'B' (ericaceous mix) suit almost the entire range, with added sharp grit or sand. Growers in their native South Africa like to use river sand over 5–7cm/2–3in. of a peaty mix at the bottom of the pot. Plastic pots are suitable, and most genera may be crowded in a pot to give a good display. Watering must be generous during the growing season, but allow pots to become fairly dry between waterings. During summer dormancy the bulbs may be left in their containers in a warm, dry place, or lifted for storage, in which case a fungicidal dust should be applied.

Among so many genera, mention can be made of only a small selection, including the amaryllidaceous *Boophone, Brunsvigia, Cyrtanthus, Gethyllis, Haemanthus, Nerine, Scadoxus;* the iridaceous *Babiana, Ferraria, Freesia, Geissorhiza, Gladiolus, Hesperantha, Homeria, Ixia, Lapeirousia, Moraea, Romulea, Sparaxis, Synnotia, Syringodea, Tritonia;* the liliaceous *Lachenalia, Massonia, Ornithogalum.* The many splendid *Watsonia* spp. prefer open ground in a neutral to acid soil, and in any case are often too large for growing in containers.

Group 4. Bulbs from the spring or summer rainfall areas of southern and central Africa, Madagascar and Mexico. The best-known examples of this disparate group are the large-flowered *Gladiolus* hybrids of horticulture and *Tigridia pavonia.* These require plenty of water coupled with (for the more northerly spp. from South Africa) night temperatures not below 16–21°C/60–70°F during their late summer growing season. Hardiness varies according to the exact place of origin, but as in the last group, most will need to be lifted for winter dormancy in eastern North America and non-Mediterranean Europe. Stringent precautions must be taken against fungal rot during dormancy: storage must be in dry, airy conditions and the bulbs should be treated with a fungicidal powder. Iridaceae from Mexico, the Transvaal and Malawi, and Mexican Liliaceae, can be difficult in cool-temperate areas like Britain where they often start growth too late in the summer and require extra warmth in the late autumn. The amaryllids are easier. Compost type 'A' is usually suitable, but some subjects require a neutral to acid pH. This geographical group includes many spectacular or intricately beautiful subjects, including the smaller tigridias (best as potplants), *Rigidella* spp. (intolerant of container treatment), *Milla* spp., *Sprekelia,* the charming little *Rhodohypoxis* and the moraeas and gladioli of Malawi and the Transvaal.

Group 5. Bulbs from the temperate regions of South America, including the high Andes. Most of these come into growth in the early spring for spring or summer, flowering after dormancy during the late summer and winter. 'Phasing' is sometimes difficult in the northern hemisphere, and the lowland South Americans will often come into growth at unexpected times. The Amaryllids require a rich medium using compost type 'A' with added garden compost or well rotted manure. They must be kept growing in full sun, with plenty of water during the summer months, and should be allowed to dry out in a sunny place before being stored for dormancy. This regime is also applicable to the horticultural 'amaryllis' hybrids (*Hippeastrum*) sold for Christmas flowering. For these there should be a resting period of at least three months before they are brought into growth in early December. The Iridaceae and Liliaceae require a lighter and grittier mixture, some of the latter (*Tristagma*) preferring deep planting in a long tom. This broad cultural group includes many fine genera of Amaryllidaceae, Iridaceae and Liliaceae, such as *Alstroemeria, Bomarea, Cipura, Conanthera, Cypella, Hippeastrum, Leucocoryne, Phaedranassa, Polianthes, Stenomesson, Tristagma* and *Zephyranthes,* and above all, that gem among bulbs, the cobalt blue *Tecophilaea.*

Group 6. The tropical zones, Australia, the coastal mist zones of western South America, and bulbs from other highly specialized habitats. Requirements are too varied and individual to be covered in a general article, and are dealt with in detail under generic headings. In attempting to grow these specialized plants outside their own climatic zones, as much attention must be paid to the atmosphere as is given to the soil. For mist-zone bulbs, and for some species of the dry-zone rhizomatous genera (*Anigozanthos* for example), air conditioning may be necessary under glass. A few species (of *Cypella* and *Neomarica,* for example) may be aquatic. The tropical group includes many good Amaryllids such as *Haemanthus, Hippeastrum, Scadoxus* and *Zephyranthes,* as well as Iridaceae such as *Dietes.* Many genera from more temperate regions have outliers in the tropics, while essentially tropical genera such as *Crinum* have certain species which can be grown outside even in northern temperate zones.

PROPAGATION

For the species (as opposed to hybrids and named cultivars, where progeny rarely comes true), it is important to grow fresh plants from seed, at least from time to time. If this is not done, cultivated stocks may become diseased or lose vigour over the years or even become reluctant to set seed: long-standing commercial stocks of *Sprekelia* , for example, are well known for their apparent inability to set seed whereas recently introduced stocks of *Sprekelia* (grown from wild seed) set viable seed freely. Virus infection can usually be eliminated from infected stocks of the species by growing them from seed. Other bulbs (for instance the smaller *Tigridia* spp.) are not long-lived in cultivation and seed should be sown as often as possible. It is generally best to sow seed as soon as it is ripe. For many (*Cyclamen* and the aril-seeded irises especially) this greatly increases the germination rate, and for many others (*Cyrtanthus* and fleshy-seeded Amaryllids such as *Nerine* and *Scadoxus*) it is essential.

Most seed can be expected to produce a leaf in the first season after planting, but certain lilies may form only a bulblet and a root during the first season. Others, such as the aril-seeded irises, may lie dormant in the soil for many years before germination, especially if the seed is not fresh. Seed should not be sown too thickly since it is often advisable to retain seedlings in their original pot for two years or more. Most bulbs can be expected to take around four or five years from seed sowing to flowering, but there are many on either side of this range. The sowing medium is similar to that used for mature bulbs but should be kept more open with added grit: a top dressing with sharp sand or grit discourages liverworts and damping off as well as slugs and snails.

Cultivars are increased clonally. Vegetative propagation is in any case a faster method for almost all bulbs than growing from seed.

(a) *Bulbs.* Natural offsets are produced from the basal plate, but the rate of increase can be artificially enhanced. *Fritillaria,* whether two-scaled or with rice grains, and bulbs with loose scales such as *Lilium,* can easily be propagated by picking off individual scales, treating the raw surface with a fungicide, either by soaking or dusting (methylated spirit is useful because it also dries the cut surface) and then plunging the scales in damp sand. After a few weeks each scale should produce a small bulb at its base. Autumn is the best time for this operation – use fresh, plump bulbs. The outer scale leaves are simply snapped away from the bulb which can be assisted by making a shallow cut with a sharp knife close to the basal plate. Insert scale leaves upright into a shallow container of a suitable rooting compost, or vermiculite, with the tips of the scales just showing above the medium, and seal with thin plastic film (30 micron). Thin film is important to ensure permeation of oxygen. Place the container in a protected environment at a temperature of 20–25°C/68–77°F. Bulblets are formed at the base of the scale leaves in about 4–8 weeks, the species varying considerably. Alternatively, the scale leaves may be placed in a thin (30 micron) polythene bag containing moist vermiculite (5 volumes of dry medium to 1 volume of water), filled with air, securely tied and incubated at 20–25°C/68–77°F. After bulblets form they are hardened off, sieved from the vermiculite and grown on.

This method is similar to that used by commercial growers for the wholesale production of clones of daffodils, hyacinths, etc., where the basal plate is cut into small sections, by bulb-chipping and twin-scaling.

Chipping is a process for rapid increase – suitable for bulbs that produce tightly packed scale leaves surrounding the central growing point and are slow to produce offsets naturally; for example, *Galanthus* has recently been successfully chipped. Clean bulbs are selected between midsummer and autumn: using a sharp, thin-bladed knife, cut the bulb vertically through the centre of the base plate making two equal-sized pieces. Each piece is then subdivided, ensuring that each piece or chip retains a portion of the basal plate. Up to 16 chips may be obtained from one bulb. The chips are treated with fungicide, preferably a liquid preparation ensuring adequate penetration between the scale leaves. Once the chips have been allowed to drain (5–10 minutes) they can be placed in a thin (30 micron) polythene bag containing moist vermiculite or perlag (1 part chips to 2 parts vermiculite or perlag). To avoid virus transmission, the knife should be sterilized between dealing with each bulb. Alternatively, the chips may be placed in stratified layers up to a depth of 150mm/6in. in a tray using a suitable medium such as pine sawdust, perlite or vermiculite. Ensure that the final layer of chips is topped off with the selected material. If the combined layers are too deep, overheating may occur. Seal the tray with thin (30 micron) plastic film, allowing a generous air gap above the medium to provide the chips with adequate gaseous exchange for subsequent development. Trays or bags containing the chips are ready to be placed into a dark, warm (20°C/68°F) environment, allowing about 12 weeks for the bulblets to develop; check for rotting at regular intervals, then harden off and grow on out of doors directly in the soil. Bulbs raised in this way take three to four years to reach flowering size.

Twin-scaling is similar to chipping but increased bulb production is achieved by subdividing the chipped segments. Because of the diminutive size of these divisions, greater precautions must be taken against fungal infection: aseptic techniques are therefore strongly advised.

Bulbs such as *Narcissus* are lifted between midsummer and late summer, graded for size and quality, cleaned and assessed for virus and pest infection. Single-nosed round bulbs are the easiest to cut. Before segmenting, the bulbs are further prepared by cutting the crust off the basal plate to reveal clean tissue, and removing and discarding the nose end to give the bulb a flat top, stripping away the outer brown scales and, finally, surface-sterilizing the bulbs by swabbing with industrial spirit. Using a sterilized work surface such as a piece of glass and a scalpel (sterilized after each bulb), the bulb is then cut lengthways into 6–16 segments depending upon size, for instance 8 segments for 12–14cm bulbs. Each segment is subdivided by carefully separating the top of two scale leaves, following the division down to the base and using a sterilized scalpel cut through the basal plate, thus giving two joined scales. The same procedure is followed with the remaining scales, taking care not to break away the basal plate tissue from the scale leaves. It is easiest to work from the outside scale leaves inwards. From a bulb cut into eight segments, between 32 and 40 twin-scales can be obtained, the outer and middle twin-scales having the greatest capacity to produce bulblets. Treat twin-scales with fungicide and drain off for 5–10 minutes. Carefully place into thin (30 micron) polythene bags containing moist vermiculite (8 volumes of distilled water to 100 volumes of dry vermiculite) and seal the bags, leaving a generous air gap. The bags containing the twin-scales are placed into a dark, warm (20°C/68°F) environment. Allow about 12 weeks for the bulblets to form, checking at regular intervals. Bulblets should be hardened off for about 55 days and planted out under a cool, well ventilated but frost-free environment; they take 3–4 years to reach flowering size. Both chipping and twin-scaling may be carried out successfully with a range of bulbous plants including *Hippeastrum, Hyacinthus* and *Nerine*.

Scooping and *scoring* are both techniques used to induce rapid multiplication of some bulb species, especially those that are slow in forming bulblets like *Hyacinthus*.

Scooping involves removing the basal plate and destroying the central shoot of the bulb, thus encouraging the formation of bulblets round the cut edges of the scale leaves. Scooping is achieved by using a special knife or a spoon with a sharpened edge to leave a concave depression at the base of the bulb. Because the bulblets are formed on cell tissue at the lowest point of the scale leaves, the depth of cut is important. If the cut is too deep, the basal cells responsible for meristem development will be removed resulting in poor bulblet formation. If the basal plate is not adequately removed it will inhibit bulblet formation.

The sequence of satisfactory bulblet formation is as follows. From mid- to later summer the stock bulbs are dried off, lifted, graded for size and quality, cleaned, and assessed for virus contamination (i.e. grey-looking bulbs). In later summer, selected healthy bulbs 8–12cm in diameter are scooped, treated with fungicide and placed upside-down supported on dry sand or in a wire mesh tray with the leaf bases fully exposed. A dry warm environment at 25°C/77°F for about seven days will encourage the leaf bases to callus over, after which the relative humidity should be increased to about 90% to prevent excessive desiccation of the bulbs, keeping the temperature at 25°C/77°F. After 12–14 weeks, bulblets will be visible at the base of the scale leaves. In very early winter, bulbs should be hardened off and planted, preferably in a cool protected environment and kept upside-down so that the bulblets are just below the surface of the planting medium. During the following spring the bulblets will produce leaves and develop further in size, leaving the original bulb to disintegrate. In late summer, when the foliage of the bulblets has died down, they should be lifted, separated and re-planted individually, to take 3–4 years to reach flowering size.

Scoring is almost identical to scooping, except for the preparation of the base of the bulb. Scoring is generally used on large-diameter bulbs (16–20cm) where scooping is difficult. The base of the bulb is prepared by making 2 or 3 incisions through the base plate, sufficiently deep to destroy the central growing shoot and induce the dormant axillary buds to sprout. Proliferation of the bulblets from the base of the scale leaves is far less generous than with scooping but their subsequent growth rate is greater, reducing the time needed to reach flowering size to 2–3 years.

Other bulbous plants that may be encouraged to regenerate by either scooping or scoring include *Albuca, Galanthus, Haemanthus, Hippeastrum, Lachenalia, Leucojum, Muscari, Narcissus, Nerine, Scilla, Sprekelia* and *Urceolina*.

Offsets. Tunicate bulbs may be vegetatively reproduced by removing the offsets and growing them on in suitable containers in close nursery rows for a period of 1–3 years until they have reached flowering size (as for bulblet production from leaf scales above). Scaly bulbs such as lilies may also be vegetatively reproduced by offsets, which are grown on in containers or lined out in open ground.

Bulbils and bulblets. Certain bulbous plants have the capacity of producing miniature bulbs either on aerial stems or below the soil level. The term bulbil is normally applied to those structures that are formed above ground, often on the stems of lilies and sometimes in the flowerhead, whereas in certain alliums the bulbils can replace flowers. Although bulbil development is a natural phenomenon on certain plants such as *Lilium bulbiferum, L. lancifolium* and *L.sargentiae*, others can be manipulated by simply removing the flowerhead just before flowering; bulbils will form in the leaf axils during the remainder of the growing seasons. Such lilies include *Lilium candidum, L. chalcedonicum, L. dauricum, L. × hollandicum, L. leichtlinii, L. × maculatum* and *L.× testaceum*. When the bulbils are mature (late summer-autumn), they may be gathered from the stems (this must be done before they drop naturally) and set in containers filled with an appropriate growing medium. They should finally be covered with fine crushed grit, labelled and placed in a cool protected environment such as a cold frame. Plants may take between two and three years to reach flowering size.

Another method of producing miniature bulbs on lily stems is to pull out the flowering stem carefully just before the flowers open, using a twisting motion and leaving the bulb below the soil. Pinch out the flower, apply fungicide to the stem, lay it in a shallow trench at 45° and back-fill with an open medium such as 50:50 coir and finely crushed grit. Bulblets will form in the leaf axils. By the following summer they may be lifted and replanted close together in containers or nursery rows. Bulblets may reach flowering size in 2–4 years.

Bulbils are sometimes produced in the flower heads; in such cases they must not be confused with the fleshy seeds of such genera as *Nerine* which sometimes germinate before dropping.

Corms. Corms increase by producing more than one new corm from the top of the old corm, sometimes (as with several South African Iridaceae) at the end of a long stolon. In genera such as

Gladiolus tiny cormlets (cormels) may be produced in prodigious numbers or the bulb may be entirely replaced by tiny bulbs, as too often happens with *Iris danfordiae*. They are most readily increased from the cormlets, which take 2–4 years to reach flowering size. Production can be induced by adjusting the planting depth of the corm. In most cases, it appears that shallow planting of the corm (2–5cm/1.5–2in.) stimulates cormel production.

Lift corms at the appropriate time, warm treat (30°C/85°F) for 12 hours to allow easier separation of cormels from the corm, grade and apply a suitable fungicide. Mix cormels in a moist sterile medium such as vermiculite, place in a plastic bag allowing a generous air-filled gap, seal and store in a cool (5°C/40°F) environment until ready for planting. This will prevent the cormels becoming dry and hard, which would result in slow growth the following spring. Cormels that have been allowed to become dry and hard should be pre-treated before planting by soaking them for 24 hours in warm (20°C/68°F) water, changing it about three times to prevent the water becoming anaerobic. Drain off, place cormels in a moist, clean medium and store in a cool (5°C/40°F) environment. Plant them out when root growth is visible.

Plant cormels in rows close together in spring, encourage active growth, lift at the appropriate time when foliage has died down, grade the newly formed corms and store ready for planting the following spring. At the end of the second season most of the newly formed corms should be of sufficient size to flower the following season.

Large, healthy corms may also be multiplied by division, by cutting them into sections. This should be carried out as near planting time as possible, ensuring that each piece possesses at least one developing bud. Apply an appropriate fungicide to each division, and place in a warm (30°C/85°F), ventilated environment for approximately 48 hours to allow the cut surfaces to heal, then replant. New full-sized corms may develop at the end of the growing season and be suitable for flowering the following year.

Tuberous roots. To increase tuberous-rooted plants such as dahlias, it is essential that each tuberous root should possess at least one crown bud. The crowns are lifted at the end of the growing season, washed clean of soil and allowed to dry off for a few days. Store in a dry material such as sawdust and place in a frost-free environment to prevent desiccation. Towards the end of the dormant season, the crown buds will be well developed, indicating the most suitable areas to divide the crown, each tuberous root with at least one strong bud. Apply fungicide to each division and before planting allow the cut surfaces to 'dry off' by storing them for 24 hours in a dry, warm environment (15–20°C/66–68°F). This will encourage a corky layer of tissue to form, greatly reducing the risk of rotting. Grow on the divisions in a frost-free environment, keeping the growing medium on the dry side until shoot growth is well developed, when watering should be increased.

Tubers. For single tubers with two or more 'eyes', such as *Begonia* Tuberhybrida Hybrids, *Cyclamen* and some *Tropaeolum* spp., propagation is possible (but often difficult) by division with a sharp knife followed by hardening and fungicidal treatment with methylated spirit or green sulphur. Large tubers which carry several growths should be used – division should not be attempted until these are apparent – and can be cut up into a limited number of sections (four at most), also bearing roots. They should if possible contain more than one bud or 'eye' and be of adequate size to ensure that the new plant can develop. Cut surfaces should be dusted with charcoal or sulphur dust, with a dust-for-mulated fungicide. The cuts should be allowed to dry completely before potting is carried out.

Rhizomes. Plants that produce rhizomes can be propagated by division. Crown-forming rhizomes may be treated in a similar way to herbaceous plants with fleshy crowns. Lift crowns in late winter as crown buds begin to develop, wash off soil and divide using a sharp spade or large knife, making sure that each piece is of adequate size and has at least one well developed bud, and replant. Further increase is possible by placing the lifted crowns under a cool protected environment, plunged in an open moist medium. This will encourage more crown buds to develop. By spring time, crowns may be divided into small pieces each with a visible bud; treat with fungicide and place in a warm (20°C/68°F) humid environment (80% RH) for 24 hours to heal the cut surfaces. Pot up using a well drained mixture and grow on in a cool protected environment.

Pogon irises may be easily divided immediately after flowering in summer. Carefully lift the clumps, wash off surplus soil and break or cut off the young lateral sections from the point of

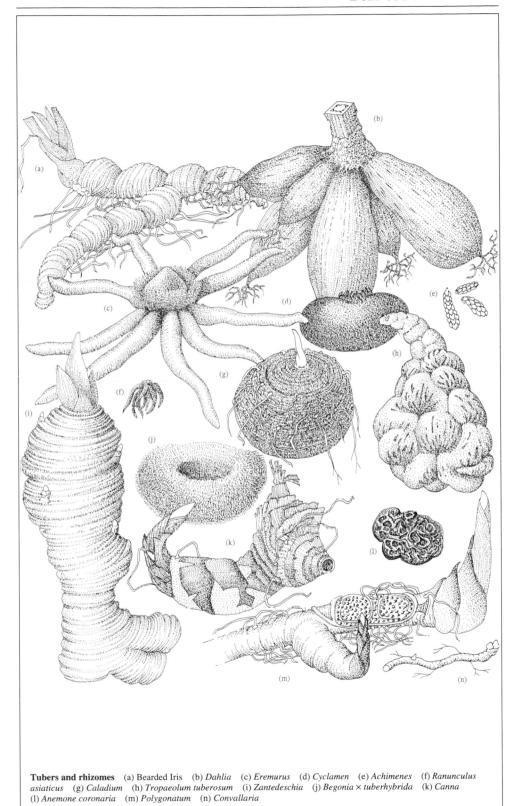

Tubers and rhizomes (a) Bearded Iris (b) *Dahlia* (c) *Eremurus* (d) *Cyclamen* (e) *Achimenes* (f) *Ranunculus asiaticus* (g) *Caladium* (h) *Tropaeolum tuberosum* (i) *Zantedeschia* (j) *Begonia × tuberhybrida* (k) *Canna* (l) *Anemone coronaria* (m) *Polygonatum* (n) *Convallaria*

attachment to the old rhizomes (which should be discarded). Trim back the old roots of the young sections and shorten the shoot growth by half to reduce water loss, then replant. To increase cultivars of pogon irises rapidly, the young lateral sections may be carefully 'diced'. Cut the rhizome vertically into sections with a sharp knife, making sure that each cut is made at the back of the remnant leaf-bases along the rhizome. Each segment should have at least one primordial axillary bud. Treat with an appropriate fungicide, place in a warm (20°C/68°F) humid environment (80% RH) for 24 hours to heal the cut surfaces, space out the segments in a shallow container (55–75mm/2–3in. deep) filled with an open moist medium and cover them with this. Cover the container with a piece of glass and place in a frame or propagator maintained at 10°C/50°F. By spring, root and shoot growth should be evident; pot up and grow on under a cool protected environment.

PESTS AND DISEASES

Virus diseases can be detected by mottling, streaking and sometimes deformities of the leaves and flowers. Occasionally these are considered desirable (as in the old 'broken' tulips) but usually viruses lead to a progressive and grave weakening of the stock. Unfortunately, there are heavily infected commercial and amateur stocks of Oncocyclus irises and *Muscari* in wide circulation. While the original host may be able to coexist reasonably well with the virus, the infection can all too easily be passed to a more susceptible host, which may be killed or become useless. Virus is spread by any leaf-biting or -sucking insect. There is no cure. Prevention is by burning all affected plants and the rigorous exclusion of insect attack by regular spraying. Cuttings and offsets from infected plants are also infected, but meristem material and seeds are usually free from disease.

Fungus infections are a major affliction. If not kept completely dry during storage, bulbs (and especially corms) are liable to a variety of fungal rots. Suitably dry storage conditions, at the appropriate temperature and the removal of earth and decayed outer bulb scales, are the most important safeguards, but dusting with a fungicidal powder may be advisable for valuable stocks or when the conditions are doubtful. Among the numerous fungal infections affecting bulbs and corms during the growing period, the most serious are those which are nearly specific to certain groups, such as ink disease of Reticulata irises. Infected bulbs must be destroyed. The most important measure is to plant 'clean' bulbs which have been treated during dormancy with a fungicidal powder or soaked when dry in a weak solution of formalin (1:300 for two hours). Fungal infections of the leaf are manifest in rusts and numerous disfiguring black and grey moulds – the most important preventive factor here is a dry, buoyant atmosphere. Systemic fungicides are helpful in some cases, but for individual and more precious plants kept under glass heavy dusting with a fungicidal powder may be more helpful.

Mites. Red spider mite (*Tetranychus telarius*) *is* one of the most damaging and difficult pests to eradicate from a hot and crowded glasshouse. An early sign is pallor, followed by fine webbing overlying leaves which develop a red-brown discolouration. Weak plants very soon have their leaves sucked dry and the bulb is weakened. Even ruthless cleaning and disinfection of an empty glasshouse rarely leads to total eradication of the pest. Regular spraying with lime sulphur was the most effective remedy, but this has been superseded. Immunity rapidly develops to systemic insecticides. The predator mite *Phytoseiulus* gives more effective control under commercial glass than in an amateur's small house. Bulb scale mite (*Tarsonemus laticeps*) manifests its presence by red streaking of the scales of dormant bulbs, followed by red streaking and blotching of the leaves. Flower stalks may be so badly affected that they can be rudimentary, or bent over at a 90° angle. Fortunately, eradication is simple, by immersing the bulb in water at a constant temperature of 44°C/110°F for one hour.

Insects. The lily beetle (*Lilioceris lilii*) has conspicuous scarlet-red adults up to 0.6cm long, with red-yellow, hump-backed larvae that cover themselves with a slimy black secretion when feeding, along with the adults, on the foliage of lilies and fritillaries. Fast becoming a widespread pest, it will quickly defoliate plants and devour emerging shoots and flowerbuds. Control with a residual contact insecticide or, where infestations are light, by picking off the adult pests by hand and blasting the larvae with a hose.

Root and shoot mealybugs of the family Coccidae feed on the roots and young shoots of (mainly) Amaryllidaceae. Besides badly weakening the plant, severe damage is done to the young leaves, scapes and flower buds. The most effective remedy is to immerse the whole plant for 12 hours in a bucket of insecticide solution. This treatment may have to be repeated, and care must be taken not to expose the leaves to sunshine until 48 hours after treatment, but persistence in eradicating this pest is worthwhile. Aphids can easily be killed by the use of insecticidal sprays.

Narcissus fly (*Merodon equestris*) attacks many genera of Amaryllidaceae and is a major pest of *Narcissus.* The adult is a large dipterous fly, usually brown with a lighter abdominal band. The eggs are laid singly in early summer beside the decaying foliage, along which the young maggot proceeds downwards. entering the bulb via the basal plate. There is total destruction of the centre of the bulb, though the stock can usually be saved from small offsets which develop from the basal plate. Bulb flies of the genus *Eumerus* are considerably smaller. They have at least two broods in the year (*Merodon* is single-brooded), laying many eggs above each bulb which consequently has a multiple infestation. For a general bulb collection out of doors it can help to remove the foliage as soon as it begins to yellow, at the same time raking or tamping down the soil to make the bulbs less obvious to the pests. Special bulbs can be heavily dusted with an insecticide powder. Netting may have to be used for glasshouses and frames during the egg-laying period.

Gastropods. Slugs can be a nuisance, sometimes eating out even a deeply planted bulb, and both slugs and snails can do immense damage to young foliage, scapes and flowers, but good control can now be obtained from the modern long-lasting molluscicides.

Nematodes. Eelworms are microscopic worms, bulb eelworms being subspecies of *Ditylenchus dipsaci,* with considerable host specificity. Dormant forms can remain in the soil for at least three years. They are, perhaps, more saprophytic than parasitic for horticultural bulbs, making their entry through already damaged tissues, but the *Narcissus* form may cause considerable damage. The main defence is good hygiene, removing all bulbs when a patch of land is cleared. If there is heavy infestation the stock should be destroyed and the land left fallow or put to other uses for at least three years.

Vertebrates. Some mammals (from baboons to badgers) are not much more than localized hazards, but deer delight in tulips, squirrels have an unerring nose for a bulb and mice can devastate a collection of crocuses. Exclusion or even trapping may have to be used.

FORCING AND EARLY FLOWERING

Because bulbs contain large quantities of stored food materials, it is possible to produce flowers out of season, largely and often entirely, at the expense of these reserves. This is particularly true for the spring-flowering bulbs, such as daffodils, tulips and hyacinths, whose vegetative parts die down in summer and whose bulbs then appear dormant until they have experienced sufficient cold to allow regrowth in the spring. In general, it is necessary to satisfy artificially a long cold requirement, which the bulbs normally experience during the winter months, after which progress to flowering can be rapid if temperatures are sufficiently high. Forcing of these plants can be regarded as a speeding-up of the natural cycle which the plants experience outdoors to allow flowering earlier than normal.

The normal post-flowering cycle of successive periods of warm–cool–warm, which occurs in summer–winter–spring, is applied to the bulbs and the growing plants by artificial means, with some shortening of the natural durations, an early start of the cool period, and a much earlier start of the final warm period leading to flowering. While much of forcing can be achieved by the gardener with unsophisticated facilities, the commercial forcers have developed fine programming of flowering dates by the use of accurate temperature-controlled stores and complex temperature schedules to provide a long sequence of flowering dates and an unbroken supply of cut or pot flowers for the market.

There is a second group of plants with bulbs, corms or other storage organs which either have no low-temperature requirement for breaking dormancy or for flowering, which can be forced at above-ambient temperatures, often out-of-season, without pretreatment or with a minimum treatment that does not involve the provision of low temperatures to the growing plant, after planting.

The recognition of the possibilities of forcing flower bulbs is credited to the Dutch grower Nicolaas Dames in about 1907 although there was a natural method of forcing hyacinths and tulips in use in the 18th century involving the moving of boxed bulbs into protected areas towards the end of winter to flower early. Dames's ideas about the early lifting of hyacinth bulbs and storing them under artificial conditions (a high temperature for about five weeks, followed by a lower temperature) led to their flowering by Christmas, and he is commemorated for this pioneering work by a bust in the garden of the Laboratory for Flower Bulb Research, Lisse, the Netherlands. This technical advance led to further investigations aimed at achieving earliness of flowering of other bulb plants, notably by Blaauw at Wageningen and van Slogteren at Lisse in the early 1930s, and their work soon showed the importance for tulips and daffodils of an extended period of low temperature before flowering could occur. Much of the enormous bulb export industry developed in the Netherlands, and to a much lesser extent in the UK, is based upon the requirements of bulbs for forcing.

In its simplest form, early flowering of daffodils, tulips and hyacinths is readily achieved by bringing into the greenhouse or the home pots of bulbs which have been kept outdoors, but with no other treatment, somewhat in advance of their natural outdoor flowering period. The extra warmth hastens development to provide early flowers. Experience has shown that if this is done too early, flowering will be marred by slow growth, short stems and irregular, unsynchronized flowering. It is recommended that the plants are not brought indoors until the flower bud is above the neck of the bulb. A few other points also need attention at this time: it is unwise to bring in frozen pots because of the risk of damage, and it is prudent to leave the pots in a cool spot for the first few days to avoid too great a shock before they are left in a warm room to flower.

Somewhat more sophisticated is an early planting of bulbs in the autumn, with some attempt to keep them cool in a plunge bed under straw or ashes, watered if necessary for cooling by evaporation. This starts the cooling period earlier, so the plants are ready to bring indoors sooner. With hyacinths it is also possible to buy specially treated bulbs, called 'prepared' bulbs – this allows flowering of some cultivars as early as Christmas.

For optimum control of flowering date, it is necessary to understand the bulb plant's periodicity and the timing of its flower initiation, factors which differ for the different species. It is probably easiest to start with the tulip.

TULIP. *Warm storage.* In the field or garden, tulip foliage dies down in June-July, and the bulbs can then be lifted. At this time the apical meristem within the bulb is producing leaves. Three or four leaves are formed, and these are followed by the formation of the floral parts. At normal temperatures the completion of flower formation occurs by late summer (mid- to late August), depending upon situation, season and cultivar, and this point of development (called Stage G) marks the time at which the artificial cold treatment can be started. It is determined by dissecting a sample of bulbs: if ready, the newly developed ovary can be seen under a hand lens like a small three-bladed ship's propeller. For the very earliest flowering, Stage G can be made to occur about a week earlier by lifting the bulbs somewhat before the time of leaf die-down, before the outer bulb skin has turned brown, and storing the bulbs, after cleaning and grading, at a temperature of 34°C/ 93°F for seven days then at 20°C/68°F until Stage G. This takes 96 weeks. This high-temperature period is often called 'curing, or 'heat curing', and it appears particularly beneficial for many species tulips. It mimics the hot, dry conditions in the original habitats of these plants.

Bulbs not required for such early forcing can be kept from lifting until Stage G at 20°C/68°F, the optimum temperature for this period of development. The largest bulbs are used for the earliest forcing, these are grades 12/13cm. For mid-season 11/12cm bulbs are used, while for late forcing 10/11cm bulbs of most cultivars are adequate.

At planting, the bulbs can be given a final health check, it being important to discard any which show signs of infection such as external discoloration, cuts or bruises caused during lifting, or any which feel soft. It is also a good precautionary measure to dust bulbs at planting with a general fungicide, if this was not done earlier, after cleaning and grading. Bulbs should not be pushed hard into the growing medium because pressure on the root plate can damage the bulb and injure the root tips which might lie just under the surface. A too compacted layer of soil under the bulb delays good rooting.

Cold treatment. A week at 17C/63°F is often given before the start of low temperature, as it improves flower quality of some cultivars, such as 'Christmas Marvel', 'Merry Widow, and 'Most Miles'. The temperature applied depends on the subsequent forcing date and method. If outdoor temperatures are used, it is necessary to store bulbs at 9°C/48°F for six weeks before they are planted, because outside temperatures are usually above this until the first week in October. Care must be taken to control the relative humidity in the store at 70–75% to prevent root development, and to ensure good air circulation. It is particularly important for tulips not to be exposed to ethylene while in store, because this causes severe damage to the developing flower. After planting, the containers and bulbs can either be returned to the cool store at the same temperature (called 'double cooling'), or be stacked on pallets outside or left on an outdoor standing ground. The cool store is preferred for early season forcing; the standing ground is the least precise method because of variability in winter temperature.

In the UK, by far the greatest sector of tulip forcing is for cut flowers rather than pot-plant production, but elsewhere, notably in the US, the converse holds. The following deals with cut-flower production, but the methods differ little from those used for pots. Bulbs are planted in boxes or trays 11cm/4.5in. deep to allow good root development, and filled with a growing medium that has a high water-holding capacity yet is free-draining. If soil is used it should be uncontaminated with pests or disease, low in soluble salts, of good structure and 6–8cm/2–3in. deep. The bulbs are placed on the surface as close together as possible and covered with a shallow layer of soil or sand. A peat-like medium can also be used in the same way if thoroughly wetted before use. For potted tulips, planting the bulbs with their flat sides facing the rim of the pot ensures that the largest, lowest leaf of each plant will be on the outside. For pot-plant production, the bulbs are usually planted less deep, with their noses just emerging from the medium. It is important to adjust the pH above 6.0 for satisfactory growth of tulips. After planting the boxes must be thoroughly watered.

The boxes are returned to the store, maintained at the same temperature; the growing medium must be kept moist, and the humidity high to encourage growth. In the store, a further refinement can be introduced by keeping the temperature at 9°C/48°F until the roots emerge from the bottom of the containers, then lowering it to 5°C/40°F. This temperature can be maintained until the shoots are 2.5cm/1in. long, when the plants can be 'held' at 10 12°C/32 36°F until transferred to the glasshouse. This technique can be useful if a batch of bulbs is being aimed at a specific marketing date, such as Easter. If a constant temperature of 9°C/48°F is used, the bulbs are held for a further several weeks before they are used for transfer to the glasshouse.

This duration of cold treatment depends on the cultivar, and the time of flowering required in the house. Each extra week at 9°C/ 48°F gives 3–4 fewer days in the house. The total number of weeks at 9°C/48°F to give a glasshouse forcing period of 21 days varies from 17 weeks for 'Trance' and 'Merry Widow', to 21 weeks for 'Apeldoorn' and 'Halcro'. For a 35-day forcing period, the numbers of weeks are 13 and 17–18 for the fastest and slowest respectively. Data are available to the growers on dates of precooling, planting and housing for a wide range of commercial tulip cultivars, to ensure successful crops of high quality flowers at different times in the forcing season. It is clearly advantageous to use cultivars with a short cold requirement for earliest forcing.

If stacks are used, rather than a cold store, boxes are stood on pallets on concrete to facilitate mechanical handling. The stack is surrounded by straw bales, and capped with loose straw under a plastic cover. Care is required to avoid rodent damage. For late forcing, it is necessary to house boxes before the shoots grow into the base of the box above and become bent. Standing grounds are now less used because of the necessary handling of heavy boxes in wet, cold conditions, the uncertainty of knowing whether the plants are ready to transfer to the glasshouse, and the difficulties of planning production to meet market demands.

Glasshouse phase. Although tulips are normally forced in glasshouses, there is little requirement for light because the food reserves in the bulb are sufficient for development to full flowering. For economic reasons, glasshouses are often lined with polythene sheet too reduce heat loss, or use can be made of insulated buildings equipped with artificial light, necessary for cultural operations and for ensuring that the plants appear a healthy dark green. The recommended temperature for this stage of forcing is 18°C/65°F. For very early forcing, 16°C/60°F is better initially, increased to 18°C/65°F. If 16°C/60°F is used, it will take longer to reach the picking stage, but flower quality is usually better.

It is important that temperature fluctuations are avoided, otherwise a condition called 'topple' occurs; this is a calcium-related physiological disorder where the flower stem collapses so that the flower hangs down. Good ventilation is essential to prevent botrytis spores germinating on the flowers and causing unsightly spotting, and too dry an atmosphere leads to bud blast. For continuity of flowering, successive 'rounds' of bulb boxes are brought into the glasshouse; on the more intensive holdings, up to seven crops can be produced, with flowers on sale from early November until the outdoor flowers are available in quantity in April/May. Before one lot is cleared, a second batch is often brought in and kept under the benches to start into growth. After commercial forcing, no attempt is made to recover tulip bulbs which have been forced: they are discarded.

Direct forcing. A completely separate method, called 'direct' or 'five-degree' forcing involves giving the whole of the low-temperature treatment to the dry (i.e. unplanted) bulbs, which are then planted directly into the border soil of a glasshouse. This method requires more skill than the traditional methods. It is used mainly for early flowering, especially of the Darwin hybrid tulips (such as 'Apeldoorn') which have a long cold requirement. Large bulbs are essential, and these are treated as above until Stage G. Thereafter they are stored at 17°C/63°F until the start of cooling which is at 5°C/40°F for 9 or 12 weeks, depending on cultivar. The bulbs are planted at the end of this period at c300 per m2/250 per yd2 and kept at 13°C/55°F initially, rising to 18°C/65°F after four weeks. Growth to flowering is 3–4 weeks slower than with the traditional method. In the Netherlands, forcing to produce flowers very early in the year (October) is achieved using 'ice tulips' which have been kept frozen from the previous season.

NARCISSUS. The forcing of most narcissi (daffodils included) is remarkably similar to that of tulips. One major point of difference, however, is the timing of flower initiation. The daffodil flower has been initiated by bulb lifting time, and its development continues to completion in about the first week in August in Lincolnshire, England, and about two weeks earlier in southwest England. The final stage, the formation of the trumpet or paracorolla, is called Stage Pc, and marks when low-temperature treatment can be started.

As with tulips, early lifting and warm storage at 35°C/95°F for five days immediately after lifting and grading are effective in encouraging early flowers; early lifting alone confers no benefit. After grading, bulbs of grades 12/14cm and 14/16cm are used for forcing. Until Stage Pc, bulbs are stored at 17°C/63°F; afterwards at 9°C/48°F for 6 weeks before planting. Planting media are the same as for tulips, except that there is no need to correct for acidity. The cold requirement of daffodils is somewhat shorter than for tulips (the main cultivars require 12–15 weeks in total) and the first forcing by a grower tends to be of daffodils from a standing ground, as this frees expensive cool stores for the tulips. Greater precision can be achieved from controlled temperature storage for the whole period.

For narcissus forcing, light is not a limiting factor, and standard glasshouses are generally used, usually plastic-lined and maintained at 16°C/60°F. The numbers of bulbs that can be accommodated is high; up to 1.7 tonnes of 14/16cm bulbs per 100m2 of glasshouse area including paths. Some cultivars, especially late season and after the first flowers have been picked, will require supporting to prevent the remainder falling over. Forced daffodil flowers are available on sale from early October until early March. Cultivars commonly forced include 'Carlton', 'Golden Harvest', 'Ice Follies' and 'Dutch Master', but there are small quantities of a wide range of other cultivars.

It is possible to reclaim narcissus bulbs after they have been forced, this being most advantageous for bulbs of the more expensive cultivars and bulbs forced late in the season. The forcing trays are taken outside and left until the foliage dies down naturally. The bulbs are then removed from the growing medium, cleaned, hot-water treated and replanted in the field. After two years they will have recovered, and can be added to general stocks or be re-forced.

Tazetta narcissi differ from the above because they have no cold requirement. Most of the 'Grand Soleil d'Or', narcissi sold in the UK, even in winter, are grown outdoors on the Isles of Scilly. Recently several tazetta narcissi cultivars have been sold in the UK for home forcing in pots, including paper-white narcissi from Israel. These bulbs should be planted thickly in pots of a well drained, sterilized planting medium, of pH 6–7 and kept at a temperature of 17°C/63°F. The first flowers are in bud in 10–40 days depending on cultivar and planting date, the later the planting, the faster the development. As the flower stems tend to be tall, they will require staking; commercial growers treat the plants with a dwarfing compound which improves their appearance. Similar species from China, called the 'sacred lily', can be grown in compost, bulb fibre, on pebbles or in a shallow sloping dish of water, and it is customary to carve the shooting bulb to modify leaf growth to a living sculpture.

HYACINTH. As almost all hyacinth bulbs are grown in the Netherlands, information on the preparation of bulbs prior to sale comes from there. Briefly, for earliest flowering, after the bulbs are lifted and air- dried at 23°C/73°F, they are treated at 30°C/85°F for two weeks, 25°C/77°F for three weeks and 23°C/73°F until the top florets are at the stage of producing their second anther whorl, followed by 13°C/ 55°F until planting. All the low-temperature treatment is given after planting.

For flowering by Christmas, it is essential to use prepared bulbs, and the best flowers are those of the largest bulbs. These should be planted in mid to late September and have their cold requirement satisfied at the temperature optimum of 9°C/48°F for 8–11 weeks, depending on cultivar. If below this temperature, growth will be retarded; if above, shoots will be long and unsightly. For later flowering, lower temperatures are used in the latter part of the forcing period. If a plunge bed is used, the bulbs must not be planted until the soil temperature has fallen to 13°C/55°F. As is well known, best results are obtained by planting bulbs in a light medium of soil, coir/sand or pre-wetted bulb fibre, with no fertilizer. Containers should be filled with bulbs but not so that they touch, with their noses peeping out, and with a reasonable depth below the bulb, or the roots will eject the plant when they reach the container wall. Frost should be avoided if at all possible, and plants should never be handled or moved to a warm place if frozen, because of the danger of the flower stem becoming detached from the bulb, and ejected as the leaves extend.

The satisfaction of the cold period can be judged by date alone only if temperature control is good and the requirement of the cultivar accurately known. Otherwise, it is prudent to wait until the shoots are 3–5cm tall with the flower bud partly out of the bulb before gradually moving the pot to warmer situations. Commercially, the earliest bulbs are forced in glasshouses at 22–25°C/66–77°F, those for flowering in January and February at 18°C/65°F and at 16°C/60°F for even later ones. To encourage taller plants and prevent the drying of the terminal flowers, it is good practice to cover shoots with opaque plastic or paper until the flower head is completely out of the bulb. An alternative system for individual plants is to use hourglass shaped hyacinth vases, on which the bulb sits with its roots in the water-filled lower part. The same temperatures are required as with solid growing media.

LILY. In the past decade lilies have become a popular forced cut flower available year-round. Commercially they are divided into two groups, the Asiatic Hybrids which are early-flowering with upright flowers and the Oriental Hybrids which have flat and recurved flowers. The former are derived from at least seven Asian species (*Lilium amabile, L. cernuum, L. concolor, L. dauricum, L. davidii, L. maculatum, L. tigrinum*) and one European one (*L. bulbiferum*), and the latter from *L. auratum, L. speciosum,* and *L. japonicum*. The Easter lily, *L. longiflorum*, is particularly important in the US, and ensuring that flowering coincides with this moveable feast presents growers with a new challenge each year. Popular cultivars include the Asiatic 'Connecticut King', 'Enchantment', 'Mont Blanc' and 'Sun Ray', the Oriental 'Star Gazer' and 'Uchida', and the *L.longiflorum* 'Osnat' from Israel.

Year-round availability is achieved by a combination of pre-cooled bulbs and the use of 'frozen-in' bulbs, which have received a cold treatment before being frozen at 1°C/30°F in boxes of moist coir protected by plastic liners. In this condition they can be kept for months, and removed for forcing in glasshouses when required. The cold requirement applied commercially is a minimum of six weeks (Asiatic hybrids) or eight weeks (Oriental hybrids) before planting. Flowers are initiated after planting, when the shoots have emerged about 2cm from the bulb.

Deep containers are required because many lilies produce stem roots above the bulb; to allow these to grow, it is usual to allow 5cm of planting medium above the tip of the bulb. The planting material should be sterile, of pH 5.5–7.0 and well drained. Unlike daffodils and tulips, there is a requirement for good light, especially in the short days of winter, a time when many commercial growers use artificial lighting to reduce the incidence of flower bud abortion and abscission in sensitive cultivars. Night temperatures of 13–17°C/55–63°F are recommended with day temperatures not exceeding 21°C/70°F. Asiatic and *L. longiflorum* lilies take 30–35 days to flower after the 'buds visible' stage, and Orientals 50–55 days.

The complexity of parentage and the wide and rapidly changing list of cultivars make lily forcing a specialized activity, but there is information available for individual cultivars, mostly from Dutch sources, on aspects of cultivation such as bulb sizes, planting densities, programming, fertilizer schedules, lighting, crop supports, fungicidal treatments, etc.

For Easter lilies, a timing system has been developed based on counting the numbers of leaves unfolded relative to the total number present in the crown of the plant below the flower, and adjusting glasshouse temperature to speed up or slow down the rate of leaf opening. The aim is to attain the 'buds visible' stage by the first Sunday in Lent, because it is a fixed number of days from that date until the flowers are ready to market in time for Easter.

While stem length is a desirable feature of cut lily flowers, those grown in pots are aesthetically more pleasing if considerably shorter, and commercial growers of pot lilies of all kinds generally apply dwarfing chemicals to achieve this.

Iris. The irises normally forced for cut-flower production are the bulbous Dutch irises developed from crosses between *Iris xiphium*, *I. tingitana* and *l.lusitanica* from Spain and Morocco. These iris are also forced on a year-round basis, out-of-season flowers being produced from 'retarded' bulbs which are stored at a temperature of 30°C/85°F. Like lilies, flower initiation occurs after planting the bulb, although they are spring-flowering. Also like lilies, irises require good light when growing to avoid bud blasting. The most commonly grown cultivars are 'Ideal' (light blue), 'Prof. Blaauw' (dark blue) and 'White Wedgwood'.

Iris bulbs benefit from warm storage after lifting. It appears to be necessary for the breaking of dormancy, and also encourages better flowering. 'Heat curing' of bulbs of a borderline size for flowering results in a greater percentage producing flowers; those that do not produce only three leaves, indicating when failure to flower occurred. Several variations of treatment of iris bulbs are in current use, depending on whether the forcing is early, mid-season or late. For early flowering of 'Ideal' (February-April) a typical sequence is 30°C/85°F (four weeks), 40°C/105°F (three days), 17°C/63°F (two weeks) then 9°C/48°F (six weeks). The last two temperatures are frequently reversed.

Miscellaneous bulbs. Many other bulbous plants with a cold requirement can be forced successfully using a period of low temperature similar to that described above for tulips. *Allium karataviense* is one such, requiring 21–22 weeks of cold before forcing at about 15°C/60°F in a well-lit greenhouse. *Crocus* spp., *Iris reticulata*, *I.danfordiae* and *Muscari* are also forced, especially on the continent and in the US, using temperature sequences similar to those used for tulip. They look their best planted thickly in 10cm/4in. or 15cm/6in. pots.

Mixed pots. A development in recent years has been the use of more than one species in the same pot marketed as a 'Spring Garden'. A simple form might include hyacinths and crocus, or up to five such as an arrangement of six bulbs of dwarf iris, six of crocus, three of tulip, one hyacinth and one daffodil in a 20cm/8in. bulb pan. It is important to clump together bulbs of the same kind, and to ensure that taller plants are at the rear of the arrangement. The bulbs are planted on the same date and the container kept at 9°C/48°F until rooting has occurred, followed by 5°C/40°F for eight weeks, then 0–2°C/32–36°F until a total cold duration of 15 weeks has been reached. The 'gardens' are then sold without use of a greenhouse period. The customer is required to keep the pot at 16–18°C/60–65°F in direct sunlight until the first flowers appear, and then in more subdued light. Use of all five species gives a two-week growing period followed by three weeks of flowering.

GLASSHOUSE FORCING. A completely separate system of forcing is used for plants which have no cold requirement for development and flowering, and this kind of forcing differs little from the growing of other house plants that require high temperatures, at least for part of the year, to ensure normal development in our climate. However, there is often some form of pre-treatment or storage of the bulbs until the time of forcing, or to ensure that their dormancy is broken, often by a period of high temperature. Plants in this category include such well known bulbs as gladioli, freesia, ixia and anemone, as well as others which are grown in cool temperate climates only under protected cultivation, like *Hippeastrum.*

Alstroemeria. The rhizomes are planted in late summer or early autumn, and the crop is grown in full light for one or two seasons in beds one metre wide. After establishment, temperatures of 10–13°C/50–55°F are maintained, and below 20°C/68°F in summer.

Freesia. Corms required for forcing should be obtained from a producer already pre-treated at 30°C/85°F. They should be planted immediately on arrival, usually in September/October and grown at 10–13°C/50–55°F in a glasshouse. Temperatures above 17°C/63°F during the growing period adversely effect flower quality. If corms are saved for a subsequent crop, they must be treated at high temperature before they will grow.

Convallaria. Lily-of-the-valley is forced from 'pips', after storage in moist coir or peat at –2°C/28°F to –4°C/25°F. They are forced in pots or trays in a low light greenhouse, maintained between 17°C/63°F and 20°C/68°F.

Hippeastrum. Although they will grow over a wide temperature range, the optimum is about 24°C/75°F. Many large bulbs will produce a second inflorescence, and some a third, depending on cultivar. After flowering, bulbs continue to grow if the foliage is retained, and the plants can be taken outdoors after the danger of frost is over. For re-forcing next season, they should be brought indoors in the autumn and stored for at least eight weeks before cutting off the foliage and starting them into re-growth. Many cultivars are available in colours including red, pink, white, orange, bicolours and picotees, and in a range of flower sizes.

Others. Other 'bulbs' that are forced commercially in greenhouses include *Anemone, Caladium, Dahlia, Oxalis, Ranunculus* and *Zantedeschia.* Although dealt with earlier, strictly, the following could also be included here: tazetta narcissi, five-degree tulips, iris and lilies, because they require no cold facilities for rooting plants before the greenhouse phase of forcing.

Bulbs Listed by Family

Illustrated genera are marked with an asterisk (*).

Agavaceae
Manfreda
Polianthes

Amaryllidaceae
× Amarcrinum
× Amarygia
Amaryllis*
Ammocharis
Apodolirion
Boophone
Brunsvigia
Calostemma
Carpolyza
Chlidanthus
Clivia
Crinum
Cyanella
Cybistetes
Cyrtanthus*
Eucharis
Eucrosia
Eustephia
Galanthus*
Gethyllis
Griffinia
Habranthus*
Haemanthus*
Hippeastrum*
Hymenocallis
Ixiolirion
Lapiedra
Lepidochiton
Leucojum*
Lycoris
Narcissus*
Nerine*
Pamianthe
Pancratium
Paramongaia
Phaedranassa
Phycella
Plagiolirion
Proiphys
Pyrolirion
Rhodophiala
Scadoxus*
Sprekelia*
Stenomesson
Sternbergia*
Strumaria
Ungernia
Urceolina
Vagaria
Worsleya
Zephyranthes*

Araceae
Amorphophallus
Arisaema*
Arisarum
Arum
Biarum
Caladium
Colocasia
Dracunculus*
Eminium
Pinellia
Remusatia
Sauromatum
Taccarum
Xanthosoma
Zantedeschia*

Asclepiadaceae
Ceropegia

Begoniaceae
Begonia

Berberidaceae
Bongardia
Gymnospermium
Leontice

Cannaceae
Canna

Compositae
Dahlia*
Liatris

Crassulaceae
Umbilicus

Dioscoreaceae
Dioscorea*

Fumariaceae
Corydalis

Geraniaceae
Pelargonium

Gesneriaceae
Achimenes*
Eucodonia
Gloxinia
Koellikeria
Sinningia

Haemodoraceae
Anigozanthos*
Macropidia

Hypoxidaceae
Hypoxis
Rhodohypoxis*

Iridaceae
Alophia

Anomatheca
Babiana*
Belamcanda
Calydorea
Chasmanthe
Cipura
Crocosmia
Crocus*
Cypella
Dierama
Dietes
Eleutherine
Ferraria
Freesia
Galaxia
Geissorhiza
Gelasine
Gladiolus*
Gynandriris
Herbertia
Hermodactylus*
Hesperantha
Homeria
Iris*
Ixia*
Lapeirousia
Melasphaerula
Micranthus
Moraea*
Nemastylis
Olsynium
Pardanthopsis
Rigidella
Romulea*
Schizostylis
Sisyrinchium
Sparaxis*
Synnotia
Syringodea
Tigridia
Trimezia
Tritonia
Tritoniopsis
Watsonia*

Labiatae
Salvia

Liliaceae
Agapanthus (Alliaceae)
Albuca (Hyacinthaceae)
Allium (Alliaceae)
Alstroemeria
(Alstroemeriaceae)
Amianthum
(Melanthiaceae)

Androcymbium
(Colchicaceae)
Androstephium
(Alliaceae)
Anthericum
(Asphodelaceae)
Aphyllanthes
(Aphyllanthaceae)
Asphodeline
(Asphodelaceae)
Asphodelus
(Asphodelaceae)
Baeometra
(Colchicaceae)
Bellevalia
(Hyacinthaceae)
Bessera (Alliaceae)
Blandfordia
(Blandfordiaceae)
Bloomeria (Alliaceae)
Bomarea
(Alstroemeriaceae)
Bowiea (Hyacinthaceae)
Brimeura
(Hyacinthaceae)
Brodiaea (Alliaceae)*
Bulbine (Asphodelaceae)
Bulbinella
(Asphodelaceae)
Bulbinopsis
(Asphodelaceae)
Bulbocodium
(Colchicaceae)*
Calochortus
(Calochortaceae)*
Caloscordum (Alliaceae)
Camassia
(Hyacinthaceae)
Camptorrhiza
(Liliaceae)
Cardiocrinum
(Liliaceae)*
Chamaelirion
(Melanthiaceae)
Chionodoxa
(Hyacinthaceae)
× Chionoscilla
(Hyacinthaceae)
Chlorogalum
(Hyacinthaceae)
Colchicum
(Colchicaceae)*
Conanthera
(Tecophilaeaceae)
Convallaria
(Convallariaceae)

Daubenya
  (Hyacinthaceae)
Dichelostemma
  (Alliaceae)
Dipcadi (Hyacinthaceae)
Drimia (Hyacinthaceae)
Drimiopsis
  (Hyacinthaceae)
Eremurus
  (Asphodelaceae)
Erythronium
  (Liliaceae)*
Eucomis
  (Hyacinthaceae)
Fritillaria (Liliaceae)*
Gagea (Liliaceae)
Galtonia
  (Hyacinthaceae)
Gloriosa
  (Colchicaceae)*
Helonias
  (Melanthiaceae)
Heloniopsis
  (Melanthiaceae)
Hemerocallis
  (Hemerocallidaceae)*
Hesperocallis
  (Agavaceae)
Hyacinthella
  (Hyacinthaceae)
Hyacinthoides
  (Hyacinthaceae)

Hyacinthus
  (Hyacinthaceae)*
Ipheion (Alliaceae)*
Kniphofia (Aloeaceae)*
Lachenalia
  (Hyacinthaceae)
Ledebouria
  (Hyacinthaceae)
Leucocoryne (Alliaceae)
Leucocrinum
  (Funkiaceae)
Lilium (Liliaceae)*
Littonia (Colchicaceae)
Lloydia (Liliaceae)*
Maianthemum
  (Convallariaceae)
Massonia
  (Hyacinthaceae)
Merendera
  (Colchicaceae)
Milla (Alliaceae)
Muilla (Alliaceae)
Muscari
  (Hyacinthaceae)*
Nectaroscordum
  (Alliaceae)
Nomocharis (Liliaceae)*
Notholirion (Liliaceae)
Nothoscordum
  (Alliaceae)
Ornithogalum
  (Hyacinthaceae)*

Paradisea
  (Asphodelaceae)
Paris (Trilliaceae)
Periboea
  (Hyacinthaceae)
Petronymphe (Alliaceae)
Polygonatum
  (Convallariaceae)
Polyxena
  (Hyacinthaceae)
Pseudogaltonia
  (Hyacinthaceae)
Puschkinia
  (Hyacinthaceae)
Sandersonia
  (Colchiacaceae)
Scilla (Hyacinthaceae)*
Stenanthium
  (Melanthiaceae)
Tecophilaea
  (Tecophilaeaceae)*
Thysanotus
  (Asphodelaceae)
Tricyrtis
  (Tricyrtidaceae)*
Trillium (Trilliaceae)
Tristagma (Alliaceae)
Triteleia (Alliaceae)*
Tulbaghia (Alliaceae)
Tulipa (Liliaceae)*
Urginea (Hyacinthaceae)
Uvularia (Uvulariaceae)

Veltheimia
  (Hyacinthaceae)
Veratrum
  (Melanthiaceae)
Whiteheadia
  (Hyacinthaceae)
Wurmbea (Colchicaceae)
Zigadenus
  (Melanthiaceae)*

Oxalidaceae
Oxalis

Primulaceae
*Cyclamen**

Ranunculaceae
Anemone
Anemonella
*Eranthis**
Ranunculus

Taccaceae
*Tacca**

Tropaeolaceae
Tropaeolum

Zingiberaceae
Cautleya
Hedychium
Roscoea

Bulbs by Geographical Region

North America
Alophia
Amianthum
Androstephium
Anemonella
Arisaema
Bloomeria
Brodiaea
Calochortus
Camassia
Chamaelirion
Chlorogalum
Dichelostemma
Erythronium
Fritillaria
Helonias
Hesperocallis
Hymenocallis
Liatris
Manfreda
Milla
Muilla
Nemastylis
Nothoscordum
Olsynium
Polygonatum
Sisyrinchium
Stenanthium
Trillium
Triteleia
Uvularia
Zigadenus

Central America and West Indies
Achimenes
Alophia
Bessera
Bloomeria
Calochortus
Canna
Cipura
Cypella
Dahlia
Eleutherine
Eucodonia
Gloxinia
Hippeastrum
Hymenocallis
Koellikeria

Manfreda
Milla
Muilla
Nemastylis
Nothoscordum
Olsynium
Petronymphe
Polianthes
Rigidella
Sinningia
Sisyrinchium
Sprekelia
Stenanthium
Tigridia
Trimezia
Tropaeolum
Zephyranthes

South America
Alophia
Alstroemeria
Bomarea
Caladium
Calydorea
Camassia
Camassia
Canna
Chlidanthus
Cipura
Conanthera
Cypella
Dahlia
Eleutherine
Eucharis
Eucrosia
Eustephia
Gelasine
Gloxinia
Griffinia
Habranthus
Herbertia
Hippeastrum
Hymenocallis
Ipheion
Koellikeria
Lepidochiton
Leucocoryne
Nothoscordum
Olsynium
Pamianthe

Paramongaia
Phaedranassa
Phycella
Plagiolirion
Pyrolirion
Rhodophiala
Rigidella
Sinningia
Sisyrinchium
Stenomesson
Taccarum
Tecophilaea
Trimezia
Tristagma
Tropaeolum
Umbilicus
Urceolina
Worsleya
Xanthosoma
Zephyranthes

Western Europe
Arum
Asphodeline
Asphodelus
Crocus
Erythronium
Fritillaria
Galanthus
Hyacinthoides
Leucojum
Lloydia
Narcissus
Paris
Polygonatum
Romulea
Scilla

Central and Eastern Europe
Arum
Asphodeline
Asphodelus
Belamcanda
Bulbocodium
Caloscordum
Colchicum
Crocus
Cyclamen
Erythronium
Fritillaria

Gagea
Galanthus
Gymnospermium
Hyacinthella
Leucojum
Pardanthopsis
Paris
Polygonatum
Puschkinia
Scilla
Tulipa
Umbilicus

Mediterranean and Southern Europe to the Aegean

Androcymbium
Anthericum
Aphyllanthes
Arisarum
Arum
Asphodeline
Asphodelus
Bellevalia
Biarum
Bongardia
Brimeura
Bulbocodium
Chionodoxa
Colchicum
Crocus
Cyclamen
Dipcadi
Dracunculus
Eminium
Eranthis
Fritillaria
Gagea
Gladiolus
Gymnospermium
Gynandriris
Hermodactylus
Hyacinthella
Lapiedra
Leontice
Leucojum
Merendera
Muscari
Narcissus
Nectaroscordum
Ornithogalum
Pancratium
Paradisea
Romulea
Scilla
Sternbergia
Tulipa
Urginea

Middle East

Anthericum
Arum

Asphodelus
Bellevalia
Biarum
Chionodoxa
Colchicum
Crocus
Cyclamen
Eminium
Fritillaria
Galanthus
Gladiolus
Gymnospermium
Gynandriris
Hermodactylus
Hyacinthella
Leontice
Leucojum
Merendera
Muscari
Ornithogalum
Puschkinia
Scilla
Sternbergia
Tulipa
Urginea
Vagaria

Central and Western Asia

Arum
Asphodelus
Belamcanda
Bellevalia
Biarum
Colchicum
Crocus
Eminium
Eranthis
Eremurus
Fritillaria
Gagea
Gladiolus
Gymnospermium
Gynandriris
Hyacinthella
Hyacinthus
Ixiolirion
Leontice
Merendera
Muscari
Narcissus
Nectaroscordum
Notholirion
Pancratium
Paris
Polygonatum
Puschkinia
Scilla
Sternbergia
Tulipa
Ungernia

East Asia (temperate)

Arisaema
Belamcanda
Caloscordum
Cardiocrinum
Cautleya
Colchicum
Eranthis
Fritillaria
Hedychium
Heloniopsis
Hemerocallis
Lycoris
Narcissus
Nomocharis
Notholirion
Pancratium
Pardanthopsis
Paris
Pinellia
Polygonatum
Remusatia
Roscoea
Sauromatum
Scilla
Stenanthium
Tricyrtis
Trillium
Tulipa
Umbilicus
Ungernia
Zigadenus

East Asia (tropical)

Amorphophallus
Arisaema
Colocasia
Dipcadi
Gloriosa
Hedychium
Nomocharis
Pancratium
Remusatia
Tacca
Thysanotus

Australia

Anigozanthos
Blandfordia
Bulbinopsis
Calostemma
Macropidia
Proiphys
Remusatia
Thysanotus
Wurmbea

New Zealand

Bulbinella
Leucocrinum

North Africa
Albuca
Androcymbium
Anthericum
Aphyllanthes
Arisaema
Colchicum
Crocus
Cyclamen
Dipcadi
Fritillaria
Gagea
Hyacinthoides
Littonia
Merendera
Narcissus
Romulea
Scadoxus
Urginea
Vagaria

Tropical Africa
Androcymbium
Anomatheca
Arisaema
Babiana
Bowiea
Camptorrhiza
Cyrtanthus
Dierama
Dietes
Drimiopsis
Eucomis
Ferraria
Galanthus
Gladiolus
Gloriosa
Kniphofia
Lapeirousia
Moraea
Remusatia
Romulea
Sauromatum
Scadoxus
Tacca
Tritonia

South Africa
Agapanthus
Albuca
Amaryllis
Ammocharis
Androcymbium
Anomatheca

Apodolirion
Babiana
Baeometra
Boophone
Bowiea
Brunsvigia
Bulbine
Bulbinella
Camptorrhiza
Carpolyza
Chasmanthe
Clivia
Corydalis
Crocosmia
Cyanella
Cybistetes
Cyrtanthus
Daubenya
Dierama
Dietes
Dipcadi
Drimia
Drimiopsis
Eucomis
Ferraria
Freesia
Galaxia
Galtonia
Geissorhiza
Gethyllis
Gladiolus
Gynandriris
Haemanthus
Hesperantha
Homeria
Ixia
Kniphofia
Lachenalia
Lapeirousia
Ledebouria
Littonia
Massonia
Melasphaerula
Micranthus
Moraea
Nerine
Ornithogalum
Pelargonium
Periboea
Polyxena
Pseudogaltonia
Rhodohypoxis
Romulea
Sandersonia

Scadoxus
Schizostylis
Scilla
Sparaxis
Strumaria
Synnotia
Syringodea
Tritonia
Tritoniopsis
Tulbaghia
Veltheimia
Watsonia
Whiteheadia
Wurmbea
Zantedeschia

Madagscar
Gladiolus
Kniphofia

Northern Hemisphere (temperate)
Allium
Convallaria
Corydalis
Iris
Lilium
Lloydia
Maianthemum
Veratrum

Temperate regions (widespread)
Anemone
Hypoxis
Oxalis
Ranunculus
Salvia

Tropical and sub-tropical regions (widespread)
Begonia
Ceropegia
Crinum
Dioscorea
Hypoxis
Oxalis
Salvia
Amorphophallus

Garden origin
× Amarcrinum
× Amarygia
× Chionoscilla

Glossary

abaxial of the surface or part of a lateral organ, turned or facing away from the axis and toward the plant's base; thus the underside of a leaf or perianth segment even when that surface may be uppermost because of the twisting of a stalk, strong incurving of petals or the hanging attitude of a branch or inflorescence; cf. adaxial.

abbreviated shortened.

aberrant unusual or atypical, differing from the normal form.

abortive (of reproductive organs) undeveloped or not perfectly developed, and therefore barren; (of seeds) failing to develop normally.

above (1) pertaining to the adaxial surface of a leaf, petal, sepal or scale; (2) pertaining to the upper portions of a stem, bulb, tuber, branch or inflorescence.

abrupt of a leaf or perianth segment tip, terminating suddenly without tapering, usually when broadly rounded or squared; 'abruptly acute' refers to parts terminating in this way but tipped with a short sharp point; 'abruptly acuminate' is used where a longer point is meant.

abscission, abscissing (abscising) (of leaves, branches, etc.) a separating or falling away, caused by disintegration of a layer of plant tissues at the base of the organ (e.g., as the result of environmental conditions or pollination leading to hormonal action), with a subsequent development of scar tissue or periderm at the point of abscission.

acaulescent of a plant whose stem is absent or, more usually, appears to be absent, being very short or subterranean.

achene a dry, small, indehiscent fruit with a tight thin pericarp, strictly consisting of one free carpel as in Ranunculaceae.

achenocarp any dry indehiscent fruit.

achlamydeous lacking a perianth.

acicular needle-shaped, and usually rounded rather than flat in cross-section.

acinaciform shaped like a scimitar.

actinomorphic of regular flowers possessing radial symmetry, capable of division in two or more planes into similar halves.

aculeate prickly, bearing sharp prickles.

aculeiform prickle-shaped.

acuminate (of leaves and perianth segments) with the tip or, less commonly, the base tapering gradually to a point, usually with somewhat concave sides.

acutangular when stems are sharply angular.

acute (of the tips or bases of leaves or perianth segments) where two almost straight or slightly convex sides converge to terminate in a sharp point, the point shorter and usually broader than in an acuminate leaf tip.

adaxial turned or facing toward the axis and apex, thus the upper, if not always the uppermost surface of an organ, sometimes used interchangeably with ventral.

adherent of parts usually free or separate (i.e. petals) but clinging or held closely together. Such parts are sometimes loosely described as united or, inaccurately, as fused, which is strictly synonymous with coherent. Some authors use this word to describe the fusion of dissimilar parts.

adnate attached by its whole length or surface to the face of an organ.

adpressed (appressed) (of indumentum, leaves, etc.) used of an organ which lies flat and close to the stem or leaf to which it is attached.

adventitious (adventive) occurring in an unusual location, originating from other than the normal place – applied to non-native plants introduced deliberately or accidentally; to buds developing along a stem rather than at leaf axils; to viviparously produced plantlets and to roots that develop not from the radicle and its subdivisions but from another part such as the stem or leaf axil.

aestivation the arrangement of floral parts before flowering.

affixed fixed upon.

afollate leafless.

alate winged, usually of stems, petioles and fruits where the main body is furnished with marginal membranous bands.

alternate (1) of leaves, branches, pedicels, etc., arranged in two ranks along the stem, rachis, etc., with the insertions of the two ranks not parallel but alternating, thus the antithesis of paired or opposite; (2) of two types of organ or structure, when one is placed in an alternating sequence with another, thus petals alternate with calyx lobes = petals placed between calyx lobes.

anastomosing of veins forming a network, united at their points of contact.

ancipitous with two sharp edges.

androdioecious a species with two forms, one with male flowers only, the other with hermaphrodite flowers.

androecium the male component of a flower, the stamen or stamens as a whole.

androgynophore a stalk-like axis subtended by the perianth and bearing stamens and pistil.

androgynous hermaphrodite or, sometimes, monoecious.

andromonoecious a species with two forms, one with only male flowers, the other with only perfect flowers, but no purely female flowers.

anfractuose (anfractuous) closely or tightly sinuous, or spirally twisted.

angular, angulate with laterally projecting angles, as in longitudinally ridged and angled stems.

anisophyllous of paired leaves differing one from the other in size or shape, a feature of some Gesneriaceae.

annual a plant which completes its entire life-cycle within the space of a year.

annular of organs of parts in a circular arrangement or forming rings.

annulate ring-shaped.

anterior of the surface or part of an organ turned away from or furthest from the axis and projecting forward or toward the base or (in the case of a flower) any subtending bract; close to abaxial but broader in definition, meaning not only 'beneath' but also lower (of two, as in the lower lip of a bilabiate flower) or furthest as in the tip of an organ, cf. posterior.

anther the pollen-bearing portion of the stamen, either sessile or attached to a filament.

anther sac a sac-shaped unit containing pollen. In many plants, the anther consists of four pollen sacs disposed in two lobes, the tissues separating the members of each pair usually break down prior to anthesis, giving rise to a biloculate (two-celled) anther.

antheriferous bearing anthers.

antheroid anther-like.

anthesis the expansion or opening of a flower, the period in which the anthers and stigmas become functional, enabling fertilization to take place.

anti- prefix meaning against or opposed to.

antipetalous opposite to or superposed on a petal, i.e. not alternate.

antisepalous opposite to or superposed on a sepal, i.e. not alternate.

antrorse turned, curved or bent upward or forward, toward the apex; cf. retrorse.

ap-, apo- prefix meaning not.

apetalous lacking petals.

apex the growing point of a stem or root; the tip of an organ or structure, most commonly used of a leaf tip.

aphyllous lacking leaves.

apical borne at the apex of an organ, farthest from the point of attachment; pertaining to the apex.

apiculate possessing an apicule.

apicule a short sharp but not rigid point terminating a leaf, bract or perianth segment.

apomict see clone.

apomictic asexual reproduction, often through viable seeds but without fusion of gametes.

apomixis the process of reproducing without fusion of gametes, ie. asexually; plants in which seeds develop from unfertilized cells are termed apomicts. The offspring of such plants are genetically uniform. The term is sometimes extended to cover other asexual (vegetative) means of increase.

aposepalous with free sepals.

appendage secondary part or process attached to or developed from any larger organ.

appendix a long, narrowed development of the spadix in Araceae.

appendiculate furnished with appendages.

applanate flattened.

appressed see adpressed.

approximate drawn very closely together, sometimes confused with *proximate*.

apterous without wings.

aquatic a plant growing naturally in water, either entirely or partially submerged.

arachnoid interlaced with a cobweb of fine white hair, as in some tightly growing succulent rosette plants.

araneous arachnoid.

arborescent with the habit or stature of a tree.

arching curved gently downwards, usually of branches, stems, large leaves and inflorescences, usually more freely than *arcuate* and less markedly than *pendent*.

arcuate curved downwards, bow-shaped, usually applied to a smaller, more rigid structure than would be described as arching, e.g. the column of an orchid.

aril a generally fleshy appendage of the funiculus or hilum, partially or entirely enveloping the seed.

arillate possessing an aril; more loosely, any outgrowth or appendage on the testa.

aristate of a leaf apex abruptly terminated in an acicular continuation of the midrib. Otherwise, awned.

aristulate bearing a small awn.

articulate, articulated jointed; possessing distinct nodes or joints, sometimes swollen at their attachment and breaking easily.

ascending rising or extending upwards, usually from an oblique or horizontal position, thus differing from erect.

asexual lacking sexual characteristics or (of reproductive processes) occurring without the fusion of gametes, thus the asexual generation of a fern is the sporophyte and asexual means of increase include apogamy, viviparity and mechanical methods such as grafting, cuttings and division.

asperous rough.

asperulous of a very rough surface, possessing short, hard projections or points.

assurgent rising, extending upwards.

astragaloid dice-shaped.

asymmetric, asymmetrical (1) irregular or unequal in outline or shape, (2) of a flower incapable of being cut in any vertical plane into similar halves.

attenuate (of the apex or base) tapering finely and concavely to a long drawn out point.

auricle an ear-like lobe or outgrowth, often at the base of an organ (i.e. a leaf), or the junction of leaf sheath and blade in some Gramineae.

auricled see auriculate.

auriculate (of the base of a leaf blade or perianth segment) possessing two rounded, ear-shaped lobes that project beyond the general outline of the organ.

autogamous self-fertilizing.

awl-shaped narrowly wedge-shaped and tapering finely to a point, subulate.

awn a slender sharp point or bristle-like appendage.

awned see aristate.

axe-shaped dolabriform.

axial relating to the morphological axis.

axil the upper angle between an axis and any offshoot or lateral organ arising from it, especially a leaf.

axillary situated in, or arising from, or pertaining to an axil.

axis a notional point or line around or along which organs are developed or arranged, whether a stem, stalk or clump; thus the vegetative or growth axis and the floral axis describe the configuration and development of buds and shoots and flowers respectively, and any stem or point of origination on which they are found.

baccate of fruit, berry-like, with a juicy, pulpy rind.

bacciform berry-shaped.

bacilliform rod- or club-shaped.

backcross a cross between a hybrid and one of its parent plants.

baculiform rod-like.

barb a hooked semi-rigid hair.

barbate bearded, with hairs in long weak tufts.

barbed of bristles or awns with short, stiff lateral or terminal hairs which are hooked sharply backward or downward.

barbellae short, stiff hairs, e.g. those of the pappus in Compositae.

barbellate furnished with barbellae.

basal at or arising from the base or point of attachment of a whole plant or organ, thus basal leaves arise from the rootstock or a very short or buried stem and a basal inflorescence arises from the rootstock or the base of a stem or storage organ.

basifixed (of an organ) attached by its base rather than its back, as an anther joined to its filament by its base.

basipetalous developing from apex to base, as in an inflorescence where the terminal flowers open first, cf. acropetal.

basiscopic directed towards the base of a frond: the first lateral vein or leaflet on a pinna branching off in a downwards direction.

beak a long, pointed, horn-like projection; particularly applied to the terminal points of fruits and pistils.

beaked furnished with a beak.

beard a tuft or zone of hair as on the falls of bearded irises.

bearded terminating in a bristle-like hair; or, more generally, possessing tufts or zones of indumentum on parts of the surface.

below pertaining to the lower, basal portions of an organ or whole plant, thus 'stems devoid of leaves below'. 'Leaves ciliate below' meaning leaves whose margins are ciliate in their lower half.

beneath pertaining to the abaxial surface of an organ, thus 'leaves tomentose beneath'.

berry a baccate, indehiscent fruit, one- to many-seeded; the product of a single pistil. Frequently applied to any pulpy or fleshy fruit.

bi- a prefix denoting two or twice; as in bifoliolate, meaning having two leaflets.

biauriculate with two auricles.

bibracteolate with two bracteoles.

bicalcarate with two spurs.

bicallose with two callosities.

bicarinate with two keels.

bicarpellate with a two-celled fruit.

bicolor distinctly two-coloured.

bicornute two-horned.

bicrenate doubly crenate.

bidentate (1) (of an apex) possessing two teeth; (2) of a margin, with teeth, the teeth themselves toothed.

biennial lasting for two years from germination to death, generally blooming in the second and monocarpic.

bifid cleft deeply, forming two points or lobes.

bifoliate having two leaves.

bifoliolate (of a compound leaf) bearing two leaflets.

bifurcate twice forked.

bilabiate of a tubular or funnelform corolla – possessing two lips.

bipinnate of compound leaves where both primary and secondary divisions are pinnate.

biseptate with two partitions.

biserrate with a row of double saw-teeth.

bisexual of flowers with both stamens and pistils; of plants with perfect (hermaphrodite) flowers.

bitten see praemorse.

bivalvate having two valves.

blade the thin, expanded part of a leaf or petal, also known as the lamina, excluding the petiole, stipe or claw; (in the strap-shaped leaves of certain monocots) the part of a leaf above the sheath.

blistered see bullate.

bloom the waxy or pruinose covering of certain fruits, leaves and stems.

blunt rounded, as in a leaf or bud tip that is neither finely tapered or pointed nor abruptly cut off. See obtuse, retuse.

boat-shaped see carinate, cymbiform, navicular.

bossed see umbonate.

bract a modified protective leaf associated with the inflorescence (clothing the stalk and subtending the flowers), with buds and with newly emerging shoots and stems.

bracteate possessing or bearing bracts.

bracteolate possessing or bearing bracteoles.

bracteole a secondary or miniature bract, often borne on a petiole or subtending a flower or inflorescence.

branchlet a small branch or twig, usually applied to the branches of the current and preceding years.

bristly see echinate, hispid and setose.

brushlike see muscariform.

bud an undeveloped organ or shoot; the rudiment of a branch, leaf cluster, inflorescence or flower, be it terminal or axillary.

bulb a modified bud, usually subterranean, consisting of a short thickened stem, serving as a storage organ. There are two principal kinds, (1) naked, composed of free, overlapping scaly modified leaves, all of them fleshy, e.g. *Lilium*; (2) tunicated, with thin, membranous, fibrous or reticulated outer and fleshy concentric inner layers, e.g. *Allium*. The 'solid bulb' is a corm.

bulb scale a component of a bulb.

bulbiferous bearing bulbs or bulbils.

bulbiform in the shape of, resembling, a bulb.

bulbil, bulblet a small bulb or bulb-like growth, arising from a leaf axil or in the place of flowers in an inflorescence.

bulbiliferous bearing bulbils.

bulbose bulb-like.

bulbous (of a stem) swollen at the base; (of a plant) with a bulb.

bullate where the surface of an organ (usually a leaf) is 'blistered' or puckered (i.e. with many superficial interveinal convexities).

cactiform with succulent stems resembling those of Cactaceae.

caducous abscising very early, soon falling.

caespitose a habit description: tufted, growing in small, dense clumps.

calcarate furnished with a spur.

calcareous (of soils) chalky, limy.

calceolate slipper-shaped; resembling a round-toed shoe in form.

calcicole a plant dwelling on and favouring calcareous soils.

calcifuge a plant avoiding and damaged by calcareous soils.

callose (1) bearing callosities; (2) hard and thick in texture.

callosity a leathery or hard isolated thickening of an organ, callus in the second sense (i.e. not as a response to wounding).

callus an abnormal or isolated thickening of tissue, either produced in response to wounding or abscission or as a stable surface feature of leaves and perianth segments.

callused bearing callus, usually in response to wounding or abscission.

calycle, calyculus the epicalyx, an involucre of bracts or bracteoles simulating and subtending the true calyx.

calyptra in flowering plants, a hood or cap-like structure terminating a circumscissile calyx or pyxis.

calyptrate bearing a calyptra.

calyx a collective term for the sepals, whether separate or united, which form the outer whorl of the perianth or floral envelope.

calyx lobe the remaining free, apical portion of sepal in a fused calyx or hypanthium.

calyx tube a tube produced by fusion of the sepals.

campanulate (of a corolla) bell-shaped; a broad tube terminating in a flared limb or lobes.

campestral growing in fields.

canaliculate channelled with a long, concave groove, like a gutter.

candelabriform (of branching patterns and stellate hairs) candelabra-like, with tiered whorls or ranks of radiating or divergent branches.

canescent hoary, or becoming so; densely covered with short, grey-white pubescence.

cano-tomentose indumentum midway between canescent and tomentose.

cap see calyptra.

capillary slender and hair-like; much as filiform, but even more delicate.

capitate (1) arranged in heads, as in the inflorescence of Compositae; (2) terminating in a knob or somewhat spherical tip.

capitellate (1) minutely head-shaped; (2) clustered in a small, compact, capitate group.

capitiform, capitose see capitate.

capitulum a head of densely clustered and sessile or subsessile flowers on a compressed axis.

capsular attached to or resembling a capsule.

capsule a dry, dehiscent seed vessel.

carina keel; the midvein of a leaf, petal or sepal, prominent to ridged beneath.

carinate of a leaf, bract or perianth segment, boat-shaped or, more usually, keeled, with a line or ridge along the centre of its dorsal surface.

carpel a female sporophyll, a simple pistil or one element of a compound pistil bearing an ovule.

carpellate, carpelled bearing or consisting of carpels; when written 2-carpellate, 3-carpellate etc., meaning composed of 2, 3, etc. carpels.

carpophore a slender stalk forming an extension of the receptacle and furnishing an axis for a carpel or carpels.

cartilaginous hard and tough in texture, but flexible.

cataphyll a reduced or scarcely developed leaf, bract-like and often sheathing emerging shoots.

caudate (of a leaf or perianth segment apex) tapering gradually into a long tail-shaped appendage.

caudex strictly, the basal axis of a plant comprising both stem and root; sometimes applied to the aerial stems of palms and superficially palm-like plants. The term is, however, most often used in connection with plants with stout, swollen or succulent simple stems (sometimes by no means distinct from the root axis), usually crowned with narrower branches, leaves or inflorescences.

caudiciform resembling or possessing a caudex, encountered in the phrase caudiciform succulents, a disparate group of horticultural importance defined only by its members' exhibiting a caudex.

caulescent producing a well-developed stem above ground.

cauline attached to or arising from the stem.

cephalanthium the capitulum or flowerhead of Compositae.

ceriferous wax-producing.

cernuous nodding, usually applied to flowers with curved or drooping pedicels attached to a straight or erect inflorescence axis; cf. nutant.

cespitose see caespitose.

chaff dry thin membranous bracts or scales.

chaffy see paleaceous.

channelled (channeled) see canaliculate and sulcate.

chartaceous (of leaf and bract texture) thin and papery.

chimaera, chimera a plant constituted of tissues of differing genetic composition; can be the result of mutation or graft-hybridization.

cilia (*sing.* cilium) fine marginal hairs.

ciliate bearing a marginal fringe of fine hairs.

ciliolate bearing a marginal fringe of minute hairs.

cincinnal pertaining to cincinni or other curled inflorescences.

cincinnus a uniparous scorpioid cyme.

cinereous ashy grey.

circinate of an unexpanded leaflet, frond or frond segment, rolled up in a close coil with the tip at its centre, like a crozier.

circumscissile a form of dehiscence in which a pod opens along a line parallel with its circumference, allowing the top to come off like a lid; see calyptra.

cirrhous (cirrose) (of the apex) terminating in a coiled or spiralling continuation of the midrib.

cladophyll (cladode) 'stem-leaf', a stem simulating a leaf, a flattened or acicular branch which takes on the form and function of a leaf, arising from the axil of a minute, bractlike, and usually caducous true leaf.

clambering of a vine climbing or growing over obstacles without the support of twining stems or tendrils.

clasping partially or wholly surrounding an organ, as a leaf-base clasps a stem.

clavate shaped like a club or a baseball bat; thickening to the apex from a tapered base.

clavellate a diminutive of clavate; club-shaped, but smaller.

claviculate bearing hooks or tendrils.

claviform club-shaped.

claw the narrowed petiole-like base of some sepals and petals.

clawed possessing a claw.

cleft of a flat organ (i.e. leaf or perianth segment), cut almost to the middle.

cleistogamous with self-pollination occurring in the closed flower.

climber any plant that climbs or has a tendency to do so, by means of various adaptations of stems, leaves or roots. See aerial root, scrambler, self-clinging, tendril, twiner.

clone the asexually produced offspring of a single parent to which it is genetically identical.

club-shaped gradually thickened upwards from a slender base, clavate.

clypeate shield-shaped.

coalescent union by growth.

coarctate crowded together.

cochlear, cochleariform, spoon-shaped.

cochleate coiled like a snail's shell.

coherent of parts usually free or separate fused together, as in a corolla tube. This term is sometimes used to describe the adhesion of similar parts; cf. adherent.

columella the central axis of a multi-carpelled fruit.

coma (1) a tuft of hairs projecting from a seed, as in Asclepiadaceae; (2) a tuft of leaves or bracts terminating an inflorescence or syncarp, i.e. the crown of a pineapple.

comate bearing a coma.

comose bearing a coma.

complanate flattened, compressed.

complete (of flowers) possessing all four whorls (sepals, petals, stamens, carpels).

compound divided into two or more subsidiary parts or orders.

compressed flattened, usually applied to bulbs, tubers and fruit and qualified by 'laterally', 'dorsally' and 'ventrally'.

con-, co-, com- prefix meaning 'with'.

concatenate linked as in a chain.

concolorous of a uniform colour.

conduplicate (of leaves) folded once lengthwise, so that the sides are parallel or applied.

confluent merging one into the other.

congested crowded.

conglomerate tightly clustered, usually into a ball.

congregate (adj.) collected into close proximity.

conic, conical cone-shaped; tapering evenly from base to apex in three dimensions.

conjugate coupled, a linked pair, as in the leaflets of a pinnate leaf.

connate united, usually applied to similar features when fused in a single structure.

connate-perfoliate where opposite sessile leaves are joined by their bases, through which the axis appears to pass.

connective the part in a stamen that connects the lobes of an anther at the point of attachment to the filament.

connivent converging, and even coming into contact, but not fused; (of petals) gradually inclining toward the centre of their flower.

constricted abruptly narrowed, contracted.

contiguous in contact, touching but not fused.

continuous an uninterrupted symmetrical arrangement, sometimes used as a synonym of decurrent.

contorted twisted or bent, in aestivation the same as convolute.

contracted narrowed and/or shortened.

contractile applied to roots which contract in length and pull parts of a plant further into the soil.

convergent see connivent.

convolute rolled or twisted together longitudinally, with the margins overlapping, as leaves or petals in the bud.

cordate heart-shaped, applied to leaves and leafy stipules, usually ovate-acute in outline with a rounded base and a deep basal sinus or notch where the petiole is inserted.

coriaceous leathery or tough but smooth and pliable in texture.

corm a solid, swollen, subterranean, bulb-like stem or stem-base; it is annual, the next year's corm developing from the terminal bud or, in its absence, one of the lateral buds.

cormel (cormlet) a small corm developing from and around the mother corm.

cormous bearing corms.

corniculate bearing or terminating in a small horn-like protuberance.

corolla the interior perianth whorl; a floral envelope composed of free or fused petals. Where the petals are separate, a corolla is termed choripetalous or polypetalous; where they are fused, the corolla is gamopetalous or sympetalous, in such cases the petals may be discernible only as lobes or teeth on the rim of a corolla tube, cup or disc.

corolliform resembling a corolla.

corona 'crown', a crown- or cup-like appendage or ring of appendages, this may be a development of the perianth (e.g. *Narcissus*), of the staminal circle, as in *Asclepias*, or located between perianth and stamens as in *Passiflora*.

coronal, coronate bearing a corona.

corrugate (adj.) crumpled or wrinkled but more loosely so than in rugose.

corymb an indeterminate flat-topped or convex inflorescence, where the outer flowers open first; cf. umbel.

corymbose, corymbiform resembling or forming a corymb.

costa a single pronounced midvein or midrib; less frequently, the rachis of a pinnately compound leaf.

costate with a single, pronounced vein, the midrib.

cotyledon the primary leaf, or seed leaf, either solitary (monocots), paired (dicots) or whorled as in some conifers, it may remain within the seed-coat or emerge and become green during germination.

crateriform shaped like a goblet; a concave hemisphere slightly contracted at the base.

crenate scalloped, with shallow, rounded teeth; bicrenate is where the teeth themselves have crenate teeth.

crenulate minutely crenate.

crinoid lily-like.

crispate curled and twisted extremely irregularly, used either of a leaf-blade or, more often, of hairs.

crispy-hairy (of hairs) wavy and curved, in dense short ringlets.

cristate crested or, less commonly, 'crest-like', ruffled.

crown (1) a corona; (2) a collective term for the main stem divisions and foliage of a tree or shrub and the branching pattern and overall habit (i.e. domed, spreading, narrowly conical, etc.) that they assume; (3) the basal portions of a herbaceous plant, usually where root or rhizome and aerial stems or resting buds meet; (4) a length of rhizome with a strong terminal bud, used for propagation as, for example, with *Convallaria*; (5) the head of a single-stemmed tree-like plant or shrub bearing a distinct apical whorl, rosette or flush of foliage; (6) the leaves and terminal buds of a low-growing plant when arranged in a fashion resembling that of the larger plants mentioned under (5), e.g. many ferns.

crumpled see corrugate.

cultivar, cv. 'a cultivated variety', a distinct assemblage of plants arising and/or maintained in cultivation which, when reproduced sexually or asexually, retains its distinguishing character. A cultivar is named with a cultivar (or fancy) epithet, a word or words in a vernacular language (unless published prior to 1959, or a botanical (Latin) epithet already established for a taxon now deemed to be a cultivar). The epithet is printed in roman characters, takes a capital first letter and is either enclosed in single quotation marks or prefixed by the abbreviation cv.

cultrate, cultriform knife-shaped, resembling the blade of a knife.

cuneate, cuneiform inversely triangular, wedge-shaped.

cupreous with the colour and lustre of copper.

cupular furnished with a cupule.

cupule a cup-shaped involucre of hardened, coherent bracts, subtending a fruit or group of fruits.

cupuliform resembling a cupule.

cusp a short, stiff, abrupt point.

cusped see cuspidate.

cuspidate (of apices) terminating abruptly in a sharp, inflexible point, or cusp.

cuspidulate minutely cuspidate.

cylindric, cylindrical elongated and virtually circular in cross-section.

cymbiform boat-shaped, attenuated and upturned at both ends with an external dorsal ridge.

cyme a more or less flat-topped and determinate inflorescence, the central or terminal flower opening first.

cymose arranged in or resembling a cyme or bearing cymes.

cymule a small and generally few-flowered cyme.

dactyloid, dactylose fingerlike.

dealbate whitened, covered with a white powder.

deciduous (1) falling off when no longer functional, as non-evergreen leaves, or the petals of many flowers; (2) a plant that sheds its leaves annually, or at certain periods, as opposed to evergreen plants.

declinate bent or curved downward or forward.

decompound a compound leaf with two or more orders of division, e.g., bipinnate, tripinnate, triternate, etc.

decumbent of a stem, lying horizontally along the ground, but with the apex ascending and almost erect.

decurrent where the base of a leaf blade extends down and is adnate to the petiole (if any) and the stem.

decurved curved downwards.

decussate of leaves, arranged in opposite pairs with adjacent pairs at right angles to each other, thus forming four longitudinal rows.

deflected bent or turned abruptly downwards.

deflexed bent downward and outwards; cf. reflexed.

dehiscence the mode and process of opening (i.e. by valves, slits, pores or splitting) of a seed capsule or anther to release seed or pollen.

dehiscent, dehiscence of a seed capsule, splitting open along definite lines to release seeds when ripe.

deltoid (deltate) an equilateral triangle attached by the broad end rather than the point; shaped like the Greek letter delta.

demersed of a part constantly submersed under water.

dendritic, dendroid ramifying finely at the apex, in the manner of the head of a tree.

dentate toothed, of the margins of leaf blades and other flattened organs, cut with teeth. Strictly, the teeth are shallow and represent two sides of a roughly equilateral triangle, in contrast to serrate, (saw-toothed), where the teeth are sharper and curved forwards, or crenate, where the teeth are blunt and rounded. Less precisely, the term is used to cover any type of toothed margin.

denticulate minutely dentate.

deplanate flattened or expanded.

depressed sunken or flattened as if pressed from above.

determinate of inflorescences such as cymes that end in a bud where the central or terminal flower opens first, thus ending extension of the main axis.

diadelphous of stamens, borne in two distinct bundles or, with several stamens united and a further solitary stamen apart from them, as in many Leguminosae.

dichasium a type of determinate inflorescence; the basic structure has three flowers (members), one terminating the primary axis, the other two carried on more or less equal secondary branches arising from beneath the primary member in a false dichotomy. The secondary members may themselves be dichasia. Such a structure is known as a *dichasial cyme* or a *compound dichasial cyme*, although the former term has been applied by some authors to the basic dichasium itself.

dichogamous (of flowers) preventing natural self-pollination by the failure of pollen dehiscence and stigma receptivity to occur simultaneously.

dichotomous branching regularly by forking repeatedly in two; the two branches of each division are basically equal.

dicotyledonous possessing two cotyledons.

dicotyledons (dicots) one of the two major divisions of the angiosperms, characterized by (usually) two cotyledons, the presence of cambium in many species and floral parts most often occurring in fours and fives.

diffuse spreading widely outwards by frequent branching.

digitate 'fingered', of a compound leaf, palmately arranged with the leaflets arising from the same point at the apex of the petiole.

digonous two-angled.

digynous with two separated styles or carpels.

dilated, dilating broadened, expanded.

dimorphic, dimorphous occurring in two dissimilar forms or shapes.

dioecious with male and female sporophylls or staminate and pistillate flowers on different plants.

disc, disk (1) a fleshy or raised development of the torus within the calyx, or within the corolla and stamens, or composed of coalesced nectaries or staminodes and surrounding the pistil; (2) (in Compositae) the central, or sometimes whole, part of the capitulum bearing short tubular florets as opposed to the peripheral ray florets; (3) the central part of the lip in Orchidaceae, often elevated and callused or crested; (4) a circular flattened organ, e.g. the disc-like tendril tips of some plants climbing by adhesion; (5) the basal plate of a bulb around which scales are arranged.

disc floret (of Compositae) a flower with a tubular corolla, often toothed, found in the centre of a radiate capitulum or occupying the whole of a discoid capitulum. See also ray floret.

disciform, discoid circular and flattened.

discoid (1) of leaves, with a round fleshy blade and thickened margins; (2) (more commonly) pertaining to the capitula of some Compositae, composed entirely of disc florets.

dissected cut in any way, a general term applicable to leaf blades or other flattened organs that are incised, lacerate, laciniate, pinnatisect or palmatisect.

distant (of leaves on a stem, stipes on a rhizome or flowers on a floral axis) widely spaced, synonymous with remote and the antithesis of proximate.

distichous (of leaves) distinctly arranged in two opposite ranks along a stem or branch.

distinct separate, not connate or in any way united, with similar parts; more generally meaning evident or obvious, easily distinguishable.

divaricate broadly divergent and spreading, a term usually applied to branching patterns where branches spread from 70° to 90° outwards from the main axis.

divergent broadly spreading from the centre.

divided a vague term meaning compound or deeply cut, lobed or cleft.

dolabriform hatchet-shaped.

doleiform barrel-shaped.

dorsal pertaining to the back of an organ, or to the surface turned away from the axis, thus abaxial. A term confused by some authors with its opposite, ventral.

dorsifixed of an organ attached by its dorsal surface to another.

dorsiventral flattened, and having separate dorsal and ventral surfaces, as most leaves and leaf-blades.

double a flower is said to be double when it has more than the usual complement of petals or petal-like elements (petaloid sepals, staminodes or colourful bracts). In flowers with tubular corollas, a further form of doubling is the hose-in-hose arrangement where additional corollas are held within each other. The capitula of Compositae are said to be double when they consist wholly of ray florets.

downy see pubescent.

drepanium a sickle-shaped cyme.

echinate covered with many stiff hairs or bristles, or thick, blunt prickles.

eciliate lacking cilia, not ciliate.

eglandular without glands.

ellipsoid elliptic, but 3-dimensional.

elliptic, elliptical ellipse-shaped; midway between oblong and ovate but with equally rounded or narrowed ends, with two planes of symmetry and widest across the middle.

elongate lengthened, as if stretched or extended.

emarginate (of the apex) shallowly notched, the indentation (sinus) being acute.

embracing clasping by the base.

emersed raised out of and above the water.

endemic confined to a particular region.

ensiform sword-shaped, straighter than lorate, and with an acute point.

entire continuous; uninterrupted by divisions or teeth or lobes, thus 'leaves entire' meaning, margins not toothed or lobed.

ephemeral very short-lived plants, or flowers lasting for only one day or less.

epicalyx an involucre of bracts surrounding a calyx, a false calyx.

epigeal *epigeal germination* describes the condition found in some Liliaceae where the cotyledon rises *above* ground at germination and the first true leaf arises soon afterwards. cf hypogeal.

epiphyte a plant which grows on another plant, but is not parasitic and does not depend on it for nourishment.

epiphytic growing on plants without being parasitic.

epruinose lacking a pruinose coating.

equilateral equal-sided.

equitant when conduplicate leaves overlap or stand inside each other in two ranks in a strongly compressed fan, as in many Iridaceae.

erect of habit, organ or arrangement of parts upright, perpendicular to the ground or point of attachment.

erinous prickly, coarsely textured with sharp points.

erose irregularly dentate, as if gnawed or eroded.

erumpent on the point of breaking through, or apparently so.

etiolated drawn out and bleached or blanched by exclusion of light.

evergreen (having) foliage that remains green for at least a year, through more than one growing season.

evolute unfolded.

exotic a plant in cultivation outside its native lands.

explanate spread out, flat.

exserted obviously projecting or extending beyond the organs or parts surrounding it, as stamens sticking out from the corolla; cf. included.

exstipulate, estipulate without stipules.

extra- (prefix) meaning 'outside', e.g. extrafloral, outside the flower proper.

extrafloral outside the true flower (as bracts, nectaries, etc.).

extrastaminal outside the stamens; mostly used of the disc.

extrorse turned or facing outwards, abaxial, often used of the dehiscence of an anther; cf. introrse.

falcate strongly curved sideways, resembling a scythe or sickle.

fall one of the drooping or spreading petals, often bearded, of an *Iris* perianth.

family the principal category of taxa intermediate between Order and genus, e.g. Rosaceae. The names of most families derive from that of the type genus (*Rosa* above) and are plural nouns ending in -aceae. Among the exceptions to this rule are Palmae, Gramineae, Leguminosae, Umbelliferae; these too have modern equivalents in Arecaceae, Poaceae, Fabaceae and Apiaceae, respectively.

farina the powdery or mealy coating on the stems, leaves, and sometimes flowers of certain plants.

farinose see farinaceous.

farinose, farinaceous having a mealy, granular texture.

fasciated (of stems or similar axes, 'bundled') where two or more narrow parts grow abnormally together lengthwise in a congested manner; (of one part) flattened and misshapen as if composed of several parts joined in that way.

fascicle a cluster or bundle of flowers, racemes, leaves, stems or roots, almost always independent but appearing to arise from a common point.

fascicled arranged in a fascicle or fascicles.

fasciculate see fascicled.

fastigiate describing the habit of trees and shrubs – often cultivars – with a strongly erect, narrow crown, and branches virtually erect and parallel with the main stem.

felted-tomentose tomentose, but more woolly and matted, the hairs curling and closely adpressed to the surface.

ferruginous brown-red, rust-coloured.

fibrillate finely striated or fibrous.

fibrillose with thread-like fibres or scales.

fibrous of a thread-like, woody texture.

fiddle-shaped see pandurate.

filament (1) a stalk which bears the anther at its tip, together forming a stamen; (2) a threadlike or filiform organ, hair or appendage.

filamentous composed of or bearing filaments.

filiferous bearing filiform appendages.

filiform (of leaves, branches etc.) filament-like, i.e. long and very slender, rounded in cross-section.

fimbriate bordered with a fringe of slender processes, usually derived from the lamina rather than attached as hairs; cf. ciliate.

fissile splitting easily.

fistulose, fistular hollow and cylindrical like a pipe.

flabellate, flabelliform fan-shaped, with a wedge-shaped outline and sometimes conspicuously pleated or nerved.

flaccid weak, limp, floppy, lax etc.

flagellate with whip-like runners, sarmentose.

flagelliform long, tapering, supple; whiplike.

fleshy-rooted used of plants with thick fleshy roots or storage organs.

flexuous (of an axis) zig-zag, bending or curving in alternate and opposite directions.

floccose possessing dense, woolly hairs that fall away easily in tufts.

flocculent, flocculose slightly floccose, woolly.

floret a very small flower, generally part of a congested inflorescence.

floriferous bearing flowers freely.

flower an axis bearing one or more pistils or stamens, or both, usually with some floral envelope; if surrounded by a perianth of calyx and corolla it is termed perfect.

foetid, fetid having an unpleasant odour.

foliaceous resembling a leaf, in appearance or texture.

foliate bearing leaves.

foliolate bearing leaflets.

follicle a dry, dehiscent, one- to many-seeded fruit, derived from a single carpel and dehiscing by a single suture along its ventral side.

form, forma [abbrev. f.] an infraspecific taxon subordinate to subspecies and variety. The lowest rank in the taxonomic hierarchy, the forma is usually distinguished by characters such as flower colour, habit, leaf division – features of importance to gardeners if 'minor' for taxonomists.

fractiflex in intermittent zig-zag lines.

free (strictly of dissimilar parts or organs) separate, not fused or attached to each other. 'Distinct' describes the separateness of similar organs.

fringed see fimbriate.

frutescent shrubby, or becoming so.

fruticose shrub-like, bearing stems or branches, but without a single main trunk.

fugacious falling off or withering rapidly; transitory.

funnelform of a corolla tube which widens gradually upward toward and into the spreading limb.

furcate forked, the terminal lobes prong-like.

furfuraceous scurfy, with soft, bran-like scales.

furrowed channelled or grooved lengthwise, a term covering both sulcate and conspicuously striate.

fuscous dusky, blackish.

fused (of parts usually free or separate) joined together to form a continuous surface; cf. coherent.

fusiform spindle-shaped, swollen in the middle and tapering to both ends.

fusoid somewhat fusiform.

fynbos a dominant vegatation type of the Cape Floral Region, characterized by low, heath and scrub-like communities in which plant families like Proteaceae, Ericaceae and Restionaceae are strongly represented, as are geophytes such as *Gladiolus*. Drought and fire are important environmental factor for fynbos.

galeate helmet-shaped, hollow and domed.

gamopetalous with petals united by their margins, forming a tubular or funnelform corolla, or at least by their bases.

gamosepalous with sepals united by their margins.

geminate paired.

gemmiparous bearing vegetative buds.

geniculate bent abruptly, in the form of a flexed knee.

geniculum a knee-like joint or node where an organ or axis is sharply bent.

genus (pl. genera) the principal rank in the taxonomic hierarchy between Family and species. The genus represents a single highly distinctive species (monotypic or monospecific genus) such as *Amaryllis* or, more often, a number of species united by a common suite of distinctive characters. The genus or generic name is italicized and takes a capital letter.

geophyte a plant growing with stem or tuber below ground, usually applied to bulbous or tuberous species from arid lands.

gibbosity a basal or apical swelling.

gibbous swollen on one side or at the base.

glabrate see glabrescent.

glabrescent (1) nearly glabrous, or becoming glabrous with age; (2) minutely and invisibly pubescent.

glabrous smooth, hairless.

gladiate sword-like.

glandular generally, bearing glands; (of hairs) bearing a gland, or gland-like prominence at the tip.

glandular-pubescent either covered with intermixed glands and hairs, or possessing hairs terminated by glands.

glaucescent slightly glaucous.

glaucous coated with a fine bloom, whitish, or blue-green or grey and easily rubbed off.

globose spherical, sometimes used to mean near-spherical.

globular composed of globose forms; sometimes used where globose is meant.

globulose diminutive of globose.

glomerate aggregated in one or more dense or compact clusters.

glomerule a cluster of capitula or grouped flowers, strictly subtended by a single involucre.

glutinose, glutinous see viscid.

granular (of a leaf) composed of granules, or minute knobs or knots; (of its surface) grainy, as if covered by small granules.

grooved a more general term for striate or sulcate.

group a category intermediate between species and cultivar used to distinguish (1) an assemblage of two or more similar cultivars and/or individuals within a species or hybrid; (2) plants derived from a hybrid of uncertain parentage; (3) a range of individuals of a species or hybrid which, although different, share certain characters that give them coherence as a unit. Group names are written in roman script, take a capital initial letter, no quotation

marks and are always linked to the word group, with a lower case initial and never abbreviated.

gynodioecious bearing perfect or pistillate flowers on separate plants.

gynoecium the female element of a flower comprising the pistil or pistils.

gynomonoecious bearing separate female and bisexual flowers on the same individual.

gynophore the stalk of a pistil which raises it above the receptacle.

habit the characteristics of a plant's appearance, concerning shape and growth and plant type (i.e. herb, shrub or tree).

habitat the area or type of locality in which a plant grows naturally.

haft the base of an organ when narrow or constricted, most often applied to the haft of the falls in *Iris* flowers.

halophyte a plant tolerant of or adapted to saline soil.

hamate hooked at the tip.

hapaxanthic with only a single flowering period.

hastate arrow-shaped, triangular, with two equal and approximately triangular basal lobes, pointing laterally outward rather than toward the stalk (see sagittate).

head a dense cluster or spike of flowers; a capitulum.

helically spirally, in a spiral arrangement.

helicoid spirally clustered, in the shape of a spring or a snail-shell.

helicoid cyme see bostryx.

helminthoid worm-shaped.

helophyte a plant growing in permanent or seasonal mud.

herb (1) strictly, a plant without persistent stems above ground, often confined to perennials with annual stems or leaves arising from a persistent subterranean stem or rootstock. More generally, any non-woody plant; (2) a plant with culinary or officinal properties.

herbaceous (1) pertaining to herbs, i.e. lacking persistent aerial parts (as in the idea of a herbaceous perennial or the herbaceous border) or lacking woody parts; (2) softly leafy, pertaining to leaves; (3) thin, soft and bright green in texture and colour, as in the leaf blades of some grasses and many other herbs.

hermaphroditic bisexual, having both pistils and stamens in the same flower.

heterogamous (1) bearing two types of flower, as in the ray and disc florets of Compositae; (2) with sexual organs abnormally arranged or developed, or with function transferred from flowers of one sex to another.

heteromorphic assuming different forms or shapes at different stages in the life-history of the plant, as opposed to polymorphic, where different forms occur at the same stage of a plant's development.

heterophyllous bearing two or more differnt forms of leaf on the same plant, either contemporaneously or at different times; sometimes used of different leaf forms exhibited by individuals of the same species.

heterostylous of species whose flowers differ in the presence or number of styles, i.e. some unisexual, some hermaphrodite.

hippocrepiform shaped like a horse-shoe.

hirsute with long hairs, usually rather coarse and distinct.

hirsutullous slightly hirsute.

hirtellous minutely or softly hirsute.

hirtuse see hirsute.

hispid with stiff, bristly hairs, not so distinct or sharp as when setose.

hispidulous minutely hispid.

hoary densely covered with white or grey hairs.

homochlamydeous with an undifferentiated perianth of tepals.

homogamous having hermaphrodite flowers, or flowers of the same sex.

homomorphic having the same shape.

hooded cucullate or, more loosely, referring to inarching parts enclosing others in the resulting concavity.

horn appendage shaped like an animal's horn, see cornute.

horny hard and brittle, but with a fine texture and easily cut.

hort., horti, 'of the garden', **hortorum** 'of gardens', **hortulanorum,** 'of gardeners'; all three are abbreviated hort., never capitalized lest the citation be mistaken for the name of a botanist. The last two of these are used to indicate either the misapplication of a name by gardeners when it is, in fact, a *homonym* of some other validly published name or to denote the origination and effective publication of a name in horticultural writings of confused authorship or of no standing as vehicles of *valid publication*. The citation horti (again shortened to hort.) usually precedes a grower's name and indicates a plant name published in a nursery catalogue, e.g. hort. Lemoine, hort. Spaeth.

hose-in-hose a form of double flower, where the corolla or corolla-like calyx – usually tubular – is duplicated with one inserted in the throat of the other.

hyaline transparent, translucent, usually applied to the margins of leaves and bracts.

hybrid a plant produced by the cross-breeding of two or more genetically dissimilar parents; the parents generally belong to distinct taxa. A natural hybrid is one arising in nature, a spontaneous hybrid one arising without the direct intervention of man but, usually, in gardens, an artificial hybrid is a cross deliberately made by man. Specific hybrids (interspecific hybrids) are those between species belonging to the same genus, intergeneric hybrids those between taxa belonging to different genera – the number of genera involved is usually denoted by a prefix, e.g. bigeneric, trigeneric, etc.

hydrophyte plants growing partly or wholly in water.

hypanthium cup-, ring- or tube-like structure formed by the enlargement and fusion of the basal portions of calyx, corolla and stamens, together with the receptacle and on which these parts are borne. Sometimes termed the floral cup or, inaccurately, the calyx tube.

hypocrateriform see salverform.

hypogeal *hypogeal germination* describes the condition found in some Liliaceae where the cotyledon remains below ground at germination, feeding a minute, growing bulb from the endosperm. Growth above ground is usually delayed by a genetic inhibitor until a cold period has passed, whereupon the first true leaf arises.

hypogynous borne beneath the ovary, generally on the receptacle; said of the calyx, corolla and stamens of a superior ovary.

hysteranthous with the leaves developing after the flowers; cf. precocious and synanthous.

imbricate (of organs such as leaves or bracts) overlapping; more strictly applied to such organs when closely overlapping in a regular pattern, sometimes encircling the axis.

immersed (1) entirely submerged in water, cf. emersed; (2) of features embedded and sunken below the surface of a leaf blade.

imparipinnate where a pinnately compound leaf terminates in a single leaflet, pinna or tendril (see paripinnate).

imperfect when certain parts usually present are not developed. Imperfect flowers are unisexual.

impressed sunken into the surface.

incised dissected, but cut deeply and irregularly with the segments joined by broad lamina.

included 'enclosed within', as in stamens within a corolla; neither projecting nor exserted.

incomplete (of flowers) lacking one or more of the four whorls of the complete flower.

incurved bending inwards from without.

indehiscent not splitting open to release its seeds or spores; the opposite of dehiscent, and generally applied to fruit types such as achenes, berries, drupes and pomes.

indeterminate used of an inflorescence with the lower flowers opening first, thus not arresting the elongation or development of the primary axes, e.g. a panicle, raceme or corymb. An inflorescence not terminated by a single flower.

indigenous native, not exotic.

indumentum a covering of hair, scurf or scales, most often used in the general sense of 'hair'.

induplicate folded inwards.

indurate hardened and toughened.

inflated bladder-like, blown up and swollen; cf. saccate.

inflexed bent inwards towards the main axis.

inflorescence the arrangement of flowers and their accessory parts on an axis.

infundibular, infundibuliform funnel-shaped.

inserted attached to or placed upon, as in 'stamens inserted on corolla'; *not* the antithesis of exserted.

insertion the point or mode of attachment for a body to its support, a leaf insertion is where the leaf joins the stem forming an axil.

intergeneric used of a hybrid produced by crossing members of two or more genera and designated by a multiplication sign before a hybrid generic name, e.g. × Chionoscilla.

intermediate used of hybrids apparently combining the characters of their parents in equal measure and standing midway between them: cf. segregate.

internode the portion of stem between two nodes.

interrupted not continuous; the disturbance of an otherwise symmetrical arrangement by, for instance, the interposition of small or undeveloped leaflets or segments.

interspecific used of hybrids between two different species belonging to the same genus, denoted by a hybrid binomial, that is, for interspecific hybrids, genus name plus multiplication sign plus hybrid epithet, e.g. *Crocosmia × crocosmiiflora*.

intricate entangled.

introduction a non-indigenous plant, usually purposefully introduced.

introrse turned or facing inwards, towards the axis, as an anther which opens towards the centre of its flower.

involucral forming an involucre.

involucrate possessing an involucre.

involucre a single, highly conspicuous bract, bract pair, whorl or whorls of small bracts or leaves subtending a flower or inflorescence.

involute rolled inward, toward the uppermost side (see revolute).

irregular zygomorphic; asymmetrical.

jointed see articulate.

jugate see paired.

jugum a pair, especially of lobes or leaflets.

juvenile the early, non-adult phases of a plant's life, evidenced by sexual immaturity and/or by different habit and foliage forms.

keel a prominent ridge, like the keel of a boat, running longitudinally down the centre of the undersurface of a leaf, petiole, bracts, petal or sepal.

keeled possessing a keel; see also carinate.

kidney-shaped reniform.

knobbed see capitate.

knotted see torulose.

labiate possessing a lip or lips, thus 'corolla bilabiate'.

labium one of the lip-like divisions of a labiate corolla or calyx.

lacerate irregularly, and more or less broadly and shallowly, cut, as if torn.

laciniate irregularly and finely cut, as if slashed.

lacrimiform, lachrymaeform tear-shaped.

lacticifer, lactifer a latex-producing duct.

lactiferous, lacticiferous containing or producing latex.

lacuna a cavity or depression, especially an air-hole in plant tissue.

lacunose pitted with many deep depressions or holes.

laevigate appearing smoothly polished.

lageniform flask-shaped.

lamellate composed of one or more thin, flat scales or plates.

lamina see blade.

lanate woolly, possessing long, densely matted and curling hairs.

lanceolate lance-shaped, narrowly ovate, but 3–6 times as long as broad and with the broadest point below the middle, tapering to a spear-like apex.

lanose woolly, see lanate.

lanuginose as lanate, but with the hairs shorter; somewhat woolly or cottony.

lanulose as lanate, but with extremely short hairs.

lateral on or to the side of an axis or organ.

latex a milky fluid or sap, usually colourless, white or pale yellow.

lax loose, e.g. of flowers in an inflorescence or a loose arrangement of leaves; or hardly coherent, e.g. loose cells in a tissue.

leaf a lateral member borne on the shoot or stem of a plant, generally differing from the stem in form and structure.

leaflet one of the leaf- or blade-like ultimate units of a compound leaf.

leathery coriaceous.

lentiginous minutely dotted, as if with dust.

lepidote, leprous covered with tiny, scurfy, peltate scales.

leprous see lepidote.

ligneous, lignose woody in texture.

ligulate (1) possessing a ligule; (2) strap-shaped, usually more narrowly so than in lorate.

ligule (1) a strap-shaped body, such as the limb of ray florets in Compositae; (2) the thin, scarious, sometimes hairy projection from the top of the leaf sheath; (3) any strap-shaped appendage.

limb a broadened, flattened part of an organ, extending from a narrower base, as in the flared upper part of a gamopetalous corolla.

linear slender, elongated, the margins parallel or virtually so.

lineate see striate.

lined see striate.

lingulate resembling a tongue.

lip (1) in, for example, Labiatae, one of the two distinct corolla divisions, one, the upper, often hooded, the other, lower, often forming a flattened landing platform for pollinators; (2) a staminode or petal modified or differentiated from the others.

lithophyte a plant that grows on rocks or stony soil, deriving nourishment from the atmosphere rather than the soil.

littoral, litoral growing on the sea-shore.

lobe see lobed.

lobed divided into (usually rounded) segments – lobes – separated from adjacent segments by sinuses which reach halfway or less to the middle of the organ (see cleft).

lobulate possessing or bearing lobules.

lobule diminutive of lobe; a small lobe.

locular, loculate furnished with locules; divided into separate chambers or compartments.

locule a cavity or chamber within an ovary, anther or fruit.

loculicidal (dehiscence); splitting longitudinally and dorsally, directly into a capsule through a capsule wall.

lorate strap-shaped.

lunate crescent-shaped.

lyrate pinnatifid, but with a large, rounded terminal lobe and smaller lateral lobes diminishing in size toward the base of the whole.

maculate blotched by wide, irregular patches of colour.

mamillate, mammillate furnished with nipple-like prominences.

marcescent withered but persisting

marginal (1) affixed at the edge or margin of an organ; (2) growing at the water's edge.

marginate with a distinct or conspicuous margin or border.

maturation the stage of development in a fruit immediately preceding ripeness.

mealy farinose.

median pertaining to the central transverse area of a leaf, thus 'median width', width through midpoint, 'median leaflet', the leaflet at the midpoint of a pinnate leaf.

membranous [membraneous], **membranaceous** thin-textured, soft and flexible.

mericarp a one-seeded carpel, one of a pair split apart at maturity from a syncarpous or schizocarpous ovary.

meristem undifferentiated tissue capable of developing into organs or special tissues.

-merous a suffix denoting number and disposition of parts, often combined simply with an arabic number, thus a 3-merous or trimerous flower has parts arranged in threes.

mesophyte a plant halfway between hydrophytic and xerophytic, i.e. the vast majority of plants growing on land and requiring regular water supplies at least when in growth.

midrib the primary vein of a leaf or leaflet, usually running down its centre as a continuation of the petiole or petiolule.

midvein see midrib.

monadelphous stamens united by fusion of their filaments into a single group or bundle.

moniliform where a cylindrical or terete organ is regularly constricted, giving the appearance of a string of beads or a knotted rope; cf. torulose.

monocarpic dying after bearing fruit (i.e. flowering) only once.

monocephalous having one flower head.

monochasial cyme as a dichasial cyme but with the branches missing from one side.

monochlamydeous with only one perianth whorl.

monocot a monocotyledonous plant. The monocots are one of the two primarily divisions of the angiosperms, the other being the dicots. They are characterized by the single, not double, cotyledon in the seed, usually the absence of cambium and thus woody tissue and, in many cases, parallel venation. The monocotyledons include Gramineae, Musaceae, Agavaceae, Liliaceae, Amaryllidaceae, Orchidaceae, Araceae, Iridaceae, Bromeliaceae, Palmae, etc.

monocotyledonous containing only one cotyledon in the seed; pertaining to monocots.

monoecious with bisexual flowers or both staminate and pistillate flowers present on the same plant; cf. dioecious.

monopetalous strictly, with one petal; often loosely used for gamopetalous.

monopodial of a stem or rhizome in which growth continues indefinitely from the apical or terminal bud, and which generally exhibits little or no secondary branching.

monospecific see monotypic.

monotypic having only one component, e.g. a genus with one species. The term is misleading for all genera, no matter how large, are based on a single type; equally, a genus with a single species may be termed monotypic yet contain many distinctive named entities (varieties and cultivars) each of which will have its own type. In such cases, the term monospecific is sometimes preferred.

morphology here, the study of plant structure. Morphological terms form the basic vocabulary of botanical description.

mother plant (1) the parent plant from which propagules are derived; (2) the seed parent of a hybrid.

mucilaginous slimy.

mucro an abrupt, sharp, terminal spur, spine or tip.

mucronate (of an apex) terminating suddenly with an abrupt spur or spine developed from the midrib.

mucronulate diminutive of mucronate.

multifid as bifid, but cleft more than once, forming many lobes.

muricate rough-surfaced, furnished with many short, hard, pointed projections.

muriculate slightly muricate.

muscariform in the shape of a broom or brush.

mutant an individual produced as a result of mutation.

navicular, naviculate shaped like a deeply keeled boat.

neck used of the upper part of a bulb, where the leaves and flower stem emerge.

nectar a sweet, liquid secretion often attractive to pollinators.

nectariferous possessing nectaries.

nectary a gland, often in the form of a protuberance or depression, which secretes and sometimes absorbs nectar.

needle a linear, stiff leaf.

needle-like see acicular.

nervation see venation.

nerved furnished with ribs or veins.

nervose see nerved.

netted reticulate, net-veined.

neuter, neutral sterile, asexual; (of flowers) lacking both pistils and stamens.

nigrescent turning black.

nocturnal opening or active only during the night.

node the point on an axis where one or more leaves, shoots, whorls, branches or flowers are attached.

nodose possessing many closely packed nodes; knobbly.

nodule a small, virtually spherical protuberance.

nut an indehiscent, one-celled and one-seeded, hard, ligneous or osseous fruit.

nutant nodding, usually applied to a whole inflorescence or stem; cf. cernuous.

nutlet a small nut or a small stone of a drupaceous fruit; as an achene, but with a harder and thicker pericarp.

obconic, obconical as conic, but with the point of attachment at the narrower end.

obcordate as with cordate, but with the sinus at the apex rather than the base.

obcuneate as cuneate, but with the point of attachment at the broad end.

obhastate as hastate, but with the triangular lobes at the apex.

oblanceolate as with lanceolate, but with the broadest part above the middle, and tapering to the base rather than the apex.

oblate spherical but dorsally and ventrally compressed.

oblique (1) (of the base) with sides of unequal angles and dimensions; (2) (of direction) extending laterally, the margin upwards and the apex pointed horizontally.

oblong essentially linear, about 2–3 times as long as broad, with virtually parallel sides terminating obtusely at both ends.

obovate ovate, but broadest above rather than below the middle, thus narrowest toward the base rather than the apex.

obovoid as ovoid, but broadest below the middle; obovate in cross-section.

obpyramidal inversely pyramidal, tapering from the apex.

obpyriform inversely pear-shaped, thus narrowing toward the base.

obsolescent (of an organ) reduced to the point of being vestigial.

obsolete extinct, or not evident; where an organ is absent, or apparently absent, from its expected location.

obtuse (of apex or base) terminating gradually in a blunt or rounded end.

oleaginous oily, though of a fleshy nature.

opercular, operculate possessing a lid or cap.

operculum the lid or cap of a capsule with circumscissile dehiscence.

opposite two organs at the same level, or at the same or parallel nodes, on opposite sides of the axis.

orbicular perfectly circular, or nearly so.

ovary the basal part of a pistil, containing the ovules; a simple ovary is derived from a single carpel, a compound ovary from two or more; a superior ovary is borne above the point of attachment of perianth and stamens, an inferior ovary is borne beneath, and a subinferior, semi-inferior or half-inferior ovary is intermediate between these two positions. See also epigynous and hypogynous.

ovate egg-shaped in outline, rounded at both ends but broadest below the middle, and 1.5–2 times as long as it is broad (see elliptic).

oviform egg-shaped.

ovoid egg-shaped, ovate but 3-dimensional.

ovule the body in the ovary which bears the megasporangium, developing into a seed after pollination.

paired usually applied to flowers or leaflets in opposite pairs; bi-, tri-, and multijugate describe compound leaves with two, three or many such pairs or leaflets.

palate the lower lip of a personate corolla, apparently closing its throat.

palea generally speaking, a small, dry bract or scale.

paleaceous bearing small, chaffy bracts or scales (paleae); more generally, chaffy in texture.

palmate with three or more free lobes or similar segments originating in a palm-like manner from the same basal point. (Of venation) three or more veins arising from the point of attachment of the petiole.

palmatifid palmately cleft rather than lobed.

palmatisect palmately cut rather than cleft or lobed into segments almost to the base of the leaf.

pandurate fiddle-shaped; rounded at both ends, one end being enlarged, and markedly constricted or indented on both sides in or around the middle.

panduriform see pandurate.

panicle an indeterminate branched inflorescence, the branches generally racemose or corymbose.

paniculate resembling, or in the form of a panicle.

pannose felt-like in texture, being densely covered in woolly hairs.

papillae small, soft, pimple-like excrescences or protuberances of various sizes.

papillate, papillose covered with small, soft pimple-like excrescences or protuberances of varying sizes.

pappus a whorl or tuft of delicate bristles or scales in the place of the calyx, found in some flowers of Compositae.

papule a relatively large pustule or papilla.

papyraceous papery.

parallel where the veins are more or less parallel to the margins, running lengthwise.

paripinnate where a pinnately compound leaf is not terminated by a single leaflet pinna or tendril.

parted divided almost to the base into a determinate number of segments; a more general term for, e.g. pinnate, palmate, etc.

parthenocarpic fruiting without fertilization having taken place.

parthenogenesis the development of a seed without fertilization having taken place.

partite see parted.

patellate see patelliform.

patelliform orbicular and thick, having a convex lower surface and a concave upper surface.

patent spreading.

pectinate pinnately divided, the segments being many, slender and long, and close together, like the teeth of a comb.

pedate palmate, but for the basal/lowest lobes on each side, which are themselves lobed.

pedicel the stalk supporting an individual flower or fruit.

pedicelled, pedicellate growing on a pedicel.

peduncle the stalk of an inflorescence.

peduncled, peduncular, pedunculate borne on or possessing a peduncle.

pellucid virtually transparent.

peltate of a leaf whose stalk is attached inside its margin rather than at the edge, usually at the centre beneath.

pendent hanging downwards, more markedly than arching or nodding but not as a result of the weight of the part in question or the weakness of its attachment or support (pendulous).

pendulous dependent, but as a result of the weakness of the support, as in a slender-stalked heavy fruit or a densely flowered weeping raceme.

penicillate brush-shaped, or like a tuft of hairs.

penninerved, penniveined, penniribbed with closely arranged veins extending from the midrib in a feather-like manner.

pentamerous with parts in groups of five, or multiples of five; often written 5-merous.

pentangular five-angled.

perennate to survive from year to year; to overwinter.

perennial a plant lasting longer than two years.

perfect a bisexual flower or an organ with all its constituent members.

perfoliate of a sessile leaf where the basal lobes are united surrounding the stem which passes through the blade. cf. connate-perfoliate.

perianth the collective term for the floral envelopes, the corolla and calyx, especially when the two are not clearly differentiated.

perigone the perianth, especially when undifferentiated, or anything surrounding a reproductive structure.

perigynous of flowers in which the perianth and stamens are apparently basally united and borne on the margins of a cup-shaped rim, itself borne on the receptacle of a superior ovary, and are thus neither above nor below the ovary.

persistent of an organ, neither falling off nor withering.

personate a sympetalous corolla with an undifferentiated limb, the upper lip arching and the lower lip prominent and addressed to it.

petal one of the modified leaves of the corolla, generally brightly coloured and often providing a place on which pollinators may alight.

petaloid petal-like in colour, shape and texture.

petiolate, petioled furnished with a petiole.

petiole the leaf stalk.

petiolulate possessing a petiolule.

petiolule the stalk of a leaflet.

phyllary one of the bracts which subtends a flower or inflorescence, composing an involucre.

phylloclad, phylloclade a stem or branch, flattened and functioning as a leaf.

phyllocladous (of stems or branches) functioning as a leaf.

phyllode an expanded petiole, taking on the function of a leaf-blade.

pilose covered with diffuse, soft, slender hairs.

pilosulous slightly pilose.

pinna (*pl.* pinnae) the primary division of a pinnately compound leaf. See pinnate.

pinnate (of a compound leaf) feather-like; an arrangement of leaflets (pinnae) in two rows along the rachis; bipinnate refers to a leaf in which the pinnae are themselves divided into rachillae and petiolules bearing leaflets (pinnules). Also applied to veins in a feather-like arrangement.

pinnately veined see penninerved.

pinnatifid pinnately cleft nearly to the midrib in broad divisions, but without separating into distinct leaflets or pinnae.

pinnatipartite see pinnatifid.

pinnatisect deeply and pinnately cut to, or near to, the midrib; the divisions, narrower than when pinnatifid, are themselves not truly distinct segments.

pinnule the ultimate division of a (generally pinnate) compound leaf; for example, a segment of a pinnately divided pinna.

pistil one of the female reproductive organs of a flower, together making up the gynostemium, and usually composed of ovary, style and stigma. A simple pistil consists of one carpel, a compound pistil of two or more.

pistillate a unisexual, female flower bearing a pistil or pistils but no functional stamens.

pistillode a sterile, vestigial pistil remaining in a staminate flower.

pitch resinous exudate.

pitted see lacunose.

placenta the tissue containing or bearing the ovules in an ovary.

placentation the arrangement of the ovules in the placenta. Several types are found: apical, where one or few ovules develop at the top of a simple or compound ovary; axile, where ovules are borne at or around the centre of a compound ovary on an axis formed from joined portions (septa); basal, where one or few ovules develop at the base of a simple or compound ovary; free central, where ovules develop on a central column in a compound ovary lacking septa or with septa at base only; lamellate, with ovules on thin extensions of the placentae into a compound ovary; marginal or ventral, with ovules borne on the wall along the ventral suture of a simple ovary; parietal, where ovules develop on the wall or on the slight outgrowths of the wall forming broken partitions within a compound ovary.

plane flat; a flat surface.

plantlet a small or secondary plant, developing on a larger plant.

pleated see plicate.

plicate folded lengthwise, pleated, as a closed fan.

plumed see plumose.

plumose feather-like; with long, fine hairs, which themselves have fine secondary hairs.

pod a general term for any dry, dehiscent fruit.

polygamodioecious (1) a plant that is functionally dioecious but contains some perfect flowers in its inflorescence; (2) a species which has perfect and imperfect flowers on separate individuals.

polygamous bearing both unisexual and bisexual flowers on the same or different plants within the same species.

polymorphic occurring in more than two distinct forms, possessing variety in some morphological feature.

polysepalous with a calyx composed of separate sepals.

porrect extending or stretching outward and forward.

posterior at or towards the back or adaxial surface.

praemorse raggedly or irregularly truncated, as if gnawed or bitten.

precocious appearing or developing early. Precocious flowers appear before the leaves; cf. hysteranthous.

procumbent trailing loosely or lying flat along the surface of the ground, without rooting.

projecting of stamens and styles and stigmas, clearly thrust outwards beyond the apical margins or (where a flared and flattened limb is present) throat of a corolla.

proliferating producing buds or off-shoots, especially from unusual organs, e.g. plants or plantlets from stolons or runners.

proliferous see proliferating.

prominent (usually applied to veins and surface features) clearly visible or palpable, standing out from the surface.

prophyll (1) the bracteole subtending a single flower or pedicel; (2) the conspicuous first bract borne on the peduncle and, sometimes, inflorescence branches of some monocots.

prostrate lying flat on the ground.

protandrous describes a flower in which pollen is released from the mature anthers before the stigma of the same flower becomes receptive; in incomplete protandry the shedding of pollen continues after the stigma becomes receptive, enabling self-pollination to take place.

protogynous of a flower in which the stigma becomes receptive before pollen is shed from the anthers of the flower.

protologue all of the appurtenances of botanical publication, i.e. diagnosis, description, synonymy, citation of specimens, illustrations, etc.

protruding exserted, e.g. with stamens or style longer than or passing clearly beyond the perianth segments.

proximal the part nearest to the axis, thus the base of a leaf is proximal; cf. distal.

proximate close together; see distant.

pruinose thickly frosted with white, rather than blue-grey bloom, usually on a dark ground colour, e.g. garnet or black.

pseudostem an erect aerial 'stem' apparently furnished with leaves but in fact composed of the packed or overlapping sheaths and stalks of essentially basal leaves.

pseudoterminal (of buds) a lateral or axillary bud which takes the place of an abscised or damaged terminal bud; (of an inflorescence or solitary flower) situated at a stem apex but in fact axillary.

puberulent, puberulous minutely pubescent; covered with minute, soft hairs.

puberulose, puberulous see puberulent.

pubescent generally hairy; more specifically, covered with short, fine, soft hairs.

pulp the juicy or fleshy tissue of a fruit.

pulverulent powdery, covered in a fine bloom.

pulvinate possessing a pulvinus; also sometimes used of cushion-like plants.

pulvinus a cushion of enlarged tissue on a stem at the insertion of a petiole, or on a rachis at the base of a petiolule; generally articulated, and sometimes responsive to environmental conditions, such as heat, light or movement.

punctate dotted with minute, translucent impressions, pits or dark spots.

puncticulate minutely punctate.

pungent ending in a rigid and sharp long point.

pustular, pustulate of a surface covered with pustules.

pustule a pimple-like or blister-like eruption.

pustuliform blister-like.

pyramidal conical, but with more angular sides.

pyriform pear-shaped.

pyxis a capsule exhibiting circumscissile dehiscence.

quadrangular four-angled.

quadrate more or less square.

quadrilateral four-sided.

quadripinnate pinnately divided into four pinnae, or groups of four pinnae.

quinate possessing five leaflets emanating from the same point of attachment.

raceme an indeterminate, unbranched and, usually, elongate inflorescence composed of pedicelled flowers.

racemiform of an inflorescence that appears to be a raceme, i.e. slender, simple and with apparently stalked flowers.

racemose of flowers borne in a raceme; of an inflorescence that is a raceme.

rachilla the secondary axis of a decompound leaf or inflorescence.

rachis (rachises,, rachides) the axis of a compound leaf or a compound inflorescence, as an extension of the petiole or peduncle, respectively.

radiate (1) spreading outward from a common centre; (2) possessing ray florets, as in the typically daisy-like capitula of many Compositae.

radical arising directly from the root, rootstock or root-like stems, usually applied to leaves that are basal rather than cauline.

ramiform branched, branch-like.

ramose bearing or divided into many branches.

ray (1) the primary division of an umbel or umbelliform inflorescence; (2) a ray flower, or a circle of ray flowers, or the corolla of a ray flower.

ray flower, ray floret a small flower with a tubular corolla and the limb expanded and flattened in a strap-like blade (ligule), these usually occupy the peripheral rings of a radiate Compositae capitulum; cf. disc floret.

receptacle the enlarged or elongated, and either flat, concave or convex, end of the stem from which the floral parts or the perigynous zone derive.

receptacular borne on a receptacle, pertaining to the receptacle.

reflexed abruptly deflexed at more than a 90° angle.

regular see actinomorphic.

remontant of a plant that flowers twice or more in a season, in distinct phases.

remote see distant.

reniform kidney-shaped; lunate, but with the concave centre of the shape attached to the base, and the ends obtuse.

repand sinuate, with less pronounced undulations.

resiniferous see resinous.

resinous containing or exuding resin.

reticulate netted, i.e. with a close or open network of anastomosing veins, ribs or colouring. A reticulate tunic in cormous plants is composed of a lattice of fibres.

reticulation a network of reticulate veins, ribs, colouring or fibres.

retrorse (usually of a minor organ attached to a larger part, e.g. a prickle on a stem, a barb on a leaf or a callus on a lip) turned, curved or bent downwards or backwards, away from the apex; cf. introrse.

retuse (of apices) emarginate, but with a small, rounded sinus, and the adjacent lobes blunt.

revolute of margins, rolled under, i.e. toward the dorsal surface, the antithesis of involute.

rhizomatous producing or possessing rhizomes; rhizome-like.

rhizome a specialized stem, slender or swollen, branching or simple, subterranean or lying close to the soil surface (except in epiphytes), that produces roots and aerial parts (stems, leaves, inflorescences) along its length and at its apex, common to many perennial herbs.

rhomboid (of leaves, tepals etc.) diamond-shaped, angularly oval, the base and apex forming acute angles, and both sides forming obtuse angles.

ribbed possessing one or more prominent veins or nerves.

rind the outer bark of a tree outside the cambium.

ripening (1) the maturescence of a fruit as developmental changes occur to prepare it for seed dispersal; (2) the hardening of wood, particularly the lignification of soft stems.

root the axis of a plant that serves to anchor it and absorb nutrients from the soil, usually geotropic, subterranean, enodose and derived from the radicle; roots may, however, be adventitious or aerial.

rootlet a small or secondary root.

rootstock see rhizome.

rosette (of leaves) radiating from a common crown or centre.

rostrate see beaked.

rosulate of leaves arranged in a basal rosette or rosettes.

rotate wheel-shaped; of a corolla with a short tube and spreading circular limb or segments.

rotund rounded, curved like the arc of a circle.

ruderal growing in waste places.

rudimentary fragmentary, imperfectly developed.

rufescent, rufous reddish-brown.

rugose wrinkled by irregular lines and veins.

rugulose finely rugose.

ruminate appearing as if chewed.

runcinate of a leaf, petal or petal-like structure, usually oblanceolate in outline and with sharp, prominent teeth or broad, incised lobes pointing backwards towards the base, away from a generally acute apex.

runner see stolon.

sac see locule.

saccate bag- or pouch-like, shaped like a round shoe.

sagittate arrow- or spear-shaped, where the equal and approximately triangular basal lobes point downward or toward the stalk; see hastate.

salverform of a corolla with a long, slim tube and an abruptly expanded, flattened limb.

sarmentose producing long, slender stolons.

saxicolous growing in or near rocky places, or on rocks.

scaberulous finely or minutely scabrous.

scabrid a little scabrous, or rough.

scabridulous minutely scabrid.

scabrous rough, harsh to the touch because of minute projections, scales, tiny teeth or bristles.

scale leaves specialized, scale-like leaves, including those covering buds or forming bulbs.

scaly possessing minute scales, attached at one end.

scandent climbing.

scape an erect, leafless stalk bearing a terminal inflorescence or flower.

scapose producing scapes or borne on a scape.

scariose see scarious.

scarious thin, dry and shrivelled; consisting of more or less translucent tissue.

scarred bearing scars where bodies have fallen off, e.g. leaf scars on stems.

schizocarp a dry, usually dehiscent syncarpous ovary which splits into separate, one-seeded halves, or mericarps, at maturity.

sclerophyll tissue abounding in schlerenchyma, composed of cells with thick, ligneous walls retaining water; a common adaptation of plants at risk from true or physiological drought and evidenced by hard, leathery or glassy leaf surfaces.

scorpioid cyme (**cincinnus**) a coiled, determinate inflorescence with flowers or branches alternating in two opposite ranks.

scrambler a plant with long stems, able to climb through shrubs and trees.

scurfy covered with tiny bran-like scales, or scale-like particles.

scutate shaped like a shield or buckler; with a concrete centre surrounded by an elevated margin.

scutelliform shaped like a small shield.

sectio, section the category of supplementary taxa intermediate in rank between subgenus and series.

secund (of flowers, leaves) where all the parts are borne along one side of the axis, or appear to be arranged in this way because of twists in their stalks.

seed leaf see cotyledon.

seedling a young plant which develops from a seed.

segment a discrete portion of an organ or appendage which is deeply divided but not compound; thus the segments of a pinnatifid leaf, or the segments (free apical portions) of a fused calyx or corolla.

selection a distinct form of a plant, sexual or asexual in origin, selected and propagated for its ornamental or economic virtues and named as a cultivar.

self-clinging used of plants that climb without the support of others, as by aerial roots or adhesive tendrils.

semiterete a semi-cylindrical form, terete on one side, but flattened on the other, as some petioles.

senescent undergoing the processes following maturity and resulting in the death of tissue.

sepal one of the members of the outer floral envelope, enclosing and protecting the inner floral parts prior to anthesis, the segments composing the calyx, sometimes leafy, sometimes bract- or scale-like, sometimes petaloid. Sepals when described as such are usually free; they may, however, be wholly or partially fused in a calyx tube, a sepaline cup or a synsepalum.

sepaline pertaining to the sepals.

sepaloid sepal-like.

septate see locular.

septicidal when, in dehiscence, a capsule splits or breaks through its lines of junction, splitting into its interior septa (partitions) and not into the locule itself.

septifragal when, in dehiscence, the valves break away from their partitions.

septum a partition or wall, particularly in an ovary.

seriate in a row or whorl; generally prefixed by a number, e.g. monoseriate, in one row, multiseriate, in many rows.

sericeous, silky covered with fine, soft, appressed hairs.

series the category of supplementary taxa intermediate in rank between section and species.

serrate essentially dentate, but with apically directed teeth resembling those of a saw; biserrate is when the teeth are themselves serrate. (See dentate.)

serrulate minutely or finely serrate.

sessile stalkless, usually of a leaf lacking a petiole.

seta a bristle, or bristle-shaped organ.

setaceous either bearing bristles, or bristle-like.

setiform bristle-shaped.

setose covered with sharply pointed bristles.

setulose finely or minutely setose.

sharp-pointed see acute, mucronate and pungent.

sheath a tubular structure surrounding an organ or part; most often, the basal part of a leaf surrounding the stem of monocot families, either as a tube, or with overlapping edges and therefore tube-like and distinct from the leaf blade.

sheathing where the tubular or convolute base of a leaf or spathe surrounds the stem or other parts.

sigmoid, sigmoidal S-shaped, curving in one direction and then the other.

simple not compound; not divided into secondary units, such as leaflets or branches, thus in one part or unbranched.

sinker a type of specialized, fleshy root produced annually by some bulbous and cormous plants. Its taproot-like shape seeks water and serves to pull the bulb deeper into the ground.

sinuate (of the outline of a margin) wavy, alternatively concave and convex. (See undulate.)

sinus the indentation or space between two divisions, e.g. between lobes.

solitary used either of a single flower which constitutes a whole inflorescence, or a single flower in an axil (but perhaps in a much larger overall inflorescence).

spadix the fleshy axis of a spike, often surrounded or subtended by a spathe. Typically the club- or tail-like inflorescence of Araceae.

spathaceous furnished with a spathe.

spathe a conspicuous leaf or bract subtending a spadix or other inflorescence, of particular importance in Araceae and Palmae, but also applied to the valves subtending scapose flowers in many other monocots.

spatheole a small or secondary spathe.

spathiform spathe-shaped.

spathulate, spatulate spatula-shaped, essentially oblong, but attenuated at the base and rounded at the apex.

species the category of taxa of the lowest principal taxonomic rank, occurring below genus level and usually containing closely related, morphologically similar individuals often found within a distinct geographical range. The species may further be divided into subspecies, variety and forma. It is the basic unit of naming, forming a binomial in combination with the generic name. The species itself is signified by a specific epithet, or trivial name.

spicate spike-like, or borne in a spikelike inflorescence.

spiciform spike-shaped.

spiculate furnished with fine, fleshy points.

spike an indeterminate inflorescence bearing sessile flowers on an unbranched axis.

spine a modified stem or reduced branch, stiff and sharp pointed.

spinescent (1) bearing or capable of developing spines; (2) terminating in, or modified to, a spine-like tip.

spinose bearing spines.

spinule a small spine.

spinulose bearing small or sparsely distributed spines.

spur (1) a tubular or sac-like basal extension of the perianth, generally projecting backwards and nectariferous; (2) a short branch or branchlet, bearing whorls of leaves and fascicled flowers and fruits from closely spaced nodes.

spurred calcarate, furnished with a spur or spurs.

squamate, squamose, squamous covered with scales.

squamulose covered or furnished with small scales.

squarrose rough or hostile as a result of the outward projection of scales or bracts with reflexed tips perpendicular to the axis; also used of parts spreading at right angles from a common axis.

stalk a general term for the stem-like support of any organ, e.g. petiole, peduncle, filament, stipe etc.

stamen the male floral organ, bearing an anther, generally on a filament, and producing pollen.

staminal attached to or relating to the stamen.

staminate of the male, a unisexual, male flower, bearing stamens and no functional pistils.

staminodal relating to a staminode.

staminode a sterile stamen or stamen-like structure, either rudimentary or modified and petal-like.

standard an erect or ascending unit of the inner whorl of an *Iris* perianth.

stellate star-like, (of hairs) with branches that radiate in a star-like manner from a common point.

sterile (of sex organs) not producing viable seed, non-functional, barren; (of shoots, branches etc.) not bearing flowers; (of plants) without functional sex organs, or not producing fruit.

stigma the apical unit of a pistil which receives the pollen and normally differs in texture from the rest of the style.

stigmatic attached or relating to the stigma.

stipe the stalk of a pistil or a similar small organ.

stipel (stipella, stipellae) the secondary stipule of a compound leaf, i.e. at the base of a leaflet or petiolule.

stipellate furnished with stipels.

stipitate provided with, or borne on a stipe or small stalk or stalk-like base.

stipular, stipuled see stipulate.

stipulate possessing stipules.

stipule a leafy or bract-like appendage at the base of a petiole, usually occurring in pairs and soon shed.

stolon a prostrate or trailing stem, taking root and giving rise to plantlets at its apex and sometimes at nodes.

stoloniferous producing stolons.

stoloniform resembling a stolon.

stramineous straw-like, in colour, texture or shape.

striate striped with fine longitudinal lines, grooves or ridges.

strict erect and straight.

strigose covered with sharp, stiff, adpressed hairs.

strigulose minutely or finely strigose.

striolated gently or obscurely striated.

stylar, styled possessing or borne on a style.

style the elongated and narrow part of the pistil between the ovary and stigma; absent if the stigma is sessile.

subgenus the category of supplementary taxa intermediate between genus and order: see sectio above.

submerged, submersed beneath the water.

subsessile with a partial or minute stalk.

subtend (verb) of a bract, bracteole, spathe, leaf, etc., to be inserted directly below a different organ or structure, often sheathing or enclosing it.

subterranean, subterraneous underground, i.e. not aerial.

subulate awl-shaped, tapering from a narrow base to a fine, sharp point.

succulent thickly cellular and fleshy, a plant with roots, stems or lvs with this quality.

sucker a shoot arising from a plant's roots or underground stem.

sulcate lined with deep longitudinal grooves or channels, often confined to parts possessing a single deep gulley, i.e. some petioles.

super-, supra- (in combined form) meaning above, greater than, superior to.

superior above, uppermost; a superior ovary is one borne above the insertion of the floral envelope and stamens, or of a hypanthium from which it is distinct.

suture a seam or groove marking the junction between organs such as the valves of a seed capsule, and/or the line of dehiscence.

symmetric, symmetrical actinomorphic.

sympetalous see gamopetalous.

sympodial a form of growth in which the terminal bud dies or terminates in an inflorescence, and growth is continued by successive secondary axes growing from lateral buds; cf. monopodial.

synandrium an androecium composed of fused or connate anthers.

synanthous (of leaves) appearing alongside the flowers; cf. hysteranthous.

syncarp an aggregate or multiple fruit produced from the connate or coherent pistils of one or more flowers, and composed of massed and more or less coalescent fruits.

syncarpous with two or more carpels fused or united in a compound pistil.

synflorescence a compound inflorescence, possessing a terminal inflorescence and lateral inflorescences.

synsepalous see gamosepalous.

synsepalum a calyx cup or tube; a discrete structure formed by the fusion of two or more sepals.

taproot the primary root, serving to convey nutrition and to anchor the plant; where a plant is described as taprooted, these long, deep, scarcely branched and usually fusiform roots persist in adult life.

teeth marginal lobes, usually relatively small, regularly disposed and with the sides tapering toward their apex, thus differing from broad lobes or very narrow divisions; see dentate, serrate.

tendril a slender modified branch, leaf or axis, capable of attaching itself to a support either by twining or adhesion.

tepal a unit of an undifferentiated perianth, which cannot be distinguished as a sepal or petal. In orchids, the term is applied to the sepals and petals minus the labellum and was originally coined for this purpose.

terete cylindrical, and smoothly circular in cross-section.

terminal at the tip or apex of a stem, the summit of an axis.

ternate (of leaves, sepals, petals) in threes; a ternate leaf is a compound leaf divided into three leaflets; in a biternate leaf these divisions are themselves divided into three parts; in a triternate leaf these parts are further divided into three.

terrestrial growing in the soil; a land plant.

tessellated chequered, marked with a grid of small squares.

tetramerous with parts in fours, or groups of four; often written as 4-merous.

thorn a sharp hard outgrowth from the stem wood.

threadlike see filiform.

throat the orifice of the tubular part of a corolla, calyx or perianth, between the tube and the limb.

thyrse, thyrsus an indeterminate, paniculate or racemose primary axis, with determinate cymose or dichasially compound lateral axes.

thyrsiform, thyrsoid thyrse-like.

tomentose with densely woolly, short, rigid hairs, perceptible to the touch.

tomentulose slightly tomentose.

tomentum a tomentose pubescence.

toothed possessing teeth, usually used of margins, often interchangeably with dentate or, qualified, as saw-toothed or bluntly toothed.

tortuous irregularly bent and turned in many directions.

torulose of a cylindrical, ellipsoid or terete body, swollen and constricted at intervals but less markedly and regularly so than moniliform.

torus a receptacle, the region in which floral parts are inserted. An elongated torus is a gynophore.

trailing (of stems) prostrate but not rooting.

trapeziform asymmetrical and four-sided, as a trapezium.

triadelphous stamens connate by their filaments in three groups or fascicles.

trichome a unbranched, hair-like outgrowth of the epidermis, often glandular-tipped.

trichotomous branching regularly by dividing regularly into three.

tridentate when the teeth of a margin have teeth which are themselves toothed.

trifid as bifid, but twice cleft into three lobe-like divisions.

trifoliate three-leaved.

trifoliolate having three leaflets (a ternate leaf is trifoliolate).

trifurcate with three branches or forked in three.

trigonal three-angled.

trigonous a solid body which is triangular but obtusely angled in cross-section.

trilobed having three lobes.

trilocular having three locules.

trimerous 3-merous, with parts in threes.

trimorphic as polymorphic, or dimorphic, but occurring in three distinct forms.

trinervate three-nerved.

tripartite divided almost to the base in three segments.

tripinnate when the ultimate divisions of a bipinnate leaf are themselves pinnate.

tripinnatifid when the leaflets of a pinnatifid leaf have pinnatifid divisions which are themselves divided in a pinnatifid manner.

tripinnatisect when the leaflets of a pinnatisect leaf are divided into pinnatisect divisions which are themselves divided in a pinnatisect manner.

triplinerved (of venation) in which a midrib produces two lateral veins from a little above its base.

tripterous three-winged.

triquetrous triangular in cross-section.

tristylous in which the styles of the flowers of a plant have three different relative lengths.

trisulcate with three grooves or furrows.

trullate, trulliform trowel-shaped.

truncate where the organ is abruptly terminated as if cut cleanly straight across, perpendicular to the midrib.

tuber a swollen, generally subterranean stem, branch or root used for storage.

tubercle a small, warty, conical to spherical excrescence.

tubercular, tuberculose see tuberculate.

tuberculate, tubercled covered with small, blunt, warty excrescences.

tuberiferous bearing tubers.

tuberous bearing tubers, or resembling a tuber.

tumid see turgid.

tunic a loose, dry, papery, membranous, fibrous or reticulate skin covering a bulb or corm.

tunicate (1) enclosed in a tunic; (2) having concentrically layered coats, the outermost being a tunic, like an onion.

turbinate top-shaped; inversely conical, but contracted near the apex.

turgid more or less swollen or inflated, sometimes by fluid contents.

twiner a climbing plant that twines around a support.

umbel a flat-topped inflorescence like a corymb, but with all the flowered pedicels (rays) arising from the same point at the apex of the main axis; in a compound umbel, all the peduncles supporting each secondary umbel (umbellule) arise from a common point on their primary ray.

umbellate borne in or furnished with an umbel; resembling an umbel.

umbelliform in the form of or resembling an umbel.

umbellule the umbel which terminates a compound umbel.

umbilicate with a more or less central depression, like a navel.

uncinate (of hairs) hooked, where the tips are acutely deflexed, or where the sides are denticulate, or bear minute, retrorse barbs.

undifferentiated of parts or tissues with no apparent characters to distinguish them – e.g. the units of an undifferentiated perianth, where sepals and petals resemble each other so closely as to be indistinguishable; cf. tepal.

undulate wavy, but of the margin's surface rather than outline (see sinuate).

unguiculate of petals and sepals, bearing a basal claw.

uni- prefix denoting one.

unicarpellate possessing a single carpel.

unifoliate a simple leaf, sometimes applied to essentially compound leaves with only a single leaflet.

unifoliolate a compound leaf of which only a single leaflet remains; can be distinguished from a simple leaf by the vestigial point of articulation between the leaflet and the petiole.

uniform of one type only (by contrast with dimorphous or polymorphic).

unijugate see paired.

unilateral one-sided; borne or arranged on one side only.

uniovular, uniovulate having a single ovule.

unisexual either staminate or pistillate; with flowers of one sex only.

united of parts usually free or separate held closely or clinging together so as to be scarcely distinguishable (e.g. stamens in tight bundles) or wholly fused forming a single whole (e.g. perianth lobes united in a tube). The term covers both adherent and coherent.

urceolate (of a corolla) urn-shaped; globose to subcylindrical but with a considerable constriction at or below the mouth.

vaginate possessing or enclosed by a sheath.

valvate (1) describing parts with touching but not overlapping margins; (2) opening by or pertaining to valves.

valve one of the parts into which a dehiscent fruit or capsule splits at maturity.

variegated marked irregularly with various colours.

varietal relating to a variety.

variety, varietas (var.) the category of taxa intermediate between subspecies and forma.

velutinous coated with fine soft hairs, more densely so than in tomentose and giving the appearance and texture of velvet.

velvety see velutinous.

venation the arrangement or disposition of veins on the surface of an organ.

ventral attached or relating to the inner or adaxial surface or part of an organ; sometimes wrongly applied to the undersurface.

ventricose unequally swollen; inflated on one side in a more pronounced manner than if gibbous.

vermiculate worm-shaped, with a pattern of impressed, close, wavy lines.

vernal appearing in spring.

vernation the arrangement of leaves in the bud, sometimes an important character for identification, as in the case of *Galanthus* where the emerging lvs have convolute (rolled), reduplicate (folded back) or flat margins if viewed in cross-section while in the sheath.

verrucose warty

verruculose finely verrucose.

versatile of an attached or supported body capable of free movement, e.g. an anther, attached to a filament by its middle and able to be rotated.

verticil a ring or whorl of three or more parts at one node.

verticillaster a false whorl where opposite cymes, being almost sessile, appear to surround the stem in a whorl.

verticillate forming or appearing to form a whorl.

vestigial of a part or organ which was functional and fully developed in ancestral forms, but is now reduced and obsolete.

vestiture, vesture see indumentum.

villous with shaggy pubescence.

virescence the appearance of green pigmentation in plant tissues not ordinarily green.

virgate long, slim and straight, like a rod or wand.

viscid covered in a sticky or gelatinous exudation.

viviparous with seeds which germinate, or buds or bulbs which become plantlets while still attached to the parent plant.

volubile twining.

whorl when three or more organs are arranged in a circle at one node or, loosely, around the same axis.

wing a thin, flat, often membranous extension or appendage or an organ.

woolly see lanate, lanuginose and tomentose.

xerophyte a plant adapted to survival in an arid habitat.

xerophytic adapted to withstand drought.

zygomorphic bilaterally symmetrical, having only one plane of symmetry by which it can be divided into two equal halves.

Temperature Conversion

$$°C = 5/9 (°F -32) \qquad °F = 9/5 °C +32$$

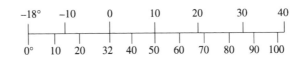

Celsius   −18°   −10   0   10   20   30   40

Fahrenheit   0° 10 20 32 40 50 60 70 80 90 100

Conversions of Measurements

Length			
	1 millimetre	=	0.0394 inch
	1 centimetre	=	0.3937 inch
	1 metre	=	1.0936 yards
	1 kilometre	=	0.6214 miles

Range of Average Annual Minimum Temperature
for each Climatic Zone

Zone	°F	°C
1	< −50	< −45.5
2	−50 to −40	45.5 to −40.1
3	−40 to −30	−40.0 to −34.5
4	−30 to −20	−34.4 to −28.8
5	−20 to −10	−28.8 to −23.4
6	−10 to 0	−23.3 to −17.8
7	0 to +10	−17.7 to −12.3
8	+10 to +20	−12.2 to −6.7
9	+20 to +30	−6.6 to −1.2
10	+30 to +40	−1.1 to +4.4
11	> +40	> +4.4

Abbreviations

anth.	anther	lf	leaf
bienn.	biennel	lvs	leaves
c	circa (before a date or measurement)	mts	mountains
cal.	calyx	N	North (e.g. N America)
C	Central (e.g. C Asia)	perenn.	perennial
cor.	corolla	pet.	petal(s)
cv.	cultivar	pubesc.	pubescent
cvs	cultivars	rhiz.	rhizome
diam.	diameter	S	South (e.g. S America)
E	East (e.g. E Indies)	seg.	segment(s)
fil.	filaments	sep.	sepal(s)
fl.	floruit (flourished)	sp.	species
fl.	flower	spp.	species (plural)
fld.	flowered	ssp.	subspecies
fls	flowers	sspp.	subspecies (plural)
f.	forma	temp.	temperature
fr.	fruit(s)	var.	variety
infl.	inflorescence	W	West (e.g. W Indies)

Bulbs

———

A to Z

Achimenes P. Browne. (From Gk *chemaino*, to suffer from cold.) HOT WATER PLANT. Gesneriaceae. Some 25 species of perennial herbs to 1m; stems unbranched to sparingly branched; rhizomes cylindrical, clad with fleshy scales. Leaves simple, opposite, in equal to strongly unequal pairs or in whorls, serrate or dentate, often fleshy, occasionally with scaly, rhizome-like structures in axils. Flowers axillary, solitary, in pairs or cymes; calyx deeply 5-partite; segments narrow, subequal; corolla tubular, funnelform or salverform, erect or oblique, sometimes spurred at base, limb actinomorphic to slightly 2-lipped, spreading to erect, upper lip 2-lobed, lower lip 3-lobed, lobes entire or erose, lower lobes largest; stamens 4, included; anthers united at apex; style extending post-anthesis. Fruit a 2-valved capsule. W Indies, Mexico to C America. Z10.

CULTIVATION Ornamentals for the glasshouse and conservatory, blooming in summer and autumn from successional plantings starting in late winter and continuing through late spring. Pot the scaly rhizomes into shallow containers of fibrous potting mix, to a depth of 2cm (3/4 in.), spaced 1cm apart, and water sparingly, temperature of 18–20°C/65–68°F. As shoots appear, water more liberally (a dry period will initiate dormancy, even before plants have flowered). Pinch shoots to encourage bushiness, and stake unobtrusively if necessary. Once in flower, plants may be moved temporarily indoors for display. Give bright, filtered light, shading from strong sunlight. Feed at fortnightly intervals when in full growth. Damp down in hot weather and syringe frequently (morning and evening) to maintain humidity. As flowering diminishes, gradually withhold water and reduce humidity until pots are dried out and the rhizomes have ripened. Remove withered foliage and store pots in a dry place with a minimum temperature of 7°C/45°F. This regime applies under glass, but these plants may also be grown successfully in the home, provided strict dormancy is enforced. As houseplants, they enjoyed a vogue at the end of the last century when the myth developed that growth could be initiated and maintained only by dousing with warm water – an error compounded by the derivation of the generic name. Propagate by division on replanting; even individual rhizome scales will give rise to new plants.Scales occasionally arise in leaf axils; these may be removed and grown on. Take stem or leaf cuttings from actively growing plants. Increase also from seed, which is small and difficult to handle.

A.antirrhina (DC.) Morton (*A.atrosanguinea* Lindl.; *A.foliosa* Morr.).
Stems to 30cm. Lvs to 10×5cm, in unequal pairs, ovate, downy, marked with red beneath. Fls solitary to yellow with maroon to purple stripes on exterior, interior yellow with red lines inside, lobes yellow above, red beneath. W Mexico, Guatemala. 'Red Cap': upright, to 75cm; lvs light green; fl. tube yellow, with red spots inside, limb deep rust red.

A.andrieuxii DC. See *Eucodonia andrieuxii*.
A.atrosanguinea Lindl. See *A.antirrhina*.

A.bella C. Morton.
Stems to 30cm, densely tomentose. Lvs to 12.5×7cm, elliptic to ovate, crenate-serrate, pubesc. Fls solitary; cor. to 3cm, violet, with 3 yellow lines inside leading to the lower lobes, W Mexico.

A.candida Lindl.
To 50cm; stems glabrate. Lvs to 8×3.3cm, in markedly unequal pairs, elliptic, apex acuminate, base cuneate, serrate. Fls 2–3 per axil; cor. to 13mm diam., erect, not spurred, white, marked with maroon outside, throat marked with yellow blotches and red lines, limb to 13mm across. Guatemala.

A.candida hort. non Lindl. See *A.longiflora* 'Alba'.

A.cettoana H.E. Moore.
Stems to 30cm, densely hairy. Lvs usually in whorls of 3–4, linear-lanceolate, serrate toward apex. Fls solitary; cor. to 2.5cm, bright purple, somewhat flattened, covered with tiny glands, limb spreading, lobes to 2cm. S Mexico.

A.coccinea (Scop.) Pers. See *A.erecta*.

A.dulcis Morton.
Stems to 60cm, densely hairy. Lvs to 11.5×5cm, ovate-lanceolate, toothed, adpressed-pubesc. above. Fls solitary; cor. to 5cm, white, throat yellow, lobes to 2cm. W Mexico.

A.ehrenbergii (Hanst.) H.E. Moore (*A.lanata* (Planch. & Lindl. ex Lem.) Hanst.).
Stems to 45cm. Lvs to 15×7.5cm, equal, ovate, crenate, sparsely hirsute above, white-tomentose beneath. Fls solitary or paired; cor. to 4cm, pale mauve, throat marked with orange and yellow lines and spots, lobes to 1.3cm. S Mexico.

A.erecta (Lam.) H.P. Fuchs (*A.coccinea* (Scop.) Pers.; *A.pulchella* L'Hérit.; *A.rosea* Lindl.).
Stems to 45cm. Lvs to 6×3cm, in pairs or whorls of 3, ovate, apex acuminate, dentate, often marked with red beneath, with

a minute axillary lf. Fls axillary, bright red, lobes to 1cm. Jamaica, Mexico to Panama. 'Mexican Dwarf': dense and bushy, to 22cm high; fls tiny, pink.

A.flava C. Morton.
Stems to 60cm, sparsely hirsute. Lvs to 8×5cm, in unequal pairs, ovate, serrate, sparsely hirsute, occasionally marked red beneath. Fls solitary to several; cor. to 2.5cm, yellow, spotted red inside, lobes entire; stigma not lobed. W Mexico.

A.foliosa Morr. See *A.antirrhina*.

A.grandiflora Schiede (*A.robusta* auct.).
Stems to 45cm. Lvs to 15×8cm, in equal pairs, ovate, dentate, sparsely hairy, marked red beneath. Fls solitary, paired or several; cor. to 4.5cm, spurred at base, maroon, throat with a light purple-spotted stripe, lobes spreading, to 2cm across. Mexico to Honduras. 'Atropurpurea': habit dwarf.

A.gymnostoma (Griseb.) Fritsch. See *Gloxinia gymnostoma*.
A.jauregia Hanst. See *A.longiflora* 'Alba'.
A.lanata (Planch. & Lindl. ex Lem.) Hanst. See *A.ehrenbergii*.

A.longiflora DC.
Stems hirsute, to 60cm. Lvs to 8×3cm, in whorls of 3 or 4, ovate to oblong or lanceolate, adpressed-hirsute, serrate, marked with red beneath. Fls solitary; cor. to 6cm, violet blue, rarely maroon or white, limb oblique, lobes to 2cm. Mexico to Panama. 'Alba' (var. *alba* F.A. Haage, Jr.; *A.jauregia* Hanst.; *A.maxima* hort.): cor. white with a large yellow spot, lobes marked with purple lines. 'Ambroise Verschaffelt' (*A.verschaffelti* hort.): as for 'Alba' but throat marked heavily with purple lines and spots. 'Margarita' (*A.margaritae* hort.): as for 'Alba' but cor. pure white, throat yellow. 'Andersonii': stems slender; lvs small, ovate, pubescent; fls axillary, pendent, salverform, mauve with a white blotch below, borne on short stalks. 'Dentoniana': fls to 3cm, pale purple, throat white blotched yellow, spotted red. 'Galatea': fls violet, stained purple on throat, with white tinges lower down; lobes separate. 'Major': lvs metallic green; fls to 7.5cm diam., lavender to pale-purple; throat yellow; tube yellow. 'Paul Arnold': lvs burgundy beneath; fls dark purple; throat white, tinged yellow, with red dots.

A.longiflora var. *alba* F.A. Haage, Jr. See *A.longiflora* 'Alba'.
A.margaritae hort. See *A.longiflora* 'Margarita'.
A.maxima hort. See *A.longiflora* 'Alba'.

Achimenes longiflora

A.mexicana Seem. (*A.scheeri* Glend.).
Stems to 60cm, hirsute. Lvs to 12.5×6.7cm, in equal pairs, ovate, dentate, hirsute. Fls solitary, to 5cm; cor. purple or blue, throat pale mauve, lobes spreading. W Mexico. Some plants offered under this name may be *A.longiflora*.

A.misera Lindl.
Stems to 20cm, pubesc. Lvs to 6×3.5cm, ovate, dentate, pubesc. Fls solitary or in pairs; cor. to 1cm, white, with three longitudinal crests; lobes marked with mauve inside. Guatemala.

A.patens Benth.
Stems to 30cm, pubesc. Lvs to 7.5×4cm, in unequal pairs, elliptic-ovate to ovate, dentate, adpressed-pubesc., marked with red beneath. Fls solitary, spurred; cor. maroon-violet, marked with yellow, spotted purple inside throat, lobes small-toothed. W Mexico. 'Major': fls with purple-pink throat.

A.pedunculata Benth.
Stem to 85cm, puberulent toward apex. Lvs to 15×8cm, in pairs, broadly elliptic, apex acuminate, coarsely dentate. Fls 1–3 on a common peduncle to 7cm; cor. to 3cm, scarlet, red-spotted in throat, short-spurred, lobes not ciliate. Mexico to Honduras.

A.pulchella L'Hérit. See *A.erecta*.
A.robusta auct. See *A.grandiflora*.
A.rosea Lindl. See *A.erecta*.
A.scheeri Glend. See *A.mexicana*.

A.skinneri Lindl.
Stems to 90m, pubesc. Lvs to 8×6cm, ovate, acutely dentate. Fls 1–2 on peduncles to 8cm or more; cor. to 3cm, broadening at apex, pink, marked with red inside, throat yellow, lobes denticulate. Guatemala.

A.tubiflora (Hook.) Britton. See *Sinningia tubiflora*.
A.verschaffeltii hort. See *A.longiflora* 'Ambroise Verschaffelt'.
A.violacea hort. See *A.*'Violacea Semiplena'.

A.warscewicziana (Reg.) H.E. Moore.
Stems to 30cm, pubesc. Lvs to 11.5×4.5cm, elliptic-ovate to ovate, dentate, viscid-pubesc., particularly beneath. Fls solitary or in pairs; cor. to 1cm, white, spotted with rust to maroon. S Mexico to El Salvador. Sometimes confused with *A.misera*.

A.Cultivars. Several hundred cvs have developed since the last century, most of them derived in part from *A.longiflora*. They range in habit from prostrate to erect – 'Pendent Purple': habit very vigorously trailing; 'Dazzler': habit bushy; 'Jubilee Gem': habit robust, vigorous, upright; 'Burnt Orange': habit erect to spreading. Some have handsome leaves, including 'National Velvet U.S.A.': lvs unusually dark glossy green; 'Jennifer Goode': lvs numerous, strikingly shiny. Flower colour ranges from mauve to crimson, rose and white – 'Ruby': fls small, deep ruby-crimson; 'Mauve Queen': fls showy; 'Charm': fls coral-pink with a crimson-velvet sheen; 'Pearly Queen': fls tinged pink and lilac with a cream centre, giving the appearance of mother-of pearl; 'Show Off': fls extremely numerous, pink-lilac; 'Glacier': fls snow-white, tinged ice-blue.

Agapanthus L'Hérit. (From Gk *agape*, love, and *anthos*, flower.) Liliaceae (Alliaceae). 10 species of perennial herbs with thickened, short, cylindric stems and thick fleshy roots. Leaves basal, linear to lorate, entire, arching, often 2-ranked, sometimes persistent, glossy and thinly fleshy to subcoriaceous. Scape stout, to 180cm; inflorescence a many-flowered terminal umbel subtended by 2 papery valves; pedicels slender, horizontal to arching; perianth large, tubular to campanulate, dark violet or deep blue to white; stamens 6, inserted on perianth tube, declinate, anthers dorsifixed; ovary superior. Fruit a trilocular capsule; seeds flat, winged, black. S Africa. Hybridization occurs so readily that all garden forms may be hybrids and it has been suggested (McNeil, 1972) that *Agapanthus* consists of one variable species.

CULTIVATION Beautiful summer- and late summer-flowering perennials grown for their umbels of long-lived blooms (excellent for cutting), ranging from pure white through pale blues to deep violet-blue. In general, the deciduous species with long, narrow leaves are hardier than evergreen species, such as *A.africanus*, which typically have broader, bright green leaves. Evergreen species are more safely grown under glass in cool temperate zones although cold-tolerance may vary with provenance; given a warm sheltered position with perfect drainage, stocks of *A.africanus* originating in the U.K., for example, may be expected to tolerate several degrees of frost. Those grouped as Headbourne Hybrids are hardy where temperatures drop to −15°C/5°F, although as with *A.campanulatus*, *A.inapertus* and *A.praecox* ssp. *orientalis*, where temperatures fall much below −5°C/23°F, a deep mulch of bracken litter will ensure survival of the rootstock. Most species, even those sufficiently hardy to survive in the open ground, thrive when overcrowded and are eminently suited to tub cultivation; grown in this way, specimens can be moved into a light, dry, frost-free situation for the winter. *A.praecox* ssp. *orientalis* is particularly suited to stream and lakeside plantings, provided that the roots are above water level.

Grow in full sun in light, fertile, well drained but moisture-retentive soil; although colonies are fairly drought-resistant once established, moisture should, ideally, be plentiful when in full growth, but reduced gradually after flowering to keep the roots almost dry in winter. In tubs, use a high-fertility loam-based mix with additional leafmould and sharp sand. Apply liquid feed from early summer until flowerheads have formed. Propagate by offsets, division of overcrowded clumps, or by seed sown ripe or in spring; seed-raised stock may take 2–3 years to flower and should be protected from frost during their first winter at least. Slugs and snails may be a problem, especially in damp springs. In dry, warm conditions, foliage may be attacked by red spider mite and thrips. Mealybugs may accumulate in the leafbases. *Agapanthus* is often infected by botrytis, and by the fungus *Macrophoma agapanthi* which causes browning of the leaf tips.

A.africanus (L.) Hoffm. (*A.minor* Lodd.; *A.umbellatus* L'Hérit., non Redouté). AFRICAN LILY; BLUE AFRICAN LILY; LILY OF THE NILE.
Lvs to 10–35×0.8–2cm, to 18, 2 ranked, evergreen, linear-lanceolate, more or less erect, canaliculate, subcoriaceous. Scape 25–60cm; spathe valves deciduous; pedicels 1.5–5cm, stiff; fls to 30 per umbel, deep violet-blue; perianth 2.5–5cm, thick and waxy, tube 9–14mm, lobes spreading, stamens shorter than perianth; style equalling stamens. 'Albus': fls white. 'Albus Nanus': habit low; fls white. 'Sapphire': fls dark blue. Z9.

A.campanulatus F.M. Leighton.
Lvs 15–40×1–2.5cm, deciduous. Scape usually 40–70cm, rarely to 100cm; pedicels 2–7cm, spreading; fls few to many, pale to dark blue, sometimes white; perianth 2–3.5cm, campanulate, tube 0.5–1cm, lobes spreading, not recurved; stamens shorter than perianth, exserted; style equalling stamens. Summer–early autumn. 'Albus': fls white. 'Iris': large heads of clear lavender-blue fls. 'Isis': to 75cm; fls deep blue, in dense heads. 'Profusion': to 90cm; fls abundant, pet. light and dark blue striped. 'Royal Blue': fls intense rich blue. 'Variegatus': lvs striped cream, fading later. ssp. *patens* (F.M. Leighton) F.M. Leighton (*A.patens* F.M. Leighton). Smaller and more slender; perianth lobes widely spreading. Z7.

A.caulescens Sprenger.
Lvs arising from a distinct pseudostem (an elongate neck) to 25cm. Basal sheathing lvs 5–15cm, upper lvs 25–60×1.5–5cm, glossy, apex acute or obtuse. Scape 60–130cm; umbel many-fld; pedicels 3–7cm, spreading and arching; perianth 3–5cm, dark or bright blue, tube to 1.9cm, lobes widely spreading, sometimes recurved; stamens exserted. Late summer–early autumn. Similar to *A.africanus* from which it may be readily distinguished by the distinct stems and exserted stamens. Z7.

A.inapertus Beauv. (*A.weilloghii* hort.).
Lvs to 70×6cm (narrower in typical form), linear, glaucous, deciduous in older plants, arising from a short, stocky pseu-

dostem. Scape to 180cm; fls many, bright blue to dark violet, sometimes white; pedicels 2–5.5cm, erect at first, later drooping; perianth 2.5–5cm, tubular, tube equalling lobes, lobes slight spreading; stamens as long as perianth; style slightly exserted when mature. Autumn. 'Albus': fls creamy white. Z7.

A.minor Lodd. See *A.africanus*.

A.nutans F.M. Leighton.
Lvs 20–50×1–4cm, glaucous deciduous. Flowering stem to 90cm; umbels few- to many-fld, fls pale blue; pedicels spreading or drooping; perianth 3.5–6cm, not opening fully, tube 1.4–2.7cm, lobes slightly spreading; stamens shorter than perianth; style almost as long as perianth. Late summer. Z7.

A.orientalis F.M. Leighton. See *A.praecox* ssp. *orientalis*.
A.patens F.M. Leighton. See *A.campanulatus* ssp. *patens*.

A.pendulus L. Bol.
Very similar to *A.nutans* except fls to 3.75cm, dark purple outside, pale blue-mauve within, always drooping or pendulous. Z7.

A.praecox Willd.
Lvs 30–70×1.5–5cm, evergreen, rather fleshy. Scape 40–100cm; fls few to many, bright to pale blue, sometimes white; pedicels 4–12cm; perianth 3–7cm, tube 0.7–2.5cm, lobes spreading; stamens and style sometimes projecting. Summer–autumn. 'Aureo-vittatus': lvs striped yellow. 'Plenus': fls double. ssp. *minimus* (Lindl.) F.M. Leighton. Lvs not exceeding 2.5cm in width; stem slender; infl. lax; fls not exceeding 5cm. ssp. *orientalis* (F.M. Leighton) F.M. Leighton (*A.orientalis* F.M. Leighton; *A.umbellatus* var. *maximus* Edwards; *A.umbellatus* Redouté non L'Hérit.). Small, forming dense clumps. Scape stout; fls seldom exceeding 5cm, to 100 per umbel. 'Albus' ('Albidus'): fls white. 'Nanus': habit dwarf. 'Variegatus': lvs striped silvery white. Z9.

A.umbellatus L'Hérit., non Redouté. See *A.africanus*.

Agapanthus   (a) *A.praecox* ssp. *minimus*   (b) *A.praecox* ssp. *orientalis*   (c) *A.pendulus*

A.umbellatus Redouté non L'Hérit. See *A.praecox* ssp. *orientalis.*

A.umbellatus var. *maximus* Edwards. See *A.praecox* ssp. *orientalis.*

A.weilloghii hort. See *A.inapertus.*

A.cultivars. 'Albatross': similar to 'Maximus Albus'; fls large, white. 'Ardernei': to 90cm; fls white, pedicels and buds flushed purple. 'Blue Giant': to 1.1m; fls rich blue. 'Blue Moon': fls pale blue, in dense heads. 'Blue Triumphator': fls clear blue. 'Bressingham White': lvs broad; fls pure white.

'Castle of Mey': tall; fls deep blue. Giant Hybrids: to 90cm; fls in a range of blue; seed race. 'Golden Rule': lvs edged gold; fls pale blue. Headbourne Hybrids (Palmer Hybrids): to 90cm, vigorous and hardy; fls range of bright colours. 'Kingston Blue': stems very upright; fls brilliant blue. 'Lilliput': dwarf, to 45cm; fls dark blue. 'Loch Hope': to 1.2m; fl. heads large, abundant, fls dark blue; late. 'Maximus Albus': fls large, white. 'Midnight Blue': to 40cm; fls deepest blue. 'Peter Pan': to 30cm; fls mid blue. 'Torbay': fls mid blue, profuse. 'Zella Thomas': to 75cm; fls rich blue. Z7.

Albuca L. (From Lat. *albucus*, asphodel; the type species has white flowers.) Liliaceae (Hyacinthaceae). Some 30 species of perennial, bulbous herbs. Bulbs tunicate. Leaves linear or lanceolate, basal, nearly terete to flat, usually glabrous. Flowers yellow or green-white, erect or nodding, borne in loose racemes; tepals 6, free, the outer spreading, the inner erect, hooded at the tips; stamens 6, the outer occasionally sterile; ovary superior; style 1. Fruit a capsule with many flattened, black seeds. Arabia, Africa, chiefly S Africa.

CULTIVATION Where frosts are light and short-lived (not more than –5°C/23°F), *Albuca* spp. are suited to the wild garden and other informal and naturalistic plantings; in cooler climates grow in the cool glasshouse of conservatory. *A.nelsonii* is one of the most attractive of the genus, bearing long spikes of slightly scented flowers that last well when cut. Grow in full sun in light, freely draining soils; in regions at the limits of hardiness give a sheltered position at the base of a warm wall, with cloche or deep mulch protection during winter. Under glass maintain a minimum temperature of 7°C/45°F with good ventilation; keep moist and apply dilute liquid feed when in full in growth and keep dry as plants enter dormancy, usually by late summer. Propagate by offsets or seed. In addition to the species listed below, *A.setosa* is sometimes offered, as are the cultivars 'Karroo Yellow' and 'The Giant'.

A.altissima Dryand.
Bulb 3.5–5cm diam., almost flat, round. Lvs 5–6, 70–90×3.5–5cm, lanceolate, glabrous, margins incurved, tapering to a long point. Fls 2–2.5cm, borne in loose raceme of 50, 30–45cm; tepals 1.5–2.5cm, white with a broad, green median stripe; outer stamens sterile; style 3-angled. S Africa.

A.aurea Jacq.
Stem 30–60cm. Lvs 6–9, 45–60cm, linear-lanceolate, flat. Fls erect; raceme to 30cm; tepals 2–3cm, pale yellow, with a green, eventually red-brown median stripe; all stamens fertile; style 3-angled. S Africa.

A.canadensis (L.) F.M. Leighton (*A.minor* L.).
Stem 20–40cm, more or less erect. Lvs 3–6, 7.5–15cm, lanceolate, grooved above, obtusely keeled, glabrous. Fls to 7, borne in a raceme, nodding; tepals 1.5–2cm, pale yellow to green-yellow, with wide, green, median stripe; outer stamens sterile; style 3-angled. S Africa.

A.cooperi Bak.
Bulb with a tuft of fibres at its apex. Stem 15 to 50cm. Lvs 2–4, 15–30cm, linear. Fls 10–12, borne in a raceme; tepals 1.5–2.5cm, with broad green, eventually red-brown stripe; outer stamens sterile. S Africa.

A.fragrans Jacq.
Close to *A.aurea*. Fls more or less pendulous, highly fragrant; tepals 1.5–2cm, yellow, with green median stripe, remaining green. S Africa.

A.humilis Bak.
Lvs 1 to 3, 7.5–15cm, narrow-linear. Fls 1 to 3; tepals 1.5cm, white, outer with green median stripe, inner unstriped, often with yellow tip; all stamens fertile; style 3-angled. S Africa.

A.major L.
Close to *A.canadensis*, but more robust. Stem 40–100cm. Lvs 20–60cm. Raceme with 6 to 12 flowers; tepals yellow with a green or brown median stripe. S Africa.

A.minor L. See *A.canadensis*.

A.namaquensis Bak.
Stem to 30cm. Lvs 10–20, 10–15cm, sub-terete, very narrow, minutely pubesc. Fls erect, 10–20cm, 6 to 10 per raceme; tepals 1.5–2cm, inner with yellow tips; outer stamens sterile; style 3-angled. S Africa.

A.nelsonii N.E. Br.
To 2.25m. Lvs 4–6, 90–120×3–5.5cm, lanceolate, bright green, gradually tapering to a point. Stem 60cm–1.5m. Fls borne in a raceme, to 30cm; tepals 3–4cm, white with a green or dull red median stripe; stamens all fertile; style 3-angled. S Africa.

A.wakefieldii Bak.
Lvs 4 or 5, 30–45cm, linear. Fls 10–12, borne on raceme of 15–23cm; tepals to 2.5cm, outer green, inner white with green median stripe; all stamens fertile; style terete. E Africa.

Allium L. (Lat. *Allium*, Classical name for garlic, from Celtic *all*, hot.) Liliaceae (Alliaceae). About 700 species of perennials and biennials, 10–150cm, many producing the characteristic smell of onions when bruised. Bulbs solitary or clustered, covered with papery or fibrous tunics, occasionally grouped on a short rhizome; aerial stems solid or hollow, unbranched. Leaves basal or sheathing, linear to elliptic, flat, grooved or terete, solid or hollow. Flowers few to many in a scapose umbel, sometimes replaced by bulbils, sheathed initially by a spathe with 1 or more bracts; petals and sepals similar, forming perianth with 6 free segments; stamens 6, filaments sometimes toothed, united at base or free, anthers longitudinally dehiscent; ovary superior, trilocular, ovules 1–8 per locule; stigma simple or trilobed. Fruit a trilocular capsule, frequently with terminal crests in American spp.; seeds numerous, black, angled, round or flat. Northern hemisphere.

CULTIVATION A huge genus predominantly found in dry, rocky terrain around the northern, Mediterranean and temperate zones of the world; the most ornamental species are, almost without exception, natives of the northern hemisphere. Some, usually those that are more leafy and of large stature, like *A.ampeloprasum*, are found in grassland and meadow or in disturbed land. *A.ursinum* and *A.triquetrum* occur in damp, shaded habitats. *Allium* includes a number of edible species: *A.cepa*, the onion and shallots, *A.fistulosum*, the Welsh onion (from the German *welsche*, foreign), *A.porrum*, the leek, *A.sativum*, garlic, *A.schoenoprasum*, chives, *A.tuberosum*, Chinese chives – cultigens of unknown wild origin.

The genus includes tall ornamentals for herbaceous or flower borders and smaller species suitable for rock gardens, terraces and pot culture. The large flowerheads of many species are suitable for drying, if cut when their stalks are ripe; some, in which the characteristic garlic perfume is muted or absent, can be grown for cutting, for example *A.aflatunense*, *A.stipitatum*, *A.moly* and the sweetly scented *A.subhirsutum*.

Typically, species from California are very brightly coloured, in shades of magenta, pink and red, as in *A.dichlamydeum*, *A.unifolium* and *A.campanulatum*. These are suitable for hot, dry positions in well-drained soils. In cool temperate areas, the smaller Californian species are best grown in pots, overwintered in frost-free conditions. Larger Californian species, like *A.unifolium* make excellent border perennials.

The tall central Asian species often have globe-like inflorescences on top of leafless stems, the foliage at the base dying back as the flowers emerge. It is advisable therefore to hide the dying foliage by planting the bulbs among shrubs which cast only light shade and which also thrive in similar hot, dry situations in nature. *A.giganteum*, *A.rosenbachianum*, *A.stipitatum*, *A.christophii* and the huge 'Globe Master' can be treated in this way. Smaller Asian species, such as *A.carinatum* ssp. *pulchellum*, *A.caesium* and *A.flavum*, need a position at the front of the border, as does *A.thunbergii*, an extremely hardy species capable of withstanding temperatures below –20°C/–4°F; it flowers in the autumn as the foliage dies back.

Smaller, clump-forming species are suitable for rock gardens, requiring good drainage and full sun, including *A.flavum*, *A.mairei* and *A.oreophilum*; the beautiful blue-flowered *A.beesianum* and *A.victorialis*, a leafy, white-flowered species, suit cooler positions on the rock garden where they need slightly more moisture and richer soils. In general, those that are native to the Himalaya need more moisture in summer than do other species.

Some central Asian species are extremely beautiful in flower but are too tender to grow safely outdoors in cool temperate climates, among them the exciting *A.schubertii*, with an inflorescence 20cm/8in. or more in diameter. Grow in half pots under glass, keep completely dry in winter and bring into growth in late winter; they require hot, dry and very sunny conditions under glass to flower well.

Several species, notably *A.ursinum*, *A.vineale* and *A.paradoxum*, will prove invasive and are best used only in less cultivated parts of the garden.

Propagate by offsets, removed when dormant, or by seed in spring at about 13°C/55°F; keep moist and well ventilated and dry progressively as foliage dies back. Pricking out and potting on is usually easiest when seedlings have become dormant. Increase also by division of clumps; spring-flowering species in summer, summer-flowering species in spring. Set mature bulbs in the soil at approximately one and a half times the depth of the bulb.

Pests and diseases which affect economic species may also affect the ornamental *Allium*; they include onion flies (*Delia antiqua*), stem eelworm (*Ditylenchus dipsaci*), and onion thrips (*Thrips tabaci*), especially under glass. Fungal diseases include smut (*Urocystis cepulae*), rust (*Puccinia allii*), smudge (*Colletotrichum circinans*) and onion white rot (*Sclerotium cepivorum*). Also bacterial soft rots (*Erwinia* spp.).

A.acuminatum Hook. (*A.murrayanum* Reg.; *A.cuspidatum* Fern.).
Stem 10–30cm; bulb 1–1.5cm wide, ovoid to spherical, tunic membranous, reticulate, with hexagonal or nearly square meshes. Lvs 2–4, narrow, channelled, linear, 1–3mm wide, shorter than stem. Fls 10–30, in a loose umbel 4–6cm wide; spathes 2, 1–3cm; pedicels 1–2.5cm; tepals 8–15mm, white to deep rose-pink, acute, 3 outer tepals entire with recurved tips, 3 inner tepals shorter, erect, slightly toothed; anth. purple; ovary with 3 crests. Fr. 4–5mm, slightly ridged; seeds 2.5mm. Spring. N America (Pacific Northwest). Z6.

A.acuminatum var. *bidwelliae* Jeps. See *A.campanulatum*.
A.acutangulum Schräd. See *A.angulosum*.
A.affine Boiss. & Heldr. See *A.vineale*.

A.aflatunense B. Fedtsch.
Stem 80–150cm, slightly ribbed; bulb 2–6cm wide, ovoid, tunic papery. Lvs 6–8, basal, slightly glaucous, 2–10cm

diam., much shorter than stem, withering before fls mature. Fls numerous in a spherical infl. with 4 spathes; pedicels 1.5–3cm; tepals 7–8mm, violet with dark central veins, becoming twisted and reflexed with age; stamens exserted, free, anth. yellow; ovary papillose on short stalk. Fr. 5mm. Spring–summer. C Asia. 'Purple Sensation': to 1m; fls intense deep violet. Z8.

A.akaka S. Gmel. ex Roem. & Schult. f. (*A.latifolium* Jaub. & Spach).
Stem 5–15cm; bulb subspherical, 1.5–3cm wide, tunic membranous. Lvs to 20×6cm, 1–3, basal, oblong-elliptic. Fls numerous, 1cm wide, in a spherical umbel 3–10cm wide produced close to ground level; spathes 1, 3–4-lobed; pedicels 8–30mm; tepals 6.5–8.5mm, elliptic becoming rigid with age, white to lilac-pink; stamens erect, longer than tepals, anth. yellow. Fr. 4–5mm. Summer. Turkey, Caucasus, Iran. Z8.

A.albidum Fisch. ex Bieb. See *A.denudatum*.

Allium (a) *A.karataviense* (b) *A.moly* (c) *A.scorodoprasum* (d) *A.insubricum*

A.*albidum* ssp. *caucasicum* (Reg.) Stearn. See A.*denudatum*.
A.*albopilosum* C.H. Wright. See A.*christophii*.
A.*album* Santi. See A.*neapolitanum*.
A.*album* var. *purpurascens* Maire & Weiller. See A.*subvillosum*.
A.*alleghaniense* Small. See A.*cernuum*.
A.*alpinum* Hegetschw. non Reg. See A.*schoenoprasum*.
A.*alpinum* Reg. non Hegetschw. See A.*narcissiflorum*.

A.*altaicum* Pall.
Stem 12–70cm, hollow, swollen in mid-region; bulbs ovoid, to 4cm wide, clustered on rhiz., tunics membranous, red-brown. Lvs 6–30×0.5–1.5cm, 2–6, hollow, terete, sheathing stem. Fls campanulate in a dense spherical umbel; spathe acuminate; pedicels thick; tepals 6–8mm, glossy yellow, acuminate; stamens exserted; style exserted. Fr. 4–6mm. Summer. Siberia, Mongolia. Z5.

A.*altissimum* Reg.
Stem 65–150cm, longer than lvs; bulb spherical, tunic membranous, grey. Lvs 15–35mm wide, 4–6, green, smooth, linear-lanceolate. Fls numerous in a dense umbel with 1 small spathe and unequal pedicels 4–6× as long as fls; tepals 6–8mm, violet with dark central vein, reflexed and twisted with age; anth. yellow. Fr. 5mm wide. C Asia. Z6.

A.*amabile* Stapf (A.*mairei* var. *amabile* Stapf).
Stem 10–20cm; bulbs slender on short rhiz., tunics fibrous, netted. Lvs 2–4, grassy, sheathing lower part of stem. Fls 2–5, funnel-shaped, often pendent, in an umbel with 1 spathe to 2cm; pedicels 1–1.5cm; tepals 1–1.5×0.15–0.2cm, recurved and keeled, deep pink to magenta with darker spotting; stamens 5–6.5mm. Fr. 4mm. Summer. SW China (Yunnan). Doubtfully distinct from A.*mairei*. Z8.

A.*ambiguum* Sm. See A.*roseum* var. *carneum*.
A.*amblyanthum* Zahar. See A.*pallens*.

A.*amethystinum* Tausch (A.*descendens* auct., non L.; A.*segetum* Schult. & Schult. f.; A.*rollii* A. Terracc.; A.*sphaerocephalon* ssp. *rollii* K. Richt.; A.*stojanovii* Kovachev).
Stem 30–120cm, upper part often tinged red; bulb spherical or ovoid, 1.5–2cm diam. Lvs to 50×0.8cm, 3–7, linear, hollow sheathing lower part of stem, often withered by flowering time. Fls numerous, tubular, in a spherical umbel, 3–5cm wide; spathe 2–7cm; pedicels 10–25mm at flowering, extending to 50mm at fruiting, outer pedicels pendent, inner pedicels erect; tepals purple; stamens exserted, fil. long-hairy. Fr. to 4mm. Summer. Balkans, Italy, Sicily, Crete. Z8.

A.*ammophilum* Heuff. See A.*denudatum*.
A.*amoenum* G. Don. See A.*roseum* var. *carneum*.

A.*ampeloprasum* L. (A.*porrum* var. *ampeloprasum* Mirb.; A.*halleri* G. Don; A.*porrum* ssp. *euampeloprasum* Breistr.).
WILD LEEK; LEVANT GARLIC; KURRAT.
Stem 45–180cm; bulb 2–6cm wide, tunic yellow, membranous, bulblets numerous. Lvs to 50×4cm, 4–10, flat, margins rough, sheathing lower half of stem, withering before flowering. Fls cup-shaped, to 500 in a 5–10cm diam. spherical umbel, with deciduous spathe 4–11.5cm long; pedicels unequal, 4–5cm; tepals 4–5.5×1.5–2.5mm, keeled, pink or dark red; stamens exserted, outer fil. simple, inner fil. with basal blade as wide as tepals; bulbils occasionally develop in place of fls. Fr. 4mm. Summer. S Europe, Caucasus, Iran, Turkey, N Africa. var. *babingtonii* (Borrer) Syme (A.*babingtonii* Borrer; A.*ampeloprasum* var. *bulbiferum* Syme; A.*scorodoprasum* var. *babingtonii* Reg.; A.*ampeloprasum* var. *bulbiliferum* Lloyd; A.*scorodoprasum* ssp. *babingtonii* K. Richt.). Numerous bulbils and few fls. SW England, Channel Is., Ireland. Z6.

A.*ampeloprasum* var. *bulbiferum* Syme. See A.*ampeloprasum* var. *babingtonii*.
A.*ampeloprasum* var. *bulbiliferum* Lloyd. See A.*ampeloprasum* var. *babingtonii*.
A.*ampeloprasum* var. *porrum* (L.) Reg. See A.*porrum*.

A.*amplectens* Torr. (A.*attenuifolium* Kellogg; A.*occidentale* A. Gray; A.*monospermum* Jeps.; A.*attenuifolium* var. *monospermum* Jeps.).
Stem 20–50cm; bulb 1–1.5cm wide, ovoid, outer tunic brown, with V-shaped reticulations, inner tunic red or white. Lvs 2–4, narrow, flat, shorter than stem, twisting with age. Fls numerous in a spherical umbel with 2–3 ovate-acute bracts 7–10mm long; pedicels 6–15mm, slender; tepals 6–7mm, acute, white to pink, becoming papery after anthesis; stamens shorter than tepals, fil. broad at base, anth. yellow or purple. Fr. 3mm with 6 shallow ridges; seeds 2mm. Spring. US (Washington to S California). Z7.

A.*anceps* var. *lemmonii* (Jeps.) Jeps. See A.*lemmonii*.

A.*angulosum* L. (A.*acutangulum* Schräd.). MOUSE GARLIC.
Stem 20–45cm, 2-angled above ground; bulbs 5mm wide, conical or cylindrical, grouped around short rhiz., tunics membranous. Lvs 10–25×1.5–6mm, 4–6, basal, channelled, keeled. Fls cup-shaped, numerous, in an hemispherical umbel, 2.5–4.5cm wide, with 2, 5-lobed spathes to 1cm long; pedicels 1–3cm; tepals 4–6×1.5–2.5mm, white to pale purple; stamens 6mm, anth. yellow at first, becoming dark purple later. Fr. 3.5mm. Summer–autumn. Europe, Siberia. Z5.

A.*angulosum* ssp. *ammophilum* (Heuff.) K. Richt. See A.*denudatum*.
A.*angulosum* var. *caucasicum* Reg. See A.*denudatum*.
A.*angulosum* var. *flavescens* Reg. See A.*denudatum*.
A.*angustipetalum* Wendelbo. See A.*rosenbachianum*.
A.*antonii-bolosii* Palau Ferrer. See A.*cupanii*.
A.*arvense* Guss. See A.*sphaerocephalon* ssp. *arvense*.
A.*ascalonicum* auct. non L. See A.*cepa*.
A.*assimile* Hal. See A.*vineale*.

A.*atropurpureum* Waldst. & Kit. (A.*nigrum* var. *atropurpureum* Waldst. & Kit.).
Stem 40–100cm; bulbs 1.5–3cm wide, spherical, tunics black, membranous. Lvs 15–35×1–4cm, 3–7, basal, linear. Fls numerous in an umbel 3–7cm wide, with 2–3 spathes to 12cm; pedicels 2–4cm; tepals 7–9×1mm, dark purple; stamens 4–5mm, anth. purple. Fr. 6–8mm. Summer. S Europe. Z8.

A.*atrosanguineum* Schrenk. See A.*monadelphum*.

A.*atroviolaceum* Boiss.
Stem 50–120cm; bulb 1–2.5cm diam., ovoid. Lvs 20×0.4–1.2cm, 3–6, sheathing stem to halfway, flat, margin denticulate. Fls many, cup-shaped, in globose umbel 3–6cm diam.; spathe 1, long-pointed; pedicels to 3cm, unequal; tepals to 5×2.5mm, dark purple, sometimes tinged green; stamens exserted, fil. 4–5mm. Fr. 2.5mm. SE & E Europe.

A.*attenuifolium* Kellogg. See A.*amplectens*.
A.*attenuifolium* var. *monospermum* Jeps. See A.*amplectens*.
A.*aureum* Lam. See A.*moly*.
A.*austinae* Jones. See A.*campanulatum*.
A.*azureum* Ledeb. See A.*caeruleum*.
A.*babingtonii* Borrer. See A.*ampeloprasum* var. *babingtonii*.
A.*bakeri* Reg. See A.*chinense*.
A.*bauerianum* Bak. See A.*nigrum*.

A.*beesianum* W.W. Sm.
Stem 15–20cm; bulbs 4–8mm wide, cylindrical, clustered, tunics fibrous, netted. Lvs 15–20×0.4–1cm, 2–4, erect, sheathing lower part of stem. Fls 6–12, pendent, campanulate or tubular, in an umbel with spathe to 1.5cm and pedicels 7–10mm; tepals 1–1.5×0.25–0.5cm, blue; stamens 7–11mm, included, blue. Fr. 3-cornered. Summer. W China (NW Yunnan, Sichuan). f. *album*. Fls white. Z8.

A.*bidwelliae* S. Wats. See A.*campanulatum*.

A.*bisceptrum* S. Wats.
Stems 10–30cm, bulbs 1–1.5cm wide, ovoid, surrounded by numerous bulblets, outer tunic grey, reticulate, inner white. Lvs 3–10mm wide, about as long as stem, 2–3, flat. Fls 15–40 in a globose umbel; spathes 5–15mm, 2, acuminate; pedicels 1–2cm; tepals 6–10mm, rose-purple, acuminate; stamens

7mm, anth. dark. Fr. 3–4mm with 6 triangular crests. Summer. US (Idaho, Utah, Nevada, S California). Z8.

A.boissieri Reg. See *A.borzczowii*.

A.bolanderi S. Wats.
Stem 10–25cm; bulb 10–12mm, ovoid, tunic finely netted, grey or brown, occasionally producing stalked lateral offsets. Lvs 2, as long as stem, 1–2.5mm wide. Fls 6–25 in an umbel with 2 acuminate spathes 10–15mm long; pedicels 1–2cm, slender; tepals 8–15mm, acuminate, white to rose-purple, margins toothed; anth. yellow. Fr. 3mm, crested; seeds 2mm. Summer. US (S Oregon, N California). var. *stenanthum* (Drew) Jeps. (*A.stenanthum* Drew). Taller. Fls white or pale pink. Z7.

A.borszczowii Reg.
Stem 10–30cm, flexuous, 2–3 per bulb; bulb 1–1.5cm diam., tunic coarsely reticulate-fibrous. Lvs 10–30×0.1–0.2cm, narrowly linear, hollow, glabrous. Fls many, campanulate, in loose rounded umbel; spathe acuminate, much shorter than umbel; pedicels unequal, to 3cm, curved, bracteolate; tepals 5–7mm, elliptic-ovate to narrow-elliptic-oblong, white or pink with purple median vein; fil. included. Fr. 4mm. Iran, Afghanistan.

A.boryanum Kunth. See *A.callimischon*.
A.brahuicum Boiss. See *A.caspium*.

A.breweri S. Wats.
Stem to 8cm, flat, 2-winged; bulbs solitary, tunic membranous. Lvs longer than stem, 3–8mm wide, curved. Fls numerous, in an umbel; pedicels longer than tepals; tepals 7–10mm, deep purple; ovary with 3 triangular crests. Summer. US (C California). Z8.

A.bucharicum Reg.
Stem 10–30cm, erect; bulb 1–3cm diam., subglobose, tunic dark grey, papery. Lvs 10–30×0.7–2cm, 3–6, margin scabrid. Fls star-shaped, many, in a loose hemispheric umbel; spathe shorter than umbel; pedicels unequal, 2–6cm; tepals 8–10mm, linear-lanceolate, acute, white with dull purple-green median vein; fil. included; ovary verruculose, stipitate. Afghanistan.

A.buhseanum Reg. See *A.schoenoprasum*.
A.bulgaricum (Janka) Prodan. See *Nectaroscordum siculum* ssp. *bulgaricum*.

A.caeruleum Pall. (*A.azureum* Ledeb.; *A.coerulescens* G. Don).
Stem 20–80cm, 3-angled; bulb 1–2cm diam., subspherical, tunic membranous. Lvs 7×0.2–0.4cm, 2–4, linear, 3-angled, keeled, sheathing lower part of stem. Fls numerous, cup-shaped in a spherical umbel 3–4cm diam., with 2 spathes to 1.5cm; pedicels 1–2cm; tepals 3.5–4.5×1–1.5mm, blue with darker central vein; anth. blue. Fr. 3mm. Summer. Siberia, Turkestan. var. *bulbiliferum* Schrenk (*A.viviparum* Karw. & Kir.). Umbels bearing bulbils. Z7.

A.caesium Schrenk (*A.urceolatum* Reg.)
Stem 25–65cm; bulb 1–1.5cm wide, ovoid, tunic leathery. Lvs 1–3mm wide, 2–4, hollow, sheathing stem. Fls numerous in an umbel, 1.5–2cm wide, with 2 spathes to 1.5cm, umbels may include some bulbils or occasionally bulbils only; pedicels 1–2cm; tepals 4–5×2mm, violet-blue with green central vein; stamens included, outer 3 stamens with broader bases and 2 basal teeth. Fr. 3–4mm. Summer. Siberia to C Asia, Pamir and Tien Shan Mts. Z7.

A.callimischon Link (*A.boryanum* Kunth).
Stem 9–38cm; bulb 1cm wide, ovoid, tunic leathery, becoming fibrous. Lvs to 30×0.1cm, 3–5, produced in autumn, sheathing stem nearly to umbel. Fls 8–25, cup-shaped, in clusters within fastigiate umbel, 2–3cm wide, requiring a year to complete development; spathe 2–4cm; pedicels 7–25mm, varying in length; tepals 5–7×1.5mm, white to pink with brown or red central veins; anth. red. Fr. 5mm. Autumn. Greece, W Turkey. ssp. **haemostictum** Stearn. Stem 4–10cm. Tepals spotted red. Crete, Peloponnese. Z8.

A.campanulatum S. Wats. (*A.bidwelliae* S. Wats.; *A.acuminatum* var. *bidwelliae* Jeps.; *A.austinae* Jones; *A.tenellum* Davidson).
Stem 10–30cm; bulbs 1.5–2cm wide, ovoid, in clusters or slender rhiz. to 10cm, tunic brown, slightly netted. Lvs to 30×0.3–0.5cm, 2–3, senescent at flowering. Fls 15–40, cup-shaped in an umbel; spathes 7–15mm, 2; pedicels 1–3cm; tepals 5–8mm, white to pale pink, acute or acuminate; stamens included, not as long as tepals, anth. red; ovary crested. Fr. crested, 3mm, tepals persisting as rigid keels; seeds 2mm. Summer. US (California, Nevada). Z8.

A.canadense L. (*A.mutabile* Michx.; *A.continuum* Small). CANADA GARLIC; MEADOW LEEK; ROSE LEEK.
Stem to 30cm, terete; bulbs ovoid, often clustered, tunic reticulate. Lvs to 5mm wide, 3, channelled, shorter than stem. Fls campanulate, in an umbel with many bulbils; spathe membranous with 3 bracts with 3–7 veins; tepals 4–7mm, white to pink, spreading; pedicels slender. Seeds glossy black. Summer. N America. var. **fraseri** F.M. Ownb. (*A.fraseri* Shinn.; *A.lavendulare* var. *fraseri* Shinn.). Tepals white, pedicels robust. var. **mobilense** (Reg.) F.M. Ownb. (*A.mobilense* Reg.). Tepals pink, pedicels slender, no bulbils in infl. Z4.

A.candissimum Cav. See *A.neapolitanum*.
A.capillare Cav. See *A.moschatum*.

A.carinatum L. (*A.flexum* Waldst. & Kit.; *A.violaceum* Willd.). KEELED GARLIC.
Stem 30–60cm; bulb 1cm diam., ovoid, tunic membranous, sometimes fibrous. Lvs 20×0.1–0.25cm, 2–4, glabrous, sheathing lower part of stem. Fls cup-shaped, to 30 in an umbel 2–5cm wide, infl. usually including bulbils; spathes slender, to 12cm, 2; pedicels 1–2.5cm, outer pedicels pendent; tepals 4–6×1.5–2mm, purple; stamens exserted, anth. purple, pollen yellow; ovary oblong. Fr. 5mm, rarely produced. Summer. C & S Europe, Russia, Turkey. ssp. **pulchellum** (G. Don) Bonnier & Layens (*A.cirrhosum* Vand.; *A.coloratum* Spreng.; *A.flavum* var. *purpurascens* Mert. & Koch; *A.pulchellum* G. Don; *A.flexum* var. *capsuliferum* Koch; *A.flavum* var. *pulchellum* (G.Don) Reg.). Stems purple. Fls numerous; bulbils absent. Summer. S Europe (SE France to W Romania, Bulgaria, N Greece). f. *album* Fls white. Z7.

A.carneum Bertol. See *A.roseum* var. *carneum*.

A.caspium Bieb. (*A.brahuicum* Boiss.).
Stem 10–20cm; bulb spherical, 2–5cm diam., tunic membranous. Lvs to 25×3.5cm, 3–6, basal, linear. Fls numerous, campanulate, in loose umbel 3–20cm diam., spathes 12–25mm, 2; pedicels 3–15cm; tepals 5–11×2–3mm, lilac tinged green; stamens to 11mm, exserted, anth. green. Fr. 6–8mm diam. developing on umbel which may expand during infructescence. Summer. SE Russia, Caucasus, C Asia. Z8.

A.caucasicum Bieb. See *A.paniculatum*.

A.cepa L. (*A.ascalonicum* auct. non L.). ONION; SHALLOT; TREE ONION. Bienn.
Stem to 100cm, hollow, lower half thick, inflated; bulb to 10cm diam., spherical, often flattened, tunic membranous. Lvs to 40×2cm, to 10, hollow, flattened, basal or sheathing lower part of stem. Fls star-shaped, numerous, in umbel 4–9cm diam., with or without bulbils; spathes to 3; pedicels to 4cm; tepals 3–4.5×2–2.5mm, white with green central vein; stamens 4–6mm, exserted. Fr. 5mm. Summer. Not known in wild. Three types are recognized: Cepa Group with solitary bulbs and no bulbils in infl. including onions; Aggregatum Group with clustered bulbs and no bulbils in infl., including shallots, multiplier onions and potato onions; Proliferum Group which produces bulbils in infl. including Egyptian onions and tree onions. Z5.

A.cernuum Roth (*A.alleghaniense* Small; *A.recurvatum* Rydb.; *A.oxyphilum* Wherry). LADY'S LEEK; NODDING ONION; WILD ONION.
Stem 30–70cm, terete or angled, sharply curved at tip; bulbs 1–2cm diam., narrow, ovoid, clustered on rhiz., tunics mem-

branous. Lvs 10–20×0.5–0.7cm, 4–6, basal, flat. Fls cup-shaped, 30–40 in a pendulous umbel, 3–5cm diam.; spathes to 1cm, 2; pedicels 8–18mm, bending upwards once fr. develops; tepals 4–6mm, white, deep pink or maroon; stamens exserted; ovary with 6 crests persisting on fr. Summer. N America (Canada to Mexico). Z6.

A.chamaemoly L. (*Saturnia cernua* Maratti).
Stem to 5cm, solid; bulb 5–10mm diam., ovoid, tunic papery. Lvs 3–27×0.2–0.8cm, 2–5, basal, linear, margins ciliate, upper surface pubesc., in spreading rosette. Fls 2–20, star-shaped, in umbel 2cm diam., close to ground; spathe 2–4-lobed; pedicels 5–10mm, recurved in fruit; tepals white with green or purple central veins; stamens 5.5mm, included. Fr. 4mm. Winter–spring. S Europe, N Africa. Z8.

A.chinense G. Don (*A.bakeri* Reg.). RAKKYO; CH'IAO T'OU.
Stem 28–30cm, solid; bulbs 1–1.5cm diam., clustered, ovoid, tunics membranous. Lvs to 30×0.1–0.3cm, 3, basal, hollow, 3- or 5-angled. Fls cup-shaped, to 18 in a hemispherical umbel; spathes 2; pedicels 1–1.5cm; tepals 5×3.5mm, obtuse, pale violet; stamens exserted. Autumn. China. Z7.

A.christophii Trautv. (*A.albopilosum* C.H. Wright). STAR OF PERSIA.
Stem 15–50cm, ribbed; bulb 2–3cm diam., spherical, tunic papery. Lvs 15–40×1–4cm, 2–7, erect, glaucous, withering before flowering with stiff hairs on margins and lower surface. Fls 2–3cm diam., numerous, star-shaped in a loose umbel 10–20cm diam.; spathe 2.5cm, apiculate; pedicels to 11cm; tepals 1–2cm, purple-violet with metallic sheen, erect with thickened central veins remaining rigid after flowering; stamens included, anth., pollen and fil. dark purple. Fr. 5–8mm. Summer. Iran, Turkey, C Asia. Hybrids include 'Gladiator': to 1.2m, fls large, lilac-mauve; 'Globus' (*A.christophii* × *A.giganteum*): stems to 35cm, fls blue, in large globose heads; 'Lucy Ball': to 1.2m, fls dark lilac in compact globose head; 'Rien Poortvliet': to 1.2m, fls lilac. Z8.

A.chrysonemum Stearn.
Stem 30–60cm; bulb about 1.5cm diam., ovoid, tunic membranous. Lvs to 15×0.2cm, 3–4, hairy, sheathing lower part of stem. Fls numerous, cup-shaped, in umbel to 4cm diam.; spathes 2; pedicels 1–1.5cm; tepals 4.5–5×2–2.5mm, pale yellow with green central vein; stamens exserted, fil. and anth. yellow. Fr. 4mm. Summer. Spain. Z7.

A.ciliatum Cirillo. See *A.subhirsutum*.
A.cirrhosum Vand. See *A.carinatum* ssp. *pulchellum*.
A.coerulescens G. Don. See *A.caeruleum*.
A.coloratum Spreng. See *A.carinatum* ssp. *pulchellum*.
A.compactum Thuill. See *A.vineale*.
A.complanatum Boreau. See *A.oleraceum*.
A.continuum Small. See *A.canadense*.
A.contortum Stokes. See *A.sativum* var. *ophioscordum*.
A.controversum Schräd. ex Willd. See *A.sativum* var. *ophioscordum*.
A.coppoleri Tineo. See *A.pallens*.

A.coryi M.E. Jones.
Stem to 30cm; bulbs ovoid, clustered, tunics fibrous, reticulate. Lvs 2–3, shorter than stem. Fls 10–25, campanulate, in an umbel without bulbils; pedicels longer than tepals, becoming rigid when fr. develop; tepals 6–9mm, chrome-yellow, occasionally tinged with red, becoming papery with thickened midribs when fr. develop. US (W Texas). Z8.

A.cowanii Lindl. See *A.neapolitanum*.

A.crenulatum Wiegand (*A.vancouverense* Macoun).
Stem 5–8cm, 2-angled, edges dentate; bulbs ovoid, oblique, tunic membranous. Lvs 3–10×0.3–0.6cm, 1–2, basal, recurved with dentate margins. Fls few, in an hemispherical umbel; spathes 8–10mm, 2; pedicels 8–15mm; tepals 6–12mm, white, pink or purple, lanceolate, acute; stamens 4mm, included; ovary and fr. 6-crested. Summer. Western N America (Vancouver Is., W British Columbia, Washington, Oregon). Z7.

A.crispum Greene. See *A.peninsulare* var. *crispum*.

A.cupanii Raf. (*A.hirtovaginatum* Kunth; *A.antonii-bolosii* Palau Ferrer).
Stem 10–25cm; bulb 7–15mm diam., ovoid, tunic fibrous, reticulate. Lvs to 10×0.05cm, 3–5, sheathing lower part of stem. Fls campanulate, to 15, in a fastigiate umbel, 2–4cm diam.; spathe 1.5–2cm, tubular at base; pedicels to 4cm; tepals 5.5–9×1.5–2mm, white to pink with dark central vein, rarely white; stamens included, anth. yellow. Fr. to 4mm. Summer. Mediterranean. Z8.

A.cusickii S. Wats. See *A.tolmiei*.
A.cuspidatum Fern. See *A.acuminatum*.

A.cuthbertii Small. STRIPED GARLIC.
Stem to 50cm; bulb solitary, tunic fibrous, reticulate. Lvs to 5mm wide, shorter than stem, 3 or more. Fls numerous in umbels without bulbils; spathes 5–7-veined; pedicels twice as long as tepals; tepals to 6mm, spreading, becoming reflexed when fr. develops, acuminate, white, withering with age; stamens exserted; ovary 6-crested. US (Atlantic coast, N Carolina to Alabama). Z8.

A.cyaneum Reg. (*A.purdomii* W.W. Sm.).
Stem 10–45cm; bulbs clustered on small rhiz., tunics fibrous, faintly reticulate. Lvs 15×0.1–0.4cm, 1–3, semi-terete, sheathing base of stem. Fls 5–18, campanulate, pendent, in an umbel; spathe 5–8mm; pedicels 4–10mm; tepals violet-blue to purple with dark blue or green central vein; stamens 5–9mm, violet or blue, exserted, inner stamens with 2 basal lateral teeth. Summer. China (Kansu). Z9.

A.cyaneum var. *brachystemon* Reg. See *A.sikkimense*.

A.cyathophorum Bur. & Franch. var. *farreri* (Stearn) Stearn (*A.farreri* Stearn).
Stem 19–42cm, 3-angled; bulbs 3–5mm, cylindric, clustered, tunics with parallel fibres. Lvs 18–24.5×0.1–0.5cm, 3–6, basal. Fls campanulate, 6–30 in a loose umbel; spathe entire or 2–3-lobed; pedicels 8–20mm; tepals 6–8×1.5–2mm, maroon; stamens 5mm, included, lower half of fil. fused into a tube. Fr. 4mm. Summer. China (Kansu). Z8.

A.cyrilli Ten.
Stem 50–60cm; bulb 1–2cm diam., ovoid, tunic membranous. Lvs 15–35×1–4cm, 3–7, basal, linear. Fls numerous, cup-shaped in an umbel, 4–7cm diam.; spathes to 2cm, 2–3; pedicels 1.5–2.5cm; tepals 6–7×1–1.5mm, tips curving inwards, white with green central vein; stamens included, united at base. Fr. 6–8mm. Summer. S Europe. Z8.

A.darwasicum Reg.
Stem 10–50cm, ribbed; bulb spherical, tunic grey, membranous. Lvs 4–16mm wide, shorter than stem, 1–2, linear, margins rough. Fls numerous, campanulate, in an umbel; spathe small; pedicels at least as long as fls, often longer; tepals white with green central vein; stamens included, lower part of fil. joined to tepals. C Asia. Z5.

A.denudatum (Delaroche f.) Redouté (*A.albidum* Fisch. ex Bieb.; *A.flavescens* Besser; *A.ammophilum* Heuff.; *A.angulosum* var. *caucasicum* Reg.; *A.angulosum* var. *flavescens* Reg.; *A.angulosum* ssp. *ammophilum* (Heuff.) K. Richt.; *A.flavescens* var. *ammophilum* (Heuff.) Zahar.; *A.albidum* ssp. *caucasicum* (Reg.) Stearn).
Stem 10–30cm, slightly ridged; bulbs narrow, to 1cm diam., clustered on rhiz., tunics membranous. Lvs to 14×0.25cm, 5–9, basal, flat, channelled. Fls numerous, star-shaped, in an umbel 1.5–2.5cm diam.; spathe to 1cm, 2-lobed; pedicels 8–15mm, rough; tepals 3.5×1–1.5mm, white to pale yellow; stamens 3–4mm, exserted, anth. yellow. Fr. 3mm. Summer. W Russia, Bulgaria, Romania. Z8.

A.descendens L. See *A.sphaerocephalon*.
A.descendens auct., non L. See *A.amethystinum*.
A.deserticola (M.E. Jones) Wooton & Standl. See *A.macropetalum*.

A.dichlamydeum E. Greene (*A.serratum* var. *dichlamydeum* Jones).
Stem 10–30cm; bulb ovoid, about 1.5cm diam., tunic membranous with horizontal zig-zag reticulations. Lvs 1–2mm wide, as long as stem, flat, 1–3. Fls campanulate, variable in number, in a close umbel; spathes 10–20mm, 2, ovate, subacuminate; pedicels thick, 1–1.5cm; tepals 9–11mm, rosepurple, acute, inner tepals erect, outer tepals spreading; stamens included, anth. yellow; ovary crested. Fr. 3–4mm, crested. Summer. US (California). Z8.

A.dictyotum E. Greene. See *A.geyeri.*

A.dioscoridis Sibth. & Small. See *Nectaroscordum siculum* ssp. *bulgaricum.*

A.douglasii Hook.
Stem to 25cm, terete; bulb solitary, tunic membranous. Lvs 6–8mm wide, shorter than stem, 2. Fls numerous in an umbel; pedicels to 30mm; tepals to 8mm, white to pink; style exserted. US (Washington, Oregon, Idaho). Z6.

A.drummondii Reg. (*A.helleri* Small; *A.nuttallii* S. Wats.; *A.reticulatum* var. *nuttallii* (S.Wats.) M.E. Jones; *A.drummondii* f. *asexuale* Ownb.).
Stem 10–20cm; bulbs 1.5cm diam., clustered, ovoid, tunic fibrous, reticulate. Lvs 10–15×0.1–0.4cm, 3 or more, basal, channelled. Fls 10–25, campanulate in an umbel; pedicels erect becoming rigid when fr. develops, tepals 4–7mm, white, pink or red, ovate to lanceolate, 4–7mm, becoming stiff and persisting on fr. Spring. N America (Texas to New Mexico, north to Nebraska). Z7.

A.drummondii f. *asexuale* Ownb. See *A.drummondii.*
A.elatum Reg. See *A.macleanii.*
A.euboicum Rchb. f. See *A.paniculatum.*

A.falcifolium Hook. & Arn. (*A.falcifolium* var. *demissum* Jeps.; *A.falcifolium* var. *breweri* Jones).
Stem 5–12×0.25–0.6cm, flattened with 2 wings; bulbs 1.5cm diam., ovoid to spherical, tunic brown, membranous. Lvs 25×0.9cm, 1–2, falcate, grey-green, recurved. Fls 10–30, campanulate in a compact umbel, 4 5cm diam.; spathes 8–10mm, 2; pedicels 6–16mm; tepals 8–15mm, deep pink to purple or green-white tinged with pink; stamens 4–9mm, included, anth. yellow; ovary crested. Fr. 4–5mm, crested. Summer. US (S Oregon to N California). Z8.

A.falcifolium var. *breweri* Jones. See *A.falcifolium.*
A.falcifolium var. *demissum* Jeps. See *A.falcifolium.*
A.fallax (F.W. Schmidt) Schult. & Schult. f. See *A.senescens* ssp. *montanum.*
A.fallax ssp. *montanum* Fries. See *A.senescens* ssp. *montanum.*
A.farreri Stearn. See *A.cyathophorum* var. *farreri.*
A.fedtschenkoanum Reg. See *A.monadelphum.*

A.fibrillum M.E. Jones.
Stem to 10cm; bulb solitary, tunic membranous, unevenly reticulate. Lvs 3–5mm wide, as long as or longer than stem. Fls numerous; pedicels at least 12mm; tepals 8–12mm, white to pale pink, thickening and persisting on fr.; ovary ridged. US (Idaho). Z5.

A.fibrosum Rydb. See *A.rubrum.*

A.fimbriatum S. Wats. (*A.fimbriatum* var. *aboriginum* Jeps.).
Stem 3–10cm; bulb 12–16mm diam., spherical, tunic membranous, dark brown. Lvs twice as long as stem. Fls 8–40, in umbel; spathes 6–12mm, 2–3, bearing apical bristles; pedicels 4–15mm; tepals 7–15mm pink to purple with darker central vein; stamens 3–10mm, anth. yellow; ovary with fringed crests; stigma with 3 slender lobes. Fr. 3–4mm, 3-lobed with 6 erect crests; seeds to 2mm. Summer. US (California). Z7.

A.fimbriatum var. *aboriginum* Jeps. See *A.fimbriatum.*
A.fimbriatum var. *purdyi* Eastw. See *A.purdyi.*

A.fistulosum L. (*Cepa fistulosum* (L.) Gray). WELSH ONION; JAPANESE BUNCHING ONION; JAPANESE LEEK.
Stem 12–70cm, hollow, central part inflated; bulbs cylindric, clustered on rhiz., tunics membranous. Lvs 6–30×0.5–1.5cm,

2–6, hollow, terete, sheathing stem. Fls campanulate, numerous or entirely replaced by bulbils in loose umbel, 1.5–5cm diam.; spathes 1–2, as large as umbel; pedicels 3–20mm; tepals yellow-white, outer tepals 6–7×2mm, inner tepals 7–9×3mm; stamens exserted, fil. 8–12mm, anth. yellow. Fr. 4mm. Summer. Not known in the wild. Z5.

A.flavescens Besser. See *A.denudatum.*
A.flavescens var. *ammophilum* (Heuff.) Zahar. See *A.denudatum.*

A.flavum L. (*A.tauricum* Rchb.). SMALL YELLOW ONION.
Stem 8–30cm; bulb ovoid, tunic membranous. Lvs 20×0.2cm, cylindric, glaucous, sheathing lower part of stem. Fls 9–60, sweetly scented, campanulate in an hemispherical umbel, 1.5–3cm diam.; spathes to 11cm, 2, acuminate; pedicels 3–25mm, outer pedicels pendulous but becoming erect as fr. develops; tepals 4.5–5×2mm, lemon-yellow; stamens exserted, fil. 6–8mm, yellow, sometimes suffused with red, green or brown; ovary globose. Fr. 4mm. Summer. C Europe to W Asia. 'Blue Leaf' ('Glaucum'): strong-growing; lvs blue; fls yellow. 'Minus': smaller, pedicels 1–1.5×fls; fil. purple. Z7.

A.flavum var. *pulchellum* (G.Don) Reg. See *A.carinatum* ssp. *pulchellum.*
A.flavum var. *purpurascens* Mert. & Koch. See *A.carinatum* ssp. *pulchellum.*
A.flexum Waldst. & Kit. See *A.carinatum.*
A.flexum var. *capsuliferum* Koch. See *A.carinatum* ssp. *pulchellum.*
A.fragrans Vent. See *Nothoscordum gracile.*
A.fraseri (F.M. Ownb.) Shinn. See *A.canadense* var. *fraseri.*

A.frigidum Boiss. & Heldr.
Stem to 25cm; bulb 5–10mm diam., ovoid, tunic papery. Lvs 5×0.1–0.3cm, 2–3, thread-like, pubesc. or glabrous. Fls 3–16 in a fastigiate umbel 1.5–4cm diam.; spathes 8–12mm, 2; pedicels 5–15mm; tepals 5–6×1–1.5mm, acute, yellow tinged with red; stamens exserted, fil. to 6mm. Fr. 5mm. Summer. Greece (Peloponnese). Z8.

A.funiculosum Nels. See *A.geyeri.*
A.fuscum Waldst. & Kit. See *A.paniculatum.*
A.gaditanum Pérez Lara ex Willk. See *A.guttatum* ssp. *sardoum.*

A.galanthum Karel. & Kir.
Stems to 50cm, lower part broad, upper part tapering; bulbs narrow, clustered on rhiz., tunic membranous, red-brown. Lvs 25–35×1cm, 2–3, cylindric, fistular, sheathing lower part of stem. Fls numerous in an umbel; pedicels 10–15mm; tepals 5mm, white; stamens joined to tepals forming a basal ring, inner fil. with 2 small basal teeth. Summer. Siberia. Z5.

A.geyeri S. Wats. (*A.dictyotum* E. Greene; *A.pikeanum* Rydb.; *A.funiculosum* Nels.).
Stems 15–50cm; bulbs 1.5–2.5cm diam., clustered, ovoid, tunics fibrous, reticulate. Lvs 10–20×0.2–0.4cm, 3 or more, channelled. Fls 10–25, campanulate in an umbel; pedicels 3–4mm, becoming rigid in fruit; tepals 4–10mm, white to pink, slightly toothed, persisting in fruit. Fr. crested. Spring. US (Texas, New Mexico, Washington, Oregon, Nevada). Z7.

A.giganteum Reg.
Stems 80–200cm, slightly ridged; bulb 4–6cm diam., ovoid, tunic brown, tough, breaking down into longitudinal fibres. Lvs 30–100×5–10cm, basal, grey-green. Fls star-shaped, numerous in a dense spherical umbel 10–15cm diam.; pedicels 6cm; spathe half length of umbel; tepals 5–7mm, purple, occasionally white, elliptic; stamens exserted. Fr. 4mm. Spring. C Asia. Z8.

A.glandulosum Link & Otto.
Stem 20–55cm, laterally compressed; bulb to 1.5cm diam., spherical, on slender rhiz., tunic membranous. Lvs to 30×0.6cm, 2–5, nearly basal, with prominent venation. Fls star-shaped in a compressed umbel, 4–9cm diam.; spathe 2-lobed; pedicels 1.5–4cm; tepals 6–9mm, maroon, lanceolate,

acute; stamens 3–5mm, basally united, spreading. Autumn. US (Texas, Arizona), Mexico. Z7.

A.glaucum Schräd. See *A.senescens* var. *glaucum*.

A.globosum DC. in Redouté (*A.stevenii* Ledeb.; *A.gmelinianum* Misch.).
Stem to 60cm; bulbs to 1.5cm diam., cylindric, clustered on rhiz., tunics brown. Lvs 5–6, acute, thread-like, sheathing lower part of stem. Fls numerous; spathe beaked, 2 or 3× as long as umbel; pedicels 7–10mm; tepals 5mm, deep pink with dark midrib; stamens 7–10mm, anth. violet; style exserted; ovary with nectaries. Summer. Caucasus. Z6.

A.gmelinianum Misch. See *A.globosum*.
A.gracile Dryand. in Ait. See *Nothoscordum gracile*.
A.grandiflorum Lam. See *A.narcissiflorum*.
A.grandisceptrum Davidson. See *A.unifolium*.
A.gredense Rivas Mart. See *A.schoenoprasum*.

A.grossii Font Quer.
Stem 30–40cm; bulbs 1.5cm diam., clustered, ovoid, tunic fibrous. Lvs linear, sheathing lower part of stem, withering before flowering. Fls numerous, campanulate, in an umbel 5.5cm diam.; spathe to 2.5cm, with 2 acuminate valves; pedicels 1–1.5cm; tepals purple with dark midrib; anth. purple, fil. to 4mm; ovary spherical. Summer. Balearic Is. (Ibiza). Z9.

A.guttatum Steven.
Stem 10–90cm; bulb 1–2cm diam., ovoid; tunic membranous or leathery. Lvs 30×0.3cm, 2–5, hollow, sheathing lower part of stem. Fls numerous, campanulate, somewhat tubular, in a dense spherical umbel 1.5–5cm diam.; pedicels to 30mm, inner pedicels erect in fruit, outer pedicels deflexed; tepals 2.5–4.5×1–1.5mm, white with green or pink veins and purple blotch; stamens exserted, anth. yellow or deep red. Fr. 3mm. SE Europe. ssp. **guttatum** (*A.margaritaceum* var. *guttatum* Steven). Tepals white with purple blotch. Aegean to Ukraine. ssp. **sardoum** (Moris) Stearn (*A.margaritaceum* Sm. non Moench; *A.sardoum* Moris; *A.gaditanum* Pérez Lara ex Willk.). Tepals white with green or pink stripe. S Europe, Portugal to Turkey. Z6.

A.haematochiton S. Wats. (*A.marvinii* Davidson). RED-SKINNED ONION.
Stem 10–40cm, slightly flattened; bulbs 2–3cm, elongate, clustered on short rhiz., tunic membranous, white to deep red. Lvs 10–20×0.1–0.4cm, several, flat, with much broader sheathing bases. Fls 10–30; spathes 2–4; pedicels 1–2cm; tepals 6–8mm, white to pink with darker central vein, acute; stamens and style included; anth. yellow. Fr. 4mm, with 6 low crests. Spring. US (California). Z8.

A.halleri G. Don. See *A.ampeloprasum*.

A.heldreichii Boiss.
Stem 20–60cm; bulb to 1cm diam., solitary, spherical, tunic membranous. Lvs 5–30×0.1–0.3cm, 2–4, hollow, cylindric, sheathing lower part of stem. Fls campanulate, numerous in a globose umbel, 2.5–4.5cm diam.; spathes 1–1.5cm, 2, persistent; pedicels to 5–15mm; tepals 10×2.5–3mm, pink, acute; stamens to 5mm, included; outer 3 fil. simple, inner 3 fil. with broad 3-toothed bases, anth. yellow. Fr. 4–5mm. Summer. N Greece. Z8.

A.helleri Small. See *A.drummondii*.
A.hirtovaginatum Kunth. See *A.cupanii*.
A.hyalinum var. *praecox* (Brandg.) Jeps. See *A.praecox*.

A.hymenorrhizum Ledeb. (*A.macrorrhizum* Boiss.).
Stem 30–90cm; bulbs to 2cm diam., conical, clustered on rhiz., tunics brown, glossy, splitting longitudinally. Lvs 30×0.6cm, 4–6, sheathing lower part of stem. Fls numerous, campanulate in a spherical or hemispherical umbel, 2–3.5cm diam.; spathe to 1.5cm, 2-lobed; pedicels 1–1.5cm; tepals 4–6×1.5–2mm, deep pink, persistent in fruit; stamens to 8mm, exserted, anth. yellow; ovaries with nectaries. Fr. 4–5mm. Summer. C Asia, W Siberia, Iran, Afghanistan. Z7.

A.illyricum Jacq. See *A.roseum*.

A.incarnatum Hornem. See *A.roseum* var. *carneum*.

A.insubricum Boiss. & Reut. (*A.narcissiflorum* var. *insubiricum* (Boiss. & Reut.) Fiori; *A.narcissiflorum* ssp. *insubiricum* (Boiss. & Reut.) Cif. & Giac.).
Stem 2-edged, 16–30cm; bulbs 5mm diam., oblong, clustered on rhiz., tunics membranous. Lvs 12–20×0.2–0.5cm, 3–4, flat, glaucous, sheathing lower part of stem. Fls 3–5, campanulate, pendent, in a fastigiate umbel; pedicels 8–20mm; spathes to 18mm, 1, acute, persistent; tepals purple, inner tepals 18×9mm, outer tepals 18×6mm; stamens included, fil. to 6mm; stigma 3-lobed. Summer. N Italy. Often confused with *A.narcissiflorum*. Z8.

A.intermedium DC. See *A.paniculatum*.
A.jacquemontii Reg. non Kunth. See *A.przewalskianum*.
A.jajlae Vved. See *A.scorodoprasum* ssp. *jajlae*.
A.japonicum Reg. See *A.thunbergii*.
A.kansuense Reg. See *A.sikkimense*.

A.karataviense Reg.
Stem 10–25cm; bulb to 5cm diam., tunic membranous. Lvs 15–23×3–15cm, 2–3, basal, broadly elliptic, glaucous, grey flushed with purple. Fls 1–1.5cm diam., numerous, star-shaped in a globose umbel to 20cm diam.; spathe to 3.5cm; tepals 5–8mm, white to pale purple-pink with darker midrib, twisted and reflexed on infructescence; stamens exserted, fil. bases triangular. Fr. deeply indented. Spring. C Asia. Z8.

A.kaufmannii Reg. See *A.monadelphum*.

A.kharputense Freyn & Sint.
Stem 30–50cm, sometimes tinged red; bulb 1.5–3cm diam., ovoid or subglobose. Lvs 2–3, 2–4cm wide, broad-lanceolate, undulate, twisted. Fls many in dense, rounded umbel 3.5–8.5cm diam.; spathe 2–3-lobed; pedicels very slender, 3–4 times length of fls, pale yellow-brown; tepals 5–6mm, linear, white or cream; fil. equalling or exceeding tepals; ovary green to black. Fr. 5mm. Turkey to Iran.

A.kochii Lange (*A.vineale* var. *kochii* H.P.G. Koch).
Stem 30–120cm; bulb to 2cm diam., ovoid, tunic fibrous. Lvs 15–60×0.15–0.4cm, 2–4, hollow, sheathing lower part of stem. Fls campanulate, numerous in an umbel to 5cm diam.; spathe pedicels 5–30mm; tepals 2–4.5×1–1.5mm, dark red; stamens exserted, inner stamens with 3 basal teeth. Fr. to 3.5mm. Summer. Europe (Baltic region), N Africa, W Asia. Z6.

A.kunthii G. Don (*A.scaposum* Benth.).
Stem to 40cm, terete; bulb solitary, tunic membranous. Lvs to 10cm, 3mm wide, 2–4, triangular in section, channelled. Fls numerous in a globose umbel; pedicels 12–20mm; tepals to 6mm, white to pink with dark red midrib. US (New Mexico, Texas), Mexico. Z7.

A.lacteum Sm. See *A.neapolitanum*.

A.lacunosum S. Wats.
Stem 10–20cm; bulb solitary, remnants of older bulbs sometimes present, tunic membranous with heavy polygonal reticulation. Lvs slender, as long as stem, 1–2, terete. Fls 8–25 in an umbel; spathes 8–12mm, 2, acuminate; pedicels 5–10mm; tepals 5–7mm, white to pink with green or red midribs; anth. yellow. Fr. 3–4mm, apex ridged. Spring. US (C & S California). Z8.

A.latifolium Jaub. & Spach. See *A.akaka*.
A.lavendulare var. *fraseri* Shinn. See *A.canadense* var. *fraseri*.

A.ledebourianum Roem. & Schult. f. (*A.uliginosum* Ledeb.).
Stem 40–80cm, robust; bulbs to 1cm diam., clustered on rhiz., tunics grey-brown. Lvs to 1cm wide, 1–2, fistular. Fls numerous, campanulate, in a dense umbel; spathe acuminate, persistent; tepals 7–12mm, glossy violet-pink with dark midrib; style exserted. Summer. Siberia. Z5.

A.lemmonii S. Wats. (*A.anceps* var. *lemmonii* Jeps.).
Stem 10–20cm, 2-edged; bulb 15–22mm, ovoid, tunic membranous, with fine oblong reticulations. Lvs 2–5mm wide, 2,

Allium   (a) *A.christophii*   (b) *A.unifolium*   (c) *A.beesianum*   (d) *A.ursinum*

flat. Fls numerous; spathes 10–17mm, 2–4, acuminate; pedicels 10–17mm; tepals 6–8mm, erect, acuminate, white to pale rose; anth. yellow. Fr. 3–4mm, crested. Spring–summer. US (California). Z6.

A.libani Boiss.
Stem to 8cm; bulb solitary, tunic membranous. Lvs 4–8×0.4–0.6cm, longer than stem, 2–3. Fls numerous; spathes 2–4, acute; pedicels 7–12mm; tepals 6mm, white with red midrib. Asia Minor. Z9.

A.lineare L.
Stem 30–60cm, terete, ribbed; bulbs to 1cm diam., clustered around ascending rhiz., tunics reticulate, brown. Lvs 18×0.35cm, 2–4, linear, flat, sheathing lower part of stem, ribbed below, margins denticulate. Fls numerous, campanulate, in a dense umbel to 3cm diam.; spathe to 1cm, acuminate, persistent; pedicels slender; tepals 4–5mm, rose-pink; style exserted. Fr. to 4mm. Summer. Russia, Siberia. Z6.

A.lineare var. **strictum** Krylov. See *A.strictum.*
A.longispathum Delaroche. See *A.paniculatum.*
A.lusitanicum Lam. See *A.senescens* ssp. *montanum.*

A.macleanii Bak. (*A.elatum* Reg.).
Stem 60–100cm, deeply ridged; bulbs 2–6cm diam., solitary, subspherical, tunic papery. Lvs to 30×2–8cm, 2–5, basal, glabrous. Fls numerous, star-shaped, in a dense spherical umbel 7–10cm diam.; pedicels 2–5.5cm; tepals 6–8mm, deep violet, acute; stamens exserted, bases united. Fr. 5mm. Spring–summer. Afghanistan, W Pakistan, Tadzhikistan. Z8.

A.macnabianum hort. ex Reg.
Stem to 30cm, terete. Lvs 25×0.6cm, linear, channelled. Fls numerous in an umbel; spathes 2, membranous; tepals deep magenta. N America. Z7.

A.macranthum Bak. (*A.oviflorum* Reg.).
Stems 20–30cm, numerous, 3-angled; bulbs 3–7mm diam., cylindric, on fleshy rhiz. Lvs 15–45×0.3cm many, basal, channelled, glabrous. Fls 3–12, occasionally to 50, pendulous, campanulate in a loose spherical umbel, 7–10cm diam.; spathe 2cm; pedicels 2–5cm; tepals 8–12×4mm, deep purple; style exserted. Fr. 4mm, 6-crested. Summer. W China, Sikkim. Z8.

A.macropetalum Rydb. (*A.reticulatum* var. *deserticola* M.E. Jones; *A.deserticola* Wooton & Standl.).
Stem 5–20cm, terete or angled; bulbs ovoid, clustered, tunic brown, reticulate, fibrous, enclosing more than one bulb. Lvs 1–3mm, wide, longer than stem, 2, concave to convex in section. Fls 10–20, campanulate in an umbel; spathes 2–3; pedicels 16–36mm, becoming rigid in fruit; tepals 8–12mm, spreading, pink with deep pink or red midrib, becoming papery and persisting on fr.; stamen bases united; ovary crested. Fr. prominently crested; seed shining black. N America (Colorado, Utah, Arizona, New Mexico and Texas). Z5.

A.macrorrhizum Boiss. See *A.hymenorrhizum.*

A.mairei A. Lév. (*A.yunnanense* Diels).
Stem 10–40cm, 2-angled; bulbs slender, clustered on rhiz., tunics fibrous, reticulate. Lvs to 25×1cm, sheathing base of stem. Fls 2–6, campanulate, erect, in an umbel; pedicels 1.5–3cm, stiff; spathes 2; tepals 8–12×1–3mm, white to pink with red spotting, recurved; stamens 5–6mm, bases united. Autumn. SW China (Xizang, Yunnan). *A.amabile*, with deep pink often pendent fls is sometimes included as *A.mairei* var. *amabile.* Z8.

A.mairei var. **amabile** Stapf. See *A.amabile.*
A.margaritaceum Sm. non Moench. See *A.guttatum* ssp. *sardoum.*
A.margaritaceum var. **guttatum** (Steven) Steven. See *A.guttatum* ssp. *guttatum.*
A.maritimum Benth. See *Muilla maritima.*
A.marvinii Davidson. See *A.haematochiton.*
A.meliophilum Juz. See *Nectaroscordum siculum* ssp. *bulgaricum.*

A.mobilense Reg. See *A.canadense* var. *mobilense.*
A.modocense Jeps. See *A.parvum.*

A.moly L. (*A.aureum* Lam.). YELLOW ONION; LILY LEEK.
Stems 12–35cm; bulb to 2.5cm diam., spherical, producing many offsets, tunic leathery. Lvs 20–30×1.5–3.5cm, 1–3, almost basal, lanceolate, glaucous, keeled beneath. Fls numerous, star-shaped in an umbel 4–7cm diam.; spathes to 3.5cm, 2; pedicels 1.5–3.5cm; tepals 9–12×4–5mm, golden-yellow above, green-yellow and keeled below; stamens included, fil. 5–6mm. Fr. covered with persistent tepals. Summer. S & SW Europe. 'Jeannine': often 2 fl. stems; fls bright yellow, in large umbels. Z7.

A.moly var. **xericense** Pérez Lara. See *A.scorzonerifolium* var. *xericense.*

A.monadelphum Turcz. ex Kunth (*A.atrosanguineum* Schrenk; *A.kaufmanii* Reg.; *A.fedtschenkoanum* Reg.).
Stem 10–60cm; bulbs to 1cm diam., solitary or clustered on rhiz., cylindric, tunics brown, fibrous. Lvs to 60×0.2–0.7cm, 1–3, cylindric, fistular, sheathing lower part of stem. Fls few, campanulate in a dense spherical umbel; spathe acuminate, persistent; pedicels unequal; tepals 7–14mm, bright yellow becoming red or dark purple with age; stamens united above junction with tepals. Fr. to 7mm. Summer. C Asia, Siberia. Z6.

A.monospermum Jeps. See *A.amplectens.*
A.monspessulanum Gouan. See *A.nigrum.*
A.montanum Schrank non F.W. Schmidt. See *A.schoenoprasum.*
A.montanum F.W. Schmidt non Schrank. See *A.senescens* ssp. *montanum.*
A.montigenum Davidson. See *A.peninsulare.*

A.moschatum L. (*A.capillare* Cav.; *A.setaceum* Waldst. & Kit.).
Stem 10–35cm; bulbs to 1.5cm diam., ovoid, clustered, tunics fibrous. Lvs 14×0.05cm, 3–6, sheathing lower part of stem, margins of lower surface slightly rough. Fls 3–12, campanulate, in a flattened fastigiate umbel, 1–3cm diam.; spathes 2; pedicels 1–1.5cm; tepals 5–7×2mm, white to pink with darker midrib, acute. Fr. to 3mm. Summer. S Europe. Z8.

A.multibulbosum Jacq. See *A.nigrum.*
A.murrayanum Reg. See *A.acuminatum.*
A.murrayanum misapplied. See *A.unifolium.*
A.mutabile Michx. See *A.canadense.*

A.narcissiflorum Vill. (*A.grandiflorum* Lam.; *A.pedemontanum* Willd.).
Stem 15–35cm, 2-edged; bulbs to 5mm diam., oblong, clustered on small rhiz., tunic composed of parallel fibres. Lvs 9–18×0.2–0.6cm, 3–5, flat, grey-green, sheathing lower part of stem. Fls 5–8, campanulate, in a fastigiate umbel, pendent in bud, becoming erect as infl. and fr. develop; spathe to 18mm, 2- or 3-lobed, persistent; pedicels 8–18mm; tepals 1–1.5cm, bright pink to purple; stamens included, fil. to 5mm; stigma 3-lobed. Fr. to 5mm. Summer. N Italy, Portugal. Z8.

A.narcissiflorum ssp. **insubricum** (Boiss. & Reut.) Cif. & Giac. See *A.insubricum.*
A.narcissiflorum var. **insubricum** (Boiss. & Reut.) Fiori. See *A.insubricum.*

A.neapolitanum Cirillo (*A.album* Santi; *A.candissimum* Cav.; *A.lacteum* Sm.; *A.sulcatum* DC.; *A.cowanii* Lindl.; *A.sieberianum* Schult. & Schult. f.). DAFFODIL GARLIC; FLOWERING ONION; NAPLES GARLIC.
Stem 20–50cm, solid, 3-angled; bulb 1–2cm diam., subspherical, tunic membranous, reticulate. Lvs 8–35×0.5–2cm, 2, basal, linear, lanceolate, keeled, sheathing lower part of stem. Fls 1.5–2cm wide, numerous, cup-shaped or stellate, in a loose fastigiate or hemispherical umbel 5–11cm diam.; spathe 1–2.5cm; pedicels 1.5–3.5cm; tepals 7–12×4–6mm, glistening white; stamens included, fil. 6mm. Fr. 5mm, covered by persistent shiny tepals. Spring. Mediterranean, S Europe, Asia Minor, N Africa. 'Grandiflorum': fls white with a dark eye, umbel large and loose. Z8.

A.neriniflorum (Herb.) Bak. See *Caloscordum neriniflorum.*

A.nevii S. Wats.
Stem to 25cm; bulb solitary, tunic finely reticulate. Lvs shorter than stem, narrow, 2. Fls several in an umbel; tepals to 6mm, light rose-pink; ovary 6-crested. US (Washington, Oregon, Idaho). Z5.

A.nigrum L. (*A.multibulbosum* Jacq.; *A.monspessulanum* Gouan; *A.speciosum* Cirillo; *A.bauerianum* Bak.; *A.nigrum* var. *multibulbosum* Rouy).
Stems 40–90cm; bulbs to 5cm diam., ovoid, tunics membranous. Lvs to 50×8cm, 3–6, basal, lanceolate. Fls 1–1.5cm diam., numerous, star-shaped, in an umbel 6–9cm diam.; spathe to 3cm, 2–4-lobed; pedicels 2.5–4.5cm; tepals 6–9×1.5–3.5mm, white, pink or purple with green midribs, becoming deflexed with age; stamens included, fil. united in basal ring, anth. yellow; ovary very dark green almost black. Fr. 6–8mm. Spring. S Europe, N Africa, Asia Minor, Cyprus. Z8.

A.nigrum var. *atropurpureum* (Waldst. & Kit.) Vis. See *A.atropurpureum.*
A.nigrum var. *multibulbosum* Rouy. See *A.nigrum.*
A.nitens Sauzé & Maillard. See *A.vineale.*

A.nutans L.
Stem 30 60cm, 2 angled; bulbs to 2cm diam., conical, clustered on short rhiz., tunics membranous. Lvs to 30×1.5cm, 6–8, basal, glabrous, glaucous. Fls numerous, cup-shaped, in a spherical umbel, to 6cm diam., pendent before fls open; spathe 2-lobed, tepals 4–6mm, rose-pink or lilac; stamens exserted, inner 3, broad basal teeth on either side, twice as broad as outer 3. Summer. Siberia. Z5.

A.nuttallii S. Wats. See *A.drumondii.*

A.obliquum L. (*A.ramosum* Jacq.).
Stem 60–100cm, terete; bulbs to 2cm diam., oblong, solitary, on rhiz., tunic red-brown, membranous. Lvs to 35×2cm, 4–10, broadly linear, sheathing lower part of stem. Fls numerous, cup-shaped to spherical, in a dense umbel 3–4cm diam.; spathe persistent; pedicels 1–2cm; tepals 4–5×2.5mm, pale sulphur-green, concave, acute; stamens exserted, fil. 8–9mm, anth. yellow. Fr. 3mm. Summer. Romania, Siberia, C Asia. Z7.
A.occidentale A. Gray. See *A.amplectens.*

A.ochroleucum Waldst. & Kit.
Stem 15–30cm; bulbs oblong to cylindrical, clustered on rhiz., tunics brown, membranous. Lvs to 2mm wide, 3–4, linear, flat, keeled, mostly basal, margins rough. Fls numerous, cup-shaped, in dense, globose umbels, 1.5–2cm diam.; pedicels equal; tepals white to yellow, with red midrib; stamens and styles exserted. Summer. Italy. Z8.

A.odorum L. See *A.ramosum.*

A.oleraceum L. (*A.virens* Lam.; *A.virescens* DC.; *A.oleraceum* var. *complanatum* Fries; *A.complanatum* Boreau). FIELD GARLIC.
Stem 25–100cm, slightly ridged; bulb 1–2cm diam., ovoid or spherical, tunic membranous. Lvs to 25×0.6cm, 2–4, linear, channelled, sheathing lower part of stem. Fls numerous, cup-shaped, inner erect, outer pendulous, in a loose umbel, 2–4cm diam., bulbils replacing some fls; spathes to 20cm, 2, acuminate, unequal; pedicels 1.5–6cm, flat; tepals 5–7×2–3mm, obtuse, white tinged green, pink or brown; stamens included. Summer. Europe. Z5.

A.oleraceum var. *complanatum* Fries. See *A.oleraceum.*
A.oliganthum Karel. & Kir. See *A.schoenoprasum.*

A.olympicum Boiss.
Stem 30–50cm; bulb to 1cm diam., ovoid, tunic black, striate. Lvs 2–3, 3–4.5mm wide, narrow-linear, flat. Fls many, campanulate, in a dense rounded umbel 3–4cm diam.; spathe-lobes narrow, exceeding umbel; pedicels subequal, 1–2cm; tepals 3–4mm, ovate, obtuse, violet-red or lilac-pink; fil. exceeding tepals, violet. Fr. 3mm, 3-angled. Turkey.

A.ophioscorodon Link. See *A.sativum* var. *ophioscorodon.*

A.oreophilum C.A. Mey. (*A.platystemon* Karel. & Kir.; *A.ostrowskianum* Reg.).
Stems 5–20cm; bulb 1–2cm diam., ovoid or spherical, tunic grey, papery. Lvs longer than stems, 2, 2–8mm wide, linear. Fls numerous, campanulate, in loose, spherical umbels; spathe 8–15mm; pedicels 7–15mm; tepals 8–11mm, pink to purple with darker midrib; stamens included, fil. 3–5.5mm, lower halves united in basal ring; stigma 3-lobed. Fr. to 4mm. Spring–summer. Turkestan, Caucasus, C Asia. 'Zwanenburg': fls deep carmine. Z8.

A.orientale Boiss.
Stems 10–40cm; bulb to 1.5cm diam., almost spherical, tunic membranous. Lvs to 40×2cm, 3–4, narrow, lanceolate, in basal rosette. Fls numerous, stellate, in hemispherical umbels to 5cm diam.; spathe to 2cm, 2–4-lobed; pedicels 1–2.5cm; tepals 5–9×2–2.5mm, narrow, lanceolate, white, with green midrib, becoming deflexed with age; stamens included, fil. to 4–5mm, bases united in basal ring, anth. yellow. Fr. to 5mm. Spring. E Mediterranean. Z8.

A.ostrowskianum Reg. See *A.oreophilum.*
A.oviflorum Reg. See *A.macranthum.*
A.oxyphilum Wherry. See *A.cernuum.*

A.pallens L. (*A.tenuiflorum* Ten.; *A.coppoleri* Tineo; *A.paniculatum* var. *pallens* (L.) Gren. & Godron; *A.serbicum* Vis. & Pančic (*A.amblyanthum* Zahar.).
Stem 10–30cm; bulb 1–1.5cm diam., tunic membranous. Lvs to 30×0.5cm, to 3–4, sheathing lower part of stem. Fls 10–70, cup-shaped in a compact umbel, 1.5–3cm diam.; spathes to 10cm, 2, acute; pedicels 5–20mm; tepals 3.5–5×1.5–2mm, white or pink; anth. yellow. Fr. to 4mm. Summer. S Europe. Z8.

A.paniculatum L. (*A.longispathum* Delaroche; *A.intermedium* DC.; *A.fuscum* Waldst. & Kit.; *A.rhodopeum* Velen.; *A.euboicum* Rchb. f.).
Stem 30–70cm; bulb to 2.5cm diam., ovoid, tunic membranous. Lvs 25×0.2cm, 3–5, sheathing lower part of stem, lower surface ribbed. Fls numerous, campanulate, in a loose 3.5–7cm diam. umbel; spathes 5 14cm, tapering, 2; pedicels unequal, 1–7cm; tepals 4.5–7×1.5–2.5mm, obtuse, white, pink or yellow-brown; stamens included or slightly protruding. Fr. to 5mm. Summer. Europe. Z5.

A.paniculatum var. *pallens* Gren. & Godron. See *A.pallens.*

A.paradoxum (Bieb.) G. Don (*Scilla paradoxa* Bieb.). FEW-FLOWERED LEEK.
Stem 15–30cm, triangular; bulbs to 1cm diam., spherical, tunics membranous. Lvs to 30×2.5cm, 1, keeled. Fls 1–10, campanulate, some umbels containing many bulbils and few or no fls; spathes 1–2.5cm, 2; pedicels 2–4.5cm; tepals 8–12×6mm, white with pale green midrib; stamens included, fil. bases united; stigma 3-lobed. Fr. to 5mm; seeds with aril. Spring. Caucasus, Iran.var. **paradoxum.** Umbel with 1 or no fls, many bulbils. var. **normale** Stearn. Umbels with to 10 fls and no bulbils. Z8.

A.parciflorum Viv. (*A.pauciflorum* Viv.).
Stem 9–30cm, 1–3; bulbs to 1.5cm diam., ovoid, tunics fibrous. Lvs to 10×0.05cm, 3–4, sheathing lower part of stem, withering by flowering time. Fls 2–10, campanulate, in a fastigiate umbel; spathe to 1.4cm, 2-lobed; pedicels unequal, 5–35mm, erect; tepals 5×1mm, pink, acute; stamens included, fil. to 3mm. Fr. to 4.5mm. Corsica, Sardinia. Z8.

A.parishii S. Wats.
Stem 10–20cm; bulbs 10–15mm, ovoid, tunics pink. Lvs much longer than stem, 1, terete above sheath enclosing base of stem. Fls 10 or more in an umbel; spathes 1–1.5cm, 2–3, ovate; pedicels 6–12mm; tepals 12–15mm, pale pink, acute, spreading; anth. yellow. Fr. 2–3mm, 6-crested. Spring. US (California, W Nevada). Z6.

A.parvum Kellogg (*A.tribracteatum* var. *parvum* Jeps.; *A.tribracteatum* var. *andersonii* S. Wats.; *A.modocense* Jeps.).
Stems 3–5cm; bulbs 10–15mm, ovoid, tunic grey-brown,

membranous. Lvs to 10×0.4cm, 2, curved. Fls 8–100 in an umbel; spathes 2; pedicels 5–10mm; tepals 7–10mm, pink to purple with darker midrib, obtuse; stamens and styles included, anth. yellow or purple. Fr. 3–4mm, 3-crested; seeds 2mm. Spring–summer. US (California, Oregon, Idaho, Utah, Nevada). Z5.

A.pedemontanum Willd. See *A.narcissiflorum.*

A.pendulinum Ten. (*A.triquetrum* var. *pendulinum* (Ten.) Reg.; *A.triquetrum* ssp. *pendulinum* (Ten.) K. Richt.).
Stem 6–25cm, triangular; bulbs to 1cm diam., spherical, tunics membranous. Lvs to 25×0.7cm, 2, keeled, soon senescent. Fls 5–9, stellate, in a loose umbel; spathes 2; pedicels to 4cm, erect becoming pendent later; tepals 3–5×1–1.5mm, white with green midrib; stamens 4–5mm; stigma 3-lobed. Fr. 4–6mm; seeds with aril. Spring. S Italy, Corsica, Sardinia, Sicily. Z8.

A.peninsulare Lemmon ex Greene (*A.montigenum* Davidson).
Stem 20–40cm; bulb to 1.5cm diam., ovoid to spherical, tunic grey-brown, with zig-zag reticulations. Lvs similar length as stem, 1–6mm wide, 2–4. Fls 6–25, in a loose umbel; spathes 1–2cm, 2, acuminate; pedicels 1.5–3cm, spreading; tepals 10–13mm, deep pink to purple, outer tepals spreading, inner tepals narrower, more erect; stamens included, anth. yellow. Fr. to 4mm, slightly crested. Spring–summer. US (California). var. *crispum* (Greene) Jeps. (*A.crispum* Greene). Inner tepals with crisp, wavy margins. Z8.

A.perdulce S. Fraser.
Stem 10–20cm, terete; bulbs ovoid, clustered, tunic dark brown, fibrous, enclosing 1 or more bulbs. Lvs as least as long as stem, to 2mm wide, 3 or more, channelled, concave to convex in section. Fls urceolate, fragrant, 5–25 per umbel; spathe membranous, 2- or 3-lobed; pedicels 7–10mm at flowering, elongating, becoming rigid as fr. develops; tepals 7–10mm, erect, deep rose to purple, persistent on infructescence; stamens 3–5mm, fil. bases united in basal cup. Spring. US (Dakota, Iowa, Texas, New Mexico). Z5.

A.pikeanum Rydb. See *A.geyeri.*

A.pilosum Sibth. & Sm.
Stem 2.5–15cm; bulb to 1cm diam., tunic leathery. Lvs 9cm, 2–4, thread-like, sheathing lower part of stem, bearing stiff spreading hairs. Fls cup-shaped, variable in number, in an hemispherical, dense umbel, 1.5–4cm diam.; spathe to 3cm, 2-lobed, caudate, persistent; pedicels 5–15mm; tepals 3–4×1–1.5mm, lilac, obtuse; stamens exserted, fil. 4–5mm, anth. yellow. Fr. 3.5mm. Summer. Greece. Z9.

A.platycaule S. Wats.
Stem 4–12cm, 3–5mm wide, compressed; bulbs 2–3.5cm, ovoid, clustered on rhiz., tunics grey. Lvs longer than stem, 8–15mm wide, 2, thick, sickle-shaped. Fls numerous; spathes 3–5, acuminate; pedicels 12–20mm; tepals 10–12mm, acute, deep pink with paler tips, folded at first, spreading later; stamens included, fils with broad bases, anth. dark. Fr. to 3–4mm; seeds 2–3mm. Spring. US (California, Nevada, Oregon). Z6.

A.platystemon Karel. & Kir. See *A.oreophilum.*

A.plummerae S. Wats.
Stem 30–50cm, terete, or slightly ridged; bulbs to 2cm, clustered on short rhiz., tunic fibrous, coarsely reticulate, enveloping more than one bulb. Lvs to 27×0.6cm, to 10, channelled, concave to convex in cross section, margins sometimes denticulate. Fls stellate, 10–25 in an erect umbel; spathe 2–3-lobed; pedicels 10–30mm, erect; tepals 5–10mm, acute, white to pink, spreading then reflexed; stamens exserted, fil. united in basal cup; ovary 6-crested. Summer. US (Arizona), N Mexico. Z8.

A.polyanthum Schult. & Schult. f.
Stem 40–80cm; bulb 1.5–2cm diam., ovoid. Lvs 10–25×0.3–2cm, 3–6, sheathing stem below, flat. Fls many in subglobose umbel 4–8cm diam.; spathe 1, long-pointed, soon deciduous; pedicels unequal, to 4mm; tepals to 5×2mm, nar-

rowly elliptic, pink, scabrid on median vein; fil. included. Fr. 3mm. SW Europe. Z8.

A.porphyroprasum Heldr. See *A.scordoprasum* ssp. *rotundum.*

A.porrum L. (*A.ampeloprasum* var. *porrum* (L.) Reg.). LEEK. Bienn., widely grown as an annual. Stem continuous with fleshy, elongated, solitary bulb. Lvs linear-lanceolate. Fls numerous in a large spherical umbel; spathe beaked; tepals white to pink. Northern temperate zones.

A.porrum ssp. *euampeloprasum* Breistr. See *A.ampeloprasum.*
A.porrum var. *ampeloprasum* Mirb. See *A.ampeloprasum.*

A.praecox Brandg. (*A.hyalinum* var. *praecox* (Brandg.) Jeps.).
Stem 20–50cm; bulbs 7–15mm diam., spherical, tunic reticulate, grey-brown. Lvs 20–50×0.1–0.5cm, 2–4, flat. Fls 6–30 in a loose umbel; spathes 1–2.5cm, 2, acuminate; pedicels 1.5–3cm, spreading; tepals 9–12mm, white with pink to purple midrib, acuminate, 3 inner tepals narrower; stamens 6–8mm, fil. bases broad, anth. yellow to red; stigma lobed. Fr. 4–5mm, slightly crested. Spring. US (California). Z9.

A.przewalskianum Reg. (*A.jacquemontii* Reg. non Kunth).
Stem 15–30cm, terete; bulbs 6–10mm diam., cylindric, clustered on rhiz., tunics fibrous, reticulate. Lvs to 35×0.1cm, 3–4, basal. Fls numerous, stellate, in an hemispherical umbel, 1.5–2.5cm diam.; spathe to 1cm; pedicels 5–10mm; tepals 4–5mm, spreading or reflexed, mauve; stamens exserted, fil. 7mm, inner fil. with broad bases and 2 lateral teeth. Himalaya, W China. Z8.

A.pseudoflavum Vved. See *A.stamineum.*
A.pulchellum G. Don. See *A.carinatum* ssp. *pulchellum.*
A.pulchrum Clarke. See *A.subhirsutum.*
A.purdomii W.W. Sm. See *A.cyaneum.*

A.purdyi Eastw. (*A.fimbriatum* var. *purdyi* Eastw.).
Stem 10–30cm; bulb 12–16mm diam., ovoid to spherical, tunic dark brown. Lf longer than stem, solitary, sheathing. Fls numerous, in an umbel; spathes 1–2cm, 3; pedicels 15–20mm; tepals to 10mm, pale pink with darker midrib; ovary 6-crested. Spring. US (California). Z8.

A.purpurascens Losa. See *A.schoenoprasum.*

A.pyrenaicum Costa & Vayr.
Stem 55–100cm; bulbs 2–3cm diam., ovoid, tunics membranous. Lvs to 45×1.5cm, 5–6, flat, linear, keeled below, sheathing lower part of stem, margins finely toothed. Fls numerous, campanulate, umbel 4–7cm diam.; spathe to 7cm, caudate; pedicels to 25mm; tepals 7–9×2mm, acuminate, white with green midrib, margins finely toothed, keel rough; stamens included, outer fil. simple, inner fil. toothed, anth. brown. Fr. to 6mm. Summer. Spain (E Pyrenees). Z7.

A.raddeanum Reg. See *A.schoenoprasum.*

A.ramosum L. (*A.odorum* L.; *A.tataricum* L. f.). FRAGRANT-FLOWERED GARLIC.
Stem 24–50cm, terete or ridged; bulbs to 1cm diam., cylindric, clustered on rhiz., tunics fibrous, reticulate. Lvs to 35cm, 4–9, hollow, sheathing lower part of stem. Fls campanulate, variable in number, umbel, 3–5cm wide, fastigiate; spathes 1–2; pedicels 1–3cm; tepals 8–10mm, lanceolate, white with dark red midribs; stamens included, fil. 4–5mm. Fr. 5–6mm. Summer. C Asia. Z7.

A.ramosum Jacq. See *A.obliquum.*
A.recurvatum Rydb. See *A.cernuum.*

A.regelii Trautv. (*A.yatei* Aitch. & Bak.).
Stem to 100cm; bulbs to 5cm diam., spherical, tunic brown, fibrous. Lvs to 5cm wide, 2–4, basal, withering before flowering, margins often rough. Fls 1–1.5cm diam. in whorls of 6, lowest 8–10cm diam., smaller toward apex, campanulate, erect; spathe to 1cm, tinged pink; pedicels unequal, 4–8cm; tepals 9–13mm, papery, pale pink to purple with darker central vein. Fr. 6–8mm diam. Summer. C Asia. Z8.

A.reticulatum G. Don non Presl & C. Presl. See *A.textile*.
A.reticulatum var. *deserticola* M.E. Jones. See *A.macropetalum*.
A.reticulatum var. *nuttallii* (S. Wats.) M.E. Jones. See *A.drummondii*.
A.rhodopeum Velen. See *A.paniculatum*.
A.rilaense Panov. See *A.vineale*.
A.rollii Terracc. See *A.amethystinum*.

A.rosenbachianum Reg. (*A.angustipetalum* Wendelbo).
Stem to 100cm, ribbed; bulb 1.5–2.5cm diam., spherical, tunic black, papery. Lvs 1–5cm wide, much shorter than stem, 2–4, glabrous. Fls stellate, umbel to 10cm diam., spherical; spathe 1; pedicels 2–6mm, maroon; tepals 6–10mm, deep purple, occasionally white, soon withering; stamens 7–10mm, exserted, persisting, prominent after tepals fade, anth. purple; ovary stalked. Fr. 5mm diam. Spring. C Asia, Afghanistan, Baluchistan, Tadzhikistan. 'Album': to 75cm; fls white, slightly tinted green. 'Purple King': stems tall; fls dark violet, stamens white, in loose, round umbel. Z8.

A.roseum L. (*A.illyricum* Jacq.). ROSY GARLIC.
Stem 10–65cm; bulbs 1.5cm diam., spherical, tunics stiff, brittle, perforated. Lvs 12–35×1–1.5cm, 2–7, sheathing lower part of stem, withering before flowering. Fls 1–1.5cm diam., 5–30, cup-shaped, umbels 2–8cm diam., fastigiate or hemispherical, containing bulbils as well as fls; spathe 1–2.5cm, 3- or 4 lobed; pedicels 7–45mm; tepals 7–12×3–5mm, white to bright pink; stamens included, fil. 5mm, anth. yellow. Fr. 4mm. Spring–summer. S Europe, N Africa, Turkey. var. **roseum**. Infl. without bulbils. var. **bulbiferum** DC. Infl. with bulbils; pedicels 0.7–4cm; fls campanulate to cup-shaped, pink or white, tepals 0.7–1.2×0.3–0.5cm; stamens included. var. **carneum** Rchb. (*A.carneum* Bertol.; *A.roseum* var. *bulbiferum* DC.; *A.ambiguum* Sm.; *A.incarnatum* Hornem.; *A.tenorii* Spreng.; *A.amoenum* G. Don). Infl. with bulbils, tepals pale pink. Z8.

A.roseum var. *bulbiferum* DC. See *A.roseum* var. *carneum*.
A.rotundum L. See *A.scordoprasum* ssp. *rotundum*.

A.rubens Schräd. ex Willd.
Stem 10–25cm, ridged; bulbs to 1cm diam., clustered on rhiz., tunics membranous. Lvs 5–20×0.1–0.2cm, 5–6, channelled, basal. Fls campanulate, umbel lax, 2–3cm diam.; spathe to 1cm, persistent; pedicels 8–12mm; tepals 4–5×2.5mm, purple, obtuse; stamens included, fil. to 4mm, anth. yellow; style included. Summer. N & C Asia, Russia (Ural Mts). Z4.

A.rubrum Osterh. (*A.rydbergii* Macbr.; *A.fibrosum* Rydb.).
Stems to 25cm; bulbs solitary, tunics fibrous, reticulate. Lvs to 6mm wide. Fls few, umbels with bulbils; pedicels to 12mm; tepals 6mm, white to pink, obtuse; stamens included; ovary 6-crested. N America (New Mexico, Arizona to British Columbia, Alberta). Z3.

A.rydbergii Macbr. See *A.rubrum*.
A.sardoum Moris. See *A.guttatum* ssp. *sardoum*.

A.sativum L. GARLIC.
Stem 25–100cm; bulbs 3–6cm diam., ovoid, containing 5–18 bulblets, often termed cloves, tunic papery. Lvs 60×3cm, 6–12, linear, flat above, keeled below, sheathing lower part of stem. Fls cup-shaped, few, buds often abortive, umbels 2.5–5cm diam., containing many bulbils; spathe 1, to 25cm, caudate; pedicels unequal, 1–2cm; tepals 3–5mm, usually white to pink, tinged with green, occasionally purple; stamens included, 3 outer fil. 6–8mm, 3 inner fil. to 2mm wide, 2–4 broad lateral teeth. Summer. Not known in the wild. Cultivated in Middle East c3500BC. var. **ophioscorodon** (Link) Döll (*A.controversum* Schräd. ex Willd.; *A.contortum* Stokes; *A.ophioscorodon* Link; *A.sativum* var. *subrotundum* Gren. & Godron). ROCAMBOLE; SERPENT GARLIC. Stems coil in 1–2 loops before fls develop. Z8.

A.sativum var. *subrotundum* Gren. & Godron. See *A.sativum* var. *ophioscorodon*.
A.scaposum Benth. See *A.kunthii*.

A.schmitzii var. *duriminium* Cout. See *A.schoenoprasum*.

A.schoenoprasum L. (*A.montanum* Schrank; *A.alpinum* DC.; *A.oliganthum* Karel. & Kir.; *A.buhseanum* Reg.; *A.raddeanum* Reg.; *A.schmitzii* var. *duriminium* Cout.; *A.gredense* Rivas Mart.; *A.purpurascens* Losa). CHIVES; CIVE; SCHNITTLAUGH.
Stems to 10–60cm; bulbs narrow, to 1cm diam., conical, clustered on short rhiz., tunics membranous, sometimes brown, leathery, or fibrous. Lvs to 35×0.6cm, 1–2, grey-green, cylindric, hollow, sheathing lower part of stem. Fls 8–30, campanulate, umbel dense, 1.5–5cm diam.; spathe to 1.5cm, 2–3-lobed; pedicels unequal, 2–20mm; tepals 7–15×2–4mm, lanceolate, white, lilac or purple, with darker midrib; stamens 5–7mm, included. Fr. 4mm. Summer. Europe, Asia, N America. 'Forescate': vigorous, to 50cm; fls rose-pink, edible. 'Fruhlau': to 25cm; early and plentiful; F1 hybrid. 'Shepherds Crook': to 5cm; lvs contorted. 'Schnittlauch': dwarf, to 20cm. var. **sibiricum** (L.) Hartm. (*A.sibiricum* L.). Stem to 40cm. Tepals deep rose becoming violet. Balkans, Siberia, Asia Minor. Z5.

A.schrenki Reg. See *A.strictum*.

A.schubertii Zucc.
Stem 30–60mm, hollow; bulb 3–4cm diam., spherical to ovoid, tunic brown, leathery, sometimes becoming fibrous. Lvs 20–45×6cm, 4–8 basal, broadly linear, wavy, glaucous, margins rough. Fls 1.5cm diam., stellate, numerous, umbel 2–4cm diam., spherical, lax; spathes 2–3cm, 2–3; pedicels unequal, 2–20cm, shorter pedicels fertile, longer pedicels infertile; tepals 6–10×2–2.5mm, white, pink or violet, with purple midribs, becoming rigid after flowering; stamens included, fil. 5–7mm. Fr. 6–8mm. Spring. E Mediterranean to C Asia. Z8.

A.scorodoprasum L. SAND LEEK; GIANT GARLIC; SPANISH GARLIC.
Stem 25–90cm; bulb 1–2cm diam., spherical, bulblets dark red, tunic membranous, sometimes becoming fibrous. Lvs 27×2cm, 2–5, linear, sheathing lower part of stem. Fls 0–12, ovoid, many replaced by purple bulbils, umbel to 1.5cm diam.; spathe to 1.5cm, soon withering; pedicels unequal, to 2cm; tepals 4–7×1.5–3.5mm, lilac to dark purple; stamens included, fil. 2.5–4.5mm, inner fil. with lateral teeth 2–3× length of central teeth, anth. yellow. Summer. E Europe, Caucasus, Turkey, N Iran. ssp. **jajlae** (Vved.) Stearn. Lvs 3–5mm wide. Umbel subglobose, bulbils absent; fls rose-violet. Crimea, Caucasus. ssp. **rotundum** (L.) Stearn (*A.rotundum* L.; *A.porphyroprasum* Heldr.). Bulb tunics black. Lvs to 1cm wide. Fls numerous, umbel spherical or hemispherical, without bulbils; tepals purple, inner paler with white margins and dark purple midrib. Fr. to 5mm. S Europe, W Russia, W Asia, Iran. Z7.

A.scorodoprasum ssp. *babingtonii* K. Richt. See *A.ampeloprasum* var. *babingtonii*.
A.scorodoprasum var. *babingtonii* Reg. See *A.ampeloprasum* var. *babingtonii*.

A.scorzonerifolium Desf. ex DC. in Redouté.
Stem 14–30cm, angular; bulb 1.5cm diam., spherical, tunic papery. Lvs 18–40×0.3–0.7cm, 1–3, basal, linear, glaucous, underside keeled. Fls to 15, stellate, umbel 4–5cm diam., fastigiate; spathe 1; pedicels 15–30mm, erect; tepals 7–10×2–4mm, yellow, lanceolate; stamens included, fil. 4–6mm; ovary angled, 6-crested. Summer. Spain, Portugal. var. **scorzonerifolium** DC. in Redouté. Umbel with many bulbils, few fls. var. **xericense** Fernandes (*A.stramineum* Boiss. & Reut.; *A.moly* var. *xericense* Pérez Lara). Umbel to 15 fls, without bulbils. Z8.

A.segetum Schult. & Schult. f. See *A.amethystinum*.

A.semenowii Reg.
Stem 10–40cm; bulbs to 1cm diam., cylindric, clustered on rhiz., tunics brown, reticulate, fibrous. Lvs 5–15mm wide, 2–3, linear, channelled, sheathing lower part of stem. Fls campanulate, few, umbel dense, spherical; spathe as long as

umbel, persistent; pedicels unequal; tepals 10–15mm, yellow becoming red later; stamens. Fr. 4–5mm. Summer. C Asia. Z6.

A.senescens L. GERMAN GARLIC.
Stem 7–60cm, flattened; bulbs to 1cm diam., conical, clustered on rhiz., tunics membranous. Lvs 4–30×1cm, 4–9, basal, flat. Fls numerous, cup-shaped, umbel 2–5cm diam., hemispherical; spathe 5–8mm, 2-lobed; pedicels 8–20mm; tepals 3.5–8×2–2.5mm, lilac; stamens exserted, fil. 4–6mm, 3 inner fil. with broad bases; ovary 3-lobed. Fr. 4mm. Summer–autumn. Europe, N Asia. 'Roseum': fls pink. ssp. **senescens**. Stems to 60cm. Lvs to 1cm wide. N Asia. ssp. **montanum** (F.W. Schmidt) Holub (A.lusitanicum Lam.; A.montanum F.W. Schmidt; A.serotinum Lapeyr.; A.fallax Schult. & Schult. f.; A.fallax ssp. montanum (F.W. Schmidt) Fries). Stems to 45cm high. Lvs to 6mm wide. Europe. var. **calcareum** (Wallr.) Hylander. Stems to 45cm. Lvs 1–6mm wide, grey, curled on surface of soil. var. **glaucum** (Schrad.) Reg. (A.glaucum Schräd.). Lvs glaucous, swirling; fls lilac. Z5.

A.serbicum Vis. & Pancǎicǎ. See A.pallens.
A.serotinum Lapeyr. See A.senescens ssp. montanum.

A.serratum S. Wats.
Stem 20–35cm; bulbs to 12mm diam., solitary, spherical, tunic grey, with horizontal V-shaped reticulations. Lvs shorter than stem, to 3mm wide, 2–4. Fls numerous, umbels dense; spathes to 1.5cm, 2; pedicels slender, 8–14mm; tepals 7–9mm, pink to purple, papery; anth. yellow becoming red; stigma 3-lobed; ovary crested. Fr. to 2mm. Spring. US (California). Z8.

A.serratum var. **dichlamydeum** Jones. See A.dichlamydeum.
A.setaceum Waldst. & Kit. See A.moschatum.
A.sibiricum L. See A.schoenoprasum var. sibiricum.
A.siculum Ucria. See Nectaroscordum siculum.
A.sieberianum Schult. & Schult. f. See A.neapolitanum.

A.sikkimense Bak. (A.cyaneum var. brachystemon Reg.; A.kansuense Reg.; A.tibeticum Rendle).
Stem to 10–40cm; bulbs 3–5mm, cylindric, clustered on rhiz., tunic fibrous, reticulate. Lvs to 30×0.5cm, 2–5, linear, flat, sheathing base of stem. Fls campanulate, pendent, variable in number, umbel pendent; spathe to 2cm; pedicels unequal, 2–6mm; tepals 6–10×3–4mm, deep blue or purple; stamens included, inner 3 with small basal teeth. Summer. Asia (Himalaya, Tibet, China). Z8.

A.speciosum Cirillo. See A.nigrum.

A.sphaerocephalum L. (A.descendens L.). ROUND-HEADED LEEK.
Stem to 90cm, terete, hollow; bulbs to 3.5cm diam., spherical, tunic membranous, sometimes becoming fibrous. Lvs 7–35×0.4–0.5cm, 2–6, hollow, sheathing lower half of stem. Fls cylindric, numerous, umbel 2–3cm diam., may contain bulbils, spathes to 2cm, 2, persistent; pedicels unequal, 2–30mm; tepals pink to dark red-brown, keeled; stamens exserted, fil. 4–7mm, inner 3 with 2 lateral teeth; style exserted. Fr. to 4mm. Summer. Europe, N Africa, W Asia. ssp. **sphaerocephalon**. Fls red. Europe, N Africa. ssp. **arvense** (Guss.) Arcang. (A.arvense Guss.). Tepals white, midrib green; pedicels smooth. Sicily, Malta, S Greece, Albania. ssp. **trachypus** (Boiss.) Richter (A.trachypus Boiss.). Tepals white, midrib green; pedicels rough. Greece. Z5.

A.sphaerocephalon ssp. **rollii** (Terracc.) K. Richt. See A.amethystinum.

A.splendens Willd.
Stem 25–50cm, terete, slightly ribbed; bulbs 3–7×0.5–0.75cm, cylindric, in pairs on ascending rhiz., tunics brown, reticulate. Lvs to 4mm wide, 3–4, linear, flat, margins rough, sheathing lower part of stem. Fls numerous, campanulate, umbel hemispherical, dense; spathe acuminate, persistent; pedicels 6–8mm; tepals to 4mm, bright pink with purple midrib; styles exserted. Fr. to 6mm. Summer. Siberia, Mongolia, Japan, China. Z5.

A.stamineum Boiss. (A.pseudoflavum Vved.).
Stem 10–35cm; bulbs to 1cm diam., solitary, tunics membranous. Lvs to 15×0.1cm, 3–4, sheathing lower part of stem. Fls cup-shaped, numerous, umbel to 7cm diam., lax; spathe to 2cm, 2-lobed, caudate; pedicels unequal, 10–40mm; tepals 5×2mm, pale purple, sometimes yellow; stamens and style exserted, fil. to 5mm, united in basal ring; ovary sessile. Fr. to 3mm. Summer. N Greece, Turkey, Asia Minor, Caucasus. Z7.

A.stellatum Ker-Gawl. PRAIRIE ONION.
Stem 30–70cm; bulbs ovoid, tunics membranous. Lvs 1–2mm wide, 3–6, basal, thick, underside keeled. Fls numerous, cup-shaped, umbel hemispherical, erect; spathes 2; pedicels 1–2cm, stiff; tepals 4–7mm, pink, ovate; stamens as long or longer than tepals; ovary 6-crested. Fr. 6-crested. Summer. N America. 'Album': fls white. Z6.

A.stellerianum Willd.
Stem 10–30cm, ridged; bulbs to 1cm diam., conical, clustered on rhiz., tunics membranous. Lvs to 21×0.15cm, 4–6, basal, margins rough. Fls cup-shaped, few, umbel spherical or hemispherical, 2–3cm diam.; spathe shorter than stem, persistent; pedicels 10–15mm, nearly equal, smooth; tepals 4–5mm, white to yellow, obtuse; stamens exserted, fil. to 10mm, anth. yellow; style exserted. Siberia, Mongolia, C Ural Mts. Z4.

A.stenanthum Drew. See A.bolanderi var. stenanthum.
A.stevenii Ledeb. See A.globosum.

A.stipitatum Reg.
Stem to 150cm, ribbed; bulbs 3–6cm diam., spherical, tunics black, papery. Lvs 2–4cm wide, 4–6, basal, pubesc., glaucous. Fls numerous, star-shaped, fragrant, in umbel 8–12cm diam.; spathes to 3cm, 2; pedicels 2.5–5cm; tepals 8–9mm, pale lilac, occasionally white, thin, papery, tapering, later reflexed and twisted; stamens included, bases united; ovary stalked. Fr. to 5mm. Summer. E Afghanistan, Pakistan, C Asia (Pamir and Tien-Shan Mts). Z8.

A.stojanovii Kovachev. See A.amethystinum.
A.stramineum Boiss. & Reut. See A.scorzonerifolium var. xericense.
A.striatum Jacq. See Nothoscordum bivalve.

A.strictum Schräd. (A.volhynicum Besser; A.schrenki Reg.; A.lineare var. strictum Krylov).
Stem 40–60cm, terete, rigid; bulbs to 10×1.5cm, cylindric, in pairs on ascending rhiz., tunics brown, reticulate. Lvs to 5mm wide, 3–4, sheathing lower third of stem, flat, rigid, margins rough, shorter than stem. Fls numerous, campanulate, umbel dense, hemispherical; spathe shorter than umbel, acuminate, persistent; pedicels 6–10mm; tepals 4–5mm, pink with purple midrib; stamens exserted, 3 inner fil. with 2 basal teeth; style exserted, stigma capitate. Fr. to 4mm. Summer. C Europe, W Asia. Z4.

A.subangulatum Reg.
Stem to 25cm; bulbs clustered on rhiz., tunic fibrous, reticulate. Lvs thread-like, margins dentate, sheathing lower part of stem. Fls numerous; pedicels 5–9mm; tepals to 6mm, purple; stamens included, fil. bases united, inner 3 fil. with 2 lateral teeth; stigma capitate. China. Z7.

A.subhirsutum L. (A.ciliatum Cirillo; A.pulchrum Clarke).
Stem 7–30cm, solid; bulbs to 1.5cm diam., spherical, tunics membranous, reticulate. Lvs 8–50×0.1–2cm, 2–3, basal, flat, margins pubesc. Fls stellate, variable in number, similar to A.neapolitanum but smaller and more delicate, umbel 2–8cm diam., loose; spathe 8–25mm; pedicels unequal, to 4cm; tepals 7–9mm, white; stamens included, anth. brown, occasionally yellow, fil. to 3mm. Spring. Mediterranean. Z8.

A.subvillosum Schult. & Schult. f. (A.vernale Tineo; A.album var. purpurascens Maire & Weiller).
Stems 10–60cm, terete; bulbs to 2.5cm diam., spherical, tunics membranous. Lvs 6–40×0.2–2cm, 2–5, basal, margins ciliate. Fls numerous, cup-shaped, umbel 2.5–4.5cm diam., hemispherical; spathe becoming 3- or 4-lobed, persistent;

pedicels to 2cm; tepals 5–9mm; white; stamens included, fil. 6–11mm, anth. yellow. Fr. 3–4mm. Spring. W Mediterranean, Canary Is., N Africa. Z8.

A.sulcatum DC. See *A.neapolitanum*.

A.suworowii Reg.
Stem 30–100cm; bulbs 2–3cm diam., spherical, tunic tough, leathery. Lvs to 3cm wide, 2–6, basal, margins rough, glaucous. Fls numerous, stellate; umbel hemispherical; spathe 3- or 4-lobed; pedicels 1–4cm; tepals 4–5.5mm, purple, linear, becoming reflexed and twisted after flowering; stamens included; ovary subsessile. Fr. to 6mm diam. Summer. C Asia. Similar to *A.rosenbachianum* but fls smaller. Z8.

A.tanguticum Reg. LAVENDER GLOBE LILY.
Stem to 40cm; bulbs ovoid, tunic fibrous, dark brown. Lvs to 3mm wide, shorter than stem, flat, linear. Fls numerous; pedicels to 1cm; tepals 3mm, purple, with darker midribs; stamens exserted, fil. to 6mm. W China.Z7.

A.tataricum L. f. See *A.ramosum*.
A.tauricum Rchb. See *A.flavum*.
A.tenellum Davidson. See *A.campanulatum*.
A.tenorii Spreng. See *A.roseum* var. *carneum*.
A.tenuiflorum Ten. See *A.pallens*.

A.textile Nels. & Macbr. (*A.reticulatum* G. Don non Presl & C. Presl).
Stem 5–30cm; bulbs to 1.5cm diam., ovoid, clustered, tunics grey, reticulate, fibrous. Lvs to 30×0.5cm, 1–3, basal, channelled, margins denticulate. Fls 15–30, campanulate, umbels erect; spathe 3-lobed; pedicels unequal, 1–2cm, becoming rigid in fruit; tepals 5–7mm, acute or acuminate, white or pink with red or brown midribs, persisting in fruit; stamens included, fil. bases united; ovary 6-crested, stigma capitate. Summer. N America.Z6.

A.thunbergii G. Don (*A.japonicum* Reg.).
Stem to 60cm; bulbs slender, clustered on rhiz., tunic fibrous. Lvs 2–3, linear. Fls numerous; pedicels 10–15mm; tepals to 5mm, purple; fil. entire; stigma exserted. Japan. 'Ozawas': low, to 30cm high; fls violet tinted red. Z8.

A.tibeticum Rendle. See *A.sikkimense*.

A.tolmiei Bak. (*A.cusickii* S. Wats.).
Stem 5–12cm, flattened; bulb 1–2cm, ovoid, tunic membranous, grey-brown. Lvs 2–8mm wide, 2, sickle-shaped. Fls 15–30; spathes 2, acuminate; pedicels 10–20mm; tepals 7–10mm, white with broad pink midrib; stamens included, bases united forming scalloped cup; ovary crested. Fr. 3–4mm. Spring–summer. US (California, Washington, Nevada to Idaho, Utah). Z5.

A.trachypus Boiss. See *A.sphaerocephalon* ssp. *trachypus*.
A.tribracteatum var. *andersonii* S. Wats. See *A.parvum*.
A.tribracteatum var. *parvum* Jeps. See *A.parvum*.

A.tricoccum Ait. WILD LEEK; RAMP.
Stem 10–40cm, terete; bulbs ovoid, clustered on rhiz., tunic fibrous, reticulate. Lvs 10–30×2.5–5cm, 2–3, basal, with narrow stalks, withering before flowering. Fls numerous, stellate, umbel loose, hemispherical; spathes 2; pedicels 1–2cm; tepals 4–6mm, white, obtuse. Summer. N America (Quebec to Virginia to Iowa). Z6.

A.triquetrum L. TRIQUETROUS LEEK; THREE-CORNERED LEEK.
Stem to 30cm, 3-angled; bulb to 2cm diam., ovoid or spherical, tunic membranous. Lvs to 50×2cm, 2–5, triangular in section, basal, loosely sheathing lower part of stem. Fls 3–15, campanulate, pendent, umbel 4–7cm diam., loose, 1-sided; spathes to 4cm, 2; pedicels to 2.5cm, 3-angled; tepals 1–2×0.2–0.5cm, white with green midrib; stamens 6–7mm, bases united; stigma 3-lobed. Fr. 6–7mm; seeds with aril, dispersed by ants. Spring. S Europe, naturalized GB. Z8.

A.triquetrum ssp. *pendulinum* (Ten.) K. Richt. See *A.pendulinum*.
A.triquetrum var. *pendulinum* (Ten.) Reg. See *A.pendulinum*.

A.tuberosum Rottl. ex Spreng. (*A.uliginosum* G. Don). CHINESE CHIVES; GARLIC CHIVES; ORIENTAL GARLIC.
Stem to 50cm, angled; bulbs to 1cm diam., cylindric, clustered on rhiz., tunics fibrous, reticulate. Lvs 35×0.8cm, 4–9, solid, sheathing base of stem, keeled. Fls fragrant, numerous, stellate, umbel 3–5cm diam., hemispherical or compressed; spathe 2-lobed; pedicels 1–3cm; tepals 4–7mm, white with green or brown stripe down centre of underside; stamens included. Fr. 4–5mm. Summer–autumn. SE Asia. Z7.

A.ucrainicum Bordz. See *A.ursinum*.
A.uliginosum Ledeb. non G. Don. See *A.ledebourianum*.
A.uliginosum G. Don. non Ledeb. See *A.tuberosum*.

A.unifolium Kellogg (*A.grandisceptrum* Davidson).
Stem to 60cm, terete; bulb 10–15mm, ovoid, withers before flowering, 2 lateral bulblets on short rhiz., tunics reticulate. Lvs 7mm wide, shorter than stem, flat, channelled, from each bulblet. Fls 5–20, campanulate, umbel 5cm diam., spherical; spathes 2; pedicels 2.5–4cm, apically thickened; tepals 1–1.5cm, deep pink; stamens included, fil. 7–9mm, anth. yellow or purple. Fr. 4–5mm. Spring–summer. US (Oregon, California). Z8.

A.urceolatum Reg. See *A.caesium*.

A.ursinum L. (*Moly latifolium* Gray; *A.ucrainicum* Bordz.). RAMSONS; WILD GARLIC; WOOD GARLIC.
Strongly scented. Stem 10–50cm, angular; bulb 4×1cm, cylindric, tunic papery, fibrous. Lvs 6–20×1–8cm, ovate-lanceolate, dark green, 2–3, basal, stalked, sheathing base of stem. Fls 6–20, stellate, umbel 2.5–6cm diam.; spathes 2, persistent; pedicels 1–4.5cm, ascending; tepals 7–12×2–2.5mm, white, acute, lanceolate; stamens included, fil. to 5mm. Fr. 3–4mm. Spring. Europe, Russia. Z5.

A.validum S. Wats. SWAMP ONION.
Stem to 50–100cm, flattened, angled; bulbs 3–5cm ovoid, clustered on rhiz., tunics membranous, deep red, with vertical reticulations. Lvs 5–12mm wide, nearly as long as stem, 3–6, flat or slightly keeled. Fls numerous; spathes 2–4, bases united, acute; pedicels 1–2cm; tepals 6–10mm, white to pink, acuminate, with basal pouches; stamens and style exserted, anth. brown. Fr. 5–7mm; seeds narrow, 4–5mm long. Summer. US (California). Z8.

A.vancouverense Macoun. See *A.crenulatum*.
A.vernale Tineo. See *A.subvillosum*.

A.victoriale L. ALPINE LEEK.
Stem 30–60cm, bulbs 1–2cm diam., cylindric, clustered on rhiz., tunics fibrous. Lvs 8–25×1.5–9cm, 2–3, lanceolate, narrow petioles sheathing lower half of stem. Fls numerous, stellate, umbel 3–5cm diam.; spathes 1–2, persistent; pedicels unequal, 1–3cm; tepals 4–5×2mm, white to yellow, deflexed later; stamens exserted, anth. yellow, fil. to 6mm; ovary with pitted nectaries. Fr. to 4mm. Summer. Europe, Asia, Aleutian Is. Z7.

A.vineale L. (*A.compactum* Thuill.; *A.affine* Boiss. & Heldr.; *A.nitens* Sauzé & Maillard; *A.assimile* Hal.; *A.rilaense* Panov). CROW GARLIC; FALSE GARLIC; STAG'S GARLIC.
Stem 30–120cm; bulbs 1–2cm diam., ovoid, tunics fibrous. Lvs 15–60×0.15–0.4cm, 2–4, hollow, sheathing lower part of stem. Fls campanulate, numerous, or few fls and many green bulbils, umbel 2–5cm diam.; spathe deciduous; pedicels 5–30mm; tepals 2–4.5×1–1.5mm, white or pink, tinged with green; stamens exserted, anth. yellow, fil. to 4mm, 3 inner fil. with 2 large lateral teeth. Fr. 3–5mm. Summer. Europe, N Africa, W Asia. Z5.

A.vineale var. *kochii* H.P.G. Koch. See *A.kochii*.
A.violaceum Willd. See *A.carinatum*.
A.virens Lam. See *A.oleraceum*.
A.virescens DC. See *A.oleraceum*.
A.viviparum Karw. & Kir. See *A.caeruleum* var. *bulbiliferum*.
A.volhynicum Besser. See *A.strictum*.
A.wallichianum Steud. See *A.wallichii*.

A.wallichii Kunth (*A.wallichianum* Steud.).
Stem 30–75cm, triangular; bulbs cylindric, poorly developed, tunics membranous. Lvs 60–90×0.8–2cm, flat, keeled, sheathing lower part of stem. Fls numerous, stellate, umbel 5–7.5cm diam., loose; spathes 2.5–4cm, 2; pedicels 2.5–4cm; tepals 7–11mm, magenta to purple, papery, reflexed; stamens included, fil. to 7mm. Fr. to 6mm. Asia (Nepal to W China). Z8.

A.yatei Aitch. & Bak. See *A.regelii*.
A.yunnanense Diels. See *A.mairei*.

A.zebdanense Boiss. & Noë.
Stem 25–40cm; bulbs 1–1.5cm diam., ovoid, tunics membranous. Lvs 3–6mm wide, flat or channelled, shorter than stem, 2. Fls 3–10, campanulate, umbel 3–5cm diam.; spathe to 1.5cm; pedicels 8–13mm, equal; tepals 9–13mm, white with red midrib, obtuse; stamens included, fil. to 7mm. Fr. to 4mm. Spring. Lebanon. Z9.

A.zenobiae Cory.
Resembles *A.canadense* var. *mobilense* but bulbs carry sessile bulblets. Stem to 30cm. Fls to 175 per 6.5cm diam. umbel; tepals lavender, to 6mm. US (S Texas). Z8.

Alophia Herb. (From Gk *a*-, without, and *lophos*, crest.) Iridaceae. About 4 species of perennial cormous herbs; corms tunicate, usually ovoid. Leaves radical or few on stems in 2 ranks, plicate, linear-lanceolate. Inflorescence a few-flowered terminal raceme subtended by 2 spathes; flowering stem sometimes branching; flowers pale blue to violet, perianth tube very short or absent, composed of 6 segments, the outer 3 slightly exceeding the inner, segments ovate with a median band of hairs; stamens 3, filaments fused at base, anthers outspread; style branches 3, cleft at apex. Fruit a capsule. S US to C & S America. Several spp. cultivated as *Alophia* are *Herbertia*. Z9.

CULTIVATION Frequently found in the wild in large colonies in clay or sandy soils on prairie and grassland, *Alophia* spp. are cormous perennials grown for their iris-like flowers, from pale to deep lavender, occasionally white, spotted with deep violet or purple brown at the base. Cultivate as for *Homeria*.

A.amoena (Griseb.) Kuntze. See *Herbertia amoena*.
A.caerulea Herb. See *A.drummondii*.
A.drummondiana Herb. See *A.drummondii*.

A.drummondii (Graham) Fost. (*A.drummondiana* Herb.; *Gelasine punctata* Herb.; *Eustylis purpurea* (Herb.) Engelm. & Gray; *A.caerulea* Herb.; *Herbertia caerulea* (Herb.) Herb.; *Herbertia drummondiana* hort.; *Herbertia watsonii* Bak.; *Trifurcia caerulea* Herb.; *Herbertia lahue* ssp. *caerulea* (Herb.) Goldbl.).

Lvs 15–30×1.25–1.5cm, narrowly to broadly lanceolate, acuminate, strongly plicate. Flowering stem 12–38cm, simple or forked; perianth seg. to 2.5cm in outer whorl, 1.5cm inner whorl, violet to indigo, fading to white spotted brown at centre and on claws, margins inrolled to central band of hairs. Early summer. S US, Mexico, Guianas.

A.lahue (Molina) Espin. See *Herbertia lahue*.

Alstroemeria L. (For Baron Claus von Alstroemer (1736–94), Swedish naturalist and pupil of Linnaeus.) LILY OF THE INCAS; PERUVIAN LILY. Liliaceae (Alstroemeriaceae). Some 50 species of herbaceous perennials producing clustered tubers or creeping rhizomes. Roots thick, fleshy, fibrous. Leaves alternate or scattered along the stem, narrowing at base to a twisted petiole. Flowers zygomorphic, showy, in a terminal, simple or compound umbel, rarely solitary; tepals 6, free, clawed, the 3 inner (lower) tepals narrower and longer than the outer; stamens 6, declinate, attached to base of tepals, anthers basifixed; style slender; downward-curving, stigmas 3-fid; ovary inferior, 3-celled. Fruit a many-seeded capsule. S America. Z9 unless specified.

CULTIVATION *Alstroemeria* spp. are valued for their handsome umbels of beautifully marked flowers, the hardier species being suited to the herbaceous border and the more tender species for pot or tub cultivation in the cool glasshouse or conservatory; they are frequently grown commercially under glass for cut flowers. With mulch protection where cold spells are prolonged, *A.aurea*, *A.haemantha* and the Ligtu Hybrids are safely grown where winter temperatures fall to between −10 and −15°C/14–5°F; *A.ligtu*, *A.hookeri*, *A.brasiliensis* and *A.violacea* are slightly more tender, but tolerant in the range −5 to −10°C/23–14°F.

Grow in any fertile, freely draining but moisture-retentive soil (performance is impaired in very dry soils) in sun or part shade; some shade is essential in warmer climates to avoid bleaching of the flowers. Left undisturbed, established clumps will spread freely by means of fleshy roots. The roots are best planted about 20cm/8in. deep, when dormant in late summer/early autumn and given a deep protective mulch, at least for their first two winters. Under glass, grow in cool conditions in deep, well crocked pots in a mix of equal parts loam, leafmould and sharp sand, increasing water gradually as growth commences so that they are evenly moist but not wet when in growth. Pot-grown specimens for cutting need stakes to support the slender stems. Keep frost-free and almost dry when dormant but not so arid that roots shrivel. Propagate by seed or division of established clumps. Sow seed when ripe or in early spring, spacing the seeds so that young seedlings may be moved with minimal root damage to their final positions.

Slugs and swift moth larvae may be destructive in the open garden, and red spider mite a pest under glass.

A.aurantiaca D. Don. See *A.aurea*.

A.aurea Graham (*A.aurantiaca* D. Don).
Stems to 1m+. Lvs 7–10cm, 40–50, lanceolate, subsessile, grey-green beneath, glabrous. Umbels 3–7-rayed with 1–3 fls per ray; tepals 4–5cm, bright orange or yellow, outer tepals

broadly ovate, obtuse, tipped green, inner tepals acute, upper part spotted and flecked red, lowermost tepal sometimes unspotted. Summer. Chile. 'Dover Orange': habit somewhat tall; fls deep orange. 'Lutea': fls yellow marked carmine. 'Moerheim Orange': habit vigorous to 1m; fls deep orange and yellow, veined darkly. 'Orange King': hardy, to 90cm; fls large in shades of orange. Z7.

A.brasiliensis Spreng.
Stems to 120cm. Lvs 5–10cm, linear, erecto-patent, glabrous, those of sterile stems 7.5–10cm, lanceolate. Umbels usually 5-rayed, fls 1–3 per ray; tepals c4cm, red-yellow, inner tepals flecked brown; stamens shorter than tepals. Summer–early autumn. C Brazil.

A.chilensis hort.
A name of doubtful standing, applied to a plant to 75cm with lvs scattered, narrowly obovate and margins minutely ciliate; umbels 5–6-rayed, fls 2 per ray; tepals pale pink to blood red, upper inner tepals yellow striped red-purple. Origin obscure.

A.haemantha Ruiz & Pav.
Stems 60–90cm. Lvs 7–15cm, narrowly lanceolate, subsessile, grey-green beneath, margin hairy. Umbel 3–15-rayed; fls 1–4 per ray; tepals 4–5cm, oblanceolate-spathulate, narrow, orange to deep vermilion, outer tepals tipped green, upper inner tepals yellow-orange striped purple, lowermost tepal orange to orange-red, striped dark red. Chile. 'Rosea': fls rose.

A.hookeri Lodd.
Resembles A.pelegrina but tepals pink, upper inner tepals blotched yellow and flecked red-purple. Peru.

A.ligtu L. ST MARTIN'S FLOWER.
Stems 45–60cm. Lvs 5–8cm, narrowly lanceolate to linear-lanceolate, erecto-patent. Umbels 3–8-rayed; fls 2–3 per ray; pedicels 5–7.5cm; tepals white to pale lilac to pink-red, obovate, upper inner tepals usually yellow, spotted and streaked white or purple or yellow and red; stamens shorter than tepals. Summer. Chile, Argentina. See also hybrids and cultivars below. var. **angustifolia** anon. Lvs narrow. Fls pale pink. var. **pulchra** anon. Fls larger; tepals acute, spotted purple in upper half. Z8.

A.pelegrina L.
Stems 30–60cm. Lvs 5–8cm, about 30, lanceolate, glabrous. Fls solitary or in 2–3-rayed umbels; tepals c5cm, off-white flushed mauve or pink with a darker central zone, inner tepals yellow at base, flecked brown or maroon. Summer–autumn. Peru. Several colour forms occur among them 'Alba' with fls white, flushed green, inner upper tepals spotted green and often blotched yellow and 'Rosea' with fls deep rose.

A.psittacina Lehm.
Stems to 90cm, spotted mauve. Lvs to 7.5cm, lanceolate, glabrous. Umbels 4–6-rayed; tepals 4–4.5cm, green overlaid with dark wine red, spotted and streaked red or maroon; stamens as long as tepals. Summer. N Brazil. A variable species; cf. A.pulchella. Z8.

A.pulchella L. f.
Similar to A.psittacina and doubtfully distinct. Plants labelled A.pulchella in gardens are usually A.psittacina or A.ligtu. Z8.

A.pygmaea Herb.
Close to A.aurea, but to only 20cm. Stem subterranean, producing a group of lvs to 2.5cm, grey-green; fls to 5cm long, yellow, inner tepals spotted red. Argentina.

A.versicolor Ruiz & Pav.
Resembles A.psittacina but smaller, stems 20–60cm, umbels 2–4-rayed; tepals 2.5cm, yellow or orange, flecked purple. Summer–autumn. Chile.

A.violacea Philippi.
Stems 50–100cm. Lvs 6–9cm, ovate-oblong, spreading, scattered, glabrous. Umbels 3–6-rayed, fls 3–5 per ray; tepals 3.5–5.5cm, bright violet, outer tepals obovate, blunt, shortly cuspidate, inner tepals oblong-acute, white at base, spotted purple, sometimes flushed orange; stamens shorter than tepals. Summer. N Chile.

A.hybrids and cultivars.
A.aurea is the parent of several hybrids, largely confined to the cut-flower trade. More frequently encountered in gardens are the Ligtu Hybrids (A.ligtu var. angustifolia × A haemantha), varying in height and habit with flowers in a range of colours from soft pink to orange and yellow, and Dr Salter's Hybrids with flowers in carmine, orange, yellow and pink, whiskered, veined or mottled dark red to purple black. Named selections include: 'Afterglow': fls deep flame orange; 'Ballerina': fls light pink; 'Parigo Charm': fls in salmon-pink, primrose-yellow and deep pink; 'Sonata': fls deep pink, scarce, often tinged green or brown with splashes with yellow and dark markings; 'Margaret': to 1m; fls deep red and 'Walter Fleming' ('Orchid'): to 1m; fls deep yellow tinged purple spotted red-purple.

× **Amarcrinum** Coutts (Amaryllis × Crinum). Amaryllidaceae. Habit similar to Crinum: bulb long-necked, leaves to 60×5cm, evergreen, distichous, narrowly strap-shaped. Flowers similar to Amaryllis, with perianth tube narrow and curved and limb slightly curved. Autumn. Garden origin. Z8.

CULTIVATION × Amarcrinum bears large heads of long-lived, fragrant, shell-pink flowers, similar to those of Amaryllis, in late summer and early autumn. The foliage, like that of the Crinum parent, remains evergreen if not subjected to severe frost. Hardy to –5°C. Cultivate as for Amaryllis.

× A.**howardii** Coutts. See × A.memoria-corsii.

× A.**memoria-corsii** (Ragion.) H.E. Moore (× Amarcrinum howardii Coutts; × Crinodonna memoria-corsii Ragion.; × Crinodonna corsii Stapf). (Amaryllis belladonna ×Crinum moorei.)

× **Amarygia** Cif. & Giac. (Amaryllis × Brunsvigia). Amaryllidaceae. Hybrids resembling Brunsvigia, but with the large flowers and hardiness of Amaryllis. Z9.

CULTIVATION As for Amaryllis.

× A.**bidwillii** (Worsley) H.E. Moore (Amaryllis belladonna × Brunsvigia orientalis.).
Similar to × A.parkeri, but fls shorter and tepals broader.

× A. **parkeri** (Will. Wats.) H.E. Moore (Amaryllis belladonna ×Brunsvigia josephinae). NAKED LADY LILY.
Fls clear deep rose suffused carmine, varying in self-crosses and back-crosses. 'Alba': fls pure white, fragrant.

Amaryllis L. (Gk name.) Amaryllidaceae. 1 species, a bulbous perennial herb. Leaves to 50cm, hysteranthous, several in 2 ranks, strap-shaped, narrowing slightly toward base, somewhat concave above, keeled beneath toward base, glabrous, glossy, mid green, rather fleshy. Scape to 60cm, stout, flushed red-purple. Flowers sweetly scented, short-stalked, 6 or more in an umbel subtended by 2 large, equal spathes which enclose the whole umbel in bud, perianth 6–10cm, purple-pink to pink, often white toward base, rarely entirely white, tube c1.2cm, funnelform, somewhat bilaterally symmetric, lobes 6, spreading, oblanceolate, acute, the inner 3 with a small, hairy, inward-pointing appendage just below apex; style and stamens deflexed,. then curving upwards toward apex; stamens 6; ovary 3-celled. Fruit a few-seeded capsule. Late summer–autumn. S Africa. Many former *Amaryllis* species are now included in *Hippeastrum*; the name persists as a popular name for the larger *Hippeastrum* hybrids. Z8.

CULTIVATION A late summer/early autumn flowering bulb which occurs naturally on the coastal hills and stream banks on the southwestern seaboard of the Cape Province, South Africa, flowering in profusion where the undergrowth has been destroyed by fire. The flower stalk appears in advance of the deciduous strap-shaped leaves, which then persist into the following summer. The beautiful and fragrant flowers, produced in late summer, bloom in a sunny border, are excellent for cutting and are suitable for cultivation in pots and tubs. The flowering season is relatively short. This plant resents disturbance.

In cultivation in temperate zones, the rest period is short, falling between mid- and late summer, and adequate warmth rather than drought appears to be the most important factor in promoting flowering. Allow the foliage to die back naturally, and remove only when completely withered. *Amaryllis* is not reliably hardy where temperatures consistently fall below –5°C/23°F since the foliage is carried through the winter. In zones at the limit of its hardiness it should be grown at the base of the south- or southwest-facing wall and given the protection of cloche or propped frame lights in winter. *Amaryllis* has survived frosts down to –19°C/–2°F, albeit with severe damage to the foliage, at the base of a south-facing wall, with a thick, dry mulch of bracken or leafmould to protect the bulbs.

Grow in deep, well-drained, sandy soil, enriched with organic matter, in full sun. Plant firmly in late summer where winters are mild, otherwise in spring, with the growing tip of the bulb at soil level; *Amaryllis* adjusts to its preferred depth and may eventually pull itself down to 20cm/8in. Apply a liquid feed at flowering time and remove blooms as they fade.

Alternatively, grow in the cool to intermediate glasshouse, minimum 5–7°C/40–45°F, in direct light and medium humidity. Shade from direct sun when flowering to avoid bleaching and to extend the life of the blooms. Plant in summer into a well-crocked pot, with at least 6cm/2.5in. of potting mix between each bulb and the sides of the pot. Use a mix of equal parts loam, leafmould or peat, and sharp sand with a little ground limestone. Water plentifully when growth commences, and feed monthly with a balanced liquid fertilizer when in growth. Reduce water as leaves begin to fade, and withold completely when dormant until growth resumes. *Amaryllis* flowers best when pot-bound; repot when necessary during dormancy.

Propagate from offsets removed during the dormant season, and grow on under glass as for mature bulbs, keeping the potting medium just moist during the first dormant season to establish good root growth. Flowering occasionally occurs in the first year, but more usually takes three years. Sow ripe seed, 5–10mm apart and just covered, *in situ* or in clay pots of loam-based propagating mix. Keep moist and germinate in bright filtered light, acclimatizing gradually to direct light. Divide established clumps when the leaves wither.

Attractive to slugs and snails and, under glass, to aphid, mealybug, whitefly and red spider mite. In cases of eel-worm infection, *Ditylenchus dipsaci*, where growth is distorted and bulbs become soft showing symptomatic brown rings when cut transversely, bulbs should be destroyed immediately by burning. They are also affected by narcissus flies (*Merodon equestris, Eumerus* spp.); burn affected stock. Bulb rot will occur if drainage is poor and dry rest requirements are neglected. Narcissus leaf scorch, *Stagonospera curtisii*, causes red-brown scorching of young leaf tips, and may be restricted by immediate removal of affected parts, followed by fungicide sprays, although the source of the infection is likely to be within the bulb itself.

A.advena Ker-Gawl. See *Rhodophiala advena*.

A.aglaiae Cast. See *Hippeastrum aglaiae*.

A.ambigua (Herb.) Sweet ex Steud. See *Hippeastrum ambiguum*.

A.andersonii (Herb.) Griseb. See *Habranthus tubispathus*.

A.andreana (Bak.) Traub & Uphof. See *Hippeastrum andreanum*.

A.araucana (Philippi) Traub & Uphof. See *Rhodophiala araucana*.

A.argentina (Pax) Ravenna. See *Hippeastrum argentinum*.

A.atamasca L. See *Zephyranthes atamasca*.

A.aulica Ker-Gawl. See *Hippeastrum aulicum*.

A.aurea Ruiz & Pav. See *Pyrolirion aureum*.

A.bagnoldii (Herb.) Dietr. See *Rhodophiala bagnoldii*.

A.barlowii Traub & Mold. See *Rhodophiala rosea*.

A.belladonna L. (*A.rosea* Lam.; *Coburgia belladonna* (L.) Herb.; *Brunsvigia rosea* (Lam.) Hann.; *Callicorea rosea* (Lam.) Hann.). JERSEY LILY; BELLADONNA LILY.
'Barberton': fls dark rose pink. 'Capetown': fls deep rose.

'Hathor': fls white. 'Jagersfontein': fls deep pink. 'Johannesburg': fls pale pink, centre lighter; free-flowering. 'Kewensis': fls deep pink. 'Kimberley': fls deep carmine pink, centre white. 'Major': stems dark pink; fls dark pink, scented. 'Pallida': robust; fls large, rose pink, abundant. 'Purpurea': fls purple. 'Rosea': fls rose, segs. striped white, pointed, late. 'Spectabilis': fls rose, interior white, umbels large.

A.bifida (Herb.) Spreng. See *Rhodophiala bifida*.

A.blossfeldiae Traub & Doran. See *Hippeastrum blossfeldiae*.

A.blumenavia (K. Koch & Bouché ex Carr.) Traub. See *Hippeastrum blumenavium*.

A.bukasovii Vargas. See *Hippeastrum bukasovii*.

A.calyptrata Ker-Gawl. See *Hippeastrum calyptratum*.

A.candida (Stapf) Traub & Uphof. See *Hippeastrum candidum*.

A.caspia Willd. See *Allium caspium*.

A.chilensis L'Hérit. See *Rhodophiala chilensis*.

A.coranica Ker-Gawl. See *Ammocharis coranica*.

Amaryllis belladonna

A.*cybister* (Herb.) Traub & Uphof. See *Hippeastrum cybister*.
A.*doraniae* Traub. See *Hippeastrum doraniae*.
A.*dryades* Vell. See *Griffinia dryades*.
A.*elegans* Spreng. See *Hippeastrum elegans*.
A.*elegans* var. *ambiguum* (Herb.) Traub & Mold. See *Hippeastrum ambiguum*.
A.*elwesii* (C.W. Wright) Traub & Uphof. See *Rhodophiala elwesii*.
A.*equestris* Ait. See *Hippeastrum puniceum*.
A.*evansiae* Traub & Nels. See *Hippeastrum evansiae*.
A.*formosissima* L. See *Sprekelia formosissima*.
A.*gigantea* Van Marum. See *Brunsvigia josephinae*.
A.*hyacinthina* Ker-Gawl. See *Griffinia hyacinthina*.
A.*immaculata* Traub & Mold. See *Hippeastrum candidum*.
A.*josephinae* Redouté. See *Brunsvigia josephinae*.
A.*lapacensis* Cárdenas. See *Hippeastrum lapacense*.
A.*leopoldii* (Dombrain) H.E. Moore. See *Hippeastrum leopoldii*.
A.*longifolia* L. See *Cybistetes longifolia*.
A.*machupijchensis* Vargas. See *Hippeastrum machupijchense*.
A.*maracasa* Traub. See *Hippeastrum maracasum*.
A.*maranensis* Ker-Gawl. See *Hippeastrum stylosum*.
A.*oconequensis* Traub. See *Hippeastrum oconequense*.
A.*organensis* Bury. See *Hippeastrum organense*.

A.*orientalis* L. See *Brunsvigia orientalis*.
A.*papilio* (Ravenna). See *Hippeastrum papilio*.
A.*pardina* Hook. f. See *Hippeastrum pardinum*.
A.× *parkeri* Will. Wats. See × *Amarygia parkeri*.
A.*pratensis* Poepp. See *Rhodophiala pratensis*.
A.*phycelloides* (Herb.) Traub & Uphof. See *Phycella phycelloides*.
A.*procera* Duchartre. See *Worsleya rayneri*.
A.*psittacina* Ker-Gawl. See *Hippeastrum psittacinum*.
A.*punicea* Lam. See *Hippeastrum puniceum*.
A.*purpurea* Ait. See *Cyrtanthus elatus*.
A.*rayneri* Hook. See *Worsleya rayneri*.
A.*reginae* L. See *Hippeastrum reginae*.
A.*reticulata* L'Hérit. See *Hippeastrum reticulatum*.
A.*rosea* Lam. See *A.belladonna*.
A.*rosea* (Sweet) Traub & Uphof non Lam. See *Rhodophiala rosea*.
A.*rutila* Ker-Gawl. See *Hippeastrum striatum*.
A.*striata* Lam. See *Hippeastrum striatum*.
A.*traubii* (Mold.). See *Hippeastrum traubii*.
A.*tubispatha* L'Hérit. See *Habranthus tubispathus*.
A.*variabilis* Jacq. See *Crinum variabile*.
A.*vittata* L'Hérit. See *Hippeastrum vittatum*.
A.*vivipara* Lam. See *Crinum defixum*.

Amianthum A. Gray (From Gk *amiantos*, immaculate, and *anthos*, flower.) Liliaceae (Melanthiaceae). 1 species, a bulbous perennial herb to 120cm. Bulbs tunicate. Leaves to 60×2cm, linear, mostly basal. Flowers in terminal, bracteate racemes to 12.5cm; tepals free, spreading, white; stamens 6. Fruit a 3-angled capsule. Summer. Eastern N America (New York to Florida, West to Missouri and Oklahoma.) Z4.

CULTIVATION As for *Zigadenus*. All parts are highly toxic.

A.*muscitoxicum* (Walter) A. Gray (*Chrosperma muscitoxicum* (Walter) Kuntze; *Zigadenus muscitoxicum* (Walter) Reg.). FLY POISON.

Ammocharis Herb. (From Gk *ammos*, sand, and *charis*, beauty, alluding to its habitat.) Amaryllidaceae. 5 species of bulbous, herbaceous perennials to 35cm. Bulb ovoid, tunicate, 2.5×3–16×20cm. Leaves prostrate, or semi-erect, distichous, in a fan, falcate to ligulate or linear, apices rounded in young leaves, later truncate, margins coarse, incised to lacerate. Inflorescence terminal, umbellate, 1- to many-flowered; scape solid, lateral; spathe 2-valved, papery, valves lanceolate, acute, 0.2×3–8.5×3cm; pedicels terete, unequal, 0.2–6cm, not lengthening after flowering; flowers regular; perianth tube cylindrical, 0.8–13cm, segments equal, flat or recurved, narrowly oblanceolate, obtuse, 0.3–1×2–13cm, red or white; stamens strongly exserted, never declinate, red or white; anthers dorsifixed; ovary obscurely angled, inferior, to 30 ovules in a cell; style straight, exserted or included. Capsule subglobose, indehiscent, to 2.5cm across; seeds subglobose or bluntly angled, pale green, 1–1.5cm. Africa. Z9.

CULTIVATION *Ammocharis* spp. occur in hot sandy habitats, flowering in their native zones in late summer and leafing up in early winter, with the onset of the winter rains. Their fragrant, trumpet-like flowers appear in autumn and early winter in cultivation. They can be grown outdoors only in regions that are frost-free, but are well suited to pot cultivation in the glasshouse or conservatory. Cultivate as for *Brunsvigia*.

A.*coranica* (Ker-Gawl.) Herb. (*Amaryllis coranica* Ker-Gawl.).
Bulb to 16cm diam. Lvs 0.5–7.5cm, to 15, falcate to ligulate, channelled, glabrous; scape to 35cm; umbel 3–56-fld; spathe valves lanceolate, to 8.5×3cm, chartaceous, acute; pedicels to 6cm; perianth basally tubular, to 2.5cm, pink to copper or crimson, veined white, seg. 2.8–5.5×0.5cm, apex spirally recurved; fil. carmine; ovary to 12mm, style carmine, exserted. Fr. to 2.5cm diam.; seeds to 1.5cm. Summer–autumn. S Africa.

A.*falcata* (Jacq.) Herb. See *Cybistetes longifolia*.

Amorphophallus Bl. ex Decne. (From Lat. *amorphus*, shapeless, and *phallus*.) DEVIL'S TONGUE; SNAKE PALM. Araceae. 90 species of cormous perennial herbs. Corm sometimes very large, to 50cm across, 50kg+, hollowed above, bearing several cataphylls at base of shoot, becoming dormant annually. Leaf solitary, produced after flower, large, to 4m+ across, 3-segmented, with segments usually bipinnatifid, occasionally viviparous, bearing cormlets; petiole erect, stout, marbled dull purple, sometimes verrucose, to 4m+. Inflorescence gigantic; *A.brooksii* Alderw. possibly largest inflorescence of any herbaceous plant, to 4.36m; peduncle stout, spotted or marbled; spathe campanulate to funnel-shaped, ventricose, margins overlapping below to form open tube, limb spreading, undulate, dark purple-red or flesh-coloured, to dull green, paler within; spadix with male and female zones of flowers adjacent; flowers unisexual, perianth absent; stamens 1–6; ovary 1–4-locular, ovules 1 per locule; spadix appendix present, equal to or exceeding spathe, even when immature, massive, to 2m, often contorted, dirty yellow, emitting strong and disagreeable odour. Old World Tropics and subtropics. Z10.

CULTIVATION Denizens of loose leafy detritus in moist, shaded habitats, *Amorphophallus* spp. are striking plants for large pots or borders in the intermediate to warm glasshouse (*A.rivieri* can be used as a houseplant or dot plant in summer bedding). They are grown for their magnificent compound foliage, marbled petioles and dramatic, if evil-smelling inflorescences. The spathe and spadix of the Titan Arum, *A.titanum*, constitute the world's largest unbranched inflorescence. The corms of *A.paeoniifolius* and *A.rivieri* are edible. In addition to those described below, *A.eichleri*, with stemless, squat, inflated spathes in bronze and flesh-pink to 7cm, is sometimes cultivated.

Allow ample space for the roots in containers and repot annually before growth resumes, planting corms 5–8cm/2–3in. deep, using a coarse, open medium comprising two parts fertile fibrous loam with one part well rotted organic matter. Grow in full sun to part shade, with a minimum temperature of 13–16°C/55–60°F, watering plentifully when in growth to keep evenly and continually moist; feed regularly when well rooted and maintain high humidity. Keep dry but not arid in winter with a minimum temperature of 10°C/50°F; 13–16°C/55–60°F for *A.rivieri*. Propagate by seed or by offsets, if produced, remove when dormant.

A.bulbifer (Curtis) Bl.
Tuber to 7cm diam. subglobose. Lvs to 60cm across, main seg. dissected to base forming few lobes, lobes to 20cm, obovate or lanceolate, bearing cormlets; petiole to 1m, dull green, irregularly marbled or spotted, dull brown to pink or dull white. Peduncle to 20cm; spathe 15–20cm, limb expanded, dull green, mottled pink externally, dull green or white, tinged pink within; spadix 7×2.5cm, equalling spathe, appendix ovoid, pink. Spring. NE India to Burma, possibly SW China.

A.campanulatus (Roxb.) Bl. ex Decne. See *A.paeoniifolius*.
A.konjac K. Koch. See *A.rivieri* 'Konjac'.

A.paeoniifolius (Dennst.) Nicols. (*A.campanulatus* (Roxb.) Bl. ex Decne.). ELEPHANT YAM, TELINGO POTATO.
Corm to 25cm thick, flattened, edible. Lvs to 60–90×60cm, occasionally 2, trifid, lateral lobes pinnate; petiole to 75cm, dark green with pale spots, sometimes verrucose. Peduncle to 20cm; spathe to 20×25cm, ovate, funnel-shaped below, externally green, spotted white, tube deep purple, verrucose within, limb green to purple, margin undulate; spadix to 30cm, appendix globose conic, to 12.5cm, deep purple, spongy. S & SE Asia to Australasia (India to New Guinea).

A.rivieri Durieu DEVIL'S TONGUE; SNAKE PALM; UMBRELLA ARUM.
Corm to 25cm diam., depressed-globose. Lf seg. 1–2× dichotomous, then bipinnate, lobes oblong-elliptic, cuspidate, to 1.3m across; petiole to 1m, brown green, mottled white. Peduncle to 60cm; spathe to 40cm, tube green, spotted green-white, limb broadly round-cordate, acute, margin undulate, green externally, dark purple within; spadix much exceeding spathe, appendix to 55cm, narrowly conic, dark red-brown. Spring. SE Asia. 'Konjac' (var. *konjac* (K. Koch) Engl.; *A.konjac* K. Koch): infl. at larger end of size range, limb oblong, widely cult. for edible corms. Indonesia to Japan.

A.titanum Becc. GIANT KRUBI; TITAN ARUM.
Corm to 1.5m diam., 50(–75)kg. Lf to 4m+ across, trifid, ultimate lobes to 40cm, ovate or oblong, abruptly acuminate; petiole to 4m, pale green, spotted white. Peduncle to 1m, spotted; spathe funnelform-campanulate, to 1.5m, 3m in circumference, margin very irregular, wavy to lobed, ribbed and fluted, green, spotted white externally, rich dark crimson within, green-yellow at base; spadix appendix to 2m+, hollow, expanded at base, tapering upwards, obtuse, furrowed, dirty dull yellow, very powerfully malodorous. Sumatra.

Androcymbium Willd. (From Gk *aner*, man, and *kymbion*, cup; the stamens are enclosed in a hollow formed by the folded blade of the tepals.) Liliaceae (Colchicaceae). Some 12 species of perennial herbs. Corms small, slightly elongated, tunics dark brown or black. Leaves basal, rosulate, to 25×2.5cm, 2–4, linear to linear-lanceolate, narrowing to the very pointed tips, margins undulate, almost always lying flat on ground (apparently stemless). Inflorescence a very short umbellate spike subtended and partly enclosed by large cupped bracts which are white or green-white, sometimes veined or flushed pink or purple; flowers small, concealed at base of bracts; tepals 6, free, green, green-white or cream, clawed, blade with conspicuously swollen yellow glands at base; stamens inserted at junction of claw and blade; styles 3, divergent near apex; ovary oblong. Seeds rounded, hard, shiny. Mediterranean to S Africa. Z9.

CULTIVATION Occurring in sandy soils in maritime habitats in Mediterranean climates, they will grow outdoors on rocky, gritty soils or in sparse turf in frost-free areas, elsewhere in deep pots in the cool glasshouse. They require a dry rest in summer. Grow in well-drained, sandy, humus-rich soils in full sun. Propagate by ripe seed sown fresh or by separation of cormels.

A.capense (L.) Krause.
Lvs 10–24cm×3–8cm, 2–3, lanceolate, undulate, pale green. Scape barely emerging above ground; bracts to 8×7cm, pale green; infl. 2–8-fld, fls cream; claw of tepals exceeding blade; styles keeled; ovary light green. S Africa (Cape Peninsula).

A.ciliolatum Schltr. & Krause (*A.fenestratum* Schltr. & Krause).
Lvs to 15cm, broadly lanceolate, margins minutely fringed. Bracts 12.5–15×7.5cm, 3–4, pale green, almost white; fls many, in small clusters. Spring. S Africa (Namaqualand).

A.eucomioides (Jacq.) Willd.
Lvs 6–15×2–8cm, 2–3, lanceolate to ovate, acute, undulate, slightly keeled, dark green. Infl. 2–5-fld; bracts shorter and broader than lvs; tepals green-white, with claw shorter than or equalling blade; styles keeled. Winter. S Africa (Cape Peninsula). May include *A.leucanthum* hort.

A.fenestratum Schltr. & Krause. See *A.ciliolatum*.

A.melanthoides Willd. BABOON'S SHOES; PYJAMA FLOWER.
Lvs narrow-linear, narrowing to a long tail 20cm long. Bracts to 7.5cm, white veined green, flushed pink; fls 6–8. S Africa.

Androstephium Torr. (From Gk *aner*, man, and *stephanos*, crown, some stamens are barren and petaloid, forming a corona.) Liliaceae (Alliaceae). 2 species of perennial herbs, related to *Bessera*. Corms fibrous-coated. Leaves basal, linear, channelled. Scape erect; flowers in a terminal umbel subtended by scarious bracts; perianth funnelform, segments 6, narrow-oblong, united below, blue; stamens 6, in a single row inserted in throat, filaments partly united into a tube of sterile stamens forming petaloid, with a corona of erect, bifid lobes between the versatile anthers; ovary sessile; style persistent. Fruit a subglobose capsule, obtusely 3-angled; seeds several per locule, black. SW US. Z8.

CULTIVATION Plant corms about 15cm/6in. deep in rich, sandy loam in full sun.Hardy to about –10°C/14°F, possibly more with perfect drainage. Propagate by offsets or ripe seed sown fresh.

A.caeruleum (Scheele) Greene (*A.violaceum* Torr.). BLUE FUNNEL LILY; BLUE BETHLEHEM LILY.
Lvs 4–6, very narrow. Scape 10–12cm, stout; umbel 3–6-fld; perianth to 3.75cm diam., tube as long as seg., pale blue to lilac or mauve. Spring. C Kansas, Oklahoma, E Texas.

A.violaceum Torr. See *A.caeruleum*.

Anemone L. (From Gk *anemos*, wind, name used by Theophrastus.) Ranunculaceae. 120 species of perennial herbs. Roots rhizomatous, fleshy or fibrous, sometimes woody. Basal leaves lobed, dissected or compound, rarely entire, stem leaves often arranged in a whorl below the inflorescence, sessile or short-petiolate. Flowers solitary or in cymes, actinomorphic, hermaphrodite, shallowly dish-shaped; perianth segments 5–20, petaloid, white, yellow, purple, red or blue; stamens numerous, free, nectar-secreting staminodes absent; carpels numerous, distinct, each with a short persistent style and pendulous ovule. Fruit of many single-seeded achenes, glabrous or densely tomentose. N & S temperate regions.

CULTIVATION The spring-flowering *A.blanda*, *A.nemorosa* and *A.apennina* occur in woodland and rocky subalpine meadow. They require moist but well-drained, humus-rich soils in the rock or woodland garden, and will tolerate dry conditions during summer dormancy. Some species, such as *A.glauciifolia* and others from Yunnan and Sichuan, require the winter protection of the cold frame in cold climates. Given suitable conditions, many species in this category, especially the rhizomatous woodland natives, will form extensive colonies if left undisturbed. *A.nemorosa* is sufficiently robust for naturalizing in thin turf, where the first cut occurs after foliage dieback. Smaller species, notably *A.blanda* and its cultivars, are well suited to pot cultivation for the alpine display house, in a gritty alpine mix with additional leafmould. Propagate by fresh seed, rhizomatous species also by careful division.

Tuberous-rooted plants (e.g. *A.coronaria*, *A.× fulgens* and *A.pavonina*) flower in spring to early summer and are well suited to areas with dry hot summers, where they grow in light sandy soils: shade in the hottest part of the day is appreciated. They require dry dormancy after flowering. They are often grown in pots or borders (De Caen, Mona Lisa and St Brigid anemones groups are a commercial cut-flower crop), or used to fill gaps and supply a long period of summer colour in a fertile but light-textured soil in sunny borders: in cold areas, mulch for winter protection or lift after flowering and overwinter dry tubers, plunged in sand under frost-free conditions, for planting out the following spring. Under glass, give a winter minimum of 10°C/150°F and pot up tubers in a sandy loam-based mix of medium fertility for flowering 3–6 months later. *A.coronaria* may be flowered under glass almost all year round from successive plantings; tubers of this and *A.× fulgens* deteriorate quickly and should be replaced every 2–3 years.

Susceptible to *Botrytis cinerea*; scabious bud eelworm (*Aphelenchoides blastophthorus*); root lesion eelworm (*Pratylenchus* spp.); symphilids (mostly under glass or in mild climates outdoors); powdery mildew; plum rust (*Tranzschelia discolor*), causing leaf distortion and preventing flowering; anemone and cucumber mosaic viruses; downy mildew (*Peronospora* spp.); anemone smut (*Urocystis anemones*), which produces swellings on the leaf stalks and leaves, bursting to release black spores, and flea beetle (*Phyllotreta* spp.) on seedlings.

A.altaica Mey.
To 20cm. Rhiz. thick, cylindrical, creeping, yellow-brown. Stems glabrous. Basal lf solitary, petiolate, petiole glabrous, seg. tapered, basal margin remaining entire, otherwise toothed, often cut; stem lvs tripartite, in whorls of 3, often further divided and toothed. Fls solitary 2–4cm diam., white veined violet inside, occasionally flushed violet outside; perianth seg. 8–9, rarely to 12. Achenes 2mm, narrowly ovoid, sparsely tomentose. Spring. Arctic Russia, Japan. Z2.

A.apennina L.
To 15cm. Rhiz. stout, creeping, almost tuberous, brown. Basal lvs divided into 3 separate seg., each deeply lobed and cut, primary divisions acute, stalked; stem lvs also in 3 seg., these deeply lobed or divided, petiole distinct. Fls 2.5–3cm diam., solitary, pedicel extending 2–3cm above the involucre; perianth seg. 8–23, oblong, blunt, erect, blue rarely flushed pink or white, basal portion hairy; anth. cream or white. Fr. globose, erect, achenes 2.5mm, ovoid. Early spring. S Europe. 'Petrovac': vigorous, fls multi-petalled, rich blue. 'Purpurea': fls soft purple-rose. var. *albiflora* Strobl. Fls white. Z6.

A.biflora DC.
To 20cm. Rhiz. congested, tuberous. Basal lvs petiolate, 3-parted, the lateral seg. sessile, central seg. on a distinct, short petiolule, all seg. further lobed and cut, lvs flattened at base to form a wing-like structure, this trifid, each seg. additionally deeply lobed. Fls usually nodding, usually 2–3 together, 2–5cm diam.; perianth seg. 5, thickly covered with flattened hairs outside, crimson, occasionally orange or yellow; anth. yellow. Achenes 2–3mm, ovoid-oblong, densely tomentose. Spring. Iran, Afghanistan, Pakistan, India (Kashmir). Z6.

A.blanda Schott & Kotschy.
To 18cm. Rhiz. thick, congested, tuberous. Basal lf absent or solitary (very rarely paired), broadly triangular, petiolate, 3-parted, each seg. unevenly lobed, acute, sessile or shortly petiolate; stem lvs 2–3, deeply lobed or divided into 3 seg., upper lf surfaces covered with flattened hairs. Fls solitary, 2–4cm diam. held 2–5cm above the involucre; perianth seg. 9–15, 14–25mm, narrow, blue, mauve, white or pink, glabrous outside. Fr. nodding; achenes 1–2mm, glabrous or sparsely pubesc. Spring. SE Europe, Cyprus, W Turkey, USSR (Caucasus). 'Atrocaerulea' ('Ingramii'): fls deep blue. 'Blue Shades': lvs very finely divided; fls pale to deep blue. 'Blue Star': fls pale blue. 'Bridesmaid': fls large, pure white. 'Bright Star': fls bright pink. 'Charmer': fls deep pink. 'Fairy': fls snow white. 'Pink Star': fls large, pale pink. 'Radar': fls magenta, centre white. 'Rosea': fls pale pink. 'Violet Star': fls large, amethyst, white outside. 'White Splendour': tall; fls large, white, exterior pink. var. *scythinica* Jenk. Fls white, exterior blue. N Turkestan. Z5.

A.blanda var. **parvula** DC. See *A.caucasica*.

A.bucharica (Reg.) Finet & Gagnep.
To 20cm, occasionally to 30cm. Rhiz. congested, tuberous. Basal lvs petiolate, 3-parted, the lateral seg. almost sessile and bifid, central seg. 3-fid, all seg. further lobed and cut; stem lvs with basal part flattened forming a 3-parted wing-like structure, each seg. further 3-parted. Fls usually in pairs, rarely solitary or in threes, 3–4cm diam.; erect; perianth seg.

5, red or violet-red, thickly covered with flattened hairs without; anth. purple. Achenes 4mm, oblong ovoid, densely tomentose. Spring. C Asia. Z5.

A.caroliniana Walter.
To 25cm. Rootstock tuberous. Lvs slender-petiolate, 3-parted, seg. further 3-fid, margins dentate; stem lvs 3-lobed, seg. sessile, cut. Fls erect, 2–4cm diam.; perianth seg. 6–20, oblong-linear, purple or white-purple, exterior pubesc. E US. Z4.

A.caucasica Rupr. (*A.blanda* var. *parvula* DC.).
Closely resembles *A.blanda*, differs in smaller, more delicate character. Tubers short, ovate. Stem 6–13cm. Stem lvs short stalked, eventually glabrous. Perianth seg. 8–11, blue or white, usually 7–13mm; style short but distinct. Caucasus, N Iran. Z5.

A.coronaria L.
To 60cm. Rhiz. congested, tuberous. Basal lvs tripartite, seg. finely dissected and individually stalked; stem lvs sessile, apex deeply cleft. Fls solitary, 3–8cm, rarely to 10cm diam.; perianth seg. 5–8, oval, almost overlapping, scarlet, blue, pink, white or bicoloured, exterior pubesc.; anth. blue. Achenes 2mm, oblong-ovoid, densely tomentose. Spring. S Europe, Mediterranean area. Over 20 cvs or groups: height 25–60cm; fls 6–10cm diam., single to semi-double, wide range of bright and pastel colours, also bicolours. Including the De Caen Group (fls single, poppy shaped, large, white, bright pink, red or purple, with black anthers; collective name for single-flowered cvs), 'His Excellency' (fls large, single, scarlet with white eye, similar to *A.× fulgens*), 'Mr Fokker' (fls single, blue), 'The Bride' (fls single, white). Mona Lisa Group (F1 hybrids; to 60cm tall; fls single, to 10cm diam., very abundant, full colour range), 'Sylphide' (fls single, mauve) and St Brigid Group (fls semi-double, many bright, pastel and bicolours; collective name for semi-double cvs), 'Lord Lieutenant' (fls semi-double, blue), 'Mt Everest' (fls white, semi-double form of 'The Bride'), 'The Admiral' (fls semi-double, deep pink) var. *coronaria*. Fls scarlet. var. *alba* (Goaty & Pons) Burnat. Fls white. var. *cyanea* (Risso) Ard. Fls blue. var. *rosea* (Henry) Rouy & Foucaud. Fls pink. Z8.

A.eranthoides Reg.
To 12cm. Rhiz. tuberous. Basal lvs petiolate, 3–5-parted, each leaflet further shallowly divided into 3 seg., seg. sessile, margins toothed; stem lvs sessile, narrowly obovate and divided into 3 seg. Fls paired, 1–2.5cm diam., golden yellow inside, yellow-green outside; perianth seg. to 8, with close flattened hairs outside. Achenes 2mm, ovoid oblong, densely tomentose. Spring. C Asia. Z5.

A.flaccida Schmidt.
5–20cm, occasionally to 30cm. Rhiz. thick, somewhat creeping, black. Stem erect, unbranched. Lvs thick, almost succulent, in mounds, bronze at first, later dark green with white markings at the lobe bases; basal lvs trilobed, petioles long, lateral lf lobes dissected, central lobe with 3 clefts, these diamond-shaped to obovate; stem lvs subsessile, resembling the basal lvs but much reduced. Fls 1–3, 1.5–3cm diam.; perianth seg. 5(–7), cream-white sometimes flushed pink. Fr. 2.5mm; achenes ovoid, white tomentose. Late spring. E Russia, China, Japan. Z6.

A.×fulgens (DC.) A. Gray (*A.stellata* Risso). (*A.pavonina* × *A.hortensis*.)
Differs from *A.pavonina* in smaller, less robust habit. Fls solitary; perianth seg. 15, scarlet, these more numerous and narrower than those of *A.pavonina*. C Mediterranean. 'Annulata Grandiflora': to 30cm; fls scarlet, centre yellow-cream. 'Multipetala': fls semi-double, perianth seg. 20+, pointed, selection of 'Annulata Grandiflora'. Z8.

A.glauciifolia Franch. (*A.glaucophylla* hort.).
To 90cm; stem naked below; rootstock thick, not fibrous. Basal lvs to 20cm, oblanceolate, pinnately lobed, sparsely long white-hirsute; stem lvs 3, linear-oblong, dentate. Fls 3.5–10cm diam., erect, usually solitary, occasionally in sparse umbels, mauve, silky-hairy externally; perianth seg. obovate, apex obtuse. Summer. China (Yunnan, Sichuan). Z7.

A.glaucophylla hort. See *A.glauciifolia*.

A.gortschakowii Karel. & Kir.
To 15cm. Rhiz. congested resembling a tuber. Basal lvs petiolate, 3-parted, the seg. sessile or nearly so, each bifid or 3-fid and additionally lobed; basal portion of stem lvs wing-like, this 3-parted, each lobe cut. Fls in pairs, rarely solitary, 1–2cm diam.; perianth seg. 5, pale yellow occasionally becoming flushed red, exterior thickly covered with flattened hairs; anth. yellow. Achenes 2–2.5mm, ellipsoid, densely tomentose. Spring. C Asia. Z4.

A.heldreichii (Boiss.) Gand. (*A.stellata* var. *heldreichii* Boiss.).
Resembles *A.hortensis*, but perianth seg. blue-grey outside, white inside. Spring. Crete. Z8.

A.hortensis L. (*A.stellata* Lam.).
To 30cm. Rhiz. congested, resembling a tuber. Basal lvs petiolate, divided into 3 seg., these free or remaining fused at the base, each seg. unevenly lobed and finely dissected; stem lvs sessile, unlobed, apical margins toothed. Fls solitary, 2–4cm diam.; perianth seg. 12–20, pink-mauve, the colour strengthening towards the apex. Achenes 2mm, oblong-ovoid, densely tomentose. Spring. C Mediterranean. Z8.

A.lancifolia Pursh.
To 8cm, closely resembling *A.quinquefolia* but larger, sturdier. Rootstock fleshy. Basal lvs 3-parted, leaflets petiolate, lanceolate, margins crenate; involucral lf ternate, margin of terminal leaflet entire. Fls solitary: perianth seg. 5, 1–2cm, white, ovate, apex pointed. Early summer. E US. Z4.

A.× lipsiensis Beck. (*A. ranunculoides* × *A.nemorosa*.)
Intermediate between parents, fls 1.5–2cm, pale sulphur yellow, often occurring where the ranges of the parents overlap. Z4.

A.nemorosa L. WOOD ANEMONE.
To 30cm. Rhiz. slender, creeping, brown. Basal lvs petiolate, trisect, lateral seg. 3-fid, deeply lobed, central leaflet deeply divided; stem lvs similar, on short, stout petioles. Fls 2–3cm diam., solitary, held 2–3cm above the involucre; perianth seg. 6–8, rarely 5–12, white, exterior occasionally flushed purple or pink, especially as they age, rarely uniformly blue; anth. bright yellow. Fr. slightly pendulous; achenes 2mm, pubesc. Early spring. Europe, widespread except in the Mediterranean. 'Alba Plena': closely resembling 'Vestal' and much confused with it, but fls smaller, petaloid stamens more irregular, tepals 6. 'Allenii': petioles maroon; pedicel brown; fls rich lilac or pale blue outside, lavender inside. 'Blue Beauty': lvs tinted bronze; fls large, pale blue, pearly beneath. 'Blue Bonnet': late flowering; fls large, blue. 'Bracteata': 16th-century variety; fls large, loose double, seg. narrow, white, outer seg. wholly or partly green. 'Grandiflora': fls large, white. 'Green Fingers': perianth seg. white, tinged green; fl. red. 'Leeds Variety': fls to 6cm diam., white, faintly flushed pink as they age, early. 'Lychette': fls large, white. 'Monstrosa': perianth seg. serrate, outer few green. 'Plena': fls double. 'Robinsoniana': pedicel maroon; fls clear grey outside, lavender within. 'Rosea': fls pink in bud, perianth seg. white at first, ageing

deep pink especially on exterior. 'Royal Blue': fls rich blue. 'Vestal': late, fl. centre a button of petaloid seg. 'Vindobonensis': fls cream. 'Virescens': fls replaced by a pyramid of small leaflike bracts. Z5.

A.palmata L.
To 15cm. Rhiz. congested, tuberous. Basal lvs petiolate, orbicular with 3–5 shallow lobes, these toothed; stem lvs sessile, 3–5-fid, seg. linear-lanceolate, connate at base. Fls solitary or occasionally paired, 2.5–3.5cm diam.; perianth seg. 10–15, oblong, obtuse, yellow often red flushed outside. Achenes 1.5mm, oblong ovoid. Spring. SW Europe. 'Alba': lvs violet beneath; fls white. 'Flore Pleno': fls double. 'Lutea': fls yellow. Z8.

A.pavonina Lam.
To 30cm, hairy. Rhiz. congested, tuberous. Basal lvs petiolate, 3-parted, each seg. deeply lobed and divided; stem lvs sessile, entire, apical margins sparsely toothed. Fls solitary, 3–10cm diam.; perianth seg. 7–9, broad, scarlet, violet, purple or pink, rarely white or yellow, the basal portion white. Achenes 2mm, oblong to ovoid, densely tomentose. Spring. S Europe, Mediterranean area. 'Barr Salmon': fls deep salmon, fading somewhat. St Bavo Group: to 30cm, strong-growing; fls rose, lavender to violet. var. *ocellata* (Moggr.) Bowles & Stearn. Fls scarlet, centre white. var. *purpureoviolacea* (Boiss.) Hal. Fls violet or pink-violet, centre white. Z8.

A.petiolulosa Juz.
To 18cm. Rhiz. congested, tuberous. Basal lvs petiolate, 3-parted, each seg. with equal petiolules, seg. also 3-parted, deeply lobed and cut; basal part of stem lvs flattened, forming a wing-like structure, this 3-lobed, the lobes 3-fid and toothed. Fls 2–4.5cm diam., slightly pendulous, occasionally solitary, usually in clusters of 2–4; perianth seg. 5, yellow, exterior flushed red, densely covered with flattened hairs outside; anth. yellow. Achenes 3mm, oblong ovoid, densely tomentose. Spring. Soviet C Asia. Z5.

A.quinquefolia L.
Resembles *A.nemorosa*. Rhiz. stout, horizontal. Stems to 30cm. Basal lf solitary, 3-parted, appearing 5-parted, rhomboidal, margins strongly irregular, dentate, generally less lobed than in *A.nemorosa*; stem lvs similar, smaller. Fls solitary; perianth seg. usually 5, occasionally 4–9, variable, 0.5–2.5cm, white, often flushed pink. US. var. *oregana* (A. Gray) Robinson. Perianth seg. 1–2cm, blue or pink. US (Washington to N Carolina). Z7.

A.ranunculoides L.
To 15cm. Rhiz. slender, creeping. Basal lf absent or solitary, 3-parted, each seg. deeply divided and lobed: stem lvs similar, short-stalked. Fls 1.5–2cm diam., solitary, held 2–3cm above the involucre; perianth seg. usually 5–6, sometimes more, elliptic, deep yellow, pubesc. outside; anth, bright yellow. Achenes 2mm, ovoid. Early spring. Europe, widespread except in the Mediterranean. 'Flore Pleno': fls semi-double, yellow: perianth seg. 12+. 'Grandiflora': fls large, to 2.5cm diam. 'Superba': lvs bronzed green; fls bright yellow. Z4.

A.rivularis DC.
To 90cm; rootstock swollen and woody. Basal lvs petiolate, 8–15cm wide, 3-parted, seg. obovate, 3-fid, lobes further cut, dentate; stem lvs sessile, base broad, apex pinnately cut. Fls in umbels, each with 2–5 fls, 1.5–3cm diam.; perianth seg. 5–8, oval, white stained blue without, glabrous without; anth. purple. Achenes oblong-cylindric, glabrous. Late spring–summer. N India, SW China. Z7.

A.stellata Risso, non Lam. See *A.×fulgens*.
A.stellata Lam., non Risso. See *A.hortensis*.
A.stellata var. *heldreichii* Boiss. See *A.heldreichii*.
A.thalictroides L. See *Anemonella thalictroides*.

A.trifolia L.
To 15cm, occasionally to 20cm. Rhiz. thin, creeping, brown. Basal lvs usually absent, if present in 3 parts on long petioles, margins toothed; stem lvs stalked, in whorls of 3, each deeply incised to form 3 leaflets, these ovate-lanceolate, acute, mar-

gins toothed. Fls solitary, 2cm diam., on long pedicels above the last whorl, erect; perianth seg. 5–8, rarely 12, elliptic, blunt, white, rarely flushed pink: anth. blue or white. Achenes c2mm, ovoid, with short stiff hairs. Spring. C Italy east to N Balkans and Hungary, west to NW Spain and Portugal. ssp. *albida* (Mariz.) Tutin. Anth. white. Achene heads pendulous. NW Spain and Portugal. Z6.

A.tschernjaewii Reg.
To 30cm. Rhiz. congested, tuberous. Basal lvs petiolate, 3-parted, seg. sessile, shallowly divided into 3 further seg.; stem lvs similar but smaller. Fls 2–3 together, 2–4.5cm diam.; perianth seg. 5, white, basal portion flushed purple-pink, exterior; pubesc.; anth. purple or violet-purple. Achenes 2–2.5mm, ellipsoid, densely tomentose. Spring. C Asia. Z5.

A.tuberosa Rydb.
To 30cm. Rhiz. tuberous. Basal lvs petiolate often solitary, 3-parted, leaflets 2.5–5cm, ovate, 3-parted, the seg. lobed and toothed; stem lvs 3, to 8cm, similarly lobed or toothed. Fls solitary; perianth seg. to 1.5cm, linear oblong, white or pink. US. Z5.

Anemonella Spach. (Diminutive of the related *Anemone*.) Ranunculaceae. 1 species, a perennial herb to 25cm, glabrous; roots tuberous. Leaves basal, 2–3-ternate; leaflets ovate to oblong, glabrous, 1–2cm, apex 3-toothed. Flowers white, 2–5, on slender pedicels in umbels, subtended by a 2–3-parted, compound, leafy involucre; calyx of 5–10 petaloid sepals, sepals 5–15mm, ovate to elliptic, spreading, soon withering; corolla absent; stamens numerous, filaments short; stigma broad, flattened atop carpel, style absent. Fruit 4–15 achenes, 8–10-ribbed. Spring. Eastern N America. Tubers edible. Z4.

CULTIVATION Woodland natives bearing fragile, cup-shaped flowers over foliage reminiscent of *Anemone* but more delicate, these are fully frost-hardy perennials for grouping in light, rich, moisture-retentive soils in acid beds, cool rock gardens and pockets of woodland. They are slow to establish and often fall prey to slug damage and overwet conditions at the roots. They can be grown in pans of a gritty alpine medium with added leafmould in cold frames or in the alpine house. Propagate from fresh seed in summer or by division of well-established plants in autumn.

A.thalictroides (L.) Spach (*Anemone thalictroides* L.; *Thalictrum anemonoides* Michx.). RUE-ANEMONE.
'Flore Pleno': fls double. 'Rosea': fls pale pink. 'Rosea Plena' ('Schoaff's Double Pink'): fls double, pale pink, long-lasting.

Anigozanthos Labill. KANGAROO PAW; CAT'S PAW; AUSTRALIAN SWORD LILY. (Derivation of name ambiguous: either from Gk *anoigo*, to open, plus *anthos*, flower, referring to the perianth which appears to be a ripped-open tube, or Gk *anisos*, unequal, and *anthos*, flower, a reference to the unequal perianth lobes.) Haemodoraceae. 11 species of evergreen or semi-deciduous perennial herbs (foliage lost to drought and fire). Rhizomes subterranean or barely protruding above soil surface, short, stout, simple or branched and clump-forming. Leaves sheathing at base, clustered to strongly equitant, erect to arching, linear-lanceolate to lorate, tapering finely, strongly conduplicate and deeply keeled to flat or subterete, grass or iris-like, glabrous or minutely bristly-pubescent, especially on margins. Flowering stem arising from axils or subterminal, erect, slender, simple or more usually branched in apical third, sparsely clothed with slender reduced leaves, glabrous or scurfy; inflorescence usually dichotomously branching with the flowers in dense secund racemes or spikes at branch tips, or a simple spike or raceme; flowers usually subtended by slender bracts; perianth zygomorphic, saccate at base then tubular, curving, gradually dilating toward limb, somewhat ventricose toward apex, splitting into 6 unequal lobes, strongly recurved toward dorsal side, opening beneath as a deep ventral cleavage (the formation of the perianth just prior to opening and its felty indumentum giving it the appearance of a slender paw, hence the popular name), exterior coarsely tomentose to felty, interior minutely downy; stamens 6, arising from a corona attached near base of lobes and clearly exserted in a 1–2-ranked arc covering upper half of perianth aperture once flower is fully open, ovary inferior, ovules 2 to many per locule, style filiform stigma entire. Fruit a dry 3-celled capsule; seed small, hard, grey-brown to black. W Australia. In the following descriptions the perianth is measured from the tips of the lobes to the apex of the ovary. Flower colour is imparted to most species not by the ground colour of the perianth (usually yellow-green) but by the vivid, often multicoloured indumentum that covers the perianth, ovary and floral axis. Although treated as distinct in this account it is the colour of these hairs that most immediately translates to the grower as the overall colour of these kangaroo paws. Z9.

CULTIVATION Grown for their racemes of curious, woolly flowers carried on sturdy but slender stems above a fan of sword-shaped leaves, *Anigozanthos* spp. are unusual and elegant perennials for the borders of gardens that are frost-free or almost so. They are most commonly grown for cutting; the blooms also have potential for dried arrangements.

In cool temperate zones *Anigozanthos* requires the protection of the cool glasshouse or conservatory. Grow in full sun, in a well drained, acid, leafy soil. Under glass, use a 3:1:1 mix of leafmould or equivalent, loam and sharp sand. Water plentifully when in full growth and keep dry but not arid during winter rest, with a minimum temperature of about 5°C/40°F. Propagate by fresh seed or division in spring. Ink spot disease can be a problem.

A.bicolor Endl. LITTLE KANGAROO PAW.
Lvs 30–40×1–1.25cm, flat, strap-shaped, glabrous or puberulous, usually with margins bristly ciliate, mid-green to grey-blue green. Flowering stems 10–60cm, simple; fls 4–10 in a terminal raceme, perianth 4–6cm, tube deeply split ventrally, exterior olive green with bright red indumentum at base, densely felted with dark indumentum (as are ovary and floral axis), interior olive to blue-green; stamens inserted in 2 ranks, anth. 2.3–2.7mm, fil.1.5–7.5mm. Spring–summer. Readily distinguished from A.manglesii by its spreading habit and smaller, more slender fls with shorter anth., this species hybridizes freely with A.manglesii and A.viridis. Hybrids are also recorded with A.humilis and A.flavidus. ssp. **minor** (Benth.) Hopper. Lvs 5–10cm. Scape 5–20cm. Perianth 3–4.5cm.

A. bicolor var. minor Benth. See A.bicolor ssp. minor.
A. bicolor var. minor hort. non Benth. See A.gabrielae.
A. coccineus Lindl. ex Paxt. See A.flavidus.

A.flavidus DC. TALL KANGAROO PAW; EVERGREEN KANGAROO PAW.
Robust, clump-forming. Lvs 35–100×2–4cm, glabrous, olive to mid-green. Flowering stems 1–3m, glabrous at base, becoming downy on branches. Infl. paniculate; perianth 3.5–5.5cm, sulphur-yellow to lime green, sometimes red, orange or pink or multicoloured, densely covered with yellow-green or red-brown hairs, lobes forward-pointing; anth. connective orange, with a gland-like appendage; ovules many per locule. Early summer–summer. A.flavidus has been used as a pollen parent in hybrids with A.onycis, A.preissii, A.pulcherrimus and A.rufus. 'Mini Red': dwarf, compact, with bright red perianth indumentum; probably a hybrid involving A.rufus. 'Pink Joey': seldom exceeding 50cm; fls smoky-pink. 'Werit-Woorata': to 50cm; fls dark red to burgundy and green.

A.flavidus var. bicolor Lindl. See A.flavidus.

A.gabrielae Domin. DWARF KANGAROO PAW.
Habit diminutive; rhiz. spreading. Lvs 3–12×0.1–0.3cm, glabrous, green to blue-green. Flowering stem 5–20cm, perianth 2.5–4cm, constricted above middle, lobes strongly recurved, green with a red or yellow base; stamens inserted in 2 ranks. Similar to A.bicolor, but smaller in all parts, with fls not curved and rather broad for their length.

A.grandiforus. Salisb. See A.flavidus.

A.humilis Lindl. COMMON CAT'S PAW.
Habit clump-forming. Rhiz. stout. Lvs 15–20×1–1.5cm, not usually persisting beyond one season, flat, falcate, glabrous or puberulous throughout, margins usually ciliate. Flowering stems 10–50cm, simple or rarely forked, flocculose. Infl. a terminal spike, to 15-fld; perianth to 5cm, yellow-green with yellow, orange-red or pink indumentum, lobes slightly recurved or with central lobes horizontal, forward-pointing and lateral lobes vertical, reflexed; stamens inserted in 3 ranks, fil.1–5–3.5mm, anth. 2–3.5mm. ssp. **chrysanthus** Hopper. Flowering stem to 40cm; fls pure sulphur yellow.

A.humilis hort. non Lindl . See A.onyeis.

A.kalbarriensis Hopper.
Readily distinguished from the similar A.humilis by its reflexed perianth lobes, usually bicoloured fls and blue-green lvs. Habit clump-forming. Rhiz. stout. Lvs 12–20×0.3–1cm, flat, falcate, blue-green, glabrous or hairy. Flowering stems 10–20cm; perianth 3–6cm, somewhat falcate, margins decurved, lobes strongly recurved, yellow-green with yellow-green indumentum, usually deepening to red at base of perianth; stamens inserted in 3 ranks, fil.1.3–3.5mm, anth. 1–6–3.5mm. Spring. Hybridizes with A.humilis and A.manglesii; A.kalbarriensis is possibly by a natural hybrid derived from a backcross of these two species.

A.manglesii D. Don.
Habit clump-forming. Lvs 10–40×0.5–1.2cm, straight, glabrous grey-green. Flowering stem 30–110cm, with sparse red hairs at base, becoming densely red-floccose toward infl. Infl. a simple, secund raceme or an open, few-branched panicle; perianth 7–12cm, curved, lobes reflexed, yellow-green with lime green indumentum often deepening to scarlet blood red especially at base of perianth, on ovary and on pedicel; stamens inserted in 1 rank, fil.to 1mm, anth. 5–12mm. Spring–early summer. ssp. **quadrans** Hopper. Perianth slightly constricted above lobes, indumentum orange-red throughout.

A.onycis A.S. George. BRANCHED CAT'S PAW.
Rhiz. short. Lvs 5–15×0.2–1.5cm, broadly keeled, conduplicate, glabrous, not usually persisting beyond one season. Flowering stems 15–30cm, floccose; infl. a lax panicle, branches racemose, 5–9-fld; perianth 5–7cm, straight, yellow green, densely covered with cream green or dull red indumentum, lobes spreading; fil.5–7.5mm, anth. 2.5–4mm. Spring.

A.preissii Endl. ALBANY CAT'S PAW.
Habit small. Rhiz. spreading. Lvs 10–25×0.1–0.5cm, subterete, tapering finely, seldom persisting beyond one season. Flowering stems 20–70cm, sparsely red-pubesc. at basc, more densely so above, simple or forked ×1; infl. a compact terminal few-fld raceme; perianth 6.4–8.2cm, curved, cream or yellow-green with lime to orange indumentum deepening to red at base, on ovary and pedicel, lobes deeply cut, slender, those in centre forward-pointing, others spreading (not reflexed); fil.6–15mm, anth. 34mm. Spring–early summer.

A.preissii var. plumosus Endl. See A.preissii.

A.pulcherrimus Hook. YELLOW KANGAROO PAW.
Differs from the closely related A.rufus in its lvs 5–15mm wide, tomentose or glabrous, and fls with yellow, never red or dark purple, indumentum. Summer. Widely grown for floristry. Has been hybridized with A.flavidus. Susceptible to ink disease.

A.rufus Labill.
Habit robust, clump-forming. Rhiz. spreading, tough. Lvs 20–40×0.2–0.6cm, flattened, conduplicate, glabrous except on bristly or scabrous margins. Flowering stem 5–150cm, pubesc. at base, thinly scurfy, becoming red-flocculose toward summit; infl. a broad dichotomous panicle, branches horizontal to ascending, red-floccose, each bearing to 10 fls in a congested, sccund, terminal raceme; perianth 3.5–5cm, straight or slightly curved, olive green with deep blood red, dark purple or, rarely, yellow indumentum throughout, lobes spreading to reflexed; fil.3–8mm, anth. 1.5–2.6mm, connective green, unappendaged; ovules 24 per locule. Spring-summer. Hybrids between this species and A.flavidus are gaining in popularity, particularly as a cut flower; the branching of the panicles is not so frequent or shapely as it is in A.rufus, but products of this cross are exceptionally vigorous.

A.tyrianthinus Hook. See A.rufus.

A.viridis Endl. GREEN KANGAROO PAW.
Habit small, compact. Lvs 5–50×0.1–0.5cm, flat to subterete, glabrous, dark or grey-green, seldom persisting beyond one season. Flowering stems to 0.8m, often rather arched with sparse floccose hairs becoming denser toward summit, usually simple; infl. a terminal raceme, to 15-fld, the axis densely woolly; perianth 5–8.5cm, curved, yellow-green with uniform sulphur yellow or lime green indumentum, lobes strongly recurved; stamens inserted in 2 ranks, fil.1.5–5.5mm, anth. 3–7.5mm. Spring–early summer. Will hybridize freely with A.manglesii and A.bicolor.

A.viridis var. major (Benth.) Geer. See A.bicolor.

A.cultivars. Anigozanthos spp. hybridize freely: the principle affinities of the relevant species and their natural and artificial crosses have been listed under each above. Hybrids developed at the Australian National Botanic gardens and held to be of particular garden merit include A.kalbarriensis × A.flavidus, A.manglesii × A.flavidus, A.onycis × A.flavidus (e.g. 'Dwarf Delight', a diminutive plant with panicles of massed orange-red fls), A.preissii × A.flavidus (e.g. 'Regal Claw', a dwarf with orange fls thickly felted in red), A.rufus × A.flavidus. In addition, see cvs listed under A.flavidus. It has been suggested that the many beautiful hybrids produced by M. Turner of Melbourne (the Bush Gems, i.e. 'Bush Baby', 'Bush Dawn', 'Bush Emerald', 'Bush Ruby', 'Bush Surprise') may be slightly more tender than those developed in Brisbane.

Anigozanthos (a) *A.flavidus* (a1) inflorescence (a2) leaf section (a3) entire flowering stem, divaricately branched
(b) *A.rufus* (b1) inflorescence (b2) flower (b3) entire flowering stem, divaricately branched (c) *A.humilis*
(c1) inflorescence simple, solitary (c2) flower (d) *A.manglesii* (d1) inflorescence, solitary (d2) habit

Anomatheca Ker-Gawl. (From Lat. *anomalus*, abnormal, *theca*, a case, referring to the warty capsule.) Iridaceae. 6 species of cormous perennial herbs, closely allied to *Lapeirousia* (in which they were formerly included) and to *Freesia*. Corm conic, round-based, with fibrous reticulate tunic. Leaves basal and cauline. Flowering stem simple or branched; bracts 2, unequal; flowers sessile, zygomorphic with segments arranged in two groups of three, the flower therefore appearing bilabiate; perianth tube straight or curved, slightly expanded towards apex; outer segments smaller than inner; anthers and style exserted from tube; ovary small, 3-locular. Capsule inflated, somewhat warty, dehiscent; seeds large, angular or rounded, red-brown. S & C Africa.

CULTIVATION As for slightly tender *Gladiolus* spp. In addition to those described below, *A.grandiflora* from Natal and S Tropical Africa is sometimes grown. It flowers in winter and spring, attains 50cm in height and produces large red flowers.

A.cruenta Lindl. See *A.laxa*.

A.laxa (Thunb.) Goldbl. (*A.cruenta* Lindl.).
To 30cm. Basal lvs several, in fan, equalling or exceeding infl.; cauline lvs smaller. Flowering stem erect, becoming horizontal above; fls 2–5, to 2cm across, red, white or pale blue, with red or purple marking at base of lower 3 seg.; perianth tube straight, pale green, striped red. S Africa, Mozambique.

A.viridis (Ait.) Goldbl.
To 35cm. Basal lvs ensiform, distichous, margin undulate or crispate. Infl. lax; fls 2–10, green, sometimes fragrant; perianth tube 2–3cm, curved, narrow below, widening above; seg. 1–2cm, reflexed. S Africa (Cape Province).

Anthericum L. (From Gk *antherikos*, for the flowering stem of the asphodel.) Liliaceae (Asphodelaceae). Over 50 species of perennial, glabrous herbs to 90cm. Rhizomes short, roots fleshy. Stem simple, to 70cm. Leaves radical, in spiral rosettes, sessile, linear, to 40cm, grass-like, canaliculate or smooth, entire, parallel-veined. Inflorescence racemose or paniculate; scape slender, to 30cm; bracts usually small, scarious; perianth rotate; flowers to 10, to 2cm, white, regular, bisexual, 3-merous; tepals connate or free, with 3 central veins; peduncles to 1.5cm, jointed; stamens 6 in 2 whorls, to 13mm, short, filiform, naked or bearded, anthers basi-fixed, yellow; ovary superior, green or yellow, 3-celled, 4–8 ovules per cell, style filiform, straight or curved. Fruit a trilocular capsule, to 1cm, not angled, cells 4–6-seeded; seeds globose, black, angled, to 3mm. Late spring–early summer. S Europe, Turkey, Africa. Z7.

CULTIVATION *A.liliago*, the most commonly cultivated species, is native to alpine meadows, where it bears spikes of small, starry white flowers on tall stems which emerge after snow melt. *A.ramosum*, which generally occurs at lower altitudes, is similar, but the flowering stems are much branched. Suitable for use on the rock garden, and in the herbaceous border, *Anthericum* spp. are also amenable to cultivation in large deep pots. The flowers last well when cut. Although the most commonly cultivated species tolerate temperatures at least to −10°C/14°F, and *A.liliago* needs cold in winter to flower well, a dry mulch to reduce extreme fluctuations is beneficial where low temperatures are not accompanied by snow cover.

Grow in sun, in fertile, well-drained soil that does not dry out excessively when plants are in growth; best on alkaline soils, *Anthericum* will also tolerate light, slightly acid soils and partial shade. Use a mix of fibrous loam, sharp sand and leafmould or well-rotted manure for pot cultivation; water plentifully when in growth and reduce after flowering. Store pots in semi-shade and do not allow to become dust-dry when dormant. Propagate by seed sown in the cold frame when ripe, under glass in spring, or by division of congested clumps in spring. Flowering may not occur in the season following division.

A.algeriense Boiss. & Reut. See *A.liliago*.
A.bulbosum R. Br. See *Bulbinopsis bulbosa*.
A.latifolium L. f. See *Bulbine latifolia*.

A.liliago L. (*A.algeriense* Boiss. & Reut.). ST. BERNARD'S LILY.
Lvs to 40cm. Scape to 60cm, unbranched; tepals to 2cm across; style curved upwards, ovary green. Fr. with pointed apex. S Europe. 'Major': stem 90cm; fls pure white, opening flat.

A.liliastrum L. See *Paradisea liliastrum*.

A.ramosum L.
Stem to 60cm. Lvs to 40cm. Scape branched, to 90cm; tepals to 1.4cm across; style straight, ovary yellow. Fr. with blunt apex. S Europe.

Aphyllanthes L. (From Gk *aphyllos,* leafless, and *anthos,* flower, referring to the rush-like stems.) Liliaceae (Aphyllanthaceae), 1 species, a fibrous-rooted perennial herb, almost like a dwarf *Ephedra* in general appearance. Stems 15–40cm, numerous, clustered, slender, terete, wiry, striate, chalky. Leaves reduced to membranous, red-brown sheaths on lower part of stem. Flowers 2cm diameter, terminal, solitary or in groups of 2–3, subtended by *c*5 red-brown scarious bracts; tepals 6, free, spreading, pale lilac to deep blue; anthers dorsifixed, introrse; ovary superior; style 1; stigma 3-lobed. Capsule 3-seeded, enclosed by bracts. Summer. SW Europe and Morocco. Z8.

CULTIVATION Occurring on hot dry hillsides, *Aphyllanthes* is a slender and distinctive perennial with rush-like foliage, grown for its charming deep blue flowers. *A.monspeliensis* is hardy to about –5°C/23°F, possibly lower with perfect drainage, and is suitable for a warm sheltered niche on the rock garden, the alpine house or frame. Grow in full sun in well drained, humus-rich, sandy soil; once planted leave the dense fibrous rootstock undisturbed. Under glass grow in deep, well crocked pots and water plentifully when in growth. Propagate by division or fresh seed sown ripe, or in spring, in a sandy propagating mix in the cool glasshouse.

A.monspeliensis L.

Apodolirion Bak. (From Gk *a-,* without, *pous,* foot and *lirion,* lily; the peduncles are short or concealed.) Amaryllidaceae. 4–6 species of perennial herbs, closely related to *Gethyllis* and differing in the stamens being in 2 ranks near the throat. Leaves to 20cm, somewhat grass-like, usually hysteranthous. Peduncle subterranean; flowers solitary; perianth narrowly funnelform, segments lanceolate; stamens in 2 ranks, inserted near throat of tube. S Africa

CULTIVATION A frost-tender genus requiring glasshouse protection and treatment as for *Gethyllis.*

A.buchananii Bak. (*A.ettae* Bak.).
Fls white tinged red. Summer.

A.lanceolatum Benth & Hook. f.
Fls white. Summer.

A.ettae Bak. See *A.buchananii.*

Arisaema Mart. (From *Arum* and Gk *aima,* blood-red; a reference to the red-blotched leaves of some species.) Araceae. About 150 tuberous or rhizomatous herbaceous perennials. Tuber rounded or rhizome elongate. Leaves solitary, paired or several, compound, trifoliate, pedate or radiate, leaflets 3–20, sometimes fewer or entire when immature; petiole emerging from several basal bracts, long, sheathed at base, sometimes forming a pseudostem, often spotted or mottled. Inflorescence solitary, adjacent to solitary leaf or emerging from pseudostem, peduncle short or long, sometimes deflexed in fruit; spathe usually borne below foliage, narrow and convolute at base, forming a tube enclosing the floral part of spadix and sometimes part of appendix, expanded toward apex into a concave or flat limb, apex hooded or erect, yellow to green to brown, red and pink, often striped on white ground; spadix with conspicuous appendix, cylindric, clavate, fimbriate or very long and slender, erect, horizontal or drooping, sometimes curved; flowers unisexual, perianth absent, stamens 1–5, united unless solitary; ovary unilocular, ovules few. Fruit an orange-red berry. E & C Africa, temperate and tropical Asia from Arabia to Japan and Malaysia, Eastern N America.

CULTIVATION Grown for their beautifully marked petioles, fine leaf blades and large hooded spathes, ranging in form from the extremely elegant and fragrant, pink-striped cowls of the frost-tender *A.candidissimum,* to the curiously reptilian *A.griffithii.* Most species are tolerant of temperatures below freezing, given a protective mulch. *A.triphyllum* is one of the hardiest species. Tropical species need the protection of the intermediate to hot glasshouse in cool temperate zones. While the hardiness may vary, cultural requirements are basically uniform for the genus. Pot tubers in deep clay pots in a mix of leafmould, neutral or slightly acid loam and grit. Overwinter in a cold frame, or plunge; bring into the alpine house or cool greenhouse for spring display. Plants that have bulked up through slightly protected container cultivation can be planted outdoors in semi-shade on peaty cool soils in the bog or woodland garden or a sheltered border, where they may be left undisturbed for many years. Protect from slugs. In addition to those described below, *A.exappendiculatum* and *A.ochraceum* are sometimes offered.

A.abbreviatum Schott. See *A.flavum.*

A.amurense Maxim.
To 45cm. Lf solitary or rarely 2, leaflets 5, entire, radiate; petiole sheathed below, forming pseudostem, dull purple. Infl. shorter than petiole; spathe longitudinally striped dark purple to green over white; spadix appendix cylindric, truncate at base, stipe distinct. Spring. N Russia (Japan, Korea, N China). Z5.

A.atrorubens (Ait.) Bl. See *A.triphyllum.*

A.candidissimum W.W. Sm.
To 40cm. Lf solitary, emerging with fl. or just after, leaflets 10–20×7–18cm, 3, median largest, suborbicular to ovate; petiole 25–35cm, surrounded by mottled pink-brown basal bracts. Peduncle 12–20cm, equalling lvs; spathe 8–15cm, tube green striped white, limb ovate, long-acuminate, slightly hooded, white striped pink; spadix appendix 5–6cm, subcylindric, tapering towards apex, first suberect then bending forwards, green. Early summer, emerging late. W China. Z6.

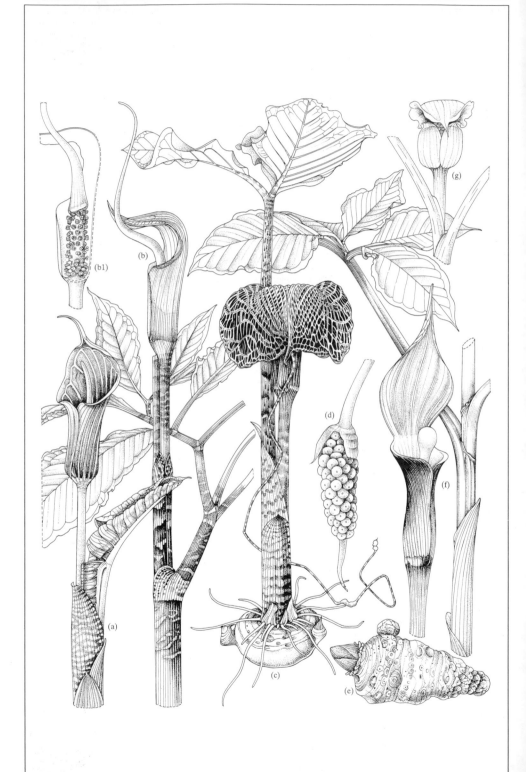

Arisaema (a) *A.candidissimum* (b) *A.tortuosum* (b1) *A.tortuosum* section of spathe showing male and female flowers
(c) *A.griffithii* (d) *A.leschenaultii* fruiting head (e) *A.speciosum* tuber (f) *A.sikokianum* (g) *A.flavum*

A.concinnum Schott.
To 50cm. Lf solitary, leaflets 15–30×2–5cm, 7–11, equal, radiate, oblanceolate, acuminate; petiole 20–50cm, green, exceeding infl. Spathe tube 5cm, cylindric, limb 5cm, ovate-lanceolate, green, longitudinally striped white, apex 2–7cm, long-acuminate, green or dark purple; spadix slender, just exceeding tube, apex thickened and roughened. Early summer. E Himalaya to Burma. Z8.

A.consanguineum Schott.
To 1m. Lf solitary, leaflets to 40cm, 11–20, radiate, lanceolate to linear-lanceolate, apex filiform. Peduncle recurved in fruit; spathe to 12cm, tube glaucous green, deep purple within, limb oblong-ovate, curved, green, sometimes tinged brown, stripes narrow, white, sometimes indistinct, apex 5–15cm, long-acuminate; spadix with sterile fls above fertile, appendix 3cm, cylindric, sparsely bristly at base, green, nearly concealed within spathe tube. Early summer. E Himalaya to N Thailand and C China (Hubei). Z7.

A.costatum (Wallich) Mart. ex Schott & Endl.
To 50cm+. Lf solitary, leaflets to 40×18cm, 3, elliptic to ovate (the median leaflets largest), dark green, edged red, lateral veins parallel, numerous, prominent beneath; petiole stout, sheath entire, forming short pseudostem. Spathe to 15cm, dark red-purple striped white, limb 1–4cm, oblong-lanceolate, incurved, apex long-acuminate; spadix appendix to 45cm, shortly stipitate, subcylindric, narrowing into filiform tail, much twisted above, reaching to ground. Early summer. C & E Nepal. Z7.

A.curvatum (Roxb.) Kunth. See *A.tortuosum*.

A.dracontium (L.) Schott.
To 80cm. Lf solitary, pedate, seg. 10–15cm, 7–15, oblong-elliptic to lanceolate, acuminate; petiole mottled, basally sheathing, basal bracts white or dull pink. Spathe poorly differentiated into tube and limb, base 5–7cm, narrow, apical portion to 5cm, ovate to oblong-ovate, short-acuminate; spadix appendix to 15cm, white at base, green, becoming filiform in apical two thirds. Spring. Eastern N America. Z4.

A.elephas Buchet.
To 30cm. Lf solitary, leaflets 3, unequal, median leaflet to 15cm, ovate, margins undulate, brown-purple. Peduncle to 15cm; spathe tube 3.5cm, limb to 12cm, obovate-oblong, dark liver-purple, striped white toward base and into tube; spadix appendix 25–30cm, exserted, curved, tapering to filiform apex reaching ground, dark black-purple. Early summer. W China (Yunnan). Z5.

A.erubescens (Wallich) Schott.
To 45cm. Lf solitary, leaflets to 17×1.5cm, 7–14, radiate, narrow-lanceolate, acuminate, margins undulate, glaucous beneath; petiole dull pink, mottled red-brown. Spathe to 15cm, tube cylindric, limb ovate, long-acuminate, incurved, margins recurved toward base, red-brown or dull green, pink and white, striped white at base and within; spadix appendix stout, erect, subcylindric, scarcely exserted from tube. Early summer. E Himalaya. Z4.

A.fimbriatum Mast.
To 45cm. Lvs 1–2, leaflets to 15cm, 3, ovate, acute, veins impressed above. Peduncle equalling petiole. Spathe tube to 6.5cm, funnel-shaped, striped green and white, limb to 11cm, erect or incurved, ovate-lanceolate, striped purple and white; spadix appendix to 10cm, red-purple, pendulous, slender, clothed with numerous filiform rudimentary sterile fls to 2.5cm. Malaysia. Z10.

A.flavum (Forssk.) Schott (*A.abbreviatum* Schott).
To 45cm, usually smaller. Lvs 2, pedate, leaflets 2.5–12cm, 5–11, oblong-lanceolate, acute, marginal veins conspicuous; petioles sheathing, forming pseudostem, finely streaked pink-brown. Peduncle equalling lvs; spathe 2–4cm, tube ovoid to subglobose, green, marked yellow, limb sharply incurved, slender-acuminate, yellow-green to yellow, purple within below; spadix included in tube, appendix 3mm, clavate. Early summer. Yemen to W China. Z7.

A.griffithii Schott (*A.hookerianum* Schott).
To 70cm. Lvs 2, leaflets 10–70×8–20cm, 3, rhombic-ovate, veins impressed above, margin yellow-green; petiole stout, spotted or blotched green or purple, far exceeding peduncle, basal bracts large. Spathe tube to 8cm, purple ribbed white, limb 10–20×10–15cm, dull purple conspicuously and openly netted green beneath (i.e. on the facing surface), interior purple to grey or green-white with eye-like purple blotches, net veins and stipes, very broadly ovate, folded over and downwards, margins dilated, forming broad lobes with an apical sinus to 7.5cm deep, tip to 10cm, acuminate, purple; spadix appendix to 1m, stipitate, purple, abruptly narrowing to tortuous capillary tail, often held in acuminate apex of spathe, reaching ground. Early summer. E Himalaya. Z8.

A.helleborifolium Schott. See *A.tortuosum*.
A.hookerianum Schott. See *A.griffithii*.

A.jacquemontii Bl.
10–70cm. Lvs 1–2, digitate, leaflets 5–15×2.5–6.5cm, 3–9, narrow-elliptic to ovate, acuminate, undulate. Infl. subequal to or exceeding lvs; spathe to 15cm, green, sometimes narrowly white-striped, limb to 7.5cm, slightly incurved, apex long-acuminate, upcurved, sometimes purple; spadix appendix stipitate, cylindric, slender, emerging from tube, upcurved, dark purple toward apex, green at base. Early summer. Afghanistan to SE Tibet. Z6.

A.japonicum Bl. See *A.serratum*.

A.kiushianum Mak.
To 40cm. Lf solitary, radiate, leaflets 10–20×2–4cm, 7–13, lanceolate, long-acuminate. Peduncle to 15cm; spathe dark purple, limb broad-ovate, strongly incurved, cuspidate, interior marked white; spadix appendix to 18cm, slender, tapering above, long-exserted. Early summer. Japan. Z7.

A.nepenthoides (Wallich) Mart. ex Schott. COBRA PLANT.
To 50cm. Lvs 2, digitate, leaflets 6–12cm, 5, narrow-elliptic, acuminate, glossy green, glaucous beneath; petiole dull yellow, spotted red-brown. Peduncle exceeding lvs, mottled dull purple; spathe tube to 7.5cm, cylindric, limb to 15cm, mottled green-brown to red-brown, striped white, triangular-ovate, incurved, forming reflexed auricles at junction of limb with tube to 2.5cm, dull green-brown, edged brown; spadix appendix stipitate, subcylindric, erect, shortly exceeding tube, green. Early summer. Himalaya to SW China, Burma. Z8.

A.praecox Koch. See *A.ringens*.

A.propinquum Schott (*A.wallichianum* Hook. f.).
To 70cm. Lvs 2, leaflets 8–20×4–15cm, 3 (median sometimes shorter than laterals), rhombic-ovate, glossy green, veins reticulate, prominent beneath; petiole spotted brown or dark green. Peduncle subequal to petioles; spathe 10–15cm, tube green-purple to purple, striped white, limb oblong, incurved, apical margins rounded, apex to 4cm, acuminate, purple, netted white toward margins; spadix appendix 8–20cm, stipitate, base thickened, tapering to filiform toward summit, long exserted. Early summer. Kashmir to SE Tibet. Z5.

A.ringens (Thunb.) Schott (*A.praecox* Koch).
To 30cm. Lvs 2, leaflets 15–20cm, 3, broad-ovate, long-acuminate, apex filiform, glossy green; petiole green or tinged purple, exceeding peduncle. Spathe tube to 3.5cm, obconic, green to purple, striped white or pale green, limb sharply incurved, helmet-shaped, purple or green, sometimes striped, auriculate at junction with tube, auricles deep chocolate or black-purple; spadix enclosed in spathe, stipitate, erect or curved, cylindric, white to pale yellow. Early spring. Japan, Korea, China. Z7.

A.robustum (Engl.) Nak.
To 60cm. Lf solitary, palmate, leaflets to 10–15×4–7cm, 5, obovate to ovate, abruptly short-acuminate; petiole sheathing for half length, far exceeding peduncle. Spathe green, striped white, or dark purple, limb 5–6cm, ovate, long-acuminate, weakly auriculate at junction with tube; spadix appendix cylindric, basally truncate. Early summer. Japan. Z7.

Arisaema (a) *A.consanguineum* leaflet, leaf plan (b) *A.concinnum* leaflet, leaf plan (c) *A.wattii* stem markings (d) *A.yamatense* ssp. *y'e*, leaflet, leaf plan, stem markings (e) *A.serratum* stem markings, leaf plan (f) *A.ringens* leaflet, leaf plan (g) *A.triphyllum* leaflet, leaf plan (h) *A.ciliatum* leaflet, leaf plan

A.sazensoo misapplied. See *A.sikokianum.*

A.serratum (Thunb.) Schott (*A.japonicum* Bl.).
To 1m. Lvs 2, pedate, leaflets to 12.5cm, 7–20, obovate to lanceolate, entire or dentate; petioles forming pseudostem for more than half length, free forward summit, pale green, densely mottled purple. Peduncle subequal to petioles; spathe 8–12cm, tube 5–7cm, cylindric, limb incurved, ovate, short-acuminate, pale green to dark purple, or purple-spotted, sometimes striped white; spadix appendix 4–5cm, cylindric to clavate, yellow-green, stipitate, erect, included in spathe. Spring. NE Asia (Japan, Korea, China, Kuril Is.). Z5.

A.sikokianum Franch. & Savat (*A.sazensoo* misapplied).
To 50cm. Lvs 2, pedate, leaflets to 15×10cm (5 in lower lf, 3 in upper lf), oblong-elliptic to broad-ovate, short-acuminate, margins finely to coarsely toothed. Peduncle 10–30cm, subequal to or exceeding petioles; spathe 15–20cm, tube funnel-shaped, interior yellow-white, dull purple at base, exterior deep purple or brown-purple, limb erect or slightly incurved, narrow-ovate, long-acuminate, green to purple-green striped green-white within, exterior darker; spadix appendix erect, emerging above tube, white, apex much thickened, club-like to subglobose, 17–25mm wide. Early summer. Japan. Z5.

A.speciosum (Wallich) Mart. ex Schott.
To 60cm. Lf solitary, leaflets 20–45×8–12cm, 3, unequal, triangular-ovate to lanceolate, acuminate, margins flushed red; petiole marbled dark purple, far exceeding peduncle. Spathe to 20cm, dark black-purple, striped white, tube ribbed, white within, limb ovate-lanceolate, long-acuminate, incurved; spadix appendix to 80cm, ovoid at base, white, long-filiform, purple toward summit. Early summer. C Nepal to SW China. Z8.

A.thunbergii Bl.
To 60cm. Lf solitary, radiate, leaflets 10–25×1–4cm, 9–17, lanceolate, acuminate. Peduncle 10–20cm; spathe red-purple to dark purple, limb ovate, strongly incurved, apex long-cau-

date-acuminate; spadix appendix 30–50cm, filiform, erect, wrinkled and thickened at base, apical portion pendulous. Spring. Japan. ssp. **urashima** (Hara) Mak. To 50cm. Leaflets to 18×3.5cm, 11–15, oblanceolate to broad-lanceolate, acuminate. Spadix appendix to 60cm, smooth not wrinkled at base. Spring. Japan. Z7.

A.tortuosum (Wallich) Schott (*A.helleborifolium* Schott; *A.curvatum* (Roxb.) Kunth).
To 150cm. Lvs 2–3, pedate, leaflets 5–17, variable, ovate to linear-lanceolate, acute; petiole mottled. Peduncle exceeding petioles; spathe to 18cm, green, occasionally purple, somewhat glaucous, tube cylindrical, limb ovate, acute, incurved or erect; spadix appendix long-exserted, 'S'-curved, erect toward apex, tapering, green to dark purple. Early summer. Himalaya (Kashmir to SW China). Z7.

A.triphyllum (L.) Torr. (*A.atrorubens* (Ait.) Bl.). JACK-IN-THE-PULPIT; INDIAN TURNIP.
To 60cm. Lvs 2 (occasionally 1 or 3), leaflets 8–15×3–7cm, 3, ovate to oblong-ovate, acute; petiole sometimes spotted purple, usually exceeding peduncle. Spathe to 20cm, green to purple, striped green or white, margins of tube reflexed, limb acute-acuminate, incurved; spadix appendix to 7cm, stipitate, erect, exserted from tube, clavate to cylindric, green to purple, or purple-flecked. Summer. Eastern N America (S Canada to Louisiana and Kansas). Z4.

A.utile Hook. f. ex Schott.
To 50cm. Close to *A.griffithii*. Lf solitary, leaflets to 25cm, 3, nearly equal, rhombic-ovate or obovate, margins flushed red, undulate; petiole spotted, far exceeding peduncle. Spathe to 15cm, dark purple, striped or netted white, tube campanulate, limb 7.5×10cm, obovate, incurved, apical sinus with interposed acuminate apex to 3cm; spadix appendix 15cm, filiform. Early summer. Himalaya (Himachal Pradesh to Bhutan). Z5.

A.wallichianum Hook. f. See *A.propinquum.*

A.yamatense (Nak.) Nak.
To 40cm. Lvs 2, pedate, leaflets 7–12×2–3cm, 7–11, broad-oblanceolate, long-acuminate. Peduncle short. Spathe green, margins of tube recurved above, limb 4–7cm, ovate to broad-ovate, short-acuminate, papillose, yellow within; spadix appendix erect, narrow-cylindric, abruptly capitellate. Spring. Japan. Z7.

Arisarum Targ.-Tozz. Araceae. 3 species of tuberous or rhizomatous perennial herbs. Leaves radical, long-petiolate, sagittate. Spathe tubular in basal third with united margins, then expanding as a hooded and forward-pointing blade; spadix shorter than or barely equalling spathe, long-appendaged; flowers unisexual, lacking peri-anth, in two contiguous zones. Mediterranean, SW Europe, Atlantic Is. Z7.

CULTIVATION *A.proboscideum* is found in moist shaded woodland, *A.vulgare* occurs in sunnier, drier habitats often in rock crevices. They are grown in the woodland or rock garden and alpine house for their curious spathes, those of *A.proboscideum* appear in spring, enclosing fungus-like appendages which attract pollinating fungus gnats.

Grow in a fertile and humus-rich soil, moist for *A.proboscideum*, slightly drier and less fertile for *A.vulgare*, which flowers in late winter and becomes dormant in spring. Transplant when dormant. *Arisarum* tolerates tem-peratures as low as –10°C/14°F for short periods, but mulch well where soil temperatures are expected to fall far below freezing. Propagate by division when dormant or by seed sown in autumn or spring.

A.proboscideum (L.) Savi. MOUSE PLANT.
Rhiz. slender. Lvs 6–15×4–10cm, sagittate to hastate, lustrous mid-green concealing all but tail-like tips of spathes; petiole 7–25cm. Peduncle 5–15cm; spathe 6–18cm, the upper two-thirds forming a slender, upturned and curling tail-like tip projecting from the strongly hooded blade, mostly chocolate brown to maroon-black fading to sunken veins in the pure white, bulbous basal portion of the tube, spadix tipped white, enclosed within spathe. Italy, Spain.

A.vulgare Targ.-Tozz. FRIAR'S COWL.
Tuber irregularly shaped, usually producing several growing points. Lf 5–12×3–10cm, solitary, deep green, sagittate, the basal lobes somewhat rounded; petiole 12–30cm, spotted pur-ple. Peduncle 6–30cm; spathe 4–6×1–1.5cm, tubular, green to silver-white striped dark purple-brown in basal two-thirds, then strongly decurved and expanded to form a dark metallic maroon or violet-black hook; spadix fleshy green to purple decurved following line of spathe and protruding. Mediterranean, Canaries, Azores.

Arum L. (From Gk *aron*, name, used by Theophrastus.) Araceae. 26 tuberous perennial herbs. Tubers horizon-tal, elongate-cylindric with shoot emerging from one end, or vertical, more or less discoid, when often com-pressed, with shoot emerging from middle of upper surface. Roots produced from base of shoot. Leaves to 40cm, radical, entire, hastate to sagittate, membranous to somewhat coriaceous, pale to dark green, sometimes spotted with black or with creamy-white to pale yellow markings; veins reticulate, with distinct marginal vein; petioles long, to 40cm, sheathing at base. Peduncle shorter than or equalling petioles, usually emerging above ground; spathe to 40cm, with margins overlapping below to form tube, contracted at throat, limb expanded above, pale green, white, yellow and deep purple, often spotted dark red or purple, withering after anthesis; spadix elongate, but usually shorter than spathe, with conic to cylindric thermogenic appendix, green to yellow to purple, often malodorous but sometimes sweetly scented; flowers unisexual, male and female zones separated by zone of filiform rudimentary sterile flowers, sterile flowers also present above male zone below appendix, important in pollination mechanism; perianth absent; stamens 3–4; ovary unilocular. Fruit an orange to red berry held in cylindric spike; seeds 1–6. Europe, especially Mediterranean, Asia to W Himalaya.

CULTIVATION A genus occurring in a range of usually semi-shaded habitats, *A.italicum* has naturalized in the hedgerows of southern England, whilst the British native *A.maculatum* is often found in deep woodland shade in natural association with *Ajuga reptans* and *Mercurialis perennis*. *Arum* spp. are frequently found on calcareous soils, *A.palaestinum* in rocky habits, *A.purpureospathum* in lime-rich soils in shade at low altitudes. *A.italicum*, *A.creticum* and *A.pictum* are suitable for the rock garden or border and, with *A.maculatum*, for the woodland garden. The more tender *A.nigrum* and *A.purpureospathum* are better suited to pot cultivation in the frost-free glasshouse or at the base of a warm but partially shaded wall. With the possible exception of the frost-tender *A.pictum*, most will tolerate several degrees of frost (to about –5°C/23°F); *A.italicum* 'Pictum' ('Marmoratum') will tolerate temperatures at least to –10°C/14°F, more with a protective mulch of well rotted manure or bracken litter.

Grown for their foliage, which provides useful winter colour, for their attractive and sometimes fragrant inflo-rescences and for the tight clusters of brightly coloured berries which follow; most flower in spring with the exception of *A.pictum*, which produces its purple brown inflorescence in autumn with the leaves. Although the berries of a number of species have been used medicinally, they are potentially poisonous; those of *A.macula-tum* are decidedly toxic.

Plant 8–10cm/3–4in. deep into moist but well drained, humus-rich soil, in sunny or semi-shaded sites that are moist during the growing period but dry during ripening and resting. For pot cultivation, allow ample room for roots, and use an open calcareous medium comprising 4 parts coir or leafmould, 2 parts composted bark, 1 part

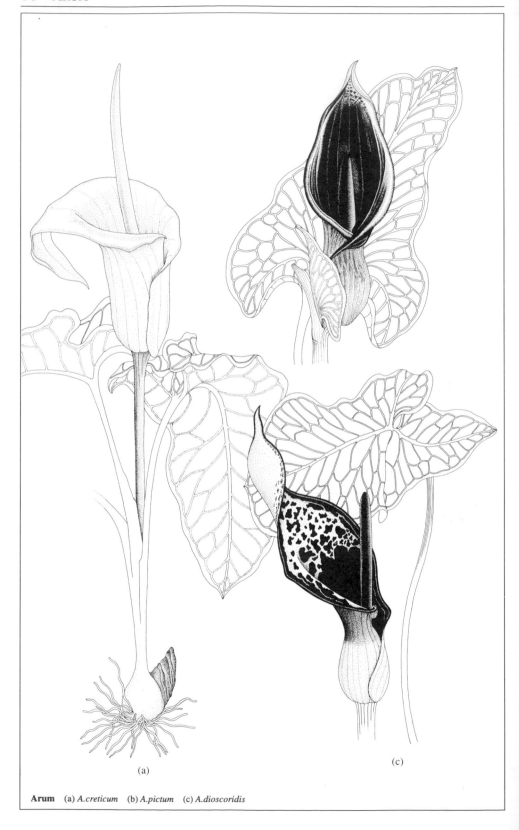

(a)

(c)

Arum (a) *A.creticum* (b) *A.pictum* (c) *A.dioscoridis*

loam and 1 part grit. Water moderately, reducing as the leaves die back in late spring. Allow a period of dry dormancy for Mediterranean species, before resuming watering in autumn.

Propagate by fresh ripe seed, cleansed of pulp before sowing (the juice is caustic and may cause skin irritation); cover with 5mm of propagating medium and 5mm of grit. Increase also by division after flowering, or by removal and replanting of the tubercles (bulbils) in autumn.

A.albispathum Steven. See *A.italicum* ssp. *albispathum.*

A.alpinum Schott & Kotschy.
Tuber vertical, to 5cm diam., 2cm thick. Lvs 9–13×3–7.5cm, sagittate to sagittate-hastate, acute to obtuse, mid-green; petiole terete, 12–18cm, green, sometimes stained purple beneath. Peduncle equalling or exceeding lvs, to 18cm; spathe to 14cm, tube oblong-cylindric, to 3cm, pale green externally, purple with white at base within, limb erect, elliptic-lanceolate, acuminate, pale green; spadix to 8cm, not more than two-thirds length spathe, appendix slender, cylindric, somewhat clavate, long stipitate, pale chocolate-brown to dull purple, to 5cm. Berries bright orange-red. Early summer. S Spain to Balkans & NW Turkey, Sweden to Crete. Often confused with *A.maculatum.* Z7.

A.concinnatum Schott (*A.marmoratum* Schott; *A.nickelii* Schott).
Tuber horizontal, 7–10cm long, 3.5cm thick. Lvs 15–55×10–32cm, sagittate-hastate to oblong-sagittate, subacute to obtuse, somewhat glossy dark green, variably blotched silver-grey above; petiole terete, to 45cm, sometimes stained purple at base. Peduncle shorter than lvs, to 14cm; spathe to 29cm, tube oblong-cylindric, to 5cm, pale green externally, tinged purple on margin, interior white below, purple above, limb erect, lanceolate-elliptic to elliptic, apex acuminate, pale green with purple margins externally, green-white with translucent patches and purple margins within; spadix shorter than or just exceeding spathe, to 27cm, appendix massively conic-cylindric to clavate-cylindric, dull yellow or occasionally pale cream-purple or purple. Infl. scented of stale urine. S Greece to SW Turkey. Z7.

A.conophalloides Kotschy ex Schott. See *A.rupicola* var. *rupicola.*
A.conophalloides var. *virescens* Bornm. & Gauba. See *A.rupicola* var. *virescens.*

A.creticum Boiss. & Heldr.
Tuber vertical, to 5cm diam. Lvs 8–26×4–18cm, emerging in autumn, hastate-sagittate, glossy dark green, basal lobes angular with rounded portion overlapping sinus; petiole 10–35cm. Peduncle exceeding petioles, to 45cm; spathe 15–25cm, bright yellow to yellow-green or green-white, tube much inflated and scarcely constricted, limb recurved and twisted; spadix equalling or exceeding spathe, appendix yellow or occasionally purple, sterile fls absent or few only below male zone. Infl. fragrant. Crete, Karpathos. A fine form is grown with spathes deep primrose; spadix bright chrome; fragrant. Z7.

A.detruncatum C.A. Mey. ex Schott. See *A.rupicola* var. rupicola.

A.dioscoridis Sm.
A variable species. Tuber vertical, discoid, 5–10cm diam., to 3cm thick. Lvs 13–45×9–27cm, oblong-hastate to narrow-sagittate-hastate, acute, mid-green, lateral veins often paler; petiole terete, 13–50cm. Peduncle usually shorter than, or seldom equalling, petioles, 3.5–10cm, occasionally longer, to 42cm; spathe 11–40cm, tube to 8cm, green suffused with purple above and on margin externally, green-white within, limb erect, lanceolate to lanceolate-elliptic, acute to acuminate, green externally, sometimes stained purple, pale green within, usually variously blotched and spotted deep purple-maroon to black purple, or unspotted (var. *syriacum* (Bl.) Engl.) or uniformly purple (var. *philistaeum* (Kotschy ex Schott) Boiss.); spadix half length of or exceeding spathe, 12–28cm, appendix stout, cylindric, subsessile to long-stipitate, dark purple, very rarely dull yellow. Infl. very malodorous, smelling of dung and carrion. Infructescence to 9cm, berries orange. Late

spring. Cyprus to Turkey, Israel and Iraq. var. *dioscoridis* (*A.dioscoridis* var. *smithii* Engl.; *A.dioscoridis* var. *liepoldtii* (Schott.) Engl.; *A.dioscoridis* var. *spectabile* (Schott) Engl.). Spathe limb 16–37cm, blotches more or less confluent, with basal two-thirds stained purple through which spots show as in the coats of melanistic leopards, apical portion yellow-green, unspotted. SW & SC Turkey, Cyprus. var. *cyprium* (Schott) Engl. Spathe limb pale green, not stained purple, with large discrete spots, especially towards base. E Aegean Is., Cyprus, Syria, Lebanon, Israel. var. *syriacum* (Bl.) Engl. Spathe limb pale green, not stained purple, blotches often absent, or if present small and scattered. Spadix appendix purple to dull yellow. SC Turkey, N Syria. var. *philistaeum* (Kotschy ex Schott) Boiss. (*A.dioscoridis* f. *atropurpureum* Hruby). Spathe limb to 14cm, uniformly purple. NW Syria. Possibly a hybrid with *A.palaestinum.* Z8.

A.dioscoridis var. *liepoldtii* (Schott.) Engl. See *A.dioscoridis* var. *dioscoridis.*
A.dioscoridis var. *smithii* Engl. See *A.dioscoridis* var. *dioscoridis.*
A.dioscoridis var. *spectabile* (Schott) Engl. See *A.dioscoridis* var. *dioscoridis.*
A.dioscoridis f. *atropurpureum* Hruby. See *A.dioscoridis* var. *philistaeum.*
A.dracunculus L. See *Dracunculus vulgaris.*

A.gratum Schott (*A.stevensii* Boyce).
Tuber vertical, to 5cm diam., 2.5cm thick. Lvs 9–18×7–12, emerging in early winter, hastate-sagittate to oblong-hastate, subacute, deep green; petiole terete, 17.5–30cm. Peduncle much shorter than lvs, often remaining below ground, to 2.5cm, striped pale-brown; spathe to 18.5cm, tube often partly subterranean, oblong-ventricose, to 3.5cm, externally pale green beneath, purple-stained above, within green-white beneath, purple above, limb cucullate, elliptic-ovate, acute, externally green flushed purple, olive-green stained purple within. Spadix less than one-third length spathe, to 6.5m, appendix clavate, stipitate, red- to green-purple. Infl. pleasantly fragrant. Spring–early summer. Syria, Lebanon, W Turkey. Z8.

A.hygrophilum Boiss.
Tuber vertical or sometimes horizontal, discoid, to 6cm diam., 2.5cm thick. Lvs emerging in early autumn. Lvs 8–45×5–14cm, lanceolate-hastate, acute to subacute, bright to dark green; petiole terete, 9–75cm, sometimes stained purple. Peduncle shorter than lvs, to 45cm; spathe to 14cm, tube ellipsoid, to 3.8cm, green or occasionally purple externally, deep purple within, limb erect or slightly cucullate, oblong- to elliptic-lanceolate, acuminate, pale-green externally, green-white within, margins purple. Spadix two-thirds length limb, to 9cm, appendix sessile, slender, deep purple. Spring. Morocco, Cyprus, Levant (Syria to Jordan). Z8.

A.idaeum Coust. & Gand.
Close to *A.creticum* and previously confused with it, sometimes known in cult. as 'white creticum'. Tuber horizontal, discoid, to 5cm diam., 2.5cm thick. Lvs emerging in early winter, oblong-sagittate, acute, 10–22.5×8–17cm, deep green; petiole terete, to 21cm, deep green much stained purple. Peduncle shorter than or equalling lvs, 5–17cm, stained purple to base of spathe tube; spathe to 11cm, tube oblong-cylindric, to 4cm, pale lime-green externally, faintly marked purple at base, margin and interior white-green, limb erect to cucullate, narrow-elliptic to lanceolate, acute, white tinged green externally, white with translucent patches within, margin narrowly bordered purple; spadix three-quarters length of spathe, to 9.5cm, appendix laterally compressed, dull deep purple, or dull yellow marbled purple; sterile fls absent. Infl. not scented. Crete (mountains). Z7.

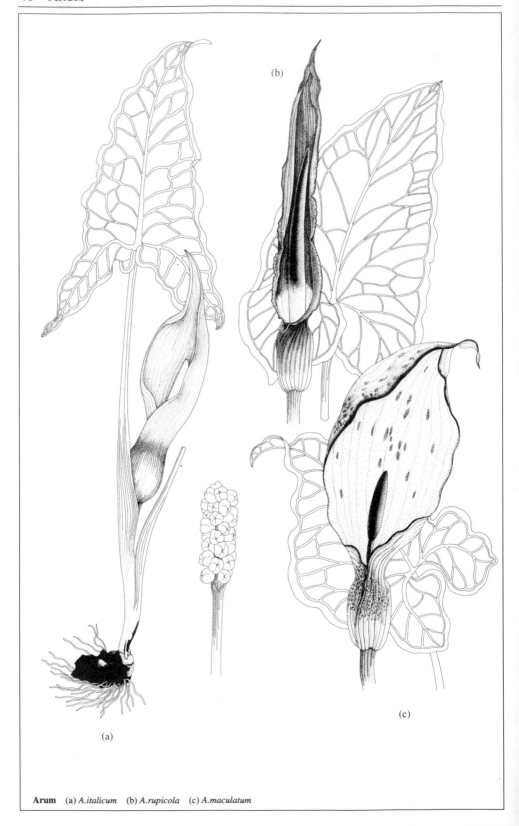

Arum   (a) *A.italicum*   (b) *A.rupicola*   (c) *A.maculatum*

A.italicum Mill.
Variable. Tuber horizontal, 5cm long. Lvs 15–35cm, emerging in autumn or early winter, sagittate to hastate, glossy dark green with various markings; petiole 15–40cm, shallowly grooved above. Peduncle to half length of, or occasionally subequal to, petioles; spathe 15–40cm, tube oblong-cylindric, 5cm, white within, limb erect, becoming cucullate, green-yellow, occasionally white, margins purple; spadix one-third to half length spathe, appendix stipitate, stout, yellow. Infructescence to 15cm, berries orange-red, very conspicuous. Late spring–early summer. S & W Europe, from Canary Is. to Cyprus, north to S England. ssp. *italicum*. Lateral lobes of lvs divergent, veins often conspicuously marked with creamy-white or yellow-green, or lvs sometimes irregularly mottled grey-green. Peduncle much shorter than petioles; spathe pale green-yellow. Seeds 3–4. Throughout range, except north. The plants cultivated as *A.italicum* 'Pictum' and 'Marmoratum' belong here. These names are not valid, never having been properly published; in addition they are a source of confusion with the species *A.pictum*, while the true *A.marmoratum* is a synonym of *A.concinnatum*. The two names seem to be generally regarded as interchangeable, despite probably belonging to distinct clones originally. Stocks in horticulture belong to several clones, clearly preventing the application of a universal cultivar name for these plants with creamy or yellow markings along the veins. At present the most distinct cultivar is 'Chamaeleon': lvs broad, marbled grey-green and yellow-green. 'Tiny': habit dwarf; lvs small, lower lvs very reduced, with cream marbling when emerging in autumn. 'White Winter': habit small, to 20cm high, lvs slender, bold white marbling; fls profuse. ssp. *neglectum* (C. Towns.) Prime (*A.neglectum* (C. Towns.) Ridl.). Lvs with basal lobes convergent or overlapping, uniform green, or with dark spots, not marked cream or grey-green as ssp. italicum. Peduncle shorter than petioles; spathe pale green-yellow. Seeds 1–2. W Europe, incl. S England. ssp. *albispathum* (Steven) Prime (*A.albispathum* Steven). Close to ssp. *neglectum*, but spathe pure white within, green externally. Crimea, SW Asia. ssp. *byzantinum* (Bl.) Nyman. Close to ssp. *neglectum* but peduncle subequal to petioles; spathe pale green, tinged purple at margin. Crete, E Balkans. Z6.

A.korolkowii Reg.
Tuber vertical, to 7cm diam., 3cm thick. Lvs 8–16×5–13cm, emerging in early winter, sagittate-hastate to oblong-sagittate, acute to obtuse, mid- to dark-green; petiole to 35cm, terete, pale green with brown-green stripes. Peduncle exceeding lvs, to 46cm; spathe 14–20cm, tube oblong-cylindric, to 3.7cm, green externally, white within, limb erect, narrow-lanceolate, acuminate, green externally, paler green with pale purple tinge within; spadix two-thirds length spathe, to 14cm, appendix stipitate, dull cream, marbled red-brown, purple-brown below. Infl. unscented. N Iran, Afghanistan, C Asia. Z6.

A.maculatum L. LORDS-AND-LADIES; CUCKOO-PINT; JACK-IN-THE-PULPIT.
Tuber horizontal, 2cm long. Lvs 7–20cm, emerging in early spring, hastate to sagittate, obtuse, glossy dark green, often with black spots; petiole 15–25cm, terete. Peduncle two-thirds length of, to equalling petioles; spathe 15–25cm, tube oblong, dull white within, limb erect, becoming cucullate, pale green, often spotted purple-black, sometimes flushed dull purple, margin purple; spadix to 12cm, half length spathe, appendix stipitate, purple or sometimes yellow. Berries orange-red; seeds 1–3. Spring. W, C & S Europe, north to Sweden and Scotland, east to Ukraine. 'Immaculatum': lvs unspotted; spathe tube interior white at base, splashed purple above, blade green, sometimes purple edged interior. 'Pleddel': lvs blotched cream. Z6.

A.marmoratum Schott. non hort. See *A.concinnatum*.
A.neglectum (C. Towns.) Ridl. See *A.italicum* ssp. *neglectum*.

A.nickelii Schott. See *A.concinnatum*.

A.nigrum Schott (*A.petteri* Schott, misapplied; *A.orientale* Bieb.).
Tuber vertical, subglobose, to 7cm diam. Lvs 10–20cm, emerging in autumn, hastate to hastate-sagittate, dull green; petiole 20–30cm. Peduncle much shorter than petioles, to 5cm; spathe 15–20cm, tube green externally, white to green or dull purple within, limb ovate- to elliptic-oblong, purple-black within; spadix less than half length spathe, appendix stout, dark purple-grey. Spring. W Yugoslavia, N Greece. Z6.

A.orientale Bieb. See *A.nigrum*.

A.palaestinum Boiss.
Tuber vertical, depressed-globose. Lvs to 20cm, emerging in spring, hastate to broadly hastate-sagittate, median lobe 12.5×10cm, ovate-oblong, basal lobes 8.5cm, broad, obtuse or acute, mid-green; petioles 20–30cm. Peduncle shorter than lvs; spathe 15–20cm, tube campanulate, scarcely constricted at apex, 4cm, green-white externally, deep purple within, limb spreading, oblong-lanceolate, often reflexed and twisted at apex, dark red-purple within; spadix two-thirds length of to subequal to spathe, appendix cylindric, dark black-purple. Spring. Israel. Z9.

A.petteri Schott, misapplied. See *A.nigrum*.

A.pictum L. f.
Tuber vertical, subglobose, to 5cm diam. Lvs 15–30cm, emerging in autumn, with or just after infl., cordate-sagittate, somewhat coriaceous, glossy dark green, finely white-veined, margin membranous, red; petiole 20–25cm, broadly sheathed below. Peduncle 5–10cm, mostly subterranean; spathe 15–25cm, tube oblong, 3.5cm, green, marked white externally, limb erect, ovate-acuminate, dark red-purple; spadix much shorter than spathe, sterile fls absent between male and female zones, appendix stipitate, dark red-purple. Autumn. Islands, W Mediterranean (Balearics, Corsica, Sardinia). Z8.

A.purpureospathum Boyce.
Tuber horizontal. Lvs 20–30×15–20cm, emerging in autumn, hastate, dark green, unspotted; petioles 20–25cm, green, stained purple below. Peduncle 6–8cm; spathe dark silky purple throughout, limb erect, becoming cucullate; spadix to not more than half length spathe, appendix slowly stipitate, very dark purple. Berries orange-red. Crete. Z8.

A.rupicola Boiss.
Very variable. Tuber vertical, discoid, 4–8cm diam., to 3.5cm thick. Lvs 8–25×4–18.5cm, emerging in early winter, oblong-sagittate to -hastate, subacute to obtuse, mid-green; petioles terete, 10–55cm, green. Peduncle exceeding lvs, 10–65cm; spathe to 40cm, tube oblong-cylindric, to 7cm, green or brown with purple margin externally, white within, limb erect and narrow but soon becoming reflexed or cucullate, apex twisted, exterior usually green with purple margin, occasionally purple or brown, green-white stained maroon to brown within; spadix subequalling or exceeding limb, to 33cm, appendix subsessile or shortly stipitate, cylindric to conic-cylindric, sometimes massive, purple to grey-lilac, or brown to yellow. Infl. not scented. var. *rupicola* (*A.conophalloides* Kotschy ex Schott; *A.detruncatum* C.A. Mey. ex Schott). Spathe limb deep wine-red, purple or maroon within. Spadix appendix dark purple to black, occasionally brown to yellow. Spring–early summer. W Asia (Turkey to Iran, Jordan, SW Russia) Mediterranean (Lesbos, Cyprus). var. *virescens* (Stapf) Boyce (*A.virescens* Stapf; *A.conophalloides* var. *virescens* Bornm. & Gauba). Spathe limb green-white within, narrowly bordered purple. Spadix appendix grey-lilac. Spring–early summer. Range as var. *rupicola* but not Jordan, Cyprus or Lesbos. Z8.

A.stevensii Boyce. See *A.gratum*.
A.virescens Stapf. See *A.rupicola* var. *virescens*.

Asphodeline Rchb. (Named from its relationship to *Asphodelus*.) JACOB'S ROD. Liliaceae (Asphodelaceae). 18–20 species of rhizomatous perennial or biennial herbs to 130cm. Rhizomes clustered, roots fibrous or fleshy; stem unbranched, erect, straight or flexuous, smooth. Leaves numerous, basal, linear to subulate, to 30cm, bases wide, membranous, sheathing, covering stem, grey-green, margins often scarious. Inflorescence usually simple; bracts membranous, 0.5–20cm; flowers numerous, almost zygomorphic, sometimes fragrant, in cylindrical racemes to 30cm; tepals 6, to 3cm, joined near base, each with 3 central veins, white tinged pink, yellow or yellow striped green; stamens 6, filaments alternately long and short, stamens and style curving downwards, anthers dorsifixed; ovary superior, trilocular. Fruit a globose capsule to 1.5cm; seeds 6, dark grey, to 0.6×0.5mm, unwinged, sharply angled. Mediterranean to Caucasus.

CULTIVATION *Asphodeline* spp. are excellent plants for the herbaceous border or for naturalizing on rocky banks. *A.brevicaulis* bears a short inflorescence of pale yellow flowers above a rosette of leaves in its second or third year. *A.lutea* is a handsome species: fragrant yellow flowers that open after midday and quickly fade are carried on stout leafy stems above fine, blue-green foliage. *A.liburnica*, also with yellow and green flowers carried later in summer, is smaller and more graceful. In *A.taurica*, the white tepals are backed by a green stripe. All are hardy to –15°C/5°F. Grow in any moderately fertile, but not too rich soil, in full sun, although *Asphodeline* spp. are tolerant of light dappled shade. Apply general fertilizer in spring, and water in drought. Propagate from seed sown in a sandy propagating mix, in the cold frame. Also by careful division, ensuring that offsets have sufficient growing points.

A.balansae Bak. See *A.damascena.*

A.brevicaulis (Bertol.) Bak.
Similar to *A.liburnica* but stem to 50cm, often flexuous; lower lvs to 15cm, narrow, subulate. Infl. usually branched; tepals pale yellow veined green, to 2cm. Asia Minor. Z8.

A.damascena (Boiss.) Bak. (*A.balansae* Bak.; *A.isthmocarpa* Bak.).
Related to *A.taurica*. Bienn. Stem to 60cm, lower half leafy. Lvs linear, rosulate, to 22cm. Infl. usually unbranched, racemose, 15–30cm; fls white to light pink, perianth lobes to 2.5cm. Fr. ellipsoid to cylindrical. Summer. Asia Minor. Z9.

A.isthmocarpa Bak. See *A.damascena.*

A.liburnica (Scop.) Rchb. (*Asphodelus liburnicus* Scop.).
Perenn. to 60cm. Stem leafy in lower half, simple. Lvs to 10cm. Infl. usually unbranched, racemose, to 22cm, bracts to 0.5cm, perianth lobes to 3cm, yellow striped green. Fr. spherical, to 0.8m. Summer. Greece, Austria, Italy, Balkans. Z7.

A.lutea (L.) Rchb. (*Asphodelus luteus* L.). KING'S SPEAR; YELLOW ASPHODEL.
Perenn. to 130cm. Stem leafy to infl. Lvs linear-subulate, tufted at base, to 30cm×0.3cm, glabrous, furrowed, silver to

dark green with paler veins, margins smooth, or rough toward apex. Infl. simple, racemose, to 20cm. Fls to 3cm, yellow, fragrant, in axils of bracts; bracts buff or red-brown, nearly equalling fls. Fr. ovate to spherical, to 1.5cm; seeds dark grey, to 0.6×0.5mm. Late spring–summer. Mediterranean, 'Florepleno': fls double, long-lasting, 'Yellow Candle' is a selected form. Z7.

A.taurica (Pall.) Endl.
Perenn. to 60cm, stem leafy except infl. Lvs to 22.5cm, narrow-subulate. Infl. racemose, dense, to 30cm; bracts longer than peduncles, tepals to 1.7cm, white with buff midvein. Fr. oblong-ovate, to 1.2cm. Summer. Greece, Asia Minor, to Caucasus. Z7.

A. tenuior (Fisch.) Ledeb.
Related to *A.taurica*. To 40cm, leafy in lower half or all leaves basal, margins of sheathing lvs ciliate. Infl. branched or simple, loosely racemose, to 10cm; perianth lobes to 2cm, white tinged pink. Fr. obovate to spherical, to 0.8cm. Summer. Turkey, Iran, Caucasus. Z8.

Asphodelus L. (From Gk *asphodelos,* of unknown origin; medieval Lat. form *affodillus,* anglicized as *affodil,* whence Daffodil.) Liliaceae (Asphodelaceae). 12 species of annuals or perennials with swollen rhizomes. Flowering stem to 2m or absent, solid or hollow, branched or unbranched. Leaves radical, linear, with membranous sheathing base, to 60cm, flat or cylindrical, entire. Inflorescence a dense raceme or panicle; bracts scarious, white or brown; pedicels jointed; flowers regular, bisexual, 3-merous, hypogynous; tepals petaloid, 6 in 2 whorls, free or joined at base, 1-veined, to 4cm across, white or rose pink with green, tan or rust midvein; stamens 6, in 2 whorls of 3, free; anthers dorsifixed; ovary superior, 3-celled. Fruit a capsule, to 2cm; seeds 6, winged. Mediterranean to Himalaya.

CULTIVATION   *Asphodelus* includes a number of tall, striking perennials that are suitable for the herbaceous border and for naturalizing in thin grass, including *A.albus* bearing simple spikes of white flowers above a clump of grass-like foliage. *A.ramosus* and *A.aestivus,* which remains evergreen in mild winters, differ in having branching flower stems. *A.acaulis* is unusual in that it bears its stemless inflorescence within the basal rosette of leaves. Demanding sharp drainage, it is grown to best advantage on the rock garden or in the alpine house. *A.fistulosus,* a short-lived perennial sometimes flowering in its first year, should be raised from seed regularly. Otherwise, cultivate as for *Asphodeline.*

A.acaulis Desf.
Perenn. Stem absent or very short. Lvs planar, to 30cm. Bracts white; tepals to 4cm across, white or pale pink with pale green midvein, Spring. N. Africa. Z9.

A.aestivus Brot. (*A.microcarpus* Salzm. & Viv.).
Perenn. Stem to 2m, solid, with short side branches, Bracts grey-green to green-white; tepals to 4cm, white with tan midvein. Capsule to 7mm. Spring–early summer. Canary Is., S Europe, N Africa, Turkey. Z8.

A.albus Mill. (*A.delphinensis* Gren. & Godron).
Perenn. Flowering stem to 1m, solid, sometimes branched, Lvs flat, to 60cm, Bracts white or dark brown; tepals to 2cm, white or rose-pink with deeper pink midvein. Capsule to 2cm. Late spring–summer. C & S Europe. Z6.

A.cerasiferus Gay. See *A.ramosus.*
A.delphinensis Gren. & Godron. See *A.albus.*

A.fistulosus L. (*A.tenuifolius* Cav.).
Annual or short-lived perenn. Stem hollow, to 70cm, branched or unbranched. Lvs to 35cm, cylindric, hollow. Bracts white; tepals to 12mm, white or rose-pink with tan midvein. Capsule to 7mm. Summer. SW Europe, Mediterranean, SW Asia; widely naturalized elsewhere. Z8.

A.liburnicus Scop. See *Asphodeline liburnica.*
A.luteus L. See *Asphodeline lutea.*
A.microcarpus Salzm. & Viv. See *A.aestivus.*

A.ramosus L. (*A.cerasiferus* Gay).
Perenn. Stem to 150cm, solid, with many long branches. Lvs to 40cm, planar, with shallow keel below. Bracts white to pale green; tepals to 2cm, white with rust midvein. Summer. S Europe, N Africa. Z7.

A.tenuifolius Cav. See *A.fistulosus.*

Babiana Ker-Gawl. (Latinized version of Afrikaans *bobbejaan*, baboon, since baboons are said to eat the corms.) Iridaceae. 50–60 species of cormous, perennial, deciduous herbs. Corm deep-seated in ground, covered with fibrous brown or red-brown tunic, usually forming a neck. Leaves usually lanceolate, plicate, hairy. Spike simple or branched, laxly or densely 3 to many-flowered; flowers regular or irregular, with long or short perianth tube, white, cream, yellow, mauve, purple, pink, red or blue, often scented; tepals 6, stamens 3, set on tube near throat; style with 3 short branches. Subsaharan Africa, from Zambia south to Cape Province. Spp. with very irregular, long-tubed flowers formerly described as *Antholyza*. Z9.

CULTIVATION *Babiana* spp. are usually found in coastal habitats, in sand dunes or other dry open areas. Most species can be grown outside in zones where winter temperatures do not fall much below –5°C/23°F, in a warm, sunny position in light, rich, and freely draining soil; for winter protection, plant at a depth of 20–25cm/8–10in. and give a deep dry mulch of bracken litter or leafmould. Alternatively, corms may be lifted in autumn and over-wintered, cleaned and dry, in frost-free conditions. Replant in early spring in a mix of equal parts loam, leafmould and sand. Plants grown permanently in pots benefit from frequent applications of dilute liquid feed just before flowering. Propagate by offsets, which are freely produced, or from fresh seed sown ripe in a light sandy propagating mix in the cool glasshouse. The seeds will germinate the following spring, and the seedlings may be planted out in the summer of the same year.

In addition to those described in full below, the following species sometimes appear in cultivation – *B.angustifolia* (*B.pulchra*), perianth lobes narrowly obovate, deep cobalt to mauve stained purple-red below (W Cape); *B.blanda*, flowers rose-pink (SW Cape); *B.cedarbergensi*s, flowers scented mauve marked yellow (W Cape); *B.dregei*, flowers deep purple-blue; *B.fimbriata*, flowers mauve and yellow (Namaqualand); *B.odorata*, flowers scented, yellow (SW Cape); *B.spathacea*, flowers white or cream marked red (W Karoo), and *B.virginea*, flowers large, white, fragrant (W Karoo).

B.ambigua (Roem. & Schult.) Lewis.
Corm 1–1.5cm diam., almost globose, neck absent or very thin. Stem short, pubesc., occasionally with 1–2 short branches, underground part 4–15cm long, aerial part 1–5cm. Lvs 3–6, 4–8cm×7–10mm, linear or lanceolate, plicate, pubesc. Spike short, densely 4–5-fld, distichous or secund; fls 2-lipped, scented, blue or mauve-blue, lower side lobes usually white or pale yellow in centre with purple W-shaped mark; tube 10–19mm, lobes clawed, lanceolate or spathulate, dorsal lobe free, 28–40×8–13mm, other lobes 20–35×6–10mm, joined for 1–5mm at base to form a lip; style branches spathulate, 5–6mm. Winter–spring. S Africa (SW Cape).

B.disticha Ker-Gawl. See *B.plicata*.
B.gawleri N.E. Br. See *B.sambucina*.

B.hypogaea Burchell.
Dwarf plants arising from deep-seated, globose corm 2–3cm diam. Lvs usually 4–7, 7–20(–30)cm long, linear, plicate, hairy. Spikes clustered at base of plant, densely 2–8-fld; fls scented, funnel-shaped, somewhat 2-lipped, blue-mauve, the lower tepals sometimes with yellow streaks and irregular purple bands; tube 35–55mm, slender, wider at throat, lobes 25–60×6–12mm, oblanceolate; style branches 5–6mm. Zambia, Zimbabwe, S Africa, Botswana, Namibia.

B.macrantha MacOwan. See *B.pygmaea*.

B.nana (Andrews) Spreng.
Corm 1–1.5cm diam., without neck. Stem short, 3–10cm high above ground, hairy, sometimes with 1–3 short branches. Lvs usually 3.5–6×1–2cm, 5–7, distichous, forming a fan, obovate or oblanceolate, usually abruptly narrowed to acute apex, hairy; petiole 1–6cm. Spike densely 2–6-fld, distichous; fls scented, irregular, broadly campanulate, blue, mauve or pink, the lower side lobes marked with yellow or white and purple; tube 12–17mm, straight; lobes 23–40×6–14mm, obovate or oblong, obtuse or emarginate, upper 3 usually slightly longer than lower; style branches 6–8mm. Winter–spring. SW Cape.

B.plicata Ker-Gawl. (*B.disticha* Ker-Gawl.).
Corm 2–3cm diam., ovoid or globose, neck 10–15cm. Lvs 6–8, distichous, 8–12×1–2cm, lanceolate, pubesc. Stem 7–20cm, sometimes with 1–3 short branches. Spike distichous, fairly densely 4–10-fld; fls scented, irregular, pale blue, violet or white, the lower side lobes usually with a yellow blotch and 2 purple dots toward base; tube 18–25mm long, slightly curved; lobes spreading, 15–25×7–10mm, the lower 3 usually slightly shorter than upper 3; stamens protruding slightly from tube; style branches 3–5mm, spathulate. Winter–spring. S Africa (W Cape).

B.purpurea (Jacq.) Ker-Gawl.
Corm 2–2.5cm diam., subglobose; neck 4–7cm. Lvs 6–7, 6–12×0.5–0.8cm, lanceolate, plicate, pubesc. Stem 10–15cm, simple or 1–3-branched. Spike distichous, laxly or fairly densely 4–10-fld; fls scented, usually regular, purple-mauve, the tube purple, outside of lobes with purple median line; tube 18–28mm long, straight or slightly curved, lobes 18–25×9–12mm, oblong or obovate, obtuse or slightly emarginate; anth. dark; style branches 3–4mm. Late winter–early spring. S Africa (W Cape).

B.pygmaea (Burm. f.) N.E. Br. (*B.macrantha* MacOwan).
Corm to 2.5cm diam., ovoid or globose, neck 3.5–10cm. Lvs 5–12×1–2cm, 4–6, distichous, lanceolate, plicate, pubesc.; petiole 1–5cm. Stem 2–6(–15)cm, usually unbranched; spike distichous, laxly 2–5-fld. Fls regular, 6–9cm diam., yellow, purple-maroon in centre, sometimes tinged with purple outside; tube 15–25mm, straight, slender but funnel-shaped at throat, lobes spreading, 30–50×17–30mm, obovate; stamens protruding from tube; style branches 2–3mm. Late winter–early spring. South Africa (W Cape).

B.ringens (L.) Ker-Gawl. (*Antholyza plicata* L.).
15–40cm; corm 1.5–2cm diam. Lvs 10–19×0.4–0.7cm, narrowly lanceolate. Spike branched, densely many-fld; fls red or maroon, laterally compressed; tube 3–4cm, upper lobe 3–3.5×0.8cm, erect, acute, other lobes about 16mm, recurved, acuminate; style branches 6–8mm. Winter-spring. Cape Peninsula.

B.rubrocyanea (Jacq.) Ker-Gawl.
Corms 1.5–2cm diam., ovoid or subglobose, neck 5–10cm. Lvs 6–10×0.5–2cm, 5–7, distichous, lanceolate, plicate, pubesc.; petiole to 6cm. Stem 5–20cm. Spike laxly to fairly densely 5–10-fld, fls spirally arranged, regular, the basal third of lobes scarlet, curving up, the apical two-thirds blue, spreading; tube 15–20mm, straight; lobes 20–24×11–14mm, clawed at base then ovate or suborbicular; style branches very short. Late winter–early spring. S Africa (W Cape).

B.sambucina (Jacq.) Ker-Gawl. (*B.gawleri* N.E. Br.).
Corm 2–3cm diam., ovoid; neck 8–10(–15)cm. Lvs 4–14cm×3–7mm, 5–6, more or less erect, linear or lanceolate, plicate, pubesc. Stem 1–2cm long above ground, angled, sometimes with 1–2 short branches underground. Spike short, densely 2–6-fld; fls scented, irregular, purple, violet or pale blue-mauve, lower side lobes with white mark near centre; tube 30–50mm, almost straight, widening from 1mm diam. at base to 3–5mm in throat; lobes 20–35×5–12(–16)mm, elliptic or obovate; style branches 4–5mm. Winter–early spring. S Africa (W Cape to Port Elizabeth).

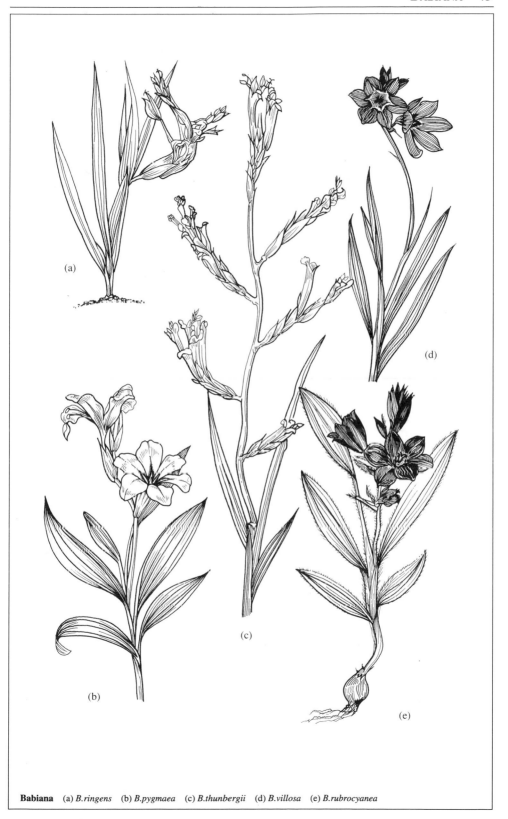

Babiana   (a) *B.ringens*   (b) *B.pygmaea*   (c) *B.thunbergii*   (d) *B.villosa*   (e) *B.rubrocyanea*

B.stricta (Ait.) Ker-Gawl.
Corm to 2.5cm diam., ovoid or globose; neck 4–9cm. Lvs 6–8, arranged in fan, 4–12×0.6–1.2cm. Stem usually erect, 10–20(–30)cm. Spike short, laxly 4–8-fld, the fls spirally arranged. Fls more or less regular, sometimes scented, purple, mauve or blue, the 2 lower or 3 inner lobes paler, sometimes yellow; tube 10–18mm, straight, rarely curved, lobes 15–25×6–13mm, oblong or obovate, equal or with outer lobes slightly shorter and narrower; style branches 2.5–3mm, filiform. Late winter–early spring. S Africa (SW Cape). var. **sulphurea** (Jacq.) Bak. Stem declinate. Fls sulphur-yellow, tube purple or blue, lobes sometimes flushed with purple outside; anth. purple-black.

B.thunbergii Ker-Gawl. (*Antholyza plicata* L. f.).
40–70cm. Lvs 15–35×0.5–0.7cm, linear. Spike branched, densely many-fld on upper side, fls bright red or pink-red with green patches on lip; tube c4cm, becoming wider above the curve, topmost seg. large, curving upwards, enclosing stamens and style, other seg. much smaller, the lower 3 partly joined, forming a lip. Winter–spring. W & NW Cape, NW Namaqualand.

B.tubata (Jacq.) Sweet. See *B.tubulosa*.
B.tubiflora var. *filifolia* Pappe ex Bak. See *B.tubulosa* var. *tubiflora*.

B.tubulosa (Burm. f.) Ker-Gawl. (*B.tubata* (Jacq.) Sweet).
Corm 2–3.5cm diam., ovoid or subglobose. Lvs 4–15cm×6–22mm, 6–8, forming a fan, lanceolate, plicate, pubesc. Stem with 7–12cm underground, the part above ground short, 1–3-branched, usually declinate. Spike secund or distichous, densely 8–12-fld; fls irregular, bilabiate, cream with red arrow-shaped or triangular marks on 3 lower lobes, tube flushed with purple or red-purple, outer lobes usually with red median line on outside; tube 65–90mm, slender in lower half, enlarged towards throat, lobes oblique, clawed at base with oblong blade, upper lobes 30–34mm, the topmost 8–14mm wide, the upper laterals somewhat narrower, lower lobes 18–23×5–9mm; style branches 6mm. Spring. S Africa (W Cape). var. **tubiflora** (L. f.) Lewis (*B.tubiflora* var. *filifolia* Pappe ex Bak.). Spike 2- to many-fld; tube 65–80mm, slender, only slightly wider towards throat, lobes 15–23×3–6mm, upper 3 slightly longer than lower 3, spathulate or clawed; style branches 3–4mm.

B.villosa Ker-Gawl.
Corm to 2.5cm diam., neck 7–10cm. Stem 12–20cm, sometimes with 1 branch. Lvs 5–7, distichous, 5–12cm×7–15mm, lanceolate or sword-shaped, plicate, hairy. Spike rather laxly 4–8-fld, distichous, fls more or less regular, deep red or red-purple; tube 12–20mmm, very slender but suddenly widened near throat, lobes 18–28×8–14mm, oblong, obtuse, the outer ones mucronate; style branches 3–5mm; anth. large, purple-black. S Africa (SW Cape).

B.villosula (Gmel.) Ker-Gawl. ex Steud.
Corm 2–3.5cm diam.; neck 4–6(–9)cm. Lvs 3–5, spreading or suberect, 4–16cm×4–14mm, lanceolate, plicate, sparsely to densely pubesc. Stem 1–5cm, erect, usually simple but sometimes branched; spike distichous, densely 2–4–(–8)fld; fls regular, pale blue or mauve, white in centre; tube 18–25(–30)mm, straight, very slender but enlarged towards throat, lobes 20–30×8–13mm, oblong or obovate, equal or the outer slightly longer than inner; stamens slightly protruding from tube; style shorter than anth. with filiform branches 4mm. Winter. S Africa (W Cape).

B.cultivars. Races are offered, mostly derived from *B.stricta* and producing flowers in a range of colours from pearly white with a dark eye through to yellow, rose, red, mauve and indigo. Some named cultivars are also listed.

Baeometra Salisb. (From Gk *baios*, small, and *metron*, measure, referring to its size.) Liliaceae (Colchicaceae). 1 species, a small perennial bulbous herb. Corms ovoid, asymmetrical; tunics brown. Stem usually sheathed below ground, scapose above, 15–30cm. Lower leaves 15–20cm, usually 6, somewhat amplexicaul, distichous, linear, upper leaves reduced, merging into bracts. Inflorescence a 1–7-flowered raceme; flowers held erect; pedicels scalloped at apex; tepals to 1.25cm, 6, free, erect, yellow inside with a purple spot at base, red outside, narrowed to a claw; stamens arising from claw, shorter than segments, anthers versatile; ovary 3-locular; styles 3. Fruit a cylindric, trigonous, septicidal capsule; seeds globose. Spring. S Africa (Cape Peninsula). Z9.

CULTIVATION Grown for its racemes of striking, brilliantly coloured flowers produced in spring, *Baeometra* is a frost-tender perennial amenable to pot cultivation in the cool glasshouse or conservatory in cool temperate zones; it is sometimes grown in summer in the border, to be lifted in autumn and stored in frost-free conditions overwinter. Grow in sun in a well drained mix of sandy loam and coir or leafmould; water plentifully when in growth and reduce after flowering as plants become dormant. Propagate by offsets or seed.

B.columellaris Salisb. See *B.uniflora*.
B.uniflora (Jacq.) G. Lewis (*B.columellaris* Salisb.).

Begonia L. (Named for Michel Begon (1638–1710), Governor of French Canada, patron of botany.) Begoniaceae. About 900 usually succulent herbs, shrubs or climbers. Roots fibrous or rhizomatous or tuberous, tubers becoming dormant in winter. Stems often swollen, conspicuously jointed, woody, to 2m+, or soft and herbaceous, or absent, leaves forming rosette at apex of rhizome. Leaves alternate, petiolate, usually asymmetric, one side shorter than other, resembling an elephant's ear, simple to lobed or occasionally compound, margin irregularly toothed, glabrous to hispid, surface smooth to rugose or bullate, membranous to coriaceous, often brightly marked red, purple, brown, grey to white; stipules 2, often large, membranous, often persistent, sometimes caducous. Inflorescence an axillary or terminal cyme or raceme, erect or pendent, few- to many-flowered; flowers unisexual, male and female adjacent in inflorescence, sometimes dimorphic in size, red, pink, white, yellow to orange, sometimes bicoloured, often double in cultivation; corolla segments (tepals) 2+2 in male flowers, 2–6 in females, of different sizes but similarly coloured, sometimes hairy externally, glabrous on inner surface, waxy in texture and of crystalline appearance; stamens numerous, massed at centre, or connate below, forming tube, anthers yellow; ovary inferior, 3–4-locular, ovules many, styles 3, free or connate below, stigmata lobed and convolute, or capitate. Fruit a loculicidal capsule, usually winged; seeds very numerous, minute, oblong. Tropics and subtropics, especially Americas. Z10 unless specified.

CULTIVATION. TUBEROUS BEGONIAS. These are found in all three continental areas. All may be grown in a free-draining, friable, soilless medium with a pH of 6.0–7.0, ideally rich in leafmould, composted bark, coir and charcoal and/or perlite. The Chinese species will accept low temperatures and are hardy in many areas. *B.grandis* ssp. *evansiana* has pink or white flowers in late summer and after flowering produces axillary bulbils. These bulbils, if started into growth the next spring, will form flowering plants in that year. This subspecies may be treated as a hardy herbaceous perennial, given the shelter of a wall. Some of the Mexican species like *B.gracilis* produce minute bulbils in large clusters enclosed in papery bracts in the leaf axils, and these usually need an extra season of growth before flowering. If grown in pots, these tuberous types need bright filtered light in the greenhouse with good air circulation to avoid powdery mildew. They should not be allowed to dry out after starting into growth. After flowering and harvesting of any bulbils, the tubers are stored dry in their pots with a winter minimum temperature of 7°C/45°F, and are repotted in spring with the first signs of growth. Bulbils should be sown on the surface of a pot or tray of damp, sifted potting medium at a temperature of 7–10°C/45–50°F and potted individually when growth starts.

B.sutherlandii from Natal, a beautiful orange-flowered species, also forms bulbils in the leaf axils after flowering. These develop tiny leaves as they mature but do not grow continuously; they should be stored in dry, frost-free conditions over winter. This species makes a good basket plant for summer use and may continue outdoors in a lightly shaded position until the first frost.

The South Asian species mostly require temperatures of 22–25°C/72–77°F and high humidity. In such tropical conditions, a very free-draining potting medium is needed. A mixture of chopped live sphagnum moss and coarse grit, with a few chopped, well-rotted oak leaves, is quite suitable. Only a medium light intensity is required, so terrarium culture is ideal. *B.picta* and *B.josephi* have beautiful foliage and rival the finer varieties of the non-tuberous *B.rex*. The old tubers of *B.picta* send out numerous thread-like runners which form small tubercles at their ends.

The tuberous species from Central America were introduced in the late 1800s and are not often seen today; these include *B.boliviensis*, *B.veitchii* and *B.davisii*. Intense hybridization, mainly by Veitch & Sons in England in the 19th century, resulted in many hybrids, the first of which was *B.'Sedenii'*. These hybrids formed the basis of the modern large-flowered hybrids so beloved of the specialist grower, and which exist in a vast range of flower colour and form, some producing flowers as large as 25cm/10in. across. Tubers may be started into growth on trays of moist coir or sawdust in early spring in a shaded greenhouse at a temperature of 15°C/60°F, placing the tubers with the convex side downwards. Once started into growth, pot into normal begonia medium, increasing the pot size at each move to a maximum of about 20cm/8in. and staking the plants as required. Keep the plants well spaced in the greenhouse and open the ventilators as much as possible to give maximum air circulation. Three flower buds will be seen to appear from each axil. Of these, the two outer female buds should be removed, leaving the central male to develop to its full potential. Because of its weight, careful staking may be needed for each bloom. Bright filtered light is needed. Specialists growing these plants for exhibition restrict growth to a single stem, usually retaining only three buds, and feed the plants intensively. Some of the smaller-flowered forms may be used as summer bedding plants in the garden in lightly shaded positions.

Some tuberous hybrids, developed from the red-flowered *B.boliviensis*, are trailing or scandent and make excellent basket plants for summer decoration in the greenhouse or garden. They are very floriferous and are available in red, pink, white, orange and yellow.

All tuberous types need to be dried off in autumn when flowering ceases and the foliage begins to die down. Once the foliage and stems have fallen away, the tubers need to be stored dry at 5–7°C/40–45°F, either in their pots or in boxes of sawdust after having been cleaned of all old planting medium. Before storing, dust the tubers with flowers of sulphur to ward off fungus. Storage temperature is 5–7°C/40–45°F. Propagation is most easily carried out as the tubers come into growth in the spring. Any excess growths that are produced from the tubers may be easily detached using a sideways pressure, and can be potted individually to grow on and form their own small tubers. Stem cuttings may also be taken during the summer months.

The latest introduction in tuberous begonias is the 'Non Stop' range, generally raised from seed sown in early spring at 25°C/77°F, to flower throughout the summer as a potplant or bedding plant in the garden. They are very floriferous, compact, and available in a wide range of colours, the individual flowers are some 5cm/2in. across. These are so easily raised from seed that tuber storage is scarcely worthwhile.

SEMI-TUBEROUS BEGONIAS Typically dwarf, shrubby plants from Africa, mostly with partite leaves and white flowers. The potting medium should consist of equal parts coir or leafmould, loam-based mix such as John Innes No.3, and coarse grit. Water moderately and feed at every other watering during the summer, in a moderate light. They stop producing flowers as the daylength decreases in autumn, after which the leaves and most of the smaller stems drop, leaving a thickened, tapering caudex partly above soil level. Watering should be reduced as this takes place. When all the foliage has fallen, store the pots dry over winter at a minimum temperature of 7°C/45°F. Repot when growth in spring recommences. Propagate by stem cuttings during summer. *B.× weltoniensis* is a pink-flowered hybrid between *B.dregei* and *B.sutherlandii*, and falls into this group. *B.dregei* is a somewhat variable, white-flowered species 30–80cm/12–30in. tall, its leaves maple-shaped, bronze-green with a red spot at the sinus. *B.partita* is a very densely branched shrub to 30cm/12in. high with deeply divided, 3cm/1in. green leaves, while *B.suffruticosa* bears deeply cut leaves on red petioles from red stems.

RIEGER BEGONIAS In 1891, Lemoine in France crossed *B.socotrana* with *B.dregei* to give *B.*'Gloire de Lorraine', the varieties of which were used extensively for many years as winter-flowering potplants. They need very careful cultivation and are not often seen today. At about the same time, in England, John Heal of Veitch & Sons crossed *B.socotrana* with a red tuberous hybrid to give *B.*'John Heal', the ancestor of the Optima or Hiemalis range of winter-flowering hybrids. These had larger flowers and a wide range of colours, but were rather straggling in growth. In 1955, Rieger in West Germany successfully improved the Optima hybrids. His efforts resulted in the range of Rieger begonias that are grown commercially on an enormous scale as flowering potplants for the home.

They are bushy plants, freely branching from the base, and are available in a wide range of colours, both single- and double-flowered. In summer, they need bright filtered light, and in winter the maximum light available. The optimum temperature range is 15–20°C/60–68°F. Higher temperatures tend to reduce flower production and give more foliage. Water with a systemic fungicide to prevent powdery mildew, and give good air circulation at all times, with a low relative humidity. Propagation is most easily carried out in summer, preferably using a plant that has gone past its peak of flower production. At this time, a number of strong basal shoots will be found, and if the plant is tipped out of its pot and the compost carefully removed these may be teased apart, some with roots already formed, to be potted into pots of the final medium.

B.× bertinii hort. ex Legros. See *B.× intermedia* 'Bertinii'.
B.bicolor Wats. See *B.gracilis*.

B.biserrata Lindl. (*B.palmaris* A. DC.).
Tuberous. Stems erect, tall. Lvs orbicular, to 20cm, palmately-lobed, lobes triangular, acute, or once-cleft between apex and base, margin toothed, ciliate, green, hairy above and on veins beneath. Fls in dense axillary cymes, not exceeding lvs; tepals white, serrate. S Mexico, Guatemala.

B.bogneri Ziesenh.
Tuberous. Stems fine. Lvs 120–150×2mm, crowded, filiform, linear, green glossy above, pale below; margin with occasional teeth; petiole 1–4cm; stipules 2–4mm, triangular, pink at first. Infl. few-fld, protandrous; male fls 4 tepals, obovate, outer pair pale pink, to 10mm, inner pair white, to 9mm, stamens 10–13, united at base; female flowers 6 tepals in 2 whorls of 3, outer whorl pink, to 6.5mm, inner whorl white-pink, to 9mm. Fr. to 1cm. Autumn–winter. Madagascar.

B.caffra Meissn. See *B.homonyma*.
B.× camelliiflora hort. See *B.*Tuberhybrida Hybrids, Camellia Group.
B.capensis hort. See *B.sutherlandii*.

B.× cheimantha Everett ex C. Weber. (*B.dregei × B.socotrana*.) CHRISTMAS BEGONIA; BLOOMING-FOOL BEGONIA; LORRAINE BEGONIA.
Roots semi-tuberous to fibrous. Stems annual, herbaceous, branching. Lvs suborbicular, base usually cordate, margin toothed, green. Fls in loose cyme exceeding lvs; peduncles, pedicels and bracts pink; fls large, generally pink, male except for terminal fl.; tepals 4. Winter. Cultivated origin, 19th century.

B.cinnabarina Hook.
Tuberous. Stems to 60cm, erect, few-branched. Lvs 10–20cm diam., obliquely ovate, palmately nerved, hairy, margin lobed, serrate; petiole 8–17cm; stipules ovate. Infl. 2–6-fld; fls fragrant, orange-red; male tepals 4, 25mm, broad-ovate, stamens very numerous; female tepals 5, 25–30mm, styles 3, bilobed. Capsule wings 3, very unequal. Summer–autumn. Peru, Bolivia.

B.× crispa hort. See *B.*Tuberhybrida Hybrids, Crispa Group.
B.crispamarginata hort. See *B.*Tuberhybrida Hybrids, Marginata Group.
B.× cristata hort. non Koord. See *B.*Tuberhybrida Hybrids, Cristata Group.

B.davisii Veitch ex Hook. f. DAVIS BEGONIA.
Tuberous, acaulescent. Lvs spreading, obliquely ovate, to 10cm, base cordate, membranous, margin crenate, sparsely hairy, glossy dark green above, crimson beneath. Infl. an erect umbel; peduncle to 10cm, peduncle and pedicels bright red; fls 6, bright red; tepals 4 in male fls, 5 in females; ovary wings unequal. Summer. Peru. Ancestor of some tuberous hybrids.

B.diversifolia Graham. See *B.gracilis*.

B.dregei Otto & A. Dietr. (*B.parvifolia* Graham, non Schott or Klotzsch).
GRAPE-LEAF BEGONIA; MAPLE-LEAF BEGONIA. Tuberous or semituberous, glabrous throughout. Stems of annual duration, to 1m, succulent. Lvs ovate or rhombic, to 7.5cm, membranous, margin shallowly lobed and dentate, pale green with grey spots and purple veins above, dull red beneath. Peduncles axillary; fls few, white, 1.5cm across. Summer. S Africa. 'Macbethii': low and fine; lvs small, very notched to lobed, veins green. 'Macbethii Obtusa': as 'Macbethii', but denser and lacking green veins. *B.suffruticosa* Meissn., a smaller plant with lvs more finely lobed and toothed with a red spot at the sinus of the lobes and fls white to pale pink, is probably a variety of this species.

B.× elatior hort. See *B.× hiemalis*.
B.evansiana Andrews. See *B.grandis* ssp. *evansiana*.
B.× fimbriata hort. non *B.fimbriata* Liebm. See *B.*Tuberhybrida Hybrids, Fimbriata Group.
B.× floribunda hort. See *B.*Tuberhybrida Hybrids, Multiflora Group.

B.froebelii A. DC.
Tuberous. Lvs numerous, orbicular, 15–30×7.5–20cm, acuminate, base cordate, margin shallowly toothed, bright green above, red beneath, with fleshy purple hairs above and

beneath. Peduncles erect, red, exceeding lvs; fls in pendent cymes, vivid crimson or scarlet, to 5cm across; tepals 4 in male fls, ovate, females with 5, smaller than males; ovary lanuginose. Late summer–winter. Ecuador.

B.×gigantea hort. non **B.gigantea** Wallich. See B.Tuberhybrida Hybrids, Single Group.

B.gracilis HBK (*B.bicolor* Wats.; *B.diversifolia* Graham). HOLLYHOCK BEGONIA.
Tuberous; tuber round, grey. Stems erect, 60–100cm, succulent, usually unbranched, glabrous. Lvs orbicular to lanceolate, small, succulent, margin crenate, pale green; bulbils present in axils. Peduncles short, axillary; fls pink, to 3cm across; males with 2 tepals large, obovate, serrate, 2 small, females with 5, small. Summer. var. *martiana* A. DC. (*B.martiana* Link & Otto). Stems 30–45cm. Lvs obliquely cordate, to 15cm, margin entire. Fls to 5cm across, fragrant; tepals entire. Mexico, Guatemala.

B.grandis Dryand. ssp. *evansiana* (Andrews) Irmsch. (*B.evansiana* Andrews). HARDY BEGONIA
Tuberous. Stems erect, 60–100cm, annual, branched, red, glabrous. Lvs obliquely ovate, large, acuminate, base cordate, margin shallowly lobed, red-hairy, copper-green above with veins red, red beneath. Fls in dichotomous pendent cymes, fragrant, pink or white, to 3cm across; tepals in male fls 4, unequal, 2 in females; ovary pink, 3-winged. Summer. Malaysia to China and Japan 'Alba': fls white. 'Claret Jug': lvs flushed red beneath; fls pink. 'Simsii': fls large. Z7.

B.hemsleyana Hook. f.
Tuberous. Stems erect, to 45cm, branches few, succulent, sparsely hairy, rose pink. Lvs orbicular in outline, 10–12.5cm across, palmately lobed, lobes 7–9, lanceolate, acuminate, margin irregularly serrate, bright green above with margin red when young; petiole to 10cm. Fls light pink, to 43.5cm; male and female in distinct cymes. Summer. China (Hunan).

B.× hiemalis Fotsch (*B.× elatior* hort.). (*B.socotrana* × B.× *tuberhybrida*.) WINTER-FLOWERING BEGONIAS.
Roots fibrous, tubers absent, but tending to die back to swollen bases and become dormant in winter. Lvs asymmetric, green to bronze. Fls single or double, white to pink, yellow, orange or red. Winter or year-round. Garden origin.

B.homonyma Steud. (*B.caffra* Meissn.).
Close to *B.dregei*. Stem to 1m, fleshy, branched. Lvs asymmetrically reniform-cordate, 5–6.5×7.5–10cm, acute or acuminate, margin angular, serrate, red-veined beneath; petiole to 7.5cm. Fls 4 in dichotomous cymes, white; ovary wings subequal. S Africa.

B.× intermedia hort. Veitch ex Van Houtte (*B.boliviensis* × *B.veitchii*.)
Close to *B.boliviensis*, differing in fls larger, light scarlet, more erect. 'Bertinii' (*B.× bertinii* hort. ex Legros). (*B.boliviensis* × B.× *intermedia*.) Tuberous. Stems several, to 30cm. Lvs obliquely ovate-lanceolate, to 12.5cm, margin dentate, hairy above and beneath. Fls many, in pairs on long pendulous peduncles, to 3cm across, vermilion. Bertinii Hybrids derived from this, correctly placed in Tuberhybrida Hybrids, Multiflora Group. Summer.

B.josephi A. DC.
Tuberous; acaulescent. Lvs peltate, ovate-acuminate, to 15cm, or 3-lobed, or orbicular with many acute lobes, margin serrate to almost entire, usually glabrous, occasionally sparsely hairy. Peduncle to 30cm, much-branched; fls numerous, to 1.5cm across, pink. Himalaya (C Nepal to Bhutan).

B.× lloydii hort. See B.Tuberhybrida Hybrids, Pendula Group.

B.ludwigii Irmsch.
Roots fibrous. Stems to 1m, very thick, swollen at base. Lvs suborbicular in outline, to 35cm across, shallowly palmately divided, lobes c7, acuminate, margin doubly serrate, white-hispid above and beneath, green with veins red at sinus above; petiole with band of hairs at apex. Peduncles 45–90cm, streaked white; fls many, cream-white with green

and pink marks externally, to 2.5cm across; tepals rounded, with margins undulate when young, 4 in male fls, 5 in females. Spring–summer. Ecuador.

B.× marginata hort. See B.Tuberhybrida Hybrids, Marginata Group.

B.× marmorata hort. See B.Tuberhybrida Hybrids, Marmorata Group.

B.martiana Link & Otto. See *B.gracilis* var. *martiana*.

B.× maxima hort. See B.Tuberhybrida Hybrids, Multiflora Group.

B.micranthera Griseb.
Tuberous. Variable; stems erect, to 50cm, branching or unbranched. Lvs obliquely ovate, to 30cm, acuminate, base cordate, shallowly lobed, hairy, margin serrate, ciliate. Peduncles erect; fls 2–3, white or pale pink, to 2.5cm across; ovary wings unequal, 1 large, 2 small. Argentina, S Bolivia.

B.× multiflora hort. See B.Tuberhybrida Hybrids, Multiflora Group.

B.× narcissiflora hort. See B.Tuberhybrida Hybrids, Narcissiflora Group.

B.octopetala L'Hérit.
Tuberous, stemless. Lvs cordate, to 20cm, lobed, toothed; petioles 30–45cm, stout, fleshy. Fls ivory-white, in 6–20-fld corymbs; peduncles 2.5–5cm; tepals 6–10 in male fls, 5–7.5cm wide (smaller in females), 6 in female fls; ovary 3-angled, 3-winged, wings unequal. Autumn–winter. Peru.

B.palmaris A. DC. See *B.biserrata*.

B.partita Irmsch.
Small and shrubby. Stem strongly swollen and rather tuberous or caudiciform at base; branches short and intricate. Lvs 5–8cm, maple-like (i.e. acuminately and palmately lobed and cut), pewter grey. Fls small, white. S Africa.

B.parvifolia Graham, non Schott or Klotzsch. See *B.dregei*.

B.× pendula hort. non *B.pendula* Ridl. See B.Tuberhybrida Hybrids, Pendula Group.

B.picta Sm.
Tuberous. Stem to 38cm. Lvs ovate, 7.5–12.5×5–7.5cm, acuminate, base cordate, margin finely biserrate, pilose above where dark green mottled with white and purple-bronze, villous on veins beneath; petiole long. Peduncle short; fls pink, 2–3cm across, fragrant; tepals in male fls 4, unequal, in females 5, equal; ovary pubesc. with 3 unequal wings. Summer or year-round. Himalaya (Pakistan to Bhutan).

B.rosiflora Hook. f. See *B.veitchii*.

B.× rosiflora hort. non *B.rosiflora* Hook. f. See B.Tuberhybrida Hybrids, Rosiflora Group.

B.sikkimensis A. DC.
Tuberous; tuber woody. Stems erect, to 45cm. Lvs weakly asymmetric, round in outline, 10–15cm across, weakly cordate, 5–7-lobed nearly to base, with lobes further incised, margin denticulate-ciliate, glabrous; petiole to 10cm, glabrous. Peduncles to 23cm; pedicels, bracts and fls bright red; fls few, to 2.5cm across; males with tepals 4, females 5. Sikkim. 'Gigantea': habit large. 'Variegata' ('Maculata'): lvs splotched.

B.socotrana Hook. f.
Semituberous. Stems annual, to 30cm, slender, sparsely branched, succulent, bearing fleshy bulb-like buds at base. Lvs peltate, orbicular, 10–25cm across, depressed in centre, margin recurved, crenate, dark green. Peduncles slender, axillary; fls few, rose-pink, 3.5–5cm across; male fls with 5 subequal tepals; females with tepals 5–6, equal, solitary and terminal in infl.; ovary green, 3-angled, one forming long wing. Winter. Socotra. Parent of many important winter-flowering hybrids.

B.suffruticosa Meissn. See under *B.dregei*.

B.sutherlandii Hook. f.
Tuberous. Stems annual, 10–80cm, trailing, red. Lvs lanceolate, 10–15cm, deeply serrate, green with margin and veins

red, pubesc. beneath; petioles slender, red. Peduncles pendulous: fls in axillary or terminal cymes, few, 2–2.5cm across, orange to orange-red; tepals 4 in male fls, unequal, 5 in females, equal; ovary wings 3, equal. Summer. Natal to Tanzania.

B.× tuberhybrida Voss. See B.Tuberhybrida Hybrids.

B.× tuberosa hort. (non *B.tuberosa Lam.*). See B.Tuberhybrida Hybrids.

B.Tuberhybrida Hybrids (*B.× tuberhybrida* Voss; *B.× tuberosa* hort. (non *B.tuberosa* Lam.).). HYBRID TUBEROUS BEGONIAS.
Many cvs derived from hybrids chiefly between the Andean spp. *B.boliviensis, B.clarkei, B.davisii, B.pearcei, B.veitchii* and possibly also *B.froebelii* and *B.gracilis*. Very variable. Tuberous; tubers large, often concave above. Stems absent or present and erect to pendulous, to 60cm, fleshy, usually hairy. Fls in axillary clusters, usually of 3, with one male between 2 females, or paired; males to 15cm across, single or double, females smaller, single; colours various, pink to dark red, white, yellow or orange, or bicoloured; tepals sometimes fimbriate, sometimes fragrant. Summer. Divided into 13 groups. (1) Single Group: fls large, tepals 4, usually flat. (2) Crispa or Frilled Group: fls large, single, tepals frilled and ruffled. (3) Cristata or Crested Group: fls large, single, with frilled outgrowth in centre of tepal. (4) Narcissiflora or Daffodil-flowered Group: fls large, double, central tepals spreading-erect, resembling corona of *Narcissus*. (5) Camellia or Camelliiflora Group: fls large, double, tepals regular, resembling a *Camellia* flower; self-coloured, not ruffled or fimbriate. (6) Ruffled Camellia Group: as (5) but fls with tepals ruffled. (7) Rosiflora or Rosebud Group: fls large, with centre resembling rose-bud. (8) Fimbriata Plena or Carnation Group: fls large, double, tepals fimbriate. (9) Picotee Group: fls large, usually double, camellia-shaped, with tepals edged with different shade or colour, or merging with main colour. (10) Marginata Group: fls as in (9), precisely edged with distinct colour. (11) Marmorata Group: fls as in (5), pink, marbled with white. (12) Pendula or Hanging-basket Group: stems trailing or pendulous; fls many, small to large, single or double. (13) Multiflora Group: plants low, bushy, compact; fls many, small, single to double.

B.veitchii Hook. (*B.rosiflora* Hook.f.).
Tuberous. Stem 30–75cm, short. Lvs 5–10cm, broadly ovate-cordate or reniform, dark green, near glabrous above, glaucous, hairy beneath, margin lobed, serrate; petiole 3–12cm, stout; stipules red, triangular. Infl. 2–4-fld; fls bright scarlet, fragrant; male tepals 4, broad ovate-elliptic, 2–3cm, stamens very numerous, free; female tepals similar to male. Capsule wings 3, largest 2–3× wider than others. Summer. Peru.

B.× weltoniensis hort. ex André. (*B.dregei* × *B.sutherlandii*.)
MAPLE-LEAF BEGONIA; GRAPEVINE BEGONIA.
Tuberous or semituberous. Stems to 1m, swollen at base, branched, red. Lvs ovate, to 7.5cm across, acuminate, shal-lowly-lobed, margin dentate, dark glossy green veined purple above, pale green beneath. Peduncles short; fls many, white or pink. Garden origin. 'Alba': fls white.

B.wollnyi Herzog.
Semituberous. Stems erect, to 30cm+, thick. Lvs large, deeply palmately lobed, margin biserrate, dark green with irregular white markings between veins. Fls with tepals green-white, ovary green-white. Winter. Bolivia.

B.cultivars
(1) *Semituberous* 'Richard Robinson' (lvs pleated, marked silver, fls white) and 'Speckled Roundabout' (lvs spiralled, pleated, deep bronze dotted silver; fls soft pink and white).
(2) *Species and first generation Hybrids* low-growing: 'Lulandii' (lvs pointed, deeply cut, bright green; fls large, pink, abundant); tall-growing: 'Torsa' (fls pink).
(3) *Tuberhybrida*, including the large-flowered single 'Bonfire' (lvs bronze; fls bright red); Crispa Marginata 'Thelma' (fls pink, edges frilly, darker); large-flowered double 'Allan Langdon' (fls deep cardinal red, abundant), 'Bernat Klein' (fls fully double, pure white, tepals slightly waved), 'Buttermilk' (fls large, cream flushed pinky apricot), 'Elaine Tarttelin' (fls deep rose pink, abundant), 'Tahiti' (fls coral orange), 'Roy Hartley' (fls salmon rose, abundant), 'Sweet Dreams' (fls soft pink), 'Falstaff' (fls rich rose pink); Picotee 'Bali Hi' (fls pale cream edged raspberry red), 'Fairylight' (fls milky white finely edged coral pink), 'Jean Blair' (fls yellow edged bright red), 'Saturn' (fls salmon-orange with darker edge); Ruffled Picotee 'Santa Teresa' (fls white, ruffle-edged pink); Grandiflora Compacta Champion Series (fls abundant, range of colours); Maxima 'Switzerland' (fls dark red, abundant); Multiflora 'Madame Richard Galle' (fls orange, abundant), 'Kupfergold' (fls copper-gold, abundant), 'Queen Fabiola' (fls rich soft red, abundant); pendula 'Jo Rene' (fls crimson to pink; abundant), 'Orange Cascade' (fls yellow flushed burnt apricot, abundant), 'Trisha' (fls picotee, yellow edged apricot, abundant); Fimbriata 'Pink Princess' (fls pale pink), 'Santa Barbara' (fls bright yellow); 'Bertinii' (fls red, abundant).
(4) *Hiemalis and Hiemalis-like*, including Aphrodite Series (fls double, everblooming, abundant, in rose, pink, peach and red), 'Bolero' (fls double, orange, everblooming, abundant), 'Fantasy' (lvs very dark, finely cut; fls deep vivid pink, everblooming, abundant), 'Man's Favorite' (fls single, white), 'Renaissance' (lvs deeply cut; fls double, frilled, dark coral red, frilled, everblooming, abundant), 'Schwabenland Orange' (bushy; lvs metallic green; fls bright apricot, abundant).
(5) *Cheimantha and Cheimantha-like*, including 'Love Me' (fls vivid lilac-pink, abundant), 'Marjorie Gibbs' (lvs round, dark matt green; fls pink, very abundant), 'White Marina' (vigorous; lvs light green; fls large, white edged soft pink).

Belamcanda Adans. (Latinized form of the Sanskrit name *mālālkanda*.) Iridaceae. 2 species of short-lived perennial herbs, resembling *Iris* in habit, to 1m. Leaves borne in fans on branching stems. Flowers with 6 equal perianth segments (unlike the falls and standards of *Iris*); style 3, slender, with a terminal stigma; stamens free. Fruit a capsule; the capsules split open and the 3 locules curl outwards, exposing large, black seeds. Eurasia. Z8.

CULTIVATION *B.chinensis* is an attractive but short-lived, summer-flowering perennial bearing deep yellow or orange iris-like blooms, spotted red or deep purple at their base, above a fan of deciduous sword-shaped leaves. The individual flowers last only for a day but are produced in succession, the petals twisting as they fade. The seed pods split open in autumn to reveal the shining black seeds, and are sometimes used in winter arrangements. Given the protection of a deep dry mulch in winter, *B.chinensis* is hardy in zones where winter temperature drop to −15°C/5°F, perhaps slightly lower, and is used in the flower border and informal plantings. Grow in sun or light shade in any well-drained and moderately fertile soil, with additional organic matter to ensure ample moisture during the growing period. Propagate in spring by seed, which should germinate within three weeks and produce plants that will flower in their second year; also by division in spring or early autumn.

B.chinensis (L.) DC. (*Pardanthus chinensis* (L.) Ker-Gawl.).
BLACKBERRY LILY; LEOPARD LILY.
Rhiz. slender, stoloniferous. Lvs to 20×1.5cm. Infl. to 1m, loosely branched; fls to 12, 4cm diam., yellow to tangerine, spotted maroon or purple; tube absent. Summer. E Russia, India, China, Japan. Leopard Lily Hybrids: fls purple, lilac, salmon, pink, orange and yellow, variously flecked and speckled.

Bellevalia Lapeyr. (For Pierre Richer de Belleval (1564–1632), who founded the Montpellier Botanic Garden in 1593.) Liliaceae (Hyacinthaceae). Some 45 species of perennial herbs. Bulbs tunicate. Leaves 2 or more, basal, with membranous, ciliate or scabrous margins. Flowers bisexual, radially or slightly bilaterally symmetric, nodding or horizontal, campanulate, funnelform or tubular, white, lilac or violet, fading to brown, borne in racemes which emerge between the leaves, subtended by very small, 2-lobed bracts; perianth deeply 6-lobed, occasionally closed at mouth; stamens 6, at the base of the tepals, inserted, filaments flat, broadly to narrowly triangular, shortly basally united; ovary 3-celled, with 2–6 ovules per cell; style single. Fruit a 3-lobed, apically obtuse, conspicuously ribbed, loculicidal capsule; with a waxy bloom; seeds blue-tinged or black, smooth, dull. Mediterranean, Black Sea, Turkestan, NE Afghanistan.

CULTIVATION As for *Muscari*.

B.atroviolacea Reg.
8–30cm. Lvs 3–6, as long as or exceeding scape, glaucous, slightly channelled and wavy, margins shortly ciliate or rough margins, outer 2cm wide. Racemes densely conical 3–6cm, becoming longer and looser in fr.; pedicels much shorter than perianth at flowering, to 2cm in fr.; fls 8–9mm, campanulate, erect in bud, overlapping and sharply nodding when open, tinged black-violet. Russia, NE Afghanistan. Z7.

B.azurea (Fenzl) Boiss. See *Muscari azureum*.

B.ciliata (Cyr.) Nees (*Hyacinthus ciliatus* Cyr.).
To 50cm. Lvs usually 3–5, to 30×3cm, lanceolate, with strongly ciliate margins, shiny. Racemes broadly conical, very loose, 10–12cm in flower, to 15×20cm in fruit; pedicels erect in bud stage, spreading to falcate during flowering, becoming straighter and horizontal; fls 9–11mm, narrow-campanulate, perianth tube brown or lilac, lobes white or green-tinted. Fr. 1.5–2cm×8mm, oblong, apex serrulate, base shortly tapered. NW Africa, S Europe, W Asia Minor. Z7.

B.dubia (Guss.) Rchb. (*Hyacinthus dubius* Guss.).
To 40cm. Lvs 2–5, channelled, trailing, outer to 1.5cm wide, margins glabrous. Racemes loose, narrow-cylindric; pedicels erect in young bud, as long as perianth in fl., spreading and then falcate, almost horizontal in fr. and then about as long as fr.; fls 6–8mm, ellipsoid to weakly campanulate, bright violet-blue with green tips in bud, perianth tube turning brown with yellow-tinted lobes when open. Fr. obovoid, 6–10mm. Portugal, Sicily to Balkan Peninsula, W Turkey. Z7.

B.flexuosa Boiss.
To 50cm. Lvs 4 or 5, usually exceeding scape, to 1.5cm wide, trailing, wavy, or in shade to 3cm wide, occasionally erect, not wavy, margins shortly ciliate or scabrous. Racemes loose, to 5cm wide in fruit, becoming cylindric; pedicels 8–20mm,

spreading or falcate in flower, ascending or horizontal in fr.; fls 7–8mm, occasionally to 10mm, widely campanulate, or broadly obconical, white in bud with green veins, sometimes tinged lilac, perianth tube becoming purple-brown when open. Fr. round or ovoid, 8–10mm. Syria, Israel, Egypt. Z8.

B.hyacinthoides (Bertero) Persson & Wendelbo (*Hyacinthus spicatus* Sibth. & Sm. non Moench; *Strangweja spicata* (Sibth. & Sm.) Boiss.).
To 15cm. Lvs 4–8, somewhat fleshy, produced in autumn, trailing, far exceeding raceme, slightly channelled, glaucous above, with shortly ciliate margins, to 5.5mm wide, narrowed at base. Racemes dense, spike-like ellipsoid to cylindric, fls 6–12, 7–12mm, campanulate, horizontal or turned upwards, perianth tube one-third to half as long as lobes, very pale blue with deeper blue to purple-blue veins; pedicels not developed; fil. very short, prominently toothed on either side at base, anth. exposed. Fr. ovoid, serrulate, to 7mm; seeds pyriform. Greece. Z8.

B.longipes Post.
Close to *B.ciliata* but lvs 3–4 with glabrous margins, fruiting raceme to 30cm wide, and pedicels becoming falcate, horizontal, or ascending immediately after anthesis. Turkey to Iran. Z8.

B.pycnantha (K. Koch) A. Los. (*Muscari pycnanthum* K. Koch; *Muscari paradoxum* misapplied).
To 40cm. Lvs 3, far exceeding scape, channelled, dark green, glaucous above, with glabrous margins, outer to 2.5cm wide. Racemes densely conical with overlapping fls, becoming ellipsoid or cylindric and loose; fls to 6mm, nodding, irregularly urceolate, lobes somewhat folded, blue-black, green-yellow on edges and inner surfaces; pedicels about as long as fls, concealed in young racemes, to 1.5cm in fr. Fr. round, 8mm diam., apex serrulate. Russia, E Turkey. Z7.

B.romana (L.) Rchb. (*Hyacinthus romanus* L.).
To 30cm. Bulb large. Lvs 3 to 6, exceeding the scape, more or less erect, somewhat fleshy, channelled with glabrous margins, outer to 1.5cm wide. Racemes loose, oblong or ovoid in flower, to 4cm wide, cylindric in fr., not widening; fls 20–30, 8–10mm, widely campanulate or broadly obconical, white becoming tinged green, violet, or brown; anth. blue-black, conspicuous. Fr. ellipsoid, 1–1.5cm. C & S Mediterranean, S France. Z7.

B.saviczii Woron. (*Hyacinthus saviczii* (Woron.) Vved.).
To 40cm. Lvs 3–6, 15–25cm, outer 5–20mm wide, oblong-lanceolate, glaucous above, margins shortly ciliate to scabrous. Racemes cylindric-oblong to ovate, becoming broadly conical in fruit, to 15×12cm; fls 15–30, 7–10mm, campanulate white, becoming grey-brown to pale grey-green; pedicels widely spreading at anthesis, falcate thereafter. Fr. obovate-oblong, 1–1.5cm, apex somewhat serrulate. Afghanistan, E & S Iran, adjacent Russia. Z7.

B.warburgii Feinbrun.
To 60cm. Lvs 3–6, shorter than scape, to 3.5cm wide, margins shortly ciliate or rough. Racemes loose, soon becoming cylindric, 7–11cm wide; pedicels 1–1.5cm, ascending in bud, becoming falcate in fl. and young fr., to 5cm in fr., eventually almost straight; fls 1–1.5cm, narrow-campanulate, white, veined green in bud, perianth tube becoming purple-brown when open. Fr. ovoid, to 1cm. Israel. Z8.

Bessera Schult. (For Dr W.S.J.G. von Besser (1784–1842), Professor of Botany at Brody.) Liliaceae (Alliaceae). 1–2 species of cormous perennials, 70–100cm, resembling *Nothoscordum* but flowers pendent, stamens exserted, staminal tube toothed at apex. Corm 2–3cm diam., globose, tunic membranous. Leaves basal, narrow-linear, concave-convex in section or terete. Inflorescence a long-stalked, terminal umbel subtended by 3–4 spreading spathe valves; flowers drooping; perianth campanulate to cylindric, tepals 3–4cm, 6, exterior scarlet to purple veined green, often only at midvein, interior ivory with margins and midvein scarlet; stamens 6, purple, exserted, united to the middle or at the base; ovary superior, trilocular. Fruit a capsule; seeds black, flattened. Mexico. Z8.

CULTIVATION With protection from frost, *Bessera* may be grown at the base of a warm south-facing wall, although in cooler regions it is more safely grown in the cool glasshouse or conservatory. Cultivate as for *Baeometra*.

B.elegans Schult. CORAL DROPS.
To 90cm. Lvs 60–80cm. Infl. 2–30-fld.

Biarum Schott. (Name used by Dioscorides for similar plant.) Araceae. About 15 species of low-growing tuberous perennials. Tuber depressed-globose or discoid, rooting around growing point. Leaves emerging from conspicuous, scarious cataphylls, hysteranthous, entire, ovate or elliptic to linear, petiolate. Peduncle very short, largely subterranean; spathe tubular at base, more or less inflated, dilated as an erect or incurved limb above, sometimes reflexed with age, oblong to oblong-lanceolate, ochre to purple-black (especially on limb and in tube above, i.e. the upper and inner surfaces), withering before fruit ripens; spadix with zones of male and female flowers, separated by rudimentary filamentous sterile flowers, appendix long, foetid but sweet-scented at base, perianth absent, stamens 1–2(–3), ovary unilocular, ovule solitary. Fruit a globose cluster of white, pale green or orange berries, sometimes striped purple. Mediterranean, W Asia. Z8.

CULTIVATION *Biarum* spp. are grown for their fascinating but frequently malodorous inflorescence carried at soil level, usually before the foliage emerges and giving rise to berries which lie on the ground like clusters of small eggs. They will succeed in the alpine house, bulb frame or for the base of a south-facing wall. Where summers are dry, they can be grown on the rock garden. Provided they are not overwet, they will tolerate winter lows of –5°C/23°F. Plant 5cm/2in deep in light, fertile and perfectly drained soils; ensure a warm dry dormancy in summer to promote flowering. Propagate by seed sown in autumn or spring at 13°C/55°F, and prick out seedlings as soon as possible; also by division when dormant or by offsets. In addition to those listed below, *B.carratracense* (Haensl.) Font Quer and *B.syriacum* (Spreng.) Riedl are also cultivated.

B.bovei Bl.
Tuber 2.5×3.5cm, subglobose. Lvs 6–13.5×2–4cm, 5–10, broad-ovate to elliptic, lateral veins 7–9 pairs; petiole 8–23cm. Spathe tube 3–4cm, limb 6–11cm, elongate-lanceolate, brown-green beneath, brown-purple above; spadix to 14cm, female zone 5–10mm, sterile zone 20–25mm, male 8–10.5mm, appendix slender, to 3mm thick, stipe absent. Berries dull orange-red. Autumn. S Turkey, Lebanon, Israel.

B.carduchorum (Schott) Engl.
Tuber 2.5×4.5cm. Lvs 7.5–14×1.5–4cm, ovate to narrow-elliptic, subobtuse to subacute; petiole 9–22cm. Spathe tube to 6×1cm, narrow, cylindric, not inflated, exterior brown-purple or dull white, interior purple to deep purple-black, limb to 19×4cm, lanceolate, green beneath, deep black-purple above; spadix to 20cm, female zone 3.5–5mm, sterile 14–24mm, male 12–22mm, appendix to 17×0.35cm, stipitate. Late summer. Turkey to Iran.

B.davisii Turrill.
Tuber 2×3cm, hemispherical. Lvs 4–6.5×1.5–3cm, ovate to obovate-elliptic, obtuse, undulate, lateral veins 7–9 pairs; petiole to 9cm. Spathe to 8cm, green-white or cream spotted pink-brown or mauve, tube strongly ventricose, large, squat, limb triangular, acuminate, hooded, strongly incurved; spadix to 7.5cm, female zone 1mm, sterile 8–10mm, male 16mm, appendix to 5×0.05cm, dull red-brown, the colour deepening toward apex. Autumn. Crete, S Turkey.

B.eximium (Schott ex Kotschy) Engl.
Tuber 3×4cm. Lvs to 17×4cm, ovate-oblong to spathulate-elliptic, subobtuse, lateral veins 12 pairs; petiole to 14cm. Spathe tube 3–4cm, ventricose, margins overlapping only at base, exterior green, interior dark purple, limb to 9×4cm, oblong-ovate, becoming strongly recurved, dull purple with small spots beneath, dark purple-black above; spadix to 12cm, female zone 5mm, sterile 10–15mm, male 10–15mm,

appendix to 8×0.75cm, sessile, cylindric. Autumn. S Turkey.

B.pyrami (Schott) Engl.
Lvs 8–12×3–5cm, ovate-elliptic, obtuse, lateral vein pairs 10; petiole 10cm. Spathe tube 4–5cm, strongly ventricose to subspherical, margins united only at base, exterior green, interior lilac to dark purple, blotched orange, limb to 20×6cm, lanceolate, acuminate, becoming recurved, green-purple, blotched or suffused black-purple within; spadix to 25cm, female zone 3.5–5mm, sterile 10–15mm, male 10–15mm, appendix to 21×0.8cm, fusiform. Autumn. S Turkey to Iraq.

B.tenuifolium (L.) Schott.
Tuber to 3×5cm. Lvs 5–20×1–2cm, linear to oblong or spathulate, margin flat or undulate, lateral vein pairs 2–3,

base tapering gradually to petiole; petiole 6–18cm, or indistinct. Spathe green beneath, dark purple above, tube to 6cm, cylindric, margins fused, limb to 30cm, erect to recurved, lanceolate-acuminate; spadix to 35cm, strongly malodorous, female zone 3mm, lower sterile zone 21–23mm, upper above male fls 13–16mm, male zone 8–15mm, appendix to 30×0.4cm. exceeding spathe, sessile, purple-black. Autumn or rarely spring, when with lvs. Portugal to Turkey. var. **abbreviatum** (Schott) Engl. Generally smaller. Spathe limb to 10×5cm, short, wide, hooded, green; spadix appendix 10cm, emerging nearly horizontally. İtaly, Yugoslavia, N Greece.

Blandfordia Sm. (For George, Marquis of Blandford, patron of botany (1766–1840).) CHRISTMAS BELLS. Liliaceae (Blandfordiaceae). 4 species of erect, rhizomatous herbaceous perennials to 1m; roots fibrous. Leaves long, linear, grass-like, striate, triangular in section, radical leaves sheathing at base, cauline leaves shorter and more distant. Inflorescence a solitary, terminal raceme; pedicels recurved; flowers showy, red, orange or yellow; perianth funnelform to campanulate, lobes 6, short, overlapping; stamens 6, included, attached to inside of tube; ovary superior, 3-celled, stigma and style 1. Fruit an ovoid, 3-angled capsule; seeds many, brown, velvety. E Australia, Tasmania. Z9.

CULTIVATION *Blandfordia* spp. occur on sandy soils or moorland to altitudes of 1200m/3900ft in their native Tasmania and Australia. Grown for the umbels or racemes of tubular or bell-shaped flowers, in warm shades of yellow, orange and red, they are reliable outdoors only in regions where temperatures do not fall much below 5°C/40°F. They are well suited, however, to pot cultivation in the cold glasshouse or alpine house, kept frost-free in winter. Grow in direct sunlight in clay pots, with an acidic potting mix of equal parts peat or leafmould, silver sand and neutral loam. Keep completely dry over winter; soak thoroughly in early spring to initiate growth. Thereafter, water moderately (i.e. allow a slight drying between waterings), reducing the supplies once flowering is over and the foliage made up. Apply dilute liquid feed occasionally when in full growth. Repot in autumn. Propagate from seed in spring, or by offsets and division.

B.aurea Hook. f. See *B.grandiflora*.

B.cunninghamii Lindl.
To 85cm. Lvs 3.5–7×0.4–0.9cm, smooth-margined. Fls 5–20 in a dense raceme; bracts 1.5–5cm, equalling pedicels; perianth 4–5cm, tubular, copper red, stained red at base, lobes 3.5mm, obtuse, yellow; stamens joined to lower half of tube. Australia (NSW).

B.flammea Lindl. ex Paxt. See *B.grandiflora*.

B.grandiflora R. Br. (*B.flammea* Lindl. ex Paxt.; *B.aurea* Hook. f.; *B.princeps* W.G. Sm.).
To 60cm. Lvs 60–80×0.1–0.5cm, margins with minute rounded teeth. Fls 7–10 in a loose spike; pedicels 4–5.5cm, much longer than bracts; perianth 4–6cm, tubular to campanulate, red with yellow lobes to entirely yellow. Spring-early summer. Australia (Queensland, NSW). Hybrids occur between *B.grandiflora* and *B.nobilis*.

B.marginata Herb. See *B.punicea*.

B.nobilis Sm.
40–70cm. Lvs 40–80×0.1–0.5cm, crowded at base, margins very finely toothed. Fls 3–15 in a loose raceme; perianth 2–3×0.8–1.2cm, tube abruptly widening a third of the way from the base, copper red to orange, often stained yellow, to entirely yellow. Spring-early summer. Australia (NSW).

B.princeps W.G. Sm. See *B.grandiflora*.

B.punicea (Labill.) Sweet (*B.marginata* Herb.). TASMANIAN CHRISTMAS BELLS.
80–100cm. Lvs 70–90×0.8–1.2cm, somewhat ligulate, coriaceous, midrib prominent, margins finely toothed. Fls 15–25, in almost opposite pairs in a loose raceme; bracts 3–4; pedicels 2–5cm, as long as bracts; perianth tubular, tapering to base, pink-scarlet, interior yellow, lobes tipped golden yellow; stamens joined to tube above the middle. Summer. Tasmania.

Bloomeria Kellogg. (For H.G. Bloomer (1821–74), pioneer Californian botanist.) Liliaceae (Alliaceae). 3 species of bulbous perennial herbs, close to *Nothoscordum* and *Brodiaea*, differing from the former in the flowering stems geniculate toward the top and the filaments broadened at the base and forming a tunic around the ovary, and from the latter in the perianth segments being free to the base. Bulb tunics fibrous. Inflorescence a many-flowered, long-stemmed umbel, jointed toward top; perianth segments 6; filaments dilated at base to form a 2-toothed cup, enclosing ovary. SW US, Mexico. Z8.

CULTIVATION Grown for the long-stemmed, spherical heads of flowers in late spring, before becoming dormant in summer, *Bloomeria* spp. are tolerant of several degrees of frost and require treatment as for *Brodiaea*.

B.aurea Kellogg. See *B.crocea*.

B.crocea (Torr.) Cov. (*B.aurea* Kellogg).
Bulb *c*1cm diam. Lvs 30×1cm, solitary, linear. Flowering stems 15–30cm; infl. a many-fld umbel; perianth 2.5cm diam., rotate, seg. 8–12mm, spreading, golden yellow with a darker central stripe. Spring. S California, Baja California.

B.maritima Macbr. See *Muilla maritima*.

Bomarea Mirb. (For Jacques Christophe Valmont de Bomare (1731–1807), a French patron of science.) Liliaceae (Alstroemeriaceae). Over 100 species of rhizomatous perennial herbs. Roots slender with tubers borne at tips. Stems long, twining. Leaves cauline, usually lanceolate. Flowers in terminal, simple or compound umbels, long-stalked, drooping; perianth tubular-campanulate, tepals obovate to oblanceolate, equal or whorled in two unequal series; stamens 6, erect, borne at base of tepals and equal in length to them, anthers basifixed; style slender, 3-fid; ovary superior, 3-celled. Fruit a 3-celled capsule; seeds orange or red, numerous. S America. Z9.

CULTIVATION Grown for their handsome umbels of brightly coloured and beautifully marked flowers, *Bomarea* species are tuberous-rooted, vining perennials for the cool glasshouse or conservatory. In favoured areas in Zone 8 they might also be tried in a sheltered, moist and slightly acid border, where their vining stems could climb and seek shade in shrubs like *Crinodendron* and *Lomatia*. Protect crowns of plants grown outdoors with bracken and straw in winter. Pot-grown specimens may spend the summer out of doors if brought in before first frosts; the stems usually die back during winter, when plants should be kept cool, almost dry and frost free; cut back old flowered growth to ground level as the leaves begin to fade.

Under glass, grow with support of wire or trellis in a light, fertile, loam-based mix, rich in organic matter and with additional sharp sand. Provide good ventilation, a minimum temperature of 5–7°C/40–45°F, and admit full light or bright filtered light in high summer. Water plentifully and liquid feed when in full growth, withdrawing water gradually to keep almost dry in winter. Propagate by careful division or by seed, in a soilless propagating mix, potting on seedlings into individual pots at 5–8cm/2–3in. high; germination takes about three weeks at 18–23°C/65–75°F.

B.acutifolia (Link & Otto) Herb.
Close to *B.shuttleworthii*. Leaves lanceolate to ovate-lanceolate, pubescent on veins beneath; outer tepals red, not spotted.

B.caldasiana Herb. See *B.caldasii*.

B.caldasii (HBK) Asch. & Gräbn. (*B.caldasiana* Herb.; *B.kalbreyeri* hort.).
Stem to 4m. Leaves to 15 × 2.5cm, oblong-acute, almost glabrescent or puberulent beneath; petiole distinct. Flowers 20–60 in a simple umbel; tepals unequal, outer 2–2.5cm, dull orange-red to red-brown, inner 2.5–3.5cm, bright yellow to orange, occasionally flecked green, brown or red. Northern S America.

B.cardieri Mast.
Stem to 4m. Leaves to 18 × 7cm, oblong-lanceolate, acuminate. Flowers to 40; umbels compound; tepals 5.5–6.5cm, equal, outer pink, finely flecked mauve inside, with a short, green, horn-like projection on the back just below apex, inner pink, occasionally green, spotted mauve. Colombia.

B.conferta Benth. See *B.patacocensis*.

B.edulis (Tussac) Herb.
Leaves to 12.5 × 2.5cm, lanceolate, glabrous or puberulent beneath. Flowers in compound umbels; tepals nearly equal, 2.5–3cm, outer pink, inner bright green or yellow, spotted purple or dark pink. W Indies, C America, Northern S America.

B.frondea Mast.
Close to *B.patacocensis*, with outer tepals yellow, and inner tepals bright yellow, spotted dark red.

B.kalbreyeri hort. See *B.caldasii*.

B.multiflora (L.f.) Mirb.
Stem puberulent. Leaves to 10cm. Flowers 20–40, in simple umbels; tepals approximately 2.5cm, equal, outer tinged red, inner red-yellow with brown flecks. Northern S America.

B.oligantha Bak.
Similar to *B.multiflora* but with flowers 6–8 per umbel.

B.patacocensis Herb. (*B.conferta* Benth.).
Stem to 5m, puberulent. Leaves to 15cm, oblong-lanceolate, puberulent beneath. Flowers 20–60, in simple umbels; tepals unequal, outer to 3.3cm, orange or crimson, inner to 6.5cm, chrome-yellow or crimson, flecked chocolate or violet, with orange tips. Andes of Colombia and Ecuador. Plants grown under this name are often *B.racemosa*.

B.racemosa Killip.
Distinguished from *B.patacocensis* by its deep red stem, scarlet outer tepals, 5–6.3cm, and scarlet inner tepals, spotted brown with yellow base, 6.3–7.5cm; pedicels stout, tomentulose, to 10cm. S America.

B.salsilla (L.) Herb.
Stem to 2m, glabrous. Leaves lanceolate to oblong. Flowers small, purple, in compound umbels; tepals equal, 1–1.5cm, crimson or purple-red, tinged green at tips. Chile.

B.shuttleworthii Mast.
Leaves to 15 × 5cm, ovate-lanceolate, glabrous beneath. Umbel compound; tepals equal, to 5cm, outer orange-red with dark spots towards the tip, inner yellow at the base with green, dark-spotted tips and a red midrib. Colombia.

Bongardia C.A. Mey. (For Heinrich Gustav Bongard (1786–1839), German botanist.) Berberidaceae. 1 species, a rhizomatous, perennial herb, to 60cm. Tuber large, nearly round. Leaves radical, spreading, 10–25cm, pinnate; leaflets sessile, oval-oblong, 3–5-cleft at apex, glaucous, often purple-red at base; flowering stems leafless. Inflorescence a lax panicle; flowers yellow; sepals 3–6, large, petaloid, tinged red, nearly round; petals 6, 8–12mm, golden. Fruit a capsule, inflated, ovoid, tinged red, 1.5cm, 2–4-seeded. S Greece, S Aegean. Leaves and rhizomes edible. Close to *Gymnospermium* and *Leontice*. Z8.

CULTIVATION Grown for its curious, marked leaves, graceful inflorescences of yellow flowers, and red-tinged, egg-shaped fruit, *Bongardia* grows best on a perfectly drained sandy soil; if moisture gathers around the neck it will rot. Hot and dry conditions are important during the dormant summer period. In temperate cultivation it is usually grown in the alpine house or bulb frame, where it may be very long-lived. In warmer zones, it will suit a sunny and dry position on the rock garden. Propagate from seed. Under natural conditions seed germinates in the autumn and, like the related *Leontice*, the tiny corm develops well below the soil surface, up to 23cm/9in. deep.

B.chrysogonum (L.) Griseb. *(Leontice chrysogonum* L.; *B.rauwolfii* C.A. Mey.).

B.rauwolfii C.A. Mey. See *B.chrysogonum.*

Boophone Herb. (From Gk *bous*, ox, and *phone*, murder – the foliage of *B.disticha* is poisonous.) Amaryllidaceae. 6 species of bulbous herbs to 30cm, glabrous or ciliate. Leaves slender-subulate or ligulate, with a pungent, onion-like odour. Inflorescence terminal, globose-umbellate, many-flowered, scapose; spathe 2-valved, valves ovate, free; pedicels straighten and lengthen after flowering, forming a many-rayed sphere that dries and detaches, dispersing seed as it rolls over the land; flowers regular; perianth tube to 1cm; tepals linear-lanceolate, to 2.5cm, red, pink or purple; stamens 6; ovary inferior, cells 1–6-ovulate. Capsule membranous, indehiscent or loculicidally dehiscent; seeds fleshy, globose, often 3-angled. S & E Africa. Z10.

CULTIVATION *Boophone* occurs naturally in dry grassland habitats in East and South Africa, protected from extremes of heat by the persistent accumulations of old foliage, and blooming in profusion in the aftermath of grassland fires; the dry flowerheads, called 'horse scarers' by the Boers, break free and are carried by the wind, dispersing their seed to germinate immediately wherever they fall on burnt ground. *B.disticha* bears large almost spherical heads of numerous starry flowers, emerging from the large bulb before the glaucous new foliage (a wide-spreading fan of strap-shaped leaves with wavy margins). Suitable for outdoor cultivation only in warm dry climates with well defined dry season, it is not hardy below 4°C/39°F. Cultivate as for *Brunsvigia*.

B.disticha (L. f.) Herb. CAPE POISON BULB. Lvs to 45cm, to 16, in 2 rows which resemble a fan, ligulate, undulate, glaucous. Scape to 30cm; umbel to 30cm diam.; pedicels to 10cm; flowers pink to red. Capsule indehiscent. Autumn. S & E Africa.

Bowiea Harv. & Hook. f. (For James Bowie (c1789–1869), a gardener at Kew who collected in Brazil and S Africa.) Liliaceae (Hyacinthaceae). 3 species of perennial bulbous herbs with deciduous twining stems. Bulbs large, globose, succulent, composed of large, closely packed concentric scales. Stems succulent, green, very slender, scrambling, twining and branching freely and intricately. Leaves small, short-lived, photosynthesis achieved by the mass of thin stems and the green bulb scales. Flowers produced on twisting racemes at the ends of the twining shoots, small, green-white or yellow. Fruit fleshy. Southern & Tropical Africa. Z10.

CULTIVATION Bizarre bulbs for the succulent house or a dry bright windowsill, minimum temperature 7°C/45°F. Sit the squat green bulb in a small pot or pan, a quarter buried in a gritty mixture suitable for succulents. Water very sparingly and then only to avoid shrivelling or growth abortion. As temperature and light increase, an elaborate, slender, lime green stem will emerge from the bulb apex and twine through any support provided. *B.volubilis* is the most commonly encountered species. It can be relied upon to produce one or two such growth flushes within a year. After fruiting, reduce water and allow the stem to die off.

B.kilimandscharica Mildbr. (*Schizobasopsis kilimandscharica* (Mildbr.) Barschus). Close to *B. volubilis*; bulb smaller, to 10cm diam. Flowers yellow-hyaline. Fruit to 3cm, pointed. Tanzania (Kilimanjaro area).

B.volubilis Harv. & Hook. f. (*Schizobasopsis volubilis* (Harv. & Hook. f.) J.F. Macbr.). CLIMBING ONION. Bulb light shining green, growing above soil level, to 20cm diam. Stems long-twining, thin, bright glossy green. Fruit to 1.4cm, blunt. S Africa.

Brimeura Salisb. Liliaceae (Hyacinthaceae). 2 species of small perennial bulbous herbs. Leaves several, glabrous. Flowers bisexual, radially symmetric in a slender-stalked raceme; perianth tubular, lobes 6, shorter than tube; stamens inserted or exserted; ovary superior, trilocular; style simple. Fruit a capsule. S Europe. Z5.

CULTIVATION Bearing small, blue, bell-shaped flowers on slender stems in late spring and much resembling diminutive bluebells (*Hyacinthoides non-scriptus*), *B.amethystina* is a charming bulb for the rock garden, for underplanting in shrub borders and for pots in the alpine house. Grow in sun or part shade in a well-drained, humus-rich soil; *B.fastigiata* prefers shade. Where winter temperatures fall below −10°C/14°F, provide excellent drainage and a protective mulch of bracken litter or leafmould. Propagate by division of established colonies as the leaves die back in early summer or by ripe seed sown fresh in a sandy propagating mix. Grow seedlings on until they enter their first year dormancy and store in dry frost-free conditions; plant out when bulblets are about 6mm in diameter.

B.amethystina (L.) Chouard (*Hyacinthus amethystinus* L.). Lvs slightly exceeding scape, to 6mm wide, channelled, bright green. Scape 10–25cm; fls c1cm, 5–15; pedicels 0.5–1.25cm, held horizontally or disposed to one side of axis, sometimes decurved, extending in fruit; perianth narrowly campanulate, bright blue, sometimes indigo or white, tube cylindric or waisted below throat, lobes to two-thirds length of tube; stamens small, not reaching throat. Late spring–early summer. NW Yugoslavia. 'Alba': fls white.

B.fastigiata (Viv.) Chouard. Lvs exceeding scape, narrowly linear, erect, dark green. Scape 5–7cm; fls 1–1.3cm diam., 1–10 in subcorymbiform raceme; lower pedicels longer than upper; perianth to 9mm, campanulate but appearing star-shaped, lilac, lilac-pink or white, lobes exceeding tube, spreading. Islands of W Mediterranean, Greece.

Brodiaea Sm. (For James Brodie of Morayshire, Scotland (1744–1824), who discovered *Pyrola uniflora* in Britain in 1800.) Liliaceae (Alliaceae). Some 15 species of perennial, cormous, slender herbs. Corm somewhat spherical, dark brown, fibrous-coated. Scape erect, rigid, slender, enveloped by leaves below ground. Leaves 2–8, linear, elongate, flat or concave above, often shrivelling before flowering, with no keel, vein impressions weak or lacking. Inflorescence a scapose umbel; flowers campanulate or funnelform, subtended by papery bracts, jointed to the pedicels; tepals 6, outer narrower than inner, widely spreading, predominantly narrower than tube below; stamens 6, erect, 3 fertile in most species, usually alternating with 3 attenuate staminodes, pressed together with – but not united to – the style; anthers basifixed; ovary superior, with no stalk, 3-celled; stigma spreading into 3 long recurved lobes; fruit a loculicidal capsule; seeds black, angled, flattened. W US, Western S America. Z8.

CULTIVATION Grown for their globose flowerheads which resemble those of *Allium*, and are produced on leafless stems in summer, often as the foliage dies back. Where winter temperatures fall much below −5°C/23°F, they require mulch protection, otherwise they are amenable to pot cultivation in the cool glasshouse or alpine house in mix of equal parts loam, leafmould and sharp sand. Suitable for the border, rock garden, for the lightest dappled shade of the woodland garden or for naturalizing in thin grass, *Brodiaea* spp. are most reliable where they can receive plenty of moisture when in growth, followed by an increasingly warm, dry period for dormancy in late summer and autumn. Grow in sun in light, fertile sandy loams that are very well drained but moisture-retentive; bulbs are susceptible to rots in wet soils. Propagate by division of established colonies, by removal of offsets which are freely produced or by ripe seed.

B.bridgesii Wats. See *Triteleia bridgesii*.

B.californica Lindl. (*B.grandiflora* var. *elatior* Benth.). Scape to 70cm. Fls blue-purple, 2–12 per umbel; pedicels to 13cm; tepals 3–4.5cm, lilac to violet or pink, recurved, ascending, overlapping to form membranous, broadly terete tube, not constricted above ovary, splitting in fruit; stamens 3, anth. 9–13mm, fil. 7–10mm; staminodes 1.6–2.7cm, erect, linear, closely folded about stamens; style 1.8–2.2cm. California.

B.candida Bak. See *Triteleia laxa*.
B.capitata Benth. See *Dichelostemma pulchellum*.
B.coccinea A. Gray. See *Dichelostemma ida-maia*.
B.congesta Sm. See *Dichelostemma congestum*.

B.coronaria (Salisb.) Engl. (*B.grandiflora* Sm.; *B.howellii* Eastw.; *Hookera coronaria* Salisb.). Scape to 30cm, rigid. Lvs 2–3, linear, sharply-tipped, channelled above, Infl. loose; fls 2–7 per umbel, blue-purple to deep mauve; perianth 2.4–4cm, tube ovoid to narrow-campanulate, thick-textured, not splitting in fruit; staminodes white, sharp-tipped, with inrolled and apically notched margins, exceeding stamens and stigma; anth. 4.5–7mm, fil. 2–4.5mm; ovary 8–10mm; style 7–11mm. NW US. Often mistaken for *B.terrestris*.

B.coronaria var. *macropoda* (Torr.) Hoover. See *B.terrestris*.
B.coronaria var. *mundula* Jeps. See *B.elegans*.
B.douglasii Piper. See *Triteleia grandiflora*.

B.elegans Hoover (*B.coronaria* var. *mundula* Jeps.). Scape to 50cm. Fls 2–12 per umbel; pedicels 5mm–10cm; perianth to 4cm; tepals to twice length of tube, deep mauve, strongly recurved; tube funnelform, thick-textured, not splitting in fruit; staminodes 6–9mm long, flat, erect, mostly shorter than stamens; anth. 4–10mm, fil. 4–6mm; ovary 9–15mm; style 7–15mm. Oregon, California.

B.grandiflora Sm. See *B.coronaria*.
B.grandiflora Macbr. non Sm. See *Triteleia grandiflora*.
B.grandiflora var. *eliator* Benth. See *B.californica*.
B.grandiflora var. *macropoda* Torr. See *B.terrestris*.
B.grandiflora var. *minor* Benth. See *B.minor*.
B.hendersonii (Greene) Wats. See *Triteleia hendersonii*.
B.howellii Eastw. See *B.coronaria*.
B.hyacintha (Lindl.) Bak. See *Triteleia hyacintha*.
B.ida-maia (Wood) Greene. See *Dichelostemma ida-maia*.
B.ixioides Hook. non (Ait.) Wats. See *Leucocoryne ixioides*.
B.ixioides (Ait.) Wats. non Hook. See *Triteleia ixioides*.
B.lactea S. Wats. See *Triteleia hyacintha*.
B.laxa (Benth.) Wats. See *Triteleia laxa*.
B.lutea Lindl. See *Triteleia ixioides*.

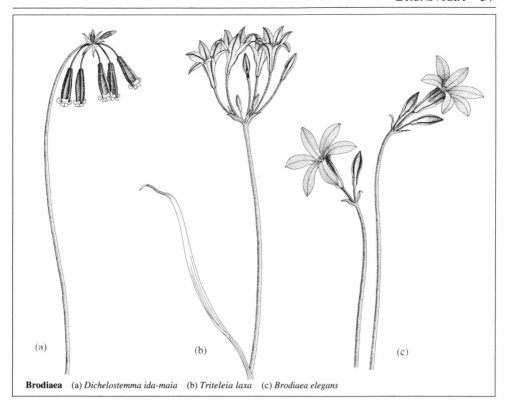

Brodiaea   (a) *Dichelostemma ida-maia*   (b) *Triteleia laxa*   (c) *Brodiaea elegans*

B.minor (Benth.) S. Wats. (*B.grandiflora* var. *minor* Benth.; *B.purdyi* Eastw.).
Scape slender, to 30cm. Lvs 0.5cm wide, channelled. Fls to 2.5cm; pedicels 1–3cm long; tepals 1.7–2.4cm, pink to violet, linear, spreading then recurved, to twice the length of apically constricted tube; anth. 1–6mm, without appendages, fil. 0.5–4mm; staminodes white, erect, folded about stamens at base, curved outward at the apex, ovary 3–5mm; style 4–9mm. California.

B.multiflora Benth. See *Dichelostemma multiflorum*.
B.peduncularis (Lindl.) Wats. See *Triteleia peduncularis*.
B.pulchella (Salisb.) Greene. See *Dichelostemma pulchellum*.
B.purdyi Eastw. See *B.minor*.

B.terrestris Kellogg (*B.grandiflora* var. *macropoda* Torr.; *B.coronaria* var. *macropoda* (Torr.) Hoover).
Scape 5mm–7cm. Tepals mauve-pink, ascending and recurved; outer whorl 2–2.4cm; tube ovoid to narrow-campanulate, usually unconstricted above ovary, thick, opaque, and not splitting in fruit; ovary 4–5mm; staminodes with slightly inrolled margins, considerably longer than distant anth. and stigma; apex unequally 3 fid, with central tooth smaller than laterals; anth. 3–5mm; fil. 1.5–3mm; style 6–9mm. W US.

Brunsvigia Heist. (For Karl Wilhelm Ferdinand, Duke of Brunswick-Lüneburg (1713–80), patron of the arts and sciences.) Amaryllidaceae. About 20 species of bulbous herbs to 50cm. Bulb ovoid, sometimes above ground; tunic membranous. Leaves synanthous or hysteranthous, radical, ligulate, glabrous or pubescent above. Scape solid; inflorescence terminal, umbellate, to 75-flowered; spathe 2-valved, membranous, brown or red-purple; pedicels lengthen after flowering; perianth declinate, zygomorphic or regular, cut nearly to base, funnel-shaped; tepals 6, flat, linear-lanceolate to oblong, flesh-pink to scarlet or claret, tips recurved; stamens and style declinate; anthers dorsifixed, versatile; stigma subcapitate; ovary 3-celled, ovules many. Capsule 3-valved, turbinate, sometimes triquetrous; seeds many, subglobose. S Africa. In habitat, the dried inflorescence breaks from the bulb and is blown around as a seed dispersal mechanism, cf. *Boophone*. Z9.
CULTIVATION *Brunsvigia* spp. are large and long-lived bulbs; those of *B.josephinae*, sometimes reach 30cm/12in. in diameter and a single bulb may live for up to 20 years. The bulbs are protected from extremes of temperature and desiccation by thick, matted layers of membranous tunic, and in their native habitats are often found blooming in profusion following bush fires. *Brunsvigia* are grown for their handsome spherical umbels of brightly coloured, funnel-shaped flowers, carried on long stout stems, which appear in late summer or autumn, before the leaves.
  Frost-tender, in temperate zones they are usually cultivated under glass, although in favoured areas they are sometimes grown in perfectly drained, deep sandy soils at the sunny base of a south-facing wall, protected with a deep dry mulch or by framelights and matting in cold weather.

Grow under glass in a potting mix of loam, leafmould and sharp sand, setting the bulb firmly with head and shoulders above soil level; plants may take two years to establish and root disturbance, which may hinder flowering for two seasons, should be avoided when possible; re-pot every fourth year. Give full sun, or part shade when flower buds begin to colour, to prolong flowering and avoid bleaching. Maintain a minimum temperature at 12°C/55°F and ensure good ventilation in summer, providing warm dry conditions with an optimum temperature of 21°C/70°F when at rest; pot-grown specimens can be moved out of doors in summer with protection from rain. After rest, allow the bulb to resume growth prior to watering, and then water liberally until leaves fade in the following season. Some authorities suggest that *Brunsvigia* should have an additional period without water between the death of the umbel and emergence of new leaves.

Propagate from offsets; these are produced in small numbers and should be allowed to reach a considerable size before potting into a sandy loam-based medium, in a closed case in warmth, watering sparingly until established. Also from ripe seed sown in sand; germinate at 18–21°C/65–70°F.

Brunsvigia are attractive to aphid, mealybug, whitefly and red spider mite. In cases of infection by eel-worm, *Ditylenchus dipsaci* (where growth is distorted and bulbs become soft showing characteristic brown rings when cut transversely), bulbs should be destroyed immediately by burning. Also infested by narcissus flies, *Merodon equestris, Eumerus* spp. – burn affected stock. Bulb rot will occur if drainage is poor and dry rest requirements are neglected. Narcissus leaf scorch, *Stagonospora curtisii*, causes red-brown scorching of young leaf tips, and may be restricted by immediate removal of affected parts followed by fungicide sprays, although the source of the infection is likely to be within the bulb itself.

B.gigantea (Van Marum) Traub. See *B.josephinae*.

B.gigantea Heist. ex Schult. non (Van Marum) Traub. See *B.orientalis*.

B.josephinae (Redouté) Ker-Gawl. (*Amaryllis gigantea* Van Marum; *Amaryllis josephinae* Redouté; *B.josephinae* var. *augustifolia* Ker-Gawl.; *B.gigantea* (Van Marum) Traub).
Bulb mainly above ground, to 30×20cm, tunicate. Lvs to 90×20cm, produced later than fls, 8–20, oblong, semi-erect, glabrous, entire. Peduncle to 45–90×5cm; spathe valves shaded red, to 15cm, keeled; umbel to 30-fld, spreading, to 1m; pedicels red-purple, to 40cm at maturity, 6-channelled; perianth scarlet, to 9cm, tube 1cm; outer tepals linear-lanceolate, inner tepals narrower, linear, 3 upper tepals strongly recurved; style longer than stamens; fil. joined to tube to 1cm from base; ovary not triquetrous, to 2.5×1.5cm. Capsule not angled, to 4×2.5cm. Summer.

B.multiflora Ait. See *B.orientalis*.

B.orientalis (L.) Ait. ex Ecklon (*Amaryllis orientalis* L.; *Haemanthus orientalis* (L.) Thunb.; *B.multiflora* Ait.; *B.gigantea* Heist. ex Schult.).
Bulb subterranean. Lvs to 45×12cm, 2–6, produced later than fls, prostrate, short-pubesc. above, apex obtuse. Scape to 50×3cm, green shaded red; pedicels to 20cm, channelled; fls irregular; perianth tube to 0.5cm; tepals to 6.5cm, linear-lanceolate, recurved, pink or scarlet; ovary to 3×2cm. Capsule triquetrous, to 9×3cm. Summer.

B.rosea (Lam.) Hann. See *Amaryllis belladonna*.

Bulbine L. Liliaceae (Asphodelaceae). (From Gk *bolbine*, star-flower.) 30–40 species of succulent and non-succulent herbs, all perennial except for *B.annua*. Leaves radical from rootstock or cauline and alternate, soft, fleshy, lanceolate or subglobose, usually persistent but deciduous during the dry season in the dwarf, caudex-forming spp. Inflorescence a terminal raceme with many small yellow flowers, rarely orange or white; stamens with bearded filaments. S & E Africa. Z9.

CULTIVATION A slightly tender genus, tolerant of thin, dry soils and easily grown in freely draining, sandy loam soils in sunny and sheltered rock gardens and borders, with some winter protection where temperatures fall much below freezing. Propagate by division and seed. Also attractive additions to xeriscapes and succulent collections.

B.bulbosa (R. Br.) Haw. See *Bulbinopsis bulbosa*.

B.diphylla Schltr. ex Poelln.
Caudex divided into 3–7 conical fleshy roots 5–10cm long, producing a main stem only 1–2mm thick, 1–2.5cm long, holding the single pairs of dimorphic lvs 1–2cm above the soil surface. Lvs highly succulent, soft, light green, tinged red, the larger lf channelled above, 3–5×1.5cm, apex obtuse, the smaller lf higher on the axis, terete, shorter and thinner. Fls 5–10, yellow; pedicels thin, red, 8–10cm. S Africa (Cape Province: Van Rhynsdorp District).

B.haworthioides R. Nordenstam.
Caudex 1.5cm diam., broadly oblong or rounded, fleshy, base 5–7-lobed. Lvs 1×0.5cm, rosulate, 12–14 in a flat spiral resembling *Haworthia venosa* ssp. *tessellata*, fleshy, carinate, blunt, lower surface convex, upper surface more or less flat with white reticulations, margins densely and finely ciliate. Infl. 15cm tall with around 10 yellow fls in a lax racemes 3–4cm long. S Africa (Cape Province: Van Rhynsdorp District).

B.latifolia (L. f.) Haw. (*Anthericum latifolium* L. f.).
Rootstock stout. Branches few. Lvs 20–35×5–7cm, in a few
aloe-like rosettes of 12–20, oblong-lanceolate, tapering,
flat, soft-fleshy, pale green, base clasping, 5–6mm thick,
margins curled upwards. Infl. to 60cm tall or more, a dense
raceme; fls yellow. S Africa (Cape Province: Somerset
South).

B.mesembryanthoides Haw.
Dwarf. Caudex subglobose, the base divided into conical
fleshy roots 1.5–2cm thick. Lvs 1.6×0.5–1×0.5–1cm, 1–2,
lemon-shaped, very soft and watery, pale green, tip translucent, broadly striate, slightly grey-pruinose. Infl. 5–15cm,
very slender, erect, with 3–6 widely spaced yellow fls. Cape
Province: Little Namaqualand.

B.succulenta Compton.
Deciduous. Caudex 3–4cm thick, tipped with tuft of spiny
scales. Lvs 6–7cm, 2–4, radical, erect, very fleshy, light green
tinged red, drying up completely during the dormant season.
Infl to 15cm; pedicel tinged red with several yellow fls near
and at apex. S Africa.

B.triebneri Dinter.
Caudex short, thick, tuberous. Lvs 15–30×0.2–0.3cm, 10–20,
subterete from a sheathed base 13mm wide, nearly flat above,
tapering, glaucous. Infl 30–40cm, racemes dense, 15cm or
more; fls white. Namibia: Great Namaqualand.

Bulbinella Kunth. (Diminutive of *Bulbine*.) Liliaceae (Asphodelaceae). 20 species of robust perennial herbs;
roots fleshy. Leaves rather succulent, in rosettes. Flowering stem exceeding leaves; flowers many in a terminal
raceme, bisexual or functionally unisexual; perianth segments 6, free, persistent; stamens 6, filaments glabrous;
ovary superior, trilocular. Fruit a septicidal capsule. New Zealand, Africa. Z8.

CULTIVATION *Bulbinella* spp. are easily cultivated on the peat terrace or rock garden in a reliably moisture-retentive, neutral or slightly acidic and freely draining soil in sun or part shade; *B.hookeri* is slightly more tolerant of
dry soils. Tolerant of light, short-lived frosts (give deep mulch protection), in cold winter areas *Bulbinella* is
amenable to pot cultivation in the cool or frost-free glasshouse as for *Anthericum*. Propagate by seed and division.

B.hookeri (Hook. f.) Cheesem.
To 60m. Lvs to 30×3cm. Raceme cylindric; fls bisexual, yellow; perianth 14mm diam., spreading. Fr. short-stalked, subtended by dried perianth remnants.

B.rossii (Hook. f.) Cheesem.
To 1.25m. Lvs to 30×6cm, oblong or oblong-lanceolate,
tapering, apex obtuse to acute, recurved. Infl. a densely fld
raceme; fls functionally unisexual, yellow; perianth 10–14mm
diam., seg. spreading in males, more erect in females, hardening and remaining erect as fr. develops. Fr. sessile. New
Zealand.

Bulbinopsis Borzi. (From *Bulbine* and Gk *opsis*, appearance.) Liliaceae (Asphodelaceae). 2 species of stem
less herbs closely allied to and formerly included in *Bulbine*. E Australia.

CULTIVATION   As for *Bulbine*.

B.bulbosa (R. Br.) Borzi.
Caudex bulbous. Lvs 15–30×0.3–0.4cm, radical, fleshy, linear, subulate, grooved on upper surface, short-sheathed at
base. Infl. 30–60cm; fls numerous, yellow, each with 6
bearded fil.

B.semibarbata (R.Br.) Borzi.
Roots fibrous. Lvs forming a dense radical rosette, to 30cm,
linear, subulate, erect or recurved. Infl. a lax raceme, 30cm+;
fls numerous, yellow; fil. 6 (3 bearded).

Bulbocodium L. (From Gk *bolbos*, bulb, and *kodya*, capsule.) Liliaceae (Colchicaceae). 2 species of perennial, cormous herbs to 10cm; tunics leathery. Leaves to 15×1.5cm, basal, bluntly tipped, linear to linear-lanceolate, somewhat cylindrical, dark green, appearing with or after flowers. Flowers violet to purple, emerging from a tubular sheath, 1–3 per corm; tepals 6, oblong-lanceolate, erect to spreading, distinctly clawed, united by basal teeth forming a short tube; stamens 6, anthers versatile. Spring. S & E Europe. Differs from *Colchicum* and *Merendera* in its style, which is trifid only at apex. Z4.

CULTIVATION   As for *Colchicum*.

B.trigynum Adam non Jank. See *Merendera trigyna*.

B.vernum L. (*Colchicum bulbocodium* Ker-Gawl.; *Colchicum vernum* (L.) Ker-Gawl.).
Lvs 3, linear-lanceolate, acute, concave above, toothed at base. Fls solitary, rarely 2–3, rose to magenta, occasionally mauve or white, claw flushed or spotted white. SW Alps to S Russia.

B.versicolor (Ker-Gawl.) Spreng.
Close to *B.vernum* from which it differs in its smaller fls and narrower lvs. E Europe, W Asia.

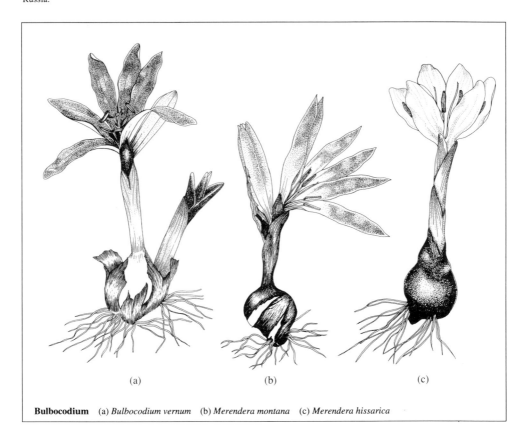

(a)   (b)   (c)

Bulbocodium   (a) *Bulbocodium vernum*   (b) *Merendera montana*   (c) *Merendera hissarica*

Caladium Vent. (From local name for these plants, *kaladi*.) ANGEL WINGS; ELEPHANT'S-EAR. Araceae. 7 species of tuberous perennials. Tubers spherical or cylindric, becoming dormant annually. Leaves usually peltate-sagittate, occasionally oblong and not peltate, base hastate to truncate or rounded, green variegated with white, pink or red, main lateral veins linked by reticulate minor venation, united to marginal vein; petiole long, sometimes streaked or spotted, glabrous or hairy. Peduncle short, not equalling petioles; spathe with margins overlapping below to form tube, limb partly expanded, constricted above tube, green to green-white; spadix included, with adjacent zones of female, sterile and male flowers, appendix absent; flowers unisexual, perianth absent; stamens 2–5, connate to form column; ovary with 2–3 incompletely separated locules, ovules 2–4; stigma sessile. Fruit a dull white berry. Tropical S America. Z10.

CULTIVATION   Used in tropical climates for bedding and in colder climates as house or conservatory potplants, Caladiums are grown for their beautifully coloured foliage, splashed, marbled and veined with red, pink and white.

Store dormant tubers at a minimum temperature of 13–16°C/55–60°F, dry but not bone dry, and check regularly for rot. Bring into growth in early spring, in a tray of moist sphagnum with gentle bottom heat and an ambient temperature of 21–23°C/70–75°F. Mist regularly and divide at this stage if necessary. As new shoots appear and the roots reach a length of about 5cm/2in., pot carefully into a coarse, open, moist but freely draining medium comprising equal parts turfy loam, leafmould and well-rotted manure with additional sharp sand. Provide a temperature of about 18°C/65°F, with high humidity, in bright light but never in full sunlight. Syringe two or three times daily; water sparingly as growth begins, increasing when leaves are fully open; liquid feed as roots fill the container. Reduce water gradually as the leaves fade in autumn. Propagate by separation of small tubers in spring, or by cutting larger tubers into sections (dusting with fungicide before starting into growth). Adult leaf colour does not become apparent until 4–5 leaves have been produced.

C.argyrites Lem. See *C.humboldtii*.

C.bicolor (Ait.) Vent. (*C.×hortulanum* Birdsey; *C.marmoratum* Mathieu; *C.picturatum* K. Koch; *C.poecile* Schott).
To 90cm. Tuber depressed-globose, to 6cm diam. Lvs 18–45×12–25cm, peltate, ovate to elliptic, base cordate to sagittate, lobes often obtuse, green with variable amounts of white, pink or red markings in spots, blotches or bands; petiole variegated. Spathe to 11cm, tube green externally, green-white within, limb dull white; male zone of spadix 2.5–6cm. Northern S America. A highly developed plant in gardens. *C.bicolor* is here interpreted as including *C.picturatum*, with narrower leaves and acute basal lobes, and *C.marmoratum* with lvs blotched grey, green and ivory on green. The three are supposedly the parents of the many hybrids grouped under the name *C.×hortulanum*. Plants with largely white-marbled lvs have been grouped under *C.×candidum*. Of these cultigens there are at least 120 modern selections, these fall into 'fancy leaf' and 'strap leaf' (lanceolate lvs derived from *C.picturatum*) categories; lvs membranous, 15–30cm, rounded-cordate to angular, margins sometimes undulate, a wide range of colours and patterns involving deep and pale green, white, red and pink. 'Fancy leaf' cvs include whites such as: 'June Bride': lvs flat, white with green edge; 'Mrs Arno Nehrling': lvs large, white with delicate dark green venation and edge, main ribs shaded red; 'White Queen': lvs white with crimson primary veins, green edge and fine tracings; and pinks such as 'Carolyn Whorton': lvs bright pink with deep green-black marbling towards edge and red ribs; 'Fannie Munson': lvs pale pink with fine green edge and some venation, main ribs deep pink; 'Pink Beauty': lvs green with pink marbling in centre and along the red ribs; 'Rosabud': lvs pink centre shading to white then green, ribs pink; and reds such as 'Freida Hemple': bushy; lvs bright red, ribs scarlet with wide dark green margin; 'Poecile Anglais': lvs dark, dull green with burgundy ribs and central shading. 'Postman Joyner': bushy; lvs pale red, veins darker, margin green; 'Red Flash': lvs dull green with vibrant red centre and ribs, blotched white. 'Strap leaf' cvs include the whites 'Candidum Junior': lvs white delicately traced with dark green veins and edge; 'Gingerland': lvs grey with white ribs, dark green edge and maroon spots; 'White Wing': lvs white with deep green edge; 'Clarice': lvs pink shaded with darker ribs, wide dark green edge and venation, blotched white; 'Miss Muffet': lvs dwarf, sage green with white ribs, soft red

heart, dark red spotting; and the red; 'Red Frill': lvs deep red shading darker towards the deep green margin. Cvs with almost entirely white lvs include 'Speciosum' with lvs quilted, midrib painted white, lateral veins spreading white, and 'Venosum' with small deep green lvs with midribs, lateral veins and inner edge ivory.

C.×hortulanum Birdsey. See *C.bicolor*.

C.humboldtii Schott (*C.argyrites* Lem.; *C.lilliputiense* Rodigas).
To 25cm. Tuber to 2cm diam., freely producing offsets. Lvs 5–10×2–4.5cm, peltate, ovate to oblong, short-acuminate, base sagittate, dull green, blotched and spotted white; petiole very slender, to 24cm, variegated. Fls not recorded. Brazil & Venezuela.

C.lilliputiense Rodigas. See *C.humboldtii*.

C.lindenii (André) Madison (*Xanthosoma lindenii* (André) Engl.).
To 80cm. Tuber freely producing offsets. Lvs 16–45×10–20cm, not peltate, hastate, main lobe oblong, acute, lateral lobes unequal, obtuse, dark green above with midrib and main veins marked white, ground colour paler towards midrib, midrib hairy; petioles sheathing below to 40cm, green, striped purple, sparsely short-hairy. Spathe to 14cm, tube white-green, limb white; male zone of spadix to 8cm, white. Colombia. 'Albescens': lvs heavily marked white at centre and on margin. 'Magnificum': lvs marked cream to white along veins and in a line inside margins.

C.marmoratum Mathieu. See *C.bicolor*.
C.picturatum K. Koch. See *C.bicolor*.
C.poecile Schott. See *C.bicolor*.

C.schomburgkii Schott.
To 45cm. Tuber spherical. Lvs to 20×15cm, not peltate, triangular, ovate, broad lanceolate to rhombic, base emarginate to truncate or rounded, variegated pink or white, margins undulate, veins silver to red; petiole to 25cm. Peduncle to 25cm; spathe tube oblong, green, 3.5cm, limb 10cm, white. Eastern S America (Guiana, Brazil). 'Changjur': stems white; lvs small, ovate, hanging downwards, light to dark green, ribs white.

C.venosum N.E. Br. See *C.schomburgkii*.
C.'Venosum'. See *C.bicolor*.

Calochortus Pursh. (From Gk *kalos*, beautiful, and *chortos*, grass, referring to the grass-like leaves.) MARI-POSA TULIP; FAIRY LANTERN; CAT'S EAR. Liliaceae (Calochortaceae). Some 60 species of bulbous, perennial herbs. Bulbs tunicate, ovoid, with membranous or occasionally fibrous-reticulate tunics. Stems leafy, occasionally scapose, often branched, frequently bearing bulbils. Leaves ensiform, usually linear, basal and cauline, the basal leaf very long, conspicuous at or withering before flowering. Flowers erect or nodding, showy, white, yellow, orange, red, lavender, purple, occasionally tinged blue or brown, borne in cymes or subumbels; perianth composed of two distinct whorls; sepals 3, glabrous, lanceolate; petals 3, obovate to oblanceolate, often bearded, usually with a somewhat flattened gland or depression near the base; stamens 6; filaments broadened at the base; anthers oblong to linear; ovary superior, 3-celled, with numerous ovules in each cell, triangular or 3-winged in section. Fruit a 3-winged or 3-angled, septicidal, erect or drooping, many-seeded capsule. N America (British Columbia to Guatemala). Z8.

CULTIVATION   Found in a range of warm, dry habitats that are usually characterized by their good, even perfect drainage – in chaparral communities and scrub for *C.amabilis*, *C.albus* and *C.pulchellus* and on slopes in mixed evergreen forest for *C.venustus* and *C.luteus*; several species occur in grassland and meadow, including *C.amoenus*. Grown for their elegant flowers carried on slender but sturdy stems in spring or summer, most are tolerant of several degrees of frost but not in combination with winter wet, nor will the bulbs tolerate damp conditions when dormant (for spring-flowering types, dormancy is in summer). Grow in a deep, freely draining and fertile soil in a sheltered position in full sun; incorporate leafmould or garden compost and sharp sand before planting on a layer of sharp sand. Bulbs frequently divide after flowering, and young bulblets may take two years to reach flowering size. Cultivation in the well ventilated bulb frame, cool glasshouse or alpine house permits greater control of moisture during dormancy. Grow in deep well crocked pots with a mix of equal parts loam, leafmould and sharp sand, with additional grit for *C.pulchellus*, *C.amoenus* and *C.coeruleus*; water moderately to plentifully when in growth and reducing as leaves wither to keep dry when dormant. Dormant bulbs are best left undisturbed and stored in their pots. Propagate by ripe seed in the cool glasshouse or frame, by offsets when dormant, or from the bulbils which form in the leaf axils.

C.albus Benth.
Stem 20–80cm, erect, stout, branched. Basal lf 30–70cm, present at flowering, stem lvs lanceolate to linear. Fls nodding, globose to globose-campanulate, white with deep red-brown spot; sep. 1–1.5cm, ovate to lanceolate, acuminate; pet. 1.5–3cm, elliptic-obovate, acute to obtuse, delicately fringed, sparsely pubesc. above the gland; gland flattened, traversed by about 5 deeply fringed membranes, extending for one-third to two-thirds of the width of the pet. at gland level; anth. oblong, obtuse or acute, usually shorter than fil. Fr. an elliptic oblong, 3-winged, nodding capsule, to 4cm. W US. var. **rubellus** Greene. Fls tinged rose. S California.

C.albus var. *amoenus* (Greene) Purdy & Bail. See *C.amoenus*.

C.amabilis Purdy (*C.pulchellus* var. *amabilis* (Purdy) Jeps.).
Stem 10–30cm, erect, rather stout, usually branched. Basal lf 20–50cm, exceeding the stem, stem lvs to 20cm, lanceolate to linear. Fls nodding, globose or globose-campanulate, deep yellow; sep. more or less spreading, usually exceeding the pet., ovate to lanceolate, acute to acuminate; pet. 1.5–2cm, triangular in outline, clawed, sharply rounded at apex, densely fringed to 1.5mm, glabrous or slightly pubesc. near the gland, gland deeply depressed, arched and bounded above by a transverse line of hairs, 2–3mm long, pointing into the centre of the depression; anth. oblong, obtuse, usually shorter than the fil. Fr. an oblong, 3-winged, nodding capsule, to 3cm. W US.

C.amoenus Greene (*C.albus* var. *amoenus* (Greene) Purdy & Bail.).
Close to *C.albus* but shorter and more slender. Stems to 50cm, erect, rather flexuous. Basal lf 20–50cm; stem lvs lanceolate, well developed. Fls nodding to erect, narrow-campanulate to globose-campanulate, deep rose-pink or purple; sep. lanceolate; pet. to 1cm; gland broad, arched, slightly depressed, extending right across the base of the pet.; anth. obtuse, about as long as fil. Fr. an elliptic, narrowly 3-winged, nodding capsule, to 3cm. W US.

C.barbatus (HBK) Painter (*C.flavus* Schult.).
Stem to 60cm, erect, flexuous, slender, often forked with somewhat spreading branches, rarely with bulbils. Basal lf linear, shorter than stem. Fls usually 2, campanulate, drooping, yellow, or pet. and often sep. tinged purple; sep. 1–2cm, obovate, obtuse, or acuminate, entire or fringed, densely

bearded with tapering, purple hairs; gland more or less circular, naked, encircled by small hairs; anth. oblong, shortly pointed, shorter than fil. Mexico.

C.benthamii Bak. See *C.monophyllus*.
C.citrinus anon. See *C.luteus*.
C.citrinus Bak. See *C.weedii*.

C.clavatus Wats.
Stem 50cm–1m, coarse, flexuous, simple or much-branched, rarely with bulbils. Lvs to 20cm, linear, reduced upward along the stem. Fls campanulate to cup-shaped, yellow, borne in an approximate umbel of 1–6, with a transverse red-brown line above the gland on the pet., with red-brown tinge on the sep.; sep. 2.5–3.5cm, ovate-lanceolate, acute; pet. 3.5–5cm, broadly obovate, covered with club-shaped hairs in lower part; gland circular, depressed, densely covered with short, much-branched processes, and surrounded by laciniate scales; anth. oblong, obtuse or acute, deep purple, about as long as fil. S Carolina.

C.coeruleus (Kellogg) Wats.
Close to *C.tolmiei*, but differing in its unbranched, stem, 3–15cm, its blue tinged fls; sep. 8–10mm; broadly obovate pet. 8–12mm; oblong, acute anth., usually slightly exceeding fil. W US.

C.coeruleus var. *maweanus* (Bak.) Jeps. See *C.tolmiei*.
C.cyaneus Nels. See *C.macrocarpus*.

C.elegans Pursh.
Close to *C.tolmiei*. Stem to 15cm, flexuous, unbranched. Fls open-campanulate, green-white, tinged purple at base above the depressed gland; gland membrane deeply fringed; anth. apiculate, usually longer than fil. Fr. an elliptic to orbicular, 3-winged, nodding capsule, 2cm. W US (Idaho, adjacent Washington and Oregon).

C.elegans Hook. f. non Pursh. See *C.tolmiei*.
C.flavus Schult. See *C.barbatus*.

C.gunnisonii Wats.
Stem slender, 20–60cm, erect, unbranched, rarely with bulbils. Fls erect campanulate, white to purple, tinged green within, with a purple stripe above the gland, borne in an approximate umbel of 1–3; sep. 2.5–3cm, lanceolate, acute; pet. 3–4cm, obovate, obtuse and rounded above, bearded near the gland, with dense, glandular, branched hairs; gland transverse, oblong, arched above, densely covered with branched processes, the

Calochortus (a) *C.clavatus* (b) *C.macrocarpus* (c) *C.venustus* (d) *C.kennedyi*

outer occasionally forming a membrane; anth. acute, lanceolate, longer than fil. US (Dakota, Mont., south to New Mexico).

C.kennedyi Porter.
Stem erect, to 50cm, usually simple and stout, rarely with bulbils. Fls campanulate, erect, borne in umbels of 1–6, vermilion to orange, often with brown-purple spot at base; sep. 1.5–2.5cm, ovate-lanceolate, acute; pet. 2.5–5cm, obovate, usually rounded above; gland circular, densely hairy, surrounded by laciniate scales. Fr. capsule lanceolate-linear, with longitudinal stripes. W US.

C.lilacinus Kellogg. See *C.uniflorus.*

C.lobbii Purdy (*C.subalpinus* Piper).
Fls broadly campanulate, more or less erect; sep. with purple glandular spot at base; pet. white to pale yellow sometimes tinted lilac, fringed with yellow hairs. W US.

C.luteus Douglas ex Lindl. (*C.citrinus* anon.).
Close to *C.venustus.* Stem erect, slender, with bulbils at base. Fls 1–4, open-campanulate, erect, dark yellow, striped red-brown, occasionally with median brown spot; gland transverse, more or less crescent-shaped, covered with short, thick processes; anth. shorter than fil. Fr. capsule lanceolate-linear. W US.

C.luteus var. **citrinus** Wats. See *C.superbus.*
C.luteus var. **oculatus** Purdy & Bail. See *C.superbus.*
C.luteus var. **weedii** (Wood) Bak. See *C.weedii.*

C.macrocarpus Douglas (*C.cyaneus* Nels.).
Stems 20–50cm, erect, rigid, simple, often with bulbils. Lvs linear, becoming tightly falcate at the tip. Fls large, open-campanulate, erect, borne in an umbel of 1–3, purple; sep. 3.5–6cm, narrow-lanceolate, glabrous, tapering, usually exceeding the pet.; pet. 3.5–6cm, acuminate, pubesc. above the gland, each with a longitudinal median green stripe; gland more or less sagittate, bound by a fringed membrane and covered with slender, usually branched processes; anth. linear, obtuse, longer than fil. W US (British Columbia to Nevada).

C.maweanus Bak. See *C.tolmiei.*

C.monophyllus (Lindl.) Lem. (*C.benthamii* Bak.).
Stem 8–20cm, slender, erect, usually branched. Basal lf 10–30cm, linear, longer than stem. Fls usually erect, spreading-campanulate, yellow; sep. 1.5–2cm, oblong, acute, about as long as pet.; pet. obovate, densely pubesc. above the gland, sparsely fringed with clavate hairs; gland naked, spreading across base of the pet., with a deeply fringed membrane below and a few short cilia above, these and the membrane densely short-papillose; anth. lanceolate, abruptly mucronate, as long as fil. W US.

C.nudus Wats.
Stem 5–15cm, erect, scapose. Basal lf 10–20cm, usually shorter than fls. Fls 1–6, open-campanulate, erect, white or pale lavender; sep. 1–2cm, elliptic-lanceolate, acuminate; pet. 1.5–2cm, erose-denticulate at apex, with irregular, fine teeth and no fringe, glabrous except occasionally for very few hairs near the gland; gland naked, transverse, shallowly arched above, bounded below by an ascending, fringed membrane, the fringe minutely papillose; anth. linear-oblong, obtuse to acute, roughly equal to fil., pale blue. Fr. an oblong, 3-winged, nodding capsule, to 2.5cm. W US.

C.pulchellus Benth.
Close to *C.amabilis,* differing in its sep. which do not usually exceed pet.; pet. 2.5–3.5cm, pubesc. within almost to the tip and lighter yellow, margin more deeply but less densely fringed. W US.

C.pulchellus var. **amabilis** (Purdy) Jeps. See *C.amabilis.*

C.splendens Benth.
Stem 20–60cm, erect, branched, occasionally bulbiliferous. Basal lvs to 15cm; stem lvs reduced. Fls 1–4, erect, campanulate, pale pink, borne in cymes of 1–4; sep. 2–2.5cm, ovate-lanceolate, acuminate; pet. 2.5–5cm, rounded with irregular, fine teeth above, sparsely pubesc. from above the gland to about the middle; gland small, circular, very near the base of

the pet., naked or more usually covered with thick, branched processes; anth. linear-oblong, obtuse to pointed, blue to purple, shorter than fil. Fr. a linear, 3-angled, erect capsule. W US.

C.subalpinus Piper. See *C.lobbii.*

C.superbus How (*C.luteus* var. *citrinus* Wats.; *C.luteus* var. *octatus* Purdy & Bail.).
Close to *C.venustus.* Stem to 70cm, erect, branched. Lvs to 25cm, smaller toward top of stem. Fls campanulate, white, cream, or yellow, streaked with purple at base, usually with median brown or maroon spot, surrounded with yellow; sep. lanceolate, tapering, usually not curled under at the tip; pet. rounded to acute, slightly hairy near the gland; gland more or less inverted V-shaped; anth. linear-lanceolate to linear-oblong. W US.

C.tolmiei Hook. & Arn. (*C.elegans* Hook. f. non Pursh; *C.maweanus* Bak.; *C.coeruleus* var. *maweanus* (Bak.) Jeps.).
Stem 5–30cm, erect, stout, somewhat flexuous, usually branched, with 1 stem lf. Basal lf 10–40cm, usually exceeding the stem. Fls open-campanulate, erect or spreading, borne in umbels of 1–10, white or cream, occasionally tinged rose or purple; sep. 8–20mm, oblong-lanceolate, acute to acuminate; pet. 1–2.5cm, obovate, pubesc. inside to the apex, sparsely fringed; gland transverse, arched above, naked, bounded below by an irregularly toothed to fringed membrane and above by a band of short, thick processes, these and the fringes papillose; anth. lanceolate, acute, shorter than fil. Fr. an elliptic-oblong, 3-winged, nodding capsule, to 3cm. W US (Oregon, Calif.).

C.uniflorus Hook. & Arn. (*C.lilacinus* Kellogg).
Stem short, simple, barely emerging above ground, with many basal bulbils. Basal lf 10–40cm, far exceeding fls, stem lvs 1–3, linear. Fls open-campanulate, erect, pale lilac, borne in loose umbels of 1–5, on very long pedicels, to 10cm; sep. 1–2cm, elliptic-lanceolate, acuminate; pet. 1.5–3cm, rounded and irregularly toothed above, sparsely pubesc. above the gland; gland naked, acute below, truncate above, with a broad fringed membrane below and a band of slender processes above; anth. oblong, obtuse or acute, shorter than fil. Fr. an oblong, 3-winged, nodding capsule, to 2.5cm. W US.

C.venustus Benth.
Stem 20–60cm, erect, rigid, usually branched, with usually 1 bulbil. Basal lvs linear, to 20cm, stem lvs reduced. Fls campanulate, erect, white to yellow, purple or dark red, borne in an umbel of 1–3; sep. 2–3.5cm, linear-lanceolate, acuminate, curled under at the tip; pet. 2–4.5cm, obovate, rounded above, sparsely pubesc. in lower part, with a median dark red spot; gland circular to diamond-shaped, densely covered with hair-like appendages; anth. linear-oblong, acute to obtuse, about the same length as fil. W US.

C.venustus var. **vestae** (Purdy) Wils. See *C.vestae.*

C.vestae Purdy (*C.venustus* var. *vestae* (Purdy) Wils.; *C.luteus* Lindl.; var. *oculatus* Purdy & Bail.).
Close to *C.venustus.* Stem to 50cm, erect, rigid. Lvs to 20cm, linear. Fls campanulate, white to tinged purple, streaked with red to purple near the base, usually with a median brown spot, surrounded by pale yellow; sep. lanceolate, usually not curled under at the tip; gland transverse, more or less doubly crescent-shaped, covered with thick, short processes. Fr. a 3-angled, erect, linear capsule. California.

C.weedii Wood (*C.luteus* var. *weedii* (Wood) Bak.; *C.citrinus* Bak.).
Stem 30–60cm, slender, erect, branched, leafy, without bulbils. Basal lf usually withering before flowering, stem lvs reduced. Fls 2, open-campanulate, erect; sep. 2–3cm, tapering, ovate-lanceolate, truncate; pet. 2.5–3cm, deep yellow, with purple dots or often margins, ciliate, broadly obovate, rounded to acute, covered with fine, yellow hairs over most of the inner surface; gland circular, nearly naked, encircled by a dense ring of hairs, which are sometimes united below to form a more or less continuous membrane; anth. linear, acute, roughly equal to fil. W US, Mexico.

Caloscordum Herb. (From Gk *kalos*, beautiful, and *skorodon*, garlic.) Liliaceae (Alliaceae). 1 species, a perennial herb, resembling *Allium* but lacking typical pungent odour when bruised and with stamen filaments fused to petals. Bulbs solitary, spherical, to 1.5cm diam., with white-papery tunics. Leaves 2–6, narrow, linear, shorter than scape, pale green, channelled above. Scape 10–25cm; flowers 10–20, stellate, in a loose erect umbel, initially sheathed by a single bract; pedicels long, slender, often upturned, unequal; tepals reflexed, 6–8×5–7mm, bright pink with darker midrib, basal third united; stamens united with perianth tube; ovary superior. N China, USSR (Pamir Mts), SE Siberia. Z7.

CULTIVATION   *C.neriniflorum* carries its lax inflorescence of starry pink flowers in late summer; the sinuous leaves, which die back at flowering. The flowers work particularly well among fine grasses on a sunny and well-drained bank. It is also suitable for cultivation in the cold or alpine glasshouse, for the rock garden, and may be naturalized in sheltered borders with the shelter of a wall or hedge. Grow in a sunny, open position in perfectly drained soils. In zones where temperatures drop much below –5°C/23°F for prolonged periods, protect with a dry mulch. Plentiful moisture is necessary in spring and early summer as growth resumes, although drier conditions are tolerated in summer and autumn. Propagate from seed sown in a sandy loam-based propagating mix under glass in spring, by division of clumps or from daughter bulbs when dormant.

C.neriniflorum Herb. (*Nothoscordum neriniflorum* (Herb.)
Traub; *Allium neriniflorum* (Herb.) Bak.).

Calostemma R. Br. (From Gk *kalos*, beautiful, and *stemma*, crown, referring to the corona.) Amaryllidaceae. 3 species of bulbous perennial herbs. Leaves basal, linear lorate, soon withering. Flowers funnel-shaped, asymmetric, in a scapose umbel surrounded by 2–3 membranous bracts; perianth deeply 6-lobed, stamens erect, inserted at throat of tube, filaments dilated and united at base, winged, wings united to form a tubular toothed corona; ovary 3-celled. Fruit a depressed-globose capsule, hard, indehiscent; seeds many. Australia. Z9.

CULTIVATION   From coastal regions of eastern Australia, grown for their irregularly funnel-shaped flowers, which emerge before the leaves. Grow in full sun in light sandy soil in frost-free regions, elsewhere, plant bulbs outside in summer and lift them in autumn to overwinter in frost-free conditions. As these bulbs flower best when undisturbed and confined at the roots, they may also be grown to advantage in pots under glass.

C.luteum Sims. AUSTRALIAN DAFFODIL.
Bulbs to 6cm diam. Lvs 4–8mm wide. Scape 15–45cm; fls 8–20 on pedicels to 2.5cm; perianth 2–2.5cm, bright yellow. Spring. S Australia, Queensland, NSW.

C.purpureum R. Br. GARLAND LILY.
Bulbs 2–4cm diam. Lvs 4–8mm wide. Scape 15–50cm; fls 8–20 on pedicels to 3cm; perianth 1.5–1.8cm, purple or pink. S Australia, NSW.

Calydorea Herb. (From Gk *kalos*, beautiful and *dorea*, gift.) Iridaceae. About 12 species of cormous perennial herbs. Leaves basal, narrowly linear or terete. Flowers short-lived, blue or yellow; tepals subequal, spreading; stamens arising at base of tepals. Warm temperate Americas.

CULTIVATION   As for *Cipura*.

C.speciosa Herb. See *C.xiphioides*.

C.xiphioides (Poepp.) Espin. (*C.speciosa* Herb.).
To c25cm; corm c2cm diam., more or less globose. Lvs 7–25cm, plicate, narrowly linear. Infl. a terminal head subtended by spathes 2.5–5cm long; fls blue, yellow in centre; tepals c2.5cm, obovate. Chile.

Camassia Lindl. (From Quamash, Native American name for these plants.) CAMASS; CAMAS; QUAMASH; CAMOSH. Liliaceae (Hyacinthaceae). 5–6 species of bulbous perennial herbs related to *Scilla* and *Ornithogalum*, readily distinguished by the perianth segments being distinctly veined (whereas 1 vein only in *Scilla*, veins in *Ornithogalum* obscure). Bulbs large, ovoid to spherical, tunics brown to black. Leaves basal, narrow-linear, keeled beneath, sheathing at base, glabrous, channelled above. Scape terete; inflorescence a terminal raceme, bracteate, densely or loosely flowered; tepals 6, spreading, persistent, white to blue-violet or purple, 3–9-veined, in some spp. twisting together after pollination; stamens 6, attached to base of tepals, filaments slender, anthers yellow, violet-blue or brown, versatile; ovary trilocular, stigma 3-lobed. Fruit a capsule; seeds black. Late spring–early summer. N & S America.

CULTIVATION Bulbous perennials for the border, and waterside plantings where the roots are well above water level. The more robust species are also suited to naturalizing in the wild garden in meadow associations. The flowers last well when cut. Most species are cold tolerant to between −10 and −15°C/14–5°F but should be given deep mulch protection where low temperatures are prolonged. With the possible exception of *C.biflora*, which occurs in dry, rocky habitats, *Camassia* spp. almost invariably underperform on dry soils. Grow in deep, fertile, humus-rich and reliably moisture-retentive loam soils in sun or with some shade at the hottest part of the day. Propagate by seed, which is freely produced, by offsets or by division of established clumps. *C.quamash* is the edible camash, its bulbs were an important food source for Native Americans.

C.cusickii S. Wats.
Bulbs to 9×5cm, ovoid to subspherical, malodorous. Lvs 40–80×2–4cm, 8–20, glaucous above, margins undulate. Scape 60–80cm; raceme to 40cm; bracts triangular-acuminate, white-green at first, becoming papery; pedicels 1.1–2.3cm, spreading at first, curving toward stem after flowering, erect in fruit; fls somewhat irregular with 1 tepal deflexed; tepals 2.5–2.7×0.4–0.5cm, linear-oblong, pale blue, not twisting together as they wither; stamens shorter than tepals, fil. white, anth. yellow. US (NE Oregon). 'Zwanenburg': fls large, deep blue. Z5.

C.esculenta Lindl. non (Ker-Gawl.) Cov. See *C.quamash*.
C.esculenta (Ker-Gawl.) Cov. non Lindl. See *C.scilloides*.
C.fraseri Torr. See *C.scilloides*.

C.howellii S. Wats.
Bulb 1.5cm diam., ovoid. Lvs 30×0.5–1cm, 3–5. Scape 30–100cm; racemes 20–25cm; bracts linear; pedicels 1.5–2.5cm, spreading at right angles; tepals 1–2cm, oblong, pale blue or purple, twisting together as they wither; stamens slightly shorter than tepals, fil. mauve, anth. yellow; ovary bright green, style equalling stamens, lilac-mauve. US (SW Oregon).

C.hyacinthina (Raf.) Palmer & Steyerm. See *C.scilloides*.

C.leichtlinii (Bak.) S. Wats.
Bulbs 1.5–4cm diam., broadly ovoid to spherical, tunics brown. Lvs 20–60×0.5–2.5cm, 4–6, bright green. Flowering stem 20–130cm, pale green; racemes 10–30cm; bracts c2cm, linear-lanceolate; pedicels 1.5–5cm, slanted upwards; fls regular; tepals 2–5cm, oblong-lanceolate, cream-white or blue to violet, twisting together as they wither; stamens to three-quarters of length of tepals, fil. blue-white, anth. yellow; ovary green-brown, style white. Western N America. 'Blue Danube': fls dark blue. 'Coerulea': fls vivid deep blue.

'Electra': fls to double size, rich blue. 'Plena': tall; fls double, rosette-form, creamy white to yellow. 'Semiplena': fls semi-double, creamy white to yellow. ssp. **leichtlinii**. Fls cream-white. Oregon. ssp. **suksdorfii** (Greenman) Gould. Fls blue to violet. British Columbia to California. 'Albocaerulea': fls deep blue-violet. 'Alba': fls white. Z3.

C.quamash (Pursh) Greene (*C.esculenta* Lindl. non (Ker-Gawl.) Cov.; *C.teapeae* St. John). QUAMASH; CAMOSH.
Bulb 2–5×1–3cm, broadly ovoid to spherical, tunics usually black. Lvs 20–50×0.5–2cm, 5–6, sometimes glaucous above. Scape 20–80cm, dark green; racemes 5–30cm; bracts narrow-acuminate; pedicels 0.5–3cm, spreading at right angles, then curving upwards, erect in fruit; fls usually irregular with 1 tepal deflexed; tepals 1–3.5cm, linear-oblong, white to pale blue to deep violet-blue, sometimes twisting together after pollination; stamens shorter than tepals, fil. white or pale blue, anth. yellow or blue; ovary bright green, style sometimes longer than stamens, mauve to white. W US to Montana and Idaho. 'Orion': fls dark steely blue, deep purple in bud, inflorescences dense. 'Purpureocoerulea': fls violet-blue. Z5.

C.scilloides (Raf.) Cory (*C.esculenta* (Ker-Gawl.) Cov., non Lindl.; *C.fraseri* Torr.; *C.hyacinthina* (Raf.) Palmer & Steyerm.). EASTERN CAMASS; WILD HYACINTH; MEADOW HYACINTH; INDIGO SQUILL.
Bulb 4×3cm, ovoid, tunic almost black. Lvs 20–60×0.5–2cm, bright green. Scape 20–80cm; racemes 8–10cm; bracts 1–2cm, linear; pedicels 0.5–3cm, slanting upwards; fls regular; tepals 0.5–1.5cm, narrow-oblong, blue, blue-violet or white, remaining free as they wither; stamens slightly shorter than tepals, fil. same colour as tepals, anth. yellow; ovary green, style white or white-blue. Central and Eastern N America. Z7.

C.teapeae St. John. See *C.quamash*.

Camptorrhiza Hutch. (From Gk *kamptos*, bent, and *rhiza*, root, referring to the bent root tuber.) Liliaceae. 1 species, a perennial herb, formerly included in *Iphigenia*. Corms ovoid, asymmetrical, often bearing a geniculate root tuber. Basal leaves 1–2, linear, canaliculate, with free tubular sheaths, upper leaves sessile, decurrent. Flowers 3–12, in a lax cyme; rachis flexuous; pedicels erect, recurved in fruit; perianth segments 6, free, deciduous, oblong, concave, margins involute, reflexed at anthesis; stamens 6, filaments swollen in the middle; ovary ovoid, style simple, stigma minute. Fruit a globose to cylindrical capsule; seeds globose, brown. S Africa to Namibia, Botswana, Zimbabwe, Mozambique. Z9.

CULTIVATION As for *Lachenalia*.

C.strumosa (Bak.) Oberm.

Canna L. (Gk and Lat. word for a type of reed.) Cannaceae. 9 species of rhizomatous perennial herbs to 5m. Rhizome horizontal, fleshy, with numerous thick roots. Leaves spirally arranged, with lamina large, to 1m, green or sometimes stained purple, glabrous to somewhat lanuginose, with open sheath decurrent to petiole; midrib prominent, lateral veins numerous. Inflorescence a terminal raceme or panicle, bracteate, upper bracts subtending solitary or paired sessile or very shortly pedicellate flowers; flowers bisexual, asymmetric, small to large and showy, to 15cm across, red, orange, yellow, pink and occasionally white, sometimes spotted; sepals 3, overlapping, free, equal, persistent in fruit; petals 3, unequal, united in basal tube; stamen 1, petaloid with solitary marginal anther, united at base to fleshy style and staminodes; staminodes 1–4, innermost (termed 'labellum') small and often recurved, outer staminodes exceeding petals; nectarial glands present; ovary inferior, 3-locular, verrucose to tuberculate, ovules numerous, style petaloid. Fruit a large verrucose to tuberculate loculicidal capsule; seeds numerous, globose to ellipsoid, black to brown, very hard. New World tropics and subtropics, N to S US, abundantly naturalized throughout tropics and subtropics.

CULTIVATION From the warm and tropical regions of America, *Canna* spp. are exotic and often brilliantly coloured; these tender, rhizomatous plants may grow to 1.2–1.85m/4–6ft in a single season. The large oval leaves spiral up the stem, and may be green, bronze or purple; the orchid-like flowers are often vividly coloured in reds, orange and yellow and are borne over a 10–12-week period from midsummer to early autumn. The canna lilies, cultivars belonging to *C.× generalis*, offer a wide range of colour and habit variations and are excellent plants for the cool greenhouse, in tubs, and in bedding displays, used as dot plants, and in mass plantings of single colours against a wall, evergreen backdrop, or at the waterside. The rosy pink, pendulous flowers of *C.iridiflora* open in late spring, and need the protection of a heated environment in temperate zones. As this species grows to 3m/10ft tall it also requires considerable headroom. In tropical regions, *Canna* spp. often bloom for much of the year and may be left undisturbed for years. Where hard and prolonged frosts occur, the rhizomes must be lifted and overwintered at a minimum of 7°C/15°F. In sheltered areas in zones 7–9 it may be possible to overwinter rhizomes *in situ* under a protective layer of leaves, ashes or glass frames. *C.indica* has proved quite resilient in these conditions, as have *C.× generalis* cvs.

Plant rhizomes outside in early summer in full sun, 45cm/18in. apart, 8–10cm/3–4in. deep. The soil should be well manured and moisture-retentive; avoid a windy site. Feed fortnightly with a phosphate-rich fertilizer. Allow the stems to blacken at the end of the season and then dig up the rhizomes; dry off for a day or so, then store in wood shavings or vermiculite. Check the rhizomes regularly, and moisten a little if there are signs of their drying out. Start the rhizomes off in early spring in pots; water sparingly until growth begins, and keep at a minimum of 16°C/80°F. The roots are easily broken, so pot on as soon as possible. Select a strong single shoot, and remove the remainder. *Canna* spp. need a constant temperature, a moist atmosphere and plenty of water – the last adjusted as the plant grows and the proportion of roots to compost increases: regular liquid feeds are required to keep the growth rate going.

Propagate cultivars by division in early spring. Also by seed; soak for 24 hours in warm water prior to sowing, or chip the seed coat; sow in late winter, into small pots using a soilless medium, at 18–20°C/65–70°F until germination occurs, then grow on at 16°C/60°F, repotting as necessary.

C.discolor Lindl. See *C.indica*.

C.edulis Ker-Gawl. See *C.indica*.

C.flaccida Salisb.
To 2m, glabrous throughout. Lvs 30–45×8–11cm, elliptic-lanceolate, apex narrowly acute to acuminate, gradually narrowing to sheath at base, glaucous. Infl. simple, fls paired, sessile; sep. 2–3cm, oblong-elliptic; cor. 8–9cm, yellow, tube 3–4cm, lobes reflexed, narrowly oblong lanceolate; staminodes 9–10cm, broadly obovate. Capsule ellipsoid, to 6cm, spiny-fimbriate. S US (S Carolina to Florida), Antilles, Panama. Z8.

C.× generalis L.H. Bail. CANNA LILY.
A large group of complex hybrids, varying in habit from short, stocky to tall and slender, in lf colour and texture from glaucous grey and leathery to dark chocolate-red and rather thin, in flower shape and colour from small with narrow segments to large and ruffled, from pale yellow to orange or scarlet. Garden origin. Bailey originally recognized *C.× generalis*, with fls to 10cm diam., not tubular at base, pet. not reflexed, staminodes and lip erect or spreading, and *C.× orchiodes* (derived in part from *C.flaccida*) with very large fls, tubular at base, with pet. reflexed, usually splashed or mottled and 3 broad, wavy staminodes exceeded by the lip. The first group included the Crozy or French cannas. With continued breeding, the distinction has become blurred and both are treated as *C.× generalis* here. 'Ambrosia': dwarf to 60cm; fls large, pink. 'America': lvs dark copper-purple; fls red. 'Black Knight': lvs brown; fls red. 'Bonfire': to 90cm; fls orange-scarlet. 'Cherry Red': lvs dark; fls bright red. 'City of Portland': to 100cm, strong grower, compact; fls rosy-pink. 'Cleopatra': lvs splashed black; combination of red and yellow fls, red and yellow bicolors often on same plant. 'Crimson Beauty': dwarf to 60cm; lvs broad; fls bright crimson. 'Cupid': fls pink in large clusters. 'Dazzler': to 120cm; fls burgundy. 'Di Bartolo': lvs brown tinged purple; fls deep pink. 'Eureka': dwarf; fls cream tinged yellow. 'Feuerzauber' ('Fire Magic'): lvs dark copper-purple; fls orange-red. 'Grumpy': miniature, compact to 50cm; fls brilliant red. 'Halloween': dwarf to 75cm; fls golden with red throats. 'J.B. Van der Schoot': to 90cm; fls yellow speckled red. 'King City Gold': fls yellow. 'King Midas': to 120cm; fls gold. 'Liebesglut': lvs dark copper-purple; fls orange-red. 'Lucifer': dwarf to 75cm; fls crimson red, broad yellow borders or edging on all segments. 'Orange Perfection': to 75cm; fls pale orange. 'Orchid': fls deep pink. 'Park Princess': dwarf to 75cm, compact; lvs glossy; fls pale pink, abundant. 'Pfitzer's Chinese Coral': dwarf to 75cm; fls pink. 'Pfitzer's Primrose Yellow': dwarf to 75cm, bushy; fls pale yellow in large clusters. Pfitzer's 'Salmon Pink': to 80cm, compact, vigorous; fls pink. 'Pfitzer's Scarlet Beauty': dwarf to 80cm, bushy; fls bright scarlet. 'Picasso': fls both yellow and red. 'President': to 120cm; lvs glossy; fls rich scarlet. 'Rosamund Cole': to 120cm; fls scarlet edged yellow, reverse golden with red overlay. 'Red King Humbert': to 2.1m; bronze-red lvs; fls brilliant orange-scarlet. 'Richard Wallace': to 120cm, vigorous grower; fls golden-yellow. 'Striped Beauty': short; lvs bright green veined in shades of cream and pale gold; fls scarlet in large truss. 'Wyoming': lvs bronze; fls orange. 'Yellow King Humbert': to 135cm; fls yellow dotted crimson. Z8.

C.gigantea Desf. ex Delaroche. See *C.tuerckheimii.*

C.glauca L.
To 1.5m. Lvs 30–50×3–15cm, narrow-ovate to narrow-ellip-tic, narrowing to apex, base cuneate, glaucous. Infl. simple, fls paired, shortly pedicellate; sep. to 2.5cm, narrowly ellip-tic-triangular, pale yellow; cor. 7–9cm, pale yellow, tube 2cm, lobes narrow-ovate; labellum strongly reflexed, outer staminodes 3, narrow-obovate to -elliptic, to 10cm. Capsule 2–6cm. Neotropics. Z10.

C.indica L. (*C.discolor* Lindl.; *C.edulis* Ker-Gawl.; *C.lanugi-nosa* Roscoe; *C.lutea* Mill.; *C.musifolia* hort.; *C.patens* (Ait.) Roscoe; *C.sanguinea* Warsc.; *C.warszewiczii* hort. ex A. Dietr.). INDIAN SHOT; QUEENSLAND; ARROWROOT; ACHIRA; TOUS LES MOIS.
To 2m, but often less. Lvs 20–50×10–18cm, narrow-ovate to -elliptic, apex acute to short-acuminate, base rounded or decurrent to sheath, green or sometimes stained red-purple. Infl. branched or simple; fls solitary or paired, sessile to shortly pedicellate; bracts waxy; sep. narrowly ovate-triangu-lar, to 1.5cm; cor. to 6cm, red to pink-red or orange, tube 1–2cm, lobes linear, to 4×0.6cm; labellum narrow-oblong-ovate, to 6×1cm, red, often spotted or edged yellow or pink, outer staminodes 2–3, narrow-elliptic to -obovate, to 7cm, red, sometimes spotted yellow. Capsule to 5cm, globose, strongly and acutely tuberculate; seeds black. Neotropics, widely naturalized elsewhere. 'Purpurea': to 2m, upright, vig-orous growth; lvs large, purple-bronze; fls small, red. Thompson & Morgan hybrids: to 90cm; lvs often bronze; fls in shades of yellow, red and cream. Z8.

C.iridiflora Ruiz & Pav.
To 3m. Lvs to 120×45cm, broad-oblong, apex acute, blue-green, lanuginose beneath when young. Infl. simple or sparsely branched, fls solitary, shortly pedicellate, pendent, deep pink or orange; sep. to 3cm, lanceolate, acuminate; cor. to 10cm, tube 6.5cm, lobes spathulate-lanceolate, reflexed at apex; staminodes 3, to 12cm, round-obovate, labellum emar-ginate at apex. Fr. oblong, to 3×2cm. Peru. Z9.

C.jaegeriana Urban.
To 5m. Lvs 50–100×13–38cm, narrow-elliptic to -ovate, apex short-acuminate, base cuneate, glabrous above and beneath, or lanuginose beneath, sheath glabrous or lanuginose. Infl. simple or branched; fls solitary or paired; pedicels to 0.5cm; sep. 2cm, triangular, orange; corolla to 6.5cm, orange, tube 2cm, lobes to 4.5×1cm; staminodes 4, to 6.5cm, obovate-elliptic. Fr. ellipsoid, covered by pink-tipped green papillae; seeds shiny black. Andes. Z9.

C.lanuginosa Roscoe. See *C.indica.*

C.liliiflora Warsc. ex Planch.
To 3m, glabrous throughout. Lvs 90–120×45cm, subhorizon-tal, oblong, acuminate. Infl. simple or occasionally branched, horizontally deflexed; fls solitary; sep. oblong, green; cor. 12–14cm, white, lobes oblong-linear, 2cm broad; staminodes 3, subequal, to 3cm broad. Panama, Bolivia. Z10.

C.lutea Mill. See *C.indica.*
C.musifolia hort. See *C.indica.*
C.× orchiodes L.H. Bail. See *C.× generalis.*
C.patens (Ait.) Roscoe. See *C.indica.*
C.sanguinea Warsc. See *C.indica.*

C.tuerckheimii Kränzl. (*C.gigantea* Desf. ex Delaroche).
Close to *C.indica.* To 3.5m. Lvs 35–100×15–40cm, narrow-ovate to -elliptic, apex short-acuminate, base cuneate to obtuse, glabrous; sheath lanuginose. Infl. branched at base, fls paired, pedicels to 3cm; sep. to 1.8cm, narrow-triangular, dull white; cor. 4–8cm, orange-red to red, tube to 3cm, lobes nar-row-ovate, to 5×1cm; staminodes 4, labellum, erect, outer sta-minodes to 8cm, narrow-obovate to spathulate. Fr. ovoid to ellipsoid, to 5.5cm. C America, much cultivated for starchy rhiz. Z9.

C.warszewiczii hort. ex A. Dietr. See *C.indica.*

Cardiocrinum (Endl.) Lindl. (From Gk *kardia*, heart and *krinon*, lily, referring to the strongly cordate leaves.) Liliaceae (Liliaceae). 3 species of large, lily-like herbs. Bulbs shallow, dying after flowering but freely producing offsets. Stems robust, erect, not rooting above bulb. Leaves broad, cordate, net-veined, long-petiolate. Inflorescence an erect terminal raceme; flowers funneliform, sometimes irregular, green to creamy white; tepals 6; stamens 6. Fruit a 3-valved capsule, valves fringed with teeth; seeds numerous, flattened. Summer. Himalaya to China, Japan. Z7.

CULTIVATION *Cardiocrinum* occurs in dense, moist forest and scrub, at altitudes of 1600–3300m/ 5200–10,725ft. *C.giganteum*, which may reach an impressive height of 4m/13ft, carries its luminous and uniquely fragrant white blooms at the tops of stout stems in late summer, maintaining their display by produc-ing large upright capsules that burst in autumn to release hundreds of flat, papery seeds. Although each indi-vidual is monocarpic, the colony is maintained by the plentiful production of daughter bulbs. *C.cathayanum*, with creamy white flowers, and *C.cordatum*, with creamy flowers sometimes spotted brown, are smaller in stature.

Cardiocrinum is eminently suited to the woodland garden, ideally planted on a slope in dappled shade. They are hardy to at least −10°C/14°F, but it may be necessary to protect the emerging young growths from frost with a dry mulch. Mulching is also advisable to protect from freeze/thaw cycles which may lift the bulbs and expose them to frost.

Grow in partial shade in deep, nutrient- and humus-rich woodland soils. All species must have ample water to grow well. The planting of different-sized bulbs with the nose just at soil level, will ensure continuity of bloom. Removal of bloomed bulbs and immediate replanting of daughter bulbs prevents overcrowding. Propagate from daughter bulbs (these take 3–5 years to flower), or from seed sown in a cool shaded frame when ripe; germina-tion is epigeal, the cotyledon usually growing out in late winter or early spring (see *Lilium*). Seed-grown plants may take seven years to flower, but are usually taller and more vigorous. Voles, mice and slugs may eat the bulbs and colonies should be inspected regularly. Pests and diseases otherwise as for *Lilium*.

C.cathayanum (Wils.) Stearn (*Lilium cathayanum* Wils.).
Stem to 1.5m, often dark purple near base, lower part of stem leafless. Lvs 10–13cm, scattered along stem, oblong-ovate, base reniform to cordate. Fls 1–5, 10–13cm, irregularly fun-neliform, tepals green-white below, cream, tipped and spotted purple above. Fr. 5.5cm. E & C China.

C.cordatum (Thunb.) Mak. (*Lilium cordatum* (Thunb.) Koidz.; *Lilium glehnii* F. Schmidt).
Stems 1.2–2m, stout, base leafless. Lvs 30×30cm, in a loose whorl toward lower half of stem, ovate, base deeply cordate, stained maroon when young. Fls 4–10, occasionally to 24, to 15cm, irregularly funneliform, cream-white, lightly fragrant;

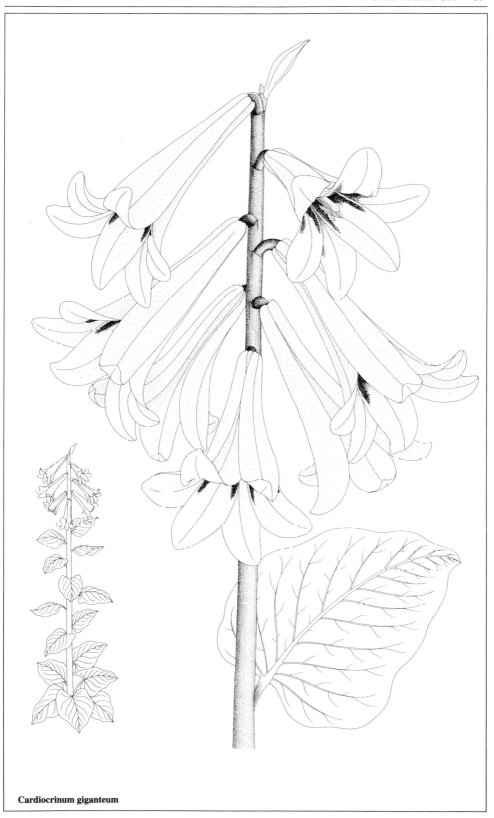

Cardiocrinum giganteum

lower tepals spotted red-brown, interior blotched yellow at base. Fr. 5.5cm. Japan, Sakhalin Is.

C.giganteum (Wallich) Mak. (*Lilium giganteum* Wallich non hort.). GIANT LILY.
Stem 1.5–4m, leafy. Lvs to 45×40cm broad-ovate, dark glossy green above, paler beneath, basal lvs in a rosette, stem leaves gradually smaller. Fls few to 20+, 15–20cm, regularly funneliform, fragrant; tepals white, sometimes tinted green, inside striped maroon. Fr. 5–6.5cm. Himalaya, NW Burma, SW China. var. **giganteum**. Fls only tinted green when young, opening from base of raceme upwards. var. **yunnanense** (Elwes) Stearn. Stem 1.5–2m, dark purple. Fls often persistently tinted green, opening from apex of raceme downwards. W & C China.

Carpolyza Salisb. (From Gk *karpos*, fruit, and *lyssa*, rage, from the peculiar method of dehiscence.) Amaryllidaceae. 1 species, a bulbous herb to 7.5–10cm. Leaves 2–5cm, 4–6, synanthous, subulate, slender. Inflorescence a 1–4-flowered umbel; scape slender, spirally twisted near base; pedicels 2–5cm, ebracteolate; spathe valves 2, linear, small; flowers 1.25cm diam., starry, pink in bud; perianth segments 12mm, 6, tubular toward base, white, outside tinted pink, basally fused into a short tube; stamens slightly exserted; ovary globose. Fruit a loculicidal capsule, c6mm diam.; seeds compressed-globose, wrinkled. Early spring. S Africa (SW Cape). Z9.

CULTIVATION As for *Ixia*.

C.spiralis (L'Hérit.) Salisb. (*C.tenella* (L. f.) Leighton).

C.tenella (L. f.) Leighton. See *C.spiralis*.

Cautleya (Benth.) Royle ex. Hook. f. (For Major-General Sir P. Cautley (1802–71), British naturalist.) Zingiberaceae. 6 species of perennial herbs. Stems leafy, arising from fleshy rhizomes. Leaves lanceolate to oblong, in 2 ranks, bases sheathing stem. Flowers yellow, borne amid conspicuous bracts in a loose terminal inflorescence on leafy stems; bracteoles absent; calyx tubular, open one side; corolla funnelform; petals 3; lateral staminodes petaloid, forming hood together with posterior petal; lip deeply 2-lobed; fertile stamen 1, short, erect, anther versatile, spurred at base. Fruit a short, 3-valved capsule, splitting readily. Summer. Himalaya. Z8.

CULTIVATION As for the hardier *Hedychium* spp.

C.gracilis (Sm.) Dandy (*C.lutea* (Royle) Hook. f.).
Stems slender, reed-like, to 40cm. Lvs 20×2cm, 4–6, glabrous, tinted purple or striped red-brown beneath, sessile. Infl. to 12-flowered, axis dark red; bracts green; cal. longer than bracts; cor. yellow.

C.lutea (Royle) Hook. f. See *C.gracilis*.

C.robusta Bak. See *C.spicata*.

C.spicata (J.M. Sm.) Bak. (*C.robusta* Bak.).
To 1m, robust. Lvs 35×10cm, glabrous, green, shortly petioled or sessile. Fls numerous, on spike; bracts 5cm, red; cal. shorter than bracts; cor. 2.5cm, yellow.

Ceropegia L. (From Gk *keros*, wax, and *pege*, fountain, in reference to the form and the waxy appearance of the flowers.) Asclepiadaceae. 200 species of perennials, climbing or erect, often with a caudex, swollen tubers or fleshy, fusiform roots. Leaves opposite, occasionally in whorls of 3, in the case of non-succulent species always well developed, usually petiolate, cordate to lanceolate especially in climbing species, usually linear to almost filiform in erect species, in succulent species well developed or smaller, reduced to scales or caducous. Flowers in a cyme or solitary, pedicellate or sessile, arising laterally between the petioles; calyx composed of 5 sepals, the 5 petals of the corolla united to form a tube which is usually longer than wide, swollen at base and cylindric or funnel-shaped in the central and upper parts, straight or curved, tips of corolla lobes often remaining united creating a lantern-like structure. Fruit a follicle, lanceolate to cylindric, pointed, glabrous; seeds flat with a tuft of silky hairs. Canary Is., Tropical & SE Africa, Madagascar, Comoro, Tropical Arabia, Himalaya, W & S China, India, Sir Lanka, Indonesia, Philippines, New Guinea, Australia (Queensland). Z10.

CULTIVATION *Ceropegia* spp. are found in almost all types of subtropical and tropical habitat, from desert to rainforest. Cultivation must be matched to the habitat from which the plants originates. Almost all spp. found in cultivation, however, tend to be more or less succulent and it is to these that the following notes apply.

The genus shows a wide diversity in shape and colour of leaf, flower and stem structure, which makes many of them excellent plants for greenhouse decoration or as house plants in temperate parts of the world. In tropical and subtropical zones, the climbing spp. can make interesting additions to trellis pergolas and walls, particularly in areas of low rainfall. All are tender and need a minimum winter temperature of 12–13°C/54–55°F. Some spp. from particularly warm areas, such as Madagascar, are better at 16°C/60°F minimum.

When grown as greenhouse plants, they require intermediate or hothouse conditions with medium to low humidity, particularly in winter, and bright filtered light in summer. When grown in pots, a well-drained, gritty potting medium should be used. The root system is often tuberous or fusiform; wide and relatively shallow pots suit the former, and standard to extra deep (e.g. long toms) suit the latter. Pot or re-pot in early spring, and water very sparingly or not at all until re-established. Rest succulents between mid-autumn and early spring, watering only to prevent excessive shrivelling. Water rapid-growing, leafy spp. sparingly in spring and autumn, moderately in summer. Water slow-growing and erect, succulent spp. sparingly at all times.

Propagate by cuttings, seed, or by tubers, which are produced at the nodes along the stem of some spp., most notably *C.linearis* and its sspp. Cuttings of climbing spp. should be taken just below a node and consist of 2–3-node tip-cuttings of mature young shoots. The most common pest is mealybug, which is best controlled using a high-volume spray/drench with a synthetic pyrethroid insecticide. Basal rot will occur in overwet conditions; stems thus affected should be used for cutting material.

C.africana R. Br. (*C.wightii* Graham & Wight).
Stems slender, trailing or erect from small tubers, the stems themselves proliferous, producing small tubers. Lvs ovate, elliptic or lanceolate, fleshy. Cor. glabrous outside, 1–2.5cm, exterior tinged green, brown-violet-striate toward the mouth, interior glabrous, lobes linear, 6–12mm, joined at the tip, with dark purple hairs inside along the keel; outer corona lobes of staminal column deeply cupular, inner lobes broad and laterally flattened. S Africa (E & W Cape).

C.assimilis N.E. Br. See *C.cancellata*.
C.barbertonensis N.E. Br. See *C.linearis* ssp. woodii.

C.barklyi Hook. f.
Differs from *C.africana* in having cor. lobe hirsute on the inside slender section, lobes equalling or exceeding tube, often twisted together for much of their length, interior hairy, particularly toward the base. S Africa (Eastern Cape).

C.cancellata Rchb. (*C.assimilis* N.E. Br.).
Stems slender, twining, from small tuber. Lvs ovate-oblong to linear, fleshy. Cor. glabrous outside, tube 12–20mm, green, interior hairy in central part, lobes 6–12mm, linear, purple brown, glabrous, united at tips. This species appears to be midway between *C.africana* and *C.linearis*. S Africa (Cape Province).

C.decidua E.A. Bruce.
Stems short, to 15cm, thin, twining, from a small round tuber. Lvs variously ovate to lanceolate. Cor. glabrous outside, papillose inside swollen basal part of tube, lobes linear widening to spathulate at tip, tips united, sometimes with a small canopy, lobes 4–6mm, interior purple-ciliate, tube ridged in line with centre of lobes for upper third of its length. Kenya to Cape Province. ssp. **pretoriensis** R.A. Dyer. Vegetatively similar to type, but longitudinal ridge on upper third of cor. tube absent; outer corona lobes forming much shallower cup. Confined to the Transvaal (in and around Pretoria).

C.galpinii Schltr. See *C.rendallii*.

C.linearis E. Mey.
Stems thin, twining or cascading, from depressed globose tubers; tubers also develop on stem nodes, especially when stems are prostrate-growing. Lvs triangular-ovate to lanceolate or linear, fleshy. Cor. exterior glabrous, tube 12–15mm, exterior light green with purple longitudinal stripes, interior of middle section dark-hirsute, lobes narrow-linear, slightly spathulately widening and united toward tips, at least twice as long as cor. tube is wide, dark purple-brown, margins with purple ciliate hairs, cor. tube not widening significantly at junction with lobes. S Africa (S Cape Province). ssp. **tenuis** (N.E. Br.) P.V. Bruyns (*C.tenuis* N.E. Br.). Cor. lobes not more than twice as long as the tube mouth is wide. Cape. ssp. **woodii** (Schltr.) H. Huber (*C.woodii* Schltr.; *C.barbertonensis* N.E. Br.; *C.hastata* N.E. Br.; *C.schoenlandii* N.E. Br.). HEARTS ENTANGLED; SWEETHEART VINE; HEARTS ON A STRING. Stems slender, glabrous, twining, pendent or creeping, forming tubers at the nodes. Lvs to 1.25cm diam., fleshy, rounded-reniform, base typically cordate, apex acute, dull purple beneath, sea green above, often with purple and grey-green markings. Cor. exterior glabrous, tube 1–2cm, exterior dull pink or light green, interior of middle section hirsute, tube widening to funnel-shaped at junction with lobes, lobes narrow-linear, spathulate, widening toward tips, 5–7mm, purple-brown, margins and interior keel with purple ciliate hairs. Zimbabwe to E Cape.

C.multiflora Bak.
Stems annual, to 90cm, from a tuber to 10cm diam., slender, twining, glabrous. Lvs fleshy, round-ovate, elliptic, lanceolate or linear. Infl. many-fld; cor. green-white, tube 12–26mm, exterior glabrous, interior hirsute, lobes 5–15mm, filiform from a triangular base, interior hairy at base, lower half projecting obliquely outward, upper half directed almost horizontally inward, tips remaining united. S Africa (N Cape, Transvaal). ssp. **tentaculata** (N.E. Br.) H. Huber (*C.tentaculata* N.E. Br.). Cor. lobes usually separating. Angola, Namibia, Zimbabwe.

C.pachystelma Schltr.
Tuber to 10cm diam.; stems slender, twining, downy. Lvs broad almost cordate, pilose, fleshy. Cor. bronze or yellow green to off-white, downy outside, tube 2–3cm, interior of middle section short-pubesc., lobes narrow-linear, 5–12mm, light brown below, red above, pubesc. throughout, or sometimes glabrescent within. Mozambique, Natal, Transvaal, Namibia. ssp. **undulata** (N.E. Br.) H. Huber (*C.undulata* N.E. Br.). Cor. lobes 8–12mm, widening to spathulate tip.

C.patersoniae N.E. Br. See *C.zeyheri*.

C.racemosa N.E. Br.
Roots fleshy, thickened, tufted; stems slender, twining, not succulent, short-hairy. Lvs broad-ovate to linear. Fl. elongated; cor. red-brown, tube 1–2cm, exterior glabrous, interior evenly hairy, a little widened at mouth, lobes long ovate, 5–12mm, interior sparsely white-hairy. Tropical Africa.

C.rendallii N.E. Br. (*C.galpinii* Schltr.).
Main tuber large; stems 8–15cm, slender, twining and bearing small tubers at nodes, or erect and remaining dwarf, glabrous or minutely downy. Lvs fleshy, ovate or linear. Cor. exterior glabrous, tube 12–20mm long on the interior middle section, lobes narrow-linear in basal half, widening above to spathulate, united to form an umbrella-shaped canopy 7–9mm across, margins obscurely 10-lobed, sparsely ciliate with purple hairs. S Africa (Orange Free State, Transvaal).

C.schoenlandii N.E. Br. See *C.linearis* ssp. woodii.

C.stentiae E.A. Bruce.
Tuber small; stems erect, to 10cm, upper part downy. Lvs fleshy, narrow-linear, glabrous. Fls 1 or few together; cor. exterior glabrous, tube 2–3cm, middle section hairy, lobes narrow-linear, as long as tube or longer, hairy toward base, tips united. S Africa (Transvaal).

C.superba D.V. Field & I.S. Collenette.
Tubers long-fusiform; stems sparsely branched, semi-succulent, twining, to 2m, 2–3mm diam. Lvs 6×1.5–2mm, minute, linear-lanceolate, caducous. Pedicel 6–15mm; cor. 6–8cm, base abruptly narrowed to a cylindric portion 2.5–3mm diam., widening to 9–12mm at mouth, interior and exterior glabrous except at mouth, lobes 23–31mm, base deltoid then replicate and narrow-linear, united at tip, tube and base of lobes dull white with pale purple spots arranged in lines, replicate portion of lobes bright green inside, base with broad, transverse, purple band. Saudi Arabia, S Yemen.

C.tentaculata N.E. Br. See *C.multiflora* ssp. *tentaculata*.
C.tenuis N.E. Br. See *C.linearis* ssp. *tenuis*.

C.turricula E.A. Bruce.
Tuber to 8cm diam.; stems 15–30cm, simple, slender, erect. Lvs to 12cm×4mm, few, non-succulent, narrow-linear. Fls few, to 4 per plant, very large for size of plant; cor. tube 3.6cm, base rounded, swollen, narrow above, expanding to a wide funnel 1.8cm diam., lobes to 2.3cm, replicate, tips united,

with long purple hairs, bases of tube and lobes dull white spotted light red-brown, base of interior of lobes white with moss green centre, edged black, tips olive. S Africa (N Transvaal).

C.undulata N.E. Br. See *C.pachystelma* ssp. *undulata*.
C.wightii Graham & Wight. See *C.africana*.
C.woodii Schltr. See *C.linearis* ssp. *woodii*.

C.zeyheri Schltr. (*C.patersoniae* N.E. Br.).
Roots fleshy, fusiform; stems twining, glabrous, usually leafless. Lvs, when present, to 1cm, small, ovate or lanceolate.

Cor. tube 2–5cm, pale green-white lobes with deltoid base then a long, narrow, straight strut terminating in an ovate-lanceolate tip which all join together, lobes almost equalling tube, bright green-hairy, particularly in lower half. S Africa (S Cape).

Chamaelirion Willd. (From Gk *chamai*, dwarf, and *lirion*, lily.) DEVIL'S BIT. Liliaceae (Melanthiaceae). 1 species, a dioecious, tuberous, perennial herb, related to *Helonias*. Stems erect, 30–70cm (males) or to 120cm (females), simple, glabrous. Basal leaves 5–20×1–4cm in a loose rosette, obovate to spathulate, stalked; stem leaves smaller, linear to lanceolate, sessile. Inflorescence a dense cylindric raceme, 4–12cm in males, often pendent towards tip, in females to 30cm, more slender, less dense; pedicels to 0.5cm; flowers *c*0.7cm across, tepals 3mm, 6, linear-spathulate, white, becoming yellow with age; stamens 6, anthers subspherical; staminodes (in females) 6; ovary superior; styles 3. Fruit a many-seeded capsule; seeds linear-oblong, broadly winged. Summer. Eastern N America. Z4.

CULTIVATION   As for *Helonias*.

C.luteum (L.) A. Gray. BLAZING STAR; FAIRY WAND; RATTLE-SNAKE ROOT.

Chasmanthe N.E. Br. (From Gk *chasma*, chasm, and *anthos*, flower.) Iridaceae. 3 species of perennial herbs. Corms renewed annually, usually fairly large, somewhat flattened, with tunic of thin fibres. Leaves several, distichous, overlapping. Spikes secund or distichous, sometimes branched; flowers irregular, vermilion, red, orange or yellow; perianth tube curved, widening abruptly from a short, tubular basal part *c*2mm diam. to a wider, cylindrical upper part, with 1–3 nectar pouches where the tube expands, segments 6, unequal, the topmost one at least twice as long as others; style and stamens lying under topmost segment, style filiform with 3 short branches. Closely related to *Crocosmia* and *Tritonia*. S Africa (Cape Province). Z9.

CULTIVATION   As for *Aristea*.

C.aethiopica (L.) N.E. Br. (*Antholyza aethiopica* L.; *Antholyza vittigera* Salisb.; *Chasmanthe vittigera* (Salisb.) N.E. Br.).
40–70cm; corms to 4.5cm diam. Lvs 6–8, usually 40–60cm×12–18mm, linear or lanceolate. Spike 15–18cm, unbranched, 7–15-fld, more or less secund; fls to 8cm long, red, maroon in throat, the tube with yellow stripes; tube 2.5–4cm, the narrow basal part 0.5–1.5cm, often spirally twisted, upper part usually 2–2.5cm long, 4–6mm wide, with 3 nectar pouches at point of expansion, mouth oblique, topmost seg. 25–35×7–10mm, oblanceolate, obtuse; lateral seg. 10–15×4–7mm, spreading or recurved, lowest seg. smaller; anth. purple or black; style 5.5–6.5cm, branches 4–5mm. Autumn–winter. SW to SE Cape, coastal areas.

C.bicolor (Gasp. ex Ten.) N.E. Br. (*Antholyza bicolor* Gasp.).
70–130cm; corm 2–2.5cm diam. at flowering time. Lvs 6–7, 50–80×2.5–3.5cm, sword-shaped, often with silky sheen. Spike 25–30cm, sometimes with 1–2 basal branches, rather laxly 12–28-fld, more or less secund. Fls to 8cm, vermilion red and yellow-green, the lobes vermilion, dark red or pink and green; tube 30–33mm, basal part 6–10mm, sometimes twisted, upper part 20–25×5–7mm, curved, topmost lobe 30–40×6–7mm, linear-spathulate, longitudinally folded, other

lobes 5–8mm, the 3 outer erect, the inner 2 spreading or recurved; style 5–8cm, branches 3mm. Winter–spring. SW Cape.

C.floribunda (Salisb.) N.E. Br. (*Antholyza floribunda* Salisb.; *C.praealta* Rehd.).
50–150cm; corms flattened, 6–7cm diam. Lvs 8–10, usually 30–50×2.5–3.5cm, lanceolate, forming a fan. Spike about 30cm, often branched at base, distichous, densely many-fld; fls to 8.5cm, orange-red or yellow; tube 3.5–5cm, basal part 9–12mm, sometimes twisted, upper part 25–30×5–8mm, curved, with 1 nectar pouch where tube expands, mouth oblique, topmost lobe 30–33×8–10mm, oblanceolate, lateral lobes 12–20×4–7mm, oblong, spreading or recurved, lowest lobe smaller; style 65–80mm, branches 7–10mm. Winter–spring. SW Cape. var. *floribunda*. Fls orange-red, tube often with yellow stripes; anth. purple. var. *duckittii* G. Lewis ex L. Bol. Fls primrose yellow, the lower part of tube slightly shorter than in var. *floribunda*; anth. yellow-brown.

C.intermedia (Bak.) N.E. Br. See *Tritoniopsis intermedia*.
C.praealta Rehd. See *C.floribunda*.
C.vittigera (Salisb.) N.E. Br. See *C.aethiopica*.

Chionodoxa Boiss. (From Gk *chion*, snow, and *doxa*, glory; the wild plants flower among the melting snow.) GLORY OF THE SNOW. Liliaceae (Hyacinthaceae). 6 species of bulbous perennial herbs allied to *Scilla*, from which they are distinguished by the tepals united at the base, and to *Puschkinia*, but with stamens free. Bulbs small, tunics brown. Leaves basal, linear, usually 2, erect or spreading. Flowers in a loose raceme, deep blue, white or pink; perianth tube short, subspherical, lobes 6, spreading; stamens 6, at apex of perianth tube, filaments unequal, compressed; ovary superior; style 1. Fruit a subspherical capsule. W Turkey, Crete, Cyprus. Z4.

CULTIVATION Small, charming and easily grown spring-flowering bulbs for the rock garden, troughs and other containers, for raised beds and in the alpine display house; most are tolerant of temperatures to –15°C/5°F and below. More robust spp. such as *C.forbesii*, *C.luciliae* and *C.sardensis* are particularly suited to underplantings in the (deciduous) shrub border and in the wild garden. The diminutive *C.albescens* (and *C.nana*) may be more safely grown in the alpine house or frame. Grow in any well-drained, moderately fertile, humus-rich soil in sun. A mulch of leafmould, garden compost or screened, well-rotted manure in autumn is beneficial. Propagate by offsets or ripe seed, and by division of established clumps.

C.albescens Speta.
Like *C.nana* but fls to 1cm, very pale pink to lavender.

C.cretica Boiss. See *C.nana*.

C.forbesii Bak. (*C.luciliae* auct.; *C.tmolusi* Whittall; *C.siehei* Stapf).
Lvs 7–28cm, few, erect to spreading. Flowering stems 8–30cm; fls 4–12 per stem, slightly drooping; perianth intense deep blue with white centre, tube 0.3–0.5cm, lobes 1–1.5×0.4–0.5cm; fil. white. W Turkey. 'Alba': fls snow white. 'Naburn Blue': fls dark blue, centre white. 'Pink Giant': fls pink with white centre. 'Tmoli': dwarf, to 10cm; fls bright blue.

C.gigantea Whittall. See *C.luciliae*.

C.lochiae Meikle.
Lvs 7–18cm, erect. Flowering stems to 18cm; fls 2–4 per stem, horizontal or drooping; perianth light blue without white zone, tube 5–7mm, lobes 12–13×4–6mm; fil. white. Cyprus.

C.luciliae Boiss. (*C.gigantea* Whittall).
Lvs 7–20cm, often recurved. Flowering stems to 14cm; fls 1–2 per stem, erect; perianth soft violet-blue with small white central zone, tube 2.5–4mm, lobes 12–20×3–8mm, fil. white. W Turkey. 'Alba': fls white. 'Rosea': fls pink.

C.luciliae auct. non Boiss. See *C.forbesii*.

C.nana (Schult. & Schult.) Boiss. (*C.cretica* Boiss.).
Lvs 8–18cm, spreading, not exceeding scape. Flowering stems to 20cm; fls 1–3 per stem, erect; perianth blue with white central zone, tube 3–5mm, narrowly conical, lobes 6–11×3mm; fil. white. Crete.

C.sardensis Whittall.
Lvs erect or spreading, channelled. Flowering stems to 40cm; fls 4–12 per stem, slightly drooping; perianth deep blue, not shading to white, tube 3–5mm, lobes 8–10×2–4mm; fil. white. W Turkey.

C.siehei Stapf. See *C.forbesii*.
C.tmolusi Whittall. See *C.forbesii*.

× **Chionoscilla** J. Allen ex Nichols. (*Chionodoxa* × *Scilla*.) Liliaceae (Hyacinthaceae). Natural hybrid, intermediate between the parents, very variable.
CULTIVATION As for *Chionodoxa*.

× *C.allenii* Nichols. (*Chionodoxa forbesii* × *Scilla bifolia*.)
Lvs exceeding scape, oblanceolate, apex acute, sheathing at base. Fls starry, perianth seg. fused at base, blue or lilac-pink, with paler central zone; fil. pale blue. Spring. Garden origin.

Chlidanthus Herb. (From Gk *chlide*, luxury, a costly ornament, and *anthos*, flower.) Amaryllidaceae. 1 species, a perennial bulbous herb. Leaves 15–40×0.9cm, hysteranthous, subsessile, linear, channelled, grey-green, apex obtuse or subacute, margins rough; membranous sheath covering one-third of leaf-length. Scape solid, to 30cm; bracts 2, to 9cm, chartaceous; inflorescence umbellate; pedicels to 1.2cm; flowers fragrant; perianth to 7cm across, trumpet-shaped, yellow, red, cinnabar or green striped pink, base tubular, to 7.5cm, free segments 6, lanceolate, shorter than tube; stamens 6, anthers dorsifixed, yellow; style straight, 3-branched, sometimes exserted; ovary inferior, 3-celled. Capsule globose; seeds flat, dark brown, often winged. Spring. Peru. Z9.

CULTIVATION *C.fragrans* is a frost-tender small bulb, native to the Andes, grown for its golden yellow, exotically perfumed flowers borne in mid- to late summer. In zones that are frost-free or almost so, plant in well drained soil at the base of a sunny wall, protecting if necessary in winter with a dry mulch of bracken litter. Otherwise, grow in a sandy loam-based medium enriched with leafmould and well rotted manure, in the cool glasshouse or conservatory, minimum 5–10°C/40–50°F. Plant in spring, with the nose just above soil level. Water plentifully when in growth and dry off in autumn after flowering, overwintering the bulbs in cool dry conditions. Pot-grown plants may be plunged in the open garden for the summer and lifted in autumn. Propagate by offsets or seed in spring.

C.fragrans Herb.

Chlorogalum (Lindl.) Kunth. (From Gk *chloros*, green, and *gala*, milk; an allusion to the colour of the sap.) SOAP PLANT; AMOLE. Liliaceae (Hyacinthaceae). 5 species of bulbous perennials. Bulb tunics fibrous or membranous. Leaves linear, mostly basal, margin undulate, cauline leaves considerably smaller. Flowers funnelform to campanulate in terminal panicles, opening in the afternoon; pedicels articulate; tepals 6, free, usually narrow-oblong, white or pink, with 3 central veins, withering and twisting together following pollination; stamens 6, not exceeding tepals, anthers versatile; ovary superior, style 1, apex 3-lobed. Fruit a trilocular capsule; seeds 1–2 per cell, black. Summer. Western N America (S Oregon to N Baja California). Z8.

CULTIVATION   As for *Camassia*.

C.angustifolium Kellogg.
To 45cm. Bulb to 6cm, tunic membranous. Lvs 30×6cm, grass-like. Tepals 0.8–1.2cm, white with a green-yellow central stripe; pedicels 3mm; stamens usually equalling tepals. N & C California.

C.pomeridianum (DC.) Kunth. SOAP PLANT; WILD POTATO.
60–150cm. Bulb to 15cm, tunic fibrous. Lvs to 75×2.5cm, flaccid, glaucous, margins scabrid, undulate. Tepals 1–2.5cm, white with a purple or green central stripe; pedicels 5–30mm; stamens two-thirds length of tepals. S Oregon to N California.

Cipura Aubl. Iridaceae. 5 species of perennial bulbous herbs related to *Tigridia*. Leaves plicate, one to several forming a fan at base and one set on flowering stem just below inflorescence. Inflorescence composed of several flower clusters enclosed in spathes; flowers short-lived, blue, violet, yellow or white; tepals 6, outer broadly clawed, inner erect, usually with a nectar-bearing area often hidden by a fold; stamens free, anthers adnate to style branches; style with 3 thick branches, with or without 1 or 2 pairs of erect crests. S Mexico to Bolivia, S Brazil and Paraguay, W Indies. Z10.

CULTIVATION   In cool temperate zones, *Cipura* spp. need glasshouse protection with a minimum temperature of 12°C. They grow well in full sun in a rich and open mix of sandy loam and leafmould; water plentifully when in growth, with a period of dry rest after flowering. Propagate by offsets, which are freely produced, or by seed sown in gentle heat in spring. Keep moderately dry in winter and repot in spring.

C.paludosa Aubl.
16–27cm. Basal lvs 1–3, 16–27cm×2–5mm, linear-lanceolate; stem lf. similar, the base clasping spathe. Fl. clusters several, sessile or with short stalks; fls usually pale blue to violet, the outer tepals white at base, sometimes white, inner tepals with yellow nectar guide sometimes edged with violet; perianth tube *c*2mm, outer tepals 25–28×13–15mm, oblanceolate, twisted, ascending or horizontal, inner tepals 15×8–10mm, obovate. Bolivia and Paraguay to S Mexico & W Indies.

Clivia Lindl. (For the Duchess of Northumberland, née Clive, *d.*1866.) KAFFIR LILY. Amaryllidaceae. 4 species of perennial, evergreen herbs, mostly stemless, a stem being only clearly differentiated in *C.caulescens*. Leaves bright green, smooth, fairly thick-textured, strap-shaped, radical, in 2 distinct, opposite ranks, sheathing at base, margins smooth or scabrous. In some species swollen leaf bases with papery blade remains form bulb-like structures. Inflorescence umbellate, subtended by several separate bracts on a solid scape; perianth tube short, funnel-shaped, segments longer than tube; stamens declinate; style slender, 3-lobed; ovary inferior, globose, 3-chambered, each locule with 5–6 ovules. Fruit a berry, red, pulpy with globose seeds. S Africa (Natal). Z10.

CULTIVATION   Native to warm, dry, forest habitats in Natal, *C.miniata* is grown for the strong warm colours of its large, fragrant flowers and robust clumps of strap-shaped evergreen leaves. *C.nobilis*, less robust in appearance, bears pendent, tubular, orange-red flowers with green tips, in spring. *Clivia* spp. are frost-tender and well suited to cultivation in large pots in the glasshouse, conservatory or home, and are noted for their tolerance of dry atmospheres and shade. They dislike root disturbance and flower best when roots are restricted. Plant in a fibrous medium-fertility loam-based mix with added leafmould and coarse sand, in bright filtered light with a minimum temperature of 10°C/50°F, rising to about 16°C/60°F when in full growth. Water plentifully when in growth, and feed weekly with liquid fertilizer as flower buds appear. Remove spent flower stems near the base and reduce water after flowering, keeping cool and dry but not arid when resting. Repot in late winter/early spring only when pot-bound; top-dress annually with fresh potting mix. For earlier flowering, maintain a temperature of 18°C/65°F, reducing to 13°C/55°F as flower buds show colour. Propagate by division or detached offsets; water plentifully, and syringe during re-establishment at 16°C/60°F. Germinate seed at 21°C/70°F in a closed case, growing on at 16°C/60°F as first seed leaves appear. Germination takes about 6–8 weeks and offspring may be variable. Sometimes infested with mealybugs.

C.caulescens R.A. Dyer.
Lf bases forming a stout pseudostem to 50cm tall. Lvs 15, to 180×2.5–5cm. Infl. to 50cm, 15–20-fld; fls drooping, slightly reflexed, to 3.5cm, yellow to salmon pink tipped with green and yellow; perianth narrowly funnel-shaped, straight or slightly reflexing, with lobes of 3.5–4cm; stamens as long as perianth, anth. 2–2.5mm. Spring.

C.×cyrtanthiflora (Van Houtte) Wittm. (*C.hybrida* hort.). (*C.miniata × C.nobilis*.)
Resembles *C.nobilis* but fls rich salmon pink or light flame-coloured; perianth tube narrow with inner perianth seg. twice as broad as outer seg.

C.gardenii Hook. f.
Lvs to 75×2.5–4cm, narrow-acuminate, entire or slightly

toothed. Infl. to 60cm, 10–14-fld; fls to 7.5cm, narrowly funnel-shaped, red, tinged orange or yellow; pedicel to 4cm; perianth lobes oblanceolate, obtuse, 3.5–5cm, margins yellow above, tips spreading, green; stamens equal to or longer than perianth, anth. to 3mm; ovary globose; style exserted. Fr. bright red, to 2.5cm. Winter–spring.

C.grandiflora Hort. See *C.miniata*.

C.hybrida hort. See *C.cyrtanthiflora*.

C.miniata Reg. (*C.grandiflora* hort.; *Imantophyllum miniatum* (Reg.) Hook. f.).
Lvs to 60×3–7cm, bright green, oblanceolate, ligulate, acute. Infl. to 45cm,12–20-fld; fls erect to spreading; pedicel 2.5–5cm; cor. tube to 13mm, bright scarlet, throat yellow, broadly funnel-shaped, outer seg. oblanceolate, inner seg. oblanceolate-oblong, lobes to 7cm, inner broader than outer; perianth longer than stamens and style; anth. to 4mm, yellow;

ovary globose. Fr. ovoid, bright red. Spring–summer. 'Aurea': fls yellow (deep yellow at base of seg.). 'Grandiflora': fls large. 'Flame': lvs wide, rich green; fls deep orange-red. 'French Hybrid': fls strong orange. Striata Group: lvs freely variegated white, cream or yellow. Several attractive variegated clones are available with stripes of various widths and colours.

C.nobilis Lindl. (*Imantophyllum aitonii* Hook. f.). GREENTIP KAFFIR LILY.
Lvs about 12, to 45×5cm, obtuse, abruptly contracted at apex, margin rough. Infl. to 25cm, 40–60-fld; fls drooping, slightly reflexed, narrower and shorter than in *C.miniata*; perianth seg. to 30×8–12mm, oblanceolate, red and yellow, tipped green, overlapping, inner seg. longer than outer seg.; stamens exserted; style longer than stamens. Spring.

Colchicum L. (Of Colchis, on the Black Sea.) AUTUMN CROCUS; NAKED LADIES. Liliaceae (Colchicaceae). 45 species of perennial herbs. Corm tunics membranous, papery or coriaceous, often extended into a persistent tubular pseudostem, occasionally with horizontal rhizomatous outgrowths. Leaves basal, linear, lorate, lanceolate or elliptic-ovate, smooth, semi-terete to ribbed or plicate, developing with or after flowering (occasionally developing as flowers fade); developing leaves and flowers enclosed in a membranous sheath. Flowers solitary or in clusters, very short-stalked, each subtended by a small bract; perianth campanulate, funnelform or star-shaped, purple, pink, white, or yellow, sometimes tessellated, perianth lobes 6, in 2 equal or almost equal whorls, sometimes winged at base, throat sometimes ridged at base of filaments, forming a short channel; stamens borne near base of perianth lobes, in 1 or 2 series, filaments slender, sometimes thickened at base, anthers dorsifixed and versatile or basifixed and rigid; styles 3, free, stigmas point-like or unilaterally decurrent along the style; ovary subterranean. Fruit a 3-celled, septicidal capsule; seeds numerous, subspherical. E Europe, N Africa to W Asia, through Afghanistan to N India and W China.

CULTIVATION   Occurring in a range of characteristically well-drained habitats, from higher-altitude spring-flowering types such as *C.szovitsii*, *C.kesselringii* and *C.luteum*, which flower at snow melt in alpine meadow and on stony or earthy hillsides, to those amenable autumn-flowering species, *C.speciosum* and *C.autumnale* of subalpine meadow which are of sufficiently robust constitution to naturalize in grass. Most *Colchicum* spp. bear their blooms before the leaves, although in many spring-flowering species the gap, if any, between blooming and emergence of the leaves is quite short. In general, those with leaves partially developed at flowering are more safely grown in the bulb frame or alpine house with protection from excess moisture, since botrytis infection of the dying flowers may spread to the emerging leaves. Grown in raised beds, at the foot of rockwork and on ledges in the rock garden, most species thrive in an open and sunny position, with some protection from the fiercest midday sun in warmer climates.

Among the hardiest species, *C.autumnale* will tolerate winter temperatures to –20°C/–4°F and below; *C.alpinum*, *C.cilicum* and *C.speciosum* are almost as hardy. With the possible exceptions of *C.variegatum* and *C.lingulatum*, which are not reliable where temperatures fall below –5 and –10°C/23–14°F, most will survive winter temperatures down to about –15°C/5°F. Grow in any moderately fertile, well-drained soil that retains sufficient moisture when plants are in leaf. Propagate by fresh seed sown ripe or by division of established clumps while dormant.

C.agrippinum Bak. (*C.variegatum × C.autumnale?*)
Vigorous sterile hybrid between *C.autumnale* and *C.variegatum*, of unknown origin. Corm to 3.5cm diam., narrow, tunic dark. Lvs to 15cm, erect, dull glaucous green, margin somewhat undulate. Fls numerous, funnel-shaped; tube to 6cm, white; seg. to 5×1.5cm, acute, heavily but indistinctly tessellated purple and white; fil. pink, red-orange at base, anth. purple, pollen yellow; styles purple, stigmatic surface white. Early autumn. Greece to SW Turkey. Z5.

C.alpinum DC.
Corm 1–2.5×1–1.5cm, subspherical to ovoid; tunics dark red-brown, membranous or rather tough-textured, neck 1–2cm. Lvs 8–15×0.2–1.4cm, 2 or 3, hysteranthous, strap-shaped to linear-lanceolate, glabrous. Fls 1 or 2, narrowly campanulate to funnelform; perianth lobes 1.7×3–0.4–1cm, narrowly oblong-elliptic, purple-pink, occasionally white; fil. 2–9mm, glabrous, anth. 2–3mm, dorsifixed, yellow, pollen yellow; styles straight, stigmas point-like. Fr. 1.5–2cm, oblong-ellipsoid. Late summer– autumn. France, Switzerland, Italy, Corsica and Sardinia. Z4.

C.ancyrense B.L. Burtt. See *C.triphyllum*.

C.andrium Rech. & P.H. Davis. See *C.stevenii*.

C.arenarium Waldst. & Kit.
Like *C.alpinum* but lvs 3–5, somewhat longer and broader, fls slightly larger. Possibly synonymous with *C.umbrosum*. Summer–autumn. EC Europe. Z6.

C.armenum B. Fedtsch. See *C.szovitsii*.

C.atropurpureum Stearn.
Close to *C.turcicum* but fls small, dark magenta-red, white in bud. Balkans, SW Turkey. Z6.

C.atticum Tomm. See *Merendera attica*.

C.autumnale L.
Corm 2.5–6×2–4cm, ovoid to subspherical; tunics dark brown, membranous to coriaceous, neck 2–4cm. Lvs 14–35×1–7cm, 3–5, coriaceous more, hysteranthous, linear-lanceolate to broadly lanceolate, erect to spreading. Fls 1–6, campanulate, sometimes narrowly so; perianth lobes 4–6×1–1.5cm, narrowly elliptic to oblong-elliptic, purple-pink to white, occasionally tessellated; fil. 1–1.6cm, glabrous,

Colchicum Flowering parts, habit outlines (a) *C.autumnale* (b) *C.speciosum* (c) *C.luteum* (d) *C.cupanii*
(e) *C.triphyllum*

anth. yellow, dorsifixed, pollen yellow; styles curved at apex, stigmas decurrent for 3–5mm. Capsule 2–6cm, oblong ovoid. Late summer–autumn. W & C Europe. Cvs include: 'Alboplenum': fls double, white. 'Album': fls small, dull white. 'Plenum': fls double, lilac-pink. Z5.

C.balansae Planch. (*C.candidum* Boiss.).
Corm 4–5×2–3cm, ovoid; tunics dull, dark black-brown, membranous to subcoriaceous, apex extended into a long, thick, persistent, strongly fibrous neck to 25cm. Lvs 18–24×4–7.5cm, 4–5, developing after flowering, erect to spreading, elliptic to oblong-elliptic, the inner lvs more strap-shaped than the outer. Fls 3–11, funnelform; perianth lobes 4.5–7.5×0.5–1.3cm, narrowly oblong-elliptic, white to purple-pink; fil. 1–1.9cm, glabrous, anth. 1–1.7cm, dorsifixed, yellow, with membranous longitudinal margins, pollen yellow; styles curved at apex, stigmas decurrent for 1.5–3mm. Fr. 3–3.5cm, ovoid. Late summer–autumn. Turkey, Greece. Z7.

C.balansae var. *macrophyllum* Siehe. See *C.cilicicum*.

C.baytopiorum C. Brickell.
Corm 2.5–3.5×1.5–2.5cm, narrowly ovoid to almost spherical, sometimes more or less horizontal with runners, irregular in shape; tunics red-brown, membranous to papery, frequently short-lived. Lvs 1–8cm at flowering, 20–32×2.5–4.5cm at maturity, 3, narrowly to very narrowly lanceolate, glabrous. Fls 1–3, rarely to 5, campanulate or funnelform, perianth lobes 2.2–4.2×0.5–1.1cm, elliptic or oblong-elliptic to oblanceolate, bright purple-pink; fil. 1–1.4cm, glabrous, anth. 5–7mm, yellow, pollen lemon yellow; styles straight, stigmas point-like. Fr. 2–2.5cm, narrowly ellipsoid. Autumn. W Turkey. Z8.

C.biebersteinii Rouy. See *C.triphyllum*.
C.bifolium (Freyn & Sint.) Bordz. See *C.szovitsii*.

C.bivonae Guss. (*C.latifolium* Sibth. & Sm.; *C.visianii* Parl.; *C.bowlesianum* B.L. Burtt, *C.sibthorpii* misapplied).
Corms 2.5–6×2.5–4cm, ovoid to subspherical; tunics mid-brown, papery to subcoriaceous, apex extended into a short neck 1–2cm. Lvs 12–30×1–4.5cm, hysteranthous, more or less erect, strap-shaped or linear-lanceolate, glabrous. Fls 1–6, campanulate, sometimes broadly so; perianth lobes 4–8.5×0.8–3.5cm, narrowly to broadly elliptic, occasionally obovate-elliptic, rosy purple, strongly tessellated, sometimes white at base, downy along ridges of fil. channels; fil. 1–2.5cm, glabrous, anth. 7–12×2–3mm, dorsifixed, purple-black or purple-brown, pollen bright yellow; styles curved and slightly swollen at apex, stigmas decurrent for 2–4mm. Fr. 3.5–4cm, oblong-ellipsoid. Late summer-autumn. S Europe from Corsica and Sardinia to W Turkey. (A parent of many garden hybrids with *C.speciosum, C.bornmuelleri* and *C.autumnale*.) Z6.

C.boissieri Orph. (*C.procurrens* Bak.).
Corm 2.5–3×0.3–1.3cm, with horizontal runners, irregular, often with tooth-like projections, occasionally irregularly ovoid or oblong-ovoid and more or less vertical, tunics pale red-brown, membranous. Lvs 11–22×0.2–0.8cm, 2–3, developing after flowering, erect or almost so, linear, margins glabrous or partly ciliate. Fls 1 or 2, campanulate to narrowly funnelform; perianth lobes 2.5–5×0.5–1.5cm, very narrowly elliptic to narrowly elliptic-obovate, bright rosy lilac; fil. 1–2cm, glabrous, anth. 5–10mm, dorsifixed, yellow, pollen yellow; style straight or slightly curved at apex, stigmas point-like. Fr. c2cm, ellipsoid. Autumn. S Greece, W Turkey. Z8.

C.bornmuelleri Freyn.
Corm 2.5–4.5×2.5–4cm, ovoid to subspherical; tunics dull mid-brown, papery to membranous, apex extended into a neck 1–8cm. Lvs 17–25×2.6–4.5cm, 3 or 4, developing after flowering more or less erect, very narrowly elliptic, glabrous. Fls 1–6, campanulate, sometimes narrowly so; perianth lobes 4.5–7×1.1–2.4cm, oblanceolate to narrowly elliptic, rosy purple (throat usually white), downy along ridges of the fil. channels; fil. 1.3–2.8cm, glabrous, anth. purple or purple-brown,

8–12mm, dorsifixed, pollen yellow; styles slightly curved, stigmatic surface 0.5–1.5mm, confined to the swollen apex of the style. Fr. 4–5cm, narrowly ovoid or narrowly ellipsoid. Late summer–autumn. Turkey. Plants grown as *C.bornmuelleri* may be white-throated variants of *C.speciosum* and can be readily distinguished by their yellow, not purple-brown anthers. Z5.

C.bowlesianum B.L. Burtt. See *C.bivonae*.

C.brachyphyllum Boiss.
Like *C.szovitsii* but lvs 4–6, narrowly ovate to lanceolate. Fls to 15. Syria, Lebanon. Z8.

C.bulbocodium Ker-Gawl. See *Bulbocodium vernum*.
C.bulbocodioides Bieb. non Brot. See *C.triphyllum*.

C.burttii Meikle.
Corm 3–5×1.5–2cm, narrowly ovoid to subspherical; tunics black-brown, coriaceous with prominent longitudinal corrugations, apex fringed with rigid fibres 1.5cm long. Lvs erect to spreading and 1–4cm at flowering, recurved and 10–15×0.8–1cm at maturity, 2–4, narrowly linear to linear-lanceolate, shortly hairy at least on margins. Fls 1–4, funnelform, becoming star-shaped; perianth lobes 1.5–4×0.3–0.8cm, narrowly oblanceolate, white or pale purple-pink; fil. 8–10mm, thinly hairy at least near base, anth. 2–3mm, dorsifixed, dark purple-black or black; styles straight, stigmas point-like. Fr. c1cm, narrowly ellipsoid, roughly hairy at apex. Early spring. W Turkey. Z7.

C.byzantinum Ker-Gawl.
Vigorous sterile hybrid, probably derived from *C.cilicicum*, first recorded by Clusius in 1601. Corm to 7cm diam., rounded, tunic red-brown. Lvs to 30×15cm, strongly ribbed or pleated, emerging in spring (cf. *C.cilicicum*, with lvs emerging in autumn), bright green. Fls numerous, pale lilac-pink; tube to 8cm, white; seg. to 5cm, oval, strongly keeled, the keel appearing as a white line within, apex spotted dark purple; fil. pale lilac-pink, anth. pale brown, pollen deep yellow; styles white, slightly exceeding stamens, stigma hooked, crimson purple. Often grown to flower as a dry corm on the windowsill before being planted out. Turkey, Syria, Lebanon. 'Album': fls white, retaining purple apices on perianth seg. and crimson stigmata. Plants similar to *C.byzantinum* are sometimes grown as *C.laetum*. Z6.

C.byzantinum auct. non Ker-Gawl. See *C.cilicicum*.
C.byzantinum var. *cilicicum* Boiss. See *C.cilicicum*.
C.candidum Boiss. See *C.balansae*.
C.candidum var. *hirtiflorum* Boiss. See *C.kotschyi*.
C.catacuzenium Stef. See *C.triphyllum*.
C.caucasicum (Bieb.) Spreng. See *Merendera trigyna*.

C.chalcedonicum Aznav.
Like *C.lingulatum* but fls deep rosy purple, tessellated. NW Turkey. Z6.

C.cilicicum (Boiss.) Dammer (*C.byzantinum* var. *cilicicum* Boiss.; *C.balansae* var. *macrophyllum* Siehe; *C.decaisnei* misapplied; *C.byzantinum* auct. non Ker-Gawl.).
Corms 4–6×3–4.5cm, subspherical to ovoid; tunics dark brown, papery to subcoriaceous, neck 5–17cm. Lvs 30–40×4–11.5cm, 4–5, developing after flowering, more or less erect, narrowly elliptic to narrowly elliptic-lanceolate, glabrous. Fls 3–25, funnelform to campanulate; perianth lobes 4–7.5×1.2–2.5cm, oblanceolate to elliptic, pale lilac to deep rose-purple, occasionally faintly tessellated, edges along fil. channels downy; fil. 2.5–3.5cm, anth. bright yellow, dorsifixed, pollen bright yellow; styles straight or slightly curved at apex, tip often dull crimson, frequently exserted, stigmas point-like or decurrent for less than 0.5mm. Capsule 3–4cm, ellipsoid to obovoid. Autumn. Turkey, Syria, Lebanon. 'Purpureum': fls very deep rosy purple. Z6.

C.corsicum Bak.
Like *C.alpinum* but lvs 3 or 4, shorter and broader; stigmas shortly decurrent. Summer–autumn. Corsica. Z7.

C.crociflorum Reg. See *C.kesselringii*.

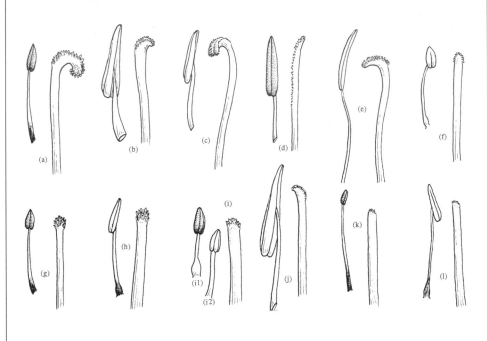

Colchium (a) *C.bivonae* anther, style tip (b) *C.speciosum* anther, style tip (c) *C.autumnale* anther, style tip (d) *C.agrippinum* anther, style tip (e) *C.luteum* anther, style tip (f) *C.triphyllum* anther, style tip (g) *C.cupani* anther, style tip (h) *C.baytopianum* anther, style tip (i) *C.szovitsii* (i1) inner anther (i2) outer anther, style tip (j) *C.macrophyllum* anther, style tip (k) *C.variegatum* anther, style tip (l) *C.boissieri* anther, style tip

C.crocifolium Boiss.
Like *C.falcifolium* but lvs glabrous or covered in rough hairs. Fls numerous, star-shaped, white and pink. Syria, Iran, Iraq. Z8.

C.cupanii Guss. (*C.glossophyllum* Heldr.).
Corms 1–2×1–1.5cm, ovoid; tunics dark brown, leathery, with a short neck. Lvs to 10cm at flowering, 7–15×0.2–1.8cm at maturity, 2 (very rarely 3), linear to linear-lanceolate, glabrous or rarely ciliate at base. Fls 1–12, funnelform to star-shaped; perianth lobes 1.8–2.5×0.3–0.5cm, narrowly elliptic, pale to deep purple-pink; fil. 6–10mm, glabrous, anth. 2–3mm, dorsifixed, purple-black, pollen yellow; styles straight, stigma point-like. Fr. 1–1.3cm, ovoid. Autumn–early winter. N Africa, France, Italy, Greece, Crete. Z8.

C.decaisnei Boiss. See *C.troodii*.
C.decaisnei misapplied. See *C.cilicicum*.
C.doerfleri Hal. See *C.hungaricum*.

C.falcifolium Stapf (*C.varians* Freyn & Bornm.; *C.serpentinum* Misch.; *C.tauri* Stef.; *C.hirsutum* Stef.; *C.szovitsii* auct. non Fisch. & Mey.; *C.szovitsii* var. *freynii* Stef.).
Corm 2–4×1.5–2cm, ovoid; tunics dark red-brown, papery to subcoriaceous, usually persistent, neck absent or vestigial. Lvs 1–8cm at flowering, 9–20×0.1–0.7cm at maturity, 3–6, narrowly linear, channelled, glabrous, roughly hairy or with margins and upper surface sparsely to densely stiffly hairy (forms treated as *C.hirsutum*). Fls 1–8, star-shaped or narrowly funnelform; perianth lobes 1.3–2.5×0.2–0.6cm, very narrowly to narrowly elliptic or narrowly oblanceolate, white to purple-pink; fil. 8–12mm, glabrous, anth. 2.5–3.5mm, dorsifixed, black, green-black or black-brown, pollen yellow; styles straight, stigmas point-like. Fr. 1–2cm, narrowly ovoid to almost spherical. Late winter–early spring. S Russia, Turkey, Iran, Iraq, W Syria. Z8.

C.fasciculare (L.) R. Br.
Like *C.falcifolium* but lvs glabrous and broader. Fls numerous, star-shaped, white and pink. Syria. Z8.

C.giganteum Arn. (*C.illyricum superbum* invalid).
Closely related to *C.speciosum* but fls broadly funnel-shaped, not campanulate. Z5.

C.glossophyllum Heldr. See *C.cupanii*.
C.hirsutum Stef. See *C.falcifolium*.

C.hungaricum Janka (*C.doerfleri* Hal.).
Corms 2–3×1–2cm, oblong-ovoid; tunics dark brown, papery to subcoriaceous, with a short neck. Lvs 3–10cm at flowering, to 20×1–2cm at maturity, 2, rarely 3, narrowly linear-lanceolate, more or less erect, ciliate, upper surface sometimes partially or entirely hirsute. Fls 1–8, campanulate to funnelform; perianth lobes 2–3×0.6–0.7cm, elliptic-lanceolate or narrowly elliptic, purple-pink to white; fil. 7–10mm, glabrous, anth. 2–3.5mm, dorsifixed, purple-black, pollen yellow or orange; styles straight or slightly curved at apex, stigmas point-like. Fr. c1cm, subspherical. Late winter–early spring. Hungary, Yugoslavia, Albania, Bulgaria, Greece. var. *albiflorum* Maly. Fls white. Z7.

C.illyricum superbum invalid. See *C.giganteum*.
C.imperator-frederici Siehe. See *C.kotschyi*.

C.kesselringii Reg. (*C.regelii* Stef.; *C.crociflorum* Reg.).
Corm 1–3×1–2cm, oblong-ovoid; tunics dark brown, coriaceous, extended into a short neck. Lvs more or less erect and 1–2cm at flowering, 7–10×0.3–1cm at maturity, 2–7, linear-lanceolate, glabrous or slightly rough at margins. Fls 1–4, narrowly campanulate to funnelform; perianth lobes 1.5–3×0.2–0.7cm, narrowly linear-lanceolate to narrowly elliptic, white with pale to deep red-purple, central stripes; fil. 3–4mm, glabrous, anth. 8–10mm, yellow, basifixed, pollen yellow; styles straight, stigmas point-like. Early spring–summer. C Asia, N Afghanistan. Z6.

C.kotschyi Boiss. (*C.candidum* var. *hirtiflorum* Boiss.; *C.imperator-frederici* Siehe; *C.persicum* Bak.).
Corm 3–5×2–3cm, ovoid; tunics dark brown, membranous to subcoriaceous, apex extended into a persistent neck 3–14cm. Lvs 10–16×3–5cm, 3–5, developing after flowering, erect to spreading, elliptic-lanceolate to oblong-elliptic, glabrous, margins slightly undulate. Fls 3–12, funnelform; perianth lobes 2.3–5.5×0.4–1.2cm, narrowly oblanceolate to oblong-elliptic, white to purple-pink, downy along bases of the ridges of the fil. channels; fil. 7–12mm, glabrous, anth. 6–12mm, dorsifixed, yellow, with membranous longitudinal margins, pollen yellow; styles curved at apex, stigmas decurrent for 2–4mm. Fr. 3–4.5cm, oblong-ovoid. Late summer–autumn. Turkey, Iran, Iraq. Z7.

C.kurdicum (Bornm.) Stef. See *Merendera kurdica*.

C.laetum Steven.
Like *C.autumnale* but fls 1–3, smaller, and stigmas shortly decurrent. Plants in cult. as *C.laetum* with numerous star-shaped, pale purple-pink fls are close to *C.byzantinum*. Z7.

C.latifolium Sibth. & Sm. See *C.bivonae*.
C.latifolium misapplied. See *C.macrophyllum*.
C.latifolium var. *longistylum* Pamp. See *C.macrophyllum*.

C.lingulatum Boiss. (*C.sibthorpii* hort.).
Corms 3–6×2–3.5cm, ovoid to subspherical; tunics black-brown, more or less leathery, extended into a persistent neck to 8cm. Lvs 3–7, hysteranthous, spreading, oblong to strap-shaped, glabrous, margins cartilaginous and usually wavy. Fls funnelform to campanulate; perianth lobes 2.5–5×0.2–1.2cm, narrowly oblanceolate to narrowly oblong-elliptic, pale to deep purple-pink sometimes faintly tessellated; fil. 6–14mm, glabrous; anth. 4–8mm, dorsifixed, yellow, pollen yellow; styles curved at apex, stigmas decurrent for 2–3mm. Fr. 1.5–2.5cm, oblong-ovoid. Late summer–autumn. Greece, NW Turkey. Z8.

C.longiflorum Cast. (*C.neapolitanum* Ten.).
Like *C.autumnale* but lvs shorter, linear-lanceolate, and fls slightly smaller. S Europe. Z7.

C.lusitanicum Brot.
Like *C.autumnale* but fls lightly tessellated; anth. pale or deep purple-black. SW Europe, N Africa. Z8.

C.luteum Bak.
Corm 1.5–3×1–2.5cm, oblong ovoid; tunics dark chestnut, papery, extended into a short neck. Lvs more or less erect and 1–3cm at flowering, 10–30×0.6–2cm at maturity, 2–5, linear-lanceolate, glabrous. Fls 1–4, funnelform to narrowly campanulate; perianth lobes 1.5–2.5×0.2–0.6cm, narrowly oblong-lanceolate, pale to deep yellow, tube sometimes purple-brown; fil. 3–4mm, glabrous, anth. 6–13mm, yellow, basifixed, pollen yellow; styles straight, stigmas point-like. Fr. 2–3cm, ovoid. Spring–summer. C Asia, Afghanistan, N India, SW China (Xizang). Z7.

C.macrophyllum B.L. Burtt (*C.latifolium* misapplied; *C.latifolium* var. *longistylum* Pamp.).
Corms 5–7×4–6cm, ovoid to subspherical; tunics dull dark brown, coriaceous, apex extended into a persistent, somewhat fibrous neck to 24cm. Lvs 24–42×11–15.5cm, 3 or 4, hysteranthous, erect to spreading, ovate to elliptic-ovate, apex subacute to bluntly acuminate, strongly plicate, glabrous. Fls 1–5; perianth lobes 4.5–7×1.5–3cm, elliptic or oblong-elliptic, spreading, lilac-purple to rosy purple, tessellated, often paler or white in throat, glabrous; fil. 2–2.5cm, glabrous; anth. 8–12mm, purple, dorsifixed, pollen grey-green, drying paler; styles shortly curved at apex, stigmas decurrent for 1.5–2.5mm. Fr. 4–5cm, ovoid. Autumn. Greece (Crete, Rhodes), SW Turkey. Z8.

C.micranthum Boiss.
Corms 2.5–3×1.3–2.7cm, subspherical to ovoid; tunics red-brown, membranous, neck 1–4cm, usually poorly developed. Lvs 10–20×0.3–1cm, 2–3, developing after flowering, almost erect, linear to very narrowly linear-oblanceolate, glabrous.

Fls 1–2, narrowly campanulate or funnelform; perianth lobes 1.8–4×0.3–1.1cm, narrowly oblanceolate, oblanceolate or narrowly linear-elliptic, white to pale purple-pink; fil. 6–10mm, glabrous, anth. 3–5mm, dorsifixed, yellow, pollen yellow; styles straight, shortly curved, slightly swollen at apex, stigmas decurrent for 1mm. Fr. 1.8–2.5cm, narrowly ellipsoid to ovoid. Autumn. NW Turkey. Z7.

C.montanum hort. See *C.triphyllum*.
C.montanum var. *pusillum* (Sieb.) Fiori. See *C.pusillum*.
C.neapolitanum Ten. See *C.longiflorum*.
C.nivale Boiss. & Huet ex Stef. See *C.szovitsii*.
C.parkinsonii Hook. See *C.variegatum*.

C.parlatoris Orph.
Corm 2–4×1.5–2cm, ovoid; tunics dark brown, leathery, neck 3–4cm. Lvs 7–10×0.1–0.4cm, 4–10, usually developing after flowering, linear to narrowly linear, glabrous. Fls 1 or 2, narrowly campanulate; perianth lobes 8–50×4–12mm, narrowly elliptic, purple-pink; fil. 1–1.2cm, glabrous, anth. 4–6mm, dorsifixed, yellow, pollen yellow; styles straight, stigmas point-like. Fr. c1cm, ovoid-oblong. Late summer–autumn. S Greece. Z8.

C.parnassicum Boiss.
Like *C.autumnale* but corm tunics membranous, lvs arched. Greece. Z8.

C.peloponnesiacum Rech. & P.H. Davis. See *C.stevenii*.
C.persicum Bak. See *C.kotschyi*.
C.procurrens Bak. See *C.boissieri*.

C.psaridis Hal.
Corm 2–5×0.4–1.2cm, irregular in shape, more or less horizontal with runners, sometimes swollen; tunics pale brown, papery or membranous. Lvs 7–9cm at flowering, 7–15×0.2–1.5cm at maturity, 2–3, erect or almost so, usually partly developed at flowering, narrowly linear to narrowly linear-lanceolate, margins glabrous or partly ciliate. Fls 1–3, star-shaped to narrowly funnelform; perianth lobes 1.1–2.7×0.2–0.6cm, very narrowly elliptic or narrowly elliptic-oblong, white to pink-purple; fil. 4–8mm, glabrous, anth. 2–3mm, black or purple black, dorsifixed, pollen yellow; styles straight, stigmas point-like. Fr. oblong-ovoid, 1.5cm. Autumn. S Greece, W Turkey. Z8.

C.pusillum Sieb. (*C.montanum* var. *pusillum* (Sieb.) Fiori).
Corm 1.5–2.5×0.9–1.7cm, ovoid to subspherical; tunics dull, dark brown, papery, neck 1–6cm. Lvs more or less erect and 1–4cm at flowering, recurved and 8–11×0.1–0.5cm at maturity, 3–8, narrowly linear, glabrous or sometimes hairy. Fls 1–6, funnelform, opening star-shaped; perianth lobes 1–2×1.5–4cm, narrowly oblanceolate to narrowly oblong-oblanceolate, pale rosy lilac to white; fil. 5–8mm, glabrous, anth. 1.5–4.5mm, dorsifixed, purple-black, brown-black or grey-brown, pollen yellow; styles straight, stigma point-like. Fr. 1–1.3cm, ovoid. Autumn. Greece, Crete, Cyprus. Z8.

C.regelii Stef. See *C.kesselringii*.

C.serpentinum Misch. See *C.falcifolium*.
C.sibthorpii Bak. See *C.bivonae*.
C.soboliferum (Mey.) Stef. See *Merendera sobolifera*.

C.speciosum Steven.
Corms 5–8×2.5–4cm, oblong-ovoid; tunics dull mid-brown, papery to subcoriaceous, extended into a persistent neck to 12cm. Lvs 18–25×5.5–9.5cm, 3–5, developing after flowering, more or less erect, narrowly elliptic to oblong-lanceolate, glabrous. Fls 1–3, campanulate (not funnelform as in the related *C.giganteum*); perianth tube green or white flushed purple, lobes 4.5–8×1–2.7cm, oblanceolate to oblong-oblanceolate or elliptic, pale to deep rose-purple, sometimes white or white at throat, downy along ridges of fil. channels; fil. 1–1.8cm, glabrous, anth. 1–1.2cm, dorsifixed, orange-yellow, pollen deep yellow; style curved but not or only slightly swollen at apex, stigmas decurrent for 2–4mm. Fr. 4–5cm, ellipsoid. Autumn. N Turkey, Iran, Caucasus. 'Album': fls large, white, throat green. 'Atrorubens': fls purple-red.

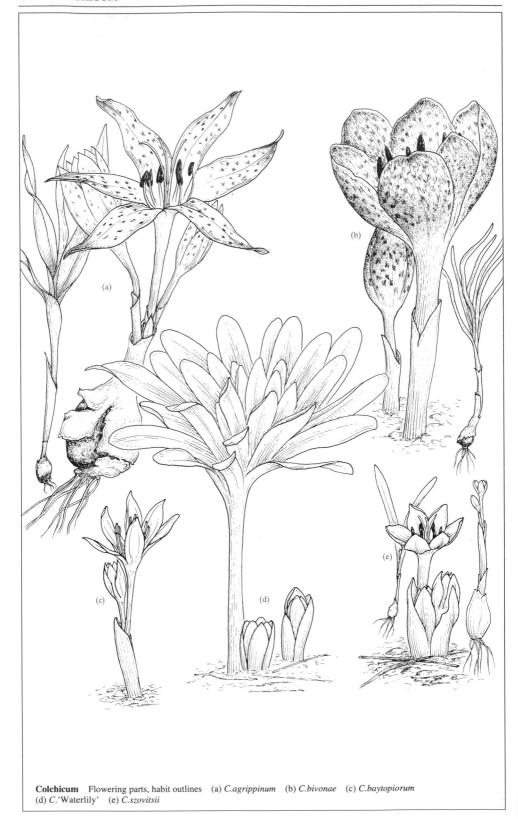

Colchicum Flowering parts, habit outlines (a) *C.agrippinum* (b) *C.bivonae* (c) *C.baytopiorum*
(d) *C.*'Waterlily' (e) *C.szovitsii*

Variants with green perianth tubes and conspicuously white-throated fls and yellow anth. are frequently but incorrectly grown as *C.bornmuelleri*, which has purple-brown anth. Z6.

C.speciosum var. *bornmuelleri* (Freyn) Bergmans. See *C.bornmuelleri*.

C.stevenii Kunth.
Corm 1.6–3×1–1.5cm, ovoid to subspherical; tunics dull, dark brown, papery to subcoriaceous, extended into a neck 1–6cm long. Lvs 1–12cm at flowering, 8–18×0.1–0.5cm at maturity, 4–12, more or less erect, recurved and often wavy, glabrous or ciliate. Fls 1–10, funnelform; perianth lobes 1.5–3×0.2–0.9cm, oblong-elliptic to oblanceolate, bright purple-pink; fil. 8–12mm, glabrous, anth. yellow; styles straight, stigmas point-like. Fr. 1–1.5cm, oblong-ovoid. Autumn–early winter. Cyprus, Turkey, W Syria. *C.peloponnesiacum* Rech. f. & P.H. Davis and *C.andrium* Rech. f. & P.H. Davis are very similar, closely related species from Greece and the Islands. Z8.

C.szovitsii Fisch. & Mey. (*C.bifolium* (Freyn & Sint.) Bordz.; *C.armenum* B. Fedtsch.; *C.nivale* Boiss. & Huet ex Stef.).
Corm 1.5–4×1–3cm, ovoid; tunic black-brown, papery to subcoriaceous, neck absent or vestigial. Lvs 2–12cm at flowering, 12–25×1.2–3.5cm at maturity, 2–3, lorate or very narrowly linear-lanceolate, more or less erect, glabrous. Fls 1–7, ovoid- or narrow-campanulate; perianth lobes 2.1–3.5×0.4–1cm, oblanceolate to very narrowly elliptic, occasionally with basal auricles, deep to pale purple-pink or white, strongly suffused purple; fil. 7–11mm, glabrous, anth. 2–5mm, dorsifixed, purple-black or green black; styles straight, stigmas point-like. Fr. 3.5–4cm, ellipsoid to spherical. Early spring–summer. Turkey, Iran, Caucasus. Z6.

C.szovitsii auct. non Fisch. & Mey. See *C.falcifolium*.
C.szovitsii var. *freynii* Stef. See *C.falcifolium*.
C.tauri Stef. See *C.falcifolium*.

C.tenorii Parl.
Like *C.autumnale* but fls slightly tessellated, stigma tips tinged purple. Italy. Z8.

C.triphyllum Kunze (*C.bulbocoides* Bieb. non Brot.; *C.biebersteinii* Rouy; *C.catacuzenium* Stef.; *C.ancyrense* B.L. Burtt; *C montanum* hort.).
Corm 1.5–2.5×1–1.5cm, oblong-ovoid; tunics chestnut, membranous, short-lived, lacking an extended neck. Lvs to 2–9cm at flowering, 11–15×0.5–1.1cm at maturity, 3, erect to spreading, linear-lanceolate, margins rough or smooth. Fls 1–6, campanulate to funnelform; perianth lobes 1.5–3×0.5–1.2cm, narrowly elliptic to oblanceolate, occasionally with auricles at base, purple-pink or white flushed purple-pink; fil. 7–9mm, glabrous, anth. 2.5–3.5mm, dorsifixed, purple-black or purple-green, pollen yellow; styles straight, stigmas point-like. Fr. 2–3cm, ovoid to oblong-ovoid. Early–late spring. NW Africa, Spain, Greece, Turkey, S Russia. Z8.

C.troodii Kotschy (*C.decaisnei* Boiss.).
Corm 3–6×2.5–4cm, ovoid; tunics dark black-brown, papery to subcoriaceous, extending into a persistent neck to 9cm. Lvs 10–30×1.2–4.5cm, 3–8, developing after flowering, erect to spreading, lorate, glabrous, ciliate or thinly hairy. Fls 2–12, narrowly funnelform to star-shaped; perianth lobes 2.8–4.5×0.4–1.1cm, narrowly oblong-lanceolate, white to pale purple-pink; fil. 1.5–2cm, glabrous, anth. 6–8mm, dorsifixed, yellow, with membranous longitudinal margins, pollen yellow; styles erect or slightly curved at apex, stigmas point-like or

obliquely decurrent for 0.5mm. Fr. 1.5–3cm, ellipsoid. Autumn–winter. Cyprus, Turkey, W Syria, Israel, Lebanon. Z8.

C.turcicum Janka.
Corm 3–5×2.5–4cm, subspherical to ovoid; tunics dark black-brown, coriaceous, with an extended persistent neck to 11cm. Lvs 9–19×1–3.5cm, 5–9, hysteranthous, more or less erect and often twisted at apex, lorate to narrowly lanceolate, somewhat glaucous, margins thinly cartilaginous, ciliate (sometimes obscurely so). Fls 1–8, campanulate to funnelform; perianth lobes 3–6×0.3–1.3cm, elliptic to narrowly obovate, red-purple, occasionally paler, sometimes lightly tessellated, downy along ridges of fil. channels; fil. 1–2.5cm, glabrous, anth. 5–8mm, yellow, perhaps sometimes tinged purple, dorsifixed, pollen yellow; styles straight, curved at apex, stigmas decurrent for 3–4mm. Fr. 2–3cm, ovoid to oblong ovoid. Late summer–autumn. Balkans, NW Turkey. Z7.

C.umbrosum Steven
Corms 1–3×1.2–2.5cm, ovoid to subspherical; tunics dark black-brown, usually coriaceous, usually with a persistent neck to 7cm. Lvs 8–17×1–2.7cm, 3–5, developing after flowering, more or less erect, strap-shaped to very narrowly lanceolate, glabrous. Fls 1–6, funnelform at first, star-shaped when fully open; perianth lobes 1.5–3×0.2–0.6cm, narrowly oblanceolate to linear-elliptic, white to purple-pink; fil. 5–8mm, glabrous, anth. 3–4mm, dorsifixed, yellow, pollen yellow; styles straight or slightly curved and swollen at apex; stigmas decurrent for 0.5–0.75mm. Fr. 2–3cm, oblong-ellipsoid. Late summer–autumn. Romania, Crimea, N Turkey. Z6.

C.varians Freyn & Bornm. See *C.falcifolium*.

C.variegatum L. (*C.parkinsonii* Hook.; *C.variegatum* var. *desii* Pamp.).
Corm 2–5×2–3.5cm, ovoid to subspherical; tunics dark brown, somewhat coriaceous, extended into a persistent neck 5–15cm. Lvs 9–15×0.7–2.5cm, 3 or 4, developing after flowering, linear-lanceolate or lorate, glabrous, margins cartilaginous, wavy. Fls 1–2; perianth lobes 2–2.7×0.5–2.5cm, spreading, lanceolate to elliptic or oblanceolate, deep red- or violet-purple, occasionally paler or white at base, strongly tessellated, frequently slightly twisted near the obtuse or acute apex, glabrous; fil. 1.5–4cm, glabrous; anth. 4–9mm, dorsifixed, purple-black or purple-brown; styles straight, occasionally slightly curved and swollen at apex, stigmas decurrent for 1.5–2mm. Fr. 2cm, oblong-ovoid. Autumn. Greece, SW Turkey. Frequently confused with *C.agrippinum* which has semi-erect rather faintly tessellated perianth lobes and which may be derived from this species. Z8.

C.variegatum var. *desii* Pamp. See *C.variegatum*.
C.vernum (L.) Ker-Gawl. See *Bulbocodium vernum*.
C.visianii Parl. See *C bivonae*.

C.cultivars.
'Autumn Queen' ('Prinses Astrid'): fls tessellated, rosy-lilac, tube ray-like; summer. 'Beaconsfield': fls tulip-shaped, lilac-pink, faintly tessellated, tube white. 'Giant' ('The Giant'): fls large, lilac-pink with faint tessellation, white in centre, tube white. 'Lilac Wonder': fls pale lilac; seg. to 7cm, narrow, tube long, soon collapsing, white. 'Pink Goblet': fls large, rounded, rosy-pink, tube pink. 'Violet Queen': fls large, blue-lilac, tessellated purple, throat and tube white. 'Waterlily': fls double, deep rose-pink, tube white.

Colocasia Schott. (From Arab. *kolkas* or *kulcas*.) COCOYAM; TARO; DASHEEN. Araceae. 6 species of evergreen perennial tuberous herbs, sometimes stoloniferous, or with stem thick and erect. Leaves peltate, entire, sagittate or ovate-cordate, large, glabrous; venation conspicuous, lateral veins pinnate, 6–8 pairs; petiole long. Inflorescence solitary or several axillary; peduncle shorter than petioles; spathe constricted, convolute at base, overlapping spadix, apical portion forming elongate, hooded or flattened limb; spadix shorter than spathe, stout or slender, with short or long appendix; flowers unisexual, perianth absent, male flowers separated from female flowers by vestigial florets, stamens 3, connate, forming column, ovary unilocular, ovules 1 to many. Fruit a berry, enclosed in persistent spathe tube; seeds numerous. Tropical Asia, some widely naturalized in Tropics and warm temperate regions. Z10.

CULTIVATION *Colocasia* spp. are grown in temperate zones as ornamentals with treatment as for *Caladium*; *C.esculenta* (taro) and *C.esculenta* var. *antiquorum* (eddo) are important staple carbohydrate foods in the humid lowland tropics, often established in low lying areas along stream and river banks, where the temperature range remains stable between 21–27°C/70–80°F and rainfall is in excess of 2500mm/100in. p.a. Both are eaten boiled, baked and roasted, the smaller, nutty flavoured cormels of eddo being particularly good roasted with meat as a substitute for potatoes; since the skins sometimes contain irritants which are destroyed on cooking, they are best peeled wearing household gloves.

Grow in a fairly heavy, fertile and moisture-retentive soil rich in organic matter, pH 5.5–6.5; improve light soils by pre-planting incorporation of compost or well rotted manure. Eddo tolerates lighter soils, slightly lower temperatures (18–25°C/65–77°F) and lower rainfall. For taro, plant side suckers, pre-sprouted tubers or portions of the corm (50–140g/1.5–4.5oz.) at 60cm/24in. spacings in rows 100cm/39in. apart; less vigorous cvs at closer spacings and in areas with a high water table, mound or ridge planting is recommended. (In the South Pacific region, the top portion of the main corm is planted, which may give rise to higher yields.) For eddo, plant small cormels (60–150g/2–5oz.), 60×.60cm/24×24in. apart, into holes prepared with organic matter and a balanced NPK fertilizer. Apply a high-potash NPK fertilizer as a monthly topdressing (additional nitrogen may be necessary for eddo). Irrigate during dry spells. The main corms of taro mature in about 220–280 days from planting and the crop is harvested by pulling up the main corm, leaving small side suckers to produce a ratoon crop. Eddo come to maturity in 150–180 days and are completely harvested; both species yield about 2kg/m^2 and may be stored for approximately 100 days in high relative humidity at 10°C/50°F. The giant taro, *Alocasia macrorrhiza*, is grown as for taro.

In temperate climates, where cultivation makes an interesting if unprofitable exercise, grow under glass with a minimum temperature of 21°C/70°F and high humidity; plant pre-sprouted corms into large pots or growing bags of soilless medium; water plentifully and watch for pests such as aphid, whitefly, red spider mite and thrips.

C.affinis Schott (*Alocasia jenningsii* Veitch; *C.marshallii* Bull).
Tuber small, rounded, offsets numerous. Lvs 10–15×7–10cm, ovate or orbicular-ovate, base rounded-retuse to cordate, apex acuminate to acute, green with purple markings between veins, glaucous beneath, veins narrow; petiole to 35cm. Peduncle to 8cm; spathe tube 2.5cm, cylindric, pale green, limb 7.5–12.5cm, linear-lanceolate, acuminate, yellow; spadix appendix 3–4cm, slender, yellow. Tropical E Himalaya (Sikkim to Burma).

C.antiquorum Schott. See *C.esculenta*.

C.esculenta (L.) Schott (*C.antiquorum* Schott). COCOYAM; TARO; DASHEEN.
Tuber rounded-turbinate, brown, large with few offsets or small with many offsets. Lvs to 80×35cm, deflexed, cordate-sagittate, basal lobes rounded or angular, apex acute, veins conspicuous; petiole to 1m, inserted close to basal sinus of lf blade. Infl. solitary or many; peduncle to 15cm, shorter than petioles; spathe 15–35cm, erect, tube green, caudate-acuminate, pale yellow; spadix shorter than spathe, appendix variable, sometimes rudimentary. Tropical E Asia, naturalized throughout tropics and warm temperate regions. Some clones never flower. 'Euchlora': lvs dark green edged violet; petioles violet. 'Fontanesii': petioles and peduncles dark red-purple or violet; lamina dark green, margin and veins violet, the coloration often staining the lamina; spathe tube dark violet. 'Illustris' (IMPERIAL TARO; BLACK CALADIUM): lvs light green, marked and stained blue-black between primary veins.

C.marshallii Bull. See *C.affinis*.

Conanthera Ruiz & Pav. (From Gk *konos*, cone, and *anthera*, anther; the 6 anthers form a cone-like structure prior to fertilization.) Liliaceae (Tecophilaeaceae). 3–4 species of bulbous perennial herbs. Corms ovoid. Leaves usually basal, sometimes clasping stems, linear. Inflorescence a panicle, often many-flowered; perianth segments 6, basally united in a short tube; anthers united to form a cone-like structure protruding from base of perianth, yellow. Late spring–early summer. Chile. Z9.

CULTIVATION   Grown for the small panicles of blue flowers in spring or early summer, *Conanthera* is not reliably cold hardy, especially when low temperatures are combined with winter wet. Grow in a warm sunny position on the rock garden, in well drained sandy soils, and protect in winter with a propped pane of glass or open cloche, or grow in the frame or alpine house. Alternatively, lift after foliage dies back and store in cool, dry and frost-free conditions. Propagate by seed or offsets.

C.bifolia Ruiz & Pav.
Corms ovoid, covered in very coarse netting extending above ground and surrounding the lower parts of the flowering stem. Lvs 25–45cm, basal, linear. Flowering stem to 30cm, usually shorter; fls in small, open 5–10-fld panicles, perianth seg. only shortly united at base, reflexed, deep blue tinted purple. Chile.

C.campanulata Lindl. (*C.simsii* Sweet).
Corms 3.8×3cm. Lvs 25–30cm, 2–3, linear, cauline, sheathing flowering stem at base. Fls campanulate, to 10 in a lax panicle; perianth seg. joined in lower third, not reflexed, strong blue, occasionally almost white to dark purple-blue. Chile.

C.simsii Sweet. See *C.campanulata*.

Convallaria L. LILY OF THE VALLEY. (From Lat. *convallis*, a valley, from the habitat.) Liliaceae (Convallariaceae). 1 species, a very variable, glabrous, herbaceous perennial. Rhizomes creeping, branching freely. Stems erect with green or violet narrow sheaths at base. Leaves 3–23×0.5–1.1cm, (1–)2–3(–4) on upper part of stem, ovate-lanceolate to elliptic, acute to acuminate, glabrous, mid-green, loosely folded and sheathing at base; petioles 1–2.4cm. Flowering stems solitary, arising from axils of basal scales; flowers 5–13 in a slender, erect to arching, secund raceme, strongly fragrant, pendent, pedicels decurved; bracts ovate-lanceolate, shorter than pedicels; perianth 5–11×5–11mm, rounded-campanulate, waxy, white to ivory, segments 6, united for half to two-thirds of their length, tips reflexed; ovary superior, 3-celled; style simple; stigma capitate. Fruit a scarlet berry. N temperate regions. Z3.

CULTIVATION   From woodland, scrub and montane meadows to altitudes of 2300m/7475ft, throughout northern temperate zones, *C.majalis* is an extremely cold-tolerant species (to −20°C/−4°F and below), valued for its long-lived and beautifully scented flowers in spring. Eminently suited to the wild and woodland garden and for groundcovering underplantings in the shrub border, lily of the valley is also commonly grown in pots, to be forced for early spring flowers for the home or conservatory.

Grow in part shade in moderately fertile, humus-rich and moisture-retentive soils; mulch with leafmould or screened, well rotted manure or compost in autumn. Site with due care, since established colonies will spread freely by means of their creeping rhizomes; *C.m.* 'Variegata' is less vigorous. Lift strong 2–3-year-old crowns for forcing in autumn, and pot up into well crocked pots in a mix of equal parts loam, leafmould and sharp sand. Overwinter in the cold glasshouse or frame and keep moist, increasing water as growth proceeds and temperatures to about 21–23°C/70–75°F. Propagate by division or ripe seed.

C.majalis L. (*C.montana* Raf.).
'Aureovariegata' ('Lineata', 'Striata', 'Variegata'): lvs striped gold. 'Fortin's Giant' ('Fortins'): tall, to 30cm; lvs wide; fls large, well scented. 'Hardwick Hall': lvs wide, edged yellow-green; fls large, white. 'Prolificans': fls tiny, congested in a tightly branched panicle, often slightly malformed. 'Vic Pawlowski's Gold': lvs held semi-erect, dark green closely striped white or clear gold. var. **keiski** (Miq.) Maxim.

Smaller, to c7.5cm. Lvs to 15cm, 2–3, elliptic-oblong. var. *rosea* Rchb. Fls pink. f. *picta* Wilcz. Sta. filaments spotted purple at base. A wide range of cultivars includes double white ('Flore Pleno') and double pink forms, others which are prolific and vigorous, as well as with variegated lvs, 'Albistriata', with longitudinal cream-white stripes.

C.montana Raf. See *C.majalis*.

Corydalis Vent. (From Gk *korydalis*, the crested lark: the flower resembles the shape of its head.) Fumariaceae. About 300 species of annual or perennial herbs, with rhizomes or tubers. Leaves basal and alternate on stems, compound, usually biternate, rarely simple, broadly triangular in outline, often glaucous; leaflets often further divided; petioles sometimes winged. Flowers tubular, in racemes, terminal or opposite leaves with a bract below each flower; petals 4, in pairs, the upper and lower, outer pair with reflexed apical lips and long basal spur, the inner pair convergent, enclosing stamens and style; stamens 6. Fruit a dehiscent capsule enclosing many black seeds. Northern temperate regions, especially the Sino-Himalayan area, and S Africa.

CULTIVATION   A large genus of attractive annuals and perennials characterized by their ferny foliage and long-spurred flowers. *Corydalis* includes such well known garden plants as the climbing *C.claviculata*, the Rock Harlequin, *C.sempervirens* and the handsome, blue-flowered *C.flexuosa*. It also boasts a number of tuberous species – of these, *C.bulbosa* and *C.solida* are beautiful spring-flowering fumitories which will soon form large colonies in wooded or semi-wooded situations where their roots will remain cool in summer. They naturalize well in association with snowdrops and winter aconites, securing a continuity of spring bloom. The remaining tuberous species originate in scree and other mountainous habitats, where they usually enter a dry dormancy in summer. They may be attempted on sheltered rock gardens and in raised beds, but fair altogether better in pans of gritty medium in the bulb frame or alpine house. Increase by division (for *C.bulbosa* and *C.solida*), or by carefully removing offsets in spring (the remaining species).

C.aitchisonii M. Popov
Tuber subspherical. Stem to 10cm, often shorter. Lvs 4, ± whorled, ternate, blue-green. Infl. a short raceme; fls to 6, to 3cm, pale yellow tipped or stained green-brown, spur long, slightly curled at tip. Central Asia.

C.ambigua Cham. & Schlecht.
Stems numerous. Lvs ternate, lobes entire; somewhat glaucous. Fls azure, in dense, showy racemes; lower outer pet. sulcate, broad-lipped, inner pet. light blue, spur deltoid, laterally compressed; floral bracts dissected. Spring to summer. Japan. Z6.

C.angustifolia (Bieb.) DC. (*Fumaria angustifolia* Bieb.).
Perenn., to 20cm. Corm 2.5cm in diam.; stem single with conspicuous basal bract. Lvs 2–3, biternate, laciniate, leaflets lanceolate-oblong. Fls to 2cm, 4–8, racemose, pale yellow or white, spur strongly recurved, to 1cm; basal floral bracts trifid, upper bracts subentire. Early spring. Caucasus. Z6.

C.bulbosa (L.) DC. (*C.cava* (L.) Schweig. & Körte).
Similar to *C.solida*, but tuber hollow and leaf at stem base absent. Perenn. to 15cm. Lvs 2, bipinnate, leaflets cuneate, lobed, lobes broader than in *C.solida*. Fls 2–2.5cm, 10–20 in erect racemes, horizontal, violet or white, spur curved sharply downwards near tip; floral bracts entire. ssp. *marshalliana* (Pallus) Chater. Fls yellow-cream. Early spring. C Europe. 'Albiflora' ('Alba'): fls white. 'Cedric Morris': fls white amid purple bracts. Z6.

C.cava (L.) Schweig & Körte. See *C.bulbosa.*

C.cashmeriana Royle.
Perenn. to 25cm. Tubers small, ovoid, scaly, in clusters. Stem unbranched. Lvs ternate, bright green, basal lvs petiolate, stem lvs subsessile, leaflets 1.5–2cm, oblong or elliptic. Fls 1–2cm, in dense, 3–8-fld racemes, bright blue, apices dark blue, spur to 1cm, curved; lower floral bracts trifid, upper bracts 3-toothed. Summer. Himalaya. Z5.

C.caucasica DC.
Tuber subspherical. Stem to 10cm, slender. Lvs 2, alternate, remote, biternate, pale green. Infl. a short raceme with small, leafy bracts; fls to 5, to 2cm, purple-pink or white (var. *albiflora* DC.). Caucasus.

C.darvasica Reg.
Tuber large. Stem to 6cm. Lvs finely and closely cut, biternate, strongly glaucous. Fls to 6, 1.8cm, cream marked brown-green with a maroon lip. C Asia.

C.emanueli C. A. Meyer.
Roots thickly fleshy, lobed. Stem short. Lvs biternately cut, mid green. Fls to 4, to 1.8cm. Cambridge blue. Caucasus.

C.glaucescens Reg.
Branching from half way up stem; branches equal. Fls nodding, broadly winged, pink to red, in erect, loose racemes, floral bracts entire, spur straight. Spring to summer. C Asia. Z8.

C.halleri (Willd.) Willd. See *C.solida.*

C.ledebouriana Kar. & Kir.
St. to 10cm. Lvs small, broadly and biternately lobed, borne near ground. Fls to 10, to 2cm, covering most of an erect raceme, deep rosy pink to wine red, especially on deflexed lower lip, spur long, upward-curving or horizontal, pure white. C Asia.

C.maracandica M. Pop. & Zak.
Differs from *C.ledebouriana* in yellow-cream fls fading to pale pink with age. C Asia.

C.macrocentra Reg.
Stem to 12cm. Lvs several, finely and remotely biternately divided, pale blue green. Infl. a loose raceme; fls to 4, to 3cm, pale gold with a long, horizpntal spur. C Asia.

C.popovii Nevski.
Lvs ternate, petiolate, lobes ovate, glaucous, blue-green. Fls in erect racemes; pet. white, upper outer pet. reflexed and dark maroon at apex, lower outer pet. with a maroon, concave lip at apex, emarginate, spurs downward-curving; pedicels to 1cm; floral bracts entire, acute. Spring. C Asia. Z8.

C.rutifolia Sibth. & Sm.
Perenn. to 20cm. Stem single, pink-tinted, glabrous, from a tuber. Lvs 2–3, opposite or in whorls, 2-ternate, leaflets ovate, entire or trifid. Fls in 6–12-fld racemes, to 2.5cm, deep crimson to violet with dark purple tips, spur ascending, inflated; floral bracts entire. Spring. Mts of Asia Minor, Europe. Z6.

C.solida (L.) Sw. (*C.halleri* (Willd.) Willd.). FUMEWORT.
Perenn., to 25cm. Tuber globose-oblong. Stem single, basally bracteate. Lvs 2–3, long-petioled, 2-ternate, leaflets deeply and unevenly dissected, lobes lanceolate-oblong. Fls to 20 in erect racemes; cal. absent; cor. to 2cm, red, often spotted darker with pale inner pet., spur tapered, downward-curving; floral bracts dissected, broadly cuneate in outline. Spring. N Europe, Asia. 'Beth Evans': clear, pale pink. 'George P. Baker': fls deep red-salmon. Z6.

C.wendelboi Liden.
Lvs in a basal rosette, biternate; lobes oblong, acute, glaucous. Scape stout; pedicels to 6mm. Fls to 2cm, pale pink to mauve, in crowded, arching racemes; outer pet. narrow, inner pet. tipped dark purple; floral bracts dissected. Summer. Turkey. Z9.

Crinum L. (From Gk *krinon*, a lily.) Amaryllidaceae. About 130 species of evergreen and deciduous bulbous herbs. Bulbs tunicated with an elongated neck of sheathing leaf bases. Leaves spirally arranged, linear or lorate, usually broad, thick. Scape solid, arising from the bulb to one side of the foliage, with 2 spathe valves; pedicels short or absent; flowers few or many in an umbel, often very fragrant, actinomorphic or zygomorphic; perianth salverform or funnel-shaped, tube long-cylindrical, straight or curved, lobes 6, linear, lanceolate or oblong, equal or subequal, spread widely, recurved or pointing forward; stamens 6, attached to the perianth tube, with long curved filaments and versatile anthers; ovary 3-celled, forming a swelling below the base of the perianth tube; style long; stigma small. Fruit a round or irregular 3-celled capsule, with a few large green thick seeds per cell. Warm and tropical regions.

CULTIVATION   *Crinum* is a large and widespread genus of handsome plants, mostly native to the coastal regions of tropical and subtropical zones and requiring glasshouse treatment in cool temperate climates. Some of the South African species, however, are suited to outdoor cultivation in sheltered temperate gardens. *C.bulbisper-mum* and *C.moorei* are among the hardiest; their hybrid offspring *C.× powellii* and its cultivars are hardier still, and will tolerate temperatures to –5°C/23°F. They are grown for their heavy umbels of sweetly fragrant, clear pink flowers, carried in succession from late summer until autumn; the pure white flowers of *C.× powellii* 'Album' are exceptionally beautiful. These three are also suitable for pot culture in the cool glasshouse. The remaining species are grown in large pots or tubs in the intermediate or hot glasshouse; tropical species such as *C.asiaticum* and *C.purpurascens* may bear their fragrant flowers almost continually throughout the year if grown under hot glasshouse conditions.

Grow cold-tolerant species in deep, well drained but moisture-retentive, fertile soils rich in organic matter; the bulbs must have sufficient moisture during the growing season. In regions at the limits of their hardiness, plant in spring with the neck of the bulb at soil level, at the base of a south- or southwest-facing wall, and give the protection of a deep mulch of bracken litter or well-rotted compost and, if necessary, a propped frame light in winter. Leave undisturbed after planting; bulbs are sensitive to transplanting and may take several years to establish and reach their potential stature. Once established, however, they reproduce rapidly from offsets, creating the overcrowded conditions that stimulate a profusion of bloom.

Grow tender species under glass in a rich, fibrous, loam-based mix with added sharp sand, leafmould and well-rotted manure. Place in direct sunlight with part-day shade or in bright filtered light; avoid full sun when leaves are young. Plant with the neck of the bulb above soil level. Water plentifully and apply a balanced liquid fertilizer monthly when in growth; reduce water after flowering and keep just moist enough to prevent foliage wilt when resting; foliage may be syringed occasionally during this period. Several species inhabit swamps, riverbanks and pond margins and may be naturalized in similar situations, either in subtropical gardens or under glass. Top-dress annually and repot when necessary in early spring, although *Crinum* flowers best when root-bound. Propagate from offsets in spring, or from fresh ripe seed sown singly in 7.5cm/3in. pots at 21°C/70°F. Pests and diseases are as for *Amaryllis*.

C.abyssinicum Hochst. ex A. Rich.
Bulb ovoid, to 8cm diam.; neck short. Lvs to 3.5×2.5cm, 6, linear, acute, glaucous, denticulate. Scape to 60cm; fls 4–6, sessile or nearly so; perianth white, tube to 5cm, lobes oblong, acute, to 8×2cm; fil. less than 2.5cm. Ethiopia (mts). Z9.

C.acaule Bak.
Bulb to 8cm diam.; neck to 9cm. Lvs to 45×1.2cm, linear, firm, glossy, channelled. Scape mostly buried, emerging to 5cm; spathe valves linear, to 13cm, green; fls 1–2, subsessile; perianth tube 10cm, cylindric, erect, lobes to 12×2cm, lanceolate, erect, recurved at one end, twice length of tube, with pale red keels; stamens half as long as lobes, anth. linear-oblong, to 8.5cm; style equalling perianth. S Africa. Z9.

C.amabile var. *augustum* (Roxb.) Herb. See *C.augustum*.

C.americanum L. (*C.roozenianum* O'Brien). FLORIDA SWAMP LILY; SOUTHERN SWAMP CRINUM.
Bulb stoloniferous, ovoid, to 10cm diam., short-necked. Lvs to 1.2m, to 12 per bulb, curved, denticulate. Scape to 75cm, erect; fls 3–6, more or less sessile; perianth erect, salverform, creamy-white, tube to 13cm, tinged green or purple, equalling or exceeding lobes, lobes linear or linear-lanceolate, to 1.5cm across; stamens spreading, conspicuous, pink or red. SW US (Georgia, Florida and westwards). 'Miss Elsie': stems to 50cm; lvs wide; fls white, exterior tinted fox brown, in large group. 'Catherine': lvs erect, pointed; stems to 90cm; fls white, fil. purple, to 6 per stem; hybrid. Z9.

C.amoenum Roxb.
Bulb globose, to 8cm diam.; neck very short. Lvs to 60×5cm, to 12, suberect, linear, spreading, bright green, tapering at the apex, margin undulate. Scape to 60cm, sometimes tinged purple; fls 6–12, fragrant; perianth tube to 10cm, straight or nearly so, green, lobes to 8×1cm, lanceolate, white, tinged red outside; fil. bright red, shorter than the lobes, ascending; style ascending. India, Burma. Z9.

C.amoenum var. *mearsii* Bedd. See *C.mearsii*.
C.aquaticum Burchell. See *C.campanulatum*.

C.arenarium Herb. WATER ISLAND SAND CRINUM.
Bulb ovate, with white-brown tunics. Lvs to 60×3.5cm, tapering, glaucous, margins scabrous. Scape to 30cm; green; spathe valves to 3.8cm; pedicel 1cm; perianth tube to 10cm, pale green mottled with red, curved, becoming erect, lobes to 7cm, white, tipped green, the outer ones to 1.8cm wide, the inner ones narrower; fil. purple, white at the base, to three-quarters the length of the limb, the inner ones smaller; style purple, with a white base, exceeding limb; stigma triangular. NW Australia. Z10. See also *C.blandum*.

C.asiaticum var. *japonicum* Bak. See *C.japonicum*.

C.asiaticum L. (*C.toxicarium* Roxb.). POISON BULB.
Bulbs clumped, to 13cm diam.; neck to 23cm. Lvs to 120×10cm, to 30 per bulb, lorate, not channelled, arching, pale blue-green. Scape to 60cm; spathe valves to 10cm; pedicels to 2.5cm; fls 20–50, white, fragrant; perianth tube to 10cm, erect, tinged green, lobes to 8×1.5cm, drooping or curving downwards; fil. tinged red, to 5cm; style ascending; ovules 1 per cell. Tropical Asia. var. *declinatum* (Herb.) Bak. (*C.declinatum* Herb.). Bud curving downwards, not erect; tips of perianth lobes tinged red. var. *procerum* (Carey) Bak. (*C.procerum* Carey). Lvs to 150×15cm. Perianth tube and lobes to 13cm, lobes tinged red below. Rangoon. var. *sinicum* (Roxb.) Bak. (*C.sinicum* Roxb.; *C.pedunculatum* hort.). ST. JOHN'S LILY. Bulb to 15cm diam.; neck to 45cm. Lvs to 15cm across with undulating edges, forming a crown to 1.5m high. Scape to 1m; perianth tube and seg. longer than in species type. China. Z8.

C.asiaticum Roxb. See *C.defixum*.
C.asiaticum var. *bracteatum* Herb. See *C.bracteatum*.

C.augustum Roxb. (*C.amabile* var. *augustum* (Roxb.) Herb.). Bulb oblong-ovate, to 18×10cm; tunics red-purple. Lvs to 75×10cm, few, canaliculate, green, purple at base. Scape equalling lvs, dark red-purple; spathe divided, green flushed purple, to 13cm; pedicel 2.5cm, red-green; fls 20–30, fragrant, rose outside, striped inside; perianth tube to 13cm, curved, dark red, lobes to 15cm, margins white, to 2.5cm; fil. ascending, 4cm shorter than limb, purple; anth. yellow; style purple; stigma minute, red. Mauritius, Seychelles. Z9.

C.balfouri Bak.
Bulb ovoid, to 8cm diam., with a short neck. Lvs to 30×5cm, about 12, lorate, bright green, closely veined, with a deltoid apex and denticulate margin. Scape to 60cm, emerging from near the top of the bulb, below the leaf rosette, compressed; spathe valves pale, lanceolate-deltoid; pedicels stout, short, each subtended by a long white filiform bract; fls 10–12, fragrant; perianth tube 5cm, cylindric, green, erect, lobes lanceolate, pure white, equalling tube, spreading horizontally, to 1.2cm wide; fil. shorter than limb; style equalling stamens, tinged red. Socotra. Z10.

C.blandum M. Roem.
Similar to *C.arenarium* but lvs broader, scape longer, perianth limb broader, lobes to 6.5, red outside, fil. white, style red above, much longer, stigmata much shorter. N Australia. Z10.

C.brachynema Herb.
Bulb to 8cm diam., ovoid, short-necked, light brown. Lvs to 60×10cm, broadly lorate, bright green, glabrous, with smooth margins. Scape to 30cm; spathe valves green, red-tipped, lanceolate; fls 15–20, subsessile, drooping, fragrant, pure white; perianth tube to 3.8cm, curved, slender, lobes to 3.8×1.9cm, spreading, equal, elliptic-oblong; stamens shortly exserted, fil. white, to 4mm, anth. yellow; style slender; stigma shortly 3-lobed. India. Z10.

C.bracteatum Willd. (*C.brevifolium* Roxb.; *C.asiaticum* var. *bracteatum* Herb.).
Bulb to 13cm diam., ovoid-cylindrical, brown, without a neck. Lvs to 45×13cm, many, spreading, striate on both surfaces, with entire margins. Scape to 30cm; spathe valves 8cm, ovate-oblong, white inside, green outside; fls 10–20, white, fragrant, with lanceolate bracts; perianth tube 5cm, lobes equalling or slightly exceeding tube, outer lobes 0.8cm wide, canaliculate-concave, the inner narrower; fil. blood-red above; style blood-red; stigma green-punctate, obscurely 3-lobed. Mauritius, E India. Z10.

C.braunii Harms.
Bulb to 12cm diam. with dirty-red scales. Lvs to 100×5.5cm, linear, each with a deep furrow along its length and sharp finely dentate white-edged margins. Scape 70cm; fls about 6, erect, sessile, with no fragrance; spathe valves to 5cm, yellow-brown, membranous; perianth tube to 15cm, furrowed, light green, upper part white, lobes to 10×0.9cm, linear, the inner surface and part of the outside white, with pink margins; fil. to 6cm, white at the base, dark red above; style to 20cm. Madagascar. Z10.

C.brevifolium Roxb. See *C.bracteatum*.

C.bulbispermum (Burm.) Milne-Redh. & Shweick.
Bulb 7.5–13cm diam., neck to 30cm. Lvs ligulate, 60–90×7.5–11cm, channelled, reflexed, margins narrowly cartilaginous, dentate. Scape 50–90cm, green; pedicels 4.5–9cm; fls 6–132, funnel-shaped, fragrant, perianth tube curved, 7–15cm, green, tinged brown-red, seg. 7–13×2–4cm, white with pink or red streak, tips reflexed; stamens declinate, exceeded by style. Summer–autumn. S Africa. 'Album': fls white. 'Cape Dawn': lvs to 2m×12cm; stalks to 2m; fls soft red to pink, in umbels to ×50cm; hybrid. 'Pam's Pink': scapes to 1m; lvs to 1.5m; fls large, rose, grouped to 12. 'Roseum': fls pink. 'St. Christopher': stems to 50cm, to 6 per bulb; lvs thin; fls cup-shaped, white, hybrid. Some of these cvs are backcrosses with *C.×powellii*. Z6.

C.campanulatum Herb. (*C.aquaticum* Burchell).
Bulb ovoid, to 4cm diam. Lvs to 1.2m, deciduous, linear, square-tipped, deeply channelled, margin dentate. Scape to 30cm, green; fls 6–8; pedicels to 2.5cm; perianth tube red-green, to 8cm, limb campanulate, equalling the tube, lobes oblong, obtuse, the free parts pointed and recurved, white suffused with pink; fil. shorter than the lobes. S Africa. Z9.

C.caribaeum Bak.
Lvs to 30×10cm, lorate-oblong, tapering at the base. Fls 3–4; perianth erect, salver-shaped; perianth tube nearly to 10cm, straight, lobes white, linear, spreading, nearly equalling tube, to 4mm wide. W Indies. Z10.

C.colensoi hort. See *C.moorei*.
C.crassifolium Herb. See *C.variabile*.

C.crassipes Bak.
Bulb large, conical, with no neck. Lvs to 120×10cm, lorate, tapering at the tip, entire. Scape stout, compressed, to 30cm; fls 15–20; pedicels to 3.5cm; perianth tube to 8cm, slightly curved, green, lobes oblanceolate, equalling tube, to 12mm across, ascending, white, tinged red below; fil. purple, nearly equalling lobes. Tropical Africa. Z10.

C.crispum Phillips. See *C.lugardae*.

C.cruentum Ker-Gawl. Bulb livid purple outside, with underground creeping stem-bases. Lvs to 120×4cm, dark green, sheathing below, acute, many-rowed, margin smooth. Scape compressed or ancipitous, green; spathe valves semi-erect, herbaceous, green and leafy, round-tipped; fls to 7, sessile, peach flushed purple, fragrant; perianth tube triangular with blunted corners, pale green, lobes elongate-lanceolate, green median stripe outside, the inner ones narrower than the outer; fil. blood-red, spreading; anthers yellow; stigma dark red-punctate. C America. Z9.

C.declinatum Herb. See *C.asiaticum* var. *declinatum*.

C.defixum Ker-Gawl. (*C.asiaticum* Roxb.; *Amaryllis vivipara* Lam.).
Bulb 5cm diam., oblong-spherical, light green, rhizomatous, with cylindrical neck. Lvs to 100×2cm, erect, linear, semi-cylindrical, concave, shiny, apex attenuate, obtuse, margin hispid with small cusps. Scape shorter than lvs, glaucous-green, tinged purple; spathe valves pale-green, to 8×2cm; fls 6–12, sessile, fragrant at night; perianth tube cylindric, to 15cm, green tinged red, lobes to 8×0.5cm, recurved-appendiculate; fil. shorter than the limb, white, red above, style fimbriate, 3-lobed. E India. Z10.

C.douglasii Bail.
Lvs to 75×12cm, several, dark green, blunt-tipped. Scape to 75cm, dark-mottled; pedicels thick; spathe valves to 12×2cm; fls about 20; perianth tube 13cm, outer lobes to 9×1.5cm, with undulate margins, purple-red, the inner lobes shorter and narrower; stamens three-quarters length of the lobes; style equalling lobes, purple; stigma short, 3-lobed. Australia. Z10.

C.erubescens Ait.
Large aquatic herb; bulb to 10cm diam., ovoid. Lvs to 90×8cm, many, curved, strap-shaped, thick and succulent; margins roughened. Scape to 60cm; spathe valves to 11cm; fls 4–12, sessile or subsessile, fragrant; perianth tube to 15cm, narrow, straight, erect, bright red, lobes lanceolate, reflexed, half the length of the tube, maroon outside, white inside; fil. wine-red, long-exserted. Tropical America. Z10.

C.erubescens HBK non Ait. See *C.kunthianum*.

C.erythrophyllum Carey ex Herb.
Bulb to 7.5cm diam. Lvs to 30×5cm, sprawling, curling, narrowing to a point, wine-red. Scape to 30cm; fls 3 or 4; perianth lobes to 10cm, white, linear-lanceolate. Burma. Z10.

C.flaccidum Herb. MURRAY LILY; MACQUARIE LILY; DARLING LILY.
Bulb to 10cm diam. Lvs to 60×3cm, linear-lorate, channelled. Scape to 60cm, green, flattened; spathe bifid, brown; pedicels

to 4cm, at an angle; fls 5–8, white, fragrant; perianth tube slightly curved, shorter than the limb, limb funnel-shaped, to 8cm diam., lobes with reflexed tips, white with green hooks, to 2cm broad; fil. green, anth. yellow; style equalling lobes, green. Australia. Z10.

C.forgetii C.H. Wright.
Lvs to 35×7cm, oblong-lanceolate, acute or short-acuminate, amplexicaul at the base, margins denticulate. Pedicel lateral, subcylindric, to 30cm; fls 5, sessile; spathe deltoid, 8cm; perianth tube 20×0.5cm, green, lobes 8–1.2cm, ligulate, acuminate, white, revolute; fil. subulate, red to 5cm; style red, slightly exceeding stamens; stigma round. Peru. Z9.

C.× herbertii Sweet. (*C.zeylanicum* 'Album' × *C.bulbispermum*.)
Bulb globose, 12.5–25cm diam., neck short, tunicated. Lvs 12–15, ensiform-acuminate, 90–180cm long, to 15cm wide at base, tapering upwards to acute apex, margins scabrid, semierect to spreading, oldest lvs prostrate, deep green to slightly glaucous. Scape to 90cm; fls 12–15, subsessile, trumpet-shaped or campanulate, to 20cm across mouth, night-opening; perianth tube curved, 10cm, seg. 8.5×2.5–3.5cm, semi-elliptic, apex acute, recurved. Garden origin. 'Gulf Pride': fls white, keels marked pink, petals broad and rounded. Z10.

C.hildebrandtii Vatke.
Bulb ovoid, to 8cm diam.; neck to 15cm. Lvs to 60×7cm, 8 or 10, lanceolate, tapering, bright green, firm, margins glabrous. Scape slender, ancipitous, to 30cm; spathe valves 2, lanceolate, reflexed; fls 6–10, sessile, pure white, erect; tube to 18cm, lobes to 8×1.2cm, oblanceolate, spreading horizontally, fil. bright purple, shorter than the limb, anth. linear, to 1.8cm; style exserted beyond perianth lobes; stigma capitate. Comoros Is. Z10.

C.humile Herb. See *C.nubicum.*

C.intermedium Bail.
Bulb to 7cm diam., neck absent. Lvs blunt-tipped with longitudinal veins. Scape compressed, glaucous, tinged red at the base; perianth lobes white with apiculate yellow tips. Australia. Z10.

C.japonicum (Bak.) Hannibal (*C.asiaticum* var. *japonicum* Bak.).
Bulb columnar, 10–20×5–7.5cm. Lvs 45–60×5–12.5cm, apex subacute, succulent, somewhat channelled, ascending, spreading, slightly recurved. Scape stout, 30–45cm; fls 15–25, white, subsessile; perianth tube straight, ascending to erect, to 7.5cm, seg. spreading, patent, to 7.5cm, recurved at apex. Summer–autumn. Japan. 'Variegatum': lvs bright green striped cream.

C.johnstonii Bak. See *C.macowanii.*

C.kirkii Bak.
Bulb globose, to 20cm diam.; neck to 15cm. Lvs to 120×12cm, to 12 or more, lorate, tapering to a point, margin with white bristles. Scapes 2–3 per bulb, compressed, to 45cm; spathe valves deltoid, red-brown, to 10cm; fls 12–15, sessile or subsessile, to 25cm; perianth tube tinged green, lobes oblong, acute, equalling tube, white with a distinct red band down the middle of each lobe; stamens declinate, shorter than limb. E Africa. Sometimes confused with *C.zeylanicum*. 'P.F. Reasoner' (*C.kirkii* × *C.bulbispermum*): lvs 1m; fls funnel-shaped, to 12cm, white with red keels; sterile. Z10.

C.kunthianum Roem. (*C.erubescens* HBK non Ait.).
Bulb ovoid, to 8cm diam.; neck short. Lvs to 90×8cm, 20, strap-shaped, spreading, margins undulate, entire. Scape to 30cm; fls 4–5, sessile or subsessile, pure white or tinged purple outside; perianth tube to 20cm, lobes lanceolate, to 6cm; fil. 5cm, red. C America. Z9.

C.latifolium L. See *C.zeylanicum.*

C.lineare L. f.
Bulb ovoid, to 9cm diam.; neck to 14cm. Lvs to 60×36cm, linear, channelled, glaucous; margin entire. Scape slender, to

30cm; spathe valves to 7cm, lanceolate-deltoid, reflexed; pedicels to 2cm; fls 5 or 6; pedicels to 2cm; perianth tube to 6cm, slender, curved, lobes to 8cm, white, tinged red in the centre, oblong or oblanceolate, acute; stamens much shorter than the lobes; styles nearly straight, equalling limb. S Africa. Z9.

C.lugardae N.E. Br. (*C.podophyllum* Hook. f.; *C.crispum* Phillips).
Bulbs ovoid, to 5cm diam.; neck to 7cm. Lvs to 75×1.8cm, linear, deep green, acute, concave, finely scabrous along the margins. Scape to 30cm, erect, somewhat compressed; spathe valves to 7cm; fls 2–6; pedicels to 1.2cm; perianth tube to 10cm, cylindric, curved, lobes to 9×2.5cm, lanceolate, white with a light pink median stripe and a green point. Central S America. Z10.

C.mackenii hort. See *C.moorei.*

C.macowanii Bak. (*C.pedicellatum* Pax; *C.johnstonii* Bak.).
PYJAMA LILY.
Bulb to 25cm diam., globulose; neck to 23cm. Lvs to 90×10cm, deciduous, 12–15, strap-shaped, thin, bright green, spreading, margins scabrous. Scape to 90cm, stout, green; spathe valves to 15cm; pedicels to 5cm; fls 10–15, nodding, fragrant, perianth tube to 10cm, curved, green at base, lobes equalling tube, to 3.5cm across, oblong, acute, pink or white, striped deep pink along middle, curving outwards at the apex; stamens white, declinate; style a little longer than the stamens. E, C & S Africa. Z9.

C.makoyanum Carr. See *C.moorei.*

C.mearsii Bedd. (*C.amoenum* var. *mearsii* Bedd.).
Bulb globose, to 8cm diam.; neck very short. Lvs to 30×2.5cm, 10–12, very smooth. Scape to 13cm; fls 6–10, white; perianth tube slender, to 13cm, lobes lanceolate, to 60×12mm. Upper Burma. Z10.

C.moorei Hook. f. (*C.makoyanum* Carr.; *C.colensoi* hort.; *C.mackenii* hort.; *C.natalense* hort.; *C.schmidtii* Reg.).
Bulb ovoid, to 20cm diam.; neck to 45cm. Lvs to 90×10cm, 12–15, deciduous, lorate, spreading, short-pointed, with distinct veins, margin entire. Scape to 90cm; pedicels to 8cm; fls 6–12, pale to deep pink, or white, fragrant; perianth tube to 8cm, curved, green or tinged red, limb funneltorm, equalling the tube, lobes oblong, 3.5cm wide, white suffused pink; fil. pink, shorter than lobes; style red towards apex. S Africa. 'Album': fls white. 'Roseum': fls pink. Z8.

C.natalense hort. See *C.moorei.*

C.nubicum Hannibal (*C.humile* Herb.).
Bulb spherical, green. Lvs to 30cm, linear, subacute, green, surface pitted. Scape to 30cm, subcylindric; spathe valves to 8cm; pedicels short; fls 6–9; perianth tube green, lobes 5cm, narrow linear-lanceolate, white; fil. purple, shorter than limb, anth. golden, 8mm; style purple, exceeding limb. Tropical Asia. Z10.

C.ornatum (Ait.) Bury. See *C.zeylanicum.*

C.parvum Bak. Bulb ovoid.
Lvs to 23×1.4cm, 5–7, linear, glabrous. Scape slender, almost equalling lvs; spathe valves lanceolate; fl. solitary, sessile; perianth tube to 8cm, cylindrical, erect, lobes to 8×1.2cm, laciniate, striped-red; anth. to 8mm. CS Africa (Zambesi River). Z10.

C.pedicellatum Pax. See *C.macowanii.*
C.pedunculatum hort. See *C.asiaticum* var. *sinicum.*
C.podophyllum Hook. f. See *C.lugardae.*

C.× powellii L.H. Bail. (*C.bulbispermum* × *C.moorei*).
Bulb ovoid, to 15cm diam., neck long, tapering. Lvs 15–18, ensiform, 65–150×7.5–10cm+, tapering to slender acuminate apex, deeply channelled, margins cartilaginous. Scape to 150cm+; pedicels to 5cm; fls 8–10, pink, fragrant; perianth tube curved, to 10cm, seg. 7.5–12.5cm×2–3.5cm, apex acute, recurved; stamens and style declinate-ascending, style red. Garden origin. 'Album': fls pure white. 'Krelagei': fls large,

dark pink, in large umbels; seg. broad. 'Harlemense': fls soft pink, in large umbels. 'Roseum': fls pale pink. Z6.

C.*pratense* Herb.
Bulb ovoid, to 13cm diam.; neck short. Lvs to 60×5cm, 6–8, linear, narrowing to a point, margin entire. Scape laterally compressed, to 30cm; fls 6–12, white; perianth tube to 10cm, tinged green, lobes lanceolate, nearly equalling tube, to 12mm wide; fil. shorter than the lobes, bright red. India. Z10.

C.procerum Carey. See *C.asiaticum* var. *procerum*.

C.*purpurascens* Herb.
Bulb ovoid, to 5cm diam., stoloniferous. Lvs to 90×4cm, 20 or more, lorate, dark green, channelled, erect or recurved, thin, margin prominently undulate. Scape to 30cm, green, tinged purple; fls 5–9, sessile; perianth tube to 15cm, slender, nearly straight, green tinged purple, lobes lanceolate, half the length of the tube, white suffused pink or purple; fil. bright red. E Guinea. Z10.

C.*pusillum* Herb.
Bulb cylindric, to 10×1cm. Lvs to 30×1cm, erect, linear, acute. Pedicels 2.5cm; fls few, erect, white to cream, sometimes tinted rose; perianth tube 8cm; lobes linear; stamens long and spreading. India (Nicobar Is.). Z10.

C.roozenianum O'Brien. See *C.americanum*.
C.scabrum Herb. See *C.zeylanicum*.

C.*schimperi* Vatke ex Schum.
Bulb to 6cm diam., depressed globose, tunic yellow-grey, neck distinct. Lvs 6–7, to 50×3cm, lorate, erect, blue-green. Scape to 20cm; spathe valve red, to 3.5cm; perianth tube to 11cm, white, lobes 7×1.8cm; stamens 5cm, anth. black, to 1.2cm; style 15cm. Ethiopia. Z10.

C.schmidtii Reg. See *C.moorei*.
C.sinicum Roxb. See *C.asiaticum* var. *sinicum*.

C.*submersum* Herb. LAKE CRINUM.
Bulb to 8cm diam., oblong-ovoid, purple-red. Lvs to 45×5cm, sharply pointed, channelled, yellow-green, margins rough. Scape 45cm, slightly compressed, green, tinged red near the base; spathe valves to 10cm, withering early; fls 8 or more, nodding before expansion, fragrant at night, with slender bracts; perianth tube to 13cm, green-yellow; lobes to 10cm, white with pink stripes and pointed red tips, oval, channelled near the base; fil. and style curving upwards, red, shorter than lobes. Brazil. Z10.

C.*sumatranum* Roxb.
Bulb ovoid, with fleshy roots. Lvs to 180×15cm, erect, broadly subulate, acute, concave, stiff; margins white, callose, hispid. Scape shorter than lvs; fls 10–20, fragrant, white, subsessile; perianth tube to 10cm, cylindrical, tinged red or green, lobes equalling tube, to 0.6cm wide; fil. ascending,

shorter than the limb. Sumatra. Z10.

C.toxicarium Roxb. See *C.asiaticum*.

C.*undulatum* Hook.
Bulb long-necked. Lvs to 45×2.5cm, ensiform. Scape shorter than lvs; spathe valves green; perianth tube to 20cm, green, twice length of the spathe, curved before the fl. expands, lobes to 7cm, undulate, fil. red. Peru, Brazil. Z10.

C.*variabile* (Jacq.) Herb. (*C.crassifolium* Herb.; *Amaryllis variabilis* Jacq.).
Bulb to 10cm diam., ovoid, without a distinct neck. Lvs 10–12, linear, weak, outer lvs to 60×5cm. Scape to 45cm; fls 10–12; pedicels to 2.5cm; perianth tube to 3.5cm, green, lobes to 8.5cm, oblong, acute, white, flushed red down the middle; fil. red, 2.5cm shorter than the lobes; style equalling limb. S Africa (Cape). Z9.

C.*wimbushii* Worsley.
Bulb round, to 7.5cm diam., with loose and brittle tunics and a short neck. Lvs to 120×63cm, 11–12, deeply channelled, spreading, with a fine point, margin entire. Scape erect, to 45cm; fls 2–6, suberect, subcampanulate, white flushed pink, fragrant; pedicels to 1.2cm; perianth tube to 9cm, slightly curved, outer lobes to 2cm wide, inner lobes to 2.5cm; fil. just shorter than the lobes, the upper half pink; style ascending, exceeding stamens; stigma capitate, not distinctly lobed. C Africa (Lake Nyasa). Z10.

C.*woodrowii* Bak.
Bulb round, to 10cm diam. with no distinct neck and brown membranous tunics. Lvs to 30×10cm, few, blunt, glabrous, bright green. Scape to 30cm, compressed; fls 6 or 7; pedicels to 2.5cm; spathe valves ovate; perianth tube to 8cm, cylindric, lobes white, lanceolate, equalling tube; fil. deep red, half as long as perianth lobes; style exceeding anth. C India. Z10.

C.yucciflorum Salisb. See *C.zeylanicum*.

C.*zeylanicum* L. (*C.latifolium* L.; *C.ornatum* (Ait.) Bury; *C.yucciflorum* Salisb.; *C.scabrum* Herb.). MILK-AND-WINE LILY.
Bulb globose, to 20cm diam.; neck to 30cm. Lvs to 90×10cm, 6–10, thin, sword-shaped, erect or spreading, subsessile, margins undulate, scabrous or dentate. Scape to 90cm, compressed, purple; spathe valves ovate-lanceolate, purple, to 8cm; fls 4–20, fragrant, exceeding spathe; perianth tube to 10cm, round to 3-angled, curved, lobes to 10×2.5cm, subequal, oblanceolate, acute, white with a broad violet-purple keel; fil. deflexed, violet-purple, 2.5cm shorter than lobes; style filiform; stigma minute, shortly trifid. Tropical Asia, E Africa. Z10.

C.cultivars.
'Ellen Bosanquet': lvs wide, fleshy; fls burgundy. 'Peach Blow': lvs dark; fls fragrant, lavender pink, interior pale, seg. recurving.

Crocosmia Planch. (From Gk *krokos*, saffron and *osme*, smell, referring to the strong smell of saffron given off by the dried flowers when immersed in water.) MONTBRETIA. Iridaceae. Some 7 species of cormous perennial herbs. Corms circular, flattened, ringed, ivory, to 2.5cm diameter, borne on short, slender stolons. Leaves linear, acuminate, often slightly recurved, in two ranks, from apex of corm and sheathing base of flowering stem, erect, glabrous or pubescent, ribbed or plicate. Flowers above leaves, semi-opposite along simple or branching spikes, erect to horizontal; perianth yellow to vermilion, often with darker markings, to 6cm, slender, tubular, curving downwards and spreading as lobes, obtuse, to 2cm across; stamens 3, free attached to perianth, ascending to meet roof of tube; anthers equal to or exceeding base of lobes; style exceeding stamens, with 3 apical branches; ovary barely enclosed by single bract. Fruit glabrous, capsular, splitting lengthwise ×3 to shed numerous small seeds. South Africa. Z7.

CULTIVATION *Crocosmia* spp. are grown for their brightly coloured, funnel-shaped flowers carried on arching, wiry stems. They occur in damp habitats: *C.aurea* in shady places in forest and along streambanks, *C.paniculata* in large colonies in moist grassland, and *C.pottsii* usually in partial shade on damp slopes, in the edge of bush and frequently along roadsides. *C.× crocosmiiflora* has naturalized as a garden escape in mild, damp regions in Europe. This hybrid and its numerous selections are the most commonly seen, being hardier, often having larger blooms than the parent species, and with an extended colour range from the lemon-yellows of *C.*'Citronella', to the strong deep red of the taller-growing *C.*'Lucifer'. In favourable conditions most species soon form large clumps, *C.× crocosmiiflora* in particular is invasive but will not bloom profusely unless congested.

Crocosmia spp. are generally hardy to –5°C—10°C/23–14°F; *C.× crocosmiiflora* will withstand temperatures to –15°C/5°F and below, with a thick dry mulch of bracken litter and shelter from cold drying winds. In general, *C.aurea* and those *C.× crocosmiiflora* cultivars with the larger flowers that favour this parent are amongst the least frost-tolerant.

Grow in sun or light, dappled shade in an open, well drained but moisture-retentive soil, enriched with organic matter and, where necessary, improved by the incorporation of sharp sand. Mulch with bracken litter in the first winter, thereafter only in regions at the limits of hardiness. It is best to avoid lifting corms where possible since the new corms seem to derive some nutrition from those that have just flowered; in very cold areas, it has sometimes been the custom to lift corms in early autumn and store them in sand, in a cool but frost-free place overwinter – this practice is, however, unnecessary given suitable mulch protection; it also severely inhibits flower production. Propagate by division of established clumps in spring (these may require routine division every third year or so to prevent congestion), or by ripe seed sown fresh into a loam-based propagating mix with additional sharp grit.

C.aurea (Hook.) Planch. (*Tritonia aurea* (Hook.) Planch.).
To 1m. Lvs to 85×2cm, glabrous, conspicuously ribbed, matt, pale green, somewhat papery, acuminate. Fls in 2 rows, semi-opposite, carried perpendicular on simple or branching scape; perianth pale to burnt orange, straight-sided, to 5cm, opening to broad lobes, each to 2.5×0.5cm; stamens exceeding lobes. Early summer. 'Flore Pleno': fls double. 'Imperialis': robust; fls large, brilliant orange-red. 'Maculata': perianth lobes with orange-brown basal spot. Z7.

C.× crocosmiiflora (Burb. & Dean) N.E. Br. (*Montbretia crocosmiiflora* Lemoine). (*C.aurea × C.pottsii*.)
Hybrid resembling *C.aurea* except in upper, apical portion of perianth which is somewhat inflated and curved, and lobes which are narrower and flush with stamens. Summer. Garden origin. A variable hybrid forming the basis for a wide range of vigorous selections. Z5.

C.masoniorum (Bol.) N.E. Br. (*Tritonia masoniorum* Bol.).
To 1.25m. Lvs to 1m×6cm, linear-lanceolate, base acuminate, glabrous, plicate. Infl. ascending then horizontal, simple or branching with fls semi-erect in 2 rows; perianth vermilion, to 5cm, narrow at base, widening to outspread lobes; stamens exceed lobes. Late summer. Z6.

C.paniculata (Klatt) Goldbl. (*Antholyza paniculata* Klatt; *Curtonus paniculatus* (Klatt) N.E. Br.).
To 1m. Lvs to 90×6cm, olive green, plicate, pubesc., tapering at base. Fls alternate on erect, branching spikes following a flexuous to jagged axis; perianth deep orange, to 6cm, curving downwards, somewhat inflated with lobes spreading to 2cm across; stamens exceed lobes. Summer. Hybrids of *C.paniculata* and *C.masoniorum* are increasingly popular.

C.pottsii (Bak.) N.E. Br. (*Tritonia pottsii* Bak.; *Montbretia pottsii* (Bak.) Bak.).
To 90cm. Lvs to 90×1.5cm, glabrous, ribbed, narrow-acuminate. Fls held densely, horizontal or erect along single side of each branch of compound spike; perianth to 3cm, widening sharply from narrow base, orange flushed red, lobes slightly flexed, each to 1×0.5cm; anth. seldom exceed base of lobes. Z6.

C.cultivars.
'Bressingham Blaze': fls widely funnel-shaped, fiery orange-red. 'Citronella': fls yellow with red-brown markings in centre. 'Emberglow': tall; fls orange-brown, upward-arching. 'Emily McKenzie': fls nodding, dark orange with red splashes in paler throat. 'Fire Bird': tall; fls orange-red outside, inside with a large yellow ring, margins and veins darker, throat tinged green. 'His Majesty': fls large, orange-scarlet. 'Jackanapes': to 60cm; fls small, bicoloured yellow and deep orange-red. 'James Coey': fls large, nodding, very dark orange-red, interior paler. 'Lady Hamilton': tall; fls large, soft orange-yellow, central zone apricot, with small maroon dots on lower perianth lobes, flushed maroon on upper lobes. 'Lucifer': tall fls large, flame-red. 'Solfatarre': fls apricot-yellow; lvs smoky bronze. 'Star of the East': tall; fls very large, soft apricot-yellow, throat paler, tips darker.

Crocus L. (Gk *krokos*, saffron, also Heb. *karkom* (Song of Solomon), Arab. *kurkum*.) Iridaceae. Some 80 species of small, cormous perennial herbs. Leaves emerging from bracts or cataphylls either at flowering time or once the flowers have withered; leaves narrowly linear to filiform, usually T-shaped in section, with a pale green or silver-white central stripe; leaf bases dilate to form a cap-like corm tunic which is papery or composed of parallel or reticulate fibres. Flowers 1–4 emerging from a sheath composed of 3 bracts: 2, the bract and bracteole, are inserted directly below the ovary; the third and largest, the prophyll, is basal; all 3 sheath components are present unless stated otherwise. Perianth funnel- to goblet-shaped, tube narrow, appearing stem-like at base, expanding above to 6 lobes in 2 overlapping whorls; filaments 3, often basally ciliate with the hairs uniting to form a ring; style trifid or divided further in apical branches. Peduncle extends after flowering; subterranean ovary ripening above ground. Capsule glabrous, ellipsoid. Mid & S Europe, N Africa, Middle East, Central Asia.

CULTIVATION   Few genera of this size include so many exquisitely beautiful species, varieties and cultivars. Saffron is obtained from the stigma of the sterile cultigen, *C.sativus*, possibly a selection in *C.cartwrightianus*. It was an important source of yellow-orange dye in the classical world (earliest surviving record, Crete 1500BC), while its medicinal value was reported in Kashmir in 500BC. *C.sativus* was introduced to Spain by the Arabs in the 10th century and soon became a major commodity. *C.nudiflorus* was brought to Britain by the Knights of St John as a saffron substitute; although farming of *C.sativus* continued in England until the 1870s. It is still extensively farmed in Spain, India, the Mediterranean, Russia and China.

Valued in gardens for their funnel-shaped, stemless blooms, which are sometimes surprisingly fragrant, *Crocus* spp. offer a range of deep, intense and glossy colours, often with beautiful textural and colour contrast between inner and outer surface of the petals, or finely marked with delicately feathered, contrasting venation. *Crocus* spp. are commonly classified into two groups, autumn- and spring-flowering, although in practice these two categories merge, so that an almost unbroken succession may be had from late summer and autumn, (e.g. *C.kotschyanus, sativus, ochroleucus, niveus*), through the dull late winter months when they are perhaps most valued, (e.g. *C.c. chrysanthus, sieberi, imperati, korolkowii*), into early spring (with *C.c. ancyrensis, reticulatus, tommasinianus*) and almost back into early summer with *C.scardicus, C.corsicus* and the myriad large-flowered cultivars of *C.vernus*. Most of the commonly grown types are very cold hardy to between –15 and –20°C/ 5 to –4°F, where the ground does not freeze for long periods.

Crocus spp. are suitable for a range of garden situations, with the most vigorous species, such as *C.speciosus* and *C.vernus*, used to great effect in the wild garden, and especially naturalized beneath deep-rooting deciduous trees and shrubs, or in grass where the first cut does not occur before foliage die back; on light, freely draining soils where turf is sufficiently fine, *C.tommasinianus, C.flavus, C.nudiflorus, C.serotinus* var. *austriacus, C.sieberi, C.versicolor* and the more robust cvs. of *C.chrysanthus* can be used to similar effect. These species also suit beds and borders, and will tolerate very low, shallow-rooting groundcover that will mask the fading foliage. The versatile *C.vernus* cvs are amongst the most useful for indoor decoration in spring, in pots or in a crocus glass, and can be gently forced for earlier blooms in pots plunged beneath 15cm/6in. of sand for 6–8 weeks in the cold frame and then brought indoors to a temperature of 10–12°C/50–54°F, either in pots or in a crocus glass. Less robust species are suited in scale to the rock garden, raised bed, or for troughs and tubs, in a gritty loam based mix with additional sharp sand and leafmould. More delicate species, and those whose perfection may be marred by rain and wind in winter can be grown in a similar mix in pots in the alpine house.

Crocus spp. occur in a range of habitats; the climatic conditions they experience under natural circumstances, especially with respect to timing and duration of rainfall, affects their facility and treatment in cultivation. Although most will thrive in a sunny position, sheltered from wind, in moderately fertile, well-drained soil, in cultural terms they may be loosely divided into three groups (although there is inevitably some overlap between groups). The first group is found in freely draining, sunny sites on soils at the coast, on open, stony hillsides, in scrub and woodland, and in rocky mountain habitats; the majority of this group occurs in the winter-rainfall climates that extend from the Mediterranean eastwards into central Asia, and experience an increase in rainfall from autumn to a mid-winter peak. They complete their growth cycle with adequate moisture, and undergo baking during dormancy in the long hot summer. These species may be extremely tolerant of low winter temperatures but are generally more safely grown in temperate maritime climates in the bulb frame or alpine house, where they are protected from excessive rainfall in summer. These include *Cc. aerius, alatavicus, aleppicus, boryi, biflorus, cambessedesii, candidus, carpetanus, cartwrightianus, cyprius, dalmaticus, fleischeri, hadriaticus, hyemalis, karduchorum, michelsonii, minimus, nevadensis, niveus, ochroleucus, olivieri, pallasii, pestalozzae, reticulatus, sieheanus, tournefortii, veluchensis* and *vitellinus*.

The second group is more amenable in cultivation, being sufficiently tolerant of damp to be grown in the open garden, given a warm, sunny position and good drainage. This tolerance may be due to very local microclimatic effects, such as those in the wild near areas of late snow melt, for example, but many of these occur naturally in those transitional maritime-Mediterranean climates that experience some summer rainfall, as on the southern shores of the Black Sea and the Caspian. For the more choice and rare varieties thorough soil preparation may be advisable, with deep cultivation, incorporating leafmould and sharp grit into the top 20cm/8in. of soil, followed by planting on a layer of sharp sand, with a covering of the same. They include *Cc. ancyrensis, angustifolius, chrysanthus, etruscus, flavus, gargaricus, imperati, malyi, medius, pulchellus, sativus, serotinus* and *versicolor*, and, if given the perfect drainage of a raised bed, *Cc. cancellatus, caspius, corsicus, danfordiae, goulimyi, fleischeri, karduchorum, laevigatus* and *longiflorus*.

The third category includes plants from maritime and other climates that experience intermittent rainfall throughout the year, with a peak in autumn and winter. They are mostly from mountain pasture, moist meadow and woodland, and shady banks in soils that seldom dry out completely; this group does not share the requirement for a warm dry dormancy and needs at least a modicum of moisture to prevent desiccation of the dormant bulbs, preferably with some shade from the hottest sun in summer. When pot-grown they prefer a retentive, fibrous and gritty medium and should be plunged in sand in the shaded frame for the summer. They include *Cc. banaticus, cvijicii, scharojanii, nudiflorus, robertianus, scardicus, tommasinianus* and *C.vernus*, and given a sheltered situation in well-drained but retentive soil, *Cc. kotschyanus, speciosus* and *vallicola*.

Corms should be planted immediately they become available, generally at 8–10cm/3–4in. spacings, at a depth of 5–8cm/2–3in., although deeper plantings may be advisable if disturbance by surface cultivations is likely; corms will usually pull themselves down to their preferred depth. The autumn-flowering species begin to form their new roots in mid-summer, spring-flowering species in late summer/early autumn; the robust *C.vernus* will tolerate delayed planting well into autumn.

Propagate by removal of cormlets, grown on in drills, by division of established colonies or by seed sown ripe; the subterranean ovary appears above ground in early to mid-summer (depending on flowering time) as seed ripens and the capsule should be collected before it splits. Sow seed in a sandy propagating mix, sufficiently thinly to accommodate young plants for two seasons, to avoid unnecessary disturbance, and move to the sheltered cold frame after germination. Pot on or set out as foliage dies down following the second season; plants will bloom in their third of fourth year. A number of species, notably *C.imperati* and *C.tommasinianus*, will self-seed freely where conditions suit.

Mice, voles, chipmunks, rabbits and pheasants may dig up and eat the corms, squirrels may eat the emerging shoots, and in areas rich in such wildlife, plantings within fine mesh cages may reduce losses. Birds, especially sparrows, may wilfully damage the flowers. The yellow or light brown wingless tulip-bulb aphids may infest corms in storage aphids and persist to form colonies which damage young shoots. *Crocus* may be affected by blue mould, *Penicillium* spp., and by many of the diseases which infect larger bulbs including, gladiolus dry rot, hard rot, scab, hyacinth black slime, narcissus basal rot, and tulip grey bulb rot. Avoid mechanical damage, which allows ingress to pathogens, by careful handling, and store in cool, dry, well ventilated conditions. In the Netherlands, crocuses are often attacked by a rust fungus, *Uromyces croci*.

C.abantensis Baytop & B. Mathew.
Tunics finely reticulate-fibrous. Lvs 5–10, to 1mm wide, appearing with fls. Fls 1–2, tube to 12.5cm, mid to deep blue, throat yellow; style trifid, orange. Prophyll absent. Spring. Turkey. Z7.

C.adanensis Baytop & B. Mathew.
Tunics papery, parallel-fibrous. Lvs to 4, to 3mm wide. Fls 1–2, tube to 10.5cm; throat white; tube white; interior of lobes lilac with cream base, exterior buff speckled violet at base; anth. yellow. Early spring. S Turkey. Z8.

C.aerius Herb. (*C.biliottii* Maw). T
unics papery, splitting lengthwise from base. Lvs to 2mm wide. Fls to 3, tube to 9cm, deep blue, often flushed, royal blue from base of lobes, overlaid with darker feather veins; style trifid, vermilion to scarlet. Prophyll absent. Mid–late spring. N Turkey. Z7.

C.aerius hort. non Herb. See *C.biflorus* ssp. *pulchricolor*.

C.alatavicus Semenova & Reg.
Outer tunics parallel fibrous, inner entire, papery. Lvs to 2mm wide, present at flowering. Fls to 5, tube to 17cm, tube white suffused violet; throat yellow, glabrous; interior white, exterior stained dark violet; style trifid, orange. Prophyll absent. Spring. Russia, W China. var. **albus** Reg. Fls white with throat yellow. var. **ochroleucus** Bak. Exterior of fls ivory to pale yellow. var. **porphyreus** Bak. Exterior flecked damson purple. Z4.

C.albiflorus Kit. ex Schult. See *C.vernus* ssp. *albiflorus*.

C.aleppicus Bak. (*C.gaillardottii* (Boiss. & Blanche) Maw).
Tunics papery at apex, otherwise parallel or, rarely, reticulate-fibrous. Lvs to 9. Fls to 4, sweetly fragrant, exterior yellow flushed mauve; anth. yellow, purple-black at base or black throughout. Winter. Asia Minor. Z7.

C.algeriensis Bak. See *C.nevadensis*.

C.almehensis C. Brickell and B. Mathew.
Resembles *C.chrysanthus* except in lvs to 3mm wide. Fls yellow to orange, suffused bronze outside. Spring. NE Iran. Z7.

C.ancyrensis (Herb.) Maw.
Tunic reticulate-fibrous. Lvs to 6, to 1mm wide, grey-green, seldom exceeding fls. Fls 1–3; tube yellow or mauve; throat yellow, glabrous; lobes 1 3×1cm; vivid yellow to pale orange; style trifid, deep orange. Prophyll absent. Spring. Turkey. 'Golden Bunch': bears up to 5 fls per corm. Z6.

C.angustifolius Weston (*C.susianus* Ker-Gawl.).
Tunic reticulate-fibrous. Lvs to 6, to 1.5mm wide, dull green, developed at flowering. Fls shorter than lvs; throat yellow, glabrous or minutely pubesc.; lobes yellow, exterior flushed or veined maroon; anth. yellow; style trifid, deep yellow to vermilion. Prophyll absent. Spring. SW Russia. Z4.

C.annulatus var. *chrysanthus* Herb. See *C.chrysanthus*.

C.antalyensis B. Mathew.
Tunic papery, splitting lengthwise into fibres. Cataphylls withering to form long neck. Lvs 3–8, appearing with fls, 1–2.5mm wide, green or grey-green, margin slightly scabrid. Fls 1–3, scented; tube 3–10cm, white or lilac above; throat yellow, pubescent; lobes 2–3.5×0.6–1.5cm, elliptic to oblanceolate, lilac-blue or white tinged blue externally, or sometimes buff externally with violet flecks; style 6–12-lobed, orange or yellow, slightly shorter than or just exceeding anthers. Early spring. SW Turkey. Z7.

C.aphyllus Ker-Gawl. See *C.nudiflorus*.
C.argenteus Sab. See *C.biflorus*.
C.asturicus Herb. See *C.serotinus* ssp. *salzmannii*.

C.asumaniae B. Mathew & Baytop.
Tunic reticulate-fibrous, fibres prolonged into neck 3–4cm long. Lvs 5–6, appearing before or with fls, 0.5–1mm wide, grey-green, glabrous. Fls 1–3, tube 5–8cm, throat white or pale yellow, glabrous; lobes 2.5–3×0.5–1cm, oblanceolate or narrow-elliptic, white, veined darker at throat, very occasionally pale lilac; style trifid, red-orange, lobes to 2cm. S Turkey. Z8.

C.athous Bornm. See *C.sieberi* ssp. *sublimis*.
C.atlanticus Pomel. See *C.nevadensis*.
C.aucheri Boiss. See *C.olivieri*.
C.aureus Sibth. & Sm. See *C.flavus*.
C.balansae Gay ex Bak. See *C.olivieri* ssp. *balansae*.
C.balcanensis Janka. See *C.veluchensis*.

Crocus   (a) *C.korolkowii*   (b) *C.chrysanthus*   (c) *C.sieberi*   (d) *C.nevadensis*   (e) *C.biflorus*   (f) *C.vernus*

C.banaticus Gay (*C.byzantinus* Herb.; *C.iridiflorus* Rchb.).
Tunics finely parallel-fibrous at base, reticulate at apex. Lvs
to 3, to 6mm wide, dark green, emerging after flowering. Fls
lilac-mauve; inner lobes to 3×1.3cm, erect; outer lobes to
5×2.5cm, patent or deflexed, darker; anth. bright yellow; style
slender, multifid, feathery, violet. Bracteole absent. Autumn.
N Romania, N Yugoslavia, SW Russia. Z4.

C.banaticus Heuff. non Gay. See *C.vernus*.

C.biflorus Mill. ssp. **biflorus** (*C.pusillus* Ten.; *C.argenteus*
Sab.; *C.praecox* Haw.; *C.biflorus* var. *parkinsonii* Sab.).
Tunic papery, tough, splitting horizontally from base as rings.
Lvs to 8, to 3mm wide, silvery green. Throat white to golden
yellow, glabrous; lobes to 3×1cm, white, lilac or pale blue
with dark mauve veins on exterior; style trifid, deep yellow.
Prophyll absent. Spring and autumn. S Europe, Asia Minor.
ssp. **alexandri** (Velen.) B. Mathew. Fls white, exterior suffused deep violet. Spring. S Bulgaria, S Yugoslavia. ssp.
melantherus (Boiss. & Orph.) B. Mathew (*C.crewei* hort. non
Hook.). Fls flecked white and feathered grey-purple on exterior; throat pale yellow; anth. damson purple to black.
Autumn. S Greece. ssp. **pulchricolor** (Herb.) B. Mathew
(*C.aerius* hort. non Herb.). Fls indigo throughout, most intense
at base of lobes; throat bright yellow. Spring. NW Turkey.
This subspecies crossed with *C.chrysanthus* has given rise to
the cultivars 'Blue Pearl', 'Blue Bird' and 'Advance'. ssp.
weldenii (Hoppe & Fur.) B. Mathew. Fls white flushed pale
lilac at base or, rarely, throughout undersides of lobes; throat
white or pale blue. Spring. Yugoslavia, Albania. Z4.

C.biflorus var. *parkinsonii* Sab. See *C.biflorus*.
C.biliottii Maw. See *C.aerius*.

C.boryi Gay (*C.ionicus* Herb.; *C.cretensis* Körn.;
C.marathonisius Heldr.).
Tunics thin, papery, splitting longitudinally from base. Lvs
3–9, to 3mm wide, appearing with fls glabrous green, rarely
ciliate. Fls to 4; tube 5–15cm, ivory, exterior sometimes
veined or flushed mauve; lobes to 5×2cm, often smaller, obovate, obtuse; anth. to 1.8cm, white; style below or equal to
anth., multifid, burnt orange. Prophyll absent. Autumn. W &
S Greece, Crete. Z8.

C.boulosii Greuter.
Tunics splitting longitudinally, terminating in tuft of coarse
fibres. Lvs 5–8, to 1mm wide, appearing with fls, glabrous
with a fine, silver-green stripe above. Fls 1, tube 6–9cm,
throat dotted papillose-pubesc.; lobes white, exterior stained
pearl-grey to blue at base of outer whorl; anth. yellow flushed
purple, to 1cm; style orange, multifid. Prophyll absent. Late
winter. Libya. Z8.

C.byzantinus Herb. See *C.banaticus*.
C.caeruleus Weston. See *C.vernus* ssp. *albiflorus*.

C.cambessedesii Gay.
Lvs to 5, to 1mm wide, appearing with fls, glabrous, green
throughout or with a central white stripe. Fls 1–2, tube
6–12cm, white to mauve with exterior feather-veined purple,
interior often flushed yellow; anth. deep yellow, to 1cm; style
dark orange, shorter than anth., trifid, branches widened and
minutely crenulate or lobed at tips. Autumn–early winter.
Balearic Is. Z8.

C.campestris Pall. ex Herb. See *C.pallasii*.

C.cancellatus Herb. ssp. **cancellatus** (*C.cancellatus* var.
kotschyanus Herb.; *C.cilicicus* Maw).
Tunics fine, openly reticulate-fibrous. Lvs 4–7, to 2mm wide,
not appearing until after flowering, green, somewhat silvery.
Fls white to opal or lilac with purple veins; throat yellow,
sometimes pubesc.; lobes to 5.5×1.8cm; anth. pale yellow;
style multifid, deep orange. Prophyll absent. Autumn. S
Turkey, W Syria, Lebanon, N Israel. ssp. **mazziaricus** (Herb.)
B. Mathew. Tube to 1.5cm; lobes 3–5.5×1.–1.8cm, oblanceolate, white to lilac sometimes stained yellow at base, usually
veined violet and more cupped than in ssp. *cancellatus*.
Autumn. Yugoslavia, Greece, Turkey. Z5.

C.candidus Clark (*C.kirkii* Maw).
Lvs 1–2, 4–9mm wide, appearing with fls, ciliate, dark glossy
green. Fls to 3, tube to 7cm, white, tube stained purple-
maroon; throat yellow, glabrous; outer lobes flushed and spotted violet-grey or blue; anth. to 1cm; style 6-branched, deep
yellow, equal to or above anth. Prophyll absent. Late winter,
early spring. NW Turkey. Z7.

C.carpetanus Boiss. & Reut. (*C.lusitanicus* Herb.).
Lvs 2–4, to 3mm wide, appearing with fls and of same height,
ciliate, semi-terete, grooved beneath, largely covered above
by central silver stripe. Fls 1, tube 6–11cm, white flushing to
lilac, usually with fine mauve veins; throat glabrous, white
with yellow tint; style ivory or lilac, trifid, flattened and ruffled at tips. Prophyll absent. Spring. C & NW Spain, N
Portugal. Z8.

C.cartwrightianus Herb. (*C.sativus* var. *cartwrightianus*
(Herb.) Maw). WILD SAFFRON.
Tunics reticulate-fibrous, fine, gathering at apex as neck to
3cm long. Lvs 7–12, to 1.5mm wide, appearing with fls, dull
green. Fls 1–5, fragrant; throat pubesc.; lobes
1.4–3.2×0.7–1.2cm; white, lilac or mauve with darker veins
and a stronger purple flush at base, albino forms may occur;
style often exceeding anth., originating in throat, trifid, vermilion, branches club-shaped; style branches 1–2.7cm.
Autumn–early winter. Greece. Z8.

C.caspius Fisch. & C.A. Mey.
Tunics papery, splitting longitudinally, fibres indistinct. Lvs
4–6, to 2mm wide, appearing with fls, glabrous, grooved and
prominently veined below. Fls 1–2, tube 6–22cm, white to
rose-lilac; tube white or pale yellow, to 18cm; throat pubesc.,
vivid yellow; style light orange, trifid, held above anth., tips
widened. Prophyll absent. Autumn. Russia, Iran. Z7.

C.chrysanthus (Herb.) Herb. (*C.annulatus* var. *chrysanthus*
Herb.; *C.croceus* K. Koch; *C.skorpilii* Velen.).
Tunics tough, papery, splitting from base as whole or jagged
rings. Lvs 3–7, 0.5–2mm wide, appearing with fls, dull green.
Fls 1–4, tube 4.5–10.5cm, scented, creamy yellow to golden,
exterior occasionally striped or stained bronze-maroon; anth.
to 14mm, yellow throughout or with basal lobes almost black;
style trifid, deep yellow. Late winter–mid spring. Balkans,
Turkey. 'Advance': fls yellow, outside violet. 'Blue Bird': fls
large and rounded, pure white, exterior grey-blue. 'Blue
Pearl': fls pearly blue, base bronze, interior silver-blue with a
rich orange stigmata. 'Blue Peter': fls soft blue inside with a
golden throat, exterior rich purple-blue. 'Brassband': fls apricot yellow outside with a bronze green-veined blotch, inside
straw-yellow with a tawny glow. 'Cream Beauty': fls
rounded, on short stalks, creamy yellow. 'E.A. Bowles': pet.
perfectly rounded, old gold, throat dark bronze. 'Elegance':
fls violet outside, edge paler, inner pet. with a deep blue
blotch, inside pale violet with a bronze centre. 'Gipsy Girl':
fls large, golden yellow, outer pet. striped and feathered purple-brown. 'Ladykiller': outer pet. rich blue, narrowly edge
white, inner pet. white, blotched with inky blue, silver-white
inside. 'Snow Bunting': fls pure white with golden throat,
exterior feathered purple. 'Snow White': fls pointed, frost-
white with a gold base. 'Zenith': fls glossy violet-blue, inside
silver-blue, contrasting with gold anth. and prominent gold
throat. 'Zwanenburg Bronze': fls golden yellow, exterior dark
bronze. Z4.

C.cilicicus Maw. See *C.cancellatus*.

C.corsicus Vanucci (*C.insularis* Gay).
Tunics finely fibrous, becoming closely reticulate toward
apex. Lvs 3–4, 1–1.5mm wide, appearing with fls, glabrous,
deep green. Fls 1, tube 5.5–10.5cm, scented, interior lilac,
exterior yellow-pink with 3 mauve, feathered veins per outer
lobe; style deep orange, trifid, with flattened, pleated tips.
Spring–summer. Corsica. Z7.

C.cretensis Körn. See *C.boryi*.
C.crewei hort. non Hook. See *C.biflorus* ssp. *melantherus*.
C.croceus K. Koch. See *C.chrysanthus*.

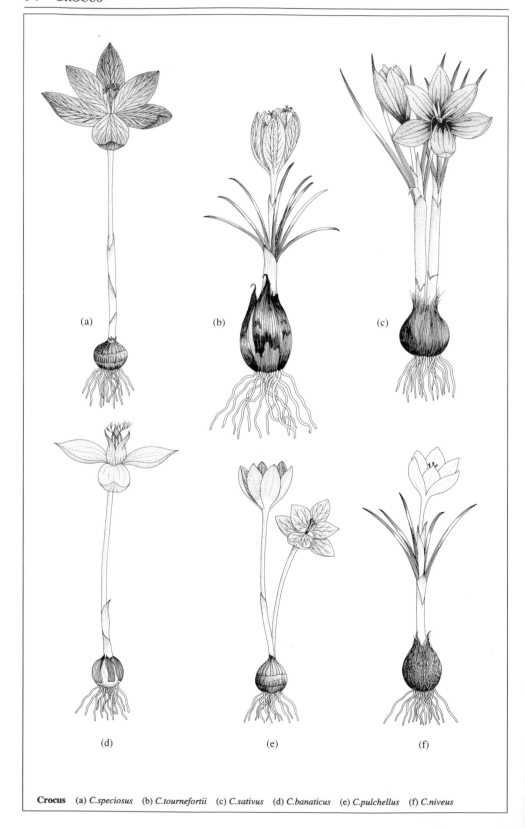

Crocus (a) *C.speciosus* (b) *C.tournefortii* (c) *C.sativus* (d) *C.banaticus* (e) *C.pulchellus* (f) *C.niveus*

C.cvijicii Košǎnin.
Tunics finely reticulate-fibrous. Lvs 2–4, appearing with fls, glabrous, to 3.2mm wide. Fls 1, tube 3.5–7.5cm, delicate yellow-golden, rarely white; tube to 3.5cm, white or pale yellow, sometimes tinted purple; throat white, sometimes stained yellow, pubesc.; style trifid, yellow-orange, branches widened at tips. Prophyll absent. Late spring–early summer. S Yugoslavia, N Greece, E Albania. Z7.

C.cyprius Boiss. & Kotschy.
Tunics splitting longitudinally and in rings from base. Lvs 3–4, to 2mm wide, appearing with fls, grooved beneath but without prominent venation, glabrous, dull green with fine white central stripe above. Fls 1–2, tube 4.5–9.5cm, scented, white-lilac, exterior flushed mauve, darkest at base of lobes and on tube; throat yellow; anth. yellow; style trifid, orange, tips enlarged. Late winter–early spring. Cyprus. Z8.

C.dalmaticus Vis.
Distinguished from the related *C.reticulatus* by its more finely reticulate tunic fibres and wider perianth lobes, and from *C.sieberi* by its broader lvs (to 3mm wide) and single fls, the exteriors pearly grey-mauve to biscuit and faintly striped purple. Late winter spring. SW Yugoslavia, N Albania. Z7.

C.danfordiae Maw.
Distinguished from the related *C.chrysanthus* and *C.biflorus* by its 1–4 diminutive fls, pale lemon or bronze-yellow, opal or white, the exterior minutely flecked silver-purple; lobes 0.9–1.5cm. Late winter–early spring. C Turkey. Z7.

C.dispathaceus Bowles. See *C.pallasii* ssp. *dispathaceus*.
C.elwesii (Maw) Schwarz. See *C.pallasii*.

C.etruscus Parl.
Tunics reticulate-fibrous. Lvs 3–4, 2–6mm wide, appearing with fls, glabrous. Fls 1–2, delicate lilac; tube white, 4.5–7cm; throat pubesc. sulphur yellow; lobes 3–4×1cm, the outer whorl ivory, nacreous or tawny, feathered purple below. Late winter–spring. N Italy. 'Zwanenburg': fls pale blue, but appearing a stronger, almost pure blue en masse. Z6.

C.fimbriatus Lapeyr. See *C.nudiflorus*.

C.flavus Weston ssp. *flavus* (*C.maesiacus* Ker-Gawl.; *C.luteus* Lam.; *C.aureus* Sibth. & Sm.; *C.lagenaeflorus* Salisb. *C.lacteus* Sab.).
Tunics papery, splitting lengthwise into fibres. Cataphylls coriaceous, withering to form slender neck. Lvs 4–8, appearing with fls, 2.5–4mm wide, green, margins ciliate or papillose, rarely glabrous. Fls 1–4, tube 7–18mm, scented, light golden yellow to apricot-yellow; tube exterior and base of lobes sometimes striped or stained brown; style trifid, yellow, rarely equal to or exceeding anth. Prophyll absent. Spring. S Yugoslavia, C & N Greece, Bulgaria, Romania, NW Turkey. ssp. *dissectus* Baytop & B. Mathew (*C.mouradii* Whittall). Differs from *C.flavus* ssp. *flavus* in its lvs, sometimes pubesc. throughout, and style divided into 6–15 branches. Spring. W Turkey. Z4.

C.fleischeri Gay.
Corm yellow, to 1.5cm diam. Tunics composed of finely plaited fibres, enclosing compressed developing cormlets. Lvs 5–8, to 1mm wide, appearing with fls. Fls 1–2, scented; tube to 5cm, throat glabrous, pale yellow; lobes 1.7–3.1cm×4–6mm, oblanceolate, white flushed mauve or maroon at base, outer lobes sometimes with central purple stripe. Style multifid, vermilion. Prophyll absent. Late winter–spring. S & W Turkey, E Aegean Is. Z6.

C.fontenayi Reut. See *C.laevigatus*.
C.gaillardottii (Boiss. & Blanche) Maw. See *C.aleppicus*.

C.gargaricus Herb. (*C.thirkeanus* K. Koch).
Corm occasionally bearing stolons. Tunics reticulate-fibrous. Lvs 3–4, to 2mm wide, appearing with fls. Fls 1, tube 5.6–10.5cm, yellow-orange; throat glabrous; style deep yellow, trifid and widening, fimbriate at tips, not exceeding anth. Prophyll absent. Spring. NW Turkey. Z7.

C.gilanicus B. Mathew.
Tunics thin, papery. Lvs 3–4, 1.5–2.5mm wide, glabrous, light green, to 10cm long, appearing long after fls. Fls 1; tube 3–7cm, white sometimes faintly veined mauve; throat pubesc., white; lobes 2–3.5×5–1cm, narrow elliptic, white veined purple, tips occasionally tinted lavender. Autumn. W Iran. Z8.

C.'Golden Yellow'. See *C.× luteus* 'Dutch Yellow'.

C.goulimyi Turrill.
Tunics smooth, tough, split, jagged at base. Lvs 4–6, 1–2.5mm wide, appearing with fls, glabrous. Fls 1–2, scented; tube white, 8–21cm; throat pubesc., white; lobes 1.5–4×1–2cm, rounded, lilac-pale mauve, inner whorl paler than outer; style trifid, white deepening to orange. Autumn. S Greece. 'Albus': fls pure white. Z7.

C.granatensis Boiss. ex Maw. See *C.serotinus* ssp. *salzmannii*.

C.graveolens Boiss. & Reut. ex Boiss.
Tunics papery or tough, splitting longitudinally from base in bands or fibres, apex sharp, fibrous. Lvs 5–8, 0.5–1.5mm wide, appearing with fls, silvery green, margins papillose or rough. Fls 2–6, malodorous, somewhat obpyriform in bud; tube 4–8cm, yellow with bronze or maroon stripes and spots; throat yellow; lobes spreading-deflexed, golden exterior marked as tube; style multifid, deep yellow. Late winter–spring. S Turkey, NW Syria, Lebanon, N Israel. Z8.

C.hadriaticus Herb. (*C.peloponnesiacus* Orph.).
Tunic fibrous, finely netted, produced as short apical neck. Lvs 5–9, to 1 mm wide, ciliate, appearing with or soon after fls. Fls 1–3; tube 3–9cm, white, yellow, maroon or mauve; throat pubesc., yellow, sometimes white; lobes 2–4.5×1–2cm, elliptic, obtuse, white suffused yellow, buff or lavender at base, occasionally tinted lilac throughout; style trifid, orange. Autumn. W & S Greece. Z8.

C.hartmannianus Holmb.
Differs from related *C.cyprius* in tunics only splitting vertically; lvs well developed at flowering and anth. dark violet-maroon. Late winter. Cyprus. Z8.

C.hermoneus Kotschy ex Maw.
Resembles the related *C.cancellatus*, differing principally in parallel fibrous tunics, splitting lengthwise, subreticulate at apex and neck. Early winter. Israel, Jordan. Z8.

C.heuffelianus Herb. See *C.vernus*.
C.hittiticus Baytop & B. Mathew. See *C.reticulatus* ssp. *hittiticus*.
C.hybernus Friv. See *C.pallasii*.

C.hyemalis Boiss. & Blanche (*C.hyemalis* var. *foxii* Maw ex Boiss.).
Tunics papery, fibrous at apex, splitting longitudinally in bands. Lvs 3–7, 2–2.5mm wide, appearing with fls, deep green, glabrous or with rough margins. Fls 1–4, scented; tube to 6cm, white sometimes flushed mauve; throat glabrous, pale yellow; lobes 2.4–4.2×0.6–1.5cm, white, base outer whorl suffused or flecked purple below, sometimes with mauve central region; style orange, multifid. Prophyll absent. Late autumn–winter. Israel, Lebanon, Syria. Z8.

C.imperati Ten. ssp. *imperati* (*C.neapolitanus* Ten.; *C.incurvus* Donn ex Steud.).
Tunics parallel fibrous, sometimes subreticulate at apex, inner tunics membranous. Lvs 3–6, 2–3mm wide, appearing with fls, glabrous, shining dark green. Fls 1–2; tube 3–10cm, white, occasionally expanding yellow or mauve; throat glabrous, deep yellow; lobes obtuse, 3–4.5×0.9–1.8cm, bright purple within, exterior tawny with to 5 feathered violet stripes. Style orange-coral, trifid. Late winter–early spring. W Italy, Capri. 'de Jager': fls lilac inside, buff and purple outer stripes. ssp. *suaveolens* (Bertol.) B. Mathew (*C.suaveolens* Bertol.). Differs from *C.imperati* ssp. *imperati* in: bracteole absent; fls smaller, each outer lobe marked with 3 purple stripes, the central, the darkest extending to tip. Late winter. W Italy. Z7.

C.incurvus Donn ex Steud. See *C.imperati* ssp. *imperati*.
C.insularis Gay. See *C.corsicus* or *C.minimus*.
C.ionicus Herb. See *C.boryi*.
C.iridiflorus Rchb. See *C.banaticus*.

C.karduchorum Kotschy ex Maw.
Tunics thin, papery, parallel-fibrous or subreticulate. Lvs 3–4, to 2mm wide, glabrous, emerging after flowering. Fls 1, fragrant; tube white, 4–9cm; throat white, pubesc.; lobes 3–4×1cm, oblanceolate, acute, pale violet fading to white at base with darker, delicate venation; anth. ivory; style spreading, multifid, exceeding anth. Autumn. SE Turkey. Z8.

C.karduchorum hort. non Kotschy ex Maw. See *C.kotschyanus* ssp. *kotschyanus* var. *leucopharynx*.
C.kirkii Maw. See *C.candidus*.

C.korolkowii Reg. ex Maw.
Outer tunics papery, splitting, parallel-fibrous, fibres often fused in points at neck. Lvs 10–20, 1–2.5mm wide, appearing with fls, green, keel prominently veined, margins glabrous or rough. Fls 3–5, scented; tube 3–10cm, golden, sometimes marked bronze or maroon; throat glabrous, yellow-metallic buff; lobes to 3×1cm, elliptic, subacute, golden yellow, outer lobes marked dark brown or maroon below; style trifid, orange, tips widened, papillose. Prophyll absent. Late winter–early spring. Afghanistan, N Pakistan, Russia. Z6.

C.kosaninii Pulev.
Related to *C.etruscus*, from which it differs in its finely parallel-fibrous tunics, reticulate only at apex, its 2, rarely 3, lvs and golden, glabrous throat. Spring. Yugoslavia. Z6.

C.kotschyanus Koch ssp. **kotschyanus** (*C.zonatus* Gay).
orms producing numerous bulblets, sometimes stolons; tunics papery, fibres parallel at base, subreticulate at apex. Lvs 4–6, to 4mm wide, glabrous, keel nearly as wide as lamina. Fls 1, scented; tube to 13cm, white; throat pubesc., white tinted yellow with 2 golden splashes at base of each lobe, sometimes fusing to form larger cleft patch; lobes 3–4.5×0.5–2cm, pale lavender with darker, parallel veins running almost to apex; style trifid, ivory to pale yellow, tips expanded and subdivided. Autumn. C & S Turkey, NW Syria, C & N Lebanon. var. **leucopharynx** B.L. Burtt (*C.karduchorum* hort.). Corms large, irregular. Fls blue-lavender, veined blue, with central white zone, yellow markings absent; anth. and style pale cream. Turkey. ssp. **cappadocicus** B. Mathew. Corm set obliquely in ground. Throat glabrous. Early autumn. Turkey. ssp. **hakkariensis** B. Mathew. Corm on its side in ground. Lobes lozenge-shaped. Autumn. SE Turkey. ssp. **suworowianus** (K. Koch) B. Mathew (*C.vallicola* var. *suworowianus* (Koch) Maw). Unscented; throat glabrous with pale yellow markings; lobes held closely, near-erect, cream with mauve veins, tone suffusing where veins converge. Early autumn. Russia, Turkey. Z5.

C.lacteus Sab. See *C.flavus*.

C.laevigatus Bory & Chaub. (*C.fontenayi* Reut.).
Tunics tough splitting at base into narrow, pointed strips. Lvs 3–4, to 2.5mm wide, barely appearing with fls, deep green, glabrous. Fls to 3, fragrant (particularly those from the Cyclades, but scarcely ever in those from Crete); tube 2–8cm, white tinted yellow or mauve toward throat; throat yellow, glabrous; lobes 1.3–3×0.4–1.8cm, obovate to elliptic, white or pale rose-lilac above, outer lobes white, mauve, bronze or yellow, with up to 3 broad dark purple or maroon feathered lines below, markings sometimes absent or exterior wholly purple; style multifid, orange, usually above anth. Prophyll absent. Autumn–early spring. Greece, Crete. Z7.

C.lagenaeflorus Salisb. See *C.flavus*.
C.lazicus (Boiss. & Bal.) Boiss. See *C.scharojanii*.

C.leichtlinii (D. Dewar) Bowles.
Tunics durable, splitting lengthwise, jagged at base, smooth or coriaceous. Lvs 6–13, to 1mm wide, usually narrower, appearing with fls. Fls to 4, fragrant; tube 4–6cm, white suffused yellow toward throat or tinted blue, appearing iridescent

green; throat golden, glabrous; lobes to 3×1cm, narrow-oblanceolate, opal to sky blue, exterior deeper blue at base or throughout; style trifid, light orange. Prophyll absent. Spring. SE Turkey. Z8.

C.libanoticus Mout. See *C.pallasii*.

C.longiflorus Raf. (*C.odorus* Biv.).
Tunics finely reticulate-fibrous. Lvs 4–6, 1–3mm wide, deep green with white central stripe, emerging at flowering. Fls 1–2, scented; tube 5–10cm, pale yellow, striped violet; throat yellow, glabrous or thinly pubesc.; lobes 2–4.5×0.5–1.5cm, lilac, exterior with darker veins, sometimes shaded bronze; style trifid, vermilion, tips widened, crenate, sometimes subdivided. Autumn. SW Italy, Sicily, Malta. Z5.

C.lusitanicus Herb. See *C.capetanus*.

C.× luteus Lam. (*C.flavus* × *C.angustifolius*.)
Ancient sterile triploid cv, the common large yellow spring crocus. Fls rich orange-yellow, paler externally, with 3 short olive-green stripes on outer lobes; anthers and style somewhat degenerate. Rapidly increasing by offsets. Garden origin, 17th century. 'Dutch Yellow' ('Golden Yellow', 'Yellow Giant', 'Yellow Mammoth'): fls large, deep yellow. 'Stellaris': resembling *C.flavus*, tunic coarsely reticulate; fls bright golden yellow, conspicuously striped and feathered dark-brown externally; sterile: anthers and style degenerate. Early spring.

C.maesiacus Ker-Gawl. See *C.flavus*.

C.malyi Vis.
Tunics finely parallel-fibrous, sometimes subreticulate at apex. Lvs 3–5, 1.5–2.5mm wide, slightly silver-green, appearing with fls. Fls 1–2; tube 4–9cm, white, occasionally flushed yellow, bronze or mauve; throat pubesc., yellow; lobes 2–4cm×0.8–1.5cm, white, often with grey-blue or bronze stain at base; style trifid, orange, tips widening, notched, held above anth. Spring. W former Yugoslavia. Z7.

C.marathonisius Heldr. See *C.boryi*.
C.marcetii Pau. See *C.nevadensis*.
C.maudii Maly. See *C.sieberi* ssp. *sublimis*.

C.medius Balb.
Tunics strongly reticulate-fibrous; cataphylls withering to form neck. Lvs 2–3, 2.5–4mm wide, appearing after flowering, dark green with silver-white central stripe, sometimes ciliate. Fls 1; tube 8–20cm, white to mauve at apex; throat glabrous, white veined violet; lobes 2.5–5×1–2cm, obovate, abruptly acute, pale blue-mauve, veined darker at base; style multifid, vermilion, branches notched and recurving. Autumn. NW Italy, SE France. Z6.

C.michelsonii B. Fedtsch.
Tunics smooth, reticulate. Lvs 4–7, 1.5–2mm wide, appearing with fls, silver-green, keel prominently veined, margins sometimes ciliate. Fls 1–2; tube 4–8cm, white suffused lilac; throat glabrous, white-lilac; lobes 2.5–4×0.5–1cm, oblanceolate, translucent white above, stained or spotted pale mauve below, but fading at margins; style trifid, white, tips widening, papillose. Prophyll absent. Spring. Russia, Iran. Z7.

C.micranthus Boiss. See *C.reticulatus* ssp. *reticulatus*.

C.minimus DC. (*C.insularis* Gay).
Tunics parallel-fibrous. Lvs 3–5, 0.5–1mm wide, dark green, appearing with fls. Fls 1–2; tube 4–11cm, white flushed mauve at apex; throat glabrous, white sometimes tinted pale yellow; lobes 2–3×0.4–0.8cm, oblanceolate, light mauve-deep purple, striped, veined or shaded darker below, on bronze background; style trifid, orange, tips, flattened, crenate-lobed. Prophyll absent. Late winter–early spring. Sardinia, Corsica, Isles Sanguinaires. Z8.

C.moabiticus Bornm. & Dinsm. ex Bornm.
Tunics finely parallel-fibrous, reticulate at apex and produced as neck. Lvs 11–13, 1–2mm wide, appearing soon after flowering, silver-green, keel margin sparsely papillose. Fls to 5; tube 2–4cm, white; throat pubesc., white tinted mauve; lobes 1.5–2.5×0.3–0.7cm, narrow elliptic, white veined purple;

style deeply trifid, burnt orange. Early winter. N Jordan. Z8.

C.montenegrinus Kerner ex Maw. See *C.vernus* ssp. *albiflorus*.

C.mouradii Whittall. See *C.flavus* ssp. *dissectus*.

C.multifidus Ramond. See *C.nudiflorus*.

C.napolitanus Mord. de Laun. & Lois. See *C.vernus*.

C.neapolitanus Ten. See *C.imperati* ssp. *imperati*.

C.nevadensis Amo (*C.atlanticus* Pomel; *C.algeriensis* Bak.; *C.marcetii* Pau).
Tunics finely parallel-fibrous, fibres often fused at apex, produced as points or narrow neck. Lvs 3–5, 1–2.5mm wide, appearing with fls, erect, glabrous, ciliate or minutely denticulate. Fls 1, scented; tube 3–8.5mm, cream tinted mauve; throat pubesc., cream or pale yellow; lobes 2–4×0.5–1cm, obtuse, cream-lilac, veined purple, sometimes tinted green below; style trifid, white, branches short, flattened, ruffled at tips. Prophyll absent. Late winter–spring. N Algeria, Morocco, Spain. Z8.

C.niveus Bowles.
Tunics finely reticulate-fibrous, extended as neck. Lvs 5–8, 1–2mm wide, glossy dark green, emerging at flowering. Fls 1–2; tube 9–18cm, ivory to dull yellow; throat golden, pubesc.; lobes 3–6×1.5–3.5cm, obovate, obtuse, white, sometimes stained lilac; style trifid, scarlet, tips flattened, lobed or fimbriate. Autumn. S Greece. Z6.

C.nudiflorus Sm. (*C.multifidus* Ramond; *C.aphyllus* Ker-Gawl.; *C.fimbriatus* Lapeyr.; *C.pyrenaeus* Herb.).
Corms sometimes stoloniferous; tunics membranous, loosely parallel-fibrous. Lvs 3–4, 2–4mm wide, appearing after flowering, long-lived. Fls 1; tube 10–22cm, white flushed mauve toward apex; throat white-mauve, glabrous or papillose; lobes 3–6×1–2cm, obtuse, pale mauve to amethyst; style multifid, orange. Autumn. SW France, N & E Spain. Z5.

C.ochroleucus Boiss. & Gaill.
Tunics thin, papery, parallel-fibrous, subreticulate at apex. Lvs 3–6, 1–1.5mm wide, just emerging at flowering, dark green. Fls 1–3; tube 5–8cm, white; throat pubesc. pale yellow-golden, spreading to base of lobes; lobes 2–3.5×1cm, elliptic, ivory; style trifid, golden yellow. Autumn–winter. Z5.

C.odorus Biv. See *C.longiflorus*.
C.officinalis G. Beck. See *C.sativus*.
C.officinalis Martyn non G. Beck. See *C.sativus*.
C.officinalis var. *sativus* (L.) Huds. See *C.sativus*.
C.olbanus Siehe. See *C.pallasii*.

C.olivieri Gay (*C.olivieri* ssp. olivieri; *C.suterianus* Herb.; *C.aucheri* Boiss.).
Tunics papery, parallel-fibrous, splitting, jagged at base, forming narrow teeth at apex. Lvs 1–4, 2–5mm wide, appearing with fls, glossy green, arching, ciliate, often pubesc. above. Fls 1–4; tube 5–7cm, yellow or maroon; throat yellow; lobes 1.5–3.5×0.4–1.2cm, yellow-orange, or striped bronze-maroon below and on tube; style divided ×6, pale orange. Prophyll absent. Late winter–spring. Balkans, Turkey. ssp. *balansae* (Gay ex Bak.) B. Mathew (*C.balansae* Gay ex Bak.). Lvs erect. Fls striped or stained brown bronze or maroon below; style divided ×12–15. Late winter–spring. W Turkey, Aegean. Z7.

C.orbelicus Stoj. See *C.veluchensis*.

C.oreocreticus B.L. Burtt.
Related to *C.cartwrightianus*. Differs in lvs barely emerging at flowering, nacreous or bronze hue to fls, fls very rarely white, usually mauve. Autumn–winter. Crete (mts). Z8.

C.orphanindis Hook. f. See *C.tournefortii*.

C.pallasii Goldbl. ssp. *pallasii* (*C.campestris* Pall. ex Herb.; *C.hybernus* Friv.; *C.olbanus* Siehe; *C.elwesii* (Maw) Schwarz; *C.thiebautii* Mout.; *C.libanoticus* Mout.).
Tunics reticulate-fibrous, produced as neck to 2cm long. Lvs 7–17, 0.5–1.5mm wide, just emerging at flowering. Fls 1–6; scented; tube 4–7cm, white or mauve; throat white or mauve,

pubesc.; lobes 2.5–5×1.–1.5cm, inner whorl smaller, rose-mauve-indigo, faintly veined darker; style trifid, vermilion. Autumn. Balkans, Middle East. ssp. *dispathaceus* (Bowles) B. Mathew (*C.dispathaceus* Bowles). Lobes strap-like, 4–7mm wide, garnet-coloured; style pale yellow. Autumn–early winter. S Turkey, N Syria. Z8.

C.pelistericus Pulev.
Tunics finely reticulate-fibrous, forming neck. Lvs 3–4, 1–2mm wide, appearing with fls, erect, matt green, central stripe absent. Fls 1; tube 3–4cm, purple; throat white, glabrous; lobes 2–3×1cm, obtuse, deep purple, shining with darker veins; style abruptly trifid, cream-orange, tips flattened, frilled, held above anth. Late spring–early summer. S Balkans, N Greece. Z7.

C.peloponnesiacus Orph. See *C.hadriaticus*.

C.pestalozzae Boiss.
Resembles *C.biflorus* except in cataphylls rigid, green, not thin; lvs narrow, 0.5–1.55mm wide; fls smaller, white or blue-mauve and fil. stained black at base, not wholly yellow. Late winter–early spring. NW Turkey. 'Caeruleus': fls slender, lilac blue; fil. with small black spot on lower internal portion and threadlike style, so that the black specks look like tiny pellets of soil fallen into throat of fl. Z7.

C.pholegandricus Orph. See *C.tournefortii*.
C.praecox Haw. See *C.biflorus*.

C.pulchellus Herb.
Differs from related *C.speciosus* in its golden yellow throat, gracefully incurving, opal blue lobes with lilac veins and cream-coloured anth Autumn–early winter. Turkey. 'Zephyr': fls very large, pale, pearly blue. Z6.

C.purpureus Weston. See *C.vernus*.
C.pusillus Ten. See *C.biflorus*.
C.pyrenaeus Herb. See *C.nudiflorus*.

C.reticulatus Steven ex Adams ssp. **reticulatus** (*C.variegatus* Hoppe & Hornsch. *C.vittatus* Raf.; *C.micranthus* Boiss.).
Tunics markedly reticulate-fibrous. Lvs 3–5, 0.5–1.5mm wide, appearing with fls, silver-green. Fls 1–2, scented; tube 3–6cm, white or mauve; throat glabrous or papillose, cream–yellow; lobes 1.7–3.5×0.5–1.5cm, outer whorl acute, white above, white, pale mauve or bronze tinted below, usually with 3–5 purple, feathered veins, inner whorl shorter, wider, obtuse, white-mauve below; anth. yellow; style trifid, vermilion, tips widened, papillose. Prophyll absent. Spring. SE Europe, SW Russia, Turkey. ssp. *hittiticus* (Baytop & B. Mathew) (*C.hittiticus* Baytop & B. Mathew). Anth. violet-black. Late winter–spring. S Turkey. Z8.

C.robertianus C. Brickell.
Tunics coarsely reticulate-fibrous. Lvs 3–4, 4–6mm wide, appearing after fls, dark green with strong central stripe, margins rough. Fls 1–2; tube 7–10cm, sometimes longer, ivory-mauve; throat glabrous or pubesc., cream-yellow; lobes 3–6×1–2cm, lilac to blue tinted mauve; style abruptly trifid, burnt orange, tips widened, slightly fimbriate. Prophyll absent. Autumn. C & N Greece. Z8.

C.salzmannii Gay. See *C.serotinus* ssp. *salzmannii*.

C.sativus L. (*C.officinalis* G. Beck; *C.officinalis* Martyn; *C.officinalis* var. *sativus* (L.) Huds.). SAFFRON.
Sterile cultigen probably selected in *C.cartwrightianus*, from which it differs chiefly in perianth lobes to 5cm and style branches to 3cm. Z6.

C.sativus var. *cartwrightianus* (Herb.) Maw. See *C.cartwrightianus*.

C.scardicus Košaanin.
Tunics finely reticulate-fibrous, produced at apex as slender, splitting neck. Lvs to 4, 0.5–1mm wide, appearing with fls, erect, glabrous, green. Fls 1; tube 2–4cm, mauve or white tinted violet; lobes 2–4×1cm, obtuse, lemon to golden yellow, the exteriors faded toward the base and stained mauve; style abruptly trifid, pale orange, tips widening, ruffled or

lobed. Late spring–early summer. Former Yugoslavia, Albania. Z6.

C.scepusiensis (Rehm & Wol.) Borb. See *C.vernus*.

C.scharojanii Rupr. (*C.lazicus* (Boiss. & Bal.) Boiss.).
Corms occasionally stoloniferous; tunics papery, fibres parallel at base, subreticulate at apex. Lvs 3–4, 1.5–3mm wide, developing after flowering and persisting into 2nd season, glabrous, green. Fls 1, seldom opening fully; tube to 10cm, yellow; throat glabrous, yellow; lobes 2.5–4×0.5–1cm, golden yellow to orange at tips; style trifid, orange. Summer–autumn. Russia, NE Turkey. Z6.

C.serotinus Salisb. ssp. *serotinus*.
Tunics markedly reticulate-fibrous, drawn toward apex, lattice-like. Lvs 3–4, 0.5–2mm wide, appearing with fls, deep green, glabrous, margins sometimes rough. Fls, scented; tube 2–5cm, white to mauve; throat pubesc., white or ivory; lobes 2.5–4×1cm, obtuse, pale mauve to lilac blue, sometimes veined purple; style multifid, burnt orange, above anth. Autumn. Portugal. ssp. *clusii* (Gay) B. Mathew. Tunics finely reticulate-fibrous. Lvs 4–7, emerging as fls fade. Throat glabrous or pubesc. Autumn. Portugal, NW & SW Spain. ssp. *salzmannii* (Gay) B. Mathew (*C.asturicus* Herb.; *C.granatensis* Boiss. ex Maw). Tunics papery, splitting longitudinally. Tube to 11cm. Autumn–winter. N Africa, Spain, Gibraltar. Z6.

C.siculus Tineo. See *C.vernus* ssp. albiflorus.

C.sieberi Gay ssp. *sieberi* (*C.sieberi* var. *versicolor* Boiss. & Heldr.; *C.sieberi* var. *heterochromus* Hal.).
Tunics finely reticulate-fibrous. Lvs 4–7, to 2mm wide, appearing with fls, glabrous. Fls to 3, scented; tube 2.5–5cm, white or mauve, usually deep yellow toward throat; throat glabrous, golden yellow or orange; lobes 2–3×1cm, obtuse, white within, tinted purple, exterior of outer whorl striped, barred or suffused mauve; style abruptly trifid, yellow-orange, tips divided or ruffled. Spring–early summer. Crete. ssp. *atticus* (Boiss. & Orph.) B. Mathew (*C.sieberi* var. *atticus* Boiss. & Orph.). Corm tunic distinctly reticulate-fibrous; cataphylls withering to leave neck. Late winter–spring. Greece. 'Bowles White': fls with pure white pet., orange throat; stigma scarlet. 'Firefly': outer pet. nearly white, inner pet. violet, base yellow. 'Hubert Edelsten': fls deep purple, blotched white at tip. 'Violet Queen': fls rounded, violet-blue on short stalks. ssp. *nivalis* (Bory & Chaub.) B. Mathew. Throat yellow, glabrous; lobes lilac. Late winter–early summer. Greece. ssp. *sublimis* (Herb.) B. Mathew (*C.maudii* Maly; *C.athous* Bornm.). Throat yellow, pubesc; lobes blue-mauve, darker at tips, sometimes white at base. Late winter–early summer. Balkans, Greece. ssp. *sublimis* f.*tricolor* B.L. Burtt. Fls with 3 distinct bands of colour: lilac, pure white and golden yellow. Z7.

C.sieheanus Barr ex B.L. Burtt.
Resembles *C.ancyrensis* and *C.chrysanthus*. Distinguished by its papery, parallel-fibrous tunics, vermilion style held above stamens and pale yellow anth. often appearing sterile. Spring. Turkey. Z7.

C.skorpilii Velen. See *C.chrysanthus*.

C.speciosus Bieb. ssp. *speciosus*.
Tunics tough, splitting as rings from base. Lvs 3–5, 3–5mm wide, initiated after fls, dark green, glabrous throughout or pubesc. above, margins sometimes ciliate or rough. Fls 1, scented; tube 5–20cm, white or pale mauve; throat glabrous, off-white, rarely, tinted yellow; lobes 3–6×1–2cm, mauve-blue above, exterior veined or spattered purple, sometimes on a paler, opal ground; style multifid, orange, much exceeding anthers. Prophyll absent. Autumn. Russia, Iran, Turkey. cvs include: 'Aitchisonii': large, pale lilac with feather venation; 'Albus': white; 'Artabir': pale lilac with strong venation; 'Cassiope': large, pale violet with yellow throat; 'Globosus': diminutive, fls lavender-blue, appearing somewhat inflated; 'Pollux': large, pale mauve with pearly exterior; 'Oxonian': indigo; 'Trotter': large, white. ssp. *xantholaimos* B. Mathew.

Lvs 1–2.5mm. Throat deep yellow, thinly pubescent; lobes 3–3.8×1–1.2cm; fil. deep yellow, style much branched, shorter than anthers. N Turkey. Z4.

C.stellaris Haw. See *C.× luteus* 'Stellaris'.
C.suaveolens Bertol. See *C.imperati* ssp. *suaveolens*.
C.susianus Ker-Gawl. See *C.angustifolius*.
C.suterianus Herb. See *C.olivieri*.
C.thiebautii Mout. See *C.pallasii*.
C.thirkeanus K. Koch. See *C.gargaricus*.

C.thomasii Ten. (*C.visianicus* Herb.).
Tunics finely reticulate-fibrous, forming apical neck to 1cm. Lvs 5–10, 0.5–1.5mm wide, barely emerging at flowering, glabrous or with margins papillose. Fls 1–3, scented; tube 3–6cm, white to mauve; throat pubesc., yellow; lobes 2–4×1cm, white to pale mauve, veined or suffused darker at base; style trifid, coral pink, widened at tips. Autumn. S Italy, Balkans. Z7.

C.tommasinianus Herb.
Tunics finely parallel-fibrous, subreticulate at apex. Lvs 3–4, 2–3mm wide, appearing with fls, glabrous, green with a conspicuous, central silver stripe. Fls 1–2; tube 3.5–10cm, white; throat white, thinly pubesc.; lobes 2–4.5×1.2cm, pale mauve to violet, occasionally white or rose, darker at apex, sometimes with silver or bronze hue below; style trifid, orange, flattened and fimbriate at tips. Late winter–spring. Balkans, Hungary, Bulgaria. 'Albus': fls white, sometimes straw-coloured externally. 'Barr's Purple': outer lobes tinged grey, inner lobes rich purple-lilac. 'Pictus': outer lobes marked mauve or purple at apex. 'Roseus': fls pink-purple. 'Ruby Giant': probably a hybrid with *C.vernus*; fls dark red-purple, especially in upper part and base of lobes. 'Whitewell Purple': fls purple-mauve externally, silver-mauve within. Z5.

C.tomoricus Markgr. See *C.veluchensis*.

C.tournefortii Gay (*C.pholegandricus* Orph. *C.orphanidis* Hook. f.).
Tunics papery, splitting from base into fine fibres. Lvs 5–10, 1–2.5mm wide, appearing with fls, deep green, sometimes ciliate. Fls 1, scented in Cretan populations; tube 3–10cm, white, rarely suffused purple; throat glabrous or pubesc., yellow to ivory; lobes 1.5–3.5×0.5–1.5cm, pale lilac, often veined darker at base of lobes, rarely white throughout; style multifid, orange-crimson, branches held above anth., arching, widening and lobed at tips. Prophyll absent. Autumn–winter. S Greece, Crete, Cyclades. Z8.

C.vallicola Herb.
Fls 1, white; lobes veined mauve and with 2 yellow spots at base, finely acuminate at apex. Late summer–autumn. Russia, Turkey. Z7.

C.vallicola var. *suworowianus* (K. Koch) Maw. See *C.kotschyanus* ssp. *suworowianus*.
C.variegatus Hoppe & Hornsch. See *C.reticulatus* ssp. reticulatus.

C.veluchensis Herb. (*C.balcanensis* Janka; *C.orbelicus* Stoj.; *C.tomoricus* Markgr.).
Tunics finely reticulate-fibrous. Lvs 2–4, 2–5mm wide, appearing with fls, dark green, glabrous. Fls 1–2, rarely scented; tube 2–10cm, white to blue-mauve; throat pubesc., white tinted mauve; lobes 2–4×0.5–1.5cm, pale lilac to purple, exterior darker at base and apex; style trifid, ivory, yellow or orange, widened and dissected at tips. Prophyll absent. Spring–early summer. Balkans, Albania, Bulgaria, Greece. Z6.

C.veneris Tapp. ex Poech.
Tunics papery, parallel-fibrous. Lvs 3–4, 0.5–1mm wide, appearing with fls, glabrous, margins sometimes rough. Fls 1–2, fragrant; tube 3–4cm, white; throat pubesc., yellow; lobes 1.5–2.5×0.5cm, acute, white, exterior of outer lobe striped or feathered purple; style finely multifid, deep golden yellow. Prophyll absent. Late autumn–early spring. Cyprus. Z8.

C.*vernus* Hill ssp. *vernus* (C.*purpureus* Weston; C.*napolitanus* Mord. de Laun. & Lois.; C.*banaticus* Heuff. non Gay; C.*heuffelianus* Herb.; C.*scepusiensis* (Rehmann & Wol.) Borb.).
Tunics finely parallel-fibrous, subreticulate toward apex. Lvs 2–4, 4–6mm wide, appearing with fls, glabrous or pubesc. Fls 1; tube 5–15cm, mauve or white if fl. colour white throughout; throat white, often suffused mauve, glabrous or pubesc.; lobes 3–5.5×1–2cm, obtuse, rarely emarginate, white, violet or blue-mauve, sometimes striped white or violet, usually with a darker, cleft-like marking near tips; style abruptly trifid, yellow-orange, widened and fimbriate at tips. Spring–early summer. Italy, Austria, E Europe. 'Early Perfection': fls violet-purple to blue with dark edges. 'Enchantress': fls light amethyst purple with silvery floss, dark base. 'Pickwick': fls white with deep lilac stripes, base deep purple. 'Remembrance': fls large, rounded, silver-purple, base flushed purple. 'Vanguard': fls light ageratum blue, exterior grey; blooms more than 2 weeks in advance of other cvs. 'Glory of Limmen': fls very large, rounded, white with short purple stripes at base. 'Haarlem Gem': fls small, silvery-lilac externally, pale-lilac-mauve within. 'Jeanne d'Arc': fls large, white, with 3 thin purple stripes, tinged violet at base. 'Kathleen Parlow': fls large, white, base and tube purple. 'Little Dorrit': fls very large, rounded, very pale silver-lilac. 'Paulus Potter': fls large, glossy red-purple. 'Purpureus Grandiflorus': fls large, deep glossy rich purple. 'Queen of the Blues': fls large, lavender-blue. 'Striped Beauty': fls pale silver-grey, striped deep mauve, base violet-purple. ssp. *albiflorus* (Kit. ex Schult.) Asch. & Gräbn. (C.*albiflorus* Kit. ex

Schult.; C.*caeruleus* Weston; C.*vilmae* Fiala; C.*siculus* Tineo; C.*montenegrinus* Kerner ex Maw). Fls usually white, sometimes marked purple. Spring–summer. Europe. Z4.

C.*versicolor* Ker-Gawl.
Tunics papery, splitting, ultimately parallel-fibrous. Lvs 3–5, 1.5–3mm wide, appearing with fls, dull green, glabrous, prominently veined below. Fls 1–2; tube 6–10cm, white or purple-striped; throat glabrous, lemon yellow or ivory; lobes 2.5–3.5×1cm, white-mauve, exterior almost always striped darker, sometimes with bronze-yellow hue; style trifid, pale orange, tips widened, indented. Late winter–spring. S France to W Italy, Morocco. 'Picturatus': fls white outside, feathered violet. Z5.

C.*vilmae* Fiala. See C.*vernus* ssp. *albiflorus*.
C.*visianicus* Herb. See C.*thomasii*.

C.*vitellinus* Wahl.
Tunics tough, papery, splitting longitudinally, leaving jagged points at apex. Lvs 2–4, 1.5–3mm wide, appearing with fls, dark, glossy green, sometimes coarse toward apex. Fls 2–6, highly fragrant; tube 4–7cm, yellow; throat yellow; lobes 2–3×0.5–1cm, obtuse, inner whorl shorter than outer, spreading or recurved, golden yellow, sometimes striped or spotted maroon-bronze; style multifid, golden to vermilion. Prophyll absent. Late autumn–early winter. Turkey, Syria, Lebanon. Z8.

C.*vittatus* Raf. See C.*reticulatus* ssp. *reticulatus*.
C.'Yellow Giant'. See C.× *luteus* 'Dutch Yellow'.
C.'Yellow Mammoth'. See C.× *luteus* 'Dutch Yellow'.
C.*zonatus* Gay. See C.*kotschyanus*.

Cyanella L. (Diminutive of Gk *kyanos*, blue.) Amaryllidaceae. 8 species of perennial herbs. Corms deep-seated with matted, fibrous tunics, deep seated forming a long thin neck. Leaves in a basal rosette and lying flat. Flowers in simple or much-branched racemes, rarely axillary and solitary; peduncles terete, bracteate; pedicels usually curved; tepals 6, free or almost so, yellow, mauve, white, pink or orange, spreading, marcescent, reflexed at anthesis; stamens 6, 5 short and of equal length, 1 longer, opposite lowest tepal, declinate, filaments basally fused, anthers yellow; ovary semi-inferior, style subulate, stigma apical. Fruit a globose to narrowly ovoid capsule, erect; seeds ovoid, black shiny. Spring. S Africa, Namibia. Z9.

CULTIVATION As for *Ixia*.

C.*alba* L. f.
Lvs to 12.5cm, numerous, in a basal tuft. Flowering stem to 25cm; fls solitary, 2.5cm diam.; tepals white flushed pale yellow, outer acute, inner rounded at apex, slightly cup-shaped. S Africa (W Cape).

C.*capensis* L. See C.*hyacinthoides*.

C.*hyacinthoides* L. (C.*capensis* L.) LADY'S HAND
Lvs 20–30cm, 5–8, mostly basal, margins undulate. Flowering stem to 30cm; fls 8–10 per branch, lightly fragrant; tepals pale lilac or blue-violet, often with a small carmine blotch at base. S Africa (Cape Peninsula).

C.*lutea* L. f. FIVE FINGERS.
Basal lvs to 15×1.5cm, narrow, margins undulate, stem lvs few, apex acute. Flowering stem to 30cm; infl. often branched, pedicels strongly arching, tepals yellow, outside of outer tepals with prominent brown veins. S Africa (SW Cape).

C.*orchidiformis* Jacq.
Lvs 12×2.5cm, prostrate or nearly so, in a rosette, green tinged grey. Flowering stems 30–40cm, naked, tinged purple above; fls to 16 per stem, on arching pedicels; tepals pale mauve with a dark carmine-mauve ring in the centre. S Africa (Namaqualand).

Cybistetes Milne-Redh. & Schweick. (From Gk *kybistetes*, one who tumbles; referring to the umbel's becoming detached and blown around when the fruit is ripe.) Amaryllidaceae. 1 species, a perennial, deciduous herb. Bulb ovoid, to 15×10cm, tunicate. Leaves to 35×1cm, usually 10 in 2 ranks, glaucous, ligulate, curving, apex truncate, margins entire to irregular, papery. Scape to 20cm, lateral, flattened to semi-terete; inflorescence umbellate, subtended by 2 persistent bracts; flowers fragrant, to 24, pedicellate; perianth tube to 1cm; lobes to 7cm, oblanceolate, obtuse, spreading, glossy rose pink to magenta; stamens 6, exserted; ovary inferior, ovules to 18 per chamber. Fruit an indehiscent capsule on an elongated pedicel, seeds subglobose. Spring. S Africa (SW Cape). Z9.

CULTIVATION *Cybistetes* bears large umbels of pale to dark pink fragrant flowers, opening white inside, in mid summer. The leaves, which emerge after flowering, persist through winter until the following spring. Cultivate as for *Brunsvigia*.

C.longifolia (L.) Milne-Redh. & Schweick. (*Amaryllis longi-folia* L.; *Ammocharis falcata* (Jacq.) Herb.).

Cyclamen L. (From Gk *kyklos*, circular, referring to the spiralling of the peduncle after flowering in some species.) PERSIAN VIOLET; ALPINE VIOLET; SOWBREAD. Primulaceae. 19 species of perennial herbs, to 20cm. Tubers usually spherical with a flattened or concave upper surface, rarely ovoid or knobbly, corky, splitting in strips or covered in fine hairs, some producing apical outgrowths (floral trunks) from which leaves and flowers develop. Leaves folded when young, variable in shape, 2–10×2–7cm, occasionally broader than long, bright green or light blue-grey to charcoal grey-green, occasionally marked with a silver-grey sheen, usually with an obcordate, dark pattern above surrounded by silver-grey blotches and patches, often tinted red or purple beneath. Flowers often fragrant, solitary, nodding, on erect then recurved pedicels; sepals 5, united; petals 5, reflexed through 90–180°, twisted away from calyx, united into a short tube at base, often auricled on tube rim, white or pale pink to deep carmine, often with a dark purple blotch at base; stamens 5, rarely exserted; peduncle usually spiralling from apex to base during fruit development, providing a spring mechanism for seed dispersal. Fruit a 5-chambered capsule; seeds sticky. Europe, Mediterranean to Iran, 1 species Somalia.

CULTIVATION Most *Cyclamen* species inhabit rocky terrain in semi-arid locations, protected by shrubs and trees. They often grow very close to the coastline and may show some tolerance of salt spray. Four exceptions are *C.purpurascens*, a woodland plant whose habitat extends north as far as Austria and Switzerland; *C.purpurascens* ssp. *ponticum*, found in the Transcaucasus; and *C.parviflorum*, from a small area of Northeast Turkey, in alpine pastures or damp shade; *C.somalense* was recently discovered in Northeast Somalia. *C.hederifolium* will stand cold to –18°C/0°F; *C.coum*, *C.parviflorum* and *C.purpurascens* to –18°C/0°F, so long as the soil is well drained. In areas regularly covered by snow during the winter these plants can survive in temperatures down to –30°C/–22°F. *C.africanum*, *C. graecum*, *C. rohlfsianum* and *C.persicum* (parent of modern florists' potplants) are frost-tender. Others, including subspecies of *C.repandum*, will stand cold up to –18°C/0°F only if the site is ideal. For these species, mulching is advisable in cold localities, as is protection from excessive winter wet in the form of a propped-up piece of glass.

Cyclamen in the garden should be grown in well drained soil, protected from wind and in light shade. They thrive if planted under trees or shrubs, which take up excess moisture and provide protection from sun and wind. Cyclamen are tolerant of a wide variety of soils within the pH range 5.5–8.0. Heavy soil should have grit and coir or leafmould added to ensure adequate porosity. Raised beds or rock gardens give ideal drainage. *C.parviflorum* and *C.purpurascens* should not dry out and watering may be required during the summer, but the other species are naturally adapted to cope with summer drought. Summer heat is normally no problem, but where summer temperatures consistently rise above 32°C/90°F, shade is vital. The frost-tender species are best grown in pots in the greenhouse except in Mediterranean climates.

Under glass, cyclamen should be grown in a well drained potting medium. Clay or plastic pots can be used. A medium level of humidity and an even temperature, similar to the conditions in the Mediterranean during the growing period, should be maintained. Adequate ventilation, plunging the pots and damping down the greenhouse in hot weather help to create the ideal environment. For the frost-tender species, the temperature must not fall below freezing point and the maximum temperature for all species should not exceed 21°C/70°F while the plants are in growth. Plants grown in pots will not stand the same drop in temperature as those planted in the ground. A three-year-old tuber will need a 9cm/3.5in. pot. As cyclamen flower better if the root run is restricted, repot only when the tuber fills the pot. *C. graecum*, which has long fleshy roots, should be grown in long-tom pots. To achieve an attractive display and restrict the root run for those species with decumbent flowers and leaves, plant in half pots.

All cyclamen, except *C.purpurascens*, are dormant during summer. Water moderately during the growing period and sparingly when dormant. *C.purpurascens* in the greenhouse is usually evergreen and should be watered moderately throughout the year. *C. parviflorum* should be watered plentifully during the growing season but only moderately when dormant. Cyclamen should be watered from the base of the pot by either standing in a water-filled pot saucer or, if plunged, watering through the plunge material. They can be moved

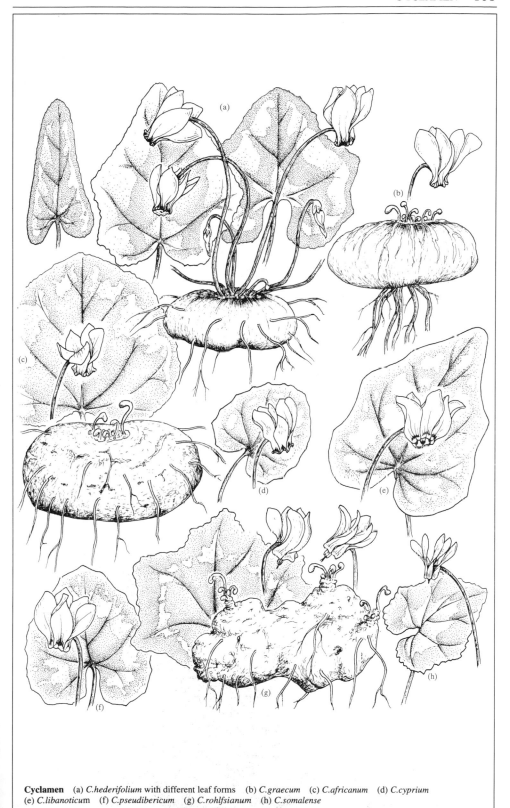

Cyclamen   (a) *C.hederifolium* with different leaf forms   (b) *C.graecum*   (c) *C.africanum*   (d) *C.cyprium*
(e) *C.libanoticum*   (f) *C.pseudibericum*   (g) *C.rohlfsianum*   (h) *C.somalense*

while in growth but it causes less disturbance to the plant if they are moved or repotted during the dormant period.

Propagation. Golden-brown ripe seed should be sown immediately the seed capsule splits in summer. Germination can be erratic, especially if the seed has become dry; soaking for 24 hours and rinsing thoroughly will remove any possible germination inhibitors. Use the same medium as for potting, provided that the fertilizer is of a slow-release type. Sow the seed 2–3cm/³/4–1¹/4in. apart, in pots or deep seed trays. The seed container should be kept in a shady place, with a temperature not exceeding but not far below 16°C/60°F, and watered frequently. Germination occurs at approximately the same time as the parent plant starts into growth after its dormant period. On germination, reduce watering. During their first year the seedlings should be kept growing as long as possible. To do this, move the seedlings into a cold shady area during the summer.

One-year-old seedlings can be potted on during their first dormant period but it is preferable to leave them until they are two years old. The florist's cyclamen is raised from seed by the following methods. They are grown commercially in a soilless medium with a pH of 5.5–6.0. Seeds are soaked and then sown in trays covered with potting medium. The trays are then covered with black plastic and a temperature of 12–15°C is maintained. Germination can take from two weeks to three months. At this stage temperature is increased to 19°C and humidity kept at a high level of 80–85% RH. At 8 to 10 weeks the plants, now bearing 3–4 leaves, are pricked out into trays and the temperature is increased to 19–21°C. Shade is kept at a minimum and fortnightly feeding with a weak liquid fertilizer begins. 8–10 weeks after pricking out they are potted up into 13cm pots (small-flowered cultivars in 8–10cm pots) with the top of the tuber just showing above the compost. Temperature is initially maintained and then reduced to 18–20°C with a minimum night temperature of 10°C. Weak low-nitrogen feeds should be given once a fortnight.

When planted deeply, tubers produce floral trunks. These twiggy extrusions from the tuber can be used as propagating material. Dip the base of the floral trunk into hormone rooting powder, insert into the potting medium and water moderately until growth appears. When planting in the garden, cover the tubers with 3–4cm/1¹/4–1⁵/8in. of free-draining compost of leafmould. In areas with frequent frosts, the frost-hardy species should be planted 8–15cm/3–6in. deep. Plants in pots need only 1–2cm/³/8–³/4in. covering of coarse grit. Cyclamen should flower in their third year and the addition of a little bonemeal during the dormant period is all that is required to prevent any nutritional deficiency.

Hybridization and breeding. In the latter part of the 19th century, plant breeders, especially in England and the Netherlands, recognized the potential value of *C.persicum* as a commercial pot plant. Originally plants were selected for size of flower and were a strong pink to purple colour. Subsequently a plant with a red hue was discovered and by the end of the century the plant breeders of Europe had, by selection, crossbreeding of cultivars and with the occurrence of chance mutations, bred a range of large-flowered plants in white, pink, salmon, purple and red. The petal shape was usually straight but doubles, butterflies with spreading wing-like lobes, frilled edges and crested forms were also produced. The diploid species with the usual chromosome number of 48 was superseded by tetraploid and hyper-tetraploid plants with increased size and vigour.

Although some of the best early exotic forms are still produced, recent breeding has concentrated on uniform plants with clear flower colour ranging from mauve, lilac, violet, pink, rose, salmon, red, cerise to scarlet and white. Additionally, the base of the flower can be a contrasting colour, white margins or stripes add even further variations. Scant attention was given to the leaves by the early breeders but recently great attention has been paid to the foliage, which rivals many plants grown for that reason alone. Plants are now bred with light or dark green backgrounds to the leaf and the natural hastate pattern in sharply contrasting green or silver. Pure silver leaves or silver leaves with midribs, ribs or edges in contrasting dark green enhance the extensive range of leaf forms. While plants used to need a period of years to reach a saleable size, now only 7–9 months is required. The marketing period has been extended from winter to autumn through to spring.

Concurrent with the recent breeding programme of large-flowered cultivars, has been the development of compact small-flowered plants closer in appearance to the typical wild species, with a range of flower colour and leaf pattern nearly as diverse as that of the large-flowered cultivars. These require a shorter period to reach flowering size, take up less bench space and are better able to withstand the conditions of modern centrally heated rooms. Crosses with wild *C.persicum* have resulted in small-flowered cultivars with perfume, a feature mainly, but not entirely, lost in the large-flowered forms. In addition, the following hybrids have been recorded: *C.africanum* × *C.hederifolium*, *C. balearicum* ×*C.creticum*, *C. repandum* ×*C.creticum* and *C.cyprium* ×*C.libanoticum*.

Recently, breeding work and selection has begun in other species, especially *C.coum*, in which several cultivars have been developed, often featuring leaves that are heavily marked with pewter or silver. In *C.mirabile*, selection can result in plants whose leaves are very conspicuously marked red on the upper surface. Several cultivars of *C.hederifolium* with combinations of leaf-markings and flower colour have been named; they require careful inspection of seedlings to be maintained as cultivars. By using ovule tissue culture, the Saitama Horticultural Experimental Station, Japan, has produced new hybrids from crossing *C. persicum* cultivars with *C.hederifolium* and *C. purpurascens*.

The development of cyclamen cultivars has produced potplants for the amateur grower that are ideal for growing in conservatories, greenhouses and in the home. The plants flower during the winter period and the

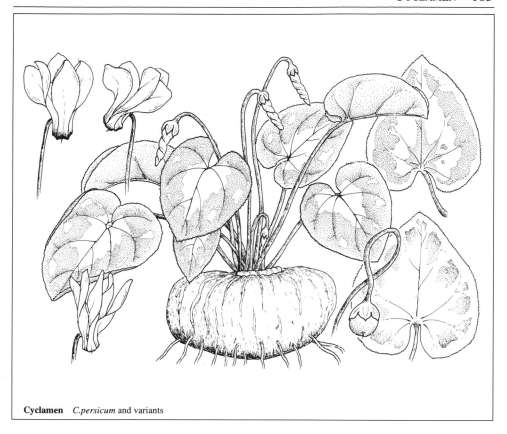

Cyclamen   *C.persicum* and variants

leaves provide decorative value for nine months of the year. Although the nurseryman must maintain rigid growing conditions to produce plants economically for an exacting market, the amateur can achieve excellent results with a little care.

Pot cyclamen thrive in light airy conditions, away from direct sunlight, high humidity, cold, draughty positions and hot, dry air. Poor growing conditions cause the leaves to turn yellow; these should be gently and completely removed by twisting the stems as they are pulled. Such distress may be due to over- or under-watering or temperatures too high or too low. Keep plants away from draughty windows and radiators. Leaf yellowing may occur in recently purchased plants, where it is caused by stress during transit from the nursery to the selling point. Always choose a fresh-looking plant and establish it, as soon as possible, in the ideal growing conditions.

Should the plant continue to deteriorate, water sparingly and allow it to go into an early state of dormancy. A natural state of dormancy usually occurs after the plant has finished flowering; it should be watered sparingly until all growth has died down and water then withheld completely. New growth will start after a dormant period of 2–3 months and the plant should be watered moderately and given weak low-nitrogen liquid feeds at fortnightly intervals. If after 2–3 months the plant is still dormant, water moderately to encourage new growth. Plants should be repotted during the dormant period, but only if they have become potbound. Do not overpot, as this or overfeeding encourages excessive leaf growth to the detriment of the flowers.

Pests and diseases. Cyclamen in the garden are relatively free from pests. Outside, netting over the tubers and under a layer of soil will protect against mice, squirrels and cats. The worst glasshouse pest is the vine weevil; if using an insecticidal drench for control, make a slanting hole in the soil with a pencil to get the drench directly under the tuber. Occasionally plants can be attacked by aphids, cyclamen mite, sciarid fly, slugs, snails, and red spider mite. Cyclamen outdoors rarely suffer from disease. Under glass, fungal diseases can occur if the greenhouse is not well ventilated or if the potting medium is too wet. To prevent botrytis, the glasshouse should be kept clean and well ventilated and any dead growth removed from the plants.

C.africanum Boiss. & Reut.
Tuber flattened to concave above, to 20cm diam., grey-brown, flaking, roots developing on all surfaces. Lvs not maturing until fruiting, to 10×10cm, circular and entire to reniform, or cordate and acute, or cordate and crenate, dark green, lightly marked with silver-grey, lustrous, light green beneath; margins tough, serrate. Fls violet-scented, to 2.5cm; pet. slightly reflexed, auricled, ovate-lanceolate to lanceolate, pale pink to dark rose-pink, with a deep red patch at base; anth. yellow, striped purple on dorsal surface. Autumn. Algeria. Z9.

C.alpinum hort. See *C.trochopteranthum.*

C.balearicum Willk.
Tuber globose, flattened at apex, rooting at base, to 2.5cm diam., hairy. Lvs to 9cm, narrowly ovate or cordate, acute, shallow-toothed, blue-grey above, heavily marked with silver-grey, crimson beneath, margins scalloped. Fls to 2cm, white veined pink, sometimes entirely pink, very fragrant; pet. lanceolate, without auricles, undulate. Spring. Balearic Is., S France. Z8.

C.caucasicum Willd. ex Steven. See *C.coum* ssp. *caucasicum.*

C.cilicium Boiss. & Heldr.
Tuber subglobose, much flattened, thinly corky, grey-brown, producing roots at base. Lvs appearing with fls, suborbicular, serrate at vein ends, crenate, grey-green to dark green, marked with silver-grey and dark blotches, purple-red beneath. Fls 1–2cm; cor. not auricled; pet. obovate, acute, slightly reflexed at apex, white to deep pink, blotched crimson at base, blotch streaking finely across pet. Autumn. SW Turkey (Cilicia). 'Album': fls white. Z7.

C.cilicium var. *intaminatum* Meikle. See *C.intaminatum.*

C.coum Mill. (*C.hiemale* Hildebr.; *C.hyemale* Salisb.; *C.orbiculatum* Mill.; *C.vernale* K. Koch).
Tuber subglobose, to 3cm diam., flattened above, rooting below, thinly corky, brown with fine dark brown hairs, floral trunks present. Lvs very variable, orbicular to reniform, 2.5–6cm diam., dark to light green, marked with lighter green spots or a silver-green band, lustrous to matt above, red, green or green-marked-red beneath; petioles to 10cm. Fls to 2cm; cor. tube rimmed white or pink; pet. elliptic to ovate-elliptic, not auricled, off-white or light pink to deep carmine, with a dark red or deep purple blotch at base; anth. yellow. Winter–early spring. Bulgaria, Turkey, Caucasus, Lebanon, Israel. 'Album': to 5×15cm; fls white, petals flushed pink with red blotch at base. 'Atkinsii': hardy growth; fls rose pink. 'Roseum': petals pink with purple spot. Pewter-leaved Group: lvs predominantly silver-grey above, with a dark green margin of varying width; they breed largely true from seed, although selection of seedlings is necessary to maintain a named cv. 'Maurice Dryden': lvs silver with dark green margin; fls white. 'Tilebarn Elizabeth': lvs small with very narrow green margin; fls bicoloured, pale pink below, darker at pet. apex, with dark basal blotch. ssp. *caucasicum* (Koch) Schwarz. Lvs cordate, dentate, with silver-grey markings. Cor. rim pale mauve; pet. acute. Caucasus. Z6.

C.creticum (Dörfl.) Hildebr.
Tuber dorsally compressed, thinly corky, grey-brown, rooting below. Lvs acute, to 4cm diam., jagged-toothed, dark grey-green, spotted with light silver-grey, purple-red beneath. Fls fragrant; pet. lanceolate, not auricled, white, sometimes, occasionally very pale pink. Spring. Crete. Z8.

C.cyprium Kotschy.
Tuber globose, flattened at apex and base, to 5cm diam., thinly corky, grey-green. Lvs broadly cordate, sharply acute or ovate-lanceolate, acuminate, to 3.5cm diam., olive-green, blotched light green near margin, hastate pattern marked with grey-green, occasionally unblotched, bright red beneath, very shallowly lobed, lobes with sharp yellow tips. Fls to 2.5cm; cor. tube narrowly campanulate; pet. sharply reflexed, folded near base, twisting toward apex, irregularly toothed at apex, auricled, pure white or pale pink with a V-shaped pink-purple blotch at base. Autumn–early winter. Cyprus. 'E.S.': lvs heavily and irregularly spotted white. Z9.

C.europaeum L. See *C.purpurascens.*

C.graecum Link.
Tuber globose, somewhat flattened, to 20cm diam., cork layer splitting in ribbons, rooting at base, floral trunks present. Lvs appearing with or after fls, obcordate, acute, dark green, with a silver-grey band within 1.5cm of margin, sometimes fainter, appearing chequered, beautifully veined lime green or silver-

grey, light green or maroon beneath, marginal teeth red-brown. Pet. much reflexed, to 1.5cm, usually not twisted, auricled, pale pink to deep carmine, with 2 maroon blotches at base, streaking across pet. to apex, auricles blue-mauve; anth. violet; peduncle coiling from base upwards after flowering. Autumn–early winter. S Greece, Aegean Is., S Turkey, Cyprus. Z9.

C.hederifolium Ait. (*C.neapolitanum* Ten.).
Tuber rounded below, flattened above, corky, dark brown, roots emerging from apex and sides. Lvs produced after or with fls, very variable, to 15cm, rounded to lanceolate, entire to shallowly lobed with acute or obtuse points, dark green to light grey-green or silver-grey, green or purple-red below, margins serrate or smooth. Fls to 2.5cm, ovate-lanceolate, acute, constricted at base, light to deep pink, with a dark red blotch at base, streaking across pet. in 2 lines, rarely pure white; mouth of cor. tube pentagonal. Late summer–early winter. S Europe to Turkey. 'Album': fls white. 'Bowles' Apollo': lvs heavily marbled; fls pink. Corfu form: fls pink, scented. 'Ellen Corker': fls white, with strong pink basal marking, turning deeper purple with age. 'Pink Pearls': fls slightly larger. Scented Strain: fls pink, sweetly scented. Silver-Leaved Group: lvs predominantly silver-grey, as in *C.coum* Pewter-leaved Group. Z6.

C.hiemale Hildebr. See *C.coum.*
C.hyemale Salisb. See *C.coum.*
C.ibericum Meikle. See *C.coum* ssp. *caucasicum.*

C.intaminatum (Meikle) Grey-Wilson (*C.cilicium* var. *intaminatum* Meikle).
Very diminutive. Tuber globose, flattened, to 3.5cm diam., velvety-pubesc., rooting from base. Lvs to 4×4.5cm, suborbicular, obtuse, emarginate, green with light marbling above, light green beneath, occasionally marked purple, margins shallowly crenate. Fls to 1cm, unscented; pet. white or pale pink, elliptic-oblanceolate, grey-veined, not blotched at base; pedicels to 16cm. WC & SW Turkey. Z8.

C.libanoticum Hildebr.
Tuber rounded, somewhat flattened, corky, grey-brown with tufted hairs, rooting from base. Lvs rounded or obcordate, occasionally acuminate, to 8cm diam., dull blue-green, dark-blotched, bright red beneath, hastate pattern dark green, undulate, basal lobes rounded. Fls to 2.5m; pedicels erect to 15cm; cor. tube campanulate, white-rimmed; pet. broadly ovate, acute, rarely twisted, pale pink to carmine, with a light red mark at base; anth. deep yellow. Winter–early spring. Syria, Lebanon. Z9.

C.mirabile Hildebr.
Tuber subglobose, to 6cm diam., deeply furrowed, corky, rooting from base. Lvs suborbicular to reniform, obtuse, to 3.5cm across, dark green, marbled grey, pink or red above, purple beneath, toothed. Fls comparatively large on erect peduncles; cal. lobes obtuse; pet. to 2.5cm long, oblong to obovate, emarginate, glandular, pale pink with a carmine blotch at base. Autumn. SW Turkey. Z7.

C.neapolitanum Ten. See *C.hederifolium.*
C.orbiculatum Mill. See *C.coum.*

C.parviflorum Pobed.
Tubers small, bright green, rooting at base. Lvs suborbicular, dull green, cordate at base, entire. Fls short-stalked; cor. tube short, pet. to 1cm, abruptly reflexed and slightly twisted, mauve-pink with purple basal blotch without a central paler spot. Winter. NE Turkey. Z7.

C.persicum Mill.
Tuber subglobose, striated, corky, rooting from base and sides, floral trunks present in older specimens. Lvs very variable, usually cordate, basal lobes overlapping, acute at apex, margins with close, fine teeth, rarely lobed, marbled or silver-grey, with a dark green central zone surrounded by a lighter or darker margin, hastate pattern with small silver-grey spots, green, rarely maroon or mottled beneath. Fls fra-

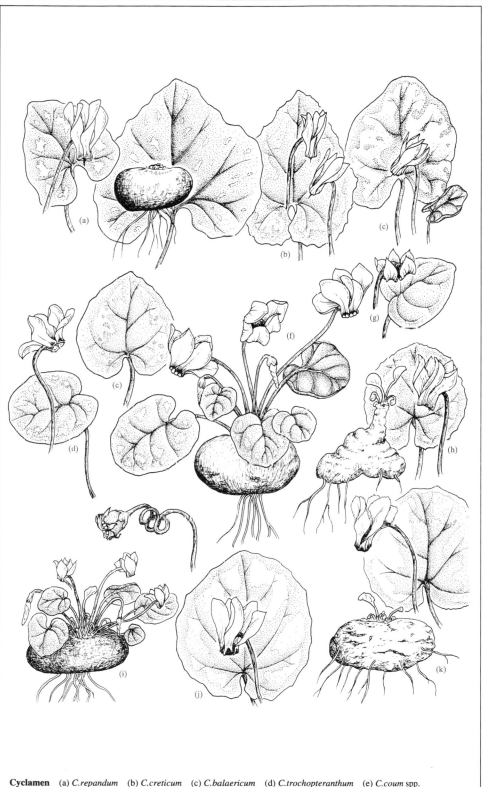

Cyclamen   (a) *C.repandum*   (b) *C.creticum*   (c) *C.balaericum*   (d) *C.trochopteranthum*   (e) *C.coum* spp. *caucasicum*   (f) *C.coum*   (g) *C.parviflorum*   (h) *C.purpurascens*   (i) *C.intaminatum*   (j) *C.cilicium*   (k) *C.mirabile*

grant, on erect peduncles to 20cm long; pet. far reflexed, twisted, oblong-lanceolate, white, pale mauve, pale pink or deep pink, with a somewhat rectangular, basal spot; peduncles not coiling after flowering. Spring. E Mediterranean, Rhodes, Crete, Libya. The florist's cyclamen, cvs range in habit from large, hearty growth to dwarf and compact; lvs from large and fleshy to silver patterned; fls from white to scarlet through salmon to pale pink, often was red centre, from simple to 'double', ruffled, twisted, sometimes scented. 'Aalsmeer Double' (large, vigorous growth; lvs fleshy), 'Boheme' (standard size, fuschia red), 'Bonfire' (compact, fls scarlet), 'Candlestick' (pale pink, with red centre), 'Double Zehlendorf' (lvs silver patterned), 'Fimbriatum' (large, vigorous growth), 'Flamenco Frills' (fls large, feathered), 'Gabi' (dwarf, dark salmon), 'Kati' (lilac, lvs silver), 'Little Dresden Mix' (lvs variegated), 'Light Fire' (lvs veined), 'Mirabelle Mix' (lvs dark), 'Rosemarie' (dwarf, light rose with white edge), 'Victoria' (pet. ruffled, white with red border and eye); scented varieties include 'Bonfire', 'Dwarf Fragrance', Scentsation Mixed, 'Swiss Dwarf', 'Vogt's Double' (fls heavy with numerous pet.). Z9.

C.pseudibericum Hildebr.
Tuber globose, flattened above, scaly, grey-brown, rooting at base, floral trunks occasionally present. Lvs obcordate, short-acuminate, to 6.5×6cm, dark green, marbled silver-grey above, red-maroon beneath, margins sharply dentate. Fls fragrant, 2.5cm; cor. tube white-rimmed; pet. broadly lanceolate to elliptic, to 1cm wide, mauve to bright magenta or pink, with cordate purple-brown blotch at base streaking across white cor. rim, not auricled; peduncles arching after flowering. Winter–spring. S Asia Minor. Z7.

C.purpurascens Mill. (*C.europaeum* L.).
Tuber globose, flattened above, corky, chestnut-brown, rooting all over surface, floral trunks occasionally produced. Lvs circular to cordate, to 8×6cm, dark green, marbled with faint to bold silver-grey blotches above; green, red or green-marked-red beneath, margins denticulate, rarely smooth. Fls very fragrant; pet. oblong, to 2cm, pink to carmine, often veined dark pink with a deep carmine blotch at base, rarely white. Late summer–autumn. C & E Europe. ssp. *ponticum* (Albov) Grey-Wilson. Lf margin with cartilaginous, 'beady' teeth. Z6.

C.repandum Sibth. & Sm.
Tuber subglobose, compressed, to 6cm diam., hairy, brown, rooting from base. Lvs broadly cordate, short-acuminate, to

12.5×12.5cm, dark green, hastate pattern bordered grey-silver, occasionally speckled white, red-maroon beneath, margins widely lobed with sharp, mucronate teeth. Fls fragrant, to 2cm; pet. linear to oblong, not auricled, white to deep carmine with a bright red basal spot; cor. tube red-rimmed; style long, exserted. Spring. C & E Mediterranean. ssp. *peloponnesiacum* Grey-Wilson. Lvs dark green, marked with silver-grey, hastate pattern often absent. Pet. carmine, magenta at tube mouth, to 3cm, twisting. Greece (Peloponnese). f. *vividum* Grey-Wilson. Fls deep purple. ssp. *rhodense* (Meikle) Grey-Wilson. Lvs grey-green, marked with silver-grey. Pet. pale pink or white, subacute to obtuse, to 2.5cm. Rhodes (Salakos region). Z7.

C.rohlfsianum Asch.
Tuber globose, becoming flattened, concave below, very corky, light brown, rooting all over. Lvs with buff-pink hairs when young, reniform, 9×11cm, bright green, patterned with silver-grey, lower surface, maroon-red, rarely green, margins finely dentate, angularly lobed, these lobes shallowly scalloped. Fls often fragrant, to 2.5cm; pet. lanceolate, acute, twisted, auricled, rose-pink with a deltoid crimson patch at base; stamens and stigma far exserted, forming a cone; pedicel curling from base to apex on fruiting. Autumn. Libya (Cyrenaica). Z9.

C.somalense Thulin & Warfa.
Tuber globose, 3–4cm diam., grey-brown, with several floral trunks to 3cm. Lvs emerging before fls, 3.5–10.5×4–12cm, broadly cordate, subobtuse, base with narrow sinus, margin unevenly dentate, deep grey-green, with conspicuous silver hastate pattern above, purple beneath; petiole to 6.5cm; pedicels to 12.5cm; fls 1.2–1.5cm, pale carmine-pink, darker at mouth; cal. to 8mm, glandular, lobes ovate-oblong, to 4mm; petals narrow, not auricled, somewhat twisted; style exserted by 1mm. Autumn to early winter. Somalia.

C.trochopteranthum Schwarz.
Similar to *C.coum* except lvs 2.5–5cm, reniform to broadly ovate, base cordate, apex truncate, dark green zoned with silver above, purple-red beneath. Fls scented, to 4cm diam.; pet. broad, twisted through 90°, thus perpendicular to ovary and propeller-like, pale pink to carmine with a darker basal blotch, blotch without a pale central spot, not 3-pronged. Winter–spring. SW Turkey, Cilician Taurus (high altitudes). Z7.

C.vernale K. Koch. See *C.coum*.

Cypella Herb. (From Gk *kypellon*, goblet or cup, referring to the shape of the flowers.) Iridaceae. 15 species of small, bulbous, perennial herbs related to *Neomarica* but with terminal, solitary or corymbose flowers, terete flowering stems and plicate leaves. Bulbs somewhat elongate, tunics pleated. Flowers ephemeral; perianth segments 6, free, outer segments obovate, spreading, inner segments far smaller, erecto-patent, recurved at apex with a bearded claw; filaments free; style exceeding stamens, style branches often rather petal-like. Fruit a capsule. Mexico to Argentina. Z9.

CULTIVATION Found in a range of habitats to altitudes of 2900m/9500ft, frequently in meadows, grassland and mossy banks (*C.herbertii* and *C.peruviana*) or in damp, marshy or periodically inundated areas (*C.armosa* and *C.curuzupensis*). *Cypella* spp. are grown for their exquisitely formed flowers, in rich shades of deep yellows or blue violets, usually exhibiting intricate marking, dotting or banding in contrasting colours on the inner segments. Although each bloom is short-lived, they are carried in succession. In frost-free zones, they are suitable for the border and rock garden. With the possible exception of the summer-flowering *C.herbertii*, which will survive out of doors in sheltered gardens where winter temperatures occasionally fall to –5°C/23°F, *Cypella* spp. are best suited to the cool glasshouse in cool temperate areas. Some spp., such as *C.peruviana*, are winter flowering. Those flowering in summer are sometimes planted outside and lifted for storage during the winter months.

Grow out of doors in a freely drained, humus-rich and moderately fertile, sandy soil in full sun; at the limits of cold tolerance, plant *C.herbertii* at the warm base of a south-facing wall (providing it does not become too arid) or in a similarly favoured niche in the rock garden; give a thick, dry mulch of bracken litter in winter.

Under glass, maintain a winter minimum temperature of 10°C/50°F, water carefully but plentifully when in growth. Store in sand and keep dry and completely frost free when dormant. Propagate by seed sown ripe into a sandy propagating mix, or by offsets and bulbils; grow on in slightly cooler and moist conditions until established.

C.armosa Ravenna.
Lvs 1–2, 12–20×0.3cm. Flowering stem to 60cm; infl. simple; fls 5–6.5cm diam., yellow; outer seg. pandurate-spathulate, somewhat reflexed; inner seg. geniculate-recurved, 1.5cm, marked yellow-orange and brown-black; stigma lobes orange. Argentina, Paraguay.

C.coelestis (Lehm.) Diels (*C.plumbea* Lindl.).
Lvs to 45×2.5cm, ensiform. Flowering stem 50–80cm; infl. simple; fls 6–8cm diam., leaden blue with a tawny flush and yellow-brown spots; outer seg. broadly spreading, inner seg. erect, blotched yellow, claw bearded; style lilac, stigma composed of short, 2-lobed arms. Late summer. Brazil, Uruguay to Argentina.

C.curuzupensis Ravenna.
Lvs to 15×30×0.1cm, linear. Flowering stem to 40cm+, unbranched; fls 1–2 per spathe. to 4cm diam., yellow, marked dull green; outer seg. ovate, 2.3×2.5cm, inner seg. 1.5cm, claw 1cm; style pale yellow. Paraguay.

C.herbertii (Lindl.) Herb.
Lvs 15–30×1.75–2.25cm, linear-lanceolate, acuminate. Flowering stem to 30cm, often branched; fls 4–6cm diam., outer perianth seg. ovate, waisted at centre, claw slender, concave above, chrome yellow to pale bronze or apricot with a central mauve stripe, inner seg. yellow spotted purple, apex reflexed, revolute. Summer. Brazil, Uruguay, Argentina. 'Pulchella': fls mostly pale mauve.

C.peruviana Bak.
Similar to *C.herbertii* but with infl. usually simple, fls bright yellow with purple, maroon or chestnut spots or broken bands in the cup formed by the base of each seg.; stigma bifid, chrome yellow, petaloid. Winter. Peru, Bolivia.

C.plumbea Lindl. See *C.coelestis*.

Cyrtanthus Ait. (From Gk *kyrtos*, curved, and *anthos*, flower, in reference to the curving perianth tube.) FIRE LILY. Amaryllidaceae. 47 species of bulbous evergreen or deciduous perennials. Bulbs subterranean or semi-exposed, ovoid, 2.5–5cm diam., clothed with membranous brown tunics. Leaves in a loose basal rosette, linear or strap-shaped, fleshy, flaccid. Inflorescence scapose, flowers in umbels or, rarely, solitary, horizontal or drooping, red, yellow or white, emerging from a spathe with 2–4 lanceolate valves; perianth funnel-shaped, waxy, often fragrant, with a narrow tube, perianth segments 6, usually spreading at tips, subequal, shorter than the tube; stamens inserted below throat of the tube; ovary ovoid, 3-celled. Fruit a membranous, oblong, 3-valved capsule; seeds many, flattened, black. Tropical Africa, S Africa.

CULTIVATION *Cyrtanthus* spp. are grown for their graceful umbels of slender tubular flowers produced in spring, summer and/or autumn; they are often strongly fragrant – the creamy yellow flowers of *C.mackenii* var. *cooperi* have a sweet, banana-like scent. *C.breviflorus* and *C.elatus* are hardy to –5°C/23°F in warm sheltered positions in well drained soils. *C.falcatus*, a distinguished native of Natal, with stout stems of nodding, subtly coloured bells, will withstand light frosts if perfectly dry when dormant and mulched by its own dead foliage. *C.brachyscyphus*, altogether smaller with fire cracker-like flowers, will take the mildest of frosts, growing well outdoors in Southern Europe and Northern California. Most other species are intolerant of frost but are well suited to pot cultivation under glass in temperate zones. Many species, especially *C.elatus*, the Scarborough Lily, make excellent house plants.

Grow in a fibrous loam-based mix with added leafmould and sharp sand, in bright indirect light and with a minimum temperature of 5–10°C/40–50°F. Water plentifully and apply dilute liquid feed weekly when in growth. Dry off deciduous species gradually after flowering; water evergreen species sparingly in winter, keeping dry but not arid when resting, at about 4–8°C/39–46°F. Top-dress with fresh medium as growth recommences; re-pot as seldom as possible. Propagate by seed or offsets in spring.

C.angustifolius (L. f.) Ait. FIRE LILY.
Evergreen. Lvs to 45×1.75cm. Scape to 45cm; fls 4–10 per umbel, pendulous; perianth to 5cm, scarlet, expanding toward the bluntly ovate, spreading lobes. S Cape.

C.brachyscyphus Bak. DOBO LILY.
Evergreen. Lvs to 25×0.5cm, to 3, linear. Scape equalling lvs; spathe valves lanceolate, to 2.5cm; pedicels to 2cm; fls 6–8; perianth bright coral red to scarlet, to 2.5cm, with a narrow funnel-shaped tube, throat to 4mm wide, perianth seg. oblong-lanceolate; stamens equalling seg. S Africa.

C.breviflorus Bak. (*Anoiganthus breviflorus* Harv.).
Deciduous or evergreen. Lvs to 30×1.5cm, 3–4, lorate, obtuse, glabrous, erect. Scape to 30cm; spathe valves 2, lanceolate; pedicels erect, to 5cm; fls 2–10 per umbel; perianth yellow or white, tube to 1cm, perianth seg. to 2cm, 5-ribbed. S Africa.

C.elatus (Jacq.) Traub (*C.purpureus* (Ait.) Herb.; *Vallota speciosa* (L. f.) T. Dur. & Schinz; *Vallota purpurea* (Ait.) Herb.).
GEORGE LILY; SCARBOROUGH LILY.
Evergreen. Lvs to 60×3cm, 6–18, lorate. Scape to 1m, glaucous, somewhat laterally compressed; spathe valves to 8cm, oblong-lanceolate; pedicels to 5cm; fls 6–9, deep pink or, more commonly, bright scarlet; perianth erect, tube to 3.5cm long by 2cm at the throat, tinged green, perianth seg. broadly spreading, to 5×2.5cm. S Africa. 'Alba': fls white.

C.lutescens var. *cooperi* Bak. See *C.mackenii* var. *cooperi*.

C.falcatus R.A. Dyer.
Bulb globose to ovoid, 5–8cm diam., producing many offsets, neck 8–12, densely covered by membranous tunics. Lvs 4, emerging with fls, falcate, 25×2–3cm, narrowing to apex, coriaceous. Scape 25–30cm, stout and purple-tinted, recurved and somewhat compressed below umbel; spathe valves 4, oblong or linear-lanceolate, to 5×1.25cm; pedicels 1cm; fls 6–15, strongly pendulous, 6cm, cream-green tinted flesh pink to brick red, or a more solid red tipped yellow-orange; perianth tube 4cm, slender, funnel-shaped, gradually expanding to a throat 1cm wide, free part of seg. obovate-oblong; stamens uniseriate or weakly biseriate, exserted. S Africa (Natal).

Cyrtanthus   (a) *C.breviflorus*   (b) *C.sanguineus*   (c) *C.obliquus*   (d) *C.mackenii* var. *cooperi*

C.mackenii Hook. f. IFAFA LILY.
Evergreen. Lvs to 30×1cm, 2–6, linear, straight. Scape to
30cm, red-brown at the base; spathe valves 2, lanceolate, to
3.5cm, green; pedicels erect, to 2.5cm; fls 4–10, ivory-white,
fragrant; perianth slender, to 5cm long by 4mm at the throat.
var. **cooperi** (Bak.) R.A. Dyer (*C.lutescens* var. *cooperi*
Bak.). Fls yellow to ivory. S Africa.

C.obrienii Bak.
Evergreen. Lvs to 30×1cm, linear, bright green, glossy. Scape
exceeding lvs; spathe valves lanceolate, scarious, to 3.5cm;
pedicels to 1.5cm; fls 7–8; perianth pale or bright scarlet,
unscented, tube curved, 3.5cm or longer by 4mm at the throat,
perianth; seg. ovate, to 4mm. S Africa.

C.purpureus (Ait.) Herb. See *C.elatus*.

C.sanguineus (Lindl.) Hook. f. (*Gastronema sanguineum*
Lindl.).
Deciduous. Lvs to 2.5×2cm, 3–4, lanceolate, petiolate, acute,
bright green. Scape to 25cm; spathe valves 2–4, lanceolate, to
8cm, green; pedicels to 5cm; fls 1–3; perianth to 10cm, bright
scarlet, tube erect or curved, spreading widely at apex, throat
2.5cm diam., perianth seg. ovate, spreading, to 5cm. E Africa,
Natal.

Dahlia Cav. (For Andreas Dahl, (1751–1789), Swedish botanist and pupil of Linnaeus.) Compositae. About 30 species of perennial herbs or subshrubs, usually tuberous-rooted, sometimes scrambling and epiphytic. Stems solitary to many, usually unbranched. Leaves usually opposite, dentate, pinnatifid or pinnate, margins often ciliate, petioles sometimes tendril-like. Capitula radiate, usually on long slender peduncles; phyllaries in 2 series, outer erect, spreading or reflexed at anthesis, usually green, fleshy, linear to ovate or obovate, inner scarious or translucent, pale, ovate, lengthening after anthesis; receptacle flat or convex; ray florets female or sterile; disc florets hermaphrodite, in many cultivars all or many replaced by ray florets. Fruit a linear to oblanceolate, obcompressed cypsela; pappus of 2 aristae. Mts of Mexico to Colombia.

HISTORY AND CLASSIFICATION. The genus *Dahlia* originates from Central and South America between Mexico and Colombia. It has a history in cultivation which long pre-dates the Spanish conquest in the 16th century. Dahlias were probably an important crop for the Aztecs. Although they were grown as double-flowered ornamentals in their gardens, it seems likely that they were first domesticated for animal fodder, and probably for their medicinal applications. The earliest surviving record, in an Aztec Herbal, the Badianus manuscript of 1582, cites their use in the treatment of urinary disorders, based on the doctrine of signatures, one of the Aztec words for dahlia being *cocoxochitl*, meaning water pipes. The long stems of the 10-metre tree dahlia *D.imperialis* (known as *acocotli*, meaning hollow pipes), were used by the Aztecs to supply domestic water from mountain springs and streams.

Dahlias were first introduced to Europe at the Royal Botanic Gardens in Madrid, in 1789, and were distributed from there throughout Europe. Progeny of *D.coccinea* and *D.pinnata*, which form the genetic nucleus of the modern hybrid dahlias, reached Kew in 1798, sent from Madrid by the Marchioness of Bute. This stock was lost, but replaced by seed sent by Lady Holland in 1804. In Europe, principally at the Jardin des Plantes in Paris, dahlias were grown experimentally as food plants. But the flavour of the tuber was described as bitter and nondescript and the experiment was soon abandoned in favour of the more familiar decorative uses.

Dahlia is a prolific and long-flowering genus, blooming reliably until first frosts in cool-temperate climates; the flowers often have a sharp bright fragrance. The border dahlias produce better blooms when grown alone but can be used in the mixed border (in the 19th century, for example, they were used to conceal the denuded bases of hollyhocks). The seed-raised bedding dahlias include dwarf forms that require no support and are used in massed bedding and for cultivation in pots and tubs.

The garden dahlia is a hybrid with highly variable progeny. By the early 1800s, nurserymen were exploiting to the full this tendency to hybridize, deriving new varieties by crossing and from chance seedlings and giving rise to the first full doubles, originally known as globe dahlias. Throughout Europe and the US the passion for dahlias in the 1840s matched the tulip mania of the 17th century both in intensity and in the prices realised by new plants.

The formation of the British National Dahlia Society in 1881 encouraged exhibition and further hybridization, producing the startling range of types which has contributed considerably to the dahlia's popularity, of great value as garden and cut flowers and as exhibition blooms. There are now Dahlia Societies throughout Europe, the US, Australia, South Africa and Israel, each of which has been engaged in the breeding of new cultivars. There are now 20,000 cultivars listed in the International Register of Dahlia Names, in the keeping of the Royal Horticultural Society, which was appointed as the International Registration Authority (IRA) in 1966. Its first task was to secure international agreement on classification, and aided by societies in Britain, Holland and the US, a system was drawn up based on ten groups. The American and the Central States Dahlia Societies use twelve groups, splitting the cactus and decorative divisions more finely, but otherwise the categories follow the recommendations of the International Registration Authority.

Group One. SINGLE-FLOWERED. Single dahlias have open-centred blooms with one or two complete outer rows of florets surrounding a disc, usually about 10cm in diameter. They are perfect for bedding purposes as most grow only to a height of about 30cm. Examples include 'Coltness Gem': a dwarf bedder, seed-sown, various colours; 'Inflammation' ('Red Lilliput'): very small plants, ideal for pot culture or patio plantings.

Group Two. ANEMONE-FLOWERED. A small group with blooms having one or more rows of ray florets surrounding a dense group of upward-pointing tubular florets. Plant height 60–90cm; blooms 7.5cm across. Examples include 'Comet': dark red with inner florets of similar colour; 'Scarlet Comet': a lighter red sport of 'Comet'.

Group Three. COLLERETTE (also spelled collarette in the US). Blooms with an open centre, surrounded by an inner ring of short florets, the 'collar', and one or two complete outer rows of usually flat ray florets. They were raised in France at the beginning of this century, have a good colour range, and are perfect for cutting. About 110cm high, blooms 10–15cm across. Many are sold as mixtures to raise from seed. Examples include 'Clair de Lune': yellow with a paler yellow collar; 'La Cierva': purple, tipped white on the outer petals with a white collar.

Group Four. WATERLILY or NYMPHAEA-FLOWERED. Fully double blooms, with broad and generally sparse ray petals which are flat or with slightly incurved or recurved margins, the overall effect being of a flat or shallow bloom, as in its namesake. 90–120cm high, blooms 10–12cm across. Examples include 'Peace Pact': pure white; 'Pearl of Heemstede': dark pink.

Group Five. DECORATIVE. Blooms fully double, showing no central disc, with broad, flat or slightly involute ray florets, sometimes slightly twisted and apex usually obtuse, plants ranging in height from 90cm to 150cm. Examples include 'Hamari Gold': a typical giant, golden bronze in colour; 'Nina Chester': small, white. Decorative dahlias can have cut or fimbriate floret tips. In the US the decorative dahlias are split into two sub-

Dahlia garden forms (a) Single (b) Anenome-centred (c) Collerette (d) Ball (e) Pompon (f) Decorative (g) Decorative (fimbriated) (h) Waterlily (i) Cactus (j) Semi-cactus (k) Peony-flowered (l) Star (m) Orchid-flowered

groups, the Formal Decoratives, with the ray florets in a regular arrangement, and the Informal Decoratives, in which the rays are generally long, twisted or pointed, and irregular in arrangement.

Group Six. BALL. These are ball-shaped or globose, sometimes slightly flattened at the top, with ray florets blunt or rounded at the tips, and cupped for more than half the length of the florets. Small Ball Dahlias have blooms 10–15cm in diameter, those of the miniature Ball Dahlias up to 10cm across. Examples include 'Opal': a blend of pink and white; 'Wootton Cupid': a dark pink miniature.

Group Seven. POMPON. Sometimes referred to as 'drum-stick' dahlias, the pompons are similar to the Ball Dahlias, but are more globose, with florets involute for their entire length, and of miniature size, up to 90cm high and up to 5cm across. Examples include 'Moor Place': purple; 'Hallmark': dark pink flushed lilac.

Group Eight. CACTUS-FLOWERED. The cactus and semi-cactus groups are largely derived from *D.hortensis*, including crosses withother species; both groups are subdivided by size, as for the decorative groups. The cactus types have fully double blooms showing no disc, with long, pointed ray florets, finely quilled (i.e. margins strongly revolute) for over half their length. Examples include 'Banker': mid-red; 'Klankstad Kerkrade': pale lemon yellow blooms, 10–15cm across. As with decoratives, the floret ends are cut or fimbriate. In the US, this group is divided into the straight cactus types with straight, slightly incurved or recurved rays, and the incurved types, whose pointed rays curve towards the centre of the bloom.

Group Nine. SEMI-CACTUS-FLOWERED. Fully double blooms, with slightly pointed ray florets which are broad at their base, revolute for less than half their length, and either straight or incurving. Plants about 120cm tall.

Group Ten. MISCELLANEOUS. A grouping of relatively small, disparate classes. It includes the Orchid cultivars, similar in form to the single dahlias except that their ray florets are revolute for at least two-thirds of their length, such as 'Giraffe', banded yellow and bronze; the Star dahlias, with small incurving flowers, formed by two or three rows of scarcely overlapping pointed rays, surrounding a central disc; the Chrysanthemum types, resembling incurved exhibition chrysanthemums, e.g. 'Akita'; and the tiny Lilliput series, with 2.5cm/1in. blooms. Other miscellaneous types include the Peony-flowered (originally Group 4 of the NDS classification) with two or more rows of flat, broad ray florets, and a centre which is open or partly covered by small twisted floral rays around the disc. This section is still considered distinct in the US and some other countries.

Subdivisions according to size are generally left to the discretion of the various national societies, since cultural conditions vary so widely as to make precise definition impossible. For example, in the UK the National Dahlia Society has adopted the size divisions, lettered A–E, but has added dimensions to suit conditions in Britain: (A) Giant: blooms of 254mm or more; (B) Large: blooms of 203–254mm; (C) Medium: blooms of 152–203mm; (D) Small: blooms of 102–152mm; (E) Miniatures: blooms up to 102mm.

Dahlias are also subject to division by colour, the range extending throughout the spectrum, stopping short of a true blue. Fourteen categories are recognized: (1) White; (2) Yellow; (3) Orange; (4) Bronze; (5) Flame; (6) Red; (7) Dark red; (8) Light pink; (9) Dark pink; (10) Lilac, lavender, or mauve; (11) Purple, wine, or violet; (12) Blends, two or more colours intermingled; (13) Bicoloured, ground colour tipped with another colour; (14) Variegated, several colours striped or splashed in one bloom.

The basic formula for classification thus outlined is used in descriptive codes for dahlias in the International Register; for example, a variety annotated 5aLtPk is a light pink, giant-flowered decorative type.

CULTIVATION Grow dahlias in an open sunny situation, avoiding the shade of tall shrubs, high walls and fences; they demand high light levels. Dahlias enjoy a rich and well drained soil, ideally created by the incorporation of garden compost or well rotted manure during autumn digging. Before planting, in spring or early summer, fork over lightly and rake in bonemeal at about 125g/m^2(4oz./yd^2). Plant unsprouted tubers 10cm/4in. deep in mid- to late spring, delaying the planting of rooted cuttings, sprouted tubers and seed-raised plants until any danger of frost has passed.

Since dahlias are gross feeders, those used for exhibition and cut flowers are best grown in beds set aside for the purpose, away from the competition of other plant roots. Plant 60cm/24in. apart, close enough to tie into marker canes and secure tall plants immediately on planting. Support canes should be approximately 30cm/12in. shorter than the expected height of the plant. Ensure protection from slugs, snails and aphids. When late frost is forecast protect with straw, large boxes or upturned pots. To encourage branching, stop plants three or four weeks after planting by removing the growing point and, at this stage, add further supports to tie in new growth. The first blooms should appear by midsummer, and continue till first frosts.

From midsummer onwards, apply a fertilizer high in nitrogen and potash, either by using a granular formulation, or by weekly liquid application, by root or as a foliar feed. Mulch dahlias with garden compost or well-rotted manure to retain moisture and suppress weed growth.

To ensure large, long-stemmed blooms, each main stem is disbudded, that is, the two ancillary buds borne below each central primary bud are removed. For exhibition purposes, where still higher standards are necessary, the disbudding process is extended to the removal of leaf-axil buds lower down on each flowering stem. During the peak flowering time (late summer and early autumn), particular attention should be given to tying in, and to the control of slugs, snails and aphids.

Bedding dahlias generally need less rigorous treatment than border cultivars and do not require staking, stopping or disbudding. Excessive feeding will encourage foliar growth at the expense of flowers; dead-heading prolongs flowering and reduces the incidence of fungal rots by removing possible sources of infection.

Dahlias are propagated from tubers or cuttings when progeny are required to be identical to the parent. Before division of the tubers in early spring, induce them into growth in boxes of moist peat and sand in frost-free conditions. The crowns must be kept clear and care taken to avoid them when watering. When the eyes begin to swell, divide the tubers into two or three pieces, each with an eye, and pot or box up in a medium-fertility loam-based mix, storing in a frost-free cold frame until conditions are suitable for planting out. These divisions will each produce a full-sized root during the season for lifting again in autumn.

To provide basal cuttings, tubers are forced at an optimum temperature range of 15–18°C/60–65°F in late winter. Take 7.5cm/13in. cuttings, severing just above the crown, and insert in a mix of equal parts of loam, peat and sharp sand, in a propagating frame or heated bench at 15–18°C, keeping moist and shaded from bright sunlight. Pot on when rooted (about one month), and protect in a frost-free frame until planting out time.

Pot tubers, or 'mini-tubers', are grown from rooted cuttings planted one to a small pot (7–10cm) and left in that pot all season, to be taken out of it in autumn. This is the method of producing the pre-packed tubers available in millions every winter and spring. Despite their small size they grow rapidly once planted, either under glass to produce cuttings for increase or outside to develop directly into garden plants.

Raise bedding dahlias from seed, sown in late winter/early spring, in loam-based propagating medium, at 16°C/60°F. Harden off in the cold frame before setting out.

Dahlias can be left in the ground only in regions that are frost-free, or almost so, but otherwise are lifted and stored over winter. Leaving tubers in the ground in frost-free climates when the plants become dormant may result in dehydration and pest attack. In areas of medium frost risk, a heap of dry mulch or garden compost over the tubers will provide additional protection.

If tubers are to be lifted, do so when they are ripe, from mid- to late autumn, preferably immediately after the first frosts when the foliage is blackened at its growing tips. Cut tops back to 15cm/6in. and dig out tubers, taking care not to damage them, removing as much soil as possible from between the fingers of the roots. Remove the remaining soil after drying, trim back the fine roots to a compact clump and cut the stem back to 2.5cm/1in.

With a sharp clean instrument such as a screwdriver, pierce the tuber through the centre of the stem so as to emerge at its base, to prevent the accumulation of excess moisture during storage. Alternatively, place the tubers upside down until the stems are quite dry. Treat with fungicide and ensure that the tubers are thoroughly dry before storing in sand, at 5°C/40°F over winter. Inspect periodically for fungal infection or deterioration, and pare back damaged parts to firm, sound flesh, dusting with fungicide before returning to store.

The foliage of dahlias may be attacked by several pests including the black bean aphid (*Aphis fabae*); the glasshouse and potato aphid (*Aulacorthum solani*); the arum lily aphid (*A.circumflexum*); onion thrips (*Thrips tabaci*) which causes flecking of flowers and silvering of leaves; capsids of the tarnished plant bug (*Lygus rugulipennis*) associated with holed and rugged leaves and deformed flowers; the common earwig (*Forficula auricularia*), which eats out holes in leaves and flowers; slugs and snails; the chrysanthemum eelworm (*Aphelenchoiles ritzemabosi*); and the glasshouse white fly (*Trialeurodes vaporariorum*). Wasps may occasionally damage dahlias by scraping the stems for nest-building materials. Stems may be girdled at ground level and tubers tunnelled by larvae of cutworms (several spp.) and roots may also be injured by the larvae of swift moths (*Hepialus* spp.) and wireworms (*Agriotes* spp.). Tubers may become infested with bulb mites (*Rhizoglyphus* spp.) after being injured first by some primary pests and occasionally plants may be attacked by the potato tuber eelworm (*Ditylenchus destructor*).

In North America, the caterpillars of the European corn borer (*Ostrinia nubilalis*) can be a serious pest; fully grown larvae up to 30mm in length are flesh-coloured with brown spots and feed at first on the young shoot tips and flowers before boring through the stems causing affected parts to wilt.

Infection by the smut *Entyloma calendulae* f. sp. *dahliae* results in pale yellow spots on the leaves; these eventually coalesce and darken; these spots contain the spores of the fungus and crop debris should be destroyed or the spores will persist in the soil. The disease is mainly a problem on closely planted, small bedding types and some control may be achieved with fungicidal sprays. Dahlias can also be affected by crown gall (*Agrobacterium tumefaciens*), grey mould (*Botrytis cinerea*), leafy gall (*Corynebacterium fascians*) and sclerotinia wilt (*Sclerotinia sclerotiorum*). Dahlia mosaic virus typically causes a yellowish or pale green vein banding although in some varieties the leaves may be distorted, wrinkled and blistered and/or the plants may be short, bushy and generally stunted. The virus is transmitted by aphids, especially *Myzus persicae*. Control is achieved by growing and multiplying only healthy stock and rogueing infected plants. Dahlias are also susceptible to cucumber mosaic virus and tomato spotted wilt virus.

D.arborea hort. ex Reg. See *D.imperialis*.

D.coccinea Cav. (*D.gracilis*; *D.yuarezii* Mast.; *D.juarezii* Van der Berg ex Mast.).
Perenn. herb to 3m. Stems usually branched, green or purple tinged, often densely pubesc. or glaucous. Lvs to 40cm, simple to 3-pinnate, ovate to elliptic or ovate-lanceolate, acute or acuminate, base tapered, round or cordate, margin dentate, dark green, glabrous or pubesc. above, pale, veins hairy beneath. Capitula few to many, in clusters of 2–3, erect or slightly nodding; outer phyllaries ovate to obovate, inner brown or scarlet or with scarlet apex; ray florets yellow, orange or scarlet to dark maroon, sometimes many-coloured; disc florets yellow, apex occasionally scarlet. Summer–autumn. Mexico to Guatemala.

D.× cultorum hort. See *D.hortensis*.

D.excelsa Benth.
Perenn. herb or shrub, to 6m. Stem thick, woody, glaucous. Lvs to 80cm, 2-pinnatisect, margins dentate, pale glaucous green beneath, acuminate, basal lvs with ovate seg., base cordate, upper lvs smaller, petioles to 20cm, amplexicaul. Capitula solitary, or 5–8 in a corymb; outer phyllaries linear, inner leaf-like, oblong, membranous; florets lilac; disc florets often more or less ligulate. Mexico.

D.gracilis Ortgies. See *D.coccinea*.

D.hortensis Guillaum. (*D.juarezii* hort.; *D.pinnata* hort.; *D.variabilis* hort.; *D.cultorum* hort.).
Perenn. herb, to 2m. Stems branched, hollow. Lvs to *c*30cm, simple or 1–2-pinnate, seg. 3–7, to 20cm, oblong to ovate or lanceolate, margins dentate, petiolate. Capitula few, axillary, in a corymb; outer phyllaries leafy, oblong to ovate, inner often brown, slightly narrower; disc floret colour very variable, red, white, yellow or orange, sometimes purple or mauve, often different colours combined in patterns. Of hybrid origin, probably between *D.variabilis* (Willd.) Desf. and *D.coccinea* Cav.

D.imperialis Roezl ex Ortgies (*D.arborea* hort. ex Reg.).
Perenn. herb or subshrub to 9m. Stems, woody, branched above, glaucous, green or tinged red. Lvs to 60cm, 2–3-pinnate; seg. to 40cm, to 15, ovate to elliptic, acute to acuminate, base tapered or round, margin dentate, pubesc. above, pale with villous veins beneath, petioles to 25cm, bases cupulate. Capitula numerous in clusters, erect or nodding; outer phyllaries pubesc., inner elliptic or ovate, brown, margins translucent; ray florets, yellow, apex occasionally red apex. Autumn–winter. Guatemala to Columbia.

D.juarezii hort. non Van Der Berg ex Mast. See *D.hortensis*.
D.juarezii Van Der Berg ex Mast. non hort. See *D.coccinea*.

D.merckii Lehm.
Perenn. herb, to 2m. Stem branched from base, mostly glabrous, usually tinged red. Lvs to 40cm, 1–2-pinnate, seg. to 16cm, *c*7, sessile or petiolate, apical seg. to 5cm, ovate to obovate, acute to acuminate, glabrous or sparsely pubesc., petioles to 16cm, bases swollen. Capitula numerous, in terminal clusters on branches; outer phyllaries ovate to lanceolate, inner slightly larger; ray florets white to purple; disc florets yellow, apex purple. Summer–autumn. Mexico.

D.pinnata Cav. (*D.purpurea* Poir.; *D.superflua* (DC.) Ait. f.; *D.variabilis* (Willd.) Desf.).
Perenn. herb to 2m. Stems branched above, scabrous, tinged purple. Lvs to 25cm, usually pinnatisect, seg. 3–5, basal to 14cm, ovate, acute, pubesc. or strigose, especially on veins, petiole to 12cm, winged. Capitula to *c*8, in clusters of 2 or 3, erect or nodding; outer phyllaries obovate, glabrous, acute, inner ovate; ray florets pale purple, yellow or pink at base. Late spring–autumn. Mexico.

D.pinnata hort. See *D.hortensis*.
D.purpurea Poir. See *D.pinnata*.
D.rosea hort. non Cav. See *D.pinnata*.

D.scapigera (A. Dietr.) Knowles & Westc. (*Georgina scapigera* A. Dietr.).
Perenn. herb, to 50cm. Stem glabrous. Lvs crowded in a basal rosette, pinnate, seg. 3–7, to 4cm, ovate to lanceolate, sessile, mostly glabrous, venation conspicuous. Capitula few, usually solitary, slightly drooping; outer phyllaries erect, linear-oblanceolate, inner elliptic to lanceolate; ray florets white to pale purple, base sometimes yellow; disc florets yellow, apex purple. Summer–autumn. Mexico.

D.superflua (DC.) Ait. f. See *D.pinnata*.

D.tenuicaulis Sorensen.
Subshrub or shrub, to 4cm. Stems much branched, woody. Lvs to 45cm, 1–2-pinnate, seg. 3–7, to 18cm, petiolate, ovate to obovate or lanceolate, margins dentate. Capitula many, usually in clusters of 12 per branch; outer phyllaries ovate to lanceolate, inner narrower; ray florets lilac. Late summer–autumn. Mexico.

D.variabilis hort. non (Willd.) Desf. See *D.× hortensis*.
D.variabilis (Willd.) Desf. non hort. See *D.pinnata*.
D.yuarezii Mast. See *D.coccinea*.

Daubenya Lind. (For Dr Charles Daubeny (1795–1867), Professor of Botany at Oxford.) Liliaceae (Hyacinthaceae). 1 species, a glabrous, bulbous, perennial herb related to *Massonia*. Leaves 5–15×3.5–7.5cm, 2, basal, lying close to the ground, ovate or oblong, strongly veined. Scape very short, barely exceeding leaf cleavage; inflorescence an umbel-like corymbose head of to 10 flowers; pedicels to 4cm; bracts to 3×2.2cm, acute, overlapping; flowers of two kinds, outer flowers to 6.5cm, usually red or yellow, sometimes orange, tube to 2.5×0.4cm, limb to 4cm, bilaterally symmetric with a large lower lip of 3 blunt, hooded lobes, and a minute, 3-lobed upper lip, lower lips forming periphery of corymb, inner flowers nearly radially symmetric, orange-yellow, tubes similar to those of outer flowers, lobes shorter, to 2cm, some intermediate flower forms also present; stamens inserted near base of perianth lobes, filaments free, anthers dorsifixed; style unbranched, as long as perianth tube; ovary trilocular, superior; seeds 2mm diam., spherical, black. S Africa. Z9.

CULTIVATION   A spring-flowering and summer-dormant bulb, it requires protected cultivation in the bulb frame in cool temperate climates. Grow in a sandy, humus-rich, loam-based mix in full sun, with moderate watering when in growth drying off as leaves fade to keep dry when dormant. Propagate by offsets.

D.aurea Lindl. (*D.fulva* Lindl.).

D.fulva Lindl. See *D.aurea*.

Dichelostemma Kunth. (From Gk *dichelos*, with two prongs, and *stemma*, garland.) Liliaceae (Alliaceae). 7 species of cormous perennial herbs, distinguished from *Brodiaea* by the leaves distinctly keeled beneath and conspicuously veined, the coloured bracts, the fertile stamens sometimes to 6 (always 3 in *Brodiaea*) and the stigma lobes short, not spreading. Corm tunic fibrous, dark brown. Leaves 2–5, long-linear, grassy, outspread to sprawling, usually shorter than scape, keeled beneath, channelled above. Scapes slender; flowers in an umbel, subtended by spathe valves; perianth campanulate; fertile stamens 3–6, inserted on inner perianth lobes; staminodes 3, inserted on outer lobes, sometimes with reduced anthers; ovary superior; style inflated toward apex, narrowly 3-winged. Fruit a loculicidal capsule; seeds long-ovoid, 3-angled, angles prominently ridged. Summer. W US.

CULTIVATION   As for *Brodiaea*.

D.californicum (Torr.) Alph. Wood. See *D.volubile*.

D.congestum (Sm.) Kunth (*Brodiaea congesta* Sm.). OOKOW. Scape 30–90cm; spathe valves pale mauve; pedicels short, bowed-ascending to erect, their fused bases collectively forming a short, distinct stalk above the spathe valves; perianth 1.4–2cm, blue-violet, tube 6-angled, somewhat constricted at throat, lobes spreading, equalling tube; staminodes 3, bifid; stamens 3. W US (Washington to California). Z8.

D.ida-maia (Wood) Greene (*Brodiaea ida-maia* (Wood) Greene; *Brodiaea coccinea* A. Gray; *Brevoortia ida-maia* Wood). FIRECRACKER FLOWER. Scape 30–90cm; spathe valves tinged red; pedicels slender, curving, slightly drooping in flower, becoming erect in fruit; perianth scarlet (sometimes yellow), tube 2–2.5cm, lobes much shorter than tube, tipped pale green, recurved in flower; staminodes white; stamens 3. W US (Oregon, California). Z7.

D.multiflorum (Benth.) Heller (*Brodiaea multiflora* Benth.). WILD HYACINTH. Scape 20–80cm; spathe valves tinged purple; pedicels erect, usually shorter than bracts; perianth violet, rarely white,

1.6–2.1cm, lobes as long as tube, widely spreading, tube tightly waisted above ovary, not angled; staminodes 3, white or tinged violet; stamens 3. W US (Oregon, California). Z7.

D.pulchellum (Salisb.) Heller (*Brodiaea capitata* Benth.; *Brodiaea pulchella* (Salisb.) Greene). BLUE DICKS; WILD HYACINTH. Scape 30–60cm; spathe valves purple-tinted, ovate, usually exceeding erect pedicels; perianth 1.2–1.8cm, white to violet, tube not constricted at throat or angled, lobes equalling or exceeding tube, not widely spreading; stamens 6 in 2 whorls, those opposite the outer perianth lobes smaller, fil. united into a short tube, connective of larger anth. dilated with 2 triangular appendages. W US (Oregon to California, east to Utah). Z5.

D.volubile (Kellogg) A.A. Heller. SNAKE LILY; TWINING BRODIAEA. Scape to 150cm, snaking and twining. Pedicels slender, spreading or pendent in flower, turning upwards in fruit; perianth to 2cm, pale to rose pink, tube 6 angled; staminodes white. California.

Dierama K. Koch. (From Gk *dierama*, funnel, referring to the shape of the flowers.) ANGEL'S FISHING ROD; WAND FLOWER; AFRICAN HAIRBELL. Iridaceae. 44 species of perennial, evergreen herbs; corm renewed annually, with fibrous tunic. Flowering stem branched in upper half, the main axis and branches terminating in a spike. Leaves linear, grassy, green, mostly basal. Inflorescence branches long, slender, arching to strongly pendulous; flowers usually funnel-shaped or bell-shaped, white to deep purple-red, usually pink or mauve, regular; tube short, cylindrical at base then bell-shaped; tepals 6, usually with a diamond-shaped mark just above the base; stamens 3, style with 3 branches. Summer. Tropical and S Africa. Z9 unless specified.

CULTIVATION   *Dierama* is usually found in the wild at fairly high altitudes, often in grassland; the species most commonly seen in cultivation are *D.pendulum*, from altitudes of 3000m/9750ft, and the closely related *D.pulcherrimum*, both found on moist rich soils. Grown for their gracefully arching, semi-evergreen foliage and pendulous sprays of crêpe-like flowers; the flowers are suspended from the long wiry stems by pedicels so slender as to be almost invisible. *D.pulcherrimum* is particularly well suited to waterside plantings. They are reliably hardy to between –5°C and –10°C/23–40°F, although well-established clumps of *D.pulcherrimum* on well drained soils have survived periods of several weeks at temperatures to –17°C/1°F. Grow in a sunny, sheltered site in deep, rich, moist but free-draining soils. *Dierama* may be slow to establish and resents disturbance, but established clumps require little aftercare. Propagate by division in spring or by seed in autumn or spring.

D.adelphicum Hilliard. Stem 60–120cm. Basal lvs few, 35–60cm×3–5mm. Infl. pendent, terminal spike rather laxly 8–11-fld, lateral spikes 5–7, 5–9-fld; bracts 10–18mm long, lightly flecked with brown. Fls 1.5–2cm, pale mauve-pink to magenta-pink, rarely white; tube 5–6mm long, tepals 11–16×5–6mm, oblong. S Africa (Transvaal).

D.cooperi N.E. Br. Stem 60–140cm, rarely to 2m, solitary or 2–3 in a tuft. Basal lvs several, 30–70cm×3–5mm. Infl. pendulous, terminal spike densely 8–13-fld, lateral spikes 3–7, 5–10-fld; bracts to 30mm, white flecked with brown; fls *c*1.5–2.5cm, bright pink or white; tube 5–7.5mm, tepals 10.5–15×4.5–6.5mm. S Africa (Natal, Orange Free State).

D.dracomontanum Hilliard (*D.pumilum* N.E. Br.). Stems 30–100cm, forming dense clumps. Basal lvs several, 30–65cm×3–6mm. Infl. pendulous, rarely almost erect; termi-

nal spike densely 4–7-fld, lateral spikes usually 3–4, 2–5-fld; bracts to 20mm, brown or brown and white; fls 2–3cm, pale to deep rose pink, mauve, purple-pink, pale coral pink or coral-red; tube 5–7mm, tepals 13–20×5–8mm. S Africa, Lesotho.

D.grandiflorum Lewis. Stems 135–150cm, solitary or a few in a tuft. Basal lvs several, 60–90cm×4–8mm. Infl. pendulous, terminal spike rather laxly 6–8-fld, lateral spikes 4–10, 3–6-fld; bracts to 3cm, white flecked with brown; fls usually 5–7cm, occasionally less; tube usually 15–24mm, blue-purple, tepals usually 33–46×10–16mm, deep pink. S Africa (E Cape).

D.igneum Klatt. Stems 45–135cm, solitary or forming small clumps. Basal lvs several, to many, 30–90cm×2.5–9mm. Infl. pendulous, terminal spike rather laxly 4–11-fld, lateral spikes usually 4–8, 2–10-fld; bracts to 25mm long, flecked with brown; fls

1.5–3.5cm, pale to deep lilac or pink, sometimes almost white; tube 5–8mm, tepals usually 13–20×5–11mm. S Africa (Cape, Transkei, Natal).

D.insigne N.E. Br.
Stems 65–150cm, solitary or a few in a tuft. Basal lvs several, 35–75cm×2–6mm. Infl. pendulous, terminal spike densely 4–12-fld, lateral spikes 2–5, 3–12-fld; bracts to 3cm, brown and solid at base, margins scarious; fls c2–3.5cm, pale pink or magenta-pink, occasionally white; tube 7–16mm, tepals 12–20×5–11mm. S Africa (Natal, Transvaal), Swaziland.

D.jucundum Hilliard.
Stems 80–95cm, forming large clumps. Basal lvs several, 45–65cm×5–7mm. Infl. pendulous, terminal spike 6–16-fld, lateral spikes 3–5, 4–6-fld; fls c2.5–3cm, openly bell-shaped, pale mauve; tube 6–9mm, tepals 18–23×8–12mm. S Africa (E Cape), Lesotho.

D.luteoalbum Verdoorn.
Stems 65–110cm, solitary or a few in a tuft. Basal lvs few, 35–60cm×3–4mm. Infl. pendulous, terminal spike 3–6-fld, lateral spikes 1–3, 1–5-fld; bracts white, sometimes lightly flecked with brown; fls 3–5cm, white or creamy-yellow; tube 10–13mm, tepals 20–35×9–18mm. S Africa (Natal).

D.pendulum (L. f.) Bak.
Stem 1–2m, solitary or forming small clumps. Basal lvs 60–90cm×4–9mm. Infl. pendulous, terminal spike rather laxly 5–9-fld, lateral spikes 3–7, 2–7-fld; fls c3–5cm, widely bell-shaped, usually purple-pink; tube 8–13mm, tepals 20–32×8–16mm. S Africa (S & E Cape). 'Album': fls white. 'Puck': habit dwarf; fls madder-pink. 'Roseum': fls rose-pink. 'Titania': habit dwarf, fls light pink. Z7.

D.pulcherrimum (Hook. f.) Bak.
Stems 90–180cm, solitary or forming small clumps. Basal lvs 50–90×0.5–1cm. Infl. pendulous, terminal spike densely 4–8-fld, lateral spikes 4–8, 2–6-fld; fls narrowly bell-shaped, 3.5–5.5cm, pale to deep magenta-pink or deep red-purple, occasionally white; tube 10–15mm, tepals 23–39×10–19mm. S Africa. 'Album': fls white. Z7.

D.pumilum N.E. Br. See *D.dracomontanum*.

D.reynoldsii Verdoorn.
Stems 1–2m, solitary or 2–3 in a tuft. Basal lvs few, 45–95cm×4–6mm. Infl. pendulous, terminal spike densely 6–12-fld, lateral spikes 3–8, 3–11-fld; bracts silvery-white; fls 2–3cm, deep wine-red; tube 6–12mm, tepals 10–20×5–9mm. S Africa (Cape, Transkei, Natal).

D.robustum N.E. Br.
Stems 70cm–2m, solitary of forming small clumps. Basal lvs several, 40–120cm×3–10mm. Infl. pendulous, terminal spike densely 6–12-fld; lateral spikes 3–7, 3–12-fld; fls c2.5–3.5cm, creamy-white, pale pink or mauve-pink, rarely deeper pink; tube 7–13mm, tepals 16–26×7–13mm. S Africa, Lesotho.

Dietes Klatt. Iridaceae. 6 species of rhizomatous perennial herbs. Rhizomes stout, creeping, sometimes elongate and ascending. Leaves linear to ensiform, leathery, equitant. Flowering stem erect, glabrous, branching and bearing bracts in upper half, leafy toward base; flowers in groups, ephemeral, the clusters subtended by a spathaceous bracts; perianth radially symmetric, segments 6, free, the outer 3 larger with claws semi-erect, blades outspread, obovate to spathulate, nectar guide conspicuous, inner segments smaller, oblong, obovate; filaments free; style short, trifid, the branches flattened, showy, petal-like, apically bifid, recurved and crested with stigmatic lobes below. Fruit a many-seeded trilocular capsule. E, C & SE Tropical Africa, coastal S Africa, 1 sp. Lord Howe Is. Z9.

CULTIVATION   *Dietes* spp. are found in the wild in habitats ranging from open grassland for *D.grandiflora*, montane and coastal cliffs for *D.robinsoniana*, and moist forest margin and dry bushland to altitudes of 2000m/6500ft in the Drakensberg for *D.iridioides*. Forming clumps of narrow evergreen leaves arising from the creeping rhizomes, they are grown for their delicate, flattened iris-like flowers (honey-scented in *D.robinsoniana*), which are carried on slender, branching, wiry stems; although individually short-lived they are borne in profusion over long periods in favourable conditions. They are generally tolerant of poor and dry soils.

Even the hardiest species, *D.bicolor*, will not tolerate temperatures much below –5°C/23°F, and should be kept dry as temperatures fall and given a dry mulch in winter; other species will not stand prolonged cold much below freezing. In essentially frost-free zones with dry summers, several spp. are valued for both informal plantings and for the strong vertical element they provide in the herbaceous border; in good conditions, the leaves of *D.robinsoniana* may reach 1.8m/6ft in length. This species is well suited to coastal gardens. In cooler temperate zones, grow *Dietes* in direct sunlight in the well ventilated cool glasshouse or conservatory.

Grow in full sun or light, dappled shade in an open but moisture-retentive, humus-rich soil; apply liquid feed and water if necessary during full growth, but reduce both water and feeding during the summer months after flowering. With the exceptions of *D.bicolor* and *D.robinsoniana*, the flowering stems in *Dietes* are perennial and should not be cut back; if this becomes necessary leave 2–3 nodes on the remaining stem to allow formation of new flowering stems. Propagate by seed or by division after flowering; divisions may not re-establish readily and should be given a period of protected cultivation.

D.bicolor (Steud.) Klatt (*Moraea bicolor* Steud.).
Lvs to 60×0.6–1.2cm, narrowly ensiform, pale green with a conspicuous, often double, central vein. Flowering stem 60–100cm; fls yellow-white, outer perianth seg. 3–4cm, blotched dark brown and burnt orange at base of blade (nectar guide), claw bearded, spotted orange. Spring–summer. S Africa (E Cape).

D.grandiflora N.E. Br. WILD IRIS.
Lvs to 70×1.75cm. Flowering stem 1–1.25m; fls white, lasting some 3 days; outer perianth seg. 4–6cm, nectar guide yellow, claw with a yellow beard, inner perianth seg. marked brown at base; fil. 1–1.3cm, anth. 0.7–1cm; style 0.5cm, style branches 1.5–2cm, tinted lilac. Spring–summer. S Africa (E Cape to Natal).

D.iridioides (L.) Klatt (*Moraea iridioides* L.; *Moraea catenulata* Lindl.; *D.vegeta* auct.).
Lvs to 60×0.5–2cm in a distinct spreading fan. Flowering stem 30–60cm with many short sheathing bracts; fls white, lasting 1 day, outer perianth seg. 2–3.5cm, downy and papillose in the centre, nectar guide yellow, claw usually spotted deep yellow or brown; fil. 0.5–1cm, anth. 0.3–0.6cm; style 0.2–0.3cm, style branches to 1cm, white suffused pale blue or mauve, or blue. Spring–summer. S Africa north through E Africa to Kenya. 'Johnsoniana': lvs erect, flowering stem taller, fls to 10cm diam. Oakhurst Hybrids: habit spreading; fls rounded, cream-white, blotched brown-yellow, with purple centre.

D.robinsoniana (F. Muell.) Klatt (*Moraea robinsoniana* (F. Muell.) Benth. & F. Muell.).
Lvs 1–2m×3–5cm, rigid, ensiform, in a robust fan. Flowering stem equalling or slightly exceeding lvs; fls pure white, ephemeral, clustered in lax corymbs; outer perianth seg. 4–5×3cm, nectar guide orange; fil. to 1cm, anth. 0.5cm; style 0.3–0.5cm, style branches 1cm, white. Spring–summer. Australia (Lord Howe Is.).

D.vegeta auct. See *D.iridioides*.

Dioscorea L. YAM. (For Dioscorides, 1st-century Greek physician and herbalist, author of *Materia medica*.) Dioscoreaceae. Some 600 species of monoecious or dioecious, scandent herbs. Stems twining, arising from tuberous roots. Leaves usually alternate, sometimes opposite, simple to palmately compound, base often cordate, axils sometimes bearing bulbils. Flowers small, usually green-like: males in small, axillary racemes, perianth campanulate, stamens 6; female flowers in spikes or spike-like racemes, opening widely, perianth deeply 6-lobed. Fruit a 3-angled or 3-winged capsule, dehiscent; seeds strongly compressed, winged. Tropical and subtropical regions. Z10 unless otherwise stated.

CULTIVATION   *Dioscorea* contains several species of great economic importance: the massive root tubers of *D.alata* and *D.batatus* are yams, cultivated throughout the tropics as sources of staple starch foods. They are also fast-growing dark green foliage cover for pergolas, fences and expanses of bare earth. Of the species listed below, only *D.balcanica* is fully hardy – an attractive herbaceous perennial producing long twining stems clothed with dark green, heart-shaped leaves and bearing drooping spikes of colourful fruit. It should be grown through shrubs in semi-shaded, damp situations. The remainder require fertile, well drained soils with full sun to part-shade and minimum temperatures of 13°C/55–60°F when in growth. Water sparingly as growth begins, increasing when in full growth. Withold water as foliage begins to yellow and store over-wintering tubers in their pots and in dry conditions with a minimum temperature of 7–10°C/45–50°F. Plants that produce small tubers, or no tubers at all (for example *D.bulbifera*), or seem likely to carry their stems and foliage over several seasons (e.g. *D.discolor*) ought not to be given a full winter rest. Support on wires or canes, or allow *D.alata* and *D.batatas* to creep. *D.amarantoides* produces dense panicles of small flowers. *D.discolor* is perhaps the most beautiful member of the genus - a luxuriant climber for shaded corners of the warm glasshouse, it carries large, quilted leaves zoned with satiny pale and dark green, patterned with silver-white and purple-red. Species hailing from dry, rocky places in Southern Africa tend to develop a large, woody exposed tuber top which resembles a domed or pyramidal caudex, fissured in *D.macrostachya*, spectacularly cracked and plated in *D.elephantipes*. The vegetative growths of these caudiciforms tend to be short-lived and lush, in strong contrast to their desiccated, corky bases. These species should be grown in a sandy free-draining mix in full sunlight. Water moderately when in growth (usually a period of 2–3 months in spring and summer), very sparingly at other times. Propagate most species by division of the dormant tuber in spring; by detached aerial tubers for *D.alata*, *D.batatas* and *D.bulbifera*, and by seed for the caudiciform species.

D.alata L. WHITE YAM; WATER YAM.
Tubers to 2.5m, ovoid-cylindrical Stem 4-winged or 4-angled, frequently with small axillary tubers. Leaves ovate to oblong, base cordate, glabrous, 7–9-nerved. Male flowers in branched spikes; female flowers in simple spikes. India to Malay Peninsula.

D.amarantoides Presl.
Stem somewhat angled. Leaves to 10×5cm, alternate, ovate-lanceolate to cordate, 7 nerved. Male flowers in a dense panicle to 40cm. Peru.

D.balcanica Kosanin.
Tuberous roots to 2cm diam. Stem to 150cm, cylindrical, twining clockwise. Leaves to 7×6cm, cordate or ovate, shortly acuminate, 9-nerved, long-petiolate. Fruiting spike to 7cm, drooping; fruit to 2.5cm diam. Balkans. Z6.

D.batatas Decne. CHINESE YAM; CINNAMON VINE.
Tuberous roots to 90cm, clavate or cylindrical. Stem somewhat angled, twining clockwise, green or green-purple, bearing small, axillary tubers. Leaves to 8cm, opposite, ovate, base cordate, 7–9-nerved, short-petiolate. Flowers white, in axillary racemes, cinnamon-scented. Temperate E Asia, naturalized US.

D.bulbifera L. AIR POTATO.
Tuberous roots small, globose, sometimes absent. Stem to 6m, bearing axillary, subspherical or angled tubers. Leaves to 25×18cm, usually alternate, sometimes opposite, ovate, base cordate, cuspidate; petiole to 14cm. Male flowers in spikes to 10cm; female flowers in spikes to 25cm. Tropical Africa and Asia.

D.cotinifolia Kunth.
Tuberous roots to 9×5cm. Stem twining anticlockwise. Leaves to 8×5cm, usually alternate, sometimes opposite, broadly ovate, subcordate or truncate at base; petiole to 3cm. Male flowers in racemes to 7.5cm; female flowers in racemes to 15cm. S Africa.

D.discolor Kunth.
Tuberous roots to 7cm diam. Stem slightly angled. Leaves to 15cm, ovate-cordate, apex cuspidate, patterned dark satiny green and lustrous light green above with a silvery white midrib and zones of silver-white, red-purple beneath. Flowers inconspicuous. Tropical S America.

D.elephantipes (L'Hérit.) Engl. (*Testudinaria elephantipes* (L'Hérit.) Burchell). ELEPHANT'S FOOT; HOTTENTOT BREAD; TORTOISE PLANT.
Tuberous roots to 90cm, exterior woody, fissured and faceted with trapezoid plates which enlarge and build up visible corky layers over the years. Stems to 6m, twining clockwise. Leaves to 6cm broad, alternate, suborbicular-cordate to reniform, shortly mucronate, 7–9-nerved. Male flowers in simple or branched racemes to 7.5cm; female flowers in simple racemes. S Africa.

D.hastifolia Nees.
Tuberous roots to 12×3cm. Stem to 9m, cylindrical, twining anti-clockwise. Leaves to 8cm, alternate, linear to linear-lanceolate or hastate. Male flowers in racemes to 8cm; female flowers in short, few-flowered racemes. W Australia.

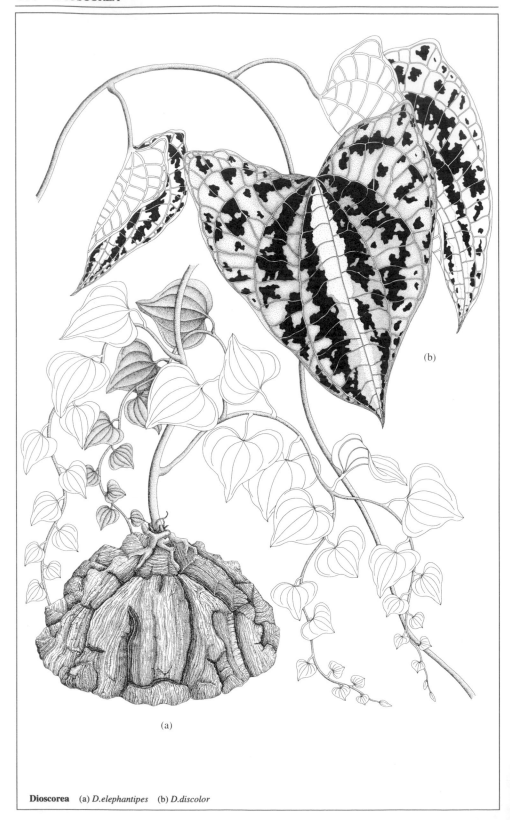

(b)

(a)

Dioscorea   (a) *D.elephantipes*   (b) *D.discolor*

D.macrostachya Benth. (*Testudinaria macrostachya* (Benth.) Rowley).
Tuberous roots to 20cm diam., deeply corrugated. Stem somewhat angled, twining clockwise. Leaves to 20 × 18cm, ovate, acuminate, base cordate, long-petiolate. Male flowers in few-flowered clusters, in racemes to 30cm; female flowers solitary, in racemes. C America.

D.trifida L.f. CUSH-CUSH; YAMPEE.
Tuberous roots small. Stems sharply angled or narrowly winged, twining clockwise. Leaves to 25cm, 3-lobed, cordate, puberulent above, pilose veins beneath. Male flowers in racemes; female flowers in spikes. S America, W Indies.

Dipcadi

Dipcadi Medik. (Oriental name for a species of *Muscari*.) Liliaceae (Hyacinthaceae). About 55 species of bulbous perennials. Bulb rounded, fleshy, enclosed and formed by leaf bases. Leaves narrow, glabrous, sheathing lower part of stem. Flowers slenderly bell-shaped or tubular, green to bronze, yellow, orange or rust, in long-stemmed loose, scapose racemes; tepals 6, slightly fleshy, bases united, inner 3 erect, outer 3 spreading; stamens 6, included; ovary superior, style 1. Fruit a 3-celled capsule. N Africa, S Africa, SW Europe, E Indies. Z8.

CULTIVATION   *Dipcadi* usually occurs in the wild in dry rocky habitats, frequently in coastal areas. *D.serotinum* is occasionally cultivated, bearing small, delicate bell-shaped flowers which fall to one side of the stem; its interesting form and subtle, subdued colours can best be appreciated in the alpine house or in sunny, well drained, frost-free pockets in the rock garden. This species is the most hardy: given perfect drainage, it tolerates temperatures to about −10°C/14°F.

D.brevifolium (Thunb.) Fourc. BROWN BELLS; CURLY-CURLY.
Bulb subglobose, pale green. Lvs to 30cm, 2–3, narrow-triangular to linear, held semi-erect. Scape to 60cm, usually shorter; fls 6–8, pale to emerald-green tinged ruby-red on outer, recurved tepals, perianth tube waisted where tepals expand. Spring–summer. S Africa.

D.fulvum (Cav.) Webb & Berth.
To 45cm; bulb spherical. Lvs basal, shorter than scape, 5–20×1–2cm, keeled. Fls 4–20, 1–1.5cm diam., in a secund raceme; tepals pink, tinged with brown. Autumn. S Spain, Morocco, Canary Is. Sometimes treated as a variety of *D.serotinum*.

D.serotinum (L.) Medik. (*Scilla serotina* L.).
Lvs to 5, linear, shorter than scape. Scape to 45cm; fls pendent, to 2.5cm, green to ochre or bronze, sometimes rusty-red or dull orange; outer tepals spreading, inner tepals straight. Spring–summer. SW Europe, N Africa.

D.umbonatum Bak. See *D.viride*.

D.viride Moench (*D.umbonatum* Bak.).
To 45cm. Lvs rolled, forming a sheath and clasping scape, often exceeding infl. Fls green to bronze; inner tepals connivent, urceolate, outer tepals strongly reflexed against pedicel. Spring–summer. S Africa.

Dracunculus

Dracunculus Mill. (Named used by Pliny for plant with curved rhizome, from Lat. diminutive of *draco*, a dragon.) DRAGON ARUM. Araceae. 3 species of tuberous herbaceous perennials. Leaves basal; petioles with overlapping mottled sheaths forming a pseudostem enveloping peduncle, blade pedate, divided into many unequal segments. Peduncle long, stout; spathe convolute at base, margins overlapping to enclose base of spadix, limb large, flat, red-purple, white or mottled; spadix nearly equalling spathe, very malodorous, floral zone short, appendix long, stout and glabrous or slender with bristly filaments, male and female flowers adjacent or separated by zone of rudimentary flowers, perianth absent, stamens 2–4, ovary unilocular. Fruit a berry; seeds to 6. Mediterranean, Madeira, Canary Is.

CULTIVATION   *D.vulgaris* will establish itself in most sheltered, well drained positions in zones 7 and over, tolerating full sun or dappled shade. The remaining two species require full sunlight in a frost-free glasshouse in very sharply draining, gritty soil with a pronounced dry rest after flowering and leaf production. Good ventilation benefits the plants and the grower (no inflorescence is more putrid than that of *D.muscivorus*, evolved as it is to attract blow flies to a simulated seabird carcass in advanced decay). General requirements otherwise as for *Arum*.

D.canariensis Kunth.
Of medium height. Lf seg. 7–11, median seg. to 15cm, pale green, unspotted; petioles to 40cm, spotted green-purple. Peduncle to 60cm+, spotted; spathe 25–35×5–6cm, white above, green beneath, margins somewhat incurved, undulate; spadix with adjacent male and female fls, male fls not included in base of spathe, appendix to 25cm, slender, yellow. Early summer. Madeira, Canary Is.Z9.

D.crinitus Schott. See *D.muscivorus*.

D.muscivorus (L. f.) Parl. (*D.crinitus* Schott; *Helicodiceros muscivorus* (L. f.) Engl.). HAIRY ARUM; DRAGON'S MOUTH.
Low-growing. Lvs to 30cm diam., irregularly divided into narrow lobes, 3 median lobes broad, deflexed, others at different angles due to twisted axis; petiole to 50cm, spotted at base. Peduncle spotted; spathe situated below lvs, tube to 15cm, limb to 35×30cm, broadly, ovate-lanceolate to suborbicular spreading to reflexed-horizontal green-white streaked purple-brown beneath, pale to deep purple-red mottled dull purple-grey or ox-blood above with red hairs particularly toward base and in tube; spadix to 15cm, dark green or yellow, stinking of carrion, with sterile fls below and above male fls, those above graduating into slender red-brown filaments which cover the appendix. Early summer. W Mediterranean Is. (Corsica, Sardinia, Balearic Is.). Z9.

D.vulgaris (L.) Schott (*Arum dracunculus* L.). DRAGON ARUM.
To 1.5m. Lvs 15–20×25–35cm, reniform in outline, seg. 9–15, lanceolate, acute, dark green spotted or striped white; petioles long, densely spotted brown-purple, forming a thick

(a)

(b)

Dracunculus (a) *D.vulgaris* (b) *D.muscivorus*

pseudostem. Peduncle exceeding petioles; spathe to 100×20cm, broadly ovate-lanceolate, acuminate, glabrous or very rarely shortly white-hairy at base, dull green beneath, dark satiny red-purple above (occasionally green, white or yellow in some wild variants), margins slightly reflexed, undulate, withering as fruit ripens; spadix with adjacent male and female fls, sterile fls above male zone, appendix nearly equalling spathe, black-red, swollen at base, tapering above, very malodorous. Berries green, becoming orange-red. Early summer. C & E Mediterranean. Z7.

Drimia Willd. (From Gk *drimys*, acrid; the juice of the roots is acrid, causing skin inflammation.) Liliaceae (Hyacinthaceae). Some 15 species of bulbous perennial herbs. Bulbs composed of fleshy stalked scales. Leaves 1 to many, lanceolate or narrow-lanceolate, flattened, grass-like, usually hysteranthous. Scape erect, terete; flowers white to green-white or green-brown, in a many-flowered elongate raceme; perianth segments connate at base, reflexed, united into a short tube; stamens 6, attached to base of tube, ovary ellipsoid, trilocular. Fruit a capsule; seed compressed or angled, black. S Africa. Z9.

CULTIVATION   Native to sandy soil in coastal scrub, *Drimia* spp. are not noted for their great ornamental value, but some are of botanical interest for the habit of growth. The bulb of *D.haworthioides* sits on the soil surface and as the foliage dies back, the leaf stalks elongate and form enlarged storage organs or bulb scales at their tips; these may persist for several years, the whole resembling the succulent leaf rosettes of *Haworthia*. Grow in the cool to intermediate glasshouse, (min. 10°C/50°F), in full sun in a mix of loam, leafmould and sand; water moderately when in growth in spring and summer and keep dry or almost so when at rest in summer. Propagate by means of the swollen bulb scales or by seed.

D.apertiflora Bak. See *Ledebouria apertiflora*.
D.cooperi Bak. See *Ledebouria concolor*.

D.haworthioides Bak.
Bulb 2–3cm high, lying on surface of soil, loosely covered with stalked scales giving it a diameter of 5–6cm. Lvs 6–8×1–1.5cm, to 10, oblong-lanceolate, usually downy and fleshy. Scape 20–40cm, glaucous; racemes 15–30-fld;

pedicels 3–8mm, bracts 1–4mm; perianth green or green-brown, 1–1.5cm, tube 0.2–0.4cm; stamens exserted. Fr. 0.7–1cm, ellipsoid. Winter. S Africa (E Cape).

D.maritima (L.) Stearn. See *Urginea maritima*.
D.ovalifolia Schräd. See *Ledebouria ovalifolia*.
D.undulata Jacq. See *Ledebouria undulata*.

Drimiopsis Lindl. (From *Drimia* and Gk *opsis*, appearance.) Liliaceae (Hyacinthaceae). 7 species of perennial herbs, related to *Ornithogalum*. Bulbs globose, sometimes scaly, turning green where exposed, otherwise off-white. Leaves 2–4, ovate to ovate-oblong, sometimes keeled, often spotted. Scape exceeding leaves; inflorescence a many-flowered, ebracteate, spiciform raceme; flowers small, green-white; perianth segments shortly united into a tube, tips slightly spreading, hooded; stamens 6, filaments triangular, attached to top of perianth tube, ovary superior, trilocular, ovules 2 per cell. Fruit a capsule; seeds few. Tropical & S Africa. Z9.

CULTIVATION   As for *Drimia*.

D.kirkii Bak.
Bulb to 3.8cm diam., tunic thin, off-white. Lvs to 15cm, oblong, sessile but narrowing toward base, apex acute, pale green with dark blotches above, paler beneath. Scape to 30cm; perianth 0.6cm, white, seg. oblong, blunt. Summer. Zanzibar.

D.maculata Lindl. & Paxt.
Bulb scaly toward neck. Lvs 10cm, ovate or ovate-oblong to cordate-oblong, somewhat fleshy, long-stalked, apex acute, bright green above, blotched deep green. Scape 20–40cm; perianth white, becoming green-white; to 0.4cm. Spring. S Africa.

Eleutherine Herb. (From Gk *eleutheros*, free, in allusion to the free filaments.) Iridaceae. 2 species of bulbous perennial herbs related to *Tigridia*. Leaves plicate, lanceolate. Inflorescence composed of flower clusters subtended by a pair of short, green, subequal spathes. Flowers white, star-like, opening in the evening; tepals free, subequal; stamens free; style with 3 filiform branches. Mexico, C & S America, W Indies; naturalized Philippines and Indochina. Z10.

CULTIVATION As for *Ixia*, but with a minimum temperature of 15–18°C/60–65°F.

E.anomala Herb. See *E.bulbosa*.

E.bulbosa (Mill.) Urban (*E.anomala* Herb.; *E.plicata* (Sw.) Klatt).
15–75cm. Infl. axis much-branched; stalks of fl. clusters 2–5.5cm long; spathes 1–2cm; tepals 10–18mm. SE Brazil and Bolivia to Venezuela and W Indies; naturalized in Philippines and Indochina.

E.latifolia (Standl. & Williams) Ravenna.
To 20cm. Infl. axis not branched; fl. clusters usually 1, stalked or subsessile, but occasionally with a second sessile, axillary cluster; spathes 1.5–2cm; tepals 12–14×6–8mm. Mexico to C & S America.

E.plicata (Sw.) Klatt. See *E.bulbosa*.

Eminium Schott. (Name used by Dioscorides.) Araceae. 7 species of tuberous, perennial herbs of dry and rocky places, resembling *Biarum* and *Dracunculus*, the former particularly in respect of flowers and fruit, the latter in respect of foliage. The leaves are borne before the inflorescence. Spathe very short-stalked or partially buried at its tubular base, expanding into a broad blade which is often deflexed or lying flat on soil surface. Fruiting heads composed of clustered berries, often developing below ground and breaking the soil surface to ripen and disperse. E Mediterranean to C Asia. Z8.

CULTIVATION *Eminium* spp. are grown for their interesting and unusual inflorescences, carried at ground level, usually in spring and summer, although those of *E.spiculatum* and its smaller but slightly earlier-flowering subspecies *negevense* are carried in February and March in habitat. The latter, holding its black spathe flat to the ground, bears an uncanny resemblance to dung when viewed from a distance. The black leathery spathe of *E.intortum* is usually described as reeking of rotting flesh. With good drainage and a period of warm, dry dormancy in late summer, they may be grown under much the same régime as *Biarum*.

E.alberti Reg.
Lvs to 25cm, usually shorter, light green, ovate-lanceolate, usually simple, sometimes lobed, withering on appearance of infl. Spathe equalling lvs, tube short, bulbous at base, green-yellow, blade broadly ovate-lanceolate, held perpendicular to tube, somewhat undulate and reflexed or spreading along soil surface, deep velvety blood red above; spadix erect terminating in a long, slender, fleshy green-brown appendage equalling or slightly shorter than spathe blade. C Asia.

E.intortum (Banks & Sol.) Kuntze.
Tuber subglobose, with a powdery white coating. Lvs to 15cm, ovate-lanceolate to hastate, grey-green, strongly divided and undulate. Spathe equalling lvs, erect, the blade undulate and incurved-hooded throughout its length, dark velvety purple above, green below; spadix appendage to half length of spathe blade, purple-black. S Turkey, Syria, Iraq.

E.lehmannii Kuntze.
Close to *E.intortum* in stature. Lvs simple, lanceolate to subsagittate. Spathe velvety black above, green below; spadix

black. Fr. white, breaking the soil surface to ripen red to violet. Iran.

E.rauwolfii (Bl.) Schott.
Close to *E.intortum*, differing in parallel, not divergent, veins in the lower part of the longer, narrower lvs. Lvs narrow-lanceolate to obscurely sagittate, sometimes spotted and flecked white or grey-green. Spathe equalling lf petioles, the tubular base squat, bright green, the blade erect, ovate-lanceolate, velvety purple-black; spadix appendage thickly club-like, glossy black. E & S Turkey, Syria.

E.spiculatum (Bl.) Schott.
Lvs to 25cm, erect, strongly undulate and pinnatifid. Spathe 10–22×8–14cm (far smaller in ssp. *negevense*), the tube usually buried, the blade ovate-lanceolate, held perpendicular to tube and along soil surface, purple-black, corrugated above; spadix black, erect, to half length of spathe. Iraq, Syria, Turkey, Negev, Sinai Peninsula.

Eranthis Salisb. (From Gk *ar*, spring, and *anthos*, flower.) WINTER ACONITE. Ranunculaceae. About 7 perennial herbs. Rhizomes short, tuberous, rounded or irregular. Basal leaves petiolate, deeply palmately lobed, arising from membranous sheath; stem leaves 3, sessile, dissected forming a ruff-like, involucral whorl below flower. Flowers solitary, terminal, yellow to white, hermaphrodite, actinomorphic; perianth segments in 2 whorls, petaloid calyx segments 5–8 as outer whorl, inner whorl of tubular, entire or 2–4-lipped nectaries; stamens numerous. Carpels usually 6, free, stalked, dry dehiscent follicles in fruit, surrounded by persistent cauline leaves; seeds numerous, in 1 row, brown. S Europe (also naturalized W & N Europe and N America), Asia (Turkey to Japan).

CULTIVATION   Found in damp woodland and shady places, *Eranthis* are valuable for the bright carpet of flower they will form in early spring under the canopy of deciduous shrubs or in light grassland. Here they will colonize and tolerate the drier conditions experienced later in the growing season, when all the foliage 'ruffs' have disappeared. Choicer plants like *E.× tubergenii* 'Guinea Gold' and *E.cilicica* make good specimens for pans in the alpine house or cold frame. Plant in summer or early autumn in humus-rich, heavy soil which remains moist at least until mid-summer. Propagate by division in spring after flowering: like *Cyclamen* and *Galanthus* spp., they are difficult to establish from dry tubers: purchase 'in the green' (i.e. bare-root but in leaf) where possible. Sow seed as soon as ripe for flowering plants in 2–3 years (hybrids such as *E.× tubergenii* are sterile). Birds may peck the flowers. Foliage is sometimes disfigured by aphids and the sooty moulds that form on the 'honeydew' they leave.

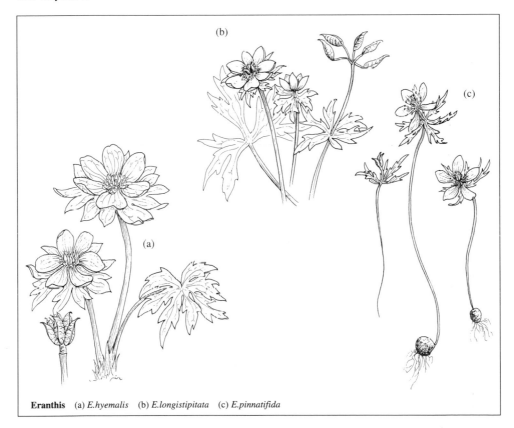

Eranthis   (a) *E.hyemalis*   (b) *E.longistipitata*   (c) *E.pinnatifida*

E.cilicica Schott & Kotschy.
Lvs tinged bronze on emergence; involucral lvs finely dissected. Fls shiny golden yellow, larger and emerging later than *E.hyemalis*. Winter. Turkey to Afghanistan. Z4.

E.hyemalis (L.) Salisb.
Glabrous perenn. to 15cm, usually far shorter (to 7cm). Rhiz. irregular when old, subglobose when young. Basal lvs emerging after fls, orbicular in outline but palmately lobed with further divisions, bright green, 3–8cm diam. Fls 2–3cm diam., yellow; sep. 6, narrowly ovate, enlarging during flowering; nectaries 6, tubular, with outer lip exceeding inner, shorter than stamens; stamens about 30. Carpels 6, short-stalked; fol-

licles 1.5cm; seeds yellow-brown. Winter. S France to Bulgaria, naturalized elsewhere. var. **bulgarica** Stef. Lvs and bracts more divided, resembling *E.cilicica*. Bulgaria. 'Aurantiaca': fls bright orange. Z5.

E.keiskei Franch. & Savat. See *E.pinnatifida*.

E.longistipitata Reg.
Resembling *E.hyemalis* but much smaller; tuber subglobose. Basal lvs 1–2, palmately, 3–5-lobed. Flowering stem 5cm; involucre divided into linear seg.; pedicel, short at first, elongating in fruit; fls, yellow, 1.5cm diam.; sep. 5–6, elliptic; nectaries tubular, entire, one-third length of sep. Carpels short-stalked. Spring. C Asia. Z6.

E.pinnatifida Maxim. (*E.keiskei* Franch. & Savat.).
To 15cm. Basal lvs reniform-orbicular, 4cm wide, 3-lobed, each lobe bifid, obtuse, pinnatifid. Fls on short pedicel, white, to 2cm across; sep. 5, ovate; nectaries yellow, 2–4-lobed, shorter than stamens. Carpels 1–5, 1cm, short-stalked; seeds brown. Spring. Japan. Z4.

E.sibirica DC. (*E.uncinata* Turcz.).
Close to *E.longistipitata*; tuber subglobose. Basal lvs 1, palmately, 3–5-lobed, lobes tripartite to middle. Flowering stem 5cm; involucre divided into linear, entire or trifid seg.; pedicels glabrous or pubescent, elongating in fruit; fls yellow,

1.5cm in diam.; sep. 5–6, elliptic or oval; nectaries broad, bilobed, one-quarter to one-third length of sep. Spring. Siberia. Z3.

E.× tubergenii Bowles. (*E.cilicica* × *E.hyemalis.*)
Vigorous sterile hybrid. Lvs tinged bronze on emergence. Fls large, rich golden yellow, appearing later than *E.hyemalis*; nectaries more numerous than in parents; anth. abortive. Carpels numerous, swelling but infertile. Winter. Garden origin. 'Guinea Gold': bracts deeply cut, lobes narrow; fls deep golden yellow, fragrant, long-lasting. Z5.

E.uncinata Turcz. See *E.sibirica*

Eremurus Bieb. DESERT CANDLE; FOXTAIL LILY. Liliaceae (Asphodelaceae). 40–50 species of perennial herbs. Rhizomes stout, thickened, bearing remains of old leaf bases. Leaves narrow, basal, forming tufts or rosettes. Scape erect, bearing a dense, narrow raceme of white, pink or yellow flowers; bracts membranous; tepals 6, sometimes fused at base, 1- or 3–5-nerved; stamens 6, sometimes exserted, anthers basifixed; ovary superior. Fruit a trilocular capsule, 0.5–3.5cm, spherical; seeds usually winged. W & C Asia. Z7.

CULTIVATION Stately plants producing tall, upright stems, each bearing a densely flowered spike- or taper-like inflorescence. In the wild, they grow in rocky semi-desert, in dry, grazed grassland or (*E.anisopterus*), in sand. The natural colour range of yellow, pink and white, is much extended in the hybrids of *E.× isabellinus* and in selections of *E.stenophyllus* to include striking golden and coppery yellows, deep pinks, oranges and brick-red. *Eremurus* spp. produce a fleshy rooted crown with a central growing-point which may rot if too wet in winter. Where possible, they should be grown on raised beds or banks where water drains quickly in winter; alternatively, set and cover the crown in sharp sand at planting time. *Eremurus* requires cold in winter to flower well, and is unsuited to cultivation in completely frost-free zones.

Grow in rich, fertile, well drained, sandy soil in full sun. Without shelter from wind, taller species and hybrids will require staking. Protect from winter wet with a mulch of sharp sand or ashes; in higher-rainfall areas an open cloche will help ensure survival. In late summer/early autumn an organic mulch may be given to established clumps, although this must be cleared away, especially in damp springs, to avoid the rotting of emerging new growth. In regions that experience late frosts, give young shoots the protection of dry bracken litter or straw; site where early morning sun does not strike frosted growth. Propagate from ripe seed in autumn, or from careful division and replanting of the crowns, as the foliage dies back in late summer.

E.aitchisonii Bak. (*E.elwesii* Micheli; *E.robustus* var. *elwesii* (Micheli) Leichtlin).
90–200cm. Lvs narrowly lanceolate, to 8cm wide, glossy green, margins rough. Scape glabrous; raceme lax; bracts linear-subulate, broad at base, ciliate; pedicels 3cm, ascending; tepals 18–25mm, pale pink to white, 1-nerved. Fr. 1.5–3.5×1.5–2cm. Summer. C Asia, E Afghanistan. 'Albus': fls white. Z6.

E.altaicus (Pall.) Steven.
To 120cm. Lvs 15–22×1.5cm, ligulate, glabrous. Racemes dense; pedicels 1.5×2.5cm, articulated at apex; tepals yellow, incurved. Fr. on erect pedicels. Summer. C Asia. Z4.

E.anisopterus (Karel. & Kir.) Reg. (*E.korolkowii* Reg.).
As for *E.bucharicus* except scape glabrous throughout, leaves with smooth margins, tepals shorter, 10mm, concave. Summer. Iran, C Asia. Z6.

E.aurantiacus Bak. See *E.stenophyllus* ssp. *aurantiacus.*

E.bucharicus Reg. 80–100cm.
Lvs linear, to 5mm wide, glabrous or finely pubesc., glaucous, margins rough. Scape sometimes pubesc. at base; raceme lax, few-fld; bracts subulate, broad at base, ciliate; pedicels 3cm, horizontal; tepals 13–15mm, white to pale pink, 1-nerved; stamens inserted. Fr. 1.5–1.8cm, subspherical, seeds broad-winged. Summer. Afghanistan, C Asia. Z4.

E.bungei Bak. See *E.stenophyllus.*

E.caucasicus hort. See *E.spectabilis.*

E.comosus O. Fedtsch.
70–180cm. As for *E.turkestanicus* except lvs to 1.5cm wide, pubesc., glaucous; bracts broadly lanceolate to ovate; pedicels 2–3cm; tepals dusky rose; fr. closely pressed to scape. Summer. C Asia to W Pakistan. Z5.

E.elwesianus hort. See *E.aitchisonii.*

E.elwesii Micheli. See *E.aitchisonii.*
E.griffithii Bak. See *E.kaufmannii.*

E.hilariae Popov & Vved.
To 1m. Lvs linear, to 40cm, glaucous, grey-pubesc., keel and margins scabrous. Bracts ciliate, equal to pedicels; tepals 12–16mm, white, yellow at base. Summer. C Asia. Z5.

E.himalaicus Bak.
To 2.5m. Lvs ligulate, to 4cm wide, glabrous. Scape glabrous; raceme dense, to 90cm; bracts narrow-linear, ciliate; pedicel to 3cm; tepals 17–20mm, white, 1-nerved; stamens equal to tepals. Fr. 12–14mm, wrinkled, seeds not winged. Late spring–summer. Afghanistan, NW Himalaya. Z3.

E.'Himrob'. (*E.himalaicus* × *E.robustus.*)
Early blooming. Lvs blue-green. Fls very pale pink. Z4.

E.inderiensis (Steven) Reg.
70–120cm. Lvs 8–15mm wide, pubesc. Scape finely pubesc.; bracts shorter than pedicels, villous; pedicels 1cm, ascending; tepals 11–12mm, subequal, red-brown, 3–5-nerved, nerves olive green. Summer. Fr. 1cm diam. C Asia, Afghanistan, Iran. Z5.

E.× isabellinus hort. Vilm. (*E.stenophyllus* × *E.olgae.*)
To 1.5m. Fls orange, pale yellow, pink, white to copper yellow. Garden origin. Shelford Hybrids: 1.25m, fls yellow, orange, pink or white suffused yellow (Foster); include 'Isobel': pale yellow, 'Rosalind': bright pink. Early summer. Highdown Hybrids: orange to buff, late-flowering, include dwarf forms (Stern). 'Feuerfackel' (Flame Torch): fls flaming orange to red. 'Moonlight': fls pale yellow. 'Schneelanze': fls pale green to white. 'White Beauty': fls pure white. Ruiter's hybrids: to 2m, brightly coloured. 'Cleopatra': fls deep orange; 'Fatamorgana': fls white to cream; 'Image': fls clear yellow; 'Obelisk': fls white; 'Parade': fls clear pink; 'Pinokkio': fls orange; 'Romance': fls tinted red; 'Sahara': fls copper. Z5.

E.kaufmannii Reg. (*E.griffithii* Bak.; *E.unaniensis* Gilli).
60–110cm. Lvs to 3.5cm wide, pubesc., glaucous. Scape pubesc.; bracts narrowly ovate-triangular, attenuate, villous; pedicels to 1cm, almost horizontal; tepals 15–22mm, 1-nerved, white, base yellow. Fr. 12mm diam., fruiting pedicels 2cm, engorged. Summer. Afghanistan, C Asia. Z5.

E.korolkowii Reg. See *E.anisopterus*.

E.lactiflorus O. Fedtsch.
To 1m. Lvs linear, to 45cm, glabrous, glaucous. Scape glabrous; raceme laxly fld; tepals golden yellow in bud, opening white with yellow base, revolute; stamens slightly exserted. Fr. 3.5cm, smooth. Summer. C Asia. Z5.

E.olgae Reg. 70–100cm.
Lvs narrowly linear, 1–1.5cm wide, glabrous, margin rough. Scape pubesc. at base; bracts linear-subulate, broad at base, glabrous; pedicels 4–6cm; tepals 12–16mm, pink, rarely white with yellow base, 1-nerved. Fr. to 14×10mm. Late summer–autumn. C Asia to N Iran. Z6.

E.regelii Vved. (*E.spectabilis* var. *marginatus* O. Fedtsch.).
To 2m. Lvs linear, glabrous. Tepals brown, 2.5cm wide, margins white; stamens exserted. C Asia. Z5.

E.robustus (Reg.) Reg.
To 3m. Lvs ligulate, to 4cm wide, glaucous. Scape glaucous; raceme to 1m, densely fld; bracts linear, wider at base, ciliate; pedicels to 4cm; tepals 18–21mm, pink, 1-nerved; stamens equal tepals. Fr. 2cm. Summer. Russia, Afghanistan. Z6.

E.robustus var. **elwesii** (Micheli) Leichtlin. See *E.aitchisonii*.

E.× shelfordii hort. See *E.× isabellinus*.

E.sogdianus (Reg.) Benth. & Hook.
80–150cm. Lvs to 1.5cm wide. Scape pubesc. at base; bracts small, subulate, villous; pedicels 5–7.5cm, spreading to ascending; tepals 10–14mm, unequal, outer tepals elliptic to narrowly ovate, sulphur green, 1-nerved, inner tepals broadly ovate, white, 3-nerved, nerves green; stamens exserted. Fr. 6–7mm. Summer. C Asia to N Afghanistan. Z6.

E.spectabilis Bieb. (*E.caucasicus* hort.)
75–100cm. Lvs linear-ligulate, to 4.5cm wide, glaucous, margins sometimes rough. Scape glabrous; raceme to 80cm; bracts linear, ciliate; pedicels 1cm, upward-curving; tepals 1cm, pale yellow suffused green, 3-nerved; stamens twice length of tepals, anth. brick-red, fil. orange-red near base, yellow above. Fr. 5–14×12mm, transversely ribbed; seeds narrowly winged. Late spring–summer. Asia Minor to W Pakistan. Z6.

E.spectabilis var. **marginatus** O. Fedtsch. See *E.regelii*.

E.stenophyllus (Boiss. & Buhse) Bak. (*E.bungei* Bak.).
30–150cm. Lvs to 12mm wide, linear, sometimes pubesc., margins rough. Scape glabrous to pubesc.; raceme dense; bracts linear-subulate, sometimes hairy; pedicels to 2cm, spreading; tepals 9–12mm, 1-nerved, clear yellow ageing brown; stamens exceeding tepals, anth. orange. Fr. 5–7mm diam., seeds broad-winged. Summer. C Asia to W Pakistan. ssp. **stenophyllus**. Lvs and scape glabrous. ssp. **aurantiacus** (Bak.) Wendelbo (*E.aurantiacus* Bak.). Lvs scabrous-pubesc. Lower part of scape pubesc.; bracts sometimes ciliate. Z5.

E.tauricus hort. See *E.spectabilis*.

E.× tubergenii Tuberg. (*E.stenophyllus* × *E.himalaicus*.) To 2.5m. Fls pale yellow. Garden origin. Z6.

E.turkestanicus Reg.
To 1m. Lvs broad-linear, glabrous. Scape glabrous; raceme 40–60cm; bracts narrow-linear, ciliate; pedicels 1cm; tepals 1cm, outer tepals sulphur yellow with brown central stripe and pale margin, 5-nerved, inner tepals white with sulphur yellow stripe, 3-nerved; stamens equal tepals, exserted as tepals age and curve inwards. Fr. smooth. Summer. C Asia. Z6.

E.unaniensis Gilli. See *E.kaufmannii*.

E.× warei hort. Reuthe. (*E.stenophyllus* × *E.olgae*.)
To 2.5m. Racemes slender. Fls small, orange. Early summer. Garden origin.

Erythronium L. (From Gk *erythros*, red, more or less the colour of *E.dens-canis*. The common name, dog's-tooth violet, refers to the bulb, which is elongated like a large canine fang.) DOG'S-TOOTH VIOLET; ADDER'S TONGUE; TROUT LILY; FAWN LILY. Liliaceae (Liliaceae). Some 20 species of perennial herbs with membranous yellow-white bulbs, these elongated and tooth-like, some species producing offsets and stolons. Leaves entire, basal, broad or narrow, mottled white, pink, chocolate or maroon, or plain. Flowers nodding, solitary to many on scape; perianth segments 6, free, sometimes strongly reflexed; stamens 6, free, shorter than petals; stigma unlobed to deeply 3-lobed. Fruit a few-seeded capsule. Spring–early summer. N US; *E. dens-canis* Europe and Asia.

CULTIVATION   From a diversity of habitats, most frequent in moist shaded woodland, but also in more inhospitable, rocky montane places where plants experience extremes of temperature in winter and summer. Some of the Western American natives experience hot dry conditions in summer, although this is usually tempered by shrub or tree cover. All require adequate moisture when in growth and most require at least a vestige of moisture when dormant.

Erythronium spp. are amongst the most elegant and graceful of spring-flowering bulbs, often with attractively marbled foliage, combining exceptional beauty with good cold-tolerance, to −15°C/5°F and below. Most species are suited to shady pockets on the rock garden and for naturalizing in the shrub and mixed border, but are perhaps seen at their best in the dappled sunlight of the woodland garden. Grow in partial shade in a well-drained, humus-rich and moisture-retentive soil; species such as *E.helenae*, *E.grandiflorum* and *E.hendersonii* appreciate perfect drainage and require drier conditions when dormant. *E.dens-canis* is sturdy enough to thrive when naturalized in thin grass. Mulch established clumps annually with leafmould. Propagate by division of established clumps as leaves fade, and re-plant immediately to avoid desiccation of the bulbs. Also by ripe seed sown fresh in a moist and humus rich propagating mix.

E.albidum Nutt. WHITE DOG'S-TOOTH VIOLET; BLONDE LILIAN.
Bulb ovoid, freely offsetting on stolons. Lvs usually mottled in cultivated plants, narrow, to 3.5cm wide. Fls solitary white inside, yellow centre, exterior tinted blue or pink; anth. ivory; stigma trifid. S Canada to Texas. var. **mesochoreum** (Kuerr) Rickett. Lvs narrower than in type, not mottled. No offsets produced. Z4.

E.americanum Ker-Gawl. YELLOW ADDER'S TONGUE; TROUT LILY; AMBERBELL.
Lvs mottled brown and white. Fls solitary, yellow exterior marked brown or purple, interior spotted; anth. to 5cm, yellow, purple or brown; stigma short-lobed. Eastern N America. Z3.

Erythronium   (a) *E.dens-canis*   (b) *E.revolutum*   (c) *E.americanum*   (d) *E.tuolumnense*

E.californicum Purdy. FAWN LILY.
Close to *E.helenae*, *E.oregonum*, *E.citrinum* and *E.howellii*. Lvs mottled brown-green. Fls 1–3, creamy white with ring of orange-brown near centre; anth. white; stigma trifid. California. Z5. *E.californicum* var. *bicolor* Purdy. See *E.helenae*.

E.citrinum S. Wats.
Similar to *E.californicum* but inner seg. yellow-green at centre and basally appendaged, stigma entire. NW California, SW Oregon. Z4.

E.dens-canis L.
Lvs mottled pink and chocolate. Fls solitary, rose to mauve; anth. lilac; stigma lobed. Europe and Asia. 'Album': fls white. 'Carneum': fls flesh pink. 'Frans Hals': lvs mottled; fls large, pale plum. 'Lilac Wonder': fls lavender, to rich purple with brown spot at base. 'Niveum': fls white. 'Pink Perfection': fls large, clear pale pink, early-flowering. 'Purple King': lvs heavily mottled; fls large, rich plum, centre mottled brown and white. 'Rose Queen': lvs mottled; fls deep pink. 'Roseum': fls rose. 'Snowflake': lvs mottled; fls pure white. 'White Splendour': fls white, centre dark, early-flowering. Z3.

E.giganteum Lindl. See *E.grandiflorum*.

E.grandiflorum Pursh (*E.giganteum* Lindl.; *E.obtusatum* Goodd.). AVALANCHE LILY.
Differs from other yellow-fld plain-lvd spp. in its 3-lobed stigma. W US. 'Album' ('Candidum'): fls white, centre yellow. 'Robustum': tall; fls large, gold. Z5.

E.hartwegii S. Wats. See *E.multiscapoideum*.

E.helenae Appleg. (*E.californicum* var. *bicolor* Purdy).
Differs from *E.oregonum* in its narrow or only slightly expanded anth. fil., and from *E.californicum* in its yellow anth. and sharply defined yellow centre. Fls white to yellow. NW California. Z5.

E.hendersonii S. Wats.
Lvs dark green, mottled, margins crisped. Fls to 10 per stem, lilac-pink with purple centre; anth. purple; stigma entire or almost so. SW Oregon, NW California. Z5.

E.howellii S. Wats.
Differs from *E.californicum* in its entire, not trifid stigma. SW California, SW Oregon. Z3.

E.montanum A. Wats. AVALANCHE LILY.
To 30cm or more. Lvs to 15cm, ovate-lanceolate. Fls 1 to several, 38mm, white, orange at base inside, tepals slightly recurved; anth. white, stigma deeply lobed. Western N America (Oregon, Washington, British Columbia). Z5.

E.multiscapoideum (Kellogg) Nels. & Kellogg (*E.hartwegii* S. Wats.; *E.purdyi* hort.).
Lvs mottled. Stolons long, subterranean, bearing many offsets. Scapes several per bulb; fls solitary; perianth seg. white, interior pale green or yellow at base; stigmatic lobes recurved; anth. white. Sierra Nevada. Z5.

E.nudopetalum Appleg. See under *E.tuolumnense*.
E.obtusatum Goodd. See *E.grandiflorum*.

E.oregonum Appleg.
Differs from *E.californicum* in fls with yellow centres, yellow anth. and flattened fil. bases. Oregon to British Columbia. Z5.

E.purdyi hort. See *E.multiscapoideum*.

E.purpurascens S. Wats.
Lvs plain bright green. Fls to 8 per raceme, white or cream with yellow centre flushing purple with age; anth. white; stigma entire. California (Cascade and Sierra Nevada Mts). Z5.

E.revolutum Sm. (*E.smithii* Orcutt).
Lvs mottled, margins crisped. Fls 1–3 per stem, deep pink with yellow centre; anth. yellow, fil. swollen; stigma trifid. N California, Vancouver Is. Z5. 'Citronella': to 25cm; lvs mottled; fls lemon yellow. 'Pagoda': to 40cm, vigorous; lvs marbled bronze; fls pale sulphur yellow, with brown centre, 3–5 per plant; hybrid of 'White Beauty'. 'Pink Beauty': fine rose fls. 'White Beauty': to 15cm; lvs heavily mottled; fls large, white, centre yellow. var. *johnsonii* (Bolander) Purdy: a name applied to forms that probably fall within the range of natural variation of the species, it is maintained in horticulture for plants with dark pink fls. Z5.

E.smithii Orcutt. See *E.revolutum*.

E.tuolumnense Appleg.
Lvs plain green. Fls solitary, small, bright yellow veined green with basally appendaged inner perianth seg.; anth. yellow; stigma entire. C California (Tuolumne region). Sometimes confused with the closely related *E.nudopetalum* Appleg., which lacks basal appendages to the perianth seg. and has white anth. Z5.

E.cultivars. 'Jeanette Brickell': fls white, free-flowering. 'Jeannine': to 30cm; fls large, clear sulphur, central pale brown ring, paler with age. 'Kondo': lvs lightly mottled; fls light yellow, centre brown. 'Miss Jessop': lvs mottled chestnut; fls pale pink.

Eucharis Planch. & Lind. (From Gk *eu*, good, and *charis*, attraction, in reference to the blooms.) Amaryllidaceae. 17 species and 2 natural hybrids of bulbous evergreen perennials. Bulbs tunicate, offsetting vigorously. Leaves persistent, ovate or elliptic to lanceolate, acute or acuminate, thin, sometimes obscurely plicate, glossy, often undulate; base narrowing to a long, dorsally sulcate petiole. Flowers in an umbel atop a solid, glaucous scape; spathe valves 2, ovate-lanceolate, green; flowers 2–10, pedicellate, drooping or decurved, each with a lanceolate bracteole, white, somewhat fleshy, green-white to white or ivory, often fragrant; perianth tube short-cylindrical, somewhat ribbed, dilating abruptly above its midpoint, sometimes tinged green at the base; perianth lobes 6, in 2 rows, spreading, the outer longer and narrower than the inner; stamens 6, broadened at the bases and fused to form a cup; style 1. Fruit a 3-lobed capsule, green or bright orange; seeds few per locule, shiny black, brown or blue. W Amazon and adjacent E Andes (Guatemala to Bolivia). Z10.

CULTIVATION *Eucharis* usually produces umbels of beautiful, white, funnel-shaped flowers in early summer. They are frost-tender, and in temperate zones must be grown under glass. Grow in direct sunlight or dappled shade, with a minimum temperature of 10°C/50°F, in a fibrous loam-based medium with added leafmould and sharp sand, with the nose of the bulb just covered. Keep dry but not arid until growth commences early in the year, then water moderately, applying a balanced liquid fertilizer weekly when in full growth. *E.subedentata* may be moved, in pots, out of doors for the summer to ripen in full sun. Propagate by offsets, either in autumn or when repotting mother plants, every third or fourth year; grow on at 15°C/60°F until established.

E.amazonica Lind. ex Planch.
Bulb to 6cm diam., tunics brown, neck to 4.5cm. Lvs to
40×18cm, 2–4, long-elliptic, tip acuminate, base subcordate,
obscurely plicate, coarsely undulate; petiole to 30cm. Scape
to 70cm; spathe valves to 6cm; fls 4–8, fragrant, pendulous;
pedicels to 15mm; tube white, curved, to 6×2cm at throat,
lobes ovate, spreading to 9cm diam., white; staminal cup to
14×30mm, cylindrical, dentate; style white, protruding by up
to 1.5cm from the cup. NE Peru.

E.amazonica hort. non Lind. See *E.× grandiflora*.

E.bakeriana N.E. Br. (*Urceolina bakeriana* (N.E. Br.)
Traub).
Bulb to 5cm diam., tunics brown. Lvs to 55×20cm, 2–4, elliptic, rather succulent, smooth. Scape to 80cm; spathe valves to
38×10mm; fls to 10, fragrant; pedicels to 30mm; tube to
40mm, lobes spreading to 6cm diam.; staminal cup to
16×15mm, subcylindrical to campanulate, dentate; style just
exceeding the anth. Capsule to 2×3cm, bright orange, leathery; seeds black. Peru.

E.bouchei Woodson & Allen (*Urceolina bouchei* (Woodson
& Allen) Traub).
Bulb subglobose, to 4cm diam., tunics brown, neck to 25mm.
Lvs to 25×10cm, 1–3, broadly elliptic, slightly succulent,
smooth, seldom undulate; petiole to 25cm. Scape to 55cm;
spathe valves to 3.5×1cm; fls 3–6, pendent, unscented;
pedicels to 10mm; tube to 45mm, curved, lobes to 32×17mm;
staminal cup to 12×15mm, subcylindrical, dentate or divided,
tinged green at base; stamens to 6mm; style exceeding anth.
by up to 1cm. Capsule to 2×3cm, bright orange, leathery;
seeds black, to 1cm. C America.

E.candida Planch. & Lind. (*Urceolina candida* (Planch. &
Lind.) Traub).
Bulb globose, to 4cm, sometimes stoloniferous. Lvs to
35×11.5cm, 1 or 2, elliptic, dark green above, deeply plicate,
coarsely undulate; petiole to 30cm. Scape to 60cm; bracts to
45×6mm; fls to 10, unscented; pedicels to 20mm; tube to
35mm, lobes spreading, to 6cm diam., sometimes recurved;

staminal cup to 11×16mm, lobed or, rarely, dentate, spotted
green or yellow-green below each stamen; style exceeding
anth. by up to 1cm. Capsule to 2.5×3cm, bright orange, leathery; seeds 1cm, black. Ecuador, N Peru, SE Colombia.

E.× grandiflora Planch. & Lind. (*Urceolina grandiflora*
(Planch. & Lind.) Traub; *E.amazonica* hort. non Lind.;
E.mastersii Bak.; *E.lowii* Bak.). AMAZON LILY; EUCHARIST
LILY; STAR OF BETHLEHEM.
A naturally occurring hybrid involving *E.amazonica*. Bulb to
5cm diam., tunics light brown, neck to 4cm. Lvs to 33×16cm,
1–3, ovate or elliptic, deeply plicate, undulate; petiole to
36mm. Scape to 50cm; spathe valves to 5×2cm; fls 2–6, declinate, fragrant; pedicel to 7mm; tube curved, to 55mm, green
at the base, lobes to 40mm, ovate, undulate, slightly overlapping; staminal cup to 7×25mm, dentate; style far exceeding
cup, green. Plant functionally sterile. Colombia.

E.lowii Bak. See *E.× grandiflora*.

E.mastersii Bak. See *E.× grandiflora*.

E.sanderi Bak. (*Urceolina sanderi* (Bak.) Traub).
Bulb ovoid, to 5cm diam., tunics light brown. Lvs to
37×17cm, ovate or elliptic, base subcordate, deeply plicate,
bright green above, undulate; petiole to 5cm. Scape to 55cm;
spathe valves to 6.5cm; fls 2 or 3, subsessile, fragrant, declinate; tube to 6cm, curved, base tinged green, lobes to 3.7cm,
somewhat overlapping, subequal; staminal cup to 24mm
diam., fused to upper portion of tube, and protruding slightly;
style far exceeding cup, white or green. Capsule green. W
Colombia.

E.subedentata (Bak.) Benth. & Hook. (*Caliphruria subedentata* Bak.; *Urceolina subedentata* (Bak.) Traub).
Lvs 4, 21×12.5cm, oblong, coriaceous; petioles to 30cm,
channelled. Scape to 45cm; fls 6–8, declinate, funnel-shaped,
to 4cm across; tube 3.5cm, urceolate in upper third, lobes
2cm, apex slightly recurved, corona absent; stamens half
length lobes, fil. with entire or dentate enlargement, style
included, stigma lobed. Colombia.

Eucodonia Hanst. Gesneriaceae. 2 species of small, saxicolous, perennial herbs. Stems somewhat succulent;
rhizomes scaly. Leaves in pseudowhorls. Flowers solitary, long-stalked; calyx small; corolla campanulate to
funnelform. C America.

CULTIVATION As for *Achimenes*.

E. andrieuxii (DC.) Wiehler (*Achimenes andrieuxii* DC.;
Gloxinia micrantha Martens & Gal.).
Stems pink-tomentose, short, few-leaved. Leaves elliptic, to
12.5×6.5cm, crenate, light-pubescent above, densely pale-
tomentose beneath. Flowers on peduncles to 6.5cm; corolla
violet, throat white and purple-spotted, corolla tube to 2cm
long, 1.5cm diam. near the limb. S Mexico.

Eucomis L'Hérit. (From Gk *eukomos*, lovely-haired, referring to the crown of bracts at the apex of the inflorescence.) PINEAPPLE LILY. Liliaceae (Hyacinthaceae). Some 15 species of perennial bulbs, related to *Scilla* and *Ornithogalum*. Bulb large, ovoid, with shiny green or purple outer layer. Leaves in a basal rosette, strap-shaped or wider, glossy, glabrous, light green flecked purple, appearing with the flowers. Scape terete; inflorescence cylindrical, a dense raceme of star-shaped green flowers, backed by bracts and crowned by a coma of leafy bracts, resembling a pineapple; perianth fused at base, with 6 oblong segments; stamens 6, usually shorter than perianth, with filaments broadened and joined in shallow cup below; ovary rounded to obovoid, 3-angled, normally green. S Tropical Africa, mainly S Africa. Z8.

CULTIVATION Bold, late summer-flowering bulbs with fresh, green, strapshaped leaves. The stout flower stalk bears a cylinder of starry blooms capped by a tuft of leafy bracts, reminiscent of *Fritillaria imperialis*, or a pineapple. *Eucomis* spp. are suitable for a warm glasshouse (4–10°C/39–50°F minimum when dormant, 10°C/50°F when in growth). In mild areas, more frost-hardy species can be tried outside and lifted in winter or protected with a heavy mulch of bracken or dry leaves. Plant about 15cm/6in. deep in autumn, in a sunny position in rich, well-drained soil. In pots, grow one bulb to a 12.5cm/15in. pot or three bulbs to larger sizes, with bulb tips just showing at surface of medium. Give bright, filtered light and good ventilation. Water sparingly when dormant, plentifully while in growth. Propagate from seed sown in spring for flowering plants in 2–5 years, or alternatively from offsets or leafy tips of flowering shoots potted in warmth in autumn.

E.albomarginata Barnes. See *E.autumnalis* ssp. *clavata*.

E.amaryllidifolia (Bak.) See *E.autumnalis* ssp. *amaryllidifolia*.

E.autumnalis (Mill.) Chitt.
To 50cm. Bulb 5–10cm long. Lvs to 45cm, linear or lanceolate to narrow-ovate, margins wavy. Raceme 5–15cm; perianth white or olive green at first, becoming deeper green; coma bracts 10–45, oblong to lanceolate, 2.5–8cm with wavy edges. Late summer. ssp. *autumnalis*. (*E.undulata* Ait.). Bulb globose. Lvs sometimes club-shaped in outline, to 30cm. Raceme to 30cm; perianth lobes to 1.3cm; coma bracts oblong 3–7cm. S Africa, Zimbabwe, Malawi. ssp. *amaryllidifolia* (Bak.) Reyneke (*E.amaryllidifolia* Bak.). Lvs linear to 50×4cm. Infl. loosely obconical, 6–23cm; raceme dense, 5–8cm; perianth lobes 6–8mm; coma bracts 13–20, lanceolate, 2.5–8cm. Late summer. S Africa. ssp. *clavata* (Bak.) Reyneke (*E.clavata* Bak.; *E.robusta* Bak.; *E.albomarginata* Barnes). Lvs to 60×10cm. Fl. stalk cylindric, 7–13cm; raceme 8–15cm; perianth lobes 1.2–1.7cm; coma bracts 15–30, ovate, 5–8cm. S Africa, Swaziland, Botswana.

E.bicolor Bak.
Lvs oblong 30–50×8–10cm, undulate. Scape cylindrical to 60cm, often flecked maroon; perianth lobes with distinct purple margin; coma bracts 30–40, ovate acuminate, 5–8cm, margins purple, closely undulate. Late summer. S Africa. 'Alba': perianth uniformly green-white.

E.clavata Bak. See *E.autumnalis* ssp. *clavata*.

E.comosa (Houtt.) Wehrh. (*E.punctata* L'Hérit.).
Bulb 7cm diam. Lvs oblong to lanceolate, to 70×6cm with numerous purple spots beneath, margins undulate. Scape 45–70cm, spotted dark purple; raceme to 30cm; perianth lobes purple; ovary purple; coma bracts lanceolate, 8–20, to 8cm, margins sometimes purple. Late summer. S Africa. var. *striata* (Houtt.) Wehrh. Leaf and scape spotting merges to form stripes.

E.nana Ait.
Bulb 5cm long. Lvs broad-lanceolate, to 60cm, base flushed purple below. Raceme 7–10cm; fls green maroon on scape stalk, spotted purple. Summer. S Africa.

E.pallidiflora Bak. (*E.punctata* var. *concolor* Bak.).
Bulb to 10cm diam. Lvs ensiform, to 70×12cm, margins tightly crispate. Scape thick, 45–75cm; raceme 24–43cm; perianth white-green, lobes to 1.6cm; coma bracts to 20, narrow-elliptic, acuminate, 3–4cm, crispate. Summer. S Africa.

E.pole-evansii N.E. Br.
Similar to *E.pallidiflora* but has larger lvs 75–120× 10–17.5cm, taller scape 90–180cm, and larger coma bracts. Possibly a vigorous variant of *E.pallidiflora*.

E.punctata var. *concolor* Bak. See *E.pallidiflora*.

E.robusta Bak. See *E.autumnalis* ssp. *clavata*.

E.undulata Ait. See *E.autumnalis* ssp. *autumnalis*.

E.zambesiaca Bak.
Bulb globose, large. Lvs 30–60×3.5–5cm, lorate, subobtuse, broadest above middle, tapering to base, margin more or less flat, not spotted or striped beneath. Scape 15–25cm; raceme 10–20cm, dense, oblong; pedicels short, erecto-patent; perianth green, lobes to 1.5cm; coma bracts small, ovate. Malawi.

Eucrosia Ker-Gawl. (From Gk *eu*, good, and *krossos*, a fringe, in reference to the staminal cup.) Amaryllidaceae. 7 species of bulbous perennial herbs; bulbs usually globose, tunicate, often large, solitary or offsetting vigorously. Leaves hysteranthous, ovate or elliptic, long-petiolate. Inflorescence an umbel borne on a glaucous, more or less solid scape, and initially enclosed by 2 ovate-lanceolate spathe valves; flowers pendulous, showy, unscented, pedicellate, each subtended by a linear bracteole; perianth narrowly campanulate, zygomorphic, with 6 subequal lobes in 2 rows, fused basally to form a tube; stamens 6, far exceeding the perianth, one usually shorter than the others; style exceeding the stamens; ovary trilocular, ovules 20–25 per cell. Fruit a glaucous turbinate capsule, ripening brown; seeds many, flat, dark brown. Ecuador and Peru. Z10.

CULTIVATION *E.aurantiaca* is rare and beautiful bulb, grown for its nodding umbels of delicately fringed orange-yellow flowers. Reduce water after flowering, and keep dry but not arid when at rest. Otherwise, cultivate as for *Hippeastrum*.

E.aurantiaca (Bak.) Pax (*Callipsyche aurantiaca* Bak.; *E.morleyana* Rose; *E.eucrosioides* var. *rauhinia* (Traub) Traub).
Bulb to 10cm diam., neck to 8cm, tunics brown. Lvs to 40×22cm, 2, ovate-elliptic, acute or acuminate, coarsely undulate; petiole to 35cm. Scape to 90cm; spathe valves to 3cm, lanceolate; fls 7–13, held horizontally; pedicels to 33mm; perianth to 4cm, yellow, to orange or pink, laterally compressed, tube to 7mm, green at the base, lobes to 2.9cm, spreading dorsally and ventrally, the 3 inner lobes forming a ventral lip-like structure; stamens to 11cm, long-declinate, ascending in the distal quarter, green; style to 11cm, green. Capsule to 30×22mm diam.; seeds many, to 6.5mm. Ecuador.

E.bicolor Ker-Gawl.
Bulb to 4.5cm diam., neck to 5cm, tunics light brown. Lvs to 24×11cm, 1–2, elliptic, short-acuminate, bright green and striate above, pale green beneath, slightly undulate; petiole to 1'/cm. Scape to 70cm; spathe valves to 4cm; fls 5–10; pedicels to 38mm, suberect; perianth strongly zygomorphic, spreading to 16mm wide, tube to 10mm, green at the base, lobes to 2.6cm, pale red tipped and medially stained yellow, 2 ascending and the others spreading laterally; stamens to 6.5cm, long-declinate, fused below into a staminal cup, yellow or red, ascending in distal quarter; style to 8cm, yellow. Capsule to 26×16mm; seeds to 1cm. Ecuador, Peru.

E.eucrosioides (Herb.) Pax (*Callipsyche eucrosioides* Herb.; *Callipsyche mexicana* Roem.).
Bulb to 7cm diam., neck to 46mm, tunics brown. Lvs to 26×21cm, 2, elliptic-ovate, obscurely plicate, dark green above, pale green beneath, coarsely undulate; petiole to 25cm. Scape to 73cm; spathe valves to 30mm; fls 7–12; pedicels to 27mm; perianth to 3cm, tube to 0.5cm, constricted at base and apex, lobes spreading to 1.4cm dorsiventrally, somewhat compressed laterally, keeled, green at the base and along the heel, otherwise orange-scarlet; stamens to 9cm, green, strongly curved, ascending in the distal quarter; style to 10cm, green. Capsule to 14×27.5mm; seeds 25 or more per locule, to 13.2mm, black-brown. SW Ecuador, N Peru.

E.eucrosioides var. *rauhinia* (Traub) Traub. See *E.aurantiaca*.

E.morleyana Rose. See *E.aurantiaca*.

E.stricklandii (Bak.) Meerow (*Phaedranassa eucrosioides* (Bak.) Benth. & Hook. f.).
Bulb 4×3cm, neck 2cm, brown. Lvs 1–2, elliptic, 21–23×11cm, short-acuminate, base shortly attenuate, smooth, bright green above; petiole 10–13cm. Scape 40–45cm; spathe valves lanceolate, 2cm; pedicels 1cm; fls 6–7, 3–4cm long, perpendicular to scape or declinate; perianth funnel-shaped-tubular, red or pink, tube subcylindric, 1cm, lobes lanceolate-spathulate, subequal, to 18mm; stamens shortly exserted. Ecuador.

Eustephia Cav. (From Gk *eu*, well, and *stephos*, crown, in reference to the circle of stamens.) Amaryllidaceae. 6 species of bulbous herbs, closely related to *Phaedranassa* but with sessile leaves and winged filaments. Bulbs tunicated. Leaves basal, erect, linear to narrow-lanceolate. Scape erect; flowers drooping, in an umbel, red or green; perianth tube short, narrowly funnel-shaped, lobes 6, long, erect; stamens 6, filaments winged; style 1; ovary 3-celled. Fruit a capsule. Andes. Z10.

CULTIVATION *Eustephia* spp. are grown for their drooping umbels of tubular flowers: those of *E.coccinea* are extremely handsome, being a warm bright red, shaded green at the base, with each segment tipped green. They are suitable for outdoor cultivation in frost-free zones but in temperate zones are amenable to pot cultivation in the cool to intermediate glasshouse or conservatory. Cultivate as for *Phaedranassa*.

E.coccinea Cav. (*E.macleanica* Herb.; *Phaedranassa rubroviridis* Bak.)
Lvs to 24×0.6cm, 3 or 4, narrow-lanceolate, acuminate, bright green. Scape slender, ancipitous, 30cm; spathe valves lanceolate; fls horizontal or drooping, to 3cm long, 2–8; pedicels to 2.5cm; perianth lobes to 3.5cm, bright red, with pale margins, green-tipped, upper quarter with a green keel; fil. white, expanding to form a corona, anth. yellow; style white. Peruvian Andes.

E.macleanica Herb. See *E.coccinea*.

E.jujuyensis hort.
Undescribed plant known in horticulture by this name. Bulb elongate, black-tunicate. Scape 45–60cm; pedicels short; fls brilliant orange-red. N Argentina (Jujuy Province).

E.pamiana Stapf.
Lvs to 35×0.5cm, about 6, erect, arching, linear, narrowly channelled, glabrous, green, sheaths streaked red. Scape to 40cm, cylindrical; fls 6, to 3cm, nodding; pedicels red or purple, to 4cm, perianth lobes to 35×7mm, united at the base for 5mm, clavate-spathulate, pink at base, green outside and above with red tips; fil. to 4.5mm, anth. purple; style 3cm; stigma obscurely 3-lobed. Argentina.

E.yuyuensis hort. See *E.jujuyensis*.

Ferraria Burm. (For Giovanni Battista Ferrari (1584–1655), Italian botanist.) Iridaceae. 10 species of small, cormous perennial herbs. Basal leaves few, linear-lanceolate, somewhat rigid, stem leaves shorter, 2-ranked, ovate-lanceolate, clasping, becoming reduced to bracts toward inflorescence. Flowering stems branched, bearing short cymes with many sheathing bracts; flowers short-lived, malodorous, yellow, red-brown, green or purple, variously marked; perianth radially symmetric, segments 6, ovate-lanceolate, more or less equal, spreading or slightly deflexed, long-clawed; filaments largely united forming a tube, anthers oblong-subulate; style branches expanded, rather petal-like, fringed. Fruit a slender capsule. Spring. Tropical & S Africa. Z9.

CULTIVATION   *F.crispa* has been known in cultivation for over 300 years; it is grown for its curious flowers, mottled in subtle shades of olive green and dark brown-purple, with extraordinary crisped and waved edges to the petals. Like most members of the genus, it is pollinated by flies and somewhat malodorous. *Ferraria* ssp. are frequently found in sand and shale, often in coastal areas and to altitudes of 500m/1625ft. *F.crispa* will withstand temperatures to about –5°C/23°F, but in zones at the limit of hardiness outdoor cultivation is reliable only in areas that do not experience late frosts. Plant deeply (15cm/6in.) in a warm, sunny and sheltered site with a protective mulch of bracken litter in winter.

In cool temperate zones *Ferraria* is more commonly grown under glass; under natural conditions the corms pull themselves down deeply into the soil and they are best planted directly into the greenhouse border, otherwise use deep pots. Grow in direct sunlight in a well drained, moderately fertile, loam-based potting mix with additional sharp sand; maintain a minimum temperature of 10°C/50°F when in growth. Water plentifully and apply dilute liquid feed when in growth, reducing water gradually after flowering until leaves wither; keep completely dry when dormant.

Propagate by seed sown in late summer or autumn in a sandy propagating mix with warmth and bright light or from offsets.

F.crispa Burm. (*F.undulata* L.).
Basal lvs 12–30cm, ensiform to linear-lanceolate, falcate, base sheathing, margins somewhat wavy. Flowering stem 18–45cm; cymes subtended by carinate, leafy bracts to 4×3cm; perianth seg. to 2.2cm, deep chestnut brown spotted and lined in a paler shade or yellow to tan spotted and lined brown, blade oblong, strongly undulate, spreading, claw erect; style branches long-fringed. S Africa (Cape Province).

F.divaricata Sw.
Basal lvs many, to 30cm, erect or spreading. Flowering stem to 20cm+, covered by leaf-bases; fls yellow, green grey-green, orange-yellow or brown, often marked purple-green or purple-blue, sweetly scented or malodorous, segments with crisped margins. S Africa (Cape Province).

F.ferrariola (Jacq.) Willd.
Lvs to 45cm. Flowering stem to 30cm, erect, flexuous, slender, occasionally branched; fls 5–6cm diam., green-white to green-blue, sweetly scented; perianth cup 1cm diam., 2cm deep; outer seg. to 4cm, with dark streaks; inner seg. to 1cm, narrow; style to 2cm+, branches bifid, pale-hairy. S Africa (Cape Province).

F.undulata L. See *F.crispa*.

Freesia Ecklon ex Klatt. (For Friedrich Heinrich Theodore Freese (d1876), a pupil of Ecklon.) Iridaceae. 11 species of perennial herbs. Corm more or less conical with reticulate tunic. Leaves iris-like, arranged in a fan. Flowering stem simple or branched, flexuous; erect, prostrate or inclined; inflorescence a horizontal, secund spike; bracts green or scarious; flowers more or less funnel- or goblet-shaped, irregular, sometimes only slightly so, sometimes 2-lipped, white, yellow or occasionally pink, sometimes flushed purple; perianth tube slender at base, widening abruptly in upper part; tepals 6, subequal or upper 3 distinctly larger than lower 3; stamens inserted on tube where it widens; style filiform with 3 deeply forked branches. S Africa, mainly Cape Province. Z9.

CULTIVATION   Valued for their usually fragrant blooms which make beautiful cut flowers, *Freesia* spp. are frost-tender bulbs, grown in the cool glasshouse for winter and early spring flowers or, using prepared bulbs, in the open garden for flowers in summer. Grow indoor bulbs in a medium-fertility loam-based mix with additional sharp sand, at 5–8cm/2–3in. spacings in prepared beds, boxes or pots, planting in succession from late summer through to winter. Water and store in the frame or cold glasshouse (5°C/40°F) and cover with a 3cm/1.5in. layer of coir, with a top dressing of gift. Gradually increase water as growth proceeds, and when corms show seven leaves raise the temperature to 10°C/50°F, provide full light and good ventilation, and feed fortnightly with a dilute liquid feed as flower buds show. Provide the support of pea sticks, slender canes or, in beds, netting. Temperatures above 15°C/60°F will result in spindly plants with quickly fading blooms. Water plentifully when in full growth and reduce as plants die back to keep completely dry when dormant; lift and store cool and dry until the following season. In mild, essentially frost-free areas, corms may be planted directly into the open ground in late summer/early autumn into fertile sandy soils in a sunny and sheltered position; in cooler zones, plant prepared bulbs in spring and lift and store as foliage fades after flowering in summer. Propagate by pre-soaked seed in the cool glasshouse or cold frame, or by offsets in autumn. Prone to aphid, red spider mite, gladiolus dry rot fungus, and fusarium wilt.

F.alba (G.L. Mey.) Gumbl. (*F.refracta* var. *alba* G.L. Mey.).
Corm conical, about 10mm wide at base. Lvs linear, of similar length to stem. Stem 12–40cm, usually branched, erect; spike 2–8-fld; fls 25–60mm, erect, almost regular, sweetly scented, white, sometimes flushed with purple outside and lined with purple in throat, sometimes with a yellow mark on lowest tepal; tube 15–40mm long; tepals spreading, upper tepals 15–18×8–12mm, oblong or ovate, lower slightly

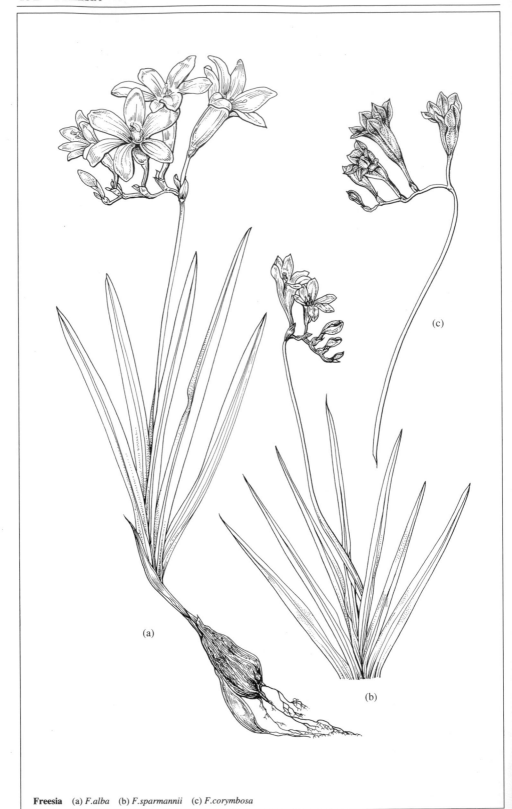

Freesia (a) *F.alba* (b) *F.sparmannii* (c) *F.corymbosa*

smaller, anth. 6–9mm. Winter–spring. W Cape.

F.armstrongii Wats. See *F.corymbosa*.

F.corymbosa (Burm. f.) N.E. Br. (*F.odorata* Ecklon ex Klatt; *F.armstrongii* Wats.).
Corms to 2.5cm wide at base. Lvs 10–20cm, linear, acute. Stem erect, to 50cm with several branches; spikes 3–10-fld; fls 25–35cm, scented or unscented, ivory, pale yellow with the lower tepals bright yellow, or pink with a yellow throat (this form was known as *F.armstrongii*); tube about 20mm; tepals unequal, the topmost to 12×12mm, cordate at base, hooded, the upper laterals to 9×6mm, ovate, the 3 lower to 7×7mm, cordate at base. Usually late winter–spring. W Cape.

F.× hybrida L.H. Ball. See *F.cultivars*.
F.× kewensis hort. See *F.cultivars*.

F.leichtlinii Klatt.
Corms 8–10mm wide. Lvs usually slightly shorter than stem, to 8mm wide, usually erect or suberect. Stem usually 8–20cm high, occasionally more. Simple or with 1–2 branches; spike 2–8-fld; fls 25–40mm, erect, bilabiate, scented, cream or pale yellow, the lower tepals orange yellow, the upper tepals sometimes flushed with purple-brown on outside; tube 15–25mm, bent at junction of narrow and wide parts; uppermost tepal 14–18×13mm, hooded, upper laterals to 8mm wide, lower tepals to 15×11mm, ovate, the edges curved up. Late winter–early spring. S Cape, from Mossel Bay to Cape Agulhas.

F.muirii N.E. Br. See *F.leichtlinii*.
F.odorata Ecklon ex Klatt. See *F.corymbosa*.
F.× ragioneri hort. See *F.cultivars*.

F.refracta (Jacq.) Klatt.
Corms 1.5–2cm diam. Lvs 15–30×0.5–1cm, linear. Stems (8–)20–45cm; spike 5–12-fld; fls 25–40mm long, bilabiate, with a spicy scent, pale yellow, yellow-brown, green or purple with orange marks on lower tepals, veined with purple in throat; tube 16–24mm; tepals unequal, upper 3, 11–14mm,

the uppermost 8–11mm wide, the laterals narrower, lower tepals horizontal or recurved, to 11×9mm, the margins curved up. Winter–early spring. S & W Cape.

F.refracta 'Leichtlinii'. See *F.leichtlinii*.
F.refracta var. *alba* G.L. Mey. See *F.alba*.

F.sparmannii (Thunb.) N.E. Br.
Corms about 1cm diam. Lvs erect, 10–16mm, linear, acute. Stems 12–18cm; spikes 3–8-fld; fls 30–40mm, scentless, tube and outside of tepals purple-flushed, inside white with yellow spot on lower tepals at junction of narrow and wide parts of tube; tube 20–27mm; tepals unequal, the topmost 11×7mm, obovate, the others to 9mm. Early spring. W Cape.

F.× tubergenii hort. See *F.cultivars*.

F.cultivars. Although species of *Freesia* were first grown in Europe in the mid-18th century, selective hybridization did not start until late 19th century, between the yellow-flowered *F.leichtlinii* and the white *F.alba*. The florist's freesias are complex hybrids involving *F.alba*, *F.corymbosa*, *F.refracta* and *F.leichtlinii*. L.H. Bailey grouped them under the hybrid epithet *F.× hybrida*; several hybrids within the complex but of more determined parentage had also been named, including *F.× kewensis* hort., an accidental cross between *F.leichtlinii* and a pink form of *F.corymbosa* that arose toward the end of the 19th century, and *F.× ragioneri*, a strain of hybrids raised in Italy and derived from *F.alba* and *F.leichtlinii*, and *F.× tubergenii*, derived from *F.corymbosa* and *F.alba*. The cultivars range in height from 10cm to 30cm, in habit from the neat and tufted to the tall and graceful, in inflorescence from short and semi-erect to long, sparsely branched and horizontal; the flowers may be single or 'double', scarcely to sweetly scented, and vary in colour from silvery white (e.g. 'Miranda') to ivory (i.e. 'Fantasy', with fls double), yellow or bronze; from soft pink (e.g. 'Aphrodite': fls double) to red (e.g. 'Pallas': fls fragrant) and mauve (e.g. 'Romany': fls double; 'Apothoase': fls pale mauve, throat white), and blue and indigo (e.g. 'Uchida': fls semi-double with a yellow throat).

Fritillaria L. (From Lat. *fritillus*, a dice-box, referring to the shape of the capsules, or alternatively to the chequered pattern on the flowers of many species, reminiscent of the traditional decoration on a dice-box.) Liliaceae (Liliaceae). Some 100 species of perennial herbs. Bulbs generally globose or ellipsoid, of 2 or more closely wrapped thick scales, occasionally with a thin, white, papery tunic, or of separate thick scales, with numerous white, rice-like bulbils at base. Leaves lanceolate or linear, a solitary basal leaf and several usually alternate, occasionally opposite or whorled stem leaves. Flowers usually pendulous, tubular to campanulate, occasionally conic or saucer-shaped; bracts alternate, or whorled, similar to leaves, but smaller; tepals 6, free, in 2 whorls, those of inner whorls broader, often tessellated; nectaries more or less conspicuous, 1 per tepal; stamens 6, with more or less basifixed anthers, rarely versatile; style solitary, more or less equal to stamens, entire or bifid. Capsule usually erect, flat-topped, sometimes 6-winged, the style deciduous; seeds usually flat. Temperate regions of Northern Hemisphere, particularly Mediterranean, SW Asia (mts), Western N America. All spp. described are spring-flowering unless otherwise specified.

CULTIVATION   *Fritillaria* is found in a variety of habitats in the Northern hemisphere. Many species from eastern Mediterranean regions through to central Asia live in dry, rocky scrub, such as *F.assyriaca*, *F.carica* and *F.raddeana*; some from these regions are found at higher altitudes in mountains and on stony hillsides congregating around late snow patches; these include *F.pinardii*, *F.armena* and *F.aurea*. Some are alpine or subalpine, e.g. *F.collina*, *F.tubaeformis* and *F.cirrhosa*, found in mountain pasture sometimes at the snow line. Japanese and Chinese spp. such as *F.verticillata* are found in open meadow and woodland, and some have developed leaf tendrils to climb through shrubs. Many Californian spp. occur on heavy, moisture-retentive clay soils, receiving abundant moisture in spring and early summer in growth, then baking during the hot summer.

Their pendent bell-shaped flowers range in size and colour from the deep mahogany reds, oranges and rich yellows of the tall, sturdy *F.imperialis* and its cvs, and the bloomed, deep purple of *F.persica*, to the tiny and exquisite blue-purple of *F.ehrhartii* and the remarkable blue-green flowers of *F.sewerzowii*. The colour range includes a large number of subtle chocolate browns, purples and yellow-greens, and many have chequered flowers, like those of *F.meleagris*.

F.meleagris, F.michailovskyi, F.persica and *F.pyrenaica*; these will thrive with full sun or light shade, in moderately fertile soils with good drainage that receive adequate moisture when plants are in leaf and do not become baked dry in summer. Those with large hollow-crowned bulbs, such as *F.imperialis*, which may hold water and rot, should be planted on their sides on a bed of sharp sand. *F.camschatcensis* and *F.imperialis* perform best on richer soils. *F.latifolia* requires a nutrient rich, leafy soil.

F.meleagris, from rich alluvial soils in flood plains and fenlands, often in very alkaline conditions, is suitable for naturalizing in grass and on banks where there is sufficient moisture when in leaf, providing that the first lawn cut does not occur until the leaves have died back in summer. Flowering is often poor in seasons following a dry spring and summer.

Most are excellent potplants for the cold glasshouse or bulb frame; a number positively require protected cultivation, especially the very small species (5–15cm/2–6in.) which are of doubtful hardiness, those which flower very early in the season (leaves and flowers may be prone to frosting), and those from hot, dry regions whose dormancy requirements are more easily accommodated with protection. Although these last require warm, dry dormancy, they should not become so dry as to risk desiccation. Grow with bright indirect or filtered light with good ventilation, in a low-fertility, loam-based mix with additional grit or sharp sand; for *F.collina* and *F.tubaeformis* add leafmould to the potting mix. The sturdy *F.crassifolia* requires a more fertile mix. Water plentifully when in full growth. Care should be taken when potting certain species, particularly those from California, which tend to form hundreds of rice-grain bulbils when moved and then take several years to flower; in general the bulbs of *Fritillaria* are fragile and succumb quickly to bruising and desiccation, so handle carefully and plant as soon as possible on receipt.

Propagate from seed when ripe or in spring, in a loam-based propagating mix with additional sharp sand; germination may take six months. Give seedlings a minimum of 5°C/40°F during the first winter. Also from rice grain or offset bulbils.

F.acmopetala Boiss.
Bulb to 3cm diam., often with subsidiary bulblets. Stem 15–45cm. Lvs 7–11, alternate, linear. Fls solitary or occasionally 3 together, broadly campanulate; tepals 2.5–4cm, lanceolate to oblanceolate, inner acute, recurved at apex, green with ferruginous markings (not tessellations); nectaries 5–11×2–4mm, 5mm above base of tepal, ovate to ovate-lanceolate, green or tinged black; style 8–12mm, smooth, 3-fid, branches 3–5mm. Capsule wingless. W Asia, E Mediterranean (Cyprus, Lebanon, Syria, S Turkey). Z7.

F.affinis (Schult.) Sealy (*F.lanceolata* Pursh; *F.mutica* Lindl.). RICE-GRAIN FRITILLARY.
Bulb to 2cm diam., with numerous subsidiary basal bulblets. Stem 15–120cm. Lvs 3–15, in 1–3 whorls, linear-lanceolate to ovate. Fls 1–4, occasionally to 12, in a raceme, pendulous, campanulate; bracts 1 per flower; tepals 2–4cm, lime-green to purple, tessellated; nectaries 1–2cm, triangular to ovate-lanceolate, prominent; style 3-fid, branches recurved. Capsule 6-winged. Late winter to late spring. NW America. Z5.

F.agrestis Greene. STINK BELLS.
Bulb composed of several large, succulent scales, to 2.5cm diam. Stem 30–60cm. Lvs 5–11×0.8–2cm, 5–12, crowded towards base, oblong-lanceolate to linear-lanceolate, glaucous. Fls 1–5, occasionally to 8, campanulate, with very unpleasant odour; tepals 25–30×7–10mm, white tinged green without, more or less purple-brown spotted within; nectaries oblong, small, green, conspicuous; style 8mm, smooth, deeply 3-fid. Capsule 4-angled, to 2cm. SW US (California). Z8.

F.alburyana Rix.
Bulb to 2cm diam., often with subsidiary bulblets. Stem 4–10cm. Lvs 3–4, alternate, lanceolate. Fls 1–2, erect, horizontal or somewhat pendulous, cupular to almost flat; tepals 2–3cm, pale pink, tessellated; nectaries 1mm, basal, elliptic, green; anth. semi-versatile; style 9–15mm, slender, smooth, 3-fid, branches 1–2mm. Capsule wingless. NE Turkey. Z7.

F.alfredae Post. ssp. **alfredae**.
Restricted to Lebanon and not in cultivation; it is a smaller, more slender plant than the cultivated ssp. described below. ssp. **glaucoviridis** (Turrill) Rix (*F.glaucoviridis* Turrill). Bulb to 3cm diam. Stem 10–35cm. Lvs 9–11, often opposite, lowest oblanceolate to ovate. Fls 1–3, narrowly campanulate; bracts usually in a whorl of 3; tepals 12–30mm, inner spathulate, green and glaucous without, lime-green within, unmarked; nectaries 5×2mm, basal, ovate, green; style to

10×3mm, stout, papillose, undivided or 3-lobed. Capsule broadly 6-winged. S Turkey. Z8.

F.armena Boiss.
Bulb to 1cm diam., globose, of 2 small scales. Stem 10–20cm, very slender. Lvs 3–4, alternate, lower lanceolate and amplexicaul, upper linear. Fls solitary, conic, rather small; tepals to 2cm, elliptic-lanceolate, ciliate at tip, deep red to dark purple-brown, tessellated; nectaries 3–5mm, basal, oblong to linear-lanceolate, small; hirsute; style to 10×3mm at most, slender, papillose, entire or 3-fid at apex, branches 1–2mm. NE Turkey. Z7.

F.askabadensis Micheli. See *F.raddeana*.

F.assyriaca Bak.
Bulb to 3cm diam., generally with bulblets or stolons. Stem 4–20cm, to 35cm in fruit. Lvs 3–9cm×3–18mm, 4–6, occasionally to 12, alternate, linear, often canaliculate. Fls 1–2, occasionally to 5, narrowly campanulate; tepals 12–25mm, obtuse or acute, tinged dull green or purple-brown; nectaries 2–4×1mm, 1mm above base of tepals, linear-lanceolate; fil. 5–11mm, stout, papillose; style 7–8×1.5–3mm, clavate. Capsule wingless. Iran; Turkey; Iraq. Z8.

F.assyriaca hort. non Bak. See *F.uva-vulpis*.

F.atropurpurea Nutt. (*F.gracillima* Smiley).
Bulb of few fleshy scales. Stem slender, 15–60cm. Lvs 5–9×0.2–0.9cm, 7–14, alternate or more or less whorled, on upper part of stem, linear to lanceolate. Fls 1–4, openly campanulate; tepals 10–20×4–8mm, oblong to rhombic, purple-brown, spotted with yellow or white, with yellow apical tuft; nectaries near base of tepal, circular, indistinct, yellow tinged brown; stamens 7–14mm; style very deeply 3-fid for more than half its length. Capsule 10–17mm, broadly obovoid, acutely angled. Late spring to summer. NW America (California to Oregon, N Dakota and New Mexico). Z4.

F.aurea Schott (*F.bornmulleri* Hausskn.).
Bulb to 2cm diam., generally with numerous subsidiary bulblets. Stem 4–15cm. Lvs 3.5–8×0.5–2cm, 5–8, alternate, lanceolate to ovate-lanceolate, glaucous. Fls solitary, very broadly campanulate; tepals 2–5×0.5×1.5cm, ovate to oblong, outer acute, inner obtuse, broader, yellow with orange or red-brown tessellations; nectaries 2mm, at angle of bell, 7mm above base of tepal, rhomboid; style 8–12mm, 3-fid, branches 2–3mm, glabrous. Capsule wingless. Late spring to summer. Turkey. Z7.

F.biflora Lindl. MISSION BELLS; BLACK FRITILLARY.
Bulb to 2cm diam., of about 3 loose, thick scales. Stem 15–40cm. Lvs mostly basal, not whorled, ovate-lanceolate,

glossy green. Fls 1–6, occasionally to 12m, campanulate; tepals 2–3.5cm, with longitudinal ridges within, brown tinged black to purple, flushed with green; nectaries linear, inconspicuous; anth. versatile; style 9mm, deeply 3-fid, branches to 5mm, recurved. Capsule hexagonal, wingless. SW US (California). 'Martha Roderick': fls rusty red and white. Z8.

F.bithynica Bak. (*F.dasyphylla* Bak.; *F.schliemannii* Sint.; *F.citrina* Bak.; *F.pineticola* Schwarz).
Bulb to 2cm diam. Stem 8–20cm. Lvs 5–8, occasionally to 12, generally opposite, oblanceolate to ovate. Fls 1 or 2, occasionally to 4, narrowly campanulate; bracts generally in a whorl of 3; tepals 17–27mm, inner obovate and cuneate, all lime-green or glaucous without, occasionally with purple markings, lime-green within; nectaries 3×1mm, basal, lanceolate, brown or green; style 7–10mm, slender, smooth, entire. Capsule usually winged. Spring. W Turkey, Greek Is. (Samos, Khios). Z8.

F.bornmuelleri Hausskn. See *F.aurea*.

F.bucharica Reg.
Bulb to 4cm diam., globose, composed of 2 large scales. Stem 10–35cm, papillose. Lvs lower 2 pairs opposite, remainder alternate, lanceolate to ovate. Fls horizontal or pendulous, 1–10, generally 4–7, in a raceme, cupulate; bracts 2 at the base of each flower stalk; tepals 14–20mm, lanceolate, white or off-white with green veins; nectaries 3mm, deeply indented; style 3–4mm, smooth and slender. Capsule winged. Soviet C Asia, NW Afghanistan. Z5.

F.burnatii Planch. See *F.meleagris* ssp. *burnatii*.

F.camschatcensis (L.) Ker-Gawl. (*Lilium camschatcense* L.; *F.camschatcensis* (L.) Fisch. ex Hook.). BLACK SARANA.
Bulb to 2.5cm diam., of many closely packed scales with numerous small bulblets around base. Stem 15–75cm. Lvs numerous, whorled below, alternate above, 5–7 per whorl, lanceolate. Fls 1–8, broadly campanulate to cupulate; tepals 20–30mm, acute, each with about 12 ridges within, purple-brown to black, occasionally tinged green or yellow; nectaries narrowly oblong, rather inconspicuous; anth. versatile; style 8–10mm, smooth, deeply 3-fid, branches 6–8mm, recurved. Capsule ovoid, obtusely-angled, wingless, 1.5–2cm. Late spring. NE Asia to NW America (E Siberia, Japan, Alaska, Canada to NW US). A double-flowered form is also in cultivation. Z4.

F.carduchorum Rix. See *F.minuta*.

F.carica Rix.
Bulb to 2cm diam. Stem 5–15cm. Lvs 3–7.5×0.6–1.8cm, 4–8, alternate, lanceolate or oblanceolate, glaucous, margins papillose, upper lvs generally twisted. Fls 1–3, narrowly campanulate or conic; tepals 13–20×4–9mm, ovate to lanceolate, obtuse, inner broader than outer, yellow fading to orange with age; nectaries 2–4×1mm, basal, narrowly ovate, small, tinged black; fil. 5–9mm, papillose; style 6–10mm, stout, papillose, entire or 3-lobed at apex, lobes to 1mm. Capsule wingless. SW Turkey. Z8.

F.caucasica Adams.
Bulb to 2cm diam., of 2 fleshy scales, white. Stem 15–40. Lvs 3–4, alternate, lower oblong-ovate, upper narrowly lanceolate, acuminate, amplexicaul. Fls solitary, campanulate to conic; tepals 18–25mm, elliptic-lanceolate, dark red-violet to purple-brown, exterior cinereous; nectaries 3–5mm, basal, linear-lanceolate, small; style 9–17mm, smooth, entire. Capsule to 2cm, oblong-ovoid, wingless. Spring to early summer. NE Turkey, Caucasus. Z7.

F.caussolensis Goaty & Pons ex Ardoino. See *F.montana*.

F.chitralensis Wallich
Like *F.imperialis* except fls 1–4, smaller, conic, buttery yellow; tepals 30–37mm; nectaries 2mm diam. N India (Chitral Valley). Z6.

F.cirrhosa D. Don.
Bulb to 3cm diam., spindle-shaped. Stem 20–60cm. Lvs whorled, 2–3 in each of 3–5 whorls, usually narrowly linear,

becoming narrower still and tendril-like toward summit of infl. Fls 1–4, broadly campanulate; upper 3 bracts reduced to tendrils; tepals 3.5–5cm, narrowly elliptic, acute, tinged purple, green or white, variously marked; nectaries at angle of bell, ovate; style 12mm, 3-fid, branches 5mm. Capsule winged. Late spring. E Himalaya, China. Z5.

F.citrina Bak. See *F.bithynica*.

F.collina Adams (*F.lutea* Bieb.).
Bulb to 2.5cm diam., spheric, of 2 fleshy scales with numerous small bulblets between scales. Stem 4–35cm. Lvs 5–9, alternate, linear to lanceolate, glossy green. Fl. solitary, very broadly campanulate to turbinate; tepals 3.5–5cm, acute, incurved at apex, dark maroon, with yellow tessellations within, exterior somewhat glaucous, inner tepals fringed along margins; nectaries 3–4×1–2mm, at angle of bell, 10mm above base of tepal, narrowly ovate, deeply indented; style 10–15mm, 3-fid, branches 2–5mm. Capsule cylindric, to 3cm, wingless. S Russia, Georgia. Z8.

F.contorta hort. ex Bak. See *F.meleagris* ssp. *burnatii* 'Contorta'.

F.crassifolia Boiss. & Reut.
Bulb to 2.5cm diam., spheric or spindle-shaped. Stem 6–20cm. Lvs generally 4, alternate, lanceolate. Fls 1–3, broadly campanulate; bracts alternate; tepals 18–24mm, tinged yellow or somewhat green, with small brown tessellations, generally with an indistinct green central stripe; nectaries 8–12×1–2mm, 3–5mm above base of tepal, linear; style 5–9mm, smooth, 3-fid, branches 2–4mm. Capsule wingless. Late spring to early summer. Anatolia. ssp. **kurdica** (Boiss. & Noë) Rix (*F.kurdica* (Boiss. & Noë; *F.karadaghensis* Turrill; *F.wanensis* Freyn). Lvs generally 5–7, linear, glaucous; inner tepals obtuse; nectary raised, forming ridge running vertically from angle of bell to near apex of tepal. Z7.

F.dasyphylla Bak. See *F.bithynica*.

F.davisii Turrill.
Bulb to 2.5cm diam., spheric or spindle-shaped. Stem 10–20cm. Lvs 3.5–11×1–3cm, 7–10, alternate, or lowest opposite and spreading, upper narrower than lower, glossy green. Fls 1–3, broadly campanulate; bracts alternate; tepals 18–24mm, inner obtuse, green, with brown or black tessellations, often heavy; nectaries at angle of bell, lanceolate; style 7mm, smooth, 3-fid, branches 3–7mm. Capsule wingless. S Greece. Z8.

F.delphinensis Gren. & Godron. See *F.tubiformis*.

F.drenovskyi Deg. & Stoj.
Bulb to 3cm diam., often with subsidiary bulblets. Stem 10–30cm. Lvs 6–7×0.5cm, 4–5, occasionally to 9, alternate, narrowly lanceolate to linear-lanceolate, glaucous. Fls 1 or 2, occasionally 4 together, narrowly campanulate; tepals 15–25×5–10mm, inner often obtuse, dark dull purple to red-brown, somewhat tinged green within, glaucous without; nectaries 2×1mm, basal, linear-lanceolate, small, green; style to 10×3mm at most, papillose, entire or 3-fid at apex, branches 1–2mm. Capsule wingless. Late spring to early summer. NE Greece, SW Bulgaria. Z6.

F.eduardi Reg. (*F.imperialis* ssp. *inodora* Reg.).
Similar to *F.imperialis* but lacking the odour characteristic of that plant. Bulb 5.5×4–5cm, spheric to ovoid, of 4 scales, inner yellow, outer brown. Stem 50–150cm. Lvs in 3–4 whorls of 4–8, oblong-lanceolate to ovate-lanceolate, semi-amplexicaul. Flowers 3–5 in a crowded umbel, erect or declined, conic to broadly campanulate; bracts 10–20 in close group above flowers; tepals 45–50mm, oblong-lanceolate, reflexed at apex, bright red; nectaries 3mm diam., basal, circular, superficial; style 30–45mm, 3-fid, branches 1–4mm, papillose towards apex. Capsule broadly 6–7×0.5–0.6cm, cylindric, winged. C Asia (Tadzhikistan), S Kashmir. Z7.

F.eggeri Bornm. See *F.persica*.

F.ehrhartii Boiss. & Orph.
Bulb to 2cm diam. Stem 8–20cm. Lvs 2.5–7×0.5–1.5cm, 6–10, generally opposite at base, alternate above, oblong-

Fritillaria (a) *F.bithynica* (a1) petal and nectary (a2) stigma (a3) capsule (b) *F.sewerzowii* (b1) flower spike (b2) bulb (b3) petal and nectary (b4) stamen (c) *F.acmopetala* petal and nectary (d) *F.messanensis* trilobed stigma (e) *F.biflora* petal and nectary (f) *F.alburyana* (f1) flower spike (g) *F.walujewii* (g1) flower spike (g2) petal and nectary (h) *F.caucasica* spp. *armena* habit (h1) section of flower (h2) stigma enlarged (i) *F.graeca* spp. *thessala* capsule (j) *F.michailovskyi* section of flower (k) *F.persica* (k1) flower spike (k2) petal and nectary (k3) stamen enlarged (l) *F.kotschyana* section of flower (m) *F.imperialis* (m1) flower spike (m2) petal and nectary (m3) seed (m4) section through flower (m5) capsule (n) *F.recurva* (n1) flower spike (n2) bulb and bulblets (o) *F.stenanthera* (o1) flower spike (o2) petal and nectary (o3) stamen (o4) stigma (05) *F.gibbosa* section showing nectary (p) *F.japonica* habit (p1) petal and nectary

lanceolate to ovate. Fls 1 or 2, occasionally to 4, narrowly campanulate; bracts generally in a whorl of 3; tepals 17–27mm, outer narrowly ovate or oblong, inner obovate-cuneate and broader than outer, dark purple-brown and yellow at apex without, lime-green within; nectaries 3×1mm, basal, lanceolate, brown or green; style 7–10mm, slender, smooth, entire. Capsule wingless. Late winter to spring. Greece (Aegean region, mts). Z8.

F.elwesii Boiss.
Bulb to 3cm diam., sometimes with numerous subsidiary bulblets. Stem 15–55cm. Lvs 4–8, alternate, linear, glaucous above. Fls 1–4, narrowly campanulate; tepals 20–30mm, inner obtuse or abruptly pointed, purple-brown with a clear green stripe; nectaries 2–3mm, at base of tepals, lanceolate, small; style 7–11mm, stout, densely papillose, 3-fid, branches 1–3.5mm. Capsule wingless. S Turkey. Z7.

F.gibbosa Boiss. (*F.pterocarpa* Stocks).
Bulb to 3cm diam., globose, with few scales. Stem to 6–30cm, densely papillose below at first. Lvs 3–7×1.5cm, 4–10, lowest occasionally opposite, ovate or lanceolate, upper much narrower, linear, acute. Fls to 25mm diam., 1–10, open saucer-shaped, horizontal or somewhat pendulous; tepals 15×10mm, inner broader, pink or rosy-purple, darker at base, spotted or blotched; nectaries to 4mm, deeply impressed; fil. 1cm; style 8–10cm, entire, smooth. Capsule to 14mm, upright, teeth to 4mm, winged. NE Iran, Afghanistan. Z8.

F.glauca Greene. SISKIYOU-LILY.
Bulb 5–10mm diam., of 2–3 large scales and a few smaller basal ones. Stem 12–18cm. Lvs 2–4cm, mostly basal, alternate, recurved, glaucous. Fls solitary, occasionally to 4 together, pendulous, broadly campanulate; tepals 15–20mm, yellow mottled with brown, occasionally all brown; nectaries 5–6mm, lanceolate to elliptic; style to 12mm, deeply 3-fid, branches 6–9mm, recurved. Capsule hexagonal, wingless. Late spring to summer. W US (California, Oregon). Z7.

F.glaucoviridis Turrill. See *F.alfredae* ssp. *glaucoviridis*.
F.gracilis (Ebel) Asch. & Gräbn. See *F.messanensis* ssp. *gracilis*.
F.gracillima Smiley. See *F.atropurpurea*.

F.graeca Boiss. & Sprun. (*F.guicciardii* Heldr. & Sart.)
Bulb to 2.5cm diam., spheric or spindle-shaped. Stem 6–20cm. Lvs 3.5–11×1–2.5cm, 7–10, alternate, or lowest opposite, glaucous. Fls 1–3, broadly campanulate; bracts alternate; tepals 18–24mm, inner obtuse, green, with brown or black tessellations, often heavy, generally with a clear green central stripe; nectaries at angle of bell, lanceolate; style 7–10mm, smooth, 3-fid, branches 3–6mm. Capsule wingless. S Greece. ssp. **thessala** (Boiss.) Rix. Generally larger; lvs not glaucous, lower opposite, intermediate opposite or alternate; bracts in a whorl of 3; tepals 28–38mm, green, generally lightly tessellated. Balkans, NW Greece. Z7.

F.graeca var. *gussichiae* Deg. & Dörfl. See *F.gussichiae*.
F.guicciardii Heldr. & Sartori. See *F.graeca*.

F.gussichiae (Deg. & Dörfl.) Rix (*F.graeca* var. *gussichiae* Deg. & Dörfl.).
Bulb to 2.5cm diam. Stem 20–30cm. Lvs 5–8, alternate, ovate to lanceolate, amplexicaul, very glaucous. Fls 1–3 in a long raceme, broadly campanulate; tepals 30mm, obtuse, not recurved at apex, green, ferruginous-marked (not tessellated); nectaries 6mm above base of tepal, ovate, green; style 9mm, smooth, 3-fid, branches 4mm. Capsule narrowly winged. Spring to early summer. Mid Balkans. Z6.

F.hermonis Fenzl in Kotschy ssp. **hermonis**.
Endemic to Mt Hermonis in Lebanon. Not in cultivation. ssp. **amana** Rix. Bulb to 2cm diam., often with subsidiary bulblets or stolons. Stem 10–35cm. Lvs 5–6, occasionally more, alternate, lanceolate or oblong. Fls 1 or 2, broadly campanulate; tepals 25–35mm, inner obtuse, all green, faintly brown- or purple-tessellated, yellow forms also recorded; nectaries at angle of bell, ovate, green or black; style 8–12mm, papillose,

3-fid, branches 3–4mm. Capsule wingless. S Turkey to Lebanon. Z8.

F.hispanica Boiss. & Reut. (*F.lusitanica* Wikstr.).
Bulb to 2.5cm diam. Stem 10–50cm. Lvs 5–7.5cm, generally 6–9, alternate, linear to narrowly lanceolate. Fls 1–3, broadly campanulate; bracts alternate; tepals 20–40mm, inner generally acute, sometimes recurved at apex, green to brown without, tinged yellow within, with brown markings or tessellations; nectaries 10–12mm, 3–4mm above base of tepal, linear to linear-lanceolate; style 8–11mm, smooth, 3-fid, branches 3–4mm. Capsule wingless. Spring to summer. Spain and Portugal. Z8.

F.imperialis L. CROWN IMPERIAL.
Malodorous, smelling of fox. Bulb to 10cm diam., compressed-spheric, with pungent foxy odour. Stem 50–150cm. Lvs in 3–4 whorls of 4–8, lanceolate. Flowers 3–5 in an umbel, broadly campanulate; bracts 10–20 in a coma, or tufted group above flowers; tepals 40–55mm, orange or red; nectaries to 5mm diam., basal on tepals, circular, large, white; style 3–4.5cm, 3-fid, branches 1–4mm, papillose towards apex. Capsule winged. Asia (S Turkey to Kashmir). 'Argenteovariegata': lvs edged white; fls rusty orange, pendent. 'Aureomarginata': lvs edged gold. 'Aurora': fls bright red-orange. 'Crown on Crown': fls red-orange, two whorls of flowers one above the other. 'Lutea': fls golden yellow. 'Lutea Maxima': tall; fls large, butter yellow. 'Orange Brilliant': fls orange, tinted brown. 'Rubra Maxima': tall; fls large, orange tinted red. 'Sulphurino': fls pale tangerine. 'The Premier': fls orange tinted yellow, veins tinged purple. Z4.

F.imperialis ssp. *inodora* Reg. See *F.eduardi*.

F.involucrata All.
Bulb to 3cm diam., globose. Stem 15–25cm. Lvs 7–10, opposite to subopposite, linear-lanceolate to linear. Fls solitary, broadly campanulate; bracts in a whorl of 3; tepals 25–40mm, obtuse, not recurved at apex, green, sometimes variously tessellated with purple-brown; nectaries at angle of bell, ovate, blackened; style 12–15mm, smooth, 3-fid, branches 5–7mm. Capsule wingless. SE France, NW Italy. Z7.

F.karadaghensis Turrill. See *F.crassifolia* ssp. *kurdica*.
F.kurdica Boiss. & Noë. See *F.crassifolia* ssp. *kurdica*.
F.lanceolata Pursh. See *F.affinis*.

F.latifolia Willd. (*F.nobilis* Bak.).
Bulb to 2.5cm diam., globose, of 2 fleshy scales with numerous small bulblets between scales. Stem 4–35cm. Lvs 5–9, alternate, ovate to lanceolate, glossy green. Flowers solitary, very broadly campanulate to turbinate; tepals 35–50mm, obtuse or rounded, incurved at apex, dark maroon, with yellow tessellations within, somewhat glaucous without; nectaries 3–4×1–2mm, at angle of bell, 10mm above base of tepal, narrowly ovate, deeply impressed; style 10–15mm, 3-fid, branches 2–5mm. Capsule to 3cm, cylindric, wingless. Late spring to summer. NE Turkey, Caucasus, NW Iran. f.**nobilis** Bak. from Caucasus and Turkish Armenia, with dull purple olive-yellow chequered flowers probably merits varietal status here. Z6.

F.libanotica (Boiss.) Bak. See *F.persica*.

F.liliacea Lindl. WHITE FRITILLARY.
Bulb to 2.5cm diam., of 4–6 loose, ovoid, succulent scales. Stem 15–35cm. Lvs 2–20, mostly basal, lower opposite, oblong-lanceolate to ovate, glossy green. Fls 2–4, occasionally to 8, openly conic to campanulate; bracts alternate; tepals 12–25mm, white, tinged green or yellow at base; nectaries oblong, small, lime-green, occasionally with purple spots; style 8mm, smooth, very deeply 3-fid, branches 4–5mm, recurved. Capsule angled, wingless. Late winter to spring. SW US (California). Z9.

F.lusitanica Wikstr. See *F.hispanica*.
F.lutea Bieb. non Mill. See *F.collina*.
F.macrandra Bak. See *F.tuntasia*.

F.meleagris L. SNAKE'S HEAD FRITILLARY; GUINEA-HEN FLOWER; CHEQUERED LILY; LEPER LILY. Bulb to 2.5cm diam., globose, of 2 large scales. Stem 12–30cm. Lvs 6–13cm, 4–6, alternate, linear to linear-lanceolate, acute. Fl. solitary or occasionally 2 together, very broadly campanulate; tepals 30–45mm, inner slightly broader than outer, all acute, white or somewhat tinged pink and tessellated all over, to pure white; nectaries 7–10mm, at angle of bell, linear, green; fil. papillose; style 13–16mm, 3-fid, branches 2–5mm, papillose. Capsule wingless. Spring–early summer. Europe (England to W Russia). Fls in shape resemble the bells lepers carried in medieval times, hence common name. Cultivated since Tudor times. Various cvs varying in flower colour (ranging from white, to grey-purple or violet or tinged green, with varying degrees of marking or tessellation) have been named, but are now rarely available. 'Alba': fls white. 'Aphrodite': fls white, large. 'Artemis': fls checked with deepest purple. 'Charon': fls dark purple. 'Emperor': fls checked grey and violet. 'Pomona': fls checked white and violet. 'Poseidon': fls purple-pink. 'Saturnus': fls pale violet tinted red. ssp. **burnatii** (Planch.) Rix (*F.burnatii* Planch.). Lvs smaller 5–8cm, obtuse; tepals purple; fil. smooth or shortly, sparsely papillose; style smooth. S & W Alps. 'Contorta': mutant form with flower contracted to a narrow bell to 5cm long, and tepals joined in lower part. Z4.

F.messanensis Raf. Bulb to 4cm diam., globose. Stem 15–45cm. Lvs 7–10, lowest generally opposite, linear. Fls solitary or occasionally to 3 together, broadly campanulate; bracts in a whorl of 3; tepals 22–42mm, inner acute and recurved at apex, green, ferruginous-tessellated; nectaries near base of tepals, ovate-lanceolate, large, green; style 10mm, smooth, 3-fid, branches 5–6mm. Capsule wingless. Mid winter to spring. C Mediterranean (N Africa, Crete, Greece, S Italy, Sicily). var. **atlantica** Maire (*F.messanensis* f. *oranensis*; *F.oranensis* Pomel). Lvs shorter, very glaucous. Atlas Mts, Morocco. ssp. **gracilis** (Ebel) Rix (*F.gracilis* (Ebel) Asch. & Gräbn.; *F.neglecta* Parl.; *Lilium gracile* Ebel). Bracts generally alternate; tepals not recurved at apex, plain green, not tessellated. Balkans. Z9.

F.michailovskyi Fomin. Bulb to 2.5cm diam. Stem 6–24cm. Lvs 5–9, alternate or lowest subopposite to opposite, lanceolate. Fls 1–4, more or less in an umbel, broadly campanulate; tepals 20–30mm, inner obtuse, purple-brown or tinged green without, the apical third bright yellow; nectaries running from angle of bell to near apex, linear, deep and prominent, yellow; style 7–9mm, smooth, 3-fid, branches 2–3mm. Capsule wingless, with dry perianth remaining attached. NE Turkey. Z7.

F.micrantha Heller (*F.parviflora* Torr.; *F.multiflora* Kellogg). BROWN BELLS. Bulb of few scales, with numerous subsidiary 'rice-grain' bulblets. Stem 40–90cm, light green. Lvs 5–15×0.3–1cm, on upper part of stem, whorled, 4–6 per whorl, linear to linear-lanceolate. Fls 4–10, broadly campanulate; tepals 12–20×4–5mm, tinged purple or white tinged green, occasionally faintly mottled, with tuft of white hairs at apex; nectaries on lower third of tepal, oblong-lanceolate; stamens 7–12mm; style 3-fid for one to two-thirds of its length. Capsule slightly broader than long, broadly winged. SW US (California). Z8.

F.minor Ledeb. See F.ruthenica.

F.minuta Boiss. & Noë (*F.carduchorum* Rix). Bulb to 3cm diam., often with numerous subsidiary bulblets. Stem 10–20cm. Lvs generally 5–7, alternate or upper 3 whorled, lanceolate, acute, 7–10×1–3cm, shining green. Fls 1–3, narrowly campanulate; tepals 16–22×7–8mm, lanceolate, acute, yellow tinged purple or red-brown, not tessellated but sometimes blotched; nectaries 2–4×1mm, basal, lanceolate, green; fil. papillose; style 4–7mm, smooth, deeply 3-fid, branches 2–4mm, reflexed when mature. Capsule wingless. Late spring to early summer. SE Turkey; NW Iran. Z8.

F.montana Hoppe (*F.racemosa* Ker-Gawl.; *F.caussolensis* Goaty & Pons ex Ardoino). Bulb to 2.5cm diam., globose. Stem 15–40cm. Lvs 8–20, lowest generally opposite, remainder alternate or in whorls of 3, linear. Fls 1–3, broadly campanulate; bracts not coiled at apex; tepals 18–26×8–12mm, elliptic, inner broader, not at all recurved at apex, green, with heavy tessellations in very dark red or purple to black, or brown; nectaries 10–15mm, 5mm above base of tepal, linear; style 8–10mm, papillose, 3-fid, branches 2–7mm. Capsule obovoid, wingless. S Europe (S France, Italy, Yugoslavia, N Greece). Z6.

F.multiflora Kellogg. See F.micrantha.
F.mutica Lindl. See F.affinis.
F.neglecta Parl. See F.messanensis ssp. gracilis.
F.nigra hort. non Mill. See F.montana.
F.nigra Mill. non hort. See F.pyrenaica.
F.nobilis Bak. See F.latifolia.

F.obliqua Ker-Gawl. Bulb to 2.5cm diam. Stem 10–20cm. Lvs to 13×2cm, 8–11, alternate or basal sometimes opposite, lanceolate, upper smaller, glaucous. Fls 1–2, occasionally to 4, conic to campanulate, generally somewhat narrowed at mouth; tepals 20–30×10–14mm, very dark purple tinged black, not marked, glaucous without; nectaries 4mm, basal, linear, green; style 10–12mm, smooth, 3-fid, branches 2–3mm. Capsule wingless. S Greece (Attiki). Z8.

F.olivieri Bak. Bulb to 2.5cm diam. Stem 20–30cm. Lvs 5–8, alternate, narrowly lanceolate, amplexicaul, green. Fls 1–3 in long raceme, broadly campanulate; tepals 3cm, obtuse, not recurved at apex, green, ferruginous-marked (not tessellated); nectaries 6mm above base of tepal, ovate, green; style 9mm, smooth, 3-fid, branches 4mm. Capsule wingless. Late spring to early summer. Iran. Z6.

F.oranensis Pomel. See F.messanensis var. atlantica.

F.orientalis Adams (*F.tenella* Bieb.). Bulb spheric, white. Stem 15–40cm. Lvs 4–13cm, 6–10, opposite or whorled at base, mid-stem lvs alternate, uppermost whorled, linear, reduced upwards. Fls solitary, broadly campanulate; tepals to 30×15mm, oblong-elliptic, obtuse, inner broader, tinged green, with heavy dull purple-brown tessellations; nectaries 10–15×2mm, 5mm above base of tepal, linear, tinged green; style 8–10mm, papillose, deeply 3-fid, branches 2–7mm. Capsule wingless. S Europe eastwards to France. Z7.

F.pallidiflora Schrenk. Bulb to 5cm diam., spheric to spindle-shaped. Stem 10–80cm. Lvs opposite or alternate, broadly lanceolate, glaucous. Fls 2.5–3cm diam., 1–6(–12), very broadly campanulate, with faintly unpleasant odour; tepals 25–45mm, rounded, pale yellow tinged green, with faint red-brown tessellations; nectaries 2mm, at angle of bell, deeply indented, ovate; style 14–17mm, smooth, 3-fid with branches 2–4mm. Capsule broadly 6-winged. Spring–early summer. E Siberia, NW China. Z3.

F.parviflora Torr. See F.micrantha.

F.persica L. (*F.libanotica* (Boiss.) Bak.; *F.eggeri* Bornm.). Bulb to 6cm high, ellipsoid, of close-fitting scales (composed of a single massive scale invested with remnants of older ones). Stem 20–50cm, leafy. Lvs alternate, lanceolate, glaucous grey-green. Fls 7–20+ in an erect, terminal raceme, narrowly campanulate; bracts 1 at base of each flower stalk or absent; tepals 15–20mm, tinged with black, grey, purple or green; nectaries to 1.5mm, 2mm above base of tepal, triangular to rectangular; style 6–8mm, slender, smooth. Capsule 1–3cm, narrowly winged. W Asia (S Turkey to W Iran, west to Jordan and Israel). 'Adiyaman': tall, to 1m; fls dull maroon. Z5.

F.pinardii Boiss. (*F.syriaca* Hayek & Siehe). Bulb to 3cm diam., often with subsidiary bulblets. Stem 6–20cm. Lvs 3–8, alternate, lanceolate, glaucous. Fls 1 or 2, occasionally 4 together, narrowly campanulate; tepals 15–25mm, inner obtuse, all tinged grey or purple and glaucous without, orange, yellow or rather green within, not tessellated; nectaries 3–5mm, basal, linear-lanceolate, small; style slender, to 10×3mm at most, papillose, entire or 3-fid at apex, branches 1–2mm. Capsule wingless. Late spring to early summer. Turkey; Syria; Lebanon. Z7.

F.pineticola Schwarz. See *F.bithynica*.

F.pinetorum Davidson.
Bulb 1–2cm diam., with numerous subsidiary 'rice-grain' bulblets. Stem 10–30cm, glaucous. Lvs 5–15×0.2–0.7cm, 12–20, somewhat whorled, linear, glaucous. Fls 3–9, erect or nearly so; tepals 14–1×2–6mm, purple, mottled with yellow-green; nectaries indistinct; stamens two-thirds length of tepal; style very deeply 3-fid. Capsule 12–15mm, winged, with horn-like projections at base and summit of each wing. SW US (California to Nevada). Z5.

F.pluriflora Torr. ADOBE-LILY; PINK FRITILLARY.
Bulb 1.3–2.5cm, of up to 8 ovate succulent scales, tinged yellow. Stem 18–40. Lvs 6–13, alternate, mostly basal, oblong-lanceolate. Fls 1–4, occasionally to 12, facing outwards, or pendulous; tepals 20–35mm, obovate, pink or somewhat tinged purple, unmarked; nectaries running two-thirds length of tepals, linear; style 1–1.5cm, entire or 3-lobed at apex. Capsule 3-ridged, wingless. SW US (California). Z5.

F.pontica Wahlenb.
Bulb to 3cm diam., globose, often with antler-like protrusion when dormant. Stem 15–45cm. Lvs about 8, opposite or sub-opposite, lanceolate to linear-lanceolate. Fls solitary or occasionally 2 together, broadly campanulate; bracts in a whorl of 3, close to flower; tepals 25–45mm, inner obtuse and somewhat recurved at apex, green, ferruginous-marbled or not (never tessellated); nectaries 3mm diam., at angle of bell, 5mm above base of tepal, circular, blackened; style 12–15mm, smooth, 3-fid, branches 5–7mm. Capsule with 6 narrow wings on angles. Balkans (S Albania, S Yugoslavia, N Greece, NW Turkey). Z6.

F.pterocarpa Stocks. See *F.gibbosa*.

F.pudica (Pursh) Spreng. YELLOW FRITILLARY.
Bulb disc-shaped, thick, of 2–4 scales with numerous subsidiary bulblets at base. Stem 8–30cm. Lvs 2–7, lowest generally opposite, upper alternate, linear to narrowly lanceolate. Fls 1–2, occasionally to 6, narrowly campanulate; tepals 10–25mm, yellow or somewhat tinged orange; nectaries basal, small, dark; style 8mm, slender, smooth, entire. Capsule wingless. Spring to early summer. Western N America. Z3.

F.purdyi Eastw.
Bulb of 3–4 ovoid succulent scales, each 8–15mm. Stem 10–40cm. Lvs mostly basal, rosulate, elliptic to oblong-lanceolate, margins generally sinuate. Fls 1–4, occasionally to 14, campanulate, pendulous; tepals 15mm, off-white or tinged pale green, strongly veined and mottled with purple-brown; nectaries 10×2mm, oblong; style 15mm, deeply 3-fid, branches to 10mm, spreading and recurved. Capsule 6-angled, wingless. Late winter to early summer. SW US (California). Z8.

F.pyrenaica L. (*F.nigra* Mill.).
Bulb globose, to 3cm diam. Stem 15–30cm. Lvs 4.5–11×0.5–1cm, 7–10, alternate, lanceolate to linear-lanceolate. Flowers solitary or occasionally 2 together, broadly campanulate; tepals 25–35mm, inner obtuse, recurved at apex, all dark purple tinged black or brown, heavily tessellated without, green tinged yellow within and brown tessellated in basal half; nectaries at angle of bell, triangular to ovate-lanceolate; style 8–9mm, slender, smooth, 3-fid, branches 2–4mm. Capsule wingless. S France, NW Spain. Z5.

F.racemosa Ker-Gawl. See *F.montana*.

F.raddeana Reg. (*F.askabadensis* Micheli; *F.imperialis* ssp. *raddeana*).
Malodorous, smelling of fox or skunk. Bulb to 10cm diam., compressed-spheric, of 4 fleshy scales. Stem 50–150cm. Lvs to 15cm, alternate, or whorled, lanceolate, pale lustrous green, glabrous. Fls 6–20 in an umbel, broadly campanulate to conic; bracts 10–20 in close group above fls, linear, recurved; tepals 40–55mm, oblong-lanceolate or inner lanceolate-rhomboid, pale yellow or tinged green with yellow-green veins, with apical tuft of white hairs; nectaries 2mm diam., basal, circular, shallow; fil. white, anth. yellow; style 3–4.5cm, 3-fid, branches 1–4mm, papillose towards apex. Capsule winged. NW Iran, Russia (Turkmenia). Z4.

F.recurva Benth. SCARLET FRITILLARY.
Bulb 2–3cm diam., disc-shaped, succulent, with some subsidiary bulblets around base. Stem 20–90cm. Lvs 9–25, in 3–5 whorls, linear to linear-lanceolate, often glaucous. Fls 3–6, occasionally 12, in a raceme, narrowly campanulate; tepals 20–35mm, recurved at tip, orange-red to scarlet, with yellow tessellations; nectaries 5–6mm, near base of tepals, lanceolate; style to 13mm, 3-fid, branches to 3mm. Capsule 6-winged. Late spring to summer. SW US (California, S Oregon). Z7.

F.rhodocanakis Orph. ex Bak.
Bulb to 2.5cm diam., globose or ellipsoid. Stem 6–20cm. Lvs 3.5–11×1.2–5cm, 7–10, alternate, or lowest opposite, glaucous. Fls 1–3, broadly campanulate; bracts alternate; tepals 18–24mm, inner obtuse, plain dark purple or purple-brown, yellow at apex and along margins, or occasionally yellow tinged green throughout; nectaries 3×2mm, at angle of bell, lanceolate; style 7–10mm, generally papillose, 3-fid, branches 3–6mm. Capsule wingless. S Greece (Idhra). Z8.

F.roylei Hook. f.
Bulb to 3cm diam., spindle-shaped. Stem 20–60cm. Lvs numerous, whorled, 4–5 in each of 6–7 whorls, linear-lanceolate to lanceolate. Fls 1–4, broadly campanulate; tepals 35–50mm, narrowly ovate, rounded, green tinged yellow, spotted or streaked with dull purple; nectaries at angle of bell, ovate, large; style 12mm, 3-fid, branches 5mm. Capsule narrowly winged. Late spring. Kashmir, Punjab. Z5.

F.ruthenica Wikstr. (*F.minor* Ledeb.).
Bulb globose, to 2.5cm diam. Stem 20–50cm. Lvs 6–9cm, 6–12, lowest generally opposite, remainder alternate or in whorls of 3, linear. Fls 1–3, broadly campanulate; bracts coiled; tepals 18–26×8–12mm, elliptic, inner broader, not at all recurved at apex, acute, blackened without, yellow tinged green within, with purple-brown tessellations; nectaries 10–15mm, 5mm above base of tepal, linear; style 8–10mm, papillose, 3-fid, branches 2–7mm. Capsule obovoid, winged. Russia, W Siberia. Z4.

F.schliemannii Sint. See *F.bithynica*.

F.sewerzowii Reg. (*Korolkowia sewerzowii* (Reg.) Reg.).
Bulb to 6cm diam., compressed-spheric, of 1–2 closely fitting scales. Stem 15–20cm. Lvs alternate or lowest opposite, lanceolate. Fls 4–12, in an elongate raceme, or occasionally solitary, narrowly campanulate, widely flared at mouth; bracts to 7×2cm, solitary at base of each flower stalk; tepals 25–35mm, tinged grey-green or purple without, and yellow to brick-red within; nectaries 1–1.5cm, linear, grooved; anth. versatile, fixed 2mm above base; style 1.5–2cm, undivided, slender, smooth. Capsule winged. Spring to summer. C Asia, NW China. Z5.

F.sibthorpiana (Sm.) Bak. (*Tulipa sibthorpiana* Sm.).
Bulb to 2cm diam. Stem 20–30cm. Lvs 9–17×1.5–5cm, 2–3, alternate, ovate-lanceolate, amplexicaul. Fls solitary, narrowly campanulate; tepals 18–22×7–9mm, lanceolate, inner broader than outer, yellow; nectaries 3mm, basal, linear-lanceolate, green; fil. 6mm, papillose; style 5–7mm, very stout, papillose. Capsule not winged. Greece (Symi), SW Turkey. Z8.

F.stenanthera (Reg.) Reg.
Bulb to 4cm diam., spheric, of 2 large scales. Stem 10–30cm, papillose. Lvs lower pair opposite, ovate, remainder alternate, lanceolate to linear. Fls horizontal or pendulous, 1–10, generally 4–7, in a raceme, conic, widely flared at mouth; bracts 2 at the base of each flower stalk; tepals 14–20mm, lanceolate, outer larger than inner, tinged rose pink; nectaries 3mm, visible as bulges on outside of perianth; style 5mm, slender, papillose below. Capsule with 6 horn-like wings on angles. Russia, Siberia, C Asia. Z7.

F.syriaca Hayek & Siehe. See *F.pinardii*.
F.tenella Bieb. See *F.orientalis*.
F.thessalica Sprun. & Nyman. See *F.graeca* ssp. *thessala*.

F.thunbergii Miq. (*F.verticillata* var. *thunbergii* (Miq.) Bak.).
Bulb to 4cm diam., spindle-shaped. Stem 30–80cm. Lvs numerous, lowest opposite, others alternate or whorled, linear. Fls 2–6 (occasionally 1), broadly campanulate to broadly cupulate; bracts coiled, tendril-like; tepals 23–35mm, obtuse, off-white, faintly tessellated or green-veined; nectaries 3–4mm, 2mm above base of tepal, linear-lanceolate; style 10mm, smooth, 3-fid with branches 2mm. Capsule winged. C China. Z8.

F.tristis Heldr. & Sartori. See *F.obliqua*.

F.tubiformis Gren. & Godron (*F.delphinensis* Gren. & Godron).
Bulb to 2.5cm diam., spheric, of 2 fleshy scales with numerous small bulblets between scales. Stem 4–35cm. Lvs 5–9, alternate, lanceolate to linear-lanceolate, glaucous. Flower solitary, very broadly campanulate to turbinate; tepals 35–50mm, obtuse, incurved at apex, dark maroon tinged grey without, with yellow tessellations within, somewhat glaucous without; nectaries 3–4×1–2mm, at angle of bell, 10mm above base of tepal, ovate, deeply impressed; style 12–13mm, 3-fid, branches 1mm. Capsule cylindric, to 3cm, wingless. Late spring to early summer. SW Alps. ssp. *moggridgei* (Boiss. & Reut.) Rix. Tepals rounded, yellow tinged green; nectaries 4–5mm, linear-lanceolate; style 13–17mm. SW Alps. Z6.

F.tuntasia Heldr. (*F.macrandra* Bak.).
Bulb to 2.5cm diam. Stem 10–35cm. Lvs to 13×2cm, 8–25, alternate or basal sometimes opposite, lanceolate, upper smaller, glaucous. Flowers 1–4, occasionally to 6, conic to campanulate, generally somewhat narrowed at mouth; tepals 20–30×10–14mm, very dark purple tinged black, not marked, exterior glaucous; nectaries 4mm, basal, linear, green; style

10mm, smooth, 3-fid, branches 1–1.5mm. Capsule wingless. Greece (Kithnos, Serifos). Z8.

F.uva-vulpis Rix.
Bulb to 3cm diam., usually with a few fairly large subsidiary bulblets. Stem 10–35cm. Lvs 3–5, alternate, lanceolate, shining green. Flowers solitary or occasionally 2 together, narrowly campanulate, rounded; tepals 20–28mm, inner obtuse, all grey-purple and glaucous without, tinged yellow within; nectaries basal, ovate, large; style 5–7×3–4mm, stout, papillose. Capsule wingless. W Asia (SE Turkey, N Iraq, W Iran). Z7.

F.verticillata Willd.
Bulb 2–4cm diam., spindle-shaped to globose. Stem 20–60cm. Lvs lowest opposite, others in whorls of 3–7, narrowly lanceolate to linear. Fls 1–5, broadly campanulate; bracts coiled, tendril-like; tepals to 45×15mm, oblong elliptic to oblong-obovate, concave, obtuse, off-white or tinged pale yellow, dark-striped without, faintly mauve-tessellated within; nectaries 3–4mm, 2mm above base of tepal, linear-lanceolate, deeply indented, prominent; style 10mm, smooth, 3-fid with branches 2mm. Capsule 2–3cm, obovoid, winged. C Asia, W Siberia. Z5.

F.verticillata var. *thunbergii* (Miq.) Bak. See *F.thunbergii*.

F.walujewii Reg.
Bulb to 4cm diam., spindle-shaped. Stem 20–70cm. Lvs numerous, lowest opposite, others alternate or whorled, linear-lanceolate. Fls 2–6 or solitary, broadly campanulate to broadly cupulate; bracts coiled, tendril-like; tepals to 50×15mm, oblong-elliptic, obtuse, white tinged green to pink without, white or flushed with red to purple-brown and faintly spotted or tessellated within; nectaries 4–6mm, 2mm above base of tepal, orbicular to lanceolate; style 10mm, smooth, 3-fid with branches 2mm. Capsule 3cm, winged. C Asia (Tadzhikistan), NW China. Z7.

F.wanensis Freyn. See *F.crassifolia* ssp. *kurdica*.

F.whittallii Bak.
Bulb to 1.5cm diam., occasionally with numerous subsidiary bulblets. Stem 10–20cm. Lvs 8–12×0.5–1cm, 6–7, alternate, linear to linear-lanceolate. Fls 1–2, broadly campanulate, not flared at mouth; tepals 25–32×10–13mm, narrowly ovate, acute or obtuse, green, with brown tessellations; nectaries 3mm, at angle of bell, ovate to circular; style 11mm, smooth, 3-fid, branches 5–5mm. Capsule wingless. Spring–early summer. Turkey. Z8.

Gagea Salisb. (For the amateur botanist Sir Thomas Gage (1761–1820), of Hengrave Hall, Suffolk.) Liliaceae (Liliaceae). About 50 species of small, bulbous perennial herbs, to 25cm; bulb often entwined with thickened roots. Stems erect, solitary, simple. Basal leaves 1–2, linear or linear-lanceolate, hollow, solid or flat, arising directly from bulb. Inflorescence an umbel subtended by a pair of stem leaves, or a few-flowered raceme with at least 1 leaf on the stem below the raceme, or flowers solitary; perianth cylindric-campanulate to rotate, segments free, usually yellow, rarely white; stamens 6, basally fixed. Fruit a many-seeded capsule. Europe, C Asia, N Africa.

CULTIVATION   *Gagea* spp. occur either in damp mountain grassland (*G.fistulosa*), or on scree and in rocky habitats, often in hot dry places, sometimes coastal; *G.lutea* and *G.minima* are found in damp grass and open woodlands. They are grown for their small, white, pale or golden yellow flowers carried in spring and early summer, in the rock garden or alpine house and bulb frame. The Mediterranean species may be short-lived in cool temperate cultivation, since they require shallow soils and hot dry conditions in summer for bulb ripening. These are best grown in shallow pans in a sunny bulb frame, watered copiously when in growth and dried out when dormant, with just sufficient moisture to prevent shrivelling. Most can be grown in well drained, sandy soils in full sun, with adequate moisture when in growth, in situations that are dry but not completely arid in summer. Propagate by division of bulbils or by seed in spring, under glass.

G.arvensis (Pers.) Dumort. See *G.villosa*.

G.fibrosa (Desf.) Schult. & Schult. f.
Bulb solitary, with a pale brown papery tunic and elongated sheath to 3.5cm high, usually entwined with thickened roots. Basal lvs 2, linear, flat or channelled, 2–4mm wide, exceeding infl.; stem lvs 3–5, whorled. Infl. an umbel, 4–6cm (sometimes 3–12cm), often branching near the ground; pedicels woolly, 2–8cm; fls 1–4 (or 6); seg. yellow inside, green outside, narrowly lanceolate, acuminate, 15–25×2–4mm. Fr. spherical to cylindric, to 1.5cm; seeds flat. Mediterranean, N Africa, Aegean, Caucasia. Z8.

G.fistulosa (Ramond ex DC.) Ker-Gawl. (*G.liotardii* (Sternb.) Schult. & Schult. f.).
Bulbs 2, tunics pale brown, new bulb arising just above base of old. Stem glabrous. Basal lvs 1 or 2, linear, hollow, glabrous, 6 20cm×0.3–0.5mm; stem lvs 2, opposite, broadly lanceolate, acuminate, glabrous, unequal, the lower lvs 2.5–4.5×0.3–1cm. Infl. an umbel, 4–16cm; pedicels usually hairy, 1.5–5cm, lengthening after flowering; fls 2–4, rarely 1 or 6, seg. yellow, narrowly ovate, glabrous, 10–18×2–4mm. Fr. obovoid, about 11×6mm; seeds subglobose. Spring–summer. Europe, Caucasia, Iran, Iraq. Z7.

G.graeca (L.) A. Terrac. (*Lloydia graeca* (L.) Salisb.).
Bulbs often crowded, covered with thickened roots. Basal lvs 2–4, linear, 4–12×0.1–0.2cm, flat, glabrous; stem lvs 3, alternate, linear-lanceolate, lowest 3–6×0.1–0.2cm. Fls 1–5; seg. 7–16mm, oblanceolate, obtuse, glabrous, white with 3 purple stripes; style 1.8–2.5mm; anth. 0.5–1mm. Fr. narrowly oblong-ovoid; seeds flat. Spring. Greece, Crete, E Mediterranean. Z8.

G.liotardii (Sternb.) Schult. & Schult. f. See *G.fistulosa*.

G.lutea (L.) Ker-Gawl. (*G.sylvatica* (Pers.) Loud.).
Bulb solitary, new bulb formed within old. Stem 10–30cm, glabrous. Basal lf solitary, linear-lanceolate, flat, 7–15mm wide; stem lvs 2, opposite, lanceolate, ciliate. Infl. an umbel, 10–25cm; pedicels glabrous or hairy; fls 1–7 (or to 10); seg.

yellow, tinged green, oblong-linear, 15–18mm. Fr. globose; seeds subglobose. Spring. Europe, Russian Asia. Z6.

G.minima (L.) Ker-Gawl.
Bulbs 2, in a common tunic. Stem glabrous. Basal lf solitary, lanceolate, flat, 1–2mm wide; stem lvs 1–2, opposite, lanceolate, tapered, usually glabrous. Fls 1–7; pedicels glabrous or slightly pubesc.; seg. yellow, linear-lanceolate, acuminate, 10–15mm. Fr. obovoid; seeds subglobose. Europe. Z6.

G.peduncularis (Presl & C. Presl) Pascher.
Bulb with black-brown tunic, new bulb next to old. Basal lvs 2, linear, glabrous, channelled, 6–30×0.1–0.2cm; stem lf 1, lanceolate, acuminate. Infl. a panicle, 3–14cm, hairy or glabrous; pedicels densely woolly above, 3–4cm; fls 1–7, seg. yellow, narrowly ovate or oblanceolate, usually obtuse, 8–16mm, elongating, woolly at base outside. Fr. obovoid. Spring. N Africa, Balkans, Aegean. Z7.

G.pratensis (Pers.) Dumort. (*G.stenopetala* Rchb.).
Bulbs 2 or 3, tunic pale brown, new bulb formed below old. Stem glabrous. Basal lf solitary, linear, flat or channelled, 3–15×0.2–0.4cm; stem lvs 1–2, opposite, lanceolate, tapered, sometimes ciliate. Infl. an umbel, 1–10cm, glabrous; pedicels 10–20mm; fls 1–7, seg. yellow inside, green outside, linear-lanceolate, acuminate, 9 16mm, lengthening in fr. Fr. ovoid; seeds subglobose. Spring. Europe, Crimea, Turkey. Z7.

G.stenopetala Rchb. See *G.pratensis*.

G.sylvatica (Pers.) Loud. See *G.lutea*.

G.villosa (Bieb.) Duby (*G.arvensis* (Pers.) Dumort.).
Bulb with hard brown tunic, new bulb next to old. Basal lvs 2, linear, D-shaped in cross section, glabrous or hairy, 16cm×1–2.5mm, exceeding infl.; additional lvs often present with bulbils in their axils at ground level; stem lvs opposite, rarely with bulbils in their axils, to 9mm wide. Infl. subumbellate, 1–10cm, hairy or glabrous; fls 1–15, seg. yellow, narrowly ovate, 7–10cm, elongating, sometimes hairy at base outside. Fr. ovoid; seeds subglobose. Spring. Europe, N Africa, Turkey, Iran. Z7.

Galanthus L. (From Gk *gala*, milk, and *anthos*, flower; 'snowdrop' derived from German *Schneetropfen*, pendants or eardrops fashionable in 16th and 17th centuries.) SNOWDROP. Amaryllidaceae. About 15 bulbous perennials. Bulbs externally covered by brown, scarious remains of scales; internally 3 fleshy scales surround the shoot, producing offsets to form clumps. Shoot surrounded by sheathing tube, thick below, membranous and often green-veined above. Vernation flat, convolute or reduplicate (important in identification); leaves paired, occasionally 3, ligulate or linear to elliptic-oblong, narrow or broad, glaucous to glossy green, usually shorter than scape at flowering time, expanding later. Scape cylindric or compressed, emerging between the leaves, green to glaucous, terminated by a spathe of 2 bracteoles united by membranes; flowers solitary, borne on short slender pedicel emerging from spathe; perianth segments 6, unequal, 3 outer segments oblanceolate to oblong-elliptic, apex acute to subacute, or rounded, base unguiculate, usually pure white, occasionally marked green at tip, 3 inner segments much shorter, cuneate, emarginate to form sinus, marked green at apex or base or both, often ridged within, markings occasionally yellow or absent; double forms occur; anthers 6, yellow, conic, poricidal, filaments short, white; style exceeding anthers, filiform; stigma capitate; ovary 3-locular, globose, green to glaucous, forming fleshy capsule. Seeds oblong, obtuse, to 3.5mm, light brown, with paler fleshy caruncle. W Europe (*G.nivalis* often naturalized) to Iranian Caucasus and Caspian Sea.

CULTIVATION Grow in cool dappled shade in moist but well drained, humus-rich soils that do not dry out excessively in summer; a mulch of leafmould is beneficial. *G.reginae-olgae* requires more sun and protection from cold winds than other species. In pots, grow in a mix of equal parts loam, leafmould and sharp sand, in a cool shaded frame in summer, bringing into the alpine house in early winter. Most species are reliably hardy to at least −15°C/5°F. *G.ikariae* is more tender and will suffer below −5°C/23°F. They may be flowered by Christmas by potting up in spring after flowering and bringing in from the frame to the cold glasshouse in early autumn. Propagate by division immediately after flowering (preferably), or in late summer and autumn when bulbs are dormant. Also by ripe seed in the cool shaded frame. Flowers may be expected after four years.

Bulbs are sometimes attacked by stem eelworm, *Distylenchus dipsaci*, causing discoloration, rotting and death of the bulbs, and by the larvae of the large narcissus fly, *Merodon equestris*, which tunnel into the bulbs and destroy then. Remove and burn all affected stock. Grey mould caused by *Botrytis galanthina* is seen on *Galanthus* spp. when infected shoots first appear above the ground and are covered with the grey mycelium and spores of the fungus. The rot extends into the bulbs and some control of the disease can be obtained by dipping dormant bulbs in a systemic fungicide. Small black sclerotia develop on the affected bulbs and contaminate the soil, so that any bulbs bearing these resting stages of the fungus should be discarded. *Galanthus* may also be affected by the same organisms which cause gladiolus dry rot, *Stromatinia gladioli*, and narcissus leaf scorch, *Stagonospora curtisii*.

G.allenii Bak.
Bulb globose, 1.8×1.6cm. Vernation convolute; lvs broad, dull deep green, somewhat glaucous, 6×2cm at flowering, later to 17×2.5cm+, concave at apex. Scape to 12cm; fls almond-scented; outer seg. obovate, 2×1.5cm, inner seg. 9mm, marked green at apex only; ovary globose, green, 5mm in diam. Winter. Caucasus, NW Iran. Z6.

G.alpinus Sosn. (*G.schaoricus* Kem.-Nat.). Bulb ovoid, large. Vernation reduplicate; lvs broad, lanceolate-spathulate, acute, to 9×2cm, dark green, glaucous. Scape to 8cm; fls scented of bitter almonds; outer seg. broadly spathulate, obtuse at apex, 1.5–2cm, inner seg. 7mm, with small apical green spot. Winter. Caucasus. Z6.

G.bortkewitschianus Koss.
Close to both *G.alpinus* and *G.caucasicus*. Lvs narrow, glaucous deep green, strongly hooded at apex. Fls to 1.5cm, with marking on inner seg. narrow. Sterile triploid of very restricted range. Winter. Caucasus. Z6.

G.bulgaricus Velen. See *G.gracilis*.
G.byzantinus Bak. See *G.plicatus* ssp. *byzantinus*.
G.cabardensis Voss. See *G.lagodechianus*.

G.caucasicus (Bak.) Grossh.
Variable. Bulb globose, to 4cm. Vernation convolute; lvs 2–3, broad, oblong or becoming wider above, to 15×2cm+, glaucous, recurved when mature. Scape to 14cm; fls sometimes large; outer seg. obovate, to 2cm+, inner seg. 9mm, marked green at apex; ovary subglobose, green, 4mm diam. Winter. Caucasus. var. **hiemalis** Stern. Fls smaller. Flowering late autumn and early winter. 'Lady Beatrix Stanley' (*G.caucasicus* 'Plenus' hort.): probably a hybrid involving *G.caucasicus*; lvs glaucous pale green, erect; fls double; outer seg. narrow, 'claw-like', to 22×7mm, inner seg. in regular rosette, minutely green-spotted at apex. 'Straffan' (*G.caucasicus* 'Grandis' Burb.): vigorous and beautiful, often with 2 scapes per shoot (collected during Crimean War, selected in Ireland). Z5.

G.cilicicus Bak. See *G.nivalis* ssp. *cilicicus*.
G.corcyrensis (G. Beck) F. Stern. See under *G.reginae-olgae*.

G.elwesii Hook. f. (*G.maximus* Velen.).
Variable. Bulb globose, to 3cm. Vernation convolute; lvs broad, oblong or becoming wider above, 7.5–9.5×1–3cm at flowering, greatly expanding later, when to 30cm, glaucous, hooded at apex. Scape usually short, about 10cm when flower appears, enlarging during anthesis to 20cm+ in some forms; fls honey-scented; outer seg. broad-obovate or rounded, often widely flared in sunshine, to 3cm, inner seg. half length outer seg., marked green at apex and base; ovary subglobose, green, 5mm diam. Winter. Balkans, W Turkey. 'Colesborne': probably *G.elwesii* × *G.caucasicus*; scape short; fls large; inner seg. green from apex to base; ovary elongated, narrow. Z6.

G.elswesii ssp. *minor* D.A. Webb. See *G.gracilis*.

G.fosteri Bak.
Bulb globose, to 2.5cm. Vernation convolute; lvs broad, to 25×2.6cm, deep green, recurved. Scape to 20cm; fls small from immature plants, larger when older; outer seg. oblong-spathulate, to 2.5cm, inner seg. marked green at apex and base; ovary subglobose, green, 4.5mm diam. Winter. S Turkey, Lebanon. Z5.

G.gracilis Čelak. (*G.graecus* hort. non Boiss.; *G.elwesii* ssp. *minor* D.A. Webb; *G.bulgaricus* Velen.).
Bulb globose, to 2cm. Vernation flat; lvs narrow, twisted, about 6cm×7mm at flowering, glaucous. Scape to 10cm; fls sometimes violet-scented; outer seg. obovate, to 2.5cm, inner seg. marked green at apex and base; ovary oblong, yellow-green, 6×4mm. Winter. Bulgaria, Greece, Turkey. Z6.

G.graecus hort. non Boiss. See *G.gracilis*.

G.ikariae Bak. sensu lato (*G.latifolius* Rupr. non Salisb.; *G.platyphyllus* Traub & Mold.; *G.woronowii* A. Los.).
Variable, formerly split into several taxa including the broad-leaved ssp. *latifolius* (Rupr.) Stearn. Bulb globose, to 3cm.

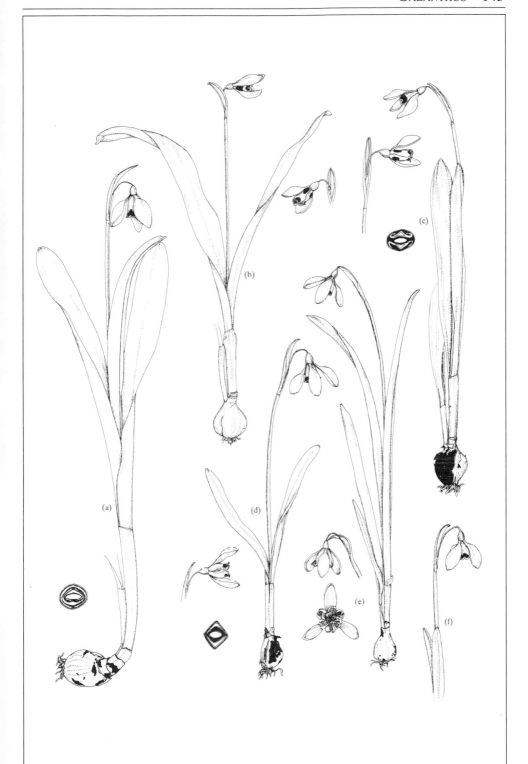

Galanthus   (a) *G.caucasicus*, stem TS   (b) *G.elwesii*, flower (petal missing)   (c) *G.plicatus*, flower (petal missing, stem, TS)   (d) *G.reginae-olgae*, flower (petal missing), stem TS   (e) *G.nivalis* 'Flore pleno' flower   (f) *G.nivalis* spp. *imperati*

Vernation convolute; lvs ligulate to broad, widest above, to 16×3cm, recurved or erect, bright glossy green. Scape to 15cm; fls variable in size; outer seg. oblong-spathulate, to 3cm, inner seg. with apical green mark; ovary subglobose, green, to 5mm diam. Winter. Aegean Is., Turkey, Caucasus. Z6.

G.imperati Bertol. See *G.nivalis* ssp. *imperati*.

G.kemulariae Kuth. See *G.lagodechianus*.

G.ketzhovellii Kem.-Nat. See *G.lagodechianus*.

G.krasnowii Khokhrj. Differs from *G.ikariae* by inner corolla seg. not being emarginate. Z6.

G.lagodechianus Kem.-Nat. (*G.cabardensis* Voss; *G.ketzkhovellii* Kem.-Nat.; *G.kemulariae* Kuth.). Similar to *G.rizehensis* but lvs a brighter glossy green. Winter. Caucasus. Z6.

G.latifolius Rupr. non Salisb. See *G.ikariae*.

G.maximus Velen. See *G.elwesii*.

G.'Merlin' (*G.elwesii* × *G.plicatus*.) Lvs convolute in vernation. Fls large; inner seg. deep green all over. Various progeny of this cross, many of them named.

G.nivalis L. ssp. *nivalis*. SNOWDROP. Variable, with many selected forms. Bulb ovoid to globose, about 1.5cm. Vernation flat; lvs narrow, linear, 9cm×6mm at flowering, somewhat glaucous. Fls faintly honey-scented; outer seg. oblong, 1.5–2cm, inner seg. with apical green mark; ovary subglobose, green, 4mm diam. Winter. Europe (Spain to W Russia; possibly native GB). 'Atkinsii': vigorous, to 25cm; fls large, elongated; another clone, 'Atkinsii Backhouse', usually has one outer seg. deformed. 'Flore Pleno', ('Plenus'): fls double, with inner seg. irregular and untidy to regular and neat; ovary narrow, sterile, spreading by prolific offsets. Several clones. 'Lady Elphinstone': flowers double; inner seg. marked yellow, sometimes temporarily reverting to green. 'Lutescens': small plants; scape yellow-green; ovary and marking on inner seg. yellow. 'Magnet': vigorous, tall; fls large, held on long slender pedicels. 'Poculiformis': inner seg. lack green markings, equalling length of outer seg. 'S. Arnott' ('Sam Arnott', 'Arnott's Seedling'): vigorous, strongly scented; fls large, rounded, on stout scapes. 'Scharlokii': bracteoles long, leafy, free, resembling long ears; outer seg. marked green toward apex. 'Viridiapicis': bracteoles united by membrane; outer seg. marked green toward apex. ssp. *cilicicus* (Bak.) Gottl.-Tann. (*G.cilicicus* Bak.). Differs from ssp. *nivalis* in lvs glaucous and longer at flowering, 16–18cm, recurved. Pedicel shorter than spathe. Marking on inner tepal more elongated than in ssp. *nivalis*. Winter (earlier than ssp. nivalis). S Turkey, Lebanon. ssp. *imperati* (Bertol.) Bak. Fls larger, elongated. Winter. Italy. Z4.

G.nivalis ssp. *reginae-olgae* (Orph.) Gottl.-Tann. See *G.reginae-olgae*.

G.nivalis var. *lutescens* Harpur-Crewe. See *G.nivalis* 'Lutescens'.

G.olgae Orph. ex Boiss. See *G.reginae-olgae*.

G.platyphyllus Traub & Mold. See *G.ikariae* ssp. *latifolius*.

G.plicatus Bieb. ssp. **plicatus.** Bulb globose to ovoid, 2.5cm+. Lvs broad, widest in middle, 10×1cm at flowering, to 30×2cm later, dull green, glaucous in centre of lamina, margins reduplicate at vernation, remaining so below, slightly undulate above. Scape to 20cm; fls variable in size; outer seg. oblong, to 2.5cm, inner seg. marked green at apex only; ovary subglobose, green, 5mm diam. Winter (later than many *Galanthus* spp.). E Europe (Bulgaria and Romania to Crimea). 'Warham': lvs apple green (collected during Crimean War, later selected in Ireland). *G.plicatus* readily hybridizes with other spp., often giving fine but short-lived offspring. *G.plicatus* × *G.nivalis* = *G.× grandiflorus* Bak. Several hybrids between *G.plicatus* and *G.nivalis* 'Plenus', collectively termed Greatorex doubles. Most are vigorous garden plants, including 'Ophelia' and 'Jacquenetta': fls double, inner pet. form a regular rosette, heavily marked green. ssp. **byzantinus** (Bak.) D.A. Webb (*G.byzantinus* Bak.). Very similar to *G.plicatus* but inner seg. marked green at apex and base. N Greece, W Turkey. Z6.

G.rachelae Burb. See *G.reginae-olgae*.

G.reginae-olgae Orph. (*G.nivalis* ssp. *reginae-olgae* (Orph.) Gottl.-Tann.; *G.olgae* Orph. ex Boiss.; *G.rachelae* Burb.). Very similar to *G.nivalis*, differing chiefly in autumnal flowering and glaucous-lined lvs. Bulb globose, to 2.5cm. Lvs linear, dull green with distinct central glaucous stripe, to 14×1cm, produced after fls; vernation flat. Scape to 10cm; fls faintly scented; outer seg. to 2.5cm, inner seg. marked green at apex; ovary subglobose, green, 5mm diam. Autumn. Sicily, Greece, SW Turkey. Plants from Corfu and Sicily flowering in late autumn with their lvs showing have been named *G.corcyrensis* (G. Beck) F. Stern or *G.reginae-olgae* ssp. *corcyrensis* (G. Beck) G. Kamari, but should be regarded as part of *G.reginae-olgae* ssp. *vernalis* G. Kamari. Lvs with central glaucous stripe, to 7cm at flowering. Winter. Balkans. Z7.

G.rizehensis F. Stern (*G.transcaucasicus* Fomin). Bulb globose, to 2cm. Vernation flat; lvs linear, dull deep green, 10×0.5cm, apex obtuse, recurved. Scape to 13cm; outer perianth seg. oblong-oval, to 2cm, inner seg. marked green at apex only; ovary subglobose, green, 5mm diam. Winter. NE Turkey. Z6.

G.sandersii hort. See *G.nivalis* 'Lutescens'.

G.schaoricus Kem.-Nat. See *G.alpinus*.

G.transcaucasicus Fomin. See *G.rizehensis*.

G.woronowii A. Los. See *G.ikariae*.

Galaxia Thunb. (From Gk *galaxaios*, milky, referring to the milky sap.) Iridaceae. 12 species of perennial cormous herbs. Corms depressed-globose with fibrous tunics. Stems shortly emerging or buried, elongating in fruit. Leaves linear or broadly ensiform or oblong-ovate, sheathing at base, at summit of stem, not equitant. Flowers solitary, scarcely exceeding leaves; perianth funnelform, tube slender, cylindrical, long, lobes 6, subequal, patent, oblong-cuneate; filaments partly or wholly fused in a narrow tube, attached to throat of perianth tube; stigmas entire, sometimes bearded; ovary ovoid, sessile or subsessile. Fruit a capsule. Southwest S Africa. Z9.

CULTIVATION   *Galaxia* spp. are most frequently found in the wild in gritty, sandy soils in open and sunny places on flats and mountain slopes in the southwestern Cape Province. They are grown for their beautiful, symmetrical funnel-shaped flowers, usually bright yellow, or rose-pink with a yellow throat in *G.versicolor*. In many species the flowers are short-lived, opening for several hours in bright afternoon sunshine; the scented, individual blooms of *G.fugacissima* last only one day. *Galaxia* may be grown outside provided that the corms can be kept dry in winter, and with protection may tolerate occasional drops in temperature to between –5°C/23°F and –10°C/14°F, but in cool temperate zones they are more frequently grown in the cool glasshouse, bulb frame or alpine house, since the requirement for a period of warm dry dormancy at about 10°C/50°F is more easily accommodated with protected cultivation. Grow in a very sandy, loam-based mix with additional leafmould or equivalent, in direct sunlight; water plentifully when in growth, reducing after flowering to keep dry when dormant. Propagate by seed or offsets.

G.fugacissima (L. f.) Druce (*G.graminea* Thunb.).
Distinguished from *G.ovata* by its narrower lvs, scented, very short-lived fls, fil. sometimes free toward apex, anth. divergent. Summer. SW Cape.

G.graminea Thunb. See *G.fugacissima*.

G.ovata Thunb.
Lvs oblong-ovate, apex minutely apiculate, margins coarse, ribbed, minutely ciliate. Fls 1 per spathe, yellow; fil. to 0.5cm, united, anth. to 0.25cm, erect; style exceeding anth., stigmas bearded. Late spring-summer. SW Cape.

G.ovata var. *purpurea* Ker-Gawl. See *G.versicolor*.

G.versicolor Klatt (*G.ovata* var. *purpurea* Ker-Gawl.).
Lvs lanceolate, margin somewhat undulate, downy. Fls mauve to rose-pink (throat yellow); perianth tube 1–2.5cm, lobes 1.25–2cm; fil. 0.5–0.6cm, free at apices, anth. 0.1–0.3cm, curved; style exceeding anth., stigmas entire, sometimes undulate. Summer. SW Cape.

Galtonia Decne. (For Francis Galton (1822–1911), who travelled and wrote in South Africa and promoted the fingerprint method of identification.) Liliaceae (Hyacinthaceae). 3 species of bulbous perennial herbs. Tunics membranous. Leaves in a basal tuft, rather fleshy, linear-lanceolate to lorate, usually flattened-conduplicate, erect to flaccid, arching. Scape terete; pedicels spreading becoming erect in fruit, subtended by large bracts; flowers showy, white or green, nodding, in a lax, cylindric to conical, erect, terminal raceme; perianth persistent, funnelform-campanulate, tube exceeding lobes, widening toward limb, lobes spreading; stamens 6, shorter than lobes, widening toward limb, attached between middle and throat of tube; ovary 3 angled, oblong. Fruit a trilocular capsule; seeds numerous, angled, brown or black. Late summer. Eastern S Africa.

CULTIVATION   Grown for their elegant spires of bell-shaped flowers, *Galtonia* spp. are specially useful for flowering above faded foliage of other, earlier perennials in the herbaceous border. Also suitable for temporary placement in large containers in the cold glasshouse or conservatory for earlier bloom. *G.candicans* is the hardiest species and with deep mulch protection, may be grown where winter temperatures fall to –15°C/5°F; the remaining species are slightly less cold-tolerant, falling to between –5 and –10°C/23–14F. Grow in a sunny, sheltered position in any light, fertile, well drained soil that does not dry out when plants are in leaf. *Galtonia* spp. greatly resent disturbance. Propagate by ripe seed, sown thinly to allow seedlings to remain *in situ* for their first season's dormancy or by offsets.

G.candicans (Bak.) Decne. (*Hyacinthus candicans* Bak.).
SUMMER HYACINTH.
Lvs 50–100×5cm, 4–6, lorate-lanceolate, suberect, slightly grey-green. Scape to 120cm, stout; raceme to 40cm, slender, to 15-fld; fls drooping, fragrant; pedicels 2.5–6cm; bracts 3–4×1cm, ovate-lanceolate, acute; perianth 3cm, snow-white faintly tinged green at base of tube, lobes twice length of tube. Fr. c3cm, erect; seeds black. Orange Free State, Natal, Lesotho. Z5.

G.princeps (Bak.) Decne. (*Hyacinthus princeps* Bak.).
Similar to *G.candicans* but lvs 40×4cm, narrowly lanceolate; scape to 90cm; pedicels extending to 8cm in fruit; fls fewer in

shorter, broader racemes; perianth tube green, lobes tinted green, only slightly longer than tube. Natal, Transkei. Z8.

G.viridiflora Verdoorn.
Lvs to 60×10cm, c7, forming a short neck base, pale yellow-green, the lower lvs narrowing abruptly at apex, mucronate. Scape to 1m; racemes 15–30-fld; pedicels 2.5cm, pale green; bracts to 3cm, lanceolate, acuminate; perianth 2–5cm, pale green, lobes exceeding tube, margins white. Fr. 2.5×1.4cm, erect, 3-lobed; seeds brown. Orange Free State, Natal, Lesotho. Z8.

Geissorhiza Ker-Gawl. (From Gk *geisson*, coping, and *rhiza*, root; an allusion to the corms which appear to be covered in tiles.) Iridaceae. About 80 species of small to medium-sized perennials, closely related to *Hesperantha*. Corms symmetrical or asymmetrical, usually with hard, sometimes woody, outer coat. Leaves 1 to several. Stems nearly erect, simple or branched. Inflorescence spicate, usually several- to many-flowered but occasionally 1–2-flowered, the flowers subtended by two opposite bracts; flowers white, cream, yellow, violet, purple, pink, red or bicoloured, usually regular but sometimes slightly zygomorphic, usually with short, straight perianth tube and flat, spreading tepals; style long, slender, almost always longer than tube, with 3 short, recurved branches; stamens 3, exserted from tube. Winter rainfall area of South Africa (Cape Province) and S Namibia. Z8.

CULTIVATION   As for *Galaxia*.

G.aspera Goldbl. (*G.secunda* Ker-Gawl.).
8–35cm high. Corm to 6mm diam., ovoid or globose. Lvs usually 3, linear, erect or curved, 2–5mm wide. Stem simple or 1–3-branched, rough to the touch; spike 1–7-fld; fls star-like, white, pale to deep blue or purple; tube 1–2mm, tepals 11–15×4–6mm, obovate; style 7–8mm long, branches to 2mm. Cape Peninsula.

G.erosa (Salisb.) R. Fost. See *G.inflexa*.

G.fulva Ker-Gawl. ex Bak.
7–18cm high; corm globose, almost symmetrical, to 9mm diam. Lvs 3, the two lowest arising near base, the upper one borne on stem, terete but with 4 longitudinal grooves. Stem erect, slightly bent below lowest fl.; spike 1–3-fld; fls star-like, deep golden yellow; tube to 5mm, tepals 15–28×15mm, obovate. SW Cape.

G.hirta (Thunb.) Ker-Gawl. See *G.inflexa*.

G.humilis (Thunb.) Ker-Gawl.
Dwarf, to 14cm; corm ovoid, asymmetrical. Lvs 2–3, the lowest longer than stem, almost linear but with 2 longitudinal grooves on each surface. Stem usually simple, occasionally with 1 branch; spike 2–8-fld; fls star-like, bright yellow; tube 5–6mm, tepals to 22×14mm, obovate; style branches 3–4mm. Cape Peninsula and Cape Flats.

G.inflexa (Delaroche) Ker-Gawl. (*G.erosa* (Salisb.) R. Fost.; *G.hirta* (Thunb.) Ker-Gawl.; *Hesperantha kermesina* Klatt.)
12–30cm, rarely shorter or taller; corm to 12mm diam.; symmetrical. Lvs 2–3, usually half to two-thirds as long as stem and 3–4mm wide, almost linear but with edges extended outwards at right angles and midrib winged, the edge and midrib pubesc. Stem usually simple, spike 2–6-fld; fls star-like, pink, red or purple, or white, cream or pale yellow tinged with red

on outside; tube 1–2.5mm, tepals 10–18×8–10mm, rarely to 24mm, obovate; style branches 4–5mm. SW Cape.

G.ovata (Burm. f.) Asch. & Gräbn.
Dwarf, to 15cm; corm ovoid, asymmetrical. Lvs 2–3, 1–6cm×5–14mm, the 2 lowest basal, prostrate or semi-erect, ovate-oblong, the edge and sometimes the veins ciliate, often with minute brown dots. Spike 1–6-fld; fls white or pale pink, marked with red in centre and dark red on outside; tube 10–30mm, tepals spreading but slightly cup-shaped, 10–13×5–7mm, lanceolate or obovate. SW Cape.

G.radians (Thunb.) Goldbl. (*G.rochensis* (Ker-Gawl.) Ker-Gawl.).
Dwarf, to 16cm; corm less than 1cm diam., globose, symmetrical. Lvs 3, to 1.5mm wide, linear, or similar length to stem. Stem erect, simple or with 1 branch; spike 1–4-fld; fls slightly zygomorphic, tepals concave, red at base, the apical half deep blue-violet, the colours separated by a white band, each tepal also with a dark, pitted mark in the centre; tube 6–8mm, tepals 15–22×12–15mm; style branches 4mm. W Cape Flats.

G.rochensis (Ker-Gawl.) Ker-Gawl. See *G.radians*.
G.secunda Ker-Gawl. See *G.aspera*.

G.splendidissima Diels.
8–20cm; corm 7–10mm diam., ovoid. Lvs 3, of similar length to stem, 1–2mm wide, linear with 2 grooves on each side, slightly sticky. Stem rough to touch, simple or 1–2-branched; spike 1–6-fld; fls deep violet-blue, dark toward base of tepals, yellow in throat, cup-shaped, slightly zygomorphic, tube 2–4mm, tepals 15–22×8–13mm, ovate, the outer 3 slightly wider than inner 3; style branches 2mm, recurved. Late winter–early spring. W Cape.

Gelasine Herb. Iridaceae. (From Gk *gelasinos*, one who laughs.) 4 species of perennial cormous herbs. Corm somewhat truncate. Leaves plicate. Flowers several in a terminal cluster, regular, short-lived; perianth tube very short; segments subequal, obovate; filaments united to form a short column, anthers basifixed, spreading, style short, subulate, 3-branched, lobes linear. Capsule turbinate, 3-locular; seeds minute. Subtropical. S America. Z9.

CULTIVATION   As for *Romulea*.

G.azurea (Herb.). See *G.elongata*.

G.elongata (Graham) Ravenna (*G.azurea* Herb.).
Stems 50–60cm. Lvs basal, to 60×3cm, narrowly lanceolate. Fls cup-shaped; tepals bright blue with a white blotch at the base; tepals *c*2cm, obovate, cuspidate. Uruguay, S Brazil.

G.punctata Herb. See *Alophia drummondii*.

Gethyllis L. (From Gk diminutive of *gethuon*, leek.) Amaryllidaceae. 12 species of bulbous, stemless herbs resembling *Crocus*. Leaves emerging as the fruit forms, linear to lanceolate, to 15cm, flat, crisped, spirally twisted or reflexed, glabrous or rough. Inflorescence a scapose raceme; perianth salverform, cylindric, tube to 8cm long; tepals to 6cm, 6, equal, white to pink or red; stamens 6 to many, to 4cm, anthers basifixed; style straight, equal to or longer than stamens; ovary 3-celled, hidden by spathe, ovules many; stigma capitate. Fruit clavate, succulent, yellow, fragrant; seeds globose. Summer. S Africa. Z9.

CULTIVATION   Frost-tender bulbs bearing their sweetly scented crocus-like flowers in summer, followed by spirally twisted narrow leaves. Suited to the rock garden in frost-free zones, or for temporary planting in similar situations in colder areas. Otherwise, grow in pots in the cool glasshouse, 2.5cm/1in. deep, in a mix of equal parts of loam, leafmould and sharp sand. Plant in spring and water very sparingly until growth commences; water plentifully when in growth, and dry off in autumn to overwinter in frost-free conditions. Propagate from offsets removed when re-potting overcrowded clumps in spring; they take two years to reach flowering size. Also by seed sown when ripe.

G.afra L.
Lvs to 5cm, to 20, linear, spirally twisted, ribbed, glabrous. Tepals oblong to oblanceolate, to 2cm across; style longer than stamens. Fr. to 7.5×3cm.

G.ciliaris L.
Lvs 20, later than fls, linear, spirally twisted, ciliate.Tepals oblong-lanceolate, to 1.5cm across; style equal to stamens. Fr. to 7.5×1.5cm.

Gladiolus L. (From Lat. *gladiolus*, diminutive of *gladius*, a sword, referring to the leaf shape.) Iridaceae. About 180 species of cormous perennial herbs. Corms with woody or fibrous tunics, globose or ovoid, occasionally rhizome-like. Leaves 1 to several, linear or ensiform, iris like, sometimes equitant, usually deciduous, rarely evergreen. Inflorescence a spike, simple or branched, 1- to many-flowered, usually secund but occasionally distichous; flowers zygomorphic, sometimes scented, white, green, yellow, orange, red, pink, mauve or purple, often striped or blotched with another colour; perianth tube long or short, tubular or funnel-shaped, usually curved, lobes 6, subequal or unequal; stamens 3; style 3-branched. Africa, mainly S Africa, Madagascar, Europe, Arabia, W Asia. Z9 unless specified.

CULTIVATION   Of the almost 200 known species and subspecies of *Gladiolus*, relatively few are cultivated outside their native regions. Those most commonly seen in modern gardens are the legion large-flowered, frost-tender hybrids developed predominantly from the South African species first introduced to Europe in the late 17th century, although the cultivation of Eurasian species, *G. communis*, *G.c.* ssp. *byzantinus* and *G.italicus* considerably predates these introductions. *G.italicus*, familiar to Gerarde as corne flag, corne sedge or corne gladin (*Herball*, 1597), still grows wild as a cornfield weed throughout its natural range from France south to North Africa, eastwards to Central Asia and Iran.

It seems likely that modern hybrids derive from only seven species all native of South Africa, these are *G.cardinalis*, *G. carneus*, *G. cruentus*, *G.dalenii*, *G.oppositiflorus*, *G. papilio* and *G. tristis*. The 19th century practice of conferring spurious Latin names to these hybrids has done much to obscure their parentage and confuse their horticultural classification. The earliest hybrid, appearing in about 1823, and forerunner of the modern early summer-flowering gladioli, was *G.×colvillei*, the cross between *G.cardinalis* and *G.tristis*, named for its hybridist, the Chelsea nurseryman James Colville. The beautiful white-flowered chimera, *G.×colvillei* 'The Bride', still grown, appeared in the early 1870s. Smaller-flowered variants of this group are often called Nanus Hybrids. The early hybridization of *G. cardinalis* ×*G.carneus* producing the Ramosus Hybrids (*G.ramosus* hort., now *G.×insignis*), eventually gave rise to over 100 variants, deservedly popular as cut flowers, for flower border and forcing; these are now usually sold as Charm Hybrids.

The introduction of *G.dalenii* to Europe in 1825 by Prof. Reinwardt of Leyden proved a major contribution to the development of modern hybrids. Unlike the earlier, spring-flowering introductions, *G.dalenii* carried its large flowers on tall spikes in summer, producing them from corms that stored well over winter for spring plantings. *G.dalenii*, used in crosses with other South African species, produced several hybrid series, including *G.×gandavensis*, from van Houtte at Ghent in 1841, later *G.×brenchleyensis* from John Hooker (a name of no botanical standing derived from Hooker's hometown of Brenchley), and *G.×nanceianus* hort. ex Bak. from Victor Lemoine at Nancy during 1877–82. Working with *G. papilio* and *G.×gandavensis*, Lemoine produced notable hybrids with distinct lip blotches, also using *G.papilio* in producing *G.×lemoinei* hort. ex Bak., the first of the 'blue' gladioli, with large purple or brown markings at the base of the yellow or orange lower segments.

From Germany, Max Leichtlin contributed a range of blue, purple and violet flowered types, known as Leichtlinii Hybrids, and by crossing the dark red *G.cruentus* with *G.×gandavensis*, also produced the Cruentus Hybrids whose further developments by John Lewis Childs in New York, were named *G.×childsii* hort. A range of interspecific hybrids was widely distributed in the latter part of the 19th-century under these names, many playing an important part in the further developments of the exhibition gladioli. The *G.×childsii* hybrids provided the basis for an extremely significant breakthrough during later work by Amos Kunderd, since from these, in 1903, he produced the first gladiolus with ruffled florets, 'Kunderdii Glory'. Kunderd's subsequent programmes gave rise in 1923 to the 'orchid flowered' types, with laciniated and double petalled forms. The production of ruffled forms continues to be a primary aim of many modern breeders and American and Canadian growers have since maintained a leading position in their production.

In the late 1890s a species named *G.nebulicola* Ingram (now included in *G.dalenii*) was used by British growers, notably James Kelway and Frank Unwin, in creating the wide range of Primulinus Hybrids. Although the exact identity of this colour variant is now unclear, its salient features were its hooded florets, supple and slender stems and the distinctive cloudy orange-yellow colouration. A deep golden-yellow flowered form of *G.dalenii*, then known as *G.× xanthus* Lewis, was also involved in the parentage of this group.

By the early 1900s, *Gladiolus* cultivars were numbered in their thousands. The British Gladiolus Society was formed in 1926 and held its first specialist show the following year. The American Gladiolus Society was established in 1910, to be absorbed in 1945 into the North American Gladiolus Council. During the 1930s in Canada, Professor Palmer produced a number selectively line-bred cultivars including 'Picardy', named 'Gladiolus of the Century' because it has been extensively used to produce superb offspring with a considerable role in further developments of large-flowered gladiolus.

Postwar developments included the crossing of Nanus and Primulinus hybrids by Unwin's (Cambridge, England), to give the Peacock hybrids, and work by Konijnenburg and Mark in Holland to produce the Butterfly hybrids, from crossings of small-flowered cultivars; their beautifully marked flowers are particularly valued for cutting. Leonard Butt, in Ontario, produced the first of the Ruffled Miniatures.

More recently, attention has been focused on improving flower scent using Cape species, notably *G.tristis* and *G. callianthus*, as the genetic source of fragrance. Significant work in this area was done by Capt. T.T. Barnard in creating the scented Purbeck Hybrids in Dorset. In America, a number of selections of fragrant sports of garden hybrids have been made, including 'Acacia', 'Yellow Rose', and 'Cliffie'. At higher levels of sophistication, the doubling of chromosome numbers in garden hybrids offers great potential in creating new strains.

The species *Gladiolus* fall broadly into four groups, the largest being the frost-tender, winter and spring-flowering natives of South Africa. The half-hardy summer-flowering species from southern and central Africa (formerly the Natalensis Group) are primarily *G.dalenii* variants. Eurasian species native to southern and western Europe and the Mediterranean are generally the hardiest in cultivation, but some African species are also resilient and cold-hardy, including *G.callianthus* and others formerly classified in *Acidanthera*.

The complexities of hybridization that have produced modern garden hybrids render their classification by species origin impracticable. They are grouped by size (in imperial measurements), colour and flower form according to the classification system developed for exhibition purposes by the North American Gladiolus Council, which is accepted in the US, Canada, the UK, Australia and New Zealand. Some groups of cultivars are unclassified and are not used for exhibition purposes; this does not imply inferiority for garden use.

Unclassified. Spring-flowering cultivars derived from interspecific hybrids primarily of South African origin. Height 60–75cm/24–30 in., stems flexible, florets 6–7 4–5cm/1.5–2 in. wide, in pink, cream and red. In mild areas with a minimum ground temperature of –6°C/21°F, planted about 8cm/3 in. deep, corms may be left *in situ* over winter for late spring flowers, best with the protection of a dry mulch, otherwise grown under glass. Examples: Nanus cultivars: 'Elvira', 'Guernsey Glory', 'Impressive'; *G.×colvillei* 'The Bride'; Charm cultivars: 'Comet', 'Charm', 'Robinetta'.

Primulinus Hybrids. Hybrids of species in the *G. dalenii* Group. Used in gardens as cut flowers and for showing. Height 90–140cm/36–56 in., stems slender and flexible, sometimes branched, flowers 14–19, alternately spaced and fully separate. Flower form includes a small basal lip or petal, wider lateral petals, the top petal with a pronounced hood. Flower maximum size 9cm/3.5 in. wide (the larger Prim-Grandiflora, above 10cm/4 in. wide is now obsolete). Where Primulinus hybrids are used for exhibition, the trinomial classification number (see below) is prefixed by the letter P, e.g. P254. Plant early to mid-spring for mid- to late summer flowers. Lift and store in frost-free conditions over winter. Examples: Gg.'White City', 'Leonora', 'Hastings' and 'Rutherford'.

Summer-flowering Grandiflora. This group includes the majority of the named garden gladiolus cultivars; they are planted in early spring to flower in late summer and lifted in autumn for frost-free storage. They are classified by flower size and colour, expressed by a trinomial classification. The first figure indicates the width of the largest floret when fully expanded thus: 1, miniature (under $2^1/2$in.); 2, small (2.5–$3^5/8$in.); 3, medium ($3^1/2$–$4^3/8$in.); 4, large ($4^1/2$–$5^3/8$in.); 5, giant ($5^1/2$in. and over). The second digit indicates colour thus: 0, white; 1, yellow; 2, orange; 3, salmon; 4, pink; 5, red; 6, rose; 7, lavender; 8, violet; 9, brown, tan, smokey and other combinations. The third digit, when an even number, indicates intensity of colour thus 2, light, 4, medium, 6, deep. Where the third digit is an odd number, this indicates the bloom carries conspicuous marking, as a throat blotch, streaking, stippling or as a contrasting edge to the perimeter of the outer petal. The higher the third digit, odd or even, the more intense the colour. For example, a cultivar classified as 454 would have a large-sized, medium red flower, a 457 cultivar would have a large-sized, deep red flower with a red black blotch or marked throat.

In addition, Grandiflora types are further classified by size. *Giant and Large*: height 140–190cm/55–75 in., 20–27 buds open, stems thick, close placement of flowers; flower form wide open, not hooded; petals plain, waved or frilled. Examples: (Giant) 'Amsterdam', 'Silver Jubilee', 'Parade'; (Large) 'Inca Queen', 'Prime Time', 'Drama'. *Medium*: height 100–115cm/40–45 in., 19–23 buds with 6–8 open; flower form not hooded, petals plain, waved, frilled or ruffled. Examples: 'Apollo', 'Atlantis', 'Mr. Fox'. *Small and miniature*: height 90–130cm/36–50 in., 12–17 buds with 5–6 open, stems slender, flower placement close and alternate, petals usually waved or ruffled. Examples: (Small) 'Georgette', 'Holland Pearl'; (Miniature) 'Small Wonder', 'Firestorm', 'Natty'. *Miscellaneous*: includes mutant forms of Grandiflora cvs that are of interest but do not con-

Gladiolus   (a) *G.citrinus*   (b) *G.dalenii*   (c) *G.×colvillei*   (d) *G.papilio*   (e) *G.nanus*   (f) *G.stellatus*
(g) *G.nerineiodes*   (h) *G.orchidiflorus*   (i) *G.alatus*

form to standard classification for exhibition purposes. They are generally referred to as Exotics and include Fancies, Face Ups, Dragons, and Doubles and come in a wide colour range sometimes in unusual combinations. Height about 90cm/36in.; buds 11–17 with 4–6 open, placement imprecise; petals frilled, ruffled, crinkled or laciniate. Examples: 'Bridesmaid', 'Gloriosa', 'Jester', 'Ripple', 'Hocus Pocus', 'Fudge'.

Most gladioli require a sunny site, with protection from wind, in a well-drained, neutral to slightly acid soil, pH 6.5–7.0. Heavy soils are improved by incorporation of compost, leafmould, and sharp sand and in addition, corms may be bedded on to a layer of sharp sand when planting. For exhibition and cut flowers, the ground should be well cultivated in autumn, to a depth of 25–30cm/8–12in., with a spring application of bonemeal or balanced fertilizer incorporated into the top spit.

Plant corms of summer-flowering hybrids and cultivars in early spring in mild weather, later blooms may be had from late spring/early summer plantings; successional planting at 10–14 day intervals prolongs the flowering season. Corms may be advanced before planting by standing in trays in good light at a temperature of 12–15°C/55–60°F, 2–3 weeks before planting out, and in dry springs, may be pre-soaked before planting; a preplanting fungicidal dip is recommended. Set corms 10–15cm/4–6 in. deep, depending on size, with the same distance between corms. Blooms for exhibition are better set at 20cm/8 in. spacings. In general, giant and large-flowered cultivars may be expected to flower approximately 100 days after planting, smaller flowered cultivars within about 80 days.

Water regularly, especially in dry seasons, and apply high potash/low nitrogen fertilizers at ten-day intervals when in full growth, as a top dressing or as foliar feed. Keep plants weed free, preferably by hand weeding and hoeing after emergence, since chemical herbicides may cause distortion of flower and foliage. Support tall plants by staking from mid-summer onwards, delaying introduction of canes until the orientation of flower buds becomes obvious; tie in at 20cm/8 in. intervals with soft twine or raffia.

Blooms for indoor decoration are best cut early in the morning, when 2–4 blooms have opened fully, from well-watered plants (especially important in frilled and ruffled miniatures). At least four mature leaves must be left for subsequent development of corms.

The Eurasian spp., including *G.byzantinus, G. communis, G. italicus* and *G.illyricus*, can be grown permanently outdoors in mild temperate gardens, where winter temperatures do not fall much below −5 to −10°C/23–14°F (lower temperatures apply to situations with perfect drainage); the last may establish itself in grassland in more favoured gardens. *G.papilio, G.tristis, G.cardinalis* and *G.dalenii* may be overwintered *in situ* in mild winter areas given mulch protection from frost, otherwise are suitable for the cool glasshouse. The subtly coloured *G.papilio* and the popular white *G.callianthus* (*Acidanthera*) are two of the more unusual species commonly encountered in dry sunny gardens. The winter-flowering South African spp., flowering at any time between autumn and very early spring, are suited to pot cultivation in the cool to intermediate glasshouse or conservatory, but may require supplementary lighting at daylengths below 8–9 hours as flowers stems and bud develop. In general porous clay pots are to be preferred, especially if small corms are to be stored dry when dormant in their pots. Black plastic pots should be avoided: overheated corms suffer.

Although giant and large-flowered cvs are generally unsuited to pot cultivation, small and miniature types, along with the Primulinus and Nanus cvs, make excellent subjects for culture in deep pots, in a moderately fertile and freely draining potting mix. Species *Gladiolus* may be better grown in a leaner mix, comprising a low-fertility loam-based medium with one quarter by volume sharp sand, perlite or vermiculite. Early-flowering types such as *G.×colvillei* may be overwintered in pots in the cool glasshouse or frost free frame, to be gently forced at 10°C/50°F for early blooms. Give good light and ventilation, water plentifully when in full growth and apply a dilute liquid feed at weekly intervals as the roots fill the pot, withdrawing water gradually after flowering to dry off completely as foliage fades.

The foliage of the hardier spring and summer-flowering types, such as *G.×colvillei*, Nanus Hybrids and the Eurasian spp., fades about six weeks after blooming and should be removed at ground level. Summer flowering gladioli remain green well into autumn, but corms should be lifted before first frosts; remove all stems and foliage close to the crown with a clean sharp knife. Detach cormlets and dry off both corms and spawn in well ventilated conditions at about 18–24°C/65–75°F. Store only sound, healthy corms after cleaning and dusting with fungicide and insecticide against the gladiolus thrip, in dry, cool but frost-free conditions; check regularly during storage and discard any that are soft, mildewed or desiccated.

Propagate by species by seed, or by cormlets, named hybrids and cultivars by cormlets, selecting larger cormlets at lifting. After drying and cleaning, store in frost-free conditions overwinter and plant in early spring after pre-soaking. Water plentifully and feed when in full growth until mid summer, removing any flower spikes to ensure good corm growth. Lift in mid-autumn, store again overwinter. They should bloom in their second season. Propagation is also possible by cutting large mature corms into sections, each with at least one shoot or eye. Use a sharp sterile knife to reduce risk of infection, treat with fungicide powder and plant in early spring in shallow beds outdoors in warm climates or under glass in cooler zones. New cormlets should have formed by mid autumn to be lifted and stored.

Sow seed thinly, when ripe in autumn, or in early spring in a moisture-retentive medium, at 15°C/60°F, in large pots or boxes so that seedlings may remain undisturbed until cormlets have formed. Water moderately during their first season and dry off in autumn; cormlets may then be lifted or overwintered in their pots provided these are kept dry and frost free.

The gladiolus thrip, *Taeniothrips simplex* causes characteristic silvery speckling on leaves and flowers. Adults and larvae occur on leaf bases in flowers and in flower buds. Apply systemic insecticide in early summer and at three-week intervals. Adults may also overwinter on corms, laying eggs as temperatures rise in spring. A measure of control is obtained by stripping off loose scale leaves and dusting with an appropriate insecticide before storing and again in spring. Also affected by aphid (including the tulip bulb aphid), wireworm, leatherjackets, swift moth larvae, keel slugs, nematodes (including the potato tuber eelworm), and bulb mites. Foliage is sometimes attacked by caterpillars of the single shades moth.

Core rot or botrytis rot is caused by the fungus *Sclerotinia draytonii* (conidial state, *Botrytis gladiolorum*): extensive brown rots are seen at the centre of the corm and spores produced from infected shoots cause leaf and flower spotting. The disease will spread from corm to corm in damp storage conditions and the black sclerotia which form on the corms can also survive in the soil to perpetuate the disease. In dry rot caused by *Stromatinia gladioli*, shoots which at first appear healthy turn yellow then brown and are easily pulled away from the corm base to reveal a mass of black sclerotia. These sclerotia remain in the soil as a major source of reinfection. The fungus also causes a dry rot of stored corms.

Hard rot, caused by *Septoria gladioli*, results in brown spots on the leaves and spores washed down into the soil and can infect the corms, producing hard dark-coloured lesions which are often concealed by the scales. This fungus does not spread from corm to corm in store, but can persist in the soil on crop debris. In fusarium yellows, caused by *Fusarium oxysporum* f. sp. *gladioli* the symptoms are similar to those of dry rot in that the leaves yellow and die back, but there are no sclerotia at the base of the shoots. The fungus attacks the roots which turn brown and die; corms in storage may eventually become black and mummified. Some infected corms remain symptomless, and give rise to diseased plants. The fungus can live on in the soil. Scab and neck rot is caused by the bacterium *Pseudomonas gladioli*. The leaf tips shrivel when the numerous red brown spots at the base of the leaves enlarge and cause rot; yellow spots on the corms exude a gum containing the bacteria. Infected corms or bacteria present in the soil perpetuate the disease.

Sites where any of these diseases have occurred are best kept free of bulbs or corms for several years. Corms must be stored in cool, dry, well ventilated conditions and any that are diseased or damaged must be destroyed. Nothing can be done to control these diseases in the growing plant, although the leaf and flower spotting caused by the botrytis stage of *Sclerotinia draytonii* can be prevented by fungicide spraying.

In common with many bulbs and corms *Gladiolus* spp. are affected by blue mould, *Penicillium* spp. including *P.gladioli*, and are susceptible to the fungus *Mycosphaerella macrospora*, which causes a serious leaf disease of irises and other members of the Iridaceae. Bean yellow mosaic virus causes a yellow leaf mottle and dark streaks on the flowers, while cucumber mosaic virus causes a greyish leaf mottle and white blotches on the flowers. Both are transmitted by aphid and may lead to a reduction in cormlet numbers. Tobacco ringspot virus causes yellow spots on the leaves and white streaks in the flowers; tomato ring spot causes a general stunting. The last two viruses are carried by ectoparasitic soil nematodes.

G.abbreviatus Andrews (*Antholyza abbreviata* (Andrews) Pers.; *Homoglossum abbreviatum* (Andrews) Goldbl.; *Petamenes abbreviatus* (Andrews) N.E. Br.).
Stems 30–65cm. Lvs 1, basal, to 40×0.5cm, X-shaped in cross-section. Spike 3–8-fld; bracts to 7cm, red, pink or orange; fls 5.5–9cm, red, dark red, brown-red or orange-red; tube 38–56mm, abruptly widening about halfway along and with a smaller nectar-sac at the point; topmost tepals 22–28×13–15mm, upper laterals 8–10×7–8mm, the lower 3 much smaller. S Africa (SW Cape).

G.alatus L.
Corm to 1.5cm diam., more or less globose. Stem 8–35cm, usually simple but occasionally branched, sometimes with the basal part creeping underground and producing cormlets in leaf axils. Lvs to 40×1cm, 4–5, linear, usually rough to touch. Spike 1–10-fld, secund; fls scented, 2-lipped, brick-red to orange, apices of the lower lobes yellow or lime green; lobes clawed, uppermost lobe 30–48mm, sometimes hooded, upper laterals 20–30×20–30mm, spreading, lower lobes spathulate, deflexed, much shorter and narrower. Late winter–spring. S Africa (winter rainfall region of Cape Province).

G.angustus L. LONG-TUBED PAINTED LADY.
Corm to 2cm diam., globose. Stem slender, 20–75cm, rarely branched. Lvs 3–5, the longest 15–75×0.3–0.87cm, linear. Spike secund, laxly 2–10-fld; fls funnel-shaped with a long tube, white, cream or pale yellow, sometimes pink-tinged, with red or purple diamond- or spade-shaped marks on lower lobes; tube 4–7cm, straight or slightly curved; uppermost lobe hooded, 25–35×13–20mm, oblong, the 3 lower lobes 18–28×5–10mm, elliptic. Spring–summer. S Africa (Cape Peninsula).

G.arcuatus Klatt.
Corm 1–2cm diam., somewhat globose. Stem to 35cm, unbranched. Lvs 3–5, the largest 12–30cm×1–4mm, linear, curved. Spike 2–9-fld, more or less secund, the rachis twisted;

fls scented, 2-lipped, mauve or purple, the basal half of the lower lobes yellow or lime green; tube 12–14mm, slightly curved; lobes clawed, the blades more or less elliptic, dorsal lobe 23–33×10–15mm, the upper laterals and 3 lower lobes somewhat shorter and narrower. Late winter–early spring. S Africa (Namaqualand), Namibia.

G.atroviolaceus Boiss.
Stem 35–70cm. Lvs 3, the lowest 30–40cm×0.4–0.8mm, narrowly linear, grass-like. Spike secund, densely 4–10-fld; fls deep violet-purple, sometimes almost black, tube curved. Spring–summer. Greece, Turkey, Iraq, Iran. Z7.

G.aureus Bak. (*Homoglossum aureum* (Bak.) Oberm.). GOLDEN GLADIOLUS.
Stems 50–60cm. Fls pale to golden yellow, opening fully only when weather is warm. Winter–spring. S Africa (SW Cape).

G.blommesteinii L. Bol.
Corm 1–2cm diam., ovoid or subglobose. Stem 30–70cm, slender, unbranched. Lvs about 4, the lowest and longest about as long as stem but only 0.5–2mm wide. Spike secund, 1–4-fld; fls funnel-shaped, pale to deep pink, mauve or blue-mauve, the basal half of the lower lobes yellow or cream with red or purple striations; tube 14–20mm, curved; lobes elliptic, 25–35mm long, the dorsal slightly larger than others, the apical half of the lower lobes deflexed, upper 3 13–19mm wide, lower 3 8–12mm wide. Late winter–spring. S Africa (SW Cape).

G.bonae-spei Goldbl. & De Vos (*Homoglossum merianellum* (Thunb.) Bak.).
Stems 30–70cm. Basal lf 22×0.5cm, linear, pubesc. Spike 2–6-fld; fls 5–7.5cm, gold, orange-red or red; tube 28–47mm, with a small nectar-sac about half way along, where the tube widens abruptly; tepals obovate, apiculate, the topmost 18–25×10–18mm, the other slightly smaller. S Africa (Cape Peninsula). var. **aureum** Lewis. Fls golden-yellow or orange-

Gladiolus　(a) *G.callianthus*　(b) *G.liliaceus*　(c) *G.saundersii*　(d) *G.caryophyllaceus*　(e) *G.undulatus*
(f) *G.brevifolius*　(g) *G.bullatus*

yellow, sometimes tinged with red. Spring. var. *merianellum* (Devos) Goldbl. & De Vos. Fls red or orange-red.

G.brevifolius Jacq.
Corm 1–4cm diam. Stem 15–65cm, slender, unbranched. Basal lf 1, 30–60cm×2–8mm, linear, spirally twisted, not usually developed by flowering time; stem lvs 1–3, mostly sheathing. Spike fairly laxly or densely 3–20-fld, secund; fls sometimes scented, 2-lipped, pale to deep pink or mauve, rarely white, dull yellow or brown, green-brown or grey-blue and yellow, the lower lobes usually with yellow and pink, red or mauve marks; tube 10–15mm long, funnel-shaped, curved; dorsal lobe hooded, 20–30×10–20mm, obovate, upper lateral lobes slightly shorter and narrower, lower 3 lobes somewhat recurved, sometimes clawed, 15–25×5–10mm, joined at base for 2–3mm. Autumn. S Africa (SW Cape). var. *brevifolius*. Stem less than 60cm. Spike 3–10-fld; fls not or very slightly scented, over 3cm long, pink, mauve or white. var. *minor* Lewis. Stem usually less than 30cm, occasionally to 45cm. Fls scented, less than 3cm, pink, mauve, occasionally white. var. *obscurus* Lewis. Stem to 75cm. Fls small, dull yellow-grey or brown, green-brown or grey-blue and yellow. var. *robustus* Lewis. Stem usually over 60cm; spike 12–20-fld. Fls pink, mauve-pink, occasionally white.

G.brevitubus Lewis.
Corm 8–12mm diam., ovoid. Stem 15–50cm, slender, unbranched. Lvs 3–4, the lowest usually longer than spike, 1–3mm wide, linear, erect. Spike densely 2–6-fld, secund; fls small, 2.5cm, scented, almost regular, pale to deep salmon-pink, orange or brick red, sometimes yellow in centre, or with a yellow mark on lower lobes; tube funnel-shaped, 3mm long; lobes spreading, 12–22×6–10mm, oblong or obovate. Spring–summer. S Africa (SW Cape).

G.bullatus Thunb. CALEDON BLUEBELL.
Corm to 2cm diam., ovoid or globose. Stem 35–70cm, slender, unbranched. Lvs 3–4, sheathing stem with a short, free blade. Spike secund, 1–2-fld; fls about 5cm long, bell-shaped with the lower lobes longer and projecting forwards, pale to deep mauve-blue, the lower lobes with yellow transverse marks and the basal half paler with purple spots; tube 10–13mm, funnel-shaped, curved; 3 upper lobes 20–33×14–28mm, obovate to orbicular, lower lobes 30–40×9–16mm, spathulate, joined at base for 7–10mm. Late winter–spring. S Africa (SW Cape).

G.byzantinus Mill. See G.communis ssp. byzantinus.

G.callianthus Marais (*Acidanthera bicolor* Hochst.).
Stem 70–100cm long, slender, arched. Lvs linear, about half as long as stem. Spike 2–10-fld; fls scented, white with dark red or purple marks in throat; tube 18cm, slender, slightly curved; lobes 2–3cm, subequal, spreading; anth. purple. Early autumn. East Tropical Africa, from Ethiopia southwards. Z8.

G.cardinalis Curtis. WATERFALL GLADIOLUS; NEW YEAR LILY.
Corm to 3cm diam., subglobose. Stem 60–115cm, robust, usually unbranched. Lvs 5–9, the largest 40–90×1.5–3cm, sword-shaped, rather lax. Spike secund, 5–12-fld, the fls facing stem apex; fls large, crimson or scarlet with a white or cream diamond-shaped mark bordered with mauve on lower 3 lobes, occasionally also on upper lateral lobes; tube 3–4cm, slender, becoming funnel-shaped; dorsal lobe hooded, the others spreading, upper lobes 40–55×18–30cm, the dorsal wider than the laterals, lower lobes 35–48×13–17mm, elliptic to oblong-spathulate, joined at base for 5–6mm. Summer. S Africa (SW Cape).

G.carinatus Ait.
Stem slender, 20–100cm tall, rather flexuous. Lvs 3, the lowest of similar length to stem but only 1–8mm wide, linear, grass-like. Spike secund, rather laxly 2–9-fld; fls sometimes scented, 4–6cm long, funnel-shaped, bell-shaped or bilabiate, pale to deep blue or violet-mauve, pale to deep pink or pale to deep yellow, the lower lobes with an irregular yellow transverse band with purple spots above and below; tube 12–18mm, curved; dorsal lobe 25–38×15–25mm, hooded,

obovate, upper laterals slightly smaller, lower lobes clawed, spathulate, 25–35cm. Winter–spring. S Africa (W Cape).

G.carmineus C.H. Wright. HERMANUS CLIFF GLADIOLUS.
Stem 16–60cm long, unbranched, usually flexuous. Lvs 2–3, arising at base after flowering, to 65×1.5cm, linear, grass-like, glaucous; stem also with 3–6 semi-sheathing lvs. Spike 2–6-fld, more or less secund; fls to 9cm diam., deep pink or carmine red with white or cream mark bordered with darker pink on lower lobes; tube 30–45mm long, straight or somewhat curved; lobes 35–58×18–30mm, the dorsal hooded, the rest spreading, the 3 lower slightly smaller than the upper 3. Late summer–autumn. S Africa (Southern Cape).

G.carneus Delaroche. PAINTED LADY.
20–100cm. Lvs about 5, to 60×2cm, but usually smaller, linear or sword-shaped. Spike laxly 3–12-fld, sometimes branched, distichous; fls to 8cm, funnel-shaped, white, cream, mauve or pink, usually with yellow, red or purple markings on lower lobes, or with dark blotches in throat; tube 2–4cm long, slender, curved, widening near throat; lobes usually spreading, of similar length to tube, ovate, the upper 3 larger than lower 3. Spring–summer. S Africa (W Cape).

G.caryophyllaceus (Burm. f.) Poir.
Stem stout, usually 50–75cm, rarely branched. Lvs 4–6, the largest about half as long as stem, 1–2cm wide, usually sparsely hairy. Spike secund or distichous, rather laxly 2–8-fld; fls large, scented, bell-shaped or funnel-shaped, pale to deep pink or mauve, the lower lobes spotted or streaked with red or pink, the outside of the lobes with a darker central line; tube usually 35–50mm, curved, funnel-shaped towards throat; lobes usually obovate, dorsal 30–40×10–25mm, the others 25–35×9–18mm, the lower 3 joined for 5–7mm at base. Late winter spring. S Africa (SW Cape).

G.citrinus Klatt.
Stem 6–25cm, very slender. Lvs 2–3, glabrous or very slightly hispid, erect, rigid, semi-terete, longer than stem. Spike 1–3-fld; fls more or less regular, erect, funnel-shaped, bright yellow, purple-maroon in throat, flushed with purple on outer lobes; tube 14–20mm; lobes 20–35×10–14mm, subequal, oblong or obovate, obtuse or emarginate. Late winter–spring. S Africa (Cape, Paarl and Stellenbosch districts).

G.×colvillei hort. (*G.tristis* × *G.cardinalis*.)
A group of hybrids raised by the nurserymen Colvilles of Chelsea in 1823, from which were later derived the Nanus Hybrids. Early spring. 'Albus': fls white, lowest tepals striped yellow; anth. tinged blue. 'Roseus': fls pale pink. 'Ruber': fls carmine-red. Z8.

G.communis L. BYZANTINE GLADIOLUS.
50–100cm. Lvs 30–50×0.5–1.5cm, linear. Spike more or less distichous, usually with 2–3 branches, laxly 10–20-fld. Fls pink, the lower lobes usually streaked or blotched with white or red; tube somewhat curved. S Europe. ssp. *byzantinus* (Mill.) A. Hamilt. BYZANTINE GLADIOLUS. Stem 50–100cm. Lvs 4–5, 30–70×1–2.5cm, linear. Spike densely 10–20-fld, distichous, sometimes with 1–2 branches; fls 4–5cm long, deep purple-red with narrow, paler marks outlined in dark purple on lower lobes; tube slightly curved, lobes broad, overlapping. Spring–summer. S Spain, Sicily. 'Albus': fls white. 'Ruber': fls vivid cerise. Z6.

G.comptonii Lewis.
Stem to 75cm, slender, unbranched. Lvs 4, usually 40–60cm×1.5–4mm, linear, minutely hispid. Spike secund, 1–3-fld; fls funnel-shaped, bright yellow with red-brown streaks and dots in the throat; tube curved, 10–14mm; lobes lanceolate or ovate-lanceolate, reflexed at about the middle, dorsal lobe 36–46×12–17mm, the others slightly smaller. Winter. S Africa (W Cape).

G.crassifolius Bak.
Corms to 5cm diam., globose. Stems to 1m. Lvs 5–11, forming to fan, to 70×2cm, linear, stiff. Spike densely many-fld, sometimes with a basal branch, distichous in bud but secund

in flower; fls 25–40mm long, narrowly bell-shaped, white, pink, mauve, purple, red or orange, the lower lateral lobes with a dark mark near apex; tube 8–15cm long, curved; upper lobes somewhat hooded, to 30×12mm, oblong or obovate, lower lobes about 15×6mm. Autumn. Eastern S Africa, Lesotho, Zimbabwe, Mozambique, Malawi.

G.cruentus Moore.
Stem 30–90cm long, stout, unbranched. Lvs 4–5, distichous, to 45×2.5mm, sword-shaped, the lower half sheathing. Spike 3–10-fld, secund or distichous. Fls large, bell-shaped, scarlet, the tube paler on outside, pale yellow flecked with red in throat, the lower lobes marked with white; tube 35–40mm, somewhat curved; lobes spreading, usually subequal, 30–50×18–30mm, obovate or spathulate. Summer. Drakensberg Mts in S Africa and Lesotho. Z8.

G.cunonius (L.) Gaertn. (*Anomalesia cunonia* (L.) N.E. Br.; *Antholyza cunonia* L.).
Corm *c*1cm diam. Stems 15–50cm. Lvs distichous, the lower ones 15–35×0.3–0.9cm, spirally twisted toward apex. Spike 3–8-fld; fls crimson, the 3 lower lobes yellow; tube 15mm, topmost lobe clawed, 35–42mm, blade 13–15mm wide, upper lateral lobes 14×7–9mm, more or less erect, obtuse or emarginate, lower 3 lobes 4–5×3mm. Spring. S Africa (SW Cape).

G.dalenii van Geel (*G.psittacinus* Hook.; *G.primulinus* Bak.; *G.natalensis* (Ecklon) Reinw. ex Hook.).
A widespread and very variable species. Corm to 5cm diam., globose or somewhat flattened, producing many sessile cormlets, sometimes also with cormlets at ends of runners. Stem to 1.5m high, occasionally with a branch. Lvs 5–12, forming a fan, 30–60×1–5cm, linear or sword-shaped. Spike few to many-fld, distichous in bud, secund in flower; fls zygomorphic, green, yellow, orange, red, pink or purple, self-coloured or striped or mottled with another colour; tube 25mm long, curved; upper lobes forming hood, the dorsal covering mouth of fl., 30–50mm long, ovate or obovate, lower lobes smaller, recurved, lanceolate. Summer. Throughout tropical Africa and summer rainfall regions of S Africa. 'Hookeri': very tall, fls large, yellow; produced late in season.

G.debilis Ker-Gawl. PAINTED LADY.
Stem 30–65cm, slender, unbranched. Lvs 3–4, lowest longer than stem but only 1–2mm wide, linear. Spike 1–4-fld; fls small, trumpet-shaped, white or pale pink spotted or streaked with red in throat, sometimes with the tube dark red; tube 10–20mm long, straight, lobes spreading, upper one 15–35mm, ovate, lower 3 slightly smaller. Spring. S Africa (SW Cape).

G.dracocephalus Hook. f. See *G.dalenii*.

G.equitans Thunb.
Stem 15–45cm, stout, usually unbranched. Lvs 3–4, the largest 10–30×1.5–4.5cm, sword-shaped or lanceolate-oblong. Spike 3–9-fld, secund, the rachis twisted; fls scented, 2-lipped, orange or vermilion, the basal part of lower lobes yellow or lime green, the dorsal lobe with 2 white papillate ridges bordered with red; tube 12–16mm long, curved, slender; dorsal lobe 33–45×24–28mm, arched, concave, obovate, the upper laterals slightly shorter and narrower, lower lobes 30–35×10mm, deflexed, clawed, spathulate, joined for 3–5mm at base. Late winter–spring. S Africa (W Cape).

G.floribundus Jacq.
Corm to 4.5cm diam., ovoid, with neck 3–9cm, often producing stolons with cormlets at ends. Stem 15–55cm, stout, branched or unbranched. Lvs 5–7, the longest 12–40×0.5–2cm, linear or sword-shaped, the sheathing bases mottled purple-red. Spike 2–14-fld, secund or distichous; fls variable in size and shape, white, pink, salmon or mauve with dark median line on lobes and sometimes with purple marks on lower lobes and in throat; tube short and curved or long and straight, lobes 20–50mm long, oblong or ovate, subequal or the upper ones slightly larger. Spring. S Africa (Cape Province). ssp. *floribundus* Fls white, cream, pale pink or mauve; lower perianth lobes much smaller than upper. ssp.

fasciatus (Roem. & Schult.) Oberm. Fls pink or pink and white in arching spray, spike usually with 1–2 branches; tube short, lobes spreading, the edges crisped and undulate. ssp. *milleri* (Ker-Gawl.) Oberm. Fls cream or pale yellow, flushed with pink or mauve on outside and with purple or red median line on basal half of lobes; perianth almost regular. ssp. *miniatus* (Ecklon) Oberm. Fls salmon-pink; perianth regular, tube slender, not funnel-shaped. ssp. *rudis* (Lichtenst. ex Roem. & Schult.) Oberm. Fls with purple, arrow-shaped marks on lower lateral lobes.

G.× gandavensis hort. (*G.dalenii* × *G.oppositiflorus*.)
A group of hybrids raised in Belgium around 1837, claimed to be between *G.dalenii* and *G.cardinalis*, but now believed to be as above.

G.garnieri Klatt.
30–50cm, dormant in winter; lvs several, linear. Fls pale salmon pink, usually with yellow blotch on lower lobes. Summer. Madagascar.

G.gracilis Jacq.
Stems 20–75cm, slender, unbranched. Lvs 3–4, the lowest and longest mainly sheathing with a short, free blade, usually subterete and 1–2mm wide, but sometimes flat, to 4mm wide, about as long as stem. Spike laxly 1–8-fld, secund; fls usually scented, funnel-shaped or somewhat 2-lipped with the lower lip projecting, pale blue, mauve or pale pink with a band of yellow or cream dotted and streaked with purple on lower lobes; tube 14–17mm, curved, slender at base then funnel-shaped; upper lobes 20–35×10–20mm, obovate, lower lobes slightly longer, clawed, spathulate. Winter–spring. S Africa (SW Cape).

G.grandis Thunb. See *G.liliaceus*.

G.huttonii (N.E. Br.) Goldbl. & De Vos (*Homoglossum huttonii* N.E. Br.).
Stems 25–85cm. Basal lf 20–60×0.1–0.4cm, X-shaped in cross-section. Spike 2–7-fld; fls 7–10.5cm, upper tepals red or orange-red, lower tepals yellow, orange-yellow or red with yellow mid-line; tepals elliptic, the 3 upper 25–38×10–22mm, the topmost the largest, the 3 lower 10–22×6–12mm. Winter–early spring. S Africa (coastal areas of S & E Cape).

G.illyricus Koch.
Stem slender, 25–50cm. Lvs 4–5, 10–40×0.5–1cm, glaucous, sword-shaped. Spike 3–10-fld, distichous, usually simple but sometimes with 1 branch; fls 4–5cm, magenta-purple, the lower 3 lobes with white, lanceolate marks; tube curved; tepals 25–30mm long, obovate, the lower 3-clawed; anth. shorter than fil. Spring–summer. W Europe, north to S England, Mediterranean, Asia Minor, Caucasus. Z6.

G.imbricatus L.
Stem 30–80cm. Lvs usually 3, 15–35×1–1.5cm. Spike densely 4–12-fld, secund, usually simple but sometimes with 1–3 branches. Fls pale crimson to red-purple or magenta, the lower lobes each with a white, lanceolate mark outlined in purple; tube curved near apex; lobes overlapping, the tips reflexed, anth. shorter than fil. or of similar length. Spring–summer. C & S Europe. Z6.

G.inflatus Thunb. TULBAGH BELL.
A variable species; stem 25–60cm high, slender, unbranched. Lvs 3, the lowest usually of similar length to stem, 0.5–1mm diam., more or less terete, the apex spine-like. Spike secund, densely 1–6-fld; fls 3.5–5.5cm long, usually bell-shaped, pale to deep pink, blue-mauve, grey-blue, rarely almost white, usually with a cream or yellow mark outlined in purple on lowest lobe, sometimes also with dark or yellow mark on lower lateral lobes; tube 9–25mm, curved; upper lobes 18–30×10–25mm, the dorsal the largest, obovate, the laterals elliptic, lower lobes 20–30×8–15mm, clawed, spathulate, joined for 4–7mm at base. Spring–summer. S Africa (W Cape). ssp. *inflatus* Perianth 2–3cm, pink, not opening wide; tube short and curved or long and almost straight. ssp. *intermedius* Lewis. Perianth 2–4cm, blue to mauve or grey-mauve, opening wide; tube short and curved.

Gladiolus Horticultural Classes   (a) Giant Exhibition   (b) Miniature Exhibition   (c) Large Exhibition   (d) Large
Exhibition, frilled   (e) Ruffled Miniature   (f) Medium Exhibition   (g) Ruffled Exotic   (h) Butterfly   (i) Small
Exhibition   (j) Exotic 'Jester'   (k) Exhibition spike of Large Exhibition ('Grandiflora')

G.× insignis hort. (*G.carneus* × *cardinalis.*)
A group of richly coloured, winter-growing, early-flowering hybrids raised around 1835 by Colvilles of Chelsea.

G.italicus Mill. (*G.segetum* Ker-Gawl.). FIELD GLADIOLUS.
Stem 40–110cm. Lvs 3–5, 20–50×0.5–1.5cm. Spike laxly 5–15-fld, more or less distichous, unbranched; fls 3–4cm, purple-pink to magenta, the lower lobes each with a pink, lanceolate blotch outlined in purple; tube slightly curved; lobes spreading, lanceolate; anth. longer than fil. Spring–summer. S Europe. Z6.

G.liliaceus Houtt. (*G.grandis* Thunb.; *G.versicolor* Andrews). LARGE BROWN AFRIKANER.
Stem 25–90cm, fairly slender, unbranched. Lvs usually 3, the lowest slightly longer than stem, to 3mm wide, linear. Spike laxly 1–5-fld, secund; fls large, strongly scented at night, very variable in colour, usually dull yellow flecked with brown, pink, red or purple, occasionally green-cream, sometimes with red in throat, after dark changing to deep mauve or blue; tube 4–6cm long, curved; lobes spreading, the tips recurved, subequal or the dorsal largest, 33–55×9–20mm, the lowest 3 joined for 5–10mm at base. Late winter–summer. S Africa (W Cape).

G.maculatus Sweet.
Stem 30–80cm, slender, unbranched. Basal lf to 40×0.5cm, filiform, withered by flowering time; stem lvs 3–5, mostly sheathing. Spike secund, laxly 1–4-fld; fls scented, 5–10cm, narrowly bell-shaped, of variable colour: dull yellow, pink or brown flecked with red, purple or dark brown, or pink or white, sometimes spotted in throat; tube 3–5cm long, curved, slender in basal half; lobes of similar length to tube or slightly shorter, ovate, the edges sometimes undulate, the dorsal largest, hooded. Autumn–winter. S Africa (W Cape).

G.natalensis (Ecklon) Reinw. ex Hook. See *G.dalenii.*
G.nebulicola Ingram. See *G.dalenii.*

G.nerineoides Lewis.
Stem 35–40cm long, slender, unbranched. Basal lf 1, 35–40cm×5–6mm, hairy, not developed at flowering time; stem lvs 3, 2–9cm long, mainly sheathing, the lowest minutely hairy, the others glabrous. Spike densely 4–7-fld; fls erect, salmon-pink to rich orange-red; tube 30mm long, straight or slightly curved; lobes more or less equal, somewhat recurved, 18–20×7–9mm, oblong; stamens short, not protruding from tube. Summer–autumn S Africa (SW Cape).

G.ochroleucus Bak.
Corm to 4cm diam., often with sessile cormlets. Stem 45–100cm, sometimes with 1 branch. Lvs 6–12, distichous, about 30×1.5cm, sword-shaped, often evergreen. Fls 3.5–7.5cm long, white, cream, yellow, pink or mauve, often veined with a darker colour; tube 15–35mm long, curved, slender at base, becoming funnel-shaped; lobes spreading, of similar length to tube but with outer lobes slightly longer, oblong, ovate or lanceolate. Autumn. S Africa (E Cape). var. **ochroleucus**. Fls 4–5cm, white, cream, yellow or pink; lobes oblong or ovate. var. **macowanii** (Bak.) Oberm. Fls 7–9cm long, pale to deep pink with darker throat; lobes lanceolate.

G.odoratus L. Bol.
Corm to 4cm diam. Stem 30–80cm, fairly slender, unbranched. Basal lf 1, 25–65×1–2cm, sword-shaped, not developed at flowering time; stem lvs 3–4, sheathing for most of their length. Spike laxly or fairly densely 3–13-fld, more or less secund; fls scented, dull yellow or yellow-brown, spotted and striped with purple or red; tube 20–25mm long, curved, funnel-shaped towards throat; lobes 20–30mm long, the edges slightly crisped near apex, dorsal lobe hooded, obovate, 14–18mm wide, the rest 7–12mm wide, sometimes clawed, the lower 3 joined for 3–4mm at base. Autumn–winter. S Africa (W Cape).

G.oppositiflorus Herb.
Stem to 1.5m tall. Lvs about 8, forming a fan, to 100×2–3cm, linear, minutely pubesc. Spike 10–35-fld, secund or distichous, sometimes branched. Fls to 10cm long, funnel-shaped,

somewhat 2-lipped, white or pale to deep pink, with dark blotches in throat and dark median line on each lobe; tube 50mm long, curved; lobes spreading, about 5cm, ovate-lanceolate, acute or acuminate. Summer–autumn. S Africa (E Cape).

G.orchidiflorus Andrews.
Corm to 2.5cm diam., producing cormlets, sessile or on stolons. Lvs 3–8, distichous, grass-like, the largest to 40×0.5cm. Spike sometimes branched, 5–15-fld, more or less secund; fls scented, 3–5cm long, 2-lipped, green, yellow-green or cream, usually tinged and blotched with purple, the lobes with purple median line; tube slender, curved, cylindrical; lobes clawed, dorsal 20–35mm long, arched, almost linear, the others somewhat spathulate, spreading or recurved. Winter–spring. S Africa (W Cape, Orange Free State).

G.ornatus Klatt. PINK BELL.
Corms very small, 6–12mm diam. Stem 30–60cm, slender, unbranched. Lvs 3, the lowest longer than spike, linear or subterete, 0.5–1.5mm wide, the basal half sheathing. Spike secund, laxly 1–4-fld; fls funnel-shaped or bell-shaped, pale to deep pink, the lower lobes with yellow, spar-shaped marks outlined in red; tube 15–20mm, curved; lobes 25–35mm, upper 3 13–20mm wide, elliptic, lower 3 spathulate, 8–15mm wide, joined for 3–6mm at base. Winter–spring. S Africa (W Cape).

G.palustris Gaud.
Stem 25–50cm high. Lvs 2–3, 10–40×0.5–1cm, linear. Spike laxly 1–6-fld, secund, unbranched; fls magenta-purple; tube curved. Spring–summer. C Europe. Z6.

G.papilio Hook. f.
Corm to 3cm diam., often with cormlets at ends of stolons. Stem 50–90cm high, unbranched. Lvs 7–8, the basal ones distichous, about half as long as stem and 0.5–2cm wide, sword-shaped. Spike fairly laxly 3–10-fld, secund or somewhat distichous; fls funnel-shaped or bell-shaped, yellow, usually tinged with purple on outside and on lower lobes, or dull purple, the lower lobes edged with yellow-green; tube 15–25mm, curved; lobes 25–33mm, the upper 3 obovate, the dorsal largest, the lower 3 narrower, spathulate. Summer–autumn. Eastern S Africa, from Transkei to N Transvaal. Z8.

G.primulinus Bak. See *G.dalenii.*

G.priorii (N.E. Br.) Goldbl. & De Vos (*Antholyza priorii* N.E. Br.; *Antholyza revoluta* Bak. pro parte; *Homoglossum priorii* (N.E. Br.) N.E. Br.).
Stems 30–80cm. Basal lf c22–0.1–0.3cm, narrowly linear. Spike 1–6-fld, usually 2–3-fld; fls 5.5–9cm, bright red or pink-red, yellow in throat; tube 40–50mm, abruptly expanded at about halfway; tepals ovate, acuminate, the 3 upper 20–35×8–18mm, the topmost largest, 3 lower 20–30× 6–10mm. Winter. S Africa (SW Cape).

G.pritzelii Diels.
Corms small, less than 2cm diam. Stem 30–50cm tall, rarely more, unbranched. Lvs 3–4, the lowest of similar length to stem, 1–3mm wide, usually hairy. Spike 1–3-fld, secund; fls nodding, bell-shaped, the lower lobes projecting, scented, yellow with dark yellow or brown patches on lower lobes, often tinged on outside with red or grey; tube 7–12mm long, sharply curved in middle; lobes 20–30mm, usually cuspidate, dorsal lobe hooded, 14–20mm wide, upper laterals 12–18mm wide, rhomboid, lower lobes 9–12mm wide, obovate or spathulate, joined for about 5mm at base. Winter–spring. W Cape.

G.psittacinus Hook. See *G.dalenii.*

G.punctatus Schrank.
Stem 25–80cm, slender, unbranched. Lvs 3, the lowest with basal half sheathing, the blade reaching about halfway up stem, 2–6mm wide, glabrous or hairy. Spike 1–8-fld, secund; fls 4–5cm, funnel-shaped, pale to deep pink or mauve, the lower 3 lobes streaked with orange, red or purple and the lower laterals usually white or yellow in basal half; tube

12–30mm, curved; lobes 20–30mm, obovate, the lower 3 slightly longer and narrower than upper 3, and joined for 5–8mm at base. Winter–spring. S Africa (Cape winter rainfall area). var. **autumnalis** Lewis. Autumn flowering.

G.purpureo-auratus Hook. f. See *G.papilio.*

G.quadrangularis (Burm. f.) Ait. (*Antholyza quadrangularis* Burm. f.; *Homoglossum quadrangulare* (Burm. f.) N.E. Br.). Stems 50–90cm. Basal lf 20–60cm×4mm, X-shaped in cross-section. Spike 3–10-fld; fls 6.5–8.5cm, pale to bright red, occasionally pink; tube with narrow basal part 13–15mm, widening abruptly to an upper part 20–30mm long, with a small nectar sac where it widens; tepals ovate, acute, 3 upper 18–30×6–16mm, the topmost largest, 3 lower 9–18×3–8mm. Spring. S Africa (SW Cape).

G.quadrangulus (Delaroche) Barnard. Corms small, to 15mm diam. Stem 15–30cm, very slender. Lvs 3, the lowest about as long as spike, linear, with a long sheathing base. Spike laxly or fairly densely 1–7-fld; fls scented, regular, tube yellow, lobes pale lilac, pale blue, pale mauve or almost white with small dark dots at the base; tube 7–10mm, funnel-shaped; lobes subequal, 16–20×7–10mm, oblong, obtuse, the 3 outer lobes sometimes to 14mm wide. Winter–spring. S Africa (Cape Flats).

G.recurvus L. Corm to 15mm diam. Stem 30–50cm tall, slender, unbranched. Lvs 3–4, the lowest 2 sheathing for most of their length, the blades 5–12cm long, 1mm wide, almost terete. Spike secund, laxly 1–4-fld; fls scented, cream, pale yellow, pale grey-green or grey-mauve, the lower lobes often paler, with purple streaks and spots; tube 28–33mm long, curved, narrow; lobes recurved, undulate towards apex, dorsal lobe 25–30×13–16mm, obovate, concave, other lobes 20–26×6–10mm, oblong or obovate, the lower 3 joined at base for 3–4mm. Winter–spring. S Africa (SW Cape).

G.rogersii Bak. Stem 30–65cm, occasionally to 1m. Lvs 3–5, the lowest semi-sheathing, the blade linear, about as long as stem. Spike usually 1–5-fld, occasionally with up to 14, secund, rarely branched; fls to 5cm long, nodding, bell-shaped, pale to deep blue, mauve or purple with dark streaks and yellow marks on lower lobes, tube 9–20mm long, sharply curved in middle, funnel-shaped towards throat, dorsal lobe 20–30×16–28mm, hooded, broadly obovate or almost orbicular, upper laterals similar but slightly smaller; lower lobes at least as long as dorsal lobe, 7–15mm wide, spathulate. Winter–spring. S Africa (SE Cape).

G.saccatus (Klatt) Goldbl. & De Vos (*Anomalesia saccata* (Klatt) N.E. Br.; *Antholyza saccata* (Klatt) Bak.). Stems 25–80cm. Basal lvs 5–6, deciduous. Fls bright red, very irregular; topmost tepals 40mm long, upper laterals short and narrow, forming pouch-like spur with 3 lower tepals. Winter. S Africa (W Cape, Namaqualand), Namibia.

G.saundersii Hook. f. Stem 40–90cm, usually unbranched. Lvs 7–8, distichous, sword-shaped, the longest 25–60×0.5–2.5cm. Spike laxly 3–12-fld; fls large, salmon-red, scarlet or vermilion, the 3 lower lobes white or cream in basal half; tube 30–40mm long, curved near apex then funnel-shaped; upper lobes 35–70×20–35mm, elliptic, lower lobes similar but shorter and narrower. Summer–autumn. S Africa (E Cape), Lesotho. Z8.

G.schweinfurthii (Bak.) Goldbl. & De Vos (*Antholyza schweinfurthii* Bak.; *Homoglossum schweinfurthii* (Bak.) Cuf.; *Petamenes schweinfurthii* (Bak.) N.E. Br.). Basal lvs 3–6, lanceolate, soft-textured. Bracts large, 2.5–3.5cm, partly enclosing fls; exposed part of fl. red, enclosed part pale; topmost tepals 18–25mm, upper laterals smaller, lower 3 much reduced. Ethiopia, Somalia, SW Arabia.

G.scullyi Bak. Corm to 4cm diam., often with sessile cormlets. Stem 10–70cm, fairly slender, sometimes branched. Lvs 4–7, of

similar length to stem, 1–10mm wide, linear. Spike fairly laxly 2–10-fld, usually secund, the rachis twisted; fls scented, about 5cm, two-lipped, tube and basal half of lobes cream, yellow or lime green, apical halves pale to deep mauve, blue, pink, red or maroon-purple; tube erect, 11–17mm, slender at base then funnel-shaped; lobes clawed, the upper 3 erect, forming hood, 25–35×10–18mm, the claw short, the blade ovate, lower lobes 19–32mm long including claw 5–10mm long, joined at base for at least half their length; blade deflexed, 7–11mm wide. Winter–spring. S Africa (Cape winter rainfall area).

G.segetus Ker-Gawl. See *G.italicus.*

G.sempervirens Lewis. Corm small, to 15mm diam., usually with short rhizomes attached. Stem 40–50cm, leafy, usually unbranched. Lvs 9–16, to 30×1–2cm, lanceolate or sword-shaped, distichous, usually evergreen. Spike laxly 4–8-fld, secund; fls to 12cm, bright scarlet with white, diamond-shaped marks on lower lobes; tube 25–50mm, curved; upper lobes 50–65×25–33mm, broadly elliptic, acute, lower lobes 50–55×18–25mm, joined for 3–4mm at base, elliptic, acute. Late summer–autumn. S Africa (Cape Province, coastal areas with rain all year round).

G.sericeovillosus Hook. f. Corms to 4cm diam. Stem to 2m tall. Lvs about 7, forming fan, to 200×2m, linear, sometimes hairy. Spike to about 40-fld, distichous, sometimes branched; fls 4–6cm, 2-lipped, cream, yellow, pink, mauve or maroon, sometimes speckled, with yellow or green marks outlined in a darker colour on lower lobes; tube 20mm, curved; upper lobes 25–30mm, lanceolate, the dorsal somewhat hooded, lower lobes slightly shorter and narrower. Summer–winter. S Africa (NE Cape, Orange Free State, Natal, Transvaal), Swaziland.

G.splendens (Sweet) Herb. (*Anomalesia splendens* (Sweet) N.E. Br.; *Antholyza splendens* (Sweet) Steud.). Stems 50–60cm high. Basal lvs 2, lanceolate, deciduous. Fls bright red; topmost tepals c40mm, upper laterals somewhat smaller; lower 3 much reduced in size. Winter–early spring. S Africa (W Karoo).

G.stefaniae Oberm. Corm 2m diam., globose. Stem about 40cm tall. Lvs 1–3, to 35×0.8cm, linear, developing after flowering. Spike 2–3-fld; fls large, more or less regular, red, the lower 3 each with a white line; tube 4cm, funnel-shaped; dorsal lobe 65×32mm, ovate-lanceolate, other lobes similar but slightly smaller. Similar to *G.sempervirens*, but dormant in summer and so not evergreen, and with fewer lvs and fls. Autumn. S Africa (SW Cape).

G.stellatus Lewis. Corms less than 2cm diam., producing 1–2 ovoid cormlets on basal stolons. Stem 15–75cm tall, slender, sometimes branched. Lvs 5–7, the longest usually reaching base of spike, 1–2mm wide, linear or subterete. Spike fairly laxly 3–18-fld, secund or distichous; fls scented, rather star-shaped, almost regular, white to pale blue, mauve or grey-mauve, sometimes with mauve median line; tube 4–6mm, straight; lobes subequal, 13–20×4–8mm, shortly clawed then lanceolate, acute or acuminate. Winter–spring. S Africa (SW Cape).

G.tenellus Jacq. Stem 10–45cm long, very slender. Lvs 3, lowest with sheath half as long as stem and with rigid, more or less terete blade overtopping the spike, glabrous or minutely hairy. Spike 1–4-fld; fls suberect, scented at night, funnel-shaped, white, cream or pale to bright yellow, often tinged with purple, mauve or red on outside, with purple or red lines on lower lobes, and often yellow in centre; tube 13–24mm long, slightly curved; upper lobes 20–42×8–16mm, oblong or elliptic, lower lobes of similar length but narrower, sometimes clawed, joined for 2–3mm at base. Winter–spring. S Africa (SW Cape).

G.tristis L. MARSH AFRIKANER. Corms to 3cm diam. Stem 40–150cm high, unbranched. Lvs 2–4, lowest of similar length to stem, 1.5–5mm wide, cruci-

Gladiolus   (a) *G.carneus*   (b) *G.cardinalis*   (c) *G.communis* spp. *byzantinu*s   (d) *G.italicus*   (e) *G.tristis*
(f) *G.oppositiflorus*   (g) *G.carmineus*   (h) *G.debilis*

form in cross-section, often spirally twisted near apex. Spike laxly 1–20-fld, secund; fls scented at night, narrowly bell-shaped, white, cream or pale yellow, often tinged with green, usually flushed or dotted with mauve, red, brown or purple, and with basal half of lower lobes yellow-green; tube 4–6cm, curved; lobes 30–33mm long, the dorsal 15–23mm wide, elliptic, the others slightly narrower, the lower 3 joined for 5–7mm at base. S Africa (Cape winter rainfall area). var. *tristis*. Spike 1–8-fld; fls cream or pale yellow heavily marked with dark grey-green, brown or purple. Late winter–spring. var. *aestivalis* (J. Ingram) Lewis. SUMMER MARSH AFRIKANER. Stem to 1.5m high; spike to 20-fld, fls funnel-shaped. Summer. var. *concolor* (Salisb.) Bak. Spike 1–8-fld; fls cream or pale yellow, sometimes tinged with green. Spring. Z7.

G.undulatus L.
Corms to 3cm diam., ovoid, often forming cormlets. Stem 30–100cm tall. Lvs usually 5, 25–75×0.5–2cm, linear or sword-shaped. Spike laxly 4–9-fld, sometimes with a short branch, distichous; fls to 10cm long, bell-shaped from a long, tapering tube; white, green-white, cream or pink, the lower lobes marked with deep pink or red; tube 5–7cm, straight or slightly curved; lobes shorter than tube, lanceolate or ovate, acuminate, the dorsal hooded, the lowest recurved. Spring–summer. S Africa (SW Cape).

G.varius L. Bol.
Stem to 1m. Lvs 2–7, distichous, to 60×0.5cm, linear. Spike densely 3–14-fld, secund; fls funnel-shaped or bell-shaped, pale to bright pink with lilac-purple mid line on lower lobes; tube 1–5cm; lobes to 4cm, lanceolate or ovate. Late summer–autumn. S Africa (Transvaal), Swaziland. var. *varius*. Fls magenta-pink, to 7cm long; tube long, slender and curved; lobes long. var. *micranthus* (Bak.) Oberm. Fls white or pink, to 4cm; tube and lobes short.

G.versicolor Andrews. See *G.liliaceus*.

G.vigilans Barnard.
Stem 20–40cm. Lvs 4, lower 2 to 40cm long, terete. Spike 1–3-fld; fls 5–6cm long, funnel-shaped, oblique, rose-pink with pale spade-shaped mark on lower lobes; tube to 40mm, slender; upper lobes to 25×20mm, ovate, the dorsal somewhat wider than laterals, lower lobes much smaller, spreading and recurved. Early summer. S Africa (Cape Peninsula).

G.virescens Thunb.
Corm to 15mm diam., often with a few very small cormlets. Stem 10–30cm, fairly slender, sometimes branched. Lvs 3, the lowest 20–60cm×1.5–3mm, linear or sometimes terete. Spike secund, 1–7-fld; fls sometimes scented, 2-lipped, dull yellow-green with brighter yellow patch on basal half of lower lobes, usually with the upper lobes brown- or purple-veined, or white, cream, pink or mauve with darker veins; tube 10–13mm; lobes very unequal, dorsal 30–40×10–18mm, spathulate; upper laterals 19–27×14–22mm, ovate from a short claw; lower lobes 22–28×6–15mm, spathulate, joined

for 4–6mm at base. Late winter – spring. S Africa (Cape winter rainfall area).

G.watermeyeri L. Bol.
Stem 10–40cm long, sometimes branched. Lvs 3–4, the lowest to 40×1cm, linear or sword-shaped. Spike secund, 1–6-fld; fls scented, 2-lipped, upper lobes cream or pale green flushed and veined with purple, lower lobes lime green, the apices cream; tube 12–14; lobes unequal, dorsal 26–35×10–14mm, ovate, arched, concave, upper laterals 20–25×14–22mm, broadly ovate, somewhat spreading, lower lobes deflexed, 20–28mm long, the lowest ovate, 10–18mm wide, the lower laterals spathulate, 4–5mm wide. Winter–spring. S Africa (W Cape).

G.watsonioides Bak. (*Antholyza watsonioides* (Bak.) Bak.).
Infl. secund, several-fld; bracts large; fls bright red, slightly drooping; perianth tube 3–4cm long, slender, curved; tepals subequal, 2–3cm. Kenya, Tanzania (mts).

G.watsonius Thunb. (*Antholyza revoluta* (Pers.) Bak. pro parte; *Homoglossum watsonium* (Thunb.) N.E. Br.).
Corms to 2.5cm wide, with hard, woody tunic. Stems 40–100cm. Basal lf 45–100×0.1–0.5cm, midrib and margins thickened. Spike 2–6-fld; fls 7.5–0cm, bright red or orange-red, yellow in throat; tube 4–5.5cm with a small nectar-sac about halfway along, where it abruptly widens, upper 3 lobes 25–35×8–16mm, the topmost widest, 3 lower 20–35×7–10mm. Spring. S Africa (SW Cape).

G.xanthus Lewis. See *G.dalenii*.

G.cultivars.
Miniature Hybrids: 50–90cm; florets to 5cm in diameter, usually frilled, closely arranged. 'Amanda Mahy': fls orange-pink, lower tepals flecked pale mauve. 'Charm': fls pink with broad yellow-green blotches. 'Hot Sauce': fls heavily frilled, light red with yellow markings. 'Nymph': fls white-pink, blotches cream, marked china rose. 'Robineau': fls bright red, edged cream on lowest tepals. *Butterfly Hybrids*: to 1.2m; florets to 10cm in diameter, often conspicuously blotched on throat, densely arranged. 'Chartres': fls purple with darker blotches. 'Georgette': fls cherry red with rich yellow centre. 'Mme Butterfly': fls shell-pink with salmon and purple throat. 'Mykonos': fls salmon-yellow blotched red. *Primulinus Hybrids*: to 9cm; florets to 7.5cm in diameter, top petals hooded, loosely arranged. 'Lady Godiva': fls white. 'Joyce': fls pale cerise with yellow throat. 'Pegasus': fls yellow; tipped red. 'Red Star': fls star-shaped, vivid purple-orange with paler centre. *Large Flowered Hybrids*: habit vigorous, erect to 1.2m; florets to 18cm in diameter, somewhat triangular, borne in spikes to 50cm; extremely wide range of colours. 'Applause': fls pink. 'Blue Conqueror': fls deep violet-blue with paler centres. 'Ebony Beauty': fls velvety black-red with white stamens. 'Fidelio': fls purple. 'Hunting Song': fls orange-red. 'Jacksonville Gold': fls bright yellow. 'Minuet': fls clear white. 'Vesuvius': fls bright scarlet-red. 'White Friendship': fls pure white.

Gloriosa L. GLORY LILY; CLIMBING LILY; CREEPING LILY. Liliaceae (Colchicaceae). 1 species, a tuberous, perennial herb, related to *Sandersonia* and *Littonia*, climbing by means of tendrils at leaf tips. Tubers narrow or thick, irregularly cylindric, red-brown. Stems to 2.5m, 1–4 per tuber, simple or sparsely branched, slender, twining, glossy bright green. Leaves 5–8cm (excluding terminal tendril), ovate-lanceolate to oblong, apex acuminate, apex finely tapering, often to a tendril to 3–5cm long (if uncoiled), glossy bright green, pliable. Flowers solitary, on long pedicels in leaf axils, usually angled downwards; tepals 6, 4–10 × 2.5–3cm, narrow-lanceolate to spathulate, acuminate, spreading, usually bowed at centre and gently but distinctly reflexed at tip, yellow to red or purple or bicoloured, margins often incurved, undulate or crisped; stamens 6, slender, spreading, anthers to 1cm, versatile; style 3-branched, bent at base at right angle to the ovary. Fruit a capsule. Summer–autumn. Tropical Africa and Asia. Z10. All parts are toxic. The several 'species' of *Gloriosa* are now treated as variants of *G.superba*. They vary in height and attitude of stems, the development of leaf tendrils, colour and shape of tepals.

CULTIVATION   A beautiful, slender climbing herb, clinging by means of tendrils, *G.superba* is grown for its exotic, brilliantly coloured blooms. It is relatively easily grown in the cool glasshouse or conservatory in cool temperate zones. In frost-free climates these plants are used as sprawlers or climbers for sunny situations in freely draining soils, showing useful tolerance of nutritionally poor soils.

Grow in full sun in a freely draining, fertile, loam-based mix with additional sharp sand and screened, well rotted garden compost. Support the climbing stems on pea sticks, a cane frame or a wire hoop, water plentifully and feed fortnightly with dilute liquid feed when in full growth, with a minimum temperature of 8–10°C/46–50°F. Pot-grown specimens may be moved out of doors for the warm summer months. Withhold water as growth ripens and dies back in late summer/early autumn; store the long, narrow tubers in their pots in dry, frost-free conditions. Repot every 1–2 years either in late winter with heat or in early spring. Propagate by seed sown in a sandy propagating mix in late winter with gentle bottom heat, by careful division in spring, or be offsets. Aphids may be a pest under glass.

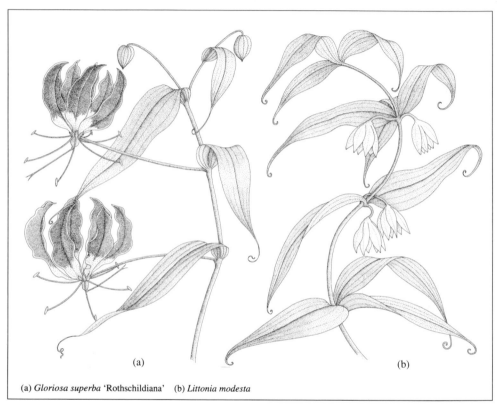

(a)   (b)

(a) *Gloriosa superba* 'Rothschildiana'   (b) *Littonia modesta*

G.abyssinica Rich. See *G.superba* 'Abyssinica'.
G.carsonii Bak. See *G.superba* 'Carsonii'.
G.rothschildiana O'Brien. See *G.superba* 'Rothschildiana'.
G.simplex L. See *G.superba* 'Simplex'.

G.superba L.
The typical plant is described below as *G.*'Superba'. 'Abyssinica' (*G.abyssinica* Rich.): stems 45–60cm; tepals 5–7.5cm, red centrally banded gold, especially at base, not crisped. 'Carsonii' (*G.carsonii* Bak.): stems to 90cm; tepals broad, purple-red, edged yellow, strongly reflexed, margins undulate, not crisped. 'Citrina': tepals citron yellow tinted or striped claret. 'Grandiflora': like 'Simplex', but tepals larger, golden-yellow. 'Greeneae': tepals smooth, straight, yellow

tinted copper. 'Rothschildiana' (*G.rothschildiana* O'Brien): stem to 250cm; tepals 7.5–10cm, scarlet fading to ruby or garnet, yellow at base and in central stripe, strongly recurved – the largest and finest form. 'Simplex' (*G.simplex* L.): small; tepals spathulate, yellow-green turning deep orange and yellow, margin not crisped. 'Superba' (*G.superba* L.): stems to 180cm; tepals narrow, closely undulate and crisped, reflexed, yellow-green turning deep rich orange and red. 'Superba Lutea': tepals yellow, tightly crisped. 'Verschuurii' (*G.verschuurii* Hoog): stems to 150cm; tepals to 9cm, thick, reflexed, undulate, vivid crimson, yellow at margins and base. 'Virescens': tepals smooth, clear yellow.

G.verschuurii Hoog. See *G.superba* 'Verschuurii'.

Gloxinia L'Hérit. (For Benjamin Peter Gloxin (*fl.* 1785), a botanical writer of Colmar.) Gesneriaceae. About 8 species of terrestrial herbs, occasionally shrubs to 1m. Rhizomes creeping, often fleshy-scaly. Stems erect, mostly unbranched. Leaves opposite, in equal or subequal pairs, orbicular, ovate or elliptic. Flowers axillary, solitary or occasionally in pairs; sepals green, united at base, oblong; corolla funnelform, limb oblique, spreading, lobes 5, unequal, obtuse; stamens 4, included; anthers all coherent; disc annular, entire to 5-lobed. Fruit obovoid, bivalved; seeds spirally striate. C & S America.

CULTIVATION   As for *Achimenes*. The florist's Gloxinia is developed from selected forms of *Sinningia speciosa* and hybrids thereof.

G.guttata (Lindl.) Mart. See *Sinningia guttata*.

G.gymnostoma Griseb. (*Achimenes gymnostoma* (Griseb.) Fritsch).
To 60cm, stoloniferous; stolons scaly. Lvs to 7.5×4.3cm, ovate, pubesc. Fls solitary; sep. narrowly deltoid, to 1.2cm; cor. to 3.4cm, rose-pink, limb spotted with red, 5-lobed, upper 2 lobes exceeding lower 3. Argentina.

G.micrantha Martens & Gal. See *Eucodonia andrieuxii*.

G.perennis (L.) Druce. CANTERBURY BELLS.
Stems glabrous. Lvs of the same pair connected by transverse ridges, to 20×15cm, ovate-cordate, acute, serrate-crenate,

green and hispid above, pale red and glabrous beneath. Lower fls solitary in lf axils, upper fls in a many-fld raceme; cal. tube to 1cm, ribbed, glabrous, sep. to 1.5cm; cor. to 4cm, pubesc., pale purple, obtuse. Colombia to Peru.

G.'Redbird'.
Habit tall; stem grey, square in section; lvs ovate, dark green, glossy; fls tubular, inflated, orange-red, spotted red on yellow inside.

G.speciosa Lodd. See *Sinningia speciosa*.

Griffinia Ker-Gawl. (For their collector, William Griffin (*d*1827).) Amaryllidaceae. 7 species of bulbous, perennial herbs. Leaves broad, usually petiolate. Flowers numerous, borne in scapose umbels; perianth 6-lobed, funnel-shaped, horizontal or downward-pointing, sometimes tubular, 3 upper segments broader than others, directed upwards, 2 lower segments spreading at right angles, the third directed downwards; stamens 6, rarely 5, anthers oblong, versatile; ovary trilocular, ovules 2 per valve. Fruit a 2-valved capsule; seeds often solitary, with pale testa. Brazil. Z10.

CULTIVATION   Frost-tender bulbs grown for their large umbels of strikingly beautiful white or lilac flowers carried on stout stems in winter or early spring, sometimes into early summer. In temperate zones, *Griffinia* spp. are suitable for container cultivation in the intermediate glasshouse or conservatory, with a winter minimum of 10°C/50°F. Grow in a loam-based mix with added leafmould and well rotted manure, in bright filtered light or part-day shade. Water plentifully when in growth, reduce after flowering and keep dry but not arid during rest. Repot approximately every three years, after flowering. Propagate from offsets when repotting, or by ripe seed, surface-sown on to a loam-based propagating mix at 18°C/65°F. Water from below, and pot on the following spring.

G.dryades (Vell.) M. Roem. (*Amaryllis dryades* Vell.).
To 45cm. Bulb 10–12cm diam. Lvs 12–15cm, oblong to lanceolate; petiole 15–20cm. Fls 10–13 in a large, loose umbel, purple, lilac, white at centre; stamens shorter than perianth seg., 1 ascending, anth. purple. Early summer. S Brazil.

G.hyacinthina (Ker-Gawl.) Ker-Gawl. (*Amaryllis hyacinthina* Ker-Gawl.).
To 60cm. Bulb globose, 5–7.5cm diam. Lvs 15–22.5cm, ovate to oblong; petiole 15–22.5cm. Fls exceeding lvs, 9–10 per umbel, 4.5cm diam.; upper perianth seg. white, spreading to blue at apex; stamens much shorter than perianth seg., 1 ascending. Early summer. Brazil. 'Micrantha': fls small, to 2.5cm. 'Maxima': lvs broadly ovate to oblong; fls 10–12 per umbel, large to 12.5cm diam., white, tipped deep blue.

G.intermedia Lindl.
To 30cm. Bulb ovoid. Lvs oblong, acute, cuneate at base, narrowing into a long petiole, produced with fls. Fls 6–10 in an umbel; perianth 3.5cm, pale lilac, tube short, funnel-shaped; stamens shorter than perianth seg., 1 ascending. Early summer. Brazil.

G.liboniana Lem.
To 30cm. Bulb 2.5cm diam. Lvs 7.5–10cm, 5–6, produced with fls, oblong-acute, sessile. Pedicel 2-ridged to subterete;

fls 2.5–3cm, 6–8 in an umbel, pale lilac; perianth seg. oblanceolate, tube scarcely developed; stamens 5, shorter than perianth, upper stamen suppressed. Early summer. C Brazil.

G.ornata T. Moore.
To 45cm. Bulb ovoid, 7.5–10cm diam. Lvs to 30cm, 6–8, elliptic to oblong, margins strongly revolute; petiole short, sulcate, with clasping base. Scape 2-ridged to subterete; fls 20–24 in an umbel, opalescent to nearly white; stamens shorter than perianth, 1 ascending. Early summer.

G.parviflora Ker-Gawl.
To 30cm. Bulb ovoid, 5–7.5cm diam. Lvs to 15cm, 3–4, present with fls, oblong, acute; petiole 15cm. Fls 2–3cm, 10–15 in an umbel, pale lilac; perianth seg. lanceolate, clawed; stamens shorter than perianth, 1 ascending. Early summer. Brazil.

G.rochae G.M. Morel.
Bulb globose, 3cm diam. Lvs 3–4, oblong, 10–12×4–5cm, acute, attenuate at base to petiole, bright green, reticulated by veins; petiole 5–6cm. Scape to 20cm, compressed, bluntly 2-edged; spathe valve solitary, 2cm; pedicels 1cm; fls 6–8, horizontal to ascending, 3cm long, bright lilac; perianth bilabiate, with tube very short, seg. lanceolate, 2.5×0.5cm, reflexed; style subequal to perianth. Brazil.

Gymnospermium Spach. Berberidaceae. Around 4 species of perennial, rhizomatous herbs. Rhizomes tuberous. Leaves few, ferny, ternately divided; leaflets pinnately lobed, glabrous. Inflorescence a terminal raceme; sepals 6, petaloid, yellow; petals 6, very small, nectary-like; stamens 6, longer than petals. Fruit an inflated capsule, dehiscing at apex; seed with a membranous coating. Europe to C Asia. Z7.

CULTIVATION Related to the slightly larger *Bongardia*, the more delicate *Gymnospermium* arises from a large tuber and bears dense racemes of yellow flowers that unfurl in spring before the ferny foliage emerges. Native of the scrub and rocky hillside of Russia and Central Asia, where it flowers soon after snow melt, *Gymnospermium* is a fine plant for the unheated alpine house or sunny bulb frame and is grown in stony or gritty, free-draining soil. Culture as for *Bongardia*. Seed germinates easily.

G.alberti (Reg.) Takht. (*Leontice alberti* Reg.).
20–25cm. Tuber nearly round, slightly compressed. Basal lvs long-petioled, 2 per growth; flowering stem lvs 5cm, very short-petioled. Raceme 5–15-fld; bracts ovate, to 10mm; pedicel 6–13mm; fls 12–18mm across; sep. oblong-elliptic, veins red-brown on back; pet. folded at base, reduced to nec-taries, 3-lobed at tip; ovary stalked. Fr. nearly round, 3–4-seeded. Spring. C Asia.

G.altaicum (Pall.) Spach (*Leontice altaica* Pall.).
Similar to *G.alberti* except 5–20cm, sep. plain yellow, ovary not stalked. Black Sea.

Gynandriris Parl. Iridaceae. 9 species of perennial herbs distinguished from *Iris* by their rootstock, which is a corm surrounded by netted-fibrous tunics. Leaves narrow and channelled, flat or tightly coiled, usually only 1–2 per corm. Flowers in terminal and axillary cymes, short-lived, resembling those of *Iris* and *Moraea*; perianth segments free, tube absent; bracts transparent, papery; stamens partly united, closely adpressed to the underside of petaloid style branches; style of 3 flat branches, concealing anthers, stigma at base of style crests; ovary extended upwards as a slender sterile beak, on which the perianth is directly inserted. Fruit a many-seeded capsule. Southern Africa, Mediterranean, east to Pakistan.

CULTIVATION *G.sisyrinchium* grows wild in arid and semi-arid areas, in garigue and grassy pastures, on stony slopes to 2000m/6500ft and on sand, especially near the coast. The South African species are found in similar habitats, often on poor soils. Since they are not the most showy species in a family which includes many of extraordinary beauty, they are uncommon in cultivation; nevertheless, *Gynandriris* retains a charm and delicacy that is absent in many horticulturally improved Iridaceae and is of interest to the botanist and valued by collectors. The small lavender blooms of *G.sisyrinchium*, blotched yellow or white at their base, carry a faint scent of violets, although, as with others in the genus, they are short-lived, opening only after midday to fade by the following morning.

The Mediterranean species tolerate cold to about –5°C/23°F, and need plentiful moisture when in growth but require a summer baking to ensure flowering, and where summers are likely to be wet may best be accommodated in the bulb frame to provide completely dry conditions during dormancy. The South African species are more safely cultivated in frost-free conditions, especially the winter-flowering *G.setifolia*, which comes into growth in autumn and goes dormant in spring. Plant deeply, at about 15cm/6in., in a well-drained, gritty soil in a warm sunny position. Propagate by seed in a sandy propagating mix, in early spring, growing on in good light at about 10°C/50°F. Also by offsets from the corm.

G.monophylla Boiss. & Heldr. ex Klatt.
Similar to *G.sisyrinchium* but to only 5cm. Stem usually simple. Lvs 1, rarely 2, narrow, prostrate or coiling on the ground. Fls 2–2.5cm diam., pale slate-blue, falls with orange-yellow signal stripe bordered with white. Spring. E Mediterranean. Z8.

G.pritzeliana (Diels) Goldbl.
7–25cm. Lvs 2, to 42cm, coiled, prostrate, with central longitudinal white line on inner surface. Infl. branched from base, branches adpressed; fls solitary, mauve-blue, falls broad-obovate, 3×1.5cm, with white signal stripe, yellow at base; standards reflexed. S Africa. Z9.

G.setifolia (L. f.) R. Fost.
5–20cm. Lvs 3–4, linear, to 30cm, spreading. Infl. unbranched; fls 1–4, sessile, yellow, pale blue or lilac, seg. subequal, oblanceolate, falls with yellow signal stripe, standards reflexed. Winter. S Africa. Z9.

G.simulans (Bak.) R. Fost.
10–45cm. Lvs 1–2, linear, erect. Infl. branched, branches short, or fls sessile on main axis; fls to 2cm, lilac, with white spots, falls obovate, spreading. S Africa. Z9.

G.sisyrinchium (L.) Parl. (*Iris sisyrinchium* L.).
10–40cm. Lvs usually 2, base long and sheathing, blade flexuous, usually prostrate. Infl. 1–4 compact cymes; fls 1–6 per cyme, 3–4cm diam., violet blue to lavender, falls 2–4cm, blade with a white or white and orange signal patch. Spring. Portugal, Mediterranean to SW Asia and Pakistan. Z8.

Habranthus Herb. emend Sealy. (From Gk *habros*, graceful, and *anthos*, a flower.) Amaryllidaceae. 10 species of perennial herbs. Bulb tunicate, ovoid or globose, often long-necked. Leaves basal, linear, grass-like, evergreen or deciduous appearing with or after the flowers. Flowers solitary or, sometimes, paired, borne terminally on a hollow scape; spathe sheathing the pedicel, usually bifid above; pedicel joining the flower at an angle; perianth zygomorphic, infundibuliform, oblique or declining, tube short, lobes subequal; stamens 6, declining, 4 different lengths, with a corona of scales between the stamens, anthers versatile; ovary 3-locular; stigma 3-fld. Fruit a subglobose, 3-locular, many-seeded capsule. Temperate S America, especially Argentina, Uruguay and adjacent regions of Brazil and Paraguay. Z9 unless stated.

CULTIVATION   Frost-tender bulbs grown for their usually single, trumpet-shaped flowers in warm shades of red, yellow, pink and copper. *Habranthus versicolor* (which flowers in winter) and *H.brachyandrus* are sometimes grown at the base of a south- or southwest-facing wall in sheltered gardens with little or no frost. *H.tubispathus* is reliably hardy in zone 8, especially if established in a dry, sheltered and sunny position – excellent results have, for example, been achieved with plants allowed to naturalize on the thinnest of soils between the paving slabs of sun-drenched patios and roof gardens. All others are suitable for pot cultivation in the cool glasshouse or conservatory (min. 7°C/45°F) and flower better when slightly pot-bound. Grow in a fibrous loam-based mix with additional leafmould, well-rotted manure and lime rubble. Plant firmly with neck and shoulders above soil level; plant spring-flowering species in autumn, autumn-flowering species in early spring; increase water as growth commences, feeding weekly with liquid fertilizer as flower spikes appear. Gradually reduce water as foliage dies back; keep plants dry but not arid, and frost-free when dormant. Propagate by offsets and also from fresh ripe seed, which, at 16°C, germinates quickly, within two weeks and soon reaches flowering size. Seed of *H.tubispathus* sown directly on the final planting site will result in far hardier and more floriferous plants. Established plants will also seed themselves freely.

H.andersonii Herb. See *H.tubispathus*.
H.andicola (Poepp.) Herb. See *Rhodophiala advena*.
H.andicola (Poepp.) Herb. See *Rhodophiala andicola*.
H.bagnoldii Herb. See *Rhodophiala bagnoldii*.

H.brachyandrus (Bak.) Sealy (*Hippeastrum brachyandrum* Bak.).
Lvs to 30cm. Scape slender, to 30cm; spathe valves linear, to 5cm; pedicel equalling spathe; fls solitary, nearly erect, 9cm, brilliant or pale pink, tube short, deep red-black at base, lobes oblong-lanceolate, acute, 1.2cm wide; stamens at least 2.5cm; stigma deeply trifid. S Brazil. Z8.

H.cardinalis (C.M. Wright) Sealy. See *Zephyranthes bifolia*.

H.concolor Lindl. (*Zephyranthes concolor* (Lindl.) Benth. & Hook. f.).
Lvs hysteranthous, ligulate, to 30×1.5cm. Scape 15–30cm, very stout; spathe 3.5–5cm; pedicel to 6cm; fl to 6.5cm long, pale green-white, or creamy-white, green in throat; perianth seg. erect, to 2.5cm wide; style exceeding stamens, stigma deeply 3-fid. Spring–summer. Mexico.

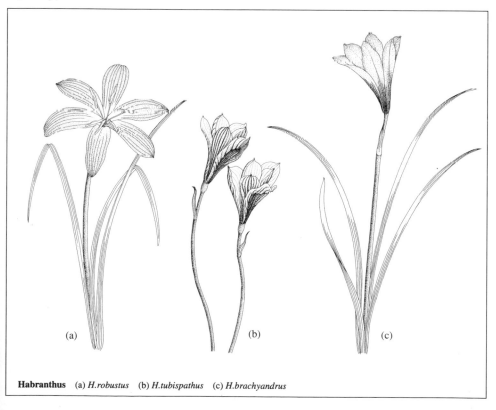

Habranthus   (a) *H.robustus*   (b) *H.tubispathus*   (c) *H.brachyandrus*

H.plumieri (Hume ex Moldenke) (*Zephyranthes plumieri* Hume ex Moldenke).
Lvs hysteranthous, filiform, to 22.5cm×1.5mm. Scape 10–20cm, slender; spathe to 3cm; pedicel to 2.5cm perianth 5–6cm, funnel-shaped, tube slender, to 1.5cm, style much exceeding stamens, stigma deeply 3-fid. Spring. W Indies.

H.gracilifolius Herb. (*Zephyranthes gracilifolius* (Herb.) Bak.).
Lvs to 45cm, 4 or 5, hysteranthous, nearly cylindrical, lustrous. Scape to 45cm; spathe valves to 3.5cm, pink-white, the upper third bifid; fls 1 or 2, at 45° to the pedicel; pedicel to 4.5cm; perianth to 5.5cm, tube short, green; lobes acuminate, pink or white, corona of scales between the stamens closing the tube; stamens 6, declinate, the longest exceeding the perianth lobes, fil. same colour as the lobes; style declinate, exceeding stamens, pink. Capsule to 1.8×1cm. Uruguay, Argentina.

H.juncifolius Traub & Hayward.
Lvs to 75×0.5cm, cylindrical. Fls 2–4, to 5.5cm, tube short, red-green, lobes white flushed pink. Argentina.

H.longipes (Bak.) Sealy (*Zephyranthes longipes* Bak.).
Lvs linear, glabrous. Scape fragile, to 30cm; spathe valves 2, convolute, to 3cm; pedicel to 10cm; fls pale red, to 8cm, tube short, narrowly funnelform, lobes lanceolate, spreading; stamens one-third length of perianth; style deeply trifid. Capsule 1.2cm diam., globose. Uruguay.

H.phycelloides Herb. See *Phycella phycelloides*.

H.robustus Herb. ex Sweet (*Zephyranthes robusta* (Herb.) Bak.).
Lvs fleshy, linear, 4mm broad, with longitudinal cavities. Scape to 30cm; spathe bifid in upper third; pedicels exceeding spathe; fls 1 or 2, declinate, to 7cm, tube green, lobes subequal, to 1.2cm wide, elliptic, acute, pink; stamens declinate, the longest half as long as perianth lobes. Argentina, S Brazil.

H.texanus (Herb.) Herb. ex Steud. See *H.tubispathus*.

H.tubispathus (L'Hérit.) Traub (*Amaryllis tubispatha* L'Hérit.; *H.andersonii* Herb.; *Zephyranthes andersonii* (Herb.) Bak.; *Amaryllis andersonii* (Herb.) Griseb.; *H.texanus* (Herb.) Herb. ex Steud.).
Lvs to 15cm, narrow, ligulate, appearing after the fls. Scape to 15cm, tinged red; spathe to 3cm, bifid in the upper third, grey-pink; pedicel equalling or exceeding spathe; fls solitary, perianth to 3.5cm, tube to 3mm, lobes obovate, cuspidate, orange, yellow or golden above, grey-pink, with darker copper, bronze or brown stripes on the underside; corona inconspicuous. Capsule to 1cm diam. Argentina, S Brazil, Uruguay, S Chile. Z8.

H.versicolor Herb. (*Zephyranthes versicolor* Bak.).
Lvs to 30×0.6cm, 3 or more, acute. Scape to 12cm, red fading to green; spathe to 3cm, red; pedicel 3.6cm, green; fls 5cm, rose, fading to white suffused with rose, red at the tip and streaked with red below, lobes to 1.8cm wide, with a red stripe on each side of the midrib near the base and a green central nerve, tube closed by a bearded or dentate membrane; stamens and style white; style to 3cm. Uruguay, Brazil. Z8.

Haemanthus L. (From Gk *haima*, blood, and *anthos*, flower, referring to the colour of the flowers.) Amaryllidaceae. 21 species of deciduous or evergreen bulbous herbs. Leaves 2–6, synanthous or hysteranthous, distichous, ligulate to lanceolate or elliptic, green or patterned red or green, glabrous or pubescent. Inflorescence an umbel, compact or loose; scapes slender to robust, glabrous or pubescent, sometimes spotted-red; spathe to 13-valved, spreading to erect, fleshy or scarious, white, pink, or red; flowers actinomorphic, white to pink or red; perianth tube cylindrical or campanulate, lobes oblong to lanceolate; anthers dorsifixed; ovary subglobose, 3-locular; style filiform. Fruits clustered, ovoid to globose berries, white, yellow, pink or red. S Africa, Namibia. Z9.

CULTIVATION From dry savannah, *Haemanthus* spp. are frost-tender bulbs grown for their exotic appearance, bearing striking globose flowerheads with coloured bracts and a remarkably dense boss of stamens that has a marked resemblance to a shaving brush. The umbels are carried on stout, often spotted stems; some species also have attractively marked leaves. *H.coccineus* is spectacular in leaf and flower; in autumn, the boss of long yellow stamens is held in a coral-red cup of fleshy bracts at the top of a short, red-spotted stem, and is followed by a pair of large leaves, hairy beneath and sometimes barred with deep red-purple; these lie flat on the soil surface.

Plant with the bulb neck at or just above soil level, in well crocked pots of humus-rich loam-based potting medium, with added coarse grit and well rotted manure. Maintain a winter minimum temperature of 10°C/50°F and grow in bright filtered light, but move into part shade as the flower buds colour, to preserve colour and prolong flowering. They will tolerate slightly lower temperatures when grown as house plants, but must have good light. Feed with dilute liquid fertilizer and water plentifully when in active growth. Dry off deciduous species as leaves yellow; keep evergreen species dry but not arid during rest. *Haemanthus* spp. flower better when underpotted and resent disturbance; re-pot only when absolutely necessary, as growth re-commences after rest. Propagate by offsets, removed as new growth begins and grown on in a closed case until established, or from ripe seed.

H.albiflos Jacq. (*H.albomaculatus* Bak.).
Lvs evergreen, erect, oblong, ligulate or elliptic, to 40×11.5cm, flat or channelled, light green sometimes spotted white, usually pubesc., margins ciliate, apex obtuse or acute. Scape to 35cm, green, glabrous or pubesc.; umbel compact, to 7cm diam.; spathe to 8-valved, erect, oblong to obovate to 4×3cm, white veined green, stiff, margins with retrorse hairs; fls to 50, white; pedicels to 1cm, green; perianth to 2.3×0.7cm; tepals to 1.8×0.25cm; fil. strongly exserted, white, anth. yellow-orange; ovary subglobose to 3mm, green; style equals fil. Fr. ovoid, to 1cm diam., white, orange or red; seeds to 0.5cm, white. S Africa.

H.albomaculatus Bak. See *H.albiflos*.
H.carinatus L. See *H.coccineus*.

H.coarctus Jacq. See *H.coccineus*.

H.coccineus L. (*H.carinatus* L.; *H.coarctus* Jacq.; *H.tigrinus* Jacq.). CAPE TULIP; BLOOD LILY.
Lvs 2–3, recurved to prostrate, synanthous; ligulate to elliptic, to 45×15cm, flat or lower part channelled, fleshy, bright green above, dull or glaucous beneath, sometimes barred maroon, green or white, glabrous or pubesc. Scape robust, to 37cm, cream to light green or pale red streaked dark red; umbel to 10cm across, compact, part-enclosed by spathes, thus cyathiform to campanulate, narrower in middle or spreading to obconical; spathe 6–9-valved, irregularly oblong to elliptic, 2–6×1.5–5cm, coral, vermilion or scarlet, fleshy; fls to 100, coral to scarlet with white markings; pedicels to 2cm, white to pale red; perianth to 3cm, tube to 0.5cm, lobes

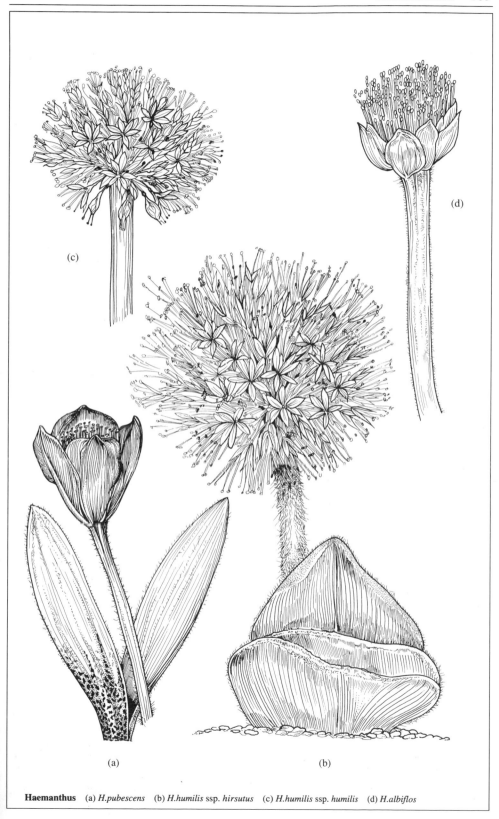

(c)

(d)

(a)

(b)

Haemanthus   (a) *H.pubescens*   (b) *H.humilis* ssp. *hirsutus*   (c) *H.humilis* ssp. *humilis*   (d) *H.albiflos*

swollen at base, oblong to spathulate, to 2.5×0.3cm; style and stamens equal, fil. strongly exserted, scarlet tipped white; ovary pale green, to 0.5cm across. Fr. to 1.5cm diam., white to deep pink; seeds 1–3, ovoid, to 1cm across, claret. Late summer. S Africa.

H.coccineus Forssk. See *Scadoxus multiflorus* ssp. *multiflorus*.

H.humilis Jacq.
Lvs 2–3, prostrate to erect, borne with flowers, elliptic to lanceolate, to 30×15cm, pubesc. Scape to 30cm, pale green or maroon, pubesc.; umbel loose or compact, obconical to hemispherical, to 12cm across; spathe 5–10-valved, reflexed, triangular, to 3×1.5cm, pink, scarious; fls to 120, white to pink; pedicels to 3cm, green; perianth to 2.5cm, tube to 1cm, lobes lanceolate to 2cm, slightly spreading; stamens included or strongly exserted; ovary to 2mm across; style equals fil. Berries ovoid, to 1cm across, green-white to orange; seeds white, ovoid, to 0.5cm across. Summer. S Africa. ssp. **humilis** (*H.nelsonii* Bak.). Umbel loose, hemispherical; spathe to 7-valved; fls white to pink, perianth to 1.5cm, tube to 0.6mm, lobes to 1cm; stamens equal to tepals or exserted by 0.8cm. Summer. ssp. **hirsutus** (Bak.) D. Snijman. Lvs pubesc., umbel stiff, obconical to hemispherical; fls pale pink to white, perianth to 2.6cm, tube to 1.2cm, lobes 2.1cm, stamens exserted by to 1.5cm. Early summer.

H.insignis Hook. See *Scadoxus puniceus*.
H.kalbreyeri Bak. See *Scadoxus multiflorus* ssp. *multiflorus*.
H.katherinae Bak. See *Scadoxus multiflorus* ssp. *katherinae*.
H.longitubus Wright. See *Scadoxus multiflorus* ssp. *longitubus*.
H.lynesii Stapf. See *Scadoxus multiflorus* ssp. *multiflorus*.
H.magnificus (Herb.) Herb. See *Scadoxus puniceus*.
H.mannii Bak. See *Scadoxus multiflorus* ssp. *longitubus*.
H.natalensis Poepp.. See *Scadoxus puniceus*.

H.nelsonii Bak. See *H.humilis* ssp. *humilis*.
H.orientalis Thunb. See *Brunsvigia orientalis*.

H.pubescens L. f.
Lvs 2–3, prostrate or recurved, hysteranthous, ligulate to oblong, to 20×4.5cm, smooth or striate, dark green, glabrous or white-pubesc. above, light green, glabrous or sparsely villous beneath, margin ciliate, green, apex acute to obtuse. Scape to 28cm, red, glabrous; umbel compact to 6cm across; spathe to 5-valved, erect, valves lanceolate to obovate, fleshy, to 8×3cm, red, apex white; pedicels to 0.3cm, white or red; perianth to 3cm, tube to 0.5cm, lobes erect, linear to oblong, to 2.5×0.2cm, apex obtuse; fil. strongly exserted, red, apex white; ovary to 0.3cm across, pale green, subglobose; style equals stamens. Fr. to 2.2cm, globose, white to pink; seeds spherical, to 0.5cm, green to claret-coloured. Autumn.

H.rouperi hort. See *Scadoxus puniceus*.
H.sacculus Phillips. See *Scadoxus multiflorus* ssp. *multiflorus*.

H.sanguineus Jacq.
Lvs 2, prostrate, hysteranthous, elliptic to oblong, to 40×28cm, flat, coriaceous, dark green and scabrid above, paler, glossy beneath, margin cartilaginous, red or hyaline, smooth or denticulate, apex obtuse. Scape to 27cm, furrowed, flushed claret; umbel narrow in middle, cyathiform or spreading, to 8cm across; spathe to 11-valved, valves ovate to lanceolate, to 7×5cm, lateral valves keeled and falcate, red-pink, obtuse to acute; fls 25, red to salmon pink marked white; pedicels to 3.2cm; perianth to 3.2cm, tube to 1cm, lobes oblong-lanceolate, to 2.4×0.5cm, acute; stamen strongly exserted; ovary subglobose, pink, style equals stamens. Berries ovoid, to 2cm, cream to claret to translucent; seeds ovoid, to 0.8cm across, claret. Late summer.

H.tenuiflorus Herb. See *Scadoxus multiflorus* ssp. *multiflorus*.
H.tigrinus Jacq. See *H.coccineus*.

Hedychium J.G. Koenig.

Hedychium J.G. Koenig. (From Gk *hedys*, sweet, and *chion*, snow: *H.coronarium* has fragrant white flowers.) GINGER LILY; GARLAND LILY. Zingiberaceae. About 40 species of erect, perennial herbs with stout, fleshy rhizomes and numerous reed-like stems. Leaves linear-lanceolate to oblong-lanceolate, in 2 ranks, sessile or on short petioles. Flowers fragrant, in dense, more or less cylindrical spikes; bracts spaced or imbricate; bracteoles tubular; calyx tubular, irregularly toothed; corolla tube slender, petals 3; lip long with 2 entire lobes; lateral staminodes petaloid; stamen filaments long and slender; anthers without spur at base; ovary inferior and 3-celled. Fruit a capsule. Tropical Asia, Himalaya and Madagascar.

CULTIVATION Rhizomatous perennials of the forest edges and moist places, grown for their very showy, fragrant flowers, those of the white ginger (*H.coronarium*) and the yellow gingers (*H.flavescens* and *H.flavum*) often appearing in Hawaiian floral garlands. The Himalayan spp., particularly *H.coccineum H.spicatum* and *H.densiflorum*, are hardy to –2°C/28°F if grown at the foot of a south-facing wall or given a mulch as winter protection.

H.gardnerianum makes a particularly fine plant for the cool conservatory or subtropical bedding scheme; less commonly seen but just as suitable are *H.greenei*, *H.flavum* and *H.forrestii*. All others require a minimum temperature of 18°C/65°F with high humidity, high fertility and plentiful water. *H.coronarium* hails from streamside habitats and will tolerate very wet conditions when in full growth in warm weather. Liquid feed pots throughout growth. Reduce water considerably in winter and allow plants to become dormant, cutting out old, flowered growths. Propagate by division in spring or from seeds sown fresh at 18°C/65°F. *H.greenei* is viviparous and can be propagated by planting its bulbils.

H.acuminatum Roscoe. See *H.spicatum* var. *acuminatum*.
H.angustifolium Roxb. See *H.coccineum* var. *angustifolium*.
H.aurantiacum Wallich ex Roscoe. See *H.coccineum* var. *aurantiacum*.
H.carneum Roscoe. See *H.coccineum* var. *aurantiacum*.

H.chrysoleucum Hook. f. (*H.coronarium* var. *chrysoleucum* (Hook. f.) Bak.).
To 1.5m. Lvs 40×8cm, oblong-lanceolate, tapering finely, sessile. Fls fragrant, 2–6 per bract; bracts 3cm, ovate to lanceolate, imbricate; cal. hidden by bract; cor. white, tube 8cm; lip 3.5cm across, 2-lobed, white tinged orange-yellow or pink; lateral staminodes spreading, white, yellow at base; stamen as long as lip, deep orange. Summer. India. Z9.

H.coccineum Sm. (*H.carneum* Roscoe). RED GINGER LILY; SCARLET GINGER LILY.
To 3m. Lvs 30–50×3.5cm, linear-lanceolate, acuminate. Fls 2–4 per bract; bracts oblong, to 2.5cm, not imbricate; cor. pale to deep red or orange; lip 1–2cm wide, red and yellow to mauve; lateral staminodes to 2cm; stamen longer than lip. Variable to fl. colour and lf size. Autumn. Himalaya. 'Tara': bold spikes of orange fls, styles conspicuously exserted, orange. var. **angustifolium** Roxb. (*H.angustifolium* Roxb.). Lvs narrower. Fls brick-red or salmon pink. var. **aurantiacum**

Roxb. (*H.aurantiacum* Wallich ex Roscoe). Lvs narrower. Fls orange. Z9.

H.coronarium J.G. Koenig. BUTTERFLY LILY; GARLAND FLOWER; WHITE GINGER.
To 3m. Lvs 60×11cm, lanceolate, acuminate, downy beneath. Fls very fragrant, in an ellipsoid spike to 20×11cm; bracts 4–6cm, imbricate, 2–6 fls per bract; cor. tube to 7cm, white, lip obcordate, 2-lobed, 5cm across, white with yellow-green centre; staminodes white; stamen shorter than lip, white. Spring. India. 'F.W. Moore' (*H.coronarium* × *H.coccineum*): spikes showy, fls fragrant, amber yellow, base of seg. blotched orange-yellow. var. **maximum** Roscoe (*H.maximum* Roscoe). Lvs broader and fls larger; bracts conspicuously ciliate; fil. tinged pink. var. **urophyllum** (Lodd.) Bak. (*H.urophyllum* Lodd.). Lip entire. Z9.

H.coronarium var. *chrysoleucum* (Hook. f.) Bak. See *H.chrysoleucum*.

H.coronarium var. *flavescens* (Roscoe) Bak. See *H.flavescens*.

H.densiflorum Wallich.
To 5m. Lvs 30–40×5–6cm, oblong or oblong-lanceolate, glabrous. Fls vermilion, in dense, cylindric, 20cm-long spikes; bracts 1.5cm, exceeding cal. and cor. not imbricate, 1 fl. per bract; lip 7mm across; stamen longer than lip, red. Himalaya. 'Assam Orange': stem shorter; fls vivid burnt orange, very fragrant. 'Stephen': infl. larger, more lax, less narrowly cylindrical; fls dirty yellow or pale orange; cor. tube exserted; fil. deep orange. Z8.

H.ellipticum Buch.-Ham. ex. Sm.
To 2m. Lvs elliptic or oblong with short spike, 30×13cm. Fls in dense 10cm spike; cor. 2-lobed, yellow-white, lip white, fil. purple. N India. Z10.

H.flavescens Roscoe (*H.coronarium* var. *flavescens* (Roscoe) Bak.). YELLOW GINGER.
To 3m. Lvs 60×8cm, lanceolate, acuminate, downy beneath. Fls in dense 20cm spike; bracts 3.5cm, imbricate, each subtending 4+ fls; cor. pale yellow, pet. green, linear; lip red-yellow at base; staminodes yellow; fil. longer than lip, yellow. Bengal. Z10.

H.flavum Roxb.
Lvs 30cm, oblong-lanceolate, glabrous above, paler beneath. Fls in dense 15cm spikes; bracts 5×5cm, imbricate; cor. yellow or orange; lip broadly obovate, sometimes 2-lobed, yellow with orange patch at centre and base; fil. yellow. N India. Z9.

H.forrestii Diels.
To 1.25m. Lvs 30 50×5cm, lanceolate. Fls in 20–25cm cylindric spike; bracts 4–5cm, spreading, 2–3 fls per bract; cor.

narrow-lobed, white or white flushed pink; lip, 3cm across, 2-lobed; staminodes elliptic; stamen not longer than lip. SW China (Yunnan). Z9.

H.gardnerianum Ker-Gawl. KAHILI GINGER.
To 2m+. Lvs 25–40×10–15cm. lanceolate. Fls white and yellow, in dense 25–35cm spike; bracts 3–5cm, oblong, 1–2 fls per bract; cor. tube 5.6cm; lip cuneate, 1–2cm diam., 2-lobed, yellow; lateral staminodes 2.5–3cm; fil. bright red. Summer–autumn. N India, Himalaya. Z8.

H.glaucum Roscoe. See *H.gracile*.

H.gracile Roxb. (*H.glaucum* Roscoe).
To 60cm. Lvs 12.5×3.25cm, lanceolate, acuminate, glaucous beneath. Fls in 10cm spike; cor. tube 2.5cm; pet. 2cm, greenwhite; lip small; fil. red. India. Z9.

H.greenei W.W. Sm.
To 2m. Lvs 20–25×5cm, oblong-acuminate. Fls in 12cm spike; bracts 5–7cm, ovate, imbricate, 2–3 fls per bract; cor. red, tube 2.5cm; lip 2-lobed, deep red; fil. longer than lip, bright red. Infl. may form bulbils. W Bhutan. Z10.

H.maximum Roscoe. See *H.coronarium* var. *maximum*.

H.speciosum Wallich.
To 2.5m. Lvs 30×9cm, lanceolate. Infl. 30cm; bracts 3–4cm, oblong-ovate, not imbricate; fls 2 per bract; cor. yellow; lip 2.5×1.5cm, oblong, entire; staminodes linear, shorter than pet.; fil. longer than lip, red. Summer. Himalaya. Z9.

H.spicatum Sm.
To 1m. Lvs 10–40×3–10cm, lanceolate or oblong-lanceolate, acuminate, sparsely hairy beneath, subsessile. Infl. to 20cm, lax; bracts 2.5cm, lanceolate, not imbricate; fls 1 per bract, cal. longer than bract; lip 1.5–2cm diam., 2-lobed, yellow; lateral staminodes spathulate, white and pink, fil. shorter than lip, red-orange. Autumn. Himalaya. var. **acuminatum** (Roscoe) Wallich (*H.acuminatum* Roscoe). Lvs distinctly stalked, downy beneath. Spike few-fld; staminodes and fil. purple. Z9.

H.thyrsiforme Buch.-Ham.
To 2m. Lvs 35×10cm, lanceolate, acuminate, pale green, pubesc. beneath. Fls in dense 10cm spike; cor. white; lip 2-lobed, white; lateral staminodes white; fil. longer than lip, white. India. Z9.

H.urophyllum Lodd. See *H.coronarium* var. *urophyllum*.

H.yunnanense Gagnep.
Lvs 40–8×10cm, entire, glabrous. Bracts orange, 1 fl. per bract; cor. tube 5cm, slender; pet. 3cm, linear, twisted; lip deeply divided, obovate; fll. 4.3cm. Yunnan, Indochina.

Helonias L. (From Gk *helos*, swamp, the natural habitat of the plant.) Liliaceae (Melanthiaceae). 1 species, an evergreen perennial to 45cm. Rhizomes horizontal, tuberous. Leaves 15– 45×3–5cm, petiolate, forming basal rosettes. Scapes 35–45×0.8–1cm, hollow, bracteate; flowers 25–30, fragrant, stellate, 15mm wide, in dense, conical, terminal racemes 8–15cm long; tepals 6, pink; stamens 6, exserted, anthers blue; ovary 3-celled, superior; styles 3. Fruit a trilocular capsule; seeds numerous, carrying white appendages. Spring. N America. Z8.

CULTIVATION *H.bullata* grows in swamps and bogs from southern New York as far south as North Carolina. Grown for its erect flowering stems of fragrant pink flowers, carried in dense cylindrical heads in spring, it is admirably suited to bog garden and waterside plantings and is occasionally pot grown under glass for early flowering. It is hardy at least to –15°C/5°F. Grow in moist to saturated, fertile, humus-rich, acidic soils in sun or light dappled shade. For forcing, pot up after flowering, plunge in the cold frame and bring under glass in late winter to temperatures of 10°C/50°F, keeping moist at all times. Apply liquid feed in summer. Propagate by division after flowering or by seed when available.

H.bullata L. SWAMP PINK.

Heloniopsis A. Gray. (From *Helonias* and Gk *opsis*, appearance.) Liliaceae (Melanthiaceae). 4 species of rhizomatous, perennial, evergreen herbs. Rhizomes short, tuberous, horizontal. Leaves in a basal rosette, petiolate, oblong or lanceolate with scarious sheaths. Flowering stems simple, erect; flowers terminal, nodding, solitary or few in a loose umbellate raceme; perianth segments 6, equal, spreading, united only at base; filaments subulate, stamens 6, purple-blue; ovary superior, trilocular; stigma entire, purple (cf. *Helonias*). Fruit a capsule; seeds many, with white appendages at each end. Japan, Korea, Taiwan.

CULTIVATION Hardy to between −10 and −15°C/14–5°F, *Heloniopsis* is grown for the nodding heads of flowers carried above the basal rosettes of evergreen leaves in spring. Grow in a moisture-retentive, humus-rich soil in light shade with some protection from cold winds to avoid leaf scorch. Propagate by division of established clumps or by seed sown when ripe or in spring.

H.breviscapa Maxim. See *H.orientalis* var. *breviscapa*.
H.japonica Maxim. See *H.orientalis*.

H.orientalis (Thunb.) Tan. (*H.japonica* Maxim.).
To 20cm+. Lvs 8–10×2.5cm, oblanceolate, acute, tinged brown toward apex, narrowed toward base. Pedicels 1–1.5cm,

longer than fls, curved, becoming erect in fruit; racemes 2–10-fld; perianth seg. 1–1.5cm, narrowly spathulate, pink or violet, persistent; stamens shortly exserted, anth. blue-violet. Spring. Japan, Korea, Sakhalin Is. var. **breviscapa** (Maxim.) Ohwi (*H.breviscapa* Maxim.). Fls smaller, pale pink or white.

Hemerocallis L. (From Gk *hemere*, day, *kallos*, beauty; the flowers only live for one day.) DAYLILY. Liliaceae (Hemerocallidaceae). Some 15 species of rhizomatous, clump-forming, perennial herbs. Roots fibrous or somewhat tuberous, often enlarged at each end. Leaves basal, linear, sessile, tapered, 2-ranked, usually falcate, basally flat or folded, deciduous or persisting well into winter. Flowers bracteate, borne in a close raceme on a long smooth scape, sometimes branched at summit; perianth funnelform to campanulate, yellow to red-orange; tepals 6, uniting to form a narrow, basal tube, free parts spreading, inner often wider; stamens 6, deflexed, inserted at mouth of tube; ovary superior, 3-celled, ovules many. Fruit a 3-valved, few-seeded, loculicidal capsule. E Asia, Japan, China.

CULTIVATION Daylilies are long-lived border perennials whose emerging pale green foliage provides interest from early spring; their flowers are produced in succession over a long period in summer, each lasting for only a day. Some are effective grown at woodland margins or at the waterside; some form very dense clumps and may be useful for groundcover, and others have uses in large landscaping schemes on sloping sites, their tough roots rapidly binding the ground. Low-growing remontant cultivars are suitable for container growing, (e.g. *H.*'Stella d'Oro', *H.*'Happy Returns'). They will grow in most fertile garden soils including sand and heavy clay but do best at a pH of 6–7.

Abundant blooms will be produced when planted in a soil liberally enriched with well-rotted manure. Shortly before they break dormancy in late winter they should be given a balanced fertilizer, followed every four weeks with a balanced foliar or soluble feed. The last application of fertilizer prior to flowering should contain an increased ratio of phosphate to promote the production of buds. Copious watering is required to maximize both the size and number of blooms, though the ground must be free-draining. If grown in waterlogged ground or rough grass they produce more foliage and less flower.

Most daylilies require long periods of full sun. Some species and older hybrids (*Hh.* 'Corky', 'Golden Chimes', 'Lemon Bells') will tolerate part shade, but the palest, pastel forms, especially pink-toned cultivars, may not open fully unless exposed to long periods of strong sunlight ('Dance Ballerina Dance'). Some dark red and deep purple cultivars, which absorb most light, benefit from part shade in tropical and subtropical climates.

Unless naturalized, plants should be lifted and divided every three years to maintain vigour and promote flowering. Divide cultivars in spring, or after flowering when the foliage should be shortened by two-thirds, or from plantlets produced on the flower-scape. Most species, except some forms of *H.fulva*, produce fertile seed, although the seedlings may not resemble the parent.

Plant in spring or autumn, except in hard winter areas (Zones 2–3), when spring planting is essential. Bare-rooted plants should be soaked in a weak solution of liquid fertilizer overnight before planting. Plants should be spaced no less than 30cm/12in. apart and their roots spread over a mound in the planting hole which should not allow the crown to lie more than 2.5cm/1in. below the surface.

Young foliage is particularly susceptible to slug and snail damage but daylilies are also prone to attack by the gall midge (*Contarinia quinquenotata* (Loew)) which is manifested by the presence of small white maggots in the flower bud; the daylily aphid (*Mygus hemerocallis*) which leaves white flecks on the foliage in spring; spider mites; thrips, nematodes (eelworm) and cutworm may also be troublesome.

Daylilies can be affected by 'spring sickness' which rots the new inner leaves. This is more likely to be a problem in temperate climates and will prevent flowering for at least a year. It is seldom a problem where continental winters are the norm. Crown rot is also a problem in these regions. It is caused by ground heaving which happens at times of alternate freezing and thawing. It can be prevented by mulching.

Daylilies hybridize readily and some 20,000 are now registered with the International Registration Authority, and this figure is being increased by some 400–800 new named cultivars each year. The American Hemerocallis Society has categorized daylily cultivars in several useful ways. Plants are classed as Evergreen, Semi-Evergreen or Dormant. Evergreen sorts are best suited to Zones 6–9; many will not thrive in cold climates especially if there is no snow cover. Dormant sorts are suited to Zones 2–6 and may not perform well in warmer climates. Semi-evergreen sorts are best suited to temperate climates but some can do well in hotter or colder regions. Some Evergreens will acclimatize to colder conditions as they mature. It is a matter of trial and error.

Leaves vary from graceful and grasslike (*H.minor*) to coarse, strap-like (*H.fulva*) varying from 30cm/12in. (*H.*'Eenie Weenie') to 1.5m/5ft (*H.altissima*). Mature foliage colour ranges from blue-green to mid or dark-green, sometimes yellowish, although excessive yellowness can denote an unhealthy plant. *H.fulva kwanso* 'Flore Pleno' has leaves with unstable longitudinal variegation.

Daylilies are further categorized according to height of flower-scape which, for garden value, should be proportional to height of leaf-mound. Dwarf: below 30cm/6in.; Low: 30–60cm/12–24in.; Medium: 60–90cm/24–36in.; Tall: over 1m/39in. Daylilies are also categorized by flower size expressed as a diameter. Miniature: less than 7.5cm/3in.; Small-flowered: 7.5–11.5cm/3–5in.; Large-flowered: over 11.5cm/5in. They are further classified by flower colour and pattern as selfs, blends, polychrome, bi-tone, reverse bi-tone, bicolour, reverse bicolour, banded, eye-zoned, edged, haloed, tipped or watermarked. Throat and eye colour can be an attractive contrast. The perianth consists of six segments arranged in threes, the outer, narrower sepals lying below the petals. The midribs of the segments may differ in colour from the segment; the stamens may also differ in colour from the segments giving added garden value. Flowers of heaviest substance are found in tetraploid cultivars where the colours are usually brighter and the blooms more prolific. Some of the species' characteristic gracefulness can be lost in tetraploid varieties. Bloom texture varies from smooth, satiny to velvety and creped, and may have an overlay known as diamond dusting. The edges may be ruffled. The species and their hybrids with brown-backed sepals tend to have brown scapes (*H.dumortierii, H.*'Golden Chimes').

Natural flower form is trumpet-shaped but the flowers of modern hybrids may be circular, triangular, star-shaped, flat or spider-like. Those with more than six segments are known as doubles or camellia forms.

Flower colour in the species ranges from lemon-chrome (*H.lilio-asphodelus*) to tawny-orange (*H.fulva*). Hybridizers have raised cultivars in almost every colour except true blue and pure white, although some daylilies appear virtually white if exposed to sufficient strong sunlight (*H.*'Gentle Shepherd', *H.*'Joan Senior'). All daylilies have a yellow undertone to a greater or lesser degree which makes some cultivars difficult to use in association with other border plants. Heavy rain can cause the pigment to scatter in some rich red varieties.

Most species are diurnal (*H.aurantiaca, H.dumortieri, H.middendorffii*). Nocturnal species (*H.citrina, H.thunbergii*) open their flowers in late afternoon and remain open all night. *H.lilio-asphodelus* is an extended bloomer, the flower sometimes remaining open up to 16 hours. Both diurnal and nocturnal types can also have this characteristic. *H.lilio-asphodelus* and *H.citrina* are very strongly fragrant, *H.middendorffii* and *H.thunbergii* less so, a characteristic inherited by some of their offspring.

The season of blooming is categorized as Extra Early, Early, Early-midseason, Midseason, Late-midseason, Late and Very Late. Some are remontant, either flowering early and repeating in autumn, or flowering over a quick succession of bloom periods. Repeat blooming is often influenced by geographical and climatic conditions and adequate moisture.

A small selection of the 20,000-odd cultivars appears at the end of this entry. Many of these are tetraploid. Most are at least ten years old but several, still standing the test of time, have been available since the 1960s.

H.altissima Stout.
Roots coarsely fibrous, some swollen. Lvs to 150×3cm. Scapes to 2m, branched toward apex, remontant; fls to 10×10cm, pale yellow, nocturnally fragrant; perianth tube to 3.7cm. Summer and autumn. China. Z6. Tallest of all spp., rare in cultivation but important in hybridization.

H.aurantiaca Bak.
Habit moderately vigorous. Rhiz. spreading, main roots enlarged. Lvs 60–80×1.5–2.5cm, glaucous, falcate, persisting into winter. Scapes taller than foliage, forked, but sparsely branched above; fls to 20, 10–13cm, sessile, densely clustered, widely funnelform, orange and often flushed with purple; perianth tube less than 3cm. China. Z6.

H.citrina Baroni.
Roots fleshy, elongated, tapering. Scapes erect, branched above, taller than foliage; lvs 20–65, 9–12cm, fragrant, pale lemon, tinged brown behind, borne in a raceme, opening at night; perianth tube to 4cm; tepals narrow. China. Z4.

H.dumortieri E. Morr.
Habit vigorous, forming a dense clump. Roots very fleshy, mostly swollen. Lvs 35×1.5cm, falcate. Scapes unbranched, spreading, shorter than or slightly exceeding lvs; fls 2–4, 5–7cm, flat-funnelform, almost sessile, borne in a tightly clustered raceme, subtended by broad, cup-shaped bracts which conceal pedicels; inner tepals less than 2cm wide; perianth tube to 1cm. Japan, E USSR, Korea. Z4.

H.flava L. See *H.lilio-asphodelus*.

H.forrestii Diels.
Roots fleshy, cylindric, conspicuously enlarged at each end.

Lvs 30×1.5cm, not falcate, narrow, arching at ends. Scapes erect, slender, ascending, branched, mostly shorter than lvs; fls 4×8, to 7cm, not fragrant, yellow, borne in a raceme; bracts conspicuous; perianth tube to 1cm. China. Z5.

H.fulva L.
Rhiz. spreading, main roots fleshy. Lvs 70×3cm, falcate, erect, green. Scapes erect, taller than foliage, branched, forked; fls 10–20, 7–10cm, widely funnelform, rusty orange-red, usually with darker median zones and stripes, borne in racemes; perianth tube 2.5cm. Origin uncertain, perhaps Japan or China. Z4.

H.graminea Andrews. See *H.minor*.
H.graminifolia Schldl. See *H.minor*.

H.lilio-asphodelus L. (*H.flava* L.).
Rhiz. spreading, roots enlarged. Lvs 50–65×1–1.5cm, falcate. Scapes closely branched above, weak, ascending, taller than foliage; fls 8–12, 7–8cm, fragrant, shortly funnelform, yellow; perianth tube to 2.5cm. Z4.

H.middendorffii Trautv. & Mey.
Main roots cylindrical and fibrous, some slightly enlarged. Lvs 30×1–2.5cm, falcate, soft. Scape erect, unbranched, slightly taller than foliage; fls 8–10cm, few, fragrant, yellow, borne in a tightly clustered raceme, subtended by conspicuous, cup-shaped, enfolding bracts; perianth tube to 2cm; tepals to 2.5cm. N China, Korea, Japan, E USSR. Z5.

H.minor Mill. (*H.graminea* Andrews; *H.graminifolia* Schldl.).
Forming a dense clump. Roots slender, mostly fibrous, occasionally a few enlarged, crown compact. Lvs

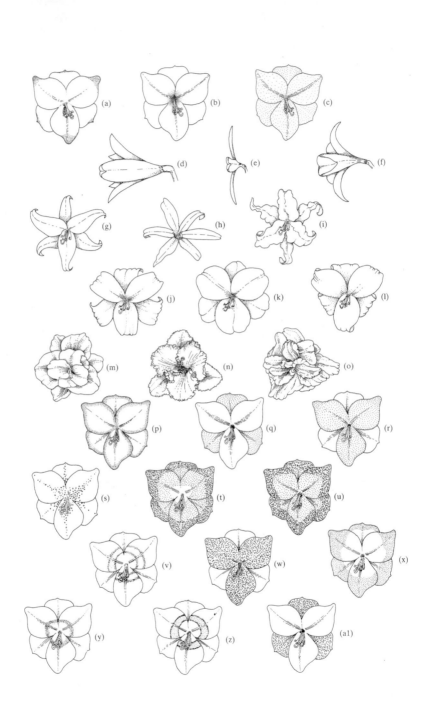

Hemerocallis flower forms (a) tipped (b) throat (c) prominently veined (d) trumpet shaped (e) flat
(f) recurved (g) star-shaped (h) spider (i) orchid form (j) flaring (k) round (l) triangular (m) layer-on-layer
(n) ruffed (o) hose-in-hose (p) edged (q) reverse bi-tone (r) bitone (s) dotted (t) polychrome (u) blended
(v) banded (w) bicolor (x) watermark (y) eyed (z) halo (a1) reverse bicolor

30–45cm×5–9mm, falcate. Scapes erect, taller than foliage, forked or shortly branched above; fls 2–5, 5–7cm, shortly funnelform, lemon yellow, tinged brown outside, borne in a raceme; tepals narrow; perianth tube less than 2cm. Japan, China. Z4.

H.multiflora Stout.
Roots fleshy, crown compact. Lvs 60×1cm, falcate, dark green. Scapes erect, slender, much branched, glaucous above, taller than foliage; fls numerous, 75–100, 7–8cm, glistening chrome yellow within, tinged brown-red without; perianth tube to 2cm; tepals narrow. China (Honan). Z4.

H.thunbergii Bak.
Habit vigorous, compact. Roots slender, cylindric, somewhat fleshy, and sometimes enlarged. Lvs 30–60cm×5–8mm, falcate, narrow, dark green. Scapes erect, rigid, branched near apex; fls 3–15, 9–11cm, fragrant, shortly funnelform, yellow, borne in a raceme, opening in the morning; perianth tube to 3cm; tepals narrow. China, Korea. Z4.

H.cultivars.
Dwarf (below 30cm/12in.). 'Buffy's Doll': pink-buff with rose-wine eye-zone. 'Eenie Weenie': light yellow with fluted edges. 'Little Grapette': flowers rounded, grape-purple.
Medium (30–60cm/12–24in.). 'American Revolution': medium-sized velvety black/red flowers. 'Ava Michelle': rich yellow, green throat, ruffled edges. 'Becky Lynn': rose-pink, deeper shaded rose eye-zone, fragrant. 'Berlin Red': rich ruby red, gold throat; weatherproof. 'Bertie Ferris': small-flowered persimmon self. 'Brocaded Gown': pale lemon-cream, very ruffled. 'Burning Daylight': tall, deep orange which glows in the evening. 'Catherine Woodbery': pale lavender pink blooms, lime green throat, fragrant. 'Cherry Cheeks': deep cherry-red, white midrib, yellow throat contrasting with black-tipped stamens. 'Chestnut Lane': light golden-brown with chestnut-brown eye-zone, golden throat. 'Chicago Apache': ruffled, deep scarlet self. 'Chicago Royal Robe': deep purple with contrasting green throat. Slightly fragrant. 'Christmas Is': low-growing; brilliant scarlet with strikingly contrasting green throat. 'Dancing Shiva': low-growing; shell pink with a blue cast, yellow-green throat. 'Double Pink Treasure': creamy-pink double. 'Fairy Tale Pink': delicate shell-pink of heavy substance with ruffled edges. 'Gentle Shepherd': low-growing, near white. 'Golden Chimes': small golden-yellow flowers on well-branched scapes; the dark brown buds make a striking contrast. 'Golden Prize': large, bright glowing golden-yellow flowers; slightly fragrant. 'Hope Diamond': wide creamy-yellow petals with blush overlay; good texture and ruffled edges. 'Joan Senior': the nearest to pure white flower, with contrasting yellow-green throat; wide ribbed-textured petals with ruffled edges. 'Kindly Light': classic citron-yellow spider, long, narrow recurved segments. 'Lusty Lealand': large blooms of rich, deep red with contrasting golden throat and reverse of petals. 'Luxury Lace': low-growing, producing a mass of creamy-lavender-pink flowers with lime-green throat. 'Mauna Loa': flaming salmon-orange with contrasting green throat; rounded, ruffled and crimped flowers. 'Real Wind': vivid pink-orange self, with wide, deep rose eye-zone. 'Ruffled Apricot': large ruffled apricot self. 'Siloam Baby Doll': apricot, rose eye-zone, green throat; small flower. 'Siloam Button Box': creamy yellow, maroon eye-zone, green throat, small flower. 'Stella d'Oro': low growing, remontant rounded canary-yellow flowers with orange throat. 'Yellow Petticoats': clear yellow double.

Tall (over 1m/39in.). 'Elaine Strutt': flowers trumpet-shaped, clear mid-pink. 'Marion Vaughan': pale lemon-yellow with green throat; fragrant; long-blooming. 'Mormon Spider': large flowered pale polychrome blend of yellow, pink and lavender. 'Whichford': highly scented, narrow trumpet-shaped flowers in palest green-yellow.

Herbertia Sweet. (For Dr William Herbert (1778–1847), Dean of Manchester and expert on bulbous plants.) Iridaceae. 6 species of perennial cormous herbs, allied to *Tigridia* and *Alophia*. Leaves usually radical, sometimes sheathing stems, lanceolate, plicate. Scape erect, simple or sparsely branched, successively bearing 1–2 short-lived flowers either at its summit or the tips of branches, each subtended by 2 spathes concealing pedicel and ovary; perianth shortly tubular, composed of 6 segments, the 3 outer broadly triangular-ovate, acute, spreading or reflexed, far exceeding the 3 inner segments, which are rounded and erect; stamens 3, united; style trifid at apex. Fruit a capsule. Temperate S America. Z9.

CULTIVATION *Herbertia* spp. are grown for their iris-like flowers, in shades of blue-violet carried on long, slender branching stems; they are individually short lived but carried in succession over a period of several weeks. Those of *H.lahue* are particularly fine, being a lavender blue blotched with deeper violet at their base. In zones that are frost-free or almost so, they are suited to the warm and well-drained sunny border; where temperatures occasionally fall to about –5°C/23°F, they can be grown outside with a deep protective mulch of bracken litter. Cultivate as for *Homeria*. Propagate by seed or by offsets.

H.amatorum Wright (*Trifurcia amatorum* (Wright) Goldbl.).
Corm globose, brown. Lvs 15–22×0.4–0.8cm, linear-lanceolate, tapering to base. Scapes 30–50cm, branches few, slender, to 12cm; outer perianth seg. 3–3.5×2.5cm, obovate, reflexed, violet, centrally striped white toward base and on claw, with a yellow basal nectary, inner seg. 1–1.5×0.25–0.6cm, violet, spotted brown at base, spreading, claw ciliate; anth. yellow; stigma mauve. Spring. Southern S America.

H.amoena Griseb. (*Alophia amoena* (Griseb.) Kuntze).
Corm ovoid to globose. Lvs 7.5–25cm, linear-lanceolate. Scapes to 30cm; fls violet, 1–2 per spathe; outer perianth seg. to 2cm. Argentina, Uruguay.

H.caerulea (Herb.) Herb. See *Alophia drummondii*.
H.drummondiana hort. See *Alophia drummondii*.

H.lahue (Molina) Goldbl. (*Alophia lahue* (Molina) Espin.; *Trifurcia lahue* (Molina) Goldbl.).
Corm ovoid to globose, brown. Lvs 5–10cm×0.3–0.5cm, narrowly lanceolate, usually subfalcate. Scape 8–15cm, simple or with a single branch; outer perianth seg. 1–1.5×0.5–0.8cm, oblanceolate, spreading, violet stained blue near base, inner perianth seg. 5–5.5×0.2–0.3cm, oblanceolate, violet, interior glandular near base; anth. yellow; stigmas mauve. Spring. S Chile, Argentina.

H.lahue ssp. *caerulea* (Herb.) Goldbl. See *Alophia drummondii*.

H.pulchella Sweet (*Trifurcia pulchella* (Sweet) Goldbl.).
Corm ovoid to globose, brown. Lvs 10×0.5cm, linear-ensiform, acute. Scape 8–15cm, simple or with 1 branch; outer perianth seg. 2.5–2.8×1–1.2cm, spreading or reflexed, blue to lilac or purple tinted pink, often with a central white stripe, claw white and bearded, flecked or flushed violet, inner seg. mauve; anth. yellow, stigmas tinted red. Spring. Southern S America to S Brazil.

H.watsonii Bak. See *Alophia drummondii*.

Hermodactylus Mill. Iridaceae. 1 species, closely related to *Iris*, differing mainly in having a unilocular ovary (trilocular in *Iris*). Rootstock creeping, of irregularly shaped, rather finger-like tubers. Leaves to 50×0.2–0.4cm, usually shorter, linear, square in cross-section, grey-green. Flowering stem 15–40cm, covered in sheathing leaves; flowers 1–2 per stem, scented, 4–5cm diam., pale olive to apple green, the outer segments (falls) velvety brown-black, tube about 5mm, falls 5cm, oblong, standards much shorter and narrower; style arms broad, erect, acutely 2-lobed, translucent olive. Late winter–early spring. S Europe, from France eastwards, Balkans, Greece, Turkey, Israel.

CULTIVATION   *H.tuberosus*, occurring naturally in scrub and on grassy banks and hills, bears its fragrant curiously coloured blooms in late winter or spring, depending on its location. It is undemanding in cultivation, well suited to dry chalky soils, and will form large clumps where conditions suit. Although hardy to –15°C/5°F, it is sometimes given cold glasshouse protection in regions where the spring weather may spoil the flower. Grow in sun in any well drained soil. The flowers last fairly well when cut and kept in a cool room, and are a welcome sight in late winter. Propagate by division in late summer. Slugs and snails may be a problem.

H.tuberosus (L.) Mill. (*Iris tuberosa* L.). MOURNING WIDOW; SNAKE'S HEAD IRIS; WIDOW IRIS.

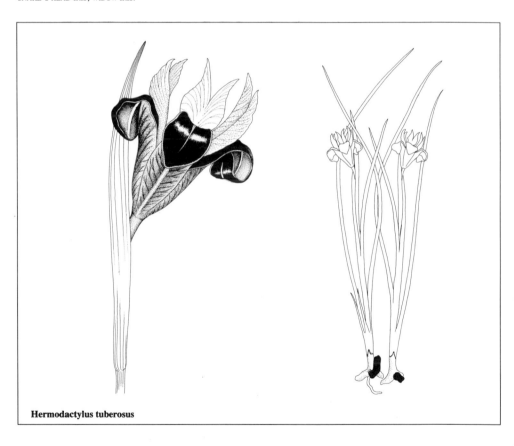

Hermodactylus tuberosus

Hesperantha Ker-Gawl. (From Gk *hespera*, evening, and *anthos*, flower.) Iridaceae. About 55 species of small to medium-sized perennial herbs, closely related to *Geissorhiza*. Corms ovoid to globose, symmetrical or asymmetrical, with hard woody tunics. Leaves 3 to several, mostly basal but often with 1 forming a cauline sheath, linear, smooth or ribbed, sometimes hairy. Scape erect, rarely subterranean; spike 1- to several-flowered; flowers usually star- or somewhat saucer-shaped, regular, usually white or pale mauve but sometimes red, purple, blue or yellow, in most species opening in the evening and at night, tube straight or curved, tepals 6, usually subequal; style usually divided at apex of tube, branches 3, long and slender. Subsaharan Africa, with most species in S Africa. Z9.

CULTIVATION   As for *Ixia*.

H.baurii Bak.
Small plants, 15–20cm; corm globose. Lvs 3–4, forming a fan. Spike laxly few-fld; fls 1–2cm diam., bright pink, tube 10–15mm, tepals spreading, to 10mm. Summer. S Africa (E Cape, Natal, Transvaal), Lesotho.

H.buhrii L. Bol. See *H.cucullata*.
H.cinnamomea (L. f.) Ker-Gawl. See *H.spicata*.

H.cucullata Klatt (*H.buhrii* L. Bol.).
Corms 1–1.5cm diam., ovoid, asymmetrical. Lvs 7–10×0.5–1cm, 3–4, sword-shaped. Scape to 30cm, simple or branched, erect; spike 1–10-fld; fls scented, white with the outer tepals red outside, opening in the evening, tube 6–9mm, tepals 15–20×5–10mm, ovate; style branches to 8mm. Winter–spring. S Africa (W Cape).

H.falcata (L. f.) Ker-Gawl. (*H.lutea* Ecklon ex Bak.).
Corm to 1.5cm diam., triangular, symmetrical. Lvs 3–5, usually 5–8cm×4–8mm, sword-shaped. Scape 6–30cm, simple or with up to 3 branches near base; spike 3–8-fld, occasionally 1-fld; fls white, cream or pale to deep yellow, the outer tepals flushed with red, pink or brown on outside, white forms scented, night-blooming, yellow forms unscented and day-flowering, tube 4–9mm, tepals 12–18×5–7mm, ovate; style branches 6mm. Winter–early spring. S Africa (W Cape and as far east as Port Elizabeth).

H.kermesina Klatt. See *Geissorhiza inflexa*.

H.longituba (Klatt) Bak.
15–30cm; corm to 18mm diam., ovoid or globose. Lvs 3–4, 5–9mm wide. Scape usually unbranched, erect; spike 1–6-fld; fls scented, white, often tinged with pink or brown outside, opening in the evening, tube 10–18mm, straight, tepals 15–22×8–10mm, ovate, the outer 3 slightly longer and narrower than inner 3; style branches to 16mm. Winter–early spring. S Africa (Karroo, E Cape, Orange Free State).

H.lutea Ecklon ex Bak. See *H.falcata*.
H.metelerkampiae L. Bol. See *H.vaginata* var. *metelerkampiae*.

H.muirii (L. Bol.) Lewis.
Corm 6–8mm diam., somewhat bell-shaped. Lvs 2–4, erect, 3–8cm×1.5–2mm, linear. Scape 10–20cm, erect, unbranched; spike 1–3-fld; fls cream or pale pink, rather irregular, tube 15–25mm long, curved, tepals 15–25×6–9mm, elliptic; style branches to 15mm. Spring. S Africa (W Cape).

H.pilosa (L. f.) Ker-Gawl.
Corm 5–12mm diam., ovoid, asymmetrical. Lvs 3, 8–20cm×1–10mm, hairy, narrowly linear. Scape 10–32cm, erect, usually unbranched, glabrous or sparsely hairy; spike usually 3–6-fld, rarely 1-fld or with up to 12, fls white, magenta-pink, violet, blue or purple, tube 6–10mm, tepals 10–15×3–5mm, elliptical; style branches 6–11mm. Winter–spring. S Africa (SW Cape, W Karroo).

H.radiata (Jacq.) Ker-Gawl. (*H.tysonii* Bak.).
10–60cm; corms 7–14mm diam., asymmetrical. Lvs 3–4, shorter than stem, 2–3mm wide, linear. Scape erect, unbranched; spike (1-)6–15-fld, secund, the fls facing downwards; fls white or green-white, often tinged with red-brown or purple on outside, tube 10–18mm, somewhat curved, tepals 7–15×5mm, slightly reflexed; style branches 7–10mm. Winter–spring or spring–summer. S Africa (Cape, E Karroo, Drakensberg), Swaziland.

H.spicata (Burm. f.) N.E. Br. (*H.cinnamomea* (L. f.) Ker-Gawl.).
Corms 1–1.5cm diam., bell-shaped. Lvs usually 3, linear or terete, the edges sometimes crisped. Scape 12–30cm, rarely to 50cm, erect, unbranched; spike 4–20-fld, secund; fls white, the outer seg. purple-brown on outside, tube 4–6mm, tepals 4–9mm long, narrowly ovate; style branches about 3mm. Late winter–spring. S Africa (W Cape).

H.stanfordiae L. Bol. See *H.vaginata* var. *stanfordiae*.
H.tysonii Bak. See *H.radiata*.

H.vaginata (Sweet) Goldbl. (*H.metelerkampiae* L. Bol.; *H.stanfordiae* L. Bol.).
12–18cm high; corm more or less globose but asymmetrical. Lvs 4–5, 5–9cm×8–10mm, falcate. Scape erect, simple or with 2–3 branches near base; spike 1–4-fld; fls about 6cm diam., bright yellow or yellow and brown, opening mid-afternoon and closing early evening, tube 5–8mm, tepals 30–35×15–17mm, lanceolate; style branches about 5mm. Late winter–early spring. S Africa (W Karroo). var. *metelerkampiae* (L. Bol.) R. Fost. Fls bicoloured, yellow with dark brown in throat and on apical half of tepals. var. *stanfordiae* (L. Bol.) R. Fost. Fls clear yellow.

Hesperocallis A. Gray. (From Gk *hesperos*, western, and *kallos*, beauty.) Liliaceae (Agavaceae). 1 species, a bulbous perennial herb. Bulb tunicate. Stems to 30cm, leafy. Leaves to 30×2cm, linear, margins undulate-crispate, white. Inflorescence a robust terminal raceme subtended by scarious bracts; flowers fragrant, funnelform, to 7cm, lobes twice length of tube, white, outside broadly striped green; stamens 6, filaments attached to perianth, anthers versatile. Fruit a capsule, strongly 3-lobed, many-seeded; seeds compressed, matt black. SW US (S California, W Arizona). Z9.

CULTIVATION   Native of desert and semi-desert, where the bulbs are often found at great depth, *Hesperocallis* is especially useful for semi-desert or Mediterranean-type gardens. They are intolerant of temperatures below freezing – certainly in combination with wet – but in cool temperate zones may be grown in the cool glasshouse or conservatory. Plant in a gritty medium and position in full sunlight. *Hesperocallis* needs no water when dormant and should be watered carefully and moderately when in growth. Propagate by seed and offsets.

H.undulata A. Gray DESERT LILY.

Hippeastrum Herb. (From Gk *hippeus*, a rider, and *astron*, a star; reference unclear.) AMARYLLIS; KNIGHT'S STAR LILY. Amaryllidaceae. About 80 species of perennial herbs. Bulb tunicate. Leaves basal, linear or strap-shaped. Scapes stout, leafless, hollow; flowers tubular to funnelform or salverform, 2 to several held horizontally or drooping in an umbel, umbel subtended by 2 large, equal free spathes persisting in flower: perianth tube often long, dilating at the throat, throat often closed or with scales or a corona, perianth lobes 6, erect and spreading, the inner 3 sometimes narrower than the others, white, red or orange-pink to deep crimson or striped combinations of these colours; filaments 6, often with small scales in between. Fruit a 3-valved capsule; seeds black, flattened or compressed. Americas.

CULTIVATION The genus *Hippeastrum* is most commonly represented in cultivation by those large-flowered species and their many named hybrids which bear their exotic and beautiful flowers on stout stems in winter and early spring. As with many florists' flowers that have been subject to intensive breeding the origin of most hybrids is now obscure, although most derive from *H.vittatum*. The cross between this species and *H.reginae*, first accomplished in 1799 by an English watchmaker, Mr Arthur Johnson, gave rise to *H.× johnsonii* and its robust and free-flowering selections amenable to cultivation in the cool glasshouse or conservatory. Hybrids are now grown in a range of colours, from the brilliant deep red of *H.*'Red Lion' and strong orange-scarlet of *H.*'Orange Sovereign', through the flamboyant salmon pink of *H.*'Bouquet' to the less vivid but equally attractive pure white of *H.*'White Dazzler' and the softer, white flushed pink of *H.*'Apple Blossom'. Many *Hippeastrum* species have equally beautiful colours and, in addition, are often possessed of a grace and elegance that intensively bred hybrids lack.

Most *Hippeastrum* spp. require protected cultivation in cool temperate climates, although *H.argentinum* and *H.× acramannii* may be cultivated outside given a south-facing wall, well-drained soil and a thick dry mulch of bracken litter to protect the bulb in winter.

Grow tender species under glass in bright filtered light, in a free-draining, medium-fertility, loam-based mix (e.g. 3:1:1 loam, leafmould, sharp sand). Plant firmly with the neck and shoulders above soil level, winter-flowering species in late summer/early autumn, summer-flowering species in early spring. Maintain a minimum temperature of 13–16°C/155–60°F and water sparingly until growth commences, when temperatures may be increased to 16–18°C/160–65°F for earlier flowers, although flowering is prolonged at lower temperatures. Water plentifully when in active growth, syringe the leaves with soft water, and feed weekly with a dilute liquid fertilizer. Remove the scape at its base when flowering is over. Leaves continue their development after flowering, and feeding and watering should be continued until growth ceases and leaves yellow, usually by mid-summer. Reduce water gradually and withhold completely when dormant, keeping bulbs dry and warm, not below 5–7°C/40–45°F, until growth resumes. *Hippeastrum* spp. are very sensitive to root disturbance, and are re-potted only every three of four years, before the new cycle of growth begins. Remove as much soil as possible from the fleshy roots before repotting firmly, and watering in thoroughly.

Propagate by offsets, and by seed sown when ripe at 16–18°C/60–65°F; if grown on without dry rest during their first year, seedlings mature and flower more quickly, and may flower in their second or third year from sowing. Red spot disease is caused by the fungus *Stagonospora curtisii*, which is also responsible for narcissus leaf scorch. Watery red lesions occur on the bulbs, leaves and flower stalks and red scabs form on the outer scales of the bulbs. Emerging foliage and flower buds can be sprayed with a copper-based fungicide; for those cvs which are sensitive to copper use dithiocarbamate fungicide. The leaves of plants affected by tomato spotted wilt virus show numerous pale yellow or white spots which may coalesce and form large patches so that the leaves die. Control vector insects and destroy affected plants. Basal rot sometimes results from poor drainage and/or overwatering. Also susceptible to red spider mite (*Tetranychus* spp.) soft scale (*Coccus hesperidum*), various thrips and mealybugs (*Pseudococcus* spp.). The bulbs may be infested by the bulb scale mite, *Steneotarsonemus laticeps*, and by bulb flies, especially the large narcissus fly, *Merodon equestris*.

H.× ackermannii Lem. See *H.× acramannii*.

H.alberti Lem. See *H.reginae*.

H.× acramannii hort. (*H.× ackermannii* hort. ex Vilm.). (*H.aulicum × H.psittacinum.*)
Intermediate between parents. Scape to 60cm; fls 15cm, lobes acute, margin somewhat undulate, green in throat, white at centre, remainder bright scarlet with white margins.

H.aglaiae (Cast.) (*Amaryllis aglaiae* Castellanos).
Bulb globose, 5×4.5cm, neck 7cm. Lvs evergreen, 20–35×1–2.5cm, obtuse, narrowed to base, slightly channelled, green. Scape 50cm, glaucous, tapering upwards; spathe valves to 4.5×1cm, scarious at anthesis; pedicels 2.5–4.5cm; fls 2–3, green-yellow below, butter-yellow above; perianth tube 5mm, with short scales at throat, outer lobes 70×25mm, spathulate, acute, inner lobes to 22mm broad, lowermost to 14mm broad; stamens included, fil. white, ascending, style equalling perianth, stigma trifid. Argentina & Bolivia.

H.ambiguum Herb. (*Amaryllis ambigua* (Herb.) Sweet ex Steud.; *H.elegans* 'Longiflorum'; *Amaryllis elegans* var. *ambiguum* (Herb.) Traub & Mold.). AMBIGUOUS KNIGHT'S STAR LILY.
Fls 4–5; perianth tube declinate, to 7.8cm, white, lobes each with 2 stripes of Tyrian rose, throat with many long hairs;

style exceeding fil., equalling perianth; stigma trifid. Argentina, Peru, Brazil, Ecuador, Costa Rica.

H.andreanum Bak. (*Amaryllis andreana* (Bak.) Traub & Uphof).
Bulb 10–11cm diam., neck short, producing many offsets. Lvs hysteranthous, lorate. Scape to 38cm, brown-violet, somewhat compressed and 2-edged; spathe-valves lanceolate, to 5cm, rose-red; pedicels 2.5–3.8cm; fls 4–6, 10cm long; perianth tube very short, corona absent, perianth lobes oblanceolate-acute, to 2cm broad, pale red with streaks of darker red; stamens much shorter than perianth, exceeded by style, stigma capitate. Colombia.

H.argentinum (Pax) Hunz. (*Amaryllis argentina* (Pax) Ravenna).
Lvs to 25×30cm, lorate, channelled, pale green, slightly glaucous. Scape to 30cm, slightly compressed, pale green; spathe valves to 6cm, joined at base for 0.5cm; pedicels to 6cm; fls to 15×8cm, 2, trumpet-shaped, fragrant; perianth tube green, to 55mm, lobes oblanceolate, green at the base, otherwise white, with undulate margins, outer lobes to 92×33mm, apiculate, inner lateral pair to 87×25mm, lower inner pair equalling lateral pair but narrower; fil. closely fascicled, white with a green base, to 8cm; style straight or slightly

ascending, to 14cm; stigma trifid with spreading lobes to 3mm. Argentina, Bolivia.

H.aulicum (Ker-Gawl.) Herb. (*H.robustum* A. Dietr.; *H.morelianum* Lem.; *Amaryllis aulica* Ker-Gawl.). LILY OF THE PALACE.
Bulb ovoid, to 10cm diam.; neck short. Lvs 6–9, blunt-tipped to 60×5cm, bright green. Scape to 60cm, stout, terete, fls usually 2, crimson, to 15cm, throat green, lobes obovate, pointed, the 2 upper inner ones much broader than the others, corona in the throat green; stamens shorter than the perianth; fil. red; stigma trifid. Brazil, Paraguay. var. *platypetalum* Lindl. More vigorous, with broader perianth lobes.

H.advenum (Ker-Gawl.) Herb. See *Rhodophiala advena*.
H.andicolum (Poepp.) Bak. See *Rhodophiala andicola*.
H.araucanum Philippi. See *Rhodophiala araucana*.
H.bagnoldii (Herb.) Bak. See *Rhodophiala bagnoldii*.
H.bifidum (Herb.) Bak. See *Rhodophiala bifida*.

H.blossfeldiae (Traub & Doran) (*Amaryllis blossfeldiae* Traub & Doran).
Bulb 8.5×8.8cm, neck 1.8cm, light brown. Lvs 3–5, linear, 73–78×2.5–4cm, apex subacute, deep green. Scape to 35cm, hollow, somewhat flattened above; spathe-valves 2, long-lanceolate, green; pedicels to 5cm; fls 4–5; perianth tube to 5cm, green or yellow, lobes to 8cm, light nasturtium red; stamens declinate-ascending, fil. and style white in lower half, pink above. Brazil (coastal areas).

H.blumenavium (K. Koch & Bouché ex Carr.) Sealy.
Bulbs globose or subglobose, to 4cm diam. Lvs to 13×7.5cm, to 7, lanceolate-elliptic to oblanceolate-ovate; petiole short. Scape to 25cm, tinged mauve below; fls 4 or 5, drooping, to 8cm; perianth lobes spreading, to 8cm diam., white, with longitudinal lines and bands of red-purple, margins undulate; stamens curving downwards. SE Brazil.

H.barbatum Herb. See *H.puniceum*.
H.brachyandrum Bak. See *Habranthus brachyandrus*.

H.bukasovii (Vargas) (*Amaryllis bukasvoii* Vargas).
Bulb subglobose, 6–8cm long. Lvs 5–7, hysteranthous, 38–40cm, subterete; spathe valves 2, lanceolate; pedicels to 3cm, fls 2, 10×12–14cm, perianth tube 1cm, perianth scales minute, throat with large green-white star, lobes obovate, acute, to 3.8cm wide at middle, lowest narrower, all dark red with conspicuous yellow-green tip to 3cm; stamens shorter than lobes, style exceeding seg., stigma 3-lobed. Peru.

H.breviflorum Herb.
Bulb ovoid, to 7.5cm diam. Lvs to 43×3.75cm, green. Scape to 90cm, cylindrical, glaucous; spathe valves lanceolate; fls 5–6; pedicels slender, to 7.5cm; perianth limb to 3.75cm, funnelform, tube shorter, seg. oblanceolate-oblong, acute, white with a red keel, the outer ones to 2cm broad, the inner to 1.25cm; stamens and style longer than limb, anth. small, oblong; stigma trifid. Argentina.

H.calyptratum (Ker-Gawl.) Herb. (*Amaryllis calyptrata* Ker-Gawl.).
Bulb to 10cm, pear-shaped, tunics grey. Lvs to 60×5cm, 8–10, channelled, with a sharp keel below, deep green, crimson on underside near the base. Scape 60cm, hollow, green, somewhat glaucous; spathe valves boat-shaped, to 8×3cm; bracteoles 2, to 5×0.3cm; pedicels 4cm; fls 2 or rarely 3, green, held horizontally; perianth tube to 2.5cm, conical, the 2 outer lobes claw-like, curving inwards, with a prominent midrib, the inner lobes rolled outwards; stamens pale pink, to 15cm; style to 18cm; stigma trifid. Brazil.

H.candidum Stapf. (*Amaryllis candida* (Stapf.) Traub. & Uphof; *Amaryllis immaculata* Traub & Mold.; *H.immaculatum* (Traub & Mold.).
Bulb globose, 7.5cm diam., black-purple. Lvs hysteranthous, ligulate, to 30(+)×2.5cm, subacute, tapering to base, shallowly channelled, somewhat glaucous. Scape to 70cm, dark purple below, glaucous above; spathe-valves 6cm, red-scarious; pedicels 4cm; fls 6, fragrant, pendent, funnel-shaped, to

20cm long; perianth tube to 10×0.5cm, green, outer lobes oblanceolate, 9–12×2cm, apex recurved, margin crisped, pure white, inner lobes narrower, to 16mm broad; stamens include, anthers golden-yellow. Argentina (Tucuman province).

H.chilense (L'Hérit.) Bak. See *Rhodophiala chilensis*.
H.correiense (Bury) Worsley. See *H.organense*.
H.crocatum Herb. See *H.reginae*.

H.cybister (Herb.) Benth. & Hook. f. (*Sprekelia cybister* Herb.; *Amaryllis cybister* (Herb.) Traub. & Uphof).
Bulb ovoid, 5cm diam., brown. Lvs hysteranthous, lorate, 2.5–3.2cm broad, green. Scape to 60cm+, subterete, glaucescent, purple below; spathe valves lanceolate, dull red; pedicels stout; fls 4–6, 7.5–10cm long; perianth tube very short, with incurved corona, lobes tapering upwards to acute apex, bright crimson, tinged green at apex and externally, upper 3 twisted upwards, lower 3 close together; stamens exceeding perianth, fil. green, stigma small, minutely 3-lobed. Bolivia (Andes).

H.doraniae (Traub) (*Amaryllis doraniae* Traub).
Bulb round, 4×4cm, neck 1.5cm. Lvs emerging with fls, developing fully later. Scape 35cm, hollow; spathe valves 2, 6cm, lanceolate, yellow-green; pedicels 3.2cm; fls 2–4, trumpet-shaped, 12×9.5cm, borne horizontally, becoming declinate; perianth tube green, lobes lanceolate, margins somewhat undulate, green in lower third, carmine-rose above, paler at apex; stamens fasciculate, declinate-ascending. Venezuela.

H.elegans (Spreng.) H.E. Moore (*Amaryllis elegans* Spreng.; *H.solandrifolium* (Lindl.) Herb.).
Lvs to 2.5cm broad. Scape to 60cm; fls 2–4, pale green, to 25cm; tube to 12.5cm; stigma capitate. S America.

H.elegans 'Longiflorum'. See *H.ambiguum*.
H.elwesii C.M. Wright. See *Rhodophiala elwesii*.
H.equestre Herb. See *H.puniceum*.

H.evansiae (Traub & Nels.) H.E. Moore (*Amaryllis evansiae* Traub & Nels.).
Bulb to 5.2cm diam., rhizomatous. Lvs to 38.5×4.9cm, 3–7, lorate to broad oblanceolate. Scape to 22.5cm, nearly terete, sometimes slightly compressed; spathe valves 2, lanceolate, to 7cm; fls 2 or 3, held horizontally; pedicels to 6.8cm; perianth tube to 7cm, throat green, corona absent, lobes with undulate or smooth margins, chartreuse green or straw yellow, outer 3 to 9.3×3.7cm, broadly or narrowly elliptic, inner 3 to 9.4×1.8cm, narrowly elliptic, stamens just exceeding perianth tube, style exceeding stamens. Capsule to 3×1.8cm; seeds many, discoid, black. Bolivia.

H.forgetii Worsley.
Resembling *H.pardinum* but fls only partially striped, unspotted, lobes narrower; pedicel to 8cm; perianth dull crimson, lobes to 15cm across, keeled in lower half, base green; stamens included in perianth; stigma 3-lobed. Peru.

H.fulgidum Herb. See *H.reginae*.
H.ignescens Reg. See *H.reginae*.
H.immaculatum (Traub & Mold.). See *H.candidum*.

H.×johnsonii hort. (*H.reginae* × *H.vittatum*.)
Intermediate between parents. Bulb to 7.5cm diam. Lvs ligulate, to 75×3.5cm. Scape to 60cm; fls 4, funnel-shaped, to 12.5×10cm, bright scarlet with narrow white streaks, green at base within and externally.

H.lapacense (Cardenas) (*Amaryllis lapacensis* Cárdenas).
Bulb globose, to 7×7cm; tunics brown. Lvs to 60×4cm, spathulate-lanceolate, slightly grooved, acute. Flowering stem to 60cm, white beneath, green above; spathe valves lanceolate, 5cm; bractlets white, 4cm; pedicels 5cm, green; fls 2, actinomorphic; perianth tube 3mm, outer lobes to 10×3.7cm, inner to 9.5×3.5cm, all lanceolate, white, with green bases and keels, streaked crimson inside; paraperigone hairy, white; stamens 5.5cm, fil. light green at the base, white in the middle, purple on top; style 9.5cm; stigma 3-lobed, dark purple. Bolivia.

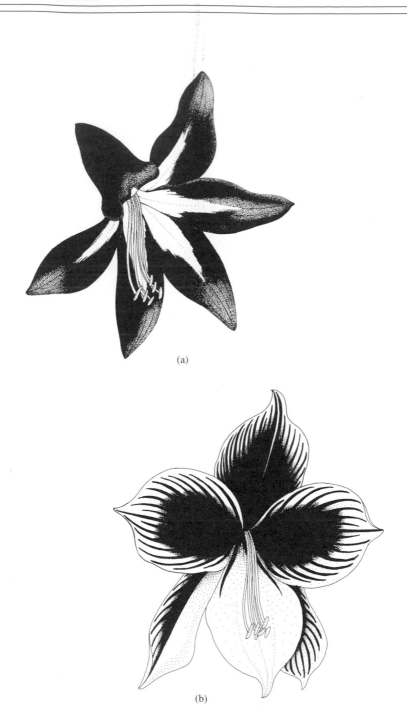

(a)

(b)

Hippeastrum   (a) *H.reginae*   (b) *H.papilio*

H.leopoldii Dombrain (*Amaryllis leopoldii* (Dombrain) H.E. Moore).
Bulb globose, to 8cm diam.; neck short. Lvs to 5cm, strap-shaped. Scape to 5cm, nearly terete; fls usually 2, large, regular, to 18cm; perianth tube without a corona or constriction at the throat, lobes obovate, to 5cm across, dull crimson below, green-white at the tip, bright red between with a forked white mark at the base and a green-white throat; stamens exceeding perianth; fil. white; style protruding. Bolivia.

H.machupijchense (Vargas) D.R. Hunt (*Amaryllis machupi-jchensis* Vargas).
Bulb subglobose, 7cm long, neck to 7cm. Lvs 5–7, hysteranthous, to 70×3cm. Scape 25cm or more, green, red at base; spathe valves lanceolate, 6–7cm; pedicel 6cm; fls 1 2, 18×16cm, tubular-campanulate; perianth tube 4–6mm, pale green, corona obscure, lobes narrow-elliptic or obovate, to 10×3cm, acute, pale green externally with margin red, dark red within, with pale green throat and longitudinal streaks; stamens slightly shorter than lobes, fil. green below, dark red above, style equalling seg. Peru.

H.maracasum (Traub) H.E. Moore (*Amaryllis maracasa* Traub).
Lvs to 52×3.9cm, to 7, lanceolate, acute, concave above, margins recurved downwards, glaucous with a white bloom. Scape to 64cm, tinged-red at base; spathe valves 2, to 6.5cm, lanceolate, acute; fls 2; pedicels 5.5cm; perianth tube to 14×11cm, brick red with darker red reticulation and a green star in the throat, with white bristles above the stamens, lobes in 4 sizes, the 2 lowest to 11×3.2cm, sickle-shaped, the uppermost to 12×6cm, the other 3 narrower; stamens and style within the perianth tube; stigma white, trifid. Brazil.

H.morelianum Lem. See *H.aulicum.*

H.oconequense (Traub) H.E. Moore (*Amaryllis oconequensis* Traub).
Bulb globose, to 8.7cm diam., neck short. Lvs to 20×2.8cm, to 8, sheathing below, oblanceolate, acute. Scape to 9cm, elongating to 24cm in fruit; spathe 2-valved, white, acuminate, 5cm; bracteoles 4, much shorter, white; pedicels to 6.5cm; fls 4, to 10.5×5cm, red inside, the outside red above, red-brown below; stamens and style exserted, declinate-ascending; stigma lobes globose. SE Peru.

H.organense (Hook. ex Herb.) (*H.correiense* (Bury) Worsley; *Amaryllis organensis* Bury).
Close to *H.aulicum.* Bulb large with short neck. Lvs 5–6, lorate, to 45×3.8cm, glaucous. Scape to 46cm; spathe-valves lanceolate, to 10cm; fls 2, to 15cm; perianth tube 1.3cm, with incurved green corona at throat, lobes oblong, acute, crimson, with green keel in lower portion, outer lobes to 4.4cm broad, inner lobes narrower; stamens and style subequal to perianth lobes, fil. red. Brazil (Organ Mts).

H.papilio (Ravenna) (*Amaryllis papilio* Ravenna).
Bulb ovate, 9×5.5cm, pseudoneck 4–5cm, dark brown. Lvs 5, synanthous, lorate, 30–50×3.5cm, channelled, spreading, recurved. Scape slightly compressed, to 33cm, somewhat glaucous, purple at base; spathe valves marcescent, to 10.5cm, subequal; pedicels to 5.5cm; fls 2, somewhat declinate, to 9×13.5cm, laterally compressed, pale green or green-white streaked, veined and stained dark red to maroon; perianth seg. oblanceolate, in outer whorl to 14×2.7cm inner whorl 9.5×4.4cm, margins somewhat undulate, acuminate; fil. declinate, fasciculate, style declinate-ascending, exceeding stamens, stigma 3-fid. S Brazil.

H.pardinum (Hook. f.) Dombrain (*Amaryllis pardina* Hook. f.).
Bulb globose, to 8cm diam., neck short. Lvs to 60×5cm, 5–7, narrowing at the base, appearing after the fls. Scape to 3.5cm, glaucous; fls usually 2, to 18cm; perianth tube less than 2.5cm, throat constricted or closed, lobes to 13cm, oblong, acute, cream or yellow-green and dotted with crimson, the lowest inner lobe the narrowest; stamens growing downwards, shorter than the perianth; stigma capitate. Peru.

H.petiolatum Pax.
Bulb globose, to 4cm, without a neck. Lvs to 20×2.5cm, lanceolate, acute, narrowing at the base to petiole of 2cm. Scape to 20cm; spathe valves 2, marcescent, lanceolate, to 3cm; fls to 7cm, 1–2, scarlet; pedicels inclining, to 2.5cm; perianth short, the throat with small scales between the bases of the fil., lobes oblong, acute, to 1.5cm broad; fil. unequal, some shorter than the perianth, anth. versatile, linear, to 2mm; style filiform, exceeding stamens; stigma bifid with erguidos lobes, to 2mm. Argentina.

H.phycelloides (Herb.) Bak. See *Phycella phycelloides.*
H.pratense (Poepp.) Bak. See *Rhodophiala pratensis.*
H.procerum (Duchartre) Lem. See *Worsleya rayneri.*

H.psittacinum (Ker-Gawl.) Herb. (*Amaryllis psittacina* Ker-Gawl.).
Bulb to 10cm diam., neck long. Lvs to 45×35cm, 6–8, lorate, slightly glaucous, appearing with the fls. Scape stout, to 60cm; fls 2–4; perianth tubes short, throat constricted, lobes to 13cm, oblong, acute, with undulate crimson margins, main part green-white striped crimson, the lower middle lobes narrower than the others and pointing downwards; stamens shorter than the perianth; stigma 3-lobed; style red. S Brazil.

H.puniceum (Lam.) Urban (*Amaryllis punicea* Lam.; *H.equestre* Herb.; *Amaryllis equestris* Ait.; *H.ignescens* Regel; *H.pyrrochroum* Lem.; *H.spathaceum* Sims). BARBADOS LILY.
Bulb globose, to 5cm diam. Lvs to 3.5×5cm, 6–8, strap-shaped, appearing after the fls. Scape to 5cm; fls to 13cm long and 10cm diam., bright red, scarlet or pink with green-yellow throats; stamens shorter than perianth lobes. Mexico to Chile, Bolivia, Brazil to W Indies. 'Semiplenum': fls semi-double to double, bright red.

H.pulverulentum Herb. See *H.reginae.*
H.pyrrochroum Lem. See *H.puniceum.*

H.reginae (L.) Herb. (*Amaryllis reginae* L.; *H.stenopetalum* A. Dietr. ex Koch; *H.alberti* Lem.). MEXICAN LILY.
Bulb globose, to 8cm diam. Lvs appearing after the fls, to 60×5cm, tapering at the base. Scape to 50cm; fls 2–4, drooping, red; perianth tube to 2.5cm, lobes to 13cm, obovate, acute, the lowest innermost one narrower than the others, all bright red with a large green-white star in the throat; stamens shorter than the perianth. Mexico to Peru and Brazil, W Indies and W Africa.

H.reticulatum (L'Hérit.) Herb. (*Amaryllis reticulata* L'Hérit.).
Bulb subglobose, neck short. Lvs appearing with the fls, to 30×5cm, oblanceolate, thin, bright green. Scape to 30cm; fls 3–6, to 8cm diam.; perianth tube to 2.5cm, throat not constricted, lobes to 10cm, obovate, mauve or red-purple with crimson stripes and cross lines; stamens shorter than the perianth, drooping. S Brazil.

H.rhodolirion (Philippi) Bak. See *Rhodophiala rhodolirion.*
H.robustum A. Dietr. See *H.aulicum.*
H.roseum (Sweet) Bak. See *Rhodophiala rosea.*
H.rutilum (Ker-Gawl.) Herb. See *H.striatum.*
H.solandrifolium (Lindl.) Herb. See *H.elegans.*
H.spathaceum Sims. See *H.puniceum.*
H.stenopetalum A. Dietr. ex Koch. See *H.reginae.*
H.sub-barbatum Herb. See *H.reginae.*

H.striatum (Lam.) H.E. Moore (*H.rutilum* (Ker-Gawl.) Herb.; *Amaryllis rutila* Ker-Gawl.; *Amaryllis striata* Lam.).
Lvs lorate, to 2.5cm broad, bright green. Scape to 30cm; fls 2–4, to 10cm, crimson keeled green to halfway up the lobes; stigma trifid. Brazil.

H.stylosum Herb. (*Amaryllis maranensis* Ker-Gawl.). LONG-STYLED KNIGHT'S STAR LILY.
Bulb globose, to 8cm diam., tunic pale, neck short. Lvs 4–6, appearing with the fls, to 5cm wide, bright green. Scape to 5cm; fls 3–8, light red or pink, to 10cm diam.; perianth tube to 12mm, green, throat not constricted, lobes oblanceolate-

acute, pink-brown, veined and speckled a deeper colour; stamens slightly protruding; style exceeding limb by 3cm. Guyana, Brazil.

H.texanum Bak. See *Habranthus tubispathum*.

H.traubii (Mold.) H.E. Moore (*Amaryllis traubii* Mold.). Bulb 3.6cm diam., neck 1.5cm. Lvs evergreen, lorate, to 25×1.7cm, tapering to obtuse apex and base, coriaceous, glossy green, red-brown at base below and on margin when young. Scape 28cm, compressed, red below, green above; spathe-valves lanceolate, 4.6cm, scarious; pedicels to 2.5cm; fls 4, variable in size; perianth tube triquetrous, to 2.3cm, brown-green, lobes lanceolate, acute, white-green in lower third, rose above, to 7.4×3.2cm; stamens and style shortly exserted, stigma capitate, obscurely trifid. Peru.

H.vittatum (L'Hérit.) Herb. (*Amaryllis vittata* L'Hérit.). Bulb globose, to 8cm. Lvs appearing after the fls, to 60cm, 6–8 bright green. Scape to 90cm; fls 3–6, to 12cm diam.; perianth tubes to 2.5cm, lobes obovate-oblong, to 4cm across, keel white, lobe margins irregular and white, striped red in between. Peruvian Andes.

H.cultivars. 'Appleblossom': fls white flecked soft pink. 'Beautiful Lady': fls pale mandarin red. 'Best Seller': stem short; fls cerise. 'Bouquet': fls salmon. 'Byjou': fls soft burnt apricot. 'Cantate': fls milky deep red. 'Christmas Gift': fls white. 'Dazzler': fls pure white. 'Dutch Belle': fls opal rose. 'Ludwig's Goliath': fls large, bright scarlet. 'Lydia': fls pale salmon. 'Oskar': fls rich deep red. 'Orange Sovereign': fls pure orange. 'Picotte': fls white rimmed red. 'Red Lion': fls dark red. 'Royal Velvet': fls deep velvety red. 'Star of Holland': fls scarlet with white star at throat. 'Susan': fls large, soft pink. 'United Nations': fls white striped vermilion. 'Valentine': fls white with pink veins, heavier towards edges. 'White Dazzler': fls pure white.

Homeria Vent. (From Gk *homereo*, to meet together: the filaments are united in a sheath around the style.) Iridaceae. 31 species of cormous, herbaceous perennials. Corms with reticulated fibrous tunics. Leaves basal and usually solitary, overtopping flowers, or on flowering stem, linear-ensiform. Flowering stem leafy, erect, branched; flowers showy, fugacious, subtended by 2 bracts, several produced in long-lasting succession, usually orange-red, bronze, golden or mauve, radially symmetric; perianth segments 6, free, connivent to outspread, forming a cup, inner segments slightly smaller than outer segments with a basal nectary extending sometimes to claw; stamens opposing outer perianth segments, filaments fused; style 3-branched, branches entire, compressed, sometimes crested. Fruit a flat-topped or beaked capsule. Summer. S Africa. Z9.

CULTIVATION Native to sand flats and other sandy habitats; in its native regions and in parts of Australia, where it is widely naturalized, *H.collina* is often regarded as a weed species, since it is toxic to livestock. *Homeria* spp. are grown for their attractive, almost symmetrical cup-shaped flowers carried on slender stems. The fragrant blooms of *H.collina* show a good range of pastel colours in soft yellows, peach and salmon pinks. Most spp. are frost-tender, although they can be grown outside in sheltered sites in regions where temperatures do not fall much below –5°C/23°F, given a deep mulch overwinter to protect the corms. Alternatively, lift in autumn or grow in the cool glasshouse. Grow in a well drained, humus-rich soil in full sun, planting corms 5–10cm/2–4in. deep, with some sharp sand at their base. Under glass use a medium-fertility, loam-based mix with additional leafmould and sharp sand; maintain good ventilation and a minimum temperature of 5–7°C/40–45°F, water plentifully when in growth and dry off gradually as flowers fade. Store in a cool dry place. Propagate by seed in autumn, leaving seedlings in their panicle for the first year, also by division or offsets.

H.breyniana (L.) Lewis. See *H.collina*.

H.breyniana var. *aurantiaca* (Zucc.) Lewis. See *H.flaccida*.

H.collina (Thunb.) Salisb. (*H.breyniana* (L.) Lewis). Lf to 30×0.4–1cm, usually flagging or trailing on ground. Flowering stem 16–38cm, simple or sparsely branched; fls pale golden yellow to peach or pink, scented, outer seg. to 3.5cm, the claw papillose at base, inner seg. slightly smaller with deep golden, green-edged nectaries; fil. to 0.6cm, slightly downy at base, anth. to 0.5cm; style branches 0.5–0.6cm. SW Cape.

H.collina var. *aurantiaca* (Zucc.) Bak. See *H.flaccida*.

H.collina var. *ochroleuca* (Salisb.) Bak. See *H.ochroleuca*.

H.elegans (Jacq.) Sweet. Similar to *H.collina*, from which it differs in its broader lf, outer perianth seg. which are yellow with large blue-green, orange-tipped blotch toward their apices and the anth. to 1cm. SW Cape.

H.flaccida Sweet (*H.collina* var. *aurantiaca* (Zucc.) Bak.; *H.breyniana* var. *aurantiaca* (Zucc.) Lewis). Lf to 25×1.3cm. Flowering stem 40–60cm, sparsely branched; fls yellow to peach with distinct golden or sulphur-yellow nectaries, outer perianth seg. to 4cm, claws sometimes minutely papillose; fil. to 0.8cm, sometimes sparsely papillose, ciliate at base, anth. 0.8–1cm; style branches to 0.7cm. SW Cape.

H.lineata Sweet. See *H.miniata*.

H.miniata (Andrews) Sweet (*H.lineata* Sweet). Closely related to *H.ochroleuca*, from which it differs in having 2–3 lvs and fls tawny red, apricot to pink golden or white; outer perianth seg. 1.5–2.25cm, nectaries rhombic, spotted green, claw downy; fil. ciliate near base, anth. to 0.2cm, not divergent (cf. *H.ochroleuca*). SW Cape.

H.ochroleuca Salisb. (*H.collina* var. *ochroleuca* (Salisb.) Bak.). Lvs 1(–3). to 30×1.5cm. Flowering stem 40–80cm, with 1 or several branches. Fls pale yellow, occasionally stained orange at centre, rather muskily scented; outer perianth seg. to 4cm, slightly exceeding inner seg., nectaries spreading; fil. to 1cm, glabrous, anth. 0.4–0.8cm; style branches to 0.6cm. SW Cape.

Hyacinthella Schur. (Diminutive of *Hyacinthus*.) Liliaceae (Hyacinthaceae). Some 20 species of small, bulbous, perennial herbs. Bulbs tunicate. Leaves occasionally 1 or 3, mostly 2 per bulb, slender, basal, conspicuously veined. Flowers more or less campanulate, blue to pink, occasionally white, in terminal scapose racemes; perianth 6-partite, persistent in fruit; stamens 6, emerging just below the base of the tepals; filaments just exceeded by or slightly exceeding anthers; ovary superior, with 3 cells, each containing 2–4 ovules. Fruit a depressed, rounded, 3-valved, loculicidal capsule, to 5mm diam., with 1–2 black, wrinkled seeds per cell. E Europe to W Asia and Israel. Z8.

CULTIVATION   Diminutive spring-flowering bulbs suitable for perfectly drained, sunny positions on the rock garden, or in the alpine house and bulb frame where they can be given protection from wet when dormant in summer. Cultivate as for *Muscari*.

H.azurea (Fenzl) Chouard. See *Muscari azureum*.

H.dalmatica (Bak.) Chouard. See *H.pallens*.

H.glabrescens (Boiss.) Persson & Wendelbo.
To 15cm. Lvs to 2cm wide, glabrous, spreading. Fls to 6mm, tubular to campanulate, deep violet-blue, on pedicels to 7mm, borne in fairly loose racemes. CS Turkey.

H.heldreichii (Boiss.) Chouard.
To 10cm. Close to *H.glabrescens*, but differing in its slightly wavy lvs and almost sessile fls. SW to CS Turkey.

H.hispida (Gay) Chouard.
Lvs to 1.2cm wide, erect or spreading, conspicuously white-pubesc. on both surfaces and margins. Fls 5–6mm, more or less campanulate, dark blue-violet, borne in a loose raceme. CS Turkey.

H.lineata (Steud.) Chouard (*Hyacinthus lineatus* Steud.).
Lvs to 15mm wide, spreading, with long hairs beneath and on margins, ciliate, often with conspicuous, raised veins. Fls to 6mm, almost campanulate, light blue to deep violet-blue, borne in a dense raceme on distinct pedicels, to 1.2cm in fr. W Turkey.

H.nervosa (Bertol.) Chouard.
Lvs to 2cm wide, glabrous, erect, with minutely pubesc. margin. Fls to 1cm, tubular to narrow-campanulate, sessile, pale blue, borne in a fairly dense raceme. SE Turkey, through Syria, Jordan and Iraq, to Israel.

H.pallens Schur. (*H.dalmatica* (Bak.) Chouard).
Lvs to 6mm wide, linear-lanceolate, glabrous with rough margins, channelled, often arched. Fls to 0.5cm, narrow-campanulate, pale to medium blue, borne in a fairly dense raceme. Balkans.

Hyacinthoides Heister ex Fabr. (From *Hyacinth* and Gk -*oides*, resembling.) Liliaceae (Hyacinthaceae). Some 4 species of perennial herbs. Bulb renewed each year, composed of tubular, coalescent scales. Inflorescence a terminal scapose raceme; flowers bracteate and bracteolate; bracts 2 per flower, linear-lanceolate, tinged blue; tepals free to the base, erect or spreading, mostly blue; stamens filaments free, inserted in tepals; anthers versatile; ovary superior, 3-celled; style simple; stigma swollen at tip. Fruit a capsule with globose, black seeds. W Europe, N Africa. Z5.

CULTIVATION   Occurring in a variety of habitats, woodland, heath, seacliffs, hedgerow and sometimes in montane habitats to 1500m/4900ft. *H.non-scripta*, the bluebell, is best known as a spring-flowering colonizer of oak and beech woodland. *H.hispanica* is of more robust appearance and hybrids between the two are common. Eminently suited to mass plantings in woodland, where still air will hold their beautiful fragrance, or other sites in cool semi-shade, especially for naturalizing in grass below shrubs where they will self-seed once established. *Hyacinthoides* spp. are sometimes used as short-lived cut flowers in spring.

Grow in any humus rich, moisture retentive soil in semi shade; flower colour will bleach in sun. *Hyacinthoides* spp. tolerate a range of soil types and prefer heavier soils. Propagate by division of established colonies, (bulbs will be found quite deep in the soil), or by seed sown when ripe or in spring in the shade cold frame.

H.hispanica (Mill.) Roth.
Close to *H.non-scripta*. Lvs 5 or 6, to 2.5cm wide, glabrous, ascending. Fls 6–8, unscented, widely campanulate, borne in a rather loose, not 1-sided raceme, upper fls remaining erect or spreading; lower pedicels to 2.5cm; tepals spreading, not curved at the tips; fil. all inserted below the middle of the perianth, anth. blue. SW Europe, N Africa. Plants cultivated as *H.hispanica* are often hybrids between this species and *H.non-scripta*. 'Alba': fls white. 'Danube' ('Donau'): fls dark blue, abundant. 'Excelsior': tall, fls large, blue violet, with marine blue stripe. 'La Grandesse': fls pure white. 'Mount Everest': fls white, in a broad spike. 'Myosotis': fls porcelain blue, with sky blue stripe; broad spike. 'Queen of the Pinks': fls deep pink. 'Rosabella': fls soft pink. 'Rose': fls violet pink, in a large spike. 'White City': fls white.

H.italica (L.) Chouard ex Rothm.
Flowering stem 10–40cm. Lvs 10–25cm×3–12mm, linear to linear-lanceolate. Fls 6–30, borne in dense, conical, erect, not 1-sided racemes; tepals 5–7mm, minutely pubesc. at the tip, spreading widely, blue-violet, occasionally white; fil. inserted at base of the perianth, anth. blue. SE France, NW Italy, Spain, Portugal.

H.non-scripta (L.) Rothm. BLUEBELL.
Lvs 20–45cm×7–15mm, linear to linear-lanceolate, subacute, concave. Flowering stem 20–50cm; fls 6–12, fragrant, in loose, 1-sided, erect then drooping racemes; bracts 2, tepals 1.5–2cm, oblong-lanceolate, erect below, giving fl. a tubular appearance, curved at the tips, violet-blue, occasionally pink or white; outer fil. inserted at about the middle of the perianth, the inner inserted near the base, anth. cream. W Europe. 'Alba': fls white. 'Rosea': fls pink.

Hyacinthus L. (An ancient Gk name used by Homer, the flowers being said to spring from the blood of the dead Hyakinthos.) HYACINTH. Liliaceae (Hyacinthaceae). 3 species of bulbous perennial herbs. Bulbs tunicate, ovoid. Leaves 2 or more per bulb, linear to broadly linear-lanceolate or oblong-ovate, glabrous, margins smooth, emerging rolled, later spreading. Inflorescence a shortly scapose many-flowered cylindrical raceme; bracts small, 2-lobed; perianth tubular-campanulate, united for half to two-thirds its length, lobes 6, spreading to recurved; stamens included, attached at mid-point of tube; ovary superior, trilocular; style much shorter than perianth tube. Fruit an almost spherical capsule; seeds 2–3 per locule, black, crinkled. Early spring. W & C Asia.

CULTIVATION *H.orientalis* and *H.litwinowii* are suited to the sunny rock garden or bulb frame in sandy, well drained soils. Those most commonly grown are highly fragrant and showy cultivars derived from *H.orientalis*, the Dutch hyacinths, and the looser-flowered Roman hyacinths, from *H.o.* var. *albulus*, which, with successional planting and selection, may be seen in bloom from Christmas until late spring. The Multiflora Group, producing several slender stems, with individual blooms more loosely set are also suitable for indoor and outdoor use. These cultivars are available in a wide colour range and are used in traditional spring bedding, in beds and borders and in tubs and other containers.

Outdoor bulbs are planted in autumn into an open and sunny position in any well drained moderately fertile soil. Prepared bulbs for forcing are potted in autumn, usually into a proprietary bulb mix, and require a period of about 8–10 weeks, in cool, dark, moist conditions to develop a good root system, temperatures at this stage should not exceed 7–10°C/45–50°F. When necessary to apply water, avoid wetting the shoot, as this may cause the bulb to rot. On emergence of the shoot tips temperatures can at once be increased to 10°C/50°F and thereafter light and warmth can be increased steadily as growth progresses. Alternatively on shoot emergence, place pots in a dark cupboard, at 18–21°C/65–70°F, and water plentifully. Bring into subdued light as flower bud emerges clear of the neck of the bulb, usually when the shoot is between 6–8cm/2–3in. high and increase light levels as growth progresses and the stem elongates. Forced hyacinths may be planted out after blooming in the open garden, and will flower in subsequent years, although blooms will decline in quality. Bulbs forced in a bulb glass are best discarded after flowering.

Propagate species by ripe seed sown thinly in a loam-based propagating mix in the cold frame so that seedlings may remain *in situ* during their first season's dormancy. Cultivars are increased by cutting out a cone of tissue from the bulb base, or by cutting crosswise slits through the base, both treatments resulting in the formation of large numbers of bulbils.

Hyacinth fire caused by the fungus *Botrytis hyacinthi* was so-called by Dutch growers because it could spread through the fields 'like fire'. Beginning at the tips the leaves become brown and shrivelled. In damp conditions a grey mould develops on the affected parts and the flowers may be destroyed. If detected early enough the disease can be controlled by fungicide sprays. In the disease known as black slime, caused by *Sclerotinia bulborum*, the leaves turn yellow and fall over just after flowering and they can be pulled away easily because they are rotten at the base. The bulb scales are dry and dark grey but under moist conditions a white, fluffy mycelial growth develops from them. Black sclerotia sometimes up to half an inch are formed between and within the scales and can remain in the soil to perpetuate the fungus. In grey bulb rot caused by *Rhizoctonia tuliparum*, which is mainly known as a serious disease of tulips, the shoots are unlikely to emerge at all. This is a dry rot which progresses from the neck of the bulb downwards and as in black slime disease the fungus persists in the soil as sclerotia. Hyacinth bulbs are susceptible to soft rot (*Erwinia carotovora*) and to yellow disease (*Xanthomonas hyacinthi*). Both of these bacterial diseases result in a complete breakdown of the bulb tissue so that the above ground parts fail to emerge or die prematurely. When bulbs affected by *Xanthomonas* are cut across concentric rings of yellow spots which contain the bacteria are visible. Control of the various bulb diseases is mainly a matter of planting healthy bulbs in uncontaminated soil and the early removal of any which subsequently appear diseased. The aphid-transmitted virus diseases hyacinth mosaic and ornithogalum mosaic can cause a conspicuous yellow or grey leaf mottling and affected plants should be destroyed to prevent the diseases from spreading.

Hyacinths may be attacked by polyphagous aphids, bulb flies especially the large narcissus fly (*Merodon equestris*), bulb mites (*Rhizoglyphus* spp.), slugs and the stem eelworm (*Ditylenchus dipsaci*).

H.amethystinus L. See *Brimeura amethystina*.
H.candicans Bak. See *Galtonia candicans*.
H.ciliatus Cyr. See *Bellevalia ciliata*.
H.corymbosus L. See *Polyxena corymbosa*.
H.dubius Guss. See *Bellevalia dubia*.
H.kopetdaghi Czerniak. See *H.transaspicus*.
H.lineatus Steud. See *Hyacinthella lineata*.

H.litwinowii Czerniak.
10–25cm. Lvs 15–17×1.5–5cm, 3–4, ovate-lanceolate to ovate, sometimes spreading and somewhat undulate, glaucous above. Fls 3–13, not fragrant; perianth 1.8–2.5cm, green-blue, tube constricted above ovary, lobes longer than tube, upper parts narrowed, spreading and recurved beyond anth., palest blue, centrally banded deeper blue outside; fil. longer than anth. Seeds unwinged. Russia, E Iran.

H.orientalis L. COMMON HYACINTH.
About 30cm. Bulb large, ovoid to depressed-globose, tunic purple or pearly off-white. Lvs 15–35×0.5–4cm, 4–6, linear-lanceolate, bright green, hooded at apex. Scape thick, hollow, erect until fruiting, thereafter prostrate; fls 2–40, waxy, remotely and gracefully disposed in the wild form, heavily scented; perianth 2–3.5cm, pale blue to deep violet, pink, white or cream, tube as long as or exceeding lobes, constricted above ovary, lobes oblong-spathulate, spreading or recurved; anth. longer than fil., not attaining throat of tube. Fr. 1–1.5cm, conic to spherical, fleshy; seeds winged. C & S Turkey, NW Syria, Lebanon. Over 60 cvs: height 14–20cm; stems 10–15cm, single or multiple; lvs c2–4cm wide; fls single or double, white to cream, pink, blue to purple, densely to loosely packed, perianth lobes usually shorter than tube, as in ssp. *orientalis*. 'Amethyst': fls lilac. 'Anna Marie': fls light

(a)

(b)

Hyacinthus   (a) *H.orientalis*   (b) *H.litwinowii*

pink. 'Appleblossom': miniature; fls shell pink. 'Ben Nevis': fls double, large, ivory white, compact. 'Blue Jacket': fls navy, striped purple. 'Carnegie': fls white, compact, late-flowering. 'City of Haarlem': primrose, late-flowering. 'Delft Blue': fls soft blue. 'Distinction': fls deep burgundy to purple. 'Gipsy Queen': fls pale salmon orange. 'Hollyhock': double, crimson, compact. 'Jan Bos': fls cerise. 'Lord Balfour': miniature; fls claret tinted violet. 'Multiflora White': multiple stems, to 4; fls sparse, white. 'Myosotis': fls palest blue. 'Ostara': large, purple-blue. 'Pink Pearl': fls deep pink, paler edges. 'Sunflower': miniature; fls bright yellow. ssp. *orientalis*. Lvs rarely to 1.1cm wide. Fls 2–12; perianth 2–3cm, pale violet-blue at base shading to white above, lobes to four-fifths length of tube. Plants naturalized in S Europe have broader lvs and bear to 18 fls per stem. ssp. *chionophilus* Wendelbo. Lvs 1.2–1.5cm wide, rarely to 3.6cm wide; peri-anth lobes equalling tube, otherwise like ssp. *orientalis*. C Turkey.

H.princeps Bak. See *Galtonia princeps*.
H.revolutus L. f. See *Ledebouria revoluta*.
H.romanus L. See *Bellevalia romana*.
H.saviczii (Woron.) Vved. See *Bellevalia saviczii*.
H.spicatus Sibth. & Sm. non Moench. See *Bellevalia hyacinthoides*.

H.transcaspicus Litv. (*H.kopetdahi* Czerniak).
Lvs 7–16×0.4–1.5cm, 2–3, linear to lanceolate, channelled. Fls 1.3–1.5cm, 4–10, violet-blue; perianth tube cylindric, lobes shorter than tube, sharply divergent or spreading; fil. exceeding anth., anth. held outside throat of perianth, blue-black. Seeds unwinged. Turkmenistan, NE Iran.

Hymenocallis Salisb. (Ismene Salisb.; Elisena Herb.). SPIDER LILY. (From Gk *hymen*, membrane, and *kalos*, beauty, in reference to the corona uniting the stamens.) Amaryllidaceae. 30–40 species of deciduous or ever-green bulbous perennial herbs. Leaves basal, sessile and lorate, or sometimes petiolate and ovate to oblong. Scapes solid topped with an umbel of several conspicuous fragrant white or ivory flowers, initially enclosed by 2 or more separate spathe valves; perianth straight or sometimes funnelform, broadly so or only above, with 6 narrow spreading lobes; stamens 6, fused below into a conspicuous serrate cup or corona inserted into the top of the perianth tube. Fruit a fleshy 3-celled capsule; seeds usually 2 per cell, large, green. Americas. *Ismene* Salisb. and *Elisena* Herb. differ in minor aspects of flower morphology and are probably best treated as subgenera of *Hymenocallis*. The subgenera may be distinguished by the shape of the corona; erect in *Hymenocallis* and *Ismene*, sharply bent in *Elisena*, and the free parts of the filaments which are erect or hanging outwards in *Hymenocallis* and *Elisena*, incurved in *Ismene*.

CULTIVATION Occurring in grassland and rocky habitats, *Hymenocallis* spp. are frost-tender bulbs grown for their fragrant, beautifully constructed flowers, with the elegantly reflexed, narrow, outer segments that give rise to their common name, spider lilies. A number of the deciduous species, particularly those from high altitudes in the Andes, such as *H.amancaes*, *H.harrisiana* and *H.narcissiflora*, are almost hardy, and are sometimes grown outdoors in sheltered cool temperate gardens that are nearly frost-free, in a sunny position on well drained soil, protected with a thick dry mulch of bracken litter or leafmould in winter. In most temperate gardens, however, they are best lifted in autumn and over-wintered in a dry frost-free place or, better still, grown permanently in pots in the cool glasshouse. The evergreen species are generally native to the subtropics and tropics and are best grown in the intermediate to warm glasshouse, minimum temperature 10–15°C/50–60°F. *H.speciosa* thrives under hot glasshouse conditions, at 15–18°C/60–65°F.

Grow in a light, well drained potting mix of equal parts loam, leafmould and sharp sand, in sun or in bright filtered light; evergreen species, in particular, should be protected from strong sunlight. Water plentifully when in growth and continue watering and liquid-feeding after flowering, as for *Hippeastrum*. Keep evergreen species just moist when resting; allow deciduous species to dry off when leaves yellow, overwintering dry bulbs at about 10°C/50°F. Propagate from offsets or by seed.

H.adnata Herb. See *H.caribaea*.

H.amancaes (Ruiz & Pav.) Nichols.
Bulb to 5cm diam. Lvs lorate, dark green, the bases sheathing and forming a thick false stem to 23cm, free parts to 45×5cm. Scape to 30cm; fls 2–5; perianth tube narrow, to 7cm, tinged green, lobes to 8cm, linear, bright yellow; staminal cup to 6×9cm, funnelform to campanulate, green-striped, dentate, free parts of fil. to 2cm, pointing inwards. Peru. Z9.

H.americana (Mill.) Roem. See *H.littoralis*.
H.amoena (Salisb. sec. Ker-Gawl.) Herb. See *H.ovata*.
H.andreana (Bak.) Nichols. See *Lepidochiton quitoensis*.
H.borskiana De Vries. See *H.tubiflora*.
H.calathina (Ker-Gawl.) Nichols. See *H.narcissiflora*.

H.caribaea (L. emend. Ker-Gawl.) Herb. (*H.adnata* Herb.).
Lvs to 60×7.5cm, many, evergreen, broad ensiform or suboblong, tapering at the apex and the base, sessile, shiny. Scape to 60cm, angled; fls 8–10+, sessile; perianth tube to 6.5cm, lobes to 11cm; staminal cup to 3cm, funnelform, with erect margins, fil. to 5cm; ovary with 2 ovules per cell. West Indies. Z10.

H.caroliniana (L.) Herb. (*H.occidentalis* in part (Le Conte) Kunth).
Bulb to 6.5cm diam., subglobose; tunics grey. Lvs to 45×1.7cm, to 12, lorate, tapering to an acute apex and at the base. Scape 70cm; spathe valves to 5cm; fls 5–10; perianth tube to 5.5cm, lobes to 8cm; staminal cup funnelform, margins erect and dentate, to 4.5cm, fil. to 1.4cm, anth. to 1.7cm; ovary with 2 ovules per cell. US (Georgia to Indiana and Louisiana). Z7.

H.caymanensis Herb. See *H.latifolia*.
H.choretis Hemsl. See *H.glauca*.

H.concinna Bak. (*H.dillennii* Roem.; *Pancratium mexicanum* L.).
Lvs to 30×4.6cm, 4, deciduous, oblong-elliptic to ensiform, acute, with a petiole-like base sheathing the stem. Scape to 30cm; spathe valves to 5.5cm; fls 2–8, sessile; perianth tube to 5cm, lobes to 67×5mm, spreading-recurved; staminal cup funnelform, to 2×2cm, fil. to 3cm. Ovary with 2 ovules per cell. Mexico. Z10.

H.cordifolia Micheli.
Bulb to 8cm diam.; neck of sheathing leaf bases, to 13cm. Lvs 4, ovate, cordate at base, to 36×14.8cm, bright green with a paler midrib; petiole to 14cm. Scape to 42cm; spathe valves to 6cm, triangular, deflexed at anthesis; fls 12, spreading to ascending; pedicels 1cm; perianth tube to 11cm, green at the base, white above, lobes to 80×6mm, white, spreading,

decurved; staminal cup to 2×2cm, funnelform, toothed, white, fil. to 4cm, green, anth. 1.5cm, orange; style exceeding stamens by 2cm. Mexico. Z10.

H.crassifolia Herb.
Lvs 6–8, lorate, 60×5cm, obtuse, bright green. Scape 60cm; fls 4, sessile, white; perianth seg. linear, 8cm. SE US. Z7.

H.crassifolia Herb. See *H.latifolia*.

H.deflexa (Herb.) Bak. (*Ismene deflexa* Herb.).
Lvs ensiform, 30×5cm, acute. Scape 2-edged; fls 3–4, sessile; perianth tube curved, 3.5–5cm, seg. linear, 7.5–10cm; corona funnel-shaped, to 7.5cm long, with recurved processes to 2.5cm. Peru. Z9.

H.dillennii Roem. See *H.concinna*.

H.eucharidifolia Bak.
Lvs to 30×9cm, 4, broad oblong-elliptic, acuminate, narrowing to a petiole-like base. Scape to 30cm; fls 4–5, sessile; perianth tube to 10cm, lobes to 2.5cm; staminal cup to 3×2.5cm, funnelform, with erect, minutely dentate margins, fil. to 3cm; ovary with 2 ovules per cell. Origin unknown. Z10.

H.expansa (Herb.) Herb.
Lvs to 77×7.5cm, many, evergreen, broad oblong-ensiform or narrowly and obliquely oblong-elliptic or oblong-lanceolate, tapering at either end. Scape to 80cm; fls 10–20, sessile; perianth tube to 10.6cm, lobes to 14.5cm; staminal cup narrow-funnelform, to 3.5cm deep, mouth to 2.4cm diam., with erect, fluted, dentate margins, fil. to 6cm; ovary with 2–3 ovules per cell. W Indies. Z10.

H.×festalis hort. ex Schmarse (*Ismene × festalis* hort.). (*H.longipetala × H.narcissiflora*.)
Lvs 9, to 90×6.5cm, the lowest third sheathing to form a false stem. Scape sharply ancipitous, 10cm; fls 4, held horizontally, pure white, fragrant; perianth tube curved, 4cm, lobes to 11.5×1.3cm, curved, the outer ones more deeply channelled and narrower; staminal cup to 5×6.5cm, with reflexed teeth, free ends of fil. to 4cm; style stout, exserted 8cm beyond staminal cup. Garden origin. Z9.

H.fragrans (Salisb.) Salisb.
Lvs to 33×8cm, 7–10, evergreen, elliptic, acute, cuneate at the base; petioles to 7×2cm. Scape to 45cm; fls 12; pedicels to 5mm; perianth tube to 8cm, lobes to 10cm; staminal cup funnelform, to 3cm high, with erect, entire margins, fil. to 4.5cm; ovary with 2 ovules per cell. W Indies. Z10.

H.glauca (Herb.) Bak. (*Choretis glauca* Herb.; *H.choretis* Hemsl.; *H.horsmannii* Bak.).
Lvs to 45×8cm, 3 or 4, deciduous, erect, elliptic or elliptic-lorate, obtuse, glaucous. Scape to 35cm; spathe valves erect, narrow, to 5cm; fls 2–4, sessile; perianth tube to 15cm or longer, lobes to 90×7mm; ovary with 2 or 3 ovules per cell. Mexico. Z10.

H.guianensis (Ker-Gawl.) Herb. See *H.tubiflora*.

H.harrisiana Herb. (*Ismene harrisiana* hort.).
Lvs to 27×5.1cm, 3–5, oblanceolate to oblong, apex obtuse and apiculate, or acute, tapering to a petiole-like base which sheathes the scape. Scape to 23cm; fls to 6; perianth tube to 13cm, green-tinged, lobes to 7.5cm, white; staminal cup funnelform, to 1.5×1.8cm, margins spreading, fil. to 3.5cm; ovary with 2 ovules per cell. Mexico. Z10.

H.horsmannii Bak. See *H.glauca*.
H.humilis S. Wats. See *H.palmeri*.
H.keyensis Small. See *H.latifolia*.
H.lacera Salisb. See *H.rotata*.

H.latifolia (Mill.) Roem. (*H.caymanensis* Herb.; *H.keyensis* Small; *H.crassifolia* Herb.). CAYMAN ISLANDS SPIDER-LILY; CHRYSOLITE LILY.
Bulb subglobose. Lvs to 80×8cm, fleshy, sessile, linear or linear-oblong, acute or obtuse, tapering at base. Scape flattened, ancipitous, equalling lvs; fls 6–12, sessile; spathe valves lanceolate, acuminate, to 7cm; perianth tube to 16cm, lobes to

10cm, linear, arching; staminal cup to 3cm; style slender, equalling perianth. Florida, Cuba, Haiti, Cayman Is. Z10.

H.liriosome (Raf.) Shinn.
Lvs synanthous, linear, 60×2–4cm, glossy light green. Scape sharply ancipitous; fls to 20cm across, snowy-white, tinged yellow in throat; perianth tube 6–8cm, green or yellow. SE US. Z7.

H.littoralis (Jacq.) Salisb. (*H.americana* (Mill.) Roem.; *H.senegambica* Kunth & Bouché in part).
Lvs to 120×3.8cm, many, evergreen, lorate, or broadly lorate in the middle and tapering at either end, bright green. Scape 60cm, fls 5–11; perianth tube to 17cm, green-tinged, lobes to 12.5cm, linear, ascending and adpressed to staminal cup at base, then spreading-decurved; staminal cup funnelform with spreading margins, to 3.5cm, fil. to 6cm; ovary with 4–5 ovules per cell. Colombia, Surinam, Mexico. 'Variegata': lvs to 50cm, bright green striped and edged cream. Z10.

H.longipetala (Lindl.) Macbr. (*Elisena longipetala* Lindl.).
Lvs to 90×3.5cm, 6, linear, bright green with a smooth margin. Scape exceeding lvs; fls 5–10; pedicel rigid, to 1.2cm; perianth tube funnelform, to 9mm, lobes to 10cm, linear, narrow, acuminate, with undulate margins, semi-transparent, white; staminal cup funnel-shaped, to 3.5cm, white, membranous, with a reflexed dentate margin; stamens 6, declinate, subequal, free parts of fil. to 6cm; style filiform, declinate; stigma simple. Peru. Z9.

H.× macrostephana Bak. (probably *H.narcissiflora × H.speciosa*).
Bulb ovoid, 5cm diam., neck long. Lvs 8–9, evergreen, oblanceolate, 50–90×6–8cm, obtuse, tapering to base, bright green. Scape 30–45cm; pedicels short; fls 8–10, fragrant; perianth tube to 8.5cm, green below, white above, seg. linear-lanceolate, 9–11cm, white to pale green-yellow, outer whorl with thickened green apices; corona funnel-shaped, to 6×7.5cm, bluntly toothed, white; free part of filament 2.5cm, style exserted 4.5cm beyond corona. Late winter. Garden origin. Z9.

H.mexicana Herb. See *H.harrisiana*.
H.moritziana Kunth. See *H.tubiflora*.

H.narcissiflora (Jacq.) Macbr. (*H.calathina* (Ker-Gawl.) Nichols.; *Ismene calathina* (Ker-Gawl.) Herb.) BASKET FLOWER; PERUVIAN DAFFODIL.
Bulb spherical. Lvs 6–8, sheathing at the base to form a thick false stem, the free parts to 60×5cm. Scape equalling lvs; fls 2–5, pedicellate; perianth tube funnelform above, to 10cm, spreading, green, lobes to 10×1.2cm, lanceolate; staminal cup striped green, to 5cm long and more than 5cm diam., striped green, with rounded spreading toothed processes, fil. to 12mm, pointing inwards; style exceeding limb. Bolivian Andes. 'Minor': lvs and peduncle shorter than in type. 'Festalis': fls white, central crown recurved and frilled, outer pet. cream. 'Sulphurea': fls deep ivory to pale yellow. Z9.

H.occidentalis (Le Conte) Kunth in part. See *H.rotata*.
H.occidentalis (Le Conte) Kunth in part. See *H.caroliniana*.

H.ovata (Mill.) Sweet (*H.amoena* (Salisb. sec. Ker-Gawl.) Herb.).
Lvs to 28×11cm, 5–8, broadly elliptic, acute, cuneate at the base. Scape to 45cm; fls 5–10; perianth tube to 5cm, green, stout, lobes to 10×0.7cm, white, spreading-recurved; staminal cup funnelform, to 2.5×2cm, toothed or entire, white, fil. green, to 4cm; anthers orange, to 1.5cm. W Indies. Z10.

H.palmeri S. Wats. (*H.humilis* S. Wats.). ALLIGATOR LILY.
Bulb ovoid, to 3cm diam.; neck to 5.5cm; tunics dark grey. Lvs to 30×0.6cm, 3, linear. Scape to 25cm; spathe valves to 4.5cm; fls solitary, sessile; perianth tube 8cm, yellow-green, lobes to 10cm, filiform, linear, spreading from base; staminal cup funnelform, with erect dentate margins, to 3.5cm, fil. 4cm. Florida. Z9.

H.pedalis Herb. (*H.senegambica* Kunth & Bouché in part).
Bulb to 6cm diam., subcylindrical. Lvs to 45×7cm, evergreen,

many, oblong-oblanceolate, acuminate, tapering at the base. Scape to 45cm, compressed, glaucous; spathe valves to 10cm; fls to 15; perianth tube to 18cm, green and glaucous, lobes to 10cm, linear-lanceolate, spreading; staminal cup funnelform, fil. to 7cm, white at the base, apex green; style green, exceeding stamens. Fr. ovoid; seeds to 3cm, 2, green. Eastern S America. Z9.

H.quitoensis Herb. See *Lepidochiton quitoensis.*

H.rotata (Ker-Gawl.) Herb. (*H.lacera* Salisb.; *H.occidentalis* (Le Conte) Kunth in part).
Bulb with grey-brown tunics. Lvs to 68×3.6cm, 7–8, deciduous, lorate to ensiform, obtuse, more or less narrowing in the basal part, glaucous. Scape 60cm; spathe valves 6.5cm; fls 2 or 3, sessile, very fragrant; perianth tube to 9.5cm, lobes to 9.5cm, spreading from the base; staminal cup to 5cm, base green and tubular, expanding to funnelform to wide cupular or rotate, white, fil. 2–3cm; ovary with 2–6 ovules per cell. Florida, W Indies. Z10.

H.schizostephana Worsley.
Lvs to 31×8.7cm, 6–8, oblong-elliptic, acute, cuneate at the base; petioles to 10cm. Scape to 30cm, compressed; fls 10–20, sessile; perianth tube to 5.5cm, lobes 7cm; staminal cup to 1.5cm, vase-shaped, cut between fil., fil. to 4cm; ovary with 2 ovules per cell. Brazil. Z10.

H.senegambica Kunth & Bouché in part. See *H.littoralis.*
H.senegambica Kunth & Bouché in part. See *H.pedalis.*

H.speciosa (Salisb.) Salisb.
Lvs to 65.5×15.5cm, evergreen, broad-elliptic, shortly acute, the base cuneate; petioles to 17cm, broad. Scape to 40cm, glaucous, ancipitous; fls 7–12, spreading, green-tinged; pedicels to 1cm; perianth tube to 9cm, lobes to 15cm; staminal cup funnelform, to 5cm, dentate between fil., fil. nearly erect, to 5cm; ovaries with 2 ovules per cell. W Indies. Z10.

H.tenuiflora Herb.
Lvs to 68×6.4cm, about 6, evergreen, broadly lorate in upper half, acute, with a narrow lorate basal part, arching. Scape to 55cm; fls 9–16, sessile; perianth tube to 14cm, slender, green-tinged, lobes to 11cm, very narrow; staminal cup funnelform, with erect margins, to 2cm high, fil. to 5.5cm; ovary with 3–5 ovules per cell. Guatemala, Ecuador. Z10.

H.tenuifolia (Bak.) Nichols. See *Lepidochiton quitoensis.*

H.tubiflora Salisb. (*H.undulatum* (HBK) Herb.; *H.guianensis* (Ker-Gawl.) Herb.; *H.borskiana* Vriese; *H.moritziana* Kunth).
Lvs to 37.5×15cm, 7–12, evergreen, elliptic or lanceolate-elliptic to ovate, acuminate or cuspidate, veins widely spaced; petioles to 30cm. Scape to 60cm; fls to 20; perianth tube to 20cm, lobes to 13.5cm; staminal cup funnelform, margins erect or only slightly spreading, to 2cm, fil. to 6.5cm; ovary with 4–5 ovules per cell. Northeast S America. Z10.

H.undulatum (HBK) Herb. See *H.tubiflora.*

H.virescens (Lindl.) Nichols.
Lvs 4–5, bright green, semierect, the lower half sheathing the stem, free part to 10×2cm, striate. Scape ancipitous, exceeding lvs, erect, glabrous, yellow-green; spathe valves 3–4, to 5cm; fls pale green; perianth tube to 4cm, slightly drooping, cylindric, lobes to 4cm, concave, acute, off-white inside, virescent outside; staminal cup with lobes 1cm, shorter than limb, ovate-cuneate, greener at the base, fil. equalling lobes, green, anth. yellow, linear, 6mm; style filiform, green below, white above. Peru. Z9.

H.cultivars. 'Sulphur Queen': fls primrose, throat yellow, striped green. 'Zwanenburg': to 60cm; lvs bright green; fls white flushed green, trumpet-shaped, outer seg. reflexed.

Hypoxis L. (Spiloxene Salisb.). (From Gk *hypo*, beneath, and *oxys*, sharp, referring to the base of the capsule; a Gk plant name which does not refer to any particular characteristic of these plants.) STAR GRASS. Hypoxidaceae. About 150 species of perennial herbs. Roots fleshy, from an annual corm. Leaves basal, sheathing, or occasionally on stem, sometimes ridged, often hairy. Inflorescence a 2–12-flowered raceme or solitary, scapose; tepals 6, outer 3 wider than inner, outside hairy, green; ovary inferior; ovules several per cell; style short; stigma 3-lobed. Capsule opening by a cap; seeds elongate or spherical, black or brown. N America, Africa, Australia, Tropical Asia. Z9 unless specified.

CULTIVATION *Hypoxis* ranges widely both geographically and in habitat type and only few species are extensively cultivated; the Australian spp. are grown mainly by enthusiasts and most, if not all, are demanding in cultivation. *H.hygrometrica*, found in moist grassland and forest clearings, is the most widely distributed and most often attempted. In South Africa *H.rooperi*, of open rocky grasslands, and *H.capensis* are the most highly regarded. The widely distributed *H.angustifolia* is also very pretty, bearing upturned golden yellow blooms amongst its slender basal leaves. The North American *H.hirsuta* is found in sparse, dry woodland and thickets on sandy soils and with other American is most commonly grown in collections of native plants, sometimes naturalized in fine turf.

Hypoxis is grown for its small, open star-shaped flowers; they are well suited to the rock garden or in cool temperate regions to the alpine or cool glasshouse. Most species will grow well in Mediterranean climates that experience little or no frost; even the hardiest species, which include *H.hirsuta*, will not tolerate temperatures much below −5°C/23°F. They greatly resent transplanting and disturbance.

Grow in a light, freely draining soil in full sun or in light dappled shade. Under glass, plant into well crocked pots with a sandy loam-based mix with additional leafmould. Water thoroughly and place in the shade frame or under the greenhouse bench and cover to keep evenly moist. Move gradually to a position in full sun and keep well ventilated as the shoots appear; water sparingly until the roots are growing well, and thereafter moderately. Keep moist when in growth and then gradually dry off and store dry in a shaded and frost free position. Protect from slugs and snails. Propagate by seed and offsets.

H.angustifolia Lam. (*H.biflora* Bak.).
Corm oblong to globose, 0.8–2cm thick. Lvs 6–12, 10–15×3.75–5cm, linear, grass-like, base lanceolate, sparsely pilose to glabrous. Peduncles 5–15cm, 2-fld; pedicels 1.25–2.5cm, bracts minute, linear-subulate; ovary turbinate, densely pilose. Capsule turbinate, 0.6–0.85cm. S Africa.

H.baurii Bak. See *Rhodohypoxis baurii.*
H.baurii var. *platypetala* (Bak.) Bak. See *Rhodohypoxis baurii* var. *platypetala.*
H.biflora Bak. See *H.angustifolia.*

H.capensis (L.) Druce (*H.stellata* (Thunb.) L. f.; Spiloxene capensis (L.) Garside; *H.elata* Schult.). WHITE STAR GRASS. Glabrous. Corm 1–2cm. Lvs 10–30×1cm, basal, outer with midrib pronounced, laterally folded; stem lvs few, sheathing. Fls solitary on 5–25cm stem; tepals 1–3cm, white or yellow with iridescent purple basal spots; stigma equal to stamens. Seeds spherical. Spring–Summer. S Africa.

H.colchicifolia Bak. (*H.latifolia* hort. non Wight). Corm 6–8cm diam., spherical. Lvs 30–60×3–5cm, basally sheathing, borne on stem, leathery, ribbed, hairless. Infl. 10–12 fls, in leaf axils; fls 3cm diam.; perianth to 1cm diam., densely hairy outside, yellow; style short. Spring–summer. S Africa (Natal, Transvaal).

H.decumbens L. (*H.mexicana* Roem. & Schult.). Corm globose, 1.25cm thick. Outer lvs scariose, brown; lvs 6–12, 7.5–30×0.2–1.3cm, linear, sparsely pilose to glabrous. Peduncles 1–4 fld, 5–15cm, pedicels densely pilose; ovary densely pilose; perianth limb *c*0.8cm, seg. lanceolate and acute, yellow, green and pilose dorsally. Capsule 1.25–2cm, glabrous. Americas.

H.elata Schult. See *H.capensis*.
H.elata sensu Hook. f., non Schult. See *H.hemerocallidea*.
H.erecta L. See *H.hirsuta*.

H.goetzei Harms.
Lvs 6–12×2–3.5cm, ovate to lanceolate, glabrous above, fringed on margin and main vein beneath. Fls 5–12 in each raceme; bracts linear-lanceolate; pedicels 3–9mm; fls 22–27mm, pale yellow, tepals lanceolate, hirsute outside; anth. linear, fil. short, glabrous; ovary obconical, hairy.

H.hemerocallidea Fisch., Mey. & Avé-Lall. (*H.elata* sensu Hook. f., non Schult.).
Corm 8–10cm diam., spherical. Lvs 45–60×3–5cm, borne at base of scape, ribbed, leathery, veins and margins hairy. Infl. 6–12 fls, racemose in leaf axils; fls 3.5cm diam.; yellow; outer 3 tepals hairy on outside. Spring–summer. S Africa.

H.hirsuta (L.) Cov. (*H.erecta* L.).
Corm oblong. Lvs to 30cm×1cm, basal, ribbed, hairy. Scape borne between lvs, densely hairy; infl. 3–7 fld, a corymbose raceme; tepals to 1cm, outer 3 hairy outside, yellow. Spring–summer. Eastern N America. Z5.

H.hygrometrica Labill. GOLDEN WEATHER GRASS; GOLDEN STAR.
Corm 6–10mm, oblong. Lvs 6–15cm, basal, filiform, sparsely hairy outside. Infl. solitary or a 2–3-fld corymbose raceme; scape basally hairy; tepals to 1.5cm, yellow, glabrous or slightly hairy; style long. Spring–summer. SE Australia.

H.latifolia Hook. non Wight. See *H.colchicifolia*.

H.leptocarpa (Engelm. and A. Gray) Small.
Closely resembles *H.hirsuta*. Lvs to 8×1.5cm, almost glabrous, flat, thin, flaccid. Scape pubesc., 1–3-fld; outer 3 tepals linear to lanceolate-elliptic, inner 3 linear-lanceolate, to 0.8cm; anth. 1.5mm. Capsule to 11mm, club-shaped to ellipsoid, glabrous or lightly pubesc. Spring–summer. SE US.

H.mexicana Roem. & Schult. See *H.decumbens*.

H.micrantha Pollard.
Resembles *H.hirsuta*, differs in lvs 2–6mm wide; infl. 1–2-fld. Southeast N America.

H.multiceps Buchinger.
Corm globose, to 5cm thick, setose. Lvs 5–6, 15–30×1.9–2.5cm, lanceolate, rigid, leathery, striate, white-setose. Peduncles 7.5–15cm, 2–4-fld, hispid; pedicels to 1.9cm, bracts linear; ovary turbinate, densely setose-hairy; perianth limb to 1.9cm, yellow, densely villous outside. S Africa.

H.neocanaliculata (Garside) Geer. (*Spiloxene canaliculata* Garside).
Resembles *H.capensis*, differs in lvs rounded in section, midrib absent; perianth orange, basal spot not iridescent; seeds curved, elongate. Spring–summer. S Africa (Cape).

H.nitida Verdoorn.
Corm 8–20×6–8cm, densely setose. Lvs 12–15, 18–23×1–2cm, in 3 vertical ranks, erect, becoming arcuate, then suberect and twisted, shiny, glabrous, midrib and margin white ciliate, 37–70-veined. Peduncle to 15cm, grey or sandy-pubesc.; racemes to 12-fld, to 14cm; pedicels absent or to 1.2cm, bracts 2.5cm, pilose; fls 3–5cm, tepals to 2×1.2cm, oblong-ovate, chrome yellow inside, outer 3 green and hairy outside, inner 3 chrome-yellow with green keel outside. Seeds shiny, smooth, black. S Africa.

H.platypetala Bak. See *Rhodohypoxis baurii* var. *platypetala*.

H.rooperi T. Moore.
Corm to 7.5cm thick, oblong, lightly setose. Lvs 12–18, 30–45cm, lanceolate, leathery, glabrous beneath, white pilose above, setose. Infl. a corymbose raceme, bracts linear; pedicels to 2.5cm; perianth limb to 2cm, oblong or lanceolate, dorsally villous; ovary obconical, 0.6cm, setose; style glabrous. Capsule to 1cm, densely setose. S Africa (Cape, Natal, Transvaal, Lesotho).

H.stellata (Thunb.) L. f. See *H.capensis*.

Ipheion Raf. Liliaceae (Alliaceae). 10 species of tufted, bulbous (not cormous, cf. *Dichelostemma* and *Brodiaea*), herbaceous perennials, most parts smelling of garlic if bruised, the leaves especially. Bulbs small, tunics membranous; roots fleshy. Leaves basal, linear. Flowers 1–2 per scape, subtended by a basally united, 2-valved, papery spathe; perianth salverform, tube narrowly campanulate to funnelform, lobes ovate-acute, spreading; stamens 6 in 2 series, 3 inserted at base of tube, 3 near middle, filaments slender, not dilated, anthers dorsifixed; ovary superior; stigma small, obscurely 3-lobed. Fruit a many-seeded capsule. S America. In his protologue, Rafinesque identifies *Ipheion* as the asphodel of antiquity. He is probably referring to the plant *iphyon*, which occurs in Theophrastus and is spelt iphion in the index to Johannes Bodaeus' edition of the *Historia Plantarum* (Amsterdam, 1644). In one place (*Historia Plantarum* VI,6,11) *iphyon* is described as a plant growing from seed with a woody root, and in another (*HP* VI,8,3) as summer-flowering. Most authors have understood *iphyon* to be *Lavandula*, although interpretations vary and are given ample scope by the vagueness of the description and the looseness of ancient taxonomic concepts.The latter passage is taken up word for word by Pliny in his Natural History (XI,67), where some manuscripts have the variant name tiphyon. *Tiphyon* also occurs in Theophrastus (*HP* VII,13,7) as a bulb whose flowers appear before its leaves and stems, and (*De Causis Plantarum* I,10,5) as a late summer-/autumn-flowering herbaceous (i.e. bulbous) plant. It has been suggested that the names *iphyon* and *tiphyon* are used interchangeably in Theophrastus.The name *tiphyon* could be a corruption, possibly ancient, of the name iphyon (? coalescence of the Greek article *to* and *iphyon*). Theodorus Gaza, whose Latin translation of Theophrastus dates to 1491, rendered *tiphyon* as iphyum in both places. Thistleton-Dyer considered *iphyon* to be *Lavandula angustifolia* (in which he followed Bodaeus, whom he held in high esteem) and *tiphyon* to be *Scilla autumnalis*. That there was probably confusion already in antiquity can be seen from the fourth century lexicographer Diogenianus (as cited in Hesychius, either directly or through the intermediate source Cyrillus) and the eighth century lexicographer Suidas. Rafinesque seems to have recognized that *iphyon* and *tiphyon* were semantically, if not perhaps botanically, equivalent, and from the many identifications given to this name, to have chosen the bulbous incarnation (probably *Scilla autumnalis* or, very generally speaking, an asphodel) appropriately enough as a classical model for the blue-flowered, bulbous, South American *Ipheion*.

CULTIVATION   Grown for the beautiful star-shaped flowers carried on slender stems amongst the long, narrow leaves, *I.uniflorum* is cold-tolerant to about –10°C/14°F, but may need mulch protection where frosts are prolonged. Plant in a well drained gritty soil in dappled or full sun in a protected position – the foot of a south-facing wall, a sunny terrace or a sheltered rock garden. Propagate by seed in spring, cultivars by offsets in late summer as the foliage dies back. Susceptible to attack by slugs and snails.

Ipheion uniflorum

I.uniflorum (Graham) Raf. (*Triteleia uniflora* Lindl.; *Milla uniflora* Graham; *Brodiaea uniflora* (Lindl.) Engl.; *Beauverdia uniflora* (Lindl.) Herter). SPRING STARFLOWER. Lvs 20–25×0.4–0.7cm, grey-green, or glaucescent pale green, linear-lorate, flaccid, midvein sunken above, keeled beneath. Scapes to 20cm, slender, erect to arching, arising in succession from lf axils; bracts green-brown, scarious; fls 4cm diam. opening in sunshine, solitary, salverform, tepals oblong-ovate, acute, shortly united below into a tube, white tinged blue to violet-blue, often with darker midvein; stamens orange. Spring. Uruguay, temperate Argentina, naturalized GB and France. 'Album': fls large, pure white. 'Froyle Mill': fls dark violet. 'Rolf Fiedler': fls clear blue, regular in form, on stout scapes. 'Wisley Blue': fls pale blue, darker toward apices of seg. Z6.

Iris L. (From the Gk messenger Iris who came to earth via a rainbow.) FLAG; FLEUR-DE-LIS; SWORD LILY. Iridaceae. About 300 species of rhizomatous or bulbous perennial herbs varying in size from 15cm to over 2m. Rhizomes horizontal or near vertical, compact or spreading by means of stolons; bulbs (where present) covered in a netted, leathery or papery tunic; roots thin and wiry to very swollen. Flowering stems branched or unbranched, hollow or solid, rounded or flattened. Leaves mostly basal, in fans or from the bulb centre, some borne along the stem or in a tuft at the stem apex, quadrangular, channelled or flat in cross section, linear to ensiform, with or without a waxy bloom. Flowers 1 to several in bracteate heads; perianth tubular, segments 6, the outer 3 (falls) narrowed basally into a haft, sometimes with a beard of coloured hairs or crested or ridged, often with a patch of different colour (the signal), the inner 3 (standards) narrowed basally into a claw, sometimes much-reduced and bristle-like, falls usually spreading or reflexed upwards, stamens 3, filaments free, borne at the base of the falls, style with 3 petaloid arms, these usually arching over the falls and bilobed at apex. Fruit a leathery, 3–6-angled, ribbed or smooth capsule; seeds sometimes arillate. North temperate zones.

CULTIVATION   The genus *Iris* includes some 300 species of perennial herbaceous plants confined to the northern hemisphere but occurring in a wide range of habitats. The underground system or most irises consists of fibrous roots and some form of storage organ, typically a swollen rhizome or a bulb; the rhizome may grow on the surface, as in the familiar bearded iris, or below ground, as in Spurias and other groups. Leaves may be in flat fans or channelled, or may be circular, or even square, in cross-section. The flowers vary greatly in size and colour but basically are comprised of six petals arising from a perianth tube; the three inner petals are known as standards and the three outer ones as the 'falls'. In some groups there is a tuft of hairs in the centre and lower part of the falls petal — the beard; in others there is a ridge, usually dissected and coloured yellow, resembling a cockscomb and called a crest; in others there is only a smooth ridge. These obvious characteristics can be used by the gardener to distinguish between the bearded or Pogon irises, the crested or Lophiris, and the non-bearded or bearded iris, Limniris. Cultivation of irises varies greatly according to the group involved.

Bearded irises. Several of the bearded iris species are good garden plants suitable for the mixed border and of these *I.germanica* and its white-flowered var. *florentina* and *I.pallida*, with its two variegated-leaf forms 'Argentea' and 'Aurea', are well known. Some of the smaller species such as *I.suaveolens* and *I.pumila* are suitable for the rock garden; others like *I.attica* and *I.timofejwii* will require protection in a bulb frame in wet-winter areas.

Considerable variations in flower colour, either self colours or bitones, occur in these species and also in related species, particularly *I.lutescens* (formerly known for many years as *I.chameiris*). Many selected forms and hybrid cultivars of these dwarf bearded irises are available and are excellent plants for the smaller garden, flowering before the taller hybrid cultivars.

To flower well, bearded irises require a sunny situation and well drained soil. The soil should ideally be in the pH range 6.0–7.5; they do not require lime, but ground limestone should be worked in if the soil is acid. They will tolerate a higher pH and can grow well on chalky soils. Some humus should be incorporated but avoid fresh manure or green compost, which may cause rhizome rot. Raise the soil level in wet places or if the soil is heavy.

Although iris rhizomes can be transplanted at any time, for the best results move only when absolutely necessary and then after flowering during summer dormancy. The latest date is determined by local conditions, ranging from late summer in temperate zones to mid-autumn in hot-summer areas. For planting on sandy soils, dig a hole allowing the roots to fall straight down, push the nose of the rhizome into the side of the hole and fill in with soil, ensuring that no space is left beneath the rhizome. On heavy soil, place the rhizome on a mound or ridge within the planting hole, with the roots spread out around, cover with soil and firm in. Under most conditions leave the top surface of the rhizome exposed, but cover thinly in hot areas, to avoid sun scorch. Shorten the leaf fan to prevent wind-rocking. Water in and keep moist until new growth is seen. Apply low-nitrogen compound fertilizers during soil preparation and subsequently in early spring and autumn.

Established plants only need watering during prolonged hot, dry weather or in very arid areas. Cultivate shallowly, i.e. the most careful pricking over with a fork or a light hoeing, to avoid damage to rhizomes and offshoots; remove weeds and grasses. Stake flower stems of tall bearded irises in exposed areas. Cut off old flower stems cleanly at the rhizome; remove dead leaves by a sharp sideways pull and cut out diseased or damaged leaves. Do not trim off leaves of established plants in summer. After 3–4 years, when the clump becomes crowded, dig up and separate into single rhizomes; discard the central ones without leaves. Replant in groups with noses together, in fresh soil.

Propagate species by seed or by detached rhizomes; with garden-grown seed take care to avoid accidental hybridization. Sow seeds thinly in a soil-based medium with a quarter extra grit; cover with coarse grit and leaves exposed to the weather. Named cultivars are propagated by vegetative means only.

Principal diseases of bearded iris are rhizome soft rot (*Erwinia carotovora*) and scorch. For rot, remove infected tissue, cutting back to firm rhizome, and allow to dry, then dust the new surface with a fungicide. If the infection is grave (affecting more than half the rhizome), discard the material altogether. The cause of scorch is uncertain but leaves suddenly turn red-brown as if burnt; the rhizome remains firm but roots wither and the plant dies. This can occur at any time; it is not believed to be contagious, but affected rhizomes should be removed and destroyed. Leaf spots are either bacterial or fungal, usually occurring after flowering. Clean growing conditions are the best preventative, and spraying early in the year with a systemic fungicide will help in wet seasons.

Irises are affected by common garden pests like aphids, slugs and wireworms, which should be controlled. In hot summer areas of the US the iris borer moth (*Macronoctua onusta*) and several other insects can be a serious problem, but can be controlled by use of systemic insecticides.

There is an enormous number of named hybrid cultivars of bearded iris resulting from repeated crossing of diploid and tetraploid species and varieties for over a hundred years. For horticultural purposes these were first divided into three classes according to height – dwarf, intermediate and tall – and flowering season, but a more precise grouping is now in use. This comprises: Miniature Dwarf Bearded (MDB) up to 20cm/8in., the first to flower; Standard Dwarf Bearded (SDB), 21–40cm/16–27in.; Intermediate Bearded (IB), 40–70cm/16–27in.; Miniature Tall Bearded (MTB), 40–70cm/16–27in.; Border Bearded (BB), also 40–70cm/16–27in., and the Tall Bearded (TB), over 70cm/27in. The MTB and BB cultivars flower with the TBs.

Many terms are in use to classify the colour combinations of bearded irises. Among those more commonly used are: Amoena (pleasing), having white or tinted white standards and coloured falls; Plicata (pleated), with a pale background and dotting or veining of a darker colour; Variegata (by association with the species *I.variegata*), having yellow or near-yellow standards with darker falls of red, brown or purple.

Many iris species will occasionally flower for a second time later in the year and this trait has been developed by the hybridizers, particularly of the bearded cultivars, to establish varieties which will bloom again, often repeatedly, until the first frost. To sustain this additional growth in one season, remontant irises may require a further application of fertilizer after the first flowering and should be watered in dry summers; more frequent replanting will be necessary to maintain vigour.

The Oncocyclus group of rhizomatous irises occurs in areas of dry, often hot summers and dry, cool or cold winters, in western Asia from central Turkey to Israel. The winter months may be spent under snow or in desert conditions followed by a growth and flowering period in spring and a long summer dormancy. Oncocyclus irises cannot be grown in the open garden except in places where the climatic conditions resemble the plant's habitat. Elsewhere they are grown either in raised beds or in deep pots under glass or plastic cover to protect them from winter and summer rain. Soil should be gritty, free-draining and with pH above 6.5, with a low-nitrogen fertilizer added. Allow full sun and ventilation at all times. Give some water to start growth in autumn and again in early spring; continue to water and feed until the foliage begins to die down after flowering. The flowers are large, often in vivid colours with striking patterns. Germination of seed is often slow and erratic.

Oncocyclus irises are very susceptible to virus diseases, which are usually lethal; aphids, which are the carriers, should be controlled at all times.

The closely related Regelia group is distinguished by having a beard on the standards as well as on the falls and occurs in Iran, northern Afghanistan and adjacent Soviet Central Asia; they grow on open rocky hillsides and have a long summer dormancy. They are best suited to bulb frame culture like the Oncocyclus, but are easier to grow; some species, such as *I.hoogiana,* can be grown outside in temperate climates in a well drained sunny site if given protection from heavy winter rain.

Many hybrids have been made between Oncocyclus and Regelia irises; classified as Regeliocyclus, these are easier to grow than either parent yet retain their strange beauty. They are good plants for the alpine house. Hybrids between Oncocyclos or Regelia irises with bearded iris species or cultivars are called Arilbreds and are suitable for garden use in temperate areas with low rainfall.

Beardless irises. One section of the beardless iris, *Lophiris,* has a frilly crest on the falls and these are collectively known as the Evansias. They are diverse in size and habitat, occurring in North America and East Asia; many are of garden value although some are frost tender. In general, they are creeping plants with branched rhizomes growing in moist soil, often in open woodlands. Both *I.cristata* and the smaller *I.lacustris* from North America are plants for the rock garden or peat bed. The beautiful *I.gracilipes,* from the mountain woodlands of Japan, enjoys a peaty soil in dappled shade. *I.japonica*, with fans of broad glossy leaves and a long succession of bright frilly flowers, grows in semi-shade in most good soils. *I.tectorum* from central China spreads quickly in an open sunny position; the white form is susceptible to virus but in cultivation its hybrid progeny tend to be white and virus-free.

In the extensive section *Limniris*, the first group of horticultural value is the Sibiricae. They occur in central and eastern Asia, growing in mountain meadows or open woodlands. They are easy garden plants in temperate regions, requiring a fertile soil which does not dry out during the growth period in spring and early summer. They are not true waterside plants, as often supposed, and do well in a mixed border, if given a topdressing of compost in autumn. Of the species, *I.chrysographes* with its many colour forms ranging from red-violet to black and the yellow *I.forrestii* are valuable garden plants and often hybridize. Hybrids between the Sibiricae and the Californicae (see below) are also known and are called Cal Sibs.

Many selected hybrids are available, both diploid and tetraploid, the latter having stouter, more upright foliage and larger flowers of heavier substance with broad flaring falls in clear rich colours. Propagation of species and hybrids is by division of clumps, discarding the old central area and keeping the remainder moist until established. All are easy from seed sown in a soil-based medium.

Infestations of blackfly on the fans at ground level should be removed, as should small black slugs. Botrytis rot is prevented by a systemic fungicide. In the Eastern and Midwest US, Sibiricas are attacked by the iris borer and the iris weevil; both are controlled by a systemic insecticide.

The Californicae comprise 11 species known as the Pacific Coast Irises (PCIs), which occur in California, Oregon and Washington, growing in neutral or slightly acid, well drained soil in lightly wooded areas. All are very variable in colour and hybridize freely where the species overlap, and also in cultivation. They are easy to grow as garden plants, but they develop chlorosis and lose vitality in alkaline soils. *I.douglasiana* is the most tolerant; *I.munzii* and some others are frost tender. Propagate by careful division when the plant is showing renewed growth some months after flowering, and keep moist and shaded until established. They are readily raised from seed in a soil-based medium, but the offspring are likely to be hybrids. There are many cultivars available in a wide range of colours.

The Laevigatae series are plants of wet places, ditches and swamps spread throughout Europe, Asia and North America, and make excellent plants in cultivation for the margins of ponds or streams; they are tall with broad leaves and stout subterranean rhizomes, favouring soils rich in humus. Included in this group are *I.pseudacorus*, known as the Yellow Flag in Europe, and *I.versicolor*, the Blue Flag of the eastern North America. *I.laevigata* from eastern Asia is often grown in containers set on shelves in garden ponds; the flower is blue or white and there is a form with variegated leaves. Several other colour forms are in commerce and 'Rose Queen' is an attractive pink. Propagation is by division of clumps and is best carried out in early autumn but is possible in mid-spring.

I.ensata (syn *I.kaempferi*) has been cultivated in Japan for centuries and many new forms, including tetraploids, are now being raised in the US and Europe. The flowers are large, sometimes double, with spreading standards, in a wide range of colours. They flower late in the iris season, often into mid-summer; soil should be slightly acid and rich in humus. These irises are often grown as a pool marginal plants in containers, and are probably best removed from the water and kept drier in winter. The Japanese irises, as these are often called, will develop chlorosis if grown in alkaline soils but some of the Higo strain or the CaRe (calcium resistant) varieties will survive up to pH 7.4.

The irises of this group are occasionally attacked by the larvae of the iris sawfly (*Rhadinoceraea micans*), which eat the foliage leaving only threads of the vein structure. If the plants are in or near a pond take care to use a chemical control that is known not to be harmful to fish and other pond life.

The Hexagonae series, often called Louisiana irises, are a showy, late-flowering group of waterside irises coming from the swamp area of the southern US. They are robust plants with branched flower stems, often in a zig-zag form, and are very popular garden plants in the southern US and Western Australia, where the high summer temperatures necessary for active growth are attained; many superb hybrids have been raised from species crossing. They are not successful in cool-temperate climates, although the bright blue *I.brevicaulis* and coppery red *I.fulva* will flower if planted in a humus-rich soil below pH 7 and kept moist while in growth, with generous liquid feeding. The hybrid between them, *I.× fulvala*, will also grow under the same conditions.

The Tripetalae series includes the iris with the widest distribution, *I.setosa*. In this series the standards are tiny and the flower appears to have only three petals. Ranging from Japan to Alaska and eastern Canada, *I.setosa* exists in many variants, of which the small ones, such as *I.alpina*, *I. arctica* and *I.canadensis*, are good for the rock garden. All are under 15mm/¹/2in. tall with blue flowers, these miniatures are stable when propagated from seed.

The Spuriae series – tough plants with woody rhizomes – are very diverse in habitat and in size, varying from 25–150cm/10–60in. tall. The taller species are herbaceous and are good plants for the back of a mixed border on deep soils with ample humus, but do not usually thrive on acid sands. Some of the smaller species such as the yellow *I.kerneriana* are rock-garden plants requiring good drainage, while the plum-scented *I.graminea* is happy in a humus-rich soil in part shade. There are two general groups, one typified by *I.orientalis*, which goes dormant after flowering, and the other including *I.spuria* itself, which retains its leaves until winter. Many excellent hybrid plants have been raised with a range of bright colours, both self- and multi-coloured.

Propagation is by division in autumn or possibly early spring, planting the rhizome below the surface in a rich deep soil and keeping moist until established. New plantings may be slow to flower but can remain undisturbed for many years.

No serious diseases or pests occur, but as the flowers produce large quantities of nectar they can become infested with aphids.

I.foetidissima is a widespread native plant of Western Europe and North Africa which will grow almost anywhere or in any soil. This iris is much prized by flower arrangers for the scarlet seeds that are displayed when the capsules split in autumn; forms with white or yellow seeds are known. Slow-growing white- and cream-variegated forms occur. *I.f.* var. *citrina* produces larger, clear topaz-yellow flowers. This species is very susceptible to a virus disease which causes streaks in the leaves, but new plants free from virus are easily raised from seed.

The last member of the *Limniris* is *I.unguicularis*, which in one of its many forms can be found in flower from early autumn to mid-spring. It occurs in the eastern Mediterranean and North Africa and is therefore adapted to a warm sunny position in the garden, ideally against a south-facing wall on a sharply draining, neutral to alkaline soil. A topdressing of potash or bone meal in early autumn and spring will promote flowering; old leaves should be removed periodically. To propagate, divide clumps in spring after flowering and keep watered until established; this species is, however, best left undisturbed for many years. Seed capsules will sometimes be found in the clumps at ground level; these will germinate if sown in a soil-based medium by the following autumn. *I.unguicularis* ssp. *cretensis* is a very distinct dwarf form occurring in Crete and the Peloponnese, with short narrow leaves and strikingly marked violet flowers with prominent veining on a white haft on the falls; it requires a hot dry situation to flower freely. There are many varieties, among which 'Alba' (creamy-white), 'Mary Barnard' (violet-blue), 'Marginata' (with white edging to the lilac falls and standards) and 'Walter Butt' (fragrant, pale lavender) are recommended.

The related *I.lazica* from the Black Sea coast enjoys slight shade and moister conditions, and will flower in late spring.

Pests include slugs and the larvae of the angleshades moth, which eat the ends of flower buds while still at ground level.

The bulbous irises of the Xiphium series occur in Western Europe and North Africa, usually on alkaline soils; as there is a dormant period after flowering, several of the species need bulb frame culture in wet summer areas. *I.xiphium* occurs over a wide range of habitats, and both the species type and the many named colour forms called Spanish Irises are reliable garden plants, the leaves appearing in autumn. Hybrids between *I.xiphium* and *I.tingitana,* known collectively as Dutch Irises, are also good garden plants, and are widely used for the cut-flower market throughout the year; colours range from white and yellow to deep purple.

I.latifolia (*I.xiphioides*), wrongly designated the English Iris in the 16th century and still so-called, is an exception, growing in damp grassy places in the Pyrenees. An easy plant for the border, it prefers a soil which does not dry out. Many colour forms are available in blue, violet, purple and white.

Section Scorpiris, the Juno irises, is one of the largest groups with over 55 species, but most of them are difficult in temperate areas. They occur in western Asia ranging from Turkey to central Russian Asia and south to Jordan with the one exception of *I.planifolia* found in Southwest Europe and North Africa. They are fleshy-rooted, bulbous plants with channelled leaves in one plane. The flowers are attractive, the falls large and brightly coloured, the standards very small, often reduced to bristles.

The majority of the Junos grow in areas of hot dry summers and cold winters with snow cover, and unless this can be achieved naturally then overhead protection from summer and winter rain is essential for cultivation. Grow in deep pots in an unheated, well-ventilated alpine house or plant out in a bulb frame. A free-draining soil with added dolomitic limestone is recommended; feed with balanced fertilizer in the growing period from mid-autumn until the leaves turn yellow after flowering. Never wet the foliage, as water trapped in the channelled leaves may cause rot.

Some of the Junos are more tolerant of damp, for example *I.aucheri, I.bucharica, I.magnifica* and probably *I.cycloglossa* will thrive in the open garden in cool-temperate areas in well-drained loam. The smaller forms of *I.bucharica* are excellent plants for the rock garden, flowering in early spring. Propagate from small young bulbs which can be carefully separated when replanting, or from seed, but artificial cross-pollination may be necessary as many species are self-sterile.

The dwarf bulbous irises forming the subgenus Hermodactyloides are often called the Reticulata group, referring to the netted tunics covering the bulbs. They occur in Turkey, Iran, Soviet Central Asia and south to Jordan. In temperate gardens both *I.histrioides* and *I.reticulata* will flourish in a sunny position in well-drained soil, and can be left undisturbed for years; an annual topdressing of a low-nitrogen fertilizer in autumn will encourage flowering. There are many colour forms available and also some named hybrids. The yellow *I.winogradowii* is a high mountain plant which likes plenty of moisture during the growing season and, unlike the other reticulatas, does not require a summer dry period. A hybrid with *I.histrioides* named 'Katharine Hodgkin' is a hardy bulb which increases rapidly in the open garden on a raised bed.

I.danfordiae will flower well in the first season but then breaks up into many tiny bulblets and should be replaced annually; only if planted deeply in a bulb frame can flowering colonies be formed.

The remaining members of the group are best grown in a bulb frame, using a medium-fertility soil-based mix with the addition of sharp grit and ground dolomitic limestone. Pot culture is not recommended since reticulata irises do not persist very long under these conditions. Propagation is by bulb offsets or from seed, which germinates freely.

All the Reticulata irises are susceptible to a fungus (*Mystrosporium adustum*) known as ink disease which rapidly kills the bulb and will spread through a whole colony. The use of a systemic fungicide before planting, or watered on later, is usually satisfactory.

Irises, particularly *I.pseudacorus* and *I.laevigata*, are frequently attacked by the blue-grey larvae, up to 20mm long, of the iris sawfly *Rhadinoceraea micans*. Control may be achieved by spraying with appropriate contact insecticides. The foliage may also become infested with the gladiolus thrips (*Thrips simplex*) and polyphagous species of aphids, which besides causing direct damage transmit various viruses; damage may also be caused by slugs and snails. Irises may be attacked by several eelworms, including the potato tuber eelworm (*Ditylenchus destructor*), the stem eelworm (*D.dipsaci*) and the scabious bud eelworm (*Aphelenchoides blastophthorus*). Subterranean pests include cutworms, bulb flies (*Merodon equestris* and *Eumerus* spp.) and the caterpillars of swift moths (*Hepialus* spp.). Bulbs in store may become infested with the tulip bulb aphid (*Dysaphis tulipae*). In North America, caterpillars of the iris borer (*Macronoctus onusta*) can be a serious pest; the grey-white larvae, up to 30mm/1.2in. long when fully grown, tunnel into leaves and shoots and are associated with bacterial rotting of the tissues.

Leaf spot caused by the fungus *Mycosphaerella macrospora* attacks both bulbous and rhizomatous irises and produces brown, oval spots which may coalesce so that the leaves die prematurely. Ink disease caused by *Drechslera iridis* affects bulbous irises and takes its name from the black streaks resembling ink splashes, which occur when it infects the outer scales of *I.reticulata*. It is now mainly known as a foliage disease, resulting in black blotches on the leaves which the turn yellow and die. Both these diseases can be controlled by sprays of dithiocarbamate fungicides.

In fusarium basal rot (*Fusarium oxysporum* f. sp. *gladioli,* cf. fusarium yellows of gladioli), roots are either absent or brown and rotten and plants arising from infected bulbs are yellow and stunted. The disease can be controlled by dipping bulbs in a suspension of systemic fungicide.

Grey bulb rot caused by *Rhizoctonia tuliparum* is mainly known as a disease of tulips; it is a dry rot which progresses from the neck of the bulb downwards and shoots are unlikely to emerge at all. The causal fungus persists in the soil as sclerotia so susceptible host plants (colchicum, crocus, hyacinth, iris, ixia, lilies, narcissi and tulip) should not be grown in contaminated land for several years. Botrytis rot (*Sclerotinia convoluta*, conidial stage *Botrytis convoluta*) is a disease of rhizomatous irises. The rhizomes may be completely rotted and a grey mycelial growth of *Botrytis* (cf. grey mould) as well as large black sclerotia may appear on the rotted tissue. Infected plants should be destroyed. Soft rot (*Erwinia carotovora*) and white root rot (*Rosellinia necatrix*) can affect both bulbous and rhizomatous irises, while blue mould (*Penicillium corymbiferum*) enters bulbs damaged during lifting and can cause a storage rot. Aphid-transmitted mosaic viruses affect both bulbous and rhizomatous irises to cause leaf yellowing and flower-colour breaks.

A CLASSIFICATION OF *IRIS*

Subgenus IRIS. Plants with well developed rhizomes, sometimes slender and stolon-like; roots not swollen and tuber-like. Falls with a distinct beard of long hairs.

1. Section *Iris* (The Bearded or Pogon irises). Rhizome stout, giving rise to fans of leaves. Flowering stems simple or branched, 2- to several-flowered; falls and standards well developed, hairs on falls multicellular. Seeds lacking fleshy appendage.

2. Section *Psammiris* (Spach) J. Tayl. Rhizomes usually stoloniferous. Flowering stems simple; flowers to 5cm diam., yellow or sometimes purple-lavender, 1–3 per stem; falls bearded, hairs unicellular. Seeds with a fleshy appendage.

3. Section *Oncocyclus* (Siemssen) Bak. Rhizomatous. Flowering stems simple, 1-flowered; flowers to 5cm diam. or more, solitary, variously coloured, rarely yellow; falls bearded, hairs unicellular. Seeds with a fleshy, often white appendage.

4. Section *Regelia* Lynch. Plants from mountainous habits. Flowering stems simple, normally with 2 flowers produced from 2 bracts. Falls and standards bearded. Seeds with a fleshy appendage.

5. Section *Hexapogon* (Bunge) Bak. Semi-desert plants. Flowering stems simple, with 3 or more flowers produced from 3 or 4 bracts; falls and standards bearded. Seeds with a fleshy appendage.

6. Section *Pseudoregelia* Dykes. Usually dwarf plants from mountainous habitats. Rhizome compact, nonstoloniferous. Flowering stems simple. Falls bearded, lilac or purple prominently blotched dark lilac or purple, hairs unicellular. Seeds with a fleshy appendage.

Subgenus LIMNIRIS (Tausch) Spach. (The Beardless irises). Rhizome well developed, sometimes slender and stolon-like; roots not swollen and tuber-like. Falls without beard but sometimes with cockscomb-like crests.

7. Section *Lophiris* (Tausch) Tausch. (The Evansia irises). Woodland plants, creeping with widely spreading rhizomes often ascending as cane-like stems. Leaves usually in an apical fan, thin and soft-textured, green. Falls with 1 or more ridges or crests, usually dissected like a cockscomb.

8. Section *Limniris* Series *Chinensis* (Diels) Lawrence. Rhizomes thin, wiry, often wide-creeping. Leaves prominently ribbed. Capsules triangular.

9. Series *Vernae* (Diels) Lawrence. Plants small. Flowers blue. Capsule 3 cornered; seeds globose, with a fleshy appendage.

10. Series *Ruthenicae* (Diels) Lawrence. Plant low, compact, clump-forming. Capsule to 1.5cm; seeds soon released, pyriform, with a fleshy appendage.

11. Series *Tripetalae* (Diels) Lawrence. Standards much-reduced, often bristle-like.

12. Series *Sibiricae* (Diels) Lawrence (The Siberian irises). Leaves narrow. Flowering stems hollow, stigma triangular. Capsule triquetrous or rounded in section; seeds deltoid.

13. Series *Californicae* (Diels) Lawrence. (The Pacific Coast irises). Plants from dry habitat. Leaves tough. Stigma triangular. Capsule with 3 ribs, triquetrous or cylindrical.

14. Series *Longipetalae* (Diels) Lawrence. Plants from calcareous soils. Stems persisting for a year or more after flowering. Stigma bidentate. Capsule 6-ribbed, each end tapered.

15. Series *Laevigatae* (Diels) Lawrence. Robust, moisture-loving. Stigma bilobed. Capsule triquetrous or subcylindrical, 3-ribbed, thin-walled; seeds shiny.

16. Series *Hexagonae* (Diels) Lawrence (The Louisiana irises). Very robust plants from marsh and swampland. Stems with leaf-like spathes and large flowers. Capsules 6-ribbed; seeds large, corky.

17. Series *Prismaticae* (Diels) Lawrence. Plants from wet grassy habitats. Rhizome thin, wide-creeping. Stems tall, bracts brown. Capsule triquetrous.

18. Series *Spuriae* (Diels) Lawrence. Stigma bidentate. Capsules triquetrous, 6-ribbed; seeds with a loose shiny coat.

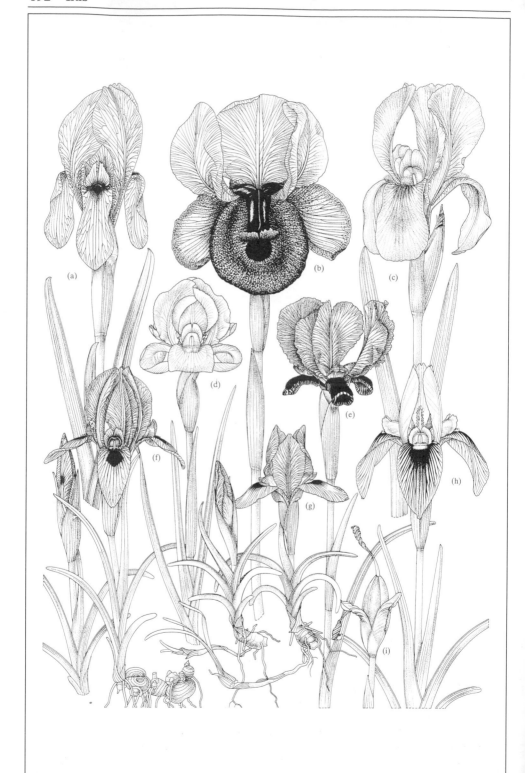

Iris: Oncoreglio Group (a) *I.korolkowii* f. *leichtliniana* (b) *I.iberica* spp. *elegantissima* (c) *I.hoogiana*
(d) *I.acutiloba* spp. *lineolata* (e) *barnumae* f. *urmiensis* (f) *I.sprengeri* (g) *I.paradoxa* (h) *I.afghanica*
(i) *I.lineata*, seed cap

19. Series *Foetidissimae* (Diels) Lawrence. Plants evergreen. Leaves wide. Seeds scarlet, remaining attached to capsule.

20. Series *Tenuifoliae* (Diels) Lawrence. Rhizome with shiny brown leaf bases at apex. Perianth tube to 14cm; stigma bilobed. Capsule ellipsoid to cylindrical, often 6-ribbed; seeds wrinkled.

21. Series *Ensatae* (Diels) Lawrence. Plants from salt marshes. Perianth tube to 3mm; ovary 6-grooved, beaked. Capsule conspicuously 6-ribbed; seeds shiny, globose.

22. Series *Syriacae* (Diels) Lawrence. Rhizome almost vertical, covered with spiny fibres.

23. Series *Unguiculares* (Diels) Lawrence. Plants low. Perianth tube to 16cm; style branched, with golden marginal glands.

24. **Subgenus NEPALENSIS** (Dykes) Lawrence. Rootstock with small growing point to which the plant dies back during winter and to which some storage roots are attached. Leaves prominently veined. Flowers fugaceous; falls with a linear crest or uncrested.

25. **Subgenus XIPHIUM** (Mill.) Spach (The Spanish irises). Bulb tunics papery to tough and coriaceous, not netted. Roots thin, fibrous. Leaves channelled. Stem to 90cm, simple, 1–3-flowered; falls unbearded; standards upright, not greatly reduced.

26. **Subgenus SCORPIRIS** Spach (The Juno irises). Bulbs with papery tunics, not netted-fibrous, usually with thickened fleshy roots when dormant. Leaves channelled. Standards much reduced, sometimes bristle-like, often horizontal or deflexed; falls beardless, with a central, raised ridge.

27. **Subgenus HERMODACTYLOIDES** Spach (The Reticulata irises). Dwarf, bulbous plants. Bulb tunics fibrous and netted. Leaves quadrangular to subcylindrical in cross section.

The numbers in square brackets below indicate the subgenus or section to which each species belongs. The descriptions should be read with the general description of the relevant group in mind.

I.acutiloba Mey.
[3.] Stem 8–25cm, unbranched. Lvs narrow sickle-shaped, 2–6mm wide. Fls solitary, 5–7cm diam., white yellow, strongly veined and lined brown-grey; falls with one central and one rust-black spot, bearded, beard hairs sparse, long, purple-brown, falls and standards more or less pointed. Seeds with large arils. Spring–early summer. Transcaucasus. ssp. *lineolata* (Trautv.) B. Mathew & Wendelbo. Falls with only one spot.

I.aequiloba Ledeb. See *I.pumila*.

I.afghanica Wendelbo.
[4.] Stem 15–35cm, unbranched. Lvs curved. Fls usually solitary, 8–9cm diam., cream-white, veins dense, purple-brown; falls bearded, signal patch purple, apex pointed, beard hairs dark, long, standards yellow, beard tinged green, apex pointed. Seeds arillate. Spring. Pakistan, E Afghanistan.

I.alata Poir. See *I.planifolia*.

I.alberti Reg.
[1.] Bearded iris 30–70cm. Lvs broad, erect, grey-green, tinged purple at base. Fls 1–3, 6–8cm diam.; bracts somewhat inflated, margins papery; perianth lilac to violet-purple, fall haft veined red-brown, beard white to pale blue, tips yellow. Late spring. Kazakstan.

I.albicans Lange.
[1.] Robust bearded iris 30–60cm; rhiz. stout. Lvs in fans, broadly lanceolate, 1.5–2.5cm wide, grey-green, tips abruptly narrowed, incurved. Fls 1–3, sessile, 8–9cm diam., sweetly scented; bracts broad, blunt, base flushed green or purple, apex papery, transparent; perianth white or blue, fall haft green-yellow, beard white, tips green, standard haft green-yellow. Saudi Arabia, Yemen. *I.germanica* 'Florentina' is distinguished by its brown papery bracts. 'Madonna': fls blue.

I.albomarginata R. Fost.
[26.] To 30cm. Bulb tunics papery; roots fleshy or thickened. Lvs channelled, to 3cm wide at base, grey-green with white margin, apex abruptly narrowed. Fls 2–5; perianth blue, tube 4cm, fall blade with white central ridge surrounded by yellow zone, haft not broadly winged, standard reduced, to 2.5cm, oblanceolate, deflexed. Spring–early summer. Russia.

I.alexeenkoi Grossh.
[1.] To 30cm. Similar to *I.pumila* but lvs larger (11–12×1.5cm); fls solitary, 7–8cm diam., purple-blue, perianth tube to 10cm, beard yellow.

I.× altobarbata Murray.
Name sometimes applied to the tall bearded irises.

I.amoena DC.
Name applied to a group of rhizomatous, bearded irises with white standards and coloured falls, probably derived from *I.variegata*.

I.antilibanotica Dinsm.
[3.] To 40cm. Lvs to 10cm, falcate. Fls solitary, large; falls rich purple with central black blotch, veins purple, beard yellow, standards violet. Seeds with large aril. Spring–early summer. Syria.

I.aphylla L.
[1.] To 30cm. Lvs deciduous, in fans, outer lvs curved, inner lvs upright, 0.5–2cm wide. Flowering stems branched from middle or near base; bracts 3–6cm, inflated, sometimes purple tipped; fls 1–5, 6–7cm diam., pale to deep purple to blue-violet, beard hairs blue-white, tips yellow. Spring. C & E Europe to W Russia and N Caucasus.

Aril Irises (Regeliocyclus Hybrids).
'Ancilla': fls white veined purple, falls flaked and netted purple. 'Chione': standards white veined lilac blue, falls veined grey, blotched black-brown. 'Clotho': standards deep violet with black beard, falls brown, veins and blotch black. 'Dardanus': standards tinged lilac, falls cream blotched matt purple. 'Theseus': standards violet with darker veins, falls ivory marked deep violet. 'Thor': fls grey veined purple, blotch bright purple. 'Vera': fls chocolate-brown tinged purple with blue beard. Aril-Median Irises: (Aril × Miniature Tall Bearded irises). 'Canasta': to 28cm; standards pale violet, falls rich beige with deep red signal and veining, the latter paling at edges, beard brown-bronze. 'Little Orchid Annie': to 30cm; standards pale amethyst veined and shaded green-gold, ruffled, midrib green, falls orchid edged yellow-green, signal and veining red, beard dark yellow. Arilbred Irises (Aril × Tall Bearded irises). 'Lady Mohr': to 75cm; standards light mauve-blue, falls yellow and green with deep red markings, beard brown. 'Loudmouth': to 25cm; fls deep red, falls with black signal. 'Nineveh': standards purple shaded pink, falls violet-red, beard dark brown. 'Saffron Charm': fls in blend of deep yellow, grey and lavender.

I.elizabethae Siehe. See *I.sprengeri*.

I.arctica Eastw. See *I.setosa* var. *arctica*.

I.assadiana Chaudhary, Kirkwood & Weymouth.
[3.] To 15cm. Rhiz. small; stolons to 12cm. Lvs strongly curved, 5–10×1cm. Fls 5.5–7.5cm diam., dark maroon, veins deeper; signal patch velvety, beard hairs short and purple, and long and off-white or yellow, tips sometimes purple; style branches light orange-red streaked purple. Syria.

I.atrofusca Bak.
[3.] Rhiz stout. Lvs erect, *c*1cm wide, pale green. Fls solitary, 8–9cm diam.; falls deep purple-brown, signal patch central, black, beard hair short, dense yellow; standards usually paler, claret-coloured. Seeds with large aril. Spring. Israel.

I.atropurpurea Bak.
[3.] 15–25cm tall. Rhiz. often stoloniferous. Lvs *c*15cm, falcate. Fls solitary, showy, 8cm diam.; perianth very deep black-purple, standards usually paler than falls, signal patch yellow, beard hairs short, yellow. Seeds with large aril. Spring. Israel. var. *eggeri* Dinsm. Non-stoloniferous. Lvs less curved; fls purple-brown. var. *gileadensis* Dinsm. Fls brown, veined and dotted red.

I.atropurpurea Dinsm. See *I.bostrensis*.

I.attica (Boiss. & Heldr.) Hayek.
[1.] Similar to *I.pumila* but smaller, 5–10cm high. Lvs in fans, 4–7×0.4–0.7cm, strongly falcate. Fls solitary, 3.5–4.5cm diam.; perianth tube to 7cm, yellow or purple or bicoloured; outer bracts somewhat keeled. Spring. Greece, S Balkans, W Turkey.

I.aucheri (Bak.) Sealy.
[26.] To 40cm. Roots fleshy. Lvs 25×2.5–4.5cm, completely concealing stem until fruiting. Fls 3–6, blue, rarely almost white; tube to 6cm; fall blade with central yellow ridge, margin wavy, haft broadly winged; standards 2–3.5cm, horizontal to deflexed, obovate. Late winter–spring. SE Turkey, N Iraq, N Syria, Jordan, NW Iran. Crossed with *I.persica* to produce *I.*'Sindpur'.

I.aurantiaca Dinsm.
[3.] To 50cm. Fls solitary, 12–15cm diam., yellow spotted brown, appearing bronze, signal patch maroon, beard broad, dense, hairs yellow, tips purple. Seeds with large aril. Late spring. Syria. var. *unicolor* Mout. Signal patch and spotting absent.

I.bakeriana Fost.
[27.] To 15cm. Bulb tunics netted. Close to *I.reticulata*, distinguished by lvs cylindric, 8-ribbed; fls solitary, white, tipped violet on falls with a cream ridge surrounded by violet spots and veins, haft spotted and veined violet, standards and style branches lilac. SE Turkey, N Iraq, W Iran.

I.baldschuanica B. Fedtsch.
[26.] Similar to *I.caucasica* but roots very swollen; plant to 15cm; lvs concealing stem until flowering, after which they are thrust up on top of the short stem, 15–20×5–6cm, grey-green; fls 1–3, cream; tube to 10cm; fall blade with central yellow ridge, haft margins downturned; standards horizontal to slightly deflexed, lanceolate; style branches tinged pink-brown. Spring. Russia, NW Afghanistan.

I.balkana Janka. See *I.reichenbachii*.

I.barnumae Bak. & Fost.
[3.] 10–30cm. Lvs curved, grey-green. Fls solitary, 7–8cm diam., deep purple-violet, sparsely veined, beard narrow, hairs yellow, sometimes tipped purple, cream or white, signal patch obscure. Seeds with large aril. Late spring. E Turkey, NE Iraq, Iran. f. *urmiensis* (Hoog) B. Mathew & Wendelbo (*I.urmiensis* Hoog). Fls yellow, without spots or veins. f. *protonyma* (Stapf) B. Mathew & Wendelbo. Falls brown-purple, beard hairs purple-black, thick, forming broad, square-ended strip, standards purple-violet. ssp. *demavendica* (Bornm.) B. Mathew & Wendelbo (*I.demavendica* (Bornm.) Dykes). More robust, lvs upright, fls larger, blue-violet, beard narrow, white-cream. Iran.

I.basaltica Dinsm.
[3.] To 70cm. Lvs erect to subfalcate, to 2cm wide, tough. Fls solitary, 15cm diam. or more, falls green-white heavily veined and dotted black-purple, signal patch rounded, dark, beard brown-purple, tips yellow, standards white or light green, markings faint. Seeds with large aril. Spring. Syria.

I.battandieri Fost. See *I.xiphium* 'Battandieri'.

Bearded (Pogon) Irises. (1) *Border Bearded* (stems to 70cm; fls large). 'Brown Lasso': standards butterscotch, falls pale violet and brown. 'Carnival Glass': fls red-brown, occasionally tinged blue or red. 'Impelling': fls bright pink and yellow with an orange beard. 'Impetuous': fls sky-blue, ruffled, beard white. 'Marmalade Skies': fls apricot-orange. 'Whoop Em Up': fls vivid golden-yellow, falls clear chestnut-red, rimmed with bright yellow. (2) *Intermediate Bearded* (stems to 70cm; fls abundant). 'Annikins': fls deep violet blue. 'Black Watch': fls very dark velvety black-purple. 'Golden Muffin': standards ruffled, yellow, falls amber-brown edged yellow. 'Indeed': standards clear lemon-yellow, falls translucent white edged bright yellow with a white beard. 'Silent Strings': fls clear blue. 'Why Not': fls bright apricot-orange with darker beard. (3) *Miniature Dwarf Bearded* (stems to 20cm, to 2 fls per stem). 'April Ballet': standards light blue with a violet-blue spot. 'Egret Snow': standards pure white, falls occasionally flecked blue. 'Jasper Gem': rust-red bicolor. 'Orchid Flare': fls pink with white beard. (4) *Miniature Tall Bearded* (stems to 70cm; fls 8 or more). 'Carolyn Rose': fls cream-white lined rose-pink. 'Dappled Pony': standards dark blue, falls white heavily flecked violet. 'Smarty Pants': fls yellow with red stripes on falls. 'Surprise Blue': fls lavender blue with white hafts. (5) *Standard Dwarf Bearded* (stems to 40cm; fls 3 or 4 per stem). 'Austrian Sky': fls blue with darker markings on falls. 'Blue Denim': fls blue, flaring with a white beard. 'Gingerbread Man': fls deep brown with a bright blue beard. 'Green Halo': fls pale olive-green with a darker 'halo'. 'Melon Honey': fls melon-orange with a white beard. 'Toots': fls velvet burgundy with a yellow beard. (6) *Tall Bearded* (over 70cm high; fls large, usually ruffled). 'Broadway': standards golden-yellow, beard orange, falls white. 'Going My Way': fls white striped violet-purple. 'Jane Phillips': fls large, pale blue. 'Love's Allure': standards grey-lilac flecked purple, falls edged sandy gold. 'Red Lion': fls deep brown-burgundy. 'Vanity': fls light pink flashed white with a pink-red beard.

I.belouinii Boiss. & Cornault.
[1.] Similar to *I.germanica* but lvs dormant in winter. Morocco.

I.biggeri Dinsm.
[3.] To 50cm. Lvs almost straight. Fls solitary, large, falls with red-violet dots merging at base, signal patch deeper, beard hairs white tipped purple, standards paler, veins fine, purple. Seeds with large aril. Spring. Israel.

I.biliotii Fost.
[1.] 60–80cm, 2–3-branched, branches to 10cm. Fls fragrant; bracts acute, grey-green, tips translucent, papery; falls red-purple, haft white veined brown-purple, beard white tipped yellow, standards blue-purple. Late spring. Turkey.

I.bismarckiana Reg.
[3.] To 50cm. Rhiz. stoloniferous. Lvs short, to 2.5cm wide, in a sturdy fan. Fls solitary, 10–12cm diam., cream yellow densely spotted and veined red brown or purple; signal patch large, black-purple, beard deep purple; standards large, rounded, white spotted and veined purple-blue. Seeds with large aril. Spring. NE Israel, S Syria.

I.bloudowii Bunge.
[2.] Similar to *I.humilis*, 15–35cm high; rhiz. not stoloniferous, growing point clad in numerous brown fibres; lvs larger, to 3×1.3cm; fls 2–3, 5cm diam., yellow stained purple-brown at base; bracts inflated; beard yellow. Seeds with fleshy aril. Spring. C & E Russia, China.

I.boissieri Henriq (*I.diversifolia* Merino).
[25.] 30–40cm. Bulb tunic not netted; roots somewhat fleshy. Lvs narrow, appearing in autumn. Fls solitary, deep purple, perianth tube to 5cm, beard a narrow band of yellow hairs. Summer. N Portugal, NW Spain.

I.bosniaca Beck. See *I.reichenbachii*.

I.bostrensis Mout. (*I.atropurpurea* Dinsm.).
[3.] 10–15cm. Lvs to 5mm wide. Fls 6–8cm diam., yellow-green or light brown, strongly spotted and veined dark purple-brown, signal patch dark maroon and velvety, beard hairs dense, yellow tipped purple. Seeds with large aril. Spring. S Syria.

I.bracteata Wats.
[13.] 20–30cm. Lvs very thick, to 1cm wide; bract-like lvs along length of stem usually tinged pink to purple-red. Fls 2 per stem, 6–7.25cm diam.; bracts sheathing stalk and ovary; perianth tube 0.5–1cm, falls spreading, cream to yellow veined brown or red-purple, central zone deep yellow. Early summer. W US (S Oregon, N California).

I.brandzae Prodan. See *I.sintenisii* ssp. *brandzae*.

I.brevicaulis Raf. (*I.foliosa* Mackenzie & Bush; *I.lamancei* (Gerard) Lynch).
[16.] To 50cm. Rhiz. long, to 15×3cm. Lvs 3–6, to 45×2–3cm, taller than fls. Flowering stems flexuous; fls terminal and axillary, usually 2 per bract pair, to 11cm diam., pale blue to blue-violet, falls large, to 9×3cm, broad-ovate, reflexed, banded yellow in centre, haft usually veined white-green, standards smaller, spreading. Seeds large, corky. Summer. C US (Mississippi Valley). 'Brevipes' (*I.brevipes* Alexander): falls ovate, pale mauve-pink, veined lilac, standards pale violet to pale blue-violet. 'Flexicaulis' (*I.flexicaulis* Small): falls obovate, dark violet, standards narrow-spathulate, violet. 'Mississippiensis' (*I.mississippiensis* Alexander): falls suborbicular, pale violet, veined green-brown, standards pale violet with white base.

I.brevipes Alexander. See *I.brevicaulis* 'Brevipes'.

I.bucharica Fost. (*I.orchioides* hort. non Carr.).
[26.] To 40cm. Lvs to 20×3.5cm at flowering, later elongated on expanded stem, shiny green, channelled, margins white. Fls 2–6 in upper lf axils; perianth tube to 4.5cm, golden yellow to white, fall with central ridge yellow surrounded by green to dull purple suffusion or markings, standards spreading, trilobed or lanceolate. Spring. Russia, NE Afghanistan.

I.bulleyana Dykes.
[12.] 35–45cm, hollow, unbranched. Lvs 45×1cm, linear, glossy above, glaucous beneath. Fls 1–2, 6–8cm diam., falls obovate, spreading, dotted streaked and veined bright blue-purple on cream ground, haft green-yellow, standards oblanceolate, shorter than falls, lilac. Summer. W China, N Burma.

I.caespitosa Pall. & Link.
[10.] Lvs to 13cm, narrow, grasslike, in clumps to 20cm diam. Fls solitary, aromatic, dark violet. Fr. to 1.5cm, smooth; seeds teardrop shaped with fleshy aril. Spring. E Europe. Possibly a dwarf variant of *I.ruthenica*.

I.camillae Grossh.
[3.] 20–40cm. Lvs narrow-falcate. Fls solitary, to 8cm diam., light yellow to blue-violet, falls smaller than standards, light yellow to blue-violet, sometimes bearded yellow and with a violet signal patch. Seeds with large aril. Transcaucasia. 'Caerulea': fls light blue. 'Lutea': fls light yellow. 'Pallida': falls intensely veined, standards white. 'Speciosissima': falls bronze, veins dark, signal patch almost black, beard yellow, standards blue. 'Spectabilis': falls cream, veins thick deep brown, signal patch black-brown, standards white. 'Sulphurea': falls golden yellow, signal patch red-purple, standards blue.

I.caucasica Hoffm.
[26.] To 15cm. Lvs 5–7, falcate, channelled, 10–12×2cm, concealing stem at flowering, margins white, glossy above, glaucous beneath. Fls 1–4, green to yellow, tube to 4cm; falls obovate, central ridge yellow; standards oblanceolate, horizontal. Late winter–spring. C & NE Turkey, NE Iraq, NW Iran, Russia. var. **multiflora** Grossh. To 10 fls. S Transcaucasia.

I.cedretii Dinsm. ex Chaudhary.
[3.] To 40cm, unbranched. Lvs straight to curved, 1–2cm wide. Fls solitary, 8–11cm diam., white, thickly covered with fine red-brown veins and spots, falls with rounded signal patch, deep red-brown, bear brown-purple, hairs long. Seeds with large aril. Spring. Lebanon.

I.chamaeris Bertol. See *I.lutescens*.

I.chrysographes Dykes.
[12.] To 50cm. Rhiz. stout. Lvs 50–1.5cm. Fls 1–4 on hollow, branched or unbranched stems, fragrant, 5–10cm diam., dark red-purple streaked gold on falls; falls deflexed; standards spreading. Late spring–summer. W China, NE Burma. Hybridizes with *I.forrestii* and *I.sibirica*. 'Black Night': fls indigo-violet. 'Inshriach': fls almost black. 'Margot Holmes': fls purple-crimson lined yellow at throat. 'Rubella': fls burgundy.

I.chrysophylla Howell.
[13.] To c20cm. Lvs 3–5mm wide. Fls 6–7cm diam., usually 2 per closely held bract pair, cream to palest yellow veined darker yellow; tube 4.5–12cm, narrow at base, widening at apex; seg. narrow, acute; style lobes long, tips pointed. Late spring–summer. W US (Oregon, N California). 'Alba': fls white. 'Caerulea': fls blue.

I.citrina anon. See *I.tenuissima*.

I.clarkei Bak.
[12.] Rhiz. stout. Stems to 60cm, 1–3-branched. Lvs to 2cm wide, glossy green above, glaucous beneath. fls 2 per branch, 5–10cm diam., blue violet to red-purple; falls with large, white, central signal patch, veined violet; haft slightly yellow; standards bent to horizontal. Late spring–early summer. E Himalaya.

I.colchica Kem.-Nat. See *I.graminea*.

I.collettii Hook.
[24.] To 5cm. Fls subsessile, solitary or 2 per branch, to 3cm diam., fragrant, light blue, with yellow-orange crest; tube to 10cm. Spring–summer. SW China, N Burma.

I.confusa Sealy.
[7.] Vigorous clump-forming, to 1.5m. Stems green, cane-like with annular scars, procumbent and branching, then ascending, with an apical fan of bright green sword-shaped lvs to 5cm across. Flowering stems to 90cm, branched; fls to 5cm diam., many, short-lived, white spotted yellow or mauve; falls 2.5×5cm, crest yellow, signal patch yellow. Spring. W China.

I.cretensis Janka. See *I.unguicularis* ssp. *cretensis*.
I.cretica Bak. See *I.unguicularis* ssp. *cretensis*.

I.cristata Sol.
[7.] Rhiz. small, much branched. Lvs around 4, to 15×1–3cm at flowering, linear. Fls 1–2 per spathe, subsessile, 3–4cm diam., pale lilac to purple; tube to 10cm; falls obovate, blunt, reflexed, 1×1cm, central patch white, crest of 3 crisped yellow ridges; standards erect, oblanceolate, shorter and narrower than falls. Early summer. NE US. 'Alba': fls white. 'Caerulea': fls blue.

I.croceu Jacq.
[18.] Rhiz. woody. Roots wiry. Lvs to 75×1.5–2cm, sword-shaped, leathery. Flowering stems to 1.5m, branched; fls 12–18cm diam., in terminal clusters, dark golden yellow; fall oblong, margins crisped; standards oblanceolate, erect, margins slightly crisped; style branch lobes narrow-triangular. Fr. capsule narrow-beaked at apex, 6-ribbed. Seed coat papery. Kashmir.

I.cycloglossa Wendelbo.
[26.] Bulb ovate-oblong, 4×2cm, tunics papery. Roots long and slender. Stem to 50cm, branched or unbranched. Lvs to 6, to 30×1.5cm, well-spaced along stem, glabrous. Fls 1–3, 8–10cm diam., lilac, aromatic, tube to 4.5cm; falls 7cm, orbicular, reflexed, centre white, blotched yellow, without ridge; standards to 4cm, obovate, erect, becoming horizontal with age. Spring. NW Afghanistan.

I.cypriana Bak. & Fost.
[1.] Similar to *I.germanica* but fls larger, to 15cm diam., scarcely scented, outer bract brown, dry and papery, falls wedge-shaped. Cyprus.

I.damascena Mout.
[3.] To 15–30cm. Lvs curved, to 1cm wide. Fls solitary, 7–9cm diam., white, thickly veined and spotted purple-brown; signal patch deep purple, small, beard hairs sparse, purple; standards more faintly veined purple; style branches to 5cm. Seeds with large aril. Spring. Syria.

I.danfordiae (Bak.) Boiss.
[27.] To 15cm. Bulb tunic netted, tiny, producing offset bulblets. Lvs 1–15cm, taller than fls, quadrangular. Fls solitary, to 5cm diam., yellow; tube to 7.5cm; falls lightly spotted green in centre and lower part, ridge deeper yellow-orange; standards reduced, bristle-like, 3–5mm. Early spring. Turkey.

I.darwasica Reg.
[4.] To 40cm. Rhiz. shortly stoloniferous, clad in fibrous remains of old lf bases. Lvs linear, to 30×0.4–0.8cm, glaucous. Fls 2, 5–6cm diam., lilac veined purple; falls elliptic-lanceolate, 6×1cm, beard blue-purple; standards oblong, to 6cm, apex rounded, claw sometimes bearded. Spring. Russia.

I.decora Wallich.
[24.] To 10–30cm, branched or unbranched. Lvs erect, linear, prominently ribbed, 2–5mm wide, overtopping fls. Fls 1–3, lightly scented, 4–5cm diam., pale lilac to deep red-purple; tube 3.5–5cm; falls spreading, crest wavy, orange-yellow, apex white or purple, haft white or yellow; standards oblanceolate, spreading, shorter than falls; style branch margins toothed or crisped. Summer. Himalaya.

I.delavayi Micheli.
[12.] Lvs to 90cm, grey-green. Flowering stems to 1.5m, 1–3× branched, hollow; fls 2 per branch, 7–9cm diam., light to deep purple-violet; fall blade wide, rounded, notched, signal area white; standards obliquely inclined, lanceolate, small. Summer. W China. Hybrids formed with *I.wilsonii* have purple fls, falls yellow veined blue-purple.

I.demavendica (Bornm.) Dykes. See *I.barnumae* ssp. *demavendica*.
I.diversifolia Merino. See *I.boissieri*.

I.doabensis B. Mathew.
[26.] 10–15cm. Bulb tunic papery, roots very swollen. Lvs 20×4cm, shiny green, enclosing stem. Fls 1–5, with fruity scent, bright deep yellow; tube 2–4cm; fall crest slightly darker, haft margins downturned; standards ovate, somewhat angular, slightly reflexed, to 1cm. Spring. NE Afghanistan.

I.douglasiana Herb.
[13.] Lvs to 100×2cm, dark green, base stained red, ribbed. Flowering stems 15–70cm, branched; fls 2–3, 7–10cm diam., lavender to purple, veins darker; tube to 3cm; falls yellow in centre; standards erect, lanceolate, clawed; lobes of style branches toothed. Fr. triangular in cross-section, apex blunt-beaked. Summer. W US (S Oregon, California). 'Alba': fls white. 'Southcombe Velvet': fls deep violet.

I.dragalz Horvat. See *I.variegata*.

I.drepanophylla Aitch. & Bak.
[26.] 10–30cm. Bulb tunics papery. Roots short, very swollen. Lvs enclosing stem at flowering, expanding to 20×2.5cm, curving strongly, the elongating stem revealing internodes, lvs channelled, margins hairy. Fls 2–8 in upper lf axils, 4–5cm diam., yellow to green; fall crest prominent darker yellow, fall haft margins narrow, downturned; standards much reduced, bristle-like, a little deflexed. Spring. Russia, NE Iran, N & W Afghanistan. ssp. *chlorotica* B. Mathew & Wendelbo. Fls silvery green; fall crest white to pale yellow-green. NE Afghanistan.

I.dykesii Stapf.
[12.] Similar to *I.chrysographes* but more vigorous and larger; lvs sheath stem for most of its length, to 2cm wide, grey-green; fls larger, bright dark violet-purple, veins in fall centre white and yellow; anth. larger, fil. shorter. Summer. China.

I.elizabethae Siehe. See *I.sprengeri*.
English Iris. See *I.latifolia*.

I.ensata Thunb. (*I.kaempferi* Sieb.). JAPANESE WATER IRIS.
[15.] Aquatic or marginal; rhiz. stout. Lvs shorter than flowering stems, 20–60×0.4–1.2cm, leathery midrib prominent. Flowering stems 60–90cm; fls 3 or 4 per branch, 8–15cm diam., purple to red-purple; tube 1–2cm; fall haft yellow, blade elliptic-ovate, also suffused yellow; standards smaller, erect. Summer. Japan, N China, E Russia. A large number of cultivars, many of which originate from Japan, with a few (such as some of the Higo Hybrids) just beginning to enter western gardens; fls to 20cm in shades of white, pink, blue and violet often mottled or flecked; single to double; often with spreading standards. 'Alba': fls pure white. 'Blauer Berg' ('Blue Mountain'): fls bright sky blue, abundant; middle to late season. 'Gei Sho Ne': habit unusually short; fls violet; middle to late season. 'Good Omen': growth strong; fls double, violet tinged red, abundant; early season. 'Major': habit tall to 46cm; fls darker. 'Moonlight Waves': fls white with lime-green centre. 'Peacock Dance': falls white, veins red-violet, signal patch yellow; standards dark red-purple; style branches purple. 'Prairie Love Song': fls white, signal patch yellow. 'Raspberry Rimmed': fls white, margins red-pink, signal patch yellow. 'Returning Tide': fls pale blue, signal yellow. 'Sorcerer's Triumph': fls double, white, veins red-purple, signal orange. 'Stranger in Paradise': fls white, margins pink, signal patch yellow. 'Summer Storm': fls to 18cm diam., violet tinged red, veined blue; late flowering. 'The Great Mohgul': fls black-purple. 'Unschuld' ('Innocence'): fls clear white, perianth seg. undulate; early flowering. 'Variegata': lvs striped white; fls purple. 'Aichi-no-Kagayaki' (*I.ensata* × *I.pseudacorus*): fls large, bright yellow, veins brown. 'Chance Beauty' (*I.ensata* × *I.pseudacorus*): fls large, bright yellow, veins red-brown.

I.eulefeldii Reg. See *I.scariosa*.
I.extremorientalis Koidz. See *I.sanguinea*.

I.falcifolia Bunge.
[1.] Slender, 10–20cm. Rhiz. compact, without stolons, roots fleshy; forming dense tufts, shoot bases clad in fibrous lf remains. Lvs grey-green, curved, 2–4mm wide. Fls 2–5 per set of 3–5 bracts, 3–4cm diam., lavender, veins darker; beard white. Seeds with fleshy appendage. Spring. C Asia.

I.fernaldii R. Fost.
[13.] Slender 20–45cm, rhizomatous. Roots wiry. Lvs grey-green, 7–9mm wide, base tinged purple. Fls 2, 7–8cm diam., light primrose with darker yellow line running down centre of falls, sometimes faintly tinged or veined purple, tube 3–6cm, widened at throat; style lobes usually 1.5cm, apex blunt. Summer. W US (California).

I.filifolia Boiss.
[25.] 25–45cm. Lvs almost thread-like, channelled, 30×0.3cm, appearing in autumn, outer scale lf blotched purple and white, sheathing shoot. Fls 1–2 on unbranched stem, rich red-violet; tube 2.5cm; fall striped yellow in centre. Summer. S Spain, NW Africa.

I.fimbriata hort.
Plants offered as this may be *I.japonica* or *I.tectorum*.

I.flexicaulis Small. See *I.brevicaulis* 'Flexicaulis'.

I.foetidissima L. ROAST BEEF PLANT; GLADWYN; GLADDON IRIS; STINKING GLADWYN.
[19.] Lvs evergreen, sword-shaped, in a basal fan, deep green, to 2.5cm wide. Flowering stem 30–90cm, somewhat flattened, 2–3-branched; fls to 5 per branch, 5–7cm diam., malodorous; falls obovate, 2cm wide, blade blue-lilac to topaz or yellow, veins purple, centre fading to white, haft bronze to brown, winged; standards smaller, oblanceolate, erect, flushed lilac. Seeds scarlet, bead-like, persisting in split capsule. Summer. S & W Europe, N Africa, Atlantic Is. 'Fructo-alba': seed coat white; rare. 'Variegata': lvs striped cream, variegated all year round; rarely, if ever, fruits. var. *citrina* Syme. Fls pale yellow and mauve. var. *lutescens* Maire. Fls pure clear yellow.

I.foliosa Mackenzie & Bush. See *I.brevicaulis*.

I.fontanesii Godron. See *I.tingitana* var. *fontanesii*.
I.fontanesii var. *mellori* C. Ingram. See *I.tingitana* var. *mellori*.

I.formosana Ohwi.
[7.] Similar to *I.japonica* but very invasive, spreading by slender stolons, stems short, erect, to 10cm; infl. branching, fls larger, somewhat compressed, lilac-blue, fall crest yellow. Taiwan.

I.forrestii Dykes.
[12.] Lvs narrow-linear, shiny above, glaucous below, shorter than stem. Flowering stem 35–40cm, unbranched; fls 2, scented, 5–6cm diam., yellow lined purple-brown on fall haft; falls oblong-ovate, blade 5cm; standards erect, oblanceolate. Summer. W China, N Burma.

I.fosteriana Aitch. & Bak.
[26.] 10–15cm. Bulb long, slender, tunics dull olive. Lvs few, to 17×0.4–0.8cm, lanceolate, silver-edged, tips acuminate, enclosing stem at first. Fls 1–2, to 5cm diam.; tube to 4cm; fall and blade orbicular, to 5cm, pale yellow, crest conspicuous, yellow, sometimes on deeper yellow, patch brown-veined; standards obovate, deflexed, purple; style branches pale yellow. NE Iran, Turkmenistan, NW Afghanistan.

I.fulva Ker-Gawl.
[16.] To 90cm; rhiz. slender, green. Lvs 1.5–2.5cm wide, green, ensiform. Fls to 6.5cm diam., bright red to rust, orange or rarely deep yellow; tube to 2.5cm; falls and standards hanging downwards, falls oblanceolate, to 2.5cm wide, blunt, narrowed to a claw, standards broad, truncate, notched, to 5×2cm. Summer. C US (Mississippi Valley)

I.×fulvala Dykes. (*I.fulva* × *I.brevicaulis*.)
Fls purple-red.

I.galatica Siehe.
[26.] 5–12cm, almost stemless. Bulb tunics papery. Roots slender. Lvs 3–4, distichously arranged, channelled, not fully developed at flowering, expanding to 12×1.2cm. Fls 1–2, 5–10cm diam., red-purple or silver-purple or yellow-green with purple falls; tube to 6cm; fall crest conspicuous, orange or yellow; standards to 2cm, paler than falls, horizontal, shape variable. Spring. Central N Turkey.

I.gatesii Fost.
[3.] 40–60cm. Lvs linear, straight, 0.5–1cm wide. Fls solitary, 13–20cm diam., extremely strong, ground colour cream, opal blue or, more usually, pearl grey, heavily overlaid with maroon or blue-mauve veins and stippling, beard yellow or maroon, signal patch absent or small and dark. Seeds with a large aril. Summer. N Iraq, SE Turkey.

I.germanica L.
[1.] Rhiz. stout. Lvs 2-ranked, equitant, 30–40×2.5–4.5cm, grey-green. Flowering stem 60–120cm, with 1–2 branches of 5cm length; fls 9–10cm diam., in various shades of blue, violet, white, beard yellow, standards sometimes paler than falls; bracts broad, apex purple-brown, translucent, base purple or green. Late spring. Widely naturalized; either a Mediterranean native or an ancient fertile hybrid. 'Amas': falls deep blue-purple, standards paler blue, prominent blue-white beard tipped orange. 'Askabadensis': tall, flowering later; falls red-purple, veins on hafts yellow-brown, beard tipped yellow, standards paler blue. 'Karput': lvs edged red-purple; falls narrow, black-purple, standards paler red-purple. 'Nepalensis': falls and standards both dark purple-red tipped orange; beard blue-white grading to white. Katmandu. 'Sivias': fls more blue; beard white, hairs scarcely tipped yellow. var.*florentina* (L.) Dykes. Smaller than species type. Fls scented, palest blue-white; veins on haft of falls yellow, beard yellow.

I.giganticaerulea Small.
[16.] Rhiz. large and thick. Stems rigid, 70–180cm, unbranched; stem lvs long, to 65×3cm. Fls to 15cm diam., light blue to dark indigo, centre white, fall signal ridge yellow, blades horizontal to just deflexed, 9×4cm, standards erect. Seeds corky. Spring. S US (Louisiana, Texas, Mississippi). 'Miraculosa': fls white.

I.glaucescens Bunge. See *I.scariosa*.
I.glockiana Schwarz. See *I.suaveolens*.

I.goniocarpa Bak.
[6.] 10–30cm. Rhiz. compact. Lvs upright, grassy, 2–3mm wide. Fls solitary, flat, to 3cm diam., colour varied, lilac to blue-purple with darker blotching or mottling; tube very short; beard compact, hair tips orange; falls rounded. Fr. triangular in cross section; seeds arillate. China, Himalaya.

I.gormanii Piper. See *I.tenax*.

I.gracilipes A. Gray.
[7.] 10–15cm; dwarf, clump-forming, rhiz. shortly stoloniferous. Stems slender, branching. Lvs grassy, ensiform, to 30×0.5–1cm. Fls 3–4cm diam., pink to blue-lilac veined violet; bracts joined at base; tube 1.5cm, falls obovate, to 2.5×1.5cm, notched, centre white, crest wavy, yellow and white. Fr. subglobose. Early summer. China, Japan. 'Alba': fls white.

I.graebneriana Sealy.
[26.] To 40cm. Bulb tunics papery. Lvs distichously arranged, shiny green above, grey-green beneath, margins white. Fls 4–6, 7cm+ diam., blue sometimes tinged violet; tube to 6cm, fall blade deeper blue, centre ridge white on veined white ground, standards obovate, to 2.5cm, tips pointed. Spring. Russia.

I.graminea L. (*I.colchica* Kem.-Nat.).
[18.] Stem 20–40cm, strongly flattened or 2-winged. Lvs borne on stem, uppermost lvs taller than fl. Fls 1–2, fruit-scented, 7–8cm diam., falls rounded, 12mm wide, violet, blade white at centre veined violet, haft winged, occasionally tinged green or yellow; standards erect, purple, 5mm wide; style branches purple, base tinged green or brown. Fr. ellipsoid, to 4cm, 6-ribbed. Summer. NE Spain to W Russia, N & W Caucasus. var. *achteroffii* Prodan. Fls yellow-white. var. *pseudocyperus* (Schur) Beck. Larger. Fls unscented. Romania & Czechoslovakia.

I.grant-duffii Bak.
[23.] 25–30cm. Rhiz. vertical, apex clad in many spiny remains of lf bases. Stems unbranched. Lvs 35×0.5–1cm, grey green, veins prominent, margins white. Fls solitary, to 6cm diam., slightly scented; tube 5mm; falls 6–7cm, sulphur-yellow with signal patch orange, sometimes streaked black, haft veins often purple; standards to 7cm, similar colour to falls. Late spring. Israel, Syria.

I.grossheimii Woron.
[3.] 13cm. Fls 7–8cm diam., claret to deep brown, veins brown-purple; signal patch large, black-brown, standards larger than falls. Seeds with large aril. Caucasia.

I.halophila Pall. See *I.spuria* ssp. *halophila*.

I.hartwegii Bak.
[13.] 10–30cm. Lvs deciduous, 2–6mm wide. Fls usually 2, 6–8cm diam., cream-yellow to lavender, veins often darker; bracts localized 4cm apart on stem, divergent; tube short, 5–10cm; seg. narrow. Summer. W US. ssp. *australis* (Parish) Lenz. To 40cm. Lvs tough, grey-green, base pink; fls violet and purple. S California. ssp. *columbiana* Lenz. Lvs bright green, c1cm wide. Fls pale yellow with darker yellow veins. C California. ssp. *pinetorum* (Eastw.) Lenz. Fls undulate, cream veined yellow.

I.haynei (Bak.) Mallet.
[3.] To 40cm. Fls solitary, 10–12cm diam., fragrant, with dark brown veins and dots on a pale ground giving overall grey-lilac colour, standards purple, signal patch rounded, black-brown. Seeds with large aril. Spring. N Israel.

I.heldreichii Siehe. See *I.stenophylla*.

I.heweri Grey-Wilson & B. Mathew.
[4.] 10–15cm. Rhiz. thin; stolons to 5cm. Lvs curved, narrow, to 5mm wide. Fls 1–2, 5cm diam.; falls dark purple-blue, haft off-white, veined purple, beard lilac; standards purple, beard paler. Late spring. NE Afghanistan.

Iris: Juno Group (a) *I.cycloglossa* (b) *I.magnifica* (b1) seed (×4) (b2) swollen tuberous root (×0.6) (b3) seed capsule (c) *I.persica* (d) *I.nicolai* (e) *I.aucheri* (f) *I.planifolia*

I.hexagona Walter.
[16.] 30–90cm, branching. Stem lvs long, *c*2.5cm wide. Fls several, 10–12cm diam., lilac; bracts to 15cm; tube to 2.5cm; falls obovate, clawed, to 11×5cm, deflexed, signal area yellow, haft often marked white-yellow and green; standards upright, narrower, apex more pointed. Seeds large, corky. Summer. SE US.

I.hippolyti Vved.
[26.] Bulb tunics papery. Roots much swollen, 10cm. Lvs sheathing stem, 1–1.5cm wide, distichously arranged, channelled. Fls 1, pale violet; tube *c*4cm; fall blade centre yellow, crest white, entire, standards 1.5cm, haft winged. Kyzyl Kum Desert.

I.hispanica Steud. See *I.xiphium.*

I.histrio Rchb. f.
[27.] Bulb offsetting, tunic netted. Lvs 30–60cm, 4-angled. Fls 1 per spathe, 6–8cm diam., falls lilac, streaked and spotted, ridge yellow surrounded by a pale, bluer spotted area, standards lilac, oblanceolate, unmarked. Winter–early spring. S Turkey, Syria, Lebanon. var. *aintabensis* (G.P. Bak.) B. Mathew. Altogether smaller, fls pale blue. S Turkey.

I.histrioides (G.F. Wils.) S. Arn.
[27.] Lvs 4-angled in section, not or scarcely developed at flowering time, extending to 50cm. Fls 6–7cm diam., blue, fall blade pale spotted blue with a yellow ridge. Early spring. Central N Turkey. 'Golden Harvest': fls yellow. 'Imperior': fls dark blue. 'Major': fls showy purple-blue, spotted white on falls. A plant with much larger, dark violet blue fls with almost horizontal falls has also been offered as *I.histrioides* 'Major'. 'White Excelsior': fls 6 8cm diam., white. 'White Perfection': fls large, white. var. *sophenensis* (Fost.) Dykes. Fl. seg. narrower, dark violet-blue, lightly spotted; fall ridge yellow. See also under *I.winogradowii.*

I.× hollandica hort. The Dutch Irises. *I.xiphium × I.tingitana*, possibly with the influence of *I.latifolia*. See *I.xiphium.*

I.hoogiana Dykes.
[4.] 40–60cm. Rhiz. stout, producing long stolons. Lvs erect, almost straight, tinged purple, to 50×1.5cm. Fls 2–3 per pair of bracts, 7–10cm diam., scented, plain grey-blue; tube to 2.5cm; falls and standards bearded yellow. Late spring. Russia. 'Alba': fls white, with a faint overlay of pale lavender-blue. 'Bronze Beauty': habit vigorous; stems tall; fls grey-violet, falls deep rich violet, edged cinnamon-brown. 'Noblense': fls blue-violet, crest golden yellow. 'Purpurea': fls deep purple.

I.hookeri G. Don. See *I.setosa* ssp. *canadensis.*

I.hookeriana Fost.
[6.] Similar to *I.kamaonensis* but with flowering stems to 12cm and fls scented like lily of the valley, lilac to indigo with darker markings, white in some forms, perianth tube 2–3cm. Late spring. W Himalaya.

I.humboldtiana anon. See *I.tenuissima.*

I.humilis Georgi.
[2.] 5–25cm, stoloniferous. Lvs erect, 2–7mm wide, tips curved inwards. Fls 1–2, 3–4cm diam., flattened in appearance; falls longer than standards, yellow, veined purple, beard orange, blades spreading horizontally; standards yellow or purple, veined purple. Seeds with fleshy aril. Spring. E Europe, Russia.

I.humilis M. Bieb. See *I.pontica.*

I.hymenospatha B. Mathew & Wendelbo.
[26.] To 12cm. Bulb neck long and papery; roots thin, scarcely fleshy. Lvs 3–4, 4–9mm wide, narrowing gradually to apex, channelled, dark green above, margin white, veins beneath prominent, silver. Fls 1–3, more or less stemless, almost white, veins violet; tube to 7cm, falls winged, crest faint yellow on blue-violet, standards oblanceolate, to 2×0.5cm, horizontal. Spring. S Iran.

I.hyrcana Woron. ex Grossh.
[27.] Similar to *I.reticulata* but bulb almost spherical, producing numerous bulblets. Fls light blue with few markings, crest bright yellow, narrow.

I.iberica Hoffm.
[3.] To 20cm. Rhiz. compact. Lvs 2–6mm diam., grey-green, linear-falcate. Fls solitary, to 6.5cm, tube to 3.5cm, falls reflexed from base, white densely veined brown and spotted, signal patch black-brown, velvety, beard hair purple-brown, standards to 8.5cm, erect, white to pale lilac, obscurely veined. Late spring. SW Asia. ssp. *elegantissima* (Sosn.) Fed. & Takht. Falls cream to ivory spotted and veined maroon, blade deflexed almost vertically, standards white, sometimes veined brown at base. Spring. NE Turkey, NW Iran, Russia. ssp. *lycotis* (Woron.) Takht. Fls densely veined purple on pale ground, falls not deflexed to vertical but curving out at an angle, signal patch velvety, brown. Spring. NE Iraq, SE Turkey, NW & W Iran, Russia.

I.imbricata Lindl.
[1.] Similar to *I.taochia* but larger, to 60cm; lvs flat, apex narrowed abruptly to a short pointed tip; fls larger, 7–9cm diam., always yellow with yellow beard. Spring–summer. Iran to E Transcaucasia.

I.innominata Henderson.
[13.] To 25cm. Lvs slender, 2–4mm wide, dark green, base tinged purple. Fls 1–2 per stem, 6.5–7.5cm diam., cream-yellow to orange or pink-lilac to dark purple, veins darker; bracts sheathing to 3cm; tube to 6.5mm, falls to 6.5mm, margins of falls and standards frilly, standards shorter, style lobes broad, margins toothed. Summer. W US. Used in hybridizing, see section on Pacific Coast hybrids. 'Lilacina': fls lavender. 'Lutea': fls yellow. 'Spinners': fls soft brown-yellow, veined and marked rich brown.

Japanese Irises. See *I.ensata, I.laevigata.*

I.japonica Thunb.
[7.] 45–80cm. Rhiz. stoloniferous; stems erect, branched. Lvs to 45cm, in fans, ensiform, shiny green. Fls 3–4 per branch, 4–5cm diam., appearing flattened due to spreading perianth lobes, margins fringed, white to light blue-lilac; falls 2cm wide, blade with orange frilly crest on purple blotched area, standards lilac. Spring. C China, Japan. 'Ledger's Variety': lvs dark green, glossy; fls frilled, white, marked purple, crest orange. 'Rudolph Spring': fls pale purple-blue marked orange. 'Variegata' ('Aphrodite'): lvs conspicuously striped white and marked purple.

I.jordana Dinsm.
[3.] To 45cm. Lvs erect, concealing stem. Fls 12–15cm diam., solitary, white densely streaked and dotted purple, maroon or rosy pink, signal patch velvety purple-black, beard hairs long, cream-yellow. Seeds with large aril. Spring. Israel.

I.juncea Poir.
[25.] To 40cm; bulb tunic shell-like, splitting at apex into stiff points. Lvs to 60cm×0.5–3mm, slender, rush-like, appearing in autumn. Fls usually 2, scented, bright yellow; tube 3.5–5cm, fall blade orbicular, 2.5cm wide; standards oblanceolate, spreading, shorter than falls, 12mm wide. Summer. N Africa, S Spain & Sicily. var. *mermieri* Lynch. Fls sulphur-yellow. var. *numidica* anon. Fls lemon-yellow. var. *pallida* Lynch. Fls large, soft yellow.

I.junonia Schott & Kotschy.
[1.] 50–65cm, similar to *I.germanica*. Lvs grey-green, 30–35×4–5cm, deciduous. Infl. 4-branched; fls smaller than *I.germanica*, white or cream to dark yellow, pale blue to lavender, beard yellow, haft white, often veined brown-purple. Early summer. Cilicia.

I.kaempferi Sieb. See *I.ensata.*

I.kamaonensis Wallich ex D. Don.
[6.] To 45cm. Rhiz. thick, knobbly, roots fleshy. Lvs to 45×1cm, shorter at flowering, more or less linear. Fls fragrant, 4–5cm diam., stemless; tube 5–7.5cm, cylindrical, purple-

striped; falls lilac mottled darker, ovate-oblong, beard dense, hairs white, tips yellow; standards paler, upright, clawed. Seeds with fleshy aril. Late spring. Himalaya.

I.kashmiriana Bak.
[1.] To 125cm. Stems robust, 1–2-branched. Lvs to 60×2–3cm, straight, glaucous, conspicuously ribbed. Fls 2–3 per branch, 10–12cm diam., fragrant, white to pale lilac-blue; bracts green, to 11cm; tube 2.5cm; falls to 9.5cm, beard dense, hairs white, tipped yellow; standards to 9cm, small beard on lower part; lateral fls pedicellate. Spring. Kashmir, Afghanistan. 'Kashmir White' ('Alba'): fls white.

I.kerneriana Bak.
[1.] Rhiz. slender, with fibrous remains of old lf bases. Lvs linear, to 5mm wide, slightly shorter than flowering stems. Fls 2–4 per branch, 7–10cm diam., deep cream to pale yellow; bracts somewhat inflated; fall blade elliptic, to 2cm wide, with deep yellow central blotch, strongly recurved, tip almost touching stem, haft narrow, 5mm; standards erect, margins wavy, notched. Fr. to 3×1.5cm, squat, beak to 1cm. Summer. N & C Turkey.

I.kirkwoodii Chaudhary.
[3.] To 75cm. Lvs curved, drooping, 1–1.5cm wide. Fls 8–12cm diam., white to pale green, dotted and veined dark purple, falls to 8cm, ovate, signal patch round, dark purple, beard hairs long, purple to maroon; standards pale blue, veins and speckling darker. Late spring. N Syria, N Turkey. var. **macrotepala** Chaudhary. Falls larger than species type, c10cm, beard purple and/or gold. ssp. **calcarea** Dinsm. ex Chaudhary. Fls 8cm diam.; falls obovate, signal patch velvety, maroon, beard hairs sparse, long, maroon, standards light blue, veined darker purple.

I.klattii Kem.-Nat. See *I.spuria* ssp. *musulmanica*.

I.× kochii Kerner ex Stapf.
Similar to *I.germanica* but to 45cm, 1–2-branched; falls and standards similarly coloured deep blue-purple; fall haft lightly veined brown-purple. N Italy. Possibly a hybrid of *I.germanica × I.pallida* ssp. *cengialtii*.

I.kolpakowskiana Reg.
[27.] To 25cm. Bulb yellow, tunics netted; roots not fleshy. Lvs 3–4, narrow, channelled, short at flowering, later to 25cm. Fls on short stems, usually pale lilac-blue to palest purple; tube to 7cm; fall blade dark red-purple, ridge yellow-orange, haft white. Late winter. Russia.

I.kopetdagensis (Vved.) B. Mathew & Wendelbo.
[26.] Similar to *I.drepanophylla* but with lf margins more or less glabrous and fall haft narrower and shallowly U-shaped in section (not winged). NE Iran and adjacent Russia, NW & C Afghanistan.

I.koreana Nak.
[8.] Similar to *I.minutiflora*. Lvs to 35×1.3cm, veins prominent. Flowering stem shorter than lvs; fls 2, flat, tube long, falls obovate, to 4cm wide, horizontal, yellow, hafts ridged, standards elliptic, nearly erect, apex notched, yellow, haft narrow, suffused brown. Spring. Korea (NE Manchurian Plateau).

I.korolkowii Reg.
[4.] 40–60cm. Rhiz. thick, stoloniferous, with fibrous lf base remains. Lvs linear, 0.5–1cm wide, base tinged purple. Fls 2–3 per spathe, 6–8cm diam., appearing elongated, cream-white lightly veined deep maroon, falls oblong, to 4×2.5cm, acute, deflexed, signal patch dark green to black-brown, beards inconspicuous, standards acute, erect. Early summer. Russia, NE Afghanistan. 'Concolor': fls bright blue-purple. 'Violacea': fls cream veined red-violet.

I.kuschakewiczii B. Fedtsch.
[26.] 10–15cm. Bulb tunic papery. Lvs 4–5, enclosing short flowering stem, dark green, channelled, 1–1.5cm wide, margin white. Fls 1–4, 6.5–8cm diam., palest violet; tube 3.5–4.5cm; fall crest white, dark violet markings to sides, haft slightly winged; standards 3-lobed. Spring. C Asia.

I.kuschkensis Grey-Wilson & B. Mathew.
[26.] Similar to *I.lineata* and *I.darwasica*; 30–50cm. Rhiz. stout. Lvs 6–8mm wide, erect. Fls 2, 6cm diam., purple-bronze, veins of a deeper colour, falls and standards bearded pale purple, falls broad, rounded, to 5cm, standards to 4.5cm. Spring. NW Afghanistan.

I.lactea Pall.
[21.] 6–40cm. Rhiz. tough. Lf base remains red-brown. Roots wiry. Lvs to 40×0.3cm, ribbed. Fls 2–3, fragrant, 4–6cm diam., blue to purple, tube 2–3mm, falls oblanceolate, to 2cm wide, white-yellow veined darker, standards shorter and narrower than falls; ovary long, narrow, beaked, ribbed. Early summer. S Russia, China, Mongolia, Himalaya.

I.lacustris Nutt.
[7.] Similar to *I.cristata* but generally smaller, to 5cm; rhiz. more compact. Lvs to 1cm wide. Fls sky blue; to 2cm, crest frilly, gold, falls white-blotched. Late spring–summer. N America.

I.laevigata Fisch.
[15.] Aquatic or marginal, to 45cm. Similar to *I.ensata* but stouter. Stems sometimes 1-branched. Lvs 1.5–4cm, without prominent midvein. Fls 2–4, 8–10cm diam., blue-violet, tube to 2cm; fall haft pale yellow, standard erect, smaller than falls. Summer–autumn. E Asia. Some 30 cvs; fls in a range of colours from white through yellow and pink to blue. 'Alba': fls white, style branches mauve. 'Albopurpurea': falls purple, mottled white around edges, standards white. 'Atropurpurea': fls red-purple. 'Colcherensis': fls white, fall centre blue. 'Lilacina': fls light blue. 'Midnight': fls very deep blue, pet. lined white. 'Montrosa': fls very large, deep blue centred white. 'Mottled Beauty': fls white, falls spotted pale blue. 'Regal': fls red-purple. 'Rose Queen': fls soft old rose; falls broad, drooping. 'Snowdrift': fls double, white, style branches light violet. 'Variegata': lvs striped green and white; fls pale blue.

I.lamancei hort. ex Lynch. See *I.brevicaulis*.

I.latifolia Mill. (*I.xiphioides* Ehrh.). ENGLISH IRIS.
[26.] To 80cm. Lvs appear in spring, to 65×0.8cm, channelled, grey-white above. Fls 1–2 per bract pair, 8–10cm diam., violet-blue, tube 5mm, falls with central yellow blotch, broad, ovate-oblong, to 7.5cm, haft winged, standards to 6cm, oblanceolate. Late spring–summer. Spain and Pyrenees. Many cvs including: 'Almona': fls light blue-lavender. 'Blue Giant': standards blue-purple, speckled darker, falls deep blue. 'Isabella': fls pink-mauve. 'La Nuit': fls dark purple-red. 'Mansfield': fls magenta-purple. 'Mont Blanc': fls white. 'Queen of the Blues': fls rich purple-blue.

I.lazica Albov.
[23.] To 25cm. Rhiz. tough, branching. Lvs evergreen, in fans, to 1.5cm wide. Fls sessile, tube 7–10cm, falls purple-blue, blade orbicular, spotted lavender with central yellow stripe, haft narrow, white, dotted and veined lavender; standards lavender, not marked. Autumn–spring. NE Turkey, Russia.

I.leichtlinii Reg. See *I.stolonifera*.
I.lepida Heuff. See *I.variegata*.
I.leucographa Kerner. See *I.variegata*.

I.lineata Fost. ex Reg.
[4.] 15–35cm; stolons short. Lvs erect, 3–6mm wide. Fls green-yellow, veins brown-purple, beard tinted blue, falls and standards to 5cm, narrow, apices pointed. SW Russia (Tadjikstan), NE Afghanistan.

I.linifolia (Reg.) O. Fedtsch.
[26.] Bulb tunics papery; roots short, much-swollen. Stem 5–10cm. Lvs curved, linear, 4–7mm wide, channelled. Fls 1–2, pale yellow; tube 4cm; fall blade darker, crest divided white, haft 6mm wide, unwinged, margins almost parallel; standards much reduced, to 1cm, deflexed, 3-lobed. Spring. Russia.

I.loczyi Kanitz.
[20.] Unbearded dwarf, tufted to 30cm. Rhiz. small, nearly vertical, persistent lf bases forming tussocks to 40cm wide. Lvs 10–30×0.2–0.4cm, tough. Fls 4–6cm diam., tube 10–14cm; falls pale cream, veins violet, centre tinged yellow, standards light blue to purple. Fr. subsessile, stout, beak slender. NE Iran to C Asia.

I.longipetala Herb.
[14.] 30–60cm. Rhiz. spreading, robust. Lvs dark green, 6–9mm wide, ensiform, equalling or slightly shorter than flowering stems; flowering stems unbranched, solid, thick. Fls 3–8 in a head at the end of the stem, 6–7cm diam., white veined violet, tube 5–13mm, funnel-shaped, falls drooping, to 3cm wide, sometimes with a bright yellow signal area, standards erect, veins more sparse, to 7.5×2cm, notched. Fr. capsule tapering to both ends. Late spring–summer. W US.

I.longiscapa Ledeb.
[5.] Similar to *I.falcifolia* but lvs more or less straight, narrower, 0.5–1.5mm wide. Fl. 4cm diam. Soviet C Asia.

I.lorea Jank.
Differs from *I.sintenisii* in lvs paler green; style arms green (papery in *I.sintenisii*). Italy.

I.lortetii Barbey.
[3.] To 50cm. Lvs linear, to 1.5cm wide, tips abruptly narrowed, thin. Fls solitary, 8–9cm diam.; falls 7.5cm wide, pale grey-lilac, spotted and striped red-brown, signal patch deep crimson, beard hairs sparse, red, standards to 10cm wide, upright and curving inwards, pale-grey, finely veined and dotted red-brown, margins wavy. Seeds with large aril. Late spring. S Lebanon.

Lousiana Hybrids Hybrids of the Series *Hexagonae* (including *I.fulva*) are becoming increasingly popular in the US. Mostly tender, the flowers come in a wide range of colours including shades of yellow, pink, red, brown, purple and blue. 'Black Gamecock': habit vigorous; fls blue-black with line signal. 'Mme. Dorothea K. Williamson' (*I.fulva* × *I.brevicaulis*): hardy, vigorous; stems horizontal; fls very large, plum-purple. 'Gold Reserve': fls golden-orange veined red. 'May Roy': standards pale pink, falls pink tinged purple. 'Roll Call': to 90cm; fls violet with green styles. 'Sea Wasp': to 110cm; fls blue with yellow line signal.

I.lupina Fost. See *I.sari*.
I.× lurida Ait. See *I.× sambucina*.
I.lusitanica Ker-Gawl. See *I.xiphium* 'Lusitanica'.

I.lutescens Lam. (*I.chamaeris* Bertol.)
[1.] Variable quick-growing, to 30cm. Rhiz. stout. Lvs 30×0.5–2.5cm, equitant, straight to curved. Fls 1–2, 6–8cm diam., yellow, violet, purple, white or bicoloured, bracts to 5.5cm, tube to 3.5cm, falls oblong-spathulate, to 7.5×2cm, beard yellow, standards oblong, erect or converging, to 7.5×2.5cm, margins crisped. Early to mid-spring. NE Spain, S France and Italy. 'Campbellii': habit very dwarf to 15cm; fls bright violet-blue, falls darker. 'Jackanapes': fls blue and white. 'Nancy Lindsay': habit dwarf; fls pale yellow.

I.macrosiphon Torr.
[13.] 15–25cm. Lvs slender, linear, to 30cm, finely ribbed, grey-green. Fls fragrant, 3.5–8.5cm, 2 per stem, 5–6cm diam., enclosed within contiguous bracts, scented, white to yellow or light lavender to dark violet, veins usually fine, tube 3–9cm, widened at apex, falls obovate, wedge-shaped, 2cm wide, signal area white. Early summer. W US.

I.magnifica Vved.
[26.] 30–60cm. Bulb tunics papery. Lvs many, remote, 3–5cm wide, channelled, pale green, lustrous. Fls 3–7, to 8cm diam., pink-lilac, tube 4–4.5cm, falls yellow at centre, crest white, fall haft widely winged, to 2.5cm wide, standards obovate, to 3cm, horizontal to deflexed. Late spring. Russia.

I.mangaliae Prodan. See *I.variegata*.

I.mariae Barbey.
[3.] 15–25cm. Rhiz. small, clad with fibrous bases of old lvs.

Lvs 3–6mm wide, curved. Fls 8–10cm diam., lilac to pink, fall haft, beard and signal patch dark purple, standards larger than falls, veins dark. Seeds with large aril. Spring. Israel.

I.marschalliana anon. See *I.pontica*.

I.marsica I. Ricci & Colasante.
[1.] To 80cm. Rhiz. stout. Lvs equitant, to 5cm wide. Flowering stem branched; bracts to 6.5cm, fls 8–9cm diam., pale to dark violet with veining on fall haft, tube to 3.5cm, beard yellow or white. Late spring-early summer. C Appennines.

I.masiae Stapf ex Fost.
[22.] Similar to *I.grant-duffii* but taller, 25–70cm. Lvs 6–8, rigid, longer and narrower, 60×0.3–0.5cm. Fl. seg. smaller and narrower, falls and standards to 6cm, blue-violet, veins conspicuous, fall centre and haft white. Mid–late spring. SE Turkey, N & C Inland Syria and adjacent Iraq.

I.meda Stapf.
[3.] To 25cm. Lvs slender, to 4mm wide, straight to curved, glaucous. Fls solitary, 5–7cm diam., seg. margins wavy, cream to lilac, heavily veined golden brown; signal patch large, deep brown, beard dense, yellow, standards longer than falls, erect. Seeds with large aril. Spring. W Iran.

I.melanosticta Bornm.
Similar to *I.masiae* but fls yellow, fall blade thickly lined with black. Spring. S Syria.

I.mellita Janka. See *I.suaveolens*.

I.mesopotamica Dykes.
[1.] Similar to *I.germanica*. Lvs dark green, lightly tinged grey, 5cm wide. Flowering stems to 120cm, branched; bracts dry and papery toward apex; fls pale blue, centre tinged red, falls obovate, beard white to orange, standards obovate, paler than falls.

I.microglossa Wendelbo.
[26.] 10–40cm. Bulb tunics papery; roots long and thickened. Lvs to 25×1.5–2.5cm, blue to grey-green above, margins white, finely hairy, internodes visible. Fls 1–4, c4.5–5.5cm diam., light blue-lavender to almost white, crest white to light yellow, tube 3–4.5cm, fall haft wings broad, standards horizontal, to 2cm, lanceolate. Spring. NE Afghanistan.

I.milesii Fost.
[7.] Rhiz. fat, green. Flowering stems branched, 30–75cm. Lvs die back in winter, in fans, 30–60×4–7cm, pale green. Fls 6–8cm diam., short-lived, pink-lilac, falls mottled darker purple, spreading, margins often wavy, fringed, yellow or orange, standards oblique. Summer. Himalaya.

I.minutiflora Mak.
[8.] Dwarf, to 10cm. Rhiz. thin, wiry. Lvs linear, 15cm×2–3mm at flowering, lengthening to 40cm, ribbed. Fls solitary, to 2.5cm diam., flattened, tube 2.5cm, falls spathulate, yellow, sometimes spotted brown-purple, standards smaller, lighter yellow, spreading, haft suffused brown. Fr. triangular in section. Spring. Korea, China, Japan.

I.mississippiensis Alexander. See *I.brevicaulis* 'Mississippiensis'.

I.missouriensis Nutt.
[14.] To 75cm. Similar to *I.longipetala* but lvs more slender, to 7mm wide, absent in winter, usually taller than fls. Fls 2–3 per bract pair, 5–8cm diam., on pedicels to 20cm, white, lilac, lavender or blue; falls obovate, deflexed, veined, signal patch yellow; standards oblanceolate, upright. Late spring-summer. W US. 'Alba': fls white.

I.× monnieri DC. (Possibly a hybrid of *I.orientalis* × *I.xanthospuria*.)
Similar to *I.orientalis*; to 120cm; stems stout. Lvs to 60cm, lanceolate. Fls lemon-yellow, fragrant; fall blade rounded, 4.5cm wide, apex notched; standards spreading, oblanceolate-spathulate, 7.5×2.5cm; style arms short, recurved, broadly triangular. Summer. Turkey, Crete.

I.munzii R. Fost.
[13.] Robust, to 75cm. Lvs 1.5–2cm wide, grey-green. Fls 2–4, 6–7.5cm diam., light blue to dark red-purple, veins often darker; bracts widely spreading; tube 7–10mm; falls and standard margins often undulate-crisped. Summer. W US.

I.musulmanica Fomin. See *I.spuria* ssp. *musulmanica*.

I.narbutii O. Fedtsch.
[26.] To 15cm. Bulb long and thin, tunics tough; roots slightly swollen. Lvs 4–6, deep green, glossy, curved, channelled, enclosing stem. Fls 1–2, 5cm diam., tube 4–5cm, falls pale yellow to light violet, blotched deep velvety violet, crest white on yellow area, haft to 7mm wide, unwinged, standards obovate, deflexed, to 3.5cm, bright violet. C Asia.

I.nectarifera Güner.
[3.] To 40cm. Rhiz. bearing long, thick stolons. Lvs to 1cm wide, curved. Fls 8–9cm diam., ivory to pale yellow, finely but conspicuously veined bronze or chestnut, signal patch maroon, beard slender, dense, yellow. Spring. Syria, Iraq.

I.× neglecta Hornem. See *I.× sambucina*.

I.×nelsonii Randolph. (*I.fulva* × *I.giganticaerulea*.) ABBEVILLE IRIS.
Robust, rhizomatous; stems branched, to 110cm, leafy. Lvs 50–75×1–3cm, tips decurved, pale green. Fls to 12cm diam., red to purple or yellow, falls 6–8cm, with or without signal patch, reflexed, standards reflexed.

I.nertschinskia anon. See *I.sanguinea*.

I.nicolai Vved.
[26.] To 15cm. Bulb tunics papery; roots very swollen. Lvs hardly developed at flowering, sheathing stem, later to 25×5–6cm on elongated stalk, tips curved in. Fls 1–3, 5–6cm diam., slate-blue to white, tube to 11cm, fall tip blotched dark purple, crest golden with dark violet vein either side, haft margin turned down, standards obovate, horizontal, margins rolled in, to 2.5cm, flushed purple. Spring. Russia, NE Afghanistan.

I.nigricans Dinsm.
[3.] Rhiz. small; stem to 30cm. Lvs narrow, strongly recurved, sheathing base of stem. Fls solitary, 8–10cm diam., white ground heavily veined brown-purple, falls obovate, haft broad, signal patch black, beard dark purple, on pale ground, standards oval, white, heavily veined deep purple. Seeds with large aril. Spring. Jordan.

I.odontostyla B. Mathew & Wendelbo.
[26.] To 13cm. Bulb long-necked, tunic papery, reaching above ground; roots wiry. Lvs 4–5, hiding stem, later to 18×1.5cm, channelled, margins white. Fls solitary, 5–5.5cm diam., grey-violet; tube 4cm; fall blade rounded, hafts widely winged, crest yellow-orange on white ground; style arms with toothed lobes. Afghanistan.

I.orchioides Carr.
[26.] Bulb tunics papery; roots fleshy. Lvs 5–7, 18×1–3cm, straight to curved, pale green, channelled, concealing stem until after flowering. Fls 3–4, 5cm diam., light yellow suffused mauve, tube 3–6cm, fall haft broadly winged, 2cm wide, crest deep yellow, toothed, on dark yellow ground veined green or mauve, standards to 15mm, trilobed or linear. Russia (Syr Daryn and Tien Shan mountains). *I.orchioides* of gardens is usually *I.bucharica*.

I.orchioides hort. non Carr. See *I.bucharica*.

I.orientalis Mill.
[18.] To 90cm, branched. Lvs to 90×1–2cm. Fls 2–3 per pair of papery bracts, 10cm diam., white; fall blade rounded, signal area large, yellow, haft narrow, slightly pubesc., standards to 8.5cm, erect. Summer. NE Greece, W Turkey.

I.orientalis Thunb. non Mill. See *I.sanguinea*.

Pacific Coast or **Californian Irises**. (*I.douglasiana* × *I.innominata*, etc.)
'Arnold Sunrise': fls white flushed blue, fall marked with

orange. 'Banbury Fair': standards off-white, falls pale lavender flecked lavender at centre. 'Blue Ballerina': fls white, falls marked with purple. 'Broadleigh Rose': fls marked with shades of pink. 'Lavender Royal': fls lavender with darker flushes.

I.palaestina (Bak.) Boiss.
[26.] Similar to *I.planifolia* but fls usually somewhat transparent, green-white or blue-tinted, stigma not bilobed. Winter. E Mediterranean; coastal Israel, Lebanon.

I.pallida Lam. DALMATIAN IRIS.
[1.] Stems branched, to 120cm. Lvs glaucous, 20–60×1–4cm, usually not deciduous. Fls 2–6, fragrant, 8–12cm diam., soft lilac-blue, bracts silvery, papery; beard yellow. Late spring-early summer. W Yugoslavia. 'Argentea Variegata': Lvs conspicuously striped blue-green and white. 'Aurea Variegata' ('Aurea', 'Variegata'): lvs striped yellow. ssp. *cengialtii* (Ambr.) Fost. 30–45cm; lvs greener, usually deciduous; fls deep blue-purple, bracts papery, brown, beard hairs white, tipped orange or yellow. NE Italy.

I.pamphylica Hedge.
[27.] 10–20cm. Bulb tunics netted. Lvs 4-angled, to 55cm after flowering. Fl. seg. narrow; falls deep brown-purple to green, mottled purple or olive green, blotched bright yellow in blade centre, haft green, veined purple, standards light blue to green, base dappled purple-brown, style arms arched. Fr. pendent. Late winter-spring. SW Turkey.

I.panormitana Tod. See *I.pseudopumila*.

I.paradoxa Steven.
[3.] 10–25cm. Lvs linear, falcate, 2–4mm wide. Fls showy, tube to 2cm, falls to 4cm, oblong, horizontal, much smaller than standards, pale purple, beard very dense, velvety, black-purple, veins black-purple, standards to 10cm, rounded, apex notched, erect, white densely dotted deep blue-violet giving dark overall appearance; style branches 2–3cm. Seeds with large aril. E Turkey, N Iran, Russia. f. **atrata** Grossh. Falls and standards violet-black. f. **paradoxa** Falls purple-black, standards dark violet. f. **choschab** (Hoog.) B. Mathew & Wendelbo. Falls narrow, black-purple-maroon, banded pale violet; standards palest mauve heavily veined purple. f. **mirabilis** Gawrilenko. Falls golden yellow, beard dark, yellow as orange; standards pale yellow and/or pale blue.

I.persica L.
[26.] Dwarf. Bulb tunics papery; roots thin. Lvs 3–4 in tufts, to 10×0.5–1.5cm, linear, recurved, green above, grey beneath, margin white. Fls 1–4 on very short stem, 5–6cm diam., violet-scented, somewhat translucent, colour variable, green-blue, silver, yellow or brown, tube 6–8cm, falls oblong-spathulate, 1cm wide, crest yellow, blade dark purple-brown, haft wide-winged, standards horizontal, to 2.5cm. Winter–spring. S & SE Turkey, N Syria, NE Iraq.

I.petrana Dinsm.
[3.] Similar to *I.nigricans* but lvs straighter, fls smaller, to 8cm diam., dark lilac, veins sparse, signal patch very dark black-purple, beard dense, hairs tipped purple; style arms brown-lilac. Jordan.

I.planifolia (Mill.) Fiori & Paol. (*I.alata* Poir.; *I.scorpioides* Desf.).
[26.] 10–15cm. Bulbs large, tunics papery; roots fleshy. Lvs many, densely arranged enclosing stem, lanceolate, acuminate, to 30×1–3cm, glossy green. Fls 1–3, 6–7cm diam., lilac purple, tube 8–15cm, falls oblong, to 5×2.5cm, darker veins around yellow crest, haft winged; standard oblanceolate, to 2.5cm, horizontal, margins usually toothed. Winter. Spain and Portugal, Sardinia, Sicily, Crete, N Africa. 'Alba': fls white. 'Marginata': fls deep blue, fall margins white.

I.polysticta Diels.
[18.] To 30cm. Rhiz. apex clad in old lf bases. Lvs 2–4mm wide, stiff, grooved, as tall as stem. Fls 6cm diam., blue-mauve, tube wide, falls spreading, narrow, to 1cm wide, pale,

veins prominent, haft centre spotted, standards also very narrow; ovary beaked. Summer. China.

I.pontica Zapal. (*I.humilis* Bieb.; *I.marschalliana* anon.).
[18.] Dwarf, tuft-forming. Lvs 20–40×0.25cm, grassy, exceeding flowering stem. Flowering stem 4–10cm; fls solitary, 5–6cm diam., violet, veined darker, fall blade orbicular, haft winged, centre pale green-yellow veined violet. Fr. produced near ground level. C & NE Romania, W Ukraine, Caucasus.

I.porphyrochrysa Wendelbo.
[26.] To 10cm. Bulb tunics papery; roots long, thick. Lvs 3–5, 10–15×0.5–1cm, grey-green, hiding stem. Fls 1–3, to 5.5cm diam., bronze; tube to 4cm; fall blade dark yellow, crest orange, haft narrow, unwinged; standards bronze, reflexed, much-reduced, bristle-like. Afghanistan.

I.prismatica Pursh ex Ker-Gawl.
[17.] Rhiz. slender. Lvs grassy, to 70×0.2–0.7cm, glaucous. Flowering stems solid, wiry, to 80cm, with a branch with solitary fl. and a terminal cluster of 2–3 fls; fls to 7cm diam.; pale violet veined blue; pedicels to 4cm; tube to 3mm, falls spreading, blade ovate, haft green-white veined violet, standards oblanceolate, suberect. Fr. capsule to 5cm on elongated pedicels. Summer. E US.

I.pseudacorus L. (*I.pseudacorus* var. *acoriformis* (Boreau) Lynch). YELLOW FLAG.
[15.] Robust, marginal or aquatic. Stems branched, to 2m. Rhiz. stout, clad in remains of old lvs. Lvs to 90×3cm, grey-green, midrib prominent. Fls 4–12, 5–12cm diam., bright yellow veined brown or violet; tube to 1.5cm, falls rounded, to 4cm wide, blotched deeper yellow; standards oblanceolate, erect, to 3cm. Early–midsummer. Europe to W Siberia, Caucasus, Turkey, Iran, N Africa. 'Alba': fls creamy white, with brown veins near tips. 'Gigantea': stems to 2.5m; fls large, golden yellow. 'Golden Fleece': fls deep yellow without darker veins. 'Mandschurica': fls matt yellow. 'Variegata': lvs striped yellow at first. var. *bastardii* (Boreau) Lynch. Fls pale yellow; fall blade not blotched deeper yellow. See *I.ensata* for hybrids.

I.pseudacorus var. *acoriformis* (Boreau) Lynch. See *I.pseudacorus*.

I.pseudocaucasica Grossh.
[26.] To 13cm. Similar to *I.aucheri* but lvs grey-green beneath, fls to 4, 5–6cm diam., pale blue or green yellow, fall crest yellow, fall blade-winged. Early summer. SE Turkey, NE Iraq, N & NW Iran, Russia.

I.pseudopumila Tineo (*I.panormitana* Tod.).
[1.] Similar to *I.pumila* but taller, to 25cm. Lvs grey-green, persisting, to 1.5cm wide, curved or straight. Flowering stem to 3cm; fls solitary, 6–8cm diam., shades of purple, yellow or white, sometimes bicoloured, bracts swollen, to 12cm, enclosing tube, tube to 7.5cm. Spring. Sicily, Malta, Gozo, SE Italy, Balkans.

I.pumila L. (*I.aequiloba* Ledeb.; *I.taurica* Lodd.).
[1.] Dwarf, to 15cm. Lvs almost straight, grey-green, to 15×1.5cm, dying away in winter. Fls usually solitary, rarely 3 in some forms, mostly purple-violet, some white yellow or blue; bracts to 10cm, enclosing tube, tube 5–10cm, beard blue or yellow. Spring. SE & EC Europe to Urals. A parent of the dwarf bearded cvs. var. *elongata* anon. Stems longer than in type, to 12cm.

I.purdyi Eastw.
[13.] To 35cm. Lvs glossy deep green, base suffused pink. Fls 2, 8cm diam., appearing flat due to spreading seg., cream, sometimes tinged mauve, tube 3–5cm, falls veined and spotted purple or pink. N California.

I.reginae Horvat. See *I.variegata*.
Regeliocyclus Hybrids. See Aril Irises.

I.regis-uzziae Feinbrun.
[26.] To 10cm. Lvs 5–7, broad, to 4cm wide, crowded together at base, curved, hiding stem. Fls 1–2, 5–6cm diam.,

light blue, blue-mauve or somewhat transparent yellow-green; tube 4cm; falls with central yellow ridge, haft wing wide; standards horizontal, to 2.5cm, spathulate. Winter–early spring. Israel, S Jordan.

I.reichenbachii Heuff. (*I.balkana* Janka; *I.bosniaca* Beck; *I.skorpilii* Velen.).
[1.] Similar to *I.suaveolens* but taller, to 30cm; lvs wider, to 1.5cm wide; fls terminal, 1–2, sometimes also one lateral, 6cm diam., yellow or purple-brown, veins often darker, tube shorter, to 2.5cm; beard white, tipped blue, purple or yellow, standards large, often wider than falls. Spring–early summer. Balkans.

I.reticulata Bieb.
[27.] Bulb pear-shaped with netted tunic and producing bulblets after fls. Lvs 4-angled, very narrow, to 30×0.2cm, synanthous or hysteranthous. Fls solitary, sessile, dark violet blue to paler blue to red-purple; tube 4–7cm; falls 5cm, often yellow-ridged, haft 2.5cm; standards erect, oblanceolate, 6cm. Early spring. N & S Turkey, NE Iraq, N & W Iran, Russia.

Reticulata Hybrids (derived from *I.histrioides* and *I.reticulata* and hybrids between them). 'Alba': fls white. 'Cantab': fls very pale Cambridge blue, crested yellow. 'Clairette': standards sky-blue, falls deep blue marked white. 'Edward': fls dark blue marked orange. 'Gordon': fls light blue with orange blotch on white ground lightly striped blue. 'Harmony': standards blue, falls royal blue blotched yellow and white. 'Ida': standards light blue, falls paler, blotch pale yellow on white ground slightly spotted blue. 'Jeannine': fls violet, falls blotched orange with white-and-violet striped patches; fragrant. 'Joyce': standard lavender-blue, falls deep sky-blue with yellow markings and grey-brown stripes. 'J.S. Dijt': fls dark red-purple; fragrant. 'Natascha': fls white tinged blue, falls veined green with golden-yellow blotch. 'Pauline': fls purple-violet with dark purple falls blotched blue and white. 'Purple Gem': fls violet, falls black-purple blotched purple and white. 'Royal Blue': standard deep velvet blue, falls blotched yellow. 'Spring Time': standards pale blue, falls dark blue tipped white, with purple spots and yellow midrib. 'Violet Beauty': standards velvet-purple, falls deep violet with orange crest.

I.× robusta E. Anderson. (*I.versicolor* × *I.virginica*.)
Intermediate between parents. 'Gerard Darby': lvs rich purple at base; fls blue borne on purple stems.

I.× rosaliae Prodan. (*I.variegata* × *I.pallida*.)
Used extensively in early breeding programmes but probably no longer in cult.

I.rosenbachiana Reg.
[26.] Similar to *I.nicolai* but lvs bright glossy green, to 5cm at flowering, later to 25cm, tips curving outwards. Fls 1–3, light purple; falls blotch deep purple, crest orange. Winter–early spring. C Asia. var. *baldschuanica* is smaller, with pale primrose flowers veined and blotched brown-purple.

I.rossii Bak.
[8.] Somewhat clump-forming, to 15cm. Rhiz. tough, thin; stolons short, bristly. Lvs linear, to 2.5mm, ribbed, glaucous beneath, equalling flowering stems, ultimately to 30cm. Fls solitary, 3–4cm diam., somewhat flat, bracts green, leaf-like, tube to 7cm, falls obovate, spreading, purple, haft short, white, veins and spots violet, centre suffused yellow, standards obovate, spreading, purple. Spring. N China, Korea, Japan.

I.rubromarginata Bak. See *I.suaveolens*.
I.rudskyi Horvat. See *I.variegata*.

I.ruthenica Ker-Gawl.
[10.] Forming grass-like tufts to 20cm. Rhiz. short-creeping. Lvs erect, bright green, 15cm at flowering, later to 30cm, 2.5mm wide. Fls 1–2, fragrant, short-stemmed, to 5cm diam.; falls broadly ovate, white marked violet, spreading, 1cm wide; standards erect, lanceolate, 6mm wide. Seeds pear-

shaped with white appendage. Late spring. E Europe through C Asia to China and Korea.

I.samariae Dinsm.
[3.] Similar to *I.lortetii* but fls to 10cm diam. on stems to 30cm; falls cream, veined and spotted purple, not as reflexed; beard brown-yellow to purple; standards purple-pink. Late spring. NW Jordan.

I.× sambucina L. (*I.× lurida* Ait.; *I.× neglecta* Hornem.; *I.× squalens* L.). (*I.variegata × I.pallida.*)
Rhiz. stout. Stem to 60cm, branched. Fls many, bracts green, suffused purple, falls red or violet-brown, haft strongly veined, beard orange or yellow, standards violet-brown, often tinged yellow. Summer. N Italy, Balkans.

I.sanguinea Hornem. ex Donn (*I.orientalis* Thunb. non Mill.; *I.extremorientalis* Koidz.; *I.nertschinskia* anon.).
[12.] Similar to *I.sibirica* but lvs as tall as or taller than unbranched flowering stems to 75cm. Fls 2, blue-purple marked white; bracts green at flowering. Fr. capsule thin. Early summer. SE Russia, Korea, Japan. 'Alba': fls white. 'Kobana': fls usually narrow, white. 'Snow Queen': fls ivory.

I.sari Schott ex Bak. (*I.lupina* Fost.).
[3.] To 30cm. Lvs 9×0.6–1.2cm at flowering. Fls solitary, 7–10cm; tube 4cm; falls lanceolate, 8×4cm, yellow or green, sometimes blue, veins brown-red, signal patch red-brown, margins wavy, beard yellow; standards wider and longer, ground colour as for falls, suffused red-brown, margins wavy. Late spring. C & S Turkey.

I.scariosa Willd. ex Link (*I.glaucescens* Bunge; *I.eulefeldii* Reg.).
[1.] Clump-forming, dwarf, to 20cm. Rhiz. clad in brown fibres. Lvs almost straight, pale glaucous green. Fls 2, 4–5cm diam., red-purple, lilac or pale yellow, bract dry, translucent, tube 3cm, purple-brown, fall veined deep red-purple or yellow, beard white on blade, yellow on haft. Spring. Russia.

I.schachtii Markgr.
[1.] Stems to 30cm, to 3-branched. Lvs glaucous. Fls solitary, to 6cm diam., green-yellow, beard yellow or blue, bracts green suffused purple, margins translucent, somewhat swollen, tube to 2cm, fall haft veined green, brown or purple. Spring. C Turkey.

I.schelkownikowii Fomin.
[1.] Dwarf, similar to *I.acutiloba* but fls fragrant, larger, lilac or fawn, veins darker, fine, signal patch purple, beard yellow, standards darker and larger than falls. Russia (Azerbaijan).

I.scorpioides Desf. See *I.planifolia*.

I.serotina Willk.
[25.] 40–60cm. Lvs narrow, channelled, appearing in autumn, dying before flowering; stem lvs small, bract-like, also dying before flowering. Fls 1–2 on unbranched stem, violet-blue, tube to 1cm, fall centre yellow, standard reduced, to 1cm, extremely narrow. Late summer. SE Spain.

I.setosa Pall. ex Link.
[11.] 15–90cm. Rhiz. stout, clad with old lf bases. Stems usually 2–3-branched; stems bracts with purple margins. Lvs to 50×2.5cm, deciduous, base suffused red. Fls to 15, 5–9cm diam., tube to 10mm, falls orbicular, 2.5cm diam., light blue-purple to purple, haft narrow, palest yellow, veins blue-purple, standards greatly reduced so that fls appear to have only 3 petals, bristle-like, erect. Late spring–early summer. Northeastern N America, E Russia, N Korea, Japan, Aleutian, Sakhalin & Kurile Is. to Alaska. 'Kosho-en': fls white. 'Nana': fls purple. f. **alpina** Komar. Stems short. Siberia. f. **platyrhyncha** Hult. Fls solitary, standards larger than in type. Alaska. f. **serotina** Komar. Fls solitary, sessile. Siberia. var. **arctica** (Eastw.) Dykes (*I.arctica* Eastw.). Dwarf; fls purple, white-variegated. Alaska. var. **nasuensis** Hara. Stems to 1m; lvs wider; fls larger. Japan. ssp. **canadensis** (Fost.) Hult. (*I.hookeri* G. Don). Dwarf; stems simple, to 15cm. Lvs few. Fls usually solitary, lavender-blue. Eastern N America. ssp.

hondoensis Honda. Stems to 75cm; fls large, rich-purple. ssp. **interior** (Anderson) Hult. Lvs narrow. Bracts violet, papery. Alaska.

I.shrevei Small. See *I.virginica* var. *shrevei*.

I.sibirica L.
[12.] Stems 1–2-branched, 50–120cm, taller than lvs. Lvs narrow, to 4mm wide. Fls to 5, to 7cm diam.; bracts brown at flowering; falls blue-purple, veined and marked white and gold, haft paler but darker-veined. Fr. shortly elliptic. Late spring–summer. C & E Europe, NE Turkey, Russia. 'Alba': fls white.

Siberian Hybrids (*I.sibirica × I.sanguinea*).
Over 150 cvs; fls in a wide range of colours from white and yellow through pink and red to violet. 'Ann Dasch': fls dark blue, falls marked yellow. 'Anniversary': fls white with yellow hafts. 'Butter and Sugar': fls white and yellow. 'Caesar's Brother': fls dark pansy purple. 'Ego': fls rich blue. 'Ewen': fls burgundy, tetraploid. 'Helen Astor': fls dark plum tinged rosy red, conspicuous white veins near throat. 'Mrs Rowe': fls small, grey-pink. 'Papillon': fls pale blue. 'Ruffled Velvet': fls red-purple marked yellow. 'Sparkling Rose': fls rose-mauve, falls flecked blue. 'Tropic Night': fls blue-violet. 'Wisley White': fls white.

I. ×sindpers Hoog. See *I.*'Sindpur'.

I.'Sindpur'. (*I.×sindpers* Hoog) (*I.aucheri × I.galactica.*)
Bulbous Juno iris to 25cm. Fls green-blue.

I.sintenisii Janka.
[18.] To 35cm. Rhiz. clad in old lf bases. Lvs linear, acuminate, 45×0.2–0.5cm. Fls 1–2, fragrant, to 6cm diam., fall blade elliptic, to 12mm wide, white, veins dense, purple, standards blue-purple, erect, oblanceolate. Fr. 3cm including beak, stout, beak slender. Summer. SE Europe, N Turkey, SW Russia. ssp. **brandzae** (Prodan) D.A. Webb & Chater (*I.brandzae* Prodan). Lvs 1.5–3.5mm wide. Fls less densely veined. Romania.

I.sisyrinchium L. See *Gynandriris sisyrinchium*.

I.skorpilii Velen. See *I.reichenbachii*.

I.sofarana Fost. (*I.susiana* f. *sofarana* (Fost.) Sealy).
[3.] 30–40cm. Lvs to 2.5cm wide. Fls to 13cm diam., cream, densely veined and spotted purple, signal patch rounded, black-purple, beard not dense, deep purple, standards paler than falls. Seeds with large aril. Late spring. Lebanon. f. **franjieh** Chaudhary. Fls white, veined and spotted yellow. ssp. **kasruwana** (Dinsm.) Chaudhary. Standards veined almost as densely as falls, signal patch pear-shaped.

I.speculatrix Hance.
[7.] 20–35cm. Lvs 100cm+, grassy, glossy green, conspicuously cross-veined, base white. Flowering stem small-lvd; fls 2, short-lived, to 5cm diam., tube 1cm, falls obovate, 1.5cm wide, mauve-lilac, ridge yellow, undissected, surrounded by white mottled purple, with purple border, standard spreading, obovate, 1.5cm wide, mauve-lilac. Spring–summer. SE China, Hong Kong.

I.sprengeri Siehe (*I.elizabethae* Siehe).
[3.] Dwarf, to 20cm. Rhiz. stoloniferous. Lvs 3–5mm wide. Fls to 6cm diam., yellow, veins purple-brown, tube to 1.5cm, signal patch large, red-purple, beard yellow; standards white, veins red-purple and black; style branches dull yellow, veined and spotted red-brown, to 3cm. Late spring. C Turkey.

I.spuria L.
[18.] To 50cm. Lvs 30×1.2cm. Fls violet-blue, yellow or white, fall blades rounded, to 2.5cm diam., standards oblanceolate. Summer. Europe, Asia, Algeria. ssp. **spuria**. To 80cm. Fls 6–8cm diam., lilac or blue-violet, veins violet; falls to 6cm, striped yellow in centre, haft exceeding blade. Summer. C Europe. ssp. **carthaliniae** (Fomin) B. Mathew. To 95cm. Fls 4–5, sky blue or white, veined deeper blue. Russia. ssp. **halophila** (Pall.) B. Mathew & Wendelbo (*I.halophila* Pall.). 40–85cm. Fls 4–8, 6–7cm diam., white, dull light yellow to bright yellow, veined deeper, falls to 6cm, haft longer than

blade. S Romania, Russia. ssp. *maritima* (Lam.) Fourn. 30–50cm. Fls to 4, bract green, falls to 4.5cm diam., veins dense, purple, blade deep purple, haft longer than blade, centrally striped green. SW Europe. ssp. *musulmanica* (Fomin) Takht. (*I.klattii* Kem.-Nat.; *I.musulmanica* Fomin; *I.violacea* Klatt). 40–90cm. Fls light violet to dark lavender-violet, veins darker, fails to 8cm, blade striped yellow, base tinged yellow, haft equalling or exceeding blade. E Turkey, N & NW Iran, Russia. ssp. *notha* (Bieb.) Asch. & Gräbn. 70–90cm. Fls 3–5, violet-blue, fall haft striped yellow, exceeding blade. Russia.

Spuria Group. Over 70 cvs; fls white and yellow through orange, red and brown to blue. 'Connoisseur': fls lavender blue. 'Elixir': fls saffron. 'Imperial Bronze': fls deep yellow veined brown. 'Protégé': standards blue, falls white veined blue. 'Red Oak': fls brown-purple. 'Shelford Hybrid': fls blue.

I.× squalens L. See *I.× sambucina*.

I.stenophylla Hausskn. ex Siehe & Bak. (*I.tauri* Siehe ex Mallet; *I.heldreichii* Siehe).
[26.] 6–12cm. Bulb tunics papery, roots fleshy. Lvs 4–5, concealing stem, to 20×1cm after flowering, curved, green, sometimes glaucous beneath. Fls 1–2, fragrant, to 5cm diam., violet, tube to 9cm, falls spreading, blade deeper blue-violet, crest yellow surrounded by white spotted violet, haft wide-winged, standard spreading, to 2.5cm, spathulate to trilobed. Early spring. S Turkey. ssp. *allisonii* B. Mathew. Lvs 6–10, broader than in type, 1.5cm wide, margins wavy; fls bluer.

I.stocksii (Bak.) Boiss.
[26.] To 30cm. Bulb oblong, tunics papery, persistent, forming a long neck; roots slender, fleshy. Lvs well developed at flowering, to 15×1.5cm, lanceolate, enclosing stem until after flowering. Fls 1–4, 5.5cm diam., pale blue-violet, veins dark mauve; tube 3–5cm; falls obovate, crest yellow, haft wide-winged; standards obovate, horizontal. Spring. C & S Afghanistan, W Pakistan.

I.stolonifera Maxim. (*I.vaga* Fost., *I.leichtlinii* Reg.).
[4.] 30–60cm. Rhiz. stoloniferous. Lvs upright, blue-green, to 60×0.5–1.5cm, prominently veined. Fls 2–3, to 8cm diam., light to deep brown purple; falls and standard blades marked pale to dark blue, both bearded, beard hairs yellow or blue. Late spring. Russia. 'Compacta': fls brown. 'Zwanenburg Bronze': fls with frilled margins.

I.stylosa Desf. See *I.unguicularis*.

I.suaveolens Boiss. & Reut. (*I.mellita* Janka; *I.rubromarginata* Bak : I glockiana Schwarz).
[1.] Dwarf, 8–15cm. Lvs in fans. Fls 1–2 on short stems, 5cm diam., yellow, purple, maroon or yellow and brown, bract keeled, tube to 4.5cm, beard yellow, blue in purple forms. Spring–early summer. SE Europe, NW Turkey.

I.subbiflora Brot.
[1.] 25–40cm. Lvs nearly straight, to 2.5cm wide, reduced lvs on stem. Fls 1–2, 7–8cm diam., deep violet or blue; bract tinged purple; tube to 5cm; falls obovate, reflexed, to 4×2.5cm, beard blue or white, or yellow on haft; standards erect, 5×2.5cm. Spring–summer. Portugal, SW Spain. var. *lisbonensis* (Dykes) Dykes. Stem lvs absent; bracts green.

I.susiana L. MOURNING IRIS.
[3.] Similar to *I.sofarana* and *I.basaltica* but with lvs almost straight; fls to 12cm diam., pale lilac-grey heavily veined deep purple, falls and standards similarly sized and shaped, blade round, to 8cm wide, signal patch velvety purple-black, beard deep brown-purple. Late spring. Origin unknown, possibly Lebanon.

I.susiana f. *sofarana* (Fost.) Sealy. See *I.sofarana*.
I.susiana f. *westii* (Dinsm.) Sealy. See *I.westii*.
I.taitii Fost. See *I.xiphium* 'Taitii'.

I.taochia Woron. ex Grossh.
[1.] Compact, to 30cm. Lvs to 2.5cm wide, tips tapering. Fls 2–5, 5–6cm diam., light to bright yellow, dull purple to violet, bracts inflated, green, papery, beard white, sometimes tipped

yellow, fall haft white or yellow, veins brown-purple. NE Turkey.

I.tauri Siehe ex Mallet. See *I.stenophylla*.
I.taurica Lodd. See *I.pumila*.

I.tectorum Maxim. ROOF IRIS.
[7.] Rhiz. stout. Stems sometimes branched, to 40cm. Lvs thin, ribbed, glossy dark green to 30×2–2.5cm. Fls 2–3 per spathe, to 10cm diam., somewhat flat, blue-lilac, veined and patched darker, falls 2.5cm wide, crest well-divided, frilly, white, spotted darker; standards and falls spreading, margins wavy. Early summer. C & SW China, possibly Burma, naturalized Japan. 'Alba': fls white, sparsely veined yellow. 'Variegata': lvs boldly striped and streaked cream.

I.tenax Douglas ex Lindl. (*I.gormanii* Piper).
[13.] To 30cm. Lvs green, tinged pink at base. Fls 1–2, 7–9cm diam., palest yellow to lavender or red-purple; bracts narrow, divergent, tube short, to 1cm, falls lanceolate, 2.5cm wide, reflexed, with a white or yellow central patch of purple, standards lanceolate, 6mm wide. Early summer. NW US. Used in hybridizing; see Pacific Coast hybrids. ssp. *klamathensis* Lenz. Evergreen. Fl. tube longer than in type, 1–2cm; fls straw to light pink-orange, veined red-purple or brown. SW California.

I.tenuifolia Pall.
[20.] 10–30cm. Rhiz. nearly vertical, apex clothed in fibrous brown lf remains. Lvs narrow, tough, to 40×0.3cm, glaucous. Fls 1–2, 4–6cm diam.; tube to 8cm, fall blade narrow, 1.5cm wide, pointed, heavily veined violet, centrally striped pale yellow, standards narrow, 1.5cm wide, pointed, blue-violet. Late spring. SE Russia through C Asia to Mongolia and W China.

I.tenuis S. Wats.
[7.] To 35cm. Rhiz. wide-spreading. Flowering stems branched. Lvs 30×1–1.5cm. Fls 1 per branch, 3–4cm diam., falls 3cm, white with some yellow marks, veins blue-purple, ridge yellow, undivided, standards erect, blue-white. Late spring. W US (Oregon).

I.tenuissima Dykes (*I.humboldtiana* anon.; *I.citrina* anon.).
[13.] To 30cm. Stems leafy. Lvs grey-green, 4–6mm wide. Fls 2, 6–8cm diam., cream, tube to 6cm, apex much widened; falls spreading, to 8cm diam., veined brown-purple; style lobes narrow, pointed, reflexed. Early summer. W US. ssp. *purdyiformis* (R. Fost.) Lenz. Stem lvs bract-like. Fls cream to light yellow, lightly veined. N Sierra Nevada.

I.tigrida Bunge ex Ledeb.
[6.] Dwarf, to 15cm. Rhiz. clump-forming, apices clad with old fibrous lf bases; roots fleshy. Lvs many, erect, to 10×10cm, usually shorter than flowering stems. Fls 1–2 per stem, to 5cm diam., lilac to dark blue, mottled purple, fall centre white streaked purple, beard white, tips sometimes yellow. Seeds with fleshy aril. SE Russia, Mongolia, NW China.

I.tingitana Boiss. & Reut.
[25.] To 60cm. Lvs appearing in autumn, to 45cm, curved, silver-green. Fls blue; tube to 3cm; falls obovate, somewhat pointed, to 7.5cm, ridge orange-yellow; standards to 10cm. Late winter–spring. NW Africa. A parent of Dutch iris. var. *fontanesii* (Godron) Maire (*I.fontanesii* Godron). Flowering later than species type; fls deeper violet-blue. var. *mellori* anon. (*I.fontanesii* var. *mellori* Collingw.). To 90cm. Fls purple, falls rounded.

I.timofejewii Woron.
[1.] Dwarf, 10–25cm. Rhiz. stout. Lvs to 5cm wide, falcate, grey-green. Fls 1–2, to 5cm diam., deep violet-red, tube 4–5cm; beard white, tips purple. E Caucasus.

I.tridentata Pursh (*I.tripetala* Walter).
[11.] To 70cm. Stems unbranched or 1-branched; stem lvs shorter than stems. Fls 1–2, fragrant, to 10cm diam., tube 2.5cm, fall blade rounded, 3.5cm diam., violet with darker veins, signal patch white with central yellow patch, haft white, veins reticulate; standards oblanceolate, reduced,

1.5cm, erect, violet. Seeds flat, semicircular. E US (N Carolina to Florida).

I.tripetala Walt. See *I.tridentata*.

I.trojana Kerner ex Stapf.
[1.] Similar to *I.germanica* but with long-branched stems 70cm+. Fl. buds long, pointed, bract somewhat narrow; fls large, 10cm diam., fragrant, falls obovate, reflexed, purple, beard white, tips yellow, haft lightly veined; standards obovate, lighter blue. Early summer. W Turkey. Used in hybridization programmes to produce plants with well-branched infl.

I.tubergeniana Fost.
[26.] To 15cm. Bulb tunics papery, somewhat thickened. Lvs 4–6, to 2.5cm wide, edged white, curved, sheathing stem. Fls 1–3, to 6cm diam., yellow; tube to 5cm; fall crest fringed, surrounded by veins and dots of green-violet, haft narrow-winged, standards 1.5cm, trilobed, deflexed. Spring. Soviet C Asia.

I.tuberosa L. See *Hermodactylus tuberosus*.

I.'Turkey Yellow'.
[18.] 50–100cm. Lvs 1–1.8cm across, shorter than or equalling fls. Fls 9–11cm diam., pure deep yellow. C & S Turkey. A wild collection as yet unnamed but used in developing new Spuria cultivars.

I.unguicularis Poir. (*I.stylosa* Desf.).
[23.] Almost stemless. Rhiz. tough, branching. Lvs evergreen, in tufts, linear-ensiform, to 60×1cm. Fls solitary, short-stemmed, fragrant, tube very long, to 20cm; falls obovate, reflexed, 2.5cm wide, white veined lavender, central band yellow, haft linear, veins dark, standards size and shape as falls, erect, lilac; style branches yellow-glandular above. Winter-spring. Algeria, Tunisia, W Syria, S & W Turkey. ssp. *cretensis* (Janka) A.P. Davis & Jury (*I.cretensis* Janka; *I.cretica* Bak.). Dwarf. Lvs grassy, to 3mm wide. Fl. seg. to 5.5cm, purple-blue, fall blade and haft white veined violet, blade striped orange in centre. S Greece, Crete. ssp. *carica* f. *angustifolia* (Boiss. & Heldr.) A.P. Davis & Jury. Lvs narrower than type; fls small, lilac-blue, falls with white centre, margins blue-lilac, standard white at base. 'Alba': fls white, falls with central green-yellow line. 'Ellis's Variety': lvs narrow; fls bright violet-blue. 'Marginata': fls lilac, margins white. 'Mary Barnard': fls violet-blue. 'Oxford Dwarf': fls deep blue, falls white veined purple, with central orange line, tips lavender. 'Speciosa': lvs short, narrow; fls fragrant, deep violet, central yellow stripe. 'Starker's Pink': dwarf; lvs shorter, narrower; fls pink-lavender. 'Variegata': fls mottled and streaked purple on lavender ground. 'Walter Butt': fls large, robust, fragrant, pale silver-lilac; late autumn-winter.

I.urmiensis Hoog. See *I.barnumae* f. *urmiensis*.
I.vaga Fost. See *I.stolonifera*.

I.variegata L. (*I.rudskyi* Horvat; *I.reginae* Horvat; *I.lepida* Heuff.; *I.leucographa* Kerner; *I.mangaliae* Prodan; *I.dragalz* Horvat; *I.virescens* Delarb.).
[1.] 20–50cm. Stems branched. Lvs dark green, sword-shaped, ribbed, to 30×3cm. Fls 3–6, 5–8cm diam., bract swollen, tinged green-purple, tube to 2.5cm, falls obovate, 2cm wide, reflexed, white to light yellow, veined red-brown, beard bright yellow, standards oblong, erect, bright yellow; style branches yellow. Spring–summer. C & SE Europe. Forms with brown-red falls occur. Used in hybridizing; parent plant of the miniature tall bearded hybrids. See also under *I.× sambucina*.

I.vartanii Fost.
[27.] Dwarf. Bulb producing 'rice-grain' offsets. Stems to 3cm. Lvs exceeding fls, quadrangular in cross-section, to 20cm at flowering. Fls almond-scented, slate blue, fall blade veined darker, crest yellow; hafts very narrow; style branches long and narrow. Autumn-winter. Israel, possibly Syria. 'Alba': fls white.

I.verna L.
[9.] To 6cm at flowering. Lvs equitant, sword-shaped, to 15×1cm after flowering, glaucous, purple at base. Fls to 5cm diam., bright blue-lilac, tube 2–5cm, falls obovate, 4×1cm, centre striped orange with brown spots, standard obovate, erect. Spring. SE US.

I.versicolor L.
[15.] Marginal. Rhiz. stout, creeping. Stems 20–80cm, branched. Lvs 35–60×1–2cm. Fls several per branch, 6–8cm diam., violet to red-purple, falls wide-spreading, blade oval, 8–2.5cm, blotched green-yellow, surrounded by white veined purple, haft white, purple-veined, standards oblanceolate, smaller, 4cm, paler, erect. Seeds small and glossy. Summer. E US. 'Gerald Derby' (*I.versicolor* × *I.virginica*): stems taller; fls large, purple-blue. 'Kermesina': fls red-purple. 'Rosea': fls pink.

I.vicaria Vved.
[26.] Bulb large, similar to *I.magnifica* but 20–50cm. Lvs 5–7, arching, 15×1.5–3cm. Fls 2–5, 4–5cm diam., light blue-violet, crest wavy, white or yellow on yellow patch, haft unwinged, dark-lined, standards to 2.5cm, dark veined. Spring. C Asia.

I.violacea Klatt. See *I.spuria* ssp. *musulmanica*.
I.virescens Delarb. See *I.variegata*.

I.virginica L. SOUTHERN BLUE FLAG.
[15.] Similar to *I.versicolor* but flowering stems usually unbranched, often curved, collapsing to ground at fruiting. Lvs 1–3cm wide, soft, tips drooping. Fls 1–4, blue, fall centre yellow-hairy (not bearded). Fr. capsule 4–7cm. Summer. E US. 'Alba': lvs wide, fls white. 'Giant Blue': fls large, blue. 'Wide Blue': lvs blue-green; fls blue. var. *shrevei* (Small) E. Anderson (*I.shrevei* Small). Flowering stem branched. Fr. 7–11cm.

I.warleyensis Fost.
[26.] 20–45cm. Roots slightly thickened. Lvs 6–7, channelled, spaced along stem, to 20×3cm. Fls to 5, 5–7cm diam., pale to dark violet to blue-purple, tube 5cm, fall blade orbicular, margins white, crest white to yellow, on yellow ground, dissected, haft unwinged, standard deflexed, linear to trilobed, to 2cm. Spring. Russia. 'Warlsind' (*I.warleyensis* × *I.aucheri*): to 25cm; falls yellow, blade blotched purple-blue, ridge yellow, standards and styles white.

I.wattii Bak.
[7.] 1–2m, similar to *I.confusa* but stems much-branched. Fls 2–3 per branch, large, 6cm diam., falls reflexed, 5×3.5cm, lavender-lilac, centre white spotted deep yellow and dark lilac, crest orange, or white spotted yellow, standards horizontal, 4×2cm. Spring–summer. India, W China.

I.wendelboi Grey-Wilson & B. Mathew.
[26.] Dwarf, to 10cm. Bulb tunics papery. Lvs well developed at flowering, to 20×1cm, glaucous, arching, concealing stem until after flowering. Fls 1–2, to 5.5cm diam., deep violet, tube 3cm; falls not winged, crest bright golden yellow, frilly, standards much reduced, to 5mm. Spring. SW Afghanistan.

I.westii Dinsm. (*I.susiana* f. *westii* (Dinsm.) Sealy).
[3.] To 30cm. Lvs almost straight, to 1cm wide. Fls solitary, 12–15cm diam., falls pale yellow, veined and blotched purple, signal patch dark brown, beard hairs sparse, long, purple, standards pale lilac veined and spotted deeper blue-lilac. Seeds with large aril. Late spring. Lebanon.

I.willmottiana Fost.
[26.] To 20cm. Bulb tunics papery; roots thickened. Lvs glossy green, concealing stem until fruiting. Fls 4–6, to 7cm diam., deep lavender to bright blue or white, tube 5cm, fall blade blotched white and deeper lavender, haft winged, crest white, slightly wrinkled, standards 1.5cm. Spring. Russia.

I.wilsonii C.H. Wright.
[12.] To 75cm. Flowering stems unbranched. Lvs glaucous, equalling flowering stems. Fls 2 per branch, fragrant, 6–8cm

diam., pale yellow, falls obovate, veined and spotted brown-purple, standards oblique, margins undulate; pedicels to 10cm at fruiting. Summer. W China.

I.winogradowii Fomin.
[27.]   To 15cm. Differs from *I.histrioides* in producing 'rice-grain' bulblets and pale primrose fls spotted green on the fall haft and centre of blade. Early spring. Russia. 'Frank Elder' (*I.winogradowii* × *I.histrioides*): fls pale blue slightly shaded yellow. 'Katherine Hodgkin' (*I.winogradowii* × *I.histrioides*): fls yellow veined blue and faintly tinged pale blue.

I.xiphioides Ehrh. See *I.latifolia*.

I.xiphium L. (*I.hispanica* Steud.). SPANISH IRIS.
[25.]   Stems to 40–60cm. Lvs 20–70×0.3–0.5cm, channelled, appearing in autumn. Fls 1–2, usually blue or violet, sometimes white, yellow or mauve, tube 1–3mm, fall blade centre usually orange or yellow, haft unwinged. Spring–early summer. Spain, Portugal, SW France, S Italy, Corsica, Morocco, Algeria, Tunisia. Hybridized with *I.tigitana* to produce Dutch irises. 'Battandieri' (*I.battandieri* Fost.): fls white, ridge on fall blades orange-yellow. 'Blue Angel': fls bright blue, central falls marked yellow. 'Bronze Queen': fls golden brown, suffused purple and bronze. 'Cajanus': fls yellow. 'King of the Blues': fls blue. 'Lusitanica' (*I.lusitanica*

Ker-Gawl.): fls yellow. 'Praecox' (*I.xiphium* var. *praecox* Dykes): flowering earlier; fls large blue. 'Professor Blaauw': fls bright violet-blue. 'Queen Wilhelmina': fls white. 'Taitii' (*I.taitii* Fost.): fls pale blue. 'Thunderbolt': falls bronze-brown, blotched yellow, standards purple-brown.

I.xiphium var. *praecox* Dykes. See *I.xiphium* 'Praecox'.

I.yebrudii Dinsm. ex Chaudhary.
[3.]   To 20cm. Lvs short, rigid, slightly curved, glaucous. Fls 9cm diam., falls pale yellow veined and spotted brown-purple, signal patch small, deep purple, beard hairs long, purple, standards pale yellow, veins open, purple. Syria. ssp. *edgecombei* Chaudhary. Fls larger than species type, 10–12cm diam., falls marked red-purple, signal patch deep red-purple, beard hairs purple, tipped yellow, standards white, densely veined maroon.

I.zaprjagajewii N. Abramov.
[26.]   Dwarf, to 15cm. Bulb tunics papery; roots radish-like. Lvs short at flowering, broad, to 4cm wide, glaucous, sheathing stem. Fls 1–3 on stem to 4cm, 5.5cm diam., white, tube to 9cm, tube and seg. base sometimes tinged blue, fall margins decurved, crest yellow, standards slightly reflexed, reduced to 1cm. Spring. C Asia.

Ixia L. (From Gk *ixia*, the name of a plant noted for the variability of its flower colour.) Iridaceae. 45–50 species of perennial herbs, usually deciduous and winter-growing. Corms small, ovoid to globose, with tunics of usually reticulate fibres, sometimes producing sessile cormlets, or stolons ending in one or more cormlets. Stem erect, usually slender and wiry, branched or unbranched. Leaves few, distichous, usually 1–4 basal and 1–2 cauline. Spike laxly or densely few to many flowered; flowers almost always regular, very variable in colour; perianth tube straight, long or short, slender to campanulate, lobes more or less equal, usually joined for 1–2mm at base; stamens arising on tube, included or exserted; style with 3 branches. S Africa (Cape Province). Z9.

CULTIVATION   Where temperatures seldom fall below freezing, they can be planted in a sunny, south-facing border or under a south wall, planted about 10–15cm/4–6in. deep with a winter covering of bracken litter or leafmould. Plant in autumn to bloom in spring and summer, or in spring for later summer blooms. In pots, set 6–8 corms firmly into 12cm pot in a mix of sandy loam and leafmould; plunge in a cool frame, watering very sparingly during winter until the flower spikes appear, then give full light and good ventilation. Continue to water until foliage begins to die back, then dry off gradually and store dry in cool but frost-free conditions. Offsets usually flower in their second year. Sow seed in autumn. Seedlings should remain in the same pans for their first year; seed-raised plants usually flower in their third or fourth year.

I.aristata Thunb. See *I.campanulata*.

I.aristata Ker-Gawl. non Thunb. See *I.longituba*.

I.aulica Ait. See *I.latifolia*.

I.aurantiaca Klatt. See *I.polystachya* var. *lutea*.

I.campanulata Houtt. (*I.aristata* Thunb.; *I.crateroides* Ker-Gawl.; *I.speciosa* Andrews).
Stem 10–35cm, occasionally with 1 long branch near base. Lvs 5–10, 15–20×0.2–0.5cm, linear-subulate. Spike short, densely 1–9-fld; fls widely bell- or cup-shaped, white, sometimes flushed with red, or crimson; perianth tube 2–3mm, filiform, lobes 12–25×8–12mm, obovate; stamens arising in throat, 9–13mm; style branches 3–4mm, linear. Spring–early summer. SW Cape.

I.capillaris L. f.
Stem 20–45cm, very slender, simple or with 1–3 short branches. Lvs 3, 6–18cm×1–2mm, finely linear or filiform, often spirally twisted. Spike laxly 1–4-fld, branches 1–3-fld; fls white, pale blue or mauve, sometimes pale green in throat; perianth tube 5–7mm, lobes 10–15×4–6mm, oblong; stamens arising near base of tube, usually exserted; style shorter than stamens, branches 2–3.5mm, linear or linear-spathulate. Winter–spring. SW Cape.

I.cochlearis Lewis.
Stem 15–45cm, unbranched. Lvs 5–6, 10–30cm×1–3mm, finely linear. Spike 3–8cm, rather laxly 4–12-fld, rachis usually flexuous; fls salmon-pink or rose-pink with dark median veins; perianth tube 10–18mm, gradually widening towards

throat, lobes 10–17×6–8mm, oblong, obtuse; stamens well exserted from tube; style of similar length, branches 1–2mm, spathulate. Early summer. SW Cape.

I.columellaris Ker-Gawl. See *I.monadelpha*.

I.conferta Fost.
Stem 15–35cm, unbranched. Lvs 5–6, distichous, 7–24×0.3–1.1cm, lanceolate or sword shaped. Spike capitate, densely 2–10-fld; fls purple or red with purple-black blotch in middle; perianth tube 6–9mm, slender, cylindrical, lobes 13–25×8–17mm, oblong or ovate, sometimes slightly clawed; stamens set at mouth of tube; style reaching base of fil., branches *c*3mm, purple, linear or oblanceolate. Late winter–early spring. W & SW Cape. var. *ochroleuca* (Ker-Gawl.) Lewis. Fls white to yellow with brown or purple-black stain in middle; plant and fls usually larger than in type. Spring. SW Cape.

I.crateroides Ker-Gawl. See *I.campanulata*.

I.curta Andrews.
Stem 15–40cm, simple or with 1 short branch. Lvs 4–6, 8–25×0.3–0.6cm, narrowly lanceolate, sometimes spirally twisted. Spike short, 3–8-fld; fls cup-shaped, but lobes spreading in bright sunshine, orange with brown or green-brown blotch often edged with red in middle, outer lobes often red-tinged outside; perianth perianth tube 10–15mm, cylindrical, lobes 20–25×10–15mm, usually obovate; stamens set at top of tube, fil. 3–4mm, joined, anth. 9–10mm; style reaching about middle of anth., branches 2–3mm, spathulate. Spring. SW Cape.

Ixia   (a) *I.scillaris*   (b) *I.monadelpha*   (c) *I.framesii*   (d) *I.viridiflora*

I.dubia Vent.
Stem 20–75cm, sometimes with 1–2 short branches. Lvs 5–7, 10–50cm×1.5–8mm, linear. Spike capitate, densely 3–15-fld; fls orange or golden-yellow, usually dark brown or purple in centre, outer lobes flushed with red outside; perianth tube 6–14mm, filiform or narrowly cylindrical; lobes 15–22×6–12mm, oblong, obtuse; stamens set at mouth of tube, 9–13mm long; style shorter than stamens, branches 3–5mm long, linear or oblanceolate. Spring–summer. S & SW Cape.

I.flexuosa L.
Stem 35–65cm, almost filiform, with 1–3 short branches. Lvs 3–5, 5–35×0.2–0.5cm, linear or subulate, usually spirally twisted. Spike usually short, densely 3–15-fld, the rachis flexuous; fls slightly scented, white, pale pink or mauve, sometimes yellow in centre, white fls often with purple veins; perianth tube 4–6mm, filiform, lobes 10–16×5–8mm, oblong, obtuse; stamens set at mouth of tube, 7–9mm; style shorter, branches 2–4mm, linear or oblanceolate. Winter–spring. S & SW Cape.

I.framesii L. Bol.
Stem 15–38cm, very slender, unbranched. Lvs 3–4, 12–40×0.1–0.2cm, linear. Spike short, densely 2–12-fld; fls salmon-pink or red-pink with a darker circle in middle; tube 15–20mm, filiform at base, gradually widening toward throat, lobes 15–24×8–12mm, oblong, ovate or obovate, obtuse; stamens set in tube, anth. wholly or partly exserted; style shorter than stamens, branches 2–3mm, linear. Spring. SW Cape.

I.grandiflora Delaroche. See *Sparaxis fragrans.*
I.incarnata Jacq. See *I.latifolia.*

I.latifolia Delaroche (*I.aulica* Ait.; *I.incarnata* Jacq.; *I.scariosa* Thunb.).
A variable species. Stem 10–60cm, usually branched. Lvs 3–4, 8–28×0.2–2cm, linear or lanceolate. Spike laxly or fairly densely 1–7-fld; fls pale to deep pink, mauve, violet, purple or magenta; perianth tube 6–20mm, widening from a slender base, lobes 11–20×5–9mm, oblong, obtuse; stamens well exserted from tube; style of similar length, branches recurved, 1–3mm, linear, oblanceolate or spathulate. Spring–summer. S & SW Cape, Namaqualand.

I.lelpoldill Lewis.
Stem 11–25cm, sometimes with 1–2 short branches. Lvs 3, 7–20×0.3–0.5cm, narrowly lanceolate. Spike short, densely 2–4-fld; fls white, base of lobes maroon-red, tube yellow; perianth tube 10–12mm, filiform at base, gradually widening to 3–6mm diam. at throat, lobes 15–17×14mm, suborbicular with very short claw; stamens arising in tube, the upper half of anth. exserted; style reaching base of anth., branches c2mm, spathulate. Spring. S Cape.

I.leucantha Jacq. See *I.polystachya.*
I.longifolia Berg. See *I.paniculata.*

I.longituba N.E. Br. (*I.aristata* sensu Ker-Gawl.).
Stem 35–75cm, sometimes with 1–3 short curved branches. Lvs 5–6, the 3 lowest 10–30×0.8–1.4cm, lanceolate or sword-shaped, often spirally twisted, upper lvs sheathing. Spike 4–7cm, rather laxly 6–12-fld; fls pale to deep pink, occasionally white, the outer lobes darker on outside; perianth tube 18–32mm, almost cylindrical but slightly wider at throat, lobes 12–20×7–10mm, oblong, obtuse, the inner 3 slightly narrower; stamens well exserted from tube; style shorter, branches 3–6mm, filiform or linear-spathulate. Spring–summer. S & SW Cape.

I.maculata L.
Stem 18–50cm, unbranched. Lvs 5–8, 10–35×0.2–0.7cm, linear, lanceolate or subulate, usually spirally twisted. Spike capitate, densely 4-many-fld; bracts conspicuous, to 1.5cm long, red-brown, papery; fls orange or yellow-orange with dark brown, black or purple mark in centre, usually with yellow or orange star in middle; outer lobes usually red on outside; perianth tube 5–8mm, cylindrical or filiform, lobes 15–30×8–12mm, spreading, oblong, obtuse; stamens arising

at mouth of tube, fil. 3–5mm, anth. 7–9mm; style reaching about half-way up anth., branches 3–5m, linear. Spring. W & SW Cape. var. **nigro-albida** (Klatt) Bak. Fls white, with black central mark. var. **ornata** Bak. Fls white, tinged purple externally, with deep crimson central mark.

I.micrandra Bak.
Stem 20–60cm, filiform, unbranched. Lvs 2–3, 12–30cm, c1mm or less wide, filiform. Spike short, 2–6-fld; fls white, pale to deep pink or mauve; perianth tube 3–5mm, filiform, lobes 10–20×5–7mm, oblong, obtuse; stamens set at top of tube, very short, 3–5mm; style shorter than stamens, branches 3–4mm, filiform. Winter–spring. SW Cape.

I.monadelpha Delaroche (*I.columellaris* Ker-Gawl.).
Stem 15–40cm, usually with 1–2 short, curved branches. Lvs 4–7, 8–28×0.3–1cm, lanceolate or sword-shaped, usually spirally twisted. Spike short, densely 4–12-fld; fls of variable colour, white, pale pink, mauve, violet, pale to deep blue, purple, with a green, brown or red-brown circular mark in middle, usually edged with a band of another colour; perianth tube 10–18mm, slender, lobes 13–20×6–11mm, oblong, obtuse; stamens set at mouth of tube, fil. 3–6mm, usually at least partly joined, anth. 7–8mm; style slightly shorter than anth., branches 2–3mm, spathulate, the tips recurved. Spring–summer. SW Cape. var. **columnaris** (Andrew) Bak. Fls uniform claret-red, without central mark; seg. narrow. var. **grandiflora** (Pers.) Bak. Fls large, lilac, with dull blue throat. var. **latifolia** (Klatt) Bak. Lvs not twisted, broad. Fls lilac, with green-brown throat. var. **purpurea** (Klatt) Bak. Fls claret-red, perianth lobes narrow-oblong.
I.monadelpha var. *curta* Ker-Gawl. See *I.curta.*

I.odorata Ker-Gawl.
Stem 20–55cm high, sometimes with 1–2 short branches. Lvs 3–6, usually 12–18×0.15–1cm, linear or lanceolate, often spirally twisted. Spike 2.5–6.5cm, densely 5–18-fld; fls yellow, the outer lobes sometimes tinged with red on outside; perianth tube 7–11mm, filiform at base but widening near throat, lobes usually of similar length to tube, about 5mm wide, oblong; stamens set near throat, 8–10mm; style reaching top of tube, branches 5–7mm, linear. Spring–summer. SW Cape.

I.paniculata Delaroche (*I.longifolia* Berg).
Stem 30–100cm, usually with 1–2 branches. Lvs 15–60cm×3–12mm, linear or lanceolate. Spike 4–14cm, laxly or densely 5–18-fld; fls cream or pale yellow, the outer lobes often tinged pink or red outside; perianth tube 4–7cm, gradually widening from base to throat, lobes 15–25×3–8mm; stamens sometimes included in tube, sometimes exerted, style also of variable length, branches c2mm, spathulate, the tips recurved. Spring–summer. W & SW Cape.

I.patens Ait.
Stem 18–50cm, sometimes with 1–2 short branches. Lvs 5–7, 10–35×0.6–1.2cm, lanceolate. Spike to 10cm, rather laxly 5–15-fld; fls pink, rose-purple or crimson, rarely white, sometimes with a small round white or green mark in centre; perianth tube 4–6mm, filiform, lobes 16–24×5–12mm, oblong, obtuse; stamens set at top of tube, 10–14mm; style slightly shorter, branches 3–4mm, narrowly oblanceolate. Spring. SW Cape.

I.polystachya L. (*I.leucantha* Jacq.).
Stem 30–100cm, slender, sometimes with 1–4 branches. Lvs 5–8, distichous, more than half as long as stem, 2–14mm wide, linear or lanceolate, grass-like. Spike laxly or densely few to many-fld; fls slightly scented, white, pale to deep mauve, golden or orange-yellow, sometimes with yellow, blue, mauve, green or purple mark in centre; perianth tube 5–14mm, usually filiform, lobes 10–25×5–9mm, oblong, obtuse; stamens set at mouth of tube, 7–11mm; style shorter, branches white, yellow or blue, 3–4mm, linear. Spring–summer. S & SW Cape. var. **polystachya.** Fls white to mauve, with or without a central stain, outer lobes often green- or blue-tinged on outside. var. **lutea** (Ker-Gawl.) Lewis (*I.aurantiaca* Klatt). Fls golden yellow or orange-yellow,

rarely with dark mark in centre, outer lobes sometimes red- or purple-tinged outside.

I.rapunculoides Delaroche.
A very variable species. Stem 25–75cm, sometimes with to 7 branches. Lvs 2–6, 10–30×0.2–1.8cm linear, lanceolate or sword-shaped. Spike laxly or fairly densely 1–7-fld; fls white, mauve-pink, pale blue or purple, the tube often yellow or green; perianth tube 5–13mm, rather bell-shaped, lobes 10–20×3–9mm, lobes spreading or the whole fl. bell-shaped; anth. slightly exserted from tube; style of similar length, branches c1mm, linear. Winter–spring. W Karroo, Namaqualand.

I.scariosa Thunb. See I.latifolia.

I.scillaris L.
Stem 20–50cm, sometimes with 1–3 long, erect branches. Lvs 3–7, distichous, 7–25×0.5–2.5cm lanceolate or sword-shaped. Spike long, laxly 7–25-fld; fls slightly irregular, scented, white, mauve, pale to deep pink or magenta, usually with a small, green mark in centre; perianth tube 3–4mm, filiform, lobes spreading or reflexed, 8–16×5–8mm, oblong or obovate; stamens asymmetrical, set at top of tube; style as long as tube, branches c3mm, recurved. Winter–spring. S & SW Cape, Namaqualand.

I.speciosa Andrews. See I.campanulata.
I.spectabilis Salisb. See I.viridiflora.

I.splendida Lewis.
Stem 30–60cm, slender, unbranched. Lvs 4–5, 18–45×0.2–0.3cm, linear. Spike capitate, 5–7-fld; fls pale pink, erect; perianth tube 22–28mm, gradually widening to throat, lobes 15–18×6–8mm, oblong, obtuse; stamens usually included in tube; style shorter, branches c1.5mm long, filiform. Spring. W Cape.

I.vanzijliae L. Bol.
Stem 18–40cm, sometimes with 1 short branch. Lvs 5, 4–16×0.4–1.2cm, lanceolate, spirally twisted, the edges undulate. Spike short, densely 2–7-fld; fls pink or mauve-pink with darker mark in centre; perianth tube 8–10mm, filiform, straight or curved, lobes 13–20×8–11mm, obovate, obtuse; stamens set in throat, fil. 3mm, anth. 6–7mm; style shorter than anth., branches 2.5mm, linear. Winter–spring. SW Cape.

I.viridiflora Lam. (I.spectabilis Salisb.).
Stem 50–100cm, occasionally with 1–2 short, erect branches. Lvs 5–7, 40–55×0.2–0.5cm, linear. Spike 12–30cm, usually laxly 12 to many-fld; fls sea-green with purple, purple-black or red blotch in centre; perianth tube 6–9mm, filiform, lobes spreading, 16–25×7–11mm, oblong, obtuse; stamens set in throat, fil. purple, 3–4mm, anth. purple or yellow, 9–13mm; style reaching top of tube, branches 3mm, linear. Spring. SW Cape.

I.cultivars. 'Blue Bird': inner pet. white, outer pet. with broad violet streak tipped dark purple, centre black shaded purple. 'Bridesmaid': fls white centred red, abundant. 'Castor': fls violet purple splashed yellow. 'Giant': fls ivory tipped purple with dark centre. 'Hogarth': fls cream centred purple. 'Hubert': fls orange centred magenta. 'Mabel': fls large, outside cyclamen purple, outer pet. shaded brown-red. 'Marquette': fls rich yellow tipped purple, centre dark purple. 'Rose Emperor': fls pale pink, outer pet. darker pink, centre deep carmine. 'Rose Queen': fls entirely pale pink. 'Uranus': fls dark lemon-yellow centred red. 'Venus': fls magenta with dark centre. 'Vulcan': fls carmine red and orange.

Ixiolirion (Fisch.) Herb. (From *Ixia* and Gk *lirion,* lily, for its resemblance to *Ixia.*) Amaryllidaceae. 4 species of bulbous perennial herbs. Leaves mostly basal, in a rosette, usually persisting in winter. Inflorescence an umbel or loose raceme; perianth radially symmetric, segments 6, free or united toward base in a short tube, usually deep blue or violet; stamens 6, shorter than perianth, attached to base of segments or base of tube; ovary 3-celled. Fruit a many-seeded capsule; seeds black. SW & C Asia.

CULTIVATION *Ixiolirion* spp. occur in fields and on rocky hillsides to altitudes of 2700m/8775ft. They are grown for their grassy foliage and for their delicate umbels of starry blue-violet flowers carried on slender stems in spring and early summer; they last well when cut. They are hardy to –15°C/5°F, but need a warm and sheltered position in a rich and perfectly drained soil, where they can be baked in summer and protected from excessive winter wet, and are well suited to the rock garden or plantings in raised beds, thus providing the necessary drainage. *I.tataricum* is sometimes pot-grown in the cool conservatory or glasshouse, in a mix of equal parts loam, leafmould and sharp sand.

Plant 15cm/6in. deep in late summer/early autumn, incorporating well rotted manure before planting; a mulch of bracken litter or leafmould is beneficial, and in high rainfall areas a propped pane of glass or open cloche will protect from rotting. Propagate by removal of offsets after flowering, or by seed in autumn.

I.kolpakowskianum Reg. (*Kolpakowskia ixiolirioides* Reg.).
Similar to *I.tataricum* but lvs linear, fls usually solely in an umbel, perianth 2–2.5cm, united into a long, slender tube at base, white to violet, Spring–summer. C Asia. Z7.

I.montanum (Labill.) Herb. See I.tataricum.
I.pallasii Fisch. & Mey. See I.tataricum

I.tataricum (Pall.) Herb. (*I.montanum* (Labill.) Herb.; *I.pallasii* Fisch. & Mey.).
Bulb to 2.5cm diam., ovoid. Stem to 40cm, 2–3-lvd. Basal lvs 3–8, linear-lanceolate. Fls in an umbel sometimes with to 4 fls below it arranged as if in a raceme; perianth funnelform, tepals 2–5cm, spreading or recurved, blue or violet-blue with 3 darker central lines. SW & C Asia, Kashmir. A very variable species that may include *I.ledebourii* Fisch. & Mey. (Ledebourii group): fls bright violet. var. **macranthum** hort. Fls deep blue tinted purple. 'Sintensii': fls pale blue.

Kniphofia Moench. (For J.H. Kniphof (1704–1756), German botanist.) REDHOT POKER. Liliaceae (Aloeaceae). About 68 species of perennial herbs with short thick rhizomes forming large clumps or having a few crowns from which arise clusters of linear to grasslike leaves, often fleshy, sometimes strap-like, sometimes keeled, rarely caulescent (*K.caulescens*, *K.northiae*). Leaves usually keeled or V-shaped in section (broad and flat in *K.northiae*). Scape erect, slender, usually exceeding leaves, bearing in the apical quarter a dense or lax spike-like raceme; flowers 4–45mm, tubular-cylindric to funnel-shaped, white to yellow, green, yellow-brown, orange, salmon-pink, to brilliant red; pedicels 1–8mm, each subtended by a small, papery, persistent bract, oblong and rounded at the apex to narrow and acute or acuminate. S Africa, mts of E Africa, Tropical Africa and Ethiopia, Madagascar (2 spp.), Yemen (1 sp.). All species described are from South Africa unless stated otherwise. Z8 unless specified.

CULTIVATION Summer- and autumn-flowering, generally sturdy perennials for the sunny border, valued for their strong form and stout spikes of often brilliantly coloured flowers which last well when cut. Species and cultivars vary in height and form, ranging from those that make slender and elegant clumps of rush-like foliage, as with *K*. 'Modesta', those with broader dark green or glaucous leaves as with *K.uvaria*, and those with grass-like foliage and more delicate spikes of flower, as in *K.galpinii*. *Kniphofia* spp. are best known for their range of hot reds and oranges, although numerous cultivars are available in softer and more unusual colours as with the creamy 'Snow Maiden', soft yellows of 'Maid of Orleans', buff yellows with 'Tubergeniana', and beautiful creamy jade with 'Green Jade'. Most are cold-tolerant to temperatures of –15°C/5°F, although at these low temperatures, plants require a warm and sheltered position, and should be mulched deeply at their roots with leafmould or bracken litter, with the crowns protected with evergreen prunings to allow good air circulation. In the northern US, plants are sometimes lifted to overwinter in a moist soilless medium in frost-free conditions, most resent root disturbance and mulch protection is preferable wherever possible. Grow in full sun in deep, fertile and freely draining, preferably sandy soil, with sufficient organic matter to ensure an adequate supply of moisture when in growth. Propagate by seed or division, cultivars only by division. Thrips occasionally cause mottling of the foliage.

K.aloöides Moench. See *K.uvaria*.

K.angustifolia (Bak.) Codd.
Small. Lvs grasslike. Infl. graceful, lax; fls 20–30mm, white to yellow, orange and coral. *K.rufa* Bak. may be a hybrid derived from this species.

K.breviflora Bak.
Dwarf. Lvs grasslike. Fls 7–11mm, yellow or white.

K.bruceae Codd.
Robust. Infl. dense, cylindric; fls orange-red, somewhat funnel-shaped, 25–30mm. Introduced to Europe *c*1800 and hybridized with *K.uvaria* or *K.linearifolia* to produce the modern Redhot Pokers represented by *K.* × *praecox* Bak.

K.burchellii (Herb. ex Lindl.) Kunth. See *K.uvaria*.
K.carinata C. H. Wright. See *K.pumila*.

K.caulescens Bak. ex Hook. f.
Robust, forming short red-brown stems to about 30cm. Lvs to 1m, glaucous, recurved, keeled below. Infl. dense, oblong-cylindric; buds tinged red; fls creamy white, tinted peach, somewhat funnel-shaped, 22–24mm; stamens well-exserted. Z7.

K.citrina Bak.
Related to *K.uvaria* but smaller; infl. globose; fls ivory to yellow-green, 22–27mm.

K.composa Hochst. See *K.pumila*.
K. elegans Engl. See *K.schimperi*.

K.ensifolia Bak.
Robust, to 2m. Infl. dense, cylindric; buds red to red-green; fls white, somewhat funnel-shaped, 15–20mm; stamens well-exserted.

K.foliosa Hochst. (*K.quartiniana* A. Rich.).
Medium-sized. Infl. dense, cylindric; fls yellow, orange or red, 20–30mm; stamens shortly exserted. Ethiopia.

K.galpinii Bak.
Medium-sized. Lvs narrow, almost grasslike. Infl. small, dense, red at the apex shading to orange-yellow; fls 27–35mm. Sometimes confused with *K.triangularis* but may be distinguished by the more fibrous lvs, bicoloured infl., and fls with perianth lobes not flared. Z7.

K.galpinii hort. non Bak. See *K.triangularis*.

K.gracilis Harv. ex Bak. (*K.sparsa* N.E. Br.; *K.woodii* Wats.).
Variable species of medium stature. Lvs narrow. Infl. fairly dense to very lax; fls yellow, or yellow to ivory, 12–18mm.

K.insignis Rendle.
Medium-sized. Infl. fairly dense, with pink buds grading down to pink to white; fls 30–40mm. Ethiopia. Z9.

K.isoetifolia Hochst.
Medium-sized. Infl. fairly dense, globose; fls 30–40mm, creamy white, yellow, pale salmon-orange or red, opening from the top of the raceme downwards (as in *K.pumila*) instead of from base upwards as in other *Kniphofia* spp. Ethiopia. Z9.

K.kirkii Bak.
Robust. Infl. dense, oblong; fls orange-pink, coral or red-orange, 35–42mm. Tanzania. Z9.

K.laxiflora Kunth (*K.natalensis* Bak.).
Medium-sized. Infl. lax to medium-lax; fls 25–35mm, pale yellow or yellow-green to orange, salmon-pink, coral-red or orange-red.

K.leichtlinii Bak. See *K.pumila*.

K.linearifolia Bak.
Robust, allied to *K.uvaria* but infl. larger, ovoid, buds bright to dull red, shading to orange-yellow or green-yellow; fls 28–35mm.

K.longicollis Bak. See *K.rooperi*.
K.macowanii Bak. See *K.triangularis*.

K.multiflora J. M. Wood & M. Evans.
Robust, to 2m in flower. Infl. slender, elongated; buds often tinged red; fls short, spreading, 8–12mm, white to pale yellow.

K.natalensis Bak. See *K.laxiflora*.
K.nelsonii Mast. See *K.triangularis*.

K.northiae Bak.
Robust, often forming a short thick stem. Lvs broad, flat. Infl. dense, oblong; buds tinged red; fls creamy white to pale yellow, somewhat funnel-shaped, 22–30mm.

K.pallidiflora Bak.
Small. Lvs narrow. Infl. small, lax; fls white, funnel-shaped, 9–12mm, distinctly widening toward the mouth. Madagascar. Z9.

K.pauciflora Bak.
Small. Lvs grasslike. Infl. small, lax; fls pale yellow, somewhat funnel-shaped, 14–18mm.

K.× *praecox* Bak. (*K.uvaria* or *K.linearifolia* × *K.bruceae*).
RED HOT POKER
Variable, hybrids displaying characters according to the par-

Kniphofia   (a) *K.pauciflora*   (b) *K.× praecox* flower   (c) *K.breviflora* flower   (d) *K.pauciflora* flower
(e) *K.ensifolia* flower   (f) *K.× praecox*   (g) *K.linearifolia*

ents; *K.linearifolia* has oblong, rounded bracts while *K.bruceae* has narrow, acuminate, bracts. Summer–winter, according to cv. Z7.

K.primulina Bak.
Probably a form of *K.praecox* but fls lacking red pigment.

K.pumila (Ait.) Kunth (*K.carinata* C.H. Wright; *K.composa* Hochst; *K.leichtlinii* Bak.).
Small to medium-sized. Infl. dense, oblong to cylindric; fls opening from the top of the infl. downwards, somewhat funnel-shaped, yellow to orange, 12–18mm; stamens well-exserted.

K.quartiniana A.Rich. See *K.foliosa.*

K.rooperi (T. Moore) Lem. (*K.longicollis* Bak.).
Robust; allied to *K.uvaria* but infl. large, globose, bright red to green-yellow; fls 35–42mm.

K.sarmentosa (Andrews) Kunth.
Medium-sized. Lvs. glaucous. Infl. fairly dense, oblong; fls pink-red, 25–35mm.

K.schimperi Bak. (*K.elegans* Engl.).
Medium-sized. Infl. lax, oblong; fls yellow, orange or red. 15–30mm. Ethiopia. Z10.

K.sparsa N. E. Br. See *K.gracilis.*

K.splendida E. A. Bruce.
Robust. Infl. cylindric; fls yellow-orange. 20–25mm; stamens well-exserted.

K.triangularis Kunth (*K.galpinii* hort. non Bak.; *K.macowanii* Bak.; *K.nelsonii* Mast.).
Small to medium-sized. Lvs narrow to grasslike. Infl. small, dense; fls coral-orange, 25–35mm; perianth lobes spreading. This species has probably contributed the coral colours found in some cultivated *Kniphofia* hybrids.

K.tuckii Bak.
Closely resembles *K.ensifolia* but shorter, to 120cm, with red buds.

K.tysonii Bak.
Robust, related to *K.uvaria* but infl. cylindric; fls shorter (20–28mm); stamens well-exserted.

K.uvaria (L.) Oken (*K.alooides* Moench; *K.burchellii* (Herb. ex Lindl.) Kunth).
Medium-sized. Infl. oblong to ovoid, dense; fls brilliant red to green-yellow, 30–40mm. The first species to be brought into cultivation in Europe, later mixed with more robust spp. with larger infl. such as *K.linearifolia* and the hybrids described as *K.× praecox.* Z5.

K.woodii Wats. See *K.gracilis.*

K.cultivars.
Over 60 cvs grouped into dwarf and tall; height for dwarfs 50–90cm, for tall 100–180cm, colours white to yellow, orange and red, or bicoloured. 'Ada': dwarf; fls primrose. 'Alcazar': tall; fls bright orange-red. 'Amberlight': fls golden amber; spikes compact. 'Apple Court'; fls cream tipped with coral pink; spikes large. 'Apricot': to 75cm; fls buff yellow; spikes slender. 'Atlanta': tall; fls sunset yellow, profuse, early. 'August Gold': fls golden yellow; spikes large. 'Bee's Orange': fls rich orange-yellow; spikes dense. 'Bee's Sunset': to 90cm; lvs narrow; fls soft orange. 'Bee's Yellow': fls chrome yellow; later flowering. 'Bressingham Comet': dwarf, to 50cm; fls orange tipped red. 'Bressingham Dwarf': fls deep flame orange. 'Bressingham Flame': to 75cm; fls deep orange. 'Bressingham Glow': to 50cm; fls very bright orange; late flowering. 'Bressingham Torch'; fls flame orange; flowering intermittently throughout season. 'Brimstone': dwarf; fls yellow from green bed; late flowering. 'Bronceleuter': to 60cm; fls clear bronze. 'Burnt Orange': to 75cm; brown tinge in bud opening to deep orange fls; spikes slender. 'Buttercup': fls clear yellow; early flowering. 'Canary Bird': dwarf; fls yellow. 'Candlelight': to 50cm; lvs long and narrow; fls clear yellow; spikes slender. 'Cardinal': to 80cm; fls red. 'Comet': fls cream turning soft orange-red at apex. 'Cool Lemon': dwarf, to 60cm. 'Corallina': to 65 cm; fls orange-brown. 'Dr E. M. Mills': to 120cm; fls red. 'Earliest of All': fls coral red; spikes long. 'Early Buttercup': fls bright yellow; spikes large; early flowering. 'Erecta': fls bright coral red; spike inverted. 'Enchantress': dwarf; fls coral and red, bicoloured. 'Evered': to 70cm; fls red; very long flowering. 'Express': fls dull green-yellow tipped red; spikes triangular. 'Fiery Fred': to 120cm; fls orange-red. 'Fireflame': dwarf; fls burning red. 'Firefly': fls orange red. 'Fireking': fls orange-red; late-flowering. 'Fyrwerkeri': to 80cm; fls orange-red. 'Green Jade': to 120cm, hardy; fls bright green; late flowering. 'Gold Else': to 75cm; fls yellow; spikes slender; early flowering. 'Goldfinch': to 90cm; fls amber-yellow. 'Ice Queen': fls cream tinged green; spikes tall. 'Indian': fls dull brown-red. 'Jenny Brown': to 90cm; fls peach and cream blotched pink. 'John Benary': to 150cm; spikes loose, fls deep scarlet. 'Lemon Ice': to 90 cm; buds lemon opening to near white. 'Little Elf': to 75cm; lvs long and narrow; fls flame orange. 'Little Maid': dwarf; spikes ivory tipped soft yellow. 'Lye End'; spikes long, fls light pink-scarlet. 'Maid of Orleans'; dwarf; fls palest ivory, abundant. 'Modesta'; dwarf, to 60cm; fls cream and coral. 'Nobilis': tall; fls deep orange. 'Percy's Pride': to 90 cm; fls green-yellow. 'Pfitzeri': fls scarlet tinged carmine; spikes large. 'Prince Igor'. tall; fls bright cherry. 'Redstart'. to 90 cm, fls clear orange; flowering throughout season. 'Royal Standard': fls bright yellow and vermilion. 'Safrangvogel': fls salmon pink. 'Samuel's Sensation': to 150cm; fls carmine shading to yellow at base; spikes very long; somewhat later flowering. 'Scarlet Cap': to 90cm; fls scarlet and yellow. 'Shining Sceptre': to 120cm; fls bright yellow to off-white. 'Slim Coral Red': to 75cm; buds shaded darker; spikes compact, narrow. 'Snow Maiden'; dwarf; fls flushed rose. 'Spanish Gold': tall; fls rich mustard. 'Springtime'. to 100cm, robust; fls buff yellow and coral red. Stark's Hybrids: fls red and yellow. 'Sunningdale Yellow': dwarf; fls yellow, long-lasting. 'Torchbearer': dwarf; fls cream-primrose. 'Tubergeniana': dwarf; fls soft primrose. 'White Fairy': dwarf; fls white, abundant. 'Wrexham Buttercup': tall; fls clear lemon. Z7.

Koellikeria Reg. (For Professor Koelliker of Würzburg, author of 'A list of Wild Plants of Zurich'.) Gesneriaceae. 3 species of perennial herbs with scaly rhizomes. Leaves opposite, soft, downy. Inflorescence racemose; flowers small, bracteate; calyx lobes 5, narrow, approximately equalling tube; corolla tubular, 5-lobed, bilabiate, upper 2 lobes short, lower 3 larger and more or less dentate or fimbriate; stamens 4, anthers united; ovary semi-inferior. Fruit a capsule. C & S America (Costa Rica to Bolivia). Z10.

CULTIVATION   As for *Achimenes*, however, growth sometimes continues when the plants might be expected to be dormant, in which case continue to water over the winter period at a somewhat reduced rate and repot in spring.

K.argyrostigma (Hook.) Reg.
Stems pilose, to 30cm. Lvs clustered toward stem apex, to 6.5cm, obovate to broadly elliptic, obtuse or rounded at apex, broadly cuneate at base, crenate, petiolate, deep velvety green with white spots, pilose, membranous. Infl. terminal, elongate, erect; cor. 5mm, white or cream with red spots and purple throat. Costa Rica to Peru.

K.erinoides (DC.) Mansf.
Rosulate, low-growing, to 20cm. Lvs decussate, to 10cm, ovate to obovate, dentate, velvety green with white spots and veins flushed red, hairy. Infl. terminal or axillary, slender, to 30cm; cor. 1cm, strongly bilabiate, tube ruby red above, white below, upper lip short, garnet, lower lip to 3mm, creamy white, margins ciliate, throat with small yellow spot. Venezuela.

Lachenalia Jacq. f. ex Murray. (For Werner von Lachenal, late 18th-century Swiss botanist, frequently mentioned in Haller.) Liliaceae (Hyacinthaceae). Some 90 species of bulbous perennial herbs. Bulbs fleshy, usually pearly white; tunics thin, fragile. Leaves synanthous, paired, numerous or solitary, erect to arching or lying flat on soil surface, highly varied in shape: lorate-lanceolate, linear and grass-like, or broadly ovate-acute, glossy glabrous, pubescent or glaucous, sometimes tuberculate, each segment often spotted or banded darker green, red or purple-brown. Inflorescence scapose, erect and terminal, spicate, subspicate or racemose; peduncle stout or slender, usually solid, glaucescent, sometimes spotted, banded or strongly tinted; flowers zygomorphic, tubular or campanulate, pendulous to erect; perianth segments free, 6, in 2 whorls, the outer whorl shorter, forming a fleshy tube or cup, each segment often with a marked apical swelling, the inner whorl protruding, usually broader and more showy, with lips coloured and recurved; stamens 6, arising from base of perianth, usually declinate, exserted or included; ovary superior, trilocular; style simple, stigma capitate. Fruit a capsule, dehiscing lengthways; seeds numerous, black, shiny. S Africa (Namaqualand to SE Cape), Namibia; all species described are from the SE Cape Province unless otherwise specified. Z9.

CULTIVATION   A large and ornamental genus of frost-tender South African bulbs. Some species bear tubular blooms in many flowered racemes in vibrant yellows, orange or red; these are usually bird-pollinated. Others, with sweetly scented bell-shaped flowers, often in white, pink or blue, are bee-pollinated. In general terms, species from the Cape flower in winter and very early spring, those from more northerly, summer rainfall areas flower in early summer. *L.aloides* and its variants have long been cultivated, often for early blooming at Christmas or New Year; *Lachenalia* spp. sometimes remain in flower for 6–8 weeks.

In zones where temperatures seldom fall below freezing and bulbs will remain dry when dormant, *Lachenalia* spp. are grown in sunny sheltered positions, with a dry mulch, out of doors but will require some protection from sun at the hottest parts of the day. Otherwise grow in the cool glasshouse or conservatory in a medium-fertility loam based mix, in direct sunlight. Plant in late autumn and water sparingly as growth commences, plentifully when in full growth. Dry off as leaves wither and keep almost completely dry when dormant. Propagate by ripe seed when available; seedlings may flower in the season following first dormancy. Offsets and bulbils are also produced.

L.aloides (L.f.) Engl. (*L.tricolor* Jacq. f.).
A highly variable species. Lvs 2, lorate-lanceolate, glabrous, glossy or glaucous, often heavily blotched green or purple above. Infl. seldom exceeding 28cm, racemose, peduncle often mottled and tinted red-brown; fls pendulous, tubular to funnelform, outer seg. half length of inner, fleshy, lemon yellow to apricot or white, sometimes flushed orange, scarlet or blue-green from the base, apical swellings bright green, inner seg. 2–3.5cm, protruding, reflexed, tipped cinnabar red, magenta, scarlet or green or self-coloured; stamens included or inserted to 2mm. Winter-early summer. var. *aloides*. Lvs to 18cm, rather glaucous, plain green or mottled red-brown. Flowering stem 15–26cm; outer seg. yellow-orange, apical swelling bright green, inner seg. deep yellow, tips wide, stains red. 'Pearsonii' (*L.pearsonii* hort. non (Glover) W. Barker). Lvs to 15cm, glossy green spotted red-brown above. Flowering stem to 18cm, stout, strongly mottled red-brown; outer seg. to 1.5cm, apricot, apical swelling lime green, inner seg. to 3cm, apricot to gold, the tips broad, reflexed, stained red to maroon; stamens inserted. A popular garden plant developed in New Zealand and possibly of hybrid origin. The true *L.pearsonii* is a narrow-lvd plant with small, campanulate white fls tipped brown or opal; it hails from the Great Karasberg and is not cultivated. var. *aurea* (Lindl.) Engl. Lvs sometimes blotched or spotted maroon. Flowering stem 6–25cm, dark maroon; fls golden yellow, apical swelling on outer seg. lemon yellow to lime green. 'Nelsonii': lvs spotted purple; fls bright yellow tipped green. var. *luteola* (Jacq.) (*L.tricolor* var. *luteola* Jacq.). Lvs glaucous, densely marked purple-brown above. Outer perianth seg. pale yellow shading to green with lime green apical swellings, inner perianth seg. yellow-green, uppermost fls often sterile, unopened and tinted vivid red. var. *quadricolor* (Jacq.) Engl. Stoloniferous, increasing from bulbils. Lvs glaucous, usually blotched maroon. Flowering stem 9–20cm; outer perianth seg. scarlet or orange-red at base, fading to yellow or apricot with large lime green apical swellings, inner perianth seg. golden or sulphur yellow with broad magenta or crimson tips. var. *vanzyliae* W. Barker. Lvs ovate-lanceolate to lorate, usually marked maroon above. Flowering stem 8–26cm; fls subtended by conspicuous pale bracts, outer perianth seg. grey-blue at base fading to white, with grey-green apical swellings, inner perianth seg. olive green, tipped and edged grey-white.

L.arbuthnotiae W. Barker.
Lvs 1–2, lanceolate, coriaceous, green or maroon, sometimes densely spotted maroon above. Infl. 18–40cm, dense, spicate, fragrant; fls oblong in outline, bright yellow fading to dull red subtended by narrow white bracts, apical swelling on outer perianth seg. pale green, inner seg. protruding; stamens included or exserted to 2mm. Late winter-spring.

L.bachmanii Bak.
Resembles *L.contaminata* but lvs 2, linear, conduplicate, unmarked, infl. 15–30cm, inner perianth seg. only slightly protruding with dark red mark near tip.

L.bulbifera (Cyr.) Engl. (*L.pendula* Ait.).
Robust, variable. Bulb large, fleshy. Lvs to 30×4cm, 1–2, narrowly to broadly ovate, lanceolate or lorate, often heavily spotted on upper surface, sometimes producing bulbils on basal margins. Infl. 8–30cm, racemose; pedicels 2mm+; fls cylindrical, pendulous, orange to red, apical swelling on outer perianth seg. dark red or brown, inner seg. slightly longer, tips green, flanked by purple shading; stamens included or exserted to 2mm. Winter-spring.

L.carnosa Bak. (*L.ovatifolia* L. Guthrie).
Robust. Lvs 2, ovate to broadly ovate, lanceolate, with depressed longitudinal veins on upper surface, sometimes with green or brown pustules above. Infl. 8–25cm, spicate; fls urceolate-oblong, white, swelling on outer perianth seg. green or maroon, inner seg. protruding, tips white or magenta; stamens included or exserted to 2mm. Spring.

L.contaminata Ait. WILD HYACINTH.
Variable. Lvs to 20×0.3cm, numerous, grass-like, linear, channelled above, semi-terete, erect to horizontal; peduncle usually marked maroon. Infl. 6–25cm, dense, subspicate; fls campanulate, white, apical swelling on outer perianth seg. maroon-brown, inner seg. protruding, striped maroon near tips; stamens sometimes exserted. Spring.

L.elegans W. Barker var. *elegans*.
Lvs 1–2, lanceolate, sometimes spotted or with thickened brown margins. Infl. 18–24cm, spicate; fls oblong-urceolate, outer perianth seg. bright blue at base shading to rose, apical swelling brown, inner seg. protruding, white with pink spot near tips; stamens included or exserted to 2mm. var. *flava* W. Barker. Lf usually solitary, lanceolate to ovate-lanceolate,

Lachenalia (a) *L.aloides* (b) *L.carnosa* (c) *L.bulbifera* (d) *L.trichophylla* (e) *L.orthopetala*

glaucous, blotched dark green above, margins maroon, crispate. Infl. 15–25cm, spicate; fls spreading, urceolate, bright yellow tipped maroon, apical swelling on outer perianth seg. pale green, margin of inner seg. narrow, white, membranous. Winter. var. *membranacea* W. Barker. As for var. *flava* but lvs 1–2, infl. 15–20cm, inner perianth seg. protruding, pale green stained brown near tips, margin broad, white, membranous. Early spring. var. *suaveolens* W. Barker. As for var. *elegans* except infl. 10–27cm, fragrant, fls spreading, outer perianth seg. pale blue or green at base shading to pink to dark maroon, apical swelling dark maroon, upper half of inner perianth seg. dark maroon, margins white, membranous. Early spring.

L.glaucina Jacq. See *L.orchioides* var. *glaucina*.

L.glaucina var. *pallida* Lindl. not *L.pallida* Ait. See *L.orchioides* var. *orchioides*.

L.juncifolia Bak. var. *juncifolia.*
Lvs 2, filiform to linear, sometimes terete, base usually banded or marked maroon. Infl. 7–23cm, racemose; fls oblong-campanulate, outer perianth seg.. usually white tinged pink, apical swelling purple, deep pink or green, inner perianth seg. protruding with pink keels; stamens exserted 2mm+. Late winter-spring. var. *campanulata* W. Barker. Infl. 8–30mm; fls white, campanulate, apical swelling on outer perianth seg. deep rose, inner seg. with deep rose keels; stamens less exserted than in var. *juncifolia.*

L.liliiflora Jacq.
Lvs to 23×1cm, 2, lanceolate, densely tuberculate above. Infl. 10–20cm, subspicate to racemose, pedicels c2mm; fls oblong campanulate, white, apical swelling on outer perianth seg. brown, inner seg. slightly protruding, tips dark magenta; stamens included or exserted to 2mm. Spring.

L.massonii Bak. See *L.trichophylla.*

L.mathewsii W. Barker.
Lvs 2, glaucous, narrow-lanceolate, tapering, apex terete. Infl. 10–20cm, subspicate; fls yellow, oblong-campanulate, apical swelling on outer perianth seg. bright green, inner seg. protruding with central green spot near tip; stamens exserted 2mm+. Spring.

L.mediana Jacq.
Variable, close to *L.pallida* and *L.orchioides*. var. *mediana.* Lvs 2, lanceolate. Infl. 20–40cm, subspicate, pedicels about 2mm; fls oblong or oblong-campanulate, pale, opalescent; outer perianth seg. pale blue at base shading to dull white, swelling green or purple, inner perianth seg. dull white, marked green or purple near tip; stamens included or exserted to 2mm. Spring. var. *rogersii* (Bak.) W. Barker (*L.unifolia* var. *rogersii* Bak.). Lf solitary, broader than in var. *mediana*, undulate to crispate, base clasping, banded dark maroon or magenta. Fls blue to pink.

L.mutabilis Sweet.
Lf to 20×2cm, solitary, sometimes glaucous, occasionally spotted or banded maroon on clasping base, often crispate; peduncle swollen below infl. Infl. 10–45cm, spicate; fls with outer perianth seg. pale blue shading to white, apical swelling dark brown, inner seg. dark yellow with brown markings near tips; apex of rachis bright blue; stamens included or exserted to 2mm. Winter.

L.namaquensis Schltr. ex W. Barker.
Stoloniferous, producing bulbils at ground level. Lvs 1–2, linear-lanceolate, plicate. Infl. 8–23cm, spicate, floriferous; fls urceolate-oblong, outer tepals palest blue at base, shading to magenta, apical swellings green-purple or maroon, the upper pair of inner perianth seg. protruding, white, tipped magenta, the lower pair magenta; stamens included or exserted to 2mm. Winter-spring. Namaqualand.

L.orchioides (L.) Ait. var. *orchioides* (*L.glaucina* var. *pallida* Lindl.).
Lvs to 28×2cm, 1–2, lanceolate or lorate, coriaceous, sometimes spotted brown above. Infl. 8–40cm, spicate, fls fragrant,

oblong-cylindrical, fading to dull red, outer perianth seg. pale blue at base shading to green-yellow or cream, apical swellings green, inner perianth seg. protruding, tips often recurved; stamens included or exserted to 2mm. Winter-spring. var. *glaucina* (Jacq.) W. Barker (*L.glaucina* Jacq.). As for var. *orchioides* but less strongly scented, outer perianth seg. blue at base, shading to purple, with apical swelling dark purple, sometimes entirely blue with dark blue swelling.

L.orthopetala Jacq.
Lvs 10–15×0.6cm, 4–5, linear, grass-like, deeply channelled above, sometimes spotted green or brown above; petiole slender, dark maroon. Infl. 9–27cm, subspicate, dense, fls oblong-campanulate, upward-facing, white, sometimes with a pale maroon central stripe, outer perianth seg. with dark maroon apical swelling, inner marked dark maroon at tips; stamens included or exserted to 2mm; style projecting. Spring.

L.ovatifolia L. Guthrie. See *L.carnosa.*

L.pallida Ait.
Lvs 15–23×2–3cm, 1–2, upper surface sometimes tuberculate. Infl. 12–30cm, subspicate; fls numerous, oblong-campanulate, cream to yellow, fading to dull red, outer perianth seg. with brown or green apical swelling, inner seg. protruding; stamens included or exserted to 2mm. Late winter–spring.

L.pearsonii hort. non (Glover) W. Barker. See *L.aloides* 'Pearsonii'.

L.peersii Marloth ex W. Barker.
Lvs 1–2, lorate, green to maroon. Infl. 15–30cm, racemose; fls white fading to dull pink, swelling on outer perianth seg. green or green-brown, inner seg. protruding, tips recurved; stamens included or exserted to 2mm. Early summer.

L.pendula Ait. See *L.bulbifera.*

L.purpureocaerulea Jacq.
Lvs 15–20×1cm, 2, lanceolate or lorate, densely tuberculate above. Infl. 10–28cm, subspicate; fls widely campanulate, fragrant, outer perianth seg. blue to white at base shading to magenta or purple, apical swelling green-brown, inner seg. broader, slightly longer, magenta, tips darker; stamens exserted 2mm+. Early summer.

L.pustulata Jacq.
Lvs to 28×2.5cm, 1–2, lanceolate or lorate, often tuberculate above. Infl. 15–35cm, racemose; fls oblong-campanulate, usually cream or straw-yellow, apical swelling on outer perianth seg. green, inner seg. with dark pink or pale green central mark at tips; stamens exserted 2mm+. Later winter–early summer.

L.reflexa Thunb.
Lvs to 15×3cm, 1–2, bright green, glaucous, lanceolate to lorate, usually reflexed, sometimes heavily spotted above, margins sometimes thickened, usually undulate, peduncle short, clasped by leaf bases. Infl. to 20cm, subspicate, fls cylindrical, erect, green-yellow fading to dull red, outer perianth seg. with green or yellow-green apical swelling, inner seg. protruding; stamens included or exserted to 2mm. Winter.

L.roodeae Phillips. See *L.splendida.*

L.rosea Andrews.
Lf usually solitary, sometimes marked maroon or brown above. Infl. 8–30cm, racemose, fls oblong-campanulate, outer perianth seg. blue to rose pink, often variegated, apical swelling brown or deep pink, inner seg. rose pink; stamens included or exserted to 2mm. Winter–mid summer.

L.rubida Jacq.
Lvs 1–2, lanceolate or lorate, often spotted green or dark purple above. Buds appearing before lvs are fully mature. Infl. 6–25cm, subspicate, pedicels about 2mm; fls pendulous, cylindrical, outer perianth seg. bright pink to ruby red, or pale yellow, heavily spotted ruby-red, apical swelling yellow-green or pink-red, inner perianth seg. exceeding outer, tips purple, marked white; stamens included or exserted to 2mm. Autumn–winter (the earliest flowering species).

L.salteri W. Barker.
Lvs 2, lanceolate, coriaceous, upper surface sometimes blotched brown. Infl. 15–35cm, subspicate; fls oblong-campanulate, cream to red-purple, outer perianth seg. often pale blue at base, apical swelling brown-purple, inner perianth seg. protruding, pink; stamens exserted 2mm+. Early summer.

L.splendida Diels (*L.roodeae* Phillips).
Lvs 2, lanceolate. Infl. 6–25cm, spicate; fls oblong-campanulate, outer perianth seg. pale blue at base shading to white or pale lilac, apical swelling green-brown, inner perianth seg. protruding, dark lilac with central purple stripe; stamens exserted 2mm+. Winter.

L.trichophylla Bak. (*L.massonii* Bak.).
Lf solitary, cordate, stellate-hairy. Infl. 8–20cm, spicate; fls oblong-cylindric, pale yellow, outer perianth seg. sometimes flushed pink, apical swellings green, inner seg. protruding; stamens included or exserted to 2mm. Spring.

L.tricolor Jacq. f. See *L.aloides*.
L.tricolor var. *luteola* Jacq. See *L.aloides* var. *luteola*.

L.unicolor Jacq.
Lvs to 15×1.5cm, 2, lanceolate or lorate, usually densely tuberculate above, dark green to maroon. Infl. 8–30cm, racemose; fls oblong-campanulate, cream with green apical swelling on outer perianth seg. to pink, lilac, magenta, blue or purple with darker swellings; stamens conspicuously exserted. Spring. Closely related to *L.pustulata*.

L.unifolia Jacq.
Lf 15–20×0.5–1cm, solitary, linear, widening at base and loosely clasping peduncle, base banded maroon and magenta. Infl. 10–35cm, racemose; fls oblong-campanulate, outer perianth seg. blue at base, shading to white, pale yellow or pink, apical swellings brown, green-brown or deep pink, inner perianth seg. protruding, white. Winter–early summer.

L.unifolia var. *rogersii* Bak. See *L.mediana* var. *rogersii*.

L.violacea Jacq. var. *violacea*.
Lvs 1–2, lanceolate, sometimes spotted maroon, undulate to crispate. Infl. 10–35cm, racemose, peduncle often swollen below infl., fls numerous, campanulate, outer perianth seg. pale blue-green shading to pale magenta or purple, apical swellings brown, inner seg. purple to violet; stamens purple, exserted 2mm+. Winter–spring. var. *glauca* W. Barker. Lf solitary, lanceolate, undulate. Infl. 10–23cm, coconut-scented, as for var. *violacea* but outer perianth seg. grey-blue shading to pale magenta, apical swelling slightly darker, inner tepals pale magenta.

L.viridiflora W. Barker.
Lvs 2, lanceolate, pale green, longitudinally veined above, sometimes spotted dark green, occasionally tuberculate. Infl. 8–20cm, subspicate, fls cylindrical-ventricose, outer perianth seg. viridian to turquoise with viridian central stripe and apical swelling, inner perianth seg. protruding, tips white, with viridian central stripe; stamens included or exserted to 2mm. Winter.

Lapeirousia Pourr. (For Philippe Picot de Lapeirouse, botanist at the University of Toulouse, late 18th century.) Iridaceae. About 38 species of perennial herbs. Corms bell-shaped with flat base and hard, woody tunics. Leaves 2 to several, iris-like, deciduous in dry season. Stem 2–3-angled, sometimes winged, usually branched. Inflorescence a spike, branched or unbranched. Flowers regular or zygomorphic, usually brightly coloured; perianth forming a long or short tube, tepals 6, subequal or unequal; stamens 3; style with 3 usually forked branches. Tropical & S Africa. Z9.

CULTIVATION   As for *Ixia*.

L.anceps (L. f.) Ker-Gawl.
Stem erect, 10–30cm, usually much-branched; branches flattened, 2–3-winged, the wings somewhat serrate. Basal lvs 1 to few, the lowest linear, ribbed, upper ones sword-shaped. Spike about 6-fld, distichous; bracts small, 5–7mm; fls irregular, white or pink, the lower 3 seg. marked with red; tube 25–80mm, very slender; tepals 10–30mm, narrowly lanceolate, the upper 3 larger, erect or reflexed, the lower 3 each with a small tooth at the base. Late winter–spring. S Africa (Cape Province).

L.compressa Pourr. See *L.fabricii*.

L.corymbosa (L. f.) Ker-Gawl.
5–45cm. Basal lvs 1 or more, 8–30cm, linear, often ribbed, the edge sometimes undulate or crisped. Stem branched, flattened, 2-winged. Panicle several-fld, each branch 2-fld; fls regular or slightly irregular, white, yellow, blue or violet, the seg. often with a dark mark at base; tube 4–15mm, tepals usually also 4–15mm, lanceolate or narrowly ovate, obtuse or acuminate. Late spring–summer. S Africa (Cape Province). ssp. *corymbosa*. To 20cm high with 1 basal lf. Fls blue, marked with white in throat, rarely cream, less than 20cm; tepals 7–10mm, tube 4–10mm. ssp. *alta* Goldbl. Over 30cm tall, usually with more than 1 basal lf. Tepals shorter than perianth tube. ssp. *fastigiata* (Lam.) Goldbl. (*L.purpureolutea* (Klatt) Bak.). To 20cm high, basal lf 1, the edge usually crisped. Fls over 20mm, violet not marked with white, or cream or yellow with purple marks.

L.denticulata (Lam.) Lawrence. See *L.fabricii*.

L.divaricata Bak.
Plants 7–25cm tall. Basal lf 1, 10–35cm, linear to awl-shaped, ribbed. Stem branched near base or unbranched; spike 5–12-fld. Fls irregular, somewhat 2-lipped, white or cream, often pink-tinged; perianth tube to 15mm long, slender at base then curving and becoming wider; tepals lanceolate, acute, the top one longest, to 16mm, erect; upper laterals reflexed, lowest 3 tepals 12mm. Late winter–spring. S Africa (W Cape).

L.erythrantha (Klotzsch ex Klatt) Bak. (*L.sandersonii* Bak.; *L.rhodesiana* N.E. Br.).
A variable species; plants 15–45cm high, corms to 1.5cm wide at base. Lvs 3–4, linear or lanceolate, about half length of stem. Stem flattened, 2–3-angled, branched. Infl. paniculate, many-fld; fls slightly irregular, violet-blue with white, arrow-shaped mark outlined in purple on lower tepals, or crimson; tube 6–14mm, slender, slightly curved; tepals subequal, 6–11×2–4mm, lanceolate-spathulate; anth. white, red, blue or purple. Summer. Southern tropical Africa.

L.fabricii (Delaroche) Ker-Gawl. (*L.compressa* Pourr.; *L.denticulata* (Lam.) Lawrence).
15–25cm, rarely more. Basal lf 1, of variable length, linear or sword-shaped, ribbed. Stem branched, flattened and 2-winged, the wings serrate. Spike to 8-fld; fls large, irregular, cream or yellow with red marks, often pink-tinged on outside. Tube 30–50mm long, slender, constricted near apex, then wider; tepals subequal, 13–20mm long, the topmost erect or reflexed, the others spreading, the 3 lowest often narrower and forming a lip. Spring–early summer. S Africa (Cape Province).

L.fissifolia (Jacq.) Ker-Gawl. See *L.pyramidalis*.

L.jacquinii N.E. Br.
Dwarf, 8–12(–20)cm. Basal lf 1; stem flattened, 3-angled. Infl. laxly to 10-fld, bracts large, to 20mm long. Fls irregular, violet with cream marks, the tube paler; tube 30–40mm, erect, slender, somewhat curved and wider near apex; tepals subequal, oblong, acute, the topmost slightly larger and hooded,

the others spreading. Late winter–spring. S Africa (Cape Province).

L.laxa (Thunb.) N.E. Br. See *Anomatheca laxa*.

L.purpureolutea (Klatt) Bak. See *L.corymbosa* ssp. *fastigiata*.

L.pyramidalis (Lam.) Goldbl. (*L.fissifolia* (Jacq.) Ker-Gawl.). Dwarf 5–12cm, sometimes branched. Basal lvs usually 1, linear or lanceolate, ribbed. Infl. many-fld, at first distichous, later spirally arranged; fls white, pale to deep blue or carmine red, the lower seg. marked with white or cream; tube 20–40mm, slender, curved; topmost tepal erect, hooded, ovate; upper laterals spreading; lower 3 forming platform at right angles to tube, often with small calli near base. Winter–spring. S Africa (Cape Province).

L.rhodesiana N.E. Br. See *L.erythrantha*.

L.sandersonii Bak. See *L.erythrantha*.

L.silenoides (Jacq.) Ker-Gawl.
5–12(–20)cm, often branched at base. Basal lf 1, to 10cm long, linear to lanceolate, ribbed. Spike fairly densely several to many-fld; fls irregular, magenta or cerise with cream-yellow markings on lower seg.; tube 30–50mm long, slender, curved; tepals subequal, broadly ovate; upper 3 erect, lower 3 geniculate and forming a lip, each with red spot in centre. Winter–spring. S Africa (Cape Province).

Lapiedra Lagasca. Amaryllidaceae. 2 species of bulbous perennial herbs. Leaves few, basal. Flowers erect, in a 4–9-flowered umbel; spathe of 2 bracts; tepals 6, free, equal, spreading; filaments as long as the basifixed anthers. Fruit a flattened, spherical, 3-lobed capsule, surrounded by the persistent, withered perianth; seeds few. W Mediterranean. Z8.

CULTIVATION   Occurring in rocky habitats in the western Mediterranean, *Lapiedra* bears its short-lived, small white flowers in succession in late summer, before the emergence of the leaves which persist until the following spring. A warm dry period of summer dormancy is essential. They grow well when restricted at the root in pans in the alpine house or frame. They will also thrive in hot, dry positions on the rock garden. Plant 7.5cm/3in deep in spring. Otherwise cultivate as for *Ixiolirion*.

L.martinezii Lagasca.
Bulb to 5cm diam. Lvs to 25×1cm, appearing after fls, with a pale band on upper surface. Tepals 8–12mm, white with a green stripe on the outside. Late summer. S Spain, N Africa.

Ledebouria Roth. (For Carl Friedrich von Ledebour (1785–1851), German botanist.) Liliaceae (Hyacinthaceae). Some 16 species of bulbous perennial herbs. Leaves basal, frequently striped or spotted red or green. Inflorescence an axillary raceme, slender, often flexuous; bracts inconspicuous; flowers small or minute, green or purple; perianth segments recurved; filaments free; ovary superior, expanding to a wide base below, conical or broadly conical, stipitate, ovules basal, 2 per locule. S Africa. Z9.

CULTIVATION   Grown for their leaf coloration and green-mauve flowers in sunny positions in the cool greenhouse or conservatory in a moderately fertile potting mix. They associate well with succulents and cacti.

L.apertiflora (Bak.) Jessop (*Drimia apertiflora* Bak.; *Scilla apertiflora* (Bak.) C.A. Sm.).
Bulbs to 6cm, frequently tinged pink towards apex. Lvs 4 to 7, to 35×2.5cm, erect, sublinear, base attenuate. Fls numerous, in an erect or flexuous raceme; perianth seg. green, grey or marked pink. S Africa.

L.concolor (Bak.) Jessop (*Drimia cooperi* Bak.; *Scilla concolor* Bak.).
Bulbs to 5cm, epigeal. Lvs 2 to 6, to 15×5cm, erect or erect-spreading, oblong-lanceolate to ovate, often undulate. Fls numerous, mostly green, in a suberect raceme; perianth seg. green, grey or marked pink. S Africa.

L.cooperi (Hook. f.) Jessop (*Scilla cooperi* Hook. f.).
Bulbs to 4cm, usually absent. Lvs 1–3, to 25×2cm, erect, somewhat fleshy, oblong to ovate-oblong or linear, base slightly narrowed, sometimes with brown longitudinal stripes. Infl. suberect; perianth seg. pale purple or with a green keel. S Africa.

L.floribunda (Bak.) Jessop (*Scilla floribunda* Bak.).
Bulbs to 15cm. Lvs 4 or 5, to 35×15cm, suberect, lanceolate to oblong-linear. Infl. suberect; perianth seg. grey or green with pink. S Africa.

L.hypoxidioides (Schönl.) Jessop (*Scilla hypoxidioides* Schönl.).
Bulbs to 4cm, sometimes pink towards apex. Lvs 2–4, to 15×3.5cm, firm, suberect, oblong-lanceolate to oblong-ovate, densely covered with silky hairs above and beneath. Infl.

L.inquinata (C.A. Sm.) Jessop (*Scilla inquinata* C.A. Sm.).
Bulbs to 6.5cm, with glossy, dark outer scales, sometimes tinged pink. Lvs to 15×3.5cm, erect, ovate-lanceolate, glaucous, mostly without spots, narrowed near base. Infl. suberect to flexuous, 50–150-fld; perianth seg. green, grey or marked pink. S Africa.

L.luteola Jessop.
Bulbs to 5cm, scales producing abundant threads, inner scales yellow. Lvs 4–10, to 8cm, erect or curving, narrowly to linear-lanceolate, firm, spotted or with indistinct transverse markings. Infl. suberect, 30–60-fld; perianth seg. to 4mm, green, grey or marked pink. S Africa.

L.marginata (Bak.) Jessop.
Bulbs to 8cm, exterior scales glossy, dark, often speckled pink. Lvs 4–10, to 16×3cm, firm, erect, with prominent venation. Infl. mostly flexuous, 50–150-fld; perianth seg. green, grey or marked pink. S Africa.

L.ovalifolia (Schräd.) Jessop (*Drimia ovalifolia* Schräd.; *Scilla ovalifolia* (Schräd.) C.A. Sm.).
Bulbs to 2.5cm. Lvs 3–5, to 3.5×1cm, erect-spreading or spreading, base narrowed, margins involute near base. Infl. to 9cm, to 20-fld; pedicels spreading; fls striped pink. S Africa.

L.ovatifolia (Bak.) Jessop (*Scilla ovatifolia* Bak.).
Bulbs to 4cm, scales truncate, imbricate, producing abundant

threads, exterior scales inconspicuous or absent. Lvs 2–5, to 25cm, ovate, with a wide base. Infl. mostly flexuous, densely 50–150-fld; perianth seg. green, grey or marked pink. S Africa.

L.revoluta (L. f.) Jessop (*Hyacinthus revolutus* L. f.). Bulbs to 7.5cm, spherical, exterior scales glossy, dark often speckled pink. Lvs 4–8, to 15×3cm, suberect or spreading, lanceolate to narrowly ovate, usually attenuate, often with dark spots above. Infl. suberect, to 100-fld; perianth seg. green. S Africa.

L.socialis (Bak.) Jessop (*Scilla socialis* Bak.). Bulbs to 2cm, ovoid, often purple, produced into a neck. Lvs few to several, to 10×2cm, erect-spreading or spreading, slightly fleshy, lanceolate, narrowed into a petiole-like base,

with a silver sheen and some dark green blotches above, green or deep pink-purple beneath. Infl. suberect, to 25-fld; perianth seg. pale purple with green keels. S Africa.

L.undulata (Jacq.) Jessop (*Drimia undulata* Jacq.). Bulbs to 5cm, with several dry outer scales which often form a neck; roots often forming fusiform tubers. Lvs 2 to 6, to 15×2cm, suberect to spreading, firm, lanceolate or linear-lanceolate. Infl. erect, lax; perianth seg. green, sometimes striped pink. S Africa.

L.viscosa Jessop. Bulbs to 10×2cm, sometimes marked pink. Lvs 1 to 3, to 23×3cm, erect, spathulate-oblanceolate, viscid. Infl. erect, lax, 20–30-fld; perianth seg. grey, green or marked pink. S Africa.

Leontice L. (From Gk *leon*, lion, alluding to the apparent lion's footprint pattern on the leaves.) Berberidaceae. 3–5 species of rhizomatous, perennial herbs, close to *Bongardia* and *Gymnospermium*. Rhizome tuberous. Leaves alternate, 2–3 times pinnately divided or cut; flowering stem leaves few. Inflorescence a raceme, sometimes branching; flowers yellow; sepals 6–9, petaloid; petals 6, smaller than sepals, blunt at tip; stamens 6. Fruit a dry, inflated capsule, 1–4-seeded. SE Europe to E Asia.

CULTIVATION *Leontice* occurs in steppes and semi-deserts from the Balkans to Central Asia, in exposed rocky places, sometimes on limestone and often as a weed of cultivated ground. Long-stalked yellow flowers in dense clusters appear in early spring over the fleshy blue-grey leaves. Hardy to at least –5°C/23°F, *Leontice* will grow outside in warm dry areas in perfectly drained soil, given a dry period for dormancy in late summer, but is best grown in a bulb frame or alpine house in damp and dull climates. Plant tubers at least 20cm/8in. deep. Propagate from seed. Seed-grown specimens may take several years to reach flowering size. In the wild, the large seeds germinate in autumn and pull themselves down to depths of 21–36cm/8.5–15in. before the cotyledons emerge. In addition to the species described below, *L.armeniaca* Boiv., *L.ewersmannii* Bunge and *L.incerra* Pall. are sometimes grown. The first seldom exceeds 7cm; the second differs from *L.leontopetalum* in its elliptic-lanceolate leaflets; the third attains 16cm, has bi- to triternate leaves and slightly fleshy, broad leaflets to 5cm long. *L.albertii* Reg. See *Gymnospermium alberti*.

L.altaica Pall. See *Gymnospermium altaicum*.
L.chrysogonum L. See *Bongardia chrysogonum*.

L.leontopetalum L.
20–80cm. Tuber. large, knobbly. Lvs to 20cm wide, 2–3× ternately divided, somewhat glaucous and fleshy, seg. ovate-

obovate, rarely cordate, 25–40cm. Infl. many-fld, terminal or lateral, dense, becoming lax; pedicel spreading; sep. round to obovate, early deciduous, around 8mm; pet. one-third length of sep.; stamens two-thirds length of sep. Fr. ovoid, 2–4cm, papery. Spring. E Mediterranean, Aegean. Z6.

Lepidochiton Sealy. Amaryllidaceae. 2–3 bulbous perennial herbs closely related to *Hymenocallis*. Leaves usually 5–9, synanthous, linear, keeled, weakly sheathing at base. Scape with solitary flower subtended by 3 linear-lanceolate bracts; flower large, sessile, somewhat declinate, fragrant; perianth crateriform, white or yellow; perianth tube long, cylindric, green; segments lanceolate, recurved, subequal; staminal cup large, widely spreading, rotate or campanulate, margin laciniate or coarsely lobed, striped green or yellow along filamental traces, free part of filaments short, incurved; style exceeding stamens, stigma capitate; ovary 3-locular, ovules 16–20 per locule. Capsule oblong, dehiscent; seeds 1–5, fleshy. S America.

CULTIVATION As for *Hymenocallis*.

L. andreana (Bak.) Nichols. See *L.quitoensis*.

L.quitoensis (Herb.) Sealy (*L.andreana* (Bak.) Nichols.). Bulb globose, 3.5cm diam., neck 3–7cm, grey-brown. Lvs deciduous, 5–7, 30–60×1.5–3cm, keeled along midrib, glossy bright green above, dull green beneath. Scape 5–35cm, ancipitous, emerging after lvs; spathe valves linear 3–5cm; fls 15–20×13–20cm wide; perianth tube erect, curved at throat,

green, seg. white, keeled at base, outer whorl 9–13×1.2cm, apiculate, inner whorl to 15×1.8cm; staminal cup 4.5–6.5×7–9cm, irregularly 2-lobed or bifid between fil., margin laciniate to coarsely dentate, striped green along filamental traces, yellow in throat; free filaments to 2.5cm, style to 23.5cm. Ecuador.

Leucocoryne Lindl. (From Gk *leukos*, white, and *koryne*, club, referring to the sterile anthers.) Liliaceae (Alliaceae). 12 species of bulbous perennial herbs, many with characteristic smell of garlic. Bulbs to 2cm wide, with dark brown tunics. Leaves basal, linear, often channelled, senescent before flowering. Flowers 2–12, funnel-shaped, in umbels with 2 spathes; perianth segments 6, similar, white, blue or violet, lower parts fused into a basal tube, upper parts free, spreading; stamens 6, 3 joined to perianth within basal tube, staminodes 3, club-shaped, joined to perianth at mouth of basal tube. Chile. Z9.

CULTIVATION   Grown for their loose heads of scented, soft blue flowers carried over long periods in spring and early summer, *Leucocoryne* spp. start into growth early in the year; the grass-like foliage dies down at or slightly before flowering, and bulbs enter dormancy during summer and autumn. They are suitable for outdoor cultivation only in areas that are essentially frost-free. Plant in full sun and in well-drained soil. Otherwise, grow in a frost-free glasshouse; a minimum winter temperature of 5–7°C/40–45°F is suitable. Grow in direct sun, in well-crocked pots with a medium-fertility loam-based mix with additional sharp sand. Water sparingly in spring when growth resumes, and reduce after flowering for a dry rest period. Top dress annually and repot every second or third year if necessary. Propagate from seed sown when ripe, or under glass in spring. Also by offsets, although these are not produced in quantity.

L.alliacea Lindl.
15–30cm. Lvs several, grass-like, 15–20cm. Fls to 18mm, basal tube to 8mm; tepals narrow, acute, white, tinged green. Spring.

L.ixioides (Hook.) Lindl. (*Brodiaea ixioides* Hook.). GLORY OF THE SUN.
To 45cm. Lvs to 45cm, slender, grass-like. Fls 6–9 in a loose fragrant umbel; pedicels 2–6.5cm; tepals 12–15mm, free portions white or, more usually, deeply edged lilac to violet-blue, basal tube white; stamens and staminodes yellow-white, slender. Spring.

L.ixioides var. *purpurea* (Gay) Bak. See *L.purpurea*.

L.odorata Lindl.
Distinguished from *L.ixioides* only by pedicels to 2cm, tepals smaller, pale blue.

L.purpurea Gay (*L.ixioides* var. *purpurea* (Gay) Bak.).
To 50cm. Lvs to 30cm, grass-like. Fls 2–6 per umbel; bracts channelled, 5–6cm; pedicels 2.5–4cm; tepals obovate, 2.5–3×1cm, white tinted purple, ageing mauve-indigo; staminodes yellow tipped purple. Spring.

Leucocrinum Nutt. ex A. Gray. (From Gk *leukos*, white, and *krinon*, a type of lily.) SAND LILY; STAR LILY; MOUNTAIN LILY. Liliaceae (Funkiaceae). 1 species, a perennial herb. Rhizomes subterranean; roots fleshy. Leaves 10–20×0.2–0.6cm, narrowly linear, radical, forming tufts, the bases sheathed by membranous bracts. Flowers white, fragrant, in clusters on 0.5–3cm subterranean stems barely breaking soil surface; perianth salverform, tube slender, 6-lobed, lobes 1.4–2cm, narrowly oblong; stamens 6, near mouth of perianth tube, anthers yellow, style 1, slender; stigma shallowly 3-lobed. Fruit a capsule, seeds black, angled. Spring–early summer. W US (Oregon to New Mexico).

CULTIVATION   Grown for the fragrant white flowers carried at ground level in spring and early summer, *Leucocrinum* is cold tolerant to between –20°C/–4°F. Grow in sun in a well drained but moisture-retentive alkaline soil. Propagate by seed.

L.montanum Nutt. ex A. Gray.

Leucojum L. (From Greek *leukos*, white, and *ion*, violet, a reference to the delicate fragrance, name first applied by Theophrastus to *Matthiola* and a white-flowered bulbous plant; other miscellaneous applications until Fuchs's *De Historia Stirpium*, when attached to *L.vernum*, but later again variously applied.) SNOWFLAKE. Amaryllidaceae. About 10 species of bulbous perennials, resembling and related to *Galanthus*. Bulbs globose to ovoid, with brown, membranous, outer scales. Leaves at first enclosed by a membranous sheath, filiform to linear or broadly ligulate, emerging with or before flowers. Scape slender and solid or stout and hollow; terminal spathe with 1–2 bracteoles, united by membranes; flowers emerging from spathe on pendulous pedicels, 1–5+ per scape; perianth segments free, equal, oblanceolate or oblanceolate-oblong, acute or apiculate, white, sometimes spotted green or yellow at apex, or tinged pink; anthers yellow, conic, opening by apical pores; filaments white, short; style filiform to clavate, exceeding anthers; ovary inferior, globose, 3-locular, green. Seeds black or brown, smooth or carunculate or with air pockets. W Europe to Middle East, N Africa.

CULTIVATION   Grown for their pendent white flowers, which bear a superficial resemblance to those of *Galanthus* but generally have a firmer, more waxen texture. The common name snowdrop, which usually refers to *Galanthus*, is applied to *Leucojum* in the southern US. *Leucojum* spp. occur in a variety of habitats; *L.vernum* grows in moist woodland and on shaded hillsides, blooming there at snow-melt; *L.aestivum* in wet fields and woods and in swamps, especially near rivers. The remaining species are more typically found in drier habitats such as on the Mediterranean dunes under pines (*L.trichophyllum*) or on dry rocky grassland (*L.nicaeense*, *L.roseum*). *L.autumnale* grows in the wild in open woodland, or scrub and in dry rocky grassland.

L.vernum and *L.aestivum* are suited to naturalizing in damp rough grass, or for growing in damp pockets in the rock garden; the latter thrives in moist, rich, heavy soils, especially by pond or streamside, and is tolerant of

(a) (b) (c) (d) (e) (f)

Leucojum (a) *L.aestivum* (b) *L.vernum* (c) *L.tricophyllum* (d) *L.autumnale* (e) *L.nicaeense* (f) *L.roseum*

waterlogged conditions. Grow in partial shade, or in sun where soils remain permanently moist. *L.autumnale*, for the sunny border front, path edging and for warm sunny locations on the rock garden, is one of the least demanding of the smaller species for growing in the open, given a well-drained sandy soil. *L.nicaeense*, *L.trichophyllum* and *L.roseum*, although sometimes grown in the open in similar warm and perfectly drained situations, are eminently suited to cultivation in the alpine house or bulb frame, where their delicate beauty can be appreciated at close quarters, and where their requirement for hot dry dormancy in summer and protection from winter wet is more easily accommodated. Propagate by division in spring or autumn, after flowering, or by seed sown when ripe.

L.aestivum L. SUMMER SNOWFLAKE; LODDON LILY.
Bulb ovoid, to 4cm diam. Lvs ligulate, obtuse at apex, to 50×2cm, glossy deep green. Scape to 60cm, stout, hollow, somewhat flattened with 2 membranous wings; spathe solitary, lanceolate, green-membranous, to 5cm; fls 2–7, faintly chocolate-scented; pedicels to 6cm; seg. broad-oblong, to 2cm, white, marked green just below apiculate apex; style clavate; ovary oblong-oval, green, to 8mm diam. Seeds black, testa loose, forming air pockets. Spring. Europe including GB to Iran. 'Gravetye' ('Gravetye Giant'): robust, vigorous, to 75cm; fls 5–7; seg. to 2.5cm. var. *pulchellum* (Salisb.) Fiori (*L.hernandezii* Cambess.). Smaller in all parts than type. Scape lacking transparent wings; fls 2–4; seg. to 14mm. Flowering earlier than type. Balearic Is., Sardinia. Z4.

L.autumnale L.
Bulb globose to ovoid, about 1cm diam., forming many offsets. Lvs filiform, to 16cm at maturity, pale green, appearing after fls. Scape slender, green- to red-brown, usually about 15cm; spathe solitary, linear to lanceolate; fls 1–4, on slender pedicels; seg. oblong, apiculate or toothed, 1cm, crystalline white faintly flushed pink at base; style filiform; ovary globose, green, 3mm in diam. Seeds soon ripening, black. Summer–autumn. W Europe (Portugal, Spain, Sardinia, Sicily, Crete), N Africa. 'Cobb's Variety': to 20cm; fls white flushed pink. var. *oporanthum* (Jordan & Fourr.) Maire. Lvs absent at flowering. Scape to 25cm; all seg. 3-toothed. Morocco. Plants in commerce under this name are var. *pulchellum*. var. *pulchellum* (Jordan & Fourr.) Dur. & Schinz. Lvs present at flowering. Outer seg. 3-toothed; inner seg. entire, acute. Morocco, Gibraltar. Z5.

L.hernandezii Cambess. See *L.aestivum* var. *pulchellum*.
L.hiemale DC. See *L.nicaeense*.

L.longifolium (M. Roem.) Gren. & Godron.
Bulb ovoid, to 1cm diam. Lvs 2–3, slender, to 25cm, green. Scape slender, to 20cm; spathes 2, linear, 2.5cm; fls 1–3; seg. oblanceolate, 9mm, white; style slender; ovary globose, green, 3mm diam. Spring. Corsica. Z7.

L.nicaeense Ardoino (*L.hiemale* DC.).
Bulb globose, to 2cm diam. Lvs 2–4, narrow-linear, to 30cm, often curled, deep green, slightly glaucous, appearing in autumn. Scape to 15cm, usually less; spathes 2, linear, to

2cm; fls 1–3, on short pedicels; seg. oblanceolate, 3 outer seg. apiculate, to 12mm, white, spreading; style slender, just exceeding stamens; ovary subglobose, 3mm diam., green, with 6-lobed disc. Seeds black, carunculate. Spring. S France, Monaco. Z7.

L.roseum Martin.
Bulb globose, to 1.5cm diam. Lvs narrow-linear, to 10cm, deep glossy green, appearing with or after fls. Scape to 15cm; spathes 2, linear; fls usually solitary; seg. oblanceolate, to 9mm, pale pink, deepest along median line; style filiform; ovary globose, deep green, 3mm in diam. Seeds deep brown. Summer–autumn. Corsica, Sardinia. Z7.

L.trichophyllum Schousb.
Bulb ovoid, to 1.5cm diam. Lvs filiform, to 20cm, green, in the wild often withered before flowering. Scape slender, to 25cm; spathes 2, lanceolate; fls 2–4 on slender pedicels to 4cm; seg. oblanceolate-oblong, 3 outer seg. apiculate, to 2.5cm, white or flushed pink to purple, especially at base; style filiform, exceeding anth.; ovary turbinate, green, to 5mm diam. Winter spring. S Portugal, SW Spain, Morocco. Z7.

L.valentinum Pau.
Bulb globose, about 2cm diam. Lvs narrow-linear, to 25cm, grey-green, appearing after fls. Scape to 15cm; spathes 2, linear; fls 1–3; seg. broad-obovate, apiculate, to 1.5cm, milk-white; style filiform; ovary turbinate, with 6-lobed disc. Autumn. C Spain, Greece. Z7.

L.vernum L. SPRING SNOWFLAKE.
Bulb ovoid, to 3cm+ diam. Lvs stout, ligulate, to 20×2cm, deep green, extending after flowering. Scape stout, hollow, to 20cm, deep green; spathe membranous; fls solitary, occasionally 2; seg. broad-oblong, acute, 2×1cm, white, marked green or yellow just below apex; style clavate; ovary subglobose, green, 6mm diam. Winter. France to EC Europe, naturalized England. var. *vagneri* Stapf. Robust. Scape to 25cm; fls paired. Hungary. ssp. *carpathicum* (Loud.) E. Murray. Fls solitary; seg. marked yellow at tips. Poland, Romania. Yellow markings usually constant in ssp. *carpathicum*, but sometimes occur in other vars, especially in newly opened fls. Z5.

Liatris Gaertn. ex Schreb. BUTTON SNAKE ROOT; GAY FEATHER; BLAZING STAR; SNAKE ROOT. Compositae. About 35 species of perennial herbs arising from corms or much-flattened rootstocks. Leaves alternate, linear to ovate-lanceolate, simple, glandular-punctate, radical leaves elongate, stem leaves numerous, reduced above. Capitula discoid, clustered in corymbose spikes or racemes; phyllaries imbricate in several series, lancolate to orbicular, herbaceous, margins ciliate or deeply erose; receptacle flat; florets hermaphrodite, tubular, purple to rose-purple, rarely white. Fruit a somewhat cylindric, basally attenuate, c10-ribbed cypsela; pappus of plumose or barbellate bristles. Eastern N America.

CULTIVATION   With the exception of *L.spicata*, which occurs on streambanks and ditchsides, most *Liatris* spp. are found in prairie or open forest glades on dry stony soils. Valued for their late summer and autumn flowers, which are unusual in opening from the top of the spike downwards, *Liatris* is suited to the herbaceous and cut-flower border and to native plant collections and other more informal situations. Flowering is prolonged by removing spent blooms at the tip of the spike, and when cutting for indoor display, care must be taken not to remove too much foliage to ensure good development of the tubers. Most species are tolerant of poor dry soils in cultivation but perform best on fertile, well drained and moderately retentive soils, with emphasis on good moisture-retention for *L.spicata*. Tubers are prone to rot in soils that are excessively wet in winter and also make a desirable food source for various rodents. Propagate by division or seed sown ripe in autumn.

L.acidota Engelm. & A.Gray.
To 80cm. Stems 1–4, stiffly erect, glabrous or puberulent. Lvs to 40 × 0.5cm, linear-lanceolate, shorter above. Capitula numerous, loosely clustered in a spike, sessile; phyllaries few, glabrous, adpressed, ovate to oblong-lanceolate, sometimes purple-tinged; florets red-purple . Fr. to 5mm; pappus c7mm. Coastal Louisiana and Texas. Z9.

L.aspera Michx.
To 1.1m. Stems usually 1, sometimes several, glabrous below with scattered hairs above, often rough throughout. Lvs to 15 × 2cm, rhombic-lanceolate to linear-lanceolate or almost linear, especially above, long-petiolate, glabrous and often rough, upper beocming sessile. Capitula at least 20, in a long open spike, sessile or pedunculate; phyllaries glabrous, with broad scarious margins, slightly wrinkled, inner oblong-spathulate, rounded, sometimes strongly wrinkled; florets usually purple, rarely white. Fr. to 6mm; pappus to 8mm. Z5.

L.callilepis hort. See *L.spicata.*

L. × creditonensis Gaiser. (*L.ligulistylis* × *L.squarrosa.*)
To c50cm. Stems 12 or more, glabrous below, sparsely pubesc. above. Lvs to 20 × 1cm, linear-lanceolate, uppermost grading into the phyllaries. Capitula few to many in a racemose infl.; phyllaries laxly erect, oblong, apex subarcuate, acute, most herbaceous, with scarious, slightly revolute margins; florets pale purple. Fr to 5mm; pappus c6mm. Garden origin. Z4.

L.cylindracea Michx.
To 60cm. Stems 1 to several, mostly glabrous, sometimes hirsutulous. Lvs to 20 × 0.5cm, linear, rigid, glandular-punctate, mostly glossy, glabrous, mostly radical. Capitula few to several in a lax, corymbose infl., often only the terminal developing; phyllaries mostly glossy, rigid, ovate and rounded, apex abruptly pointed, outer sometimes spreading; florets purple or rarely white. Fr. to 6mm; pappus c10mm. Late summer–early autumn. S Ontario and W New York State to Missouri. Z4.

L.elegans (Walter) Michx.
To 1.2m. Stems 1–2, finely pubesc. and leafy. Lvs to 10×0.5cm, linear to linear-lanceolate, glabrous, reduced upwards, upper soon deflexed. Capitula few to many, subsessile, in cylindrical or pyramidal racemose infl.; phyllaries lanceolate, outer short, herbaceous, inner red-pink, elongated and petaloid; florets white or purple. Fr. to 6mm; pappus to 11mm. Autumn. S & SE US. Z7.

L.glabrata Rydb. See *L.squarrosa.*

L.gracilis Pursh.
To 1m. Stems slender to stiff, often thick, usually purple. Fr. to 4mm; pappus to 6mm. Autumn. CE & SE US. Z6.

L.helleri Porter.
To 20cm. Stems 1–2. Lvs to 30 × 1cm, radical, linear-lanceolate, attenuate to long, winged petioles, stems lvs gradually reducing upwards. Capitula few to many, in dense clusters to 7cm; phyllaries oblong-ovate, with a narrow scarious rim and finely ciliolate margin; florets purple. Fr. to 3.5mm; pappus to 4mm. N Carolina. Z7.

L.ligulistylis (Nels.) C.B. Lehm.
To 60cm. Stems 1 or several, glabrous below and adpressed white-pubesc. above, or mostly pubesc., red-tinged. Lvs to 15 × 1.5cm, lanceolate-oblong or oblanceolate, usually long-petiolate, glabrous to sparingly hispidulous on midvein beneath, or densely pubesc. on both surfaces, more ciliate, reduced abruptly upwards. Capitula few, in a racemose cluster, shortly pedunculate; phyllaries glabrous, erect, with irregular, spathulate, broadly lacerate, scarious, often coloured tips, outer oblong to orbicular, shortest; florets purple. Fr. to 6mm; pappus to 10mm. Autumn. S Manitoba and Wisconsin to N New Mexico. Z3.

L.montana hort. See *L.spicata.*

L.novae-angliae (Lunell) Shinn.
To 60cm. Stem glabrous or sparingly pubesc., somewhat striate. Lvs to 15 × 1cm, numerous, often twisted, glabrous or

sparsely hairy along lower midrib, or hairy beneath and margin ciliate, lower amplexicaul, upper linear-lanceolate, sessile, gradually reduced. Capitula few to many in a simple raceme; phyllaries rounded to ovate or linear, outer herbaceous, slightly pubesc., margins ciliate, sometimes coloured, inner narrower, often coloured; florets purple, rarely white. Fr. to 7mm; pappus c8mm. SW Maine to Pennsylvania. Z4.

L.pumila Lodd. See *L.spicata.*

L.punctata Hook. SNAKEROOT.
To 80cm. Stems numerous, glabrous, striate. Lvs to 15 × 0.6cm, numerous, glabrous, rigid, linear, glandular-punctate, gradually reduced above. Capitula numerous, crowded in a usually dense spike, to 30 × 3cm; phyllaries herbaceous, thick, glandular punctate, closely adpressed except for apices, outer short, rigid, ovate-acuminate or cuspidate, inner oblong, apices acute to mucronate or lanceolate-acuminate, margins ciliate; florets purple, rarely white. Fr. to 7mm; pappus to 11mm. Autumn. E Canada to SE US and New Mexico. Z3.

L.pycnostachya Michx. BUTTON SNAKEROOT.
To 1.5m. Stems 1 to many, stiff, striate, generally hirsute. Lvs to 10 × 0.5cm, linear, hirsute or glabrous, gradually reducing up stem. capitula crowded in very dense spikes to 30 × 3cm, sessile; phyllaries green or purple-tinged, lanceolate-acuminate or oblong, usually laxly spreading; florets red-purple, sometimes white. Fr. to 7mm; pappus to 7mm. Autumn. SE US. Z3.

L.scariosa (L.) Willd.
To 80cm. Stems 1 to several, usually densely pubesc. Lvs few to many, to 15 × 5cm, broadly oblanceolate, oblong to ovoid, base attenuate, amplexicaul, gradually reducing up stem. Capitula few to many, in particular infl; phyllaries leathery, mostly recurved, outer ovate, mostly herbaceous, sometimes coloured; florets purple. Fr. to 5mm; pappus c9mm. SE US. 'Alba': fls white. 'Gracious': to 1.5m; fls snow-white. 'Magnifica'('Alba Magnifica'): fl. heads very large, white. 'September Glory': to 1.25m; fls deep purple. 'White Spires': fls in long white spikes. Z3.

L.spicata (L.) Willd. (*L.callilepis* hort; *L.montana* hort.; *L.pumila* Lodd.). BUTTON SNAKEWORT.
To1.5m. Stems stiff, glabrous, rarely hirsute. Lvs to 40 × 2cm, linear-lanceolate or linear. Capitula clustered in a dense spike, to 70cm, sessile or pedunculate, to 1.5cm; phyllaries adpressed elliptic-oblong, glabrous, margins scarious, purple-tinged at anthesis; florets red-purple. Fr. to 6mm; pappus to 7mm. Late summer. E US. 'Alba': fls white. 'Blue Bird': fls vivid blue. 'Floristan': to 90cm; fls white ('Floristan Weiss') and deep violet ('Floristan Violet'); seed race. 'Kobold' ('Goblin'): dwarf to 40cm; fls bright violet. 'Picador': fls ranging from white to violet; seed race. 'Snow Queen': to 75cm; fls snow-white. T&M Border Mixed: to 1.5m, fls from white to dark blue; seed race from named selections of *L.scariosa* and *L.spicata.* Z3.

L.squarrosa (L.) Michx. (*L.glabrata* Rydb.).
To 60cm. Stems several to numerous, glabrous, softly pubesc. or hairy. Lvs to 25 × 0.7cm, linear, rigid, glandular-punctate, glabrous or hirsute, gradually reduced upwards. Capitula 1 to few in a raceme, or many in a branched panicle; phyllaries leaf-like, glabrous or hirsute, inner narrowly linear, outer elongate triangular-lanceolate, apex more or less squarrose; florets red-purple. Fr. to 6mm; pappus to 12mm. Summer–early autumn. CE & SE US. Z4.

L × weaveri Shinn. (*L.aspera* × *L.punctata.*)
To 50cm. Stems slender, 12–24, glabrous below, white-pubesc. above. Lvs to 15 × 1cm, linear to narrowly linear-lanceolate, glandular-punctate, reduced gradually upwards. Capitula numerous, in a dense spike-like infl., to 30cm long; phyllaries linear-lanceolate, erect and moderately loose, outer herbaceous, oblong-triangular, inner oblong, with a narrow, scarious, erose, pale margin; florets purple. Fr. c5mm; pappus 8mm. Ontario, probably elsewhere. Z2.

Lilium L. (Lat. form of Gk *leirion*, used by Theophrastus for the Madonna Lily.) LILY. Liliaceae (Liliaceae). About 100 species of perennial monocots, to 3m. Stems subterranean forming bulbs, with white or yellow fleshy scales, sometimes purple when exposed to light. Bulbs of 5 types: concentric, central growing point with overlapping scales (e.g. *L.medeloides*); subrhizomatous, growing horizontally in only one direction with declining basal plate (e.g. *L.washingtonianum*); rhizomatous scales forming extensive mats (e.g. *L.pardalinum*); stoloniferous, developing new bulbs at apices of one or more horizontal stolons (e.g. *L.canadense*); stoloniform, developing horizontal stems before shoots appear above ground (e.g. *L.wardii*). Some species stem-rooting, roots developing on underground stems above bulbs. Stems unbranched above ground; bulbils develop in leaf axils or on lower leafless portion. Leaves linear or lanceolate, whorled, horizontal or with recurved tips; veins parallel; petioles very short or absent. Flowers in a terminal raceme or umbel, occasionally solitary, erect (cup-shaped), horizontal (funnel-shaped or bowl-shaped), pendulous (bell-shaped or turk's-cap with recurved tips), to 10–30cm wide; tepals 6, free, inner usually broader, white, yellow, orange, red or maroon, interior surface often spotted, nectary and filament of stamen at base of each tepal; anthers versatile; stigma 3-lobed, style 1, ovary superior. Fruit a 3-celled capsule, seeds numerous, flat, in 2 rows per cell. Temperate northern hemisphere.

CULTIVATION   All lilies have a bulbous rootstock comprised of a base upon which are few to numerous scales, always without any outer protective sheath. There are several types of bulb: concentric, with the scales firmly clustered around a central growing point, as in *L.dauricum*; rhizomatous, where the base elongates in one direction and the new growing point is set away from the old, as in *L.pardalinum*; and stoloniferous, where during the growing season a stolon or horizontal stem is thrust out by the current bulb at the end of which a new concentric bulb is formed, as in *L.canadense*. Another term, stoloniform, depicts a type of growth where the stem wanders some distance underground before emerging; new bulbs often arise at intervals on the section below ground: *L.nepalense* is typical of this type. Most hybrid lilies have concentric bulbs, except those derived from western American species, which are generally rhizomatous. Some Asiatic Hybrids have stoloniform stems.

Most lilies grow in acidic soils, but some grow in alkaline soils (or even on both alkaline and acid) and on limestone formations. The following are considered as lime-loving or lime-tolerant: *Ll. amabile, bolanderi, brownii, bulbiferum, callosum, canadense* var. *editorum, candidum, cernuum, chalcedonicum, concolor, dauricum, davidii, duchartrei, hansonii, henryi, humboldtii, lankongense, leucanthum, longiflorum, martagon, monadelphum, pardalinum, parryi, pomponium, primulinum, pyrenaicum, regale, sulphureum*. Hybrid lilies based on these species may be considered lime tolerant and often accept a wider range of soil types than their parents. A few lime-loving species, such as *L.henryi* and *L.candidum*, appear to do less well when grown in acid soils.

Lilium spp. grow in a variety of conditions, but most enjoy an open free-draining loamy soil, with a high humus content. Some demand drier conditions at times other than in spring when in full growth. A few are native to bogs, ditches or streamsides, but still require free-draining sites in spring, tolerating wetter conditions at other seasons.

As nearly all lilies like deep planting – *L.candidum* being a notable exception – the soil should be well worked to the necessary depth. The subsoil should be broken up, but not brought to the surface, to improve drainage and to allow free run for basal roots. Coarse grits and gravels (free of sticky sand) may be added to the subsoil, and bulbs may be planted on a layer of sharp sand, if the subsoil is heavy. Topsoils may be improved with leafmould, coir and other well-decomposed vegetable matter with the addition of grits and sharp sand, so that the surface will always absorb light rains and artificial watering without lateral run-off when dry. If the quality of drainage is in doubt, the whole bed should be improved rather than creating good conditions immediately below the bulbs, producing pockets which will fill with water in winter with disastrous results. If drainage cannot easily be improved, raised beds may be the only answer, but in such conditions the bulbs must be provided with regular and adequate moisture when necessary. Soil moisture should be plentiful in late winter and spring, easing gradually in summer so that, following flowering, the soil is moist enough for the bulb to replenish itself.

Because lily bulbs have their outer scales exposed, they are easily damaged and can quickly lose moisture by evaporation, rendering them more susceptible to pathogens. The aim should be to obtain high-quality bulbs in firm fresh condition with sound fleshy basal roots at the correct time for planting outdoors. In cool-temperate areas planting time is early to mid-autumn, or into later autumn in warmer regions. If this is not possible, planting should be delayed until late winter or early spring. Bulbs received in winter months should be potted up, and nurtured and protected until spring. On receipt bulbs should be examined and any damaged badly marked outer scales removed. If flaccid, the bulbs should be placed in cool moist sawdust for 10–14 days to absorb water and plump up. If the bulbs have obviously been out of the ground for some time or shows signs of rot or other moulds, particularly near the base, they should be washed clean and then immersed in a fungicide solution for 20 minutes. If the bulbs are uncommon or expensive, it is a wise precaution to take off two or three scales to propagate some new bulblets (see below).

Many lilies produce roots from the subterranean portion of the stem allowing them to take up extra moisture and nutrients at the height of their activity; even so, those not normally stem-rooting still require deep planting to gain stability for the stems. However, planting should not be deeper than soil conditions and cultivation allow and usually 8cm/3in. of soil above the bulb is adequate. Many lilies have the ability, when established, to adjust their depth in the soil by contractile roots, stolons, rhizomatous bulbs or stoloniform stems.

Sprinkle a balanced fertilizer over the planting area at $140g/m^2$ ($4.5oz/yd^2$) and also the extracted portion, mixing it into the soil. Thin sandy soils often need a more complete fertilizer including trace elements. Fresh organic manure should be kept away from the bulbs and young root growth. If there is a fear of soil-borne pests, a dressing of insecticidal dust may be mixed with the soil, and for subterranean slugs, a drench of metaldehyde liquid should be given in advance. When planting, spread the basal roots carefully. Mark the outline of the area with short sticks and fill in with the loam. Should conditions seem over-dry, controlled watering is helpful to compact the soil around the bulbs and give them a good start.

The often-quoted advice to keep the roots in the shade while allowing the heads in the sun is generally sound. Many of the Asiatic species, like *L.pumilum* and *L.dauricum*, will accept full sun. Most of the Oriental species and hybrids will appreciate dappled shade for some of the day; this applies also to forms of *L.martagon* and Western American species. The Caucasian lilies will take full sun as in the wild but must have adequate moisture, and as will *L.candidum* and other southern European species used to the heat of sun at lower latitudes. Lilies are best not grown in one bed together but in small groups interspersed with shrubs, dwarf conifers and strong-growing perennials. These plants will help in producing a barrier between the groups and restrict the movement of aphids, the main vector in carrying lily virus diseases. Lilies will also look more natural in these surroundings, continuing the floral sequence into late summer and, if *L.speciosum* and *L.formosanum* can be flowered successfully, in early autumn.

In early spring, as growing shoots emerge, slugs must be carefully controlled. The succulent stems are very vulnerable and if the top is eaten out or the stem eaten through, all is lost for the year and the bulb loses its vigour. Extra feeding with a high-potash fertilizer to promote flower quality, and a mulch of decayed leafmould over moist soil to promote stem roots, are desirable. The plants should be watered if soil moisture declines, without waiting for the soil to dry out. Water plants at ground level rather than over the foliage, as wetting the leaves may encourage botrytis, even in cool dry conditions.

Most lilies, other than those which are stoloniferous or stoloniform, may be grown in containers, the Asiatic and Oriental and hybrid trumpet lilies are particularly suitable. Bulbs must not be crammed into pots: as a guide, three *L.concolor* fit into a 15cm/6in. pot, one large *L.auratum* hybrid or three *L.chalcedonicum* will go into a 23cm/9in. pot, while three or four medium-sized *L.auratum* hybrids could go into a 30cm/12in. pot. Space the bulbs at equal distance, allowing 2cm/1in. between them or at least to avoid their touching, and keep the bulbs at least 1cm/0.5in. from the sides of the pot. If deeper than average pots are available, so much the better. To maintain very good drainage throughout the season, cover the base of the pot with a layer of dust-free sherds and grit with 2–3cm/1in. of potting medium above. When the stem starts to emerge fill the remainder of the container with rich open compost in two stages. This ensures good new basal root growth while providing fresh nourishment for the stem roots. This method may be used to start plants to be transferred to urns and large tubs. It is also helpful in bringing soft, poorly rooted bulbs back into prime condition, although wherever possible high-quality bulbs should be used for container cultivation. Loam-based mediums with good aeration, drainage and a high humus level are best, but soilless mediums can be used if compaction is avoided, adequate moisture is always provided, and the appropriate liquid feeding carried out.

In frost-prone areas in zones lower than 8, certain lilies should be grown under glass, among them *Ll. alexandrae, bakerianum*, *brownii* var. *australe, catesbaei, iridollae, longiflorum, neilgherrense*, *nepalense*, *nobilissimum, primulinum*, *sulphureum, wallichianum**. (Those marked * are stoloniform and are not considered suitable for normal pot culture.) In colder areas the following species may be added to the list: *Ll. candidum, formosanum, leucanthum, maritimum, occidentale, parryi, philippinense, pomponium, sargentiae, speciosum*.

The more tender lilies with stoloniform stems (marked * above) are not suitable for pot culture and may be grown in greenhouse borders in specially prepared soil with a high humus level. If this is not practical, then they may be planted in broad boxes with plentiful drainage provided. Depth of soil is not so much the criterion as lateral spread. It should be recognized that some lilies, like *L.speciosum*, require a long growth season and so do not perform satisfactorily where this is not available. Others, for instance *L.pomponium*, need a hot flowering and ripening season to grow well in subsequent years.

PROPAGATION   Lilies may be increased by seed, from above-ground stem bulbils and below-ground stem bulblets, by division of the main bulb and by scaling the bulb.

Division. Following maturity, most lilies will produce two or possibly three stems in the subsequent year. In remaking the beds in autumn or late winter, advantage can be taken of this and the bulbs carefully split up by prising apart or by cracking the basal plate with firm hold and deft motion before replanting. (If gross proliferation has occurred, then inherent disease – possibly virus – should be suspected and the bulbs discarded.)

Bulblets. Many lilies will produce these on the underground portion of the stem. When the stem has died down or begun to wither, wrench the stem from the bulb, holding the bulb firm. Most of the bulblets will also come away and can be picked out from among the stem roots; others may need to be eased out from the top soil. Those of sufficient size may be replanted around the main bulbs or grown on elsewhere. The smaller bulblets should be treated as for bulbils.

Bulbils. These occur most commonly on *L.lancifolium* and many Asiatic Hybrids, also *L.bulbiferum* in the typical form, *L.sargentiae, L.sulphureum*, and casually on other lilies, particularly when flowering is frustrated. When bulbils are few in number, planting may be in a pot of suitable size, potting on as soon as necessary or planting outdoors according to suitability of the season. Larger numbers of hardy kinds may be planted outside immediately into drills 2.5cm/1in. deep made in friable humus-rich soil. Once covered over, water well and keep free of weeds, avoiding damage to the single leaves arising from the bulbils which often have brittle petioles. Oriental Hybrids may often have a few stem bulbils arising in leaf axils near the base of the stem, frequently with a leaflet and extending root while still on the stem. These are best grown on in pots under glass for a season.

Scales (scaling). This is the most important method of propagation for producing large numbers of a particular cultivar. The method is very simple. The required number of firm clean scales is snapped off the base of the bulb. The scales are kept in conditions that prevent any dehydration, as in trays of moist sharp sand, or sealed in polythene bags. A callus grows on the base of the scale and in a few weeks one or more small bulbs will develop on the callus. When large enough, the bulblets are carefully prised from the scales and grown on in a sterilized medium. Scales of some lilies may produce bulblets freely, others are slow, difficult and the bulblets small in size and number. Numbers may usually be increased, especially with broad scales, if the base is cut to a depth of, say, 5mm every 5mm of its length. A similar effect is often produced when the scale is dipped in rooting hormone. The more bulblets produced per scale the smaller each individual will be and the more aftercare it will need in the early stages of growing on. Likewise, whereas the outer scales of a bulb may respond strongly, the innermost scales, being softer and smaller, are more likely to rot off, so if these are used they should first be treated with a fungicide solution. Small numbers of scales may be placed in thin polythene bags to which a small amount of moist sterilized sharp sand or sawdust has already been added. With most air excluded, the bags should be tightly folded over at the top two or three times, pleated in and tied firmly to prevent escape of moisture. Each bag should be clearly named and dated.

Asiatic, Oriental, Caucasian, Martagon, European and Eastern North American lilies benefit from being kept in a dark moderately warm (18–23°C/65–73°F) cupboard. Most Asiatic species and hybrids will usually grow away freely, according to season and conditions, but the other kinds should be given a cool period, equivalent to a winter season, as advocated for seeds below. These lilies should be scaled in the relatively dormant period from after flowering until early spring. Western American lilies should be scaled in autumn and late autumn/early winter. The small, numerous scales of these bulbs make cutting unnecessary; the often jointed scales may easily be snapped into separate portions and usually each section will provide a new bulblet. These should be kept in cool conditions (3–10°C/37–50°F) in dark or reasonably dark conditions, allowing them to initiate bulblets, and as the winter progresses into early spring, produce young leaves without recourse to refrigeration. At this stage they are easy to pot up (leaving the scales attached), 1cm apart in 15cm/6in. half-pots in sterilized medium, preferably with additional sharp sand. Watered in, they will grow in this medium for the season, requiring occasional liquid feeds, the stronger kinds being transferred as a whole into deep pots when necessary and practical to maintain their active growth. Asiatic spp. and hybrid lily bulbs may be treated likewise, teasing them gently from the scales with, or preferably without, top growth yet showing. Bulblets from their dormancy period in the refrigerator should be potted up in similar manner.

It is essential to take the greatest care of all bulblets and to avoid handling the roots, exerting minimal pressure. If leaflets must be handled, hold only the tip. After spending a season in pots, the new small bulbs should be suitable for planting outside in nursery beds, the tender kinds for planting in large pots. Other containers which may be used for scales are half-pots, deep seed trays and propagating trays, using an open medium of equal parts peat/sharp sand or similar material; if refrigeration is to be given, convenience and ease of storage are key factors – the quantities of compost required at this stage are minimal.

Seed is often the best and easiest means of propagating the species. Seed from hybrid lilies, produce either seed parent accurately, but produce a variable new race of hybrids. Seed will produce virus-free seedlings.

Seed germination may be epigeal or hypogeal. If epigeal, the cotyledon rises above ground, similar in action to the germination of an onion seedling, with the first true leaf, normally broader, appearing soon after. If hypogeal, the cotyledon remains below ground at germination, feeding a tiny growing bulb from the endosperm; usually a genetic delay mechanism inhibits growth above ground until a cold period, representing winter, has passed. Thus the first sign of the seedling is a true leaf in spring. The species in each group are listed below. It will be noted that a few members of the epigeal group exhibit delay characteristics, whereas it is very rare for hypogeal seed to be witnessed above ground without previous delay, except in respect of the Western American species which, despite their differing native climatic conditions, germinate in a cool (winter) period, emerging in the spring with a true leaf following in a seemingly continuous process.

EPIGEAL GERMINATION   (a) Immediate: *Ll. amabile, arboricola, bakerianum, brownii, callosum, candidum, catesbaei* (?), *cernuum, concolor, dauricum, davidii, duchartrei, formosanum, henrici, henryi, lankongense, leichtlinii, leucanthum, longiflorum, mackliniae, maculatum, nanum, neilgherrense, nepalense, oxypetalum, papilliferum, philadelphicum, philippinense, primulinum, pumilum, pyrenaicum, regale, sargentiae, sherriffiae, sulphureum, taliense, tigrinum, wallichianum, wardii.* (b) Delayed: *Ll. carniolicum, chalcedonicum, ponticum.* (c) Autumnal/winter: *L.pomponium.*

HYPOGEAL GERMINATION   (a) Immediate: *Ll. iridollae* (?), *medeoloides* (?), *parryi.* (b) Delayed: *Ll. auratum, bulbiferum, canadense, ciliatum, distichum, grayi, hansonii, japonicum, kesselringianum, ledebourii, martagon, michauxii, michiganense, monadelphum, polyphyllum, rubellum, speciosum, superbum, tsingtauense.* (c) Autumnal/winter: *Ll. alexandrae*, bolanderi, columbianum, humboldtii, kelleyanum, kelloggii, maritimum, nobilissimum*, occidentale, pardalinum, parvum, pitkinense, rubescens, vollmeri, washingtonianum, wigginsii.* (*Oriental species germinating in similar manner to those on the American Pacific coast.)

'Epigeal' seeds should be sown according to conventional methods. Ordinary seed trays are too shallow, whereas half-pots and other plastic containers of similar depth are very suitable. Adequate drainage may be ensured by covering the base of the container with potting grit to 1cm depth before adding a medium-fertility loam-based mix, or one with slow-release fertilizers, with sharp sand added to approximately 20% of the whole. This allows the seedlings to be retained in the original container for a full season, or even for two seasons if necessary, should *en bloc* potting-on to deeper containers be feasible. The consistency of the compost should allow the roots of the seedlings to be freed one from another with relative ease and so produce the least damage when transplanted. Peat-based mediums are not usually so suitable even with extra sand added and will require more frequent liquid feeding.

This method is also suitable for 'hypogeal' seeds, but then conventional germination would require two growing seasons. 'Hypogeal' seeds may be treated in far less space and time by germinating them in thin polythene bags, each containing a small quantity of a moist sterilised perlite mixture. Seed may be freed of superficial fungus spores by immersion in household bleach. Whereas good quality fresh seed should conventionally be thinly sown, many seeds may go into one bag with relatively little compost, sufficient only for ensuring moist seed, but the resulting seedlings must be pricked out individually, with great care, with their initial leaf and fragile root. The bags should be tightly sealed, labelled with name and date and, except for western American kinds which need cool conditions, kept in a warm cupboard (18–23°C/65–73°F). Germination varies, but will take at least three weeks, possibly as much as six or more, and then the bulbs will increase in size over about a further three weeks. Older seed would take longer than indicated. When the tiny bulbs look plump and white, the polythene bags – after indicating the date on the label – may be transferred to a refrigerator. The precise time required in these cool (not freezing) conditions varies. Two months may be sufficient for many species, but a period closer to three months ensures regular growth once the seedlings have been pricked out. (Keeping the bags in the refrigerator over-long will not necessarily inhibit or delay growth of the seedlings. When ready they will send forth their first leaves and, with lack of light, these will be soft and etiolated; losses following pricking out could be considerable.) Using sterile compost, half-pots are large enough for first growth.

When roots fill the pot, seedlings may be transferred *en bloc* to a pot of full depth and, if the seedlings are particularly vigorous, a wider one, with fresh sterile compost in the base and around the sides. Further growth in these conditions will produce seedlings large enough to handle easily to place in nursery beds, or even in their final position depending on species and garden conditions. The best time to do this is spring when the young bulbs will grow fast. Choose moist mild conditions, when night frosts are not imminent. An outdoor site for seedlings should be in semi-shade with fair protection from harsher winds. The free-draining friable loam should have a high humus content, preferably with a pH 5.5–6.5, suitably free of pests and weeds.

MICROPROPAGATION *Tissue culture* has a number of advantages for the lily grower: it can produce a continuing supply of bulblets; it can take reproductive tissue from many parts of the plant; it can (but not necessarily) produce virus-free material from a virus-infected plant; it can aid the production of difficult hybridization; cultures can be put on 'ice' and so stored in a 'bank', thus helping conservation and the storage of genetic material.

Various kinds of material may be used for tissue culture. (a) The seed embryos, best taken from green seed pods, being at this stage virtually sterile and easily removed. (b) Basal pieces of bulb scale up to 5mm cube from clean outer scales; contamination is generally high from this source as soil-borne pathogens are often growing *inside* the tissue. (c) Flower buds, either using tepal sections or ovary sections. The process takes longer than with other material – small buds are quicker – but the material is generally less contaminated and yields a fair proportion of virus-free stock, when this is the aim. (d) Basal portions of young leaves taken well before flowering time. (e) Shoot tips – traditional meristem cultures – though these are not normal nor best with lilies.

The tissue, once it has been cleaned properly, needs to be grown on agar-nutrient mediums containing, as necessary, growth regulators or 'hormones', auxins for cell division and cytokinins for cell division and shoot initiation. The dry mediums are available as proprietary products. The aim is to produce a reasonable amount of callus on which bulblets will grow, and for those bulblets to grow leaves in due course. Variations in the growing medium are necessary at particular stages to achieve this, aided by variations in light and temperature. Careful weaning from cultures to outdoor life is required, maintaining sterile conditions as carefully and closely as possible in the early days. Bulblet cultures will normally need a cool period of up to eight weeks before active growth recommences.

All-Year-Round Cultivation. The production of lilies for sale as cut flowers and pot-grown plants at all seasons is based on micropropagation at specific intervals from the desired time of maturity. The interval varies according to the variety involved. This AYR cultivation is widely practised, especially in the Netherlands and California.

PESTS AND DISEASES Attacks by aphids must be dealt with promptly, they lurk behind partly exposed young flower-buds and under fresh unfolding foliage. Botrytis may normally be controlled, if dealt with promptly with appropriate fungicide, preferably systemic, on a regular basis. Spray when the foliage is dry, thoroughly wetting the undersurface of the leaves, as this is where infection originates. *L.candidum* is particularly vulnerable and can carry the disease on its overwintering basal foliage, so it should be sprayed before stem growth begins and, if signs are visible, in autumn.

Basal rot (*Fusarium oxysporum*) may attack and destroy bulbs, especially where another pathogen is present, so it is best to plant high-quality bulbs fresh and clean, giving them good cultivation, never too wet or too dry, nor allowing them to be exposed or out of the ground for any longer than absolutely necessary. New bulbs should not be planted in soil where others may have died. Remedial action with affected bulbs is to cut away and burn all dead and rotting parts, sterilizing the remainder in 2% formalin or immersing in a suitable fungicide solution. Fortunately, many newer hybrids are more resistant, and with better commercial practice and the use of virus-free stocks this disease is less formidable than heretofore.

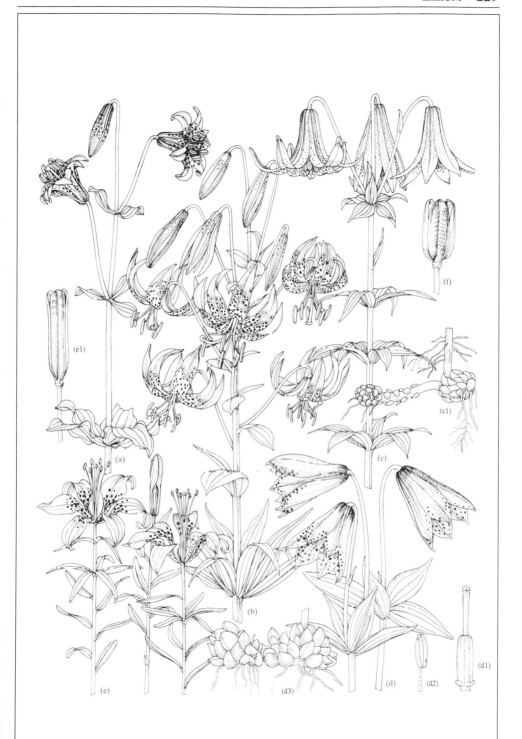

Lilium   American species   (a) *L.parvum* f. *crocatum*   (b) *L.superbum*   (c) *L.canadense*   (c1) rhizomatous bulb
(d) *L.grayi*   (d1) stigma and style   (d2) stamen   (d3) bulb   (e) *L.philadelphicum*   (e1) *L.philadelphicum* var. *andinum*,
capsule   (f) *L.pardalinum* capsule

L.albanicum Griseb. See *L.pyrenaicum* ssp. *carniolicum* var. *albanicum*.

L.alexandrae (Wallace) Coutts. UKE-YURI.
Stems to 1m; bulbils above and below ground; stem-rooting; bulbs concentric, to 15cm wide, scales white, lanceolate, acute. Lvs 20×4cm, lanceolate to ovate, 3–5-veined, petiolate. Fls 1–5, fragrant, 16×10cm, bowl-shaped, horizontal or erect; tepals to 18×3–4cm, white with green bases and tips, exterior occasionally striped pink; stamens shorter than pistil; anth. and pollen brown; style pale green, stigma brown. Fr. 5cm; seeds brown, 7×5mm. Summer. Japan, Ryukyu Is. Z5.

L.amabile Palib. (*L.fauriei* Lév. & Vaniot).
Stems to 90cm, pubesc., stem-rooting; bulbs concentric, 4×3cm, scales white, broad. Lvs to 9cm, scattered, lanceolate, 3-veined, absent on lower part of stem, numerous towards top. Fls 1–5, turk's-cap, in a raceme, malodorous; pedicels 2.5–5cm, pubesc.; tepals 5.5cm, red with dark purple spots, 2–3 fleshy papillae on upper surface; anth. dark brown; pollen red; stigma red-brown. Fr. 3×2cm. Summer. Korea. var. *luteum* anon. Fls yellow. Z5.

L.artvinense Misch. See *L.pyrenaicum* ssp. *ponticum* var. *artvinense*.

L.atrosanguineum anon. See *L.maculatum*.

L.auratum Lindl. GOLDED-RAYED LILY OF JAPAN; MOUNTAIN LILY; YAMA-YURI.
Stems 60–150cm, sometimes to 225cm, purple-green, stem-rooting; bulbs concentric, 10cm diam., scales pale yellow, lanceolate. Lvs to 22×4cm, numerous, scattered, lanceolate, dark green, 5–7-veined, petiolate. Fls 6–30, 30cm wide, bowl-shaped, horizontal or slightly pendulous, in a raceme, very fragrant; tepals 12–18×4–5cm, white with yellow or crimson central streaks and crimson-spotted, fleshy papillae on basal part, tips recurved; pollen chocolate to red. Fr. 8cm; seeds 11×9mm. Short-lived, requiring lime-free soil in full sun with shade provided by low-growing plants. Summer–autumn. Japan (Honshu Is.). 'Apollo': central band and spots ruby-red. 'Crimson Beauty': cherry red, margin white. 'Praecox': heavily spotted; early flowering. 'Rubrum': pet. band crimson. 'Tom Thumb': dwarf. Crossed with *L.speciosum*, *L.japonicum* and *L.rubellum* to give rise to a wide range of cvs. var. *platyphyllum* Bak. Stems to 2.3m. Lvs broadly lanceolate. Fls larger, fewer spots on tepals. var. *rubrovittatum* Duchartre. Band on tepals yellow at base, deep crimson at apex. var. *virginale* Duchartre. Stems to 2m. Albino form, tepals white, streaked yellow, spotted pale yellow or pink. 'Album': fls white. Z6.

L.×aurelianense Debras. (*L.henryi* × *L.sargentiae*.)
Stems to 2.5m, stem-rooting. Lvs 12×3.5cm, lanceolate, 3-veined, bulbils in axils. Fls to 12, scented, 12.5cm wide, horizontal or slightly pendulous. Autumn. Garden origin. Many cvs, white to apricot and pink fls, some not lime-tolerant.

L.australe Stapf. See *L.brownii*.
L.avenaceum Fisch. See *L.medeloides*.

L.bakerianum Collett & Hemsl. (*L.lowii* anon.).
Stems 60–90cm, usually hairy, stem-rooting; bulbs stoloniform, 3.5×5cm, scales white, 2×1cm, lanceolate. Lvs 10×1.5cm, scattered on upper part of stem, linear to lanceolate, 1–3-veined. Fls 1–6, bell-shaped, pendulous; tepals 7×1.5cm; anth. orange. Fr. 3.5cm. Summer. N Burma, SW China (Sichuan, Yunnan). Z8.

L.batemanniae Wallace. See *L.maculatum*.
L.biondii Baroni. See *L.davidii* var. *unicolor*.
L.bloomerianum Kellogg. See *L.humboldtii*.

L.bolanderi S. Wats. (*L.howellii* I.M. Johnst.).
Stems to 140cm, glaucous green, marked brown; bulbs concentric, 5cm wide, scales to 5×9cm, yellow, lanceolate. Lvs to 5×1.5cm, in whorls, sessile, oblanceolate, 1–3-nerved. Fls 1–18, 6.5cm wide, funnel-shaped, pendulous; tepals 3–4.5×1cm, maroon, interior spotted dark red or purple, exte-

rior green at base, tube yellow, spotted chocolate; anth. purple; pollen deep yellow; stigma purple. Fr. 4cm. Summer. W US (S Oregon, N California). Z5.

L.brownii Miellez.
Stems to 1m, green tinged dark brown, stem-rooting; bulbs concentric, 7cm wide, scales ovate, cream. Lvs to 25×2cm, scattered, lanceolate, 5–7-veined. Fls fragrant, 1–4, funnel-shaped; tepals 12–15×2.5–6.5cm, interior white, exterior purple, tinged green; anth. brown; pollen red-brown. Fr. 5cm. Summer. China, Burma. var. *australe* (Stapf) Stearn (*L.australe* Stapf). Stems to 3m. Interior of tepals white, exterior flushed green. SE China, Hong Kong. var. *viridulum* Bak. (*L.brownii* var. *colchesteri* (Van Houtte) Elwes). Stem green. Fls strongly scented, exterior of tepals tinged yellow-green and pale purple, tube interior yellow, fading to white. China. Z6.

L.bulbiferum L. (*L.bulbiferum* var. *chaixii* (Maw) Stoker; *L.chaixii* Maw). FIRE LILY.
Stems 40–150cm, ribbed, green, occasionally spotted purple, woolly toward top, stem-rooting, green bulbils in lf axils; bulbs concentric, 9cm wide, scales lanceolate, white. Lvs 10×2cm, lanceolate, scattered, 3–7-veined. Fls usually to 5, occasionally to 50, erect, cup-shaped, tepals 6–8.5×2–3cm, bright orange, bases and tips deeper in colour, interior spotted maroon; anth. brown; pollen orange. Grows in well-drained soil in summer shade. Summer. S Europe. var. *croceum* (Chaix) Pers. (*L.croceum* Chaix). Tepals orange, bulbils absent. Z7.

L.× burbankii anon. (*L.pardalinum* × *L.parryi*.)
Stems 1–2m. Lvs in whorls. Fls horizontal, fragrant; tepals reflexed, 8cm, yellow, spotted chocolate-brown, tips red. Summer. Garden origin. Z5.

L.callosum Sieb. & Zucc. SLIMSTEM LILY.
Stems to 90cm, green, stem-rooting; bulbs concentric, 2.5cm wide, scales oval, white. Lvs 8–13×0.3–0.8cm, scattered, linear, 3–5-veined, apices thickened. Fls to 10, pendulous turk's-cap, 4cm wide, in a raceme; pedicels 7cm; tepals 3–4cm, orange-red, spotted black toward base; pollen orange. Fr. 4×2cm. Late summer. China, Japan, Korea, Taiwan, Russia (Amur region). Z6.

L.camschatcensis L. See *Fritillaria camschatcensis*.

L.canadense L. (*L.canadense* var. *flavum* Pursh). MEADOW LILY; WILD MEADOW LILY.
Stems to 1.5m, green, stem-rooting; bulbs stoloniferous, scales white or pale yellow. Lvs 15×2cm, lanceolate to oblanceolate, mostly in whorls, veins 5–7. Fls 10–12, bell-shaped, pendulous, in an umbel; pedicels to 20cm; tepals 5–7.5×1–2.5cm, yellow, basally spotted maroon, apices recurved; pollen yellow to red-brown. Fr. 3cm. Plant in moist but well-drained soil. Summer. Eastern N America (Quebec to Alabama). 'Chocolate Chips': tepal exterior and tips crimson, fading to orange then yellow toward the interior base, spots large. 'Fire Engine': tepals slightly recurved, exterior and interior tips crimson, fading to orange then yellow near the base; pollen burnt-orange. 'Melted Spots': lvs whorled; fls yellow-orange, spots dense on the basal two-thirds. 'Peaches and Pepper': fls peach-orange; tepals recurved, finely spotted. var. *coccineum* Pursh (*L.canadense* var. *rubrum* T. Moore). Fls red, throat yellow. var. *editorum* Fern. Lvs broader than var. *L.canadense*. Fls red, tepals 8–13mm wide. Appalachian Mts. Z5.

L.candidum L. MADONNA LILY; WHITE LILY.
Stems 1–2m, dark maroon; bulbs concentric, 9cm wide, scales white or pale yellow, ovate. Basal lvs 22×5cm, 3–5-veined, produced in autumn, retained in winter, stem lvs scattered, 7.5×1cm, lanceolate. Fls 5–20, funnel-shaped, fragrant, in a raceme; tepals 5–8×1–4cm, white, interior base yellow, tips recurved; pollen bright yellow. Fr. not usually formed in cult. Summer. Balkans, E Mediterranean. var. *plenum* West. Fls double. Very rare. var. *salonikae* Stoker. Stems dark green. Fls fertile; tepals widely spreading; pollen pale yellow. W Greece. Z6.

L.carniolicum Koch. See *L.pyrenaicum* ssp. *carniolicum*.
L.carniolicum ssp. *ponticum* P.H. Davis & D.M. Henderson. See *L.pyrenaicum* ssp. *ponticum* var. *ponticum*.

L.catesbaei Walter. LEOPARD LILY; PINE LILY; TIGER LILY. Stems 30–60cm; bulbs concentric, 2.5cm wide, scales lanceolate, white. Lvs to 10cm, alternate, lanceolate, acute. Fls 1–2, erect, cup-shaped; tepals 5–12×1–2.5cm, bottom half of tepals narrowed into a claw, interior deep yellow, tips recurved, scarlet, exterior pale yellow to green; pollen orange-red; stigma dark red. Late summer. SE US. Z5.

L.cathayanum Wils. See *Cardiocrinum cathayanum*.
L.centifolium Stapf. See *L.leucanthum* var. *centifolium*.

L.cernuum Komar. NODDING LILY.
Stems to 60cm, green, sometimes spotted brown, ribbed, stem-rooting; bulbs 3×3cm, scales imbricate, lanceolate to ovate, thick, white, smooth. Lvs 8–15×0.1–0.5cm, scattered, mostly crowded on centre third of stem, 1–3-veined, sessile. Fls 1–14, turk's-cap, 3.5cm wide, fragrant, in a pendent raceme; pedicels spreading, 6–10cm; tepals lilac, purple, pink or occasionally white, spotted purple; pollen lilac. Fr. 2cm; seeds 6–7×4.5mm. Summer. Korea, NE Manchuria, Russia (Ussuri region). Z3.

L.chaixii Maw. See *L.bulbiferum*.

L.chalcedonicum L. (*L.heldreichii* Freyn) SCARLET TURK'S-CAP LILY, RED MARTAGON OF CONSTANTINOPLE.
Stems 45–150cm, stem-rooting; bulbs concentric, 7.5×10cm, scales pale yellow, lanceolate. Lvs to 11.5×1.5cm, edged silver, spirally arranged, sessile, 3–5 veined. Fls to 12, pendulous turk's-cap, 7.5cm wide, slightly scented; tepals scarlet, recurved, without spots; pollen scarlet. Fr. 3×2cm. Summer. Greece, S Albania. 'Maculatum': scarlet, spotted black. *L.chalcedonicum × L.× testaceum* has produced a number of cvs including 'Apollo', 'Hephaistos' and 'Zeus'. Z5.

L.chinense Baroni. See *L.davidii* var. *willmottiae*.

L.ciliatum P.H. Davis.
Stems 60–150cm, white-hairy on upper part until fls drop, stem-rooting; bulbs 10–12cm wide, scales yellow, narrow. Lvs 7–12.5×1.5cm, spirally arranged, glabrous, margins hairy. Fls 5–8, sometimes to 21, turk's-cap, 5cm wide, scented; tepals ivory, cream or pale yellow, interior purple-brown toward base, upper portion finely spotted; pollen orange-red. Fr. 2.5cm. Summer. NE Turkey. Z5.

L.colchicum Steven. See *L.monadelphum*.

L.columbianum Bak. (*L.nitidum* Bull; *L.parviflorum* Hook.).
COLUMBIA TIGER LILY; OREGON LILY.
Stems to 2.5m; bulbs concentric, 4×4cm, scales white, lanceolate. Lvs 5–14×1–4cm, oblanceolate, 3–5-veined, upper lvs scattered, lower lvs in whorls. Fls 6–10, occasionally to 40, pendulous turk's-cap, 7.5cm wide, in a long-pedicellate raceme; tepals 3.5–6.5×0.8–1.2cm, recurved, yellow to orange-red, base spotted maroon; anthers 6–11mm, pollen deep yellow to brown. Summer. Western N America. 'Ingramii': fls large, many deep orange. Z5.

L.concolor Salisb. MORNING STAR LILY.
Stems 30–90cm, green flushed purple, lightly pubesc., stem-rooting; bulbs concentric, 2×2cm, scales ovate-lanceolate, white, closely overlapping. Lvs 8.5×1.5cm, scattered, linear or linear-lanceolate, 3–7-veined, ciliate on margins and below. Fls 1–10, erect, star-shaped, 8.5cm wide; pedicels erect, 5cm, 2 basal leafy bracts; tepals 3–4×1cm, recurved, scarlet, glossy, unspotted; pollen red. Fr. 2cm. Summer. China (Hubei, Yunnan). 'Racemosum': stems taller than type of species; more vigorous. var. **partheneion** (Sieb. & De Vries) Bak. Fls red, streaked green and yellow, black spots few. var. **pulchellum** (Fisch.) Reg. (*L.pulchellum* Fisch.). Stems green, not pubesc. Fls spotted, buds woolly. Summer. NE Asia. Z4.

L.cordatum (Thunb.) Koidz. See *Cardiocrinum cordatum*.
L.× creelmannii hort. See *L.× imperiale*.
L.croceum Chaix. See *L.bulbiferum* var. *croceum*.

L.dahuricum Elwes. See *L.dauricum*.

L.× dalhansonii Baden-Powell. (*L.hansonii × L.martagon* var. *cattaniae*.)
Stems 1.5–2m, stem-rooting. Fls turk's-cap, 3cm, malodorous; tepals recurved, dark maroon, to pink, white or yellow, spotted darker; style purple. Summer. 'Backhouse hybrids': fls cream, yellow, pink to maroon with darker spots. Damson': fls plum-purple. 'Destiny': fls yellow, spotted brown; tepal tips reflexed. 'Discovery': fls turk's-cap, rose-lilac, base white, tinged pink, spotted deep crimson, tips darker, exterior pink with a silvery sheen.

L.dauricum Ker-Gawl. (*L.pennsylvanicum* Ker-Gawl.; *L.formosum* Lem.; *L.dahuricum* Elwes; *L.davuricum* Wils.).
Stems to 75cm, ribbed, green, spotted red-brown, woolly, stem-rooting; bulbs 1.5×2cm, stoloniferous, scales 1×0.6cm, white, lanceolate. Lvs 5–15×0.5–0.3cm, scattered, linear to lanceolate, 3–5-veined, margins hairy, whorl of small lvs below fls. Fls 1–6, erect, cup-shaped, to 10cm wide, in an umbel; pedicels hairy, to 9cm, spreading; tepals 5–10×1.5–3.5cm, recurved, oblanceolate, vermilion to scarlet, spotted brown-red, base yellow, narrow; pollen red. Fr. 5cm. Summer. NE Asia. Z5.

L.davidii Elwes (*L.thayerae* Wils.).
Stems 1–1.4m, green, spotted brown, stem-rooting; bulbs concentric or stoloniferous, 4×4cm, scales white, pink when exposed to light, ovate or ovate-lanceolate. Lvs 6–10×0.2–0.4cm, numerous, linear, acute, dark green, 1-veined, margins finely toothed and inrolled, basally white-hairy. Fls 5–20, turk's-cap, unscented, pendulous, in a raceme, buds hairy, pedicels to 15cm, horizontal, stiff; tepals to 8cm, vermilion spotted purple; pollen orange or scarlet. Fr. 3.5×2cm. Summer. W China (Sichuan, Yunnan). var. **unicolor** (Hoog) Cotton (*L.biondii* Baroni). Stems shorter, to 1m; bulbs not stoloniferous. Lvs more numerous and longer, very crowded. Fls paler, spots red, mauve or absent. Summer. N China. Italy. var. **willmottiae** (Wils.) Raffill (*L.sutchuenense* Franch.; *L.chinense* Baroni). Stems to 2m, arching; bulbs stoloniferous. Lvs to 6mm wide. Fls to 40. Summer. China (Shensi, Hupei, Sichuan, NW Yunnan). Preston Hybrids, Patterson Hybrids, Fiesta Strain and North Hybrids developed from *L.davidii*. Z5.

L.davimottiae.
Name given to hybrid between *L.davidii* var. *davidii* and *L.davidii* var. *willmottiae*.

L.davuricum Wils. See *L.dauricum*.

L.distichum Nak. in Kamib. KOCHANG LILY.
Resembles *L.tsingtauense* but tepals recurved and bulb scales jointed. Stems 60–120cm, hollow, lower part ribbed, stem-rooting; bulbs to 3×4cm, concentric, scales 1.5–2×0.4–0.6cm, white, lanceolate, jointed. Lvs 8–15×2–4cm, obovate-elliptical, in 1–2 whorls lower part of stem, none below, sparsely scattered above. Fls 3–8, turk's-cap, horizontal or slightly pendulous, in a raceme; pedicels 6–8cm; tepals 3.5–4.5×0.6–1.3cm, recurved, pale orange usually with darker spots. Fr. 2×1.5cm. Summer. E Russia, N Korea, NE China. Z5.

L.duchartrei Franch. (*L.farreri* Turrill). MARBLE MARTAGON.
Stems 60–100cm, green flushed brown, ribbed, white-hairy in lf axils, stem-rooting; bulbs stoloniferous, 2.5–4cm wide, scales white, ovate, acute. Lvs 10.5×1.5cm, dark green above, pale green beneath, lanceolate, scattered, sessile, margin rough, veins 3–5. Fls to 12, turk's-cap, pendulous, fragrant, in an umbel; pedicels 7–15cm; tepals recurved, interior white, spotted deep purple, tubes green at base, exterior white flushed purple, ageing red; pollen orange. Fr. purple, 2.5×1.5cm; seeds 1.8cm. Summer. W China (NW Yunnan, W Sichuan, SW Kansu). Z5.

L.elegans Thunb. See *L.maculatum*.
L.excelsum Endl. & Hartinger. See *L.× testaceum*.
L.farreri Turrill. See *L.duchartrei*.
L.fauriei Lév. & Vaniot. See *L.amabile*.

L.formosanum Wallace.
Stems 30–150cm, purple-brown toward base, 1–3 per bulb, stem-rooting; bulbs 3×4cm, stoloniferous, white tinged purple, scales oblong-ovate, acute. Lvs 7.5–20×1cm, scattered, dark green, oblong-lanceolate, spreading, margins recurved, 3–7-veined, scattered, crowded near base. Fls 1–2, sometimes to 10, in umbels, fragrant, funnel-shaped, horizontal; pedicels 5–15cm, erect; tepals 12–20×2.5–5cm, interior white, exterior white flushed purple, tips recurved, nectary furrows green; anth. yellow to purple; pollen brown or yellow. Fr. 7–9×2cm; seeds 0.5cm. Often grown as bienn. Summer–autumn. Taiwan. var. **pricei** Stoker. Stems 30–60cm. Fls 1–2, more deeply coloured than type. Summer. Taiwan. Z5.

L.formosum Lem. See **L.dauricum**.
L.forrestii W.W. Sm. See **L.lankongense**.
L.fortunei Lindl. See **L.maculatum**.
L.giganteum Wallich non hort. See *Cardiocrinum giganteum*.
L.glehnii F. Schmidt. See *Cardiocrinum cordatum*.

L.grayi S. Wats.
Stems to 1.75m; bulbs stoloniferous, scales white, fleshy, to 1cm. Lvs to 5–12×1.5–3cm, lanceolate or oblong-lanceolate, sessile, in whorls. Fls 1–8, unscented, bell-shaped; pedicels to 20cm; tepals 6.25×0.5cm, interior light red with yellow base, spotted purple, exterior crimson, darker towards base, upper part spreading, lower part forming a tube 3×0.5cm; anth. yellow; pollen orange-brown; style red, stigma green. Fr. 4cm; seeds 9×7mm. Summer. E US (Alleghany Mts). 'Gulliver's Thimble': fls bright crimson. Z5.

L.hansonii Moore.
Stems to 120cm, green, stem-rooting; bulbs 7×6cm, stoloniferous, scales yellow-white, purple when exposed, triangular to ovate. Lvs 18×4cm, dark green, oblanceolate to elliptic, 3–5-veined. Fls 3–12, turk's-cap, fragrant, pendulous; tepals 3–4×1.5cm, thick, recurved, oblanceolate, deep orange-yellow, spotted purple-brown toward base; anth. purple; pollen yellow; style green. Fr. 3.5×3.5cm, rarely produced. Summer. E Russia, Korea, Japan. Z5.

L.harrisii Carr. See **L.longiflorum** var. *eximium*.
L.heldreichii Freyn. See **L.chalcedonicum**.

L.henrici Franch.
Stems to 90cm, smooth, green flushed brown; bulbs concentric, 5×4.5cm, scales 1.5–3.5×1.0–1.5cm, lanceolate, purple. Lvs 10–12×0.7–1.2cm, numerous, lanceolate, margins rough. Fls 1–7, in a raceme, bell-shaped, pendulous; pedicels 3.5–6cm; tepals 3.5–5×1–2cm, apically recurved forming a short basal tube, white suffused purple, tube dark purple within, anth. and pollen yellow. Summer. China (NW Yunnan, W Sichuan). Z5.

L.henryi Bak.
Stems 1–3m, green marked purple, stem-rooting; bulbs 8–18×7–15cm, concentric, scales 3.5–4.5×1.5cm, thick, white, red when exposed, acute, lanceolate, imbricate. Lvs 8–15×2–3cm, shiny, scattered, upper lvs ovate, sessile, basal lvs lanceolate, petiolate, 3–5-veined, crowded below fls, some axils bulbiliferous. Fls 4–20, turk's-cap, pendulous, in a raceme; pedicels 5–9cm, horizontal, 1–2 leafy bracts below fls; tepals 6–8×1–2cm, orange, spotted black, lanceolate, recurved; anth. deep red. Fr. 4×2cm, seeds golden brown, 9×6mm. Summer. China (Hubei, Jiangxi, Gouzhou). 'Citrinum': fls pale lemon-yellow, spotted brown. Z5.

L.× hollandicum Bergmans (*L.umbellatum* hort.). (*L.maculatum × L.bulbiferum*.) UMBEL LILY.
Stems 70–130cm, stem-rooting. Lvs crowded, veins 3. Fls erect, cup-shaped, to 7.5cm wide, in umbels; tepals yellow, orange or red. Summer. Garden origin. Z5.

L.howellii I.M. Johnst. See **L.bolanderi**.

L.humboldtii Duchartre (*L.bloomerianum* Kellogg.)
Stems to 2.25m, green flushed purple, non-rooting; bulbs subrhizomatous, scales white, purple when exposed, lanceolate-ovate, unjointed, 7cm. Lvs to 12.5×3cm, oblanceolate, in

whorls of 10–20. Fls 10–15, occasionally 80, pendulous, turk's-cap, in a raceme; pedicels horizontal; tepals 6.5–10×1.5–2.5cm, recurved, yellow to orange, spotted maroon and purple; pollen brown. Fr. to 5cm. Summer. US (California: Sierra Nevada). var. **ocellatum** (Kellogg) Elwes (var. *magnificum* Purdy). Tepals tinged red, the spots ringed red, eye-like. Z5.

L.× imperiale Wils. (*L.× princeps* Wils.; *L.× sargale* Crow; *L.× creelmannii* hort.). (*L.regale × L.sargentiae*.) SARGALE LILY.
Stems to 120cm, grey-green. Lvs alternate, linear, 1–5-veined, axils of upper lvs bulbiliferous. Fls bowl-shaped; tepals recurved, interior white, basal tube yellow, exterior purple; anth. orange-brown. Summer. Z5.

L.iridollae M.G. Henry. POT-OF-GOLD LILY.
Stems to 175cm; bulbs stoloniferous, 2cm wide. Lvs 9.0×2.3cm, usually whorled, obovate, basal rosettes of lvs persisting through winter. Fls 1–8, pendulous, turk's-cap; tepals 10×2.5cm, yellow, spotted brown, apex speckled red; anth. red-brown. Late summer. SE US (S Alabama, N Florida). Z4.

L.isabellinum Kunze. See **L.× testaceum**.
L.jankae Kerner. See **L.pyrenaicum** ssp. *carniolicum* var. *jankae*.

L.japonicum Houtt. (*L.krameri* Hook. f.; *L.makinoi* Koidz.). BAMBOO LILY; SASA-YURI.
Stems 40–90cm; bulbs 4cm wide, scales white, pink when exposed, ovate, imbricate. Lvs 15×2.5cm, scattered, lanceolate, 3–5-veined, margins rough; petiole to 1cm. Fls 1–5, fragrant, funnel-shaped, horizontal; tepals 10–15×2–3.5cm, oblanceolate to oblong, pink, occasionally white; anth. brown; pollen red or brown. Fr. 4cm, seeds brown, 8.5×7mm. Summer. Japan. 'Albomarginatum': lf margins white. 'Album': fls white. var. **platyfolium** anon. More vigorous, with broader lvs. Z5.

L.kelleyanum Lemmon (*L.nevadense* Eastw.; *L.shastense* Eastw.).
Stems to 1m, occasionally to 2m; bulbs stoloniferous, scales white. Lvs 5–15×1.5–3.5cm, lanceolate to elliptic, sometimes in 2 whorls of 7–16. Fls pendulous, turk's-cap, fragrant; tepals 2.5–5×1cm, yellow or orange, maroon or basally spotted brown, apex sometimes red; anth. brown. Summer. W US (California, S Oregon). Z5.

L.kelloggii Purdy.
Stems 30–125cm; bulbs 5×4cm, concentric, scales 5×1cm, white, lanceolate. Lvs to 10×2cm, in whorls of 12 or more, sessile, lanceolate or oblanceolate, acute, 1–3-veined. Fls to 20, pendulous, turk's-cap, fragrant, in a raceme; pedicels slender with leafy bracts, 3.5cm; tepals 5.5×1cm, reflexed, mauve-pink or white with dark purple spots and central yellow stripe toward base; anth. and pollen orange, stigma green. Fr. 5×2cm; seeds 5mm. Summer. W US (S Oregon, NW California). Z5.

L.kesselringianum Misch.
Stems to 1m; bulbs 5×5cm, concentric, scales yellow. Lvs lanceolate, 9–13×1–1.5cm. Fls 1–3, 9–14cm wide, bell-shaped; tepals 9cm, recurved, pale cream to yellow, spotted purple; anth. brown; pollen orange. Summer. Republic of Georgia, NE Turkey. Z5.

L.krameri Hook. f. See **L.japonicum**.

L.lancifolium Thunb. (*L.tigrinum* Ker-Gawl.). DEVIL LILY; KENTAN; TIGER LILY.
Stems 60–150cm, dark purple with white hairs, stem-rooting; bulbs to 7×8cm, scales ovate, white, overlapping; black bulbils in lf axils. Lvs 12–20×1–2cm, numerous, lanceolate, scattered, 5–7-veined, margins rough. Fls to 40, in a raceme, pendulous, turk's-cap, to 12.5cm wide, unscented; pedicels to 10cm, stiff; tepals 7–10×1–2.5cm, lanceolate, recurved when first open, gradually spreading, interior orange, spotted deep purple; anth. orange-red to purple; pollen brown.

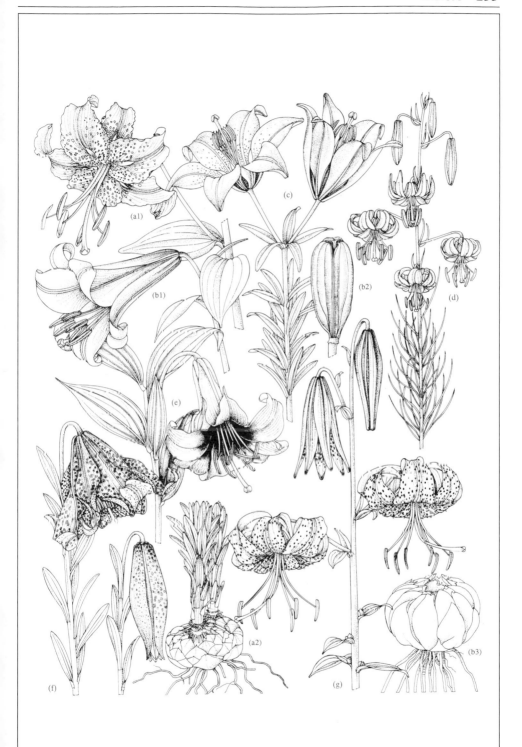

Lilium   Asiatic species   (a) *L.speciosum* var. *rubrum*   (a1) flower   (a2) bulb   (b) *L.leucanthum* var. *centifolium*
(b1) flower   (b2) capsule   (b3) bulb   (c) *L.maculatum*   (d) *L.pumilum*   (e) *L.nepalense*   (f) *L.bakerianum*
(g) *L.lancifolium*

Summer–early autumn. E China, Japan, Korea. 'Flore Pleno': fls double; tepals 24–36, narrow; stamens absent. 'Yellow Tiger': fls lemon-yellow, spotted dark purple. var. *flaviflorum* Mak. (*L.tigrinum* var. *flaviflorum* Mak.). Fls yellow. Japan. var. *fortunei* (Standish) V. Matthews (*L.tigrinum* var. *fortunei* Standish). Stems to 2m, densely woolly. Fls 30–50, tepals orange-red. Korea (Dagelet Is.), China (Lushan Mts). var. *splendens* (Van Houtte) V. Matthews (*L.tigrinum* var. *splendens* Van Houtte). Stems black with shiny bulbils. Fls to 25, larger; tepals bright orange-red, spotted black. Japan. Z4.

L.lankongense Franch. (*L.forrestii* W.W. Sm.).
Stems to 120cm, rough, ribbed, green, stem-rooting; bulbs 4cm wide, stoloniferous, scales white, pink on exposure, ovate, acute. Lvs 10×0.8cm, numerous, sessile, scattered, crowded near base, oblong-lanceolate, acute, 3–7-veined, margins rough. Fls to 15, 5cm wide, in a raceme, pendulous, turk's-cap, fragrant; pedicels recurved, green, 12.5cm; tepals 4–6.5×1–2.5cm, rose-pink, spotted purple, green central stripe, recurved, acute; anth. purple; pollen brown. Fr. to 4×2cm, seeds to 8mm. Summer. W China (SE Xizang). Z5.

L.ledebourii (Bak.) Boiss.
Stems slender to 1.25m, green, smooth, stem-rooting; bulbs concentric, 11×7–9cm, scales white turning yellow when exposed. Lvs scattered, spirally arranged, lower 11–12×2cm, upper narrower, 5-veined. Fls 1–5, fragrant, turk's-cap; tepals 6–7×1.3cm, creamy white to yellow, centrally spotted dark purple or red; anth. and pollen red. Fr. 4×2cm; seeds to 250. Summer. NW Iran, Azerbaijan. Z5.

L.leichtlinii Hook. f.
Stems to 120cm, green with a few white hairs in lf axils, stem-rooting; bulbs stoloniferous, 4×4cm, scales white, ovate, imbricate, 1.5cm. Lvs to 15×1cm, numerous, scattered, linear-lanceolate, 1–3-veined, margins rough. Fls 1–6, in a raceme, unscented, pendulous turk's-cap, buds white-hairy; tepals to 8×2cm, lemon yellow spotted maroon, lanceolate, tips recurved; anth. and pollen red-brown. Summer. Japan. var. *maximowiczii* (Reg.) Bak. (*L.maximowiczii* Reg.; *L.pseudotigrinum* Carr.; *L.leichtlinii* var. *tigrinum* Nichols.). Stems to 2.5cm; bulbs stoloniferous, 4×4cm, scales white. Lvs numerous, linear-lanceolate, 3–7-veined. Fls 1–12; tepals bright orange-red, spotted purple-brown; anth. and pollen red. Japan, C Korea. Z5.

L.leucanthum (Bak.) Bak var. *centifolium* (Stapf) Stearn (*L.centifolium* Stapf).
Stems 2–3m, glaucous; bulbs concentric, to 8×6.5cm, scales 5×2cm, dark yellow to red-brown, imbricate, ovate. Lvs 15–20cm, dark green, ascending, recurved, scattered, linear to lanceolate, 1-veined, non-flowering lvs shorter and 3-veined. Fls to 18, scented, funnel-shaped, horizontal or slightly pendulous; pedicels horizontal, 6–12cm; tepals 14–18×3–6cm, interior white with yellow basal tube, exterior flushed purple-red, green toward base, recurved toward tip; anth. red-brown; pollen brown. Fr. 6×2.5cm; seeds 1cm. Summer. W China (W Kansu). Z5.

L.linifolium Hornem. See *L.pumilum*.

L.longiflorum Thunb. EASTER LILY.
Stems to 1m, green, stem-rooting; bulbs 4×6cm, scales creamy yellow, oblong-lanceolate, imbricate. Lvs to 18×1.5cm, numerous, scattered, lanceolate or oblong-lanceolate. Fls to 6, funnel-shaped, scented, in an umbel; pedicels horizontal, to 12cm; tepals to 18cm, white, forming a basal tube, tips slightly recurved; pollen yellow; stigma green. Fr. 7cm. Summer. S Japan, Taiwan. 'Albomarginatum': lvs blue-green, margins white. 'Gelria': fls white; tepals slightly recurved at apex; pollen yellow. 'Holland's Glory': fls white, to 20cm. 'White America': fls white, tips and nectary green, pollen deep yellow. 'White Europe' (Georgia, 'Avai No. 5'): fls white; tepals strongly recurved, throat venation lettuce-green, exterior green-white below, venation cream above, pollen lemon-yellow. var. *eximium* (Courtois) Bak. (*L.harrisii* Carr.). Tepals more recurved, basal tube narrower. Japan. 'Howardii' ('Romanii'): fls pure white, firm-textured. var.

takeshima Duchartre. Stems taller, purple-brown. Fls flushed purple outside; pollen orange. Japan (Takeshima Is.). 'Erabu No Hikari' ('Erabu'): taller, more floriferous. Z5.

L.lowii anon. See *L.bakerianum*.

L.mackliniae Sealy.
Stems to 40cm, green, sometimes tinged purple, stem-rooting; bulbs 4.5×4–6cm, concentric, scales brown, ovate-lanceolate, 3×2cm. Lvs 3–6×0.4–1cm, spiral, horizontal, linear-lanceolate or elliptic-lanceolate. Fls 1–6, in a raceme, pendulous, bell-shaped; pedicels 3–6cm; tepals 5×2cm, interior rose-pink, exterior purple-pink; anth. purple; pollen yellow-orange or brown. Fr. 3×2cm; seeds brown, 8×7mm. Late spring–summer. NE India (Manipur). Z5.

L.maculatum Thunb. (*L.elegans* Thunb.; *L.thunbergianum* Schult. & Schult. f.; *L.fortunei* Lindl.; *L.batemanniae* Wallace; *L.atrosanguineum* anon.).
Considered by some to be *L.dauricum* × *L.concolor*. Stems to 60cm, ribbed, stem-rooting; bulbs concentric, 4cm wide, scales white, unjointed. Lvs 5–15×1.5cm, lanceolate to elliptic, scattered, 3–7-veined. Fls cup-shaped, erect; tepals 8–10cm, yellow, orange or red, variably spotted. Summer. Japan. 'Alutaceum': fls deep apricot, spotted purple-black. 'Aureum': fls orange-yellow, spotted black. 'Bicolor': fls brilliant orange, margins bright red, spots few, faint. 'Biligulatum': fls deep chestnut-red. 'Sanguineum': stems to 40cm; fls solitary, orange-red. 'Wallacei': fls apricot with raised maroon spots. Z4.

L.makinoi Koidz. See *L.japonicum*.
L.martagon var. dalmaticum Elwes. See *L.martagon* var. *cattaniae*.

L.× marhan Bak. (*L.hansonii* × *L.martagon* var. *album*.)
Stems to 1.5m. Fls pendulous, turk's-cap, 5–6cm wide; tepals thick, orange-yellow, spotted red-brown. Summer. Garden origin. Z5.

L.maritimum Kellogg. COAST LILY.
Stems 30–70cm, occasionally 2m, dark green; bulbs 5×3.5cm, rhizomatous, scales white, 3.5cm wide. Lvs 12.5×1.5cm, linear to oblanceolate, scattered, with a central whorl. Fls 1–12, pendulous, wide bell-shaped, in a raceme; pedicels arching; tepals 4.5cm, apically recurved, deep crimson or orange, spotted maroon inside; pollen brown. Fr. to 4cm. Summer. W US (N California coast). Z4.

L.martagon L. MARTAGON; TURK'S-CAP.
Stems to 2m, purple-green, stem-rooting; bulbs concentric, ovoid, 7.5cm wide, scales yellow, oblong or lanceolate, acute. Lvs to 16×6.5cm, oblanceolate, 7–9-veined, in whorls of 8–14. Fls to 50, in raceme, pendulous, recurved, turk's-cap, 5cm wide, fragrant; pedicels short; tepals 3–4.5×0.6–1cm, dull pink, spotted maroon; pollen yellow; stigma purple. Fr. 3.5×2.5cm. Summer. NW Europe, NW Asia. var. *albiflorum* Vukot. Fls white with pink spotting, rare in cultivation. Yugoslavia. var. *album* Weston. Stem green. Fls white, not spotted. var. *cattaniae* Vis. (var. dalmaticum Elwes). Stems and buds hairy. Fls maroon, unspotted. Balkans. var. *caucasicum* Misch. Stems to 2.5m. Fls lilac-pink. var. *hirsutum* Weston. Stem hairy, purple. Lvs downy beneath. Fls purple-pink, spotted. var. *pilosiusculum* Freyn. Stems purple, hairy. Lvs narrow, margins hairy. Fls deep red, sparsely spotted; bracts and buds hairy. Mongolia, Siberia. var. *sanguineopurpureum* G. Beck. Fls dark maroon, spotted. Balkans. Z4.

L.maximowiczii Reg. See *L.leichtlinii* var. *maximowiczii*.

L.medeoloides A. Gray (*L.avenaceum* Fisch.). WHEEL LILY.
Stems to 75cm, hollow, stem-rooting; bulbs 2.5×2.5cm, concentric, scales 2cm, white, jointed, acute, easily detached. Lvs to 12×3.5cm, lanceolate, sessile or short-petioled, 1–2-whorled, a few scattered. Fls 1–10, turk's-cap, 5cm wide, unscented, in a raceme or umbel; pedicels erect, arched; tepals lanceolate, 4.5×1cm, recurved, apricot to orange-red, usually with darker spots; anth. purple; pollen orange-red. Fr. 1.5×1.5cm. Summer. China, Japan, S Korea, Russia. Z5.

L.michauxii Poir. CAROLINA LILY.
Stems to 1m, green, sometimes spotted, stem-rooting; bulbs stoloniferous, scales white, lanceolate to ovate. Lvs to 11.5×2.5cm, fleshy, glaucous, oblanceolate to obovate, in whorls of 3–7. Fls 1–5, pendulous, turk's-cap, to 10cm wide, scented; tepals to 10cm, lanceolate, recurved, orange-red to pale crimson, yellow toward base, inner surface spotted purple or black; anth. brown; pollen red. Fr. 4×2cm. Early autumn. SE US. Z6.

L.michiganense Farw.
Stems to 1.5m; bulbs stoloniferous, 3×3cm, each flowering once only, scales thick, yellow, flushed pink or brown. Lvs 9–12cm, lanceolate or elliptic-lanceolate, in up to 4 whorls of 4–8. Fls 3–6, occasionally to 25, pendulous turk's-cap, 7.5cm wide; pedicels to 24cm, curved; tepals 7×2cm, recurved, orange-red, spotted deep crimson, basal tube green; pollen orange-brown. Summer. Central N America. Z4.

L.monadelphum Bieb. (*L.szovitsianum* Fisch. & Avé-Lall.; *L.colchicum* Steven). CAUCASIAN LILY.
Stems 100–150cm, stem-rooting; bulbs 4–8cm wide, scales yellow-white, lanceolate. Lvs 12.5×2.5cm, lanceolate or oblanceolate, spirally arranged, 9–13-veined. Fls 1–5, occasionally to 30, fragrant, pendulous, turk's-cap; tepals 6–10×1–2cm, recurved, yellow, interior spotted purple or maroon, exterior flushed purple-brown; pollen orange-yellow. Summer. NE Turkey, Caucasus. var. *armenum* (Misch.) P.H. Davis & D.M. Henderson. Inner tepals acute, 1–1.6cm wide. NE Turkey, Armenia. Z5.

L.montanum Nels. See *L.philadelphicum*.
L.myriophyllum Franch. See *L.sulphureum*.

L.nanum Klotzsch (*Nomocharis nana* Wils.).
Stems 6–45cm; bulbs concentric, 4×2cm, scales white, imbricate, lanceolate. Lvs to 12×0.5cm, linear, scattered, 3–5-veined. Fls solitary, pendulous, bell-shaped; tepals to 1–4×0.3–1.6cm, pale pink to purple with fine dark purple or brown mottling; anth. yellow-brown. Summer. Himalaya, W China. var. *flavidum* (Rendle) Sealy. Fls pale yellow. Z5.

L.neilgherrense Wight. See *L.wallichianum* var. *neilgherrense*

L.nepalense D. Don.
Stems to 1m, smooth, green; bulbs to 9cm wide, stoloniferous, scales white, pink on exposure, ovate-lanceolate. Lvs to 14×3cm, oblong-lanceolate, 5–7-veined. Fls 1–3, slightly pendulous, funnel-shaped, with a musky nocturnal scent; pedicels ascending, to 10cm; tepals to 15cm, recurved, ribbed, green-white to green-yellow, base red-purple; anth. purple; pollen orange-brown. Summer. Bhutan, Nepal, N India. var. *concolor* Cotton. Fls green-yellow, throat not red. Bhutan. Z5.

L.nevadense Eastw. See *L.kelleyanum*.
L.nitidum Bull. See *L.columbianum*.

L.nobilissimum (Mak.) Mak.
Stems purple-green, to 1.7m, stem-rooting; bulbs concentric, to 15cm wide, scales creamy white. Lvs to 12×5cm, scattered, dark green, short-petioled, lf axils bulbiliferous. Fls 1–3, vertical, 15×13cm, funnel-shaped, fragrant; tepals white; anth. green; pollen yellow. Summer. S Japan. Z6.

L.occidentale Purdy. EUREKA LILY.
Stems 70–200cm, smooth, green tinged purple; bulbs rhizomatous, scales jointed. Lvs to 13×1.5cm, in whorls, linear-lanceolate to lanceolate, 7-veined. Fls 1–5, occasionally 20, in a raceme, pendulous, turk's-cap, to 7cm wide; pedicels arching, to 15cm; tepals 3.5–6×1.5cm, reflexed, crimson with green-yellow throat, or vermilion with orange throat and brown spots; anth. purple; pollen orange-red. Fr. 2.5×1cm; seeds 6–7mm wide. W US (Coast of S Oregon and N California). Z5.

L.oxypetalum (Royle) Bak. (*Nomocharis oxypetala* Royle).
Stems to 25cm, bright green; bulbs concentric, to 5cm high, scales lanceolate, 1cm wide. Lvs to 7.5×1.25cm, scattered, sessile, elliptic, whorl immediately below fl. Fls 1–2, cup-shaped, pendulous; pedicels very short; tepals to 5.5cm, ovate, lemon-yellow, often spotted purple; pollen orange. Fr. 3×2cm; seeds pale brown, 9×7mm. Summer. NW Himalaya. var. *insigne* Sealy. Fls purple. Z4.

L.papilliferum Franch. LIKIANG LILY.
Stems to 90cm, green mottled purple, stem-rooting; bulbs 3×2.5cm, stoloniferous, scales white, lanceolate-ovate to ovate. Lvs to 10×0.8cm, scattered, linear or linear-oblong. Fls 1–3, 7.5cm wide, in a raceme, fragrant, pendulous, turk's-cap; pedicels stiff; tepals 4×1.5cm, reflexed, apex acute, deep purple or maroon with lighter central stripe, exterior green; anth. brown; pollen orange-yellow. Fr. 4×2cm. Late spring–late summer. SW China. Z5.

L.× pardaboldtii Woodcock & Coutts. (*L.humboldtii* × *L.pardalinum*.)
Stems to 150cm. Lvs whorled. Fls pendulous, turk's-cap; tepals orange-red, spotted dark crimson. Summer. Bellingham Hybrids: rhizomatous, orange-fld (US).

L.pardalinum Kellogg. LEOPARD LILY; PANTHER LILY.
Stems 2–3m; bulbs rhizomatous, 4cm wide, forming large clumps, scales to 2cm, numerous, brittle, yellow-white, pink on exposure, jointed. Lvs to 18×5cm, in whorls of to 16, elliptic or oblanceolate, glabrous, to 3-veined. Fls to 10 in a raceme, unscented, pendulous, turk's-cap, to 9×9cm; pedicels arching; tepals reflexed, lanceolate, acute, orange-red to crimson, spotted deep maroon toward base, some spots outlined yellow; anth. red-brown; pollen orange. Summer. W US (S Oregon, N California). 'Californicum': fls deep orange, spotted maroon, tips scarlet. 'Johnsonii': stems tall; fls finely spotted. var. *angustifolium* Kellogg (*L.roezlii* Reg. non Purdy). Lvs narrow. US (California around San Francisco). var. *giganteum* Woodcock & Coutts. Stems to 2.5m. Fls to 30; tepals crimson and yellow, densely spotted. *L.pardalinum* 'Red Sunset' is a synonym of *L.pardalinum* var. *giganteum*. Z5.

L.× parkmanii T. Moore. (*L.auratum* × *L.speciosum*.)
Lvs broad. Fls fragrant, bowl-shaped, to 20cm wide; tepals recurved, crimson, margins white. Summer. 'Allegra': fls white with sparse pink papillae. 'Empress of China': fls white, spotted pink. 'Empress of India': fls deep red, margin white. 'Empress of Japan': fls white with a golden band, spotted deep maroon. 'Excelsior': fls china-rose, pet. tips and narrow margins white. 'Imperial Crimson': fls deep crimson, margin white. 'Imperial Silver': fls white with small maroon spots. 'Jillian Wallace': fls rose, margin white, interior spotted deep crimson. 'Pink Glory': fls shell-pink to salmon-pink, golden spots few.

L.parryi S. Wats. LEMON LILY.
Stems to 2m, glabrous; bulbs to 4×4cm, rhizomatous, scales numerous, 3-pointed, brittle, yellow-white. Lvs to 15cm, oblanceolate, 3-veined, margins slightly rough. Fls to 15, occasionally many more, fragrant, horizontal, funnel-shaped; pedicels long, sharply angled; tepals to 7–10×0.8–1.2cm, oblanceolate, apically recurved, lemon-yellow, base sparsely spotted maroon; anth. orange-brown; pollen red. Fr. to 5cm. Summer. SW US (S California, S Arizona). Z5.

L.parviflorum Hook. See *L.columbianum*.

L.parvum Kellogg. SIERRA LILY.
Stems to 2m; bulbs 3.5×3.5cm, rhizomatous, scales thick, white, lanceolate, acute. Lvs 12.5×3cm, mostly in whorls, lanceolate or linear, 1–3-veined. Fls to 30, bell-shaped, borne horizontally in a raceme; pedicels to 6cm; tepals to 4cm, oblanceolate, recurved, red, interior spotted deep maroon. Fr. to 1.2mm. Summer. W US (Oregon to C California). f. *crocatum* Stearn. Fls yellow or orange. Z4.

L.pennsylvanicum Ker-Gawl. See *L.dauricum*.

L.philadelphicum L. (*L.montanum* Nels.). WOOD LILY.
Stems to 1.25m; bulbs 2.5cm wide, stoloniferous, scales
1.35cm, white, ovate. Lvs 5–10×1.5cm, mostly in whorls of
6–8, oblanceolate, margins sometimes rough, 3–5-veined. Fls
1–5, cup-shaped, erect, in an umbel; tepals to 7.5cm, oblanceolate, orange to vivid orange-red, spotted purple, edges revolute; pollen deep red. Fr. 2.5cm; seeds brown, 8×7mm.
Summer. Eastern N America. var. *andinum* (Nutt.) Ker-
Gawl. Lvs to 5mm wide, scattered. US and S Canada (Rocky
Mts). Z4.

L.philippinense Bak.
Stems 30–40cm, occasionally to 1m, green, purple towards
base; bulbs 3.5×4cm, stoloniferous, scales white, acute, lanceolate. Lvs to 15×0.6cm, scattered, linear. Fls 1–6, scented, to
25cm, funnel-shaped; tepals to 5cm wide, oblanceolate to
spathulate, apices spreading, interior white, exterior flushed
green and purple; anth. yellow; pollen yellow. Summer.
Philippine Is. (N Luzon). Z9.

L.pitkinense Beane & Vollmer.
Stems 1–2m, glabrous; bulbs rhizomatous, occasionally
stoloniferous, scales unjointed. Lvs scattered and in 2–3
whorls, linear or lanceolate, 3-veined. Fls 1–3, occasionally to
8 in cult., unscented, in an umbel or raceme; pedicels long,
arched; tepals scarlet, yellow toward base, spotted dark purple; anth. purple; pollen brown. Summer. W US (California).
Z5.

L.polyphyllum D. Don.
Stems 1–2m; bulbs 7.5×2.5cm; scales sharply acute, pink.
Lvs to 12×2cm, scattered, linear to oblong-lanceolate. Fls
1–6, sometimes to 30, fragrant, turk's-cap, 11cm wide, in an
umbel or raceme; tepals recurved, white or pink, sometimes
spotted red, base yellow-green; pollen orange; seeds
7mm wide. Summer. Afghanistan, W Himalaya. Z7.

L.pomponium L.
Stems to 1m, base spotted purple; bulbs concentric, 6.5cm
wide, scales white, yellow on exposure, ovate lanceolate,
acute. Lvs to 12.5×2cm, numerous, crowded, linear, margin
silver-ciliate. Fls to 6, pendulous, turk's-cap, 5cm wide, in a
raceme, malodorous; pedicels long; tepals recurved, bright
scarlet, base spotted black inside, outside purple-green toward
base; pollen orange-red. Fr. 4×2.5cm. Summer. Europe
(Maritime Alps). Z4.

L.ponticum K. Koch. See *L.pyrenaicum* ssp. *ponticum* var.
ponticum.
L.ponticum var. *artvinense* P.H. Davis & D.M. Henderson.
See *L.pyrenaicum* ssp. *ponticum* var. *artvinense*.

L.primulinum Bak. OCHRE LILY.
Stems to 2.4m, green spotted brown, or brown, stem-rooting;
bulbs 3–4×3.5cm, stoloniform, scales to 5×1.5cm, cream, purple on exposure, ovate-lanceolate, acute. Lvs to 15×4cm,
scattered, lanceolate, 1–3-veined. Fls 2–8, occasionally 18,
fragrant, funnel-shaped, pendulous; pedicels to 15cm,
decurved below fls; tepals 6–15×1–5cm, oblong-lanceolate,
recurved, yellow, sometimes with purple-red markings;
pollen   brown.   Fr.   2.5–3.4cm;   seeds   winged.
Summer–autumn. W China (Yunnan), N Burma, Thailand.
var. *primulinum*. Tepals entirely yellow, upper half recurved.
N Burma. var. *burmanicum* (W.W. Sm.) Stearn. Stems
120–240cm. Lvs to 4cm wide. Tepals 6.5–15cm, upper third
recurved, base purple-red. N Burma, Thailand. var.
ochraceum (Franch.) Stearn. Stems to 120cm. Lvs 2cm wide.
Tepals 6cm, red-purple toward base, upper two-thirds
recurved. Z4.

L.× princeps Wils. See *L.× imperiale*.
L.pseudotigrinum Carr. See *L.leichtlinii* var. *maximowiczii*.
L.pulchellum Fisch. See *L.concolor* var. *pulchellum*.

L.pumilum DC. (*L.tenuifolium* Schrank; *L.linifolium*
Hornem.). CORAL LILY.
Stems 15–45cm, occasionally 90cm, green, stem-rooting;

bulbs concentric, 4×2.5cm, scales white, imbricate, ovate-
lanceolate. Lvs to 10×0.3cm, scattered, sessile, linear, 1-
veined. Fls to 7–20, scented, pendulous, turk's-cap, in a
raceme; buds woolly; tepals 5×5cm, oblong-lanceolate,
reflexed, scarlet, base sometimes dotted black; pollen scarlet.
Fr. 3×1.5cm. Summer. N China, N Korea, Mongolia, Siberia.
'Golden Gleam': fls apricot yellow. Z5.

L.pyrenaicum Gouan.
Stems 15–135cm, green, sometimes spotted purple, often
stem-rooting; bulbs 7×7cm, scales oblong-lanceolate, yellow-white, pink on exposure. Lvs to 12.5×2cm, linear-lanceolate, acute, margins sometimes silver or ciliate. Fls to 12,
pendulous, turk's-cap, 5cm wide, in a raceme; pedicels to
12.5cm; tepals recurved, green-yellow, streaked and spotted
dark maroon; pollen orange-red. Fr. 3.5×2.5cm. Summer.
Europe (SE Alps, Pyrenees, Balkans, NE Turkey), Georgia.
'Aureum': fls deep yellow. ssp. *pyrenaicum*. Stems
30–135cm, green, sparsely spotted purple. Lvs 7–15×
0.3–2cm, 3–15-veined. Fls to 12; tepals 4–6.5cm, yellow,
interior lined and spotted dark purple. N Spain. ssp.
pyrenaicum f. *rubrum* Stoker (*L.pyrenaicum* var.
rubrum hort.). Fls orange-red. ssp. *carniolicum* (Koch) V.
Matthews (*L.carniolicum* Koch). Stems to 120cm, green,
stem-rooting; bulbs 7.5×6.5cm, scales ovate-lanceolate, yellow-white. Lvs 3–11×0.4–1.7cm, 3–9-veined, pubesc.
beneath. Fls 6–12; tepals 3–7cm, yellow, orange or red,
sometimes spotted purple. SE Europe. var. *albanicum*
(Griseb.) V. Matthews (*L.albanicum* Griseb.). Stem to 40cm.
Fls yellow. Lf veins not pubesc. Albania, NW Greece,
Balkans. var. *jankae* (Kerner) Matthews (*L.jankae* Kerner).
Stems to 80cm. Lf veins pubesc. below. Fls yellow. N
Bulgaria, NW Italy, C Romania, Balkans. ssp. *ponticum* (K.
Koch) V. Matthews (*L.ponticum* (K. Koch)). Stems
15–90cm. Lvs 3–8×0.8–2cm, 7–15-veined, pubesc. beneath.
Fls 5–12, tepals 7–10mm wide, deep yellow or deep orange,
interior red-brown, spotted purple toward base. NE Turkey,
Georgia. var. *artvinense* (Misch.) V. Matthews (*L.artvinense*
Misch.; *L.ponticum* var. *artvinense* (Misch.) P.H. Davis &
M.D. Henderson). Fls deep orange; tepals 5–6mm wide. NE
Turkey, Republic of Georgia. Z3.

L.regale Wils.
Stems 50–200cm, grey-green flushed purple, stem-rooting;
bulbs 6.5–15.5cm wide, concentric, scales thick, imbricate,
lanceolate to ovate-lanceolate, acute, deep red. Lvs
5–13×0.4–0.6cm, scattered, sessile, linear, 1-veined. Fls
1–25, fragrant, horizontal, funnel-shaped, in an umbel;
pedicels 2–12cm, spreading; tepals 12–15×2–4cm, apically
recurved, white, interior of basal tube yellow, exterior purple;
anth. and pollen golden; style and stigma green. Fr. purple,
5–7×2.5cm; seeds to 7mm. Summer. W China (W Sichuan).
'Album': fls almost pure white; anth. orange. 'Royal Gold':
fls yellow. Z5.

L.rhodopaeum Delip.
Stems to 80–100cm; bulbs concentric, 2–8–4cm wide, scales
white or pale yellow, linear-lanceolate. Lvs numerous, alternate, linear, acute, hairy on margins and on veins beneath. Fls
1–5, funnel-shaped, pendulous, strongly scented; tepals
8–12cm, lemon yellow, recurved; anth. and pollen scarlet.
Summer. Bulgaria, Greece. Z6.

L.roezlii Reg. non Purdy. See *L.pardalinum* var. *angustifolium*.
L.roezlii Purdy non Reg. See *L.vollmeri*.

L.rubellum Bak.
Stems 30–80cm, stem-rooting; bulbs concentric, 3cm wide,
scales white, lanceolate. Lvs 10×3.5cm, scattered, petiolate,
ovate-lanceolate to oblong-elliptic, 5–7-veined. Fls 1–9, very
fragrant, horizontal, funnel-shaped; tepals 7.5cm, oblanceolate to oblong, apically recurved, rose-pink, base sometimes
spotted maroon; pollen orange-yellow, style green. Fr. 2.5cm.
Summer. Japan (N Honshu). Z6.

Lilium European species (a) *L.candidum* (b) *L.chalcedonicum* (b1) single leaf (c) *L.martagon* flower spike
(c1) seed (c2) capsule (c3) bulb (d) *L.monadelphum* (e) *L.pyrenaicum* (f) *L.bulbiferum*, bulbils in leaf axils

L.rubescens S. Wats. (*L.washingtonianum* var. *purpureum* hort.; *L.washingtonianum* var. *rubescens* S. Wats.). CHAPARRAL LILY.
Stems to 3m, green flushed purple; bulbs 6×5.5cm, rhizomatous or subrhizomatous, scales 5×2cm, white flushed purple. Lvs to 12×3.5cm, lanceolate to oblanceolate, scattered and in 1–4 whorls. Fls 1–30, occasionally 100 or more, fragrant, broadly funnel-shaped, 10cm wide, in an umbellate raceme; tepals 3.5–6.5cm, apically recurved, white, finely spotted purple, ageing to purple; pollen and stigma yellow. Summer. W US (NW California, S Oregon). Z6.

L.× sargale Crow. See *L.× imperiale*.

L.sargentiae Wils.
Stems to 1.5m, purple, stem-rooting; bulbs concentric, 4×15cm, scales thick, lanceolate to ovate-lanceolate, acute, imbricate, yellow-white with wine-red apices. Lvs 10–20×0.5–2cm, fleshy, scattered, sessile, linear-oblong to oblong-lanceolate, basally addressed, 3–7-veined, axils bulbiliferous. Fls 2–5, fragrant, funnel-shaped, 13–18cm wide, horizontal or pendulous, in a corymb or umbel; pedicels horizontal or ascending, 3–10cm; tepals 12–15cm, interior white with yellow basal tube, exterior suffused green or purple; anth. purple; pollen brown. Fr. 5–6cm. Summer. W China (Sichuan). Z6.

L.shastense Eastw. See *L.kelleyanum*.

L.sherriffiae Stearn.
Stems 35–90cm, green flushed purple, stem-rooting; bulbs 2.5×2cm, concentric, scales 2.5×0.8cm, lanceolate or ovate-lanceolate, acute. Lvs 3–13×0.3–0.6cm, scattered, linear-lanceolate or linear. Fls 1–2, narrow funnel-shaped; tepals recurved, acute, dark purple outside, inside tessellated golden yellow–green toward apex; pollen yellow. Summer. Bhutan, Nepal. Z6.

L.speciosum Thunb.
Stems 120–170cm, green tinged purple, stem-rooting; bulbs 10×10cm, concentric, scales white, yellow or brown, imbricate, lanceolate, acute. Lvs to 18×6cm, scattered, lanceolate, petiolate, 7–9-veined. Fls to 12, fragrant, pendulous, turk's-cap, 15cm wide, in a raceme; pedicels to 10cm; tepals to 10×4.5cm, white, base flushed carmine, spotted pink or crimson, recurved, lanceolate or ovate-lanceolate, margins wavy; pollen dark red. Late summer. China, Japan, Taiwan. 'Grand Commander': fls deep pink tinted lilac, edged white, spotted red. 'Krätzeri': fls white, exterior with central green stripe. 'Melpomene': fls deep carmine, segments edged white. 'Uchida': fls brilliant crimson, spotted green, tips white. var. **album** Mast. ex Bak. Stems purple-brown. Fls white. var. **gloriosoides** Bak. Tepals spotted scarlet. China (Kiangsi, Anwhei), Taiwan. var. **magnificum** Wallace. Fls rose, spotted deep crimson, margins paler; pollen red. var. **roseum** Mast. ex Bak. Fls rose. var. **rubrum** Mast. ex Bak. Stems purple-brown. Fls carmine. Z6.

L.sulphureum Bak. (*L.myriophyllum* Franch.).
Stems 150–200cm, ribbed, green, mottled with purple, stem-rooting; bulbs 10×10cm, concentric, scales dark purple, lanceolate-ovate. Lvs to 20×2cm, scattered, linear-lanceolate, 3–7-veined, axillary brown bulbils. Fls 1–15, fragrant, pendulous or horizontal, funnel-shaped; tepals to 25×6cm, apically recurved, interior surface creamy white with yellow basal tube, exterior flushed pink; anth. brown; pollen orange-brown. Fr. 10×2.5cm; seeds golden brown, winged. Late summer. Burma, W China (Yunnan). *L.sulphureum × L.regale* is known as *L.× sulphurgale*. Z6.

L.superbum L. TURK'S-CAP LILY.
Stems 1.5–3m high, green, mottled purple, stem-rooting; bulbs concentric, stoloniferous, scales white, ovate, imbricate. Lvs 3.5–11×0.8–2.8cm, lanceolate or elliptic, 3–7-veined, in whorls of 4–20 and scattered. Fls to 40, pendulous, turk's-cap in a raceme; pedicels ascending, bracteolate; tepals recurved, orange flushed red, spotted maroon toward green base; anth. red, 1.6–2cm; pollen orange-brown. Summer. E US. Z3.

L.sutchuenense Franch. See *L.davidii* var. *willmottiae*.
L.szovitsianum Fisch. & Avé-Lall. See *L.monadelphum*.

L.taliense Franch.
Stems to 140cm, dark purple or green, mottled purple, stem-rooting; bulbs 4.5cm wide, stoloniferous, scales ovate, acute, cream with purple markings. Lvs to 12.7×0.6cm, scattered, sessile, linear-lanceolate, 3-veined. Fls to 12, scented, pendulous turk's-cap, in a raceme; pedicels horizontal, stiff, tepals 5.7×1.2cm, recurved, lanceolate, white, interior spotted purple; anth. mauve-white; pollen yellow. Fr. 2.5×2cm; seeds brown, winged, 8×6mm. Summer. W China (NE Yunnan). Z5.

L.tenuifolium Schrank. See *L.pumilum*.

L.× testaceum Lindl. (*L.isabellinum* Kunze; *L.excelsum* Endl. & Hartinger). (*L.candidum × L.chalcedonicum*.) NANKEEN LILY.
Stems to 100–150cm, purple with grey bloom. Lvs 5–10cm, scattered, linear, margins ciliate, veins pubesc. beneath. Fls 6–12, scented, pendulous, turk's-cap; tepals to 8cm, yellow to pale orange, interior spotted red; anth. red; pollen orange. Summer. Garden origin. Z6.

L.thayerae Wils. See *L.davidii*.
L.thunbergianum Schult. & Schult. f. See *L.maculatum*.
L.tigrinum Ker-Gawl. See *L.lancifolium*.
L.tigrinum var. *fortunei* Standish. See *L.lancifolium* var. *fortunei*.
L.tigrinum var. *flaviflorum* Mak. See *L.lancifolium* var. *flaviflorum*.
L.tigrinum var. *splendens* Van Houtte. See *L.lancifolium* var. *splendens*.

L.tsingtauense Gilg.
Stems to 120cm, glabrous, hollow, stem-rooting; bulbs to 4×4cm, scales 2–2.5×0.6–0.8cm, white, lanceolate, imbricate. Lvs to 15×4cm, glabrous, oblanceolate, petiolate, often in 2 whorls. Fls 2–7, in a raceme, unscented, erect, bowl-shaped; pedicels to 8.5cm, tepals to 5×1.5cm, orange or vermilion with purple spotting; anth. and pollen orange. Fr. ribbed; seeds brown, 8×7mm. Summer. NE China, Korea. var. **carneum** Nak. Fls red, unspotted. var. **flavum** Wils. Fls yellow, spotted red. Z6.

L.umbellatum hort. See *L.× hollandicum*.

L.vollmeri Eastw. (*L.roezlii* Purdy non Reg.).
Stems to 1m; bulbs rhizomatous, scales white, ageing to yellow. Lvs to 15cm, scattered or in 1–2 whorls, elliptic-linear. Fls 1–10, turk's-cap, in a raceme; long, arching; tepals to 8×1cm, reflexed, red-orange with dark margins, dark purple or black spots ringed with yellow on inner surface; pollen orange-red. Summer. W US (S Oregon, N California). Z5.

L.wallichianum Schult. & Schult. f.
Stems to 2m, green, tinged purple, stem-rooting; bulbs stoloniferous, 9cm wide, scales lanceolate, white. Lvs 25×1.2cm, scattered, linear or lanceolate. Fls 1–4, scented, horizontal, funnel-shaped, 20cm wide with basal tube to 10cm; tepals 15–30cm, apically recurved, interior creamy white, exterior tinged green; pollen yellow. Fr. to 4cm. Summer–autumn. Himalaya. Ireland. var. **neilgherrense** (Wight) Hara (*L.neilgherrense* Wight). Stems to 90cm. Lvs to 12×3cm, lanceolate. S India. Z5.

L.wardii F. Stern.
Stems to 1.5m, dark green flushed purple, stem-rooting; bulbs 5cm wide, stoloniform, scales ovate, imbricate, light brown speckled red, becoming purple on exposure. Lvs 3–8×0.6–2cm, scattered, sessile, glabrous, 3-veined, oblong to linear-lanceolate, apex acute. Fls to 35, fragrant, pendulous, turk's-cap, in a raceme; pedicels stiff, horizontal; tepals 5–6.5×1.5cm, pink with purple basal median line and spotting, recurved; anth. mauve; pollen yellow. Fr. 4×1.5cm; seeds brown, 8×6mm. Summer. W China. Z5.

L.washingtonianum Kellogg.
Stems 2.5cm; bulbs subrhizomatous, scales lanceolate, acute,

white, to 5cm. Lvs to 15×3.5cm, in whorls, oblanceolate, margins wavy. Fls to 20, scented, to 11cm wide, bowl-shaped, horizontal, in a raceme; pedicels bracteate, erect; tepals 8×2.5cm, oblanceolate, white, spotted purple at base, apex acute, recurved; pollen yellow. Fr. cylindrical, furrowed. Summer. W US (NW California, S Oregon). var. *purpurascens* Stearn. Fls opening white, becoming pink then purple. Z4.

L.washingtonianum var. *purpureum* hort. See *L.rubescens*.
L.washingtonianum var. *rubescens* S. Wats. See *L.rubescens*.

L.wigginsii Beane & Vollmer.
Stems to 90cm, stem-rooting; bulbs rhizomatous, scales entire or jointed, producing bulbils. Lvs to 22×2cm, linear-lanceolate. Fls solitary or in a raceme, pendulous, turk's-cap; pedicels arching; tepals to 7cm, reflexed, yellow with variable purple spotting; pollen yellow. Summer. W US (N California, S Oregon). Z4.

L.wilsonii Leichtlin.
Stems to 1m; bulbs 5.5×3.5cm, concentric, scales white. Lvs 10×2.5cm, lanceolate, 5–7-veined. Fls cup-shaped, erect, 12.5cm wide, tepals recurved, to 10cm, orange-red with basal central yellow stripe, dark spotting. Summer. Japan. Z5.

LILY HYBRIDS AND THEIR CLASSIFICATION

The vast majority of the hybrids slot easily into the various divisions, such as Orientals, Asiatics, Martagons, etc. In 1963 the Royal Horticultural Society Lily Committee drew up a Horticultural Classification for show, exhibition, catalogue and registration purposes. This classification has stood the test of time, although in recent years the barriers between the various divisions, which at one time seemed almost inviolable, have been broken, as hybridizers with particular skills have created 'bridge-builders' between one division and another. Notable within these has been *L.henryi*, which was originally crossed with the trumpet lily, *L.leucanthum* ssp. *chloraster* to produce *L.×kewense* (flowered 1900). This was followed by Debras's cross in 1925 with *L.sargentiae* and named *L.×aurelianense*. In the 1950s Woodriff crossed *L.henryi* with *L.speciosum* ssp. *rubrum* to achieve *L.*'Black Beauty', and in the 1970s North eventually obtained a successful cross with an Asiatic hybrid which he named *L.*'Eureka'. Another link between different divisions has been *L.longiflorum* and various Asiatic hybrids. These few instances may show a trend which will continue and flourish with genetic engineering.

In *The New RHS Dictionary of Gardening* (1992), it was observed of recent departures and successes in lily hybridization that 'these few instances may show a trend which will continue ...'.

As recently as summer 1994, John Bryan confirmed this view:

When I came to the United States, some 30 odd years ago, I worked with Jan de Graaff in Oregon. Just a few years before I arrived, the Mid Century Hybrids had been introduced. At the time of the introduction of these hybrids, including the great 'Enchantment', (they were) absolute show stoppers. Such vigour, vibrant colours and high bud count had not been seen before. But the Asiatic Hybrids ... were just part of the revolutionary wave. Outstanding new Trumpet Lilies, particularly 'Golden Splendor', 'Pink Perfection' and 'Black Dragon' soon became garden favourites. Today these are many Asiatic Hybrids, many in colours we just dreamed about, white and pink, for example, and two-toned flowers, some with 'brush marks' on the petals, which now outnumber other types. Now we have plants with double the chromosome count ... giants if you will. New techniques have allowed hybridizers almost to disregard the boundaries of various types of lilies. Trumpets are now being crossed with Orientals; Asiatics with Trumpets ... coloured Easter Lilies, yellow Orientals, ... dwarf and tall-growing lilies of many shapes and sizes will soon be launched in the market. I find it interesting to see all such developments.

It means that horticultural classifications have to be reclassified to accommodate the new forms and types.

There follow two classifications, the first (presented in synopsis) is provisional and intended to reflect the very latest developments in lily breeding. It differs from the second (based on the *International Lily Register*), largely in removing certain classes whose distinctiveness has been blurred by new plants that cross old boundaries.

Division 1. Asiatic Hybrids.
1.A. upright-facing flowers
1.B. outward-facing and pendent flowers

Division 2. Martagon Hybrids.

Division 3. Candidum Hybrids.

Division 4. American Hybrids.

Division 5. Longiflorum Hybrids.

Division 6. Chinese Trumpet and Aurelian Hybrids.
6.A upright-facing flowers
6.B. outward-facing and pendent flowers

Division 7. Oriental Hybrids.
7.A. trumpet-shaped flowers.
7.B. bowl-shaped flowers.
7.C. flat-faced flowers.
7.D. recurved flowers.

Division 8. All hybrids not described by any previous division.

Division 9. Species - all true species and their botanical variants.

Division 1: Asiatic Hybrids – derived from such species or hybrid groups as *Ll.cernuum, davidii, lancifolium, leichtlinii, maculatum, ×hollandicum, amabile, tigrinum, pumilum, concolor* and *bulbiferum*.

1(a): Early-flowering with upright flowers, single or an umbel. 'Apeldoorn': 80cm; flowers bright orange-red. 'Connecticut King': to 1m; flowers golden-yellow. 'Connecticut Star': flowers yellow, with yellow orange throat, sparsely flecked purple. 'Cote d'Azur': flowers deep pink with paler centre. 'Enchantment': 75cm; flowers bright nasturtium red, to 15 per stem. 'Golden Chalice'. 'Joan Evans': flowers orange, with basal spots inside petals. 'Marilyn Monroe': to 1.2m; flowers yellow. 'Ming Yellow': to 1.2m; leaves glossy; flowers broad, somewhat recurved, bright golden yellow. 'Mont Blanc': flowers broad, open, cream-white, spotted brown. 'Peach Blush': to 90cm; flowers rose-pink, darker at the base, sparsely spotted maroon. 'Rainbow Hybrids'. 'Sterling Star': to 1.2m; flowers white with a cream tinge and brown spots.

1(b): Flowers outward-facing. 'Brandywine': to 1m; flowers deep orange with red spots. 'Corsage': to 1.2m; flowers pale pink with an ivory-white centre, spotted burgundy, tinged yellow and cream outside. 'Fireking': to 90cm; flowers bright orange-red with purple spots. 'Paprika'. 'Prosperity': flowers lemon-yellow. 'Tamara': flowers red with yellow-orange centre and grey-purple flecks. 'Valencia'.

1(c): Flowers pendent. 'Amber Gold'. 'Adagio'. 'Black Butterfly': 90cm; flowers deep burgundy-red. 'Citronella': to 1.5m; lemon-yellow, with small, feint, black spots, to 30 per stem. 'Connecticut Yankee': stems 1.2m; flowers vivid orange-red, unspotted. Fiesta Hybrids: flowers golden-yellow to bright red. Harlequin Hybrids: to 1.5m; flowers salmon-pink, with shades of cream, lilac, rose, and purple. 'Lady Bowes Lyon': flowers rich red with black spots. Tiger Hybrids: flowers dark red.

Division 2: Martagon Hybrids. Hybrids of Martagon type of which one parent has been a form of *L.martagon* or *L.hansonii*. Backhouse Hybrids: flowers ivory, yellow, cream, pink, and burgundy, occasionally flecked pink. 'Marhan': to 1.3m; flowers orange with red-tinged spots, or bright yellow with dark purple-brown spots. 'Paisley Hybrids'.

Division 3: Candidum Hybrids – derived from *L.candidum*, *L.chalcedonicum*, and other related European species (but excluding *L.martagon*). 'Apollo': to 75cm; flowers dwarf, pure white. 'Ares': flowers bright orange-red. 'Artemis': flowers pale pink to rich yellow-orange. 'Prelude': flowers orange-red, darker red at tips.

Division 4: Hybrids of American species. Bellingham Hybrids: flowers bicoloured orange-yellow and red, with deep brown spots. 'Bellmaid Hybrids': flowers golden-yellow, tinged orange, eventually turning red, with median spots. 'Buttercup'. 'Shuksan'.

Division 5: Longiflorum Hybrids – derived from *L.longiflorum* and *L.formosanum*. 'Formobel': flowers . very large, white, flushed green on the throat. 'Formolongi': flowers snow-white. This category excludes forms and polyploids of either parent species.

Division 6: Trumpet Hybrids. Hybrid Trumpet Lilies and Aurelian Hybrids derived from Asiatic species including *L.henryi*, but excluding those derived from *Ll.auratum, speciosum, japonicum,* and *rubellum*.

6(a): Chinese Trumpets. Flowers trumpet-shaped. 'African Queen': 1.5m; flowers large, rich apricot orange. 'Black Dragon': flowers white inside, very dark rich purple-red outside. 'Black Magic': flowers snow-white inside, purple-black outside. 'Golden Clarion': flowers golden-yellow. 'Golden Splendour': flowers deep golden-yellow; petals with one dark burgundy stripe outside. 'Green Dragon': flowers snow-white inside with yellow flush at base, striped brown and green outside. 'Limelight': flowers lime-yellow. Olympic Hybrids: flower white outside, shade cream or fuchsia-pink inside, occasionally tinged green. 'Pink Perfection': 1.5m; flowers very large, deep purple-pink, fragrant.

6(b): Flowers bowl-shaped. 'First Love': flowers golden-yellow, edged pink, with pale-green throat. 'Heart's Desire': flowers flushed yellow through cream to white, occasionally with orange throat. 'New Era': flowers large, white, tinged green.

6(c): Flowers pendent, flat, or only petal tips recurved. 'Christmas Day': flowers cream, with bright orange and clear green centre. 'Golden Showers': flowers golden-yellow inside, brown outside. 'Summer Song': flowers yellow.

6(d): Sunburst type. Flowers star-shaped, distinctly recurved 'Bright Star': flowers ivory-white, with light orange star in centre. 'Golden Sunburst': flowers vivid golden-yellow, veined green outside. 'Good Hope'. 'Magic Fire': flowers deep apricot. 'Mimosa Star': flowers yellow, fragrant. 'T.A. Havemeyer': flowers deep orange with dark ivory tips and green throat. 'White Henryi': flowers white, flushed deep orange on throat.

Division 7: Oriental Hybrids. Hybrids of Far Eastern species, such as *Ll.auratum, speciosum, japonicum* and *rubellum,* including any of their hybrids with *L.henryi.* 'Dominique': flowers red-purple, with red spotted throat and somewhat crinkled petals. 'Empress of Mars': flowers blood-red, tipped white. 'Omega': flowers white, with a median band of salmon-pink on each petal. 'Suzanne Sumerville': flowers white, blotched pale pink and lavender.

7(a): Flowers trumpet-shaped.

7(b): Flowers bowl-shaped. 'Bonfire': flowers carmine inside with a silver edge, silver-white outside with a very pale pink flush. 'Casablanca': flowers very large, pure white, very fragrant. 'Empress of China': flowers pure white, with heavy dark red or burgundy spots inside. 'Empress of India': flowers carmine, edged white. 'Empress of Japan': flowers pure white, banded gold, spotted deep burgundy. 'Imperial Jewel': flowers white with red throat.

7(c): Flowers flat. 'Imperial Red Band': flowers very large, with a deep red stripe on each petal. 'Imperial Pink': flowers large, pink. 'Imperial Salmon': flowers large, salmon-pink. 'Imperial Silver': flowers large, pure white, spotted burgundy. 'Jillian Wallace'. 'Spectre': flowers pale to deep pink. 'Stargazer': flowers very wide, rich carmine, spotted crimson. 'Troubador': flowers very large, heavily spotted, rich carmine at centre, edged pink and white.

7(d): Flowers recurved. 'Jamboree': flowers carmine with darker spots, edged white. 'Journey's End': flowers very large, carmine, tipped and margined white, spotted red. 'Pink Solace': fls off-white, turning red, with yellow-green throat. Rangotito hybrids: flowers white through pink to deep rich red, occasionally with burgundy spots or white margin.

Littonia Hook. (For Dr S. Litton, former Professor of Botany in Dublin (mid-19th century).) Liliaceae (Colchicaceae). Some 8 species of perennial, tuberous-rhizomatous, climbing herbs. Stems prostrate to erect, flexuous, simple. Leaves alternate or opposite above, ternate or quinate, often almost whorled below, lanceolate, tendrilous at apex. Flowers campanulate, nodding, axillary, solitary in leaf axils, with pedicel occasionally borne just below leaf; tepals 6, separate, free almost to the base, not spreading widely, with basal, nectar-bearing scale; stamens 6, anthers basifixed, versatile; style simple, straight. Fruit a loculicidal, 3-valved capsule; seeds globose, brown. S Africa, Arabia. Z9.

CULTIVATION   Scrambling or climbing understorey herbs of woodland and scrub, grown for their brilliant flowers often followed by attractive seed pods. In mild sheltered gardens, *L.modesta* will survive mild winters, or can be lifted and stored in frost-free conditions over winter, otherwise it needs protected cultivation as for *Gloriosa*.

L.modesta Hook.
Tuber 3cm diam. Stem to 1.2m, unbranced, slender, often prostrate or runner-like. Lvs bright emerald, linear to ovate-lanceolate, alternate or opposite and narrow above, whorled, glabrous, ending in tendril below. Fls bright orange-yellow; pedicels short, to 5cm; tepals lanceolate, tapering, sharply-tipped. S Africa. var. **keitii** Leichtlin. Stem branched, fls abundant.

Lloydia Salisb. ex Rchb. (For Edward Lloyd (1660–1709), keeper of the Ashmolean Collection, Oxford.) Liliaceae (Liliaceae). About 12 species of rhizomatous, creeping perennials to 15cm. Bulbs with a thin, brown papery tunic. Leaves basal and cauline, narrow-linear. Flowers 1–2, terminal, white or yellow; perianth segments 6, free, spreading, with a gland at base; stamens inserted at perianth base, anthers attached to filament at base; ovary trilocular, superior. Fruit a 3-grooved capsule; seeds several per chamber, in 2 ranks, roughly triangular. Temperate N Hemisphere. Z5.

CULTIVATION   *L.serotina*, from arctic, tundra and rocky alpine habitats to altitudes of 3000m/9750ft, is a delicate species grown for its slender, thread-like leaves and small, bell-shaped, white flowers in summer. It is very cold-hardy but sometimes proves difficult to maintain in cultivation. Grow in light shade or bright indirect light, in perfectly drained but moisture-retentive soil, so that bulbs receive adequate moisture in summer, when in growth, but can be drier in winter. A gritty or gravelly acid soil that approximates to those of its native rock ledges is ideal. Sow seed when ripe in the cold frame.

L.graeca (L.) Salisb. See *Gagea graeca*.

L.longiscapa Hook.
Similar to *L.serotina* but fls larger, drooping; perianth seg. marked purple or red at base. Summer. Himalaya, W China.

L.serotina (L.) Salisb. ex Rchb. SNOWDON LILY
To 15cm. Bulb tunic fibrous. Basal lvs 2–3, stem lvs 2–5, to 20cm. Fls erect, to 1.5cm, white, pale yellow at base on exterior surface, veined red-purple; perianth seg. ovate-lanceolate, obtuse. Spring–summer. Temperate N Hemisphere.

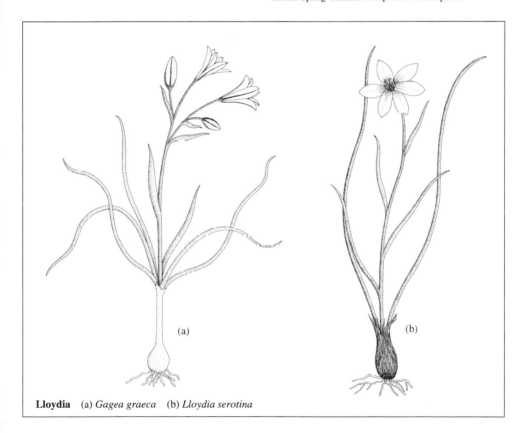

Lloydia   (a) *Gagea graeca*   (b) *Lloydia serotina*

Lycoris Herb. (For a beautiful Roman actress, the mistress of Mark Anthony.) Amaryllidaceae. 10–12 species of bulbous perennial herbs. Bulbs ovoid to ellipsoid, short-necked, sheathed with membranous tunics. Leaves basal, linear or lorate, usually hysteranthous. Scape solid, robust; inflorescence a terminal umbel, subtended by 2 free spathes; perianth bilaterally or radially symmetric, lobes 6, free, usually united into a short tube at base, spreading, strongly recurved, somewhat undulate, covered in minute scales; stamens 6, erect or ascending, inserted near throat of perianth tube, deflexed, anthers versatile. Fruit a spherical to ovoid capsule; seeds black-brown. China, Japan. Z7.

CULTIVATION Often found flowering in profusion at the edges of cultivated fields in China and Japan; *L.sanguinea* grows on sparsely wooded slopes and on mountain foothills. Sharing their common name of spider lily with the genus *Hymenocallis*, *Lycoris* spp. bear showy and elegant flowers with narrow reflexed petals in late summer and early autumn; the leaves emerge after the flowers, although sometimes, as in *L.squamigera*, not until spring. *L.aurea*, *L.radiata* and *L.squamigera* will tolerate temperatures to at least –15°C/5°F; *L.sprengeri* and *L.incarnata* are almost as hardy, and where conditions allow a period of dry warmth during their summer dormancy and winter wet is not excessive, they can successfully be grown out of doors. All are amenable to pot cultivation in the cool glasshouse or conservatory. *Lycoris* is particularly sensitive to root disturbance, and may take several years to become well established; topdressing is therefore preferable to repotting whenever possible, and plants may remain in the same pot for up to 4–5 years. Propagate by offsets or from ripe seed. Otherwise, cultivate as for *Amaryllis*.

L.africana (Lam.) M. Roem. See *L.aurea*.

L.albiflora Koidz.
Very similar to *L.radiata* and probably only a variety of that species. Lvs to 1.25cm across; fls white. Z7.

L.aurea (L'Hérit.) Herb. (*L.africana* (Lam.) M. Roem.). GOLDEN HURRICANE LILY; GOLDEN SPIDER LILY.
Bulb 5–6cm diam., ovoid. Lvs to 60×1.2–1.8cm, lorate, fleshy, glaucous. Scape to 60cm; spathes 3–5cm; pedicels 8–15mm; fls 5–6, erect; perianth 9.5–10cm, golden-yellow, funnelform, tube 1.5–2cm, lobes recurved at tips, margins very wavy; stamens slightly exserted. Spring–summer. China, Japan.

L.incarnata Comes ex Spreng.
Habit as *L.aurea* but scape to 45cm, fls fragrant, pale flesh-pink or rose, perianth lobes neither reflexed nor wavy. China.

L.radiata (L'Hérit.) Herb. SPIDER LILY; RED SPIDER LILY.
Bulb 2.5–3.5cm diam., broadly ellipsoid. Lvs 30–60×0.6–0.8cm, linear-lorate, dark green, somewhat glaucous. Scape to 50cm; spathes 2–4cm; pedicels 6–15mm; fls 4–6, nodding; perianth 4–5cm, rose-red to deep red, tube 6–8mm, lobes strongly reflexed and margins very wavy; stamens well exserted. Summer–autumn. Japan. The superficial

resemblance of this plant to *Nerine sarniensis* has led to its confused naming in horticulture and may account for the enormous distribution long ascribed to the Guernsey Lily. 'Variegata': fls crimson, edged white as they fade. 'Alba': fls white, perianth lobes tinged yellow at base.

L.sanguinea Maxim.
Bulb 2.5cm diam., ovoid. Lvs *c*1cm wide, linear, dark green. Scape to 50cm; spathes 2–4cm; pedicel *c*5cm; fls 4–6, erect; perianth 5–6cm, dull red, funnelform, tube 12–15mm, lobes slightly recurved, margins not crisped; stamens not exserted. Summer. China, Japan.

L.sprengeri Bak.
Resembles *L.squamigera* but shorter, scape to 30cm; fls many, erect, perianth tube very short, margins of lobes not wavy. Japan.

L.squamigera Maxim. MAGIC LILY; RESURRECTION LILY.
Bulb 4–5cm diam., ovoid. Lvs 30×1.8–2.5cm, lorate, borne in spring. Scape to 70cm; spathes 2–4cm; pedicels 1–3cm; fls 6–8, slightly nodding, fragrant; perianth 9–10cm, pale rose-pink flushed or veined lilac or purple, funnelform, tube 2.5cm, lobes recurved at tips, margins slightly wavy; stamens not exserted. Summer. Japan.

Macropidia J. L. Drumm. ex Harvey. (Gk, with large seeds). A genus of one species, very similar to and formerly included in *Anigozanthos*, from which it differs chiefly in its deepiy cut perianth and large seeds. Leaves persistent, to 30cm, sword-shaped, conduplicate and loosely equitant, mid to deep green. Inflorescence a stout-stemmed, loosely branched panicle to 1m, covered in dark scurfy hairs; flowers to 3cm, tubular and curving, deeply lobed, bright lime green to sulphur yellow thickly covered in black felty hairs. Summer. Z9. SW Australia.

M.fuliginosa. BLACK KANGAROO PAW.

Maianthemum Wigg. (Unifolium Haller). (From Gk *maios*, the month of May, and *anthemon*, blossom.) Liliaceae (Convallariaceae). 3 species of perennial, rhizomatous herbs. Rootstock slender, creeping. Stems erect, glabrous, or minutely pubescent, with basal scales. Leaves 2 or 3, alternate above. Flowers white, borne in terminal racemes; flower-stalks slender, bracted; tepals 4, free, spreading or deflexed, deciduous; stamens 4; ovary superior or 2-celled, with 2 ovules per cell; style simple, short; stigma slightly 2-lobed. Fruit a 1- or 2-seeded berry. Northern temperate regions.

CULTIVATION   A charming plant from humus-rich slightly acid soils in moist and shaded habitats, *Maianthemum* makes a good groundcover in the wild and woodland garden, but may prove too invasive for more carefully manicured areas. It tolerates hot summers only if given a cool, damp root run. Propagate by division.

M.bifolium (L.) Schmidt. FALSE LILY OF THE VALLEY.
Stems 5–20cm, upper part hairy. Lvs 3–8×2.5–5cm, broadly cordate-ovate, thinly-textured, with a broad sinus, apex acute to acuminate, persistent, distinctly stalked. Fls 8–20 per raceme, white; pedicels solitary or twin, slender, jointed near apex; tepals 1–3mm. Fr 5–6mm, pale green and spotted at first, eventually red. W Europe to Japan. Z3.

Manfreda Salisb. (For Manfred 'de Monte Imperiale', ancient author on simples.) Agavaceae. 18 species of perennial herbs, with succulent roots, fleshy subterranean stems or bulbous rootstocks. Stems very short or absent. Leaves rosulate, basal, flexible, margins often sinuate, small, green, often blotched with red, brown or purple, not evergreen. Inflorescence spike-like, lax, several-flowered; flowers bisexual, radially symmetric; perianth segments 6, united below to form a generally long and narrow tube, lobes subequal or equal, spreading or reflexed, green, yellow or tinged purple; stamens 6, filaments attached to perianth tube, long-exserted, anthers versatile; ovary inferior, 3-celled with numerous ovules in each cell; style club-shaped, 3-lobed at apex, long-exserted. Fruit an erect capsule, apically dehiscent; seeds copious, black. SE US to Mexico.

CULTIVATION   The slender and scarcely succulent foliage of *Manfreda* is usually marked with pink or brown, and is quite distinct from the firm fleshy leaves of the related *Agave*. Plant in an open, sandy medium in deep pots or beds in full sunlight (minimum temperature 7°C/45°F). The foliage is softer than that of most of the Agavaceae and is more prone to red spider mite; spray regularly with clean water in summer to reduce risk of infestation.

M.longiflora (Rose) Verh.-Will. (*Runyonia longiflora* Rose; *Polianthes runyonii* Shinn.).
Rootstock short, thick. Stems bulbous. Basal lvs 5–7, 10–25×2cm, spreading, elongate, linear, minutely serrate, spotted dark green or brown, stem lvs 2–3, bract-like. Flowering stem 30–100cm, erect, simple, green tinged purple; fls few, solitary in axils of bracts; perianth slender, salverform, white tinged green at first, brick red in age, tube 35mm, seg. spreading, oblong. Fr. small, subglobose, 35mm diam.; seeds flattened. Spring–summer. S Texas, N Mexico.

M.maculosa (Hook.) Rose (*Agave maculosa* Rose; *Polianthes maculosa* (Hook.) Shinn.).
Lvs 15–30×1–2cm, few, linear-lanceolate, recurved, concave, minutely irregularly dentate, margins hyaline, glaucous with brown or somewhat green markings, thick and fleshy. Flowering stem 90–120cm; infl. lax, 20–30cm; fls 10–18, subsessile, 4–5cm, fragrant; perianth lobes oblong, shorter than tube, white tinged green, flushed pink with age; stamens slightly exserted, fil. attached at top of perianth tube, anth. 9–16mm. Fr. 2–2.5×2–2.5cm. Spring–summer. Southern N America (Texas, Mexico).

M.variegata (Jacobi) Rose (*Agave variegata* Jacobi; *Polianthes variegata* (Jacobi) Shinn.).
Lvs 20–45×2–4cm, few, lanceolate, slightly tapered to base, gradually tapered to apex, obtuse, margins incurved, glaucous with brown markings, succulent, deeply grooved. Flowering stem 90–130cm; fls 4cm, subsessile, fragrant, perianth lobes at least to length of tube, narrow, green tinged brown; stamens to 5cm, fil. attached at top of perianth tube, anth. 8mm. Fr. 15–22mm, much longer than broad. Spring. Southern N America (Texas, Mexico).

M.virginica (L.) Salisb. (*Agave virginica* L.; *Polianthes virginica* (L.) Shinn.).
Lvs 60×2.5–5cm, 6–15, oblong-spathulate, gradually tapered to base, abruptly tapered at apex, margins sinuate, dark green with red stripes, thick, flaccid, somewhat grooved. Flowering stem 80–180cm; infl. about 30-fld, 30–50cm; lower pedicels to 8mm; fls 2.5–5cm, fragrant; perianth seg. linear-oblong, yellow tinged green or brown; fil. attached to base of perianth tube, anth. 12mm. Fr. 1.5–2cm, longer than broad. Summer. S US (Maryland to Missouri, Florida & Texas).

Massonia Thunb. ex L. f. (For Francis Masson (1741–1805), who collected in South Africa.) Liliaceae (Hyacinthaceae). 8 species of bulbous perennial herbs. Leaves 2, usually opposite, ovate, oblong or suborbicular, rather fleshy, spreading and lying close to or directly upon soil surface. Scape very short, barely emerging from leaf cleavage; flowers fragrant, in a rounded, corymbose umbel-like head, subtended by large scarious bracts; perianth tube erect, cylindric, lobes 6, spreading or reflexed; stamens attached to mouth of tube; ovary superior; style usually exceeding stamens. Fruit a winged or deeply lobed capsule, longitudinally dehiscent; seeds many, black. Late autumn–early winter. S Africa. Z9.

CULTIVATION Late autumn and early winter-flowering bulbs for sunny rockeries in essentially frost-free, mediterranean-type climates, or for the cool glasshouse (min. 7°C/45°F), *Massonia* spp. are curious rather than beautiful, holding the almost stemless flowers close against the pair of leaves which lie on the soil surface. Grow in full sun in a sandy potting mix and water moderately when in growth, reducing water after flowering for a period of dry dormancy. Propagate by surface-sown seed or by removal of offsets when dormant.

M.amygdalina Bak. See *M.echinata*.

M.angustifolia L. f. See *Polyxena angustifolia*.

M.bolusiae Barker. See *M.echinata*.

M.bowkeri Bak. See *M.jasminiflora*.

M.brachypus Bak. See *M.depressa*.

M.depressa Houtt. (*M.brachypus* Bak.; *M.latifolia* L. f.; *M.sanguinea* Jacq.).
Bulb 2–3.5cm, ovoid. Lvs 7–15×4–10cm, orbicular to oblong, acute, glabrous or with sparse marginal hairs. Fls 20–30, green, yellow, white, cream or pink to red or brown, occasionally flecked purple; tube 1–1.5cm, lobes 0.8–1cm, linear-lanceolate; fil. as long as tube, cream, yellow or green, occasionally tinged red or purple, anth. 2.5–4mm, yellow or purple. Cape Province.

M.echinata L. f. (*M.amygdalina* Bak.; *M.bolusiae* Barker; *M.longifolia* var. *candida* Ker-Gawl.; *M.scabra* Thunb.).
Bulb 1–2cm, ovoid. Lvs 2–8×1–4cm, ovate to oblong, acute or obtuse, usually hairy, at least on margins. Fls 5–20, yellow, white or pink; tube 0.5–0.7cm, lobes 0.4–0.8cm, lanceolate, reflexed; fil. white, anth. 0.5–1.25mm, yellow or purple. Cape Province.

M.ensifolia Ker-Gawl. See *Polyxena pygmaea*.

M.jasminiflora Bak. (*M.bowkeri* Bak.).
Bulb 1–2cm, ellipsoid. Lvs 3–6×1.5–5cm, ovate to broadly oblong, acute, glabrous or occasionally with marginal hairs, rarely papillose. Fls to 15 (usually fewer), fragrant, white or pink; tube 0.8–2cm, slender, lobes 0.4–0.8cm, reflexed; anth. 1–1.5mm, green, blue, dark purple or black. Cape Province, Orange Free State, Lesotho.

M.latifolia L. f. See *M.depressa*.

M.longifolia var. *candida* Ker-Gawl. See *M.echinata*.

M.odorata Hook. f. See *Polyxena odorata*.

M.pustulata Jacq.
Bulb 1–2.5cm, ovoid or spherical. Lvs 3–10×2–7cm, ovate-orbicular to oblong, acute, pustular-papillose above, especially toward apex, margins often minutely ciliate or finely toothed. Fls 15–25, pink, white, yellow or tinged green; tube 0.6–1.1cm, lobes 0.45–1cm, linear-lanceolate, reflexed; fil. 0.4–1.2cm, white, anth. 1–1.75mm, yellow or tinged red. Cape Province. Close to *M.echinata* but distinguished by lvs papillose above.

M.sanguinea Jacq. See *M.depressa*.

M.scabra Thunb. See *M.echinata*.

M.violacea Andrews. See *Polyxena pygmaea*.

Melasphaerula Ker-Gawl. (From Gk *melas*, black, and *sphaerula*, a Latinized diminutive of a sphere, referring to the corms.) Iridaceae. 1 species, a perennial herb. Corms to 1cm diam., globose or conical, often with cormlets at base, with dark, leathery fibrous tunic. Stem 20–50cm, straggling, branched, branches to 7cm. Leaves 5–25×1cm, 6–7 lanceolate, grass-like, sheathing the basal half of stem. Spikes flexuous, laxly 3–7-flowered; flowers small, irregular, white or cream, usually purple-veined; perianth segments 6, 10–15×2–4mm, joined for 1mm at base, either spreading and stellate or 2-lipped; stamens short, arched; style 6mm, 3-branched, branches 2mm; ovary sharply 3-angled. Close to *Sparaxis*, differing in the angled ovary. S Africa (SW Cape). Z9.

CULTIVATION As for *Ixia*.

M.graminea Ker-Gawl. See *M.ramosa*.

M.ramosa (L.) N.E. Br. (*M.graminea* Ker-Gawl.).

Merendera Ramond. (From *quita meriendas*, Spanish for *Colchicum*.) Liliaceae (Colchicaceae). Some 10 species of perennial, stemless herbs to 4cm; corm oblong to ovoid, sometimes with a neck, enclosed by a leathery or thin-textured, black or dark brown tunic. Leaves 3–15, usually to 6, basal, linear to linear-lanceolate, partially developed at flowering. Flowers white or magenta or mauve, solitary or grouped, emerging from spathaceous bracts; tepals 6, linear to narrowly obovate with a long narrow claw, initially valvate, later spreading; stamens borne near base of tepals, anthers versatile or basifixed, pollen yellow; ovary subterranean, styles 3, free to base (cf. *Colchicum, Bulbocodium*). Mediterranean, N Africa, W Asia, outliers in Middle East and NE Africa.

CULTIVATION   With the possible exception of *M.montana*, which thrives outdoors in cool temperature zones, the remaining species are more safely grown in the bulb frame or in pans in the alpine house where the flowers and dormant bulbs can be protected from rain. Propagate by seed, when ripe for spring-flowering species, or in spring for those which bloom in autumn.

M.aitchisonii Hook. See *M.robusta*.

M.androcymbioides Valdes.
Close to *M.attica* but with anth. yellow and lvs slightly broader. Balkan Peninsula, Turkey. Z8.

M.attica (Tomm.) Boiss. & Sprun. (*Colchicum atticum* Tomm.; *M.rhodopea* Velen.; *M.brandegiana* Markgr.).
Corm 1.5–2×1–2cm, oblong-ovoid, tunic leathery, black-brown to black, neck 1–2cm. Lvs to 18×0.3–0.8cm after flowering, 2–6, linear to linear-lanceolate. Fls 2–6, white to lilac; tepals 15–27×2.5mm, linear to narrow-elliptic, usually with basal teeth; fil. to 8mm, anth. 2–4mm, black, deep purple-black or green-white, versatile. Autumn. Balkan Peninsula, Turkey. Z8.

M.brandegiana Markgr. See *M.attica*.
M.bulbocodium Ramond. See *M.montana*.
M.caucasica Bieb. See *M.trigyna*.
M.eichleri Boiss. See *M.trigyna*.

M.filifolia Cambess. (*M.linifolia* Munby).
Corm 1.5–2×1.2cm with long neck 1–5cm. Lvs 15×0.1–0.3cm, 5–15, linear, glabrous, developing after flowers or as they fade. Fls solitary, rose to red-purple; tepals 20–40×2–8mm, narrow-elliptic to narrow oblong-elliptic; fil. 4–7mm, anth. yellow, basifixed. Capsule to 12mm, ellipsoid-oblong. Spring. SW Europe, W Mediterranean, N Africa. Z8.

M.hissarica Reg.
Close to *M.robusta*, from which it differs in its solitary white fls and 2 lvs per corm. Z8.

M.kurdica Bornm. (*Colchicum kurdicum* (Bornm.) Stef.).
Corm 2–4×1.5–2cm, oblong-ovoid, narrow, almost horizontal, tunics brown, thin-textured. Lvs 4–12cm at flowering, expanding to 17cm, 3, lanceolate to narrow-lanceolate. Fls 1–2, pale to deep purple; tepals 3–3.5×0.5–1cm with basal auricles; fil. to 9mm, anth. 3–4mm, yellow. Capsule 2–3cm, ellipsoid. Spring. SE Turkey, NE Iraq. Z8.

M.linifolia Munby. See *M.filifolia*.
M.manissadjianta Aznav. See *M.trigyna*.

M.montana Lange (*M.bulbocodium* Ramond; *M.pyrenaica* (Pourr.) Fourn.).
Corm 2–3×1.5–2.75cm, tunic leathery, dark brown, neck to 2cm. Lvs to 44×0.4–1cm, 3 or 4, appearing after flowers, lin-

ear, channelled, somewhat falcate. Fls 1–2, pale magenta to rosy purple; tepals 26×3–11mm, narrow-elliptic to narrow oblong-oblanceolate, subacute, erect to spreading; fil. 4–6mm, anth. 5–10mm, yellow, basifixed. Capsule to 2.5cm, ellipsoid-oblong. Autumn. Iberian Peninsula, C Pyrenees. Z6.

M.navis-noae Markgr. See *M.trigyna*.
M.persica Boiss. & Kotschy. See *M.robusta*.
M.pyrenaica (Pourr.) Fourn. See *M.montana*.
M.raddeana Reg. See *M.trigyna*.
M.rhodopea Velen. See *M.attica*.

M.robusta Bunge (*M.persica* Boiss. & Kotschy; *M.aitchisonii* Hook.).
Corm 3–6×2–3cm, tunics tough, dark brown, neck 1–3cm. Lvs to 5cm at flowering, to 25cm at maturity, 3–6, linear-lanceolate, concave above, dark green. Fls 1–4, deep pink to pale lilac or white, flask-shaped, fragrant; tepals 18–40×2–9mm, oblong-elliptic to linear-elliptic, keel tinted red to orange below; anth. 8–12mm, green-yellow, basifixed. Capsule to 3cm, oblong-ovoid. Spring. C Iran, C Asia, N India. Z8.

M.sobolifera Mey. (*Colchicum soboliferum* (Mey.) Stef.).
Corm 2–8cm, small and narrow, borne at the end of a horizontal shoot, tunics brown. Lvs linear, 3, 2–10cm at flowering, 10–21×0.3–1.3cm thereafter. Fls 1, occasionally black-violet, versatile. Capsule to 2cm, ovoid-oblong. Spring. E Europe, Iran and adjacent C Asia. Z6.

M.trigyna (Adams) Stapf (*Bulbocodium trigynum* Adams non Jank.; *M.caucasica* Bieb.; *Colchicum caucasicum* (Bieb.) Spreng.; *M.raddeana* Reg.; *M.eichleri* Boiss.; *M.manissadjianii* Aznav.; *M.navis-noae* Markgr.).
Corm to 3.5×2cm, oblong-ovoid; tunics black or black-brown, coriaceous; neck 2–3cm. Lvs to 17×0.3–1.8cm, 3, narrow lanceolate, emerging at flowering, glabrous, blunt-tipped, tapering into tube. Fls 1–3, rose to white; tepals 20–30×4–9mm, free, erect, disintegrating after spreading, oblong or narrow-elliptic, usually toothed at base; anth. 2–4mm, brown to yellow, versatile. Capsule to 3cm, ovoid-ellipsoid. Spring. E Turkey, Iran, Caucasus. Z7.

Micranthus (Pers.) Ecklon. (From Gk *mikros*, small, and *anthos*, flower.) Iridaceae. 3 species of perennial herbs. Corms small, globose, with tunics of coarse, matted fibres. Leaves 3–5, partly sheathing. Spikes distichous, flowers numerous, small, blue, irregular, closely imbricate; tube slightly curved, widened towards throat, lobes more or less equal, obtuse, spreading; stamens inserted near top of tube, usually arched; style branches 6, short. S Africa (SW Cape). Z9.

CULTIVATION   As for *Watsonia*.

M.junceus (Bak.) N.E. Br. 2
0–70cm, usually unbranched. Lvs 3–4, the 2 lowest long, terete, 1–2mm diam., the lowest with axillary bulbils. Spike to 25cm, often with bulbils in the bracts in the basal half; fls slightly scented, pale to deep blue; tube 4–5mm, lobes 5–6mm, oblong. Similar to *M.plantagineus*, except for lvs. Summer.

M.plantagineus (Pers.) Ecklon.
25–40cm, sometimes branched. Lvs 3, the 2 lowest usually 10–25×0.5–1cm, the blade flat, but in some populations longer and only 2–3mm wide, lowest lf often with bulbils at base. Spike to 20cm; fls slightly scented, pale to deep blue; outer lobes sometimes tipped with red; tube 4–5mm, lobes 5–6mm, oblong. Summer.

M.tubulosus (Burm.) N.E. Br.
20–35cm, unbranched. Lvs 3–5, usually brown at flowering time, the lowest 2–3 with tubular, inflated blades 5–15cm×3–7mm. Spike 7–17cm, often with bulbils in lower bracts; fls scented, blue, sometimes almost white; tube 5–6mm, lobes 5–6mm, oblong. Summer.

Milla Cav. (For Juliani Milla, gardener to the Spanish court in Madrid, 18th century.) Liliaceae (Alliaceae). 6 species of perennial herbs. Corm small, with thinly-textured coat, roots fleshy. Stem erect. Leaves 2–7, linear, flat to almost terete. Inflorescence a scapose umbel, erect to spreading, subtended by 4 chaffy spathes. Flowers 2–4 per umbel, rarely solitary, with long pedicels; tepals united to above the middle, forming a long tube, striped green on white, pink, or blue; lobes 6, shorter than tube; stamens 6, emerging at mouth of tube, protruding beyond corolla; ovary 3-celled, borne on a long stalk. Fruit a loculicidal capsule; seeds black, flat. S US, C America.

CULTIVATION   As for *Ipheion*.

M.biflora Cav.
To 30cm. Lvs 2–7, 10–50cm, narrow-linear, channelled above and rounded beneath to almost terete, blue-green. Fls 1–6, occasionally 8, snow-white within, green without, fragrant; perianth seg. 6, 1.5–3.5cm, erect to spreading, overlapping to form a long, campanulate tube white or tinged with lilac, with 3, 5, or 7 green central veins or 1 broad central stripe. SW US, C America.

M.uniflora Graham. See *Ipheion uniflorum*.

Moraea Mill. (For Robert More, 18th-century botanist and natural historian. Originally spelt *Morea*, but changed to *Moraea* by Linnaeus in 1762, possibly in honour of his father-in-law Johan Moraeus, a Swedish physician.) Iridaceae. About 120 species of perennial herbs, usually deciduous, rarely more or less evergreen. Rootstock a corm rooting from apex, covered with membranous, fibrous or almost woody tunics. Leaves 1 to several, basal or borne on stem. Stem simple or branched; inflorescence of one to several flowers in terminal clusters enclosed by paired spathes. Flowers usually yellow or purple-blue but sometimes white, cream, pink, orange or red, often with nectar guides of a contrasting colour at base of outer, and sometimes also inner, tepals; tepals 6, free; outer 3 usually with a more or less erect claw with nectary at base and spreading or reflexed blade, inner 3 sometimes similar to outer 3 but smaller, sometimes tricuspidate, occasionally much reduced or even absent; stamens 3, lying opposite outer tepals, filaments free or partly joined, usually forming column surrounding style, anthers adpressed to style branches; style with 3 branches, usually flat and petaloid, each with pair of terminal, projecting crests. Fruit a globose or cylindrical capsule. Subsaharan Africa from Ethiopia to S Africa. Z9 unless specified.

CULTIVATION   *Moraea* spp. occur in coastal and mountain habitats in the Cape, Natal and the Transvaal, with a number of species occurring in more tropical climates. Those from tropical Africa and Madagascar require temperatures in excess of 12–15°C/53–60°F, those species from the Southwest Cape, which grow in winter and flower in spring or early spring, also need protection from frost in cool temperate climates but are well suited to cultivation in the cool glasshouse or conservatory. In general, species from the Eastern Cape, which flower in summer, are frost-hardy, withstanding winter temperatures between –5 and –10°C/23–14°F.

All need full sun and a fertile, sandy and well drained medium with plentiful moisture when in growth, and to be kept dry when dormant. Sow seed in spring for species that grow during summer, in autumn for winter-growing species.

M.alpina Goldbl.
Dwarf to 12cm, sometimes branched. Lf 1, absent or starting to develop at flowering time, terete, less than 1mm diam. Fls violet to deep blue with orange-yellow nectar guides on outer tepals; outer tepals 12–18mm, the blade 6–10×5–7mm; inner tepals 11–13mm, lanceolate, usually reflexed; style branches 6–8mm, crests 2–3mm. Spring–summer. S Africa (Natal, Drakensberg), Transkei, Lesotho. Z8.

M.angusta (Thunb.) Ker-Gawl.
20–40cm, unbranched. Lf 1, arising from stem just above ground, longer than plant, stiff, terete. Fls pale yellow, usually brown- or grey-tinged, or grey-blue; outer tepals with yellow nectar guides; outer tepals 30–50mm, the claw longer than blade, inner tepals 25–35mm long, at first erect, reflexing later; style branches to 20mm long, crests of similar length or longer. Late winter–summer. S Africa (SW Cape).

M.arenaria Bak. See *M.serpentina*.

M.aristata (Delaroche) Asch. & Gräbn. (*M.glaucopis* (DC.) Drapiez).
25–35cm, sometimes with 1 branch. Lf 1, basal, longer than plant, to 5mm wide, linear, glabrous. Fls white, outer tepals with concentric crescents of green, blue-violet or black at base; outer tepals 30–35mm, claw to 12mm, hairy, blade about 20×15mm, horizontal, inner tepals 15–20mm, tricuspidate with long, central cusp; style branches 7–8mm, crests 6–7mm. Spring. S Africa (Cape Town, almost extinct in wild).

M.bellendenii (Sweet) N.E. Br.
50–100cm, usually branched. Lf 1, basal, longer than plant but not erect, to 10mm wide, linear, glabrous. Fls yellow speckled with brown-purple in centre; outer tepals 22–33mm, claw 9–13mm, blade 14–18mm long and wide, the edges curving up, inner tepals tricuspidate, 8–10mm long, not including central cusp 2–4mm long, coiled inwards; style branches 6mm, crests 3–8mm. Spring. S Africa (SW Cape, east to Plettenberg Bay).

M.bicolor Steud. See *Dietes bicolor*.

M.caeca Barnard ex Goldbl.
Slender, 20–40cm, occasionally 1-branched. Lf 1, longer than plant, to 3mm wide, linear, channelled, glabrous. Fls lilac-purple, the outer tepals with yellow claws and yellow or black nectar guides at base of blades; outer tepals 23–28mm, claw 8–12mm, pubesc., blade not quite so long and 18–22mm wide, horizontal, inner tepals spreading, tricuspidate, to 18mm including central cusp 5–8mm long; style branches 5mm, crests to 7mm. Spring. S Africa (SW Cape).

M.calcicola Goldbl.
Slender, 30–40cm, stem slightly pubesc., sometimes with 1 branch. Lf 1, basal, longer than stem but usually trailing, 3–5mm wide, linear, channelled, hairy on outer side. Fls slightly scented, blue-violet, outer tepals with triangular blue-black nectar guides; outer tepals 25–35mm, spreading, claw 8–10mm, hairy, inner tepals 14–22mm, tricuspidate, the central cusp long, narrow and spreading; style branches 6–8mm, crests about 4mm. Spring. S Africa (W Cape).

M.catenulata Lindl. See *Dietes iridioides*.

M.ciliata (L. f.) Ker-Gawl.
Dwarf, 2.5–20cm, unbranched, the stem subterranean. Lvs 3–4, arising at ground level at base of infl., erect, usually longer than infl., 3–35mm wide, usually pubesc., the edges ciliate, often undulate or crisped. Fls scented, white, yellow, pale brown or blue with yellow nectar guides on outer tepals, opening at midday, withered by evening; outer tepals 20–35mm, blade 10–25mm, slightly reflexed, inner tepals 16–30mm, erect or spreading, linear or narrowly lanceolate; style branches 7–15mm, crests of similar length. Winter–spring. S Africa (Cape Province).

M.edulis (L. f.) Ker-Gawl. See *M.fugax*.
M.filicaulis Bak. See *M.fugax* ssp. *filicaulis*.

M.fugax (Delaroche) Jacq. (*M.edulis* (L. f.) Ker-Gawl.).
12–50cm, branched. Lvs 1 or 2, subopposite, arising on stem just below lowest branch, usually longer than stem, trailing, linear or filiform, channelled. Fls scented, white, yellow or blue, opening midday and fading in evening; outer tepals 20–40mm, blade horizontal or reflexed, of similar length to claw, inner tepals 20–35×5–8mm, blade spreading or erect; style branches 12–20mm, crests 6–18mm. Late winter–spring, occasionally to summer. S Africa (S & W Cape). ssp. *fugax*. Lvs 1 or 2, linear, channelled. Fls yellow, white or deep blue; outer tepals 27–40mm; spathes 35–65mm. ssp. *filicaulis* (Bak.) Goldbl. (*M.filicaulis* Bak.). Lvs 2, filiform. Fls white or cream sometimes tinged with pink or violet, or deep violet; outer tepals 20–26(–35)mm; spathes 20–40mm.

M.gawleri Spreng.
To 45cm, usually with 3–5 branches. Lvs 1–3, 1 or 2 basal, the topmost borne at lowest branch, shorter than stem, 1–6mm wide, linear, erect or spreading and coiled, the edges sometimes wavy or crisped. Fls cream, yellow or brick-red, often with darker veins, sometimes with style branches and crests paler; outer tepals 12–28mm long, the blade more than twice as long as claw, 5–14mm wide, reflexed, inner tepals 10–20mm long, reflexed; style branches 5–8mm, crests erect, lanceolate. Winter–spring. S Africa (Cape winter rainfall area).

M.gigandra L. Bol.
20–40cm, occasionally with 1 branch; stem pubesc. Lf 1, basal, as long as or longer than stem, linear, glabrous or somewhat pubesc. Fls large, most often blue-purple with bright blue nectar guides bordered with white at base of outer tepals, rarely orange or white with nectar guides of a different colour; outer tepals 30–45mm long, claw 6mm, blade horizontal, to 35mm wide, inner tepals 9–15mm, tricuspidate, the central cusp long and narrow; style branches to 6×2mm, crests short; anth. large, 13–15mm, overtopping style crests. Spring. S Africa (SW Cape), almost extinct in the wild.

M.glaucopis (DC.) Drapiez. See *M.aristata*.

M.gracilenta Goldbl.
30–80cm, with many branches. Lf 1, longer than stem but trailing, linear, channelled, arising at base of lowest branch. Fls scented, opening mid to late afternoon, fading by early evening, mauve blue; outer tepals 20–30mm, blade of similar length to claw, 6–8mm wide, reflexed, inner tepals 18–28×5–6mm, the blade spreading; style branches 7–9mm, crests 7–12mm, linear-lanceolate. Spring–summer. S Africa (SW Cape).

M.huttonii (Bak.) Oberm.
Robust plants to 1m, occasionally with 1–2 short branches, forming clumps. Lf 1, usually longer than stem, 0.5–2.5cm wide, linear. Fls scented, yellow with darker yellow marks at base of outer tepals; style crests with brown or purple blotch; outer tepals to 55mm, blade to 35×20mm, spreading, inner tepals to 45mm, lanceolate, erect; style branches to 15×8mm, crests 10–13mm. Spring early summer. S Africa (E Cape, Natal, SE Transvaal, Transkei), Lesotho.

M.insolens Goldbl.
To 35cm tall, usually branched, forming small clumps. Lf 1, usually longer than stem, 2–4mm wide, linear, channelled. Fls bright orange-red or rarely cream, claws and nectar guides dark brown; outer tepals to 30mm long, blade to 20mm wide, much longer than claw, spreading or slightly reflexed, inner tepals similar but smaller, to 25×15mm; style branches 4mm long, crests 1–2mm, triangular; anth. 8mm, overtopping style crests. Spring. S Africa (SW Cape); only 1 small population is known in the wild.

M.iridioides L. See *Dietes iridioides*.

M.loubseri Goldbl.
15–20cm, usually with 1 branch; stem finely pubesc. Lf 1, basal, usually longer than plant, 2–3mm wide, linear, channelled, pubesc. on outer side. Fls violet-blue, black and bearded in centre, with dark blue nectar guides on outer

Moraea (a) *M.neopavonia* (b) *M.gigandra* (c) *M.spathulata* (d) *M.serpentina*

tepals; outer tepals 20–24mm, claw to 10mm, covered with black hairs, inner tepals 15–20mm, tricuspidate, the central cusp long and slender; style branches 6mm, crests 1–2mm, triangular. Very rare in wild. Late winter–spring. S Africa (W Cape).

M.moggii N.E. Br.
Slender, to 70cm, unbranched. Lf 1, longer than stem, to 1.5cm wide, linear, flat or channelled above, channelled beneath. Fls white, cream or yellow, the outer tepals with bright yellow nectar guides bordered with purple veins; outer tepals 40–75mm, blade to 50×33mm, reflexed, inner tepals 60×25mm, erect; style branches to 20mm, crests 10–20mm. Summer–autumn. S Africa (E Transvaal, NE Natal), Swaziland.

M.natalensis Bak.
15–45cm, branched. Lf 1, arising near top of stem, to 20cm, narrowly linear to subterete. Fls lilac to violet-blue, outer tepals with yellow nectar guides bordered with purple; outer tepals 14–20mm, blade to 14×10mm, reflexed, inner tepals to 15mm, linear-lanceolate, blade also reflexed; style branches, including crests, to 11mm. Summer. S Africa (Natal, Transvaal), Zimbabwe, Zambia, Malawi, Mozambique, Zaire.

M.neopavonia R. Fost. (*M.pavonia* (L. f.) Ker-Gawl.).
Slender, 30–60cm, sometimes with 1 branch, the stem pubesc. Lf 1, basal, longer than plant, 3–5mm wide, linear, channelled, pubesc. on outer side. Fls large, 6–8cm diam., orange, rarely orange-red, the outer tepals with deep blue nectar guides, sometimes speckled, the claws speckled with deep blue; outer tepals 22–40mm, claw 10–12mm, blade 20–28×12–18mm, inner tepals entire or tricuspidate; style branches 5–8mm, crests 1–2mm; anth. 9–12mm, overtopping style branches and crests. Spring. S Africa (W Cape).

M.papilionacea (L. f.) Ker-Gawl.
10–15cm, usually with few to several branches. Lvs 2–4 arising near base, of similar length to plant, sometimes longer, to 7mm wide, linear, usually hairy, the edges ciliate. Fls scented, pale yellow or salmon-pink, the outer tepals with yellow nectar guides edged with yellow, green or red; outer tepals 22–28mm, claw 8–10mm, blade 8–14mm wide, spreading or reflexed; inner tepals 20–22mm, blade 5–8mm wide, reflexed, style branches 5–9mm, crests 8–15mm long, lanceolate. Late winter–spring. S Africa (SW Cape).

M.pavonia (L. f.) Ker-Gawl. See *M.neopavonia*.

M.polyanthos L. f.
10–45cm, usually branched in upper half. Lvs 2–3, the lowest basal, longer than stem, 3–6mm wide, linear, channelled. Fls scented, white, lilac or pale to deep purple-blue, all tepals with yellow nectar guides; claws forming cup, holding stamens; outer tepals 23–40mm, claw 10–12mm, blade 8–10mm wide, obovate, spreading or slightly reflexed, inner tepals 18–55×6–10mm, blades also spreading, style branches 4–5mm long, the apices forked; crests absent. Winter–spring. S Africa (Cape winter rainfall area).

M.polystachya (Thunb.) Ker-Gawl.
To 80cm, branched; corm to 5cm diam. Lvs 3–5, as long as or longer than stem but usually trailing, 6–20mm wide, linear, flat or channelled. Fls pale blue or violet with yellow or orange nectar guides on outer tepals; outer tepals 36–55mm, claw 15–20mm, blade 13–25mm wide, spreading or reflexed; inner tepals 30–45×15mm, blade erect or reflexed; style branches about 10mm long, crests about 20mm; ovary often veined with red. Autumn–winter. S Africa (Cape, W OFS, W Transvaal), Namibia, Botswana.

M.ramosa (Thunb.) Ker-Gawl. See *M.ramosissima*.

M.ramosissima (L. f.) Druce (*M.ramosa* (Thunb.) Ker-Gawl.).
Large, branched, 50–120cm; corm to 18mm diam., surrounded by small cormlets; roots spiny; stem with axillary cormlets towards base. Lvs numerous, mostly basal, 30–50×1.5–3cm, somewhat channelled. Fls bright yellow,

outer tepals with darker yellow nectar guides, opening late morning and fading in late afternoon; outer tepals 30–40mm, blades about 15mm wide, reflexed, inner tepals to 35mm, also reflexed; style branches 20–25mm, crests prominent. Spring–summer. S Africa (S & W Cape).

M.robinsoniana (F. Muell.) Benth. & F. Muell. See *Dietes robinsoniana*.

M.schimperi (Hochst.) Pichi-Serm.
20–50cm, unbranched, often forming clumps. Lf 1, 9–15mm wide, linear, channelled below, shorter than stem at flowering, later much longer. Fls purple-blue, outer tepals with yellow nectar guides; ovary usually maroon-red; outer tepals 40–65mm, claw and blade of similar length, blade spreading or slightly reflexed, inner tepals 35–45mm, lanceolate, erect; style branches 15–20mm, crests 10–20mm. Spring–early autumn. Widespread in tropical Africa.

M.serpentina Bak. (*M.arenaria* Bak.).
4–20cm, usually with several branches. Lvs 1–5, usually basal but occasionally borne on stem, linear, sometimes pubesc., wavy or coiled. Fls white to yellow, inner tepals sometimes flushed with violet or mauve-pink, outer tepals with large, deep yellow nectar guides; outer tepals 24–30mm, blade 14–20×15–24mm, somewhat reflexed, inner tepals 20–30mm long, erect, oblanceolate; style branches about 6mm, crests 4–8mm, lanceolate. Spring. S Africa (NW Cape).

M.spathacea (Thunb.) Ker-Gawl. See *M.spathulata*.

M.spathulata (L. f.) Klatt (*M.spathacea* (Thunb.) Ker-Gawl.).
Robust, 50–90cm, usually unbranched, often forming clumps. Lf 1, basal, longer than stem, to 1.5cm wide, linear, flat or channelled. Fls yellow, outer tepals with darker yellow nectar guides; outer tepals 35–50mm long, blade 20–35mm, spreading or reflexed, inner tepals erect, 30–40mm; style branches to 18mm, crests to 10mm. Flowering time variable. S Africa (Cape summer rainfall area, E Transvaal, Transkei), Lesotho, Swaziland, Zimbabwe, Mozambique. Z8.

M.speciosa (L. Bol.) Goldbl.
40–75cm high, branching toward apex; corm large, to 4cm diam. Lvs several, basal and cauline, about half length of stem, to 4cm wide, channelled, the edges undulate. Fls erect or drooping, pale blue-mauve, all tepals with yellow nectar guide; tepal claws forming cup including fil., outer tepals 30–45mm, claw 12–15mm, blade to 17mm wide, spreading or reflexed, inner tepals similar but blades slightly narrower; style branches 2–6mm; crests absent. Winter–spring. S Africa (S & W Cape).

M.stricta Bak. (*M.trita* N.E. Br.).
15–25cm, usually with 3–6 branches; corms to 3cm diam., often with cormlets attached. Lf 1, basal, usually absent at flowering time, later about 60cm long, 1.5mm wide, terete. Fls lilac or violet-blue, outer tepals with yellow or orange nectar guides; outer tepals to 24mm, blade 11–14×5–8mm, lanceolate or obovate, reflexed, inner tepals 15–18×2–4mm, more or less erect, linear or lanceolate; style branches 7–8mm, crests 3–6mm. Winter–spring. E Ethiopia to E Cape. Z8.

M.thomsonii Bak.
Slender, 15–30cm, usually with 3–6 branches. Lf 1, basal, usually absent or just starting to grow at flowering time, to 60cm long, 1.5mm wide, terete. Fls pale blue-violet, all tepals with yellow nectar guide; outer tepals 20–24mm, claw 9–10mm, blade 11–14×5–8mm, spreading, lanceolate or obovate, inner tepals 16–18mm, blade about 7mm wide, lanceolate, spreading; style branches 7–8mm, crests very small. Winter–spring or early summer. Tanzania, Malawi, S Africa (E Transvaal).

M.tricolor Andrews.
Small plants 5–15cm, unbranched. Lvs usually 3, slightly shorter than plant, glabrous or pubesc., the margins ciliate. Fls yellow, pink, red or pale purple, outer tepals with yellow nectar guides sometimes bordered with maroon; opening mid

Moraea (a) *M.tripetala* (b) *M.speciosa* (c) *M. loubseri* (d) *M.tricolor*

morning, fading late afternoon; outer tepals 20–25mm, blade 8–13mm, spreading, lanceolate; inner tepals similar but narrower; style branches to 5mm, crests 8–10mm long, triangular. Winter–spring. S Africa (SW Cape).

M.tripetala (L. f.) Ker-Gawl.
10–50cm, sometimes branched. Lf 1, rarely 2, basal, usually longer than stem and trailing, linear or lanceolate, sometimes pubesc. Fls usually pale to deep blue or purple, sometimes yellow or pale pink, outer tepals with white or yellow nectar guide; outer tepals lanceolate, 20–35mm, claw to 15mm, hairy, blade spreading or reflexed; inner tepals very small, usually filiform but sometimes tricuspidate, occasionally absent; style branches 7–10mm, crests linear-lanceolate, 5–15mm. Late winter–summer. S Africa (Cape winter rainfall area).

M.trita N.E. Br. See *M.stricta*.

M.vegeta L.
10–30cm, usually with several branches. Lvs several, longer than plant, linear, glaucous grey-green. Fls relatively small, dull-coloured, yellow, brown, pink or blue, outer tepals with yellow nectar guide; outer tepals lanceolate, 20–25mm, blade

to 18mm, reflexed, inner tepals similar but smaller; style branches 7–8mm, crests 7–10mm. Spring. S Africa (SW Cape).

M.villosa (Ker-Gawl.) Ker-Gawl.
15–40cm, stem hairy, branched or unbranched. Lf 1, basal, as long as or longer than plant, linear, channelled, pubesc. on outside. Fls white, cream, pink, lilac, orange or purple, outer tepals with yellow nectar guides edged with 1 or 2 broad outer bands of darker colour; outer tepals 28–40mm, claw 8–12mm, blade suborbicular, 20–28mm long and wide, spreading horizontally or slightly reflexed, inner tepals 16–30mm, tricuspidate, the central cusp long, narrow and spreading; style branches 5–7mm long, to 8mm wide, crests 5–8mm, erect. Late winter–early spring. S Africa (W Cape). ssp. *villosa*. Stem usually branched. Fls pink, blue or purple (rarely cream or green); outer tepals 30–40mm, blades more or less horizontal. ssp. *elandsmontana* Goldbl. Stem usually unbranched. Fls orange, nectar guides edged with dark blue (rarely white with brown nectar guides); outer tepals 28–31mm, blades curved up, rather cup-shaped.

Muilla S. Wats (Anagram of the closely related *Allium*.) Liliaceae (Alliaceae). 5 species of herbaceous perennials to 60cm, resembling *Allium* but lacking characteristic odour. Corms covered with fibrous tunics, developing from subterranean stems. Leaves few, nearly terete. Flowers numerous, stellate in scapose umbels with more than 1 spathe; tepals 6, white to green with darker midrib, bases united, forming perianth tube, upper parts free; stamens 6, inserted at base of perianth tube; ovary with many ovules. Fruit globose, 3-ridged. SW US, Mexico. Z8.

CULTIVATION   As for *Allium*.

M.maritima S. Wats. (*Hesperocordium maritimum* Torr.; *Allium maritimum* Benth.; *Nothoscordum maritimum* Hook. f.; *Bloomeria maritima* Macbr.; *M.serotina* Greene).
To 50cm high. Corm to 2cm diam. Lvs to 60cm. Fls 4–70; spathes 3–6, lanceolate; pedicels 1–5cm; tepals 3–6mm, white, tinged with green, midrib brown; anth. purple. Fr. 5–8mm. Spring–summer. US (California), Mexico.

M.serotina Green. See *M.maritima*.

Muscari Mill. (From Gk *moschos*, musk, alluding to the scent of some species.) GRAPE HYACINTH. Liliaceae (Hyacinthaceae). 30 species of bulbous perennial herbs. Bulbs tunicated, ovoid, sometimes producing offsets. Leaves 1–4, basal, linear, sometimes sulcate, rather fleshy. Inflorescence a dense, scapose, terminal raceme, uppermost flowers often sterile, forming a tuft (coma); bracts minute; perianth united into a tube, cylindric, campanulate, tubular or urceolate, blue to yellow to white, limb comprising 6 small lobes, acute, reflexed, often of a different colour; stamens 6, anthers included; ovary superior, 3 celled. Fruit a 3-angled capsule; seeds 2 per cell, black, shiny or wrinkled. Spring. Mediterranean, SW Asia.

CULTIVATION   Early spring-flowering bulbs, they are well suited to naturalizing at woodland edge and for lining borders or paths in full exposure. Many species can be treated as temporary bedding plants for spring display; the more choice and unusual species deserve positions on rock gardens or on the tops of banks and walls, where their sweet musky fragrance can be appreciated at close quarters. *M.macrocarpum* and *M.muscarimi* are both powerfully scented; these two Asian spp. must have good drainage and full sun to flower well, and may be pot grown in a medium-fertility, loam-based mix, to be brought indoors when in full bloom.
    M.comosum is a large and beautiful Mediterranean species, made conspicuous by the coma of sterile florets above the fertile flowers; in the cultivar 'Plumosum' the inflorescence consists of finely shredded, violet blue, sterile florets. Amongst the easiest and most prolific species are *M.armeniacum*, *M.aucheri*, *M.botryoides*, *M.comosum*, *M.latifolium* and *M.neglectum*, these last two, in some forms, with particularly beautiful, deep navy blue flowers. These vigorous species may become invasive but in any case look best in large, bold groups.
    Topdress established clumps with bonemeal in spring; lift and divide when overcrowded, incorporating fresh top soil before replanting. Propagate by offsets after flowering or by seed sown when ripe.

M.armeniacum Bak. (*M.szovitsianum* Bak.; *M.cyaneoviolaceum* Turrill).
Lvs to 30×6cm, 3–5, sometimes to 7, linear to linear-oblanceolate, sometimes paler above. Racemes 2.5–7.5cm, fls crowded and overlapping; fertile fls 3.5–5.5×2.3–3.5mm, perianth obovoid to oblong-urceolate, azure, sometimes flushed purple, rarely white, lobes paler than tube or white, sterile fls few, smaller and paler than fertile, rarely of the same colour. SE Europe to Caucasus. 'Album': fls white. 'Argaei': fls bright blue. 'Argaei Album': fls white; spike small; late-flowering. 'Blue Spike': to 15cm, vigorous; infl. branched, fls large, fully double, profuse, soft blue. 'Cantab':

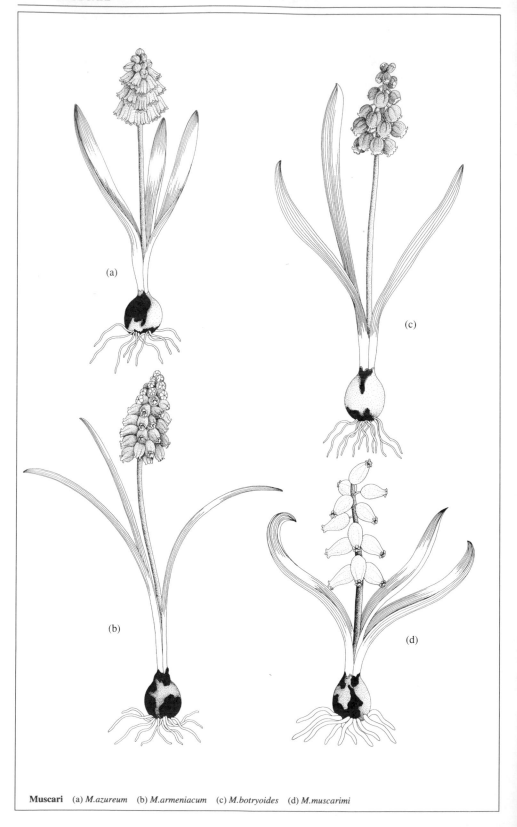

Muscari (a) *M.azureum* (b) *M.armeniacum* (c) *M.botryoides* (d) *M.muscarimi*

Muscari (a) *M.comosum* (b) *M.neglectum* (c) *M.macrocarpum*

strong-growing; stalks short; fls pale Cambridge blue. 'Dark Eyes': fls bright blue, rimmed white. 'Heavenly Blue': fls vivid blue. 'Saphir': fls dark blue, rim white, long-lasting, sterile. 'Sky Blue': fls pale turquoise, rim white, compact. Z4.

M.atlanticum Boiss. & Reut. See *M.neglectum*.

M.aucheri (Boiss.) Bak. (*Botryanthus aucheri* Boiss.; *M.tubergenianum* Turrill).
Lvs 5–20×0.2–1.5cm, usually 2, erect to spreading, falcate to narrowly spathulate, pale green and glaucous above, tip hooded-incurved. Raceme dense, ovoid or cylindric; fertile fls 3–5×2–5mm, perianth subspherical or ovoid, bright azure, rarely white, lobes paler blue or white, sterile fls paler, as many as fertile fls or fewer. Turkey. The variant formerly known as *M.tubergenianum* is commonly cultivated and has a prominent coma of pale sterile fls. Z6.

M.azureum Fenzl (*Bellevalia azurea* (Fenzl) Boiss.; *Hyacinthella azurea* (Fenzl) Chouard).
Lvs 6–20×0.3–1.5cm, 2–3, erect to spreading, narrowly oblanceolate, tip often incurved, glaucous and paler above. Racemes 1.5–3cm, dense, ovoid; fertile fls 4–5mm, perianth campanulate, not constricted, bright blue with a darker stripe on the lobes, sterile fls few, smaller and paler than fertile; anth. blue. E Turkey. 'Album': fls pure white. 'Amphibolis': fls pale blue, larger, earlier. Z8.

M.botryoides (L.) Bak.
Lvs 5–25×0.5–1.3cm, 2–4, erect, spathulate, often ribbed above, apex abruptly contracted, hooded or tapering. Raceme dense at first, later loose and cylindric; fertile fls 2.5–5mm, perianth subspherical, azure, rarely white, lobes white. C & SE Europe. 'Album': fls pure white, sweetly scented. 'Caeruleum': fls bright blue. 'Carneum': fls flesh pink. Z3.

M.comosum (L.) Mill. (*M.pinardii* Boiss.). TASSEL HYACINTH.
Bulbs to 3.5cm, without offsets, tunics pink. Lvs 3–7, erect to spreading, linear, channelled. Raceme loose; fertile fls 5–9mm, perianth oblong-urceolate, brown-olive, lobes cream or yellow-brown, sterile fls subspherical or obovoid, rarely tubular, bright violet, on fleshy, bright violet, ascending pedicels, forming a conspicuous terminal tuft. S & C Europe, N Africa, SW Asia; naturalized Europe. 'Plumosum' ('Monstrosum'): inflorescence much-branched, consisting only of sterile fls and their stalks, all mauve blue. Z4.

M.cyaneoviolaceum Turrill. See *M.armeniacum*.

M.latifolium T. Kirk.
Lvs 7–30×1–3cm, 1, rarely 2 together, erect, broadly oblanceolate, apex acuminate, often hooded. Raceme dense at first, becoming loose; fertile fls 5–6mm, perianth oblong-urceolate, tube strongly constricted toward apex, deep violet, lobes concolorous, recurved; sterile fls blue. S & W Asia. Z4.

M.luteum Tod. See *M.macrocarpum*.

M.macrocarpum Sweet (*M.luteum* Tod.).
Bulbs 2–4cm diam., roots thick. Lvs to 30cm. Racemes to 20cm, loose, 20–30-fld; fertile fls 8–12mm, fragrant, perianth oblong-urceolate, blue-violet becoming bright yellow, lobes brown or yellow, sterile fls small, uppermost, tinged purple-brown, few or absent. Aegean Is., W Turkey. Z7.

M.massayanum Grunert.
Bulbs 2–6cm diam., without offsets, tunics ivory. Lvs to 25×1–2.5cm, linear, falcate or sinuous, thick, glaucous, apex incurved. Flowering stem to 22cm, stout, tinted mauve; raceme dense, cylindric; fertile fls to 1.1cm, pink to violet at first, later pale green- or yellow-brown, lobes dark brown, sterile fls pink or violet on ascending to spreading pedicels, forming a dense tuft. E Turkey. Z7.

M.moschatum Willd. See *M.muscarimi*.

M.muscarimi Medik. (*M.moschatum* Willd.).
Bulb 2–4cm diam., roots thick. Lvs 10–20×0.5–1.5cm, pale grey-green. Flowering stem erect to prostrate, not exceeding lvs; fls muskily scented, fertile fls 8–14mm, perianth narrowly urceolate, purple at first, becoming pale green to ivory, strongly contracted toward apex, then expanded to form a brown corona, sterile fls purple-tinged, rarely present. SW Turkey. Z6.

M.neglectum Guss. ex Ten. (*M.racemosum* Lam. & DC.; *M.atlanticum* Boiss. & Reut.). COMMON GRAPE HYACINTH.
Bulb 1–2.5cm diam., sometimes with offsets. Lvs 6–40×0.2–0.8cm, erect and spreading to prostrate, channelled to subterete, bright green, sometimes red-brown at base. Raceme dense in flower, loose in fruit; fertile fls 1.5–3.5×3.5–7.5mm, perianth ovoid to oblong-urceolate, strongly constricted toward apex, deep blue-black, lobes white, recurved, sterile fls smaller and paler blue, rarely white. Europe, N Africa, SW Asia. A very variable species. Z4.

M.pallens Bieb.
Bulb ovoid, small. Lvs to 20cm+, equalling to exceeding scape, linear, acute, becoming enlarged above. Flowering stem 15–20cm; raceme short, oblong, dense; pedicels short; fls nodding, perianth oval, white or blue tinged violet, teeth reflexed; sterile fls small, capsule compressed, valves obcordate. Caucasus.

M.paradoxum misapplied. See *Bellevalia pycnantha*.
M.pinardii Boiss. See *M.comosum*.
M.pycnanthum K. Koch. See *Bellevalia pycnantha*.
M.racemosum Lam. & DC. See *M.neglectum*.
M.szovitisianum Bak. See *M.armeniacum*.

M.tenuiflorum Tausch (*Leopoldia tenuiflora* Heldr.).
Like *M.comosum* but with 3–7 narrower lvs; fls fewer, pale grey-brown, lobes pale cream, sterile fls bright violet. C Europe (Germany). Z5.

Narcissus L. (A Gk plant-name said to be derived from *narke*, numbness, torpor, from its narcotic properties; in Gk mythology the youth Narcissus, who fell in love with his own reflection in a pool, was turned into a lily by the gods.) DAFFODIL. Amaryllidaceae. About 50 species of perennial bulbous herbs. Leaves 1 to several, lasting from late winter to early summer, basal, erect, spreading or prostrate, linear, rush-like or strap-shaped. Flowers yellow or white, sometimes fragrant, erect to drooping, solitary or in an umbel of 2–20, subtended by a one-valved, usually scarious membranous spathe, borne on a leafless scape; perianth tubular at the base, with 6 segments, almost always with a conspicuous corona in the form of a trumpet or a smaller ring or cup, often a different colour from the segments; stamens 6, usually in 2 whorls, attached to the perianth tube; ovary 3-celled, with many ovules. Fruit an ellipsoid to almost spherical capsule; seeds many, sometimes with an appendage. S Europe and Mediterranean; also N Africa, W Asia, China and Japan.

CULTIVATION   Narcissi (which include all daffodils; see classification below) are among the most popular garden plants, grown in beds and borders, rock gardens, in grass and woodlands, and in pots. They are also excellent as cut flowers. Their flowering period extends from late autumn to early summer though the main flowering period is in spring. In the wild, species are found in cool-temperate climates in a great variety of habitats including coastal areas, meadows, woodlands, river banks, rocks and alpine turf, at altitudes from sea level to over 3000m/9840ft.

Most daffodils of garden origin will grow in almost any soil or situation, though their preference is for soil which stays moist but well-drained during the growing season. Full sun or some sun during parts of the day is usually desirable but most cultivars will tolerate some shade. Light shade from deciduous trees or shrubs suits most cultivars, and is preferable to full sun for late-flowering cultivars in warmer areas. Most daffodils are hardy enough to survive even when the ground is frozen solid to a depth of several centimetres in midwinter, but they will benefit from the insulating effect of snow-cover or a mulch of leaves. They are also tolerant of quite severe frost on leaves and even flowers, but members of the Tazetta division are less hardy and need protection in colder areas.

Generally, bulbs should be planted to one-and-a-half times their own depth. In light soils they can be planted rather deeper. Shallow planting produces more increase and smaller bulbs; deeper planting less increase but larger bulbs. The soil, unless recently dug to a depth greater than planting depth, should be loosened with a fork to allow penetration by roots, and the bulbs then pressed firmly in. Bulbs should be divided by pulling them apart at the basal plate before planting. For clumps it is advisable to plant bulbs at least 15cm/6in. from their neighbours in every direction. Bulbs can be established in sward either by removing the turf before planting or by using a bulb planter. Clumps in borders may be left for three years after planting, and often much longer. Bulbs in grass can be left undisturbed for many years.

Most cultivars are tolerant of either acid or alkaline soils. Species will, of course, favour a soil type close to that of their habitat – e.g. acid to neutral soils, pH 5.5–7.0, for most forms of *Narcissus bulbocodium*, *N. triandrus*, *N. asturiensis* and *N. cyclamineus*; alkaline, pH 7.0–8.0, for *N.jonquilla* and *N.tazetta*. Where the right conditions can be provided many species can colonize by offsetting and self-seeding. When daffodils are grown in grass it is advisable not to cut the grass until 4–6 weeks after the flowers have faded, but it can then be cut with little damage to the bulbs, even if the leaves are still green. Where it is desirable to lift bulbs for storage, wait until the leaves have turned yellow. Unless replanted immediately the bulbs should be dried off and stored in single layers in a cool, dry, dark place. Care should be taken not to damage or bruise the bulbs, and they should not be exposed to strong sunlight or damage will follow. When dry, the bulbs should be cleaned of old tunics and soil, any showing signs of damage or disease should be discarded, and offsets should be detached for propagation. The best time for planting is late summer or very early autumn, or even earlier for *N.poeticus* and its hybrids, which have virtually no resting period. Later planting, deferred even until late autumn, reduces the length of the growing season but can give reasonable results. When possible bulbs should be planted in soil which has been well cultivated.

Daffodils are well suited to pot cultivation, either for exhibition or decorative purposes. Deep pots should be used to allow plenty of room for roots. Either soil-based or soilless potting medium can be used. The medium needs to be free-draining, and perlite can usefully be added. Four or five double-nosed bulbs can be put in a 25cm/10in. pot, three double-nose or 4–5 single-nosed in a 22cm/9in. pot. Bulbs should be pressed in firmly and the medium over and around the bulbs should also be pressed firm. A mass of flowers can be produced by 'double-banking' the bulbs, placing one layer half way down the pot, infilling with soil, and placing another layer between the noses of the lower ones.

After planting the pots should be stood outdoors for at least 12 weeks, and should be plunged and covered with a protective layer. The plunge bed should allow free drainage. The protective layer should provide insulation, but should be of a substance through which shoots can grow without obstruction such as light soil, leached ash, straw or pine needles. Bulbs should be kept adequately watered while in the plunge bed, but not too wet. The time for taking them out depends on when flowers are required and the conditions to which they are moved, for example whether to a heated or unheated greenhouse or indoors. It is essential that they should be kept cool, especially at first, otherwise they will grow lax and the flowers may abort. If plastic pots are used, special care must be taken not to allow the soil to overheat. Leaves and stems may well require staking. After removal from the plunge, pots should be watered frequently and never be allowed to become dry, and can be fed with weak tomato (high potash) fertilizer. Humidity needs to be medium to high. After flowering, unless the bulbs are discarded, they should be carefully removed from their pots and planted with as little disturbance of their roots as possible in a lightly shaded place outside and kept well watered. They can then be lifted in the normal way and replanted in the garden. The bulbs are unlikely to be suitable for growing in pots again until they have had a season to recover.

For home decoration, bulbs can be grown in bulb fibre, but this provides no nutrient at all and the bulbs will be exhausted unless they are planted out as above after flowering. The fibre should be kept moist at all times. For very early flowering in pots, bulbs which have been specially prepared by pre-cooling should be obtained.

The smaller species and miniature hybrids perform especially well in pots, either in the cold or alpine house or in frames. A high-fertility soil-based potting medium is suitable for most, preferably mixed with coarse grit or fine chippings in the proportion two parts medium to one of grit. An ericaceous mix with extra bulky material is best for species which grow in acid soils. Small bulbs (e.g. *N.bulbocodium*) can be planted 12 to a 12cm/5in. pot, about 7cm/3in. deep. Good ventilation is essential throughout the growing season. Bulbs should be started into growth by watering plentifully in late summer or early autumn. They should then be kept moist through the winter and again watered copiously through the spring until the leaves begin to yellow, after which little or no water will be required. Species from hotter areas can be 'baked', i.e. given full sun exposure and minimal moisture; they are still best plunged, however, in summer. Those from cooler regions are better left outside, plunged in a shady place and uncovered.

For daffodils in the garden, two parts bonemeal and one part hoof-and-horn meal are beneficial to provide slow-release phosphate and some nitrogen. This mixture may be combined with the soil at planting time or scattered at any time afterwards at 175–225g/m². Alternatively, a slow-release nitrogen compound can be used as an autumn dressing. Wood ash applied in early spring is useful for providing potassium. In spring a balanced liquid fertilizer or one containing extra potash may be used, but is rarely necessary for bulbs grown outside. In normal seasons rainfall will provide all the water needed, but daffodils need moisture in early autumn to initiate growth, and they appreciate abundant water in the period of rapid growth up to and through flowering.

Propagation of daffodil cultivars is achieved by letting the bulbs divide naturally, which is a slow process. It can be speeded up by twin-scale propagation, a time-consuming method. The bulb is sterilized for five minutes in 1% formaldehyde and then cut into segments, usually 36 or 48 for a good-sized bulb. Each segment is then cut so that pairs of fleshy leaf scales are created, attached to their own portion of basal plate. The twin scales are further disinfected by dipping for 30 minutes in a weak solution of fungicide (e.g. 0.2% benomyl). They are then placed in polythene bags containing damp vermiculite. The bags are sealed with an air space above the vermiculite and stored at 20°C/68°F for 12 weeks, by which time small bulbs should have formed. These can then be grown on like daffodil seedlings and should reach flowering size in 3–4 years. Blades used for twin-scaling should be sterilized or discarded after each operation to avoid the transmission of viruses from bulb to bulb. Some cultivars respond to this method better than others. It has not been used for species to any extent. Most species are slow to increase by division and are propagated by seed.

Most cultivars readily set seed if hand-pollinated, but will not breed true. The seed should be collected when the capsule begins to turn yellow or the old flower falls away. Seed should be sown immediately or in early autumn at the latest. It is best sown in pots or boxes which are at least 15cm/6in. deep, in a light sandy medium and shallowly covered. Germination occurs in winter and the first leaf appears in late winter or early spring. The seedlings should be kept watered to prolong their growing season, and are better not planted out into open ground until the end of their second growing season. Two-year-old bulbs can be planted out about 10cm/4in. deep and about 10cm/4in. apart. They can then be left undisturbed until they flower, usually in their fourth or fifth year, and for a year or two after so that selections can be made. It is unwise to give names to new cultivars until they have flowered several times so that their consistency can be assessed. Names should be registered with the Royal Horticultural Society, the International Registration Authority for the genus.

The smaller species can easily be raised from seed in the same way, but the sowing containers should be shallower and the medium grittier. If thinly sown they can be left in their original pot until they flower, after three or four years in good conditions.

Over the last century, breeders have greatly widened the available range of colours and combinations of colours as well as the sizes and shapes. Although yellow trumpet daffodils are perhaps still the most popular, pure white daffodils are now common, cultivars with deep red or orange cups are often sunproof or nearly so, and cultivars with deep pink cups or cups paler than the perianth are no longer novelties. Many cultivars bred from *N.cyclamineus, N. triandrus* and members of the Jonquil and Tazetta divisions are attractive and satisfactory garden plants.

Miniature daffodils are increasingly popular. There is no universally accepted definition of a miniature. The Royal Horticultural Society defines them for exhibition purposes as having flowers no more than 5cm/2in. in diameter when flattened out. Other societies issue what they call Approved Lists. Some of the best miniatures for garden purposes are now propagated commercially on a very large scale. Daffodils larger than miniatures but less than standard size are now being termed intermediates, but again there is no generally accepted definition.

Daffodils are increasingly popular for competitive exhibition. The qualities sought after are poise, horizontally held flowers on stiff upright stems, broad flat untwisted petals of tough substance and satin-smooth quality, strong colours or pure whites, symmetry and consistency.

CLASSIFICATION Although the usage of the cut flower trade and of some bulb catalogues is to call narcissus cultivars with long coronas (or 'trumpets') daffodils, and those with short coronas (or 'cups') narcissi, this is not a tenable distinction when so many have coronas of medium length. 'Narcissus' and 'daffodil' are treated here as synonyms.

Narcissus (a) *N.papyraceus* (b) *N.poeticus* (c) *N.cyclamineus* (d) *N.pseudonarcissus* (e) *N.bicolor*
(f) *N.pseudonarcissus* ssp. *nobilis* (g) *N.pseudonarcissus* ssp. *moschatus* (h) *N.asturiensis* (i) *N.viridiflorus*

The RHS has pioneered classification of daffodils since 1908 and since 1955 has been International Registration Authority for the genus. Under the current (1989) system of classification daffodils fall into 12 divisions. Within each division daffodils are further distinguished by code letters for their colours: White or Whitish = W; Green = G; Yellow = Y; Pink = P; Orange = O; Red = R.

The colour code consists of two letters or groups of letters separated by a hyphen. The letter(s) before the hyphen describe the perianth segments (or 'petals'), the letter(s) following it describe the corona. For purposes of colour coding perianth segments and coronas are divided into three zones, none of which need be in specific proportions. If the perianth segments are substantially of a single colour one letter is used. If they are of more than one colour two or three letters are used, describing the outer zone before the midzone and/or base. If the corona is substantially of a single colour one letter is again used. Otherwise three letters are always used, describing the eye zone before the midzone and rim. In double daffodils the code letter(s) before the hyphen describe not only the outer whorl of perianth segments but also any extra perianth segments (of the same colour) interspersed with the corona segments.

The full classification consists of the division followed by the colour code. For example a daffodil with yellow petals and yellow trumpet is 1 Y–Y; one with mainly yellow petals having a white base and a medium cup having a white eye zone and midzone and a yellow rim is 2 YW–WWY; and one with white petals and a short cup having a green eye zone, yellow midzone and orange rim is 3 W–GYO.

Division 1. *Trumpet daffodils of garden origin.* One flower to a stem; corona ('trumpet') as long as, or longer than the perianth segments ('petals'). 'Arkle' (1Y–Y): fls yellow, trumpet deep yellow. 'Ballygarvey' (1W–Y): petals wide and pointed, trumpet rich chrome. 'Bravoure' (1W–Y): perianth pure white, trumpet long, yellow. 'By Jove' (1Y–Y): fls vivid gold, petals broad, trumpet narrow. 'Dutch Master' (1Y–Y): stem thick; fls golden yellow, trumpet frilled. 'Empress of Ireland' (1W–W): fls very large, white. 'Hero' (1Y–O): perianth rich gold, trumpet orange. 'Honeybird' (1Y–W): perianth pale lemon flushed white, trumpet white with yellow base and rim. 'King Alfred' (1Y–Y): tall; fls golden yellow. 'Little Gem' (1Y–Y): dwarf, to 12cm; fls yellow. 'Lunar Sea' (1Y–W): perianth light lemon, trumpet fades to white. 'Mount Hood' (1W–W): perianth wide, white, trumpet ivory; long–lasting. 'Primeur' (1Y–Y): fls gold. 'W.P. Milner' (1W–W): dwarf, to 20cm; perianth frilled, soft cream, trumpet white flushed lemon.

Division 2. *Large-cupped daffodils of garden origin.* One flower to a stem; corona ('cup') more than one-third, but less than equal to the length of the perianth segments ('petals'). 'Ambergate' (2O–O): perianth vibrant tangerine, cup strong orange. 'Ann Abbott' (2W–P): fls delicate, perianth white, cup pale pink touched yellow, darker pink at rim. 'Apropos' (2W–YYP): perianth white, cup orange-yellow with frilled salmon pink edge. 'Binkie' (2Y–W): perianth sulphur yellow, cup becoming pale cream edged yellow. 'Camelot' (2Y–Y): perianth rounded, thick, cup frill-edged. 'Carlton' (2Y–Y): tall; perianth clear yellow, cup lighter. 'Ceylon' (2Y–O): perianth yellow, cup orange turning brilliant red. 'Charter' (2Y–W): tall; perianth lemon, cup yellow turning white. 'Dailmanach' (2W–P): fls large, perianth white, cup long, apricot pink. 'Daydream' (2Y–W): perianth pale yellow, cup white with cream edge. 'Desdemona' (2W–W): fls purest white, stamens pink. 'Falstaff' (2Y–R): perianth metallic gold, cup deep orange-red. 'Fortune' (2Y–O): tall, to 45cm; perianth bright yellow, cup long, vivid red-orange. 'Golden Aura' (2Y–Y): fls large, brilliant yellow. 'Ice Follies' (2W–W): perianth soft white, cup wide and crinkled, pale primrose fading to white. 'Passionale' (2W–P): tall, to 40cm; perianth snow white, cup soft pink. 'Professor Einstein' (2W–R): perianth white, cup flat and frilled, brilliant orange. 'Red Hill' (2W–R): perianth white, flushed yellow at centre, cup orange-red. 'Salome' (2W–PPY): perianth white, cup long, deep pink finely edged yellow. 'Satin Pink' (2W–P): perianth white, cup pale creamy pink. 'Silver Standard' (2W–Y): perianth white, cup crinkled, creamy yellow fading with age. 'Stainless' (2W–W): fls delicate, pure white. 'Vulcan' (2Y–O): perianth yellow, cup deep scarlet.

Division 3. *Small-cupped daffodils of garden origin.* One flower to a stem; corona ('cup') not more than one-third the length of the perianth segments ('petals'). 'Amor' (3W–YYO): perianth white, cup wide, primrose shading to orange at rim. 'Audubon' (3W–WWP): perianth white, cup cream with coral pink band. 'Barrett Browning' (3W–O): perianth rounded, white with a flush of lemon at centre. 'Birma' (3Y–O): perianth golden yellow, cup deep orange. 'Doctor Hugh' (3W–GOO): perianth white, cup orange with a green hue at base. 'Edward Buxton' (3Y–OOR): perianth white, cup orange. 'Gold Frills' (3W–WWY): perianth white, cup open and crinkle-edged, white with fine yellow rim. 'Lollipop' (3W–Y): tall; perianth, rounded, white, cup frilled, pale lemon. 'Lovable' (3W–W): fls pure white, cup neat.

Division 4. *Double daffodils of garden origin.* One or more flowers to a stem, with doubling of the perianth segments or the corona or both. 'Acropolis' (4W–R): tall; white with occasional orange-red segments. 'Cheerfulness' (4W–Y): creamy white, centre segments yellow, fragrant. 'Dick Wilden' (4Y–Y): tall; yellow, centre segments darker, early-flowering. 'Double Event' (4W–Y): fls rounded, pure white with yellow segments interspersed in centre. 'Erlicheer' (4W–Y): white with centre segments yellow, long-lasting. 'Eystettensis' (4Y–Y): to 20cm; double, segments regularly arranged, pale yellow; corona absent. 'Pencrebar' (4Y–Y): dwarf to 20cm; camellia-form, yellow. 'Petit Four' (4Y–PPY): tall; perianth pale cream, centre segments soft pink-apricot. 'Rip van Winkle' (4Y–Y): dwarf to 12cm; sunny yellow. 'Swansdown' (4W–W): perianth white, cup full of delicate white segments. 'Tahiti' (4Y–O): tall; perianth golden, centre segments brilliant red-orange. 'Unique' (4W–Y): perianth white, centre segments wavy, yellow. 'White Lion' (2W–Y): white petals interspersed with buff to yellow segments.

Division 5. *Triandrus daffodils of garden origin*. Characteristics of *N.triandrus* clearly evident: usually two or more pendent flowers to a stem; perianth segments reflexed. 'April Tears' (5Y–Y): fls yellow, cup lighter coloured. 'Arish Mell' (5W–W): tall; fls pure white. 'Hawera' (5Y–Y): to 7 fls per stem; fls bright yellow. 'Ice Wings' (5W–W): fls snow white, trumpet long. 'Liberty Bells' (5Y–Y): tall; to 3 fls per stem; fls rich lemon. 'Thalia' (5W–W): tall, to 40cm; 3 or more fls per stem; fls pure white. 'Tuesday's Child' (5W–Y): to 3 fls per stem; perianth white, cup sulphur.

Division 6. *Cyclamineus daffodils of garden origin*. Characteristics of *N.cyclamineus* clearly evident: usually one flower to a stem; perianth segments reflexed; flower at an acute angle to the stem, with a very short pedicel ('neck'). 'Beryl' (6W–YYO): perianth primrose, cup orange. 'Charity May' (6Y–Y): fls vivid pure yellow, long-lasting. 'Dove Wings' (6W–Y): perianth clear creamy yellow ageing to white, cup yellow. 'February Gold' (6Y–Y): perianth clear yellow, cup deeper yellow, profuse. 'February Silver' (6W–W): perianth white, cup creamy white. 'Foundling' (6W–P): perianth recurved, white, cup deep rose. 'Jack Snipe' (6W–Y): perianth creamy white, cup yellow. 'Jenny' (6W–W): perianth white, cup narrow, pale yellow, becoming white. 'Jetfire' (6Y–R): perianth yellow, cup red and deepening with age. 'Jumblie' (6Y–O): to 3 fls per stem; perianth yellow, cup yellow-orange. 'Peeping Tom' (6Y–Y): perianth deep yellow, cup yellow. 'Tête-à-Tête' (6Y–Y): dwarf, to 20cm, multi-headed; fls bright yellow.

Division 7. *Jonquilla daffodils of garden origin*. Characteristics of the *N.jonquilla* group clearly evident: usually 1–3 flowers to a rounded stem; leaves narrow, dark green; perianth segments spreading not reflexed; flowers fragrant. 'Baby Moon' (7Y–Y): fls rich yellow. 'Bellsong' (7W–P): perianth opening blush pink fading to ivory, cup bright pink. 'Bobbysoxer' (7Y–YYO): perianth yellow, cup yellow with orange rim. 'Lintie' (7Y–O): perianth yellow, cup dark orange. 'Pipit' (7Y–W): perianth pale lemon, cup fading to white. 'Pueblo' (7W–W): fls white. 'Sugarbush' (7W–YYW): perianth white, cup yellow and white. 'Suzy' (7Y–O): to 4 fls per stem; perianth yellow, cup intense orange. 'Sweetness' (7Y–Y): fls rich gold, petals pointed. 'Trevithian' (7Y–Y): to 3 fls per stem; fls lemon.

Division 8. *Tazetta daffodils of garden origin*. Characteristics of the *N.tazetta* group clearly evident: usually 3–20 flowers to a stout stem; leaves broad; perianth segments spreading not reflexed; flowers fragrant. 'Avalanche' (8W–Y): to 15 fls per stem; fls white, cup soft yellow. 'Chinita' (8Y–YYR): perianth rounded, primrose, cup shallow, yellow with wide red rim. 'Cragford' (8W–R): perianth white, cup vibrant orange. 'Geranium' (8W–O): perianth soft white, cup rich orange, scented. 'Grand Soleil d'Or' (8Y–O): to 5 fls per stem; perianth gold, cup orange, strongly scented. 'Minnow' (8Y–Y): to 20cm high; to 5 fls per stem; perianth creamy yellow, cup flat, pure yellow. 'Paper White' (8W–W): to 5 fls per stem; fls pure white. 'Scarlet Gem' (8Y–O): perianth yellow, cups rich red-orange. 'Silver Chimes' (8W–W): perianth white, cup white with a strong cream flush from the base.

Division 9. *Poeticus daffodils of garden origin*. Characteristics of the *N.poeticus* group without admixture of any other: usually one flower to a stem; perianth segments pure white; corona usually disc-shaped, with a green or yellow centre and a red rim; flowers fragrant. 'Actaea' (9W–GWO): fls large, perianth wide, white, cup canary yellow edged in red, flush of green at base. 'Cantabile' (9W–GGR): perianth white, cup green with fine red rim. 'Felindre' (9W–GYR): perianth white, cup green and yellow, edged red.

Division 10. *Species, wild variants and wild hybrids*. All species and wild or reputedly wild variants and hybrids, including those with double flowers. Species and natural varieties.

Division 11. *Split-corona daffodils of garden origin*. Corona split rather than lobed and usually for more than half its length. 'Baccarat' (11Y–Y): fls rich lemon yellow, corona darker. 'Broadway Star' (11W–W): fls white, cream streaked orange and yellow. 'Canasta' (11W–Y): perianth white, corona very large, rich yellow. 'Cassata' (11W–W): perianth white, corona white with hint of lemon. 'Orangery' (11W–OOY): perianth cream-white, corona orange with yellow rim. 'Pearlax' (11W–P): perianth white, corona apricot-pink. 'Valdrone' (11W–Y): perianth white, corona lemon.

Division 12. *Miscellaneous daffodils*. All daffodils not falling into any one of the above divisions. 'Nylon' (12W–W): fls creamy white. 'Tarlatan' (12W–W): fls soft white.

PESTS AND DISEASES Most narcissus pests are common to both Europe and North America. These include bulb flies (*Merodon equestris* and *Eumerus* spp.), the stem eelworm (*Ditylenchus dipsaci*), the root lesion eelworm (*Pratylenchus* spp.), the bulb mite (*Rhizoglyphus* spp.), the bulb scale mite (*Steneotarsonemus laticeps*, a tarsonemid mite), slugs and millepedes. In some areas, particularly those in the vicinity of oil seed rape crops, narcissus blooms may become invaded by pollen beetles. Bulbs may be eaten by mice in the field and during storage where they may also become infested with the tulip bulb aphid (*Dysaphis tulipae*).

A basal rot, caused by the fungus *Fusarium oxysporum* f. sp. *narcissi*, is the most important disease of narcissi in Britain. During the growing season the fungus enters the bulbs through the roots or root plate and there may be some yellowing of the leaf tips. The main problem occurs during storage: a chocolate-brown soft rot spreads up through the scales from the base and a mass of pink spores may be produced on the basal plate. In leaf scorch, caused by the fungus *Stagonospora curtisii*, there appears a red-brown leaf tip necrosis as well as brown spots elsewhere on the leaf and on the spathes, flower stalks and flowers. Most of the infection takes place as the shoot passes through the neck of the bulb because the fungus survives in the bulb scales.

Narcissus smoulder disease, caused by the fungus *Sclerotinia narcissicola* (conidial state *Botrytis narcissicola*), also causes brown spots on the leaves and flowers. In wet conditions a grey mould growth appears on the

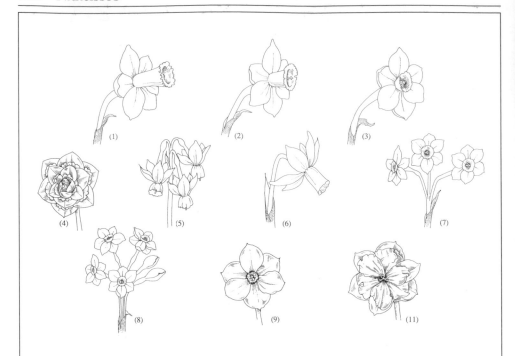

Daffodils (Numbers refer to the divisions of the official Classification) (1) Trumpet (2) Large-cupped (3) Small-cupped (4) Double (5) *N.triandrus* derivatives (6) *N.cyclamineus* derivatives (7) Jonquils (8) *N.tazetta* derivatives (9) *N.poeticus* derivatives (11) Split-cupped These relate to cultivars of garden origin. Div. 10 comprises the wild species, and Div. 12 miscellaneous cultivars.

spots and produces conidia which spread the disease further. It is small black sclerotia between the bulb scales and in the soil which cause the primary infection as the shoots emerge. Narcissus fire is caused by the fungus *Sclerotinia polyblastis* (conidial state *Botrytis polyblastis*) which overwinters as sclerotia on plant debris. The flowers are disfigured and eventually destroyed by small brown spots, while elongated red-brown blotches later form on the leaves to result in the 'fire' phase of the disease. As with smoulder disease, conidia produced on the dead tissue continue to cause secondary infections during the growing season.

Narcissus white mould (*Ramularia vallisumbrosae*) causes sunken, grey or yellowed spots and streaks on the leaves, which become covered with powdery masses of white spores. These spores spread the disease during the growing season and the fungus overwinters by producing small, black sclerotia in the infected tissue.

Narcissi can be affected by grey bulb rot caused by *Rhizoctonia tuliparum*, which is mainly known as a serious disease of tulips. This is a dry rot which progresses from the neck of the bulb downwards and the shoots are unlikely to emerge at all. As in so many of these diseases the fungus persists in the soil as sclerotia.

Most of the diseases can be controlled to some extent during the growing season by removing heavily infected leaf tissue and spraying with dithiocarbonate or other fungicides. But selection of healthy bulbs, routine dormant bulb treatment (dips in systemic fungicides or in hot water (44.4°C/112°F for three hours) plus formalin (0.2% commercial formaldehyde), careful handling and proper storage conditions are the main control measures. Narcissi can also be affected by blue mould (*Penicillium* spp.) and white root rot (*Rosellinia necatrix*), as well as several virus diseases, including those caused by narcissus degeneration virus, narcissus latent virus, narcissus mosaic virus, narcissus tip necrosis virus, narcissus yellow stripe virus, arabis mosaic virus and cucumber mosaic virus. Some of the viruses are transmitted by aphids, some by eelworms and some by contact. The gardener should obtain virus-free stocks and discard any obviously affected plants.

N.abscissus (Haw.) Schult. & Schult. f. See *N.bicolor*.
N.albescens Pugsley. See *N.pseudonarcissus* ssp. *moschatus*.
N.alpestris Pugsley. See *N.pseudonarcissus* ssp. *moschatus*.

N.assoanus Dufour (*N.requienii* Roem.; *N.juncifolius* auct.; *N.pallens* Freyn ex Willk.). RUSH-LEAVED JONQUIL.
Bulb to 3cm, subglobose, dark. Lvs to 20×0.2cm, cylindric, slightly striate on outer surface, spreading or prostrate, green. Scape 7–25cm, terete, smooth; pedicels 1.5–2cm, included in spathe; fls 2–3, to 2.2cm diam., horizontal or slightly ascending, yellow, fragrant; perianth tube 1.2–1.8cm, straight; seg. obovate, 0.7–1×0.7cm patent, incurved, imbricate at base; corona cup-shaped, conical,

0.5×1.1–1.7cm, crenate, deeper yellow than seg. S France, S & E Spain. Z7.

N.asturiensis (Jordan) Pugsley (*N.minimus* hort.).
Bulb to 2cm, globose, pale. Lvs 8×0.6cm, glaucous-green, spreading, channelled. Scape 7–14cm, not erect, nearly terete, striate, solid; fl. solitary, to 3.5cm across, usually drooping, soft yellow; spathe to 2.8cm, remaining green; pedicel to 10mm; perianth tube to 8mm, green-yellow; seg. to 1.4×0.4cm, usually twisted, deflexed; corona 1.7cm, widened below, constricted at middle, mouth spreading, fimbriate. N Portugal, NW & NC Spain. 'Giant': larger in all parts, to 20cm. Z4.

N.aureus L. See *N.tazetta* ssp. *aureus*.

N.barlae Parl. See *N.papyraceus* ssp. *panizzianus*.

N.bertolonii Parl. See *N.tazetta* ssp. *aureus*.

N.bicolor L. (*N.abscissus* (Haw.) Schult. & Schult. f.).
Bulb to 3cm with short neck, pale. Lvs 30–35×1.1–1.6cm,
green or glaucous, erect, flat. Scape 35cm, compressed,
sharply 2-edged; fl. solitary, horizontal or ascending; spathe
to 54cm; pedicel 2–2.5cm; perianth tube 1cm,
green- to orange-yellow, broad; seg. 3.5–4cm, cream or pale
sulphur-yellow, spreading or deflexed, imbricate, not twisted;
corona to 4cm, yellow, almost parallel, 1.5–2cm diam., mouth
with little or no flange, lobed or dentate. Pyrenees and
Corbières. Z6.

N.× biflorus Curtis. See *N.× medioluteus*.

N.broussonetii Lagasca.
Bulb to 4cm, neck long, brown. Lvs 4, 28×0.9cm, glaucous,
erect, lightly striate but keel absent. Scape to 40cm, compressed, lightly striate; fls 1–8, ascending, white, to 3.5cm
diam., fragrant; pedicel 1cm; perianth tube to 2.8cm, funnel-
shaped, white; seg. 1.6×1.2cm, patent or incurving, slightly
imbricate; corona rudimentary; stamens exserted, bright yellow. Autumn. Morocco. Z8.

N.bulbocodium L. ssp. **bulbocodium**. HOOP PETTICOAT DAF-
FODIL; PETTICOAT DAFFODIL.
Bulb to 2×1.5cm, globose, pale to dark. Lvs
10–30(–40)cm×1–5mm, semi-cylindric, erect, ascending or
prostrate, dark green. Scape 2.5–20cm, terete, faintly striate; fl. solitary, horizontal, pale yellow to deep golden-yellow, often green-tinged, to 4.5cm diam.; spathe to 3.5cm;
pedicel 2.5–20mm, or absent; perianth tube 6–25mm, yellow, often tinged green, especially below; seg. much
shorter than corona, 0.6–2cm×0.5–5mm, often tinged
green; corona funnel-shaped, 0.9–3.2×0.7–3.4cm, yellow,
margin of mouth spreading or incurved, entire to dentate or
crenate; anth. included in corona or slightly exserted; style
and filaments usually concolorous with corona, style sometimes long-exserted. W France, Spain, Portugal, N Africa
(usually on acidic soil in habitat). var. **bulbocodium**
(including *N.bulbocodium* 'Tenuifolius' (*N.tenuifolius*
Salisb.)). Plants usually dwarf, bulb dark 1.v4 2–3, prostrate or spreading. Fls golden-yellow; pedicel 0.4–2cm,
perianth to 3cm long. var. **conspicuus** (Haw.) Bak. Plant
robust. Lvs erect. Fls dark yellow to citron, 3–3.5cm long,
corona 2cm diam. Includes var. *citrinus* hort., loosely
applied to large-flowered pale yellow plants, but not var.
citrinus Bak. ssp. **obesus** (Salisb.) Maire (*N.obesus* Salisb.)
Bulb globose, dark. Lvs to 30×0.2cm, more or less prostrate, sinuous, channelled on inner surface, lightly striate on
outer. Scape 10cm, terete, smooth; pedicel 7mm; fl. to
3.5cm diam., horizontal or ascending, bright yellow; perianth tube to 2.5cm, conic, yellow; seg. 1.4×0.5cm, patent,
twisted; corona to 1.8×2cm, mouth crenate or slightly
incurved, deeper yellow than seg.; anth. biseriate, upper 3
in corona. WC Portugal. Z6.

N.bulbocodium ssp. **romieuxii** (Braun-Blanquet & Maire)
Emberger & Maire. See *N.romieuxii*.

N.calathinus L. See *N.× odorus*.

N.campernelli hort. ex Haw. See *N.× odorus*.

N.canaliculatus hort. See *N.tazetta* 'Canaliculatus'.

N.cantabricus DC. WHITE HOOP PETTICOAT DAFFODIL. ssp.
cantabricus (*N.clusii* Dunal).
Bulb to 2.5×2cm, globose, dark. Lvs 2, or 4–5 in var. folio-
sus (Maire) Fernandes, ascending or spreading, to
15cm×1mm, semicylindrical, slightly channelled and faintly
or not striate. Scape 5–10cm, terete; fl. solitary, ascending, to
40mm diam., pure- or milk-white, fragrant; pedicel absent or
5–17mm; perianth tube to 2.4×1.2cm, funnel-shaped, white,
green below; seg. 1.2×0.5cm, white, nearly patent; corona to
1.5×4cm, entire or crenate or undulate; anth. included, yellow, style and filaments white, style exserted. S Spain, N
Africa (Morocco, Algeria). var. **petunioides** Fernandes.

Scape 6cm; fls pure white, horizontal; corona nearly flat,
3–4cm diam., deeply crenate, margin recurved. Algeria. ssp.
monophyllus (Dur.) Fernandes. Differing from ssp. *cantabricus* in lf solitary, 27cm×1mm. Scape 3–8cm; pedicel absent;
fl. horizontal or ascending, to 4.5cm diam. S Spain, N Africa.
Z8.

N.cavanillesii A. Barra & G. Lopez. See *N.humilis*.

N.clusii Dunal. See *N.cantabricus* ssp. *cantabricus*.

N.confusus Pugsley. See *N.pseudonarcissus* ssp. *major*.

N.corcyrensis (Herb.) Nyman. See *N.tazetta* ssp. *corcyrensis*.

N.cupularis (Salisb.) Schult. See *N.tazetta* ssp. *aureus*.

N.cyclamineus DC.
Bulb to 15mm, globose, pale. Lvs 12(–30)cm×4–6mm, bright
green, spreading, keeled. Scape to 20cm, terete, smooth; fl.
solitary, drooping or pendent, deep yellow; spathe green,
becoming scarious; pedicel 10mm; perianth tube 2–3mm,
green; seg. sharply reflexed, obscuring ovary 2×0.4cm,
twisted or not twisted; corona 2cm, slightly constricted just
below flared margin, 12-lobed or fimbriate. NW Portugal,
NW Spain. Z6.

N.dubius Gouan.
Bulb to 3cm with distinct neck, dark. Lvs 50cm×7mm at
flowering, spreading, dark green, inner face flat, outer striate.
Scape 15–25cm+, elliptic; fls 2–6, ascending, 16mm diam.,
white; spathe to 4cm; pedicel 4.5cm; perianth tube
1.6×0.2cm, green, white at distal end; seg. 7×6mm, apiculate,
patent, slightly imbricate; corona 4×7mm, cup-shaped, crenate; anth. biseriate. S France, SE Spain. Z7.

N.elegans (Haw.) Spach.
Bulb to 3.5×3cm, globose, dark. Lvs 12–25cm×3–5mm, erect,
glaucous, striate on outer surface, apex hooded. Scape
20cm+, compressed, striate, scabrid; fls 2–7, horizontal,
2.5–3.5cm diam., fragrant; spathe 4cm, scarious; pedicels
unequal, to 5cm; perianth tube 1.6×0.2cm, green; seg.
1.5×0.3–0.7cm, white, patent, becoming twisted with age,
slightly imbricate; corona 1×2mm, green, becoming dull
orange; anth. biseriate. Autumn. W & S Italy, Sicily, Corsica,
Sardinia, N Africa (Morocco to Libya). Z8.

N.fernandesii Pedro.
Close to *N.wilkommii* and *N.gaditanus*. Bulb small, globose,
dark. Lvs 33cm×3mm, green, erect to spreading or prostrate, finely striate, channelled at base. Scape 17cm, terete,
finely striate; fls 1–5, ascending, 2.8cm diam., yellow;
pedicel 2–4cm, exceeding spathe; tube 2×0.3cm, sometimes
slightly curved, green except for distal end; seg. 1.2×0.7cm,
apiculate, patent but reflexed at base, imbricate at base;
corona 6×8mm, slightly deeper yellow than seg., parallel
sided above, crenate; anth. biseriate. C Portugal, SW Spain.
Z8.

N.× gracilis Sab. See *N.× tenuior*.

N.gaditanus Boiss. & Reut. (*N.minutiflorus* Willk.).
Bulb small to medium-sized, globose, dark. Lvs 20cm×2mm,
ascending or prostrate, dark green, tip rounded, channelled at
base, outer surface striate. Scape 9–14cm, terete, finely striate; fls 1–3, ascending, 1.4–1.6cm, diam.; pedicel 1.5cm;
perianth tube 1.5×0.3cm, green or yellow, straight or slightly
curved; seg. 5×4mm, apiculate, yellow, reflexed, slightly
imbricate at base; corona 3–5×6–7mm, yellow, cup-shaped,
entire; anth. biseriate. S Portugal, S Spain. Z8.

N.hispanicus Gouan. See *N.pseudonarcissus* ssp. *major*.

N.hedraeanthus (Webb & Heldr.) Colmeiro.
Bulb to 1.5×1cm, globose, dark. Lvs 2 or more, to
6×0.1–0.15cm, erect to spreading, dark green. Scape shorter
than lvs, curved or ascending; fl. solitary, horizontal or
ascending, pale yellow, 2.4cm diam.; spathe dark brown;
pedicel absent; perianth tube 1.4×0.5cm, pale yellow, base
green; seg. 1.2×0.2cm, patent or spreading, not twisted;
corona 0.7×1cm, margin often slightly expended, crenate;
anth. exserted; style and filaments concolorous with corona,
style long exserted. S Spain. Z8.

N.humilis (Cav.) Traub (*N.cavanillesii* A. Barra & G. Lopez; *Tapeinanthus humilis* (Cav.) Herb.; *Braxireon humile* (Cav.) Raf.; *Carregnoa humilis* (Cav.) Gay).
Bulb to 1.5cm, globose, dark. Lvs to 20×0.1cm, solitary or occasionally 2, usually not produced by flowering bulbs, erect, channelled at base. Scape 7–20cm, slender; pedicel 0.6–1.6cm; fl. solitary, 2.5cm diam., ascending, yellow; perianth tube absent; seg. 1–1.8×0.2–0.3cm; corona absent; fil. spreading, anth. uniseriate. Autumn. S Spain, Algeria, Morocco. Z8.

N.× incomparabilis Mill. (*N.× leedsii* hort.; *N.× nelsonii* hort. ex Bak.). (*N.poeticus* × *N.pseudonarcissus.*)
Bulb to 3cm(+)cm. Lvs to 35×1.2cm, glaucous, linear, flat. Scape to 45cm, compressed; spathe to 3.5cm; fl. solitary, to 8cm diam.; perianth tube to 2.5cm, narrowly obconic, widening to throat; seg. narrow-obovate, 2.5–3×1.2–1.6cm, patent, pale yellow; corona to 2.2×2cm, deep orange-yellow, margin undulate, lobulate. Wild in S & SC France, also of garden origin and widely naturalized. Z4.

N.× intermedius Lois. (*N.jonquilla* × *N.tazetta.*)
Lvs 4, subcylindric, to 45×0.8cm, deeply channelled, bright green. Scape to 40cm, subterete; spathe to 4cm, scarious; pedicels to 4cm; fls 3–6, to 3.5cm diam., fragrant; perianth tube to 2cm, tinged green; seg. ovate, to 1.4cm, imbricate, bright lemon-yellow; corona 4mm high, orange yellow. W Mediterranean. Z8.

N.italicus Ker-Gawl. See *N.tazetta* ssp. *italicus.*
N.italicus ssp. *lacticolor* (Haw.) Bak. See *Narcissus tazetta* ssp. *italicus.*

N.jonquilla L. JONQUIL.
Bulb to 3×2.5cm, globose, dark, with short neck. Lvs 2–4, erect to spreading, to 40–45×0.8cm, channelled at base, cylindric towards apex, striate, green. Scape to 40cm, terete or subterete, finely striate; spathe to 5cm, scarious; pedicels 4.5–9cm; fls 1–6, to 3cm diam., ascending; perianth tube to 3cm, slightly curved, pale green , seg. elliptic, to 1.3cm, apiculate, patent, imbricate, yellow; corona cup-shaped, 7–10×2–4mm, yellow, margin shallowly lobed or somewhat crenate. S & C Spain, S & E Portugal, naturalized elsewhere. var. *henriquesii* Fernandes. Lvs to 25×0.3cm. Scape to 21cm; pedicel to 3.5cm; fls 1–2, to 3.8cm diam., horizontal; perianth tube to 1.8cm, straight; seg. to 1.7cm, patent, not imbricate, margins curving inwards; corona cup-shaped, parallel-sided near margin, to 0.6×1cm, 6-lobed. C Portugal. Z4.

N.jonquilloides Willk., non Willk. ex Schult. f. See *N.willkommii.*
N.juncifolius auct. See *N.assoanus.*
N.juncifolius ssp. *rupicola* Dufour. See *N.rupicola.*
N.× leedsii hort. See *N.× incomparabilis.*
N.lobularis hort. See *N.minor.*

N.longispathus Pugsley.
Bulb to 3cm, dark, with neck. Lvs 20–40(–60)×1cm, erect, striate, glaucous. Scape 10–45(–175)cm, compressed, striate; spathe to 10cm, green; pedicel 5cm; fls 1–3, 4–9cm diam., ascending; perianth tube 1.5cm, green; seg. 2–3cm, patent, sometimes twisted, slightly imbricate, yellow; corona subcylindric, margin expanded, crenate, yellow. SE Spain. Z8.

N.major Curtis. See *N.pseudonarcissus* ssp. *major.*
N.maximus hort. See *N.pseudonarcissus* ssp. *major.*

N.× medioluteus Mill. (*N.× biflorus* Curtis; *N.× poetaz* hort. ex L.H. Bail.). (*N.poeticus* × *N.tazetta.*) PRIMROSE PEERLESS.
Bulb to 6×4.5cm. Lvs to 70×1cm, glaucous, flat. Scape to 60cm, compressed; pedicels to 3.5cm; fls 2, occasionally 1 or 3, 3–5cm diam., fragrant; perianth tube to 2.5cm, cylindric, broader at throat; seg. broad-obovate to 2.2cm, white; corona to 5×12mm, bright yellow, margin crenate, white-scarious. S France, naturalized elsewhere. Z7.

N.minimus hort. See *N.asturiensis.*

N.minor L. (*N.nanus* Spach; *N.pumilus* Salisb.; *N.provincialis* Pugsley; *N.lobularis* hort.).
Bulb to 3cm, globose, pale brown, with neck. Lvs 3–4, erect, 8–15×0.4–1cm, sage-green or glaucous, flat or channelled. Scape 14–20cm, terete; spathe to 4cm, scarious; pedicels 7–12mm; fl. solitary, to 3.7cm diam., horizontal or ascending; perianth tube 1–1.8cm, yellow or green-yellow; seg. ovate-lanceolate, 1.5–2.2cm, somewhat twisted, drooping, yellow, often with deeper median streak; corona 1.7×2.5cm, plicate, dilated at mouth, margin frilled. Pyrenees, N Spain. Z4.

N.minutiflorus Willk. See *N.gaditanus.*
N.moschatus L. See *N.pseudonarcissus* ssp. *moschatus.*
N.nanus Spach. See *N.minor.*
N.× nelsonii hort. ex Bak. See *N.× incomparabilis.*
N.nevadensis Pugsley. See *N.pseudonarcissus* ssp. *nevadensis.*
N.nobilis Haw. See *N.pseudonarcissus* ssp. *nobilis.*
N.obesus Salisb. See *N.bulbocodium* ssp. *obesus.*
N.obvallaris Salisb. See *N.pseudonarcissus* ssp. *obvallaris.*

N.× odorus L. (*N.calathinus* L.; *N.campernelli* hort. ex Haw.). CAMPERNELLE JONQUIL. (*N.jonquilla* × *N.pseudonarcissus.*)
Bulb to 3cm. Lvs to 50×0.8cm, strongly keeled, bright green. Scape to 40cm, terete or nearly so; spathe to 7cm, scarious; pedicels to 3cm; fls 1–4, ascending, bright yellow, very fragrant, perianth tube to 2cm; seg. to 2.5×1.3cm; corona to 1.8×2cm, regularly lobed to subentire. Garden origin; naturalized S Europe. 'Rugulosus': selected cv, larger than the type. 'Plenus': fls double, regular to form. Z6.

N.ornatus Haw. See *N.poeticus.*

N.pachybolbus Durieu.
Bulbs 10×5–7cm, globose, dark. Lvs 7, to 50×3.8cm, flat or slightly twisted, finely striate on both surfaces, pale green. Scapes to 7 per bulb, 30(–50)cm, compressed; pedicels to 4cm; fls 3–17, to 1.8cm diam., white; perianth tube 1.4cm; seg. ovate-oblong, 7mm, obtuse, imbricate; corona 2–3mm high, entire. Morocco, Algeria. Z9.

N.pallens Freyn ex Willk. See *N.assoanus.*
N.pallidiflorus Pugsley. See *N.pseudonarcissus* ssp. *pallidiflorus.*
N.panizzianus Parl. See *N.papyraceus* ssp. *panizzianus.*

N.papyraceus Ker-Gawl. (*N.tazetta* ssp. *papyraceus* (Ker-Gawl.) Bak.). PAPER-WHITE NARCISSUS.
Bulb to 5×3.5cm, globose, dark. Lvs to 30×1.7cm, erect, keeled, glaucous. Scape to 40cm+, sharply keeled, striate; spathe to 5cm, scarious; pedicels 4cm; fls 2–20, 2.5–4cm. diam., ascending, fragrant; perianth tube 15×3mm, green below, white above, seg. white, to 1.8cm, ovate, apiculate, imbricate; corona cup-shaped, 3–6×8–11mm, entire or slightly notched, white. Winter–spring. ssp. **polyanthus** (Lois.) Asch. & Gräbn. (*N.polyanthus* Lois.). Lvs green, to 25×1.5–2cm. Scape subterete; pedicels to 4.5cm; fls 3–12(–20), 2.5–4cm diam., horizontal; corona entire, pale sulphur-yellow when young, becoming white. W Mediterranean. ssp. **panizzianus** (Parl.) Arcang. (*N.panizzianus* Parl.; *N.barlae* Parl.). Lvs to 55×1cm, erect, glaucous. Scape to 28cm, compressed; pedicels 3cm; fls 2–8, 2–2.5cm diam. SE France, SW Spain, Portugal. Z8.

N.× poetaz hort. ex L.H. Bail. See *N.× medioluteus.*

N.poeticus L. (*N.ornatus* Haw.). POET'S NARCISSUS; PHEASANT'S-EYE NARCISSUS.
Bulb to 4×3.5cm, pale, with long neck. Lvs 4, to 45×0.6–1cm, erect, channelled, green or somewhat glaucous. Scape 35–50cm, compressed, striate; spathe to 5cm, scarious; pedicel 2.5cm; fl. solitary, 4.5–7cm diam., horizontal to ascending, fragrant; perianth tube cylindric, 2.5×0.4cm, green; seg. suborbicular to cuneate, to 3×2.2cm, more or less patent, imbricate, white, yellow at base externally; corona flat and discoid, to 2.5×14mm, yellow with red frilled margin; anth. biseriate, upper 3 exserted. Capsule broadly ellipsoid. Late spring. France to Greece. var. **recurvus** (Haw.) Fernandes PHEASANT'S

Narcissus   (a) *N.requienii*   (b) *N.bulbocodium*   (c) *N.cantabricus*   (d) *N.jonquilla*   (e) *N.hedraeanthus*
(f) *N.romieuxii*   (g) *N.triandrus*   (h) *N.rupicola*   (i) *N.rupicola* ssp. *watieri*

EYE NARCISSUS. Perianth seg. strongly reflexed, pure white; corona discoid, with throat green, margin red. Capsule spherical. Late spring. var. **hellenicus** (Pugsley) Fernandes. Lvs 50×1cm, erect, pale green. Scape to 50cm; fl. 4.5cm diam., somewhat ascending; seg. rounded, becoming reflexed; corona 3mm high, yellow, throat green, margin scarlet. Greece. ssp. **radiiflorus** (Salisb.) Bak. (*N.radiiflorus* Salisb.; *N.poeticus* ssp. *angustifolius* (Haw.) Hegi). Lvs 5–8mm wide. Perianth seg. to 3cm, narrow, green-white, unguiculate, scarcely imbricate; corona to 2.5×10mm, shortly cylindric, sometimes wholly red (var. *poetarum* Burb. & Bak.); stamens all partially exserted. S & C Europe, W Balkans. Z4.

N.poeticus ssp. *angustifolius* (Haw.) Hegi. See *N.poeticus* ssp. *radiiflorus*.

N.polyanthus Lois. See *N.papyraceus* ssp. *polyanthus*.

N.portensis Pugsley. See *N.pseudonarcissus* ssp. *portensis*.

N.provincialis Pugsley. See *N.minor*.

N.pseudonarcissus L. WILD DAFFODIL; LENT LILY; TRUMPET NARCISSUS.
Bulb 2–5cm, pale brown, with neck. Lvs 8–50×0.5–1.5cm, erect, ligulate, usually glaucous. Scape 12–50(–90)cm, erect, 2-edged, striate; spathe to 6cm, scarious; pedicel 2–20mm; fl. usually solitary, occasionally 2–4, horizontal to drooping, sometimes ascending, concolorous or bicoloured, fragrant; perianth tube 1.5–2.5cm; seg. 1.8–4cm, patent to erect-patent, sometimes twisted, white to deep yellow; corona 1.5–4.5cm, white to deep yellow; margin subentire to 6-lobed. W Europe to N England. ssp. **pseudonarcissus**. Lvs 12–35×0.6–1.2cm, erect, glaucous. Scape 20–35cm; pedicel 3–12mm; fl. solitary, horizontal or drooping, to 6.5cm diam.; perianth tube 1.5–2.2cm, yellow, usually tinged green; seg. 2–3.5cm, twisted, deflexed, slightly imbricate, white to sulphur yellow, usually darker than seg. W Europe except Portugal & S Spain. ssp. **major** (Curtis) Bak. (*N.major* Curtis; *N.hispanicus* Gouan; *N.confusus* Pugsley; *N.maximus* hort.). Lvs 20–50×0.5–1.5cm, erect, twisted, glaucous blue. Scape to 50cm; pedicels 0.8–3cm; fl. solitary, to 9.5cm diam., concolorous, deep yellow; perianth tube 1.8cm, green-yellow; seg. 1.8–4cm, twisted, inner deflexed, outer reflexed; corona 2–4cm, margin expanded. Spain, Portugal, S France, naturalized elsewhere. ssp. **moschatus** (L.) Bak. (*N.moschatus* L.; *N.tortuosa* Haw.; *N.albescens* Pugsley; *N.alpestris* Pugsley). Lvs 10–40×0.5–1.2cm, erect, glaucous. Scape 15–35cm; pedicel 1–2.5cm; fl. solitary, 5–6cm diam., horizontal or drooping, usually white; perianth tube 8–15mm, green; seg. 2–3.5cm twisted; corona 3–4cm, slightly flanged at margin. Pyrenees. ssp. **nevadensis** (Pugsley) Fernandes (*N.nevadensis* Pugsley). Lvs 12–30× 0.5–1cm, erect, glaucous. Scape to 30cm, somewhat compressed; pedicel 2–3.5cm; fls 1–4, 5cm diam., ascending; perianth tube 1.5cm, green-yellow; seg. 1–2×1cm, deflexed, not twisted, slightly imbricate, white with yellow central streak; corona 1.5–2.5cm, subcylindric, margin slightly expanded, yellow. S Spain (Sierra Nevada). ssp. **nobilis** (Haw.) Fernandes (*N.nobilis* Haw.). Lvs 15–50×0.8–1.5cm, glaucous. Scape 15–30cm, somewhat compressed, striate; pedicel 8–15mm; fl. solitary, horizontal or ascending, 8–12cm diam.; perianth tube to 2.5cm, bright yellow; seg. 3–4cm, more or less patent, twisted, imbricate, white with yellow mark at base on reverse; corona 3–4cm, margin expanded, deeply dentate. N Portugal, NW & NC Spain. ssp. **obvallaris** (Salisb.) Fernandes (*N.obvallaris* Salisb.). TENBY DAFFODIL. Lvs 30×0.6cm, erect, glaucous. Scape 20cm; pedicel 2mm; fl. solitary, 4cm diam., horizontal; perianth tube 1cm, yellow with green stripes; seg. to 3cm, nearly patent, slightly twisted, yellow; corona to 3.5cm, margin dilated, 6-lobed, sometimes reflexed. S Wales but true origin unknown; similar plants recorded from C Spain. ssp. **pallidiflorus** (Pugsley) Fernandes (*N.pallidiflorus* Pugsley). Lvs 15–40×0.5–1.2cm, erect, slightly glaucous. Scape 30cm; pedicel 2mm; fl. solitary, horizontal or drooping, 7.5cm diam.; perianth tube 2.5cm, green, with yellow streaks; seg. 3–4cm, twisted, slightly imbricate, pale yellow with darker median streaks; corona 3–4cm, margin expanded, recurved, pale yellow, slightly deeper than

seg. Pyrenees, Cordillera Cantabrica. ssp. **portensis** (Pugsley) Fernandes (*N.portensis* Pugsley). Lvs 8–12×0.5–0.7cm, suberect, nearly flat, glaucous. Scape 12–20cm, compressed, 2-edged; pedicel 0.5–1.5cm; fl. solitary, drooping, horizontal or ascending, concolorous, deep yellow; perianth tube to 2.2cm, green; seg. 2–3cm, narrow, deflexed, median veins green; corona obconic, 2.5–3.5cm, margin 6-lobed or crenulate, but not expanded. N Portugal, NW & C Spain. Z4.

N.pumilus Salisb. See *N.minor*.

N.radiiflorus Salisb. See *N.poeticus* ssp. *radiiflorus*.

N.requienii Roem. See *N.assoanus*.

N.romieuxii Braun-Blanquet & Maire (*N.bulbocodium* ssp. *romieuxii* (Braun-Blanquet & Maire) Emberger & Maire).ssp. **romieuxii**.
Bulb 1cm, globose, dark. Lvs to 20×0.1cm, erect or spreading, dark green, weakly striate. Scape 10–20cm, terete; spathe scarious, usually brown; pedicel absent; fl. solitary, 2.5–4cm diam., horizontal or ascending, pale to medium yellow; perianth tube to 2.5cm, green at base, yellow above; seg. to 1.3×0.4cm, nearly patent; corona 1.5×3cm, margin 6-lobed and crenate; anth. exserted, exceeded by style, pollen bright yellow, fil. and style yellow. N Africa. var. **mesatlanticus** Maire. Strictly indistinguishable from ssp. *romieuxii*, but the plant in commerce under this name has pale yellow flowers. 'Julia Jane': Selected form with wide corona, resembling *N.cantabricus* ssp. *cantabricus* var. *petunioides*, but fl. pale yellow. ssp. **albidus** (Emberger & Maire) Fernandes. Bulb globose, dark. Lvs to 22cm, suberete with shallow channel, erect, green. Scape to 9cm, terete; pedicel 4mm; fl. solitary, to 3cm diam., ascending; perianth tube 1.7cm, green at base, white above; seg. 9×3mm, patent, white; corona 0.9×2cm, margin crenate, white; stamens widely separated, slightly exceeded by style, fil. and style white. Algeria. Z7.

N.rupicola Dufour (*N.juncifolius* ssp. *rupicola* (Dufour). ssp. *rupicola*.)
Bulb to 2.5cm, globose, pale. Lvs 18×0.3cm, erect, 2-keeled, glaucous. Scape 14–23cm, terete, striate; pedicel absent or very short; fl. solitary, to 3cm diam., ascending; perianth tube 2.2cm, green or green-yellow; seg. to 1.5×1.1cm, patent, imbricate, apiculate, yellow; corona 3–5×6–18mm, conic or reflexed, deeply 6-lobed to crenate or subentire, yellow; anth. and style included in tube. Spain, Portugal. ssp. **watieri** (Maire) Maire & Weiller (*N.watieri* Maire). Fls white; pedicel 2mm. Morocco (High Atlas). Z8.

N.scaberulus Henriq.
Bulb to 2.2×1.8cm, globose, pale. Lvs 7–30×0.2cm, erect or prostrate and sinuous, 2-keeled, margin often scabrid, glaucous. Scape 5–25cm, terete, striate; pedicel to 2.5cm; fls 1–5, 1.8cm diam., ascending; perianth tube to 1.4cm, green; seg. to 7×5mm, apiculate, patent or slightly reflexed, slightly imbricate, deep orange-yellow; corona cup-shaped, 5×7mm, margin often incurved minutely crenulate or entire, deep yellow; anth. biseriate. NC Portugal. Z8.

N.serotinus L.
Bulb 1.5–2cm, globose, dark. Lvs 1–2, 10–20×0.1–0.5cm, erect or spreading, dark green, sometimes with longitudinal white stripes, absent from bulbs that have flowered. Scape 13–30cm, terete, finely striate; spathe 1.5–3.5cm, tubular below, hyaline; pedicel 7–2cm; fls solitary or occasionally 2–3, to 3.4cm diam., ascending, fragrant; perianth tube to 2cm, dark green; seg. oblong-lanceolate, to 1.6×0.7cm, patent or sometimes recurved, twisted, white; corona minute, to 1.5×4mm, 6-lobed, dark yellow to orange. Autumn. Mediterranean. Z8.

N.tazetta L. BUNCH-FLOWERED NARCISSI; POLYANTHUS NARCISSUS.

ssp. **tazetta**. Bulb to 5×3.5cm, globose, dark. Lvs 20–50×0.5–2.5cm, erect, twisted, keeled, glaucous. Scape 20–45cm, stout, slightly compressed; spathe to 5cm, scarious; pedicels unequal, 2.5–7.5cm; fls 1–15, 4cm diam., horizontal, fragrant; perianth tube cylindric, 2cm, pale green; seg. broad-ovate, 0.8–2.2cm, patent, incurving, white; corona cup-shaped, 0.5×1cm, bright to deep yellow; stamens biseriate, upper 3 included in corona. S Portugal, Mediterranean, east to Iran, probably introduced further east, where fully naturalized in Kashmir, China and Japan. ssp. *aureus* (Lois.) Bak. (*N.aureus* L.; *N.bertolonii* Parl.; *N.cupularis* (Salisb.) Schult.). Perianth seg. deep yellow to golden yellow; corona deep yellow to orange. SE France, Italy, Sardinia, Algeria, naturalized elsewhere. ssp. *corcyrensis* (Herb.) Bak. (*N.corcyrensis* (Herb.) Nyman). Fls 1–2; perianth seg. narrow, sometimes reflexed, pale yellow; corona yellow. Corfu. ssp. *italicus* (Ker-Gawl.) Bak. (*N.italicus* (Ker-Gawl.; *N.italicus* ssp. *lacticolor* (Haw.) Bak.). Perianth seg. cream or very pale yellow; corona deeper yellow. NE Mediterranean, N Africa. 'Canaliculatus' (*N.canaliculatus* hort.): to 20cm; lvs narrow, erect, glaucous, striate; fls small; seg. white, corona ochre yellow; sometimes shy-flowering, origin unknown. Z8.

N.tazetta ssp. *papyraceus* (Ker-Gawl.) Bak. See *N.papyraceus*.

N.tenuifolius Salisb. See *N.bulbocodium* var. *bulbocodium*.

N.× tenuior Curtis (*N.× gracilis* Sab.). (*N.jonquilla* × *N.poeticus.*)
Close to *N.jonquilla*. To 30cm. Lvs linear, flat. Fls 2–3, to 5cm diam.; corona flat, to 5mm, deeper yellow than perianth seg. Probably garden origin. Z4.

N.tortuosa Haw. See *N.pseudonarcissus* ssp. *moschatus*.

N.triandrus L. ANGEL'S TEARS.
Bulb to 2×1.7cm, globose, dark. Lvs 15–30×1.5–5mm, keeled or striate, flat or channelled, erect or decumbent, sometimes curled at tip, green, or slightly glaucous. Scape 20–30cm,

elliptic, slightly keeled; spathe to 4cm; pedicel to 4cm; fls 1–6, pendulous, white to bright yellow, usually concolorous; perianth tube 1.5cm, green below, yellow above; seg. sharply reflexed, lanceolate to linear-oblong, 1–3cm, often with deeper median streak; corona cup-shaped, 0.5–1.5(–2.5) × 0.7–2.5cm, entire, somewhat undulate; anth. biseriate, upper 3 exserted beyond corona. Spain & Portugal, NW France. var. *albus* (Haw.) Bak. Typical of wild populations and should not be separated from the species. var. *concolor* (Haw.) Bak.Fls deep yellow and lvs 2mm wide; the name is loosely applied in horticulture to any yellow-flowered plant. Z4.

N.viridiflorus Schousb.
Bulb to 3×3cm, globose, very dark. Lvs 30–60×0.4cm, cylindric, hollow, erect or spreading, striate, glaucous dark green, not usually produced by flowering bulbs. Scape 9–25(–40)cm, terete or elliptic, striate; spathe to 5cm; pedicel to 7cm; fls 1–5, ascending, 2.5cm diam., dull green, malodorous; perianth tube 1.5cm; seg. linear-oblong, 1–1.6×0.2cm, acute, patent or reflexed; corona 1×4mm, 6-lobed; stamens bright yellow, upper 3 included in corona, pollen bright yellow. SW Spain, Morocco. Z8.

N.watieri Maire. See *N.rupicola* ssp. *watieri*.

N.willkommii (Samp.) Fernandes (*N.jonquilloides* Willk., non Willk. ex Schult. f.).
Bulb to 3×2.5cm, globose, dark. Lvs to 37×0.3cm, erect, flattened at base, rounded above, glaucous dark green. Scape to 18cm, terete, smooth; pedicels to 2.2–4cm; fls usually solitary, 3cm diam., horizontal; perianth tube to 1.6cm, straight, green-yellow; seg. broad-elliptic, 0.6–1.3×0.7cm, apiculate, patent, or reflexed and curving inwards, slightly imbricate, yellow; corona cup-shaped, 0.6×1cm, deeply 6-lobed, yellow. S Portugal, SW Spain. Z8.

Nectaroscordum Lindl. (From Gk *nektar* and *skorodon*, garlic, a reference to the large nectaries on the ovary.) Liliaceae (Alliaceae). 3 species of onion-scented, herbaceous perennials to 120cm, resembling *Allium* but outer tepals with 3–7 veins; pedicel apices swollen beneath flowers; ovary many-ovuled. Bulbs solitary, subterranean, tunics membranous. Leaves linear, sheathing base of stem. Flowers numerous in a scapose umbel; perianth segments free; stamens 6; ovaries with 5 or more ovules per cell. S Europe, W Asia, Iran. Z7.

CULTIVATION Attractive bulbs for naturalizing in the open woodland or herbaceous border, they carry nodding, subtly coloured flowers atop tall stems in early summer. The strap-shaped leaves, which emerge in spring, die back at or shortly after flowering. As the generic name suggests, the whole plant smells strongly of garlic when crushed. Hardy to at least 13°C/5°F. Grow in any light, well-drained soil that is neither excessively dry nor waterlogged, in sun or part shade. In sunny, favourable conditions, they may become invasive. Propagate from seed in early spring; in suitable conditions seed may be sown *in situ*. Also from offset bulbils.

N.bulgaricum Janka. See *N.siculum* ssp. *bulgaricum*.

N.siculum (Ucria) Lindl. (*Allium siculum* Ucria). SICILIAN HONEY GARLIC.
Bulbs solitary, ovoid, to 3cm diam., tunics membranous. Lvs 3–4, 30–40×1–2cm; basal lvs deeply channelled, keel sharp-edged. Scapes to 120cm; fls 10–30, 1.5–2.5×2cm, bell-shaped, pendulous, in loose umbels; pedicels unequal, pendent at first, erect on fruiting; tepals to 15×9mm, typically

nearly white, flushed flesh-pink and dark red, green toward base below; ovary tinted pink. Spring–summer. France, Italy. ssp. *bulgaricum* (Janka) Stearn (*N.bulgaricum* Janka; *Allium dioscoridis* Sibth. & Sm.; *Allium bulgaricum* Prodan; *Allium meliophilum* Juz.). Tepals white to yellow, flushed pale pink and green above, edged white, flushed green below. E Romania, Bulgaria, Turkey, Crimea. Z6.

Nemastylis Nutt. (From Gk *nema*, thread, and *stylos*, column, referring to slender style.) Iridaceae. 7 species of perennial herbs; rootstock a tunicate bulb. Leaves long, linear, plicate. Flowers short-lived, in few-flowered clusters subtended by spathes; tepals 6, similar; stamens 3, filaments separate or joined only at base; style short, with 6 long, spreading, divided branches. N & Tropical America. Z9.

CULTIVATION As for *Tigridia*.

N.acuta (Bartr.) Herb. (*N.geminiflora* Nutt.). PRAIRIE IRIS. 15–60cm, sometimes branched; bulb to 2cm diam., globose or ovoid, with dark brown, scaly tunic. Lvs 3–4, to 30cm. Infl. 2–3-fld; fls 4–6cm diam., blue-violet, opening in early morning; tepals spreading, obovate. Spring. Southern US.

N.floridana Small.
To 1.5m but often less, sometimes branched. Lvs to 45cm,

narrowly linear. Fls to 5cm diam., violet, white in centre, opening in afternoon. Late autumn. SE US (Florida).

N.geminiflora Nutt. See *N.acuta*.

N.tenuis ssp. *pringlei* (Wats.) Goldbl.
Stem unbranched. Fls scented, pale blue; outer tepals obtuse, inner acute. Mexico.

Nerine Herb. (From Gk Nereis, the name of a sea nymph.) Amaryllidaceae. About 30 species of bulbous perennials. Bulb globose or ovoid-pyriform, tunicated, sometimes produced into a neck. Lvs strap-shaped appearing with or soon after the flowers. Flowers 4–20+ on a slender or stout scape, often curiously scented; perianth funnel-shaped, usually zygomorphic, white, pink or bright red, erect or decurved, lobes 6, free, narrow-oblong to linear-lanceolate, falcate, more or less crisped, tips usually strongly recurved and rolled; stamens 6 inserted at the base of the perianth lobes, suberect or declinate, 2 lengths; style filiform, straight or declinate, stigma simple or trifid; ovary globose, 3-lobed. Fruit a globose, 3-celled capsule; seeds 1 or a few to a cell, globose. S Africa, Lesotho, Botswana, Swaziland. Z9 unless specified.

The tale of the Guernsey Lily, *N.sarniensis*, is one of profound botanical and geographical confusion and perhaps even political intrigue. Plants resembling and usually identified as *N.sarniensis* were grown and illustrated in the 17th century. Cornut based the first supposed illustration of *N.sarniensis* on a plant growing in the garden of Jean Morin in Paris in 1634. Cromwellian Major-General John Lambert grew a *Nerine*-like plant in his garden at Wimbledon in the 1650's and probably took his most treasured bulb with him to Guernsey when exiled there following the Restoration. In the 1680's, Robert Morison, Professor of Botany at Oxford suggested that the bulb had become naturalized on the Guernsey coast following the shipwreck of a vessel coming from Japan. So much for the 'facts', now the problems. Cornut's plant was named 'Narcissus Japonicus Rutilo Flore'; *Nerine sarniensis* is South African. John Lambert's 'Nerine' was called the 'golden tulip'; *N. sarniensis* is never yellow.

Did Morison's 'Nerine' hail from Japan or had it been picked up *en route* by a vessel that called at the Cape having left Japan? One commentator, believing the Lambert plant to be true *Nerine*, explains Morison's stated distribution for the plant – Japan – and the Guernsey shipwreck saga as a ruse intended to conceal the plants' association with Lambert (Morison was a Royalist). This rather subtle interpretation depends on a certain degree of colour-blindness – Lambert's plant was golden; moreover, all signs point to the Japanese origin of the plant supposed to have been *Nerine sarniensis* at this early date. An alternative and mercifully simpler explanation of the Japanese (sic) origin of the Guernsey Lily is that the plant was long confused with the superficially similar *Lycoris radiata*, a Japanese native. This would have been in Morin's mind, and Morison's. A splendid red (or perhaps yellow) herring: the exiled Lambert's 'Golden Tulip' could not have been *Nerine sarniensis*. *Lycoris radiata* 'Alba', however, has white and yellow flowers, whilst *L. aurea* (again, Japanese) is pure gold. What we have is a web of coincidence and mistaken identity, by no means an uncommon situation in botany, but one with an unusual solution – the true Guernsey Lily, cast ashore ex Cape, neither Japanese nor golden, is *Nerine sarniensis*.

CULTIVATION *Nerine* is a genus of predominantly frost-tender bulbs grown for their long-lived, autumn blooms, carried in delicate umbels, each flower having the characteristically narrow, undulate perianth segments that give the spider-like appearance also seen in the related genera *Hymenocallis* and *Lycoris*. In many species, notably *N.sarniensis*, the flowers have a beautiful iridescent quality. The flowers last well when cut, and *Nerine* spp. are grown commercially on a large scale for this purpose. The leaves emerge after flowering, and persist over winter into the following spring or summer.

In cool-temperate zones, most species are cultivated in the cool glasshouse, since they are not tolerant of temperatures below freezing; *N.masonorum*, a dainty species for warm sheltered pockets in the rock garden in areas with mild winters, is well suited to cultivation in the alpine house in cooler zones. *N.bowdenii* will grow where winter temperatures drop to −15°C/5°F, although it will not tolerate these low temperatures in combination with winter wet, and in regions at the limits of its hardiness should be grown at the base of a south-facing wall in perfectly drained soil, with the additional protection of a dry mulch of bracken litter or leafmould. In northern Britain, large and well established clumps are most commonly seen at the base of south-facing house walls, in the rain shadow of the eaves. *N.sarniensis* may be treated similarly, but is rather more susceptible to cold and set.

Nerine (a) *N.filamentosa* (b) *N.duparquetiana* (c) *N.bowdenii* (d) *N.undulata* (e) *N.sarniensis*

N.bowdenii Will. Wats. (*N.veitchii* hort.).
Bulb to 6×5cm, ovoid-pyriform, neck sometimes attaining 6cm. Lvs to 30×3cm, pale to dark green, glossy, appearing after fls. Scape to 45cm, hollow toward apex, spathe valves 2, thin; fls 6–7, muskily scented; pedicels to 5cm; perianth lobes to 7×0.8cm, candy pink to deep rose, rarely white, darker at midrib, margins undulate; stamens shorter than lobes; style equalling lobes, stigma obscurely 3-lobed; ovary glabrous. Fr. to 1cm diam., irregularly 3-lobed. S Africa (E Cape, Natal). 'Alba': fls white with a blush of pink. 'Hera' (*N.bowdenii* × *N.sarniensis*): fls rich pink. 'Mark Fenwick' ('Fenwick's Variety'): vigorous; fls soft cyclamen pink, early-flowering. 'Pink Triumph': fls deep pink. 'Wellsii': fls dark pink, seg. crinkled. Z7.

N.curvifolia Herb. See *N.fothergillii*.

N.duparquetiana Bak.
Lvs usually prostrate, slender. Scape to 25cm; fls to 13; pedicels to 6cm, slender; perianth lobes to 4.5×0.5cm, white, suffused or ribbed red-pink and sometimes tinted yellow, conduplicate, strongly recurved and twisted; stamens exceeding lobes, strongly forward-projecting. S Africa (N Cape, Kalahari).

N.filamentosa Barker.
Bulb to 2.7cm diam., subglobose to ovoid-pyriform with a slender neck to 2.5cm. Lvs to 10cm, 3–5, very slender, lax, sometimes sprawling and curling at tips, appearing with fls. Scape to 20cm, usually shorter, to 0.45cm diam.; spathe valves to 4.5cm, narrow; fls to 8; perianth lobes to 2cm, bright rose, narrow-lanceolate, strongly recurved and rolled at tips; fil. far exceeding perianth, anth. dark red to black-purple. S Africa (E Cape).

N.filifolia Bak.
Bulb to 2.5cm diam., globose, with pale tunic overtopping the neck. Lvs to 20cm, 6–10, appearing with fls, very slender, suberect. Scape to 30cm, slender, somewhat glandular-pubesc.; spathe valves to 2.5cm; fls 8–10; pedicels to 3.5cm; perianth 2.5cm, deflexed, white, rose pink, magenta or bright crimson, lobes to 3cm wide, oblanceolate, clawed, crisped; stamens declinate, shorter than lobes, anth. red; style equalling the longer stamens; ovary hairy. S Africa (E Cape, Transkei, Orange Free State, Swaziland, E Transvaal).

N.flexuosa Herb.
Bulb subglobose, to 3.5cm. Lvs to 2cm wide, 4–6, appearing with the fls, linear-lorate, arching, bright green, sometimes rough and pustular. Scape to 1m, slender, slightly glaucous, flexuous; spathe valves and pedicels to 5cm; fls 10–20, pale pink or white; perianth lobes to 3×0.4cm, crisped, oblanceolate; stamens declinate, shorter than the lobes, anth. to 4mm, claret red; style declinate, equalling the stamens. 'Alba': fls white, edges somewhat ruffled. S Africa.

N.fothergillii M. Roem. (*N.curvifolia* Herb.).
Bulb subglobose with membranous red-tinged tunics. Lvs 6–8, falcate, obtuse, glabrous, base canaliculate. Scape to 60cm with sheathing leaf bases, erect, glabrous; spathe to 3.5cm, valves acute, red; fls 15, scarlet; perianth lobes 2cm, subundulate, strongly recurved, somewhat spiralling; filaments erect, scarlet, slightly exceeding perianth, anth. deep. violet; style filiform, suberect. S Africa.

N.humilis Herb.
Bulb to 3.5cm diam.; ovoid, tunics membranous. Lvs to 30×1.5cm, about 6, appearing with the fls, linear, suberect, channelled above. Scape to 35cm, slender, slightly glaucous; spathe valves to 3.5cm, green, equalling pedicels; fls 10–20, bright pale pink to deep rose; perianth lobes to 3cm, oblanceolate, acute, crisped; stamens declinate, the longer 3 equalling the lobes, anth. 3mm, purple; style declinate, equalling the lobes. S Africa (W, SW & S Cape).

N.masonorum Bol.
Dwarf. Bulb short-necked. Lvs to 20cm×1.5mm, thread-like. Scape to 30cm, downy; pedicels to 3cm, densely pubesc.; fls 4–15; perianth pale to deep rose-pink, perianth lobes to

1.5cm, recurved, undulate, with a deep pink longitudinal stripe; stamens deflexed, with 2 lanceolate processes at the base; style deflexed; ovary glabrous. S Africa (Cape Province).

N.sarniensis Herb. GUERNSEY LILY.
Bulb 5cm diam., ovoid, tunic pale brown. Lvs to 30×2cm, about 6, appearing after fls, suberect, not curved, bright green, glabrous. Scape to 45cm, somewhat compressed; spathe valves to 5cm, crimson; pedicels to 5cm; fls 10–20, erect, pale rose-red to scarlet, pink, rarely white, scarcely zygomorphic, perianth lobes to 3.5×1.3cm, lanceolate, strongly recurved at tips, only slightly crisped; fil. boldly erect, bright red, 1.2cm longer than lobes, anth. usually pale; styles to 5cm, straight; ovary glabrous. Coastal S Africa. 'Kirstenbosch White': fls pure white. Z8.

N.undulata Herb.
Bulb to 2.5cm diam., ovoid; tunics membranous, pale. Lvs to 45×1.2cm, 4–6, appearing with the fls, linear, bright green. Scape to 45cm, slender; spathe valves to 3.5cm, equalling pedicels; fls 8–12, pale candy pink or rose; perianth lobes to 2×0.2cm, oblanceolate, strongly crisped; stamens declinate, equalling lobes, anth. ultimately dark; style declinate. Fr. to 6mm diam., deeply lobed; seeds 1 per cell. S Africa.

N.veitchii hort. See *N.bowdenii*.

N.cultivars.
Scape height can exceed 90cm, but new dwarfs are under 15cm. The most usual hybrids (i.e. using *N.sarniensis*) range between 30cm and 60cm. The range of colours shows a great variety of red; there are no blue or yellow fls but excellent white and pink, through to very dark red and the most brilliant scarlet. Bicolours, mostly pink and white are increasingly common. Flowering season extends from June (with some of the progeny of *N.hirsuta*) to late November and, with suitable treatment, into December. *N.sarniensis* hybrids peak in mid-October, *N.flexuosa* hybrids in late October and November. The number of flowers in the head varies widely, again reflecting the range found amongst the species. Selective breeding has given emphasis to larger flowerheads with more individual flowers. 10–15 flowers is normal for the better cultivars but more recent forms may have as many 24, giving a more rounded head.

Very short. 'Hero': to 34cm; flowerheads 16cm diam.; fls 12, 7cm wide, red-violet. 'Hotspur': to 34cm; flowerheads 10cm wide; fls 13, 6cm wide, deep magenta. 'Ixanthia': to 30cm; flowerheads 5.5cm wide; fls 11, 5cm wide, pink-carmine. 'Kate Cicely': to 30cm; fls 8, 8cm wide, flame. 'Latu': to 36cm; flowerheads 14cm wide; fls 14, 6cm wide, white, red-ribbed. 'Patina': to 38cm; flowerheads 11cm wide; fls 11, 5cm wide, pale pink. 'Phoebe': to 30cm; flowerheads 13cm wide; fls 6, 5.5cm wide, blue-violet. 'Priscilla': to 37cm; flowerheads 13cm wide; fls 13, 6cm wide, pink. 'Pym': to 36cm; flowerheads 12cm wide; fls 7, 6.5cm wide, pink.

Very early (July-August). 'Anna Fletcher': to 51cm; flowerheads 12.5cm wide; fls 11, 6cm wide, apricot. 'Catherine': to 51cm; flowerheads 17cm wide; fls 14, 5cm wide, light red. 'Diana Wharton': to 42cm; flowerheads 13cm wide; fls 8, 6.5cm wide, mid-red. 'Fothergillii Major': to 51cm; fls 12, 14cm wide, fls 12, 6cm wide, deep orange-red. 'Glensavage Gem': to 78cm; flowerheads 21cm wide; fls 13, crimson. 'Hera': to 90cm; flowerheads 21cm wide; fls 16, 8cm wide, rose-carmine. 'Miss Eva Godman': to 42cm; flowerheads 16cm wide; fls 8, 6cm wide, light red. 'Mrs Bromely': to 60cm; flowerheads 12cm wide; fls 11, 6cm wide, red-orange. 'Paula Knight': to 60cm; fls 12, 7cm wide, china rose. 'Plymouth': to 60cm; flowerheads 16cm wide; fls 12, 7cm wide, mid-red.

Very tall. 'Blush Beauty': to 120cm; flowerheads to 16cm wide; fls 14, 7cm wide, very pale pink. 'Guy Fawkes': to 72cm; flowerheads 15cm wide; fls 14, 6.5cm wide; light cerise. 'Kilwa': to 84cm; flowerheads 17cm wide; fls 14, 7cm wide; magenta. 'Kingship': to 75cm; flowerheads 15cm wide;

fls 17, 5cm wide; cerise-purple. 'Mansellii': to 72cm; flowerheads 16cm wide; fls 18, 6cm wide; mid-cerise. 'Mischief': to 75cm; flowerheads 14cm wide; fls 14, 7cm wide; cerise-mauve. 'Namba': to 120cm; flowerheads 19cm wide; fls 17, 4cm wide; mid-pink. 'Parbet II': to 123cm; flowerheads 19cm wide; fls 10, 7.5cm wide; pink, deep pink. 'Rushmere Star': to 72cm; flowerheads 16cm wide; fls 10, 7cm wide; bright magenta. 'Supremo': to 108cm; flowerheads 24cm wide; fls 15, 7cm wide; white/pale pink.

Very late (late October and November). 'Ancilla': to 66cm; flowerheads 12cm wide; fls 15, 6cm wide; purple-red. 'Bennet Poe': to 54cm; flowerheads 13cm wide; fls 13, 6.5cm

wide; mid-cerise. 'Cranfield': to 75cm; flowerheads 15cm wide; fls 16, 6cm wide; cerise. 'Konak': to 75cm; flowerheads 14cm wide; fls 12, 5cm wide; white/purple. 'Koriba': to 66cm; flowerheads 12cm wide; fls 12, 7cm wide; cerise. 'Kymina': to 75cm; flowerheads 14cm wide; fls 14, 7cm wide; pale pink. 'Mansellii': to 72cm; flowerheads 16cm wide; fls 18, 6cm wide; mid-cerise. 'Namba': to 120cm; flowerheads 19cm wide; fls 17, 4cm wide; mid-pink. 'Pink Triumph': to 60cm: flowerheads 15cm wide; fls 15, 6cm wide; fuschia pink. 'Wombe': to 57cm; flowerheads 16.5cm wide; fls 14, 6cm wide; orange-red. 'Zeal Giant': fls vivid deep pink, in large heads.

Nomocharis Franch. (From Gk *nomos*, pasture, and *charis*, loveliness, referring to the plant's beauty.) Liliaceae (Liliaceae). 7 species of bulbous perennial herbs. Bulb scaly, ovoid to oblong, composed of several scales; scales erect, lanceolate, overlapping, fleshy, pale yellow. Bracts 1–4, remote, oblong to lanceolate, leafy, to 5cm in lower of part of stem. Leaves in 2–9 whorls of 3–9 on upper half of stem with 1 or 2 leaves between each whorl, or scattered along stem in pairs or triads toward apex, linear to lanceolate or oblong-ovate, acute to acuminate. Flowers 1–9, terminal in uppermost leaf axils, flat to bowl-shaped, white to pink or pale yellow, often spotted purple or maroon; perianth segments 6, not united, margins entire to subserrate or fimbriate; inner segments grooved, with basal nectary; stamens 6; filaments often fleshy, to 1.5cm long; anthers fixed laterally on a fine acicular appendage at filament apex; stigma 3-lobed. Fruit a chambered capsule; seeds many, ovate, narrow-winged. Summer. W China, SE Tibet, Burma, N India. Z7.

CULTIVATION Most species require acid, cool and shady conditions, similar to those given for the woodland species of *Lilium*; they are well suited to the peat terrace and woodland garden, where the optimal cool, humid and stable conditions prevail. Grow in light dappled or semi-shade in well-drained, peaty or leafy soils, with plenty of cool, fresh moisture at the roots. Propagate by seed, which has epigeal germination; see *Lilium*.

N.aperta (Franch.) Wils.
To 80cm. Bulbs ellipsoid, to 3.5cm. Lvs scattered along stem, 6.5–10×1–2cm, sessile, elliptic to lanceolate, acute, sometimes slightly pubesc. Fls flattened, to 10cm across, pale pink to red; outer perianth seg. 2–5×1–2cm, entire, pink to deep pink, spotted red in lower half, usually blotched maroon at base and pale green near tip, nectaries with fleshy excrescence; inner perianth seg. 2.5–4×1.3cm, always blotched; fil. to 1.5cm, maroon tipped yellow, anth. to 6mm; style to 1.3mm. Fr. cylindric, 2×2cm. Summer. W China (Yunnan, Sichuan).

N.farreri (W.E. Evans) R. Harrow.
To 1m. Bulb ellipsoid or subspherical, to 4cm. Lvs whorled, 3.5×2cm, linear to lanceolate, acuminate, dark green above, paler beneath. Fls to 20, saucer-shaped, drooping at first, later flattened and upright or horizontal, white to pink; outer perianth seg. elliptic to ovate, 2.5–5.5×1–2.5cm, entire, blotched dark maroon at base with finer spots toward centre; inner perianth seg. ovate to broadly ovate, 2.5–5.5×1.5–3.5cm, entire or subserrate, maroon at base with a pale green patch toward centre and a few finer blotches; nectaries grooved; fil. to 11mm, purple, anth. to 6mm; style to 10mm. NE Burma.

N.×finlayorum Synge. (*N.farreri* × *N.pardanthina*.)
Garden hybrid to 70cm. Lvs 4–12 per whorl. Fls 2–7, white to pink; perianth seg. outspread, usually red-maroon spotted only in lower half, occasionally spotted throughout, entire to subserrate.

N.mairei Lév. See *N.pardanthina*.

N.meleagrina Franch.
To 85cm. Bulb ovoid, to 3.5cm. Lvs in 3–6 whorls, lanceolate, acuminate, to 13×3cm, dark green above, paler beneath, margins sometimes slightly hispid. Fls nodding, flattened, to 9.5cm diam., white, occasionally flecked pink below, blotched purple above; outer perianth seg. to 5.5cm, blotched purple at base; inner perianth seg. to 6cm, entire to fimbriate, purple at base; gynoecium sometimes absent. W China (Yunnan, SE Xizang).

N.nana Wils. See *Lilium nanum*.

N.× notabilis Sealy. (*N.saluenensis* × *N.farreri*.)
Garden hybrid to 42cm. Bulb ovoid, to 2.5cm. Lvs scattered, elliptic to ovate, acute, 4–5×1–3cm, lustrous green above, paler beneath. Fls nodding, saucer-shaped, to 6cm diam., pink to mauve, spotted maroon, usually in lower half; outer perianth seg. with a deep crimson basal blotch and smaller markings above this; inner perianth seg. similar to outer seg. in colour; nectaries with black markings; stamens purple, light yellow at apex, to 12mm; anth. to 6mm; style to 12mm.

N.oxypetalum Royle. See *Lilium oxypetalum*.

N.pardanthina Franch. (*N.mairei* Lév.).
To 90cm. Bulb ovoid, to 3cm. Lvs whorled, sessile, elliptic to lanceolate, 2.5–10.5×0.5–2.5cm. Fls 1–24, nodding to erect, flattened, to 8.5cm diam.; outer perianth seg. 2.5–4.5×1.5–2.5cm, entire, white to pink, blotched purple, dark maroon at base; inner perianth seg. 2.5–4.5×2.5–3.5cm, blotches more numerous than in outer seg., apex fimbriate; fil. to 8mm, purple, anth. to 4mm, red-maroon; style to 1cm. Fr. cylindric, 2.5–3×2–2.5cm, brown. W China (Yunnan, Sichuan). f. *punctulata* Sealy. Perianth seg. less densely spotted, spots only at base, margins shallow-fimbriate to subscrrate. W China (W Yunnan).

N.saluenensis Balf. f.
To 85cm high. Bulb ovoid, to 3cm. Lvs scattered along stem, sessile, elliptic to elliptic-oblong, 2–4cm long, dark green above, pale green beneath, veins distinct. Fls 2–5, horizontal or drooping, saucer-shaped, to 6.5cm diam.; outer perianth seg. 3.5–4.5×1.5–2.5cm, entire, rose pink, paler in lower part, dark maroon patch at base with small spots over lower half; inner perianth seg. 4–4.5×1.5–2.5cm, entire; fil. to 11mm, purple, anth. to 8mm, green-blue; style to 6mm. W China (Yunnan, SE Xizang), NE Burma.

N.synaptica Sealy.
Similar to *N.saluenensis*. Fls white, tinted purple, spotted dark maroon throughout; perianth seg. with a dark purple, yellow-fringed, basal blotch. India (Assam).

Nomocharis (a) *N.aperta* flowering stem (a1) stigma and style (a1) petal (b) *N.meleagrina* inner petal (c) *N.farreri* flowering stem (c1) inner petal (c2) stamen and style (d) *N.×finlayorum* (3) *N.pardanthina* f. *punctulata* inner petal (f) *N.pardanthina* flowering stem (f1) inner petal (f2) stamen (f3) stigma (g) *N.×notabilis* flowering stem (h) *N.saluenensis* inner petal (h1) stigma (h2) stamen

Notholirion Wallich ex Boiss. (From Gk *nothos*, false, and *leirion*, lily; these plants have been placed in both *Lilium* and *Fritillaria* but are now considered separate from both.) Liliaceae (Liliaceae). 4 species of bulbous perennials. Bulb composed of pale, fleshy scales enclosed in a thin, brown, ribbed tunic formed from the bases of the previous year's leaves, bulbiliferous. Leaves produced in autumn and winter, basal and cauline, linear-lanceolate. Racemes 1–30-flowered, subtended by a short, linear bract; flowers trumpet-shaped to spreading, red, pink or pale purple, sometimes tipped green; perianth segments 6, free, tips recurved, occasionally spotted green; stamens 6, anthers versatile; stigma distinctly trifid. Fruit a 3-chambered capsule; seeds small, wingless. Summer. Afghanistan to W China. Z7.

CULTIVATION Grown for their delicate, trumpet-shaped flowers, carried on slender stems. *N.thomsonianum*, found in scrub and rocky habitats to altitudes of 2300m/7475ft in the western Himalaya, is prone to frost damage, since it leafs up early in the season. For this reason it is more commonly cultivated in cool temperate zones in large containers in the cool glasshouse. Use a potting mix of rich woodland soil with silver sand and leaf-mould; grow in bright, filtered light and water plentifully when in full growth. Withold water when dormant but keep just sufficiently moist to avoid desiccation. *N.macrophyllum, N.campanulatum* and *N.bulbuliferum*, which come into growth later, are more hardy and appear to grow better where summers are reasonably cool. Grow in well-drained, humus-rich soils in light, dappled shade. Seed, which has epigeal germination, is the best means of increase, despite the plentiful production of bulbils; see*Lilium*.

N.bulbuliferum (Lingl.) Stearn (*N.hyacinthinum* (Wils.) Stapf).
To 1.5m. Lvs 7–13, to 45×1cm. Fls horizontal, trumpet-shaped, to 4cm, pale lilac; perianth seg. recurved, spreading, the upper 3 ascending, 2 horizontally outspread, 1 descending, 2–4×1–1.5cm, tipped green. Nepal to W China.

N.campanulatum Cotton & Stearn.
To 80cm. Lvs 8–13, to 30cm. Fls to 20, pendulous, to 5cm, crimson to maroon; perianth seg. tipped green. N Burma, W China (Xizang, Yunnan).

N.hyacinthinum (Wils.) Stapf. See *N.bulbuliferum*.

N.macrophyllum (D. Don) Boiss.
To 40cm. Stems flimsy. Lvs 3–5 linear-lanceolate, to 45×2.5cm. Fls 1–7, horizontal to nodding, trumpet-shaped, to 5cm, pale pink to light mauve throughout; perianth seg. widespread. Himalaya.

N.thomsonianum (Royle) Stapf.
To 1m. Lvs 8–12, to 45×2cm. Fls 10–30, horizontal to ascending, trumpet-shaped, to 6.5cm, pale mauve; perianth seg. reflexed at tips, 5–6.5×0.5cm. W Himalaya, Afghanistan.

Nothoscordum Kunth (From Gk *nothos*, false, and *skorodon*, garlic.) FALSE GARLIC; GRACE GARLIC. Liliaceae (Alliaceae). 20 species of herbaceous perennials, resembling *Allium* but lacking characteristic odour. Bulbs tunicate. Leaves basal. Flowers numerous in loose umbels; spathe 1, 2-lobed; tepals 6, persistent, united at base, free at apex; ovary superior, cells with several ovules, style terminal. Fruit a 3-celled capsule; seeds black, angular. Americas.

CULTIVATION *Nothoscordum* spp. usually have white flowers, sometimes with a marked brown line running down each petal. *N.bivalve* is non-invasive and will grow in damp exposed places, tolerating temperatures to –10°C/14°F. *N.gracile* has deliciously scented flowers above straggling glaucous foliage and may be considered one of the most persistent and invasive weeds introduced to British gardens. It produces many tiny offset bulbils which fall off into the soil when the bulb is dug up; it also provides copious fertile seed which germinates readily in the poorest of soils. Grow in semi-wild, remote areas of the garden where few other species will grow and where its inevitable spread will not cause nuisance.

N.bivalve (L.) Britt. (*N.striatum* (Jacq.) Kunth; *Allium striatum* Jacq.).
To 20cm. Lvs 3–4, to 4mm wide. Fls 4–8, almost stellate, tepals white to yellow, with a green midrib, lanceolate, spreading widely, united below for a very short distance. Spring. S US. Z5.

N.fragrans (Vent.) Kunth. See *N.gracile*.

N.gracile (Ait.) Stearn (*Allium gracile* Ait.; *N.fragrans* (Vent.) Kunth; *Allium fragrans* Vent.).
30–75cm; bulbs ovoid, tunics membranous. Lvs 6–8, 20–40cm×7mm+. Fls 8–15, fragrant, funnel-shaped; tepals 9–15mm, white to lilac, streaked brown and pink below, midrib pink or mauve, obtuse, united in a short tube, ascending. Fr. 6–10mm. Spring–summer. S America, Mexico. Z7.

Olsynium Raf. (From Gk meaning hardly united, referring to the stamens.) Iridaceae. About 12 species of perennial herbs with fibrous roots closely related to *Sisyrinchium*. Leaves mostly basal, usually linear or lanceolate. Flowers enclosed in spathes; perianth bell-shaped; tepals equal, 6; stamens joined only at base; style with 3 short branches. Fruit a capsule; seeds brown, seeds brown, more or less angular. N & S America. Z9.

CULTIVATION Graceful perennials for cool, semi-shaded positions in peat pockets on the rock garden or peat bed. They will survive frosts to –20°C/4°F and become dormant in late spring, but nonetheless require permanent moisture.

O.biflorum (Thunb.) Goldbl. (*Phaiophleps biflora* (Thunb.) R. Fost.; *Synphyostemon biflorus* (Thunb.) Dusén; *Synphyostemon narcissoides* (Cav.) Miers ex Klatt).
Stem 10–70cm. Basal lvs 1–5, 4–22cm×1–2.5mm, linear, cauline lvs 1–3. Infl. 2–7-fld; fls scented, cream, striped with maroon; tube 7–20mm, cylindrical to cup-shaped; tepals 10–18×5–7.5mm, oblong-ovate. Spring. Patagonia.

O.douglasii (A. Dietr.) E. Bickn. (*O.grandiflorum* (Douglas ex Lindl.) Raf.; *O.inflatum* Suksd.; *Sisyrinchium douglasii* A. Dietr.; *Sisyrinchium grandiflorum* Douglas; *Sisyrinchium inflatum* (Suksd.) St. John). GRASS WIDOW; PURPLE-EYED GRASS.
Stems 15–30cm high, flattened but not winged. Basal lvs bract-like, stem lvs to 1cm. Spathes terminal, 2–3-fld; fls pendent, bell-shaped, 15–20mm, wine-red, purple-pink or white; tepals oblong-obovate. Western N America.

O.filifolium (Gaudich.) Goldbl. (*Sisyrinchium filifolium* Gaudich.).
Stem 15–20cm; lvs rush-like. Fls erect, white with red-purple lines. Spring. Falkland Is.

O.grandiflorum (Douglas ex Lindl.) Raf. See *O.douglasii*.
O.inflatum Suksd. See *O.douglasii*.

Ornithogalum L. (Name used by Dioscorides, from Gk *ornis*, bird, and *gala*, milk.) Liliaceae (Hyacinthaceae). Some 80 species of bulbous perennial herbs. Bulbs usually subterranean, globose, tunics white or brown, rarely part-exposed, green and fleshy. Leaves in a rosette, linear to lanceolate or obovate, sometimes with a silver-white median stripe above, margins smooth or hairy. Inflorescence a scapose raceme or corymb, pyramidal to subcylindric, 2- to many-flowered; bracts usually conspicuous; tepals 6, equal or unequal in 2 distinct whorls, white, rarely yellow, orange or red, outside usually marked with a green stripe, usually widely spreading, rarely erect; stamens 6, filaments flattened, often broadened at base, sometimes winged; ovary superior, cylindric to spherical, yellow-green or purple-black; style terminal. Fruit a trilocular, many-seeded capsule. S Africa, Mediterranean.

CULTIVATION *Ornithogalum* has two main centres of distribution, in South Africa and around the Mediterranean, but includes a number of more northerly European natives which are robust and cold-hardy in cultivation, some of which may become invasive where conditions suit, such as *O.umbellatum* and *O.nutans*. The South African species are generally frost-tender and are planted temporarily in the summer borders of cool temperate gardens or grown in pots in the cool glasshouse. They include a number of species that are extremely valuable as long-lived cut flowers, especially *O.thyrsoides* which, if arranged when in bud, may last for several weeks in a cool room.

Vigorous species like *O.nutans*, *O.umbellatum* and *O.montanum* are suitable for naturalizing in short turf or thin grass or beneath shrubs. Taller species such as *O.pyrenaicum* and *O.nutans* also suited to the wild garden or other naturalistic plantings. The hardiest species, *O.umbellatum* and *O.pyrenaicum*, withstand temperatures to between –15 and –20°C/5 of to –4°F; *O.montanum*, *O.nutans* and *O.orthophyllum* are almost as tolerant, surviving temperatures at the warmer end of this range. *O.pyramidale*, *O.narbonense*, *O.oligophyllum* are hardy where temperatures seldom fall below –10°C/14°F. The beautiful *O.arabicum*, once widely cultivated as a cut flower crop, suits warm sunny borders, but where temperatures fall much below freezing are more satisfactory in containers of medium-fertility, loam-based mix in the cold glasshouse.

Grow in any moderately fertile, well-drained soil in sun; *O.nutans* and *O.umbellatum* tolerate partial shade. Propagate by seed sown when ripe in the cold frame; sown thinly they can remain *in situ* during their first summer dormancy and may be planted out as small bulbs form in their second or third year. Increase also by offsets when dormant.

O.apertum (Verdoorn) Oberm.
Lvs 10–20, glaucous, flat, narrow, tightly spiralled and coiled. Scape to 20cm, 8–20-fld; tepals white or yellow, with broad green central band. S Africa (Namaqualand, SW Cape Province). Z9.

O.arabicum L. (*O.corymbosum* Ruiz & Pav.).
Bulb subterranean, broadly ovoid, bearing numerous bulblets. Lvs to 60×2.5cm, 5–8, broadly linear, more or less erect, dark green, thickly textured. Scape 30–80cm; raceme cylindric to subspherical, 6–25-fld, fls fragrant; tepals 1.5–3.2cm, white or cream, withering but not reflexing in fruit; fil. broadening below; ovary black or purple-black. Mediterranean. cf. *O.saundersiae*. The name *O.corymbosum* or var. *corymbosum* is usually applied to exceptionally floriferous specimens, bearing larger fls in corymbose racemes; the hardiness and vigour of such plants is often superior. Z9.

O.aurantiacum Bak. See *O.multifolium*.
O.aureum Curtis. See *O.dubium*.
O.balansae Boiss. See *O.oligophyllum*.
O.caudatum Ait. See *O.longibracteatum*.

O.conicum Jacq. (*O.lacteum* Jacq.).
Very similar to *O.thyrsoides* but flowering stems 40–100cm, lvs with smooth margins, fil. barely expanded at base. Early spring. S Africa (Cape Province). Z9.

O.corymbosum Ruiz & Pav. See *O.arabicum*.
O.dichotomum Labill. See *Thysanotus dichotomus*.

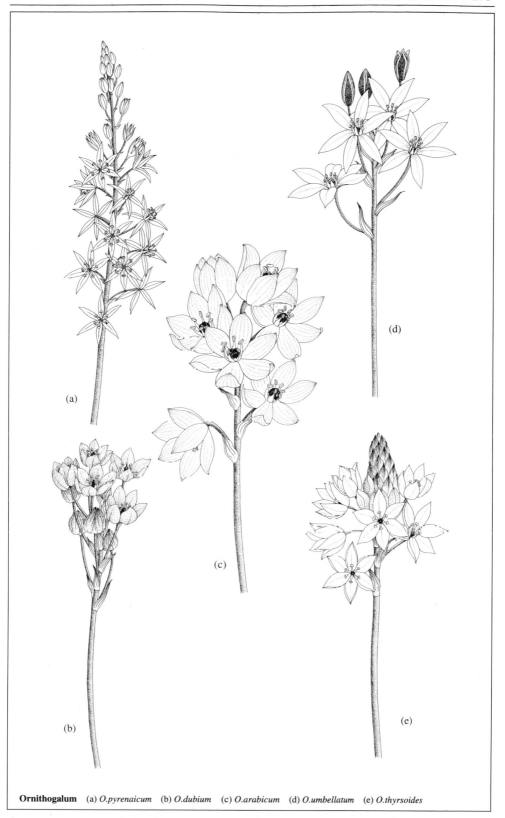

Ornithogalum   (a) *O.pyrenaicum*   (b) *O.dubium*   (c) *O.arabicum*   (d) *O.umbellatum*   (e) *O.thyrsoides*

O.dubium Houtt. (*O.miniatum* Jacq.; *O.aureum* Curtis).
Bulb subterranean. Lvs to 10×2cm, 3–8, lanceolate to ovate-lanceolate, yellow-green, margins hairy. Scape to 30cm; raceme crowded, corymbose, cylindric to subspherical, 20+-fld; tepals 1.2cm, orange, red, yellow or, rarely, white, often tinged green or brown at base within; ovary yellow-green. Winter–spring. S Africa (Cape Province). Z9.

O.flavescens Lam. See *O.pyrenaicum*.
O.lacteum Jacq. See *O.conicum*.

O.longibracteatum Jacq. (*O.caudatum* Ait.). SEA ONION; FALSE SEA ONION; GERMAN ONION.
Bulb with upper part exposed; tunics green and fleshy, bearing many bulblets. Lvs to 60×4cm, 8–12, strap-shaped, long-acuminate fleshy, flaccid, pale green. Scapes 1–1.5m; raceme triangular to cylindric, 60–300-fld; bracts far exceeding fls; tepals to 9mm, white, outside with a green stripe; fil. broadening toward base; ovary yellow-green. S Africa (Cape Province, Natal). Z9.

O.maculatum Jacq. SNAKE FLOWER.
Lvs to 15cm, fleshy, blue-green. Scape 10–50cm, usually *c*15cm; infl. to 8-fld; tepals yellow or orange, but outer whorl often with tips blotched black or brown. Spring. S Africa (SW Cape). Z9.

O.miniatum Jacq. See *O.dubium*.

O.montanum Cyr.
Bulb to 2.5cm diam., ovoid, subterranean, tunics usually brown. Lvs linear, 10–15cm, several, pale green usually with a white line above. Scape to 60cm; raceme to 10cm broad, somewhat corymbose, cylindric, 10–20-fld, fls drooping; tepals 2–3cm, not widely spreading, translucent white, outside with a broad green stripe; fil. of inner 3 stamens winged; ovary green, shorter than style. Europe (Balkans, Italy), SW Asia. Z6.

O.multifolium Bak. (*O.aurantiacum* Bak.).
Bulb *c*1.25cm diam. Lvs to 7cm, *c*10, slender, terete, glabrous, somewhat twisted. Scape to 25cm, usually *c*15cm; infl. 5–10-fld; fls fragrant, bright yellow to orange yellow. Spring. S Africa (Cape Peninsula).

O.narbonense L.
Lvs to 90×1.25cm, linear. Scape to 90cm; fls to 5cm diam. in loose, many-fld racemes; tepals keeled, milk white, midvein green. cf. *O.pyramidale*. Spring. Mediterranean, Caucasus, NW Iran. Z7.

O.nutans L.
Bulb to 4cm diam., ovoid, subterranean, bulblets numerous. Lvs 30–40cm, lorate, rather limp, several, pale green, with a white line above. Scapes to 60cm; raceme cylindric, 1-sided, 10–20-fld; fls nodding; tepals 2–3cm, translucent, white, broadly striped green outside, not widely spreading; fil. of at least 3 inner stamens winged, wings terminating in teeth at either side of anth.; ovary green; style shorter than ovary. Spring. Europe, SW Asia, naturalised in E US. Z6.

O.oligophyllum Clarke (*O.balansae* Boiss.).
Bulb subterranean. Lvs to 15cm, linear-lanceolate to narrowly obovate, broad and blunt at apex, somewhat glaucous.

Racemes corymbose, 2–5-fld; tepals 1–1.6cm, white to ivory edged pure white with a broad yellow-green stripe outside; pedicels 1–3cm, erect to spreading in fruit. Spring. Balkans, Turkey, republic of Georgia. Z6.

O.orthophyllum Ten. (*O.tenuifolium* Guss.).
Similar to *O.umbellatum* but not producing bulblets; pedicels spreading to ascending in fruit, the lower 2–3.5cm. Spring. S & C Europe to N Iran. Z6.

O.pruinosum F.M. Leighton. CHINCHERINCHEE.
Lvs to 17cm, to 6, deep blue-green. Scape to 35cm, occasionally to 60cm; infl. a dense, many-fld spike, usually 35cm; fls white, fragrant. S Africa (Namaqualand, SW Cape Province). Z9.

O.pyramidale L.
Bulb to 3.7cm diam., ovoid, subterranean. Lvs to 45×1.25cm, glossy green, glaucous, withering before flowering ends. Scape 30–120cm; raceme cylindric to pyramidal, 30–50-fld; tepals 1.1–1.5cm, translucent white with a green stripe outside; ovary green; style shorter than ovary, base thickened and conical. Spring. C Europe, Balkans. cf. *O.narbonense*. 6.

O.pyrenaicum L. (*O.flavescens* Lam.). BATH ASPARAGUS; PRUSSIAN ASPARAGUS; STAR OF BETHLEHEM.
Close to *O.pyramidale* but smaller and more delicate; tepals 9–13mm, pale yellow with a narrow green stripe outside; style longer than ovary. Spring. Europe, W & S Turkey, Caucasus. Z6.

O.saundersiae Bak. GIANT CHINCHERINCHEE.
Bulb large, globose, subterranean. Lvs 60×5cm, 6–8, erect to flaccid, lorate, dark green and glossy above. Scape 30–100cm; raceme corymbose, pyramidal, many-fld; pedicels long; tepals 1–1.5cm, white or cream; fil. conspicuously broadened below; ovary black or green-black, persistent and reflexed in fr. Early spring. S Africa (E Transvaal, Natal, Swaziland) cf. *O.arabicum*. Z9.

O.tenuifolium Guss. See *O.orthophyllum*.

O.thyrsoides Jacq. CHINCHERINCHEE; WONDER FLOWER.
Bulb subterranean. Lvs to 30×5cm, 6–12, linear to narrow-lanceolate, ascending, withering before flowering ends, margins ciliate. Raceme corymbose, pyramidal to subspherical, many-fld; fls very long-lasting; tepals 1–2cm, translucent white to ivory tinted bronze or green at base; fil. of inner stamens broadly expanded at base; ovary yellow-green; style as long as ovary. Spring–early summer. S Africa (Cape Province). 'Album': fls snow white, with a somewhat darker 'eye' crowded in showy raceme. 'Aureum': fls topaz to golden. 'Flavescens': fls golden. 'Flavissimum': fls golden to ochre. Z9.

O.umbellatum L. STAR OF BETHLEHEM.
Bulb to 3.25cm diam., subglobose, subterranean, bulblets numerous. Lvs to 30×8cm, several, linear, tapering to apex, with a broad white line on midvein. Raceme broad corymbose, 6–20-fld; tepals 1.5–2.2cm, lustrous pure white with a green stripe outside; pedicels becoming horizontal, rigid in fruit, the lower 5–9cm. Spring. Europe, N Africa, Middle East. Z5.

Oxalis L. (From Gk *oxys*, acid, referring to the sour taste of leaves.) SORREL; SHAMROCK. Oxalidaceae. 800 species of annual or perennial, stemmed or stemless herbs and shrubs, often with tuberous or bulbous underground parts; very rarely aquatic plants. Leaves radical or cauline, palmate; leaflets usually 3, sometimes more or phyllodic, often folding down at night; stipules adnate to petiole bases or absent. Flowers with a tristylic, heteromorphic arrangement of parts, on axillary peduncles; often in cymes or contractions of this to umbellate, 1- to many-flowered; bracteoles in pairs subtending pedicels and cyme branches, many and crowded in umbellate inflorescences; pedicels articulate below calyx and/or their base; petals usually partly fused at base, white, pink, red or yellow, stamens 10 in two whorls of 5, filaments fused in a tube; carpels 5, fused, styles 5, free. Fruit a dehiscent capsule; seed in a fleshy aril which ejects the seed from locule when ripe. Cosmopolitan but centres of diversity in S Africa and S America.

CULTIVATION   Although a number of species are potential weeds (e.g. *O.articulata, O.corniculata, O.corymbosa, O.exilis, O.latifolia* and *O.pes-caprae*) that spread by means of seed and underground bulbils and may prove difficult to eradicate, *Oxalis* includes a number of beautiful ornamentals for a diversity of situations in the garden. Most species are low and spreading, the flowers and sometimes the leaves close up at night or in shade. Relatively few are reliably frost-hardy, but these include *O.adenophylla* and *O.enneaphylla* (particularly valued for their neatly pleated glaucous foliage, suited to the sunny raised bed and large trough or for well-drained, humus-rich, sandy niches on the rock garden), *O.magellanica* and *O.depressa* (for the well-drained interstices of paving or partially shaded bases of walls and rockwork), *O.acetosella, O.oregana* and *O.violacea* (for naturalizing in the wild and woodland garden in moisture-retentive, humus-rich soils with shade or dappled sunlight). *O.corniculata* var. *atropurpurea* is hardy and attractively bronzed but should be used only where self-sown seedlings will not cause nuisance.

Most of these will tolerate temperatures as low as −15°C/5°F, and thrive in temperate climates where summers are relatively cool, or where they can be given shade from the hottest sun in summer. Some of the annuals, including *O.rosea* and *O.valdiviensis*, are suitable for hanging baskets, window boxes and other containers, requiring a moderately fertile and retentive potting mix in sun or part shade. Some from the Cape and temperate South America may tolerate a few degrees of short-loved frost but are most safely grown in the alpine house in zones that experience severe or prolonged frosts; in positions where the root is protected from severe cold, as in rock or pavement crevices, they may re-emerge in spring. These include *O.bowiei, O.hirta, O.laciniata, O.latifolia, O.lobata, O.purpurata* and *O.tetraphylla*; all are easily grown in well-crocked pans or pots in a gritty, leafy alpine mix. Most other species from these regions are suitable for outdoor cultivation only in warm, essentially frost-free climates, otherwise requiring slightly warmer glasshouse conditions, among them the excellent purple-leaved houseplant *O.triangularis*. The bulbous/tuberous species need a sunny position in pots of moderate fertility, loam-based mix with additional sharp sand and leafmould; maintain good ventilation, with a minimum temperature in the range 7–10°C/45–50°F. Liquid feed weekly and water moderately when in growth, allowing the medium to dry partially between waterings. Keep cool, dry and frost-free when dormant and repot annually as growth resumes, in late winter for spring-blooming bulbous types, in early spring for summer-flowerers and in late summer for those that bloom in autumn; repot herbaceous species in spring.

Propagate by ripe seed, division, or offsets. Soft-stemmed species may be increased by cuttings in sand in a shaded closed case with gentle bottom heat, woody species by semi-ripe cuttings in similar conditions, rooting is enhanced by use of rooting hormone.

O.acetosella L. WOOD-SORREL; CUCKOO BREAD; ALLELUIA.
Creeping perenn., 3–12cm; rhiz. slender, scaly, pale green. Lvs trifoliate, petioles erect to 8cm; leaflets to 1.5×2cm, obcordate, pale green, sparsely hairy. Fls solitary, borne slightly above the lvs, 1.5–2cm across; pet. white, veined purple. Fr. 3–4mm, ovoid to spherical. Spring. N temperate America, Europe and Asia. var. *purpurascens* Mart. ('Rosea', 'Rubra'). Fls rose with purple veining. Z3.

O.adenophylla Gillies. SAUER KLEE.
Stemless perenn., 10–15cm, from a brown, scale-covered, tuberous base. Lvs numerous, erect to spreading; petioles 5–12cm, red-brown; leaflets c6×6mm, 9–22, obcordate, silver-grey, glabrous. Peduncles as long as lvs, 1–3-fld; fls c2.5cm across, lilac-pink to violet with darker veins and 5 purple spots in the white throat; sep. without orange calli. Late spring–early summer. Chile, W Argentina (Andes). 'Minima': lvs small. Z5.

O.ambigua A.Rich.
4–12cm. Lvs to 2.5cm, tufted; petioles ciliate; leaflets 3, to 0.75cm obselloid, blue green flecked purple, ciliate. Fls solitary, to 1.5cm diam., white usually with yellow in throat and exterior tinted pink. Summer. S Africa. Z9.

O.amplifolia (Trel.) Knuth. See *O.drummondii*.

O.articulata Savigny (*O.floribunda* Lehm.).
Stemless perenn. to 10–40cm; rhiz. to 14×2cm, little-branched, dark brown, tuberous, semi-woody, glabrous

becoming cylindrical with articulations. Lvs 6–25cm, numerous, basal, petioles erect to sprawling, glabrous or with adpressed hairs; leaflets 3, 10–25×20–35mm, obcordate, green usually with punctate margin below, glabrous above, hairy beneath. Peduncles very numerous, to 40cm, erect to spreading; infl. a 5–10-fld umbellate cyme held well above the lvs; fls to 2cm across, bright mauve pink; sep. with 2 orange apical calli. Summer–autumn. Paraguay. var. *hirsuta* Progel. Lvs hairy above. 'Alba' (*O.floribunda* var. *alba* Nichols.): fls white. Z8.

O.asinina Jacq. See *O.fabaefolia*.

O.bifida Thunb. (*O.filicaulis* Jacq.).
Perenn. with a weak, erect or procumbent, branched stem to 30cm; bulb scaly. Petioles slender, 1.5–4cm, congested at the stem apices; leaflets 3, 5–6×5–6mm, narrowly obcordate, divided to the middle or more, green, punctate with black marginal spots, glabrous above, sparsely hairy beneath. Fls solitary on peduncles 2.5–8cm long, c12mm across, purple-red with a yellow-green throat; sep. with purple-black apical calli. Spring–summer. S Africa (Cape Province). Z9.

O.binervis Reg. See *O.latifolia*.
O.bipunctata Graham. See *O.corymbosa*.
O.bowieana Lodd. See *O.bowiei*.

O.bowiei Lindl. (*O.bowieana* Lodd.; *O.purpurata* var. *bowiei* (Lindl.) Sonder; *O.floribunda* Lehm. (misapplied)).
Stemless perenn., 20–30cm with glandular hairs on the peti-

oles, peduncles and cal. Bulb elongate with a smooth brown tunic covering pale brown flesh inside, and with a long, white, fleshy, contractile root. Petioles 5–15cm, stout, erect; leaflets 3, to 5×5cm, rounded to broadly obcordate, shallowly notched, rather thick and leathery, green, sometimes purple beneath, more or less glabrous above, more densely hairy beneath. Peduncles 10–30cm, erect, bearing 3–12-fld umbels, fls 3–4cm across, bright rose-red to pink, with a yellow-green throat; sep. with no calli. Summer–autumn. S Africa (Cape Province). Z8.

O.caprina L. GOAT'S-FOOT; WOOD-SORREL.
Nearly stemless, or very short-stemmed, almost hairless perenn., 15–20cm. Bulb scaly with a slender vertical rhiz. Lvs basal or at stem apex; petioles 2–5cm, erect to spreading; leaflets 3, 5–10×5–15mm, widely triangular in outline, deeply divided to about the middle, lobes obovate. Peduncles to 20cm, longer than petioles, weak, bearing 2–4-fld umbels; fls pale violet, rarely white, with pale green throat; sep. with 2 orange apical calli. Spring–early summer. S Africa (Cape Province). Z9.

O.cathariensis N.E. Br. See *O.regnellii*.
O.cernua Thunb. See *O.pes-caprae*.
O.convexula Jacq. See *O.depressa*.

O.corniculata L. (*O.repens* Thunb.). PROCUMBENT YELLOW SORREL; CREEPING YELLOW OXALIS; CREEPING OXALIS.
Creeping, much-branched, mat-forming, short-lived perenn., with many prostrate to ascending, slender stems 10–30cm long, from a short, vertical taproot. Lvs numerous along stem, petioles erect, 1–8cm, somewhat hairy, with fused rectangular stipules; leaflets 3, 5–15×8–20mm, obcordate, green, usually glabrous above and hairy beneath. Peduncles axillary, 1–10cm, bearing 2–6-fld umbels; flowers c1cm across, light yellow, sometimes with a red throat; sep. without calli. Fr. cylindrical, 12–15mm long, erect on deflexed pedicels. Spring–autumn. Cosmopolitan weed, origin unknown. var. *atropurpurea* Planch. (var. *purpurata* Parl.; *O.tropaeoloides* Schlechter). Foliage purple-bronze and all parts suffused with purple. var. *villosa* (Bieb.) Hohen. Lvs hairy above and beneath. Z5.

O.corniculata L. (misapplied). See *O.dillenii*.
O.corniculata var. *microphylla* Hook. See *O.exilis*.
O.corniculata var. *purpurata* Parl. See *O.corniculata* var. *atropurpurea*.

O.corymbosa DC. (*O.bipunctata* Graham; *O.martiana* Zucc.; *O.debilis* Kunth).
Stemless perenn., 15–40cm, with round bulb producing numerous loosely scaly, sessile bulbils with 3 nerves per bulb scale. Petioles 10–35cm, erect to spreading, with white patent hairs 0.5–2.5mm long; leaflets 3, 25–45×30–62mm, broadly obcordate, rounded, green, with dark spots beneath, sparsely hairy. Peduncles 15–40cm, erect, with white patent hairs as petioles; infl. a 8–15-fld, irregularly branched cyme; fls c1.5cm across, red to purple with darker veins and a white throat; sep. with 2 apical calli. Spring–early summer. S America (Brazil, Argentina). 'Aureo-reticulata': lvs with yellow veining, probably virus-induced. Z9.

O.crenata Jacq. See *O.tuberosa*.
O.debilis Kunth. See *O.corymbosa*.
O.deppei Lodd. See *O.tetraphylla*.
O.deppei Lodd. (misapplied). See *O.tuberosa*.

O.depressa Ecklon & Zeyh. (*O.convexula* Jacq.; *O.inops* Ecklon & Zeyh.).
Bulbous, nearly stemless perenn., 4–12cm, with an underground, slender, vertical rhiz. 5cm long or more, from bulb to soil surface. Petioles 8–20mm, glabrous, erect to spreading in a crown at soil surface; leaflets 3, 3–10×5–16mm, rounded to triangular-ovate, grey-green, sometimes dark-spotted, glabrous or sparsely hairy. Peduncles 1–10cm, erect; fls solitary held above the leaves, 1.5–2cm across, bright pink to rose-violet, with a yellow throat; purple and white forms are known; sep. without calli. Summer. S Africa (Cape Province). Z5.

O.drummondii A. Gray (*O.vespertilionis* Torr. & A. Gray; *O.amplifolia* (Trel.) Knuth).

Bulbous, stemless perenn. to 20cm or more, bulb of open, papery, 3-nerved scales. Petioles 5–16cm, erect to spreading, glabrous; leaflets 3, V-shaped, deeply lobed to up to four-fifths of their length, lobes to 30×5mm. Infl. a 3–10-fld umbel held well above the lvs; fls c2cm across, purple; sep. with fused red apical calli. A variable species. Spring–summer. Mexico. Z9.

O.elongata Jacq. See *O.versicolor*.

O.engleriana Schlechter.
Deciduous, 8–18cm, similar in habit to *O.gracilis*, but with still narrower stem and lvs in strictly terminal rosettes with to 6 finger-like leaflets. Fls to 1.5cm diam., rose-pink. S Africa. Z9.

O.enneaphylla Cav. SCURVY GRASS.
Stemless perenn. to 14cm, with slender, creeping, horizontal rhiz. 5×2cm, covered in thick white scales with bulbils in their axils. Petioles 1.5–8cm, erect, occasionally hairy; leaflets 9–20, 4–12×2–8mm, obcordate, partially folded upwards, somewhat fleshy, glaucous blue, shortly hairy; fls solitary, held just above lvs, c2cm across, white to red, fragrant; sep. without calli. Spring–summer. Falkland Is., Patagonia. 'Alba': fls white. 'Ione Hecker' (*O.enneaphylla* × *O.laciniata*): lvs with rather narrower seg. and deeper green; fls large, to 3cm across, vivid blue at edge darkening to dark purple at centre. 'Minutifolia': dwarf form less than 5cm high. 'Rosea': to 6cm, fls rose-pink. 'Rubra': fls red. Z6.

O.enneaphylla var. *patagonica* (Speg.) Skottsb. See *O.patagonica*.
O.europaea Jordan. See *O.stricta*.

O.exilis A. Cunn. (*O.corniculata* var. *microphylla* Hook.).
Very similar to a small form of *O.corniculata*, to 4cm tall and stems to 15cm long. Petioles 6–13mm; leaflets 3–5×3–7mm, green. Fls solitary. Fr. 5–8×3mm, globose-cylindrical, sparsely hairy. Spring–summer. Australia, New Zealand. Z8.

O.fabaefolia Jacq. (*O.asinina* Jacq.).
Glabrous, bulbous, stemless perenn. to 15cm tall; bulb to 4cm, ovoid; rhiz. long, brown, with membranous scales, the upper large and prominent. Petioles 1.5–10cm, with leaf-like wings orbicular to ligulate in outline; leaflets 2–5, 1.5–5cm, ovate to obovate or oblanceolate, rather thick with cartilaginous margin. Peduncles 1–7cm, erect; fls solitary, to 3cm across, yellow, white or mauve; sep. with brown apical calli. Summer–autumn. S Africa. Z9.

O.filicaulis Jacq. See *O.bifida*.
O.floribunda Lehm. See *O.articulata*.
O.floribunda Lehm. (misapplied). See *O.bowiei*.
O.floribunda Lehm. (misapplied). See *O.lasiandra*.
O.floribunda Lehm. (misapplied). See *O.rosea*.
O.floribunda Lehm. (misapplied). See *O.rubra*.
O.floribunda var. *alba* Nichols. See *O.articulata* var. *hirsuta* 'Alba'.
O.fulgida Lindl. See *O.hirta* var. fulgida.

O.furcillata Salter.
Deciduous, 6–8cm. Similar in habit to *O.gracilis*, but with white, hairy stems and congested lvs with shorter petioles and strongly cleft leaflets. Fls to 2cm diam., solitary, white, yellow in throat. Summer. S Africa. Z9.

O.gracilis Eckl. & Zeyh.
Deciduous perenn., 50–30cm. Stems simple, slender, bronze, arising from bulb, flimsy. Lvs in remote of strictly terminal whorls, amber-red in fall; petioles to 2cm, wiry; leaflets. 3, to 1cm, narrow, folded, cleft. Fls to 1.5cm diam., solitary or clustered, salmon pink to apricot. Summer. S Africa. Z9. cf. *O.polyphylla*.

O.grandiflora Jacq. See *O.purpurea*.

O.hirta L. (*O.hirtella* Jacq.; *O.multiflora* Jacq.).
Erect, decumbent or trailing, bulbous perenn.; stems to 30cm, branching above; bulbs to 15mm diam., small, round, each producing one deciduous stem; all parts of plant hairy. Lvs almost sessile; leaflets 3, 10–15×1.5–3mm, linear to oblong with an apical notch, green. Peduncles 1–5cm long, borne in

upper leaf axils; fls solitary, c2.5cm across, variable in colour from red to violet and purple, or paler to white, rarely yellow, with a yellow throat; sep. without calli. A very variable species. Autumn. S Africa (Cape Province). 'Gothenburg': to 25cm; fls deep pink. var. *fulgida* (Lindl.) Knuth (*O.fulgida* Lindl.). Fls purple. var. *rubella* (Jacq.) Knuth (*O.rubella* Jacq.). Fls deep red. Z9.

O.hirtella Jacq. See *O.hirta*.

O.imbriciata Eckl. & Zeyh.
Deciduous, 6–15cm. Lvs dense, tufted; petioles to 1cm, red-tinted; leaflets. 3, to 0.5cm, obcordate, rounded, retuse, blue-green. Fls solitary, to 1.5cm diam., white to magenta or red-purple on stalks far exceeding lvs. Summer. S Africa. Z9.

O.incarnata L.
Bulbous, glabrous, perenn. with erect to sprawling slender stems 10–50cm long; bulb to 2cm diam., rounded. Petioles 2–6cm in whorls up the stems; leaflets 3, 8–20×5–15mm, obcordate, translucent green with dark marginal spots beneath; leaf axils may bear red-brown bulbils. Peduncles 3–7cm, erect; fls solitary, 2cm across, white or very pale lilac, with darker veins and a yellow throat; sep. with several converging apical calli. Autumn. Namibia. Z9.

O.inops Ecklon & Zeyh. See *O.depressa*.
O.intermedia Rich. (misapplied). See *O.latifolia*.

O.kumiesbergensis auct.
Deciduous, 2–3cm. Lvs in rosettes; petioles to 1.5cm; leaflets 3, to 0.8cm, folded, blue-green. Fls to 1.5cm diam., pink on stalks exceeding lvs. Summer. S Africa. Z9.

O.laciniata Cav. (*O.squamosoradicosa* Steud.).
Rhizomatous, stemless perenn., 5–10cm; rhiz. branching freely just below ground level forming an elongate chain of tiny, linked, scaly bulbils. Lvs arising from apex of rhiz.; petioles 2.5–7cm, erect, tinged pink; leaflets 8–12, to 2cm, obcordate, folded length-wise, glaucous green with purple, undulate margin, glabrous to softly hairy. Peduncles as long as lvs; fls solitary, c2.5cm across, very variable in colour, violet, crimson to lilac, blue and paler, all with darker veins and green throat, sweetly scented; sep. without calli, tips reddened. Late spring–summer. Patagonia. 'Ione Hecker': see *O.enneaphylla*. Z8.

O.lactea Hook. See *O.magellanica*.

O.luslundra Zucc. (*O.floribunda* Lehm. (misapplied)).
Bulbous, stemless perenn., 15–30cm or more, with a thick tap-root densely covered in scaly bulbils at the apex; bulb scales 15–35-nerved. Petioles to 15cm, erect, stalks red-green with sparse to abundant patent hairs c2mm long; leaflets 5–10, to 5×2cm, narrowly wedge-shaped to strap-like, apex rounded, usually shallowly notched, green, glabrous. Peduncles twice as long as petioles, erect, succulent, with long, spreading hairs as the petioles; infl. a 9–26-fld umbel; fls c2cm across, crimson to violet, with a yellow throat; sep. and bracts with red apical calli. Summer–autumn. Mexico. Z9.

O.latifolia HBK (*O.binervis* Reg.; *O.intermedia* Rich. (misapplied); *O.vespertilionis* Zucc.).
Bulbous, stemless perenn., 7–25cm, producing numerous bulbils on short underground runners off the parental bulb; bulbils scaly, scales 5–11-nerved. Petioles 8–23cm, erect to spreading; leaflets 3, to 7×7cm, broadly deltoid to obcordate, dark green, glabrous. Peduncles to 25cm; infl. a 6–32-fld pseudo-umbel; fls 1.5–2cm across, violet-pink or paler, with a green throat; sep. with 2 orange-brown apical calli. Summer–autumn. Mexico to Peru; widely naturalized, can be a troublesome weed. Z9.

O.libyca Viv. See *O.pes-caprae*.

O.lobata Sims.
Stemless, bulbous perennial, 8–10cm, with tuberous roots; bulb to 2.5cm diam., round, densely covered in brown, woolly scales. Petioles 4–5cm, erect; leaflets 3, 5×6mm, obcordate, light green, glabrous, usually maculate, the lateral pair somewhat folded lengthwise. Peduncles almost twice the height of lvs; fls solitary, about 1.5cm across,

golden-yellow, dotted and veined red; sep. with apical calli. Late summer–autumn. Chile. The lvs appear in spring then die down; they reappear with the flowers in the autumn. Z8.

O.magellanica Forst. f. (*O.lactea* Hook.).
Reminiscent of a small *O.acetosella*; a prostrate, stoloniferous, carpet-forming perenn. to 4cm; rhiz. slender, scaly, bearing leaves and peduncles from the apex. Petioles 2–4cm, erect, sparsely hairy; leaflets 3, 5×5mm, obcordate, bronze-green, glabrous. Peduncles short, 1.5–3.5cm, erect; fls solitary, 1cm across, pure white; sep. without calli. Late spring–summer. S America, Australia; can become a garden pest. 'Nelson' ('Flore Pleno'): lvs tinged bronze; fls double, white. 'Old Man Range': lvs distinctive, grey tinged pink in summer; fls white, abundant. Z6.

O.martiana Zucc. See *O.corymbosa*.

O.massoniana Salter.
Deciduous, 4–24cm. Fls brick red with yellow throat. Close to *O.pardalis*. Summer. S Africa. Z9.

O.melanosticta Sonder.
Small, nearly stemless, bulbous perenn. to 2.5cm; bulbs 6.5–8.5mm, scaly. Petioles 1.5–2.5cm, erect to spreading, very hairy; leaflets 3, 7–11×5–9mm, obcordate to rounded, rather thick, green with orange spots (which blacken on drying), usually hairy on both surfaces, margins densely white ciliate. Peduncles as long as the petioles or shorter, erect, densely hairy; fls solitary, to 2cm across, yellow; sep. densely hairy, without calli. Late spring–summer. S Africa. Z9.

O.multiflora Jacq. See *O.hirta*.

O.nelsonii (Small) Knuth.
Resembling *O.tetraphylla* but differing in bulb scales 5–12-nerved, plant with sparse to abundant hairs; leaflets 5 or 6, usually entire; fls larger, 1.5 to 2.5cm across, deep purple. Summer. Mexico. Z9.

O.obtusa Jacq.
6–10cm. Fls pink red, yellow or white. Summer. S Africa. Z9.

O.oregana Nutt. ex Torr. & A. Gray. REDWOOD SORREL.
Perenn. reminiscent of a robust *O.acetosella*, rising to 6–20cm from a horizontal, creeping, brown, rhiz. Petioles 3–20cm, erect with patent hairs; leaflets 3, 2.5–3.5×2.7×4.5cm, widely obcordate, green, glabrous above, margins and undersurfaces with long hairs. Peduncles as long as or just longer than petioles, erect, hairy; fls solitary, 2–2.5cm across, pale lilac or darker, occasionally white; sep. hairy, without calli. Fr. 7–8mm, globose. Spring–autumn. Western N America. Z7.

O.palmifrons Salter.
Deciduous, 2–4cm. Lvs flat spread in a symmetrical, ground-hugging rosette, multifoliate with numerous leaflets in palm-like arrangement. Fls white. Summer. S Africa. Z9.

O.pardalis Sond.
Deciduous, 4–7cm. Fls white, yellow, lilac, deep pink, purple or red-purple. Summer. S Africa. Z9.

O.patagonica Speg. (*O.enneaphylla* var. *patagonica* (Speg.) Skottsb.).
Stemless perenn. to 5cm with a semi-jointed, creeping rhiz.; rhiz. covered below with rounded orange scales, and above with narrow brown scales congested at the apex. Petioles 2–5cm, erect; leaflets 10–14, 7–8×3–5mm, obcordate, divided to base and folded lengthwise, glaucous grey, densely hairy. Peduncles 1.5–3.5cm, glaucous grey, hairy; fls solitary, 2.5cm across, red, pink to pink blue; sep. and pet. somewhat hairy, sep. without calli. Late spring–summer. Patagonia. Z8.

O.pectinata Jacq. See *O.flava*.
O.pentaphylla Sims. See *O.polyphylla*.

O.pes-caprae L. (*O.cernua* Thunb.; *O.libyca* Viv.). BERMUDA BUTTERCUP; ENGLISH-WEED.
Bulbous, stemless, glabrous, perenn., flowering to 20–40cm; bulbs with white, fleshy, contractile root and slender vertical

stem to the soil surface, stem and crown bearing numerous sessile bulbils. Lvs numerous; petioles 3–12cm, erect to spreading, somewhat succulent; leaflets 3, 16–20×23–32mm, obcordate, bright green often maculate. Peduncles twice as long as petioles, erect; infl. a 3–20-fld umbellate cyme; pedicels somewhat nodding; fls 2–2.5cm across, deep golden yellow; sep. with 2 orange apical calli. Spring–early summer. S Africa (Cape Province). Widely naturalized in milder climates and can be a serious weed of cultivation. Seed is very rarely set in Europe but reproduces asexually by producing numerous bulbils. 'Flore Pleno': double-fld. Z9.

O.polyphylla Jacq. (*O.versicolor* Jacq., non L.; *O.pentaphylla* Sims).
Erect stemmed, bulbous perenn., 5–30cm; bulb to 2–3cm, ovoid, pale to dark brown; stem to 20cm, rather rigid. Lvs numerous, congested at the apices of the stems; petioles 1–5cm; leaflets 3–7, 1–3cm, linear, minutely emarginate, glabrous above, sparsely pubesc. or glabrous beneath, with 2 conspicuous orange-red apical calli. Peduncles 3–10cm, pubesc.; fls solitary, 1.5 to 3cm across, purple, rose-pink to rose-flesh colour or white, throat yellow; sep. with two orange apical calli. A very variable species probably including *O.gracilis*. Summer. S Africa (Cape Province). Z8.

O.pulchella Eckl. & Zeyh.
Deciduous, 3–16cm. Lvs tufted; petioles to 2cm, slender; leaflets 3, to 0.8cm, obovate-cuneate, rounded, sage green. Fls to 3cm diam., solitary, salmon- or rose-pink, throat often yellow. Summer. S Africa. Z9. Close to and possibly synonymous with *O.obtusa*.

O.punctulata Knuth. See *O.versicolor*.

O.purpurata Jacq.
Bulbous perenn., 10–30cm high with no aerial stem; bulb without contractile root, rhizomatous with slender vertical stem to the soil surface and crown; fleshy underground stolons bear apical bulbils or occasionally further crowns. Lvs numerous; petioles to 30cm, erect to spreading, glabrous to pubesc.; leaflets 3, 1.5–5×2.7cm, obcordate, rounded, dark green and glabrous above, dark purple (variable) and hairy beneath, margins ciliate. Peduncles 10–30cm, erect sparsely hairy; infl. a 3–10-fld umbel; fls 2.5cm across, purple to violet with a yellow throat, sep. with 2 orange apical calli. A very variable species. Summer. S Africa (Cape Province). Z9.

O.purpurata var. *bowiei* (Lindl.) Sonder. See *O.bowiei*.

O.purpurea L. (*O.variabilis* Jacq.; *O.grandiflora* Jacq.; *O.speciosa* Jacq.).
Bulbous perenn. to 15cm with no aerial stem; bulb to 17mm diam., smooth, rounded, black-brown; slender vertical stem from bulb to soil surface and crown. Petioles 2–8cm, usually spreading to prostrate, white-pubesc.; leaflets 3, 4–40×4–30mm, rhomboid to orbicular, or widely obovate, dark green above, maculate or deep purple beneath, glabrous except for a densely, long-ciliate margin. Peduncles erect, equal or shorter than lvs; fls solitary, 3–5cm across, rose-purple, deep rose to violet and pale violet, yellow, cream or white, all with a yellow throat; sep. without calli. Autumn–winter. S Africa (Cape Province). A very variable species particularly in leaf shape and flower size and colour. 'Bowles' White': fls white. 'Ken Aslet': to 7cm; lvs large, silky; fls yellow. Z8.

O.racemosa Savigny. See *O.rosea*.

O.regnellii Miq. (*O.cathariensis* N.E. Br.).
Stemless, rhizomatous perenn. 10–25cm; rhiz. about 5cm long, simple or sparsely branched, vertical, densely covered in tubercle-like deltoid scales about 4mm diam. pressed against it. Lvs quite numerous; petioles 10–15cm, erect to spreading, glabrous; leaflets 3, to 25×50mm, broadly deltoid, emarginate, green suffused purple above, vivid purple beneath, sometimes with dark blotches. Peduncles few, 1–4, 10–20cm long, erect to spreading; infl. a 3–7-fld umbel; fls 1.5–2cm across, pale pink to white. Spring–summer. Peru, Brazil, Bolivia, Paraguay, Argentina. Z9.

O.repens Thunb. See *O.corniculata*.

O.rosea Jacq. (*O.delicata* Pohl; *O.racemosa* Savigny; *O.floribunda* Lehm. (misapplied); *O.rubra* 'Delicata' (misapplied)).
Erect stemmed annual flowering to 20–40cm, glabrous, often reddened at base, entirely herbaceous; stem 10–35cm, not thickened, much branched and leafy throughout. Petioles to 3cm, spreading; leaflets 3, to 11×11mm, obcordate, pale green, occasionally reddened beneath. Peduncles numerous, to 10cm, erect to spreading; infl. a lax bifurcating cyme of 1–3 fls; fls 1–1.5cm across, pink with darker veins and a white throat, rarely entirely white; sep. red-tipped but without calli. Fr. to 8mm, round, seed set readily. Spring. Chile.

O.rubella Jacq. See *O.hirta* var. *rubella*.

O.rubra A. St.-Hil. (*O.floribunda* Lehm. (misapplied); *O.rubra* Jacq. (misapplied)).
Clump-forming, stemless perenn. to 40cm, from a semi-woody, tuberous crown; tubers round to cylindrical, covered with red-brown scales, branched in tight clusters, in old plants may rise above soil surface. Lvs numerous; petioles to 30cm, spreading to erect; leaflets 3, c18×15mm, obcordate, green, maculate, particularly around sinus, glabrous above, hairy beneath, ciliate. Peduncles to 40cm, erect; infl. a 6–12-fld umbellate cyme; fls 1–1.5cm across, red to pink; sep. with several apical calli. Summer. S Brazil to Argentina. 'Alba': fls white. 'Lilacana': fls lilac-purple. Z9. *O.rubra* 'Delicata' (misapplied). See *O.rosea*. *O.rubra* Jacq. (misapplied). See *O.rubra*.

O.smithiana Ecklon & Zeyh.
Stemless, rather weak perenn., 10–20cm, glabrous; bulb to 2cm, round-ovate, red-brown with contractile root. Lvs 2–20; petioles 5–18cm, slender; leaflets 3, 1–4.5cm, polymorphous, sometimes heterophyllous, 2-lobed to middle or below almost to base, obcordate to obtriangular in outline, lobes linear, spreading, green, densely punctate above. Peduncles as long or longer than lvs; fls solitary, 2–3cm across, rose-lilac or white, throat yellow-green; sep. with 2 orange apical calli. Spring–summer. S Africa. Z9.

O.speciosa Jacq. See *O.purpurea*.
O.squamosoradicosa Steud. See *O.laciniata*.

O.tenuifolia Jacq.
Slender stemmed bulbous perenn. 6–24cm, often caespitose; bulb to 3cm, ovoid, black-brown; stem erect, pubesc., with dense rosettes of lvs in upper parts and numerous short, abortive branches above. Lvs almost sessile, appearing fasciculate; leaflets 3, 4–9mm, linear, somewhat folded or with a rolled margin, emarginate, glabrous above, yellow-pubesc. beneath, maculate at apex and on margins. Peduncles numerous, 1–6cm, yellow pubesc., erect; fls solitary, 2–3cm across, purple to white with purple margin and yellow throat; sep. with apical calli. Winter. S Africa. Z9.

O.tetraphylla Cav. (*O.deppei* Lodd.). LUCKY CLOVER; GOOD LUCK LEAF; GOOD LUCK PLANT.
Bulbous, stemless perenn., flowering to 15–50cm; bulb large, 1.5–3.5cm, covered in hairy scales with fleshy contractile root. Petioles 10–40cm, erect to spreading, sparsely to moderately hairy; leaflets 4 (rarely 3), 2–6.5×2–3cm, strap-shaped to obtriangular, entire or shallowly emarginate, green, usually with a V-shaped purple band near the base pointing to the apex, usually glabrous above, hairy beneath. Peduncles 15–50cm, erect; infl. a 5–12-fld umbel; fls 1–2cm across, red to lilac-pink, rarely white, all with green-yellow throat; sep. with red apical calli. Summer. Mexico. 'Iron Cross': seg. formed by the coloured band on the leaflets entirely purple. Z8.

O.triangularis A. St. Hil.
Loosely similar to *O.regnellii*, but more tender with larger leaves flushed a deep wine red to purple, with a darker zone at the base of each segment. Brazil.

O.tropaeoloides Schlachter. See *O.corniculata* var. *purpurata*.

O.tuberosa Molina (*O.crenata* Jacq.; *O.deppei* Lodd. (misapplied)). OCA.
Erect to decumbent, succulent-stemmed perenn. to 25cm; rhiz. greatly branched, tips swollen into fleshy tubers 4×3cm,

covered in small triangular scales; stems fleshy, to 30×1cm, green-purple, densely pubesc., leafy in the upper part. Petioles 7–10cm, spreading, glabrous or sparsely hairy; leaflets 3, to 25×22mm, widely obcordate, green or suffused purple (particularly beneath), densely pubesc., rather thick. Peduncles 15–17cm, spreading, from upper leaf axils; infl. a 5–8-fld umbel; fls to 2cm across, yellow; sep. without calli. Summer. Colombia. Long cultivated as root crop oca of the high Andes, once grown in Europe as potato substitute. Three colours of tuber are grown: yellow, white and red; the red and yellow types have lost the ability to flower. Z7.

O.valdiviana hort. See *O.valdiviensis*.

O.valdiviensis Barnéoud (*O.valdiviana* hort.).
Compact, erect-stemmed annual, flowering to 10–25cm or more, glabrous with a thick fleshy taproot; stems (2–)5–10cm, densely leafy, unbranched. Petioles 4–14cm, erect; leaflets 3, 12–20×10–20mm, broadly obcordate with a narrow sinus, pale green, thin. Peduncles 8–18cm, from upper leaf axils; infl. a forked cyme of 4–14 fls; fls 1–1.5cm across, yellow, usually with brown veins; sep. often with a red margin, no calli. Fr. 6mm, globose, pendulous. Chile. Readily sets seed and may become a pest in glasshouses. Z9.

O.variabilis Jacq. See *O.purpurea*.

O.versicolor L. (*O.elongata* Jacq.; *O.punctulata* Knuth).
Bulbous perenn. rising to 8–20cm high, or more shade, almost glabrous or sparsely pubesc.; bulbs 1.5–2.5cm, ovoid.

black-brown; stems 3–15cm, erect to spreading, simple, somewhat woody. Lvs in apical clusters of 8 to 20; petioles 0.5–4cm; leaflets 3, to 12×2mm, cuneate-linear to linear, apex emarginate, glabrous to hairy, apex and margins maculate. Peduncles few, 1–4, to twice as long and thicker than petioles, more or less erect, glabrous to pubesc.; fls solitary, 2–3cm across, white to purple-white, throat yellow, margin purple-violet; sep. with apical calli. A variable species. Summer–autumn. S Africa (Cape Province). 'Candy Cane': compact; lvs small, round; fls white striped red. var. *flaviflora* Sonder. Fls yellow. Z9.

O.versicolor Jacq., non L. See *O.polyphylla*.
O.vespertilionis Torr. & A. Gray, non Zucc. See *O.drummondii*.
O.vespertilionis Zucc., non Torr. & A. Gray. See *O.latifolia*.

O.violacea L. VIOLET WOOD SORREL.
Stemless, bulbous perenn. flowering to 20cm or more, usually glabrous; bulb 1cm diam., brown, round, scaly, scales 3-nerved. Petioles 7–13cm, erect; leaflets 3, 8–20×10–28mm, obcordate, green, orange maculate around sinus. Peduncles 9–25cm, erect, much longer than petioles; infl. an umbel of 2–8(–16) fls; fls 1.5–2cm across, lavender, pink or paler (rarely white), all with green throat; sep. without calli. Spring–autumn. N America. Z5.

Pamianthe Stapf. (For Major Albert Pam (*d*1955), English horticulturist, and Gk *anthe*, flower.) Amaryllidaceae. 2 or 3 species of bulbous herbs. Bulbs globose, stoloniferous, tunicate, with a long stem-like neck of sheathing leaf-bases. Leaves evergreen or deciduous, linear with a rounded keel. Flowers 1–4 in a terminal umbel on a somewhat compressed scape; spathe valves linear; perianth white or ivory flushed green, with a long cylindrical tube, lobes 6, subequal; stamens 6, filaments short and incurved, fused at the base into a campanulate corona with 6 short lobes; anthers versatile, exserted from the corona; style basally joined to perianth tube by 3 wings; ovary inferior, 3-celled. Fruit a capsule; seeds many, pale brown, winged at the apex. Northern S America. Z10.

CULTIVATION *P.peruviana* is an evergreen bulb grown for its arching, strap-shaped leaves and large, white and exquisitely fragrant flowers in early spring. *Pamianthe* is frost-tender, but eminently suited to the glasshouse or conservatory, with a winter minimum temperature of 10°C/50°F. Plant in a fibrous, loam-based medium in late summer/early autumn with the neck of the bulb at soil level, and water sparingly until growth commences. Grow in bright indirect light and water moderately when in growth; reduce water after flowering to keep just moist enough to prevent wilting. Pot-grown plants may be moved outdoors for the summer, when danger of frost is passed. Top-dress in autumn, and re-pot every third or fourth year.

Propagate by offsets. Seeds take 12–15 months to mature on the plant, but germinate rapidly if sown when ripe in a warm and humid closed case.

P.peruviana Stapf.
Lvs to 50×4cm, 5–7, spreading. Scape exceeding lvs; fls 2–4, fragrant, perianth tube to 13cm, green, lobes to 13cm, white or flushed cream, the inner ones to 3cm wide, oblanceolate with a central green stripe; corona to 8cm, lobes bifid or mucronate, free portions of fil. to 12mm. Peru.

Pancratium L. (Name in Dioscorides for a bulbous plant.) Amaryllidaceae. About 16 species of bulbous perennial herbs. Leaves basal, 2-ranked, linear to lorate. Flowers 3–15 in a scapose umbel, or, rarely solitary, usually subtended by 2 scarious spathes, large, white, fragrant; perianth more or less funnelform, tube often enlarged at throat, lobes narrow, linear-lanceolate, spreading or almost erect; staminal corona conspicuous, basally united to base of filaments, anthers dorsifixed; ovary 3-celled, stigma capitate. Fruit a capsule; seeds numerous, black, angled. Canary Is., Mediterranean to Tropical Asia, W Africa to Namibia. Distinguished from *Hymenocallis* by its numerous seeds with thin, dry, black testa.

CULTIVATION The species most commonly grown in temperate gardens are those from warm Mediterranean habitats, where bulbs ripen fully in hot dry conditions in summer. Handsome plants grown for their strongly fragrant, white flowers in summer, they are suitable for the cool glasshouse or conservatory, or for outdoor cultivation given a warm sheltered position in full sun at the base of a south-facing wall. *P.illyricum* is hardy to –5°C/23°F; *P.maritimum* is almost as hardy although the foliage is susceptible to frost, and in cool temperate gardens, the hot dry conditions necessary for bulb ripening are seldom achieved. Plant outdoors 15–30cm/6–12in. deep on a base of sharp sand, otherwise grow under glass as for *Amaryllis. P.zeylanicum* requires warm glasshouse conditions, as for *Hippeastrum*. Propagate by offsets or from ripe seed.

P.amboinense L. See *Proiphys amboinensis.*
P.aurantiacum HBK. See *Stenomesson aurantiacum.*
P.australasicum Ker-Gawl. See *Proiphys amboinensis.*

P.canariense Ker-Gawl.
Resembles *P.illyricum* but lvs broader, pedicels much longer (to 3cm), corona teeth shorter, and free part of fil. scarcely as long as anth. Early autumn. Canary Is. Z9.

P.coccineum Ruiz & Pav. See *Stenomesson coccineum.*
P.flavum Ruiz & Pav. See *Stenomesson flavum.*

P.illyricum L.
Bulb large, covered with purple-black scales. Lvs 50×1.5–3cm, broad, ligulate, deciduous, glaucous, strongly veined. Scape to 40cm; pedicels 1–1.5cm; fls fragrant; perianth white, sometimes ivory or cream at base of seg. and on corona, tube *c*2cm, lobes 5cm, linear-oblong to narrowly elliptic; corona much longer than perianth, teeth paired, long and narrow, alternating with stamens; free part of fil. much longer than anth. Late spring-early summer. W Mediterranean Is. (Corsica, Sardinia). Z8.

P.latifolium Ruiz & Pav. See *Urceolina latifolia.*

P.maritimum L.
Resembles *P.illyricum* but bulb scales pale, bulb very long-necked; lvs longer and narrower, persistent; fls highly fragrant; perianth tube to 7.5cm, very slender; corona two-thirds length of perianth, with short triangular teeth alternating with stamens; free part of fil. about the same length as anth. Summer. Mediterranean, SW Europe. Z8.

P.mexicanum L. See *Hymenocallis concinna.*
P.variegatum Ruiz & Pav. See *Stenomesson variegatum.*
P.viridiflorum Ruiz & Pav. See *Stenomesson viridiflorum.*

P.zeylanicum L.
Lvs lorate-lanceolate, fresh green, not glaucous. Scape to 30cm; fls solitary; pedicels short; perianth lobes narrowly lanceolate longer than tube, fused at base, free and recurved toward apex; style exceeding stamens. Summer. Sri Lanka. Z10.

Paradisea Mazz. (For Count Giovanni Paradisi of Modena (1760–1826.) Liliaceae (Asphodelaceae). 2 species of hardy perennials allied to *Anthericum*. Roots fleshy and fibrous; rhizomes short, clustered. Leaves basal. Scapes slender, bracteate; flowers to 20, showy, funnelform to campanulate, in lax racemes; tepals 6, free, clawed, white with apical spots, 3-veined; stamens and style upward-curving, anthers versatile. Capsule 3-valved; seeds small, numerous, ridged. Summer. S Europe (mts). Z7.

CULTIVATION Closely related to *Anthericum* and found in similar alpine meadow habitats, these are beautiful rhizomatous perennials grown for their grey-green, grasslike foliage and loose racemes of translucent, white, saucer-shaped flowers in early summer; they are fragrant and suitable for cutting. *P.liliastrum* makes an attractive clump-forming addition to the herbaceous border, leafing up in spring and dying back in autumn. *P.lusitanicum*, taller, tougher and with smaller flowers, will form dense spreading clumps and is useful for colonizing banks and open or partially shaded woodland. *Paradisea* is hardy to –15°C/5°F, probably more.

Grow in sun or dappled shade in fertile well-drained soils that do not become too dry in summer. Top-dress established clumps with garden compost or well-rotted manure in autumn. Propagate by division after flowering or in early spring, or by seed in spring in the cold frame.

P.liliastrum (L.) Bertol. (*Anthericum liliastrum* L.). ST BRUNO'S LILY; PARADISE LILY.
Stem 30–60cm. Lvs 4–7, linear, 12–25×1cm. Raceme secund; fls 3–10; tepals 3–5cm, white with green apical spot; pedicels not articulated. Fr. 13–15mm. S Europe. 'Major': more robust, fls larger.

P.lusitanicum (Cout.) Samp. (*P.liliastrum* var. *lusitanicum* Cout.).
To 150cm, more robust than *P.liliastrum*. Lvs to 2cm wide. Fls white, to 2cm, in 2-ranked racemes; pedicels articulated. Portugal.

Paramongaia Velarde. (From Paramonga, a locality in Peru where *P.weberbaueri* was collected.) Amaryllidaceae. 1 species, a deciduous bulbous herb. Bulbs to 6.5cm diam., tunicate, lacking a neck. Leaves to 75×5cm, 6–8, narrow-linear, bright green or glaucous, appearing with or after the flowers. Flowers solitary or sometimes 2, to 18cm diam., bright yellow, fragrant, on an erect scape to 60cm; spathe valves linear, separate; perianth tube 10cm, cylindrical, lobes to 8×1.8cm, 6, spreading; anthers versatile, not exserted, from the large trumpet-like corona; style exserted from the perianth tube, not winged. Fruit to 3.6cm, a capsule; seeds many. Peru. Z10.

CULTIVATION From coastal zones and on the steep rocky hillsides of Peru to altitudes of 2700m/8775ft, the bulbs often pulling themselves down to depths of 30cm/12in. In autumn *P.weberbaueri* bears magnificent long-lasting blooms, strongly fragrant and of an intense deep yellow, on a stout stem which may reach 75cm/30in. in height. It is frost-tender, but well suited to the warm glasshouse or conservatory. Plant deeply in well-crocked pots in a slightly acid medium comprising equal parts loam, leafmould and sharp sand, with added charcoal. Grow in full sun and water plentifully when in full growth, maintaining a minimum temperature of 18°C/65°F with high humidity and good circulation of air. Feed well-rooted specimens with dilute liquid feed when in growth. Reduce water as leaves begin to yellow and keep dry when dormant in summer, at a temperature of 21–24°C/70–75°F. Plants flower best when pot-bound; topdress annually in autumn as growth resumes. Propagate from offsets, or from seed.

P.weberbaueri Velarde. COJOMARIA.

Pardanthopsis Lenz. (From *Pardanthus* (Gk *pardos*, panther and *anthos*, flower) and Gk *opsis* appearance.) Iridaceae. 1 species, a perennial herb closely resembling *Iris*, to 1m. Rhizomes slender producing many swollen roots. Leaves to 8 in fans, to 30×2.5cm. Inflorescence branching frequently, bearing thin spathes; flowers to 6 per spathe, ephemeral, to 4.5cm diam.; falls larger than standards, ivory spotted and striped maroon from base, flecked purple in centre; claw striped purple; style branches bilobed; perianth segments spiral tightly as they fade. Fruit cylindrical. Summer. Siberia, N China, Mongolia. Z7.

CULTIVATION A short-lived deciduous perennial grown for its beautifully marked and spotted ivory-white flowers, carried on branching stems in summer above a fan of blue-green, white-edged leaves. The individual blooms open during the afternoon, lasting for the day, the petals twisting spirally as they fade; *P.dichotoma* frequently flowers so freely over long periods that it exhausts itself and dies, but in favourable conditions will renew itself by self seeding. It is hardy in zones where temperatures fall to –15°C/5°F to –20°C/–4°F. Grow in a sunny border in any well-drained soil that remains adequately moist during the growing season but allows moderately dry conditions during dormancy. Propagate by seed sown ripe in the cold frame; plants flower at about a year-old.

P.dichotoma (Pall.) Lenz (*Iris dichotoma* Pall.).

Paris L. (From Lat. *par, paris*, equal, on account of the supposed regularity of its leaves and flowers.) Liliaceae (Trilliaceae). 4 species of deciduous herbaceous perennials. Rhizomes creeping. Stem erect, glabrous, to 40cm. Leaves 4–12 in a whorl near apex of stem. Flowers solitary, terminal; sepals 4 6, green; petals 4– 6, yellow, linear; stamens 4–10, filaments flat, anthers basifixed; ovary superior; styles slender, 4, free. Fruit a fleshy, indehiscent purple-black capsule. Spring–summer. Europe to E Asia.

CULTIVATION *Paris* spp. are found throughout temperate Europe and Asia, from Siberia to the Mediterranean. *P.quadrifolia*, Herb Paris, grows naturally on calcareous soils in damp, shaded woodland, often in natural association with *Polygonatum multiflorum*, Solomon's Seal, and *Mercurialis perennis*, Dog's Mercury; in Britain, it is an indicator of ancient woodland.

Cultivated for its unusual yellow green flowers, borne in spring and early summer, and its symmetrically arranged foliage, *Paris* also bears poisonous blue-black berries in autumn. It is suited to the woodland or wild garden, or for shaded parts of the rock garden, and is hardy to at least –15°C/5°F. Plant rhizomes 12cm/4.5in. deep in moisture-retentive, humus-soils enriched with leafmould, and in dappled shade. Propagate by division or by seed sown ripe in autumn.

P.apetala Hoffm. See *P.incompleta*.

P.bashanensis Wang & Tang (*P.quadrifolia* var. *setchuanensis* Franch.).
Differs from *P.quadrifolia* in its narrower but longer lvs and reflexed sep. which are half as wide (3–4mm). China (Sichuan, Hubei). Z7.

P.dahurica Fisch. ex Tersch. See *P.verticillata*.
P.hexaphylla Cham. See *P.verticillata*.
P.hexaphylla f. *purpurea* Miyabe & Tatew. See *P.verticillata*.

P.incompleta Bieb. (*P.apetala* Hoffm.; *P.octyphylla* Hoffm.).
Rhiz. slender, creeping. Stem weak, to 33cm. Lvs 6–12, oblong-lanceolate to obovate, prominently 3-veined, base narrowed into short petiole, 6–10cm, pale green. Pedicel shorter than lvs; sep. 4, pale green, sessile, lanceolate, 2.5–4cm, spreading; pet. absent; stamens 8, fil. 5–15mm anth. 5–8mm, free portion of connective absent; ovary globose, dark purple; styles 4, much longer than stamens, 12–23mm. Turkey, Caucasus, Armenia. Z7.

P.obovata Ledeb. See *P.verticillata*.
P.octyphylla Hoffm. See *P.incompleta*.

P.quadrifolia L. HERB PARIS.
Stems glabrous, 15–40cm. Lvs usually 4, ovate with short petiole; if lvs more or less than 4, then other parts equal number of lvs. Fls erect, pedicel 2–8cm, yellow-green; sep. 4, green, lanceolate, 2.5–3.5cm, pet. 4, equalling sep, very narrow, flattened, acute; stamens erect, fil. short, equal to anth.

connective long; ovary globose, 4-celled; styles 4, shorter than stamens. Europe, Caucasus, Siberia, temperate E Asia. Z6.

P.quadrifolia var. *setchuanensis* Franch. See *P.bashanensis*.
P.quadrifolia Thunb. non L. See *P.tetraphylla*.

P.tetraphylla A. Gray (*P.quadrifolia* Thunb. non L.; *P.yakusimensis* Masam.).
Rhiz. slender, creeping. Stem erect, slender, to 40cm. Lvs 4–5, sessile, 3-nerved, oblong to elliptic, 4–10×1.5–4cm, acute, Pedicel 3–10cm; sep. similar in shape to lvs, green, 1–2cm×3–8mm, reflexed; pet. absent, stamens 8, anth. 3–4mm, as long as fil., connective not extended beyond anth.; ovary ovoid, styles 4, slender, longer than stamens. Japan. Z8.

P.verticillata Bieb. (*P.dahurica* Fisch. ex Tersch.; *P.hexaphylla* Cham.; *P.hexaphylla* Cham. f. *purpurea* Miyabe & Tatew.; *P.obovata* Ledeb.; *P.verticillata* f. *purpurea* Miyabe & Tatew.).
Rhiz. slender. Stem erect, to 40cm. Lvs subsessile, 5–8, ovate to lanceolate, Pedicel 5–15cm, erect; sep. 4, ovate to lanceolate, 24×1–1.5cm, green; pet. 4, filiform, 1.5–2cm×11–27mm, reflexed, yellow; stamens 8–10, slightly longer than pet., fil. anth. and free portion of connective about same length, 5–8mm; ovary ovoid to quadrangular, dark purple brown; styles 4, short, recurved. Caucasus, Siberia, E Asia. Z7.

P.verticillata f. *purpurea* Miyabe & Tatew. See *P.verticillata*.
P.yakusimensis Masam. See *P.tetraphylla*.

Pelargonium L'Hérit. (From Gk *pelargos*, stork; the beak of the fruit resembles that of the stork.) Geraniaceae. About 250 species of subshrubs, herbaceous perennials and annuals; roots sometimes tuberous. Stems sometimes succulent or swollen. Leaves alternate, palmate or pinnate, simple or compound, usually lobed or toothed, often hairy, sometimes fleshy, sometimes aromatic; stipules present, sometimes persistent; petioles often long, sometimes persistent. Flowers bisexual, usually irregular, occasionally fragrant, often white, pink or purple, rarely yellow or brown, arranged in a pseudoumbel; calyx of 5 sepals with a spur formed at the base of the posterior sepal, the lower end of which is swollen with a nectiferous gland and joined to the pedicel; corolla of usually 5, free petals, sometimes 2 or 4, usually clawed, 2 upper petals usually larger than the lower 3; stamens 10, of which no more than 7 bear fertile anthers; stigmas 5. Fruit of 5, 1-seeded mericarps. Most from S Africa with a few from tropical Africa, Australia and Middle East. 7). Z10.

CULTIVATION   Grow in a free-draining gritty potting medium, in a brightly lit, dry, well ventilated position, minimum temperature 5°C/40°F. Water carefully to avoid waterlogging and keep nearly dry during periods of low temperatures and low light intensity. Tuberous *Pelargonium* species usually die back entirely and should be kept dry while dormant. Gradually recommence watering when growth starts again (or in order to activate new growth).

Propagate by root cuttings. Use thick roots taken from near the base of the plant and cut into 5–8cm/2–3in. lengths. Place upright in a damp medium with a minimum temperature of 13°C/55°F. Small tubers may also be detached and potted on under similar conditions.

P.echinatum Curtis. CACTUS GERANIUM; SWEETHEART GERANIUM.
Erect subshrub, to 50cm with tuberous roots and succulent branched stems covered with persistent spiny stipules. Lvs ovate, lobed, to 6cm diam., grey-green above, paler and tomentose below. Infl. 3–8-fld; fls 15–20mm diam., usually white with dark red blotches on 2 upper pet.; spur 3–4cm; fertile stamens 6–7. Spring. Western S Africa. 'Miss Stapleton': fls bright purple-pink.

P.heracleifolium Lodd. See *P. lobatum*.

P.incrassatum (Andrews) Sims (*P.roseum* (Andrews) DC.).
Herb with large underground tuber. Lvs basal, narrowly ovate, 3–6×2–5cm, deeply pinnatifid, silver-pilose to canescent. Infl. a large pseudoumbel, 20–40-fld, on stem to 30cm; fls bright magenta, 2 upper pet. spathulate, to 20mm, 3 lower pet. much smaller with inrolled edges; spur to 4cm. Spring. S Africa (Western Cape).

P.lobatum (Burm. f.) L'Hérit. (*P.heracleifolium* Lodd.).
Herb with large underground tuber and very short stem. Lvs apparently basal, softly hairy, to 30cm diam., usually less in cultivation, 3- or more lobed. Infl. branched with several clusters, each 5–20-fld; fls strongly scented at night, 2cm diam.; pet. rounded, very dark purple with yellow-green margin; spur to 3cm; fertile stamens 6. Spring. S Africa (S & SW Cape).

P.pinnatum (L.) L'Hérit.
Herb bearing a cylindric, taproot like, subterranean tuber to 25cm, usually shorter. Lvs to 30cm, slender, basal, erect, villous, finely pinnate, in a loose rosette; pinnae elliptic, to 2cm, borne in alternate whorls of 2–3. Scape slender, erect; infl. umbellate, open; fls to 3cm diam., delicate; upper pet. buff, veined rose and dark violet, apically blotched violet, lower pet. bronze suffused rose pink. Winter. S Africa.

P.reniforme Curtis.
Erect subshrub with tuberous roots, becoming woody at base with age, sometimes reaching 1m. Lvs reniform, to 3cm diam., grey-green with velvety texture above, silvery grey beneath; petioles long, to 5cm+. Infl. branched, leafy, with 3–12-fld clusters; fls 1–2cm diam., deep magenta or deep pink; 2 upper pet. narrow-oblong, marked deep purple; spur 1–2cm; fertile stamens 6–7. Spring–summer. S Africa (E. Cape).

P.roseum (Andrews) DC. See *P.incrassatum*.

P.triste (L.) L'Hérit.
Herb with turbinate to ovoid, woody, fissured, subterranean or exposed tuber. Stem very short, jointed, rather succulent. Lvs apparently basal, variable but usually oblong in outline, to 45cm, finely 2–3-pinnate or pinnatifid, hairy. Infl. a 5–20-fld, flat-topped, radiate, scapose umbel; fls to 1.5cm diam., sweetly scented at night; pet. obovate, usually brown-purple with a dull yellow or cream margin but sometimes yellow or brown; spur to 3cm; fertile stamens 7. Spring–early summer. S Africa (NW to S Cape).

Periboea Kunth. (For Periboea, one of the wives of Neptune.) Liliaceae (Hyacinthaceae). 2 species of perennial herbs. Bulbs tunicate. Leaves basal, linear, channelled, fleshy. Inflorescence a few-flowered raceme; perianth lobes 6, basally united into a tube, rose to lilac, falling early; stamens 6 in 2 series, arising from perianth tube. Fruit a 3-valved capsule; seeds globose, black, 1–2 per locule. S Africa. Z9.

CULTIVATION   As for *Hyacinthus*.

P.corymbosa (L.) Kunth (*Hyacinthus corymbosus* L.).
Lvs to 12cm, 3–6. Flowering stem to 7.5cm; fls to 1.5cm, in 4–8-fld corymbose raceme; perianth lilac-rose, tube to 0.75cm; stamens exserted.

Petronymphe H.E. Moore. (From Gk *petros*, rock, and *nymphe*, nymph.) Liliaceae (Alliaceae). 1 species, a perennial herb. Corm tunic membranous. Leaves to 60cm, linear, 5–7-keeled. Scape to 60cm, arched toward summit; inflorescence an umbel, to 14–flowered, subtended by 3–4 spreading bracts; pedicels to 7.5cm, slender; perianth to 5cm, tubular, pale yellow lined green, lobes 6, 0.5cm, spreading; stamens 6, inserted at throat of tube, filaments pale yellow, anthers blue-violet; ovary superior, 3-celled, on a short stalk united to the perianth tube at 3 angles. Mexico. Z8.

CULTIVATION As for the warmer-growing *Allium* species.

P.decora H.E. Moore.

Phaedranassa Herb. (From Gk *phaidros*, bright, and *anassa*, lady, referring to the beauty of the flowers.) QUEEN LILY. Amaryllidaceae. About 6 species of bulbous, herbaceous perennials. Leaves 1–4, stalked, narrow to broadly oblong, appearing at same time as or after flowers. Flowers showy, drooping, in scapose umbels; perianth narrow, funnel-shaped or nearly cylindric, with narrow, spreading lobes at apex, red marked with green or bi-coloured; flowers differ from those of *Urceolina* in having corona of hyaline teeth between the 6 anther filaments; stamens exserted. Fruit a globose, deeply furrowed, 3-valved capsule containing many small black seeds. S America; native to Andes but cultivated in Costa Rica. Z8.

CULTIVATION Widely cultivated in their native regions, *Phaedranassa* spp. are rarely grown in Europe, although in temperate zones they make beautiful plants for the cool glasshouse or conservatory or, in mild areas, for well-drained, sheltered borders, at the base of a south wall. In spring or early summer, they bear umbels of brilliantly coloured, narrowly tubular flowers with anthers protruding from the rim of the bell; in *P.carnioli* they are bright red, flushed green at the base and marked with green and yellow at the lips. The leaves appear with or slightly later than the flowers.

Plant in autumn, with the bulb neck at soil level, in a mix of equal parts loam, leafmould, and sharp sand; keep cool and just moist until growth begins, then water moderately and grow in full light at a minimum temperature of 7°C/45°F. Dry off as foliage dies down in late summer or autumn, and keep cool and dry over winter until growth resumes in early spring. Propagate by offsets and seed.

P.carnioli Bak.
To 60cm. Bulb to 5cm diam. Lvs 1–3, ovate, to 60cm including 20cm-long petiole. Fls 6–10; perianth to 5cm, straight, glaucous crimson, tipped green with yellow fringe; seg. largely united; stamens shortly exserted, fil. white. Spring–summer. S America.

P.chloracra Herb. See *P.dubia*.

P.cinerea Ravenna.
25–30cm. Bulb 3.7–6×2–6cm, neck to 8cm. Lvs 2, elliptic-lanceolate, to elliptic, 29–51cm, short-acuminate, tapering at base, olive-green or grey above, somewhat glaucous; petiole 11–17cm. Fls 7–17; perianth 3.2–5.5cm long, coral-pink, green at apex, separated by narrow white band, tubular; stamens exserted, fil. white, anth. green with yellow pollen. Ecuador.

P.dubia HBK (*P.chloracra* Herb.; *P.viridiflora* Bak.).
To 45cm. Fls 5cm long or more, purple-pink, tipped green; perianth lobes revolute; stamens exserted by 7mm. Spring–summer. Peru. var. *obtusa* Herb. (*P.obtusa* Herb.). Perianth seg. obtuse, not acute. Peru.

P.eucrosioides (Bak.) Benth. & Hook See *Eucrosia stricklandii*.

P.lehmannii Reg.
Lvs solitary, elliptic-lanceolate, acute, dark green above, glaucous green below. Fls 3; perianth to 2.5cm, scarlet, seg. shortly spreading; stamens exserted by 1.5–2cm. Spring–summer. Colombia.

P.obtusa Herb. See *P.dubia*.

P.rubroviridis Bak. See *Eustephia coccinea*.

P.schizantha Bak.
Fls with very short green tube; perianth seg. convergent at tips, to 3cm, bright red, fading to pink at apices. Late autumn. Ecuador.

P.tunguraguae Ravenna.
Bulb ovoid, 5.5×4.5–5cm, neck short, brown. Lvs 3 or less, hysteranthous, lanceolate or oblanceolate, 29–40×5.3–8cm, glossy dark green; petiole 6–9cm. Scape terete, solid, to 54cm; fls 6–8; perianth to 3.2cm long, coral-red, apex green, seg. connate at base to 3.5mm. Ecuador.

P.ventricosa Roezl. ex Wallace. See *P.dubia*.

P.viridiflora Bak.
To 66cm. Bulb 4–5×3–4cm, neck 6cm, brown. Lvs 2–3, hysteranthous, narrow-lanceolate, 25–40×4–5cm, bright green above; petiole 6–9cm. Fls 5; perianth to 1cm, yellow-green, campanulate-tubular, seg. oblanceolate, to 2.4cm. Ecuador and possibly Peru.

Phycella Lindl. Amaryllidaceae. About 7 species of bulbous herbs. Leaves narrow-linear. Flowers 2–12, in drooping scapose umbels, scapes hollow; perianth declinate, funnel-shaped with a short tube, lobes 6, stamens 6, in 2 rows, inserted into the bases of the lobes, declinate, subequal, each with 2 subulate processes at the base; stigma obscurely 3-fid or capitate. Fruit a capsule with many flat black seeds. S America. Z9.

CULTIVATION   Frost-tender bulbs, grown for their brightly coloured umbels of drooping, funnel-shaped flowers. Cultivate as for *Hippeastrum*.

P.bicolor Herb.
Lvs linear, 46–60cm, obtuse, tapering to base. Scape 30–45cm, terete, slender; spathe valves lanceolate, to 3.8cm, equalling pedicels; fls 4–9, ascending; perianth to 5cm, bright red, green-yellow at base, tube short, with 6 minute teeth at base, lobes oblanceolate, connivent; stamens unequal, declinate, not exserted, style exserted. Autumn. Chile.

P.phycelloides (Herb.) Traub (*Habranthus phycelloides* Herb.; *Hippeastrum phycelloides* (Herb.) Bak.; *Amaryllis phycelloides* (Herb.) Traub & Uphof).
Lvs to 30cm, linear, narrow, glaucous. Scape to 25cm; spathe valves linear, exceeding pedicels; fls 3–6, erect; perianth to 7cm, brilliant red, yellow in the centre, tube to 2cm, lobes ovate-lanceolate, connivent except for the apex; stamens equalling perianth, with ciliate processes; style exserted; stigma obscurely trifid. Chilean Andes.

Pinellia Ten. (For Giovanni Vincenzo Pinelli (1535–1601), of the Botanic Garden, Naples.) Araceae. 6 species of low perennial herbs. Tuber globose to depressed globose, 2–4cm diam. Leaves basal, synanthous, simple to compound with 3–7-segments; petioles slender, bulbils sometimes borne on leaves at junction of veins and petiole or on the lower part of the petiole. Peduncle shorter than or exceeding petioles, solitary and not forming part of the same shoot as the leaves; spathe persistent, margins overlapping below to form a tube, limb expanded above, oblong, concave, flat or channelled, green, sometimes striped purple; spadix with zone of female flowers adnate to base of spathe tube, male zone free, not adjacent to female; perianth absent; stamens 1–2; ovary unilocular, ovules solitary; sterile appendix present, slender, elongate, sigmoid, long-exserted from spathe, ascending. Fruit a single-seeded berry. China, Japan. Z6.

CULTIVATION   As for *Arum*.

P.cordata N.E. Br.
Lvs 3–5cm, lanceolate, base cordate, green with veins marked in cream; petioles short, purple, bulbiliferous at junction of lamina and petiole. Spathes to 3cm, strongly incurved, green with purple veins; spadix long-exserted, erect, to 7cm above the spathe, pleasantly fragrant of fruit. Summer. China.

P.integrifolia N.E. Br.
Lvs 3.5–7.5cm, 1–3, ovate to oblong, acute; petiole to 15cm. Spathe to 3.5cm, limb lanceolate; spadix sigmoid, appendix exserted to 3.5cm. Summer. China, Japan.

P.pedatisecta Schott.
Lvs pedate, seg. 7–11, median seg. to 18cm, ovate-lanceolate to lanceolate. Peduncle shorter than petioles; spathe to 19cm, limb to 15cm; appendix shorter than spathe, yellow-green. Summer. N & W China.

P.ternata (Thunb.) Breitenb. (*P.tuberifera* Ten.).
Lvs simple when young, compound with 3 leaflets when adult; leaflets 3–12×1–5cm, sessile, ovate-elliptic to oblong; petiole bulbiliferous. Peduncle to 40cm; spathe to 7cm, green, tube 1.5–2cm, limb lanceolate, curved at apex, glabrous externally, puberulent within; spadix appendix to 10cm, slender, erect, clasping with apex of spathe, green, purple below. Summer. Japan, Korea, China.

P.tripartita (Bl.) Schott.
Lvs pedatisect, seg. 8–20×2–12cm, 3, ovate, abruptly short-caudate. Peduncle to 50cm; spathe 6–10cm, green externally, purple within, tube to 3cm, limb lanceolate, obtuse, apex slightly curved, papillose within; appendix 15–25cm. Summer. S Japan.

P.tuberifera Ten. See *P.ternata*.

Plagiolirion Bak. (From Gk *plagios*, oblique, and *lirion*, lily, from the form of the flower.) Amaryllidaceae. 1 species, a perennial herb. Bulb round, long-necked. Leaves to 15×7.5–10cm, 2–3, basal, apex obtuse, bright green above, darker beneath, petiolate. Flowers to 12, in an umbel, white, small, zygomorphic, with 1 segment pointed downwards, 5 ascending. Summer. Colombia. Z9.

CULTIVATION   As for *Eucharis*.

P.horsmannii Bak.

Polianthes L. (From Gk *polios*, bright, and *anthos*, flower.) Agavaceae. 13 species of perennial herbs with thick, elongate, bulb-like bases, often from a short rhizome with thickened roots. Leaves few, thinly succulent, lanceolate or linear, thin, entire; stem leaves much reduced. Inflorescence terminal, bracteate, a spike-like raceme; flowers mostly in pairs; perianth tube long, cylindrical to narrowly, funnel-shaped, bent near base, segments 6, short, unequal; stamens 6, filaments thread-like, short, anthers linear, erect, dorsifixed; style thread-like, stigmas 3-lobed, ovate, sickle-shaped; ovary inferior, 3-chambered. Fruit a capsule, crowned by persistent perianth; seeds flat, with a loose testa. Mexico. Z9.

CULTIVATION Tuberose has long been valued for its spikes of very strongly scented, waxen-white flowers; its fragrance is sometimes considered too overpowering for use in confined spaces, although the flowers were traditionally cut and used to decorate churches in Italy, the cooler temperatures prolonging the life of the bloom and, no doubt, muting the intense fragrance. Essential oil of tuberose is extracted by cold enfleurage from the flowers and used extensively in perfumery; 1150g of flowers yields 1gm of oil. The Aztecs used tuberose oil to flavour chocolate.

Frost-tender tuberous perennials, they usually flower in midsummer. Given protection and a minimum temperature of 15°C/60°F, with successional plantings they may be forced to flower almost throughout the year. In cool temperate climates, *Polianthes* is grown in the warm, sheltered flower border, to be lifted and dried off in autumn and stored in sand to overwinter in frost free-conditions. Otherwise, grow in bright direct sunlight in the glasshouse or conservatory. Plant singly into a 15cm/6in. pot, into a mix of fibrous loam with additional well-rotted manure and leafmould or equivalent; give bottom heat at about 15–18°C/60–65°F, keeping the potting mix just moist until the leaves appear. Water plentifully when in full growth, and feed fortnightly with liquid fertilizer. Dry the plants off after the leaves fade in winter. Propagate by seed or offsets in spring.

P.geminiflora (La Ll. & Lex.) Rose (*Coetocapnia geminiflora* Link & Otto; *Bravoa geminiflora* La Ll. & Lex.). To 60cm; rhiz. bulbous, 2.5–3cm diam. Basal lvs 5–6, 30–40×1.5cm, linear, stem lvs 4, shorter, lanceolate, erect, adpressed to stem. Infl. 30–50cm; raceme 8–30cm; bracts thin, dry; perianth bright red-orange, to 2.5cm, free seg. ovate, green, to 2cm. Summer.

P.maculosa (Hook.) Shinn. See *Manfreda maculosa*.
P.runyonii Shinn. See *Manfreda longiflora*.

P.tuberosa L. TUBEROSE.
To 1m; rhiz. tuberous. Basal lvs to 45×1.5cm, in rosettes, thin, linear, bright green to grey-green, deeply grooved below, stem lvs 8–12, reduced, clasping. Fls very fragrant, in a lax spike; bracts green, lanceolate; perianth pure waxy white, 3–6cm, free seg. oblong-lanceolate, spreading, showy. Only known as a cultigen; cultivated in pre-Columbian Mexico. 'Excelsior Double Pearl': an improved form of 'The Pearl'. 'Single Mexican': fls single, to 5 spikes, long-lasting; possibly typical. 'The Pearl': fls double, highly fragrant. var. **gracilis** Link & Otto. Habit more slender, lvs narrower, perianth with long slender tube, seg. linear.

P.variegata (Jacobi) Shinn. See *Manfreda variegata*.
P.virginica (L.) Shinn. See *Manfreda virginica*.

Polygonatum Mill. SOLOMON'S SEAL. (From Gk *polys*, many, and *gonu*, joint, referring to the many-jointed rhizome; name used by Dioscorides.) Liliaceae (Convallariaceae). Some 30 species of mostly hardly, rhizomatous, perennial herbs. Rhizome horizontal, jointed, with many scars. Stems erect to arching. Leaves alternate, opposite, or whorled, ovate, lanceolate, or linear. Flowers green to yellow, nodding or pendulous, axillary along stems, solitary or emerging sometimes in loose racemes or subumbels; perianth terete, marcescent, deciduous, with 6 erecto-patent lobes; stamens 6. Fruit a blue-black, or red, several-seeded berry. N US, Europe, Asia.

CULTIVATION Occurring predominantly in woodland habitats, frequently on calcareous soils, *Polygonatum* spp. are valued for their graceful, usually arching habit, fine foliage and for the small pendant waxy flowers which are often faintly scented, more noticeably so in *P.odoratum*. The flowers last fairly well when cut and *P.multiflorum* is sometimes forced under glass for this purpose. Ranging in size from the small, densely rhizomatous *P.hookeri*, for the peat terrace, sink garden and alpine house, through low-growing types such as *P.× hybridum* 'Striatum' (less vigorous than the species), to *P.biflorum*, which on rich moist soils may reach heights of 1.8m/6ft and more.

Most are valued for form and textural contrasts in the foliage garden and shaded herbaceous or mixed border, and are eminently suited to naturalizing in the woodland garden. With the possible exceptions of *P.falcatum* and *P.stenanthum*, which need deep mulch protection where temperatures fall to between –5 and –10°C/23–14°F, most are tolerant of temperatures to at least –15°C/5°F; the hardiest species, the whorled Solomon's Seal, *P.verticillatum*, *P.sibiricum*, *P.multiflorum*, *P.odoratum* and *P.pubescens* are reliable down to –20°C/–4°F. All benefit from a deep mulch of leafmould or bracken litter where low temperatures are prolonged to protect the shallowly rooting rhizomes.

Polygonatum spp. are tolerant of a range of conditions except heat and drought but are best grown in a fertile humus-rich, moisture-retentive but well drained soil in cool semi-shade or shade. Leave undisturbed once planted and allow to establish large clumps for best effects. In addition to the species described below, *P.kingianum* is sometimes cultivated in cool to intermediate glasshouses and conservatories. This is a magnificent plant, semi-scandent and resembling a giant *P.verticillatum* (to 4m), but with large flowers of a dusky pink marked crimson. Propagate by division or by seed in autumn, germination may be slow and offspring may not come true. Larvae of the saw fly will strip foliage in summer, and slugs may also be a problem.

P.biflorum (Walter) Elliott (*P.canaliculatum* (Muhlenb.) Pursh); *P.commutatum* (Schult.) Dietr.; *P.giganteum* Dietr.)
Stem 40cm–2m, erect or arched, slender, glabrous. Lvs 4–18cm, alternate, sessile, narrow-lanceolate to broadly elliptic, glabrous or minutely puberulent and glaucous beneath. Fls drooping, solitary or clustered 1–4 per peduncle; perianth 1.1–2.3cm, green-white, terete, tepals 3–4mm; stamens borne about half-way up the tube, fil. filiform, glabrous, occasionally minutely warty. E US, SC Canada. Z3.

P.canaliculatum (Muhlenb.) Pursh. See *P.biflorum*.
P.commutatum (Schult.) Dietr. See *P.biflorum*.

P.falcatum Gray.
Stem to 85cm. Lvs to 23cm, narrow-lanceolate to ovate-elliptic, alternate, sickle-shaped, sometimes minutely rough on veins beneath. Fls 2–5, drooping; perianth 1.1–2.2cm, white, terete; stamens borne about half-way up the tube, fil. usually glabrous, occasionally puberulent or warty, 5–7mm. Japan, Korea. Often cultivated as *P.pumilum*. Z6.

P.giganteum Dietr. See *P.biflorum*.

P.hirtum (Poir.) Pursh (*P.latifolium* (Jacq.) Desf.; *Convallaria latifolia* (Jacq.)).
Stem 20–120cm, erect, angular, sparsely puberulent above. Lvs 10–15, 7–15cm, alternate, lanceolate to ovate, puberulent beneath. Fls to 2cm long, white, drooping from axils, solitary or borne in axillary peduncles of 1–5; tepals with green tips, forming cylindric tube, 1–2.5cm; fil. glabrous or glandular. EC and SE Europe, W Russia, NW Turkey. Z5.

P.hookeri Bak.
Stem to 10cm, often much shorter, glabrous. Lvs alternate, 1.5–2cm, linear to narrow elliptic, glabrous beneath, emerging on stem in apical clusters Fls solitary in leaf-axils, erect, *c*2cm, purple or lilac; perianth 1.1–1.2cm, pink to purple, occasionally green-yellow, tepals free, 4–5mm, spreading; stamens borne about half-way up to the tube, fil. glabrous. E Himalaya, China. Z6.

P.humile (Maxim.).
Close to *P.hirtum*, differs in its solitary or paired fls. Z5.

P.× hybridum hort. (*P.multiflorum × P.odoratum*.)
Intermediate between the parents; the most common sp. in cult. 'Flore Pleno': fls double. 'Striatum' ('Variegatum'): lvs striped creamy white, somewhat undulate. Z6.

P.japonicum Morr. & Decne. See *P.odoratum*.
P.latifolium (Jacq.) Desf. See *P.hirtum*.
P.macranthum (Maxim.) Koidz. See *P.stenanthum*.
P.macrophyllum Sweet. See *P.verticillatum*.

P.multiflorum (L.) All. (*Convallaria multiflora* L.). SOLO MON'S SEAL.
Stem to 90cm, terete, arched, glabrous. Lvs 5–15cm, alternate, elliptic-oblong to ovate, amplexicaul, glabrous beneath; petioles very short. Fls white, drooping, borne 2–5 per axillary peduncle; perianth 9mm–2cm, constricted in the middle, with green tip; stamens borne near mouth of tube, fil. sparsely puberulent. Europe, Asia. Z4.

P.odoratum (Mill.) Druce (*P.japonicum* Morr. & Decne.; *P.officinale* All.; *P.vulgare* Desf.).
Stem to 85cm, glabrous, angular, arched. Lvs 10–12, lanceolate to ovate, alternate, ascending, glabrous beneath. Fls 2–4 per axillary peduncle, drooping, fragrant; perianth white, 8–20mm with green tip, terete or spreading at mouth of tube; stamens borne near mouth of tube, fil. glabrous, occasionally minutely warty. Europe, Asia. 'Gilt Edge': lvs edged yellow. 'Grace Barker': lvs striped creamy white. 'Variegatum': stems red when young; lvs narrowly edged creamy white. var. **thunbergii** (C. Morris & Decne.) Hara Stems to 1.1m. Lvs to 15cm. Z4.

P.officinale All. See *P.odoratum*.

P.pubescens (Willd.) Pursh.
Close to *P.odoratum*, differs in fls yellow-green, tepals contracted at base and spreading, minutely warty inside; fil. densely warty. E to SC Canada, South to Georgia and North Carolina. Z3.

P.roseum (Ledeb.) Kunth.
Stem to 70cm, glabrous, terete, sulcate. Lvs 7–15cm, ascending, linear to narrow-lanceolate, acuminate, sub-petiolate, upper opposite or ternate, whorled in clusters of 3 at tips of stems, often minutely rough on veins beneath. Fls erect, rose, solitary or in pairs, borne in lf axils; perianth 1.1–1.2cm, tube terete, finely toothed, tepals narrowly reflexed; stamens borne about half-way up the tube, fil. papillose. W Siberia, C Asia. Z3.

P.sibiricum Delaroche.
Close to *P.verticillatum*. Stems to 1m. Infl solitary or clustered to 30 per peduncle. W Siberia, C Asia. Z3.

P.stenanthum Nak. (*P.macranthum* (Maxim.) Koidz.).
Stem to 120cm, glabrous, terete. Lvs 8.5–17.5cm, lanceolate to ovate, alternate, glabrous beneath. Fls drooping, solitary or clustered in peduncles of 2–4; perianth 2.1–3.6cm, white, cylindric, tepals free, 4–7mm; stamens borne near mouth of tube, fil. warty. Japan, Korea. Z7.

P.stewartianum Diels.
Close to *P.verticillatum*. Lvs always whorled, 5–10cm and apically tendrilous. Tepals purple-pink; stamens borne near the mouth of the tube. Europe, temperate Asia. Z6.

P.verticillatum (L.) All. (*P.macrophyllum* Sweet).
Stem 20–100cm, erect, angular, glabrous or occasionally sparsely puberulent. Lvs 6.5–15cm, opposite or whorled, alternate lower down, sessile, linear-lanceolate to narrow-ovate, minutely rough on veins beneath. Fls to 1.5cm, green, campanulate, drooping, solitary or in clusters of 2–3, perianth 5–10mm, white, constricted in the middle; stamens borne about half-way up tube, fil. glabrous. Europe, temperate Asia, Afghanistan. Z5.

P.vulgare Desf. See *P.odoratum*.

Polyxena Kunth. (For Polyxenus (Priam), King of Troy.) Liliaceae (Hyacinthaceae). 5–6 species of dwarf perennial herbs. Bulbs with a dense mat of soft branching roots and tubular, membranous, truncate tunics extending into a neck. Leaves to 10–15×cm, 2, basal, opposite, ovate to linear, canaliculate, spreading above, sheathing below, glabrous. Flowers fragrant in a terminal corymb; peduncle concealed by sheathing leaf bases; bracts small, membranous; pedicels short; perianth salverform, tepals 6, marcescent, fused into a long narrow tube, lobes spreading; stamens 6, in 2 series, filaments fused to base of tube; ovary trilocular, style terete, stigma apical. Fruit a rounded, 3-valved, capsule; seeds globose, black, shiny. Early spring. S Africa. Z9.

CULTIVATION   As for *Massonia*.

P.angustifolia Bak. (*Massonia angustifolia*; *Neobakeria angustifolia*; *Neobakeria namaquensis*).
Lvs 10×2.5cm. Scape 7.5–16cm; fls white. Cape Province.

P.corymbosa (L.) Jessop (*Hyacinthus corymbosus*).
Lvs linear. Scape to 5cm; fls carmine with paler exterior. Cape Peninsula.

P.odorata Nichols (*Massonia odorata*).
Lvs to 12×0.6cm. Scape very short; fls white, held more or less between lvs. Cape Province. Closely resembles *Massonia*.

P.pygmaea Kunth (*Massonia ensifolia*; *Massonia violacea*).
Lvs to 10×2.5cm. Scape 10–15cm; fls lilac. Cape Province.

Proiphys Herb. (From Gk, *proi*, early, and *phyo*, to bring forth, referring to the premature germination of the seed.) Amaryllidaceae. 3 species of perennial herbs; bulbs subglobose, tunicated. Leaves basal, elliptic to ovate, expanding after flowering, midvein prominent, primary veins looped; petiole channelled above. Inflorescence umbellate; involucral bracts 2–4, ovate; perianth funnel-shaped, white, lobes 6, elliptic to obovate, apiculate, spreading, fused at base; stamens 6, inserted at throat of perianth tube, filaments united and expanded in basal half into a distinct corona, anthers versatile; ovary inferior, globose, 1- or 3-locular; stigma small. Fruit subglobose, 1–3-seeded; seeds globose, smooth, green. NE Australia. Z10.

CULTIVATION   *Proiphys* spp., grown primarily for their umbels of pure white flowers, also have attractively arching, evergreen long-stalked leaves. Although frost-tender they are well suited to pot cultivation in temperate zones. *P.cunninghamii* needs a minimum temperature of 12°C/54°F while *P.alba*, from more tropical climates, needs minimum temperatures of 16–18°C/60–64°F. Pot singly in autumn, with the nose of the bulb at soil level, in a well-drained mix of fibrous loam, leafmould and well-rotted manure. Water plentifully when in growth, reducing after flowering so that plants are just moist enough to prevent flagging, when at rest in winter. Propagate by seed or offsets. Pests and diseases as for *Amaryllis*.

P.alba (R. Br.) Mabb. (*Eurycles alba* (R. Br.) F. Muell.).
Bulb 2–4cm diam. Lvs 10–35×2–10cm, elliptic to ovate, apex acute to acuminate, base cuneate; petiole 7–35cm. Scape to 60cm; umbel 10–30-fld; bracts 2–3cm, 3–4; perianth tube 8–15mm, lobes 6–24mm; fil. united for 3–12mm. Queensland.

P.amboinensis (L.) Herb. (*Pancratium amboinense* L.; *Pancratium australasicum* Ker-Gawl.; *Eurycles sylvestris* Salisb. ex Schult. & Schult. f.).
Bulb to 8cm diam. Lvs 20–30×15–35cm, reniform or broadly ovate, apex emarginate to short-acuminate, base cordate, mar-

gin undulate; petiole 15–60cm. Scape 15–90cm; umbel 5–25-fld; bracts 3–10cm, 3–4; perianth tube 2.5–3cm, lobes 2.5–4cm; fil. united for 2–3mm. W Australia.

P.cunninghamii (Ait. ex Lindl.) Mabb. (*Eurycles cunninghamii* Ait. ex Lindl.). BRISBANE LILY.
Bulb to 5cm diam. Lvs 10–25×8–13cm, ovate, apex acute or shortly acuminate, base rounded; petiole 10–25cm. Scape 25–80cm; umbel 5–12-fld; bracts 1.5–5cm, 2–3; pedicels to 4.5cm; perianth tube 8–12mm, lobes 15–18mm; fil. united for 12–16mm. SE Queensland, NSW.

Pseudogaltonia Kuntze. (From Gk *pseudes*, false, and *Galtonia*.) Liliaceae (Hyacinthaceae). 1 species, a perennial herb. Bulbs large, scaly, forming a fibrous neck. Leaves 6–10, synanthous, in a rosette, erect, broadly linear, apex acuminate, base clasping, margin entire, glaucous green, glabrous, soft. Flowers 10cm in an erect, dense raceme, far exceeding leaves; bracts linear-acuminate, membranous, with a small lateral bracteole; pedicels long, ash-grey at apex; tepals pale glaucous green, basally united into a slightly curved cylindric tube, lobes spreading, ovate, obtuse, half length of tube; stamens 6, slightly exserted, from throat of tube; ovary ovoid, style terete, stigma apical. Fruit an ovoid capsule; seeds rounded, flattened, shiny, black. S Africa (N Cape), Namibia, Botswana, Angola. Z10.

CULTIVATION   Grow in sun in a freely draining, medium-fertility, loam-based mix with additional sharp sand, keep moist when in leaf (from late winter/early spring) and apply a dilute liquid feed until the flower spikes show. Dry off gradually as foliage fades and keep dry overwinter at about 7°C/45°F. Propagate by seed sown when ripe or by bulbils.

P.clavata (Mast. ex Bak.) Phillips.

Puschkinia Adams. (For Count Apollo Apollosovich Mussin-Pushkin (*d*1805), Russian chemist who collected plants in the Caucasus and Ararat.) Liliaceae (Hyacinthaceae). 1 species, a perennial herb, closely related to *Chionodoxa* and *Scilla*, bulbs small, tunicate, brown. Leaves to 15×0.5cm, 2–3, basal, linear-lorate. Flowering stems 5–20cm, naked; flowers in a loose raceme, pale blue with darker stripes, rarely white or tinged green, subsessile or, on lower stems, on pedicels to 1cm; perianth short-tubular, 7–10mm, lobes 6, erect or slightly spreading; stamens 6, filaments united in a 6-lobed cupular corona, anthers borne on corona and alternating with corona lobes; ovary superior; style 1. Fruit a 3-valved, spherical capsule. Spring. Caucasus, Turkey, N Iran, N Iraq, Lebanon. Z5.

CULTIVATION   Charming small bulbs native to montane meadow and stony habitats to 3000m/9840ft. Cold-tolerant to about –20°C/–4°F, they are fairly undemanding in cultivation, thriving in sun or partial shade in gritty, well-drained, humus-rich soil. Flowering is usually better where bulbs can dry out in summer. They are sometimes grown in the alpine display house. Propagate by offsets when dormant in late summer or by seed in autumn.

P.hyacinthoides Bak. See *P.scilloides*.
P.libanotica Zucc. See *P.scilloides* var. *libanotica*.

P.scilloides Adams (*P.hyacinthoides* Bak.).
'Alba': fls pure white. var. **libanotica** (Zucc.) Boiss. (*P.libanotica* Zucc.). Fls smaller; corona lobes sharply acute.

Pyrolirion Herb. (From Gk *pyr*, fire, and *lirion*, lily, from the colour of the flowers.) Amaryllidaceae. 4 species of perennial herbs. Bulbs ovoid, with bulbils. Leaves long, narrow, suberect. Flower solitary, scapose; scapes hollow, spathe tubular and sheathing below, divided into 2 free and opposite segments above; perianth tube erect, narrow and cylindrical in the basal part, the upper part swollen, limb of 6 subequal lobes, not spreading, with a reflexed apex; filaments erect, subequal, inserted in the mouth of the tube, with incumbent anthers; style declinate; stigma trifid, with spathulate lobes. Andes. Z9.

CULTIVATION   Rare in cultivation, *Pyrolirion* may prove difficult to flower. It is particularly susceptible to bulb rot when grown in wet soils. Cultivate as for *Zephyranthes*.

P.aureum (Ruiz & Pav.) Herb. (*Amaryllis aurea* Ruiz & Pav.). GOLDEN FLAME LILY.
Lvs to 10×0.8cm, acuminate, channelled, arching, bright yellow-green. Scapes terete, lightly striate, glossy; spathe oblong, deeply bifid; pedicel 1cm; perianth golden, tube to 3.5×0.8cm, widening to a turbinate throat with denticulate scales, lobes to 6×0.8cm, lanceolate, deflexed, acuminate; fil. equal, 2.5cm shorter than perianth lobes; stigma with spread lobes. Peru.

P.aureum Edwards non (Ruiz & Pav.) Herb. See *Zephyranthes flava*.
P.flavum Herb. See *Zephyranthes flava*.

Ranunculus L. (Name used by Pliny, derived from Lat. *rana*, a frog; some species grow in wet places.) BUT-TERCUP; CROWFOOT. Ranunculaceae. About 400 species of annual, biennial or perennial herbs, sometimes submerged aquatics. Roots fibrous or tuberous. Leaves 2-ranked or spiralling, often forming basal rosette, with some cauline, or mostly cauline, sometimes dimorphic, especially in aquatic spp., stipulate or exstipulate, laciniate to palmately lobed to entire, linear to orbicular, glabrous to hairy, sometimes glaucous. Flowers solitary or in cymose panicles, terminal or axillary, dioecious, actinomorphic, white, yellow, pink to red; sepals 3–7, variable in colour, sometimes caducous; petals usually 5, but to 15+, occasionally reduced or absent, often glossy, with nectariferous depression at base. Stamens numerous, spirally arranged, shorter than petals; carpels numerous, also spiral, with 1 ovule. Fruit a head of compressed or sub-globose achenes, smooth to rugose or bristly, often beaked; some poisonous, with acrid sap. Temperate and boreal regions worldwide, mountains in Tropics. Some are weeds; several are dangerous to cattle, but usually avoided.

CULTIVATION Cultivars of the lesser celandine (*R.ficaria*) are available in double, white, orange and pale creamy flowered forms, and with bronzed foliage. These are worth cultivating in shady, moist soils below trees and shrubs where their foliage will die back in early summer. In cold areas, frost-sensitive, fleshy-rooted spp. from warmer regions such as *R.calandrinioides*, *R.cortusifolius* and *R.bullatus* may survive in warm, sunny, sheltered spots on freely draining soils, but are often best in the frame or alpine house: here they may be summer-dormant.

Plant in spring or autumn, 30–90cm/12–36in. apart. Repot plants under glass every 2–3 years in spring and give deep pots to thongy-rooted spp. such as *R.calandrinioides*. Grow the more frost-tender *R.asiaticus* and cultivars as for tuberous-rooted anemones. These bear flowers suitable for cutting of two sorts: the Persian Group with neat, shapely plants and well-formed flowers, and the taller Turban Group which are hardier but make larger-flowered, coarser plants. Propagate by division in spring and autumn or from fresh seed sown in cold frames after flowering. Susceptible to powdery mildew, especially in hot, dry weather where plants are closely spaced: treat with a systemic fungicide.

R.asiaticus L.
Pubesc. perenn.; some roots tuberous, fascicled. Stems simple or branched, to 45cm. Outer basal lvs 3-lobed, lobes stalked, further divided and toothed; inner lvs 2–3-sect. Fls few to several, red, pink, purple, yellow to white, 3–5cm across; sep. spreading, becoming reflexed; pet. obovate, obtuse; anth. purple-black. Head of achenes to 1cm; achenes ovate, beak broad, hooked. Spring–summer. SE Europe (west to Crete), SW Asia. Very variable; seed races are offered with fls of mixed colours; the fls may be double or semi-double. At one time a very popular florists' flower. Bloomingdale Hybrids: habit dwarf; fls double in shades of pink, yellow, rose, red and white; seed race. 'Color Carnival': tall, robust; fls large, double, in wide range of colours; 'Picotee': compact; fls double, very large, ruffled, in pink, red, orange, white and yellow, picotee edge; 'Pot Dwarf': fls semi-double and double, in scarlet, pink, salmon, orange and white; 'Superbissima': tall; fls large. Tecolote Hybrids: robust; fls exceptionally large. Victoria Hybrids: fls large, fully double in wide range of colours. Z9.

R.brevifolius Ten.
Close to *R.thora*, but smaller in all parts; to 10cm. Basal lvs several, grey; cauline lf solitary, 3-sect. Fls 1–2, to 2.5cm across. Achenes 3–4mm, beak long, curved. Spring–summer. Italy, Balkans. Z7.

R.broteri Freyn. See *R.bulbosus* ssp. *gallecicus*.

R.bulbosus L.
Pubesc. perenn.; roots fibrous; stems 15–50cm, swollen and bulb-like at base, with enlarged, overlapping petiole bases. Basal lvs ovate, 3-lobed, middle seg. stalked or sessile, seg. further divided and toothed, persisting over winter; cauline lvs progressively reduced, uppermost with linear-lanceolate lobes. Fls several, golden yellow, occasionally sulphur yellow (e.g. 'F.M.Burton'), to 3cm across; sep. yellow-green, strongly reflexed; pet. 5, obovate-cuneate, glossy. Receptacle hairy; achenes obovate, dark brown, 3mm, beak short, hooked. Spring–summer. Europe to W Asia, N Africa, naturalized N America, New Zealand. Z5. 'F.M. Burton': fls single, light lemon. 'Pleniflorus' ('Flore Pleno') (*R.speciosus* 'Plenus'; *R.gouanii* 'Plenus'): botanical status uncertain; rootstock thick, shortly rhizomatous; stems to 30cm; lvs glossy green; fls double, chrome-yellow with green centre, to 4cm across. ssp. *gallecicus* (Freyn ex Willk.) P.W. Ball & Heyw. (*R.broteri* Freyn). Rootstock not or scarcely swollen, roots fusiform. Basal lvs with seg. obovate-cuneate, sessile or short-stalked; cauline lvs small, with entire seg. Fls solitary or few. Spring. NW Spain. Z7.

R.bullatus L.
Perenn.; roots tuberous; stems simple, to 30cm. Lvs all basal, ovate, crenate, hispid below, bullate. Fls 1–2, yellow, 2.5cm across, violet-scented; sep. green, pubesc.; pet. 5–12, oblong. Achenes inflated, beak short, curved. Autumn–spring. Mediterranean to NW Spain and Portugal. Z7.

R.calandrinioides Oliv.
Perenn.; rootstock thick, unbranched, roots fleshy; stems several, to 15cm, flushed pink below. Lvs to 6.5cm, basal, long-petiolate, lanceolate to ovate-lanceolate, entire, margins undulate, glaucous green, veins parallel. Fls 1–3, white or flushed pink, to 5cm across; sep. tinged red, thin, 1.5cm; pet. thin. Achenes short-beaked. Winter–spring. Morocco. Z7.

R.chaerophyllos sensu Coste, non L. See *R.paludosus*.

R.cortusifolius Willd. (*R.cortusaefolius* hort.).
Villous perenn.; some roots tuberous; stems robust, to 1.2m. Basal lvs leathery, orbicular-cordate, shallowly lobed, with lobes further divided and toothed, to 30cm broad; cauline lvs progressively reduced, uppermost bract-like, sessile. Fls numerous in corymb, golden-yellow, to 5cm across, sweetly scented, sep. spreading. Summer. Azores, Canaries, Madeira. Z9.

R.creticus L.
Pubesc. perenn.; some roots tuberous; stems branched, to 30cm. Basal lvs reniform, crenate, shallowly lobed; cauline lvs 3-lobed, lobes lanceolate, entire. Fls several, yellow to 3cm across. Receptacle almost glabrous; achenes pubesc., flattened, 4–5mm, beak short, hooked. Spring. Crete. Z8.

R.ficaria L. LESSER CELANDINE; PILEWORT.
Glabrous perenn., 5–30cm; root tubers prolific, fusiform or clavate, 1–2.5cm. Basal lvs rosulate, cordate, angled or crenate, 1–4cm, dark green, often with brown or silver markings, long-petiolate; cauline lvs smaller, petioles shorter. Fls solitary to few, brilliant golden-yellow, fading to white, 2–3cm across; sep. 3, green; pet. 8–12, narrow-ovate. Receptacle hairy; achenes spherical, carinate, finely pubesc., to 2.5mm, beak minute. Spring. Europe, NW Africa, W Asia, naturalized N America. Very variable and many cvs selected, usually from wild populations. Most of those below belong to ssp. *ficaria*. 'Albus': lvs with a dark mark; fls very pale yellow, fading white, blue-green below. 'Bowles Double': fls double,

green centre on opening, later paler yellow. 'Brazen Hussy': lvs chocolate brown; fls golden. 'Collarette': anth. petaloid, forming a tight anemone centre. 'Cupreus' ('Aurantiacus'): lvs heavily silvered with a prominent dark mark; fls coppery-orange. 'Double Bronze': fls double, yellow, with bronze backs to pet., a few normal stamens present. 'Double Cream': fls double, upper surface of pet. creamy, lower surface tinged grey; a few normal stamens present. 'E.A. Bowles': fls golden yellow, anemone-centred. 'Flore Pleno': fls double, yellow, pet. reverse tinged green; stamens absent. 'Green Petal': many narrow, wavy-edged green and yellow staminodes; pet. absent. 'Hoskin's Miniature': small; lvs slightly marked silver. 'Lemon Queen': fls simple, pale yellow, petal reverse tinged bronze. 'Major' ('Grandiflorus'): very large in all parts; fls to 42mm across. 'Randall's White': lvs without a dark mark; upper surface of pet. pale cream, lower surface purple-blue. 'Salmon's White': lvs with a dark mark; upper surface of pet. very pale cream, lower surface purple-blue. 'Whiskey Double Yellow': fls double, yellow, pet. reverse tinged yellow and bronze. ssp. *bulbilifer* (L.) Lambinon. Bulbils borne in stem leaf axils. Potentially a pernicious weed. ssp. *ficariiformis* Rouy & Foucaud. Large in all parts. Fls 3–5cm across; sep. white-yellow. S Europe. Z5.

R.flabellatus Desf. See *R.paludosus*.
R.fumariifolius Desf. ex DC. See *R.millefoliatus*.
R.gouanii 'Plenus'. See *R.bulbosus* 'Pleniflorus'.

R.illyricus L.
Sericeous perenn. to 50cm; root-tubers ovoid. Lvs linear-lanceolate, to 3-lobed, lobes entire or further divided, seg. linear lanceolate. Fls numerous, pale yellow, 3cm across; sep. somewhat reflexed. Receptacle glabrous; achenes triangular, compressed, nearly winged, 3mm, beak straight. Spring. C & SE Europe. Z6.

R.kochii Ledeb.
Close to *R.ficaria*, 5cm. Lvs rounded, entire. Fls golden-yellow, to 2cm across; 12–15+. Spring. Mts Turkey, Iraq, Iran. Z6.

R.millefoliatus Vahl (*R.fumariifolius* Desf. ex DC.).
Pubesc. perenn.; root-tubers ovoid, or shortly oblong; stem almost leafless, 15–30cm. Basal lvs 2–3-pinnatisect, lobes linear-lanceolate, acute. Fls usually solitary, golden-yellow, 2–3cm across, almost flat; sep. glabrous spreading. Receptacle glabrous; achenes rounded, keeled 3.5mm, beak broad, hooked. Spring–summer. S & EC Europe, N Africa, W Asia. 'Grandiflorus': fls larger. Z6.

R.monspeliacus L.
White-woolly or -silky perenn. to 50cm.; root-tubers cylindric or fusiform. Basal lvs variable, ovate-cordate, 3-lobed and dentate, or trifid with stalked, oblong-cuneate, laciniate lobes; cauline lvs 3-lobed, lobes linear. Fls several, golden yellow, 2.5cm across; sep. reflexed. Receptacle glabrous; achenes ovoid, compressed, sparsely downy, beak curved. Spring. W Mediterranean. Z8.

R.nyssanus Leichtlin. See *R.psilostachys*.

R.paludosus Poir. (*R.flabellatus* Desf.; *R.chaerophyllos* sensu Coste, non L.).
Variable pubesc. perenn. to 50cm; rootstock stout, fibrous, root-tubers fusiform. Basal lvs 3-lobed to trifid, middle lobe long-stalked, lobes further divided, seg. narrow, dentate. Fls few, golden-yellow, to 2cm across; sep. spreading. Receptacle glabrous; achenes 2mm, sparsely pubesc., keeled, beak long, hooked at apex. Spring. W Europe (to Channel Is.), Mediterranean. Z7.

R.psilostachys Griseb. (*R.nyssanus* Leichtlin).
Perenn.; root-tubers fusiform; stems simple or little-branched, to 30cm. Basal lvs to 10cm across, suborbicular and shallowly 3-lobed or deeply cut, seg. obovate-cuneate, dentate, all sericeous below. Fls 1–14, glossy yellow, 2–3cm across; sep. reflexed, sericeous without. Achenes ovoid, verrucose, beak curved. Spring. Balkans, W Turkey. Z6.

R.rupestris Guss. (*R.spicatus* Presl).
Pubesc. perenn. to 30cm; root-tubers fusiform. Basal lvs reniform or orbicular, shallowly 3-lobed, lobes shallowly-divided, crenate, densely hirsute. Fls 1–4, yellow, to 4cm across. Receptacle pubesc.; achenes obovate, glabrous or bristly, beak broad, recurved and hooked. Spring. Spain, Portugal, Sicily. Z7.

R.speciosus 'Plenus'. See *R.bulbosus* 'Pleniflorus'.
R.spicatus Presl. See *R.rupestris*.

R.thora L.
Perenn. 10–30cm; roots tuberous. Basal lvs reniform, entire at base, coarsely toothed towards apex, glaucous, glabrous, petiolate, emerging after flowering; cauline lvs sessile, small, uppermost lanceolate, 3-lobed. Fls 1–few, yellow, 1–2cm across; sep. glabrous; pet. ovate. Receptacle hairy; achenes few, glabrous, rounded, 4mm, beak short, hooked. Spring. Europe (mts, Spain to Balkans). Z5.

Remusatia Schott. (For Abel Remusat (1785–1832), orientalist and physician.) Araceae. 4 species of tuberous perennial herbs. Tuber rounded, bearing spike-like bulbiliferous shoots (rather than flowering stems) bearing cataphylls and clusters of hooked bulbils. Leaves solitary, entire, peltate, long-petiolate. Inflorescence solitary, emerging with leaf (true flowering very sporadic); spathe thick-textured, convolute-tubular at base, limb broad or narrow, erect or spreading and reflexed, deciduous; spadix short, sessile, female zone short, cylindric, male zone clavate, exserted, male and female zones separated by zone of sterile flowers; stamens 2–3; ovary unilocular, ovules many. Fruit small red berries. Tropical Africa, Himalaya through SE Asia to N Australia. Z10.

CULTIVATION An unusual aroid which rarely flowers, increasing itself instead by producing small, hooked bulbils on sterile, modified 'inflorescences'; its general requirements are as for *Amorphophallus*.

R.vivipara Schott.
Tuber 7.5cm diam., depressed-globose; bulbiliferous shoots to 30cm, ascending, simple or with short branches, bulbils many, hooked. Lf 12.5–45×7.5–30cm, orbicular-ovate or cordate, acute or acuminate, dark green with paler veins; petiole to 50cm. Peduncle to 15cm; spathe tube 5cm, green, limb to 7.5cm, reflexed, lime-green to golden yellow; spadix to 3.5cm, cream-white. Berries red. Late spring. Range as for the genus. In many examples of this species, the reproductive function is reduced to vivipary: the bulbiliferous spike is almost always produced, whereas flowering is often suppressed or the spadix will tend to bear only sterile fls.

Rhodohypoxis Nel. (From Gk *rhodon*, rose, and *Hypoxis*.) Hypoxidaceae. 6 species of usually dwarf perennial herbs with no true stem but a short pseudostem and both fibrous and fleshy roots. Leaves basal, spreading or erect, elliptic to filiform, hairy. Scape sometimes absent, the ovary lying at or below soil level, bearing the perianth on a beak; flowers solitary or few; perianth lobes 6, outer 3 broader than inner 3, fused at base as tube, inner 3 clawed, a pronounced inflexed curve at this position sealing the tube entrance; stamens adnate to tube; stigma 3-parted; ovary with 3 cells; ovules numerous per cell. Fruit a capsule, breaking up in the soil or opening by means of a lid; seeds ellipsoid to spherical, black. SE Africa. Z8.

CULTIVATION Diminutive alpines are grown for their charming flowers, carried throughout the season from early spring into autumn, with a colour range from pure white to clear deep pinks and crimson. Found in high altitude habitats in the Drakensberg, *R.baurii* occur to altitudes of 2400m/7800ft on open grassy slopes that are frequently mist covered, in damp peaty soils; *R.b.* var. *confecta* is also found in short damp turf, frequently amongst rock outcrops at 1900–2500m/6175–8125ft, although it is more common at the higher levels. *R.b.* var. *platypetala* is more characteristically found in drier conditions, while *R.milloides* grows in marsh and flushes at similar heights.

Rhodohypoxis is eminently suited to plantings in pockets of acid soil in the rock garden, or in sinks and troughs, provided with plentiful moisture during spring and summer; although they will withstand cold, they are intolerant of winter wet, demanding dry conditions when dormant. When grown outside, protect with a propped pane of glass. Otherwise grow in the alpine house or bulb frame.

Grow in sun in a light, freely draining, lime-free potting mix, with additional sharp sand and leafmould; water plentifully when in growth, avoiding the foliage, and keep almost completely dry in winter. Pot-grown specimens may be plunged out of doors in summer. Repot annually as growth resumes. Propagate by offsets or by division of established clumps; also by seed, which may show considerable and interesting variation.

R.baurii (Bak.) Nel (*Hypoxis baurii* Bak.). RED STAR. Pseudostem to 3cm. Lvs 2.5–11× to 1cm, linear to lanceolate, folded, keeled, hairy, more so on upper surface. Scape to 15cm (usually far shorter), hairy; fls solitary or in twos, white, pink or red; perianth tube to 2.5mm, lobes ovate-elliptic, to 2cm, hairy. Late spring. S Africa. var. *baurii*. Lvs narrower, suberect; fls red or deep pink. Found in wetter areas. var. *confecta* Hilliard & B.L. Burtt. Lvs to 7.5cm, erect bright green. Fls white to red, often white ageing to red. Included in the parentage of many cultivars. var. *platypetala* (Bak.) Nel (*Hypoxis platypetala* Bak.; *Hypoxis baurii* var. *platypetala* (Bak.) Bak.; *R.baurii* f. *platypetala* (Bak.) Milne-Redh.; *R.platypetala* (Bak.) Gray). Lvs broader, spreading, grey/green; fls white pale pink. Found in drier areas. *R.baurii* × *Hypoxis parvula* is a cross that occurs naturally between close-growing wild populations. White variants of *Hypoxis parvula* are known to cross with *R.baurii* var. *baurii* and *R.baurii* var. *platypetala*. Yellow forms of *Hypoxis parvula*

Rhodohypoxis baurii

have crossed with *R.baurii* var. *confecta*.

R.milloides (Bak.) Hilliard & B.L. Burtt.
Underground axis to 2cm; crown fibrous; stolons numerous. Pseudostem 1–5cm. Lvs 4–10, 2.5–17× to 1cm, linear, lanceolate, keeled, folded acuminate, erect, hairy except on tip,

light green. Fls solitary or in twos, deep crimson or cerise, sometimes white or pink; perianth tube narrowly bell-shaped, outer seg. 10–20×4–10mm, elliptic, hairy at base. S Africa (Natal).

R.platypetala (Bak.) Gray. See *R.baurii* var. *platypetala*.

Rhodophiala C. Presl (From Gk *rhodo*, red, and *phiale*, a shallow cup, a reference to the broadly funnelform, red flowers). Amaryllidaceae. 31 bulbous perennials, closely related to *Hippeastrum*. Bulb small, with distinct neck. Leaves narrow-linear, 2–12(–20)mm broad. Scape hollow, leafless; spathe-valves 2, rarely monophyllous or valves slightly united at base, bracteoles very small to minute; pedicels variable in length; flowers in an umbel of 1–6, funnel-shaped or nearly tubular; perianth tube usually very short, less than 5mm, occasionally to 20mm, perianth segments of different sizes, longer than tube, yellow to bright pink or red; stamens 6, fasciculate with style, declinate-ascending; anthers oblong, versatile; stigma distinctly or obscurely 3-lobed, or capitate. Fruit a capsule; seeds discoid, winged, dark brown or black. Summer to autumn. Andes (Chile, Argentina, Bolivia). Z9.

CULTIVATION   Plant in a well drained loamy medium. Most are best suited to the alpine house or bulb frame, although *R.advena* and *R.pratensis* will tolerate winter lows of –5°C/23°F/23°F with some crown protection in a perfectly drained sunny border. Otherwise as for *Hippeastrum*.

R.advena (Ker-Gawl.) Traub (*Hippeastrum advenum* (Ker-Gawl.) Herb.; *Amaryllis advena* Ker-Gawl.).
Bulb ovoid, to 4cm diam., neck short, somewhat glaucous. Scape to 50cm, slender; spathe-valves to 5cm, pedicels 2–7cm; fls 2–6, borne more or less horizontally, open-funnel-shaped, to 5cm long, red, pink or yellow; perianth tube 5mm, with perianth scales small, seg. oblong, acute; stamens to two-thirds length perianth, style subequal to perianth. Chile.

R.andicola (Poepp.) Traub (*Hippeastrum andicola* (Poepp.) Bak.; *Habranthus andicola* (Poepp.) Herb.).
Lvs linear, glaucous, smooth. Scape 15–20cm, glaucous; spathe valves elongate; fl. solitary, erect, 5cm long; perianth tube 6–8mm, seg. subequal, brilliant violet; stamens short, deflexed. S Chile.

R.araucana (Philippi) Traub (*Hippeastrum araucanum* Philippi; *Amaryllis araucana* (Philippi) Traub & Uphof).
Bulb 2.7cm diam. Lvs synanthous, 30×0.4cm. Scape 30cm, 2mm thick, spathe-valves 3.2cm; fls 2, erect, funnel-shaped, rose pink; perianth tube 5mm; stamens and style much shorter than perianth. Chile.

R.bagnoldii (Herb.) Traub (*Habranthus bagnoldii* Herb.; *Hippeastrum bagnoldii* (Herb.) Bak.; *Amaryllis bagnoldii* (Herb.) Dietr.).
Bulb globose, 5cm diam., black. Lvs linear, 30×0.6cm, obtuse, somewhat glaucous. Scape 30cm, slender; spathe valves lanceolate, 5cm; pedicels to 5–7.5cm; fls 4–6, erect or ascending, openly funnel-shaped, 3–5.5cm, yellow, often tinged red; perianth tube 5mm, not closed by perianth scales, seg. oblong, to 1.2cm broad; stamens shorter than perianth, style equal to perianth, stigma 3 fld. Chile.

R.bifida (Herb.) Traub (*Hippeastrum bifidum* (Herb.) Bak.; *Amaryllis bifida* (Herb.) Spreng.).
Bulb globose, 3.8cm diam., neck 5–7.5cm, dark brown. Lvs 2–3, linear, 30cm, somewhat glaucous. Scape subterete, 9–30cm; spathe-valves lanceolate, 5–7.5cm; pedicels 2.5–5cm, slender; fls 2–6, erect or ascending, 5cm long, bright red; perianth tube very short with corona at throat, seg. oblanceolate, to 8mm wide; stamens declinate, half length seg., exceeded by style, stigma trifid. Argentina, Uruguay.

R.chilensis (L'Hérit.) Traub (*Amaryllis chilensis* L'Hérit.; *Hippeastrum chilense* (L'Hérit.) Bak.).
Bulb globose, 2.5–3.8cm diam., neck to 7.5cm, dull brown; lvs 2, synanthous, narrow-linear, 15–23cm. Scape 15–23cm;

spathe-valves linear, 3.8cm; pedicels to 2.5cm; fls 2, erect or ascending, to 5cm, bright red or yellow; perianth tube very short, seg. oblong, 9mm wide, acute; stamens shorter than seg., style equalling seg., stigma 3-fid. S Chile.

R.elwesii (C.W. Wright) Traub (*Hippeastrum elwesii* C.W. Wright; *Amaryllis elwesii* (C.W. Wright) Traub & Uphof).
Lvs synanthous, linear, 26×0.5cm. Scape terete, 6mm diam., spathe-valves oblong, 6×8mm, deciduous; pedicels 4cm; fls 2, yellow with throat red; perianth tube 1cm, with perianth scales above insertion of stamens, seg. elliptic, 4×1.8cm; stamens shorter than seg., style long-exserted, stigma 3-fid. Argentina.

R.pratensis (Poepp.) Traub (*Amaryllis pratensis* Poepp.; *Hippeastrum pratense* (Poepp.) Bak.).
Bulb ovoid, to 4cm diam., neck short, dark brown. Lvs synanthous, linear, 30–45×0.6–1.2cm. Scape stout, 30–60cm; spathe-valves lanceolate, 5cm; pedicels 2.5–3.8cm; fls 2–5, ascending or horizontal, bright red or violet purple; perianth tube very short with minute scales in throat, seg. oblanceolate, 6.4×1.3cm, subobtuse; stamens declinate, half length perianth seg., style equalling seg., stigma capitate. Chile.

R.rhodolirion (Bak.) Traub (*Rhodolirion andinum* Philippi; *Hippeastrum rhodolirion* (Philippi) Bak.).
Lvs hysteranthous, linear. Scape to 45cm, stout; spathe valves lanceolate, to 5cm; pedicels 2cm; fls solitary, openly funnel-shaped to 7.6cm long, bright red to pink with darker veins or white, yellow in throat; perianth tube 2cm, green; stamens declinate-ascending, half length seg., exceeded by style. Chile.

R.rosea (Sweet) Traub (*Hippeastrum roseum* (Sweet) Bak.; *Amaryllis rosea* (Sweet) Traub & Uphof non Lam., *Amaryllis barlowii* Traub & Mold.).
Bulb ovoid, less than 2.5cm diam., neck short, dark brown. Lvs 3, synanthous, narrowly linear, glaucous. Scape 15cm, slender; spathe valves to 4cm, exceeding pedicels; fls 1–2, nearly horizontal, 5cm long, bright red; perianth tube very short, green, oblong-lanceolate, acute; stamens shorter than seg., exceeded by style, stigma 3-fid. Chile (Is. of Chiloe).

Rigidella Lindl. (Lat. diminutive of *rigidus*, rigid, referring to the pedicels, which become erect in fruit.) Iridaceae. 4 species of perennial bulbous herbs. Leaves few, radical, long, broadly lanceolate, sometimes narrowing to a long petiole, plicate, becoming progressively reduced to narrowly acuminate, spathaceous bracts on the flowering stalk. Flowering stems erect, simple or sparsely branched; flowers 1 to many per spathe, fugacious, on slender nodding pedicels, bright red, lacking a tube, cup-shaped at base, outer lobes 3, slender-clawed, blades ovate-acute, spreading or reflexed, inner lobes ovate, small, erect; stamens 3, filaments fused as a cylindrical tube, exserted, enclosing style; stigmas 3, deeply cleft. Fruit a thin-walled capsule. Mexico to Guatemala. Distinguished from *Tigridia* by the small, erect, ovate inner perianth segments; in *Tigridia* they are larger, pandurate and spreading. Z9.

CULTIVATION   Grown for their brilliant but short-lived blooms, carried in succession over a long period where temperatures do not fall much below −3°C/26°F to −5°C/23°F for long periods, *Rigidella* spp. may be grown in full sun, in a humus-rich, fertile and well-drained soil at the sheltered base of a south-facing wall. A deep mulch of bracken litter will help secure the essential dry winter rest. Ensure sufficient moisture in spring and early summer when in growth and feed established colonies if necessary as growth commences. In cooler zones, lift and store in dry, frost-free conditions over winter or grow in the cool glasshouse or conservatory in deep pots or in the border. Propagate by seed in spring in a sandy propagating mix.

The hybrid between *R.orthantha* and *Tigridia pavonia* is an extremely vigorous and attractive plant, flowering freely over long periods and successful in the cool glasshouse, possibly also out of doors in favoured temperate climates.

R.flammea Lindl.
Basal lvs 90–125cm, broadly ensiform, sheathing stem at base, stem lvs few, reduced. Flowering stems 1–1.5m; flowers pendent in pseudo-umbels, outer perianth seg. to 6cm, cup to 2cm, scarlet spotted or striped purple or black above claw, inner perianth seg. to 1cm, yellow tipped red; style branches to 0.4cm. Mexico.

R.immaculata Herb.
Differs from *R.flammea* in its narrower, synanthous, not hysteranthous basal lvs, shorter flowering stem and unmarked scarlet fls. Mexico, Guatemala.

R.orthantha Lem.
Basal lvs to 100×8.5cm, stem lvs 1–2. Fls scarlet, erect, outer perianth seg. to 6cm, cup to 1cm, inner seg. to 3cm; style branches to 7.5cm. Mexico, Guatemala.

Romulea Maratti. (For Romulus, founder and first King of Rome.) Iridaceae. Some 80 species of small, crocus-like, perennial, cormous herbs. Corms asymmetric at base with brown crust-like or tough tunic. Basal leaves 1–6, usually 2, linear-filiform to narrow-subulate, the sheaths sometimes dilated, glabrous, 4-ridged or -grooved. Scapes erect or elongate-recurved (in fruit), sometimes lacking, emerging from ground at flowering time; flowers erect, subtended and partly enclosed by an outer bract and inner bracteole, 1 per spathe; perianth tube shortly funnelform, segments equal, erecto-patent; stamens 3, attached to throat, shorter than or exceeding style, sometimes infertile; stigmas 3, bifid, branches filiform. Fruit a trilocular, oblong, thin-walled capsule. Spring. Mediterranean, north to SW England; S Africa, and at high altitudes, in C & E Africa north to the Mediterranean. Distinguished from *Crocus* by the corm, which is asymmetric at base, the long-stemmed flowers and short perianth tube.

CULTIVATION   *Romulea* spp. range widely in habitat, from coastal regions on cliff tops and fixed dunes, in sandy maquis, and at higher altitudes, near snow melt in the Lebanon at 2000m/6500ft, for *R.nivalis*, and in the Drakensberg at over 2000m/6500ft for *R.macowanii*; most habitats are characterized by their excellent drainage and warm dry summers. With the exception of the summer-flowering *R.macowanii*, *Romulea* is a predominantly spring-flowering genus grown for its small crocus-like flowers carried on short and slender stems. The individual blooms are short-lived (about 3–4 days), and frequently open only at midday, closing in the evening. Providing that they can be kept dry in summer when dormant, the Europeans and Asiatics are the hardiest species, tolerating short periods of low temperatures in the range −5°C/23°F to −10°C/14°F; they are best given placement at the base of a south-facing wall or niche in the rock garden. *R.bulbocodium*, *R.tempskyana* and *R.ramiflora* are slightly more cold-tolerant. The South African species, with the possible exception of the alpine *R.macowanii*, are probably more safely grown under glass or in the bulb frame in cool temperate zones. Grow in full sun, in well-drained, very sandy soil. Under glass use a loam-based mix with additional sharp sand and leafmould; grow in direct sunlight, with good ventilation and water moderately when in growth, drying off gradually as the foliage dies down. Propagate by seed in autumn, or in spring for *R.macowanii*, also by offsets.

R.atranda Lewis.
Basal lvs to 40×0.1cm, erect or curved, conspicuously channelled. Fls 3–4cm diam., magenta-rose, with dark purple zone above yellow throat; anth. black, purple or yellow. S Africa (Cape Province).

R.bulbocodioides auct. See *R.flava*.

R.bulbocodium (L.) Sebast. & Mauri (*R.grandiflora* Tod.; *R.clusiana* (Lange) Nyman).
Basal lvs 6–15×0.06–0.2cm, usually 2, erect or recurved, linear, conspicuously channelled. Fls 1–6 per scape; bracts green, margin hyaline, bracteole green or purple-flushed in central region, otherwise very thin-textured; perianth 2.25–5cm, bright violet, rarely white, tube 0.3–0.8cm, yellow, orange or white within or at throat, perianth seg. elliptic-lanceolate; fil. ciliate at base; styles white, equal to or exceeding anth. Mediterranean, Portugal, NW Spain, Bulgaria. var. *crocea* (Boiss. & Heldr.) Bak. Fls yellow. var. *leichtliniana* (Heldr.) Bég. Fls white, throat yellow. var. *subpalustris* Bak. Fls tinted purple-blue, throat white. Z7.

Romulea   (a) *R.bulbocodium*   (b) *R.nivalis*   (c) *R.atranda*   (d) *R.flava*

R.clusiana (Lange) Nyman. See *R.bulbocodium*.

R.columnae Sebast. & Mauri.
Basal lvs 5–10×0.06–0.15cm, erect or recurved, grooved above. Scape short; fls 1–3; bract exceeding perianth tube, green, margins hyaline, bracteole mostly thin-textured, transparent; perianth 1–1.5cm, white tinted lavender or blue or violet, often with darker veins, tube 0.25–0.5cm, yellow within, perianth seg. oblong-lanceolate, acute, strongly 3-nerved; fil. usually glabrous, anth. tips exceeding style and attaining midpoint of perianth. W Europe (SW England to Mediterranean). Z8.

R.corsica Jourd. & Fourr. See *R.ligustica*.

R.dichotoma (Thunb.) Bak.
Basal lvs to 20×0.1–0.2cm, 1–2, usually erect, sometimes recurved; stem lvs 1–2. Scapes 4.5–30cm, erect, branching near summit; fls several, terminating on branches; bract green, margin shallowly hyaline, bracteole green, tinted red toward apex, margin broadly hyaline; perianth 2.5–4cm, pink with darker veins in throat, tube 0.3–0.5cm, yellow within and at throat, seg. 0.6–1cm across; fil. minutely ciliate at base, anth. seldom attaining midpoint of perianth, equalling or fractionally exceeding stigmas. S Africa (Cape Province). Z9.

R.flava (Lam.) De Vos (*R.bulbocodioides* auct.).
Basal lf to 15×0.3cm, 1, hollow, sheathing, glabrous or minutely ciliate; stem lvs 1–3. Scapes concealed by lf bases or elongate, conspicuous; pedicels 1.5–7cm; fls 1–4; bract carinate, green, margin shallow, hyaline, bracteole very thin-textured with a brown central stripe; perianth 2.25–4cm, yellow-green, occasionally white or tinted blue or pink, tube 0.3–0.7cm, yellow within and at throat, seg. 0.3–1.2cm across; fil. ciliate at base, anth. tips scarcely attaining midpoint of perianth, equalling stigmas. S Africa (Cape Province). Z9.

R.grandiflora Tod. See *R.bulbocodium*.

R.hirta Schltr.
Basal lvs 0.2–0.5cm across, 3–6, distinctively 4-winged, usually ciliate. Scape short, concealed by lf bases; pedicels 4–20cm; fls 1–4; bract green, margin shallow, hyaline, bracteole slender, mostly thin-textured; perianth 1.6–3.5cm, pale yellow, usually banded brown at centre of seg., tube to 0.5cm, seg. 0.5–0.8cm across; fil. downy at base, anth. tips not exceeding midpoint of perianth, equalling or exceeding stigmas. S Africa (Cape Province). Z9.

R.ligustica Parl. (*R.corsica* Jourdan & Fourr.).
Basal lvs exceeding scape, to 0.15cm across, erect or recurved. Fls 1, rarely 2–3 per scape; bract green, margin narrow, hyaline, bracteole mostly thin-textured, transparent; perianth 2–3.25cm, mauve to violet, tube 0.5–0.7cm, striped violet within and at throat; fil. downy at base, anth. not attaining midpoint of perianth seg. but exceeding stigmas. Corsica, Sardinia, Italy. Z9.

R.linaresii Parl.
Basal lvs to 0.15cm wide, terete, recurved to sprawling. Fls 1–2 per scape; bract green, margin hyaline, to 0.1cm deep, bracteole thin-textured, transparent, except for green centre; perianth 1.25–2.25cm, violet, tube 0.4–0.7cm, deep purple within and at throat, seg. erecto-patent, oblanceolate, acute or obtuse; fil. downy at base, anth. exceeding midpoint of perianth seg. and exceeding style. Sicily, Greece, W Turkey. Z8.

R.longituba Bol. See *R.macowanii*.
R.longituda var. *alticola* Burtt. See *R.macowanii* var. *alticola*.

R.macowanii Bak. (*R.longituba* Bol.).
Basal lvs 0.05–0.01cm wide, 3–6, subterete. long, suberect, recurved or sprawling. Scapes short, concealed by lf bases; fls 1–3 per scape; pedicels to 8cm, often perianth; bract green, thinly textured at base, bracteole thin-textured, margin broad, white, apex green; perianth 3–10cm, golden yellow, tube 2–6cm, deep orange-yellow within and at throat, seg. 0.5–1.5cm across, acute or obtuse; fil. hairy at base, anth. equalling midpoint of perianth and equalling stigmas. S Africa (Drakensberg), Lesotho. var. *alticola* (Burtt) De Vos

(*R.longituba* var. *alticola* Burtt). Perianth tube to 6.5cm; seg. to 3.5×1cm. S Africa, Lesotho (mts). Z9.

R.nivalis (Boiss. & Kotschy) Klatt.
Basal lvs to 0.2cm across, erect, rigid, 8-ridged. Fls 1–3 per scape; bract green, with 0.1cm-deep hyaline margin, bracteole green with broad thin margin; perianth to 2.5cm, lilac to mauve, tube to 0.3cm, yellow within and at throat, seg. lanceolate-obtuse; anth. attaining midpoint of perianth, not exceeding stigma. Lebanon. Z9.

R.ramiflora Ten.
Basal lvs 15–30×0.07–0.15cm, stout, erect or recurved. Scape elongate (ultimately to 30cm); fls 1–4 per scape; pedicels to 10cm at fruiting stage; perianth 1–2.5cm, exterior yellow-white or green-tinted, deepening to pale lilac, throat white or yellow, seg. purple; fil. sometimes glabrous, anth. attaining two-thirds length of perianth, equalling stigma. Mediterranean. ssp. *gaditana* (Kunze) Marais. Lvs slender, curled. Fls 2–3cm, violet-purple, throat pale green, outer seg. green externally, inner seg. violet externally, all reflexed at apex; stigma white, glandular-hairy, slightly exceeding stamens. SW Spain. Z9.

R.requienii Parl.
Basal lvs to 0.1cm across, terete, nearly prostrate. Fls 1–3 per scape; bract green, margin narrowly hyaline, bracteole thin-textured, transparent except for slender green central zone; perianth to 2.5cm, dark violet, tube to 0.8cm, sometimes paler or white within and at throat, seg. to 0.6cm across, oblanceolate-obtuse; anth. attaining at least two-thirds length of perianth, style exceeding anth. Corsica, Sardinia, Italy. Z8.

R.rosea (L.) Ecklon.
Basal lvs 0.1–0.25cm across, erect or arching to sprawling, sheathing at base, ciliate on ribs. Scape short, unbranched, not lengthening at fruiting stage; pedicels to 15cm; bract green, margin narrow-hyaline, bracteole with deep thin transparent margins, streaked brown; perianth 1.25–4cm, rosy-purple, pink or white, tube to 0.5cm, tinted yellow within and at throat, sometimes suffused blue, seg. 0.3–1cm across; fil. downy at base, anth. attaining midpoint of perianth. S Africa (SW Cape Province). var. *australis* (Ewart) De Vos. Fls pale lilac-pink, occasionally white, throat yellow; outer seg. yellow externally, sometimes with 3–5 longitudinal streaks. Cape Province, naturalized Australia, St Helena, Channel Is. var. *elegans* (Klatt) Beg. Fls white, throat yellow; outer seg. red, red-purple or red-green externally. S Cape Province. var. *reflexa* (Ecklon) Beg. Fls magenta to pink-lilac, occasionally white, throat orange or yellow, sometimes tinged violet-blue, outer seg. green-red with dark markings or longitudinal lines externally. W Cape Province. Z8.

R.sabulosa Bég.
Basal lvs to 0.1cm across, erect to recurved. Scapes short, concealed by lf bases, 1–4-fld; pedicels 4–14cm; bract rigid, green, narrowly edged brown, bracteole bicarinate, green, margin transparent to white at base; perianth to 3–5.5cm, bright scarlet, tube 0.2–0.4cm, with a dark white- or pink-edge blotch within and at throat, seg. 1.25–2cm across, acute or obtuse; fil. glabrous or minutely downy at base, anth. never attaining midpoint of perianth but exceeding stigmas. S Africa (Cape Province). Z9.

R.saldanhensis De Vos.
Basal lvs to 60cm, filiform, ascending or curved. Scapes to 35cm. Fls 3cm diam., glossy deep- or golden-yellow, with narrow dark streaks in throat; seg. obovate, 3×1.4cm, outer seg. yellow externally, marked brown. S Africa. Z9.

R.tempskyana Freyn.
Basal lvs to 0.1cm across, usually recurved. Fls 1 per scape; bract green with a shallow hyaline margin, bracteole thin-textured, transparent except for slender green central zone; perianth 2–3.5cm, mauve to violet, tube 0.8–1.7cm, slender, mauve within and at throat, seg. to 0.5cm across, lanceolate, ultimately reflexed; fil. glabrous, anth. attaining midpoint of perianth seg.; style purple, exceeding anth. Greece, SW Turkey, Cyprus, Israel. Z8.

Roscoea Sm. (For William Roscoe (1753–1831), founder of the Liverpool Botanic Garden.) Zingiberaceae. Some 17 species of perennial, fleshy-rhizomatous herbs, to 50cm. Leaves lanceolate or oblong, with parallel veins, borne spirally or 2-ranked, base often ligulate. Flowers in terminal condensed spikes on leafy shoots or distinct, leafless stalk, purple, blue or rarely yellow, 1 per bract; bracts overlapping; bracteoles absent; calyx split down on one side; corolla tube long, petals 3, posterior erect, incurved, wider than lateral petals which are spreading. Fruit elongated, slow to open. China, Himalaya. Z8.

CULTIVATION Grown for their showy flowers produced in summer, especially fine in *R.purpurea*. Hardy to –20°C/–4°F provided they are planted at least 15cm/6in. deep with a protective mulch; they are best sited on a sheltered peat bank or woodland garden in part shade and in a well drained, acid loam rich in leafmould. Plant in early spring and propagate by division at the same season. Water while in growth if early summer drought is prolonged.

R.alpina Royle (*R.longifolia* Bak.; *R.intermedia* Gagnep.).
To 30cm. Lvs 1–4, 10cm, acuminate, not usually fully developed at flowering. Fls in short infl. hidden in terminal lvs, pink or mauve; cal. green; cor. tube projects from cal.; posterior pet. circular, 2cm diam.; lip narrow, 2-lobed; staminodes 6–12×4–8mm, circular to elliptic. Summer. Kashmir, Nepal. Z6.

R.alpina hort. non Royle. See *R.scillifolia*.

R.auriculata Schum.
To 55cm; stem flushed purple. Lvs to 25cm, 3–10, linear to broad-lanceolate, auriculate at base. Fls bright purple, infl. enclosed in upper lf sheath, 1 opening at a time; posterior pet. 3.5×2cm; staminodes 1.5–2cm, white. Summer–autumn. F. Nepal, Sikkim. 'Beesiana' (*R.auriculata* × *R.cautleoides*): stem to 45cm; lf bases strongly auriculate; fls yellow, sometimes streaked mauve. Z6.

R.auriculata hort. See *R.purpurea*.

R.capitata Sm.
To 40cm. Lvs 20×2cm, usually 7, lanceolate. Fls 5–7, blue or purple, in dense, spike; bracts green; cal. 2.5cm; cor. 5cm; lip 2cm. Himalaya. Z8.

R.capitata var. *scillifolia* (misapplied). See *R.scillifolia*.

R.cautleoides Gagnep. (*R.chamael* Gagnep.; *R.yunnanensis* Loes.).
To 55cm. Lvs 15×2.5cm, 1–4, acuminate, glabrous, greygreen above, sessile, not always fully expanded at flowering. Infl. carried clear of lvs, subtended by tubular bracts; fls 6–7, pale yellow; cor. tube longer than cal.; dorsal pet. obovate, abruptly acute, hooded; lip 3–4cm, obovate, 2-lobed, deflexed; staminodes 1–2cm. 'Kew Beauty': lvs dark green; fls orchid-like, pale yellow. Z6.

R.chamaeleon Gagnep. See *R.cautleoides*.

R.humeana Balf. & Sm.
To 34cm. Lvs 2–20cm, 4–6, oblong to ovate, glabrous, sessile, expanded at flowering. Fls 2–4, purple or lilac, in short infl. hidden in lf sheaths; bracts concave, rounded, hairy at apex; cal. exceeding bracts; posterior pet. 2.5–4.5×2–3cm, arching, longer than lateral pet.; lip large, obovate, deeply 2-lobed; staminodes 2.5cm diam., square, reduced, clawed. Spring–summer. SW China (Yunnan, Sichuan). Yellow-fld forms occur. Z7.

R.intermedia Gagnep. See *R.alpina*.
R.longifolia Bak. See *R.alpina*.
R.procera Wallich. See *R.purpurea*.

R.purpurea Sm. (*R.procera* Wallich; *R.purpurea* var. *procera* (Wallich) Bak.).
To 30cm, stem flushed purple. Lvs to 25cm, 4–8, acuminate, sessile. Infl. hidden in upper lf sheaths, pale purple or white with dark purple markings; posterior pet. 3–6×1–3cm, narrow, arching, lip to 6cm including claw, obovate, 2-lobed; staminodes slender, 2.5–4cm. Summer–autumn. Himalaya, Sikkim. Z6.

R.purpurea var. *procera* (Wallich) Bak. See *R.purpurea*.
R.purpurea hort. See *R.auriculata*.

R.scillifolia (Gagnep.) Cowley (*R.alpina* hort. non Royle).
To 37cm. Lvs 6–12cm, 1–5, not fully developed at flowering. Infl. carried clear of lvs on an exposed stalk; fls pink; bract tubular, pubesc. at apex, longer than cal.; posterior pet. 1.4–2cm, elliptic; lip to 2cm, narrow, 2-lobed or entire. Summer. SW China (Yunnan). Z8.

R.sikkimensis auct. See *R.auriculata*.
R.sinopurpurea Stapf (invalid). See *R.cautleoides*.
R.yunnanensis Loes. See *R.cautleoides*.

Salvia L. (From Lat. name used by Pliny, derived from Lat. *salvare*, to save or heal, alluding to the supposed medicinal properties of certain species.) SAGE. Labiatae. Some 900 or more species of perennial or, occasionally, annual or biennial herbs, shrubs or subshrubs. Stems erect or ascending, glabrous to glandular and/or variously pubescent. Leaves sessile or petiolate, opposite, simple or lyrate or pinnatisect. Flowers in 2–40-flowered, approximate or distant verticillasters, these disposed in terminal or axillary racemes, spikes, panicles, or, rarely, cymes; pedicels erect to spreading; bracteoles and non-foliaceous bracts usually present; calyx 2-lipped, tubular or ovoid to bell- or funnel-shaped, often dilated and membranous in fruit, lips eventually convergent, upper lip truncate to obsoletely or distinctly 3-toothed, teeth unequal, lower lip 2-toothed, teeth equal; corolla 2-lipped, tube straight or curved, often invaginate or distended, occasionally annulate or squamate, smooth to papillose or rugose, upper lip hooded, erect, plane or falcate, entire to emarginate or bifid, lower lip spreading, 3-lobed, lateral lobes reduced, middle lobe often emarginate; stamens 2, included or exserted, staminodes 2 or absent; style 2-lobed or -branched, glabrous or pubescent. Fruit of 4 nutlets, globose to ovoid and more or less trigonous, often mucilaginous, smooth. Cosmopolitan.

CULTIVATION Suited to sunny or semi-shaded borders or shrub underplantings on loamy soils, generally undemanding and pest-free.

S.yunnanensis C.H.Wright.
Rhizomatous, tuber-bearing perennial herb to 30cm. Lvs to 75×25mm, petiolate, entire to pinnate-pinnatifid, glabrous to sparsely pubescent and purple beneath, terminal segments ovate to linear or oblong, margin toothed to notched, lateral segments reduced, 2–3 pairs. Verticillasters 3–6-fld, in simple spikes; calyx glandular; corolla to 25mm, blue or violet to purple, exterior pubescent. China. Z8.

Sandersonia Hook. (For John Sanderson (?1820–91), honorary secretary of the Horticultural Society of Natal.) Liliaceae (Colchicaceae). 1 species, a perennial herb with tuberous roots. Stems to 75cm, erect. Leaves to 10cm, sessile, cauline, alternate, often tendril-tipped. Flowers solitary in axils of upper leaves; pedicels 2–3cm, decurved; perianth 2–2.5cm, rounded-campanulate to urceolate, orange, lobes 6, fused except at outward-curving tips, with 6 short nectariferous spurs at base; stamens to 0.8cm, at base of lobes; ovary superior; style trifid. Fruit a capsule. Summer. S Africa (E Cape). Z9.

CULTIVATION As for *Gloriosa*.

S.aurantiaca Hook. CHINESE LANTERN LILY; CHRISTMAS BELLS.

Sauromatum Schott. (Named used by Dodoens, derived from the Gk *sauros*, lizard, a reference to the spathe and the petioles which resemble a mottled lizard skin.) Araceae. 2 species of tuberous, perennial herbs. Tubers squat-cylindric to depressed-globose, somewhat rough, light brown, the upper surface smooth producing roots, sometimes offsets and, on withering of leaf, giving way to new tuber; growing point, narrowly conical, enclosed in tightly rolled, glossy, maroon-flecked bracts, developing very rapidly. Leaf usually solitary, produced after flowers, pedate, long-stalked. Spathe short-stalked, the base bulbous, then tubular with margins fused, expanding to a narrow, oblong-lanceolate blade, soon recurved and withering; spadix terminating in a long, slender, fleshy appendage, far exceeding spathe and emitting a foul stench; flowers lacking perianth, unisexual, the males and females in two distinct and proportionate zones, separated by a long section of sterile, rudimentary flowers. E & W Africa, E Asia. Z9.

CULTIVATION *Sauromatum* spp. occur predominantly in humus-rich soils in shaded habitats, although *S.venosum* is also found along sunny river valleys in the Western Himalaya at 1000–2300m (3264–7550ft). Grown for the magnificent but foul-scented inflorescence in late spring/early summer and for the curiously saurian leaf stalks which follow, gradually unfurling to reveal the single large handsome leaf. *S.venosum* makes an interesting specimen for the cool glasshouse or for a warm and sunny, essentially frost-free situation in the garden. Tubers are sometimes grown as malodorous and malevolent-looking curiosities without soil or water in the house, their spathes developing with astonishing rapidity. They should be planted and fed immediately after flowering.

Grow in a fertile and well drained medium, rich in organic matter. Water as the new leaf appears and withhold water as it dies down. Keep dry but not arid when dormant in winter, maintaining a minimum temperature of 5–7°C/40–45°F. In the open, plant 15cm/6in. deep in full sun. Propagate by removal of offsets or by seed (when available).

S.guttatum (Wallich) Schott. See *S.venosum*.

S.nubicum Schott.
Very close to *S.venosum*, but lf seg. broader, spathe blade narrower. E & W Africa.

S.venosum (Ait.) Kunth (*S.guttatum* (Wallich) Schott).
MONARCH OF THE EAST; VOODOO LILY; RED CALLA.
Tuber to 12cm diam. Petiole to 70cm, erect, terete, pale green usually mottled dark green or maroon, lf seg. 7–15 per lf, each to 40×12cm, becoming progressively smaller to sides of a pedate arrangement, oblong-lanceolate, dark, glossy green with veins impressed above. Peduncle to 6cm, stout; spathe tube 5–10×2–3.5cm, blade 30–70×8–10cm, somewhat fleshy, soon becoming reflexed, twisted and undulate, exterior a pearly grey to livid flesh tone, interior yellow-green to ochre spotted and mottled blood-red to dark maroon; spadix appendage to 35cm, narrowly cylindric, fleshy pink or green darkening to metallic maroon or bronze apex. Himalaya, S India.

Scadoxus Raf. (Compound name derived from Gk *skiadion*, parasol (i.e. umbel), and *doxa*, glory.) Amaryllidaceae. 9 species bulbous or rhizomatous herbs most clearly differing from *Haemanthus* in their leaves, which are not 2-ranked and lack distinct midveins. Leaves to 12, spirally arranged, entire, elliptic to ovate, membranous, glabrous, apex obtuse, acute or acuminate, bases tapered, rounded or truncated; petioles spotted, sheathing stem, forming a neck. Scape emerging earlier than or with leaves, lateral, axillary, solid, base terete, angular above, spotted; spathe valves 4 to many, erect, persistent or soon withering; inflorescence 10–200-flowered, showy, conical to spherical; flowers mostly erect, occasionally drooping; perianth tubular, tepals 6, linear to lanceolate, erect or spreading, apices glandular-hairy; corona absent, stamens 6, long, exserted, anthers yellow or red; ovary 3-locular; style longer than stamens. Fruit an orange to red berry; seeds 1–3, pale. Tropical Arabia and Africa to S Namibia and E Cape. Z10.

CULTIVATION Cultivate as for *Haemanthus*, maintaining slightly higher temperatures at 10–15°C/50–60°F, and with higher humidity.

S.multiflorus (Martyn) Raf.
Lvs 5, to 32×20cm, lanceolate to ovate. Neck to 60cm. Scape to 75cm; spathe valves to 6×1.5cm, colourless or tinged red, soon withering; infl. hemispherical to spherical; perianth tube 0.5–2.6cm, tepals linear, to 4mm, spreading, scarlet, fading pink; anth. to 3mm. Spring–summer. Tropical & S Africa, Yemen. ssp. *multiflorus* (*Haemanthus sacculus* Phillips; *Haemanthus kalbreyei* Bak.; *Haemanthus tenuifolius* Herb.; *Haemanthus lynesii* Stapf; *Haemanthus coccineus* Forssk.). Perianth tube to 1.5cm; tepals to 2.5mm. ssp. *katherinae* (Bak.) Friis & Nordal (*Haemanthus katherinae* Bak.). To 1.2m. Lvs undulate. Perianth tube 1.6–2.6cm; tepals to 4mm across. ssp. *longitubus* (Wright) Friis & Nordal (*Haemanthus longitubus* Wright; *Haemanthus mannii* Bak.). To 65cm. Perianth tube 1.5–2.6cm; tepals 1.4–3.5mm across. W Africa.

S.pole-evansii Oberm.
Lvs 24–52×3–12cm; neck to 85cm. Scape to 120cm; fls 30–70, pink or scarlet; perianth tube 4–5mm, tepals elliptic, 2.2–5×0.5–1cm, spreading; stamens 1.2–1.3cm. Berries 1–2cm across, scarlet. E Zimbabwe.

S.puniceus (L.) Friis & Nordal (*Haemanthus magnificus* (Herb.) Herb.; *Haemanthus insignis* Hook.; *Haemanthus magnificus* var. *insignis* (Hook.) Bak.; *Haemanthus magnificus* var. *superbus* Bak.; *Haemanthus natalensis* Poepp.; *Haemanthus rouperi* anon.). ROYAL PAINT BRUSH.
Lvs 7–12, to 3×12cm, oblong to elliptic, margins undulate, stalks forming bulb neck to 50cm. Scape to 40cm; spathes conspicuous, erect to spreading, outer spathes 6 or 7, lanceolate to rhombic, to 10×5cm, inner spathes paler, narrower; infl. conical, resembling a single flower with many colourful stamens; fls 100; perianth tube to 1.2cm, tepals linear, erect, to 27×2mm, scarlet to green-yellow. Berries to 1cm across, yellow, Spring–summer. E & S Africa.

(b)

(a)

Scadoxus   (a) *S.puniceus*   (b) *S.multiflorus* ssp. *katharinae*

Schizostylis Backh. & Harv. (From Gk *schizo*, to split and *stylis*, style.) KAFFIR LILY. Iridaceae. 1 species, a perennial herb to about 60cm; rootstock a short, slightly swollen, corm-like rhizome. Leaves to 40×1cm, several, basal, 2-ranked and overlapping, sword-shaped. Spike distichous, 4–10-flowered; flowers salverform, almost regular, scarlet, pink or white; tube to 3cm, slender, abruptly widened at throat, lobes subequal, about 3.5×1.5cm, ovate; stamens 3, set in throat, filaments free, about 15mm, very slender, anthers large; style as long as tube, slender, branches 3cm, very slender. Summer to early winter. S Africa, Lesotho, Swaziland. Z6.

CULTIVATION Found in moist habitats in the wild by streamside and riverbank, *S.coccinea* requires a sunny position in moist soils, including sodden, heavy clay. Hardy to between −5 and −10°C/14°–23°F, it is also grown in the cool glasshouse, for long-lasting cut flowers. Apply an organic mulch to conserve moisture. Under favourable conditions, plants quickly become congested and should be divided every few years; propagate also by seed.

S.coccinea Backh. & Harv. (*S.pauciflora* Klatt).
'Alba': to 45cm; fls white faintly tinged pink. 'Cardinal': habit vigorous; fls large, red; early flowering. 'Jennifer': stems erect; fls large, clear pink. 'Major' ('Gigantea', 'Grandiflora'): to 60cm; fls scarlet, abundant. 'November Cheer': to 60cm; growth strong; fls deep pink. 'Pallida': fls large, very pale pink. 'Professor Barnard': to 50cm; fls dusky red. 'Rosalie': fls pink. 'Sunrise': fls large, pink. 'Tambara': fls large, soft rose-pink. 'Viscountess Byng': fls red; late flowering. 'Zeal Salmon': hardy; fls large, clear salmon-pink.

S.pauciflora Klatt. See *S.coccinea*.

Scilla L. (Gk and Lat. name for *Urginea maritima*.) Liliaceae (Hyacinthaceae). Some 90 species of perennial or annual, bulbous herbs. Bulbs tunicate, composed of numerous, free scales which are renewed annually. Leaves basal, few to several, linear to elliptic, loriform, mostly glabrous, occasionally channelled, emerging before, after, or at the same time as flowering. Scapes erect, glabrous, 1–4 per bulb. Flowers few to numerous, borne in terminal scapose racemes or corymbs on jointed pedicels, blue to purple or white, subtended by a single, usually small bract, or bractless; tepals 6, nearly equal, distinct, or very shortly connate towards the base, often conspicuously 1-nerved; stamens 6, with filaments free, inserted at the base of the tepals, anthers dorsifixed; ovary superior, subspherical to ovoid, 3-celled, ovules 1–12 per cell; style single with straight, small, truncate stigma. Fruit a 3-lobed or 3-angled loculicidal capsule, with few spherical or oblong, occasionally angled black seeds in each cell. S Africa, Asia, Europe.

CULTIVATION Best known are the amenable spring-flowering and early summer species: they include some of the most beautiful of early flowers for rock garden, scree and raised beds. Some are grown in the alpine display house, where the early-flowering species achieve a perfection of bloom seldom seen in the open. Some, such as *S.bifolia* and *S.siberica*, are suitable for naturalizing in short grass or in the wild garden and others, such as *S.bifolia* and *S.messeniaca*, for underplantings with shrubs. Several species need slightly more attention to drainage or are grown in the bulb frame including *S.mischtschenkoana* and *S.persica* and, in the slightly shaded frame, *S.cilicica*. *S.siberica* performs best in rich, sandy soils. Most are cold-tolerant to at least −10°C/14°F, *S.rosenii* and *S.hohenackeri* to −15°C/5°F. With *S.scilloides* hardiness varies according to provenance, the hardiest variants are tolerant to −15°C/5°F. *S.siberica* will tolerate temperatures of −20°C/−4°F, probably even lower; *S.peruviana* needs protection in regions experiencing temperatures below about −5°C/23°F. The South African species, often with extremely attractive foliage, need cool glasshouse protection in cool temperate zones. Grow in freely draining but humus-rich soils, with adequate moisture when in growth, in sun or dappled shade. Propagate by offsets (not freely produced but indicated by the presence of additional leaf clusters at the base of the stem), by seed when ripe or by division of established clumps as the foliage dies back.

S.adlamii Bak. See *Ledebouria cooperi*.
S.amethystina Vis. See *S.litardieri*.

S.amoena L.
Bulb 1.5–2cm diam., with a dark purple-brown tunic, tinged white beneath. Scapes 1–5, 15–20cm, weak, angled. Lvs 4 to 7, 15–22×1–2cm, flaccid, strap-shaped, ascending, glabrous, usually emerging before flowering, often tinged red near the base. Fls rotate, erect, borne in a loose raceme of 3–6, bractless, blue; stalks 6–15mm, lower longer than the perianth; tepals 9–12mm, lanceolate, mauve-blue with deeper blue midribs; fil. lanceolate, anth. blue. Fr. a globose capsule, with 6–8 seeds per cell, each cell with a scarcely developed appendage. Origin uncertain but naturalized SE Europe. Z7.

S.apertiflora (Bak.) C.A. Sm. See *Ledebouria apertiflora*.

S.autumnalis L.
Bulb 1.5–3cm diam., ovoid, with brown- or pink-tinged tunic, occasionally with a few membranous scales. Scapes 1–3, 5–30cm, scabrous. Lvs 5–12, 2–18cm×1–2mm, grooved above, almost terete, emerging usually after flowering. Fls 5–25, borne in a bractless, open raceme, elongating in fruit; pedicels 3–10mm, ascending or spreading; tepals 3–5mm, spreading, lilac to pink. Fr. an ovoid-globose, obscurely 3-angled capsule, to 4mm, with 2 black finely roughened seeds per cell, to 2×1mm. S, W & C Europe, NW Africa to C Asia, Iran, Iraq. 'Alba': fls white. 'Praecox': fls large, purple-blue; very robust. 'Rosea': fls pink. Z6.

S.bifolia L.
Bulb 0.5–2.5cm diam., with brown tunic, pink beneath. Scape solitary, 7.5–15cm, terete, partially enclosed at the base by a sheath of leaves. Lvs 5–20×0.3–1.5cm, 2, rarely 3, linear to linear-lanceolate, apically cucullate, appearing at the same time as flowering, concave on face. Fls 1–10, borne in a narrowly 1-sided or deltoid, loose, mostly nodding raceme 2.5–4cm diam.; lower pedicels 1–4cm, upper less than 1cm; bracts, if present, ovate-lanceolate to 1mm; tepals 5–10×1–3mm, ovate to elliptic, apically cucullate, blue to purple-blue. Seeds subglobose to 2mm, tinged brown, with an irregular, white appendage. Summer–autumn. C & S Europe, Turkey. Z6.

S.campanulata Ait. See *Hyacinthoides hispanica*.
S.chinensis Benth. See *S.scilloides*.

S.cilicica Siehe
Bulb 1.25–2.5cm diam., tunic dull violet. Lvs 13–40×1–2cm, 4–6, broadly linear, appearing before fls. Scapes 14–38cm,

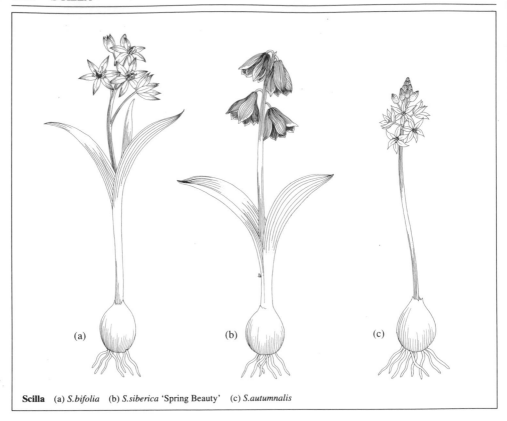

Scilla (a) *S.bifolia* (b) *S.siberica* 'Spring Beauty' (c) *S.autumnalis*

2–4, erect. Raceme lax; fls 2–8; pedicels ascending, shorter than seg.; bracts 2–5mm, ovate, bifid; seg. 9–16×3–4mm, spreading, pale or lavender-blue; fil. to 1mm wide; ovary 3mm, subglobose. Seeds black, with black caruncle. Turkey.

S.concolor Bak. See *Ledebouria concolor*.
S.cooperi Hook. f. See *Ledebouria cooperi*.
S.floribunda Bak. See *Ledebouria floribunda*.
S.hispanica Mill. See *Hyacinthoides hispanica*.

S.hohenackeri Fisch. & Mey.
Bulb 1.5–2cm diam., ovoid, with grey-brown, thinly-textured tunic. Scape 5–20cm. Lvs 3–5, 10–25×0.3–1cm, linear, V-shaped in cross-section, emerging at flowering. Fls borne in a loose raceme of 4–12, on spreading or curving pedicels, 1–1.5cm, the same length as tepals, to 2.5cm in fruit; bracts 5–6mm, conspicuous, spurred below, fringed and 2-lobed above; tepals 1–1.5×0.2–0.3cm, oblanceolate, pale blue, becoming falcate with age; fil. pale blue, anth. green-blue. Fr. a pale brown, 3-angled capsule, with 2–4 shiny black seeds per cell. S Iran, Russia. Z6.

S.hypoxidioides Schönl. See *Ledebouria hypoxidioides*.
S.inquinata C.A. Sm. See *Ledebouria inquinata*.
S.italica L. See *Hyacinthoides italica*.

S.lilio-hyacinthus L.
Bulb 3–5cm, no tunic, composed of loose, imbricate, yellow tinged scales. Scapes 2 or 3, 5–10cm. Lvs 6–10, 15–30×1–3cm, linear, acute, shiny, emerging at flowering. Fls 5–20, campanulate, borne in a dense, conical raceme, 3–8cm, on ascending, blue-violet stalks, 8–12mm; bracts 1–2.5cm, ovate, thinly-textured, tinged white; tepals 9–12mm, ovate to elliptic, bright violet-blue, occasionally white; stamens 7–9mm; fil. pale, 1–2mm, lanceolate, anth. deep blue; ovary subglobose. Fr. a narrowly 3-angled capsule with obovoid, black seeds. France, Spain. Z6.

S.litardieri Breistr. (*S.pratensis* Waldst. & Kit.; *S.amethystina* Vis.).
Bulb 1.5cm diam., ovoid, tunic brown. Scape 5–15cm. Lvs 3–6, 25–30×0.4–0.8cm, narrow-ligulate, glabrous, narrowed at both ends, emerging at flowering. Fls 3–15, campanulate, borne in dense, narrow, conical racemes, 5–15cm, on ascending, spreading, pale blue-violet pedicels, 8–12mm; bracts to 1cm, ovate; tepals 4–6mm, ovate, tinged pink or blue-violet; stamens 3–5mm; fil. pale blue, anth. deep violet-blue; ovary with 3 or 4 ovules per cell. Fr. a capsule to 4mm diam., with brown or black seeds, to 3×1–2mm. Former Yugoslavia. Z6.

S.messeniaca Boiss.
Bulb 2–3cm diam., ovoid, tunic pale brown. Scapes solitary or paired, 5–15cm, angled. Lvs 5 to 7, 15–25×1–2.5cm, broadly linear, forming a basal sheath around the scapes, emerging at flowering. Fls 7–20, borne in a dense, ovate-oblong raceme, 4–12cm long; bracts to 1mm, linear, occasionally bifid; lower pedicels 4–8mm, ascending or spreading; tepals 6–8mm, lilac-blue, linear, somewhat spreading, apically obtuse; ovary subglobose, with 2 ovules per cell; stamens 4–6mm, fil. pale blue, anth. dark violet-blue. Fr. a subglobose capsule to 7mm with 3 broad angles. S Greece. Z8.

S.mischtschenkoana Gross (*S.tubergeniana* Stearn).
Bulb 1.5–3cm diam., ovoid or subglobose, with grey-brown, thinly-textured tunic. Scapes 1–3, 5–10cm, terete. Lvs 3–5, 4–10×0.4–2cm, linear to oblanceolate, flat, not channelled, emerging at flowering. Fls 2–6, widely campanulate, borne in a loose raceme, 6–12cm, on ascending stalks to 2.5cm; bracts oblong, to 5mm; tepals 1–1.5×0.4–0.8cm, oblong-elliptic, obtuse, white-blue with a darker median stripe; stamens 6–11mm, white, basally widened; anth. grey-blue; fil. white; ovary subglobose, with usually 6 ovules per cell; style exceeding ovary. Fr. a subglobose capsule to 9mm, with

brown or black globose seeds, each with a conspicuous, pale appendage. Iran, Russia. Z6.

S.monophyllos Link.
Bulb 1–2cm diam., ovoid, tunic pale brown. Scape 5–15cm, slender, flexuous. Lf usually solitary, 10–25×1–3cm, broadly lanceolate to elliptic, strap-shaped, acute, ascending, forming basal sheath around scape, emerging at or marginally before flowering. Fls 3–15, campanulate, borne in a loose raceme, 5–10cm, on ascending pedicels, 1–1.5cm; bracts 4–7mm, linear-lanceolate, acuminate; tepals 6–9mm, elliptic, pale violet-blue; stamens 3–5mm; fil. linear, pale-violet; anth. blue; ovary subglobose with few ovules per cell. Spain, Portugal, NW Africa. Z9.

S.natalensis Planch.
Bulb 7–10cm diam., ovoid or sub-globose, with a brown tunic. Scape 30–45cm, stout, erect, terete. Lvs 4–8, to 20cm at flowering, to 30–60×7–10cm at maturity, lanceolate, strap-shaped, acuminate, ascending. Fls 50–100, borne in a dense raceme, 15–30cm, on ascending, blue pedicels, 2–4cm; bracts to 1cm, solitary; tepals 6–10×3–4mm, elliptic-oblong, obtuse, spreading, light violet-blue or occasionally pink or white; fil. white, basally widened; ovary ovoid, usually white, with 10–12 ovules per cell; style the same length as ovary. Eastern S Africa, Lesotho. Z9.

S.non-scripta (L.) Hoffsgg. & Link. See *Hyacinthoides non-scripta*.
S.nutans Sm. See *Hyacinthoides non-scripta*.
S.ovalifolia (Schräd.) C.A. Sm. See *Ledebouria ovalifolia*.
S.ovatifolia Bak. See *Ledebouria ovatifolia*.

S.persica Hausskn.
Bulb 2.5–3cm diam., broadly ovoid to sub-globose, with violet-purple inner tunic, dark brown outer. Lvs 3–7, 30–45×1–1.5cm, slightly keeled, linear, acutely tipped with rolled bases, forming a tube, emerging at flowering. Scapes 1–3, 20–40cm. Fls 20–80, borne in a compact, conical raceme 5–10cm long, to 25cm in fruit; bracts 2–7mm, fringed or 2-lobed above; pedicels 1.5–4cm, becoming thick in fruit; tepals 7–8mm, lanceolate to elliptic, narrow-concave, spreading, bright blue; ovary subglobose, 3mm diam. with 2 or 3 ovules per cell. Seeds 4×2.5mm, dark brown. W Iran, N Iraq. Z8.

S.peruviana L.
Bulb 6–8cm diam., ovoid, tunic brown with woolly outer scales. Scapes 15–25cm, solitary, occasionally paired, stout. Lvs 5–15, 40–60×1–4cm, linear to lanceolate, strap-shaped, narrowed to base and tip, with sparsely bristly-ciliate margins. Fls 40–100, borne in a very dense, deltoid raceme, 5–20cm; lower bracts 3–8cm, solitary, persistent, subulate, papery; lower pedicels 3–5cm, tinged green, to 10cm in fruit; tepals 8–15mm, deep violet-blue to dull purple-brown, or white; stamens lanceolate-elliptic, pale blue, anth. yellow; ovary subglobose. Fr. an ovoid, acuminate capsule, with 3 or 4 seeds per cell. SW Europe, W Africa. Close to *S.hughii* Tineo ex Guss., which differs in its larger habit and deep violet fls. 'Alba': fls white. Z8.

S.pratensis Waldst. & Kit. See *S.litardieri*.

S.puschkinioides Reg.
Bulb 1–2cm diam., ovoid, with grey-tinged tunic. Scape 10–15cm, terete. Lvs 2–5, 10–15×0.3–0.6cm, broadly linear, obtuse, emerging at flowering. Fls 2–8, erect, 'starry', borne in a short raceme; pedicels 3–10mm, exceeding the bracts; tepals 1–1.5cm×2.5–3.5mm, oblong, acute, tinged white or pale blue, with a darker median stripe; stamens 8–12mm, fil.

awl-shaped, white, anth. blue; ovary ovoid. Fr. a flat, globose capsule. Russia. Habit close to *S.bifolia*. Z6.

S.ramburei Boiss. See under *S.verna*.

S.rosenii K. Koch.
Bulb 1–2.5cm diam., ovoid, with dark brown-violet tunic. Lvs 2–3, 10–15×0.6–1.5cm, apically cucullate, ovoid, emerging at flowering. Scapes 1–4, 10–25cm, terete. Fls borne in short racemes, pendent, single, paired, occasionally few, on arching pedicels, 1–1.5cm; bracts 2–3mm, 2-lobed; tepals 1.5–2.5cm×4–8mm, oblong, obtuse, becoming falcate, pale blue with a darker median stripe on the outside, tinged white inside near the base; stamens 8–12mm; fil. slightly widened towards the base, white; ovary obovoid, to 5mm, with exceeding style. Seeds to 3×2mm, pale brown, each with a white appendage. Russia. Z6.

S.scilloides (Lindl.) Druce (*S.chinensis* Benth.; *S.sinensis* (Lour.) Merrill; *Barnardia scilloides* Lindl.).
Bulb 1.5–2cm diam., ovoid, with a black tinged tunic. Scape 20–40cm, slender, straight or slightly angled. Lvs 2–7, 15–25×0.4–0.7cm, acute, linear, flaccid, channelled, apically obtuse and slightly cucullate. Fls 40–80, borne in a dense, oblong raceme, 7–12cm, on ascending, often twin pedicels, 4–8mm; bracts 1–2mm, linear; tepals 3–4mm, narrow-oblong, acute, spreading, mauve-pink; fil. minutely pubesc. on edges, basally widened; ovary ovoid, minutely pubesc. on the angles, with few ovules. Fr. an obovoid-spherical capsule to 5mm, with black seeds. China, Korea, Taiwan, Japan, Ryukyu Is. Z5.

S.siberica Haw.
Bulb 1.5–2cm diam., ovoid, tunic dark purple brown. Scapes 1–6, 10–20cm, fleshy, tinged mauve above, with fine ribs. Lvs 2–4, 10–15×0.5–1.5, narrowly strap-shaped, slightly cucullate, ascending, shorter than the scape at flowering. Fls borne in loose, bracteate racemes, to 1.5cm diam., rotate or broadly bowl-shaped, pendent; bracts 1–2mm, white; pedicels 8–12mm, mauve; tepals 1–2cm×4–6mm, elliptic-oblong, obtuse, bright-blue with a darker median band; stamens 5–8mm, fil. lanceolate, white below, blue above; anth. violet or grey-blue; ovary ovoid, light green with 2–12 ovules per cell, style 4–5mm, white. Fr. a subglobose capsule, 8–10mm diam., with light brown, spherical seeds, each with a long appendage. S Russia. Naturalized C Europe. 'Alba': fls white. 'Spring Beauty' ('Atrocaerulea'): upright, to 20cm; fls deep blue, long-lasting, scented. ssp. *armena* (Grossh.) Mordak. Bulb 0.7–2cm diam. Lvs 5–6×0.4–0.5cm, occasionally longer, to 28cm, 2–3, linear. Scapes 6–8cm, 1–3; fls 1–2; pedicels curved, shorter than neg.; seg. spreading, pale blue with dark blue median line. Turkey, Georgia, Armenia. Z5.

S.sinensis (Lour.) Merrill. See *S.scilloides*.
S.socialis Bak. See *Ledebouria socialis*.
S.tubergeniana Stearn. See *S.mischtschenkoana*.

S.verna Huds.
Bulb 1–2cm diam., ovoid. Scapes single or paired, shorter than lvs. Lvs 2–7, 3–20cm×2–5mm, linear, falcate, concave, obtuse, slightly channelled, emerging at flowering. Fls 2–12, borne in a somewhat dense, short, subcorymbose or deltoid raceme, with linear bracts, 5–15mm; lower pedicels 5–12mm, ascending, elongating slightly in fruit; tepals 5–8×2–3mm, narrow-oblong-ovate, light violet-blue; ovary oblong, blue. Fr. a subglobose capsule, with black, oblong seeds, each with a small appendage. W Europe. Close to *S.ramburei* Boiss., which differs in its larger, more robust habit. Z7.

S.violacea Hutch. See *Ledebouria socialis*.

Sinningia Nees. (For Wilhelm Sinning (1792–1874), Prussian horticulturalist and botanist.) Gesneriaceae. Some 40 species of perennial herbs and shrubs, usually tuberous, rarely rhizomatous. Leaves opposite or in whorls, often crowded at base of stem. Flowers solitary or clustered in leaf axils, occasionally scented; calyx 5-partite, tubular to angled or winged at base; corolla campanulate to cylindric; limb broad, spreading, 2-lipped, lower lip 3-lobed, upper lip 2-lobed, lips often indistinct; stamens 4; anthers coherent in a cross at apex; disc of 2–5 glands. Fruit a dehiscent capsule. Mexico to Argentina and Brazil. Z10.

CULTIVATION *Sinningia* spp. occur in tropical zones with seasonal rainfall, and die back to a tuber in dry periods. Grown for their large velvety flowers, they require intermediate to warm glasshouse protection and may be successfully moved to the home or cooler glasshouse when in flower. A succession of blooms may be secured throughout summer by starting tubers into growth from late winter onwards, or throughout the year given supplementary lighting.

Pot individual tubers into shallow containers with a fibrous potting medium, covering them to a depth of 2–3cm/0.75–1.25in. Apply water sparingly at first, increasing the amount as growth progresses until watering copiously when plants are in full growth. Maintain a temperature of 21–23°C/70–75°F until flowering, then move to cooler temperatures for display. Apply a balanced liquid feed monthly throughout the growing season. Frequent damping-down during hot weather is beneficial, although the foliage is easily marked by water and syringing must be carried out cautiously; bright sunlight will also damage the leaves so admit only bright indirect light. Watering from below, by immersing the base of the pot in water for a while, will avoid damaging contact of water with the foliage. Gradually withhold water after flowering until foliage dies back, and the root ball is quite dry; store tubers in a cool, dry place (at *c*7°C/45°F), until the following season.

Propagate by seed; in commerce, *S.speciosa*, the Florist's Gloxinia, flowers from seed within six months. Seed and seedlings are tiny and require careful handling, as they have a high susceptibility to fungal diseases. Sowings may be made from mid- to late winter with supplementary lighting (an extra 6–8 hours following dusk); seedlings may produce a small corm and then cease growth at this time of year. Early to mid-spring sowings are more easily accommodated. Surface sow on to a finely graded propagating mix, maintaining high humidity and a temperature of 18–20°C/65–68°F; germination will occur within 2–3 weeks. Increase temperatures to 21–23°C/70–75°F after germination and prick out into seed trays or individual pots. Maintain a constant supply of water to avoid initiation of dormancy; capillary matting provides a convenient means of doing so. Tubers may also be cut up, each segment with a bud. Cuttings of emerging shoots may be rooted in a closed case with bottom heat. Leaf cuttings may be made with tubers being produced at the cut edge, the old leaf decaying in the process.

S.aggregata (Ker-Gawl.) Wiehler (*Gesneria aggregata* Ker-Gawl.; *Rechsteineria aggregata* (Ker-Gawl.) Kuntze). Herb to 60cm. Lvs to 12.5×6.2cm, opposite, ovate, glandular-pubesc., petiole to 1.2cm. Fls solitary or in pairs; cor. tube to 2.5cm, horizontal, inflated dorsally at base, otherwise cylindric, red-orange, throat yellow-orange, spotted with red, lobes 5, acute, all equal. Brazil.

S.allagophylla (Mart.) Wiehler (*Rechsteineria allagophylla* (Mart.) Reg.). Stem to 1m. Lvs in whorls of 3 along stem, elliptic, margin crenate. Fls solitary or in cymes of 2–3; cor. much reduced, to 1.2cm, barely exceeding cal., bright red. Brazil.

S.barbata (Nees & Mart.) Nichols. (*S.carolinae* (Wawra) Benth. & Hook.). Stem erect, to 60cm, marked with red. Lvs to 15cm, oblong-lanceolate, tapering at base and apex, dark green above, maroon beneath. Fls solitary or in pairs, on pedicels to 3cm; sep. foliose, deltate; cor. to 3cm, white-pubesc., inflated dorsally at base; lobes short. Brazil.

S.bulbosa (Ker-Gawl.) Wiehler (*Gesneria bulbosa* Ker-Gawl.). Tuber large and knotty. Stem erect, to 60cm. Lvs ovate-cordate, dentate, somewhat succulent; petioles short. Fls bright red, in terminal panicles; cor. tube narrow, opening toward throat, lobes unequal, uppermost exceeding others. Brazil.

S.canescens (Mart.) Wiehler (*S.leucotricha* (Hoehne) H.E. Moore; *Gesneria canescens* Mart.; *Rechsteineria canescens* (Mart.) Kuntze). Stems to 25cm, densely tomentose. Lvs to 15×10cm, in whorls, obovate, grey-green, densely white-pubesc. Fls in cymes of 3–5 at each axil; cal. lobes tapering from deltoid base; cor. cylindric, pink to orange to red, hairy, to 3cm, lobes nearly equal, obtuse, maroon-violet, brown-black-striate. Brazil.

S.cardinalis (Lehm.) H.E. Moore (*Gesneria cardinalis* Lehm.; *Rechsteineria cardinalis* (Lehm.) Kuntze). Stems to 30cm. Lvs in pairs along stem, to 15×11cm, ovate-

cordate, somewhat crinkled, densely short-pubesc., dark green around main veins. Fls solitary or several in cymes in axils of upper lvs; sep. erect, lanceolate to 0.7cm; cor. to 5cm, bright red, pubesc., limb distinctly 2-lipped. Brazil. Dwarf Hybrids: habit small; fls trumpet-shaped, plum, magenta, carmine, purple, lilac, bicolour. 'Feuerschein': fls pale tangerine-red to carmine. 'Innocence': habit compact; lvs bright green, pubesc.; fls pure snow white. 'Splendens': branches rambling; lvs heart-shaped, broad; fls 2-lipped, tubular, bright scarlet.

S.carolinae (Wawra) Benth. & Hook. See *S.barbata*.
S.claybergiana H.E. Moore. See *S.sceptrum*.

S.concinna (Hook.) Nichols. Lvs to 6×2cm, ovate, crinkled, red-veined, otherwise green, erect hairy above. Fls sparse, solitary; sep. lanceolate, to 2mm; cor. trumpet-shaped, horizontal, lilac above, pale mauve to yellow-brown below, purple-spotted inside tube, limb broadly spreading, upper 2 lobes deep purple; lower 3 lobes paler; disc 5-glandular. Brazil.

S.cooperi (Paxt.) Wiehler (*Rechsteineria cooperi* (Paxt.) Kuntze; *Corytholoma cooperi* (Paxt.) Fritsch). Similar to *S.cardinalis* except; cor. limb broadly spreading, heavily marked with purple at margin. Brazil.

S.eumorpha H.E. Moore. Stems pubesc. marked with red. Lvs to 10×9.5cm, ovate-cordate, crinkled, pubesc. petiolate. Fls solitary or few in cymes, on peduncles to 11cm; cal. marked with red; sep. ovate-lanceolate, to 1.2cm; cor. to 3.5cm, horizontal, curved, white or faintly flushed with mauve, lobes to 1cm, throat with a purple-bordered, red-spotted yellow streak. Brazil.

S.guttata Lindl. (*Gloxinia guttata* (Lindl.) Mart.). Stems short, erect. Lvs ciosely set, oblong-lanceolate, pale green, crenate. Fls in uppermost lf axils; cal. large green; sep. foliose, covering basal third of cor. tube; cor. tube white, widening to throat; lobes cream, finely purple-spotted. Brazil.

S.helleri Nees. Stems round, fleshy, to 30cm. Lvs to 6cm, opposite, petiolate, cordate-ovate, serrate, slightly pubesc. Fls pale green-yellow; calyx inflated, campanulate; sep. equal; cor. to 5cm, funnelform, glandular-hairy, viscid, inflated between upper limb lobes, tube purple-striate inside, lobes obtuse, ovate-cordate, unequal. Brazil.

S.hirsuta (Lindl.) Nichols.
Lvs to 15×10cm, broadly ovate, crinkled, finely pubesc. Fls many; cal. lobes to 0.5cm; cor. mauve outside, darker inside, white striped and red-maculate inside tube, tube to 1.2cm, limb broadly spreading. Brazil.

S.incarnata (Aubl.) Denh. (*Besleria incarnata* Aubl.; *Rechsteineria incarnata* (Aubl.) Leeuwenb.; *S.warscewiczii* (Bouché & Hanst.) H.E. Moore).
Stems to 1.5cm. Lvs in opposite pairs or ternate, elliptic, to 12×4cm, crenate. Fls red or yellow, in terminal infl. on pedicels to 2cm; cal. to 1.4cm, lobes partially connate, acute or acuminate; cor. tubular, somewhat inflated, to 5cm, spurred at base, limb prominent, to 1×1cm. C Argentina to C Mexico.

S.leucotricha (Hoehne) H.E. Moore. See *S.canescens*.

S.macropoda (Sprague) H.E. Moore (*Rechsteineria macropoda* (Sprague) Curtis; *Rechsteineria lineata* Hjelmqv.).
Stems to 60cm, marked with red stripes. Lvs sparsely distributed in pairs, broadly ovate, to 20×15cm, crinkled, pubesc. Fls clustered at apex, axillary red-maculate, glandular peduncles to 15cm; calyx pubesc.; sep. deltoid, cor. tube cylindric expanding at apex, to 3cm, glandular hairy, red; lower limb lip marked with purple spots or lines; lobes subequal. Brazil.

S.macrorrhiza (Dumort.) Wiehler (*Rechsteineria macrorrhiza* (Dumort.) Kuntze).
Similar to *S.cardinalis*. Tuber large. Stem extending to 120cm. Lvs 10–15×8–13cm, ovate, in pairs. Fls bright red; lower limb lip red-purple-maculate. Brazil.

S.magnifica (Otto & Dietr.) Wiehler.
Similar to *S.cardinalis* except fls held in a dense terminal cluster above foliage. Brazil.

S.× pumila Clayb. (*S.pusilla × S.eumorpha*.) Rosette.
Fls to 12×3cm, light mauve, shading to deep purple. Garden origin. Sterile hybrid. Made available as a fertile tetraploid under the name 'Tetra' by use of colchicine.

S.pusilla (Mart.) Baill.
Stems very short. Lvs ovate to suborbicular, to 1.2cm, short, erect-hairy above, pale, hairy, red-veined beneath. Fls on hairy pedicels to 2.5cm; cor. to 2cm, lilac, prominently spurred; lobes unequal, lilac with purple lines; throat white. Brazil. 'White Sprite': habit dwarf; fls tubular, glistening snow-white.

S.regina Sprague. See *S.speciosa*.

S.reitzii (Hoehne) Skog (*Rechsteineria reitzii* Hoehne).
Stem to 1m. Lvs cordate, dark green above, red beneath, veins marked with white. Fls clustered in axils of full-sized lvs; calyx lobes linear, spreading; cor. horizontal, maroon, tubular, to 4.5cm; lobes marked with dark purple. Brazil.

S.richii Clayb.
Tubers small, globose. Stems ascending, swollen, 5–15cm. Lvs to 20cm, opposite, oblong, pale green, lustrous. Fls 1 or 2 in each upper lf axil on peduncles to 8cm; cor. white with short, maroon lines inside and out, pubesc. outside, disc white-glandular. Mexico.

S.× rosea (Moore & Wils.) H.E. Moore. (*S.eumorpha × S.macropoda*.)
As for *S.eumorpha* except pink fls borne in an axillary infl.

S.sceptrum (Mart.) Wiehler (*S.claybergiana* H.E. Moore; *Rechsteineria lindleyi* (Hook.) Fritsch).
Stems to 1.5m, often marked with purple. Lvs to 15×6cm, opposite or whorled, elliptic, crinkled, densely pubesc. above pale-pubesc. below. Fls in clusters near apex; sep. deltoid, to 9mm; cor. to 3cm, rose, pubesc., spurred, limb distinctly 2-lipped, spreading, lobes subequal. Brazil.

S.schiffneri Fritsch (*Paliavana schiffneri* (Fritsch) Handro).
Tuberless, erect shrub to 1.5m. Stems many. Lvs to 15×7.5cm, lanceolate, dentate, pubesc. Fls solitary or 2–3 in axils; cal. lobes narrow, spreading, to 1.2cm; cor. funnel-shaped, to 2.5cm, cream; tube lined and spotted with red inside. Brazil.

S.sellovii (Mart.) Wiehler (*Rechsteineria sellovii* (Mart.) Kuntze; *Rechsteineria ramboi* Hoehne; *Corytholoma sellovii* Mart.).
Stem erect, to 75cm. Lvs elliptic in pairs. Fls in long terminal spikes; sep. deltoid; cor. red, hairy, nodding, to 7cm, swollen at base, then constricted and inflated once more toward apex, lobes obtuse. SE Brazil, Argentina, Paraguay, E Bolivia. Some material cultivated under this name is *S.sceptrum*.

S.speciosa (Lodd.) Hiern (*Gloxinia speciosa* Lodd.; *S.regina* Sprague). FLORISTS' GLOXINIA; GLOXINIA.
Stems to 30cm. Lvs to 20×15cm, on short petioles, ovate to oblong, crinkled, finely pubesc., green above, flushed with red below. Fls solitary or 2–3 or more in axils on ascending pedicels; sep. to 2.2cm, ovate, acuminate; cor. horizontal, to 4cm+, somewhat compressed near base with a central, hairy ridge above, distinctly swollen dorsally, occasionally erect and bell-shaped purple, lavender, red or white in wild, variously coloured in cultivation; disc 5-glandular. Brazil. Fyfiana Group: fls large, campanulate, erect, white, through pink, yellow and orange, to red and violet, variously blotched and striped. Notable cvs include: 'Blanche de Meru': fls white, fringed pink; 'Boonwood Yellow Bird': lvs dark, acuminate, fls yellow; 'Chic': fls numerous, flame-red; 'Mont Blanc': fls pure white; 'Violacea': fls deep violet-blue. Maxima Group: fls large, nodding. Notable cvs include: 'Buell's Blue Slipper': lvs velvety, fls trumpet-shaped, curved, numerous, 'Buell's Queen Bee': fls lobed, white with a bright pink blotch on either side of throat; 'Kiss of Fire': fls erect, numerous, velvety with wavy lobes; 'Pink Slipper': lvs soft, light green, crenate; fls rose-pink with a dark centre and spotted throat.

S.sulcata (Rusby) Wiehler (*Rechsteineria sulcata* (Rusby) Fritsch).
Similar to *S.tubiflora*; lower part of stem with elliptic lvs, upper part with a terminal infl. of nodding, yellow, tubular fls. Bolivia.

S.tuberosa (Mart.) H.E. Moore (*Rechsteineria tuberosa* (Mart.) Kuntze).
Stem virtually absent. Lvs and infl. arising from tuber. Lvs to 45×30cm, ovate or oblong, crinkled, sparsely pubesc. Fls 1–6 in a raceme to 15cm; sep. to 0.7cm, deltoid, often flushed with red, sparsely hairy; cor. cylindric, to 3.5cm, bright red, throat marked with yellow, upper 2 lobes not recurved, lower 3 lobes spreading. Brazil.

S.tubiflora (Hook.) Fritsch (*Achimenes tubiflora* (Hook.) Britton).
Stems to 60cm+, pubesc. Lvs to 12.5×4cm, subsessile, oblong elliptic, crinkled, sparsely pubesc. Fls in a monocasial, terminal cyme, scented; sep. to 0.9cm, lanceolate; cor. white, tube cylindric, slightly curved toward apex, lobes spreading, to 1.2cm. Argentina, Paraguay, Uruguay.

S.verticillata (Vell.) H.E. Moore (*Rechsteineria purpurea* hort.; *Rechsteineria verticillata* (Vell.) L.B. Sm.).
Stems to 60cm, flushed with red, downy. Lvs in a pseudowhorl of 2–6, to 19×10cm, cordate-ovate, acutely dentate; petiole to 7cm; reduced lvs in pseudowhorls toward apex. Fls many in axils of reduced lvs on pedicels to 7.5cm; sep. to 0.5cm, deltoid; cor. to 3.8cm, cylindric, red, marked with purple, lobes all equal except lower most larger lobe. Brazil.

S.warscewiczii (Bouché & Hanst.) H.E. Moore. See *S.incarnata*.

S.× youngeana Marnock. (*S.speciosa × S.velutina*.)
Similar to *S.guttata* except cor. deep violet, lvs oblong, cordate at base, densely tomentose.

Sisyrinchium L. (Name used by Theophrastus for a plant related to *Iris*.) Iridaceae. About 90 species of herbaceous plants, usually perennial but sometimes annual; roots fibrous or fleshy usually arising from a short rhizome. Leaves linear to sword-shaped, distichous, mostly basal forming a fan. Stem usually flattened and winged, often branched and then with cauline leaves as well as basal. Inflorescence composed of a 2–8-flowered cluster enclosed in a pair of spathe bracts; flowers regular, short-lived, yellow, blue-violet, white, or pink in one species, stellate or cup-shaped; perianth tube very short; tepals 6, free; filaments usually joined for part or all of length; style with 3 undivided branches. Fruit a capsule; seeds black, globose. N, C & S America, with 1 species in Ireland. Australia, New Zealand and Hawaiian Is., probably all naturalized. This is a complex genus; the species are very similar morphologically and, therefore, are difficult to distinguish and are frequently misidentified. Species previously included in Sect. *Eriphilema* are now considered to belong in the genus *Olysnium*.

CULTIVATION *Sisyrinchium* spp. are grown in the rock garden, alpine house or herbaceous border, depending on stature; those most common in cultivation can be successfully grown out of doors in cool temperate zones, with the exception of *S.convolutum*, which require a minimum of about 10°C/50°F. Where temperatures fall much below freezing several species, such as *S.angustifolium*, *S.micranthum* and *S.chilense*, will need protection in the cold glasshouse or alpine house; most of the remaining species described are hardy to between –10 and –15°C/14–5°F. *S.idahoense* and *S.montanum* thrive in zones that experience cold to –20°C/–4°F. Grow in freely draining, sandy loam soils with additional organic matter such as leafmould; *S.californicum*, *S.bellum* and *S.angustifolium* prefer moist soils, but still need good drainage. Give a position in full sun, although most will tolerate at least part-day shade. Species such as *S.angustifolium* and *S.bellum* self-seed if conditions suit. Propagate by seed in spring or autumn or by division in early spring.

S.alatum Hook. See *S.vaginatum*.

S.albidum Raf.
Stems 15–50cm tall, flattened, with narrow or broad wings; lvs narrowly linear. Spathes sometimes tinged with purple, sometimes with denticulate keel, fls pale violet-blue or almost white with a yellow centre; tepals 6–11mm long, apiculate. South Eastern N America. Z4.

S.anceps Cav. See *S.angustifolium*.

S.angustifolium Mill. (*S.anceps* Cav.; *S.graminoides* E. Bickn.; *S.iridoides* Curtis). BLUE-EYED GRASS.
Stem 15–45cm, flattened, narrowly winged. Lvs 7–15×0.1–0.3cm, narrowly linear. Spathes usually 2–4-fld; fls about 15mm diam., blue, yellow in centre; tepals spreading, 7mm long, obovate, emarginate, mucronate. Summer. W Ireland, naturalized in Europe including parts of England; SE US. Z3.

S.atlanticum E. Bickn.
Stems 10–70cm, branched, narrowly winged. Lvs narrowly linear, pale glaucous green. Spathes green or purple-tinged, sometimes with denticulate keel; fls violet-blue with a yellow centre; tepals 8–12mm, apiculate. Eastern N America. Z6.

S.bellum S. Wats. (*S.eastwoodiae* C. Bickn.). CALIFORNIAN BLUE-EYED GRASS.
Stems 10–50cm, branched, narrowly winged, forming tufts. Lvs narrowly linear. Spathes sometimes with a denticulate keel; fls violet-blue with purple veins; tepals 10–17mm, apiculate. California. Z8.

S.bermudiana L. BLUE-EYED GRASS.
Stem 15–45cm, flattened, narrowly winged. Lvs 7–15×0.1–0.3cm, narrowly linear; fls *c*15mm diam., starry; blue, yellow in centre; tepals 7mm, obovate, emarginate, mucronate. Summer. W Indies. Z8.

S.birameum Piper. See *S.idahoense*.
S.bogotense Kunth. See *S.tinctorium*.
S.boreale (C. Bickn.) J. Henry. See *S.californicum*.
S.brachypus (C. Bickn.) J. Henry. See *S.californicum*.

S.californicum Ait. f. (*S.boreale* (C. Bickn.) J. Henry; *S.brachypus* (C. Bickn.) J. Henry).
Stems to *c*40cm, broadly winged. Basal lvs to 15×0.5cm, grey-green, sword-shaped. Spathes 2–9-fld; fls starry, to 36mm diam., bright yellow, sometimes turning orange on drying; pedicels just longer than spathes; tepals 6–18mm long, ovate or elliptic. Late spring–summer. Western US, naturalized Ireland. Z8.

S.campestre E. Bickn.
Stems to 50cm tall, often shorter, flattened, narrowly winged, pale glaucous green. Lvs shorter than stem, *c*3mm wide.

Spathes sometimes slightly scabrid, often tinged with purple. Fls pale blue to white with a yellow centre; tepals 8–10mm, apiculate. Central (Great Plains) US. Z5.

S.chilense Hook.
Stems 15–30cm; basal lvs of similar length, 2–4mm wide, linear. Fls purple, yellow in centre; tepals *c*13mm. Summer. Mexico to Southern S America, naturalized in Mauritius. Z9.

S.convolutum Nocca.
To 30cm tall, with fleshy, tuberous roots. Stems winged, usually branched. Lvs falcate, 3–8mm wide. Spathes broad, enlarged, at base; fls yellow, with brown veining; tepals to 15mm. Capsules inflated, glabrous, 3-lobed, 8–10mm diam. C America. Z9.

S.cuspidatum Poepp.
Stems 30–60cm; roots fleshy. Basal lvs 15–30cm, linear. Infl. spicate, with many-fld clusters; fls yellow, *c*20mm diam. Chile. Z9.

S.douglasii A. Dietr. See *Olysnium douglasii*.
S.eastwoodiae E. Bickn. See *S.bellum*.

S.ensigerum E. Bickn.
Stems 15–35cm, winged, branched. Lvs to 15×0.5cm, narrowly linear or sword-shaped. Spathes with finely denticulate keel, 2–4-fld; fls pale blue-violet, *c*20mm diam. Tepals 10–15mm long, apiculate. Oklahoma to Texas and Mexico. Z6.

S.filifolium Gaudich. See *Olysnium filifolium*.
S.graminoides E. Bickn. See *S.angustifolium*.
S.grandiflorum Douglas. See *Olysnium douglasii*.

S.idahoense C. Bickn. (*S.birameum* Piper).
Stems to 50cm, winged, usually unbranched, glaucous green. Lvs about half length of stem, 1–3mm wide. Fls light to dark violet-blue, yellow in centre; tepals 8–20mm, apiculate. Western US and SW Canada. 'Album': fls white. Z3.

S.inflatum (Suksd.) St. John. See *Olysnium douglasii*.
S.iridifolium HBK. See *S.micranthum*.
S.iridoides Curtis. See *S.angustifolium*.

S.laxum Otto.
Annual to *c*20cm. Fls blue or white; tepals about 10mm. Temperate S America.

S.littorale Greene.
Stems to *c*50cm tall, winged sometimes branched. Lvs linear. Fls violet-blue, yellow in centre; tepals 11–20mm, apiculate. Alaska to Washington. Z2.

S.lutescens Lodd. See *S.striatum*.

S.macrocephalum Graham.
Robust, forming clumps; stems to *c*1m, somewhat winged.

Lvs to 1cm diam. Infl. usually branched; fls yellow, tepals about 10mm. Uruguay, E Brazil, Bolivia, N Argentina. Z8.

S.micranthum Cav. (*S.iridifolium* HBK).
Annual, 5–25cm, branched at base. Stem flattened, narrowly winged, with basal and cauline lvs. Spathes 2–6-fld; fls blue or white, yellow at base of tepals, with red-purple eye; tepals *c*6mm long. Capsules small, *c*3mm, globose. C America to NW Argentina, naturalized in Australia.

S.montanum E. Greene.
Stems to *c*50cm, pale green, narrowly winged. Lvs shorter than stem, narrowly linear, to 3mm wide. Fls 25–35mm diam., starry, bright violet-blue, yellow in centre tepals 9–15mm, apiculate. Summer. Eastern N America, widely naturalized in Europe. Z6.

S.mucronatum Michx.
Stems slender, dark green, to *c*40cm, very narrowly winged. Lvs narrowly linear, less than 2mm wide. Spathes often tinged red-purple; fls violet-blue, rarely white with yellow centre; tepals 8–10mm, apiculate. Eastern N America. 'Album': fls white. Z5.

S.pachyrhizum Bak.
Stems 30–60cm high, flattened, winged, much branched, leafy; roots fleshy. Lvs shorter than stem, linear. Spathes 3–6-fld; fls yellow; tepals 6mm; fil. joined for their whole length. Brazil, Paraguay, Argentina. Z9.

S.palmifolium L.
Infl. sessile, crowded at apex of stem; fls yellow. Z9.

S.pedunculatum Hook. See *Solenomelus pedunculatus*

S.sarmentosum Suksd.
Stems 15–30cm, very slender. Lvs less than 3mm wide. Fls pale blue with a yellow centre; tepals 6–11mm, apiculate. Washington. Z7.

S.striatum Sm. (*S.lutescens* Lodd.).
Stems 40–80cm, narrowly winged. Lvs 20–40×2cm, lanceolate. Infl. spicate, with 8–20 sessile clusters of fls; fls somewhat cup-shaped, cream or pale yellow, veined with brown; tepals to 15mm; fil. joined at base. Late summer. Argentina, Chile. 'Aunt May' ('Variegata'): to 60cm, hardy; lvs narrow, green tinged grey, striped cream; fls pale yellow striped purple, trumpet-shaped, in slender spikes. Z8.

S.tenuifolium Kunth.
Variable, slender or robust, branched or unbranched; roots swollen, tuberous. Basal lvs 5–22×0.05–0.2cm, linear. Fls yellow, starry; tepals *c*15mm, oblong, acute. Capsule 5–7mm, globose, sparsely pubesc. C America. Z8.

S.tinctorium Kunth (*S.bogotense* Kunth).
Stems to 15cm tall, slender, unbranched, often broadly winged; roots fibrous. Lvs 5–8×0.2–0.3cm. Spathes terminal, 2–4-fld; fls pale yellow, somewhat bell-shaped. Capsules almost pear-shaped, pendent. S Mexico to Colombia and Venezuela. Z8.

S.vaginatum Spreng. (*S.alatum* Hook.).
Stems 30–50cm, winged, much branched, forming dense tufts; lvs cauline. Spathes 2–6-fld; fls yellow, tepals to 10mm; fil. joined at base. Brazil, Bolivia, South to Uruguay and Paraguay. Z8.

S.cultivars.
'Biscutella': to 35cm; lvs grass-like; fls yellow stained and veined dusky purple. 'E.K. Balls' ('Ball's Mauve'): lvs in fan-shaped sprays; fls mauve. 'Mrs Spivey': fls pure white, abundant. 'Pole Star' ('North Star'): to 15cm; fls white; long-flowering. 'Quaint and Queer': habit small, vigorous; fls centred yellow, outer tepals dull purple.

Sparaxis Ker-Gawl. (From Gk *sparasso*, to tear, referring to the bracts.) Iridaceae. 6 species of deciduous perennial herbs. Corms small, globose, with fibrous tunics. Stems unbranched or branched, with axillary cormlets. Leaves glabrous, ribbed. Spike laxly 1- to several-flowered; bracts scarious with brown streaks, the edge lacerate, bracteoles similar but smaller; flowers large, regular or slightly irregular; perianth tube short, narrow at base then funnel-shaped, segments 6, more or less equal, lanceolate, ovate or spathulate, stamens arising in throat, symmetrically or asymmetrically arranged; style with 3 branches. S Africa (SW Cape). Z9.

CULTIVATION   As for *Ixia*.

S.bulbifera (L.) Ker-Gawl.
15–50cm, usually with 1–3 branches, with numerous small cormlets produced in leaf axils after flowering. Lvs 5–9, distichous, shorter than stem, 4–10mm wide, sword-shaped, closely ribbed. Spike laxly 1–6-fld; fls irregular, tube yellow, green at base, seg. white or cream, the outside usually with purple median streak, rarely whole seg. plum-coloured; perianth tube 14–16mm, seg. 25–28×12mm, lanceolate, subacute; stamens asymmetrically arranged, fil. and anth. white, all 7–8mm long; style usually longer than stamens, branches filiform, about 10mm. Late winter–spring.

S.elegans (Sweet) Goldbl. (*Streptanthera elegans* Sweet).
Stem 10–30cm, unbranched, but 2–5 arising per corm, with some cormlets produced at lowest nodes. Lvs 5–9, forming a fan, 8–25×0.5–1.5cm, glabrous, sword-shaped. Fls regular, brightly coloured, perianth tube yellow, lobes vermilion fading to pink, with violet band sometimes marked with yellow at edge inside at base; tube 6–8mm, lobes 18–22×14–17mm, ovate, obtuse; stamens symmetrical, fil. yellow, 5–6mm, anth. shorter, maroon or brown; style yellow, red at tip, of similar length to stamens, branches *c*2mm. Spring. 'Coccinea': fls orange-red with near-black centre.

S.fragrans (Jacq.) Ker-Gawl. (*Ixia grandiflora* Delaroche).
Stem 1–3, 8–45cm, unbranched, with a few cormlets in lowest axils. Lvs 6–10, distichous, 3–20cm×4–13mm, lanceolate

or falcate. Spike laxly 1–6-fld; fls irregular, tube yellow, purple or black, lobes cream, yellow, red-purple or violet-purple with or without dark blotches and streaks; perianth tube 10–14mm, lobes 24–40×12–16mm, lanceolate, ovate or spathulate, subacute or obtuse; stamens white or yellow, asymmetrically arranged, fil. 7–9mm, curved, anth. slightly longer; style about as long as stamens, branches filiform, curved, 6–10mm. Late winter–spring. ssp. *acutiloba* Goldbl. To 45cm; fls purple, or yellow sometimes with the outside of lobes marked with black, perianth lobes 25–29×12mm, lanceolate, acute. ssp. *fimbriata* (Lam.) Goldbl. Very robust; tube yellow, purple outside, lobes cream or pale yellow, usually with large black blotches at base and streaked on outside with purple; perianth lobes 28–40×14–16mm, narrowly ovate, obtuse. ssp. *grandiflora* (Delaroche) Goldbl. Plants less robust; fls usually red-purple but sometimes white with purple marks, the tube yellow inside, purple outside; perianth lobes 25–30×8–14mm, spathulate, obtuse. ssp. *violacea* (Ecklon) Goldbl. (*Sparaxis violacea* Ecklon). Usually less than 20cm high. Perianth tube yellow or cream, perianth lobes white with or without violet marks, or violet with white at base and apex; lobes 22–26×12mm, spathulate, obtuse.

S.pillansii L. Bol.
Stems 2–4, 25–65cm, unbranched, with cormlets in lower axils. Lvs 8–10, distichous, to 35cm, narrowly sword-shaped. Spike laxly 4–9-fld; fls regular, tube yellow, lobes rose-pink with yel-

(a)

(b)

(c)

Sparaxis (a) *S.elegans* (b) *S.fragrans* ssp. *grandiflora* (c) *S.fragrans* ssp. *acutiloba*

low mark edged with purple at base; perianth tube 7–9mm, lobes 22–29×10–13mm; stamens symmetrical, fil. white, 7–8mm, anth. slightly longer, purple-red; style white, branches maroon-red, 3mm, widened and bilobed at tips. Spring.

S.tricolor (Schneev.) Ker-Gawl.
Stems 1–5, 10–40cm, with a few cormlets at lower nodes. Lvs 5–10, arranged in fan, shorter than stem, 1–2cm wide, sword-shaped. Spike laxly 2–5-fld; fls regular, tube yellow, lobes vermilion or salmon, almost always with black arrow-shaped mark at base; perianth tube about 8mm, lobes 25–33×10mm, lanceo-late, acute; stamens symmetrical, fil. yellow, 6–7mm, anth. 8–9mm, yellow or white; style yellow, shorter than stamens, branches 1–2mm, slightly wider and bilobed at tips. Spring. 'Alba': fls white to 5cm across, petals yellow at throat with dark centre stripe. 'Honneur de Haarlem': fls large, deep crimson, petals blotched black in middle with yellow markings. Magic Border Hybrids: habit hardy; fls large in rich selection of colours, often four colours in one bloom; seed race.

S.violacea Ecklon. See *Sparaxis fragrans* ssp. *violacea*.

Sprekelia Heist. (For J.H. von Sprekelsen (*d*1764), German botanist.) Amaryllidaceae. 1 species, a bulbous herb. Bulbs globose, to 5cm diam.; tunics brown. Leaves to 45cm, basal, deciduous, synanthous, linear, narrow. Scape to 30cm, erect, hollow, tinted red, especially at base; flowers showy, solitary, terminal, bright to deep scarlet to deep crimson or white; spathe valves to 5cm; pedicel erect; perianth segments 6, the lower 3 declinate, subequal, over-lapping and partly inrolled at their bases into a loose, waisted cylinder, their free parts narrow-lanceolate and drooping, the upper 3 segments more or less erect, outspread or reflexed, the central one to 2.5cm across, broader than the lateral segments; stamens in the cylinder, attached to the bases of the segments, filaments long, projecting down, outwards and upwards ending in large drooping versatile anthers; stigma 3-branched, exceeding stamens; ovary 6-angled, inferior. Fruit a 3-valved capsule; seeds flat, narrowly winged, black. Mexico. Z9.

CULTIVATION *S.formosissima* is a frost-tender bulb, grown for its exotic, brilliant red, orchid-like flowers, borne in spring or early summer and followed or accompanied by the slender strap-shaped leaves. In gardens that are frost-free or almost so, they are grown permanently out of doors. In cooler regions they are lifted in autumn or grown in pots in the cool glasshouse and conservatory, overwintered at 7–10°C/45–50°F. Cultivate as for the cooler-growing *Hippeastrum* species and cultivars.

S.cybister Herb. See *Hippeastrum cybister*.

S.formosissima (L.) Herb. (*Amaryllis formosissima* L.).
JACOBEAN LILY; ST JAMES LILY; AZTEC LILY; ORCHID LILY.
'Glauca': lvs very glaucous, fls small, pale red. 'Karwinskii': fls vivid scarlet, edged white. 'Ringens': lvs somewhat glaucous; fls pendent, the central seg. with a vertical golden stripe.

Sprekelia formosissima

Stenanthium (A. Gray) Kunth. (From Gk *stenos*, narrow, and *anthos*, flower; the perianth segments and panicles are narrow.) Liliaceae (Melanthiaceae). 5 species of bulbous perennial herbs. Stems slender, erect. Leaves 2–4, narrow, grass-like, mostly basal, arching, glabrous, acute; stem leaves few, bract-like, borne toward summit. Flowers bisexual or unisexual in dense or loose terminal racemes or panicles; perianth narrowly campanulate, white or white-green or dark purple, tube short, free lobes 6, linear, spreading to recurved stamens 6, at base of perianth lobes; styles 3, free; ovary superior. Fruit a 3-beaked capsule; seeds many, narrow-oblong. Western N America, Mexico, Sakhalin. Z6.

CULTIVATION Grown for the small, bell-shaped flowers carried on long slender stems, *Stenanthium* spp. are suited to the wild garden, native plant collections and other informal plantings. Most species occur on moist soils, some, such as *S.gramineum* and *S.occidentale* in woodland. Grow in a position with some shelter from wind in sandy, well-drained but humus-rich and retentive, neutral or slightly acid soil in partial shade. Most are hardy about –20°C/–4°F, but benefit from mulch in spring with leafmould or garden compost to retain moisture. Propagate by ripe seed sown fresh in a moist, sandy propagating mix.

S.angustifolium Kunth. See *S.gramineum*.

S.gramineum (Ker-Gawl.) Morong (*S.angustifolium* Kunth). Bulb oblong. Basal lvs to 30–40×1.8cm, channelled. Scapes to 1.5m, channelled; infl. a dense panicle, 30–60cm, apex dense, spicate, lower regions furnished with spreading or nodding branches; fls 1.2–1.8cm diam., variable in size on a single plant, white to white-green or purple, fragrant, starry, lower fls often male only; perianth lobes c6mm, linear-lanceolate, acuminate, briefly connate at base; stamens very short; stigmatic branches very short, spreading. Fr. pendulous. Late summer. SE US. var. **robustum** (S. Wats.) Fern. (*S.robustum* S. Wats.). Lvs to 2.5cm wide. Flowering stem to 1.8m, panicle denser than in type, with ascending to spreading branches. Fr. often erect.

S.occidentale A. Gray.
Bulb ovoid. Basal lvs 15–30×1.8cm, linear to narrowly oblanceolate, slightly keeled, ascending. Scape to 60cm; infl. a loose raceme to 20cm, sometimes with a few short branches at base; fls 1.2–1.8cm, campanulate, brown-purple, nodding; perianth lobes slender, fused for half their length; stamens half length of perianth seg.; stigmatic branches long and slender, erect. Summer. Western N America.

S.robustum S. Wats. See *S.gramineum* var. *robustum*.

Stenomesson Herb. (From Gk *stenos*, narrow, and *mesos*, middle, referring to the shape of the perianth.) Amaryllidaceae. 20 species of stemless, bulbous herbs to 30cm. Tunic extends above neck, sheathing stem and leaf bases. Leaves 3–8, radical, linear to lanceolate, oblanceolate or ligulate, acute, truncate or acuminate, lengthening after flowering, green to blue-green above, occasionally channelled or keeled below. Scape solid or hollow, terete or quadrangular; bracts 4, leafy; spathe-valves 2, leafy or membranous. Infl. 1–6 fls in an umbel, pink, green, yellow, scarlet or crimson or variegated; perianth tubular, often contracted or suddenly dilating from middle; tepals 6, ovate, hooded; cup-like corona formed from united filament bases present and toothed in some species; stamens 6, included or exserted, anthers versatile, included, sometimes cohering; style exserted; stigma capitate; ovary green, triangular. Fruit a capsule; seeds many, flat, black. High Andes. Z9.

CULTIVATION Mostly native to high altitudes in the Andes (to about 3,500m/11,375ft), *Stenomesson* spp. are frost-tender bulbs, bearing delicate umbels of pendant tubular flowers in winter, early spring or summer. They are uncommon in cultivation and are generally not as flamboyant as many other Amaryllidaceae. Cultivate under glass with a winter minimum temperature of 7–10°C/45–50°F, as for cool-tolerant *Hippeastrum*. Keep dormant bulbs just moist enough to prevent shrivelling.

S.aurantiacum (HBK) Herb. (*Pancratium aurantiacum* HBK; *S.hartwegii* Lindl.; *S.suspensum* Bak.).
To 30cm. Lvs later than fls, lanceolate, to 33×3.5cm, dark green above, paler and keeled beneath. Scape terete; spathe-valves 2, withered; pedicels to 3cm; fls 2–5, pendulous, funnel-shaped, scarlet or cinnabar; floral tube to 9mm; tepals narrowly elliptic, to 1.25cm, joined for 1cm, apex acute or obtuse; fil. of 2 lengths, to 11mm, joined for 0.5cm forming staminal cup, coronal teeth absent; style to 3.8cm longer than anth.; stigma capitate. N Peru to N Ecuador.

S.coccineum (Ruiz & Pav.) Herb. (*Pancratium coccineum* Ruiz & Pav.).
Lvs 4–5, later than fls, to 30cm, thick. Scape terete, to 30cm; spathe valves 2, lanceolate, to 3.5cm; pedicels to 4cm; fls 4–8, crimson; floral tube to 4cm; tepals to 4cm, joined to 2.3cm, abruptly dilated, free portion 1.5×0.7cm, lanceolate, acute; stamens exserted or included. Spring–summer. Peru.

S.croceum Herb.
Lvs solitary, linear-lanceolate or ovate-lanceolate, green above, paler beneath. Scape 30cm, terete, glaucous; bracts 2.5cm; fls 4, suberect, 3.5cm long, golden-yellow, tube curved, segments connivent. Spring–summer. Peru.

S.curvidentatum (Lindl.) Herb. (*S.pauciflorum* var. *curvidentatum* (Herb.) Macbr.).
Lvs oblanceolate, to 30×2.5cm; subsessile. Scape to 30cm; fls 4–6, 3.5–5cm, tube abruptly dilated from midpoint, bright yellow; stamens united to form staminal cup, a corona of bidentate teeth alternating with stamens. Spring–summer.

S.flavum (Ruiz & Pav.) Herb. (*Pancratium flavum* Ruiz & Pav.; *S.latifolium* Herb.; *Chrysiphiala flava* Ruiz & Pav.).
Like *S.curvidentatum* but lacking corona. Spring–summer. Peru, Argentina.

S.fulvum (Herb.) Ravenna. See *S.variegatum*.
S.hartwegii Lindl. See *S.aurantiacum*.

S.humile (Herb.) Bak. (*Clitanthes humilis* Herb.).
Lvs lanceolate, 30×0.5cm, glabrous, glossy, channelled; flower 1, to 8cm, scarlet; floral tube abruptly dilated from midpoint; tepals slightly spreading. Spring. Peru, Bolivia, Argentina.

S.incarnatum (HBK) Bak. See *S.variegatum*.
S.incarnatum var. *acutum* (Herb.) Bak. See *S.variegatum*.
S.latifolium Herb. See *S.flavum*.
S.luteoviride Bak. See *S.variegatum*.

S.luteum (Herb.) Bak.
Lvs linear, to 21cm. Scape equals lvs; fls 2, to 5cm, ascending, yellow; fil. winged at base but without coronal teeth. Peru.

S.miniatum (Herb.) Ravenna.
Lvs ligulate, to 40×5cm, developing after fls, margins reflexed. Scape to 30cm; fls cinnabar-red; floral tube to 1.3cm, cylindrical, then urceolate above for 2cm; tepals to 1cm, recurved; stamens strongly exserted. Spring–summer. Peru, Bolivia.

S.pauciflorum var. *curvidentatum* (Herb.) Macbr. See *S.curvidentatum*.

S.pearcei Bak.
Lvs lorate lanceolate, 45cm, tapering to acute apex, margins somewhat revolute; petiole to 7.5cm, flattened. Scape to 90cm, solid, somewhat compressed; pedicels 5–10cm; fls 6–8, pendent, funnel-shaped, tube green-yellow,, seg. primrose-yellow, tinged green externally, oblong, erecto-patent. Spring–summer. Bolivia.

S.recurvatum Bak.
Bulb 2.5–3.5cm. Lvs 3–6, linear, 30×0.8cm. Scape 30–45cm; fls 6–12 to 6.5cm, red-yellow, seg. short. S America.

S.suspensum Bak. See *S.aurantiacum*.

S.variegatum (Ruiz & Pav.) Macbr. (*Pancratium variegatum* Ruiz & Pav.; *S.luteoviride* Bak.; *S.incarnatum* var. *acutum* (Herb.) Bak.).
Lvs 4–8, remains of lf bases sheathing lower lvs and scape to 17cm, distichous, ligulate, to 75×4.5cm, channelled, rounded or acute. Scape terete, to 66cm, narrowing towards apex; spathes leafy, to 4.5×1.5cm, yellow-green, margins white; fls 6–8, subsessile, many-coloured, tawny banded red, pink, scarlet or crimson banded darker pink, or green on tepals, or variously green and yellow; floral tube to 7cm, abruptly dilated after 3cm; tepals ovate, acute, unequal, 2.4×1.1 or 3×1.4cm; stamens included, white, united for 5mm into staminal cup, then alternating with deep green teeth; anth. fused; ovary to 1.3×0.7cm, green; style exserted, white. Spring.

S.viridiflorum (Ruiz & Pav.) Benth. (*Pancratium viridiflorum* Ruiz & Pav.).
Lvs flat, sword-shaped, to 2cm across. Scape to 180cm, glabrous; spathe valves marcescent; fls 1, green, subsessile; floral tube cylindrical, slightly widened at apex, pale green; fil. projecting inwards, shorter than in *S.variegatum*, margin of staminal cup undulate, anth. yellow. Spring–summer.

Sternbergia Waldst. & Kit. (For Count Kaspar Moritz von Sternberg of Prague (1761–1838), botanist, author of *Revisio Saxifragum*, 1819.) AUTUMN DAFFODIL. Amaryllidaceae. 7–8 species of perennial herbs; bulb tunics membranous, brown or black. Leaves basal, linear or lorate to narrowly lanceolate, sometimes shallowly channelled above, sometimes keeled beneath, often twisted, borne with or after flowers. Flowering stems 1-to several, sometimes subterranean at flowering, elongating and often arching in fruit; spathe membranous, tubular below; flowers solitary, yellow or white; perianth lobes 6, basally united into a narrow cylindrical tube, in 2 whorls, oblanceolate to obovate, regular, equal; stamens 6 in 2 unequal whorls at top of tube; ovary 3-celled; stigma entire or 3-toothed. Fruit a fleshy, 3-celled, indehiscent capsule; seeds globose, dark, usually with fleshy appendages. Turkey, west to Spain and east to Kashmir.

CULTIVATION Found in exceptionally free-draining habitats, usually on calcareous soils. With the exception of *S.fischeriana* and *S.candida*, *Sternbergia* spp. are autumn-flowering bulbs grown for their usually brilliant yellow and sometimes sweetly scented flowers; *S.lutea* and *S.sicula* are the most reliable species for cultivation in the open, and are well suited to plantings on the rock garden or border front, in sunny positions and in well-drained soils, where they can be left undisturbed to form large and congested clumps. *S.candida* and *S.fischeriana*, which flower in late winter or early spring, should be planted deeply, thus discouraging prolific division which results in small, non-flowering bulbs. Although most withstand considerable cold they are intolerant of winter wet, needing relatively little moisture even when in full growth, and their need for hot, dry summer conditions is more easily accommodated in the alpine house and bulb frame.

Grow in a mix of equal parts loam, leafmould and sharp sand, and water moderately when in growth, gradually reducing water as the leaves die back, and the bulb becomes dormant. Propagate by division of offsets when dormant, or from ripe seed.

S.candida B. Mathew & Baytop.
Like *S.fischeriana*, but scape 12–20cm; spathe 5–5.5cm; perianth lobes 4.3–5×0.9–1.8cm, obovate, apex rounded, white. Winter–spring. Z7.

S.clusiana (Ker-Gawl.) Spreng. (*S.macrantha* Bak.).
Bulb 2.5–4cm diam. Lvs 5–12, appearing long after fls, 8–16mm wide, lorate, obtuse, flat, often twisted, glaucescent. Scape very short, below ground at flowering; spathe 5–10cm; perianth lobes 3.7–7.5×1.1–3.3cm, obovate to oblanceolate, bright yellow to yellow-green. Autumn. Turkey, Jordan, Israel, Iran. Z6.

S.colchiciflora Waldst. & Kit.
Bulb 0.5–1.5cm diam. Lvs 4–6, narrow-linear, erect, twisted, keeled, tip obtusely callose, 10cm, borne after flowers. Scape below ground at flowering, raising ovary above ground in fruit; spathe 2.2–4cm; perianth lobes 2–3.4×0.4–1.2cm, linear, pale yellow. Autumn. SE Spain, Italy, west to Iran. Z5.

S.fischeriana (Herb.) Rupr.
Bulb 2.5–3.5cm diam. Lvs 4–7, appearing before fls, 15×1.2cm wide, lorate, flat, scarcely keeled, dark grey-green. Scape 3–15cm, longer in fruit; spathe 2.5–4.5cm; perianth lobes 2–3.5×0.5–0.8cm, oblanceolate, bright yellow. Spring. Caucasus to Kashmir. Z6.

S.lutea (L.) Spreng. GOLDEN CROCUS.
Bulb 2–4cm diam. Lvs to 30×1.2cm, 4–6, borne with or just after fls, narrowly lanceolate, slightly channelled above, keeled beneath, bright lustrous green. Scape 2.5–20cm, longer in fruit; spathe 3–6cm; perianth lobes 3–5.5×1–2cm, oblanceolate to obovate, deep yellow. Autumn. Spain to Iran and Soviet C Asia. 'Angustifolia': lvs narrow; fls bright yellow. Some plants grown under this name are *S.sicula*. Z7.

S.lutea ssp. *sicula* (Tineo) Webb. See *S.sicula*.
S.lutea var. *angustifolia* hort. See *S.sicula*.
S.lutea var. *graeca* Rchb. See *S.sicula*.
S.macrantha Bak. See *S.clusiana*.

S.sicula Guss. (*S.lutea* ssp. *sicula* (Tineo) Webb; *S.lutea* var. *gracea* Rchb.; *S.lutea* var. *angustifolia* hort.).
Similar to *S.lutea*. Bulb 1–2.5cm diam. Lvs 6–12mm wide, appearing before fls, lorate, flat or scarcely keeled, dark grey-green. Scape to 7cm; spathe 3–6cm; perianth lobes 2–3.4×0.4–1.2cm, yellow. Autumn. Italy, Greece, Aegean Is., W Turkey. 'Dodona': lvs prostrate, narrow; fls funnel-shaped, erect, vivid yellow. Z7.

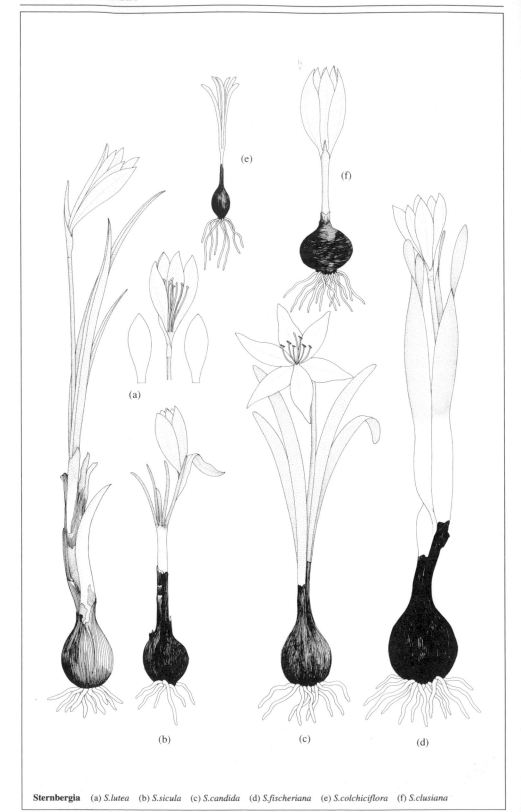

Sternbergia (a) *S.lutea* (b) *S.sicula* (c) *S.candida* (d) *S.fischeriana* (e) *S.colchiciflora* (f) *S.clusiana*

Strumaria Jacq. ex Willd. (From Lat. *struma*, a cushion-like swelling – the middle of the style is swollen.) Amaryllidaceae. 8 species of perennial, bulbous herbs. Leaves glabrous, ovate, synanthous; base enclosed in coarse sheath to 5cm long. Inflorescence umbellate, scapose; spathe 2-valved, green to green-purple; flowers stalked, sometimes scented; perianth infundibuliform; tepals 6, oblanceolate, free, to 15cm, flat or crisped; stamens exserted, free or united and joined to style at base, style and stamens equal; ovary globose, 3-celled. Capsule globose, membranous, 3-locular, to 4mm; seeds globose. S Africa. Z9.

CULTIVATION   *Strumaria* are small plants, bearing their numerous umbels of bell-shaped, white or flesh-coloured flowers in mid- to late spring. Grow under glass, as for *Hippeastrum*.

S.truncata Jacq.
Lvs to 6, erect, obtuse, to 15×1.5cm, sheath truncate. Peduncle to 30cm; fls 6–15, unscented; spathe green; tepals white to pink, to 1.5cm, stamens united at base. Spring. S Africa.

Synnotia Sweet. (For Walter Synnot (1773–1851), who sent many Cape bulbs to England.) Iridaceae. 5 species of perennial herbs, closely related to *Sparaxis*; rootstock a globose corm with a tunic of reticulate fibres. Stem branched or unbranched; leaves usually lanceolate, distichous, imbricate. Spike laxly few-flowered; flowers irregular; perianth tube curved, lobes 6, the topmost erect or arched, the others shorter, spreading or recurved; stamens arched; style with 3 short branches. Spring. South Africa (W Cape, Namaqualand). Z9.

CULTIVATION   As for *Ixia*.

S.bicolor Sweet. See *S.villosa*.
S.galeata Sweet. See *S.villosa*.

S.metelerkampiae L. Bol.
Stem branched, 15–25cm. Lvs 6–7, 5–10cm, broadly linear, arranged in a fan. Fls about 3cm diam., violet, the 3 lowest lobes with a white blotch; tube 3cm, slender, funnel-shaped in upper half; tepals spreading, outer ones 1cm, oblong obovate, inner slightly larger, edges undulate; anth. purple.

S.parviflora G. Lewis.
Stem 15–30cm, sometimes branched. Lvs 7–9, shorter than stem. Spike 2–4-fld; fls cream and yellow.

S.variegata Sweet.
Stem 15–40cm, usually unbranched. Lvs 7–8, to 15cm, ovate-lanceolate. Spike 2–7-fld; fls yellow and violet, or purple with yellow marks tube 3cm, topmost lobe erect, lateral lobes recurved.

S.villosa (Burm.) N.E. Br. (*S.bicolor* Sweet; *S.galeata* Sweet).
15–30cm, glabrous (in spite of name); corms 1–1.5cm diam. Basal lvs 6–7, 2–13cm×8–13mm, linear; stem lvs 2, semi-sheathing. Fls slightly scented, yellow-cream, the topmost lobe mauve; tube 1.5cm, widening toward throat, topmost tepal 15×11mm, other lobes shorter, the lower lateral lobes with margins incurved.

Syringodea Hook. (From Gk *syringodes*, like a small pipe or fistula, referring to the slender perianth tube.) Iridaceae. 7 species of small, cormous perennial herbs. Corms ovoid to globose, sometimes compressed, tunics tough, splitting. Leaves 1–6, filiform, terete or sulcate. Flowers 1–2, enclosed by a spathe consisting of 2 thin textured valves atop a short, usually subterranean, stalk; perianth salver- or funnelform, tube long, slender, straight or declinate, lobes spreading, sometimes cleft; filaments free, inserted in throat, anthers erect; style slender, branches 3, simple or divided. Fruit a globose capsule. S Africa. Z9.

CULTIVATION   Found in the wild in moderately heavy clays in short grassland and in open, stony ground on hillsides and mountains at over 1300m/4225ft, *Syringodea* spp. are grown for their small, charming, funnel-shaped flowers which emerge above the curled, threadlike leaves in autumn. The flowers are stemless like those of the related *Crocus*, which they resemble. The most commonly grown species, *S.pulchella*, has slightly fragrant, deep lilac blooms, veined with darker shades of purple, sometimes blotched blue at the base.

In cool temperate zones, *Syringodea* is eminently suited to cultivation in the alpine house, where flowers are longer-lived and can be appreciated at close quarters; the requirement for a warm, dry period of dormancy is also more easily met under glass. In zones where temperatures only occasionally fall below zero they can be planted in the rock garden, given the protection of a propped pane of glass as growth fades. Plant at 5cm/2in. deep in a fertile sandy loam in full sun, watering moderately when in growth and drying off completely when dormant. Propagate by seed sown in a sandy propagating mix, grown on in bright light with a temperature of about 10°C/50°F; also by offsets, although these are very small and may prove difficult to handle.

S.filifolia Bak. See *S.longituba*.

S.longituba (Klatt) Kunze.
Lvs 15–60cm, 8, slender, curled. Fls blue-purple, orange-yellow in throat; perianth tube 2–3.3cm, widening above, seg. 1–1.5×0.4–0.8cm. S Africa (Cape Province).

S.pulchella Hook.
Lvs 6.5–10cm, 4–6, rigid, arched to strongly curved, glabrous, rather coarsely textured. Fls pale purple; perianth tube 3–5cm, cylindric, becoming thicker toward limb, seg. 1–1.25cm, triangular to obovate, cleft. Autumn. S Africa.

Tacca Forst. & Forst. f. (From Indonesian *taka*, for these plants.) Taccaceae. 10 species of perennial, rosulate, terrestrial, stemless herbs to 1m, young parts pubescent. Rhizomes ascending, usually simple, cylindric, scarred by leaf bases, or with solid, starchy tubers (*T.leontopetaloides*). Leaves to 13, spaced or crowded onto rhizome, to 70×120cm, entire or palmately or pinnately lobed (*T.leontopetaloides*), ovate, obovate, oblong-ovate, ovate-lanceolate, oblong or linear-lanceolate, green to grey-green, glossy above, duller beneath, main nerves ribbed, venation reticulate; petiole erect, to 120cm, ribbed, glabrous, with purple-green, channelled, sheathing base. Inflorescence scapose, umbellate; peduncle radical or axillary, simple, erect, to 180cm; involucral bracts 4–22, to 14cm, leaflike, white, green, green to purple veined black, or black; filiform bracts 6–27 (same number as flowers), to 25cm, white, bright yellow-green, violet-green or dark purple-brown; flowers nodding, campanulate, bisexual, actinomorphic; perianth lobes 6 in 2 whorls, white, pale green or pale yellow to dark violet-brown or red, star-like, later reflexed; pedicel to 6cm, 6-ribbed, thickened in fruit; stamens 6, inserted in corolla tube, filaments short, flattened; ovary unilocular, 3-carpellate, obpyramidal, to 1.5×0.7cm. Fruits berry-like, to 5×2.5cm, fleshy, pericarp 6-ribbed, green to dark purple, pale yellow or orange; seeds filling fruit, to 8×5mm, strongly ribbed. SE Asia, W Africa. Z10.

CULTIVATION *T.leontopetaloides* is found in semi-evergreen monsoon forests, and is widely naturalized throughout the tropical Pacific as an escape from cultivation; the tubers and rhizomes of many spp. are used as starch sources. *Tacca* spp. are useful foliage plants in the humid tropics, especially in fertile, humus-rich soils beneath a tree canopy in approximation of their habitat. The foliage of all species is handsome; the blooms are both beautiful and extraordinary – each individual bell in the cluster is backed by a large ruff of dark glossy bracts, bizarrely ornamented by many long, spidery appendages.

In temperate regions, grow in filtered light in a humid glasshouse or conservatory, with a minimum temperature of 13–15°C/55–60°F. Re-root and repot every two years into a 1:1 leafmould and coarse bark mix with a slow-release fertilizer, at the same time reducing the senescent basal stem portion to maintain vigour. Water and syringe continuously, giving a monthly dilute foliar feed, except in the case of *T.leontopetaloides*, which requires a resting period of 8–10 weeks in warm, almost dry conditions, on completion of a new tuber. Propagate by division; take cuttings of the transverse portion of old rhizomes, each with an axillary eye, dust with sulphur or charcoal. Surface-sow seed at 22–27°C/72–80°F; flowering-sized plants are produced after three years. Susceptible to red spider mite, tarsonemid mite and botrytis.

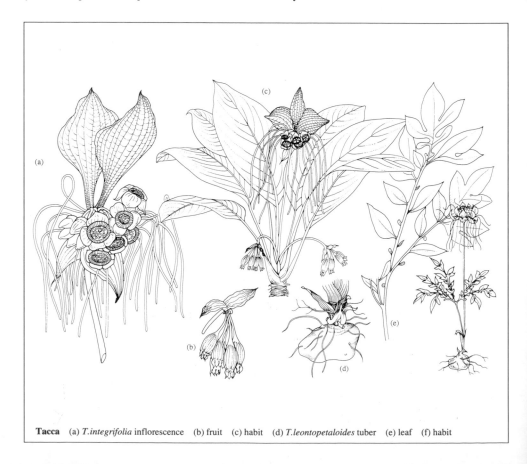

Tacca   (a) *T.integrifolia* inflorescence   (b) fruit   (c) habit   (d) *T.leontopetaloides* tuber   (e) leaf   (f) habit

T.artocarpifolia Seem. See *T.leontopetaloides*.
T.aspera Roxb. See *T.integrifolia*.
T.borneensis Ridl. See *T.integrifolia*.

T.chantrieri André (*T.macrantha* Limpr.; *T.lancifolia* Zoll. & Moritzi; *T.paxiana* Limpr.; *T.roxburghii* Limpr.). DEVIL FLOWER; BAT FLOWER; CAT'S WHISKERS.
Like *T.integrifolia*, but lvs dark green above, paler beneath, to 22×55cm. Infl. 1–2, to 25-fld; scape to 63cm; involucral bracts in 2 pairs, decussate, green to black, floral bracts filiform, to 25cm, olive green to maroon or violet-black; pedicel to 4cm; ovary to 7×5mm. Fr. to 40×12mm, lustrous green to deep cinnabar red or purple, seeds reniform, glabrous, 8–14-ribbed. Thailand.

T.choudhuriana Deb. See *T.integrifolia*.
T.cristata Jack. See *T.integrifolia*.
T.dubia Schult. See *T.leontopetaloides*.
T.gaogao Blanco. See *T.leontopetaloides*.

T.integrifolia Ker-Gawl. (*T.cristata* Jack; *T.aspera* Roxb.; *T.laevis* Roxb.; *T.lancaefolia* Zoll. & Moritzi; *T.borneensis* Ridl.; *T.sumatrana* Limpr.; *T.choudhuriana* Deb). BAT PLANT; BAT FLOWER.
Rhiz. erect, terete, to 15×3cm, roots borne mostly at base and a few directly below apical whorl of lvs. Lvs entire, base mostly attenuate but not decurrent on petiole, acuminate, to 65×24cm, grey-green, usually oblong or lanceolate; petiole to 40cm; sheath to 17cm. Infl. 1–5, to 30-fld; scape to 100cm, dark purple or red, sometimes brown, involucral bracts 4, to 14cm, outer 2 opposite, green to dark purple, inner 2 in axil of one outer bract, thinner, white or green to purple, veined black; filiform bracts to 26, to 20cm, pale green shaded violet, darkening as flowering continues to dark brown or purple; pedicel to 4cm, dark red or purple; ovary yellow-green with purple ribs, to 15×7mm, annular disc absent. Fr. triangular to circular in section, to 50×25mm, green to black tinged purple; seeds ovate, concave to convex, dorsiventrally compressed, glabrous to strongly papillose, 6–16-ribbed. E India to S China, south to Sumatra, Borneo, W Java.

T.involucrata Schum. & Thonn. See *T.leontopetaloides*.
T.laevis Roxb. See *T.integrifolia*.
T.lancaefolia Zoll. & Moritzi. See *T.integrifolia*.
T.lancifolia Zoll. & Moritzi. See *T.chantrieri*.

T.leontopetaloides (L.) Kuntze (*T.pinnatifida* Forst. & Forst. f.; *T.pinnatifolia* Gaertn.; *T.involucrata* Schum. & Thonn.; *T.dubia* Schult.; *T.gaogao* Blanco; *T.oceanica* Nutt.; *T.quanzensis* Welw.; *T.maculata* Seem.; *T.artocarpifolia* Seem.; *T.samoensis* Reinecke). INDIAN ARROWROOT.
Tuberous. Lvs palmately lobed. Africa to E Pacific (Easter Is.)

T.macrantha Limpr. See *T.chantrieri*.
T.maculata Seem. See *T.leontopetaloides*.
T.oceanica Nutt. See *T.leontopetaloides*.
T.paxiana Limpr. See *T.chantrieri*.
T.pinnatifida Forst. & Forst. f. See *T.leontopetaloides*.
T.pinnatifolia Gaertn. See *T.leontopetaloides*.

T.plantaginea (Hance) Drenth (*Schizocapsa plantaginea* Hance).
Resembles *T.integrifolia* except lf bases long-cuneate and decumbent on petiole; inner involucral bracts decussate, to 2.5×1cm; fr. to 10×7mm; seeds oblong-ovoid, subterete, 2.5×1.0×0.5mm.

T.quanzensis Welw. See *T.leontopetaloides*.
T.roxburghii Limpr. See *T.chantrieri*.
T.samoensis Reinecke. See *T.leontopetaloides*.
T.sumatrana Limpr. See *T.integrifolia*.

Taccarum Brongn. ex Schott. (From the generic names *Tacca* and *Arum*.) Araceae. 4 species of tuberous perennials. Tuber rounded, becoming dormant annually. Leaves solitary, radical, broadly hastate-ovate in outline, to 75cm across, 3-lobed and further 2–3-pinnatifid, median lobe larger than lateral lobes, margins of ultimate segments undulate; petiole long, to 120cm, green or purple, sometimes streaked white. Peduncle to 20cm; spathe to 15cm, margins overlapping beneath to form tube around female flowers, limb expanded, recurved, short and much exceeded by male portion of spadix, yellow- to lime-green or brown; spadix much exceeding spathe, to 50cm, flowers unisexual, female flowers at base, included in spathe tube, male flowers loosely distributed on apical portion, held on short stalks; ovaries with 4–6 staminodes, style long. Tropical America (seasonally dry areas). Z10.

CULTIVATION   As for *Amorphophallus*.

T.weddellianum Brongn. ex Schott.
Tuber large. Lvs to 60cm across, median seg. to 40cm long, pinnae small, light green; petiole to 120cm, purple to green streaked white. Peduncle 5–15cm; spathe to 15cm, yellow-grey-green, prominently veined; spadix to 50cm, male fls yellow, pedicels white, to 2cm, spicily fragrant. Brazil, Bolivia, Paraguay.

Tecophilaea Berter ex Colla. (For Tecofila Billiotti, daughter of Professor Colla of Turin, *c*1830.) Liliaceae (Tecophilaeaceae). 2 species of perennial herbs. Corm fibrous-coated. Scape leafless emerging from thin, papery sheath. Leaves basal linear-lanceolate, few, spreading. Flowers blue, usually solitary, salverform appearing flat and dish-shaped to broadly funnelform; tepals overlapping at base to form a short tube, lobes broadly obovate-oblong; ovary semi-inferior, 3-celled; stamens 3; staminodes 3. Andes of Chile. Z8.

CULTIVATION   A beautiful genus with exquisite clear blue flowers; rare in cultivation and gravely endangered in habitat (to 3000m/9750ft on the high stony slopes of the Santiago Cordilera) because of over-collecting. They are usually grown in the alpine or cold glasshouse, partly because of their rarity and partly because the young growth emerges early in the year and may then be susceptible to frost. Plant in a fertile, sandy potting mix; position in sun; water only when in growth, reducing gradually after flowering to allow warm, dry dormancy in summer. Withholding water in winter may delay emergence of the leaves until the onset of more clement weather. Propagate by offsets or by seed, which will develop more reliably following hand-pollination.

T.cyanocrocus Leyb.
To 15cm. Corm fibrous-coated, almost flat, 0.5cm diam. Lvs to 12.5cm, 2–3, linear to linear-lanceolate, somewhat undulate, glabrous. Fls 3–3.5cm, royal blue, veined and often tinted white in neck, sometimes with a white margin; peduncles 1–3, 2.5–5cm, slender. Chile. 'Leichtlinii': fls paler blue, with broad white central zone. 'Violacea': fls deep purple-blue.

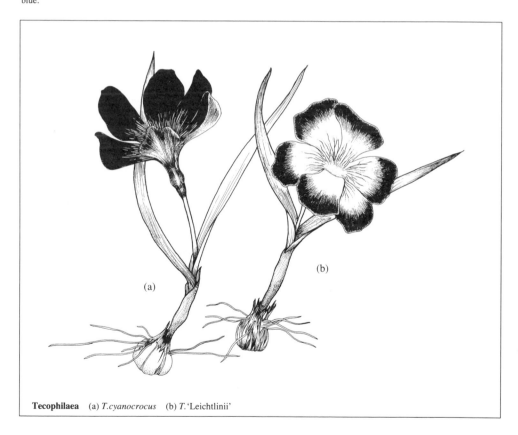

Tecophilaea   (a) *T.cyanocrocus*   (b) *T.* 'Leichtlinii'

Thysanotus R. Br. (From Gk *thysanos*, fringed, and *ous*, ear, from the fringed inner perianth segments.) Liliaceae (Asphodelaceae). FRINGE LILY; FRINGE FLOWER; FRINGE VIOLET. Some 47 species of rhizomatous or tuberous perennials. Stems simple or branched, usually naked. Leaves radical, linear, grasslike, expanded into papery, sheathing wings at base. Flowers usually in panicles or umbels; perianth segments 6, free, mauve, blue to lavender, inner whorl considerably wider than outer, margins fimbriate; stamens 6 or 3, filaments straight or twisted; anthers basifixed; ovary superior, style simple. Fruit a 3-valved, subspherical capsule enclosed within persistent perianth segments; seeds cylindric, black, with yellow aril. Australia, 2 species SE Asia.Z10.

CULTIVATION   Few species of this large, mainly Australian genus are cultivated, although several are attractive in flower. *Thysanotus* bears pink, lilac or deep violet flowers, in *T.tuberosus* and *T.multiflorus* carried in umbels on long, slender stems, their most notable feature being the conspicuously fringed outer tepals. In cool temperate zones they require protected cultivation in the intermediate glasshouse; in warm temperate climates they are suitable for rockeries and front garden positions in fertile, well-drained sandy soils. Grow in a mix of equal parts fine sand, leafmould and neutral loam, in direct sunlight; water moderately when in growth and keep almost dry when stem has withered. Propagate by offsets or from seed sown in sand in spring under glass.

T.dichotomus (Labill.) R. Br. (*Ornithogalum dichotomum* Labill.; *Chlamysporum dichotomum* (Labill.) Kuntze; *T.divaricatus* R. Br.; *T.elongatus* R. Br.; *T.flexuosus* R. Br.; *T.intricatus* Lindl.).
Rootstock rhizomatous, subspherical, to 5cm diam., aerial shoots borne from rhiz. Stems dichotomously branched, to 60cm, ridged, ridges tuberculate, hairy. Lvs 5–10, basal, 8–14cm, narrow lanceolate, margins ciliate. Infl. a 1–3-fld umbel; fls purple; outer perianth seg. oblong, to 18×3mm, inner seg. to 3.5×7mm, fimbria 2–3.5mm; stamens 6; anth. twisted. Fr. 4–5×2.5–3mm. W Australia.

T.divaricatus R. Br. See *T.dichotomus*.
T.elatior R. Br. See *T.tuberosus*.
T.elongatus R. Br. See *T.dichotomus*.
T.flexuosus R. Br. See *T.dichotomus*.
T.intricatus Lindl. See *T.dichotomus*.

T.multiflorus R. Br. (*T.prolifer* Lindl.; *T.multiflorus* var. *prolifer* Lindl.).
Lvs 3–30, radical, linear to narrowly lanceolate, sometimes channelled, glabrous, 20–30cm, margins entire, occasionally ciliate. Scapes erect, glabrous, 15–30cm; infl. a solitary umbel (or with 2 large, superimposed umbels in plants formerly classed as var. *prolifer*); fls 4–20+, bracteate; perianth seg. blue-violet, 7–17mm, outer seg. linear to narrowly oblanceolate, to 2.5mm wide, inner seg. to 8mm wide, fimbria 3–5.5mm; stamens 3, fil. twisted, anth. purple to yellow. Fr. to 4mm. W Australia.

T.prolifer Lindl. See *T.multiflorus*.

T.tuberosus R. Br. (*T.elatior* R. Br.).
Roots tuberous. Scape 20–60cm, terete. Lvs 5–15, radical, 20–30cm, glabrous, linear, channelled below with membranous wings at base, apex subterete. Scape 20–60cm, terete; infl. a 1–5-fld umbel; pedicels erect, to 2cm; perianth seg. to 2cm, outer seg. lanceolate, purple above, 3–4-veined, 2–2.5mm wide, inner seg. ovate, limbria 5mm+; stamens 6, fil. twisted. Fr. 5×2.5mm. Queensland, NSW, Victoria, S Australia.

Tigridia Juss. (From Lat. *tigris*, tiger, in this case referring to the jaguar, whose spotted pelt the distinctly marked perianth cup and inner segments resemble.) PEACOCK FLOWER; TIGER FLOWER; FLOWER OF TIGRIS. Iridaceae. 23 species of perennial bulbous herbs. Basal leaves linear-lanceolate to broadly ensiform, plicate, equitant, forming a fan, stem leaves few, reduced to 2 or 3 leaflike bracts. Flowering stem erect, not branched; flowers borne a few per spathe, large, showy, perianth shallowly cupped, lacking a tube, outer segments 3, broadly obovate, apiculate, spreading, conspicuously and broadly clawed, inner segments alternating with outer segments, far smaller, erecto-patent, obtuse, ovate, the margins undulate to gathered, appearing pandurate; filaments united in a cylindrical tube, stamens 3; stigmas 3, cleft, alternating with anthers. Fruit a capsule. Mexico, Guatemala. Z5

CULTIVATION   *Tigridia* spp. are frost-tender bulbous perennials grown for their large, exotic and brilliantly coloured iris-like flowers, the three larger outer petals usually unmarked, the surface of the inner cup blotched, spotted or banded in darker colours. The individual blooms are short-lived, but are carried in clusters of 6–8 opening in succession on long stems above a fan of sword-shaped basal leaves. In warm temperate zones, with dry winters and light frosts, they are grown for their summer flowers in beds and borders, being especially useful to fill gaps left by earlier blooms. In cool temperate climates they are given temporary positions out of doors and lifted in autumn to be dried off and stored at 8–12°C/45–55°F in sand. Otherwise they make beautiful specimens in pots or in the border of the cool glasshouse or conservatory.

Grow in a warm, sheltered site in full sun, in a fertile, well-drained, sandy or gritty soil. Plant in late spring, 10–12.5cm/4–5in. deep in light soils, more shallowly in heavier soils or if bulbs are small. Prepare soil by deep digging, incorporating well-rotted manure or garden compost and sand or grit as appropriate. Propagate from seed; in favourable areas *Tigridia* may establish themselves by self-seeding. Increase also by offsets, although they may be prone to virus and are more safely grown from seed.

T.chiapensis Molseed.
Basal lvs 40–50cm, narrow, acute, exceeding infl., stem lvs 1–3. Flowering stem to 30cm; fls to 5cm diam., erect, white, spotted purple at base, perianth cup yellow with purple spots, inner seg. to 1cm. Mexico.

T.dugesii S. Wats.
Basal lvs to 13cm. Flowering stem 9–13cm; fls 2–3 per spathe, 2–4cm diam., erect, yellow, spotted red-brown; outer seg. ovate, inner lanceolate-oblong, shorter than outer seg.; staminal tube to 5mm. Mexico.

T.durangense Molseed ex Cruden.
Basal lvs linear, to 12cm at anthesis, elongating in fruit; stem lvs absent. Flowering stem 3–15cm, elongating in fruit to 30cm; fls 2–6 per spathe, 3–4.5cm diam., erect; outer seg.

oblong, lavender to deep lilac-lavender, spotted and streaked white; inner seg. hastate, margin undulate, bright golden yellow; staminal tube to 8mm, anthers to 1cm, exserted. Mexico.

T.meleagris (Lindl.) Nichols.
Basal lvs usually absent; cauline lvs 2, the lower 20–30×0.9–1.5cm, lanceolate, upper much smaller. Flowering stem 25–60cm, branched; fls several per spathe, 3cm diam., pendent, silver-pink to dark maroon, usually spotted darker; seg. subequal, outer seg. in curved at spex, apex of inner seg. yellow; staminal column to 7mm, anthers and style included. Mexico.

T.mexicana Molseed.
Basal lvs 1-several, 30×1.3cm at anthesis, elongating later, linear; cauline lvs 1, short, linear-lanceolate. Flowering stem 10–30cm, branched; fls 2 to several per spathe, 2.5–5cm diam., yellow, spotted red-brown at centre with shallow cup; outer seg. oblong-obovate to obovate, to 3.6×2.5cm, inner seg. shorter; staminal column 6–7mm, anth. slightly exserted from cup. Mexico. ssp. **passiflora** Molseed. Fls 4–6cm diam., white, spotted purple in cup. Mexico.

T.multiflora (Herb.) Rav.
Basal lvs 40×1cm, linear; cauline lvs 1–2, lower to 30×0.8cm, upper smaller. Flowering stem to 40cm, branched; fls several per spathe, 3–4cm diam., erect, brown-orange or purple, with deep perianth cup; outer seg. to 3×1.3cm, obovate-elliptic, obtuse, inner ovate-elliptic, acute. Mexico.

T.pavonia (L. f.) DC. (*T.pringlei* Wats.).
Basal lvs preceding fls, 20–50×1.5–5cm, lanceolate, stem lvs 1–3. Flowering stem 80–125cm; outer perianth seg. 6–10cm, orange, bright pink, red, yellow or white, variously spotted red, brown or maroon at base, inner seg. to one-third length of outer seg., of similar ground colour but more distinctly marked; staminal tube 5–7.25cm, erect, exserted far beyond perianth cup; anth. erect, incurved. Mexico. Cultivars are generally available in seed mixtures; the following names are probably invalid and at least of uncertain application, but are recorded here to reflect the colour variation. 'Alba' ('Alba Grandiflora'): fls white with flesh-pink spots. 'Alba Immaculata': fls pure white. 'Aurea': fls yellow and red. 'Canariensis': to 75cm; lvs lanceolate, plaited; fls to 15cm across; pale yellow spotted red, lasting one day only. 'Carminea': fls pink-red with darker spots. 'Grandiflora': fls large in a variety of colours. 'Liliacea': fls red-purple variegated with white. 'Liliacea Immaculata': fls pure red-purple. 'Lutea': fls yellow. 'Red Giant': fls bright red with red and yellow centre. 'Rosea': fls pale pink, centre variegated with yellow. 'Rubra': fls orange-red. 'Speciosa': bright red, centred spotted, in both red and yellow. 'Watkinsonii': fls deep orange shaded yellow, often marked with red. 'Wheeleri': fls bright red, centre yellow, brightly spotted.

T.pringlei Wats. See *T.pavonia*.

T.seleriana (Loesener) Ravenna.
Basal lvs few; cauline lf 1, perfoliate at base, linear-lanceolate above. Flowering stem 2–10cm; fls 3.5–5cm diam., erect, lavender, spotted darker blue in cup; outer seg. broad-ovate to oblong-ovate, to 3×1.7cm, apex spreading or reflexed, inner seg. ovate, to 0.9cm; staminal column to 1cm. Guatemala, Mexico.

T.vanhouttei Roezl. ex Van Houtte.
Lvs to 50×2.5cm, lanceolate to lanceolate-elliptic, all similar except smaller upper cauline lvs. Flowering stem to 65cm, branched; fls many per spathe, 2–3cm diam., erect, dull yellow-green, strongly streaked purple; outer seg. elliptic to obovate-elliptic, to 2.6×1.5cm, inner seg orbicular, concave, to 1.5cm wide; staminal column to 8mm. Mexico. ssp. **roldanii** Molseed. Fls pendent, campanulate, pale yellow, veined purple; outer seg. elliptic, 2.5×1.5cm, inner seg. orbicular to oval, to 1.7cm wide. Mexico.

T.violacea Schldl.
Basal lvs emerging at flowering, extending to 50cm, linear-lanceolate, stem lf 1. Flowering stem 12–35cm; fls 3–4 per spathe, outer perianth seg. 2.5–3cm, oblong, obtuse to shortly apiculate, violet, fading to rose-purple, the claw white, dotted purple, inner seg. ovate, somewhat saccate, deflexed, white spotted purple or rose; staminal tube to 0.5cm, not projecting far beyond cup (cf. *T.pavonia*). Mexico.

Tricyrtis Wallich. (From Gk *treis,* three, and *Kyrtos,* convex; the three outer petals are bag-like at the base.) TOAD LILY. Liliaceae (Tricyrtidaceae). 10–16 species of perennial herbs. Rhizome shortly creeping. Stem 20–110cm, leafy, erect or arched, simple below or with few branches. Leaves ovate to lanceolate, alternate, sometimes amplexicaul or subsessile, somewhat plicate, occasionally with dark green spots, Inflorescence terminal or in upper leaf axils, erect, solitary, or cymose, loosely dichotomous; flowers white or yellow, with purple spots, bisexual, few, campanulate, with fairly long pedicels; tepals, style and filaments usually spotted violet to red-purple; tepals 6, lanceolate, free, outer 3 conspicuously basally saccate, occasionally short-spurred, inner 3 flat, all spreading in upper part; stamens curved outwards at the top; ovary superior, 3-celled, narrow-oblong; style single, with 3 recurved, bifid, stigmatic branches. E Himalaya to Japan and Taiwan.

CULTIVATION Handsome perennials of elegant and graceful habit, with upright or arching stems clothed with attractive stem-clasping leaves, sometimes also, as with *T.hirta* and *T.macrantha,* with conspicuous velvety down. They are grown for their subtly coloured flowers, of substantial waxen texture and curious form beautifully spotted and freckled with contrasting shades of rich chocolate, purple and maroon, *Tricyrtis* spp. usually bloom over several weeks; *T.latifolia,* bearing yellow-green flowers in terminal clusters on short slender stems in midsummer, is one of the earliest species in flower, *T.perfoliata* and other autumn-flowering spp. need a warm position in more northerly gardens if they are to bloom before the onset of severe frosts. With the possible exception of *T.formosana,* most will tolerate temperatures as low as −20°C/−4°F, although where prolonged low temperatures are not accompanied by snow cover, most species benefit from the additional protection of a deep, dry organic mulch. *Tricyrtis* spp. are well suited to plantings in the dappled shade of the woodland garden or shaded border, with smaller species such as *T.nana* suitable for shaded niches on the rock garden or peat terrace. Grow in partial shade in well-drained but moisture-retentive neutral or acid soils enriched by liberal additions of well-rotted organic matter; provide an annual mulch of the same. Where soils remain reliably moist throughout the growing season, most will tolerate greater exposure to sun, this having the advantage in cooler climates of inducing earlier flowers. Propagate by division in spring or by ripe seed sown fresh, otherwise stratify for about 12 weeks at 5°C/40°F.

Tricyrtis (a) *T.hirta* habit (a1) flower detail (a2) stigma (b) *T.latifolia* habit (b1) flower detail (b2) stigma (c) *T.macranthopsis* habit (c1) flower detail (c2) stigma (d) *T.ohsumiensis* habit, (d1) flower section (d2) stigma (d3) stamen (e) *T.formosana* (e1) root system (f) *T.perfoliata* habit

T.affinis Mak.
Close to *T.macropoda*, differs in that its fls are borne on separate stalks. Z6.

T.bakeri Koidz. See *T.latifolia*.
T.dilatata Nak. See *T.macropoda*.

T.flava Maxim. (*T.kyusyensis* Masum.; *T.yatabeana* Masum.)
Stems 20–30cm, occasionally to 50cm, erect, hairy, Lvs to 12.5cm, elliptic to oblanceolate, amplexicaul, blotched. Fls erect, 1 to few, in upper lf axils, funnelform, stalks rigid, somewhat exceeding fls and fr.; tepals to 2.5cm, yellow, with brown-red spots inside, apical bristle of outer seg. 3–4mm; anth. 2.5–3mm. Japan. Z6.

T.flava var. *nana* Mak. See *T.nana*.

T.formosana Bak. (*T.stolonifera* Matsum.)
Stems erect, somewhat hairy, spreading by stolons, Lvs 1–1.5cm, oblanceolate, pubesc, on veins beneath, lower narrowed to form tubular sheath, upper ovate, cordate, amplexicaul, Infl, branched, terminal, cymose; fls 2.5–3×1cm, widely funnelform; tepals white to pink with dense crimson spots inside, tinged yellow towards base; style as long as stigma, Taiwan. Some plants in cult. as *T.formosana* and *T.stolonifera* are probably hybrids between *T.formosana* and *T.hirta*. 'Amethystina': to 1.2m; fls clustered, amethyst, throat white, speckled maroon, blush of yellow. Z7.

T.hirta (Thunb.) Hook.(*T.japonica* Miq.)
Stems thickly hairy, to 80cm, without stolons, slightly divergent from the rootstock, Lvs 15×2–5cm, lanceolate, pale green, strongly cordate-amplexicaul, shortly acuminate, minutely pubesc, Fls 2.5–3cm, erect, funnelform, borne in lf axils, solitary or 2–3 on separate stalks, with pedicels shorter than fls; tepals 2.5–3cm, white with large purple spots, spreading or recurved only at the tips. Japan. Plants in cult. under this name are sometimes *T.macropoda*. 'Alba': less vigorous; fls white flushed green. 'Lilac Towers': as 'White Towers', but fls lilac. 'Miyazaki': to 90cm; stems arching; lvs pointed; fls white spotted lilac, all along stem. 'Miyazaki Gold': as 'Miyazaki', but lvs edged gold. 'Variegata': lvs green edged gold; fls lavender. 'White Towers': to 60cm; stems arching; fls in most leaf-axils, white. Z5.

T.japonica Miq. See *T.hirta*.
T.kyusyuensis Masum. See *T.flava*.
T.kyusyuensis var. *pseudoflava* Masum. See *T.nana*.

T.latifolia Maxim. (*T.bakeri* Koidz.; *T.puberula* Nak. & Kit.)
Stems 40–90cm, erect, hairy, Lvs 8–15×4.9cm, broadly ovate, heart-shaped at base, amplexicaul, abruptly acuminate, Infl. erect, cymose, branched, loosely terminal in upper lf axils; fls 2–2.5cm, funnelform, 2 or several per distinctly peduncled cyme; tepals 3cm, yellow to yellow-green, spotted purple, Japan, China, Z5.

T.macrantha Maxim.
To 90cm, arched, drooping, with coarse brown hairs, Lvs to 10×5cm, ovate-oblong to lanceolate, amplexicaul, heart-shaped, with markedly acuminate tip. Fls 3–4cm, axillary, pendulous, campanulate; tepals yellow with chocolate

spots inside, outer tepals short-spurred; nectarial pouch ovoid, bent, Japan, Z6.

T.macranthopsis Masum.
Rhiz. short. Stems 40–80cm, becoming pendulous in flower, Lvs 7–17×2,2.5–5cm, narrowly oblong-ovate, cordate or somewhat auriculate or amplexicaul at base, gradually acuminate at apex, glossy green, subglabrous, or hairy on veins. Fls pendulous, terminal or axillary, 14; pedicels short; perianth 3 4cm, tubular-campanulate; tepals oblanceolate, outer whorl with short broad spur, clear yellow with fine brown spots within, glabrous. Japan (Honshu) .

T.macropoda Miq. (*T.dilatata* Nak.; *T.macropeda* var. *glabrescens* Koidz.; *T.macropeda* var. *hirsuta* Koidz.).
Stem erect, to 70cm, occasionally minutely pubesc. above, Lvs 10–12.5×3.5–5cm, oblong to ovate, acuminate, rounded at base, sessile or with a very short stalk, glabrous above, minutely pubesc. beneath, Fls 1.5–2cm, erect, borne in branching cymes, mostly terminal, occasionally axillary; tepals white-purple with small purple spots, outer tepals reflexed; style half as long as stigmas, China. Z5.

T.macropoda var. *glabrescens* Koidz. See *T.macropoda*.
T.macropoda var. *hirsuta* Koidz. See *T.macropoda*.

T.maculata D. Don.
Close to T. *macropoda*, differs in its looser infl, and spreading tepals. Z5.

T.nana Yatabe. (*T.flava* var. *nana* Mak.; *T.kyusyensis* var. *pseudoflava* Masum.)
Stem 5–15cm, shortly hairy. Lvs lanceolate to ovate or elliptic, few, amplexicaul, blotched dark green, borne in basal rosette, spreading flat on ground. Fls few, 3cm diam,, almost flat, erect, solitary in leaf-axils, funnelform; tepals to 2cm, and yellow with brown-red spots, orange-brown band across base, outer with dark green tip and apical bristle to 2mm; anth. 2mm. Japan. Z6.

T.ohsumiensis Masum.
Rhiz. short. Stems 20–50cm, erect, subglabrous. Lower lvs oblong-lanceolate, acute, upper lvs 5–20×2–6cm, larger than lower lvs, elliptic to oblong, amplexicaul, glabrous, pale green. Fls erect, axillary and terminal, 1–2; pedicels slightly shorter than or exceeding length of fl.; perianth 2.5–3.5×5cm, broadly funnel-shaped; tepals narrow-ovate or obovate-oblong, primrose-yellow, faintly spotted. Japan (Kyushu).

T.perfoliata Masum.
Stems 50–70cm, arched, drooping, glabrous. Lvs 2.5–4cm, lanceolate, perfoliate, alternate, long-tapering, abruptly acuminate. Fls 4cm diam., funnelform, ascending, solitary in lf axils; tepals 2.5–3cm, yellow with red-purple spots inside, erect to widely spreading. Japan. Z6.

T.puberula Nak. & Kit. See *T.latifolia*.

T.sinonome.
Fls white spotted bright purple, autumn-flowering. Z7.

T.stolonifera Matsum. See *T.formosana*.
T.yatabeana Masum. See *T.flava*.

Trillium L. (From Gk *tris*, thrice: the leaves and floral parts occur in threes.) WOOD LILY; BIRTHROOT; WAKE ROBIN; STINKING BENJAMIN. Liliaceae (Trilliaceae). Some 30 species of deciduous, perennial herbs, to 40cm. Rhizomes stout, subterranean. Stems single, erect, procumbent or scarcely emerging from the soil. Leaves 3 in an apical whorl, sessile or petiolate, soft, glossy glabrous, elliptic to ovate with reticulate venation, sometimes mottled silver-white or purple, apex acute or obtuse, base often round to cordate, margins somewhat undulate. Flowers solitary, terminal, at junction of leaves, stalked or sessile, erect or nodding; outer sepals 3, leaf-like, lanceolate, reflexed; inner petals 3, more conspicuous, to 8cm, oblanceolate, green-yellow to white to pink and dark maroon; stamens 6, anthers basifixed; style deeply divided in three, ovary superior, 3- or 6-faceted or winged. Fruit a 3-valved, glabrous berry. N America, W Himalaya, NE Asia.

CULTIVATION   *Trillium* spp. are usually found in the humus-rich soils of moist woodland and scrub, often on limestone formations, although a number of species, such a *T.decumbens* and *T.tschonoskii*, are found in humus-rich niches in rocky wooded ravines. *T.grandiflorum* occurs in the wild in natural association with *Veratrum viride* and *Osmunda cinnamomea*, while *T.nivale* inhabits the rock ledges of riverside clearings, often flowering through snow cover.

Trillium spp. are suitable for the woodland garden or peat terrace, for pocket plantings in the rock garden and for the alpine house, where the perfection of the spring flowers can be appreciated at close quarters and protected from rain splash. *Trillium* is also used in the underplantings of shrubs, although in these circumstances the neighbouring plants should not be shallow-rooting. The smaller species can be grown in troughs. With the exception of *T.undulatum*, which needs a very acid soil, and *T.nivale*, which is calcicole, most species will thrive in soils that are neutral to slightly acid. *T.chloropetalum*, *T.cuneatum*, *T.erectum*, *T.grandiflorum*, *T.luteum*, *T.ovatum* and *T.sessile* all occur on soils that tend to the alkaline side of neutral.

Grow in dappled shade in well-aerated soil, moist but not waterlogged and rich in organic matter, preferably leafmould. Providing that the soil remains moist, *T.erectum*, *T.grandiflorum*, *T.ovatum* and *T.rivale* will grow in sun, given shade at the hottest part of the day. Give an annual mulch of leafmould or well-rotted compost in autumn. Divide carefully and replant when the foliage has died down, or propagate from cleaned, fresh seed sown 15mm/0.5in. deep in a propagating mix with added leafmould, in a cool, shaded frame. Seed-grown plants flower about five years from sowing.

T.albidum Freeman.
Related to *T.chloropetalum*. To 50cm. Lvs to 20cm, sessile, lanceolate-ovate, apex obtuse, usually mottled silver-white. Fls sessile, nestling in foliage and fragrant; sep. to 6cm, narrow-ovate, spreading to reflexed; pet. to 10×4.5cm, obovate, held semi-erect or somewhat incurving, white with basal portion flushed rose pink; stamens to 3cm, anth. exceeding green fil.; ovary sap-green. Spring. W US. Z6.

T.×amabile Miyabe & Tatew. (*T.amabile* Miyabe & Tatew.). (*T.smallii* × *T.kamtschaticum*.)
Lvs to 12cm, sessile, ovate to rhombic, acuminate. Pedicels to 6cm, erect; sep. to 3cm, mauve, elliptic; pet. to 2.5cm, dark purple, ovate-orbicular to reduced or absent, fused with or replaced by anth. to 6mm, bright mauve; ovary olive green suffused pink at apex. Spring. Japan. Z5.

T.angustipetalum (Torr.) Freeman (*T.sessile* I var *angustipetalum* Torr.).
Stem erect, glabrous, to 60cm. Lvs to 20×8.5cm, subsessile, broadly ovate, obtuse, mottled. Fls sessile, fragrance aromatic; sep. to 6m, linear-lanceolate; pet. to 5–10×1cm, narrowly lanceolate, held erect, silky, maroon; stamens mauve, to 2cm, anth. exceeding fil.; ovary deep purple, hexagonal at apex. Spring. California. Z8.

T.catesbaei Elliott (*T.nervosum* Elliott; *T.stylosum* Nutt.).
Stem to 50cm, glabrous, flushed pink-red. Lvs to 7cm, subsessile, ovate. Pedicel to 5cm, deflexed, borne below lvs, nodding; sep. reflexed; pet. to 5cm, reflexed, ovate to cordate, acuminate, rose pink or darker; ovary light green. Spring. SE US. Z8.

T.cernuum L.
Stem glabrous, to 50cm. Lvs short-petiolate, rhombic, acute. Fls on reflexed, pendent pedicels to 2cm, held among or below lvs; pet. to 2cm, undulate, white sometimes flushed rose; anth. dark purple; ovary purple to crimson. Spring. E N America. Z6.

T.chloropetalum (Torr.) Howell.
Stem thick, robust, to 50cm. Lvs 10–20cm, sessile, broadly ovate-rhombic, mottled maroon. Fls sessile, among lvs, fragrant, held erect or gracefully incurved; pet. obovate, green to yellow to purple; ovary flushed mauve, blurred hexagonal.

Spring. California. var. **giganteum** (Hook. & Arn.) Munz. Pet white to maroon and red: a white selection is most often offered. Z6.

T.cuneatum Raf. (*T.hugeri* Small; *T.sessile* hort. non L.).
Stem robust, erect to 60cm. Lvs to 20cm, sessile, broadly ovate-orbicular, obtuse or abruptly acuminate, mottled pale or silver green. Fls sessile, nestling among lvs, with musky fragrance; sep. olive green tipped purple; pet. to 5×2.5cm, wedge-shaped, maroon. Spring. SE US. Z6.

T.declinatum (A. Gray) Gleason non Raf. See *T.flexipes*.

T.decumbens Harb.
Stem minutely pubesc. to velvety papillose, to 15cm, procumbent. Lvs to 12cm, sessile, ovate-orbicular, mottled silver. Fls sessile; sep. elliptic, to 5cm, reflexed; tinged maroon; pet. to 10cm, lanceolate, held erect, cupped, margins somewhat wavy or recurved, dark maroon often tipped golden-green; ovary winged, hexagonal. Fr. blue-black. Spring SE US. Z6.

T.discolor Hook.
Stem to 18cm. Lvs to 12cm, sessile, elliptic-orbicular, acuminate or abruptly acute, pale, shining green, mottled jade. Fls sessile; sep. to 3cm, narrow, lanceolate, reflexed; pet. ovate, acute, somewhat deflexed, twisted, golden yellow with green or, rarely, violet basal patches, to 5cm; stamens to 2cm, fil. mauve; stigmas held erect or at 45°; scent aromatic; ovary dark purple, ridged, hexagonal. Spring. SE US. Z6.

T.erectum L.
Highly variable. Stem to 50cm, erect. Lvs to 20cm, sessile, broadly ovate. Fls borne upright or obliquely on pedicel to 10cm, malodorous; sep. to 5cm, light green suffused red-purple, the margins particularly; pet. to 8cm, elliptic, acute, spreading or incurved, dark garnet to white; ovary maroon. Late spring. Eastern N America. 'Ochroleucum' ('Viridiflorum'): fls tinged green. var. **album** Pursh. Pet. white, occasionally flushed rose; anth. golden yellow. f. **albiflorum** Hoffm. Fls white, stained lime green. f. **luteum** Lal. Short-stemmed (seldom exceeding 10cm); pet. green-yellow, blood red above. Z4.

T.erythrocarpum Michx. See *T.undulatum*.

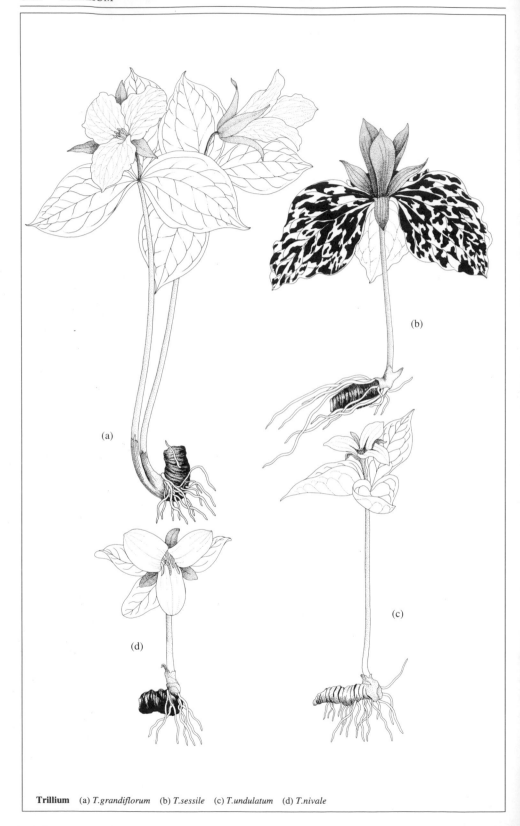

Trillium (a) *T.grandiflorum* (b) *T.sessile* (c) *T.undulatum* (d) *T.nivale*

T.flexipes Raf. (*T.declinatum* (A. Gray) Gleason non Raf.; *T.gleasonii* Fern.).
Stem to 40cm. Lvs to 20cm, sessile, ovate, acute. Fls on slender pedicel to 10cm, sharply oblique, held horizontally, level with lvs; sep. reflexed; pet. to 5cm, ovate, spreading to give flattened appearance, often reflexed at apex, white to pale pink; ovary white flushed rose. Spring. N US. Z4.

T.gleasonii Fern. See *T.flexipes*.

T.govanianum D. Don (*Trillidium govanianum* D. Don).
Stem erect to 20cm. Lvs to 10cm, ovate, acute, dark green. Fls erect on slender pedicel; sep. to 1.5cm, green flushed maroon, linear-lanceolate; pet. to 2×0.5cm, narrow, yellow-green to pale, uneven maroon. Spring. Himalaya. Z5.

T.grandiflorum (Michx.) Salisb.
Stem erect to 45cm. Lvs subsessile, ovate to orbicular. Fls erect on pedicels to 5cm; sep. to 5cm, dark green; pet. to 8cm, broad-ovate, basal portions stiffly upright and overlapping, slightly cupped then spreading widely, undulate, opening white, flushing pale pink; stamens to 2.5cm, fil. green, anth. golden yellow; styles erect. Fr. scarlet to maroon. Late spring. Eastern N America. 'Flore pleno' (f. *florepleno* anon.): fls double. 'Roseum': fls flushing pink almost immediately, ageing damask. f. *parvum* Gates. Far smaller with fls ultimately violet-pink. f. *variegatum* Sm. Pet. with bright green midrib or green throughout save margins, which are white. Z5.

T.hibbersonii auct. See *T.ovatum* f. *hibbersonii*.
T.hugeri Small. See *T.cuneatum*.

T.kamtschaticum Pall.
Stem erect to 30cm. Lvs to 15cm, sessile, ovate to rhombic, acute. Pedicel erect; sep. to 5cm, ovate-acuminate, dark green; pet. to 4.5cm, ovate, acute, white ageing faded purple. Fr. dark green, spotted maroon at apex. Early summer. E Asia. Z5.

T.luteum (Muhlenb.) Harb. (*T.sessile* L. var. *luteum* Muhlenb.; *T.viride* Beck var. *luteum* Muhlenb.).
Stem erect to 45cm. Lvs to 15cm, sessile, broadly ovate, abrupt-acuminate, mottled. Fls sessile, sweetly scented; sep. to 6cm, lanceolate, obtuse, reflexed, spreading, green; pet. to 9cm, elliptic, erect, cupped, golden or bronzy green; ovary ridged, hexagonal. Spring. SE US. Z5.

T.nervosum Elliott. See *T.catesbaei*.

T.nivale Riddell.
Dwarf, stems erect, to 5cm at flowering, to 12cm in fruit. Lvs to 3.5cm, distinctly petiolate, ovate, a deep, slightly nacreous green. Pedicel to 2.5cm, erect at first, nodding with age; sep. green, to 2cm, lanceolate, pet. to 4cm, brilliant white; ovary pale green. Early spring. SE US. Calcicole, flourishing in exposed situations. Z5.

T.ovatum Pursh.
Stem red-green, erect to 50cm. Lvs to 15cm, sessile, rhombic, acute, with 5 conspicuous, sunken veins. Fls borne erect on pedicel to 8cm, muskily fragrant, often malodorous; sep. to 5cm, green; pet. ovate, held at 0–45° to receptacle, spreading, rather than erect to spreading as in *T.grandiflorum*, white colouring later to pink or red. Spring. Western N America. 'Kenmore': fls double, pale pink. f. *hibbersonii* Tayl. & Szcz. (*T.hibbersonii* nom. illegit.). Smaller (to two-thirds size) with pet. rose pink fading to white stained pink. Spring. British Columbia. Z5.

T.petiolatum Pursh.
Stem erect to 20cm. Lvs to 15cm, petiolate, ovate, obtuse. Fls sessile; sep. to 5cm, oblanceolate, reflexed; pet. to 5cm, linear, acute, erect and incurved at apex, green flushed purple to dark maroon. Spring. Midwest US. Z5.

T.recurvatum Beck.
Stem erect to 45cm. Lvs to 8cm, lanceolate-elliptic, tapering basally to petioles, mottled. Fls sessile; sep. to 4cm, green, lanceolate, sharply reflexed, pointing downward among lvs; pet. to 5cm, erect, dark purple or, rarely, yellow-green, ovate, base clawed; ovary maroon, winged, hexagonal. Spring. E US. Z5.

T.rivale Wats.
Stem erect to 5cm, or elongating after flowering. Lvs to 3cm, ovate, acute, petioles to 2cm. Fls on erect pedicels to 5cm; sep. to 1.5cm, ovate to oblanceolate, green; pet. to 2.5cm, rhombic to ovate, white flushed pink, spotted purple toward base. Spring. W US. 'Purple Heart': basal markings of pet. form a solid, central 'eye' of colour. Z5.

T.sessile L.
Stem to 30cm, erect. Lvs to 12cm, sessile, elliptic to orbicular, with dark mottling. Fls sessile with pungent odour; sep. to 4cm, elliptic, green flushed maroon; pet. to 4.5cm, erect, lanceolate, maroon. Late spring. NE US. 'Rubrum': fls crimson-purple. 'Snow Queen': fls white. f. *viridiflorum* Beyer. Fls green-bronze to yellow. Z4.

T.sessile var. *angustipetalum* Torr. See *T.angustipetalum*.
T.sessile var. *luteum* Muhlenb. See *T.luteum*.
T.sessile hort. non L. See *T.cuneatum*.

T.smallii Maxim.
Erect to 40cm. Lvs to 12cm, sessile, rhombic, acute. Fls on pedicel to 4cm, held obliquely at opening, later upright; sep. green; pet. equal sep. in length, to 2cm, semi-erect, maroon, fleshy, sometimes reduced or absent. Spring. Japan. Z5.

T.stylosum Nutt. See *T.catesbaei*.

T.tschonoskii Maxim.
Resembles *T.kamtschaticum* except in height, seldom exceeding 20cm; pet. to 3.5cm; pedicel horizontal. Late spring. NE Asia. Z5.

T.underwoodii Small.
Erect to 20cm. Lvs to 15cm, sessile, ovate, acuminate, mottled, lax, somewhat pendent. Fls sessile, malodorous; sep. to 5cm, narrow-ovate, green, outspread or slightly reflexed; pet. to 6cm, often much smaller than sep., elliptic, mauve-maroon. Spring. SE US. Z6.

T.undulatum Willd. (*T.erythrocarpum* Michx.).
Stem erect to 30cm, pale green with basal purple flush. Lvs to 15cm, petiolate, narrow-acuminate. Fls on upright pedicel to 3cm; sep. to 1cm, dark green bordered maroon; pet. to 3cm, undulate, white or pale rose pink, dark maroon basal blotch stains venation. Fr. scarlet. Late spring. E N America. Z4.

T.vaseyi Harb.
Stem robust, thick, erect to 60cm. Lvs to 20cm, sessile, rhombic, broad. Fls on nodding pedicel, often found below lvs; pet. to 4.5cm, broad, overlapping, spreading to reflexed, dark red to maroon, obtuse. Early summer. SE US. Z6.

T.viride Beck.
Erect to 40cm, stem glabrous or minutely pubesc. Lvs sessile, variable, lanceolate to elliptic, acute to obtuse, rarely mottled, spotted white above. Fls sessile, foetid; sep. lanceolate, acuminate, to 6cm, reflexed; pet. to 6cm, often less, erect oblanceolate, flexed with margins somewhat revolute, green-yellow with maroon basal patch or entirely maroon. Spring. N US. Z4.

T.viride Beck var. *luteum* Muhlenb. See *T.luteum*.

Trimezia Herb. (From Gk *treis*, three, and *meizon*, greater; the outer flower segments are much larger than the inner.) Iridaceae. 5 species of rhizomatous perennial herbs. Rhizome swollen, bulbous, densely clothed in the matted, fibrous remains of withered leaf bases. Leaves few, usually wholly basal or a single leaf on the flowering stem, linear to narrow-lanceolate, rather rush-like. Flowers short-lived, produced in succession in 1–3 clusters subtended by terminal spathaceous bracts on a slender stem seldom exceeding leaves; perianth radially symmetric, segments free, in 2 unequal whorls, short-clawed; stamens opposing style branches, filaments free. Fruit a long-stalked dry capsule. C & Tropical S America, W Indies. Z10.

CULTIVATION A cormous genus ranging through various tropical habitats, usually in damp grassland, frequently on heavy soils, but also in savannah, rainforest and woodland; species occur from sea level to altitudes of 1700–1800m/5525–5850ft. They are grown for their beautiful yellow flowers, intricately marked with purple and brown at the base, emerging above in favourable conditions, the fan of rush-like foliage; each bloom may last only hours but they are produced in succession over long periods. For outdoor cultivation in humid tropical or subtropical zones, in cooler regions *Trimezia* are eminently suited to the warm glasshouse, where growth will be continuous. Grow in a rich, well-drained, sandy potting mix with additional organic matter in direct sunlight; maintain a minimum temperature of 13–15°C/55–60°F, with moderate humidity but in buoyant, airy conditions; keep moist at all times but water judiciously during the short days of the year. Propagate by seed or offsets.

T.martinicensis (Jacq.) Herb.
Lvs to 30cm, linear, in an erect basal fan. Flowering stem to 30cm with a single clasping lf; fls 4–6 per cluster, ephemeral, outer perianth seg. to 2cm, yellow spotted brown or purple at base, erect to incurved, inner seg. far smaller, strongly incurved. Throughout the year, though mainly in spring. S America, W Indies, naturalized elsewhere.

Tristagma Poepp. (From Gk *tri-*, three, and *stagma*, something which drips (e.g. honey which drips from the three nectary pores of the ovary).) Liliaceae (Alliaceae). 5 species of dwarf perennial herbs; bulbs tunicate. Leaves few, basal, linear. Scape unbranched; spathe 2-valved; flowers 2–5 in a terminal scapose umbel subtended by a 2-valved spathe; perianth tube cylindrical, lobes linear, involute; stamens dorsifixed, included. Chile, S Argentina. Z9.

CULTIVATION Seldom cultivated but botanically interesting on account of the very narrow, almost tubular, rolled perianth segments, grow in the cool glasshouse as for *Tecophilaea*.

T.nivale Poepp.
Bulb to 4cm, ovoid or cylindrical; tunics white, membranous. Lvs to 25×0.3cm, 3–6, linear, obtuse, glabrous, shining, bright green. Scape 5–18cm; fls olive green, erect, tube to 12.5mm, lobes half length of tube; anth. sessile, yellow; ovary sessile, stigma capitate. Midsummer. Patagonia, Tierra del Fuego, S Chile.

Triteleia Lindl. (From Gk *tri-*, three and *telos*, end; the parts of the flower are in threes.) Liliaceae (Alliaceae). Some 15 species of perennial, cormous herbs. Corm fibrous-coated, straw-coloured, flattened. Scape slender, scabrous or pubescent below. Leaves 1 to 2 per corm, narrowly linear, basal, with prominent midrib below, grooved above. Flowers jointed at the pedicel, funnelform, borne in scapose umbels, subtended by scarious, green or occasionally purple tinged spathe valves; tepals spreading; tube various; staminodes absent; fertile stamens 6; filaments equal, unequal, or unequally inserted; anthers versatile, not adpressed to style; style slender; ovary superior, shortly stalked; stigma small, 3-lobed. Fruit a loculicidal capsule, with black, angled, subglobose seeds. W US.

CULTIVATION As for *Brodiaea*.

T.bridgesii (Wats.) Greene (*Brodiaea bridgesii* Wats.). Scape to 50cm. Pedicels to 9cm. Perianth 2.5–4cm, lilac or blue, tube gradually expanded, with slender base, lobes spreading, usually longer than base; stamens inserted at mouth of tube; fil. basally dilated; anth. 3.5–4.5mm; ovary green, blue or lilac, with a stalk 3–4× its length. W US (SW Oregon, California). Z7.

T.candida (Bak.) Greene. See *T.laxa*.

T.grandiflora Lindl. (*Brodiaea grandiflora* Macbr. non Sm.; *Brodiaea douglasii* Piper). Scape to 70cm. Pedicels 1–4cm, mostly shorter than fls, elongating somewhat in fr. Perianth 1.5–3cm, bright blue or rarely white, tube rounded at base, as long as or exceeding lobes; stamens borne in 2 separate whorls; fil. slender, dilated toward base, anth. 2–4mm; ovary about twice the length of stalk, green or blue. US (British Columbia, Oregon, N Utah.). Z5.

T.hendersonii Howell ex Greene (*Brodiaea hendersonii* (Greene) S. Wats.). Scape to 35cm. Pedicels to 50mm. Spathe valves long and narrow. Perianth 2–2.5cm, lobes twice as long as tube, yellow with a dark purple midrib; tube narrow-funnelform, basally tapered; stamens inserted at mouth of tube, more or less equal; fil. thread-like, anth. 1.5–2mm; ovary green or tinged yellow, half the length of stalk. W US (SW Oregon). Z7.

T.hyacintha (Lindl.) Greene (*Brodiaea hyacintha* (Lindl.) Bak.; *Brodiaea lactea* S. Wats.; *T.lutea* Davidson & Moseley). Scape to 70cm. Pedicels to 50mm. Perianth 8–18mm, usually white, occasionally blue or lilac, bowl-shaped, lobes twice as long as tube or longer; tube spreading away from the base;

stamens more or less equal, all inserted at the same level; fil. broadly dilated at base; ovary green, white, or rarely pale blue or purple, stalk very short. W US (British Columbia to Idaho and California). Z4.

T.ixioides (Ait.) Greene (*Brodiaea ixioides* (Ait.) Wats.; *Brodiaea lutea* Lindl.). Scape to 60cm. Pedicels 1.5–7cm. Perianth 1–2.5cm, golden-yellow with dark midribs; tube about half the length of lobes; stamens borne virtually in a single whorl inserted in the throat; fil. with wings extending as teeth beyond the anth., anth. 1.5–2mm; ovary green or tinged yellow, exceeding the stalk. W US. Z7.

T.laxa Benth. (*Brodiaea laxa* (Benth.) Wats.; *Brodiaea candida* Bak.; *T.candida* (Bak.) Greene. GRASSNUT; TRIPLET LILY. Scape to 75cm. Lvs grass-like, about two-thirds the length of the scape. Pedicels to 9cm. Fls deep violet-blue, rarely white, borne in a many-fld umbel; perianth 2–5cm; tube usually slightly exceeding lobes, attenuate at base; stamens borne in 2 whorls inserted at different levels; fil. 3–6mm, thread like, anth. 2–5mm; ovary green, blue, or white, with stalk 3× as long. W US (California, S Oregon). 'Konigin Fabiola' ('Queen Fabiola'): fls pale violet blue, to 25 per umbel.

T.lutea Davidson & Moseley See *T.hyacintha*.

T.peduncularis Lindl. (*Brodiaea peduncularis* (Lindl.) Wats.). Scape to 40cm, flexuous. Lvs often longer than scape. Fls broadly funnelform, white, blue, or tinged lavender, borne in umbels of 3–15, on pedicels 2–18cm; perianth to 3cm; tube equal to or shorter than lobes; stamens borne in 2 whorls, inserted at different levels; fil. slightly dilated at the base, anth. 2–4mm; ovary yellow, equal to or exceeding stalk. Z6.

Tritonia Ker-Gawl. (From Gk *triton*, thought by Ker-Gawler to mean a weathervane, referring to the variable direction of the stamens of different species.) Iridaceae. 28 species of small to medium-sized, deciduous, perennial herbs. Corms renewed annually, usually round or ovoid, sometimes depressed or elongated, with fibrous tunics. Stem branched or unbranched, often with collar of old leaf bases at base. Leaves several, distichous, usually linear or lanceolate. Spike usually distichous in bud, secund in flower, laxly or densely few- to several-flowered; flowers usually irregular but sometimes almost regular; tube longer or shorter than segments; cream, yellow, orange, red or pink; stamens set in tube; style long, slender, curved with 3 short recurved branches; capsules papery or membranous with many seeds. Closely related to *Chasmanthe* and *Crocosmia*. Tropical & S Africa. Z9.

CULTIVATION As for the small South African spp. of *Gladiolus*.

T.aurantiaca Ecklon. See *T.deusta* ssp. *miniata*.
T.aurea (Hook.) Planch. See *Crocosmia aurea*.

T.bakeri Klatt. Stem to 80cm, simple or branched. Lvs 4–7, 15–60×0.1–0.3cm, succulent, more or less terete. Spike distichous with 1–3 branches, each laxly 3–10-fld; fls almost regular, cream, pale yellow or mauve-pink, the outer lobes with dark veins on outside; tube 2–5.5cm, straight, widening to 7mm diam. at throat, lobes spreading, 15–30×5–10mm, oblanceolate, obtuse; anth. violet. Spring–early summer. S Africa (S & SW Cape).

T.capensis (Houtt.) Ker-Gawl. See *T.flabellifolia*.

T.chrysantha Fourc. Stem 10–50cm, sometimes with 1–2 branches. Lvs 4–7,

5–20×0.2–1cm, lanceolate, acute. Spike distichous, sometimes branched, laxly 2–8-fld; fls bright yellow; tube 18–28mm, slender but widening towards throat, lobes 10–15mm long, ovate-spathulate, the topmost 9–12mm wide, often concave, the others spreading, 5–8mm wide, the lowest 3 each with a yellow callus c5mm high, sometimes set on a small pink blotch. Winter–spring. S Africa (Karoo).

T.cooperi (Bak.) Klatt. Stem to 60cm, sometimes with 1 branch. Lvs 4–6, 20–50×0.1–1cm, terete or H- or X-shaped in cross-section. Spike secund, sometimes with 1 branch, densely 5–10-fld; fls irregular, white or cream turning pink with age, often pink outside, with red or purple marks in throat; tube 3–5.5cm, often somewhat curved, widening gradually near throat, lobes 12–24mm long, upper lobes usually 10–13mm wide, elliptic or obovate, lower lobes 6–9mm wide, oblanceolate. Late spring–early summer. S Africa (S & SW Cape).

T.crispa (L. f.) Ker-Gawl.
Stem 15–45cm, simple with 1–3 branches. Lvs 3–8, 10–40×0.5–2.5cm, linear-lanceolate, the edge often crisped. Spike secund, densely few to several-fld, often slightly bent; fls irregular, cream, pale yellow, pale pink or salmon pink, red or purple in centre and with red or purple median stripe on 3 lower lobes; tube 2–7cm, somewhat curved, the lower half cylindrical, the upper half widening gradually to 7mm diam., lobes 12–25mm, upper lobes suberect, 5–13mm wide, obovate, lower lobes spreading, 3–10mm wide, oblanceolate. Spring–summer. S Africa (W & SW Cape).

T.crocata (L.) Ker-Gawl. (*T.fenestrata* (Jacq.) Ker-Gawl.).
20–50cm tall, sometimes branched. Lvs 4–8, 5–30×0.4–1.5cm, lanceolate. Spike secund or distichous, 2–10-fld; fls regular, rather cup-shaped, bright orange, orange-red or pink-orange, the 3 lower lobes with a yellow mid-line which sometimes forms a low callus, claws of lobes with hyaline margins; tube 8–15mm, curved, gradually widening to 7–10mm diam., lobes subequal, spreading, 16–28×8–17mm, spathulate. Closely related to *T.squalida*, apparently differing only in colour of flower. Spring. S Africa (S Cape).

T.deusta (Ait.) Ker-Gawl.
Stem to 50cm, sometimes 1–2-branched. Lvs 4–8, to 30×1.5cm, lanceolate. Spike few to several-fld, secund or distichous; fls regular, cup-shaped, bright orange-red or orange-salmon, the tube with a yellow, star-shaped mark inside, lobes often marked with dark or yellow blotches; tube 8–15mm, gradually widening to 7–10mm diam. at throat, lobes spreading, 16–28×8–17mm, spathulate. Spring. S Africa (S & SW Cape). ssp. *deusta*. Outer lobes with black-red basal blotch or stripe with ridge or callus in centre of each blotch; inner lobes sometimes also blotched at base. ssp. *miniata* (Jacq.) De Vos (*T.miniata* (Jacq.) Ker-Gawl.; *T.aurantiaca* Ecklon). Outer lobes without dark blotch or stripe; lower lobes often with yellow blotch sometimes edged with red, or dark spot or mid-line.

T.disticha (Klatt) Bak.
Stem 20–100cm, sometimes with 1–3 branches. Lvs 4–8, 25–70×0.5–2cm, linear or linear-lanceolate. Spikes 1–4, distichous at first, then more or less secund, laxly few- to several-fld; fls slightly irregular, funnel-shaped red, orange-red or pink, the lower lobes with a small yellow blotch sometimes edged with red; tube 8–16mm, funnel-shaped; lobes spreading, 10–20mm, elliptical and oblanceolate, topmost lobe 8–10mm wide, others 5–6mm wide, lowest lobe sometimes with low, yellow callus. Summer. S Africa, Swaziland. ssp. *disticha*. Bracts to 20mm; fls 20–35mm, red or pink; tube subequal to, or slightly longer than lobes; style 14–20mm. ssp. *rubrolucens* (Fost.) De Vos (*T.rosea* Klatt; *T.rubrolucens* Fost.). Bracts to 15mm; fls 24–35mm, red, orange-red or pink; tube equal to or slightly longer or shorter than lobes; style 18–22mm.

T.fenestrata (Jacq.) Ker-Gawl. See *T.crocata*.

T.flabellifolia (Delaroche) G. Lewis (*T.capensis* (Houtt.) Ker-Gawl.).
Stem 20–60cm, unbranched or with 1–3 branches. Lvs 6–9, 10–45×0.2–1cm, linear or linear-lanceolate, acuminate. Spikes 1–3, secund, each densely or laxly 3–7-fld; fls irregular, suberect, white, cream or pale pink with red or yellow stripe or blotch on lower 3 lobes, often magenta in throat; tube 2.5–6.5cm, widening to 10mm diam. in upper quarter, lobes unequal, 12–25mm, topmost 10–15mm wide, obovate, others 5–10mm wide, oblanceolate; anth. violet. Spring–summer. S Africa (S Cape). var. *flabellifolia*. Fls 4.2–6.0cm, usually less than 5cm; tube 2.5–4cm. var. *major* (Ker-Gawl.) De Vos (*T.rosea* (Jacq.) Ait.). Fls 6–9.5cm; tube 4.5–6.5cm.

T.flava (Ait.) Ker-Gawl. See *T.securigera*.

T.karooica De Vos.
10–20cm, sometimes with 1 branch. Lvs 6–10, forming fan, 4–15×0.3–0.7cm, falcate, reflexed or spreading. Spike distichous, usually 2–6-fld; fls scented in evening, slightly irregular, funnel-shaped, dull yellow or yellow-brown, cream, salmon pink or orange, dark-veined, flushed with pink or orange on outside; tube 25–32mm, lobes 12–18mm, obovate-spathulate, upper lobes 7–12mm wide, lower lobes 6–7mm wide, each with low, linear yellow callus 6–10mm long. Winter–spring. S Africa (Karoo).

T.laxifolia (Klatt) Benth. ex Bak.
Slender, to 60cm, sometimes with 1–2 branches. Lvs 4–7, 10–50×0.5–1cm, lanceolate or linear-lanceolate. Spike secund, rather laxly few- to several-fld, sometimes branched; fls salmon-pink, orange or brick red, the 3 lower lobes with peg-like yellow callus 3–5mm high set on a yellow blotch; tube slightly curved, 12–16mm, slender at base and becoming funnel-shaped in upper half, lobes 10–15mm, topmost 8–12mm wide, obovate, others 5–8mm wide, elliptical. Summer–autumn. Tanzania, Malawi, Zambia, S Africa (E Cape).

T.lineata (Salisb.) Ker-Gawl.
To about 80cm tall, usually less, sometimes branched. Lvs 4–8, 15–50×0.7–1.5cm, linear-lanceolate, suberect or spreading. Spike more or less secund, laxly 1–12-fld, sometimes with 1 branch; fls slightly irregular, funnel-shaped, cream, pale yellow or pale apricot with darker veins, sometimes flushed with apricot outside; tube 10–15mm, lobes 15–23mm, topmost 8–14mm wide, obovate, the others 5–10mm wide, oblanceolate, the lowest sometimes with a median yellow ridge. Winter–spring. S Africa, Lesotho.

T.masonorum Bol. See *Crocosmia masonorum*.

T.miniata (Jacq.) Ker-Gawl. See *T.deusta* ssp. *miniata*.

T.nelsonii Bak.
25–90cm, sometimes branched. Lvs 4–8, 20–90×0.15–1cm, linear, rather stiff. Spike more or less secund, often branched, rather laxly few- to several-fld; fls red or orange-red, the 3 lower lobes each with a tall yellow-green callus; tube 10–18mm, funnel-shaped, lobes 10–17×5–10mm, the topmost the widest, hooded, the others spreading or recurved. Summer–autumn. S Africa (N Transvaal).

T.pallida Ker-Gawl.
15–60cm, often branched. Lvs 5–6, 10–50×0.8–1.5cm, linear-lanceolate, acute or acuminate. Spike distichous, sometimes branched, few- to several-fld; fls irregular, suberect, white, cream or pale lilac, yellow-green in throat, the tube purple-veined; tube slightly curved, 2.5–7.5cm, tubular but widening towards throat, often somewhat pouched on lower side, lobes 1–2cm, the topmost erect, 7–13mm wide, obovate or almost orbicular, the others spreading, 4–8mm wide, oblong or oblanceolate; 3 lower lobes sometimes with low, yellow-green ridges in throat. Spring. S Africa (S & SE Cape).

T.pottsii Bak. See *Crocosmia pottsii*.

T.rosea (Jacq.) Ait. non Klatt. See *T.flabellifolia* var. *major*.

T.rosea Klatt non (Jacq.) Ait. See *T.disticha* ssp. *rubrolucens*.

T.rubrolucens Fost. See *T.disticha* ssp. *rubrolucens*.

T.securigera (Ait.) Ker-Gawl. (*T.flava* (Ait.) Ker-Gawl.).
10–35cm tall, sometimes with 1 branch. Lvs 4–7, 7–25cm×6–10mm, lanceolate or linear-lanceolate. Spike more or less secund, rather laxly 5–15-fld; fls usually apricot or orange-red, yellow in throat, but sometimes all yellow; tube slightly curved, becoming funnel-shaped in upper half, 10–20mm, lobes 12–20mm, topmost 8–15mm wide, obovate, concave, others 5–11mm wide, spreading, oblong, the 3 lowest narrower than the upper laterals and each with a high yellow callus in the throat. Spring–early summer. S Africa (S & SE Cape).

T.squalida (Ait.) Ker-Gawl.
Stem 20–50cm, sometimes branched. Lvs 4–8, 5–30cm×4–15mm, lanceolate. Spike secund or distichous, 2–10-fld; fls regular, cup-shaped, pale pink to deep mauve-

pink, sometimes almost white, often veined with deeper pink; tube 8–15mm, curved, gradually widening to 7–10mm diam., lobes subequal, spreading, 6–28×8–17mm, spathulate, the claws with hyaline margins. Spring. S Africa (S Cape).

T.watermeyeri L. Bol.
10–30cm. Lvs 3–7, 5–15×0.2–0.8cm, linear-lanceolate, the margins undulate, sometimes spirally twisted. Spike distichous, laxly 2–6-fld; fls almost 2-lipped, slightly scented,

orange or orange-pink, the upper lobes often buff or salmon inside, the lower lobes with a yellow mark edged with red in the throat; tube 10–16mm, widening in upper half, lobes unequal, topmost erect, 15–22×12–15mm, obovate, concave; upper laterals spreading, 15–18×7–10mm, oblong, lower lobes deflexed, 11–14×5 9mm, oblanceolate, each with yellow callus 3–4mm high. Late winter–spring. S Africa (Little Karoo).

Tritoniopsis L. Bol. (From *Tritonia*, and Gk *opsis*, appearance.) Iridaceae. About 20 species of perennial herbs. Rootstock a deep-seated corm, with tunic of matted, red-brown fibres forming a neck. Stem simple or branched. Basal leaves few, sometimes absent at flowering time, petiolate, firm-textured, usually linear or lanceolate, with 2–7 main veins. Spike lax or dense, few to many-flowered, distichous or spirally arranged; bracts and bracteoles firm, dry, brown or red-brown; flowers irregular (except for 1 species), often almost bilabiate; perianth tube long or short, either straight and cylindrical, or widening gradually to the throat; tepals 6, clawed; stamens arising in perianth tube; style long, with 3 short branches. Fruit a capsule, seeds winged. S Africa (Cape Province). Z9.

CULTIVATION   As for the smaller S African spp. of *Gladiolus*.

T.antholyza (Poir.) Goldbl. (*Anapalina nervosa* (Thunb.) Lewis; *Antholyza nervosa* Thunb.).
Stem 20–90cm, unbranched. Basal lvs 3–6, 15–30×1–2cm, usually developed at flowering time; petiole short, flattened. Spike c12cm, densely many-fld, usually spirally twisted; fls pink, salmon-pink or red, almost bilabiate; tube 25–30mm; tepals arising obliquely, all clawed, oblanceolate, topmost 22–30×4–5mm, projecting forwards at first, later with the blade recurved, other tepals 10–18×3–4mm, all recurved. Summer–autumn. S, W, SW & E Cape.

T.burchellii (Burm. f.) Goldbl. (*Anapalina burchellii* (N.E. Br.) N.E. Br.; *Antholyza burchellii* N.E. Br.).
Stem to 90cm, unbranched. Basal lf usually 1, to 35×1.3cm, present at flowering time; petiole long, 20 30cm, slender; terete. Spike to 18cm, densely many-fld; fls red; tube 30–40mm; tepals 20–25×6–8mm, arising obliquely, somewhat clawed, oblong or spathulate, the topmost the largest. Summer. S & SW Cape.

T.caffra (Ker-Gawl. ex Bak.) Goldbl. (*Anapalina caffra* (Ker-Bawl. ex Bak.) Lewis; *Antholyza caffra* Ker-Gawl. ex Bak.).
Stem 20–80cm, sometimes with 1 or 2 short branches. Basal lvs 3–6; petioles 3–15cm, slender; blade to 50×1cm, linear-lanceolate. Spike 7–30cm, rather laxly 7–25-fld; fls distichous, deep red or scarlet, almost bilabiate; tube 20–30mm;

tepals arising obliquely, clawed, spathulate or oblong, topmost lobe 26 33×10mm, arched, other lobes 10–16×5–7mm, eventually all reflexed. Spring–summer. S & SE Cape.

T.intermedia (Bak.) Goldbl. (*Anapalina intermedia* (Bak.) Lewis; *Antholyza intermedia* Bak.; *Chasmanthe intermedia* (Bak.) N.E. Br.).
Stem 30–45cm, unbranched. Basal lvs 3–7, appearing before fls; pet., flattened, very short, blade 10–15×1 1.5cm, sword-shaped. Spike to 24cm, fairly densely 10–25-fld; fls distichous, almost bilabiate, bright red, the 3 lower lobes with a purple-black blotch at base; tube 25–30mm; tepals arising obliquely, all clawed, topmost arched, 25–30×7–8mm, spathulate; others 12–18×4–6mm, almost oblong. E Cape.

T.pulchra (Bak.) Goldbl. (*Anapalina pulchra* (Bak.) N.E. Br.; *Antholyza pulchra* Bak.).
Stem 22–50cm, sometimes with 1 short branch. Basal lvs 3–5, often withered by flowering time; petiole short, slender; blades 20–40×0.3–0.6cm, linear. Spike 5–15cm, fairly densely 7–20-fld, the fls spirally arranged; fls carmine-red, purple-red or deep pink-red, the lower 3 lobes usually with red and white lines; tube 30–33mm; tepals not arising obliquely, shortly clawed, ovate or oblong, topmost 15–20×8–10mm, the others slightly shorter and narrower. Autumn–winter. SW Cape.

Tropaeolum L. (Coined by Linnaeus from Gk *tropaion*, Lat. *tropaeum*, trophy, i.e. a sign of victory consisting originally of a tree-trunk set up on the battlefield and hung with captured helmets and shields; as gardeners used to grow *T.majus* up pyramids of poles and netting, Linnaeus compared its rounded leaves to shields and its flowers to spear-pierced blood-stained gold helmets ornamenting such a memorial or statue of victory.) NASTURTIUM; INDIAN CRESS; CANARY BIRD VINE; CANARY BIRD FLOWER; FLAME FLOWER. Tropaeolaceae. Some 86 species of annuals and perennials, many climbing, some tuberous- or fleshy-rooted. Leaves alternate, mostly long-stalked, shield-shaped, 5-angled, or variously lobed and dissected. Flowers solitary from the leaf axils, usually long-stalked, asymmetrical, generally colourful and showy, spurred; sepals 5; petals usually 5, sometimes fewer, entire to lobed or fringed, clawed at base, upper two differ from the others and are commonly smaller; stamens 8. Fruit separates into 3 rounded 1-seeded carpels with a fleshy or spongy outer layer. S Mexico to Brazil and Patagonia.

CULTIVATION   *T.tricolorum* and *T.tuberosum* will thrive in essentially frost-free gardens, but they will survive short-lived light frost given a warm sheltered situation with good drainage; *T.tuberosum* is a short day plant and in cool temperate gardens the late flowers are likely to be spoiled by frost. The large-tubered form known as 'Ken Aslet' begins to bloom much earlier in mid summer and is more desirable for cooler climates. The tubers of these and other slightly tender species, such as *T.pentaphyllum*, may be lifted in autumn and stored in cool, dry conditions for replanting in spring. Alternatively, grow in the cool glasshouse or conservatory; *T.azureum, T.tricolorum* and *T.brachyceras* in particular make handsome climbers in this situation. Grow in good light, in a neutral or slightly acidic mix of loam leafmould and sharp sand. Water plentifully when in growth; withold moisture gradually as foliage fades. Store the tubers dry in their pots over winter.

Propagate these species by careful division or by separation of small tubers when repotting; also by basal stem cuttings in spring.

T.albiflorum Lem. See *T.leptophyllum.*

T.azureum Miers (*T.violiflorum* A. Dietr.).
Glabrous climber to 1.2m, with small tubers. Stems slender. Lvs 5-parted, to 3cm across, often less, lobes narrow, small, linear-lanceolate to obovate. Fls purple-blue, 1–2cm in diam.; pet. emarginate; spur *c*5mm, conical. Flowers variable in form. Chile. Z9.

T.brachyceras Hook. & Arn.
Slender, glabrous climber with small tubers. Stems slender. Lvs 5–7-parted, to 3cm across, often less, lobes obovate to linear-lanceolate, obtuse. Fls to 13mm, yellow, upper pet. with purple lines; pet. more or less emarginate. Chile. Z9.

T.edule Paxt. See *T.leptophyllum.*
T.elegans G. Don. See *T.tricolorum.*

T.leptophyllum G. Don (*T.albiflorum* Lem.; *T.edule* Paxt.).
Climber with large tubers. Lvs long-stalked, 6– or 7-lobed. Flowers *c*3.5cm, much overtopping lvs, orange, yellow, or pink-white; pet. notched; spur straight, *c*1.5cm, narrow, conical. Chile and Bolivia. Z8.

T.mucronatum Meyen. See *T.tuberosum.*

T.pentaphyllum Lam. (*T.quinatum* Hellen.)
Tall glabrous, tender, perenn. climber to 6m with long, beaded tubers; stems and petioles tinted purple. Lvs 5-lobed, lobes elliptical, usually obtuse, long-stalked. Fls 2–3cm, in pendent masses; upper sep. spotted, red; pet. scarlet, entire; spur conical, *c*2.5cm, red or green. Fr. spotted black. S America. Z8.

T.quinatum Hellen. See *T.pentaphyllum.*

T.sessilifolium Poepp. & Endl.
Climber with tuberous roots. Lvs 3–5-lobed, to 1.5cm diam., often less, lobes ovate. Cal. green-yellow; pet. dark red shaded with violet, bright red towards the base, to 1.5cm, spur conical, to 1.2cm. Chile. Z9.

T.tricolorum Sw. (*T.elegans* G. Don; *T.jarrattii* Paxt.).
Variable, tall, slender, perenn. climber to 2m, with small tubers. Lvs 5–7-lobed, to 3cm across, lobes usually linear, obovate, green. Fls of various colours; cal. obconical-turbinate, orange-scarlet, tipped black, yellow-red edged dark grey-green, or red with yellow interior and dull, slate-blue margin; pet. short, yellow-orange, entire; spur 1.5–2.3cm, straight or somewhat curved, red to yellow with a blue or green tip. Bolivia, Chile. Z8.

T.tuberosum Ruiz & Pav. (*T.mucronatum* Meyen).
Glabrous, perenn. climber, 2–3m, with large yellow tubers marbled with purple and red or blue-tinged stems, lf-stalks and peduncles. Lvs (3–5)5-lobed, truncate at base, long-stalked, grey-green. Fls long-stalked, cup-shaped. Sep. red; pet. about equal to sep., usually entire, upper rounded, lower narrower, all orange or scarlet; spur straight, abruptly narrowed, scarlet, 1.5–2cm. Peru, Bolivia, Colombia and Ecuador. 'Ken Aslet': fls orange. Z8.

T.violiflorum A. Dietr. See *T.azureum.*

Tulbaghia L. (For Ryk Tulbagh (*d*1771), governor of the Cape of Good Hope.) WILD GARLIC; SOCIETY GARLIC. Liliaceae (Alliaceae). 26 species of perennial free-flowering bulbous or fleshy-rhizomatous herbs with a garlic-like scent. Leaves several, sheathing at base, ligulate, glabrous, bright green or glaucous grey-green. Flowers many, star-like, borne in a loose scapose umbel, pedicellate and subtended by 2 bracts; perianth urn-shaped, with 6 nearly equal, spreading lobes, united for only half its length, mouth of tube with a fleshy corona composed of 3 free scales; anthers 6, stalkless in 2 whorls, one above the other; style short; stigma capitate; ovary superior. Fruit an ovoid, trilocular capsule containing triangular black seeds. Summer. S Africa.

CULTIVATION In areas that are essentially frost-free, *Tulbaghia* spp. are suitable for the sunny border or rockery; in cooler zones they are more commonly cultivated as houseplants or grown in large containers in the cool glasshouse or conservatory. Montane species from the high Drakensberg, such as *T.natalensis*, will tolerate temperatures of –5°C/23°F to –10°C/14°F of frost, as will *T.capensis* and *T.violacea*; these species are sometimes given front positions in the herbaceous border, or grown at the base of a warm wall, in well-drained soils in sun, with a dry mulch of bracken litter in winter. *T.alliacea* will tolerate temperatures to –5°C/23°F, but is in leaf during winter and is more safely grown under glass in cold regions. In its native regions, *T.violacea* is often used as a bedding plant.

Tulbaghia spp. are grown for their dainty flowers carried in umbels on slender stems; some are very fragrant at night, such as *T.alliacea* and *T.fragrans*. *Tulbaghia* flowers in early summer but most continue to bear flowers periodically throughout summer. Plant 2.5–5.0cm/1–2in. deep into a medium-fertility, loam-based mix with direct sunlight; water plentifully when the foliage is in active growth, reducing as flowering spikes emerge and again as plants enter dormancy. Maintain a winter minimum of 5–7°C/40–45°F, higher for natives of tropical regions. Apply general fertilizer to established plants as growth commences. Propagate by division or from seed sown when ripe or in spring.

T.acutiloba Harv.
Bulb ampulla-shaped, tunic brown. Lvs 4–6, 10–15×0.2cm, linear, strap-shaped. Scape to 15cm; pedicels to 2.5cm; bracts green, lanceolate; fls to 6, 8mm; perianth tube oblong, seg. lanceolate, green; corona annular, crenate, purple. E Cape, Transvaal. Z9.

T.alliacea L.
Bulb or rhiz. with fleshy roots. Lvs to 6, 15–22×0.3–0.6cm, linear, obtuse. Scape to 45cm; fls to 10 per umbel; pedicels to 3cm; perianth green or white, tube to 6mm, lobes oblong, 2–5×1.5mm, 3 inner lobes fused to corona for half their length; corona orange brown, fleshy, entire, crenate; style thick, stigma almost flat; stamens in 2 whorls, one in perianth throat, the other attached to base of corona; anth. oblong; ovary obovate, glabrous. Cape Province. Z8.

T.capensis L.
Lvs 10–12, 30×1–1.3cm. Scapes to 60cm; fls 6–8 per umbel; perianth olive green; corona 5mm, maroon, deeply cleft with 3 bifid lobes. Z8.

T.cominsii Vosa.
Lvs to 20×0.1cm, narrowly linear, grooved, glaucous, purple at base. Scape 22cm; fls 0.5cm diam., 6–8 in an umbel on pedicels to 1.5cm, white, with tube pale purple, fragrant at night. Spring–summer. S Africa (Cape Province).

T.daviesii C.H. Grey. See *T.fragrans*.

T.fragrans Verdoorn (*T.daviesii* C.H. Grey). SWEET GARLIC; PINK AGAPANTHUS.
Bulb ovoid 6×3.5cm. Lvs 30×2cm, 5–7, ligulate. Scape to 60cm, laterally compressed, purple-green; fls 20–40 per

umbel, sweet-scented; perianth light purple, tube to 9mm, lobes to 8mm, sometimes with ragged, involute margins; corona purple tinged pink, cylindric, to 4mm diam., split into 3 bifid lobes; style 6-grooved; stigma 2mm; stamens 6, 3 on long lobes of corona, 3 in cor. tube; ovary 3mm. NE Transvaal. Z8.

T.natalensis Bak.
Lvs 6–8, to 30cm, linear, light green. Scape 30cm; fls fragrant, 6–10 per umbel; perianth tube to 4mm, white sometimes tinged lilac; perianth lobes to 7mm; corona about 4mm, yellow-orange or green-white with 3-toothed lobes. NE Transvaal, Natal. Z8.

T.violacea Harv.
Rhiz. bulb-like. Lvs usually 5–9, to 30×1cm, erect, linear-ligulate, channelled at base, grey-green. Scape to 60cm, laterally compressed, purple green; fls 10–20 per umbel, sweet-scented, bright lilac; perianth tube to 1.5×0.5cm, cylindrical, slightly inflated at base; perianth lobes to 2cm, lanceolate or elliptic with deeper coloured median stripe; corona with 3 lobes of 1.5mm, purple tinged red or white; pedicels violet, to 4cm; stamens subsessile in 2 whorls half way down perianth tube. E Cape, Transvaal. 'Silver Lace': fls large. 'Variegata': lvs grey to blue-green, longitudinally striped cream to white. Z7.

Tulipa L. (From Turkish *tulbend*, turban, which this flower resembles.) Liliaceae (Liliaceae). Some 100 species of bulbous, perennial herbs, some stoloniferous; bulb tunics papery to coriaceous, lining glabrous to coarsely ciliate or tomentose. Stems simple, glabrous, glaucous or pubescent, sometimes tinged red. Leaves few, basal or cauline, alternate, linear-lanceolate to broadly ovate, sometimes undulate or crispate, margins often pubescent. Flowers usually solitary, rarely to 12, erect, campanulate to cup-shaped; tepals 6, free, in 2 whorls, often blotched near base; nectaries absent; stamens 6, filaments flattened, narrow, often triangular, anthers oblong-linear, basifixed; ovary superior, 3-sided, stigma 3-lobed, prominent, style short or absent. Fruit a spherical or ellipsoid capsule; seeds numerous, flat. 'Broken' colours, i.e. irregular splashes of colour, are due to virus infections. Spring-flowering, unless otherwise stated. N temperate Old World, especially C Asia.

CULTIVATION   The introduction of the garden tulip into Europe was probably due to Ogier Ghiselin de Busbecq, Ambassador of the Holy Roman Empire to Suleiman the Magnificent (1520–66), who saw them at Adrianople in 1554. Conrad Gesner described some tulips he saw growing at Augsburg in 1559. It is possible that Clusius, who certainly had seed from Busbecq, sent tulips to England from Vienna, for Richard Hakluyt wrote in 1582: 'Within these four years there have been brought into England from Vienna in Austria diverse kinds of flowers called Tulipes and these and others procured thither a little before from Constantinople by an excellent man called Mr Carolus Clusius'.

In 1593 Clusius became Professor of Botany at Leiden University and brought tulips there. These were stolen from his garden and soon became widely distributed in Holland. Apparently they were not the first to be grown in Leiden, for in 1590 John Hogeland grew tulips in Leiden from bulbs possibly obtained from George Rye, a merchant of Mechlin, who had them from an Eastern merchant in Antwerp. Whatever their exact date of introduction, the garden tulip first came to Europe from Turkey and quickly became a general favourite.

The tulip had been grown in gardens in Turkey for a long time and in considerable quantities. In 1574 Selim II sent an order to the Sherriff of Aziz for '50,000 bulbs for my Royal gardens'. High prices were paid for individual bulbs and the Sultan directed the Mayor of Stamboul to fix prices, those who sold at higher prices being sentenced to expulsion from the city. The cult of the tulip became as extravagant in Turkey during the reign of Ahmed III (1702–20) as it did in Holland during the 'Tulipmania' of 1634–7. In both countries fabulous prices were paid for special bulbs, which in Holland were the subject of intense financial speculation. Tulips have been an important crop in Holland ever since, to supply the enormous international demand for spring-flowering bulbs. Considerable numbers are now grown in parts of England, especially around Spalding, Lincolnshire, in the Western United States and in British Columbia

Even at the time of Busbecq great numbers of tulip cultivars were known. A list of 1323 kinds is given in a manuscript by Sheik Mohammed Lalizare in the reign of Ahmed III (1702–30) and there are other very lengthy Turkish lists. The pointed or dagger-shaped petal, forming an almond-shaped flower, was the ideal in Turkey but was then little valued in Europe, where a rounded broad end to the petal was more esteemed. As time passed various forms have evolved and led to the invention of classes quite different from those in existence when the tulip was first introduced

No wild species known at present can be identified with certainty as the species from which today's garden tulips originally derived. Evidence of chromosome behaviour and the invariable infertility of tulips suggest that they are all derived from one species and are not of hybrid origin, though they present features, for instance the white base of the flower many of them display, that are not known in combination with their other characters in any wild species. Sir Daniel Hall in *The Genus Tulipa* pointed out that all wild species, save the Clusiana-Stellata Group, with which the garden tulips will not cross, have yellow bases

The garden tulips therefore probably arose from a yellow-based species which gave white-based mutants under cultivation, and the intercrossing of such variants gave rise to the garden tulips of Turkey from which modern garden forms are directly derived. It has been suggested that the dwarf Duc van Tol Tulips (now classed as Single Early) are derived from a dwarf species from South Russia and called *T.armena* (*T.schrenkii*), but no direct proof is forthcoming. The Dutch and English Breeder Tulips, like the Cottage Tulips, which are all now classed as Single Late, were selected seedlings raised in gardens from the original Turkish garden tulips, and their form can be matched among the illustrations of early Turkish and Dutch garden tulips. The Parrot tulips are a later garden-raised group

The Introduction to past editions of the Classified List gives a valuable guide as to how the present classification has evolved as various distinct forms have merged or gone out of cultivation. The robust group known as Darwin tulips, noticeable for their strong tall stems and square based substantial flowers, were introduced in 1899 and provided many well-known and widely grown varieties. Crossed with *T.fosteriana*, this group has now produced the popular Darwin hybrid division and itself, together with the Cottage tulips, has been classed as Single Late. In 1923 Messrs. Zandbergen of Rijnsburg introduced a race raised by Messrs Zocher and Co of Haarlem which were probably the result of crossing Single Early varieties with Dutch Breeder, Cottage and Darwin tulips. The name Triumph tulips were given to this race by Messrs Zanbergen, and many others of similar breeding have since been added. The Lily-flowered group was separated from the Cottage tulips in 1958; their parentage is possibly *T.retroflexa* crossed with a Cottage tulip. In 1981 Fringed and Viridiflora tulips were given separate divisions in the Classified List

Nomenclature of cultivars was very confused until in 1913 a Tulip Nomenclature Committee was set up by The Royal Horticultural Society and comparative trials were instituted in its gardens at Wisley. English and Dutch growers cooperated in preparing a report which was published in 1917. Other groups of tulips were later developed in Holland at the headquarters of the Algemene Vereniging voor Bloembollencultuur (General Dutch

Bulb-Growers Society) of Haarlem, and the Committee was reconstituted to settle questions of classification and synonymy, and to draw up colour descriptions of the numerous additional cultivars which were grown there. In 1929 a tentative list of tulip names was published, with a supplement in 1930, and in accordance with the resolution adopted at the International Horticultural Conference held at Rome in 1935 this list of garden varieties of tulips serves as the basis from which their names take priority

This List has been revised on several occasions and the latest *Classified List and International Register of Tulip Names*, published in 1987 by the Koninklijke Algemene Vereniging voor Bloembollencultuur (The Royal General Association of Bulbgrowers) contains over 2300 names, of which 215 are synonyms and 120 are species. The List also includes over 600 non-commercial and historical cultivars. (For classification, see the end of this entry.)

The cultivation of tulips is rather more exacting than that of other spring-flowering bulbs. They usually dislike competition and prefer to be planted in beds that have been well prepared, and to be used as bedding plants rather than 'spring fillers' in herbaceous borders. However, it is possible to naturalize many cultivars in grass in 'meadow gardening', and species such as *T.sprengeri* and *T.sylvestris*. Tulips abhor low-lying dark sites prone to frost. They should ideally be planted half way down a slope fully exposed to light and sheltered from high winds; if this is not available, the soil in the bed is best mounded slightly, which should also help to avoid tulip fire, a disease which is very prevalent in low-lying, ill-ventilated beds

Many of the modern forms and hybrids in the Kaufmanniana, Greigii and Fosteriana groups may be left in the ground if healthy for several years but in principle all tulips are better lifted once growth has died down, and stored in an airy place until planting time at the end of autumn. Ideally they should not be planted in the same ground year after year – however, if the top 15–20cm/6–8 inches of soil is removed and disposed of in another part of the garden, the bed can be dug over in early autumn incorporating humus on light soils and drainage material on heavy soils, with the addition of bone meal or a well balanced general fertiliser low in nitrogen. Highly nitrogeneous fertilizers and fresh manure should be avoided at all costs as these encourage soft, rank growth which easily falls prey to botrytis attack, starting at the top of the plant

Tulips can be planted much later in autumn than other spring-flowering bulbs. At planting time, lightly refork the surface again and place the bulbs firmly on the surface 10–15cm/4–6in. apart and cover with 15–20cm/6–8in. of fresh soil, or make trowel holes to the appropriate depth. This deep and late planting helps to prevent slug damage. Preferably the soil structure should be a good loam, free draining and yet able to hold moisture during dry spells when the bulbs are in full growth. If it becomes necessary to water, apply lightly to the soil between the stems

The species are well suited to sunny pockets in rock gardens, and with care, can remain *in situ* for several years in a good 'alpine soil' of roughly one part each loam, leafmould and grit, needing to be disturbed only when the bulbs are obviously overcrowded

With all tulips it is essential to clear old yellow foliage away as soon as possible, raking soil over the holes left by the old stems, if the bulbs are not to be lifted

Propagation. Most modern hybrids are sterile. If seed is required the plants will have to be hand-pollinated, using more than one cultivar – only one resulting plant in many hundreds will be any improvement on the parents, and the first flowers give little indication of the final potential

Most species set seed prolifically. Seed is collected as the pod splits and stored in paper bags in a cool, dark place until autumn. A soil-based seed-raising medium mixed with equal quantities of sharp grit is placed in a pot to within 6mm of the rim and levelled. Sow the seed thinly and cover with sharp grit. After soaking stand the pots in a north-facing frame all winter. If early germination ensues, remove the pots to a light, well ventilated cold house, and keep the seedlings growing for as long as possible. In the second year the whole potful can be potted on without disturbance. During the fourth year the small bulbs should be large enough to plant out. They will flower in 5–7 years. Mature bulbs increase slowly by offsets, many of the species much faster. Offsets can be treated as 2–3-year-old seedlings

Other than slugs, which damage the bulbs and the emerging shoots, aphids are the main trouble. They infest the buds at an early stage and distort the flowers if not destroyed by hand picking or appropriate pesticides. Tulip fire (*Botrytis tulipae*) is a debilitating disease. The sclerotium of the fungus is very persistent, remaining in the soil and on the withered skins of the old bulb. The mycelium attacks the young roots as they emerge, and destroys the bulb and emerging shoots. Dusting bulbs with flowers of sulphur or soaking bulbs when lifted in a systemic fungicide, according to the manufacturer's instructions, will help to control the disease

T.acuminata Vahl ex Hornem. (*T.cornuta* Delile; *T.cornuta* var. *stenopetala* (Mord. de Laun. ex Lois.) hort.).
Bulb 2.5–3cm diam., ovoid; tunic papery, lined with long hairs, especially at base and apex. Stem glabrous, 30–45cm. Lvs to 20×5cm, 3, lanceolate, slightly undulate, glaucous. Fls yellow, sometimes streaked red; tepals 7.5–13cm, long-acuminate, tapering, apex often convoluted; fil. yellow or white, anth. red-brown. Known only in cult. (Turkey, 18th century). Closely related to *T.gesneriana* and possibly a variety of that species. Z5.

T.agenensis DC. (*T.oculis-solis* St.-Amans; *T.lortetii* Jordan). As for *T.praecox* but tunics lined with matted woolly hairs; stem to 20cm; fls red, basal blotch black, edged yellow; outer tepals 6–8.5×1–3cm, oblong to elliptic, acuminate, inner tepals 5–7.5×1.5–2cm, elliptic, acute; fil. blue, anth. black, sometimes tipped yellow. W & S Turkey, NW Iran, naturalized S France and Italy. Z6.

T.aitchisonii Hall. See *T.clusiana*.

T.aitchisonii ssp. *cashmeriana* Hall. See *T.clusiana* var. *chrysantha*.

T.aitchisonii ssp. *chrysantha* Hall. See *T.clusiana* var. *chrysantha*.

T.alberti Reg.
Bulb to 4cm diam., ovoid; tunic elongated, black to dark brown, apex densely hairy. Stem to 20cm, pubesc., tinted

claret. Lvs to 14×6cm, 3–4, closely set, broadly lanceolate, crispate, glaucous blue, margins thickened, white. Fl. solitary, glossy vermilion, orange or yellow; tepals rhombic with rounded angles, tip pubesc., inner whorl cup-shaped, outer tepals reflexed, tinged purple, tapering, tip pubesc., basal blotch black or dark purple, heart-shaped, bordered yellow; stamens 2–9cm, fil. yellow-orange, broad-triangular, anth. dark, sometimes yellow. C Asia. Z6.

T.aleppensis Hall. Stoloniferous.
Bulb 4cm diam., ovoid; stem 20cm. Lvs 4–5, to 30×6cm, glaucous, ciliate. Fl. solitary, cup-shaped, crimson; inner tepals to 7cm, outer tepals to 9cm, reflexed, basal blotch black, edged yellow. Syria, S Turkey. Z7.

T.altaica Spreng.
Bulb ovoid, 2–3cm diam.; tunic brown, coriaceous, lining hairy, especially at apex. Lvs to 15×4cm, 3, lanceolate, erect, evenly spaced, plicate, glaucous green. Stem 10–25cm. Fl. solitary, opening like a sunburst; tepals 5×3cm, oblong, acuminate, lemon-yellow, lacking a basal blotch, outside tinted red and green; fil. yellow. Related to *T.ferganica*. C Asia (Altai Mts to W Siberia). Z6.

T.armena Boiss. (*T.schrenkii* Reg.; *T.suaveolens* Roth).
Bulb to 4cm diam.; tunic tough, lining either weakly long-pubesc. or downy at base and apex. Stem to 25cm, glabrous, upper part coarsely pubesc. Lvs to 16×2.5cm, 3–6, lanceolate, glaucous, sometimes pubesc. above, recurved, undulate, margins ciliate. Fl. solitary, variable, cup-shaped to bowl-shaped, crimson, vermilion, yellow or multi-coloured; tepals to 6×3cm, rhombic to long-obovate, basal blotch black, navy or yellow-green, sometimes fan-shaped or bordered yellow; stamens yellow or black, fil. narrow-triangular. Turkey, NW Iran, Iraq, Transcaucasia. Z7.

T.aucheriana Bak.
Close to *T.humilis* and doubtfully deserving specific rank but fls star-shaped, pink, tepals 3×1cm, basal blotch yellow. Flowers later than *T.humilis*. Iran. Z5.

T.australis Link (*T.sylvestris* ssp. *australis* (Link) Pamp.).
Scarcely distinct from *T.sylvestris* but stem slender, to 0.2cm diam., outer tepals shorter, 2–3.5cm, outside flushed red. Distribution as for *T.sylvestris*.

T.baeotica Boiss. & Heldr. See *T.undulatifolia*.

T.bakeri Hall.
Scarcely distinct from *T.saxatilis* but fls deeper in colour, lilac to purple. Crete. Z6.

T.batalinii Reg.
Tepals pale yellow, golden to bronze at centre, stamens yellow, pollen yellow, otherwise very close to *T.linifolia*. 'Apricot Jewel': fls apricot-orange, interior yellow. 'Bright Gem': fls sulphur yellow, flushed orange. 'Bronze Charm': fls sulphur, feathered apricot-bronze. 'Red Gem': fls bright red, long-lasting. 'Yellow Jewel': fls pale lemon tinged pink. Z5.

T.biflora Pall. (*T.polychroma* Stapf).
Bulb to 2cm diam., ovoid; tunic papery, brown, lining silky-hairy. Stem to 10cm, glabrous, brown-green, glaucous. Lvs to 15×1cm, 2, widely spaced, linear, channelled, decurved, feathered glaucous, margins and tips claret, sometimes ciliate. Fls fragrant, 1–2, broad-campanulate; tepals to 3×1cm, narrowly rhombic, cream to ivory, outside grey-green or green-violet, inner tepals acute, base abruptly attenuate, midrib green, basal blotch yellow, fringed with yellow cilia; fil. yellow, downy, anth. yellow, oblong, mucronate, tip purple-black. Late winter–spring. Balkans, SE Russia. Z5.

T.billietiana Jordan. See *T.gesneriana*.
T.bonarotiana Reboul. See *T.gesneriana*.

T.borszczowii Reg.
Similar to *T.armena*, but tepals usually vermilion or inner tepals yellow, or outer tepals red edged yellow. Bulb 2–4cm diam., ovoid; tunic hard, coriaceous, lining densely tomentose. Stem to 20cm, glaucous, glabrous, sometimes tinged

red. Lvs to 18×4cm, 3, widely spaced, lanceolate, glaucous, reflexed, undulate, margins white, sparsely ciliate. Fl. solitary; tepals yellow, orange or vermilion, outer tepals to 6×4.5cm, rhombic, tip attenuate, pubesc., inner tepals to 7cm, obtriangular, basal blotch rhombic, black; anth. black to purple. C Asia, Iran.

T.butkovii Z. Botsch.
Differs from *T.armena* in tunics short-pubesc. within, stem downy and fls ox-blood to jasper with deep red basal blotches on tepals. Bulb to 2.5cm diam., ovoid; tunic brown, papery, lining densely golden-hairy at base and apex. Stem to 15cm; peduncle brown-green, pubesc. Lvs to 12.5×4.5cm, 3–4, closely set, broad to narrow-lanceolate, reflexed, declinate, pubesc., glaucous, crispate, margins ciliate. Fl. solitary, broad-campanulate to almost star-shaped; tepals to 5.5×2cm, coral-red, outer tepals narrow-oblong to lanceolate, obtuse, sometimes pungent, basal blotch oblong, maroon, inner tepals oblong or narrowly ovate, apiculate, tips pubesc.; basal blotch small, rectangular, brown-red; fil. triangular, red, anth. yellow or brown, pollen yellow or maroon. C Asia. Z6.

T.carinata Vved.
Bulb to 4cm diam., ovoid; tunic black-brown, leathery, lined with woolly hairs. Stem to 48cm, pubesc. in apical half. Lvs to 21×6.5cm, 3–4, broadly lanceolate, blue-green, pubesc., upper part often twisted around keel, margins ciliate, yellow or pink. Fl. solitary, resembling *T.ingens* in pointed tepals but arrangement of 2 whorls more pronounced; tepals to 9×4cm, crimson flushed pink, obovate to subrhombic, tapering to a long, downy tip, basal blotch small, yellow or black bordered yellow; fil. black, tapering, anth. black, tinged red, pollen beige to yellow-pink. C Asia. Z6.

T.celsiana DC.
Resembles *T.sylvestris* but stem shorter, to 15cm, lvs often prostrate, lying twisted along the ground, fls appearing later, outer tepals shorter, outside flushed red. Distribution in the southern range of *T.sylvestris*. Z5.

T.chrysantha Boiss. ex Bak. See *T.clusiana* var. *chrysantha*.

T.clusiana DC. (*T.aitchisonii* Hall). LADY TULIP.
Bulb 2cm diam., globose; tunic coriaceous, lining tomentose at apex. Stem to 30cm, glabrous. Lvs to 30×1cm, 2–5, linear, glaucous. Fls 1, rarely 2, opening to form a star; tepals tapering, acute, white to cream, outer tepals to 6×1.5cm, exterior carmine, edged white, elliptic, acuminate, basal blotch purple or red; fil. smooth, anth. purple. Iran to Afghanistan, naturalized S Europe. 'Cynthia': fls cream, exterior red with green edge, base purple. 'Tubergen's Gem': fls yellow, exterior red. var. **chrysantha** (Hall) Sealy (*T.stellata* var. *chrysantha* (Hall) Sealy; *T.aitchisonii* ssp. *chrysantha* Hall; *T.chrysantha* Boiss. ex Bak.; *T.aitchisonii* ssp. *cashmeriana* Hall). Fls 1–3, golden-yellow, exterior of tepals stained red or purple-brown, basal blotch absent; stamens yellow. NW India. var. **stellata** (Hook.) Reg. (*T.stellata* Hook.). Basal blotch yellow; stamens yellow.

T.cornuta Delile. See *T.acuminata*.

T.cretica Boiss. & Heldr.
Stoloniferous. Tunic sparsely hairy at base and apex. Stem to 20cm. Lvs 2–3, lanceolate, glabrous. Fls 1–3; tepals to 3×1.1cm, white flushed pink, basal blotch yellow, outer tepals spreading, inner tepals erect; stamens yellow. Crete. Z7.

T.cuspidata Reg. See *T.stapfii*.

T.cypria Turrill.
Related to *T.agenensis* but lining of bulb tunics densely tomentose; stem to 35cm. Fls deep crimson, exterior flushed green at base, basal blotch navy, usually edged yellow; fil. purple. Cyprus. Z7.

T.dasystemon (Reg.) Reg.
Bulb to 1cm diam.; tunic tawny, papery, scantily white-hairy. Stem to 5cm, glabrous; peduncle glabrous, tinted brown-claret. Lvs to 10×1cm, 2, semi-subterranean at flowering, narrowly lanceolate, blue-green, glabrous. Fl. solitary; tepals to

Tulipa   (a) *T.urumiensis* (b) *T.pulchella* (c) *T.sylvestris* (d) *T.celsiana* (e) *T.cretica* (f) *T.orphanidea*

2×0.7cm, narrowly lanceolate, bright yellow, outer tepals with a broad, brown-claret or green band along midrib on the outside, inside pure yellow, inner tepals streaked brown-green along midrib; anth. yellow. C Asia. The name *T.dasystemon* has been misapplied to *T.tarda*. Z5.

T.didieri Jordan.
Bulb 2.5–3cm diam., ovoid; tunic glabrous, lining sparsely hairy. Stem to 40cm, rarely 50cm. Lvs 15–20×3cm, 3–4, lanceolate, undulate, glabrous, glaucous. Fl. solitary; tepals usually bright crimson, occasionally white, rounded, apex acute, reflexed basal blotch black with broad pale yellow margin; anth. purple-black. S Europe. Closely allied to *T.gesneriana*. Z7.

T.dubia Vved.
Bulb 1–3cm diam; tunic papery, black or black-brown, lined with adpressed hairs. Stem abbreviated; peduncle to 25cm in flower, pubesc., glaucous, often tinged pink-brown. Lvs to 14×6cm, 2–4, in a rosette, broadly lanceolate, falcate, glaucous, margin undulate, ciliate, villous at tip. Fl. solitary; tepals to 4×1.5cm, lanceolate to rhombic to oblong, yellow, outside streaked blue-pink, widely stellate, fragrant, outer tepals rounded, acute, basal blotch orange, 3-toothed, inner tepals usually obtuse, lemon-yellow shading to orange at base; fil. long-triangular, glabrous, orange, anth. oblong, yellow, not coiled. Z6.

T.edulis (Miq.) Bak. (*Amana edulis* (Miq.) Honda).
Bulb tunic lining densely tomentose. Stem to 15cm, glabrous, with 2–3 narrow bracts beneath fls. Lvs to 25×1cm, to 6. Fls 1–2; tepals to 3×0.6cm, ivory, exterior veined claret or mauve, basal blotch purple-black edged yellow; fil. glabrous. Late winter–spring. S Japan, NE China, Korea. var. *latifolia* Mak. (Amana latifolia (Mak.) Honda; *T.latifolia* (Mak.) Mak.). Lvs shorter and wider, to 15×1.5cm. Z7.

T.eichleri Reg. See *T.undulatifolia*.

T.elegans hort. ex Bak.
Close to *T.gesneriana* and possibly not distinct from it. Tunic glabrous. Stem to 45cm, pubesc. Lvs to 25cm, lanceolate. Fls with tepals scarlet, tapering, apex acute, basal blotch yellow; stamens purple. Known only in cult. 'Alba': tepals white with pink edge. Z6.

T.etrusca Levier. See *T.gesneriana*.

T.ferganica Vved.
Bulb to 3.5cm diam., ovoid; tunic tough, coriaceous, lined with adpressed hairs near base and apex. Stem to 25cm, pubesc., glaucous, sometimes tinged red. Lvs to 16×7cm, 3–5, closely set, broadly to narrowly lanceolate, reflexed, glaucous, pubesc., margins undulate to crispate, ciliate, thickened, pale yellow. Fls 1–2, star-shaped with concave base, yellow, exterior blue-pink or pale chocolate-pink; tepals 5×2cm, lanceolate to oblong, acuminate, tip pubesc., basal blotch absent; fil. tapering above, orange-yellow, anth. oblong, orange. C Asia. Z5.

T.florentina hort. ex Bak. See *T.sylvestris*.

T.fosteriana Hoog ex W. Irv.
Bulb 2–6cm diam., ovoid; tunic black-brown, leathery, densely lined with coarse golden hairs. Stem 15–50cm, tinted pink, sometimes hairy. Lvs to 30×16cm, 3–5, widely spaced, oblong to broadly ovate, glossy green, pubesc. above. Fl. solitary, faintly scented; tepals to 18×8.5cm, lustrous vivid red, long-ovate to narrowly rhombic to broadly lanceolate, tip pubesc., basal blotch black, fan-shaped or 2–3-pointed, edged yellow; fil. glabrous, black, triangular, anth. black-violet, pollen purple-brown or yellow. Fosteriana Hybrids (*T.fosteriana* × *T.greigii* or *T.kaufmanniana*): fls large, white or yellow. 'Princeps': resembles 'Red Emperor' but stem shorter, flowers later. 'Red Emperor' ('Mme Lefeber'): fls large, tepals to 15cm, brilliant red, glossy, basal blotch black with irregular yellow border. Crossed with Darwin tulips to produce Darwin Hybrids, which include Mendel tulips (fls large, stem stout). Z5.

T.fulgens Bak.
As for *T.elegans* but stems glabrous; anth. yellow. Probably of garden origin. Z5.

T.galatica Freyn.
Tunic lined with silky hairs. Stem 15cm. Lvs to 12cm, 4, linear-lanceolate, undulate, acuminate. Fls campanulate; tepals to 7cm, obovate, apex acute, reflexed, pale yellow, exterior tinged green-brown, basal blotch yellow-grey or olive; stamens golden-yellow. Turkey (not known in the wild). Z5.

T.gesneriana L. (*T.billietiana* Jordan; *T.bonarotiana* Reboul; *T.etrusca* Levier; *T.passeriniana* Levier; *T.pubescens* Willd.; *T.scabriscopa* Strangw.; *T.sommieri* Levier; *T.spathulata* Bertol.; *T.strangulata* Reboul; *T.variopicta* Reboul).
Bulb ovoid; tunic lining glabrous or sparsely hairy near apex. Stem glabrous or finely pubesc., to 60cm. Lvs to 15cm, 2–7, lanceolate to ovate-lanceolate, glaucous, margin ciliate toward apex. Fl. solitary, cup-shaped, opening to form a star; tepals 4–8cm (inner tepals wider than outer tepals), purple to dull crimson to yellow, sometimes variegated ('broken'), sometimes with yellow or dark olive basal blotch which may be edged lemon-yellow; fil. glabrous, yellow or purple, anth. yellow or purple. E Europe, Asia Minor. A complex and variable species, from which most late-flowering cvs are derived. The name is sometimes used to include the allied Neo-tulips *T.acuminata*, *T.didieri*, *T.platystigma*, *T.mauritania*, *T.grengiolensis*, *T.hungarica*, *T.galatica*, *T.urumoffii* and *T.schrenkii*. Z5.

T.goulimyi Sealy and Turrill.
Resembles *T.ferganica* but lining of tunic densely tomentose, tepals orange to brick-red; fil. pubesc. S Greece. Z7.

T.greigii Reg.
Bulb ovoid to spherical; tunic elongated, leather to papery. Stem to 45cm, often tinged pink or brown, densely pubesc. Lvs to 32×16cm, 3–5, usually closely set and reflexed, lanceolate-oblong to lanceolate, glaucous, stained and streaked maroon above. Fl. solitary; tepals to 16×10cm, usually vermilion but sometimes claret, orange, yellow, cream or multicoloured, rhombic to oblong-obovate, angles rounded, acute, tip pubesc., basal blotch rhombic, black on red forms, red on yellow forms; fil. glabrous, black or yellow, anth. black, pollen yellow. C Asia. Z5.

T.grengiolensis Thommsen.
As for *T.gesneriana* except stem shorter, 25–40cm; tepals pale yellow, edged crimson. Switzerland. Z7.

T.grisebachiana Pant. See *T.sylvestris*.

T.hageri Heldr.
Fls dull red, exterior tinted or marked green, otherwise as for *T.orphanidea*. Range as for *T.orphanidea*. 'Splendens': fls bronze tinted red, exterior dark red. Z5.

T.heterophylla (Reg.) Bak. (*Eduardoregelia heterophylla* (Reg.) Popov).
As for *T.kolpakowskiana* but bulb tunics glabrous within; stem 5–15cm; tepals 1.5–3cm, yellow, exterior stained purple or green. C Asia. Z6.

T.hoogiana B. Fedtsch.
Bulb ovoid, to 5cm diam.; tunic densely lined with thin, silky, rippled hairs. Stem to 40cm, glabrous, glaucous, dark redbrown. Lvs to 25×10cm, 3–5, widely spaced, lanceolate to narrowly lanceolate, clasping stem below, falcate, strongly reflexed, glabrous, grey-green, margins long-hairy. Fl. solitary, fragrant at first, glossy dark crimson or orange-pink, cup-shaped; outer tepals slightly reflexed 9.5×5cm, broadly elliptic, somewhat toothed and undulate, inner tepals upright, spoon-shaped with pubesc. tip, basal blotch narrow-elliptic or sharply triangular, black to dark crimson or grey-green edged yellow; fil. black or red-lined toward apex, paler at base, anth. exceeding fil., claret, pink, beige or black, often spirally coiled, pollen brown-pink to yellow. C Asia (Turkmenistan, mts). Z6.

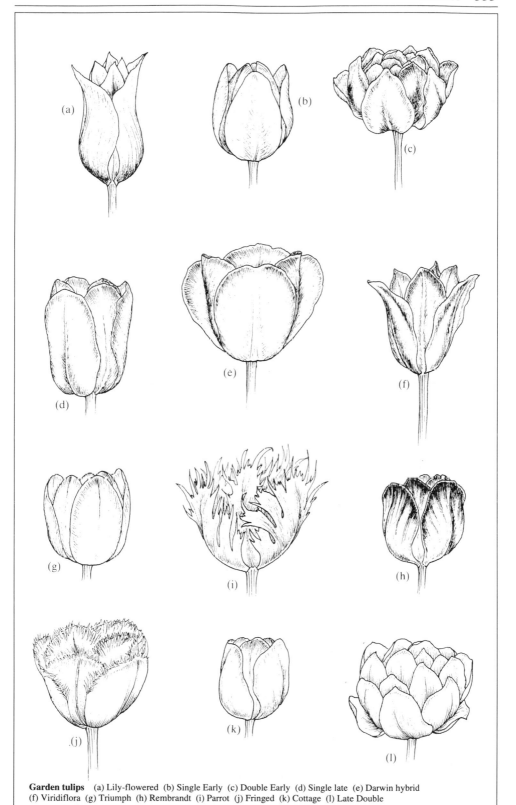

Garden tulips   (a) Lily-flowered (b) Single Early (c) Double Early (d) Single late (e) Darwin hybrid
(f) Viridiflora (g) Triumph (h) Rembrandt (i) Parrot (j) Fringed (k) Cottage (l) Late Double

T.humilis Herb.
A highly variable species. Bulb 1–2cm diam., ovoid; tunic brown tinged yellow or red, interior lightly hairy at base and apex. Stems to 20cm, 1–3. Lvs 10–15×1cm, 2–5, channelled, somewhat glaucous. Fls solitary, or to 3, cup-shaped opening to a star, pale pink, yellow at centre; tepals 2–5×1–2cm, acute inner tepals longer than outer; fil. hairy, yellow or purple, anth. yellow, pollen yellow, blue or green. SE Turkey, N & W Iran, N Iraq, Azerbaidjan. 'Eastern Star': fls rose, flamed bronze green on outer tepals, base yellow. 'Magenta Queen': fls lilac with yellow centre, exterior lush green flame. 'Odalisque': fls light purple, base yellow. 'Persian Pearl': fls cyclamen-purple, base yellow, exterior light magenta. 'Violacea': fls deep violet, centre yellow. Z7.

T.iliensis Reg.
As for *T.kolpakowskiana* but stem pubesc.; fls 1–5; tepals to 3.5×1cm, yellow, exterior stained crimson or dull yellow-green. C Asia. Z6.

T.ingens Hoog.
Bulb to 6cm diam., elongate-ovoid; tunic thin, interior sparsely pubesc., with long hairs forming a tuft at apex. Stem to 40cm. Lvs 3–6, closely spaced, narrowly lanceolate, sometimes channelled, glaucous, usually downy and undulate. Fl. solitary, opening to a star; tepals to 12×6cm, red-purple, outer tepals broadly-elliptic or subrhombic with rounded angles, tapering to a densely pubesc. tip, upper part reflexed, often minutely dentate, basal blotch black, with acute apex, inner tepals narrowly obovate or rhombic, basal blotch pronounced, black, sometimes 3-pointed or toothed, occasionally edged yellow; fil. glabrous, black or dull yellow, tapering, anth. black, brown-black or wine-red, pollen violet to purple-brown. C Asia. Z6.

T.julia K. Koch.
Bulb 1.5–3.5cm diam., thickly lined with gossamer hairs. Stems to 15cm, green tinged brown, glabrous. Lvs to 13.5×5cm, 4, lanceolate, slightly glaucous, glabrous, channelled, crispate, usually reflexed. Fl. solitary, opening to a wide cup; tepals to 5×3cm, dull crimson to orange-red, exterior tinted salmon or orange, subrhombic with rounded angles and pubesc. tip, basal blotch elliptic or obtriangular, green-black, edged yellow; fil. tapering, black, yellow at base, anth. oblong, black, pollen brown-purple. Transcaucasus, NW Iran, E Turkey. Z6.

T.kaufmanniana Reg.
Bulb 1.5–8cm diam., narrow; tunic black and leathery to tawny and papery, lining adpressed golden-hairy, indumentum denser toward apex and base. Stem to 50cm, upper part pubesc., sometimes glabrous, often tinged red. Lvs 2–20cm wide, 2–5, closely set, often rosulate, lanceolate to oblanceolate, slightly undulate, pale grey-green, veins darker, glabrous except minutely ciliate margins. Fls 1–5, star-shaped to campanulate to cup-shaped, often fragrant; tepals to 11×5cm, white or cream, sometimes shades from yellow to brick-red, outer tepals lanceolate to broad-lanceolate, often recurved, basal blotch yellow, outside red or pink along midrib, inner tepals often erect, long-elliptic or long-rhombic, obtuse, sometimes multi-coloured, midrib often green or red in lighter-coloured forms, basal blotch fan-shaped, bright yellow; fil. glabrous, yellow, anth. twisted, yellow. C Asia. Often crossed with *T.fosteriana* and *T.greigii*. 'Lady Killer': fls white, exterior central crimson flame, centre and anth. purple. Z5.

T.kolpakowskiana Reg.
Bulb 1.5–3cm diam., ovoid; tunic leathery black to brown, lined with thin adpressed hairs. Stem 15–35cm, glaucous, glabrous. Lvs to 20×3cm, 2–4, erect, deeply channelled, glaucous, margin undulate, ciliate. Buds nodding at first, later erect; fls solitary, rarely 2–4, cup-shaped, opening widely; tepals 5–8×1.5–3cm, long-rhombic, acuminate, yellow, exterior marked green, basal blotch absent; stamens yellow. C Asia (Tien Shan), Afghanistan. Frequently hybridizes with *T.ostrowskiana*. Z6.

T.kurdica Wendelbo.
Closely related to *T.orphanidea*, from which it differs in its shorter stem (6–15cm) and solitary, vivid, jasper-coloured fls with tepals blotched green-black at base. NE Iraq. Z7.

T.kuschkensis B. Fedtsch.
Bulb ovoid; tunic papery, densely lined with thin, rippled, silky hairs. Stem 14–45cm, glabrous, green, glaucous. Lvs 3–5, widely spaced, lanceolate, to 25×9cm, apical half falcate and recurved, margins crispate, ciliate. Fls resembling those of *T.hoogiana*, but with revolute outer tepals. C Asia, Afghanistan. Z6.

T.lanata Reg.
Bulb to 4cm, ovoid; tunic soft, densely pubesc. within. Stem 13–60cm, pubesc., pale green. Lvs to 16×5.5cm, 4, broadly to narrowly lanceolate, glaucous, reflexed, pubesc., margins red, undulate, ciliate. Fl. solitary; tepals to 12×6cm, exterior silver-pink, interior bright red, outer tepals rhombic, tapering to a pubesc. tip, inner tepals obovate, tip broad, pubesc., basal blotch black, elliptic to rhombic, edged pale yellow; fil. triangular, black, anth. dark purple, pollen red-purple. C Asia. Z7.

T.latifolia (Mak.) Mak. See *T.edulis* var. latifolia.

T.lehmanniana Bunge.
Bulb long-elongated; tunic lining densely tomentose. Stem to 25cm. Lvs undulate, margin smooth. Buds nodding. Fls yellow, vermilion or crimson, flushed scarlet or red-brown, basal blotch black, olive-green or purple. C Asia, Afghanistan, NE Iran. Z7.

T.linifolia Reg.
Bulb ovoid or globose, to 2cm diam.; tunic coriaceous, lining densely tomentose at apex. Stem to 30cm, glabrous. Lvs to 8×1cm, 3–8, closely set, linear, falcate, margin often wavy, usually ciliate and pink. Fl. solitary, star-shaped; tepals to 6×3.5cm, rhombic to subovate, scarlet, basal blotch blue-black, truncate, often edged cream to lemon-yellow; fil. glabrous, broadening towards base, yellow or black, anth. grey-yellow, pollen dark purple or yellow. C Asia, N Iran, Afghanistan. Z5.

T.lortetii Jordan. See *T.agenensis*.

T.marjolettii Perrier & Song.
Close to *T.gesneriana*. To 50cm. Tepals pale yellow to cream edged pink, exterior flushed rose-mauve, especially along midrib; fil. black, anth. pale yellow. SE France. Z6.

T.maurania Jordan & Fourn. See *T.mauritania*.

T.mauritania Jordan (*T.maurania* Jordan & Fourn.).
Bulb ovoid, 4cm diam.; tunic subglabrous. Stem to 40cm. Lvs 20×4–8cm, 3–4, lanceolate, undulate, slightly glaucous. Fl. solitary, campanulate; tepals oblong, 3.5–5×2.5cm, red, basal blotch yellow or black edged yellow; fil. yellow, anth. dark violet. SE France. Z6.

T.maximowiczii Reg.
Basal blotch black edged white, fil. black fading to white at apex, anth. mauve or yellow, pollen mauve; otherwise very close to *T.linifolia*. Z5.

T.micheliana Hoog.
Bulb 2–8cm diam., ovoid; tunic leathery, often elongate, lining adpressed-pubesc., especially at base and apex. Stems to 35cm, pubesc. Lvs to 30×2cm, 3–5, widely spaced, lanceolate, grey-green with garnet or maroon stripes above, somewhat downy, margin usually ciliate, undulate. Fl. solitary; tepals to 16×9cm, rhombic to obovate, vermilion or scarlet to dark crimson, wavy, glossy, acute, tip pubesc., basal blotch rectangular to elliptic, purple-black often thinly edged pale yellow, sometimes violet or 3-toothed on inner tepals; fil. short-triangular, black, glabrous, anth. broad-oblong, violet or yellow, pollen violet, purple-green or bronze. NE Iran, C Asia. Z6.

T.montana Lindl. (*T.wilsoniana* Hoog).
Bulb 1.5–2.5cm diam., ovoid; tunic stiff, coriaceous, apex thickly lined with long soft hairs. Stem 5–15cm, glabrous,

Tulipa   (a) *T.tarda*   (b) *T.saxatilis*   (c) *T.praestans*   (d) *T.clusiana*   (e) *T.undulatifolia* flowers, habit reduced

sometimes tinted red. Lvs to 15×1.5cm, 3–6, narrowly lance-olate, reflexed, channelled, glaucous, margins undulate-crispate, purple. Fls cup-shaped; tepals to 5×2.5cm, subrhom-bic to narrowly obovate, base cuneate, brilliant red, basal blotch green or purple-black; fil. conical, glabrous, black shading to claret, anth. narrow, yellow, pollen yellow. N Iran, C Asia. Z6.

T.oculis-solis St.-Amans. See *T.agenensis*.

T.orphanidea Heldr.
Bulb 2–4cm, ovoid; tunic leathery, interior pubesc. at base and apex. Stem 10–35cm, glabrous or pubesc. Lvs to 30×1.5cm, 2–7, lanceolate, glabrous, margin often claret. Fls 1–4, globose; tepals 3–5×1–2cm, elliptic, vermilion to brick-red, outside of outer tepals buff stained green or purple, basal blotch olive to black, sometimes edged yellow; stamens brown or olive. Closely related to *T.sylvestris*, producing many natural hybrids. E Mediterranean. *T.orphanidea* is a variable species encompassing such variants as *T.hageri* Heldr. and *T.whittallii* Hall which scarcely deserve specific rank. Because of their importance in gardens, however, these names have been maintained in this account. The plant usu-ally offered as *T.orphanidea* has dull orange-brown fls, the exterior suffused green and mauve. 'Flava': fls yellow, flushed red; almost indistinguishable from *T.sylvestris*. Z5.

T.ostrowskiana Reg.
Bulb 1.5–3cm diam., ovoid; tunic black, leathery, lining densely hairy, especially toward apex. Stem to 35cm; pedun-cle glabrous, blue-green, sometimes tinged red. Lvs to 15×3cm, 2–4, closely set, strongly decurved, sometimes almost prostrate, linear-lanceolate to lanceolate, channelled, falcate, reflexed, glaucous, margins undulate-crispate, white, ciliate. Fl. solitary, cup-shaped to star-shaped; tepals 5–8×1.8–3cm, long-rhombic, vermilion, orange, yellow or multi-coloured, outer tepals with an opaline lustre on exterior, particularly along midrib, often with 3-peaked yellow basal blotch, inner tepals with rounded angles, abruptly mucronate, with 2 stripes brighter than main colour parallel with midrib, basal blotch yellow, sometimes with a central brown spot; fil. narrowing toward top and base, yellow, red or brown, anth. yellow to black, pollen yellow, black, brown or claret. C Asia. Z6.

T.passeriniana Levier. See *T.gesneriana*.

T.platystigma Jordan.
Bulb ovoid; tunic brown, sparsely hairy. Lvs 20–30×5cm, 3–4, lanceolate, slightly wavy, glabrous. Stem slender, 40–55cm. Fl. solitary, campanulate, fragrant; tepals 8×3cm, elliptic, pink-violet, basal blotch or zone blue, edged orange; stamens violet. Similar to *T.didieri*, from which it is readily distinguished by the enlarged stigma. SE France. Z7.

T.polychroma Stapf.
Dubiously distinct from *T.biflora* and probably best included in that species. Stem 10–15cm. Lvs to 15cm, 1–2, channelled. Fls 1–2, nodding, white with yellow base inside, exterior green with red veins; stamens yellow, black at base. Iran, Afghanistan. Z7.

T.praecox Ten.
Bulb 3–5cm diam., stoloniferous; tunic papery, lining densely tomentose. Stem to 65cm, glabrous or puberulent. Lvs to 35×7cm, 3–5, lanceolate, glabrous, glaucous. Fl. solitary; tepals orange-red, outside streaked green, basal blotch green-brown, edged yellow, outer tepals 4–10×2–5cm, ovate to elliptic, inner tepals 4–7×1.5–3cm, ovate, midrib bordered yellow; fil. glabrous, black or green, anth. black or deep green, pollen olive or yellow. Probably Middle East, natural-ized S Europe and W Turkey. Z5.

T.praestans Hoog.
Bulb to 2cm diam., ovoid; tunic thick, coriaceous, thinly lined with adpressed hairs toward apex. Stem 10–60cm, finely canescent toward apex. Lvs 3–6, declinate, widely spaced, oblong or lanceolate, pale grey-green, midrib thick, distinctly keeled, margins sometimes undulate, ciliate. Fls 1–5, cupped;

tepals orange-red, outer tepals 7×2.5cm, broadly elliptic or subovate, tinged yellow toward base, inner tepals shorter, lanceolate, elliptic or obovate; fil. glabrous, red, anth. oblong, yellow, violet or claret, pollen grey-brown, crimson or red. C Asia. 'Fusilier': fls glowing orange-red, to 4 per stem. 'Unicum': lvs broadly edged white; fls to 5 per stem, red, base small, yellow, anthers black. 'Van Tubergen's Variety': fls red, several per stem. 'Zwanenburg': fls large, striking red. Z5.

T.primulina Bak.
Lvs grey-green. Fls 1–2, occasionally somewhat nodding; tepals off-white to ivory or pale yellow, the outer tepals suf-fused rose or pale green; anth. yellow. Algeria. Z8.

T.pubescens Willd. See *T.gesneriana*.

T.pulchella (Reg.) Bak.
As for *T.humilis* but tepals to 3×1.5cm, strongly cupped, mauve, central (basal) blotch navy edged white. Turkey. var. **albocaerulea-occulata** Tuberg. Fls white-mauve, basal blotch navy, flowers earlier than type. Z5.

T.retroflexa Bak.
Close to *T.gesneriana* and often considered a variety of that species. Tepals 7.5–10cm, golden yellow, long-acuminate, upper half reflexed; fil. yellow. SE France. Z7.

T.rhodopea (Velen.) Velen. See *T.urumoffii*.

T.saxatilis Spreng. CANDIA TULIP.
Bulb 2–3.5cm diam., globose, stoloniferous; tunic papery, hairy at apex and base. Stem 15–45cm, glabrous. Lvs 10–30×2–5cm, 2–4, glabrous, lustrous or, rarely, glaucous. Fls 1–4, fragrant; tepals 4–5×1.5–3cm, elliptic, acute, pink to mauve, basal blotch yellow edged white; stamens and pollen yellow, fil. pubesc. Crete, W Turkey. See also *T.bakeri* Hall. Material offered as *T.saxatilis* will usually have lilac fls, those named '*T.bakeri*' have deeper mauve tones. 'Lilac Wonder': fls rosy lilac, base large, lemon-yellow, anth. yellow. Z6.

T.scabriscopa Strangw. See *T.gesneriana*.
T.schrenkii Reg. See *T.armena*.

T.sharonensis Dinsm.
As for *T.praecox* and *T.agenensis* but basal tepal blotch larger, deep olive, edged yellow, covering basal half of seg. Israel. Z8.

T.sommieri Levier. See *T.gesneriana*.
T.spathulata Bertol. See *T.gesneriana*.

T.sprengeri Bak.
Bulb 2–3cm diam., ovoid; tunic tough, brown, interior glabrous or thinly sericeous. Lvs to 25×3cm, 3–6, linear, glabrous. Stem to 30cm; bud erect. Fl. solitary, brilliant red, acute, tapering toward base, outer tepals 6×1.5cm, buff-coloured beneath, inner tepals to 2.5cm wide, basal blotch absent; fil. bright red with glabrous protuberance at base, 3 long, 3 short, anth. and pollen yellow. N Turkey. Late spring–early summer. Z5.

T.stapfii Turrill (*T.cuspidata* Stapf).
Lining of bulb tunics densely tomentose. Stem to 30cm. Lvs glaucous. Fls red, basal blotch dark violet, edged yellow. W Iran, N Iraq. Z8.

T.stellata Hook. See *T.clusiana* var. *stellata*.
T.stellata var. *chrysantha* (Hall) Sealy. See *T.clusiana* var. *chrysantha*.
T.strangulata Reboul. See *T.gesneriana*.
T.suaveolens Roth. See *T.armena*.

T.subpraestans Vved.
Bulb 1.5–4cm diam., ovoid; tunic coriaceous, interior rarely pubesc. Stem to 40cm, glaucous, pubesc. Lvs 3–4, widely spaced, falcate, reflexed, coarsely undulate, lanceolate to oblong-lanceolate, margins undulate, ciliate. Fls 2–3, some-times to 6, from axils of upper lvs; tepals glossy orange-red, narrow, acute, opening to form a star, tinged yellow at base; fil. glabrous, flat, tapering, red, fading to yellow at base, anth. black, spiralling at dehiscence, pollen dark brown. C Asia. Z6.

Tulipa (a) *T.linifolia* (b) *T.julia* (c) *T.retroflexa* (d) *T.acuminata* (e) *T.batalinii*, true size as for *T.linifolia*
(f) *T.gesneriana*

T.sylvestris L. (*T.florentina* Hort ex Bak.; *T.grisebachiana* Pant.; Degen).
Bulb to 2cm diam., stoloniferous; tunic coriaceous, black to tawny, interior densely hairy at base and apex. Stem to 45cm, glabrous, sometimes tinted red at base. Lvs to 24×2.5cm, 2–4, widely spaced, declinate, linear, acuminate, channelled, dark green, glabrous, glaucous. Bud nodding. Fls 1–2, starry; tepals to 7×2.5cm, lanceolate to subrhombic, acuminate, golden, midrib bordered green, inner tepals convex, sometimes tinged pink; fil. flat, ciliate, yellow, anth. and pollen orange. Origin unknown; naturalized from Europe and N Africa to C Asia and Siberia. 'Major': fls to 3 per stem, gold, abundant, larger, with 8 petals. 'Tabriz': tall; fls large, lemon-yellow, sweetly scented. Z5.

T.sylvestris ssp. *australis* (Link) Pamp. See *T.australis*.

T.systola Stapf.
As for *T.agenensis* but lvs very waxy, nestling close to ground, tepals deep tomato-red, outside streaked grey; fil. navy, apex yellow. Iran. Z8.

T.tarda Stapf.
Bulb 1.5–3cm diam., ovoid; tunic leathery, black-brown, interior glabrous. Stem to 5–11cm. Lvs to 12×1.5cm, 3–7, closely set, lanceolate, recurved, bright green, glabrous, margins claret, often ciliate. Fls 4–15, broadly star-shaped, fragrant; outer tepals to 3.5×1cm, broadly lanceolate, acute, white, the outside, midrib edged with a broad green stripe shading to purple and yellow, inner tepals 3.5×2cm, spoon-shaped, acute, often yellow toward base; fil. conical, ciliate, yellow, anth. and pollen yellow. C Asia. Z5.

T.tetraphylla Reg.
Bulb to 3cm diam., broad-ovoid; tunic coriaceous, apex lined with coarse golden hairs. Stem to 25cm, glabrous, glaucous just below fl. Lvs to 14×9cm, 3–7, widely spaced, bases subterranean at flowering, lanceolate, reflexed, falcate, ligulate, glabrous, glaucous, margins crispate, often white-ciliate. Bud drooping. Fls 1–4, double cup-shaped; tepals to 8×3cm, yellow, outer tepals broadly lanceolate, reflexed, exterior tinted lime-green along midrib surrounded by a broad crimson band, inner tepals narrowly obovate, attenuate, apex acute, basal blotch green; fil. thick, yellow-green, anth. yellow, pollen yellow-brown. C Asia. Z6.

T.tschimganica Z. Botsch.
Bulb to 3.5cm diam.; tunic papery, dark brown, lining densely hairy at apex and base. Stem to 26cm, downy. Lvs to 24×7cm, 3–4, closely set, broadly to narrowly lanceolate, declinate, falcate, recurved, channelled, ciliate, glaucous, margins pale. Fl. solitary, conical or star-shaped; tepals yellow with crimson V-shaped markings toward centre, outer tepals to 7×3cm, broadly lanceolate to narrowly ovate, inner tepals rounded, top often notched; fil. thin, yellow, anth. 2× fil., yellow and yellow-brown, pollen yellow. C Asia. Z6.

T.tubergeniana Hoog.
Bulb 3–5cm diam., globose; tunic grey-brown, papery, thickly lined with silky hairs. Stem 5–60cm, covered with short, erect hairs, sometimes tinted red-pink toward fl. Lvs to 18×2.5cm, 3–4, closely set, lanceolate to linear, glaucous, falcate, reflexed, pubesc., undulate. Fl. solitary, resembling *T.greigii* but outer tepals upright with apex reflexed; tepals to 10×7cm, rhombic to obovate, long-acuminate, red, basal blotch elliptic, black or black-claret, edged yellow, tip acuminate; fil. thin, glabrous, black, anth. broad, dark purple, pollen yellow-brown or brown-purple. C Asia. Z5.

T.turkestanica Reg.
Very close to *T.biflora* and possibly part of that species. Stem to 30cm, white-pubesc. Lvs 2–4 exceeding infl. Fls to 12, smaller than *T.biflora*, white, centre yellow or orange, sometimes malodorous; anth. purple, brown or yellow tipped purple. C Asia. Z5.

T.undulatifolia Boiss. (*T.baeotica* Boiss. & Heldr.; *T.eichleri* Reg.).
Bulb to 4cm diam., ovoid; tunic elongate, leathery, black to

tawny, lining hairy, especially at base and apex. Stem to 50cm, pubesc. Lvs to 19×5.5cm, 3–4, widely spaced, linear to lanceolate, reflexed, glaucous, pubesc., margins crispate or undulate, ciliate. Fl. solitary, cup-shaped to broadly campanulate; tepals to 7×3.5cm, crimson to dark red, usually paler below, downy, broadly lanceolate to obovate, tapering to pubesc. tip, basal blotch elliptic to rhombic, black to purple, often edged yellow; fil. glabrous, tapering, black, anth. black to yellow, pollen dark green or yellow-brown. Balkans, Greece, Turkey, Iran, C Asia. 'Clare Benedict': fls bright red, base black, edge yellow, early-flowering. 'Excelsa': fls large, scarlet, base black, edge yellow. Z5.

T.urumiensis Stapf.
Bulb to 2cm diam., globose; interior of tunics sparsely hairy toward base. Stems 1–2, to 20cm, mostly subterranean, glabrous. Lvs 10–12×1cm, 2–4 in a flat rosette, plicate, glabrous, glaucous. Bud nodding. Fls 1–2, cup-shaped, opening to a star in sunlight; tepals to 4×1cm, yellow, outside streaked green or red; stamens and pollen yellow. NW Iran. Z5.

T.urumoffii Hayek (*T.rhodopea* (Velen.) Velen.).
Bulb tunic lining sparsely hairy. Stem to 30cm, glabrous. Lvs 3–5, glaucous, glabrous, margins ciliate toward apex. Fls usually solitary, rarely to 3; tepals to 6×2.5cm, yellow to red-brown, basal blotch black edged yellow, often absent; stamens yellow to olive-green; pollen buff to buff-green. S Bulgaria. Z6.

T.variopicta Reboul. See *T.gesneriana*.

T.violacea Boiss. & Buhse.
As for *T.humilis* but fls more rounded, tepals 3–5×2–3cm, violet-pink, basal blotch black, edged yellow. N Iran, SE Turkey. var. *pallida* Bornm. Fls paler mauve, basal blotch navy, flowers appear earlier than type; may be identical with *T.pulchella* var. *albocaerulea-occulata*. Z5.

T.viridiflora anon.
As for *T.gesneriana* but tepals green-white or yellow-green fading to cream or white at edges. May be a cv. of *T.gesneriana*. Z6.

T.vvedenskyi Z. Botsch.
Bulb to 3cm diam., ovoid; tunic dark brown, papery, lining sparsely hairy, apex densely ciliate. Stem 15–20cm, glaucous, sometimes tinged maroon, densely short-hairy. Lvs to 25×6cm, 4–5, closely set, lanceolate to narrow-lanceolate, reflexed, glaucous, crispate, sometimes sparsely pubesc. Fl. solitary, cup-shaped; outer tepals to 10×6cm, crimson, acute, tip pubesc., basal blotch yellow, often with brown spot, inner tepals obovate, upper margin undulate, tip pubesc., base yellow, basal blotch black-brown to claret; fil. glabrous, triangular, yellow to brown, anth. yellow or black-purple, pollen yellow, dark purple or brown. C Asia. 'Tangerine Beauty': fls bright red with grey-brown and lemon-yellow basal blotches, exterior light orange to flame. Z6.

T.whittallii Hall.
To 35cm, fls vivid orange-bronze, otherwise very similar to *T.orphanidea*. Z5.

T.wilsoniana Hoog. See *T.montana*.

HYBRIDS AND CULTIVARS

CLASSIFICATION. There are currently 15 subdivisions in the classification of garden tulips, a reduction from 21 in the previous classification. In the descriptions below the older group names have been inserted for completeness. The groups can be arranged into early, mid-season and late-flowering, plus the 'botanical' and other species tulips. Since the time of flowering is the decisive criterion for these groups in Holland, the actual months relevant there have been cited. At least two well known examples of cultivars are given for each subdivision, but the named varieties in some groups are very numerous. Except in double flowers, or where otherwise stated, tulip flowers are of typical inverted bell form

Tulipa   (a) *T.kaufmanniana*   (b) *T.subpraestans*   (c) *T.greigii*   (d) *T.dubia*   (e) *T.armena*

EARLY TULIPS. (1) Single Early. Over 25 cvs: height 15–40cm; fls 8–14cm long, white to deep purple with coloured edges, flecks or exterior central flame; late March–early April. 'Apricot Beauty': salmon pink flushed orange. 'Bellona': globular, butter yellow, fragrant. 'Brilliant Star': low; fls scarlet vermilion. 'Couleur Cardinal': deep red washed purple with white bloom. 'Diana': white, central flame tinted cream. 'Generaal de Wet': tall; fls gold washed and flecked dark orange, fragrant. 'Joffre': yellow with red flushes. 'Keizerkroon' ('Grand Duc'): scarlet broadly edged yellow and cream. 'Pink Beauty': deep pink edged white. 'Prince of Austria': orange flecked scarlet with tawny bloom. 'Prins Carnaval' ('Prince Carnival'): yellow with exterior red flame and feathering. 'Prinses Irene': orange with exterior purple flame. 'Van der Neer': deep purple. The original Duc van Tol tulips, rarely offered now, were around 15cm high with large pointed flowers. They were always frail and have been superseded by cultivars of varying height largely used for forcing for market and municipal displays

(2) Double Early. Over 20 cvs: height 30–40cm; fls fully double bowl-shaped, 8–10cm across, white through yellow to red with coloured edges or flecks; early to mid-April. 'Electra': deep pink-mauve edged lighter. 'Madame Testout': rose. 'Maréchal Niel': yellow tinted tawny orange. 'Monte Carlo': clear yellow. 'Mr Van der Hoef': golden yellow. 'Murillo': white flushed pale pink. 'Orange Nassau': dark red flushed brilliant red. 'Peach Blossom': deep pink with creamy exterior flame and flecks. 'Schoonoord' ('Purity'): white. 'Triumphator': rosy red. 'Wilhelm Kordes': orange-red edged white

MID-SEASON. (3) Triumph. Over 100 cvs, chiefly the result of hybridization between Single Early and various late-flowering tulips; height 45–50cm; fls single, white through yellow, orange, pink, red to deep purple, with coloured edges or flecks; late April. 'Abu Hassan': cardinal red edged yellow. 'African Queen': deep burgundy with fine white edge. 'Athlete': white. 'Douglas Bader': exterior rose, paler within on white ground. 'Dreaming Maid': raspberry pink with white edge. 'Fidelio': magenta shading to orange. 'Garden Party': carmine pink with white base and central flame. 'Lustige Witwe' ('Merry Widow'): deep red edged silvery white. 'Negrito': deep purple with grey bloom. 'New Design': cream with white edging tinted pink and apricot. 'Orange Wonder': orange-bronze with scarlet shading. 'Paul Richter': geranium red. 'Pax': white. 'Peerless Pink': satin pink. 'Reforma': sulphur yellow edged golden yellow. The Mendel tulips, now no longer included in the classification, were the less sturdy forerunners of the Triumphs, raised in the 1920s by crossing Duc Van Tol with Darwins and about 37cm tall

(4) Darwin Hybrid Tulips. Chiefly the result of hybridization between Darwin tulips (see Single Late) with Tulipa fosteriana and also other tulips and 'botanical tulips' which have the same habit. Over 60 cvs; height 60–70cm; fls single, vividly coloured yellow through orange to bright red, often with coloured edges and base; May. 'Beauty of Apeldoorn': orange, exterior flushed red, base and anthers black. 'Apeldoorn': scarlet, base black, bordered yellow. 'Daydream': golden apricot. 'Elizabeth Arden': deep pink tinted salmon. 'Golden Oxford': pure yellow edged red. 'Gudoshnik': cream flushed pink-apricot and flecked red, base and anthers black. 'Holland's Glorie': large, tepals pointed, outside deep carmine, edged red, inside mandarin red, base greenish black. 'Ivory Floradale': pale ivory yellow. 'Jewel of Spring': creamy yellow edged red outside, inside creamy yellow, anthers purple, base green-black. 'Oranjezon' ('Orange Sun'): pure orange, fragrant. 'Oxford': fls rounded, bright orange-red, base yellow. 'Spring Song': bright red tinted salmon, base white

LATE TULIPS. (5) Single Late. This class includes those originally known as Darwin and Cottage tulips: because of hybridization, it is now impossible to keep these separate. Darwin tulips were over 60cm tall, bearing large squarish flowers on sturdy stems. Cottage tulips, a shorter and much

older race, had long tepals, often waisted, some cultivars being multi-headed. Over 100 cvs; height 60–75cm; fls of rectangular outline, ivory through yellow, salmon, pink, red to black, often with coloured edges or feathering. 'Aristocrat': soft violet edged white. 'Bleu Aimable': vivid mauve. 'Clara Butt': rosy salmon pink. 'Halcro': fls oval, carmine red. 'Maureen': fls oval, marble white. 'Mrs John T. Scheepers': vivid yellow. 'Picture': bright cerise flushed lilac, edges laciniate. 'Queen of Bartigons': clear salmon-pink, base white edged blue. 'Queen of Night': deepest maroon to black. 'Renown': bright rouge red, yellow based edged blue. 'Rosy Wings': pink, very long, waisted tepals. 'San Marino': yellow with central red flame. 'Scarlett O'Hara': scarlet, base black with yellow ring. 'Shirley': ivory, spotted and finely edged purple. 'Sorbet': creamy white feathered red. 'Sweet Harmony': pale yellow edged cream. 'Wallflower': dark red, up to 5 flowers per stem. 'Zomerschoon': fls goblet-shaped, raspberry pink feathered white

(6) Lily-flowered. Over 30 cvs; height 45–60cm; fls long, waisted, tepals pointed, white to deep violet with coloured edges. 'Astor': bronze-pink. 'Ballade': violet edged white. 'Burgundy': deep violet-purple. 'China Pink': clear pink, white base. 'Elegant Lady': cream flushed yellow, edged rose. 'Golden Duchess': deep primrose yellow. 'Marilyn': low; cream feathered strawberry red. 'Mariette': large, deep pink. 'Queen of Sheba': red edged golden orange. 'Red Shine': deep ruby. 'West Point': clear primrose. 'White Triumphator': pure white

(7) Fringed. Over 15 cvs; fls with fringed tepals, fringes often crystal-like and of contrasting colour. 'Aleppo': pink and apricot, bright yellow base. 'Bellflower': pink, base white tinged blue. 'Blue Heron': violet-purple, marked white, base white. 'Burgundy Lace': claret edged white. 'Fancy Frills': pink shading to white edges, ivory white base. 'Fringed Beauty': vermilion edged gold, base black. 'Maja': golden yellow, base bronze-yellow. 'Noranda': blood red, edges tinted orange, base green-yellow. 'Redwing': cardinal red, edges lighter

(8) Viridiflora. Around 45cm tall, the tepals with varying amounts of green. 'Angel': off-white, flare apple green, reaches tepal tip. 'Artist': china rose, edges wavy. 'Esperanto': china rose, flamed green fading into red brown, base green-yellow, lvs edged white. 'Golden Artist': gold with red flushes. 'Green Eyes': yellow-green with darker markings. 'Groenland': pale pink with vivid green flare surrounded by cream. 'Humming Bird': clear yellow, flare apple green. 'Pimpernel': vivid claret. 'Praecox': pale yellow, edges wavy, early. 'Spring Green': ivory, flare pale green

(9) Rembrandt. 'Broken' tulips having striped or feathered markings. First recorded by Clusius in 1576, they became especially prized by early fanciers, and were frequently depicted by the Dutch flower-painters. The colour 'breaking' is now known to be caused by a virus, and since this can be transmitted to other tulips by aphids, and only a handful are currently listed, it is possible that they will be dropped from later classifications. However, they are historically important. They arose from 'Breeders', another classificatory group now abandoned; these were plain-coloured seedlings which were especially prone to 'breaking'. Broken tulips can be marked in brown, bronze, black, red, pink or purple on a white, yellow or red ground. The term Rembrandts included 'Bizarres' or 'Bizards', mostly marked with brown, bronze or black on yellow ground; and 'Bybloemens', striped pink, violet or purple on white ground. The markings could be described as feathered, with fine, symmetrical marks on each tepal, mainly confined to the edges but with a small 'beard' running down the centre from the top; flaked, with streaks or bands of different colour; or flamed, when feathering was augmented by a band of solid colour up each tepal centre, branching to merge with the feathering at the edge. 'Absalon': coffee brown on yellow. 'Beauty of Volendam': deep crimson on white. 'Cordell Hull': rose on white. 'May Blossom': deep maroon on cream. 'Pierette': purple on pale violet. 'Striped Bellona': vivid red on yellow

Tulipa   (a) *T.goulimyi* (b) *T.butkovii* (c) *T.ferganica* (d) *T.biflora*

(10) Parrot. Sports (mutations) from other tulips in which the large flowers are deeply laciniate or slashed, with even bands of colour. The name comes from the tepals curling around each other in bud when they resemble a parrot's beak. Over 25 cvs: height 50–60cm; fls to 20cm diam., often bicoloured, edges fringed, shredded or wavy. 'Apricot Parrot': apricot flushed pink and sometimes green. 'Bird of Paradise': deep cardinal red shading to orange tips, base bright yellow, edges shredded. 'Blue Parrot': mauve, bronzed outside, tepals ruffled. 'Black Parrot': deepest maroon, heavily fringed. 'Estella Rijnveld' ('Gay Presto'): white flushed yellow with heavy red markings, edges shredded. 'Fantasy': pale salmon edged and flecked rose, occasional green flushes, edges wavy. 'Karel Doorman': cherry red, edged yellow. 'Orange Parrot': gold and mahogany, fragrant. 'Texas Gold': deep gold, red on tips, flushes of green. 'White Parrot': white, tepal edges wavy

(11) Double Late or Peony-flowered. These have huge peony-like flowers of many tepals and are much used in pot work for bringing under glass out of inclement weather which shatters the heavy heads. Over 30 cvs; height 45–60cm; fls to 10cm diam. 'Allegretto': red tipped yellow. 'Angélique': pale pink flushed darker, edges pale and ruffled. 'Bonanza': deep red edged gold. 'Brilliant Fire': cherry flushed orange. 'Carnaval de Nice': white feathered deep red, lvs edged white. 'Eros': deep pink with faint blue hints. 'Golden Medal': compact, deep yellow. 'Golden Nizza': gold lightly feathered rich violet. 'Maywonder': rose pink. 'Mount Tacoma': compact, pure white. 'Miranda': vermilion with darker flames, base yellow. 'Wirosa': bright claret edged cream

SPECIES ('BOTANICAL TULIPS'). The first three of these groups arose from the wild species which give each group its name; however, recent interbreeding of the many original selections has almost rendered the groupings meaningless. All flower in March–April

(12) Kaufmanniana. Very early flowering with strap-shaped tepals opening flat in sunlight, hence the name waterlily tulips. Over 50 cvs: height 15–25cm; lvs plain or marked dark green-brown; fls white to currant-red with coloured edges, throat, base or central flame on exterior. tepals. 'Alfred Cortot': lvs streaked purple-brown; fls bright scarlet, base black. 'Ancilla': white with red ring and yellow throat, exterior red edged rose. 'Berlioz': red-brown edged yellow, yellow exterior. 'Chopin': lvs mottled; fls lemon-yellow, base black. 'Fair Lady': lvs mottled; fls cream, base yellow, occasional red streaks, exterior carmine edged cream. 'Franz Léhar': lvs mottled; fls lemon white, base yellow, occasional red flecks. 'Fritz Kreisler' ('Yolanda'): cream to deep pink throat, exterior salmon pink edged sulphur. 'Glück': yellow, throat gold, exterior red edged yellow-cream. 'Heart's Delight': lvs mottled; fls pink, throat gold, exterior carmine broadly edged milky pink. 'Shakespeare':

salmon streaked yellow and red. 'Showwinner': lvs mottled; fls cardinal red, base yellow. 'Stresa': lvs mottled; fls yellow, red mark at throat, exterior with currant red flame. 'The First': ivory, throat yellow, exterior with carmine flame. 'Vivaldi': lvs mottled bronze; fls sulphur, base gold, exterior carmine rose edged yellow

(13) Fosteriana. Over 30 cvs: height 20–65cm; lvs apple to dark green or variegated; fls oval to oblong, white through yellow to pink or dark red, sometimes with coloured edges central flame or base. 'Candela': fls large, oblong, rich lemon yellow, anthers black. 'Cantata': to 20cm; lvs apple green; fls deep scarlet. 'Golden Eagle': fls oval, rich yellow with exterior burnt orange flame, base black and soft orange tints. 'Juan': to 45cm; lvs mottled; fls orange-scarlet marked with red-brown bands, base yellow. 'Madame Lefeber' ('Red Emperor'): fls large, bright red. 'Orange Emperor': fls large, rich vivid orange, base yellow. 'Purissima' ('White Emperor'): to 50cm; fls large, clear creamy white with yellow centre, long-lasting. 'Robassa': lvs striped cream near edge; fls vibrant red, base bluish black edged yellow. 'Spring Pearl' ('Pink Emperor'): fls pink-red with pearl sheen, centre yellow. 'Sweetheart': yellow central flame and wide white edge, slightly frilled. 'Tender Beauty': soft yellow, tepal sides with pinky red margin. 'Zombie': carmine-rose, edges yellow, exterior yellow tinted rose, red ring and black throat

(14) Greigii. Over 40 cvs: height 20–30cm; lvs lightly to heavily mottled brown-purple; fls yellow through apricot to red, base and edges coloured. 'Cape Cod': exterior apricot edged yellow with thin red central stripe, interior flushed bronze, base black. 'Corsage': bright rose edged yellow, interior feathered gold. 'Donna Bella': cream, base black with scarlet ring, exterior carmine flame. 'Large Copper': tall; fls orange-red. 'Margaret Herbst' ('Royal Splendour'): fls large, vivid scarlet. 'Oratorio': rose, interior tinted apricot, base black. 'Oriental Splendour': fls large, deep yellow with broad scarlet flame. 'Pandour': pale yellow with red flames. 'Perlina': rose tinted orange, shading to yellow. 'Plaisir': cream with broad vermilion flame and yellow flushes. 'Red Riding Hood': fls scarlet, base black edged yellow, exterior darker. 'Toronto': multistemmed; fls deep salmon pink, interior tangerine-red, base bronze-green on yellow. 'Zampa': primrose, base bronze and green

(15) Other Species, including selections and hybrids. The most suitable for pots in a cold greenhouse, or for rockwork, include the following. *T.batalinii*: 10–15cm tall, whose dainty flowers in mid spring are pale lemon; there are several named colour forms. *T.clusiana*, the Lady Tulip: 15–20cm tall, slender and elegant, the narrow flowers white with scarlet midstripe to tepals. *T.praestans* carries up to 6 scarlet flowers on 15cm tall, many named forms in shades of pink and purple. *T.sprengeri*, the last to flower, around midsummer: 30–38 cm tall, slender green buds open to bright scarlet.

Umbilicus DC. (From Lat. *umbilicus*, navel, alluding to the shape of the leaf.) Crassulaceae. 18 species of perennial, succulent herbs. Leaves nearly round-peltate, with a dimple near the centre, at least 2cm across, glabrous, petioled; flowering stem leaves much reduced. Inflorescence a many-flowered, terminal raceme or panicle; sepals 5, small, fused below; petals 5 fused below, into a bell-shaped or tubular floral cup, lobes erect; stamens 10, occasionally 5, fused to petals below. Fruit a follicle, slender, style short or absent. S Europe to SW Asia. Z7.

CULTIVATION   *U.rupestris*, an interesting plant with round fleshy leaves with a sunken `navel' at the centre, occurs on rocks, banks and walls (not on lime), bearing spikes of tubular flowers in summer above a mound of succulent foliage. *Umbilicus* spp. are easily grown in any near-neutral, gritty, moisture-retentive but well-drained soil, in sun or light shade. They are hardy to −15°C/5°F, although the more succulent species are best pot-grown and moved into the greenhouse during the winter months. Propagate by seed or leaf cuttings.

U.erectus DC.
30–80cm. Stem much-branched, sometimes and swollen and tuber-like below. Lvs 3–7cm across, peltate-orbicular, margin broad-toothed, flowering stem lvs obovate to linear, toothed. Raceme 8–25cm, dense, many-fld, simple, occasionally branched; pedicel 1–2mm; sep. 3–4mm, linear-lanceolate; pet. 9–14mm, yellow-green, fused for half their length, lobes pointed. S Europe, N Africa, SW Asia.

U.erubescens Maxim. See *Orostachys erubescens*.

U.horizontalis (Guss.) DC.
Similar to *U.rupestris* except raceme covering less than half the stem, flowering stem lvs compact, fls horizontal, subsessile. Mediterranean var. ***intermedius*** (Boiss.) Chamberl (*U.intermedius* Boiss.; *Cotyledon intermedius* (Boiss.) Stef.). Pet. long-pointed.

U.intermedius Boiss. See *U.horizontalis* var. *intermedius*.
U.libanoticus Náb. See *Rosularia rechingeri*.
U.pallidus Schott & Kotschy. See *Rosularia aizoon*.
U.pendulinus DC. See *U.rupestris*.

U.rupestris (Salisb.) Dandy (*U.pendulinus* DC.; *Cotyledon pendulina* (DC.) Battand.). NAVELWORT; PENNY WORT.
20–40cm. Base tuberous. Lvs 15–70cm across, round, peltate, crenate; flowering stem lvs reniform, toothed. Raceme simple, covering more than half the stem; fls pendent; sep. 1.5mm, ovate; pet. 7–9mm, fused for three-quarters of their length, white-green, sometimes tinged pink; carpels tapering to style. Widespread Europe to SW Asia.

Ungernia Schott. & Endl. (For Baron Franz von Ungern-Sternberg of Dorpat (1800–1868).) Amaryllidaceae. 8 species of perennial herbs close to *Lycoris*, differing in the numerous discoid seeds. Leaves lorate. Scape solid; spathe valves 2; flowers many in an umbel; perianth regular, tube funnel-shaped, lobes 6, oblong, keeled, with many close green ribs; stamens in 2 rows near throat of perianth tube. C Asia to Japan.

CULTIVATION   As for *Amaryllis*.

U.trisphaera Bunge.
Bulb to 7.5cm diam., tunics extending 13cm above neck. Flowering stem 15–30cm; umbel 6–15-fld; fls 2.5–4cm, red; perianth lobes acute. Turkestan. Z8.

Urceolina Rchb. (From Lat. *urceolus*, a small cup or pitcher, referring to the shape of the perianth.) Amaryllidaceae. About 6 species of glabrous, herbaceous, bulbous perennials. Bulbs to 7×5cm, tunicate. Lvs to 4, ovate or elliptic to oblong, appearing with or later than flowers, bright green above, paler beneath; petioles to often sulcate. Scape solid, terete, to 45cm; spathe valves 2; inflorescence umbellate, 2–6 flowers to an umbel; perianth urceolate, to 10×7cm, yellow, cinnabar-red, orange or white, with or without a corona of short teeth; stamens and style equal to perianth or exserted; anthers versatile; ovary trilocular. Fruit a capsule. Andes. Z9.

CULTIVATION From the Andes of Peru and Bolivia to altitudes of 1900–3400m/6175–11,050ft, *Urceolina* spp. are frost-tender bulbs, grown for their interesting and moderately pretty urn-shaped flowers, carried in brightly coloured umbels in spring and early summer. They need temperatures that do not fall much below +5°C/40°F and flower better when pot-bound, so that they are well suited to cultivation in the cool glasshouse or conservatory. Keep dry but not completely arid when at rest in winter. *Urceolina* is easily propagated from the freely produced offsets. Otherwise, cultivate as for *Phaedranassa*.

U.bakeriana (N.E. Br.) Traub. See *Eucharis bakeriana*.
U.bouchei (Woodson & Allen) Traub. See *Eucharis bouchei*.
U.candida (Planch. & Lind.) Traub. See *Eucharis candida*.
U.grandiflora (Planch. & Lind.) Traub. See *Eucharis × grandiflora*.

U.latifolia Benth. and Hook. (*Pancratium latifolium* Ruiz & Pav.).
Lvs 2–4, ovate or elliptic, acute, channelled, to 25×12cm; petiole channelled, to 30cm. Fls 6–8; spathe valves scarious, lanceolate, to 5cm; pedicels declinate in flower, erect in fruit, to 5cm; perianth funnel-shaped, yellow shaded orange and tipped green; tepals erect, not recurved; corona of 6 short, rounded teeth, alternate with stamens, arising from apex of tube; stamens and style exserted, style longest; ovary inferior, dark green, globose-triangulate. Winter. Peruvian Andes.

U.mastersii Bak. See *Eucharis × grandiflora*.
U.miniata (Herb.) Benth. See *Stenomesson miniatum*.
U.pendula Herb. See *Stenomesson miniatum*.
U.peruviana (Presl) Macbr. See *Stenomesson miniatum*.
U.sanderi (Bak.) Traub. See *Eucharis sanderi*.
U.subedentata (Bak.) Traub. See *Eucharis subedentata*.

U.urceolata (Ruiz & Pav.) Green.
Lvs ovate to oblong, acute, to 50×15cm. Scape to 30cm; fls 4–6, declinate, tube to 10cm, urceolate for upper two-thirds; tepals 6, recurved, lanceolate, apex green, sometimes with white margins. Spring–summer. Peru.

Urginea Steinh. (From the Afro-Arab tribe, the Urgin.) Liliaceae (Hyacinthaceae). Some 100 species of bulbous perennial herbs. Bulbs scales free. Leaves basal, narrow-linear to broadly lorate or nearly oblong. Flowering stem with small, often persistent papery bracts; flowers white to pale yellow or pink in a terminal, many-flowered raceme; tepals 6, free, spreading; style equalling stamens. Fruit a many-seeded, 3-angled, oblong capsule; seeds brown-black, slightly winged. Mostly Africa, 3 species Mediterranean. Z8.

CULTIVATION *U.maritima* is occasionally successful out of doors in Northern Europe although it is rarely free-flowering in cooler climates. Plant with the bulb only partly buried on very free-draining gritty or sandy soils in full sunlight with protection from winter wet.

U.maritima (L.) Bak. (*Drimia maritima* (L.) Stearn). SEA ONION; SQUILL.
Bulb 5–15cm diam., ovoid-globose, protruding above soil surface or fully exposed in shifting, sandy substrates. Lvs 30–100×3–10cm, 10–20, narrow-lanceolate, rather fleshy, glaucous, glabrous. Scape 50–150cm, terete, slender, tinted red; racemes dense, 30cm+; bracts subulate, soon falling; pedicels to 3cm; fls appearing after lvs; tepals 6–8mm, oblong, white with a green or purple keel. Summer. Mediterranean, Portugal.

Uvularia L. (From Lat. *uvula*, the soft palate, referring to the drooping flowers.) BELLWORT; WILD OATS; MERRY-BELLS. Liliaceae (Uvulariaceae). 5 species of perennial, rhizomatous herbs, superficially resembling *Polygonatum* spp., to 75cm. Stems simple or branched, glabrous or pubescent, deciduous, arching. Leaves alternate, 2-ranked along stem, oblong-lanceolate to elliptic, perfoliate or sessile-divergent, to 4.5×13cm, glabrous above, sometimes pubescent beneath, margins entire or scarious to minutely serrulate. Flowers 1 to few, usually solitary, terminal or in axillary clusters, narrowly campanulate, pendulous, hanging below leaves; perianth to 5cm; tepals 6, lanceolate-ovate, slightly twisted, free, pale or deep yellow, often flushed or lined green, smooth or rough within; stamens 6, shorter than tepals; style strongly 3-cleft; ovary superior. Fruit a capsule, membranous to leathery, to 3.3cm, truncate or elliptic, 3-lobed or winged, loculicidal. S & SE US.

CULTIVATION *Uvularia* spp. grow naturally in rich deciduous woodland and thickets and are suitable for cultivation in the woodland or rock garden, or at the waterside above water level. They are grown for their delicate, suspended, bell-shaped flowers; those of *U.grandiflora*, particularly in the cv. Citrina, are often considered the most attractive. In higher-fertility soils, *Uvularia* spp. achieve greater stature and can be grown in the herbaceous border. Propagate by division of established clumps, or from ripe seed sown in the cold frame.

U.caroliniana (Gmel.) Wilbur (*U.pudica* (Walter) Fern.; *U.puberula* Michx.).
Stem to 45cm, lined with minute coarse hairs. Lvs to 7.5cm, bright green, glaucous, elliptic, sessile, margins minutely serrulate. Perianth pale yellow, to 3cm; ovary and capsule sessile. Capsule membranous, trigonal-ellipsoid, to 3.3cm. Spring–summer. Z5.

U.grandiflora Sm.
Stem to 75cm, smooth. Lvs to 13cm, perfoliate, pubesc. beneath, glabrous above. Perianth yellow sometimes tinted green, to 5cm, glabrous within; stamens longer than style. Capsule bluntly 3-lobed. Spring–summer. 'Citrina': fls larger, clear lemon yellow. Z3.

U.perfoliata L.
Stem to 60cm. Lvs to 11cm, perfoliate, oblong-lanceolate, glaucous, glabrous. Perianth to 3.5cm, interior rough; stamens shorter than style. Capsule truncate. Late spring–summer. Z4.

U.puberula Michx. See *U.caroliniana*.
U.pudica (Walter) Fern. See *U.caroliniana*.
U.sessilis Thunb. See *Disporum sessile*.

U.sessilifolia L. STRAWBELL.
Resembles *U.caroliniana* but smooth-stemmed. Lvs to 9cm, sessile, oblong-lanceolate, sap green above, pale to grey-green beneath. Tepals coarsely papillose within. Late spring–summer. Z4.

Vagaria Herb. (From Lat. *vagans*, wandering; the first recorded specimen flowered in a Parisian garden in the autumn of 1815, its origin unknown.) Amaryllidaceae. 4 species of perennial herbs. Bulbs clustered, tunic brown, enclosing scape and leaf bases. Leaves to 7, ligulate, linear, to 60cm at maturity, green banded white, apex obtuse. Scape obscurely tetragonal, solid, to 25cm; inflorescence umbellate, 3–9-flowered; bracts 2–4, to 5cm, chartaceous; pedicels to 2cm at flowering, then lengthening; flowers funnel-shaped, tube 0.5–1cm; tepals 6, equal, lanceolate, to 3.5cm, white with broad green keel below; corona of 12 acute teeth paired between filaments, to 6mm; filaments included, anthers 6, versatile; style to 3cm; stigma capitate, short; ovary 3-locular. Fruit a capsule, 3-cleft; seeds triangular, shiny black. Autumn. N Africa, Syria and Israel.

CULTIVATION *V.parviflora* is a late summer or early autumn-flowering bulb found in warm and well-drained habitats in the Middle East. It is grown for its umbels of white flowers which appear with or slightly in advance of the leaves. The bulbs are not frost-tolerant and *Vagaria* is best grown in the cool glasshouse or alpine house.

V.parviflora Herb.
Described above. Syria, Israel. Z9.

Veltheimia Gled. (For August Ferdinand, Graf von Veltheim (1741–1801), German patron of botany.) Liliaceae (Hyacinthaceae). 2 species of bulbous perennial herbs. Bulbs ovoid, scales concentric, fleshy, becoming withered, papery toward neck. Leaves in a basal rosette, oblong or strap-shaped, rather thick, glaucous or glossy, margins undulate. Scapes stout, erect, fleshy; inflorescence a crowded cylindrical raceme rather resembling *Kniphofia*; flowers nodding; pedicels short, bracteate; perianth tubular, declinate, persistent, lobes 6, toothlike; stamens 6, attached at middle of tube. Fruit a trilocular winged capsule; seeds 2 per locule, black. Spring. S Africa. Z9.

CULTIVATION Handsome frost-tender bulbs grown for their attractive undulate foliage and dense spikes of waxy, tubular flowers carried on sturdy scapes in late winter or early spring. Although *Veltheimia* spp. may experience light frosts in habitat, in cool temperate zones they need glasshouse protection and make beautiful specimens for pots in the home or conservatory. In essentially frost-free zones, they are suitable for the border and appreciate the enhanced drainage of the rockery. Grow in bright light in well-drained sandy soils. Under glass, set the bulbs with their necks just above soil level. Grow in bright indirect light or filtered light, in a freely draining loam-based medium with additional coarse sharp sand and with a minimum temperature of 5–7°C/40–45°F. Water moderately and regularly when in growth, allowing the surface of the medium to dry between waterings. Give an occasional dilute low-nitrogen liquid feed; reduce water gradually as foliage fades to allow a period of about eight weeks of almost dry dormancy in summer. Resume watering as new growth recommences. Disturbance of the roots inhibits flowering and plants need repotting only when performance becomes markedly impaired. Propagate by offsets when dormant, by seed or by leaf cuttings, mature leaves will form bulbs at the base if inserted in damp sharp sand.

V.bracteata Bak. (*V.capensis* misapplied; *V.viridifolia* Jacq.). Bulbs 7×6cm, broad-ovoid. Lvs to 35×10cm, 8–12, strap-shaped, glossy mid- to dark green throughout. Scape to 45cm, dark purple spotted yellow; raceme 7.5–12.5cm, to 60-fld; perianth 3–4cm, pink-purple, sometimes tinged yellow. Fr. narrow-obovate in profile, conspicuously 3-winged. E Cape.

V.capensis (L.) DC. (*Aletris capensis* L.; *V.glauca* (Ait.) Jacq.; *V.roodeae* Phillips). Bulbs to 13×6cm, ovoid, flattened at base. Lvs to 30×4cm, 10, lanceolate, glaucous green, margins strongly undulate, apex short-mucronate. Scape to 30cm+, flecked purple, glaucous; raceme 5–15cm; perianth 2–3cm, from white with red spots to pink with green or claret apex. Fr. rounded in profile, 3-channelled. SW Cape. 'Rosalba': fls white spotted pink. 'Rubescens': fls deeper in colour. Plants cultivated as *V.deasii* are variants of *V.capensis*, of more compact habit (to 25cm) and with shorter, grey-green, crispate lvs.

V.capensis misapplied. See *V.bracteata*.

V.glauca (Ait.) Jacq. See *V.capensis*.

V.roodeae Phillips. See *V.capensis*.

V.viridifolia Jacq. See *V.bracteata*.

Veratrum L, (From Lat. *vere,* truly, and *ater,* black, from the colour of the root.) Liliaceae (Melanthiaceae), Some 20 species of coarse perennial herbs. Rhizome thick, highly toxic. Stem stout, erect, leafy. Leaves often plicate, emerging from large sheath, uppermost usually narrow. Flowers numerous, in terminal panicles, white, green or brown to purple, pedicels short; perianth purple, green or off-white, campanulate or spreading; tepals 6, basally connate, forming very short tube or, in others, scarcely narrowed at base, oblong, spreading, many-nerved; stamens 6, anthers confluent; styles 3, Fruit a 3-lobed, septicidal capsule. N temperate regions.

CULTIVATION Occurring predominantly in the damp grassland meadows and open woodland of temperate mountain ranges, often at high altitudes, *Veratrum* spp, are grown for their mounded form, deeply pleated foliage, and, in mature specimens, statuesque flowering spikes. With the possible exception of *V.fimbriatum,* which seldom experiences freezing in habitat, most species are extremely hardy, tolerating temperatures of about –20°C/–4°F, especially if given a deep protective mulch when dormant in winter. Grow in deep, fertile, moisture-retentive soils rich in well-rotted organic matter. In reliably retentive soils, *Veratrum* will tolerate full sun but best foliage effects are obtained in partial shade with shelter from drying winds, to avoid risk of scorch and drought stress which results in yellowing foliage and early dieback.

Propagate by division, potting up divisions in a fertile loambased medium to establish in the shaded frame before setting out when roots are well grown. Alternatively, take 6mm, root sections, each with a bud, and root in a sandy propagating mix in the cold frame. Seed germination may be erratic and plants may take up to ten years to reach maturity; sow ripe seeds and overwinter in the cold frame. One small leaf is produced in the first spring which will then produce an overwintering bulb; mature leaves are not produced until the following spring. Stratification for three months at 1.6–4.4°C/35–40°F followed by warmth at about 20°C/70°F gives better germination. For *V.fimbriatum,* stratify for two months 4.4–7.2°C/40–45°F: lower temperatures may kill the embryo. Do not allow seed to dry out. Unless stored in damp sand at about 4.4°C/40°F, seed has short viability.

V.album L.
Stem erect to 20cm, downy. Lvs to 30×15cm, 10–12, basal oblong to elliptic, plicate. Fls tinted white outside, green inside, in dense racemes to 60cm long, downy. Europe, N Africa, N Asia. Z5.

V.californicum Dur.
Stout, to 2m. Lvs elliptic to ovate, upper lvs lanceolate, to 35×20cm. Fls to 2cm, campanulate, in tomentose panicles; tepals blunt-tipped, off-white, base green. W US. Z5.

V.eschscholtzii A. Gray. See *V.viride.*

V.nigrum L.
Stem 60–120cm, erect, somewhat swollen at base. Lvs to 30×17cm, broadly elliptic to linear-lanceolate, lower leaves 30×15–20cm, oblong, plicate. Fls black-purple, to 0.5cm diam., in dense racemes, panicles narrow, 30–90cm; tepals oblong to obtuse. S Europe, Asia, Siberia. Z6.

V.viride Ait. (*V.eschscholtzii* A. Gray).
Stem erect, to 2m, leafy throughout. Lvs to 30cm, elliptic to ovate, acute, smaller toward top of stem. Fls yellow-green, to 2.5cm diam. in a raceme; tepals lanceolate or oblong, ciliate, toothed, loose, lateral panicles hirsute with drooping lower bracts. N US. Z3.

V.wilsonii O. Loes. ex C.H. Wright.
Stem to 90cm. Lvs to 60×2.5cm, c10, ligulate, acute, glabrous. Fls white with green band below, about 2.5cm diam., in pyramidal panicles to 60cm long. Fr. a 3-celled capsule, seeds to 20 per capsule. S China. Z6.

Watsonia Mill. (For Sir William Watson (1715–1758), British physicist and scientist.) Iridaceae. 52 species of perennial herbs. Rootstock a corm. Leaves two to several, distichous, sword-shaped, lanceolate or linear. Stem simple or branched; spike distichous, several to many-flowered; flowers regular or zygomorphic, white, pink, orange, red, purple or maroon, rarely yellow; perianth tube curved, slender and erect near base then usually fairly abruptly enlarged and often horizontal; tepals 6, the inner 3 slightly larger than outer 3; stamens 3, the filaments inserted on the tube; style 3-branched, each branch divided and recurved. Fruit a globose, oblong or elongated capsule, seeds angular or winged. S Africa (Cape to Transvaal), Swaziland. Species with red, almost tubular flowers are believed to be pollinated by sunbirds; those with pink, open flowers by bees. Z9 unless specified.

CULTIVATION *Watsonia* spp. are slightly frost-tender, and in cool temperate zones, are more safely grown in the cool glasshouse, although with a protective mulch of bracken litter most can be grown outside in mild areas where temperatures only rarely fall to –5°C. They are generally best left undisturbed, but spring- and early summer-flowering species, which rest during late summer, are sometimes lifted and stored in a cool frost-free place in winter. The late summer and autumn-flowering species are more or less evergreen and should not be dried out. Grow in an open sunny position, but with some protection from sun at the hottest part of the day, in a light, well-drained, sandy loam with additional leafmould or equivalent and provide plentiful water when in growth. Apply a slow-release fertilizer in summer. Propagate by seeds or offsets.

W.aletroides (Burm. f.) Ker-Gawl.
25–60cm, occasionally branched. Lvs 4–5, glossy, the topmost about half as long as stem, 5–10mm wide, linear or lanceolate. Spike to 20-fld, the outer bracts overlapping; fls slightly irregular, usually orange-red, occasionally pink or purple; basal part of tube slender, 12–15mm, upper part 25–28mm, broadly cylindrical, horizontal or pendent; tepals 10×7–9mm, obovate, acute. Late winter–spring. SW & W Cape.

W.alpina G. Lewis. See *W.strubeniae*.

W.amabilis Goldbl.
8–30cm, rarely more. Lvs 4–7, lanceolate, about half the height of the plant and 5–20mm wide. Stem sometimes with 1–2 branches; spike 4–16-fld; fls slightly irregular, rose-pink, darker in centre; basal part of tube slender, 10–17mm, upper part 6–10mm, horizontal; tepals spreading, 19–25×7–13mm, ovate. Spring–early summer. SW Cape. Possibly now extinct in the wild.

W.ardernei Sander. See *W.borbonica*.
W.beatricis Mathews & L. Bol. See *W.pillansii*.

W.borbonica (Pourr.) Goldbl. (*W.pyramidata* (Andrews) Klatt).
1–2m high, usually branched; corm to 4cm diam. Lvs 5–8, to two-thirds as long as spike, 2–4cm wide, lanceolate. Spike to 20-fld, lateral spikes to 10-fld; fls slightly scented, somewhat irregular, rarely white, usually pale to deep pink or purple with white lines at base of each tepal; basal part of tube slender, 12–20mm long, upper part 8–20mm long, funnel-shaped, horizontal or slightly pendent; tepals spreading, 30–36×13–18mm, obovate or oblanceolate. Spring–summer. SW Cape. ssp. *borbonica*. Upper perianth tube 8–15mm. ssp. *ardernei* (Sander) Goldbl. (*W.ardernei* Sander). Upper perianth tube 14–20mm; fls pink in the wild, but cultivated plants are often white.

W.brevifolia Ker-Gawl. See *W.laccata*.
W.bulbilifera Mathews & L. Bol. See *W.meriana* 'Bulbilifera'.

W.coccinea Herb. ex Bak. 1
5–40cm tall, sometimes branched towards top. Lvs 4–6, 2–8mm wide, linear or lanceolate. Spike 3–6-fld; fls red, purple or pink, tepals sometimes with dark central line; basal part of tube 20–24mm, upper part 18–24mm more or less horizontal, tubular; tepals 16–23×8–12mm, obovate, somewhat spreading. Winter–spring. SW Cape.

W.comptonii L. Bol. See *W.zeyheri*.

W.densiflora Bak.
60–150cm, forming clumps. Lvs 4–5, about half as long as spike, 10–18mm wide, linear or lanceolate. Spike many-fld, bracts overlapping, brown and scarious; fls irregular, almost 2-lipped with upper 3 tepals semi-erect, lower 3 horizontal,

pink, usually with darker mid-line on tepals, rarely white; basal part of tube slender, 12–18mm, enclosed in bracts, upper part 9–12mm, narrowly funnel-shaped; tepals 18–24×7–9mm, lanceolate, apiculate. Summer. SE Cape coastal area and into Natal midlands. 'Alba': fls white.

W.fourcadei Mathews & L. Bol. (*W.stanfordiae* L. Bol.).
90–180cm with several short, erect branches towards top. Lvs 5–8, to about one-third height of plant, 1.5–4cm wide, sword-shaped. Spike 25–40-fld; fls rather irregular, pink, orange or vermilion, rarely purple, sometimes with the tube paler; basal part of tube slender, 20–30mm, upper part 22–26mm, cylindrical, horizontal or pendent; tepals 24–33×9–13mm, the inner wider than the outer, lanceolate, semi-spreading. Spring–summer. SW Cape.

W.galpinii L. Bol.
1–2m, usually with 1–2 branches. Lvs 5–7, to 30×1–2cm, lanceolate or sword-shaped. Main spike densely 30–40-fld, lateral spikes to 15-fld. Fls somewhat irregular, orange-red or mauve-pink; basal part of tube 10–13mm, very slender, upper part 4–8mm, tubular or narrowly funnel-shaped; tepals 15–20mm, lanceolate-obovate, outer 3–8mm wide, inner 3–13mm, all spreading. Summer–autumn. S Cape.

W.humilis Mill. (*W.roseo-alba* (Jacq.) Ker-Gawl.).
10–30cm, sometimes with 1 branch. Lvs 5–6, usually about half length of stem, 8–15m wide, lanceolate. Spike 6–12-fld; fls slightly irregular, white or pale pink tinged with darker pink, the tube and outside of tepals darker; basal part of tube slender, 13–30mm, upper part more or less horizontal, 10–20mm, cylindrical; tepals spreading, 15–22×7–12mm, lanceolate or ovate, the inner wider than outer. Spring–early summer. SW Cape.

W.laccata (Jacq.) Ker-Gawl. (*W.brevifolia* Ker-Gawl.).
20–65cm, the stem branched or unbranched. Lvs 4–5, one third to two thirds as long as plant, linear or lanceolate. Spike to 20-fld; fls irregular, pale pink, pale orange or purple; basal part of tube 12–15mm, slender; upper part 7–8mm, funnel-shaped, horizontal or pendent; tepals 14–16×8mm, spreading, oblanceolate or obovate. Late winter–spring. S Cape.

W.latifolia N.E. Br.
70–150cm, rarely branched; corms large, to 6cm diam. Lvs 4–6, broadly lanceolate, 5–9cm wide. Spike 15–25-fld; fls slightly irregular, maroon-red; basal part of tube 15–25mm, upper part 18–24mm, 5–6mm wide, cylindrical; tepals 20–30×4–8mm, lanceolate, the topmost largest, somewhat spreading. N Natal & SE Transvaal, Swaziland.

W.marginata (L. f.) Ker-Gawl.
To 2m, unbranched or with several short, erect branches; corms to 5cm diam. Lvs 3–4, shorter than stem, 2–5cm wide, lanceolate, the margins much thickened. Spike several to many-fld, the side branches with fewer, more or less distichous but sometimes secund. Flowers almost regular, mauve-

Watsonia   (a) *W.humilis*   (b) *W.strictiflora*   (c) *W.borbonica*   (d) *W.marginata*

pink or magenta, each tepal with a white line edged with purple towards base; sometimes white; basal part of tube 7–12mm long, slender; upper part 6–7mm almost funnel-shaped, almost horizontal; tepals 14–22×7–13mm, obovate, spreading. Spring–early summer. W Cape.

W.meriana (L.) Mill.
50cm–2m, usually with several short branches. Lvs 4–6, to about half the height of plant, 1–3.5cm wide, lanceolate. Spike to 25-fld; fls irregular, orange, red, pink or purple, rarely yellow; basal part of tube 22–25mm, upper part 20–25mm, to 6mm wide, cylindrical, horizontal; tepals 21–26mm, the outer 3 to 12mm wide, the inner to 15mm; ovate, spreading. Spring. Cape winter rainfall area. 'Bulbilifera' (*W.bulbilifera* Mathews & L. Bol.): a large-fld form with axillary cormlets; naturalized in Australia, Mauritius and Réunion.

W.pillansii L. Bol. (*W.beatricis* Mathews & L. Bol.; *W.socium* Mathews & L. Bol.).
50–120cm, occasionally with 1–3 short, erect branches. Lvs 4–6, about half length of plant, 7–18mm wide. Spike 20–35-fld; fls somewhat irregular, orange or orange-red; basal part of tube 17–25mm, upper part 18–25mm, more or less cylindrical, 6mm wide; tepals 20–26mm, the outer to 12mm wide, inner to 15mm, spreading. Summer. S & E Cape, Natal, Transkei. Z7.

W.pyramidata (Andrews) Klatt. See *W.borbonica*.
W.roseo-alba (Jacq.) Ker-Gawl. See *W.humilis*.
W.socium Mathews & L. Bol. See *W.pillansii*.

W.spectabilis Schinz.
20–50cm, rarely branched. Lvs 3–5, almost as long as stem, 2–8mm wide, linear. Spike 2–5-fld, rarely to 10-fld; fls irregular, red or orange; basal part of tube 18–22mm long, hidden by bracts, upper part 20–25mm, abruptly widened to about 10mm diam., subcylindrical, horizontal; tepals 30–35×7–12mm, the upper 3 horizontal, hooded, the lower 3 recurved. Winter–spring. SW Cape.

W.stanfordiae L. Bol. See *W.fourcadei*.

W.stenosiphon L. Bol.
20–45cm, unbranched. Lvs 3–4, to about half height of plant, 5–12mm wide, linear or lanceolate. Spike several-fld; fls irregular, salmon-orange or mauve, the lower 3 tepals sometimes with a dark, median line; basal part of tube 14–18mm long, upper part 13–16mm long, cylindrical; tepals 17–20×9–13mm, lanceolate or obovate, spreading. Spring. S Cape coast.

W.strictiflora Ker-Gawl.
24–40cm, sometimes with 1–2 branches. Lvs 5–7, about half length of spike, about 1.5cm wide, lanceolate. Spike few to several-fld; fls somewhat irregular, pink with a dark red-purple streak near base of each tepal; basal part of tube 20–35mm, slender, upper part 8–14mm, funnel-shaped, not clearly separated from lower part; tepals 22–25×11–15mm, obovate, spreading. Late spring–early summer. SW Cape.

W.strubeniae L. Bol. (*W.alpina* G. Lewis).
60–100cm, with 3–5 somewhat spreading branches. Lvs 4–5, reaching base of spike, 1.5–2cm wide, lanceolate, the margins and midvein thickened. Main spike 25–35-fld, lateral spikes

with fewer; fls irregular, pale pink; basal part of tube 7–9mm, slender, mostly enclosed in bracts, upper part 6–7mm long, funnel-shaped, horizontal; tepals 17–19×5–6mm, projecting forwards, the tips somewhat reflexed. Late summer–autumn. E Transvaal.

W.tabularis Mathews & L. Bol.
Plants to 1.5m; corms to 6cm diam. Lvs several, sword-shaped, about half as long as stem, 2–3.5cm wide. Spike 20–30-fld; fls irregular, orange-red, or pink with the inner tepals paler; basal part of tube 20–25mm, upper part 20–25mm, more or less cylindrical; tepals semi-spreading, 20–26mm, broadly lanceolate, the outer 9–11mm wide, inner 14–17mm wide. Winter. Cape Peninsula and Cape flats.

W.transvaalensis Bak.
To 50cm high, rarely branched. Lvs 3–4, usually of similar length to stem, 8–25mm wide, lanceolate, the margins and mid-vein somewhat thickened. Spike 10–16-fld; fls irregular, deep pink; basal part of tube 10–12mm, very slender, upper part 7–10mm, funnel-shaped, horizontal; tepals 20–25×6–8mm, projecting forwards with the tips recurved, lanceolate, the inner wider than the outer. Late summer–autumn. NE Transvaal.

W.versfeldii Mathews & L. Bol.
1–2m, branched. Lvs 6–8, shorter than stem, 2.5–4cm wide, lanceolate. Main spike to 24-fld, side spikes to 10-fld; fls irregular, purple-pink; basal part of tube 15–22mm, upper part 20–30mm, more or less tubular or slightly flared, horizontal or drooping; tepals 33–46×10–15mm, lanceolate, acute, spreading. Spring. SW Cape.

W.wilmanii Mathews & L. Bol.
80–150cm, usually with a few short branches. Lvs 5–7, about half length of stem, 1.5–3cm wide, lanceolate. Spike densely to about 35-fld, lateral spikes to 12-fld; fls cream, pink, red, purple or orange; basal part of tube about 15mm, upper part 15–20mm, more or less cylindrical, horizontal; tepals 18–22×7–10mm, ovate, the topmost somewhat hooded, spreading. Late spring–summer. S Cape.

W.wilmsii L. Bol.
45–75cm, sometimes with 1–2 branches. Lvs 4–5, about half length of stem, 1–2.5cm wide, lanceolate. Spike to about 25-fld; fls deep pink, the lower tepals with a darker median line. Basal part of tube 25–30mm, slender, upper part about 15mm, funnel-shaped, horizontal; tepals 22–24×6–9mm, lanceolate, the inner slightly wider than outer, projecting forwards, the tips somewhat recurved. Summer–autumn. E Transvaal.

W.zeyheri L. Bol. (*W.comptonii* L. Bol.).
To 80cm tall but often less, unbranched or with 2–4 short branches. Lvs usually 4, about half as long as stem, 12–18mm wide, linear or lanceolate. Spike few to several-fld; fls irregular, salmon-orange, the basal part of tepals with a darker mid-line; tube rather long and slender; basal part 15–18mm, upper part 16–20mm, more or less cylindrical; tepals 20–22×8–11mm, lanceolate, inner slightly wider than outer, somewhat spreading. Spring–early summer. SW Cape.

W.cultivars. 'Dazzler': fls bright red. 'Malvern': fls large, clear orchid-pink. 'Mrs. Bullard's White': fls pure white. 'Rubra': fls deep crimson.

Watsonia (a) *W.aletroides* (b) *W.galpinii* (c) *W.pillansii* (d) *W.zeyheri* (e) *W.tabularis*

Whiteheadia Harv. (For the Rev. Henry Whitehead of South Africa, (mid-19th century).) Liliaceae (Hyacinthaceae). 1 species, a perennial herb, resembling *Massonia* in having 2 leaves which are opposite and prostrate, differing in the convex, overlapping leaf bases. Bulb 4–5cm, tunicated. Leaves to 30×20cm, 2, opposite, spreading, rounded-oblong, succulent, fragile, smooth. Flowers in a condensed terminal spike to 7.5–15×1.25cm; peduncle short, tapered; involucral bracts 2.5–4cm, exceeding flowers, persistent, ovate-acuminate; perianth persistent, green, segments 6, basally fused; stamens 6, filaments fused below forming a short, erect cup, anthers basifixed; ovary 3-locular, dark green; styles short, curved, tapered to apical stigma. Fruit an obtriangular capsule with 3 transparent wings; seeds black, shiny. S Africa (NW Cape), S Namibia. Z10.

CULTIVATION   A frost-tender, winter and early spring-flowering bulb that enters dormancy in mid to late summer, when it will require warm, dry conditions. Cultivate as for *Massonia*.

W.bifolia (Jacq.) Bak. (*Melanthium massoniifolium*).

Worsleya (Traub) Traub. (For Arthington Worsley (*d*1943), English botanist.) Amaryllidaceae. 1 species, an evergreen, bulbous, perennial to 2m. Bulbs to 15cm diam. at base, cylindric-pyriform, clothed in papery brown tunics, usually several clumped together and appearing stem-like due to thick, tapering, aerial necks to 1m, these formed from sheathing leaf bases. Leaves to 100×10cm, 12–14, strap-shaped, thick, glabrous, pale green to blue-green, 2-ranked, usually decurved-arching. Flowers 4–14 in a terminal umbel borne on a stout scape exceeding leaves; spathe valves 4; pedicels 8cm; perianth horizontal, lilac to heliotrope or opalescent blue; speckled mauve within, white at base, tube to 2cm, lobes to 15×2.5, curving, acute; stamens much shorter than lobes; style exceeding stamens, stigma obscurely 3-lobed. Fruit a capsule; seeds many, black. S Brazil. Z10.

CULTIVATION   *W.rayneri*, which occurs in sunny and exposed positions in the Organ mountains in southern Brazil, is a challenging species with a reputation of being short-lived and difficult to flower. It is, however, exceptionally handsome, with strongly arching evergreen leaves and umbels of large and beautiful lilac-blue flowers. Grow in the warm glasshouse (minimum 15°C/60°F), in well-crocked pots of a loam-based mix, with additional parts of leafmould, and bark chips/perlite, and some charcoal. Water plentifully when in growth; reduce water during the winter months but never allow shrivelling of leaves. The Blue Amaryllis strongly resents disturbance and grows best if allowed to make untidy stands of crowded pseudostems. Propagate by detaching offsets.

W.rayneri (Hook.) Traub & Mold. (*Amaryllis rayneri* Hook.;
Amaryllis procera Duchartre; *Hippeastrum procerum*
(Duchartre) Lem.). BLUE AMARYLLIS.

Wurmbea Thunb. (For F. van Wurmb, Secretary of the Batavian Academy of Sciences, *c*1800.) Liliaceae (Colchicaceae). 37 species of perennial herbs. Corms tunicated, with a long neck, each bearing a single stem. Leaves 3–4, cauline, alternate, 2-ranked, loosely sheathing, lanceolate, conduplicate, recurved. Flowers crowded or distant in a short-stalked, ebracteate spike; perianth 6-lobed, united below into a short tube, lobes long and spreading, each bearing a dark glandular nectary in the form of a tuck or lamella at its base; stamens 6, borne on perianth lobes, filament base just below nectary, anthers ovate; styles 3, free, rigid, spreading. Fruit a 3-valved capsule. S Africa, Australia. Z10.

CULTIVATION   Frost-tender bulbs, grown for the short densely flowered spikes of bloom in late winter or early spring; they need deep soils, kept moderately moist when in growth, with a period of dry dormancy in late summer or autumn. Cultivate as for *Androcymbium*.

W.capensis Thunb.
Corm ovoid, tunic brown. Lvs 7.5–22cm. Flowering stem 15–30cm; fls *c*1.5cm in spikes to 10cm, lobes pale with purple margin to entirely dark purple with black glands near base; anth. yellow. S Africa. A variable species that may include *W.spicata* (Burm.) Dur. & Schinz and *W.campanulata* Willd.

W.dioica R. Br. EARLY NANCY.
Lvs 3, well-separated, broadly amplexicaul at base, tapering upwards. Flowering stem to 30cm; fls 1–11, to 11mm; lobes usually white with lilac gland; anth. red or purple. Australia.

Xanthosoma Schott. (Name Gk *xanthos*, yellow, and *soma*, body, referring to yellow inner tissue of some species.) YAUTIA; TANNIA; MALANGA. Araceae. 45–50 species of tuberous or caulescent perennial herbs. Tubers cylindric to spherical, starchy, white to orange to purple within, edible; stems stout, 1m high, sometimes pubescent or bulbiferous; sap milky. Leaves to 2m, entire, sagittate to hastate, or pedate with 3–18 segments, somewhat fleshy, dark green above, often glaucous beneath; main veins pinnate, minor veins reticulate; petiole long, to 2m, sheathed. Peduncle shorter than petioles, solitary or several; spathe to 30cm, margins overlapping to form persistent tube below, limb expanded above constricted throat of tube, cymbiform, rapidly deciduous, yellowgreen to white within, usually green externally; spadix shorter than spathe, covered with unisexual flowers, male and female zones separated by zone of sterile flowers, male zone twice as long as female, flowers often of different colours; perianth absent; stamens 4–6, connate; ovary with 2–4-locules, ovules numerous. Tropical America. Very close to *Caladium*, differing only in pollen shed in tetrads rather than monads. Z10.

CULTIVATION *Xanthosoma* spp. are grown in temperate climates primarily as glasshouse ornamentals, for their handsome foliage and sometimes for their fruitily scented inflorescences. *X.violaceum*, the Blue Tannia, is an exceptional foliage plant for the warm glasshouse and conservatory, or for favoured, humid and shady positions in the home. It produces large, arrow-shaped leaves in a shade of inky violet. *X.sagittifolium*, tannia, is an important food crop; the edible lateral cormels are a staple carbohydrate throughout the tropics, particularly in the Caribbean, Central and South America, West Africa and tropical Asia. The cormels are eaten grilled, fried, puréed in soups, and barbecued whole (the skin is best avoided), the young leaves and shoots are valued as a boiled vegetable.

In tropical zones with a rainfall of about 1000–1500mm/40–60in. p.a., grow in a well-drained, fertile soil rich in organic matter, pH 5.5—6.5, avoiding heavy clay in higher rainfall areas as *Xanthosoma* is sensitive to waterlogging. Plant small corms 3–5cm/1.5–2in. deep, at 75–90cm/30–36in. spacings on mounds or ridges 100–120cm/40–48in. apart. (In many areas, the tops of young plants are removed and inserted as cuttings.) Apply a balanced NPK fertilizer before planting with occasional topdressings when in growth. Earth up and mulch with organic matter, particularly during drier weather. Cormels will normally mature 240–350 days from planting and successional harvesting may continue for a further 150 days or more, (leave the main corm undisturbed during this period); yields of up to 2kg/m² may be obtained. In temperate climates, cultivate as for *Colocasia*.

X.atrovirens K. Koch. See *X.sagittifolium*.
X.barilletii Carr. See *X.hoffmannii*.
X.belophyllum Kunth. See *X.sagittifolium*.

X.brasiliense (Desf.) Engl. (*X.hastifolium* K. Koch).
Tubers small. Lvs 40×15cm, ovate-sagittate when plant young, hastate when adult, basal lobes spreading, oblong, with main veins naked in sinus; petiole to 40cm, sheathing to less than one-third length. Spathe tube to 5cm, oblong-ovoid, limb to 12cm, oblong-lanceolate, yellow-green; spadix with female fls yellow, sterile fls pink, male fls white. Neotropics, original range unknown, widely cult. for lvs.

X.hastifolium K. Koch. See *X.brasiliense*.

X.helleborifolium (Jacq.) Schott.
Tuberous. Lvs reniform in outline, deeply pedatisect, seg. 5–18, oblong to lanceolate, median seg. to 36×9cm; petiole to 85cm, mottled purple and green, sheath broad. Spathe tube to 6cm, elliptic-ovoid, limb oblong-ovate, to 10cm, yellowgreen to white; spadix stipitate. C America to Peru and Guianas, Caribbean Is.

X.hoffmannii Schott (*X.barilletii* Carr.).
Tuberous or with very short stem. Lvs reniform in outline, deeply pedatisect, segments to 50×53cm, 5–9, ovate, acuminate; petiole to 1m, sometimes stained purple at base, sheath broad. Spathe tube to 7cm, oblong, green externally, limb to 12cm, lanceolate, acuminate, white; spadix shortly stipitate. C America (Mexico to Costa Rica), Surinam.

X.holtonianum Schott. See *X.pilosum*.
X.jacquinii Schott. See *X.undipes*.
X.lindenii (André) Engl. See *Caladium lindenii*.
X.mafaffa Schott. See *X.sagittifolium*.

X.pilosum K. Koch & Augustin (*X.holtonianum* Schott).
Tuberous, pubesc. in most parts. Lvs 35×20cm, sagittateovate to cordate-ovate, green, often spotted white; petiole to 40cm, sheathed to more than half length. Spathe tube to 7cm, oblong, green, limb to 10cm, oblong-lanceolate, white; sterile fls violet. Costa Rica to Colombia.

X.sagittifolium (L.) Schott (*X.atrovirens* K. Koch; *X.belophyllum* Kunth; *X.mafaffa* Schott). TANNIA.
Very variable, with many regional cvs bearing specific names. Stems to 1m+, increasing with age, fleshy, edible. Lvs to 90cm, broad-sagittate-ovate, median lobe semi-ovate, acuminate, much larger than spreading, broad basal lobes, glaucous above when young, main lateral veins 8–9 per side, marginal vein conspicuous; petiole to 1m, glaucous. Spathe tube to 7cm, oblong ovoid, green, limb to 15cm, acuminate, green-white; spadix white. Neotropics; natural range unknown, widely cult. in Americas and Africa. 'Albomarginatum': dense; lvs broadly sagittate, tinted blue, veins off-white, edged white. 'Albomarginatum Monstrosum': vigorous; lvs small, divided into lobes, variegated green, white, gold and yellow.

X.undipes (K. Koch) K. Koch (*X.jacquinii* Schott).
Stem to 200×20cm. Lvs 50–200cm, broadly cordate-sagittate, veins naked in sinus for 1–5cm; petiole to 1m, sheath undulate, green. Spathe tube to 7cm, ovoid, green externally, yellow-green within, limb to 25cm, yellow-green externally, cream within; spadix with female fls orange, sterile fls white, male fls yellow. Mexico to Peru, cult. in Caribbean.

X.violaceum Schott. BLUE TANNIA; BLUE TARO.
Tubers large, pink within, edible. Lvs to 70×45cm, oblongovate, sagittate, short-acuminate, basal lobes subtriangular, glaucous when young, margin, veins and interstitial areas of blade suffused deep, bloomy violet-purple to near-black, especially beneath; petiole to 30–200cm, glaucous, dark brown-purple. Spathe tube to 10cm, oblong, green-violet externally, cream within, limb to 20cm, sulphur-white; spadix with sterile fls violet to red-brown, others white. Neotropics, natural range unknown, widely cult. and naturalized.

X.cultivars. 'Maculatum': lvs broadly sagittate, to 30cm, pale green splashed white.

Zantedeschia Spreng. (Richardia Kunth). (For Giovanni Zantedeschi (1773–1846), Italian botanist and physician.) ARUM LILY; CALLA LILY. Araceae. 6 species of rhizomatous perennial herbs to 2.5m. Rhizomes subterranean, fleshy, tuber-like, oblique, much branched. Leaves to 45cm+, borne from apex of rhizome, deciduous or evergreen, lanceolate to orbicular, base cuneate or truncate, or hastate, sagittate to cordate, apex acute or obtuse with subulate tip, usually dark green, spotted or unspotted, margin undulate, main lateral veins united with marginal vein, minor veins reticular; petioles spongy, long, often exceeding length of lamina, sheathed at base. Peduncle long, often much exceeding foliage; spathe subcylindric to funnel-shaped, convolute at base, apex often recurved, to 25cm, ivory-white, cream, yellow, to pink or rosy-purple, sometimes with a purple blotch at base within, persistent; spadix sessile to stipitate, much shorter than spathe, usually yellow, flowers unisexual, male and female zones adjacent, male much longer than female zone; perianth absent; male flowers not individually distinct; female flowers with or without staminodes, ovary 3-locular, ovules 1–8. Fruit a green to orange-red, beaked berry. Seed leathery, subglobose to ovoid, often compressed. Southern Africa (Cape Province to Angola, Malawi), some widely naturalized elsewhere. Z9 unless specified.

CULTIVATION *Z.rehmannii* occurs in shaded rocky habitats, in damp grassland and at woodland edge, *Z.pentlandii* is found on rocky hillsides. *Z.aethiopica* is a wetland species, occurring as a roadside wildflower in its native zones and widely naturalized in subtropical regions; in habitat it is sometimes found in natural association with *Hyperolius horstockii*, a small frog with the chameleon-like ability to change its colour according to its position on the plant. In recent years, cultivars with spathes in rich tones of pink, ruby, mauve, green and yellow have enjoyed popularity as pot plants and cut blooms.

Zantedeschia spp. are suitable for containers and borders in the cool to intermediate glasshouse or conservatory, and as cut flowers; *Z.aethiopica* is also useful as a focal specimen in tubs, the cool, moist, shaded border, in the bog garden and as a marginal aquatic, in up to 1m/*c*3ft of water. Most species tolerate temperatures down to about –4°C/25°F for short periods, *Z.aethiopica* is hardy to between –7 and –10°C/19–14°F, but some forms like 'Crowborough' are hardier still and plants grown as aquatics will also survive lower temperatures provided the crown is under a protective layer of ice in a sheltered pond.

Grow in moist fertile soils, rich in organic matter, in full sun or in shade, especially in drier conditions. When grown as a semi-aquatic, *Z.aethiopica* is best introduced gradually to the required depth as growth progresses. Under glass, use a high-fertility, loam-based mix, setting 'tubers' upright with the tips just at or below the medium's surface, watering sparingly as growth begins then increasing to plentiful watering in full growth, with a weekly liquid feed as roots fill the pot. With the possible exception of *Z.aethiopica*, which at suitable temperatures may be grown without a resting period, gradually withhold water from midsummer. Where winter blooms are required, *Z.aethiopica* may also benefit from enforced rest. Maintain a winter minimum temperature of 7–10°C/40–50°F for *Z.rehmannii*, 10–12°C/50–55°F for other spp.; at these higher temperatures *Z.aethiopica* can be forced for early flowers. Propagate by careful removal of suckers in spring, or by seed, pre-soaked in warm water for 24 hours and germinate at 21–27°C/70–80°F.

A leaf spot fungus, *Phyllosticta richardiae*, causes grey-black blotches on leaves, leaf stalks and spathes – remove and destroy affected parts. Cucumber mosaic virus causes irregular mottling and streaking of the foliage, tomato spotted wilt virus causes white spots and streaks on foliage and stem blotches, sometimes with distortion of the foliage; destroy affected plants and control sap-sucking vectors in spring. Also affected by a bacterial soft rot of the tubers, *Bacterium aroidae*; cut away affected parts and dust with fungicide. *Phytopthora* spp. also cause root rot, leading to browning of leaves, spathe tips and margins.

Z.aethiopica (L.) Spreng. (*Calla aethiopica* L.; *Richardia africana* Kunth).
To 250cm in shade. Lvs 45×20cm, evergreen, or deciduous in cold places, broadly ovate-cordate or hastate, coriaceous, deep green, unspotted, basal lobes broad, obtuse, somewhat upturned; petiole to 75cm+, stout, green, winged at base. Peduncle exceeding foliage, green; spathe to 25cm, rhombic-ovate, apex cuspidate, white, except base and apex tinged green externally; spadix sessile, to 9cm, pale yellow; staminodes present, conspicuous, yellow. Berries to 12mm across, orange when ripe. S Africa (Cape Province, Natal, Transvaal), Lesotho, widely naturalized in tropical and temperate regions. 'Crowborough': to 90cm; spathe large, white; selected for cold-hardiness, otherwise more or less identical to type; fully hardy when established. 'Green Goddess': to 90cm; lvs dull green; spathe large, stained green, centre mottled white. 'Little Gem': habit dwarf, to 45cm; free-flowering. 'White Sail': to 90cm; spathe very open. Z8.

Z.albomaculata (Hook.) Baill. (*Z.oculata* (Lindl.) Engl.; *Z.hastata* Engl.; *Z.melanoleuca* Engl.).
To 125cm. Lvs to 40×25cm, deciduous, oblong- to triangular- to orbicular-hastate, basal lobes short and rounded to elongate-triangular, green with white translucent spots or unspotted; petiole long, sometimes marked with purple, sometimes pubesc. at base (also in peduncle). Peduncle exceeding lvs; spathe 2.5–11.5cm, white to ivory to cream to pale yellow, occasionally coral-pink, green at base externally, blotched dark purple at base within, tube sometimes opening to base, usually convolute; spadix sessile or stipitate; staminodes absent. S Africa, Tropical E Africa. ssp. **albomaculata**. Lvs seldom unspotted. ssp. **macrocarpa** Engl. Lvs sometimes unspotted. ssp. **valida** Letty. Lvs always unspotted, ovate-cordate. Spathe to 15cm, often open.

Z.elliotiana (Wats.) Engl. (*Richardia elliotiana* Wats.).
To 150cm. Lvs to 28×25cm, deciduous, orbicular-ovate, base deeply cordate, apex apiculate, green with many translucent white spots; petiole longer than lamina. Spathe to 15cm, funnel-shaped above, campanulate beneath, apex caudate, golden yellow, duller externally. Spadix to 7cm, yellow; staminodes absent. Not known in wild, possibly of hybrid origin.

Z.jucunda Letty.
To 60cm. Lvs 17–30×5–15cm, deciduous, triangular-hastate, apex acute, with many elongated white, translucent spots, somewhat folded along midrib, spreading upwards; petiole 10–30cm. Spathe 10–16cm, tube cup-shaped, limb spreading, slightly recurved, tapering to subulate apex, golden-yellow with purple blotch at base within, deep yellow externally; spadix to 4cm. S Africa (Lulu Mts, Sekhuniland).

Z.melanoleuca Engl. See *Z.albomaculata*.
Z.oculata (Lindl.) Engl. See *Z.albomaculata*.

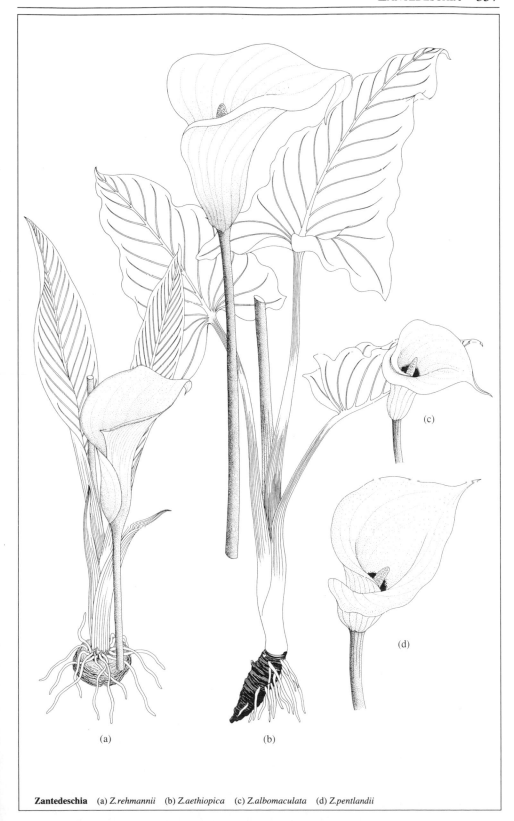

(a)   (b)

(c)

(d)

Zantedeschia   (a) *Z.rehmannii*   (b) *Z.aethiopica*   (c) *Z.albomaculata*   (d) *Z.pentlandii*

Z.pentlandii (Wats.) Wittm. (*Richardia pentlandii* Wats.; *Z.sprengeri* (Burtt) Davy).
To 60cm. Lvs 35×15cm, oblong-elliptic to oblong-lanceolate, base hastate, apex obtuse to acute, abruptly apiculate, yellow-grass-green, usually unspotted; petioles to 30cm. Spathe to 13cm, funnel-shaped, apiculus to 2cm, lemon- to chrome-yellow, with dark purple blotch at base within; spadix stipitate, 6cm. S Africa (Transvaal).

Z.rehmannii Engl. (*Richardia rehmannii* (Engl.) N.E. Br. ex W. Harrow).
To 80cm. Lvs 15–40×2–7cm, deciduous, lanceolate, apex acuminate, base cuneate, dark green, unspotted; petioles to 20cm. Peduncle channelled, expanding and arching to ground in fruit; spathe to 12×2cm, convolute for two-thirds length, forming narrow tube, slightly spreading above, apex tapering, white or pink to very dark maroon; spadix stipitate, to 6cm;

staminodes absent. S Africa (Transvaal, Natal) Swaziland.

Z.sprengeri (Davy) Davy. See *Z.pentlandii*.

Z.cultivars. 'Apple Court': habit dwarf; spathe white. 'Aztec Gold': spathe bright orange to red. 'Best Gold': spathe large, gold. 'Black Magic': spathe yellow, throat black. 'Black-eyed Beauty': spathe cream, throat black. 'Bridal Blush': spathe cream washed pink. 'Cameo': spathe peach, throat black. 'Carmine Red': spathe deep carmine. 'Dusky Pink': spathe light pink. 'Giant White': spathe white, spathes to ×18cm. 'Golden Affair': spathe bright gold. 'Harvest Moon': spathe pale lemon. 'Lady Luck': spathe rich yellow faintly washed orange. 'Lavender Petite': spathe plum edged fading to blush pink centre. 'Majestic Red': spathe strong crimson red. 'Maroon Dainty': spathe plum, throat paler.

Zephyranthes Herb. ZEPHYR FLOWER; FAIRY LILY; RAIN LILY. (From Gk *zephyros*, the west wind, and *anthos*, flower, in reference to the origin of the genus in the western hemisphere.) Amaryllidaceae. 71 species of bulbous perennial herbs, deciduous or evergreen. Leaves narrow, linear, strap- or grass-like, appearing with flowers. Flowers solitary, scapose, subtended by membranous, tubular spathe, bifid at the apex; perianth erect, or slightly inclined, white, red, pink or yellow, funnel-shaped with 6 subequal lobes, sometimes with scales in throat of tube; stamens 6, 3 long and 3 short, inserted in mouth of tube; ovary 3-celled. Fruit a globose capsule; seeds black. Americas.

CULTIVATION Predominantly frost-tender bulbs grown for their upturned crocus-like flowers carried singly at the top of the stems, which usually appear before the leaves. The spring-flowering *Z.atamasca*, from damp woodland clearings in the southeastern US, and *Z.candida*, from the marshlands of the Rio de la Plata in Argentina and flowering in autumn, are the most suitable for outdoor cultivation in temperate gardens; both are frost-tolerant to about –5°C/23°F. *Z.rosea* and *Z.grandiflora* are sometimes grown outside in milder regions or, in cooler zones, lifted in autumn and stored in cool dry conditions over winter. These and other almost hardy species, such as *Z.mesochloa*, *Z.pulchella* and *Z.treatiae*, are also amenable to pot cultivation in the cold glasshouse, and all flower better when slightly pot-bound. The remaining species are more tender and are best cultivated in the intermediate glasshouse, minimum 12°C/54°F. Grow out of doors in a warm, sheltered situation in full sun, in a free-draining but moisture-retentive soil, incorporating leafmould or well-rotted manure and grit if necessary before planting the bulbs about 10cm/4in. deep. Apply an organic mulch after flowering. Ensure that plants have plentiful moisture when in growth, but protect from excessive winter wet with a propped frame light or open cloche if necessary.

Under glass, plant in well-crocked pans in a mix of equal parts loam, leafmould and sharp sand; keep just moist until growth begins and then water plentifully until the leaves begin to fade as the plants enter dormancy. Keep dry but not arid during rest. As with most Amaryllids, an annual topdressing of fresh potting mix is to be preferred to re-potting. Propagate by offsets, or from seed which is freely produced.

Z.andersonii (Herb.) Bak. See *Habranthus tubispathus*.

Z.atamasca (L.) Herb. (*Amaryllis atamasca* L.). ATAMASCO LILY.
Bulb ovoid-oblong, to 2.5cm diam., short-necked. Lvs to 40×5cm, 4–6, light green, channelled, glossy, margins acute. Scape to 30cm; spathe erect, to 2.5cm; pedicel to 1.5cm; fl. to 8×8cm, pure white or tinged purple, funnel-shaped, lobes acute; stamens erect to spreading, much shorter than the limb; style declinate. Seeds round, black. SE US (Virginia to Florida and Alabama). Z8.

Z.aurea Benth. & Hook. f. See *Pyrolirion aureum*.

Z.beustii Schinz. See *Z.flava*.

Z.bifolia (Aubl.) M. Roem. (*Z.cardinalis* C.H. Wright; *Habranthus cardinalis* (C.H. Wright) Sealy).
Bulb to 3.5×4cm, neck 3–12cm, dark. Lvs 1–3, linear, 11–35×0.5cm, curved, tapering to apex. Scape subterete or flattened, pink below green-pink above, to 8cm; spathe membranous, 2.5cm; pedicel 2.5cm; fl. declinate, broadly funnel-shaped, 6.5cm long, cardinal red, green in throat; perianth tube 1.6cm, green, seg. to 4.5×2cm; stamens declinate, much shorter than perianth, exceeded by style, stigma 3-fid, lobes broad. Hispaniola. Z10.

Z.brasiliensis (Traub) Traub. See *Z.drummondii*.

Z.brazosensis Traub (*Cooperia drummondii* Herb.).
Bulb ovoid. Lvs to 33×0.2cm, channelled, twisted, flaccid, bright green, tinged red at base. Scape 11cm, green; spathe 1-valved, cylindric; fls sessile; perianth tube to 11cm, erect, cylindric, red with longitudinal stripes, lobes to 1cm, spreading, white with red stripes outside, the 3 outer lobes acute, the inner 3 narrower and obtuse; anth. 6mm, sessile, on mouth of tube; style shorter than anth; stigma 3-lobed. S US (Texas). Z9.

Z.candida (Lindl.) Herb. (*Argyropsis candida* (Lindl.) Roem.).
Bulb to 2.5cm diam. Lvs to 30×0.3mm, evergreen, erect, slightly fleshy. Scape to 25cm; spathe to 2.5cm, cylindric below, not divided; pedicel 1.5cm; fls to 5cm, pure white or slightly rose-tinged outside, green at the base, closing in the evening or in shade; perianth tube absent, lobes to 1.3cm broad, spreading; style equalling the stamens; stigma capitate or obscurely 3-lobed. Argentina and Uruguay (marshes of La Plata river). 'Major': fls large. Z9.

Z.cardinalis C.H. Wright. See *Z.bifolia*.

Z.carinata Herb. See *Z.grandiflora*.

Z.citrina Bak.
Bulb to 3.5cm diam., globose, stoloniferous, tunics membranous, brown. Lvs to 30×0.4cm, 3 or 4, bright green, chan-

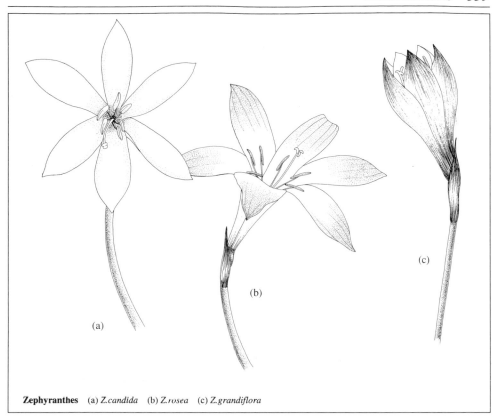

Zephyranthes   (a) *Z.candida*   (b) *Z.rosea*   (c) *Z.grandiflora*

nelled on the upper surface, tinged red-brown near base. Scape to 13cm, 2-edged, green tinged red-brown near base; spathe short, tubular; pedicel 2.5cm; perianth tube to 1.2cm, funnel-shaped, lobes to 3.5×1.2cm, oblong, subacute, connivent, bright yellow; stamens same colour as limb, fil. to 2.5cm, erect, equal; style 2.5cm, with 3 distinct rounded stigma lobes. Tropical America. 'Ajax' (*Z.citrina* × *Z.candida*): small; lvs erect, narrow, dark green, to 25cm; fls to ×5cm, dark cream to yellow, anthers yellow, solitary. Z10.

Z.concolor (Lindl.) Benth. & Hook. f. See *Habranthus concolor*.

Z.cubensis Urban. See *Z.wrightii*.

Z.drummondii D. Don (*Cooperia pedunculata* Herb.; *Z.brasiliensis* (Traub.) Traub.).
Bulb flattened-globose, deeply seated in ground. Lvs linear, to 6mm wide, twisted, prostrate, glaucous-green. Scape 12.5–20cm; fl to 7.5cm long, white, tinged red externally, fragrant, opening at night; perianth tube to 3.5cm. Texas, Mexico. Z7.

Z.eggersiana Urban. See *Z.citrina*.

Z.flava (Herb.) Bak. (*Pyrolirion flavum* Herb.; *Z.beustii* Schinz; *Pyrolirion aureum* Edwards).
Bulb to 2.5cm diam., subrotund, light brown. Lvs 1 or 2, dark green, channelled, with a narrow recurved apex. Scape to 30cm+, terete, exceeding lvs; fls to 10cm, yellow, sessile in the membranous spathe; perianth tube funnel-shaped, without scale inside, lobes lanceolate, acute, spreading; fil. inserted in neck of tube; style linear; stigma with 3 dilated minutely papillose lobes. Peru. Z10.

Z.gracilifolius (Herb.) Bak. See *Habranthus gracilifolius*.

Z.grandiflora Lindl. (*Z.carinata* Herb.; *Z.tsouii* Hu).
Bulb to 2cm diam., dark brown. Lvs to 30cm, 3, erect, acute, bright green, tinged red at base. Scape to 30cm, smooth,

bright green, coloured red at base; spathe shorter than pedicel, spreading; pedicel nearly erect, to 3.5cm; perianth to 8cm, funnel-shaped, bright pink with a white throat, tube pale green below, lobes ovate, subequal, opening nearly flat in sunshine; stamens much shorter than perianth, spreading; style filiform, clavate above, exceeding stamens but shorter than perianth. Mexico. 9.

Z.insularum Hume.
Bulb to 2.5×2.7cm, subglobose, dark brown, neck to 7cm. Lvs to 21×0.7cm, suberect becoming declinate, bright green, brown near the base, striate beneath, slightly keeled. Scape to 15cm, 1 or more, green, pink-brown towards the base; spathe 2cm, membranous, light green, tip bifid; pedicel light green, to 3cm; fls declinate, funnel-shaped, white, flushed pink outside and green at the base; to 4mm, perianth tube light green, outer lobes to 2×3.8cm, flushed pink along the centre and towards the tip outside, inner 3 slightly smaller; stamens shorter than the perianth, fil. green below, white above; style exceeding fil.; stigma trifid, to 4.5mm diam. Cult. in Florida and Cuba; origin not known. Z9.

Z.jonesii (Cory) Traub (*Cooperia jonesii* Cory).
Bulb to 3cm diam., subglobose, the base usually seated about 7.5cm below ground. Lvs to 35×3cm, slightly glaucous green, obtuse. Scape to 30cm; spathe to 4cm; perianth tube to 5.5cm, upper part pale white-green, lower part greener and tinged rose, lobes to 4cm, yellow, oblanceolate to oval; style white, to 7.5cm; stigma exceeding stamens by up to 5mm; ovary slightly or not at all stipitate. S US (Texas). Z9.

Z.lindleyana Herb.
Bulb to 1.8cm diam., globose, short-necked. Lvs to 50×0.3cm, linear, spreading. Scape to 15cm; spathe 3-fid only at the tip, to 3cm; pedicel equalling spathe; fls to 5cm, rose; lobes to 1.2cm wide; style shorter than stamens; stigma trifid; ovary stalked. Mexico (mts). Z9.

Z.longifolia Hemsl.
Bulb ovoid, neck to 5cm. Lvs to 30cm, narrow-linear. Scape to 15cm; spathe tubular in lower half, apex with 2 teeth; pedicel much shorter than spathe; fls to 2.5cm, yellow, coppery outside; perianth lobes free to the base, to 1cm wide; style not exceeding stamens; stigma trifid. Texas to New Mexico. Z8.

Z.longipes Bak. See *Habranthus longipes.*

Z.macrosiphon Bak.
Bulb 2.5cm diam., ovoid, with brown membranous tunics forming a neck. Lvs to 30×3cm, 3–4, bright green, fleshy. Scape terete, equalling lvs; spathe 2-valved, to 3.5cm; pedicel 2.5cm; perianth funnel-shaped, bright rose-red, to 6cm, lobes suberect, equalling tube, to 2.5cm wide; stamens shorter than the perianth; style reaching the base of the anth.; lobes of stigma spreading, suborbicular. Mexico. Z10.

Z.mesochloa Herb.
Bulb obovoid, black. Lvs 0.6cm wide, 8 or 9, channelled, acute. Scape 18cm, thickening at the base and becoming longer and red-speckled as the fruit ripens; spathe slightly exceeding pedicel, either looped at the end or bifid; pedicel 2.5cm; fls to 4.2cm, the lower half of tube green, the upper half white, stained red outside, mouth of tube smooth, outer lobes 1.2cm wide, the inner 3 narrower; outer fil. nearly equalling style; inner shorter; style 2.5cm shorter than the limb; stigma white, deeply 3-lobed. Argentina. Z9.

Z.plumieri Hume. See *Habranthus plumieri.*
Z.pseudocolchicum Kränzl. See *Z.pusilla.*

Z.pulchella J.G. Sm.
Bulb to 2cm diam., globose, dark brown, neck to 4cm. Lvs to 25×0.2cm, 3 or 4. Scape to 20cm; spathe to 2.5cm, slightly exceeding pedicel; fls erect, 2cm; perianth tube 5mm, lobes oblanceolate, acute, bright yellow; stamens inserted into throat, half as long as the perianth lobes; style equalling stamens; stigma capitate, 3-lobed. S US (Texas). Z9.

Z.pusilla (Herb.) Dietr. (*Haylockia pusilla* Herb.; *Z.pseudocolchicum* Kränzl.).
Bulb subglobose, to 2cm diam., pseudostem 4–8cm, brown. Lvs hysteranthous, linear, 7–15×1–2.2mm, channelled, dark green. Scape subterranean at anthesis, compressed; spathe subterranean or half-emergent above soil, 2.5–3.5cm, hyaline with brown veins; perianth tube 3.1–4.2cm, seg. oblanceolate, shortly connate at base, to 3cm, yellow. S Brazil, Uruguay, Argentina. Z9.

Z.robusta (Herb.) Bak. See *Habranthus robustus.*

Z.rosea Lindl.
Bulb to 1.8cm diam., globose, with hardly any neck. Lvs to 15×6cm, 4 per bulb, glabrous, striate, bright green. Scape to 15cm, compressed, glabrous, green; spathe glabrous, to 1.8cm, bifid at the tip; pedicel exceeding spathe; perianth rose, infundibuliform, to 3cm diam., tube 0.5cm, lower half of lobes green; stigma with 3 spreading lobes. Cuba. Z10.

Z.smallii (Alexander) Traub (*Cooperia smallii* Alexander).
Bulb 2.5cm diam., obovoid, tunics brown. Lvs to 15×0.3cm,

bright green, channelled above, ribbed beneath, acute. Scape to 20cm, erect, slightly flattened, bright green; spathe membranous, green-brown, 3.8cm; pedicel to 6mm; tube 1.8cm, abruptly widening, green, lobes lemon yellow, ovate, the outer 3 often red-tinged with a green rib near the apex and a short green apiculate hood, spreading to 2cm diam.; stamens erect, fil. to 0.5cm, green, fleshy, exceeding the stigma; style 2.5cm, green, with white apex; ovary markedly stipitate. Capsule strongly 3-lobed, 1.8cm; seeds black, thin. S US (Texas). Z9.

Z.striata Herb. See *Z.verecunda.*
Z.texana Herb. See *Habranthus tubispathus.*
Z.timida Holmb. See *Z.traubii.*

Z.traubii (Hayward) Mold. (*Z.timida* Holmb.; *Cooperia traubii* Hayward).
Bulb to 2.5×1.25cm, oblong-ovoid, with dark tunics, neck to 1.5cm. Lvs to 13×0.2cm, 3, green, channelled above, slightly keeled beneath. Scape to 14cm, compressed, green, paler at the base; spathe to 3.5cm, off-white, dotted and lined with rose; pedicel 3.5cm, pale green; perianth tube short, lobes to 4×0.6cm, acute, lanceolate-oblong, the inner ones slightly shorter, interior white, outside with a pale rose band and green veins; fil. to 16mm, green; style to 17mm, trifid, pale green. Argentina. Z7.

Z.treatiae S. Wats.
Lvs to 30×0.2cm, thick, semi-terete, deep green, matt, with rounded margins and a blunt apex. Scape to 25cm; spathe to 3.5cm; pedicel absent or to 1cm; perianth to 10cm, white becoming pink with age, lobes to 2cm broad, keels sometimes rose; style exceeding stamens; stigma trifid; ovary stalked. SE US (Florida, Georgia). Z8.

Z.tsouii Hu. See *Z.grandiflora.*
Z.tubiflora Schinz. See *Pyrolirion aureum.*
Z.tubispatha Herb. See *Habranthus tubispathus.*

Z.verecunda Herb. (*Z.striata* Herb.).
Bulb to 2.5cm diam., dark brown, neck to 5cm. Lvs to 30×0.6cm, glabrous, purple-tinged below. Scape to 12cm; spathe to 2.5cm, bifid at the apex; fls to 5cm, sessile; perianth tube to 1.5cm, green, lobes 2.5cm, white, becoming pale pink, green at the base; style to half length of lobes, white, decurrent, erect; anth. yellow. Mexico. Z10.

Z.versicolor Bak. See *Habranthus versicolor.*

Z.wrightii Bak. (*Z.cubensis* Urban).
Bulb to 2×1.8cm, subglobose, dark brown, neck to 4cm. Lvs to 25×0.4cm, green, linear, tapering, erect. Scape to 30cm, terete, green; spathe to 2.8cm, membranous, pale pink, tips bifid; pedicel to 4.5cm; fls erect, to 6cm; perianth tube to 4mm, pink, lobes to 5.5×0.12cm, elliptic-ovate, pink, the inner ones slightly smaller than the outer; stamens much shorter than perianth lobes, fil. white; stigmas trifid, white, recurved; ovary ovoid, to 5×6mm. Cuba. Z10.

Zigadenus Michx. (From Gk *zygon*, yoke, and *aden*, gland; the glands are sometimes in pairs at the base of the sepals.) DEATH CAMAS; ZYGADENE. Liliaceae (Melanthiaceae). 18 species of bulbous or rhizomatous perennial herbs. Stems erect, simple, with or without a few small leaves. Leaves mostly basal, long-linear, glabrous. Flowers in terminal panicles or racemes, green-white to yellow-white; tepals 6, persistent, free, spreading, ovate to lanceolate, each with 1–2 green glands near base; stamens 6, nearly equalling tepals; ovary superior or partly inferior, 3-celled; styles 3, persistent. Fruit a 3-lobed, septicidal capsule. Summer. N America, N Asia (1 species).

CULTIVATION   *Zigadenus* spp. contain highly toxic steroidal alkaloids which cause vomiting, respiratory difficulty and coma if ingested; they are fatal to livestock and should not be grown near herbivorous animals. That said, these summer-flowering bulbs with attractive foliage and spikes of small star shaped flowers, are well suited to moist shaded borders, to the wild and woodland garden and to native plant collections. Plants are dormant in winter and cold-tolerant to at least –15°C/5°F. Grow in partial shade in deep, humus-rich, moisture-retentive soils, with plentiful moisture in spring and summer when in full growth. *Z.paniculatus* and *Z.fremontii* tolerate drier soils in sun. Propagate by division or seed when ripe or in spring.

Z.elegans Pursh (*Anticlea elegans* (Pursh) Rydb.). WHITE CAMAS; ALKALI GRASS. Bulbous.
Stems to 90cm. Lvs to 30×1cm, mostly basal, or a few, reduced on stems, keeled beneath, semi-rigid, grey-green, closely veined. Infl. a loose raceme, sometimes branched at base; tepals 8–12mm, green-white above, green beneath, gland near base or each tepal solitary, cordate to strongly 2-lobed. Fr. conical, 2× length of perianth. Western N America (Minnesota west to Alaska and Arizona). Z3.

Z.fremontii (Torr.) S. Wats. STAR ZYGADENE; STAR LILY.
Bulbous. Stems to 90cm. Basal lvs to 60×7.5cm, margins scabrid, apex pungent, stem lvs few. Infl. a panicle or raceme, often corymbose, the lower pedicels much longer than the upper; tepals 1–1.6cm, off-white to ivory margins toothed toward apex; stamens half length of tepals, ovary superior. Fr. 1.5–3cm, oblong. Western N America (S Oregon to N Baja California). Z8.

Z.glaucus Nutt. WHITE CAMAS.
Like *Z.elegans* but lvs glaucous, blunt, not pungent at apex; bracts fleshy; tepals white to white-green, suffused brown or purple, glands green or bronze solitary, 2-lobed; fr. only slightly longer than tepals. N America (Minnesota to Quebec, south to Illinois, Vancouver). Z3.

Z.gramineus Rydb. See *Z.venenosus* var. *gramineus*.

Z.muscitoxicum (Walter) Reg. See *Amianthum muscitoxicum*.

Z.nuttallii A. Gray (*Toxicoscordion nuttallii* A. Gray) Rydb.).
DEATH CAMAS; POISON CAMAS; MERRYHEARTS.
Bulbous. Stems to 75cm, robust. Basal lvs to 45×2.5cm, linear-falcate, keeled, coriaceous. Infl. a raceme, rarely a panicle; tepals 6–8mm, yellow-white, margin toothed toward apex, basal gland solitary, obovate, green; stamens equal in length to tepals; ovary superior. Fr. ellipsoid, 3–4× longer than tepals. N America (Tennessee to Kansas to Texas). Z6.

Z.paniculatus (Nutt.) S. Wats. (*Toxicoscordion paniculatum* (Nutt.) Rydb.). SAND CORN.
Bulbous. Stems to 60cm. Basal lvs to 50×2cm, conduplicate, margins scarious. Infl. a panicle; tepals 3mm, yellow-white, inner 3 clawed, glands green; anth. yellow. W US (Washington to Montana south to California, Arizona, New Mexico). Z4.

Z.toxicoscordion var. *venenosum* (S. Wats.) Rydb. See *Z.venenosus*.

Z.venenosus S. Wats. (*Z.toxicoscordion* var. *venenosum* (S. Wats.) Rydb.). DEATH CAMAS.
Bulbous. Stems to 60(–70)cm, narrow. Basal lvs to 30×1cm. Infl. a raceme, sometimes branched near base; tepals 3–6mm, off-white, clawed, inner whorl slightly longer than outer, margin toothed toward apex; stamens exceeding tepals, anth. white. Fr. 8–15mm, cylindric. W Canada to Utah and New Mexico. var. *gramineus* (Rydb.) Walsh ex Peck (*Z.gramineus* Rydb.; *Toxicoscordion gramineum* (Rydb.) Rydb.). GRASSY DEATH CAMAS. Habit grassy. Tepals slightly longer with very short claws and obscure glands. Z4.

Names no longer in use

Acidanthera Hochst.
A.bicolor Hochst. See *Gladiolus callianthus.*

Agave L.
A.maculosa Rose. See *Manfreda maculosa.*
A.variegata Jacobi. See *Manfreda variegata.*
A.virginica L. See *Manfreda virginica.*

Amana Honda.
A.edulis (Miq.) Honda. See *Tulipa edulis.*
A.latifolia (Mak.) Honda. See *Tulipa edulis* var. *latifolia.*

Anapalina N.E. Br.
A.burchellii (N.E. Br.) N.E. Br. See *Tritoniopsis burchellii.*
A.caffra (Bak.) Lewis. See *Tritoniopsis caffra.*
A.intermedia Bak. See *Tritoniopsis intermedia.*
A.nervosa (Thunb.) Lewis. See *Tritoniopsis nervosa.*
A.pulchra (Bak.) N.E. Br. See *Tritoniopsis pulchra.*

Anoiganthus Bak.
A.breviflorus Harv. See *Cyrtanthus breviflorus.*

Anomalesia N.E. Br.
A.cunonia (L.) N.E. Br. See *Gladiolus cunonius.*
A.saccata (Klatt) N.E. Br. See *Gladiolus saccatus.*
A.splendens (Sweet) N.E. Br. See *Gladiolus splendens.*

Antholyza L.
A.abbreviata (Andrews) Pers. See *Gladiolus abbreviatus.*
A.aethiopica L. See *Chasmanthe aethiopica.*
A.bicolor Gasp. See *Chasmanthe bicolor.*
A.burchellii N.E. Br. See *Tritoniopsis burchellii.*
A.caffra Ker-Gawl. ex Bak. See *Tritoniopsis caffra.*
A.cunonia L. See *Gladiolus cunonia.*
A.floribunda Salisb. See *Chasmanthe floribunda.*
A.intermedia (Bak.) Lewis. See *Tritoniopsis intermedia.*
A.nervosa Thunb. See *Tritoniopsis nervosa.*
A.paniculata Klatt. See *Crocosmia paniculata.*
A.plicata L.f. See *Babiana thunbergii.*
A.priorii N.E. Br. See *Gladiolus priorii.*
A.pulchra Bak. See *Tritoniopsis pulchra.*
A.quadrangularis Burm. f. See *Gladiolus quadrangularis.*
A.revoluta (Pers.) Bak. pro parte. See *Gladiolus priorii.*
A.revoluta (Pers.) Bak. prop parte. See *Gladiolus watsonius.*
A.ringens L. See *Babiana ringens.*
A.saccata (Klatt) Bak. See *Gladiolus saccatus.*
A.schweinfurthii Bak. See *Gladiolus schweinfurthii.*
A.splendens (Sweet) Steud. See *Gladiolus splendens.*
A.vittigera Salisb. See *Chasmanthe aethiopica.*
A.watsonioides (Bak.) Bak. See *Gladiolus watsonioides.*

Anticlea Kunth.
A.elegans (Pursh) Rydb. See *Zigadenus elegans.*

Argyropsis Roem.
A.candida (Lindl.) Roem. See *Zephyranthes candida.*

Barnardia
B.scilloides Lindl. See *Scilla scilloides.*

Besleria L.
B.incarnata Aubl. See *Sinningia incarnata.*

Bravoa La Ll. & Lex.
B.geminiflora La Ll. & Lex. See *Polianthes geminiflora.*

Brevoortia Alph. Wood.
B.ida-maia Alph. Wood. See *Dichelostemma ida-maia.*

Caliphruria Herb.
C.subedentata Bak. See *Eucharis subedentata.*

Calla L.
C.aethiopica L. See *Zantedeschia aethiopica.*

Callicorea
C.rosea (Lam.) Hann. See *Amaryllis belladonna.*

Callipsyche Herb.
C.aurantiaca Bak. See *Eucrosia aurantiaca.*
C.eucrosioides Herb. See *Eucrosia eucrosioides.*
C.mexicana Roem. See *Eucrosia eucrosioides.*

Cepa L.
C.fistulosum (L.) Gray. See *Allium fistulosum.*

Chlamysporum Salisb.
C.dichotomum (Labill.) Kuntze. See *Thysanotus dichotomus.*

Choretis
C.glauca Herb. See *Hymenocallis glauca.*

Chrosperma
C.muscitoxicum (Walter) Kuntze. See *Amianthum muscitoxicum.*

Chrysiphiala
C.flava Ruiz & Pav. See *Stenomesson flavum.*

Clitanthes
C.humilis Herb. See *Stenomesson humile.*

Coburgia Sweet.
C.belladonna (L.) Herb. See *Amaryllis belladonna.*

Coetocapnia Link & Otto.
C.geminiflora Link & Otto. See *Polianthes geminiflora.*

Cooperia Herb.
C.drummondii Herb. See *Zephyranthes drummondii.*
C.jonesii Cory. See *Zephyranthes jonesii.*
C.pedunculata Herb. See *Zephyranthes drummondii.*
C.smallii Alexander. See *Zephyranthes smallii.*
C.traubii Hayward. See *Zephyranthes traubii.*

Corytholoma (Benth.) Decne.
C.cooperi (Paxt.) Fritsch. See *Sinningia cooperi.*
C.sellovii Mart. See *Sinningia sellovii.*

× **Crinodonna** Stapf.
× *C.memoria-corsii* Ragion. See × *Amarcrinum memoria-corsii.*
× *C.corsii* Stapf. See × *Amarcrinum memoria-corsii.*

Curtonus N.E. Br.
C.paniculatus (Klatt) N.E. Br. See *Crocosmia paniculata.*

Eurycles Salisb. ex Schult. & Schult. f.
E.alba (R. Br.) F. Muell. See *Proiphys alba.*
E.cunninghamii Ait. ex Lindl. See *Proiphys cunninghamii.*
E.sylvestris Salisb. ex Schult. & Schult. f. See *Proiphys amboinensis.*

Gastronema Herb.
G.sanguineum Lindl. See *Cyrtanthus sanguineus.*

Georgina
G.scapigera A. Dietr. See *Dahlia scapigera.*

Gesneria L.
G.aggregata Ker-Gawl. See *Sinningia aggregata.*
G.bulbosa Ker-Gawl. See *Sinningia bulbosa.*
G.canescens Mart. See *Sinningia canescens.*
G.cardinalis Lehm. See *Sinningia cardinalis.*

Haylockia Herb.
H.pusilla Herb. See *Zephyranthes pusilla.*

Helicodiceros Scholt ex K.Koch.
H.muscivorus (L.f.) Engl. See *Dracunculus muscivorus.*

Hesperocordium Lindl.
H.maritum Torr. See *Muilla maritima.*

Homoglossum Salisb.
H.abbreviatum (Andrews) Goldbl. See *Gladiolus abbreviatus.*
H.aureum (Bak.) Oberm. See *Gladious aureus.*
H.huttonii N.E. Br. See See *Gladious huttonii.*
H.merianellum (Thunb.) Bak. See *Gladiolus bonae-spei.*
H.priorii (N.E. Br.) N.E. Br. See *Gladiolus priorii.*
H.schweinfurthii (Bak.) Cuf. See *Gladiolus schweinfurthii.*
H.watsonium (Thunb.) N.E. Br. See *Gladiolus watsonius.*

Hookera Salisb.
H.coronaria Salisb. See *Brodiaea coronaria.*

Imantophyllum
I.aitonii Hook.f. See *Clivia nobilis.*
I.miniatum (Reg.) Hook.f. See *Clivia miniatum.*

Ismene Salisb. ex Herb.
I. amancaes (Ruiz & Pav.) Herb. See *Hymenocallis amancaes.*
I.calathina (Ker-Gawl.) Herb. See *Hymenocallis narcissiflora.*
I.deflexa Herb. See *Hymenocallis deflexa.*
I. × festalis hort. See *Hymenocallis × festalis.*
I.harrisiana hort. See *Hymenocallis harrisiana.*
I.longipetala (Lindl.) Meerow. See *Hymenocallis longipetala.*
I.narcissiflora M.Roem. See *Hymenocallis narcissiflora.*
I.virescens Lindl. See *Hymenocallis virescens.*

Kolpakowskia Reg.
K.ixiolirioides Reg. See *Ixiolirion kolpakowskianum.*

Korolkowia Reg.
K.sewerzowii (Reg.) Reg. See *Fritillaria sewerzowii.*

Melanthium L.
M.massoniifolium Andrews. See *Whiteheadia bifolia.*

Moly
M.latifolium Gray. See *Allium ursinum.*

Montbretia DC.
M.crocosmiiflora Lemoine. See *Crocosmia × crocosmiiflora.*
M.pottsii (Bak.) Bak. See *Crocosmia pottsii.*

Neobakeria Schltr.
N.angustifolia Schltr. See *Polyxena angustifolia.*
N.namaquensis Schltr. See *Polyxena angustifolia.*

Pardanthus Ker-Gawl.
P.chinensis (L.) Ker-Gawl. See *Belamcanda chinensis.*

Petamenes Salisb. ex J.W. Loudon.
P.schweinfurthii (Bak.) N.E. Br. See *Gladiolus schweinfurthii.*

Rechsteineria Reg.
R.aggregata (Ker-Gawl.) Kuntze. See *Sinningia aggregata.*

R.allagophylla (Mart.) Reg. See *Sinningia allagophylla.*
R.canescens (Mart.) Kuntze. See *Sinningia canescens.*
R.cardinalis (Lehm.) Kuntze. See *Sinningia cardinalis.*
R.cooperi (Paxt.) Kuntze. See *Sinningia cooperi.*
R.incarnata (Aubl.) Leeuwenb. See *Sinningia incarnata.*
R.lindleyi (Hook.) Fritsch. See *Sinningia sceptrum.*
R.lineata Hjelmqv. See *Sinningia macropoda.*
R.macropoda (Sprague) Curtis. See *Sinningia macropoda.*
R.macrorrhiza (Dumort) Kuntze. See *Sinningia macrorrhiza.*
R.purpurea hort. See *Sinningia verticillata.*
R.ramboi Hoehne. See *Sinningia sellovii.*
R.reitzii Hoehne. See *Sinningia reitzii.*
R.sellovii (Mart.) Kuntze. See *Sinningia sellovii.*
R.sulcata (Rusby) Fritsch. See *Sinningia sulcata.*
R.tuberosa (Mart.) Kuntze. See *Sinningia tuberosa.*
R.verticillata (Vell.) L.B. Sm. See *Sinningia verticillata.*

Richardia Kunth non L.
R.africana Kunth. See *Zantedeschia aethiopica.*
R.elliotiana Wats. See *Zantedeschia elliotiana.*
R.pentlandii Wats. See *Zantedeschia pentlandii.*
R.rehmannii (Engl.) N.E. Br. ex W.Harrow. See *Zantedeschia rehmannii.*

Runyonia Rose.
R.longiflora Rose. See *Manfreda longiflora.*

Saturnia
S.cernua Maratti. See *Allium chamaemoly.*

Schizobasopsis Macbr.
S.kilimandscharica (Mildbr.) Barschus. See *Bowiea kilimandscharica.*
S.volubilis (Harv. & Hook. f.) J.F. Macbr. See *Bowiea volubilis.*

Strangweja
S.spicata (Sibth. & Sm.) Boiss. See *Bellevalia hyacinthoides.*

Streptanthera Sweet.
S.elegans Sweet. See *Sparaxis elegans.*

Synphyostemon Miers.
S.biflorus (Thunb.) Dusén. See *Olsynium biflorum.*
S.narcissoides (Cav.) Miers ex Klatt. See *Olsynium biflorum.*

Testudinaria Salisb.
T.elephantipes (L.Hérit.) Burchell. See *Dioscorea elephantipes.*

Thalictrum L.
T.anemonoides Michx. See *Anemonella thalictroides.*

Toxicoscordion Rydb.
T.nuttallii (A.Gray) Rydb. See *Zigadenus nuttallii.*
T.paniculatum (Nutt.) Rydb. See *Zigadenus paniculatus.*

Trifurcia Herb.
T.amatorum (Wright) Goldbl. See *Herbertia amatorum.*
T.caerulea Herb. See *Alophia drummondii.*
T.lahue (Molina) Goldbl. See *Herbertia lahue.*
T.pulchella (Sweet) Goldbl. See *Herbertia pulchella.*

Trillidium Kunth.
T.govanianum D. Don. See *Trillium govanianum.*

Vallota Salisb. & Herb.
V.purpurea (Ait.) Herb. See *Cyrtanthus elatus.*
V.speciosa (L. f.) T. Dur. & Schinz. See *Cyrtanthus elatus.*

Index of Popular Names

Bibliography

GENERAL

Anderson, E. A. 1959. *Dwarf Bulbs for the Rock Garden*. Nelson.

Arroyo, S.C. 1984. Contribucion al Conocimiento de los Bulbos de Amaryllidaceae. *Kurtziana* 17: 55–70.

Baker, G. 1892. *Irideae*.

Bond, P. & Goldblatt, P. 1984. Plants of the Cape Flora: a descriptive catalogue. *Journal of South African Botany* suppl. vol. no. 13.

Boussard, M. 1985. Growing South African Iridaceae. *Veld & Flora* 71(2): 61–63.

Brickell, C.D., Cutler, D.F. & Gregory, M. (eds) 1980. *Petaloid Monocotyledons*. Academic Press.

Bryan, J.E. 1989. *Bulbs*, 2 vols. Portland, Oregon: Timber Press.

— 1992. *Bulbs*. New York: Hearst Books.

— 1994. *Bulbs*. New York: Macmillan.

Cotter, Sir J. L. *The Culture of Bulbs: Bulbous Plants and Tubers Made Plain*. Hutchinson.

Crockett, J. U. 1971. *Bulbs*. Time-Life.

Dahlgren, R.M., Clifford, H.T. & Yeo, P.F. 1985. *The Families of the Monocotyledons*. Heidelberg: Springer-Verlag.

Doerflinger, F. 1973. *The Bulb Book*. David & Charles.

Eliovson, S. 1980. *Wild Flowers of Southern Africa*. Macmillan South Africa.

Galil, J. 1980. Kinetics of Bulbous Plants. *Endeavour* (new series) 5(1): 15–20.

Genders, R. 1954. *Bulbs All the Year Round*. Faber.

Gould, C.J. 1957. *Handbook on Bulb Growing and Forcing*. Washington.

Grey, C.H. 1937; 1938; 1938. *Hardy Bulbs*, 3 vols. vol. 1: *Iridaceae*; vol. 2: *Amaryllidaceae, Commelinaceae, Haemodoraceae, Orchidaceae, Scitamineae*; vol. 3: *Liliaceae*.

Grey-Wilson, C., Mathew, B. & Blamey, M. 1981. *Bulbs: The Bulbous Plants of Europe and Their Allies*. Collins.

Jeppe, B. 1989. *Spring and Winter Flowering Bulbs of the Cape*. Oxford University Press.

Leak, G.W. *Cultivation of Bulbs in Bowls*. RHS Pamphlet.

McFarland, J. H., Hatton, R. M. & Foley, D. J. 1941. *Garden Bulbs in Color*. Macmillan Inc.

Macself, A.J. 1948. *Bulbs and their Cultivation*. rev. edn, Collingridge.

Mathew, B. 1973. *Dwarf Bulbs*. Batsford.

— 1978. *The Larger Bulbs*. Batsford.

— 1986. *The Year Round Bulb Garden*. Souvenir Press.

Mathew, B. & Baytop, T. 1984. *The Bulbous Plants of Turkey*. Batsford.

Mathew, B. & Swindells, P. 1994. *The Gardener's Guide to Bulbs*. Mitchell Beazley.

Ministry of Agriculture, Fisheries and Food 1967. *Flowers from Bulbs and Corms*. Ministry of Agriculture, Fisheries and Food, Bulletin 197. HMSO.

Moore, W.C. (rev. Brunt, A.A., Price, D. & Rees, A.R.) 1979. *Diseases of Bulbs*. Ministry of Agriculture, Fisheries and Food.

Nixon, M., Silberrad, U. & Lyall, S. 1909. *Dutch Bulbs and Gardens*. A. & C. Black.

Pate, J. & Dixon, K. 1982. *Tuberous, Cormous and Bulbous Plants*. Nedlands, W Australia: University of Western Australia Press.

Rees, A.R. 1972. *The Growth of Bulbs*. London & New York: Academic Press.

Rix, M. 1983. *Growing Bulbs*. London & Canberra: Croom Helm; Portland, Oregon: Timber Press.

Rix, M. & Phillips, R. 1981. *The Bulb Book*. Pan.

Rockwell, F. F. & Grayson, E. 1953. *The Complete Book of Bulbs*. New York: Macmillan.

Royal General Bulb-Growers' Society of Haarlem 1958. *A Tentative List of Bulbous and Tuberous Rooted Plants*, with supplement. Haarlem.

Schauenberg, P. 1965. *The Bulb Book*. Warne.

Shewell-Cooper, W.E. 1948. *The A.B.C. of Bulbs and Corms*. English Universities Press.

Synge, P. M. 1961. *Collins Guide to Bulbs*. Collins.

Tompsett, A.A. 1985. Dormancy breaking in bulbs by burning over. *The Plantsman* 7(1): 40–51.

Weathers, J. 1911?. *Beautiful Bulbous Plants for the Open Air*. Simpkin, Marshal Hamilton, Kent & Co. Ltd., and Frederick Warne & Co.

Wendelbo, P. 1977. *Tulips and Irises of Iran*. Tehran.

Wild Flowers of South Africa. 1980. Cape Town: Struik.

ACHIMENES

Townsend, K.J. 1984. *Achimenes*. The Plantsman 5(4): 193–205.

AGAPANTHUS

Duncan, G.D., 1983. The white form of *Agapanthus walshii* L. Bol. *Veld & Flora* 69(1): 21.
— 1985. *Agapanthus* species – their potential, and the introduction of ten selected forms. *Veld & Flora* 71(4): 122–125.
Leighton, F.M. 1965. The genus *Agapanthus* L'Héritier. *Journal of South African Botany* suppl. vol. no. 4.

ALBUCA

Baker, J.G. 1897. *Albuca*. In Thistleton-Dyer, W.T. (ed.), *Flora Capensis* 6: 451–462. Reeve & Co.

ALLIUM

Bijl van Duyvenbode, J. 1990. Breeding ornamental onions. *The Plantsman* 12(3): 152–6.
Davies, D. 1987. Onions in a damp climate. *AGS Bulletin* 55: 60–69.
— 1992. *Alliums: the Ornamental Onions*. Batsford.
Moore, H.E. 1954; 1955. The cultivated Alliums. *Baileya* 2: 103–13, 117–23; 3: 137–49, 156–67.

ALSTROEMERIA

Garaventa, A. 1971. El genero *Alstroemeria* en Chile. *Anales del Museo de Historia Natural de Valparaiso* 4: 63–108.

AMARYLLIS

Dyer, R.A. 1955. *Amaryllis belladonna. Flowering Plants of Africa* 30: t.1200.

AMMOCHARIS

Milne-Redhead, M.A. & Schweickerdt, H.G. 1939. A new conception of the genus *Ammocharis* Herb. *Journal of the Linnean Society – Botany* 52:159–190.

ANIGOZANTHOS

Geerinck, G. 1970; 1972. Revision du genre *Anigozanthos* Labill. (Haemodoraceae d'Australie). *Bulletin du Jardin Botanique de Belgique* 40: 261–76; *Growing Native Plants* 2: 30–1.

ANOMATHECA

Goldblatt, P. 1972. A revision of the genera *Lapeirousia* Pourret and *Anomatheca* Ker in the winter rainfall region of Southern Africa. *Contributions from the Bolus Herbarium* 4: 75–103.

ANTHERICUM

Obermeyer, A.A. 1962. The South African species of *Anthericum*, *Chlorophytum* and *Trachyandra*. *Bothalia* 7: 669–768.

APODOLIRION

See Müller-Doblies 1986 under *Gethyllis*.

ARISAEMA

Mayo, S.J. 1982. A survey of cultivated species of *Arisaema*. *The Plantsman* 3(4): 193–209.
Pradhan, U.C. 1990. *Himalayan Cobra-lilies (Arisaema): their Botany and Culture*. Kalimpong: Primulaceae Books.

ARUM

Boyce, P. 1993. *The Genus Arum*. HMSO.
Bedalov, M. 1980. Two *Arum* interesting to the flora of South Italy. *Journées Etud. Systém. et Biogéogr. Médit.* Cagliari C.I.E.S.M.: 101–2.
— 1981. Cytotaxonomy of the genus *Arum* (Araceae) in the Balkans and the Aegean area. *Botanische Jahrbücher für Systematik, Pflanzengeschichte und Pflanzengeographie* 102: 183–200.
— 1984. A new pentaploid of the genus *Arum* (Araceae). *Botanica Helvetica* 94(2): 385–90.
Bogner, J. 1978. A critical list of the Aroid genera. *Aroideana* 1: 63–73.
Bogner, J. & Nicolson, D. H. 1991. A revised classification of Araceae with dichotomous keys. *Willdenowia* 21: 35–50.
Bown, D. 1988. *Aroids, plants of the Arum family*. Century.
Boyce, P. C. 1986. Observations on Aroids. *AGS Bulletin* 54: 35–42.
— 1987. A new species of *Arum* L. from Crete. *Aroideana* 10(1): 6–8.
— 1987. A new subspecies of *Biarum davisii* Turrill from Turkey. *Aroideana* 10(2): 14–15.
— 1989. A new classification of *Arum* with keys to the infrageneric taxa. *Kew Bulletin* 44: 383–95.
Dormer, K. J. 1960. The truth about pollination in *Arum* L. *New Phytologist* 59: 298–301.
Hruby, J. 1912. Le Genre *Arum. Bulletin de la Société Botanique de Genève* 4: 113–60, 330–71.
Lack, A. J. & Diaz, A. 1991. The pollination of *Arum maculatum* L. – a historical review and new observations. *Watsonia* 18: 333–42.
Mayo, S. J. 1980. Aroid symposium at Selby Gardens. *Aroideana* 3: 69–71.
Mayo, S. J. & Meikle, R. D. 1985. Araceae. In Meikle, R. D. (ed.), *Flora of Cyprus* 2: 1664–71. Kew: RBG.
Mill, R. R. 1983. Araceae. In Davis, P. H. (ed.), Materials for a Flora of Turkey XXXVIII: Araceae, Dioscoreaceae, Liliaceae. *Notes from the Royal Botanic Garden Edinburgh* 41: 45–7.
— 1984. Araceae. In Davis P. H. (ed.), *Flora of Turkey* 8: 41–63. Edinburgh University Press.

Mill, R. R. & Alpinar, K. 1988. Araceae. In Davis, P. H. (ed.), *Flora of Turkey* 10: 218–21, 236.

Prime, C. T. 1960. *Lords and Ladies*. Collins.

— 1961. Taxonomy and nomenclature in some species of the genus *Arum* L. *Watsonia* 5: 106–9.

— 1980. Araceae. In Tutin, T. G. et al. (eds), *Flora Europaea* 5: 268–72. Cambridge University Press.

Takhtadjan, A. L. 1982. Araceae. *Zhizn' rastenii (Tsvetkovye rasteniya)* 6: 466–92, t.64(2). Moscow.

BABIANA

Duncan, G.D. 1982. Ten *Babiana* species for promotion. *Veld & Flora* 68(2): 47–48.

Goldblatt, P. 1971. Cytological and morphological studies in the Southern African Iridaceae: *Antholyza*. *Journal of South African Botany* 37(4): 430–432.

Lewis, G.J. 1960. The genus *Babiana*. *Journal of South African Botany* suppl. vol. no. 3.

BEGONIA

American Begonia Society 1934–. *Begonian*.

Buxton, B.R. 1946. *Begonias and How to Grow Them*. New York: Oxford University Press.

Caterall, E. 1984. *Growing Begonias*. Croom Helm.

Haegeman, J. 1978. *International List of Tuberous Begonia Names*. Melle: Institute of Ornamental Plant Growing.

— 1979. *Tuberous Begonias: Origin and Development*. Vaduz: J. Cramer.

Langdon, B. 1989. *Begonias: the Care and Cultivation of Tuberous Varieties*. Cassell.

Smith, L.B. et al. 1986. *Begoniaceae: Illustrated Key [&] Annotated Species List. Smithsonian Contributions to Botany* no. 60.

Thompson, M.L. & E.J. 1981. *Begonias: the Complete Reference Guide*. New York: Times Books.

Torode, S.J. 1984. *Begonia chlorosticta*. *The Plantsman* 5(4): 243–5.

Wall, B. 1989. Some unusual Begonias. *The Plantsman* 11(1): 4–15.

Weber, C. & Dress, W.J. 1968. Notes on the nomenclature of some cultivated Begonias (Begoniaceae). *Baileya* 16: 42–72, 113–36.

BELLEVALIA

Bothmer, R. & Wendelbo, P. 1981. Cytological and morphological variation in *Bellevalia*. *Nordic Journal of Botany* 1: 4–11.

Feinbrun, N. 1938–40. A monographic study on the genus *Bellevalia* Lapeyr. *Palestine Journal of Botany* 1: 42–54, 131–42, 336–409.

Freitag, H. & Wendelbo, P. 1970. The genus *Bellevalia* in Afghanistan. *Israel Journal of Botany* 19: 220–4.

Wendelbo, P. 1980. Notes on *Hyacinthus* and *Bellevalia* (Liliaceae) in Turkey and Iran. *Notes from the Royal Botanic Garden Edinburgh* 38: 423–34.

BLOOMERIA

Ingram, J. A monograph of the genera *Bloomeria* and *Muilla* (Liliaceae). *Madroño* 12: 19–27.

BOOPHONE

Olivier, W. 1981. The genus *Boophane*. *Bulletin of the Indige-nous Bulb Growers Association of South Africa* 31: 5–8.

Snijman, D. 1983. A new species of *Boophane* Herbert (Amaryllidaceae) from the North-Western Cape. *Journal of South African Botany* 49(3): 243–249.

BOWIEA

Rowley, G.D. 1987. *Caudiciform and Pachycaul Succulents*. California: Strawberry Press.

BRODIAEA

Hoover, R.F. 1939. A revision of the genus *Brodiaea*. *American Midland Naturalist* 22: 551–74.

— 1955. Further observations on *Brodiaea* and some related genera. *Herbertia* 11: 13–23.

Niehaus, T.F. 1971. A biosystematic study of the genus *Brodiaea* (Amaryllidaceae). *University of California Publications, Botany* 60: 1–66.

— 1980. The *Brodiaea* complex. *The Four Seasons* 6(1): 11–21.

BRUNSVIGIA

Dyer, R.A. 1950; 1951. A review of the genus *Brunsvigia*. *Herbertia* 6: 63–83; 7: 44–64.

BULBINE

Obermeyer, A.A. 1966. Two new species of *Bulbine*. *Bothalia* 9: 342–4.

BULBINELLA

Obermeyer, A.A. 1966. The identity of *Bulbinella carnosa*. *Bothalia* 9: 345.

Perry, P.L., 1987. A synoptic review of the genus *Bulbinella* in South Africa. *Journal of South African Botany* 53(6): 431–444.

CALOCHORTUS

Elliott, J.G. 1981. *Calochortus*: a survey of the species in cultivation. *The Plantsman* 2(4): 195–213.

Matthews, V. 1994. *Calochortus gunnisonii*. *The New Plantsman* 1(4): 220–4.

Ownbey, M. 1940. A monograph of the genus *Calochortus*. *Annals of the Missouri Botanic Garden* 27: 371–560.

CAMASSIA

Gould, F.W. 1942. A systematic treatment of the genus *Camassia* Lindl. *American Midland Naturalist* 28: 712–42.

CHASMANTHE

De Vos, M.P. 1985. Revision of the South African genus *Chasmanthe* (Iridaceae). *Journal of South African Botany* 51(4): 253–261.

CHIONODOXA

Meikle, R.D. 1970. *Chinodoxa luciliae*, a taxonomic note. *Journal of the Royal Horticultural Society* 95: 21–24.

Speta, F. 1976. Über *Chionodoxa* Boiss., ihre Gliederung und Zugehörigkeit zu *Scilla* L. *Naturkundliches Jahrbuch der Stadt Linz* 21: 9–79.

CHLIDANTHUS

Ravenna, P.F. 1974. Contributions to South American Amaryllidaceae VI. *Plant Life* 30: 71–3.

CHLOROGALUM

Hoover, R.F. 1940. A monograph of the genus *Chlorogalum*. *Madroño* 5: 137–47.

CLIVIA

Duncan, G.D. 1985. Notes on the genus *Clivia* Lindley, with particular reference to *C. miniata* Regel var. *citrina* Watson. *Veld & Flora* 71(3): 84–85.

Dyer, R.A., 1943. *Clivia caulescens*. *Flowering Plants of Africa* 23: t.891.

COLCHICUM

Bowles, E. A. 1924. *A Handbook of Crocus and Colchicum for Gardeners*. 2nd edn, Bodley Head, 1952; repr. Waterstone, 1985.

Burtt, B.L., Meikle, R.D. & Furse, J.P.W. 1968. *Colchicum* and *Merendera*. *RHS Lily Year Book* 31: 90–103.

Feinbrun, N. 1953. The genus *Colchicum* in Palestine and neighbouring countries. *Palestine Journal of Botany, Jerusalem series 6* 2: 71–95.

Stefanoff, B. 1926. Monographie der Gattung *Colchicum*. *Sbornik Bulgariskata Akademiya na Naukita* 22: 1–100.

Wittmack, L. 1904. *Clivia (Imantophyllum) cyrtanthiflora* van Houtte (*Clivia nobilis* and *Clivia miniata*). *Gartenflora* 53: 225–8.

CORYDALIS

Ingwersen, W. 1980. Commendable Corydalises. *The Plantsman* 2(3): 129–31.

Rix, M. 1993. *Corydalis flexuosa* from Western China. *The Plantsman* 15(3): 129–30.

CRINUM

Nordal, I. 1977. Revision of the east African taxa of the genus *Crinum*. *Norwegian Journal of Botany* 24: 177–94.

Uphof, J.C. 1942. A review of the species of *Crinum*. *Herbertia* 9: 63–9.

Verdoorn, I.C. 1973. The genus *Crinum* in Southern Africa. *Bothalia* 11: 27–52.

CROCOSMIA

De Vos, M.P. 1984. The African genus *Crocosmia* Planchon. *Journal of South African Botany* 50(4): 463–502.

Kostelijk, P. 1984. *Crocosmia* in gardens. *The Plantsman* 5: 246–53.

CROCUS

Baker, J.G. 1873. Review of the known species of *Crocus*. *Gardener's Chronicle* 1873: 107.

Baytop, T., Mathew, B. & Brighton, C.A. 1975. Four new taxa in Turkish *Crocus*. Kew Bulletin 30(2): 241–6.

Bowles, E.A. 1924. *A Handbook of Crocus and Colchicum*. 2nd edn, Bodley Head 1952; repr. Waterstone, 1985.

Brickell, C.D. & Mathew, B. 1973. Three recent discoveries in *Crocus*. *Journal of the Royal Horticultural Society* 98(8): 360–66.

Brighton, C.A. 1976. Cytological problems in the genus *Crocus* 1. *Crocus vernus* aggregate. *Kew Bulletin* 31: 33–46.

— 1976. Cytology of *Crocus olivieri* and its allies. *Kew Bulletin* 31: 209–27.

— 1977. Cytological problems in the genus *Crocus* 2. *Crocus cancellatus* aggregate. Kew Bulletin 32: 33–45.

— 1977. Cytology of *Crocus sativus* and its allies. *Pl. Syst. Evol.* 128: 137–157.

— 1980. Cytology of *Crocus vallicola* and its allies. *Notes from the Royal Botanic Garden Edinburgh* 38: 399–412.

Brighton, C.A., Mathew, B. & Marchant, C.J. 1973. Chromosome counts in the genus *Crocus*. *Kew Bulletin* 28: 451–64.

Brighton, C.A., Scarlett, C.J. & Mathew, B. 1980. Cytological studies and origins of some *Crocus* cultivars. In Brickell, C.D., Cutler, D.F & Gregory, M. (eds) 1980, *Petaloid Monocotyledons*. Linnean Society, London: Academic Press.

Burtt, B.L. 1952. *Crocus vernus*, the name and its history. In Bowles, E.A. 1924, *A Handbook of Crocus and Colchicum*: 141–52.

Fedtschenko, B. 1935. *Crocus*. In Komarov, V.L. (ed.) 1968, *Flora USSR*: vol. 4.

Feinbrun, N. 1957. The genus *Crocus* in Israel and neighbouring countries. *Kew Bulletin* 2: 269–85.

Feinbrun, N. & Shmida, A. 1977. A new review of the genus *Crocus* in Israel and neighbouring countries. *Israel Journal of Botany* 26: 172–89.

Gay, J. 1831. Nouvelles espèces de *Crocus*. *Bull. Sci. Nat. Géol.* 25: 319–21.

Grossheim, A.A. 1940. *Crocus*. In *Flora Kavkaza*: vol. 2. Leningrad.
Haworth, A.H. 1809. On the cultivation of Crocuses with a short account of the different species known at present. *Transactions of the Horticultural Society of London* 1: 122–39.
Herbert, W. 1841. Crocorum Synopsis. *Botanical Magazine* 67: tt.3861–3875.
Maire, R. 1959. *Crocus*. In *Flore de l'Afrique du Nord*: vol. 6. Paris.
Mathew, B. 1975. *Crocus*. In Rechinger, K.H. (ed.), *Flora Iranica*: part 112. Graz: Akademische Druck- und Verlagsanstalt.
— 1976. *Crocus olivieri* and its allies. *Kew Bulletin* 31(2): 201–8.
— 1977. *Crocus sativus* and its allies. *Pl. Syst. Evol.* 128: 89–103.
— 1980. *Crocus vallicola* and its allies. *Notes from the Royal Botanic Garden Edinburgh* 38: 387–97.
— 1980. *Crocus*. In Tutin, T.G., Heywood, V.H. et al. (eds), *Flora Europaea*: vol. 5. Cambridge.
— 1984. *Crocus*. In Davis, P.H. (ed.), *Flora of Turkey* 8: 413–38.
— 1982. *The Crocus*. Batsford.
Mathew, B. & Baytop, T. 1976. Some observations on Turkish *Crocus*. *Notes from the Royal Botanic Garden Edinburgh* 35: 61–7.
Mathew, B. & Brighton, C.A. 1977. Four central Asian *Crocus* species. *Iranian Journal of Botany* 1(2): 123–35.
— 1977. *Crocus tournefortii* and its allies. *Kew Bulletin* 31(4): 775–84.
Maw, G. 1886. *A Monograph of the Genus Crocus*. Dulau & Co.
Papanicolaou, K. & Zacharof, E. 1980. *Crocus* in Greece. *Botaniska Notiser* 133(2): 155–63.
Prodan, J. & Nyárády, E.I. 1966. *Crocus*. In *Flora of Roumania*: vol. 2. Bucharest.
Pulevic, V. 1977. A contribution to the knowledge of taxonomy and horology of some species of genus *Crocus* L. from Yugoslavia. *Glas. Repub. Zavod. Zast. Prirode-Prirodn. Muzeja Titograd* 10: 81–99.
— 1979. The contribution to the knowledge of genus *Crocus* L. in Yugoslavia. *Glas. Repub. Zavod. Zast. Prirode-Prirodn. Muzeja Titograd* 12: 195–212.
Rafinski, J.N. 1976. On systematic position of the Crocuses growing in the Izerian mountains. *Fragm. Flor. Geobot.* 22: 9–12.
Rees, A.R. 1988. Saffron – an expensive plant product. *The Plantsman* 9(4): 210–217.
Sabine, J. 1829. An account and description of spring Crocuses. *Transactions of the Horticultural Society of London* 7: 419–32, 433–98.
Sopova, M. 1972. The cytology of ten *Crocus* species from Macedonia. *God. Zborn.* 24: 73–81.
Stojabov, N., Stefanov, B. & Kitanov, B. 1966. *Crocus*. In *Flora of Bulgaria*, 4th edn: part 1.
Tenore, M. 1826. *Memoria sulle Specie e Varietà de' Crochi della Flora Napolitana*. Naples.
Warburg, E.F. 1957. Crocuses. *Endeavour* 16, 64: 209–16.

CYANELLA

Baker, J.G. 1896. *Cyanella*. In Thistleton-Dyer, W.T. (ed.), *Flora Capensis* 6: 6–7. Reeve & Co.

CYBISTETES

Milne-Redhead, M.A. & Schweickerdt, H.G. 1939. The genus *Cybistetes*. *Journal of the Linnean Society – Botany* 52: 190–197.

CYCLAMEN

Bowles, E.A. 1949. Cyclamen in the garden. *Journal of the Royal Horticultural Society* 74: 325–32.
Cyclamen Society. *Cyclamen* (quarterly journal).
Doorenbos, J. 1950. *Taxonomy and Nomenclature of Cyclamen*. *Lendbouwhogeschool Leaflet no. 87*. Wageningen.
Grey-Wilson, C. 1988. *The Genus Cyclamen*. Christopher Helm/Kew.
— 1991. *Cyclamen* – a reappraisal. *The Plantsman* 13(1): 1–20
Hildebrand, F. von 1898. *Die Gattung Cyclamen L.* Jena: Gustav Fischer.
Langdon, A. 1948. The Cultivation of *Cyclamen persicum*. *Journal of the Royal Horticultural Society* 72: 322.
Nightingale, G. 1984. *Growing Cyclamen*. 2nd edn, Croom Helm.
Wellensiek, S.J. et al. 1962. *Cyclamen: a Descriptive List of Cultivars*. Wageningen: Laboratorium voor Tuinbouw-plantenteelt.

CYRTANTHUS

Compton, J. 1989. *Cyrtanthus mackenii* var. *cooperi*. *The Plantsman* 11(2): 65–6.
Dyer, R.A. 1939. A review of the genus *Cyrtanthus*. *Herbertia* 6: 65–103.
Holford, F. 1989. *Cyrtanthus* in the cool greenhouse. *The Plantsman* 11(3): 170–5.
Reid, C. & Dyer, R.A. 1984. *A Review of the Southern African Species of Cyrtanthus*. California: The American Plant Life Society.

DAHLIA

Barnes, A.T. 1966. *The Dahlia Grower's Treasury*. 3rd edn, Collingridge.
Damp, P. 1981. *Growing Dahlias*. Croom Helm.
— 1987. *Classical Garden Plants: Dahlias*. Century Hutchinson.
— 1989. *Dahlias: the Complete Guide*. Marlborough: Crowood Press.
Drayson, G.F. 1958. *Dahlias*. Ward Lock & Co.
Hammett, K. 1980. *The World of Dahlias*. Kaye & Ward.
Lebar, R.R.H. 1957. *Dahlias for Everyone*. Blandford.
National Dahlia Society 1911–. *Dahlia Year Book*, later *Annual*.

Ogg, S. 1961. *Dahlias*. Penguin.

Royal Horticultural Society 1969–. *Tentative Classified List and International Register of Dahlia Names*, with supplements. RHS.

Smith, N.G. 1948. *Dahlia Cultivation*. Faber.

Unwin, C.W.J. 1957. *Gladioli and Dahlias*. Collingridge.

DAUBENYA

Hall, H. 1970. *Daubenya* Lindley. *Journal of the Botanical Society of South Africa* 56: 13–16.

Jessop, J.P. 1976. Studies in the bulbous Liliaceae of South Africa: 6. *Journal of South African Botany* 42(4): 431–2.

DICHELOSTEMMA

Hoover, R.F. 1940. The genus *Dichelostemma*. *American Midland Naturalist* 24: 463–76.

Lenz, L.W. 1976. The nature of the floral appendages in four species of *Dichelostemma* (Liliaceae). *Aliso* 8: 383–9.

Niehaus, T.F. 1980. The *Brodiaea* complex. *The Four Seasons* 6(1): 11–21.

DIERAMA

Brown, N.E. 1929. The genus *Dierama* K. Koch and Bouché. *Journal of the Royal Horticultural Society* 54(1): 193–202.

Hilliard, O.M. & Burtt, B.L. 1990. *Dierama*: a neglected genus of Iridaceae. *The Plantsman* 12(2): 106–12.

— 1991. *Dierama: the Hairbells of Africa*. Johannesburg: Acorn Books.

DIETES

Goldblatt, P. 1981. Systematics, phylogeny and evolution of *Dietes* (Iridaceae). *Annals of the Missouri Botanic Garden* 68: 132–153.

DIOSCOREA

Rowley, G.D. 1987. *Caudiciform and Pachycaul Succulents*. California: Strawberry Press.

Von Teichman et al. 1979. The genus *Dioscorea* in South Africa. *Boissiera* 24: 215–24.

DRACUNCULUS

See Bown 1988 under *Arum* above.

DRIMIA

Jessop, J.P. 1977. The taxonomy of *Drimia* and certain allied genera. *Journal of South African Botany* 43(4): 265–319.

EREMURUS

Fedtschenko, O. 1909. *Eremurus: Kritische Uebersicht der Gattung*. St Petersburg: Akademia Nauka; repr. *Cramer Plant Monographs Reprints 3*, 1968.

Wendelbo, P. 1964. On the genus *Eremurus* in south-west Asia. *Acta Universitatis Bergensis, Series Mathematica Rerumque Naturalium 5*.

Wendelbo, P. & Furse, P. 1968. *Eremurus* in south-west Asia. *RHS Lily Year Book 1969*: 56–69.

ERYTHRONIUM

Andersen, F. 1958. The genus *Erythronium*. *RHS Lily Year Book*.

Applegate, E.I. 1935. The genus *Erythronium*. *Madroño* 3: 58–113.

Parks, C.R. & Hardin, J.W. 1963. Yellow Erythroniums of the Eastern United States. *Brittonia* 15: 245–59.

Watson, S. & Woodward, R. 1974. Erythroniums. *AGS Bulletin* 42: 35–53.

EUCHARIS

Meerow, A. 1984. Two new species of pancratoid Amaryllidaceae from Peru and Ecuador. *Brittonia* 36: 19–25.

EUCOMIS

Compton, J. 1990. *Eucomis* L'Héritier. *The Plantsman* 12(3): 129–39.

Reyneke, W.F. 1972. 'n Monografiese studie van die genus *Eucomis* in Suid-Afrika. M.Sc. thesis, University of Pretoria.

FERRARIA

De Vos, M.P. 1979. The African genus *Ferraria*. *Journal of South African Botany* 45(3): 295–375.

FREESIA

Brown, N.E. 1935. *Freesia* Klatt and its history. *Journal of South African Botany* 1(1): 1–35.

Goldblatt, P. 1982. Systematics of *Freesia* Klatt (Iridaceae). *Journal of South African Botany* 48(1): 39–91.

Kragtwijk, G. 1965. Freesia-sortiment. *Tuinbouwgids* 20: 380–1.

Mackenzie, W.F. 1957. *Freesias*.

Sennels, N.J. 1951. *The Cultivated Species of Freesia*. Copenhagen: J.E. Ohlsens Enke.

Smith, D. 1979. *Freesias*. Grower Books.

FRITILLARIA

Beck, C. 1953. *Fritillaries*. Faber.

Furse, P. 1959. Fritillaries in Britain. *RHS Lily Year Book 1960*: 92–100.

Haw, S.G. 1982. The Chinese species of *Fritillaria*: their distribution, habitats and cultivation. *AGS Bulletin* 50: 148–59.

Macfarlane, R.F. 1975. *Fritillaria* in California. *Lilies 1975*: 53–66.

Obermeyer, A.A. 1966. The identity of *Fritillaria nana*. *Bothalia* 9: 345.

Rix, M. 1977. Fritillaries in Iran. *Iranian Journal of Botany* 1: 75–95.

— 1980. *Fritillaria* in Japan. *The Plantsman* 2(2): 65–6.

— 1994. *Fritillaria ruthenica*. *The New Plantsman* 1(4): 232–5.

Turrill, W.B. & Sealy, J.R. 1980. Studies in the genus *Fritillaria*. *Hooker's Icones Plantarum* 39.

GAGEA

Uphof, J.C.T. 1958; 1959; 1960. A review of the genus *Gagea* Salisb. *Plant Life* 14: 124–32; 15: 151–61; 16: 163–76.

GALANTHUS

Artiushenko, Z.T. 1966. Taxonomy of the genus *Galanthus* L. *RHS Daffodil & Tulip Year Book* 32: 62–82.

— 1974. *Galanthus* L. (Amaryllidaceae) in Greece. *Annales Musei Goulandris* 2: 9–21.

Beck, G. 1894. Die Schneeglöckchen, eine monographische Skizze der Gattung *Galanthus*. *Wiener Illustrierte Garten-Zeitung* 19: 45–58.

Bowles, E.A. 1917. Snowdrops. *Journal of the Royal Horticultural Society* 43: 28.

Davis, A.P. & Brickell, C.D. 1994. *Galanthus peshmenii*: a new Snowdrop from the Eastern Aegean. *The New Plantsman* 1(1): 14–19.

Gottlieb-Tannenhain, P. von 1904. Studien über die Formen der Gattung *Galanthus*. *Abhandlungen der Zoologisch-botanischen Gesellschaft in Wien* 2(4): 1–95.

Kamari, G. 1981; 1982. A biosystematic study of the genus *Galanthus* L. in Greece. *Botanika Chronika* 1: 60–98; *Botanische Jahrbücher* 103: 107–35.

Nutt, R. 1993. Growing Snowdrops. *The Plantsman* 14(4): 197–9.

Schwarz, O. 1963. Tentative key to the wild species of *Galanthus* L. *AGS Bulletin* 31: 131–41.

Stern, W.C. 1956. *Snowdrops and Snowflakes*. Royal Horticultural Society.

Traub, H.P. & Moldenke, H.N. 1947. The tribe Galantheae. *Herbertia* 14: 85–114.

Webb, D.A. 1978. The European species of *Galanthus* L. *Botanical Journal of the Linnean Society* 76: 307–13.

GALAXIA

Goldblatt, P. 1979. Biology and systematics of *Galaxia* (Iridaceae). *Journal of South African Botany* 45(4): 385–423.

GALTONIA

Hilliard, O.M. & Burtt, B.L. 1986. Notes on some plants from Southern Africa, chiefly from Natal. *Notes from the Royal Botanic Garden Edinburgh* 43(3): 369–370.

GEISSORHIZA

Foster, R. 1941. Studies in the Iridaceae II. A revision of *Geissorhiza*. *Contributions from the Gray Herbarium* 135: 3 78.

Goldblatt, P. 1985. Systematics of the Southern African genus *Geissorhiza* (Iridaceae – Ixiodaceae). *Annals of the Missouri Botanic Garden* 72: 277–447.

GETHYLLIS

Baker, J.G. 1896. *Gethyllis* L. In Thistleton-Dyer, W. T. (ed.), *Flora Capensis* 6: 193–6. Reeve & Co.

Du Plessis, N.M. 1973. The genus *Gethyllis* L. *Bulletin of the Indigenous Bulb Growers Association of South Africa* 21: 2–4.

Müller-Doblies, D. 1986. Enumeratio specierum generum *Gethyllis* et *Apodolirion* (Amaryllidaceae). *Wildenowia* 15: 465–471.

GLADIOLUS

Anderton, E.W. & Park, R. 1989. *Growing Gladioli*. Helm.

British Gladiolus Society 1926–. *The Gladiolus Annual*.

Creasy, L.B. 1937. Garden gladioli – their origin and history. *Journal of the Botanical Society of South Africa* 23: 10–14.

Delpierre, G.R. & Du Plessis N.M. 1973. *The Winter-growing Gladioli of South Africa*. Tafelberg, Cape Town and Johannesburg.

De Vos, M.P. 1976. Die Suid-Afrikaanse spesies van *Homoglossum*. *Journal of South African Botany* 42(4): 301–359.

Du Plessis, N.M. & Delpierre, G.R. 1977. Die Gladioli van Suid-Afrika. *Veld & Flora* 63(1): 9–12.

Fogg, G.H.W. 1957. *The Gladiolus Today*. Gifford.

Garrity, J.B. 1975. *Gladioli for Everyone*. David & Charles.

Genders, R. 1961. *Gladioli and the Miniatures*. Blandford.

Goldblatt, P. 1971. Cytological and morphological studies in the Southern African Iridaceae. *Journal of South*

African Botany 37(4): 405–412.

Hamilton, A.P. 1975. A history of the garden gladiolus. *Journal of the Royal Horticultural Society* 101: 424–8.

— 1976. The European gladioli. *AGS Bulletin* 44: 140–46.

Koenig & Crowley (eds), 1972. *The World of Gladiolus.* Edgewood, Maryland: Edgewood Press.

Lewis, G.J. & Obermeyer, A.A., with Barnard, T.T. 1972. *Gladiolus* – a revision of the South African species. *Journal of South African Botany* suppl. vol. no. 10.

North American Gladiolus Council 1942–. *Bulletin.*

— 1972. *The World of the Gladiolus.* Edgewood, Maryland: NAGC.

Park, R. 1992. Gladiolus breeding in Russia. *The Plantsman* 13(4): 215–18.

Thomas, S.G. 1955. *Gladiolus for Garden and Exhibition.* Collingridge.

Unwin, C.W.J. 1957. *Gladioli and Dahlias.* Collingridge.

GLORIOSA

Ferguson, I. 1980. *Gloriosa simplex. The Garden* 105(12): 504.

Field, D.V. 1971. The identity of *Gloriosa simplex* L. (Liliaceae). *Kew Bulletin* 25: 243–245.

— 1972. The genus *Gloriosa. Lilies and other Liliaceae 1973*: 93–5.

Karihaloo, J.L. 1986. Cytology of three species of *Gloriosa. Herbertia* 42: 2–13.

Kirtikar, K.R. 1977. The Glory Lily, *Gloriosa superba. Hornbill*: 6–7.

Narain, P. 1988. *Gloriosa*: cultivars and natural species. *Herbertia* 44: 2–12.

Onderstall, J. The fabulous Flame Lily. *Veld & Flora* 62(3): 24–5.

Percy-Lancaster, S. 1958. *Gloriosa. Bulletin of the National Botanic Garden of Lucknow* no. 26.

Percy-Lancaster, S. & A. 1966. Gloriosa. *Bulletin of the National Botanic Garden of Lucknow* no. 123.

GRIFFINIA

Traub, H.P. & Moldenke, H.N. 1949. *Amaryllidaceae Tribe Amarylleae*: 153–7.

GYMNOSPERMIUM

Takhtajan, A.L. 1970. On the genus *Gymnospermium. Botanicheskii Zhurnal* 55: 1191–3.

GYNANDRIRIS

Goldblatt, P. 1980. Systematics of *Gynandriris* (Iridaceae), a Mediterranean-southern African disjunct. *Botaniska Notiser* 133: 239–60.

HABRANTHUS

Herklots, G.A.C. 1980. Wind Flowers II: *Habranthus. The Plantsman* 2(2): 90–99.

Sealy, J.R. 1937. *Zephyranthus, Pyrolirion, Habranthus* and *Hippeastrum. Journal of the Royal Horticultural Society* 62: 195–209.

HAEMANTHUS

Friis, I. & Nordal, I. 1976. Studies on the genus *Haemanthus* IV. *Norwegian Journal of Botany* 23: 63–77.

Snijman, D.A. 1984. A revision of the genus *Haemanthus* L. (Amaryllidaceae). *Journal of South African Botany* suppl. vol. no. 12.

HEDYCHIUM

Schilling, A. 1982. A survey of cultivated Himalayan and Sino-Himalayan *Hedychium* species. *The Plantsman* 4(3): 129–49.

— 1994. Further notes on Himalayan and Sino-Himalayan *Hedychium* species. *The New Plantsman* 1(2): 114–6.

HEMEROCALLIS

Bailey, L.H. 1930. *Hemerocallis*: the Day Lilies. *Gentes Herbarum* 2: 143–56.

Stout, A. B. 1986. *Daylilies.* Sagapress Inc.

Stuntz, M.F. et al. 1957. *Hemerocallis Checklist 1893–1957.*

HESPERANTHA

Foster, R.C. 1948. Studies in the Iridaceae V. *Contributions from the Gray Herbarium* 166: 3–27.

Goldblatt, P. 1982. Corm morphology in *Hesperantha. Annals of the Missouri Botanic Garden* 69: 370–8.

— 1984. A revision of *Hesperantha* (Iridaceae) in the winter rainfall area of Southern Africa. *Journal of South African Botany* 50(1): 15–141.

Hilliard, O.M., & Burtt, B.L., 1986. *Hesperantha* (Iridaceae) in Natal and nearby. *Notes from the Royal Botanic Garden Edinburgh* 43: 407–438.

HIPPEASTRUM

Growing Amaryllis. 1958. Grower Books.

Sealy, J.R. 1937. *Zephyranthus, Pyrolirion, Habranthus* and *Hippeastrum. Journal of the Royal Horticultural Society* 62: 195–209.

Traub, H.P. 1958. *The Amaryllis Manual.* Macmillan Inc.

Traub, H.P. & Moldenke, H.N. 1949. *Amaryllidaceae Tribe Amarylleae.*

HOMERIA

Goldblatt, P. 1981. Systematics and biology of *Homeria* (Iridaceae). *Annals of the Missouri Botanic Garden* 68: 413–503.

HYACINTHELLA

Feinbrun, N. 1961. Revision of the genus *Hyacinthella* Schur. *Bulletin of the Research Council of Israel, Section D: Botany* 10D: 324–47.

Persson, K. & Wendelbo, P. 1981; 1982. Taxonomy and cytology of the genus *Hyacinthella* (Liliaceae – Scilloidaceae) with special reference to the species in SW Asia. *Candollea* 36: 513–41; 37: 157–75.

HYACINTHOIDES

Adolfi, K. 1977. Zur Unterscheidung von *Hyacinthoides non-scripta* (L.) Chouard und *Hyacinthoides hispanica* (Mill.) Rothm. *Gottinger Floristische Rundbriefe* 11(2): 33–4.

Quere-Boterenbrood, A.J. 1984. Over het vorkomen van *Scilla non-scripta* (L.) Hoffmannsegg & Link, *S.hispanica* Miller en hur hybrids in Nederland. *Gorteria* 12(5): 91–104.

HYACINTHUS

Bentzer, B. & von Bothmer, R. 1974. Cytology and morphology of the genus *Hyacinthus* L. s. str. (Liliaceae). *Botaniska Notiser* 127: 297–301.

Persson, K. & Wendelbo, P. 1979. The artificial hybrid *Hyacinthus orientalis* × *transcaspicus* (Liliaceae). *Botaniska Notiser* 132: 207–9.

Wendelbo, P. 1980. Notes on *Hyacinthus* and *Bellevalia* (Liliaceae) in Turkey and Iran. *Notes from the Royal Botanic Garden Edinburgh* 38: 423–34.

HYPOXIS

Baker, J.G. 1896. *Hypoxis*. In Thistleton-Dyer, W.T. (ed.), *Flora Capensis* 6: 174–89. Reeve & Co.

Garside, S. 1936. The South African Species of *Spiloxene* Salisb. *Journal of Botany, London* 74: 267–269.

Thompson, M.F. 1969. *Spiloxene capensis* and *S.canalicu-lata*. *Flowering Plants of Africa* 39: t. 1557, A & B.

IPHEION

Mathew, B. 1995. Two interesting bulbs from South America. *The New Plantsman* 2(1): 10–11.

Stearn, W.T. 1943. *Ipheion uniflorum*. *The Gardeners' Chronicle* (August 14th).

IRIS

American Iris Society. Annual *Bulletin*.

American Iris Society & Davidson, B.L. (ed.) 1972. *Species Manual*.

Anley, C. 1946. *Irises, their Culture and Selection*. Collingridge.

Brearley, C. 1985. The crested Irises of North America. *The Plantsman* 7(2): 114–5.

British Iris Society 1974. *An Alphabetical Table and Cultivation Guide to the Species of the Genus Iris*.
— *Iris Year Book*.

British Iris Society (Species Group). *Summary of Iris Species*.

Cave, N.L. 1959. *The Iris*. Faber & Faber.

Cohen, V.A. 1967. *A Guide to the Pacific Coast Irises*. The British Iris Society.

Davis, P.H. 1946. Oncocyclus Irises in the Levant. *Journal of the Royal Horticultural Society* 71.

Deutsche Iris- und Liliengesellschaft (now Gesellschaft der Staudenfreunde). *Year Books*. Stuttgart.

Dykes, W.R. 1924. *A Handbook of Garden Irises*. Hopkinson.
— 1913. *The Genus Iris*. Cambridge; repr. Dover, 1974.

Fedschenko & Vvedensky 1968. *Iris*. In Komarov, V.L. (ed.), *Flora USSR*: vol. 4. Leningrad.

Foster, M. 1892. *Bulbous Irises*.

Foster, R.D. 1937. A cytotaxonomic survey of the North American species of *Iris*. *Contributions from the Gray Herbarium* 119.

Grey-Wilson, C. 1971. *The Genus Iris Subsection Sibiricae*. The British Iris Society.

Grossheim, A.A. 1940. *Iris*. In *Flora Kavkaza*: vol. 2. Leningrad.

Hoog, M.H. 1980. Bulbous Irises. *The Plantsman* 2(3): 141–64.

Jones, S.K. & Hanks, G.R. 1988. Bulking up bulbous Iris. *The Plantsman* 9(4): 247–51.

Köhlein, F. 1981. *Iris*. Helm.

Lawrence, G.H.M. 1953. A reclassification of the genus *Iris*. *Gentes Herbarum* 8: 346.

Lenz, L.W. 1955. Studies in *Iris* embryo culture. *Aliso* 3: 173.
— 1958. A revision of the Pacific Coast Irises. *Aliso* 4: 1.
— 1959. Hybridization and specification in the Pacific Coast Irises. *Aliso* 4: 237.
— 1959. *Iris tenuis*. *Aliso* 4: 311.
— 1962. A key character in *Iris* for separating the Sibiricae and the Californicae. *Aliso* 5: 211.

Lenz, L.W. & Day, A. 1963. The chromosomes of the Spuria Irises and evolution of garden forms. *Aliso* 5: 257.

Lynch, R.I. 1903. *The Book of Iris*. London & New York: Bodley Head.

Maire, R. 1959. *Iris*. In *Flore de l'Afrique du Nord*: vol. 6. Paris.

Marchant, A. & Mathew, B. 1974. *An Alphabetical Table and Cultivation Guide to the Species of the genus Iris*. The British Iris Society.

Mathew, B. 1981. *The Iris*. Batsford.
— 1993. *Iris chrysographes*. *The Plantsman* 14(4): 193–6.

Price, M. 1966. *The Iris Book*. Constable & Co.

Randall, H. 1969. *Irises*. Batsford.

Randolph. L.F. (ed.) 1959. *Garden Irises*. The American Iris Society.

Randolph, L.F. 1966. *Iris nelsonii. Baileya* 14: 143.

Randolph, L.F. & F. 1955. Embryo culture of *Iris* seed. *Bulletin of the American Iris Society* 139: 7.

Randolph, L.F. & Mitra, J. 1959. Karyotypes of *Iris pumila* and related species. *American Journal of Botany* 46: 93.

Rechinger, K.H. 1975. Iridaceae. In *Flora des Iranischen Hochlandes und der umrahmenden Gebirge*. Graz: Akademische Druck- und Verlagsanstalt.

Rodionenko, G.I. 1962. *Iris*. Leningrad.

Service, N. 1988. Bearded Irises: comments on the species in section *Iris. The Plantsman* 10(1): 6–26.

— 1990. Winter flowering Irises: series *Unguiculares. The Plantsman* 12(1): 1–9.

Small, J.K. & Alexander, E.J. 1931. Botanical interpretations of the Iridaceous plants of the Gulf States. *Contributions from the New York Botanic Garden*.

Società Italiana dell'Iris 1963. *Report of the First International Symposiun on Iris*. Florence.

Stojanov, N., Stefanov, B. & Kotanov, B. 1966. *Iris*. In *Flora of Bulgaria*, 4th edn: part 1.

Taylor, J.J. 1976. A reclassification of *Iris* species bearing arillate seed. *Proc. Biol. Soc. Washington* 89, 35: 411.

The Median Iris Society (a section of the American Iris Society) 1970. *The Eupogon Iris Species. Prodan*. Westborough, Massachusetts: Mis Press-Hudson Printers.

The Median Iris Society (Publications Committee) & Warburton, B.A. 1972. *The Median Bearded Irises. Introduction and Varietal Listing*. Westborough, Massachusetts: Mis Press-Hudson Printers.

Ugrinsky, K.A. 1922. The *Iris flavissima* Pallas complex. *Feddes Repertorium* 14.

van Nes, H. 1967. *Iris im Garten*. Munich: BLV.

Warburton, B. & Hamblen, M. 1978. *The World of Irises*. The American Iris Society. Salt Lake City: Publisher's Press.

Webb, D.A. & Chater, A.O. 1980. *Iris*. In *Flora Europaea*: vol 5. Cambridge.

Wendelbo, P. 1977. *Tulips and Irises of Iran*. Tehran.

Wendelbo, P. & Mathew, B. 1976. Iridaceae. In *Flora Iranica*: part 112. Graz: Akademische Druck- und Verlagsanstalt.

Werckmeister, P. 1967. *Catalogus Iridis*. Deutsche Iris- und Liliengesellschaft.

IXIA

Lewis, J.G. 1962. The genus *Ixia. Journal of South African Botany* 28(2): 45–195.

IXIOLIRION

Traub, H.P. 1942. The *Ixiolirion* tribe. *Herbertia* 9: 53–9.

KNIPHOFIA

Codd, L.E. 1968. The South African species of *Kniphofia. Bothalia* 9: 363–513.

— 1968. New species of *Kniphofia. Bothalia* 9: 139–42.

Marais, W. 1973. The tropical species of *Kniphofia* (Liliaceae). *Kew Bulletin* 28: 465–83.

Taylor, J. 1985. *Kniphofia* – a survey. *The Plantsman* 7(3): 129–60.

LACHENALIA

Crosby, T.S. 1986. The genus *Lachenalia. The Plantsman* 8(3): 129–66.

Duncan, G.D. 1978. *The Lachenalia Handbook*. Cape Town: Kirstenbosch.

Ingram, J. 1966. Notes on the cultivated Liliaceae 4: *Lachenalia. Baileya* 14: 123–46.

LAPEIROUSIA

Goldblatt, P. 1972. A revision of the genera *Lapeirousia* Pourret and *Anomatheca* Ker in the winter rainfall region of Southern Africa. *Contributions from the Bolus Herbarium* 4: 1–74.

Lawrence, G.H.M. 1955. Notes on *Lapeirousia* in cultivation. *Baileya* 3: 131–6.

LEDEBOURIA

Jessop, J.P. 1970. Studies in the bulbous Liliaceae: 1. *Scilla, Schizocarpus* and *Ledebouria. Journal of South African Botany* 36(4): 233–266.

LEUCOCORYNE

Pizarro, C.M. 1966. *Flores Silvestre de Chile*.

LEUCOJUM

Elliott, J. 1992. *Leucojum* – the Snowflakes. *The Plantsman* 14(2): 70–9.

Stern, W.C. 1956. *Snowdrops and Snowflakes*. Royal Horticultural Society.

LILIUM

Boardman, R. C. 1906. *Lilies and Orchids*. Robert Grier Cooke.

Coldring, William. 1905. *The Book of the Lily*. Bodley Head.

de Graaff, J. 1951. *The New Book of Lilies*. Barrows.

de Graaff, J. & Hyams, E. 1967. *Lilies*. Funk & Wagnalls.

Elwes, H.J. 1877–1880. *A Monograph of the Genus Lilium*.

Feldmaier, C. 1970. *Die neuen Lilien*. Stuttgart: Ulmer; trans. as *Lilies*. Batsford.

Feldmaier, C. & McRae, J. 1982. *Lilien*. Stuttgart: Ulmer.

Fox, D. 1985. *Growing Lilies*. Croom Helm.

— 1992. *Lilies*. Royal Horticultural Society.

Grove, A. & Cotton, A.D. 1933–40. *Supplement to Elwes' Monograph of the genus Lilium*, parts 1–7.
Haw, S.G. 1985. *The Lilies of China*. Batsford.
Jefferson-Brown, M.J. 1988. *Lilies for Garden, Patio and Display*. David & Charles.
— 1990. *Lilies: their Care and Cultivation*. Cassell.
Jekyll, G. 1901. *Lilies for English Gardens*. Country Life.
Leeburn, M.E. 1955. *Lilies and their Cultivation*.
— 1963. *Garden Lilies*. Collingridge.
Leslie, A.C. (ed.) 1982–. *The International Lily Register*, with supplements. Royal Horticultural Society.
Macneil, A. & E. 1946. *Garden Lilies*. Oxford University Press.
McRae, E.A. 1987. *Lily Disease Handbook*. North American Lily Society.
Matthews, V. 1989. *Lilies*. Collingridge/Kew.
Maxwell, A.C. 1953. *Lilies in their Homes*. Collins.
North American Lily Society 1948–. *Yearbooks, Bulletins*.
Rockwell, F.F., Grayson, E.C. & de Graaff, J. 1961. *The Complete Book of Lilies*. New York: American Garden Guild & Doubleday.
Royal Horticultural Society 1932–71. *Lily Year Books*, succeeded by *Lilies and other Liliaceae*. The 1990 supplement contains the *Proceedings of the 5th International Lily Conference, 1989*.
Slate, G. L. 1930. *Lilies for American Gardens*. Scribners.
Stoker, F. 1943. *A Book of Lilies*. London & New York: Penguin.
Synge, P.M. 1980. *Lilies*. Batsford.
— 1980. Some newer hybrid Lilies. *The Plantsman* 1(4): 250–2.
Turrill, W.R. 1960–62. *Supplement to Elwes' Monograph of the genus Lilium*, parts 8–9.
Wallace, A. 1879. *Notes on Lilies and their Culture*. 2nd edn. Colchester.
Wilson, E. H. 1929. *The Lilies of Eastern Asia*. Stratford
Withers, R. M. 1967. *Liliums in Australia*. Australian Lilium Society.
Woodcock, H. B. D. & Stearn, W. T. 1950. *Lilies of the World*. Country Life.

LITTONIA

Baker, J.G. 1897 *Littonia* Hook. In Thistleton-Dyer, W.T. (ed.), *Flora Capensis* 6: 527. Reeve & Co.

LYCORIS

Traub, H.P. & Moldenke, H.N. 1949. *Amaryllidaceae Tribe Amarylleae*: 165–82.

MAIANTHEMUM

Ingram, J. 1966. Notes on cultivated Liliaceae: 3. *Maianthemum*. *Baileya* 14: 50–9.

MASSONIA

Jessop, J.P. 1976. Studies in the bulbous Liliaceae in South Africa: 6. The taxonomy of *Massonia* and allied genera. *Journal of South African Botany* 42(4): 401–37.

MERENDERA

Burtt, B.L., Meikle, R.D. & Furse, J.P.W. 1968. *Colchicum* and *Merendera*. *RHS Lily Year Book* 31: 90–103.
Stefanoff, B. 1926. Monographie der Gattung *Colchicum*. *Sbornik Bulgariskata Akademiya na Naukita* 22: 1–100.

MILLA

Moore, H.E. 1953. The genus *Milla* and its allies. *Gentes Herbarum* 8: 263–94.

MORAEA

Barnard, T. 1950. Peacock Moraeas. *Journal of the Royal Horticultural Society* 75.
Goldblatt, P. 1973. Contributions to the knowledge of *Moraea* (Iridaceae) in the summer rainfall region of South Africa. *Annals of the Missouri Botanic Garden* 60: 204–59.
— 1976. The genus *Moraea* in the winter rainfall region of Southern Africa. *Annals of the Missouri Botanic Garden* 63: 657–786.
— 1977. Systematics of *Moraea* (Iridaceae) in tropical Africa. *Annals of the Missouri Botanic Garden* 64: 243–95.
— 1986. *The Moraeas of Southern Africa*. *Annals of the Kirstenbosch Botanic Gardens* 14.

MUILLA

Ingram, J. A monograph of the genera *Bloomeria* and *Muilla* (Liliaceae). *Madroño* 12: 19–27.

MUSCARI

Speta, F. 1982. Über die Abgrenzung und Gliederung der Gattung *Muscari*, und über ihre Beziehungen zu anderen Vertreten der Hyacinthaceae. *Botanische Jahrbücher* 103: 247–91.
Stuart, D.C. 1966. *Muscari* and allied genera. *RHS Lily Year Book* 29: 125–38.

NARCISSUS

American Daffodil Society/RHS 1980. *Daffodils to Show and Grow. An Abridged Classified List of Daffodil Names*.
American Horticultural Society 1966. *The Daffodil Handbook* (special issue of the *Horticultural Magazine*).
Baker, J.G. 1875. Review of the genus *Narcissus*. In Burbidge, F.W. 1875, *The Narcissus: its History and Culture*.
— 1888. *Handbook of the Amaryllideae*.

Barnes, D. 1987. *Daffodils for Home, Garden and Show*. David & Charles.

Blanchard, J.W. 1990. *Narcissus: a Guide to Wild Daffodils*. AGS.

Bowles, E.A. 1934. *A Handbook of Narcissus*. Martin Hopkinson.

Burbidge, F.W. 1875. *The Narcissus: its History and Culture*.

Calvert, A.F. 1929. *Daffodil Growing for Pleasure and Profit*.

Daffodil Year Book, later *Daffodils* 1913–. Royal Horticultural Society.

Fernandes, A. 1953. Sobre a distribicao geografica de *N. cyclamineus* DC e *N. calcicola* Mendonca. *Bol. Soc. Broteriana*.

— 1959. On the origin of *N. romieuxii* Br-Bl & Maire. *Bol. Soc. Broteriana*.

— 1959. On the origin of *N. cantabricus* DC. *Bol. Soc. Broteriana*.

— 1963. Sobre a evolucao no subgenero *Corbularia* do genero *Narcissus* L. *Mem. Acad. Cien. Lisboa*.

— 1964. Contribution à la connaissance de la genetique de l'heterostylie chez le genre *Narcissus* L. I. Resultats de quelques croisements. *Bol. Soc. Broteriana*.

— 1965. Contribution à la connaissance de la genetique de l'heterostylie chez le genre *Narcissus* L. II. L'heterostylie chex quelques populations de *N. triandrus* var. *cernuus* et *N.t.* var. *concolor*. *Genet. Iberica*.

— 1966. Nouvelles études caryologiques sur la section *Jonquilla* DC du genre *Narcissus*. *Bol. Soc. Broteriana*.

— 1967. Contribution à la connaissance de la biosystematique de quelques espèces du genre *Narcissus* L. *Port. Act. Biol.*

— 1968. Keys to the identification of native and naturalized taxa of the genus *Narcissus* L. *Daffodil and Tulip Year Book*: 37–66.

— 1968. Sur la caryologie du *N. serotinus* L. *Collectanea Botanica*.

— 1969. Contribution to the knowledge of the biosystematics of some species of genus *Narcissus* L. *Simposio de Flora Europea*.

Fernandes, A. & Almeida M.T. de 1968. La meiose chez *Narcissus bulbocodium* × *N. concolor* Rozeira. *Port. Act. Biol.*

— 1971. Sur les nombres chromosomiques de quelques formes horticoles du genre *Narcissus* L. I. *Bol. Soc. Broteriana*.

Fernandes, A. & Franca, F. 1970. Sur la meiose d'un descendant du croisement de formes triploides de *N. bulbocodium* L. *Bol. Soc. Broteriana*.

— 1971. Sur la meiose d'une plante de *N. bulbocodium* L. à 40 chromosomes. *Bol. Soc. Broteriana*.

— 1971. Sobre a descendencia do cruzamento de triploides em *Narcissus bulbocodium*. *An. Estacion Exper. de Aula Dei.*

Fernandes, A. & Queiros, M. 1970. Sur quelques particuliarités de *N. gaditanus* Bois. & Reut. *Bol. Soc. Broteriana*.

Gray, A. 1955. *Miniature Daffodils*. Collingridge.

Hanks, G.R. & Jones, S.K. 1986. Notes on propagation of *Narcissus* by twin-scaling. *The Plantsman* 8(2): 118–27.

Hartland, W.B. 1894–1912. *Little Book of Daffodils*.

Haworth, A.H. 1831. *Narcissearum Monographia*.

Henriques, J.A. 1887. Amaryllideas de Portugal. *Bol. Soc. Broteriana, series 1.*

Jacob, J. 1910. *Daffodils*. J.C. & E.C. Jack.

Jefferson-Brown, M.J. 1951. *The Daffodil*. Faber & Faber.

— 1952. *Daffodils for Amateurs*. Faber & Faber.

— 1969. *Daffodils and Narcissi*. Faber.

— 1991. *Narcissus*. Batsford.

Kirby, A.M. 1907. *Daffodils, Narcissus and How to Grow Them*.

Ministry of Agriculture 1951. *Narcissus Flies*. Leaflet 183. HMSO.

— 1951. *Narcissus Culture*. Bulletin no. 44. HMSO.

— 1970. *Narcissus Pests*. Bulletin no. 51. HMSO.

— 1981. *Basal Stem Rot in Narcissus*. Leaflet 783. HMSO.

— 1983. *Stem Nematode on Narcissus*. Leaflet 460. HMSO.

Pugsley, H.W. 1915. *Narcissus poeticus* and its allies. *Journal of Botany* 53.

— 1933. A monograph of *Narcissus*, subgenus *Ajax*. *Journal of the Royal Horticultural Society* 58: 17–93.

Quinn, C.E. 1959. *Daffodils, Outdoor and In*. New York: Hearthside Press Inc.

Rees, A.R. 1987. The structure and growth of the *Narcissus* bulb. *The Plantsman* 9(1): 42–7.

Royal Horticultural Society 1989–. *The International Daffodil Checklist*, with supplements. RHS.

Shepherd, F.W. 1987. *Daffodils*. Wisley Handbook: Cassell/RHS.

Taylor, A.W. 1970. Narcissi of the section Pseudo-Narcissus. *AGS Bulletin* 38: 98–109.

Wells, J.S. 1989. *Modern Miniature Daffodils: Species and Hybrids*. Batsford; Portland, Oregon: Timber Press.

NEOBAKERIA

Jessop, J.P. 1976. Studies in the bulbous Liliaceae in South Africa: 6. *Journal of South African Botany* 42(4): 406–426.

NERINE

Duncan, G.D. 1984. *Nerine sarniensis* 'Kirstenbosch White' – the White Sport. *Veld & Flora* 70(2): 55-56.

Nerine Society of Great Britain 1966–. *Bulletin*.

Norris, C.A. 1974. The genus *Nerine*. *Bulletin of the Nerine Society of Great Britain* 6: 7–31.

Traub, H.P. 1967. Review of the genus *Nerine*. *Plant Life* 23, suppl.

NOMOCHARIS

Sealy, J.R. 1983. A revision of the genus *Nomocharis* Franchet. *Botanical Journal of the Linnean Society* 87: 285–323.

Wilkie, D. 1946. The genus *Nomocharis*. *RHS Lily Year Book*.

NOTHOLIRION

Woodcock, H.B.D. & Stearn, W.T. 1950. *Lilies of the World*: 373–80.

ORNITHOGALUM

Cullen, J. 1984. *Ornithogalum*. In Davies, P.H. (ed.), *Flora of Turkey* 8: 227–45.

Obermeyer, A.A. 1978. *Ornithogalum*: a revision of the Southern African species. *Bothalia* 12(3): 323–376.

OXALIS

Salter, T.M. 1944. The genus *Oxalis* in South Africa. *Journal of South African Botany* suppl. vol. no. 1.

PARDANTHOPSIS

Lenz, L.W. 1972. The status of *Pardanthopsis*. *Aliso* 7: 401.

PARIS

Mitchell, R. 1987; 1988. *Paris. The Plantsman* 9(2): 81–9; 10(3): 167–90.

PELARGONIUM

Australian Geranium Society 1978–. *Check List and Register of Pelargonium Cultivar Names*.

Clark. D. 1988. *Pelargoniums*. Collingridge/Kew.

Clifford, D. 1970. *Pelargoniums*. 2nd end, Blandford Press.

Key, H. 1985. *Pelargoniums*. Wisley Handbook: Cassell/RHS.

Taylor, J. 1988. *Geraniums and Pelargoniums*. Crowood Press.

Van der Walt, J.J.A. 1977; 1977; 1981. *Pelargoniums of Southern Africa*, 3 vols. vol. 1 Cape Town: Purnell; vol. 2 Cape Town: Juta; vol. 3 Kirstenbosch: National Botanic Gardens.

— 1985. A taxonomic revision of the type section of *Pelargonium* L'Hérit. (Geraniaceae). *Bothalia* 15: 345–85.

Webb, W.J. 1984. *The Pelargonium Family*. Croom Helm.

Wood, H.J. 1966. *Pelargoniums: a Complete Guide to their Cultivation*. Privately published.

— 1983. *Pelargoniums, Geraniums and their Societies*. Privately published.

PHAEDRANASSA

Ravenna, P.F. 1969. Contributions to South American Amaryllidaceae III. *Plant Life* 25: 55–62.

POLYGONATUM

Jeffrey, C. 1980. The genus *Polygonatum* (Liliaceae) in Eastern Asia. *Kew Bulletin* 34: 435–71.

Ownbey, R.P. 1944. The Liliaceous genus *Polygonatum* in North America. *Annals of the Missouri Botanic Garden* 31: 373–413.

POLYXENA

Jessop, J.P. 1976. Studies in the bulbous Liliaceae in Southern Africa: 6. *Journal of South African Botany* 42(4): 426–431.

Mathew, B. 1982. *Polyxena. The Plantsman* 4(3): 179–81.

PSEUDOGALTONIA

Solch, A. et al. 1970. *Pseudogaltonia. Flora of South West Africa* 147: 63–64.

PYROLIRION

Sealy, J.R. 1937. *Zephyranthus, Pyrolirion, Habranthus* and *Hippeastrum*. *Journal of the Royal Horticultural Society* 62: 195–209.

RHODOHYPOXIS

Hilliard, O.M. & Burtt, B.L. 1978. Notes on some plants from Southern Africa chiefly from Natal: VII. *Notes from the Royal Botanic Garden Edinburgh* 36(1): 43–70.

Mathew, B. 1984. *Rhodohypoxis. The Plantsman* 6(1): 49–59.

RHODOPHIALA

Traub, H.P. 1956. The genera *Rhodophiala* and *Phycella*. *Plant Life* 12: 67–76.

RIGIDELLA

Cruden, R.W. 1971. The systematics of *Rigidella*. *Brittonia* 23: 217–25.

ROMULEA

Beguinot, A. 1907; 1908; 1909. Revisione monographica del genere *Romulea* Maratti. *Malpighia* 21: 49–122, 364–478; 22: 377–469; 23: 55–117, 185–239, 257–96.

De Vos, M.P. 1972. The Genus *Romulea* in South Africa. *Journal of South African Botany* suppl. vol. no. 9.

— 1983. *Romulea*. In Leistner, O.A. (ed.), *Flowering Plants of South Africa* 7(2,2): 10–73. Pretoria: Botanical Research Institute.

SANDERSONIA

Hennessy, E.F. 1977. *Sandersonia aurantiaca*. *Flowering Plants of Africa* 44: t.1755.

SCADOXUS

Friis, I.B. & Nordal, I. 1976. Studies on the genus *Haemanthus* (Amaryllidaceae) IV. Division of the genus into *Haemanthus* and *Scadoxus* with notes on *Haemanthus*. *Norwegian Journal of Botany* 23: 63–77.

SCHIZOSTYLIS

Goldblatt, P. 1971. Cytological and morphological studies in the Southern African Iridaceae: *Schizostylis*. *Journal of South African Botany* 37(4): 384–386.

SCILLA

Anderson, E.B. & Meikle, R.D. 1962. A Lily Group discussion of Scillas and Chionodoxas. *RHS Lily Year Book* 25: 116–33.

Anderson, E.B. & Synge, P.M. 1961. Hardy Scillas. *RHS Lily Year Book* 24: 27–30.

Jessop, J.P. 1970. Studies in the bulbous Liliaceae: 1. *Scilla, Schizocarpus* and *Ledebouria*. *Journal of South African Botany* 36(4): 233–266.

Speta, F. 1980. Die frühjahrsblühenden *Scilla*-Arten des östlichen Mittelmeerraumes. *Naturkundliches Jahrbuch der Stadt Linz* 25: 19–198.

SINNINGIA

Mathew, B. 1994. *Sinningia tubiflora*: a Gesneriad for the conservatory. *The New Plantsman* 1(4): 236–7.

SISYRINCHIUM

Parent, G.H. 1980. Le genre *Sisyrinchium* L. (Iridaceae) en Europe: un bilan provisoire. *Lejeunia* 99: 1–40.

SPARAXIS

Goldblatt, P. 1969. The genus *Sparaxis*. *Journal of South African Botany* 35(4): 219–252.

— 1978. The species of *Sparaxis* and their geography. *Veld & Flora* 65: 7–9.

STENOMESSON

Ravenna, P.F. 1971. Contributions to the South American Amaryllidaceae IV and V. *Plant Life* 27: 73–84.

STERNBERGIA

Mathew, B. 1983. A review of the genus *Sternbergia*. *The Plantsman* 5(1): 1–16.

STRUMARIA

Baker, J.G. 1896. *Strumaria* Jacq. In Thistleton-Dyer, W.T. (ed.), *Flora Capensis* 6: 215–217. Reeve & Co.

SYNNOTIA

Lewis, G.J. 1956. A revision of the genus *Synnotia*. *Annals of the South African Museum* 40: 137–51.

SYRINGODEA

De Vos, M.P. 1974. Die suid-Afrikaanse genus *Syringodea*. *Journal of South African Botany* 40(3): 201–54.

— 1983. *Syringodea*. In Leistner, O.A. (ed.), *Flowering Plants of South Africa* 7(2,2): 1–9. Pretoria: Botanical Research Institute.

THYSANOTUS

Brittan, N.H. 1987. Revision of the genus *Thysanotus* R.Br. (Liliaceae). *Brunonia* 4: 67–181.

TIGRIDIA

Molseed, E. 1970. The genus *Tigridia* (Iridaceae) of Mexico and Central America. *University of California Publications in Botany* 54.

TRICYRTIS

Mathew, B. 1985. A review of the genus *Tricyrtis*. *The Plantsman* 6(4): 193–224.

TRILLIUM

Christian, P. 1980. Trilliums. *AGS Bulletin* 48: 61–5, 139–43, 189–202, 339–4.

Freeman, J.D. 1975. Revision of *Trillium* subgenus *Phyllantherum* (Liliaceae). *Brittonia* 27: 1–62.

Mitchell, R.J. 1969; 1970; 1972. The genus *Trillium*. *Journal of the Scottish Rock Garden Club* 11: 271–83; 12: 16–20, 115–23; 13: 13–19.

— 1989; 1989; 1990; 1992. *Trillium*. *The Plantsman* 10(4): 216–231; 11(2): 67–79; 11(3): 132–151; 12(1): 44–60; 13(4): 219–25.

Samejima, K. & J. 1962. Studies on the eastern Asiatic *Trillium* (Liliaceae). *Acta Horti Gotoburgensis* 25: 157–259.

— 1987. *Trillium Genus Illustrated*. Sapporo: Hokkaido University Press.

TRITONIA

De Vos, M.P. 1982. The African genus *Tritonia* Ker-Gawler (Iridaceae): Part 1. *Journal of South African Botany* 48(1): 105–163.

— 1982. The genus *Tritonia* Ker-Gawler: Part 2. Sections *Subcallosae* and *Montbretia*. *Journal of South African Botany* 49(4): 347–422.

TRITONIOPSIS

Goldblatt, P. 1971. Cytological and morphological studies in the Southern African Iridaceae: *Antholyza. Journal of South African Botany* 37(4): 430–432.

Lewis, G.J. 1960. The genus *Anapalina. Journal of South African Botany* 26(1): 51–72.

TULBAGHIA

Benham, S. 1993. *Tulbaghia*: a survey of the species in cultivation. *The Plantsman* 15(2): 89–110.

Burbidge, R.B. 1978. A revision of the genus *Tulbaghia* (Liliaceae). *Notes from the Royal Botanic Garden Edinburgh* 36(1): 77–104.

— 1978–9. The genus *Tulbaghia. Lilies and other Liliaceae 1978–9*: 78–84.

Vosa, C.G. 1975. The cytotaxonomy of the genus *Tulbaghia. Annali Botanici* 34: 47–121.

TULIPA

Blunt, W. 1951. *Tulipomania*. Penguin.

Botschantzeva, Z.P. 1982. *Tulips: Taxonomy, Morphology, Cytology*. Rotterdam: A.A. Balkema.

Classified List and International Register of Tulip Names. 1987. Holland, Hillegom: Royal General Bulbgrowers' Association (KAVB).

Dykes, W.R. 1930. *Notes on Tulip Species*. Herbert Jenkins.

Hall, A.D. 1940. *The Genus Tulipa.* Royal Horticultural Society.

Lodewijk, Tom. 1978. *Het Boek Van de Tulp.* Sijthoff.

McKay, M.B. & Warner, M.F. 1933. Historical sketch of tulip mosaic or breaking: the oldest known plant virus disease. *National Horticultural Magazine* 12: 179–216.

Royal Horticultual Society 1931–64. *Daffodil and Tulip Year Book*; with the Royal General Dutch Bulb-Growers' Society 1960: *Classified List of Tulip Names.*

Stork, A. 1984. *Tulipes Sauvages et Cultivées*. Geneva: Conservatoire et Jardins Botaniques.

Wendelbo, P. 1977. *Tulips and Irises of Iran.* Tehran.

VAGARIA

Herklots, G.A.P. 1982. *Eurycles* and *Vagaria. The Plantsman* 3: 220–9.

VELTHEIMIA

Duncan, G.D. 1982 *Veltheimia bracteata* 'Lemon Flame' – introducing the yellow form. *Veld & Flora* 68(3): 72–73.

Marais, W. 1972. The correct names for Veltheimias, the winter red-hot pokers. *Journal of the Royal Horticultural Society* 47: 483–484.

Obermeyer, A.A. 1961. *Flowering Plants of Africa* 34: t.1356.

VERATRUM

Loesener, O. 1927; 1928. Die Gattung *Veratrum. Feddes Repertorium* 24: 61–72; 25: 1–10.

Mathew, B. 1989. A review of *Veratrum. The Plantsman* 11(1): 34–61

WATSONIA

Bond, P. & Goldblatt, P. 1984. *Plants of the Cape Flora; Watsonia. Journal of South African Botany* suppl. vol. no. 13: 85–86.

Goldblatt, P. 1987. Notes on the variation and taxonomy of *Watsonia borbonica* (*W. pyramidata, W. ardernei*) (Iridaceae) in the South-Western Cape, South Africa. *Annals of the Missouri Botanic Garden* 74(3): 570–2.

— 1989. *The Genus Watsonia*. Cape Town: Kirstenbosch.

Roux, J.P. 1980. Studies in the genus *Watsonia* Miller. *Journal of South African Botany* 46(4) 365–78.

WORSLEYA

Martinelli, G. 1984. Nota sobre *Worsleya rayneri* (J.D. Hooker) Traube & Moldenke, espécie ameaçada de ertinçal. *Rodriguesia* 36: 65–71.

Traub, H.P. & Moldenke, H.N. 1949. *Amaryllidaceae Tribe Amarylleae*: 22–4.

WURMBEA

Nordenstam, B. 1978. The genus *Wurmbea* in Africa except the Cape Region. *Notes from the Royal Botanic Garden Edinburgh* 36: 211–233.

— 1986. The genus *Wurmbea* (Colchicaceae) in the Cape Region. *Opera Botanica* 87: 1–41.

ZANTEDESCHIA

Letty, C. 1973. The genus *Zantedeschia. Bothalia* 11(1&2): 5–26.

ZEPHYRANTHES

Herklots, G.A.C. 1980. Wind Flowers I: *Zephyranthes. The Plantsman* 2(1): 8–19.

— 1981. Wind Flowers III: *Zephyranthes* subgenus *Cooperia. The Plantsman* 3(2): 108–17.

Sealy, J.R. 1937. *Zephyranthus, Pyrolirion, Habranthus* and *Hippeastrum. Journal of the Royal Horticultural Society* 62: 195–209.